3 From beginning to end, a fully integrated **customer value framework** captures the essence of today's marketing.

4 The **enhanced-learning design** of the book features annotated, illustrated chapter-opening vignettes to introduce key chapter concepts. For each chapter, the Objectives Outline shows what you'll need to know and where to find it. The end-of-chapter Reviewing Objectives and Key Terms summary tie back to the chapter objectives.

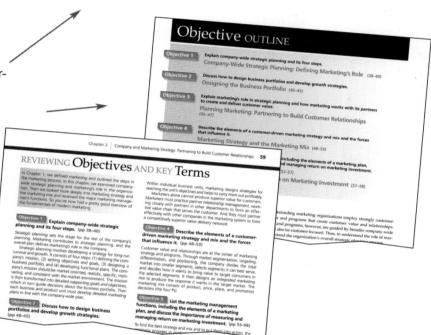

5 Updated **annotated figures** and **author comments** throughout each chapter provide the authors' insights on key points.

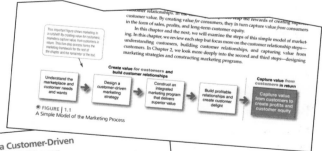

Principles of

Marketing

Principles of **Marketing**

14 | E

PHILIP **Kotler** Northwestern University

GARY **Armstrong** University of North Carolina

Pearson Prentice Hall

Boston   Columbus   Indianapolis   New York   San Francisco   Upper Saddle River
Amsterdam   Cape Town   Dubai   London   Madrid   Milan   Munich   Paris   Montreal   Toronto
Delhi   Mexico City   Sao Paulo   Sydney   Hong Kong   Seoul   Singapore   Taipei   Tokyo

Editorial Director: Sally Yagan
Director of Development: Stephen Deitmer
Editor in Chief: Eric Svendsen
Acquisitions Editor: Melissa Sabella
Editorial Project Manager: Meeta Pendharkar
Editorial Assistant: Elisabeth Scarpa
Director of Marketing: Patrice Jones
Senior Marketing Manager: Anne Fahlgren
Senior Marketing Assistant: Melinda Jensen
Senior Managing Editor: Judy Leale
Senior Production Project Manager: Karalyn Holland
Senior Operations Supervisor: Arnold Vila
Creative Director: Christy Mahon
Senior Art Director/Design Supervisor: Janet Slowik
Interior and Cover Designer: Karen Quigley
Cover Images: Matka Wariatka/Dreamstime, Imagebroker.net/SuperStock
Manager, Rights and Permissions: Hessa Albader
Acquisitions Editor, Digital Learning & Assessment: Josh Keefe
Multimedia Product Manager: Cathi Profitko
Editorial Media Project Manager: Joan Waxman
Media Project Manager: Lisa Rinaldi
Full-Service Project Management: S4Carlisle Publishing Services
Composition: S4Carlisle Publishing Services
Printer/Binder: Courier Kendallville
Cover Printer: Lehigh-Phoenix Color/Hagerstown
Text Font: 9/12.5 Palatino Lt Standard

Credits and acknowledgments borrowed from other sources and reproduced, with permission, in this textbook appear on page C1.

Microsoft® and Windows® are registered trademarks of the Microsoft Corporation in the U.S.A. and other countries. Screen shots and icons reprinted with permission from the Microsoft Corporation. This book is not sponsored or endorsed by or affiliated with the Microsoft Corporation.

Library of Congress Cataloging-in-Publication Data

Kotler, Philip.
  Principles of marketing / Philip Kotler, Gary Armstrong. -- 14th ed.
    p. cm.
  Includes bibliographical references and index.
  ISBN-13: 978-0-13-216712-3
  ISBN-10: 0-13-216712-3
  1. Marketing. I. Armstrong, Gary (Gary M.) II. Title.
  HF5415.K636 2011
  658.8--dc22

                                          2010052017

Prentice Hall
is an imprint of

10 9 8 7 6 5 4 3 2 1
ISBN 10: 0-13-216712-3
ISBN 13: 978-0-13-216712-3

www.pearsonhighered

DEDICATION

*To Kathy, Betty, Mandy, Matt, KC, Keri, Delaney, Molly, Macy, and Ben;
and Nancy, Amy, Melissa, and Jessica*

ABOUT The Authors

As a team, Philip Kotler and Gary Armstrong provide a blend of skills uniquely suited to writing an introductory marketing text. Professor Kotler is one of the world's leading authorities on marketing. Professor Armstrong is an award-winning teacher of undergraduate business students. Together they make the complex world of marketing practical, approachable, and enjoyable.

PHILIP KOTLER is S. C. Johnson & Son Distinguished Professor of International Marketing at the Kellogg School of Management, Northwestern University. He received his master's degree at the University of Chicago and his Ph.D. at M.I.T., both in economics. Dr. Kotler is author of *Marketing Management* (Pearson Prentice Hall), now in its fourteenth edition and the world's most widely used marketing textbook in graduate schools of business worldwide. He has authored dozens of other successful books and has written more than 100 articles in leading journals. He is the only three-time winner of the coveted Alpha Kappa Psi award for the best annual article in the *Journal of Marketing*.

Professor Kotler was named the first recipient of two major awards: the Distinguished Marketing Educator of the Year Award given by the American Marketing Association and the Philip Kotler Award for Excellence in Health Care Marketing presented by the Academy for Health Care Services Marketing. His numerous other major honors include the Sales and Marketing Executives International Marketing Educator of the Year Award; The European Association of Marketing Consultants and Trainers Marketing Excellence Award; the Charles Coolidge Parlin Marketing Research Award; and the Paul D. Converse Award, given by the American Marketing Association to honor "outstanding contributions to science in marketing." A recent *Forbes* survey ranks Professor Kotler in the top 10 of the world's most influential business thinkers. And in a recent *Financial Times* poll of 1,000 senior executives across the world, Professor Kotler was ranked as the fourth "most influential business writer/guru" of the twenty-first century.

Dr. Kotler has served as chairman of the College on Marketing of the Institute of Management Sciences, a director of the American Marketing Association, and a trustee of the Marketing Science Institute. He has consulted with many major U.S. and international companies in the areas of marketing strategy and planning, marketing organization, and international marketing. He has traveled and lectured extensively throughout Europe, Asia, and South America, advising companies and governments about global marketing practices and opportunities.

GARY ARMSTRONG is Crist W. Blackwell Distinguished Professor Emeritus of Undergraduate Education in the Kenan-Flagler Business School at the University of North Carolina at Chapel Hill. He holds undergraduate and masters degrees in business from Wayne State University in Detroit, and he received his Ph.D. in marketing from Northwestern University. Dr. Armstrong has contributed numerous articles to leading business journals. As a consultant and researcher, he has worked with many companies on marketing research, sales management, and marketing strategy.

But Professor Armstrong's first love has always been teaching. His long-held Blackwell Distinguished Professorship is the only permanent endowed professorship for distinguished undergraduate teaching at the University of North Carolina at Chapel Hill. He has been very active in the teaching and administration of Kenan-Flagler's undergraduate program. His administrative posts have included Chair of Marketing, Associate Director of the Undergraduate Business Program, Director of the Business Honors Program, and many others. Through the years, he has worked closely with business student groups and has received several campuswide and Business School teaching awards. He is the only repeat recipient of school's highly regarded Award for Excellence in Undergraduate Teaching, which he received three times. Most recently, Professor Armstrong received the UNC Board of Governors Award for Excellence in Teaching, the highest teaching honor bestowed by the sixteen-campus University of North Carolina system.

BRIEF Contents

Contents

Consumer Markets and Consumer Buyer Behavior 132

Business Markets and Business Buyer Behavior 164

Part 3: Designing a Customer-Driven Strategy and Mix 188

Customer-Driven Marketing Strategy: Creating Value for Target Customers 188

Products, Services, and Brands: Building Customer Value 222

13 Retailing and Wholesaling 372

14 Communicating Customer Value: Integrated Marketing Communications Strategy 406

15 Advertising and Public Relations 434

16 Personal Selling and Sales Promotion 462

17 Direct and Online Marketing: Building Direct Customer Relationships 494

Part 4: Extending Marketing 526

Creating Competitive Advantage 526

The Global Marketplace 550

Sustainable Marketing: Social Responsibility and Ethics 580

Preface

The Fourteenth Edition of *Principles of Marketing*! Still Creating More Value for You!

The goal of every marketer is to create more value for customers. So it makes sense that our goal for the fourteenth edition is to continue creating more value for you—*our* customer. Our goal is to introduce new marketing students to the fascinating world of modern marketing in an innovative and comprehensive yet practical and enjoyable way. We've poured over every page, table, figure, fact, and example in an effort to make this the best text from which to learn about and teach marketing. Enhanced by mymarketinglab, our online homework and personalized study tool, the fourteenth edition creates exceptional value for both students and professors.

Marketing: Creating Customer Value and Relationships

Top marketers at outstanding companies share a common goal: putting the consumer at the heart of marketing. Today's marketing is all about creating customer value and building profitable customer relationships. It starts with understanding consumer needs and wants, determining which target markets the organization can serve best, and developing a compelling value proposition by which the organization can attract and grow valued consumers. If the organization does these things well, it will reap the rewards in terms of market share, profits, and customer equity.

Five Major Value Themes

From beginning to end, the fourteenth edition of *Principles of Marketing* develops an innovative customer-value and customer-relationships framework that captures the essence of today's marketing. It builds on five major value themes:

1. *Creating value* for *customers in order to capture value* from *customers in return.* Today's marketers must be good at *creating customer value* and *managing customer relationships*. Outstanding marketing companies understand the marketplace and customer needs, design value-creating marketing strategies, develop integrated marketing programs that deliver customer value and delight, and build strong customer relationships. In return, they capture value from customers in the form of sales, profits, and customer loyalty.

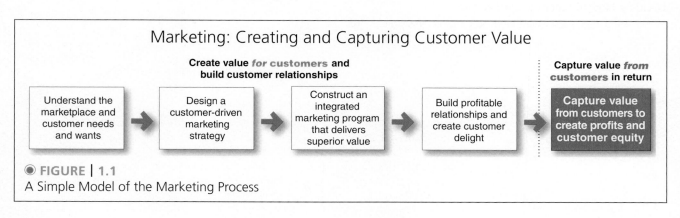

● FIGURE | 1.1
A Simple Model of the Marketing Process

This innovative *customer-value framework* is introduced at the start of Chapter 1 in a five-step marketing process model, which details how marketing *creates* customer value and *captures* value in return. The framework is carefully developed in the first two chapters and then fully integrated throughout the remainder of the text.

2. *Building and managing strong, value-creating brands.* Well-positioned brands with strong brand equity provide the basis upon which to build customer value and profitable customer relationships. Today's marketers must position their brands powerfully and manage them well. They must build close brand relationships and experiences with customers.

3. *Measuring and managing return on marketing.* Marketing managers must ensure that their marketing dollars are being well spent. In the past, many marketers spent freely on big, expensive marketing programs, often without thinking carefully about the financial returns on their spending. But all that has changed rapidly. "Marketing accountability"—measuring and managing return on marketing investments—has now become an important part of strategic marketing decision making. This emphasis on marketing accountability is addressed throughout the fourteenth edition.

4. *Harnessing new marketing technologies.* New digital and other high-tech marketing developments are dramatically changing how consumers and marketers relate to one another. The fourteenth edition thoroughly explores the new technologies impacting marketing, from "Web 3.0" in Chapter 1 to new digital marketing and online technologies in Chapters 15 and 17 to the exploding use of online social networks and customer-generated marketing in Chapters 1, 5, 14, 15, 17, and elsewhere.

5. *Sustainable marketing around the globe.* As technological developments make the world an increasingly smaller and more fragile place, marketers must be good at marketing their brands globally and in sustainable ways. New material throughout the fourteenth edition emphasizes the concept of sustainable marketing—meeting the present needs of consumers and businesses while also preserving or enhancing the ability of future generations to meet their needs.

New in the Fourteenth Edition

We've thoroughly revised the fourteenth edition of *Principles of Marketing* to reflect the major trends and forces impacting marketing in this era of customer value and relationships. Here are just some of the major and continuing changes you'll find in this edition.

- New coverage in every chapter of the fourteenth edition shows how companies and consumers are dealing with **marketing and the uncertain economy** in the aftermath of the recent Great Recession. Starting with a major new section in Chapter 1 and continuing with new sections, discussions, and examples integrated throughout the text, the fourteenth edition shows how, now more than ever, marketers must focus on creating customer value and sharpening their value propositions to serve the needs of today's more frugal consumers. At the end of each chapter, a new feature—*Marketing and the Economy*—provides real examples for discussion and learning.

- Throughout the fourteenth edition, you will find revised coverage of the rapidly **changing nature of customer relationships** with companies and brands. Today's marketers aim to create deep consumer involvement and a sense of community surrounding a brand—to make the brand a meaningful part of consumers' conversations and their lives. Today's new relationship-building tools include everything from Web sites, blogs, in-person events, and video sharing to online communities and social networks such as Facebook, YouTube, Twitter, or a company's own social networking sites.

- The fourteenth edition contains new material on the continuing trend toward two-way interactions between customers and brands, including such topics as **customer-managed relationships**, **crowdsourcing**, and **consumer-generated marketing**. Today's customers are giving as much as they get in the form of two-way relationships (Chapter 1), a more active role in providing customer insights (Chapter 4), crowdsourcing and shaping new products (Chapter 9), consumer-generated marketing content (Chapters 1, 14, and 15), developing or passing along brand messages (Chapters 1 and 15), interacting in customer communities (Chapters 5, 15, and 17), and other developments.

- This edition provides revised and expanded discussions of new **marketing technologies**, from "Web 3.0" in Chapter 1 to "Webnography" research tools in Chapter 4 to neuromarketing in Chapter 5 and the dazzling new digital marketing and on-line technologies in Chapters 1, 15, and 17.

- New material throughout the fourteenth edition highlights the increasing importance of **sustainable marketing**. The discussion begins in Chapter 1 and ends in Chapter 20, which pulls marketing together under a sustainable marketing framework. In between, frequent discussions and examples show how sustainable marketing calls for socially and environmentally responsible actions that meet both the immediate and the future needs of customers, companies, and society as a whole.

- The fourteenth edition continues its emphasis on **measuring and managing return on marketing**, including many new end-of-chapter financial and quantitative marketing exercises that let students apply analytical thinking to relevant concepts in each chapter and link chapter concepts to the text's innovative and comprehensive *Appendix 2: Marketing by the Numbers*.

- The fourteenth edition provides revised and expanded coverage of the developments in the fast-changing areas of **integrated marketing communications** and **direct and online marketing**. It tells how marketers are blending the new digital and direct technologies with traditional media to create more targeted, personal, and interactive customer relationships. No other text provides more current or encompassing coverage of these exciting developments.

- Restructured **pricing** chapters (Chapters 10 and 11) provide improved coverage of pricing strategies and tactics in an uncertain economy. And a reorganized products, services, and brands chapter (Chapter 8) helps to promote the text's coverage of **services marketing** and better applies the branding strategy discussions that follow to both products and services.

- The fourteenth edition continues to improve on its **innovative learning design**. The text's active and integrative presentation includes learning enhancements such as annotated chapter-opening stories, a chapter-opening objective outline, and explanatory author comments on major chapter sections and figures. The chapter-opening layout helps to preview and position the chapter and its key concepts. Figures annotated with author comments help students to simplify and organize chapter material. End-of-chapter features help to summarize important chapter concepts and highlight important themes, such as marketing and the economy, marketing technology, ethics, and financial marketing analysis. In all, the innovative learning design facilitates student understanding and eases learning.

An Emphasis on Real Marketing

Principles of Marketing features in-depth, real-world examples and stories that show concepts in action and reveal the drama of modern marketing. In the fourteenth edition, every chapter opening vignette and Real Marketing highlight has been updated or replaced to provide fresh and relevant insights into real marketing practices. Learn how:

- Web seller Zappos.com's obsession with creating the very best customer experience has resulted in avidly loyal customers and astronomical growth.

- Nike's customer-focused mission and deep sense of customer brand community have the company sprinting ahead while competitors are gasping for breath.

- Trader Joe's unique "cheap gourmet" price-value strategy has earned it an almost cult-like following of devoted customers who love what they get for the prices they pay.

- ESPN has built a global brand empire as much recognized and revered as megabrands such as Coca-Cola, Nike, or Google.

- Dunkin' Donuts successfully targets the "Dunkin' Tribe"—not the Starbucks snob but the average Joe.

- When it comes to sustainability, no company in the world is doing more good these days than Walmart. That's right—big, bad, Walmart.

- Four Seasons hotels has perfected the art of high-touch, carefully crafted service, prompting one customer to reflect: "If there's a heaven, I hope it's run by Four Seasons."

- The "Häagen-Dazs loves honey bees" integrated marketing campaign has helped make Häagen-Dazs more than just another premium ice cream brand—it's now "a brand with a heart and a soul."

- Hyundai hit the accelerator on marketing when the slow economy caused rivals to throttle down, making it the world's fastest growing major car company.

- McDonald's, the quintessentially all-American company, now sells more burgers and fries outside the United States than within.

- Google's odyssey into mainland China—and back out again—vividly illustrates the prospects and perils of going global.

Beyond these features, each chapter is packed with countless real, relevant, and timely examples that reinforce key concepts. No other text brings marketing to life like the fourteenth edition of Principles of Marketing.

Valuable Learning Aids

A wealth of chapter-opening, within-chapter, and end-of-chapter learning devices help students to learn, link, and apply major concepts:

- *Chapter Preview.* As part of the active and integrative chapter-opening design, a brief section at the beginning of each chapter previews chapter concepts, links them with previous chapter concepts, and introduces the chapter-opening story.

- *Chapter-opening marketing stories.* Each chapter begins with an engaging, deeply developed, illustrated, and annotated marketing story that introduces the chapter material and sparks student interest.

- *Objective outline.* This chapter-opening feature provides a helpful preview outline of chapter contents and learning objectives, complete with page numbers.

- *Author comments and figure annotations.* Throughout the chapter, author comments ease and enhance student learning by introducing and explaining major chapter sections and organizing figures.

- *Real Marketing highlights.* Each chapter contains two highlight features that provide an in-depth look at real marketing practices of large and small companies.

- *Reviewing the Objectives and Key Terms.* A summary at the end of each chapter reviews major chapter concepts, chapter objectives, and key terms.

- *Discussing and Applying the Concepts.* Each chapter contains a set of discussion questions and application exercises covering major chapter concepts.

- *Marketing and the Economy.* End-of-chapter situation descriptions provide for discussion of the impact of recent economic trends on consumer and marketer decisions.

- *Focus on Technology.* Application exercises at the end of each chapter provide discussion of important and emerging marketing technologies in this digital age.

- *Focus on Ethics.* Situation descriptions and questions at the end of each chapter highlight important issues in marketing ethics.

- *Marketing by the Numbers.* An exercise at the end of each chapter lets students apply analytical and financial thinking to relevant chapter concepts and links the chapter to Appendix 2, Marketing by the Numbers.

- *Company Cases.* All new or revised company cases for class or written discussion are provided at the end of each chapter. These cases challenge students to apply marketing principles to real companies in real situations.

- *Video Shorts.* Short vignettes and discussion questions appear at the end of every chapter, to be used with the set of mostly new 4- to 7-minute videos that accompany this edition.

- *Marketing Plan appendix.* Appendix 1 contains a sample marketing plan that helps students to apply important marketing planning concepts.

- *Marketing by the Numbers appendix.* And innovative Appendix 2 provides students with a comprehensive introduction to the marketing financial analysis that helps to guide, assess, and support marketing decisions.

More than ever before, the fourteenth edition of *Principles of Marketing* creates value for you—it gives you all you need to know about marketing in an effective and enjoyable total learning package!

A Valuable Total Teaching and Learning Package

A successful marketing course requires more than a well-written book. A total package of resources extends this edition's emphasis on creating value for you. The following aids support *Principles of Marketing, 14e:*

Videos

The video library features 20 exciting segments for this edition. All segments are on the DVD (ISBN: 0-13-216723-9) and in mymarketinglab. Here are just a few of the videos that are offered:

Stew Leonard's Customer Relationships
Eaton's Dependable Customer Service
GoGurt's Winning Brand Management
FiberOne's Exponential Growth
Nestlé Waters' Personal Selling

PEARSON
mymarketinglab™

mymarketinglab (**www.mypearsonmarketinglab.com**) gives you the opportunity to test yourself on key concepts and skills, track your own progress through the course, and use the personalized study plan activities—all to help you achieve success in the classroom.

The MyLab that accompanies *Principles of Marketing* includes:

- *Study Plan:* The Study Plan helps ensure that you have a basic understanding of course material before coming to class by guiding you directly to the pages you need to review.

- *Mini-Simulations:* Move beyond the basics with interactive simulations that place you in a realistic marketing situation and require you to make decisions based on marketing concepts.

- *Applied Theories:* Get involved with detailed videos, interactive cases, and critical-thinking exercises.

- *Critical Thinking:* Get involved with real marketing situations that might not always have a right answer but will have a best answer. This allows for great discussion and debate with your classmates.

Plus:

- *Interactive Elements:* A wealth of hands-on activities and exercises let you experience and learn firsthand. Whether it is with the online e-book where you can search for specific keywords or page numbers, highlight specific sections, enter notes right on the e-book page, and print reading assignments with notes for later review or with other materials.

Find out more at **www.mypearsonmarketinglab.com**

More Valuable Resources

CourseSmart is an exciting new choice for students looking to save money. As an alternative to purchasing the print textbook, students can purchase an electronic version of the same content and save up to 50 percent off the suggested list price of the print text. With a CourseSmart eTextbook, students can search the text, make notes online, print out reading assignments that incorporate lecture notes, and bookmark important passages for later review. For more information, or to purchase access to the CourseSmart eTextbook, visit www.coursesmart.com.

Acknowledgments

No book is the work only of its authors. We greatly appreciate the valuable contributions of several people who helped make this new edition possible. As always, we owe very special thanks to Keri Jean Miksza for her dedicated and valuable help in *all* phases of the project, and to her husband Pete and little daughter Lucy for all the support they provide Keri during this often-hectic project.

We thank Andy Norman of Drake University for his skillful development of company and video cases and help with preparing selected marketing stories; and Lew Brown of the University of North Carolina at Greensboro for his able assistance in helping prepare selected marketing stories and highlights. We also thank Laurie Babin of the University of Louisiana at Monroe for her dedicated efforts in preparing end-of-chapter materials and keeping our Marketing by the Numbers appendix fresh; and to Michelle Rai of Pacific Union College for her able updates to the Marketing Plan appendix. Additional thanks also go to Andy Lingwall at Clarion University of Pennsylvania, for his work on the Instructor's Manual; Peter Bloch at University of Missouri and ANS Source for developing the Power Points; and Bonnie Flaherty for creating the Test Item File & Study Plan.

Many reviewers at other colleges and universities provided valuable comments and suggestions for this and previous editions. We are indebted to the following colleagues for their thoughtful inputs:

Fourteenth Edition Reviewers

Alan Dick, University of Buffalo

Rod Carveth, Naugatuck Valley Community College

Anindja Chatterjee, Slippery Rock University of Pennsylvania

Mary Conran, Temple University

Eloise Coupey, Virginia Tech

Karen Gore, Ivy Tech Community College, Evansville Campus

Charles Lee, Chestnut Hill College

Samuel McNeely, Murray State University

Chip Miller, Drake University

David Murphy, Madisonville Community College

Esther Page-Wood, Western Michigan University

Tim Reisenwitz, Valdosta State University

Mary Ellen Rosetti, Hudson Valley Community College

William Ryan, University of Connecticut

Roberta Schultz, Western Michigan University

J. Alexander Smith, Oklahoma City University

Deb Utter, Boston University

Donna Waldron, Manchester Community College

Wendel Weaver, Oklahoma Wesleyan University

Previous Reviewers

Praveen Aggarwal, University of Minnesota, Duluth

Ron Adams, University of North Florida

Sana Akili, Iowa State University

Mary Albrecht, Maryville University

Mark Alpert, University of Texas at Austin

Mark Anderson, Eastern Kentucky University

Lydia E. Anderson, Fresno City College

Allan L. Appell, San Francisco State University

Laurie Babin, University of Louisiana at Monroe

Michael Ballif, University of Utah

Pat Bernson, County College of Morris

Roger Berry, California State University, Dominguez Hills

Amit Bhatnagar, University of Wisconsin

Donald L. Brady, Millersville University

Thomas Brashear, University of Massachusetts, Amherst

Fred Brunel, Boston University

Jeff Bryden, Bowling Green University

David J. Burns, Youngstown State University

Kirsten Cardenas, University of Miami

Rod Carveth, Naugatuck Valley Community College

Glenn Chappell, Coker College

Hongsik John Cheon, Frostburg State University

Sang T. Choe, University of Southern Indiana

Glenn L. Christensen, Brigham Young University

Kathleen Conklin, St. John Fisher College

Mary Conran, Temple University

Michael Coolsen, Shippensburg University

Alicia Cooper, Morgan State University

Douglas A. Cords, California State University, Fresno

Preyas Desai, Purdue University

Philip Gelman, College of DuPage

James L. Giordano, La Guardia Community College

Karen Gore, Ivy Tech Community College, Evansville Campus

Hugh Guffey, Auburn University

Kenny Herbst, Saint Joseph's University

Terry Holmes, Murray State University

David Houghton, Charleston Southern University

Pat Jacoby, Purdue University

Carol Johanek, Washington University

Eileen Kearney, Montgomery County Community College

Thomas R. Keen, Caldwell College

Tina Kiesler, California State University at North Ridge

Dmitri Kuksov, Washington University in St. Louis

Bruce Lammers, California State University at North Ridge

J. Ford Laumer, Auburn University

Debra Laverie, Texas Tech University

Kenneth Lawrence, New Jersey Institute of Technology

Richard Leventhal, Metropolitan State College, Denver

Charles Lee, Chestnut Hill College

Marilyn Liebrenz-Himes, George Washington University

Dolly D. Loyd, University of Southern Mississippi

Kerri Lum, Kapiolani Community College

Larry Maes, Davenport University

Tamara Mangleburg, Florida Atlantic University

Patricia M. Manninen, North Shore Community College

Wendy Martin, Judson College, Illinois

Patrick H. McCaskey, Millersville University

June McDowell-Davis, Catawba College/High Point University

Samuel McNeely, Murray State University

H. Lee Meadow, Indiana University East

H. Lee Meadow, Northern Illinois University

John Mellon, College Misericordia

Mohan K. Menon, University of Southern Alabama

Martin Meyers, University of Wisconsin, Stevens Point

Chip Miller, Drake University

William Mindak, Tulane University

Ted Mitchell, University of Nevada, Reno

David Murphy, Madisonville Community College

David M. Nemi, Niagra County Community College

Carl Obermiller, Seattle University

Howard Olsen, University of Nevada at Reno

Betty Parker, Western Michigan University

Vanessa Perry, George Washington University

Susan Peterson, Scottsdale Community College

Abe Qastin, Lakeland College

Paul Redig, Milwaukee Area Technical College

William Renforth, Angelo State University

Gregory A. Rich, Bowling Green State University

William Ryan, University of Connecticut

Melinda Schmitz, Pamlico Community College

Roberta Schultz, Western Michigan University

Alan T. Shao, University of North Carolina, Charlotte

Lynne Smith, Carroll Community College

Martin St. John, Westmoreland County Community College

Randy Stewart, Kennesaw State University

Karen Stone, Southern New Hampshire University

John Stovall, University of Illinois, Chicago

Jeff Streiter, SUNY Brockport

Ruth Taylor, Texas State University

Donna Tillman, California State Polytechnic University

Janice Trafflet, Bucknell University

Rafael Valiente, University of Miami

Simon Walls, University of Tennessee

Donna Waldron, Manchester Community College

Mark Wasserman, University of Texas

Alvin Williams, University of Southern Mississippi

Douglas E. Witt, Brigham Young University

Andrew Yap, Florida International University

Irvin A. Zaenglein, Northern Michigan University

Larry Zigler, Highland Community College

We also owe a great deal to the people at Pearson Prentice Hall who helped develop this book. Executive Editor Melissa Sabella provided fresh ideas and support throughout to revision. Project Manager Meeta Pendharkar provided valuable assistance in managing the many facets of this complex revision project. Janet Slowik developed the fourteenth edition's exciting design, and Senior Production Project Manager Karalyn Holland helped guide the book through the complex production process. We'd also like to thank Elisabeth Scarpa, Anne Fahlgren, and Judy Leale. We are proud to be associated with the fine professionals at Pearson Prentice Hall. We also owe a mighty debt of gratitude to Project Editor Lynn Steines and the fine team at S4Carlisle Publishing Services.

Finally, we owe many thanks to our families for all of their support and encouragement —Kathy, Betty, Mandy, Matt, KC, Keri, Delaney, Molly, Macy, and Ben from the Armstrong clan and Nancy, Amy, Melissa, and Jessica from the Kotler family. To them, we dedicate this book.

Gary Armstrong
Philip Kotler

Principles of

Marketing

Marketing
Creating and Capturing **Customer Value**

Chapter Preview

This chapter introduces you to the basic concepts of marketing. We start with the question, What is marketing? Simply put, marketing is managing profitable customer relationships. The aim of marketing is to create value for customers and capture value from customers in return. Next we discuss the five steps in the marketing process—from understanding customer needs, to designing customer-driven marketing strategies and integrated marketing programs, to building customer relationships and capturing value for the firm. Finally, we discuss the major trends and forces affecting marketing in this age of customer relationships. Understanding these basic concepts and forming your own ideas about what they really mean to you will give you a solid foundation for all that follows.

Let's start with a good story about marketing in action at Zappos.com, one of the world's fastest-growing Web retailers. The secret to Zappos' success? It's really no secret at all. Zappos is flat-out customer obsessed. It has a passion for creating customer value and relationships. In return, customers reward Zappos with their brand loyalty and buying dollars. You'll see this theme of creating customer value in order to capture value in return repeated throughout this first chapter and the remainder of the text.

Zappos: A Passion for Creating Customer Value and Relationships

Imagine a retailer with service so good its customers wish it would take over the Internal Revenue Service or start up an airline. It might sound like a marketing fantasy, but this scenario is reality for 12-year-old Zappos.com. At Zappos, the customer experience really does come first—it's a daily obsession. Says Zappos understated CEO, Tony Hsieh (pronounced *shay*), "Our whole goal at Zappos is for the Zappos brand to be about the very best customer service and customer experience." When it comes to creating customer value and relationships, few companies can match Zappos' passion.

Launched in 1999 as a Web site that offered the absolute best selection in shoes—in terms of brands, styles, colors, sizes, and widths—the online retailer now carries many other categories of goods, such as clothing, handbags, and accessories. From the start, the scrappy Web retailer made customer service a cornerstone of its marketing. As a result, Zappos has grown astronomically. It now serves more than 10 million customers annually, and gross merchandise sales top $1 billion, up from only $1.6 million in 2000. Three percent of the U.S. population now shops at Zappos.com. And despite the harsh economy, Zappos sales have continued to soar in recent years.

Interestingly, Zappos doesn't spend a lot of money on media advertising. Instead, it relies on customer service so good that customers not only come back but also tell their friends. More than 75 percent of Zappos.com's sales come from repeat customers. "We actually take a lot of the money that we would have normally spent on paid advertising and put it back into the customer experience," says Hsieh. "We've always stuck with customer service, even when it was not a sexy thing to do." Adds Aaron Magness, Zappos' director of business development and brand marketing, "We decided if we can put all the money possible into our customer service, word of mouth will work in our favor."

What little advertising the company does do focuses on—you guessed it—customer service. The most recent Zappos TV ads feature "Zappets," puppetlike characters styled after actual Zappos employees, highlighting interactions between Zappos customer service reps and customers.

Free delivery, free returns, and a 365-day return policy have been the cornerstone of Zappos' customer-centric approach. To wow customers, it even quietly upgrades the experience, from four-to-five-day shipping to second-day or next-day shipping. Its customer service center is staffed 24/7 with 500 highly motivated employees—about one-third of the company's payroll—answering 5,000 calls a day. "Those things are all pretty expensive, but we view that as our marketing dollars," says Hsieh. "It's just a lot cheaper to get existing customers to buy from you again than it is to try to convince someone [new]."

Zappos has been steadfast in its focus on customer service even as it's grown. In a sluggish economy, retailers especially should be focusing on customer service. But as Hsieh points out, it's often the first thing to go. "The payoff for great customer service might be a year or two down the line. And the payoff for having a great company culture might be three or four years down the line."

At Zappos, customer intimacy starts with a deep-down, customer-focused culture. "We have a saying," proclaims the company at its Web site. "We are a service company that happens to sell [shoes (or handbags, or clothing, or eventually, anything and everything)]." The Zappos culture is built around its 10 Core Values, ranging from "Build open and honest relationships with communication" to "Create fun and a little weirdness." Value number one: "Deliver WOW through service!"

Zappos' online success and passion for customers made it an ideal match for another highly successful, customer-obsessed online retailer, Amazon.com, which purchased Zappos in late 2009. Amazon.com appears to be letting Hsieh and Zappos continue to pursue independently the strategy that has made them so successful in the past.

To make sure Zappos' customer obsession permeates the entire organization, each new hire—everyone from the chief executive officer and chief financial officer to the children's footwear buyer—is required to go through four weeks of customer-loyalty training. In fact, in an effort to weed out the half-hearted, Zappos actually bribes people to quit. During the four weeks of customer service training, it offers employees $2,000 cash, plus payment for the time worked, if they leave the company. The theory goes that those willing to take the money and run aren't right for Zappos' culture anyway.

Hsieh says that originally the incentive was $100, but the amount keeps rising because not enough people take it. On average, only 1 percent takes the offer, and Hsieh believes that's too low. Zappos argues that each employee needs to be a great point of contact with customers. "Getting customers excited about the service they had at Zappos has to come naturally," says Magness. "You can't teach it; you have to hire for it."

When dealing with customers, Zappos employees must check their egos and competitiveness at the door. Customer service reps are trained to look on at least three rival Web sites if a shopper asks for specific shoes that Zappos doesn't have in stock and refer customers accordingly. "My guess is that other companies don't do that," Hsieh says. "For us, we're willing to lose that sale, that transaction in the short term. We're focused on building the lifelong loyalty and relationship with the customer."

Relationships mean everything at Zappos. Hsieh and many other employees stay in direct touch with customers, with each other, and with just about anyone else interested in the company. They use social-networking tools, such as Facebook, Twitter, and blogs, to share information—both good and bad. And the company invites customers to submit frank online reviews. Such openness might worry some retailers, but Zappos embraces it. As Magness points out, "You only

"A woman just called and asked if we sold dresses. I told her we had hundreds of dresses from the biggest designers. Know what she said? She said, 'I love you.' Actually, she said, 'Thank you,' but I read between the lines."

At Zappos, taking care of customers starts with a deep-down, customer-focused culture. Zappos is "happy to help, 24/7."

need to worry if you have something to hide," and Zappos seems to take even criticism as a free gift of information.

Zappos has set new standards in the industry, leading the way for a new type of consumer-focused company. "There's something about these young Internet companies," says a retailing expert. "I'm not sure exactly why—if it was because they were born in a different era, the leadership has a different worldview, or if they just have amazing access to customer data and see firsthand what customers are thinking," he says. "It seems that Zappos is really the poster child for this new age of consumer companies that truly are customer focused. A lot of companies like to say they are, but none of them is as serious as Zappos."

It's that intense customer focus that has set the stage for Zappos' growth, as the company branches out into new categories, such as electronics and home goods. "Hopefully, 10 years from now, people won't even realize we started out selling shoes online. We've actually had customers ask us if we would please start an airline or run the IRS," Hsieh says, adding, "30 years from now I wouldn't rule out a Zappos airline that's all about the very best service."[1]

Web seller Zappos is obsessed with creating the very best customer service and customer experience. In return, customers reward the company with their brand loyalty and buying dollars. The result: Zappos' sales have grown astronomically.

Today's successful companies have one thing in common: Like Zappos, they are strongly customer focused and heavily committed to marketing. These companies share a passion for understanding and satisfying customer needs in well-defined target markets. They motivate everyone in the organization to help build lasting customer relationships based on creating value.

Customer relationships and value are especially important today. As the nation's economy has recovered following the worst downturn since the Great Depression, more frugal consumers are spending more carefully and reassessing their relationships with brands. In turn, it's more important than ever to build strong customer relationships based on real and enduring value.

| **Author Comment** | Stop here for a second and think about how you'd answer this question before studying marketing. Then see how your answer changes as you read the chapter. |

What Is Marketing? (pp 4–5)

Marketing, more than any other business function, deals with customers. Although we will soon explore more-detailed definitions of marketing, perhaps the simplest definition is this one: *Marketing is managing profitable customer relationships.* The twofold goal of marketing is to attract new customers by promising superior value and keep and grow current customers by delivering satisfaction.

For example, Walmart has become the world's largest retailer—and the world's largest company—by delivering on its promise, "Save money. Live better." Nintendo surged ahead in the video-games market behind the pledge that "Wii would like to play," backed by its wildly popular Wii console and a growing list of popular games and accessories for all ages. And McDonald's fulfills its "i'm lovin' it" motto by being "our customers' favorite place and way to eat" the world over, giving it a market share greater than that of its nearest three competitors combined.[2]

Sound marketing is critical to the success of every organization. Large for-profit firms, such as Procter & Gamble, Google, Target, Toyota, and Marriott use marketing. But so do not-for-profit organizations, such as colleges, hospitals, museums, symphony orchestras, and even churches.

You already know a lot about marketing—it's all around you. Marketing comes to you in the good old traditional forms: You see it in the abundance of products at your nearby shopping mall and the ads that fill your TV screen, spice up your magazines, or stuff your mailbox. But in recent years, marketers have assembled a host of new marketing approaches, everything from imaginative Web sites and online social networks to your cell phone. These new approaches do more than just blast out messages to the masses. They reach you directly and personally. Today's marketers want to become a part of your life and enrich your experiences with their brands—to help you *live* their brands.

At home, at school, where you work, and where you play, you see marketing in almost everything you do. Yet, there is much more to marketing than meets the consumer's casual eye. Behind it all is a massive network of people and activities competing for your attention and purchases. This book will give you a complete introduction to the basic concepts and practices of today's marketing. In this chapter, we begin by defining marketing and the marketing process.

Marketing Defined

What *is* marketing? Many people think of marketing as only selling and advertising. We are bombarded every day with TV commercials, catalogs, sales calls, and e-mail pitches. However, selling and advertising are only the tip of the marketing iceberg.

Today, marketing must be understood not in the old sense of making a sale—"telling and selling"—but in the new sense of *satisfying customer needs.* If the marketer understands consumer needs; develops products that provide superior customer value; and prices, distributes, and promotes them effectively, these products will sell easily. In fact, according to management guru Peter Drucker, "The aim of marketing is to make selling unnecessary."[3] Selling and advertising are only part of a larger "marketing mix"—a set of marketing tools that work together to satisfy customer needs and build customer relationships.

Broadly defined, marketing is a social and managerial process by which individuals and organizations obtain what they need and want through creating and exchanging value with others. In a narrower business context, marketing involves building profitable, value-laden exchange relationships with customers. Hence, we define **marketing** as the process by which companies create value for customers and build strong customer relationships in order to capture value from customers in return.[4]

Marketing
The process by which companies create value for customers and build strong customer relationships in order to capture value from customers in return.

The Marketing Process

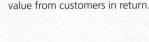 **Figure 1.1** presents a simple, five-step model of the marketing process. In the first four steps, companies work to understand consumers, create customer value, and build strong customer relationships. In the final step, companies reap the rewards of creating superior customer value. By creating value *for* consumers, they in turn capture value *from* consumers in the form of sales, profits, and long-term customer equity.

In this chapter and the next, we will examine the steps of this simple model of marketing. In this chapter, we review each step but focus more on the customer relationship steps—understanding customers, building customer relationships, and capturing value from customers. In Chapter 2, we look more deeply into the second and third steps—designing marketing strategies and constructing marketing programs.

This important figure shows marketing in a nutshell! By creating value *for* customers, marketers capture value *from* customers in return. This five-step process forms the marketing framework for the rest of the chapter and the remainder of the text.

Create value *for customers* and build customer relationships

Capture value *from* customers in return

| Understand the marketplace and customer needs and wants | Design a customer-driven marketing strategy | Construct an integrated marketing program that delivers superior value | Build profitable relationships and create customer delight | Capture value from customers to create profits and customer equity |

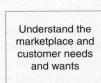
● FIGURE | 1.1
A Simple Model of the Marketing Process

Understanding the Marketplace and Customer Needs (pp 6–8)

As a first step, marketers need to understand customer needs and wants and the marketplace in which they operate. We examine five core customer and marketplace concepts: (1) *needs, wants, and demands*; (2) *market offerings (products, services, and experiences)*; (3) *value and satisfaction*; (4) *exchanges and relationships*; and (5) *markets*.

Customer Needs, Wants, and Demands

The most basic concept underlying marketing is that of human needs. Human **needs** are states of felt deprivation. They include basic *physical* needs for food, clothing, warmth, and safety; *social* needs for belonging and affection; and *individual* needs for knowledge and self-expression. Marketers did not create these needs; they are a basic part of the human makeup.

Wants are the form human needs take as they are shaped by culture and individual personality. An American *needs* food but *wants* a Big Mac, french fries, and a soft drink. A person in Papua New Guinea *needs* food but *wants* taro, rice, yams, and pork. Wants are shaped by one's society and are described in terms of objects that will satisfy those needs. When backed by buying power, wants become **demands**. Given their wants and resources, people demand products with benefits that add up to the most value and satisfaction.

Outstanding marketing companies go to great lengths to learn about and understand their customers' needs, wants, and demands. They conduct consumer research and analyze mountains of customer data. Their people at all levels—including top management—stay close to customers. For example, retailer Cabela's vice-chairman, James W. Cabela, spends hours each morning reading through customer comments and hand-delivering them to each department, circling important customer issues. At Zappos, CEO Tony Hsieh uses Twitter to build more personal connections with customers and employees. Some 1.6 million people follow Hsieh's Twitter feed. And at P&G, executives from the chief executive officer down spend time with consumers in their homes and on shopping trips. P&G brand managers routinely spend a week or two living on the budget of low-end consumers to gain insights into what they can do to improve customers' lives.[5]

Needs
States of felt deprivation.

Wants
The form human needs take as they are shaped by culture and individual personality.

Demands
Human wants that are backed by buying power.

Market Offerings—Products, Services, and Experiences

Consumers' needs and wants are fulfilled through **market offerings**—some combination of products, services, information, or experiences offered to a market to satisfy a need or a want. Market offerings are not limited to physical *products*. They also include *services*—activities or benefits offered for sale that are essentially intangible and do not result in the ownership of anything. Examples include banking, airline, hotel, tax preparation, and home repair services.

Market offerings
Some combination of products, services, information, or experiences offered to a market to satisfy a need or want.

More broadly, market offerings also include other entities, such as *persons, places, organizations, information,* and *ideas*. For example, the "Pure Michigan" campaign markets the state of Michigan as a tourism destination that "lets unspoiled nature and authentic character revive your spirits." ◉ And the U.S. Forest Service's "Reconnecting Kids with Nature" campaign markets the idea of encouraging urban young people to explore the joys of nature firsthand. Its DiscoverTheForest.org Web site helps children and their parents figure out where to go outdoors and what to do there.[6]

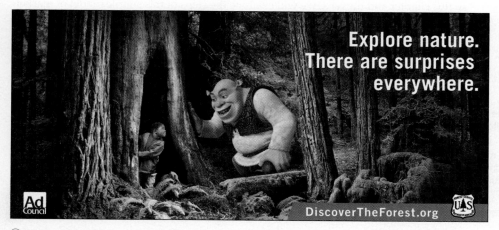

Explore nature. There are surprises everywhere.

DiscoverTheForest.org

◉ Market offerings are not limited to physical products. Here, the U.S. Forest Service markets the idea of reconnecting young people with exploring the joys of nature firsthand.

Many sellers make the mistake of paying more attention to the specific products they offer than to the benefits and experiences produced by these products. These sellers suffer from **marketing myopia**. They are so taken with their products that they focus only on existing wants and lose sight of underlying customer needs.[7] They forget that a product is only a tool to solve a consumer problem. A manufacturer of quarter-inch drill bits may think that the customer needs a drill bit. But what the customer *really* needs is a quarter-inch hole. These sellers will have trouble if a new product comes along that serves the customer's need better or less expensively. The customer will have the same *need* but will *want* the new product.

Marketing myopia
The mistake of paying more attention to the specific products a company offers than to the benefits and experiences produced by these products.

Smart marketers look beyond the attributes of the products and services they sell. By orchestrating several services and products, they create *brand experiences* for consumers. For example, you don't just watch a NASCAR race; you immerse yourself in the exhilarating, high-octane NASCAR experience. Similarly, HP recognizes that a personal computer is much more than just a collection of wires and electrical components. It's an intensely personal user experience. As noted in one HP ad, "There is hardly anything that you own that is *more* personal. Your personal computer is your backup brain. It's your life. . . . It's your astonishing strategy, staggering proposal, dazzling calculation. It's your autobiography, written in a thousand daily words."[8]

Customer Value and Satisfaction

Consumers usually face a broad array of products and services that might satisfy a given need. How do they choose among these many market offerings? Customers form expectations about the value and satisfaction that various market offerings will deliver and buy accordingly. Satisfied customers buy again and tell others about their good experiences. Dissatisfied customers often switch to competitors and disparage the product to others.

Marketers must be careful to set the right level of expectations. If they set expectations too low, they may satisfy those who buy but fail to attract enough buyers. If they set expectations too high, buyers will be disappointed. Customer value and customer satisfaction are key building blocks for developing and managing customer relationships. We will revisit these core concepts later in the chapter.

Exchanges and Relationships

Marketing occurs when people decide to satisfy needs and wants through exchange relationships. **Exchange** is the act of obtaining a desired object from someone by offering something in return. In the broadest sense, the marketer tries to bring about a response to some market offering. The response may be more than simply buying or trading products and services. A political candidate, for instance, wants votes, a church wants membership, an orchestra wants an audience, and a social action group wants idea acceptance.

Exchange
The act of obtaining a desired object from someone by offering something in return.

Marketing consists of actions taken to build and maintain desirable exchange *relationships* with target audiences involving a product, service, idea, or other object. Beyond simply attracting new customers and creating transactions, companies want to retain customers and grow their businesses. Marketers want to build strong relationships by consistently delivering superior customer value. We will expand on the important concept of managing customer relationships later in the chapter.

Markets

The concepts of exchange and relationships lead to the concept of a market. A **market** is the set of actual and potential buyers of a product or service. These buyers share a particular need or want that can be satisfied through exchange relationships.

Market
The set of all actual and potential buyers of a product or service.

Marketing means managing markets to bring about profitable customer relationships. However, creating these relationships takes work. Sellers must search for buyers, identify their needs, design good market offerings, set prices for them, promote them, and store and deliver them. Activities such as consumer research, product development, communication, distribution, pricing, and service are core marketing activities.

Although we normally think of marketing as being carried out by sellers, buyers also carry out marketing. Consumers market when they search for products, interact with

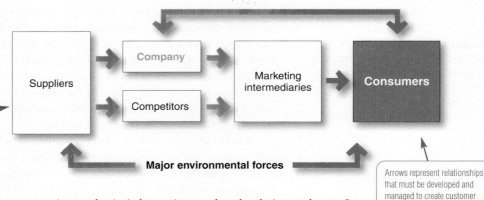

Each party in the system adds value. Walmart cannot fulfill its promise of low prices unless its suppliers provide low costs. Ford cannot deliver a high quality car-ownership experience unless its dealers provide outstanding service.

Major environmental forces

Arrows represent relationships that must be developed and managed to create customer value and profitable customer relationships.

companies to obtain information, and make their purchases. In fact, today's digital technologies, from Web sites and online social networks to cell phones, have empowered consumers and made marketing a truly interactive affair. Thus, in addition to customer relationship management, today's marketers must also deal effectively with *customer-managed relationships*. Marketers are no longer asking only "How can we reach our customers?" but also "How should our customers reach us?" and even "How can our customers reach each other?"

● **Figure 1.2** shows the main elements in a marketing system. Marketing involves serving a market of final consumers in the face of competitors. The company and competitors research the market and interact with consumers to understand their needs. Then they create and send their market offerings and messages to consumers, either directly or through marketing intermediaries. Each party in the system is affected by major environmental forces (demographic, economic, natural, technological, political, and social/cultural).

Each party in the system adds value for the next level. The arrows represent relationships that must be developed and managed. Thus, a company's success at building profitable relationships depends not only on its own actions but also on how well the entire system serves the needs of final consumers. Walmart cannot fulfill its promise of low prices unless its suppliers provide merchandise at low costs. And Ford cannot deliver a high quality car-ownership experience unless its dealers provide outstanding sales and service.

Author | Now that the company
Comment | fully understands its
consumers and the marketplace, it
must decide which customers it will
serve and how it will bring them value.

Designing a Customer-Driven Marketing Strategy (pp 8–12)

Once it fully understands consumers and the marketplace, marketing management can design a customer-driven marketing strategy. We define **marketing management** as the art and science of choosing target markets and building profitable relationships with them. The marketing manager's aim is to find, attract, keep, and grow target customers by creating, delivering, and communicating superior customer value.

Marketing management
The art and science of choosing target markets and building profitable relationships with them.

To design a winning marketing strategy, the marketing manager must answer two important questions: *What customers will we serve (what's our target market)?* and *How can we serve these customers best (what's our value proposition)?* We will discuss these marketing strategy concepts briefly here and then look at them in more detail in Chapters 2 and 7.

Selecting Customers to Serve

The company must first decide *whom* it will serve. It does this by dividing the market into segments of customers (*market segmentation*) and selecting which segments it will go after (*target marketing*). Some people think of marketing management as finding as many customers as possible and increasing demand. But marketing managers know that they cannot serve all customers in every way. By trying to serve all customers, they may not serve any customers well. Instead, the company wants to select only customers that it can serve well

It's a fuel-efficient fan favorite. Chalk it up to the smart fortwo's innate charm. Superb Mercedes-Benz engineering. Vast amounts of head and legroom. Exceptional safety ratings. And of course, its EPA-estimated 41 mpg highway. The smart fortwo is the guilt-free, 95% recyclable way to go from your driveway to virtually anywhere. And every mile, every turn, every stop along the way is fun. Sorry, big guy. Efficiency is in these days. smartusa.com

⦿ **Value propositions:** Smart car suggests that you "open your mind"—"Sorry, big guy. Efficiency is in these days."

and profitably. For example, Nordstrom profitably targets affluent professionals; Dollar General profitably targets families with more modest means.

Ultimately, marketing managers must decide which customers they want to target and on level, timing, and nature of their demand. Simply put, marketing management is *customer management* and *demand management*.

Choosing a Value Proposition

The company must also decide how it will serve targeted customers—how it will *differentiate and position* itself in the marketplace. A brand's *value proposition* is the set of benefits or values it promises to deliver to consumers to satisfy their needs. At AT&T, it's "Your World. Delivered." whereas with T-Mobile, family and friends can "Stick together." The diminutive Smart car suggests that you "Open your mind to the car that challenges the status quo," whereas Infiniti "Makes luxury affordable," and BMW promises "the ultimate driving machine."

Such value propositions differentiate one brand from another. They answer the customer's question, "Why should I buy your brand rather than a competitor's?" Companies must design strong value propositions that give them the greatest advantage in their target markets. ⦿ For example, the Smart car is positioned as compact, yet comfortable; agile, yet economical; and safe, yet ecological. It's "sheer automotive genius in a totally fun, efficient package. Smart thinking, indeed."

Marketing Management Orientations

Marketing management wants to design strategies that will build profitable relationships with target consumers. But what *philosophy* should guide these marketing strategies? What weight should be given to the interests of customers, the organization, and society? Very often, these interests conflict.

There are five alternative concepts under which organizations design and carry out their marketing strategies: the *production*, *product*, *selling*, *marketing*, and *societal marketing concepts*.

The Production Concept

Production concept
The idea that consumers will favor products that are available and highly affordable and that the organization should therefore focus on improving production and distribution efficiency.

The **production concept** holds that consumers will favor products that are available and highly affordable. Therefore, management should focus on improving production and distribution efficiency. This concept is one of the oldest orientations that guides sellers.

The production concept is still a useful philosophy in some situations. For example, computer maker Lenovo dominates the highly competitive, price-sensitive Chinese PC market through low labor costs, high production efficiency, and mass distribution. However, although useful in some situations, the production concept can lead to marketing myopia. Companies adopting this orientation run a major risk of focusing too narrowly on their own operations and losing sight of the real objective—satisfying customer needs and building customer relationships.

The Product Concept

Product concept
The idea that consumers will favor products that offer the most quality, performance, and features and that the organization should therefore devote its energy to making continuous product improvements.

The **product concept** holds that consumers will favor products that offer the most in quality, performance, and innovative features. Under this concept, marketing strategy focuses on making continuous product improvements.

Product quality and improvement are important parts of most marketing strategies. However, focusing *only* on the company's products can also lead to marketing myopia. For example, some manufacturers believe that if they can "build a better mousetrap, the world will beat a path to their doors." But they are often rudely shocked. Buyers may be looking for a better solution to a mouse problem but not necessarily for a better mousetrap. The better solution might be a chemical spray, an exterminating service, a house cat, or something else that works even better than a mousetrap. Furthermore, a better mousetrap will not sell unless the manufacturer designs, packages, and prices it attractively; places it in convenient distribution channels; brings it to the attention of people who need it; and convinces buyers that it is a better product.

The Selling Concept

Selling concept
The idea that consumers will not buy enough of the firm's products unless it undertakes a large-scale selling and promotion effort.

Many companies follow the selling concept, which holds that consumers will not buy enough of the firm's products unless it undertakes a large-scale selling and promotion effort. The **selling concept** is typically practiced with unsought goods—those that buyers do not normally think of buying, such as insurance or blood donations. These industries must be good at tracking down prospects and selling them on a product's benefits.

Such aggressive selling, however, carries high risks. It focuses on creating sales transactions rather than on building long-term, profitable customer relationships. The aim often is to sell what the company makes rather than making what the market wants. It assumes that customers who are coaxed into buying the product will like it. Or, if they don't like it, they will possibly forget their disappointment and buy it again later. These are usually poor assumptions.

The Marketing Concept

Marketing concept
A philosophy that holds that achieving organizational goals depends on knowing the needs and wants of target markets and delivering the desired satisfactions better than competitors do.

The **marketing concept** holds that achieving organizational goals depends on knowing the needs and wants of target markets and delivering the desired satisfactions better than competitors do. Under the marketing concept, customer focus and value are the *paths* to sales and profits. Instead of a product-centered "make and sell" philosophy, the marketing concept is a customer-centered "sense and respond" philosophy. The job is not to find the right customers for your product but to find the right products for your customers.

● **Figure 1.3** contrasts the selling concept and the marketing concept. The selling concept takes an *inside-out* perspective. It starts with the factory, focuses on the company's existing products, and calls for heavy selling and promotion to obtain profitable sales. It focuses primarily on customer conquest—getting short-term sales with little concern about who buys or why.

In contrast, the marketing concept takes an *outside-in* perspective. As Herb Kelleher, the colorful founder of Southwest Airlines puts it, "We don't have a marketing department; we have a customer department." The marketing concept starts with a well-defined market, focuses on customer needs, and integrates all the marketing activities that affect customers. In turn, it yields profits by creating lasting relationships with the right customers based on customer value and satisfaction.

Implementing the marketing concept often means more than simply responding to customers' stated desires and obvious needs. *Customer-driven* companies research current customers deeply to learn about their desires, gather new product and service ideas, and test proposed product improvements. Such customer-driven marketing usually works well when a clear need exists and when customers know what they want.

● **FIGURE | 1.3**
Selling and Marketing Concepts Contrasted

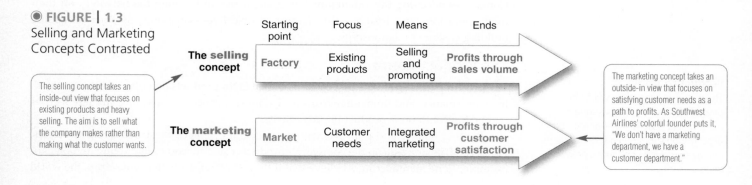

The selling concept takes an inside-out view that focuses on existing products and heavy selling. The aim is to sell what the company makes rather than making what the customer wants.

	Starting point	Focus	Means	Ends
The selling concept	Factory	Existing products	Selling and promoting	**Profits through sales volume**
The marketing concept	Market	Customer needs	Integrated marketing	**Profits through customer satisfaction**

The marketing concept takes an outside-in view that focuses on satisfying customer needs as a path to profits. As Southwest Airlines' colorful founder puts it, "We don't have a marketing department, we have a customer department."

⊙ **Customer-driving marketing: Even 20 years ago, how many consumers would have thought to ask for now-commonplace products such as cell phones, notebook computers, iPods, and digital cameras? Marketers must often understand customer needs even better than the customers themselves do.**

Societal marketing concept
The idea that a company's marketing decisions should consider consumers' wants, the company's requirements, consumers' long-run interests, and society's long-run interests.

In many cases, however, customers *don't* know what they want or even what is possible. ⊙ For example, even 20 years ago, how many consumers would have thought to ask for now-commonplace products such as notebook computers, cell phones, digital cameras, 24-hour online buying, and satellite navigation systems in their cars? Such situations call for *customer-driving* marketing—understanding customer needs even better than customers themselves do and creating products and services that meet existing and latent needs, now and in the future. As an executive at 3M puts it, "Our goal is to lead customers where they want to go before *they* know where they want to go."

The Societal Marketing Concept

The **societal marketing concept** questions whether the pure marketing concept overlooks possible conflicts between consumer *short-run wants* and consumer *long-run welfare*. Is a firm that satisfies the immediate needs and wants of target markets always doing what's best for its consumers in the long run? The societal marketing concept holds that marketing strategy should deliver value to customers in a way that maintains or improves both the consumer's *and society's* well-being. It calls for *sustainable marketing*, socially and environmentally responsible marketing that meets the present needs of consumers and businesses while also preserving or enhancing the ability of future generations to meet their needs.

Consider today's bottled water industry. You may view bottled water companies as offering a convenient, tasty, and healthy product. Its packaging suggests "green" images of pristine lakes and snow-capped mountains. Yet making, filling, and shipping billions of plastic bottles generates huge amounts of carbon dioxide emissions that contribute substantially to global warming. Further, the plastic bottles pose a substantial recycling and solid waste disposal problem. Thus, in satisfying short-term consumer wants, the bottled water industry may be causing environmental problems that run against society's long-run interests.

As ⊙ **Figure 1.4** shows, companies should balance three considerations in setting their marketing strategies: company profits, consumer wants, *and* society's interests. UPS does this well. Its concern for societal interests has earned it the number one or number two spot in *Fortune* magazine's Most Admired Companies for Social Responsibility rankings in four of the past five years.

UPS seeks more than just short-run sales and profits. Its three-pronged corporate sustainability mission stresses *economic prosperity* (profitable growth through a customer focus), *social responsibility* (community engagement and individual well-being), and *environmental stewardship* (operating efficiently and protecting the environment). Whether it involves greening up its operations or urging employees to volunteer time in their communities, UPS proactively seeks opportunities to act responsibly. UPS

⊙ **FIGURE | 1.4**
Three Considerations Underlying the Societal Marketing Concept

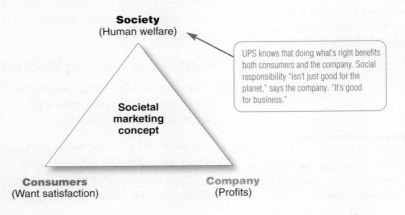

Society
(Human welfare)

UPS knows that doing what's right benefits both consumers and the company. Social responsibility "isn't just good for the planet," says the company. "It's good for business."

Societal marketing concept

Consumers
(Want satisfaction)

Company
(Profits)

knows that doing what's right benefits both consumers and the company. By operating efficiently and acting responsibly, it can "meet the needs of the enterprise . . . while protecting and enhancing the human and natural resources that will be needed in the future." Social responsibility "isn't just good for the planet," says the company. "It's good for business."[9]

Author | The customer-driven
Comment | marketing strategy
discussed in the previous section
outlines which customers the company
will serve (the target market) and how
it will serve them (the value
proposition). Now, the company
develops marketing plans and
programs—a marketing mix—that will
actually deliver the intended customer
value.

Preparing an Integrated Marketing Plan and Program (p 12)

The company's marketing strategy outlines which customers it will serve and how it will create value for these customers. Next, the marketer develops an integrated marketing program that will actually deliver the intended value to target customers. The marketing program builds customer relationships by transforming the marketing strategy into action. It consists of the firm's *marketing mix*, the set of marketing tools the firm uses to implement its marketing strategy.

The major marketing mix tools are classified into four broad groups, called the *four Ps* of marketing: product, price, place, and promotion. To deliver on its value proposition, the firm must first create a need-satisfying market offering (product). It must decide how much it will charge for the offering (price) and how it will make the offering available to target consumers (place). Finally, it must communicate with target customers about the offering and persuade them of its merits (promotion). The firm must blend each marketing mix tool into a comprehensive *integrated marketing program* that communicates and delivers the intended value to chosen customers. We will explore marketing programs and the marketing mix in much more detail in later chapters.

Author | Doing a good job with
Comment | the first three steps in the
marketing process sets the stage for
step four, building and managing
lasting customer relationships.

Building Customer Relationships (pp 12–19)

The first three steps in the marketing process—understanding the marketplace and customer needs, designing a customer-driven marketing strategy, and constructing a marketing program—all lead up to the fourth and most important step: building profitable customer relationships.

Customer Relationship Management

Customer relationship management is perhaps the most important concept of modern marketing. Some marketers define it narrowly as a customer data management activity (a practice called *CRM*). By this definition, it involves managing detailed information about individual customers and carefully managing customer "touchpoints" to maximize customer loyalty. We will discuss this narrower CRM activity in Chapter 4 when dealing with marketing information.

Most marketers, however, give the concept of customer relationship management a broader meaning. In this broader sense, **customer relationship management** is the overall process of building and maintaining profitable customer relationships by delivering superior customer value and satisfaction. It deals with all aspects of acquiring, keeping, and growing customers.

Customer relationship management
The overall process of building and maintaining profitable customer relationships by delivering superior customer value and satisfaction.

Relationship Building Blocks: Customer Value and Satisfaction

The key to building lasting customer relationships is to create superior customer value and satisfaction. Satisfied customers are more likely to be loyal customers and give the company a larger share of their business.

Customer-perceived value
The customer's evaluation of the difference between all the benefits and all the costs of a marketing offer relative to those of competing offers.

Customer Value. Attracting and retaining customers can be a difficult task. Customers often face a bewildering array of products and services from which to choose. A customer buys from the firm that offers the highest **customer-perceived value**—the customer's evaluation of the difference between all the benefits and all the costs of a market offering relative to those of competing offers. Importantly, customers often do not judge values and costs "accurately" or "objectively." They act on *perceived* value.

To some consumers, value might mean sensible products at affordable prices, especially in the aftermath of recent recession. To other consumers, however, value might mean paying more to get more. For example, despite the challenging economic environment, GE recently introduced its new Profile washer-and-dryer set, which retails for more than $2,500 (more than double the cost of a standard washer-and-dryer set). Profile ads feature stylish machines in eye-catching colors, such as cherry red. But the ads also focus on down-to-earth practicality. They position the Profile line as a revolutionary new "clothes care system," with technology that allocates the optimal amount of soap and water per load and saves money by being gentle on clothes, extending garment life. Are Profile washers and dryers worth the much higher price compared to less expensive appliances? It's all a matter of personal value perceptions. To many consumers, the answer is no. But to the target segment of style-conscious, affluent buyers, the answer is yes.[10]

Customer satisfaction

The extent to which a product's perceived performance matches a buyer's expectations.

Customer Satisfaction. **Customer satisfaction** depends on the product's perceived performance relative to a buyer's expectations. If the product's performance falls short of expectations, the customer is dissatisfied. If performance matches expectations, the customer is satisfied. If performance exceeds expectations, the customer is highly satisfied or delighted.

Outstanding marketing companies go out of their way to keep important customers satisfied. Most studies show that higher levels of customer satisfaction lead to greater customer loyalty, which in turn results in better company performance. Smart companies aim to delight customers by promising only what they can deliver and then delivering more than they promise. Delighted customers not only make repeat purchases but also become willing marketing partners and "customer evangelists" who spread the word about their good experiences to others (see Real Marketing 1.1).[11]

For companies interested in delighting customers, exceptional value and service become part of the overall company culture. For example, year after year, Ritz-Carlton ranks at or near the top of the hospitality industry in terms of customer satisfaction. ◉ Its passion for satisfying customers is summed up in the company's credo, which promises that its luxury hotels will deliver a truly memorable experience—one that "enlivens the senses, instills well-being, and fulfills even the unexpressed wishes and needs of our guests."[12]

Check into any Ritz-Carlton hotel around the world, and you'll be amazed by the company's fervent dedication to anticipating and meeting even your slightest need. Without ever asking, they seem to know that you're allergic to peanuts and want a king-size bed, a nonallergenic pillow, the blinds open when you arrive, and breakfast with decaffeinated coffee in your room. Each day, hotel staffers—from those at the front desk to those in maintenance and housekeeping—discreetly observe and record even the smallest guest preferences. Then, every morning, each hotel reviews the files of all new arrivals who have previously stayed at a Ritz-Carlton and prepares a list of suggested extra touches that might delight each guest.

◉ Customer satisfaction: Ritz-Carlton's passion for satisfying customers is summed up in its Credo, which promises a truly memorable experience—one that "enlivens the senses, instills well-being, and fulfills even the unexpressed wishes and needs of our guests."

Once they identify a special customer need, Ritz-Carlton employees go to legendary extremes to meet it. For example, to serve the needs of a guest with food allergies, a Ritz-Carlton chef in Bali located special eggs and milk in a small grocery store in another country and had them delivered to the hotel. In another case, when the hotel's laundry service failed to remove a stain on a guest's suit before the guest departed, the hotel manager traveled to the guest's house and personally delivered a reimbursement check for the cost of the suit. According to one Ritz-Carlton manager, if the chain gets hold of a picture of a guest's pet, it will make a copy, have it framed, and display it in the guest's room in whatever Ritz-Carlton the guest visits. As a result of such customer service heroics, an amazing 95 percent of departing guests report that their stay has been a truly memorable experience. More than 90 percent of Ritz-Carlton's delighted customers return.

Real Marketing ■.■

In-N-Out Burger:
The Power of Customer Delight

In-N-Out Burger opened its first restaurant in Baldwin Park, California, in 1948. It was a simple affair, with two drive-through lanes, a walk-up window, outdoor seating, and a menu that boasted only burgers, shakes, fries, and soft drinks. That was a pretty standard format for the time. In fact, another California burger stand fitting about the same description was opened that same year just 45 minutes away by the McDonald brothers. Today, however, In-N-Out is pretty much the exact opposite of McDonald's. Whereas McDonald's now operates more than 32,000 stores worldwide and pulls in more than $79 billion in annual system-wide sales, In-N-Out has less than 250 stores in four states and about $400 million in annual sales.

But In-N-Out Burger never wanted to be another McDonald's. And despite its smaller size—or perhaps because of it—In-N-Out's customers like the regional chain just the way it is. When it comes to customer satisfaction—make that customer *delight*—In-N-Out beats McDonald's hands down. It regularly posts the highest customer satisfaction scores of any fast-food restaurant in its market area. Just about anyone who's been to In-N-Out thinks it makes the best burger they've ever had.

In-N-Out has earned an almost cultlike following by doing something unthinkable: not changing. From the start, the chain has focused tenaciously on customer well-being. Its founding philosophy is as strongly held today as it was when the first In-N-Out Burger opened its doors: "Give customers the freshest, highest quality foods you can buy and provide them with friendly service in a sparkling clean environment."

Unlike McDonald's or Burger King, which introduce a seemingly unending stream of new menu items, In-N-Out's simple menu never changes. Instead, In-N-Out still focuses on what it does well: making really good hamburgers, really good fries, and really good shakes—that's it. The burgers are made from 100 percent pure, fresh beef with no additives, fillers, or preservatives. Potatoes and other fresh vegetables are hand cut daily at every restaurant, and shakes are made from—yes—real ice cream. In an industry increasingly en-

amored with technologies like cryogenically frozen ingredients and off-site food preparation, you won't find a single freezer, heat lamp, or microwave oven at an In-N-Out. Every meal is custom-made with fresh ingredients. "We serve every customer, one burger at a time," says one restaurant manager.

Although the menu might seem limited, In-N-Out employees will gladly customize a burger to each customer's tastes. In fact, over the years, a "secret menu" has emerged for customers who know the right code words (which aren't advertised or posted on the menu board). So a customer in the know might order a "Double-Double Animal Style" (double burger and double cheese, with pickles, grilled onions, extra spread, and fried mustard). Ordering a 4X4 gets you four beef patties and four slices of cheese, and a "grilled cheese" is an In-N-Out cheeseburger without the meat. Knowing the secret menu makes regulars feel even more special.

It's not just In-N-Out's food that pleases customers but also its friendly and well-trained employees. In-N-Out treats its employees very well. It pays new part-time staff $10 an hour to start and gives them regular pay raises. Part-timers also get paid vacations. General managers make at least $100,000 a year plus bonuses and a full-benefit package that rivals anything in the corporate world. Managers who meet goals are sent on lavish trips with their spouses, often to Europe in first-class seats. Managers are also promoted from within—80 percent of In-N-Out managers started at the very bottom. As a result, In-N-Out has one of the lowest turnover rates in an industry famous for high turnover.

Happy, motivated employees help to create loyal, satisfied customers. In fact, words like "loyal" and "satisfied" don't do justice to how

customers feel about In-N-Out Burger. "Delighted" or even "fanatically loyal" might say it better. The restaurant chain has developed an unparalleled cult following. When a new In-N-Out first opens, the line of cars often stretches out a mile or more, and people stand in line for an hour to get a burger, fries, and a shake. Fans have been known to camp overnight to be first in line. When the first Arizona store opened in Scottsdale, people waited in line for as long as four hours while news helicopters buzzed above the parking lot.

Ardent fans willingly go out of their way to satisfy an In-N-Out Burger craving. Jeff Rose, a financial planner from Carbondale, Illinois, always stops at In-N-Out first when he visits his mother in Las Vegas. "You have to pass it when you drive to her house," he says in his own defense. But how does he explain that he once paid an extra $40 in cab fare to visit an In-N-Out on the way to the San Diego airport?

In-N-Out doesn't spend much on advertising—it doesn't have to. Other than a small promotional budget for local billboards and some radio ads, when it comes to getting the word out, In-N-Out lets its customers do its heavy lifting. Loyal customers are true apostles for the brand. They proudly wear In-N-Out T-shirts and slap In-N-Out bumper stickers on their cars. Rabid regulars drag a constant stream of new devotees into In-N-Out restaurants, an act often referred to as "the conversion." They can't wait to pass along the secret menu codes and share the sublime pleasures of diving into a 4X4 Animal Style. "When you tell someone else what 'animal style' means," says an analyst, "you feel like you're passing on a secret handshake. People really get into the whole thing."

In-N-Out Burger delights customers by focusing on friendly service and what it does well: making really good hamburgers, really good fries, and really good shakes—that's it.

In-N-Out doesn't use paid endorsers, but word-of-mouth regularly flows from the mouths of A-list celebrities. When former *Tonight Show* host Conan O'Brien once asked Tom Hanks what he recommended doing in Los Angeles, Hanks replied, "One of the truly great things about Los Angeles is In-N-Out Burger." PGA golf star Phil Mickelson talked about the chain so much that whenever he hit a losing streak, sportswriters began suggesting that he cut back on the Double-Doubles. Once, when celebrity socialite Paris Hilton was pulled over and charged with driving under the influence, her excuse was that she was on her way to satisfy an "In-N-Out urge" (a term originating from fans cutting the "B" and the "r" off from the company name on bumper stickers).

In-N-Out Burger is privately owned and doesn't release sales and profit figures. But if the long lines snaking out the door at lunchtime are any indication, the chain is doing very well financially. In-N-Out's average sales per store are double the industry average and well ahead of leaders McDonald's and Burger King. "The more chains like McDonald's and Burger King change and expand, the more In-N-Out sticks to its guns," says the analyst. "In a way, it symbolizes the ideal American way of doing business: Treating people well, focusing on product quality, and being very successful." In-N-Out's customers couldn't agree more. When it comes to fast-food chains, delighted customers will tell you, "there's In-N-Out, and then there's everyone else."

Sources: Stacy Perman, "In-N-Out Burger's Marketing Magic," *Businessweek*, April 24, 2009, accessed at www.businessweek.com; Stacy Perman, "The Secret Sauce at In-N-Out Burger," *Businessweek*, April 20, 2009, p. 68; Dan Macsai, "The Sizzling Secrets of In-N-Out Burger," *Fast Company*, April 22, 2009, accessed at www.fastcompany.com; Michael Rigert, "In-N-Out Fans Come Out En Masse for Orem Opening," *Daily Herald (Orem)*, November 20, 2009; Lisa Jennings, "Regional Fast-Food Chains Top Satisfaction Survey," *Restaurant News*, February 15, 2010, accessed at www.nrn.com/article/regional-fast-food-chains-top-satisfaction-survey; Gil Rudawsky, "Is In-N-Out Burger Moving East?" *Daily Finance*, May 26, 2010, accessed at www.dailyfinance.com.

However, although a customer-centered firm seeks to deliver high customer satisfaction relative to competitors, it does not attempt to *maximize* customer satisfaction. A company can always increase customer satisfaction by lowering its price or increasing its services. But this may result in lower profits. Thus, the purpose of marketing is to generate customer value profitably. This requires a very delicate balance: The marketer must continue to generate more customer value and satisfaction but not "give away the house."

Customer Relationship Levels and Tools

Companies can build customer relationships at many levels, depending on the nature of the target market. At one extreme, a company with many low-margin customers may seek to develop *basic relationships* with them. For example, Nike does not phone or call on all of its consumers to get to know them personally. Instead, Nike creates relationships through brand-building advertising, public relations, and its Web site (www.Nike.com). At the other extreme, in markets with few customers and high margins, sellers want to create *full partnerships* with key customers. For example, Nike sales representatives work closely with the Sports Authority, Dick's Sporting Goods, Foot Locker, and other large retailers. In between these two extremes, other levels of customer relationships are appropriate.

Beyond offering consistently high value and satisfaction, marketers can use specific marketing tools to develop stronger bonds with customers. For example, many companies offer *frequency marketing programs* that reward customers who buy frequently or in large amounts. Airlines offer frequent-flyer programs, hotels give room upgrades to their frequent guests, and supermarkets give patronage discounts to "very important customers." For example, JetBlue Airways offers its TrueBlue members frequent-flyer points they can use on any seat on any JetBlue flight with no blackout dates. JetBlue promises its members "More award flights. More points. More to love." The airline's "Be True" marketing campaign even highlights real TrueBlue members who are nominated by JetBlue crewmembers for their TrueBlue dedication to inspiring causes.

Other companies sponsor *club marketing programs* that offer members special benefits and create member communities. ● For example, Harley-Davidson sponsors the Harley Owners

● Building customer relationships: Harley Davidson sponsors the Harley Owners Group (H.O.G.), which gives Harley owners "an organized way to share their passion and show their pride." The worldwide club now numbers more than 1,500 local chapters and one million members.

Group (H.O.G.), which gives Harley riders a way to share their common passion of "making the Harley-Davidson dream a way of life." H.O.G. membership benefits include a quarterly *HOG* magazine, the *Touring Handbook*, a roadside assistance program, a specially designed insurance program, theft reward service, a travel center, and a "Fly & Ride" program enabling members to rent Harleys while on vacation. The worldwide club now numbers more than 1,500 local chapters and more than one million members.[13]

The Changing Nature of Customer Relationships

Significant changes are occurring in the ways in which companies are relating to their customers. Yesterday's big companies focused on mass marketing to all customers at arm's length. Today's companies are building deeper, more direct, and lasting relationships with more carefully selected customers. Here are some important trends in the way companies and customers are relating to one another.

Relating with More Carefully Selected Customers

Few firms today still practice true mass marketing—selling in a standardized way to any customer who comes along. Today, most marketers realize that they don't want relationships with every customer. Instead, they target fewer, more profitable customers. "Not all customers are worth your marketing efforts," states one analyst. "Some are more costly to serve than to lose." Adds another marketing expert, "If you can't say who your customers *aren't*, you probably can't say who your customers *are*."[14]

Many companies now use customer profitability analysis to pass up or weed out losing customers and target winning ones for pampering. One approach is to preemptively screen out potentially unprofitable customers. Progressive Insurance does this effectively. It asks prospective customers a series of screening questions to determine if they are right for the firm. If they're not, Progressive will likely tell them, "You might want to go to Allstate." A marketing consultant explains: "They'd rather send business to a competitor than take on unprofitable customers." Screening out unprofitable customers lets Progressive provide even better service to potentially more profitable ones.[15]

But what should the company do with unprofitable customers that it already has? ● If it can't turn them into profitable ones, it may even want to dismiss customers that are too unreasonable or that cost more to serve than they are worth. "Like bouncers in glitzy nightspots," says another consultant, "executives will almost certainly have to 'fire' [those] customers." For example, American Express recently sent letters to some of its members offering them $300 in exchange for paying off their balances and closing out their accounts. Reading between the lines, the credit card company was dumping unprofitable customers. Sprint took similar but more abrupt actions:[16]

Sprint recently sent out letters to about 1,000 people to inform them that they had been summarily dismissed—but the recipients were Sprint *customers*, not employees. For about a year, the wireless-service provider had been tracking the number and frequency of support calls made by a group of high-maintenance users. According to a Sprint spokesperson, "in some cases, they were calling customer care hundreds of times a month . . . on the same issues, even after we felt those issues had been resolved." Ultimately, the company determined it could not meet the billing and service needs of this subset of subscribers and, therefore, waived their termination fees and cut off their service. Such "customer divestment" practices were once considered an anomaly. But new segmentation approaches and technologies have made it easier to focus on retaining the right customers and, by extension, showing problem customers the door.

Memo To: **Unprofitable Customers**

You Are Fired!

● Marketers don't want relationships with every possible customer. In fact, a company might want to "fire" customers that cost more to serve than to lose.

Relating More Deeply and Interactively

Beyond choosing customers more selectively, companies are now relating with chosen customers in deeper, more meaningful ways. Rather than relying on one-way, mass-media messages only, today's marketers are incorporating new, more interactive approaches that help build targeted, two-way customer relationships.

Two-Way Customer Relationships. New technologies have profoundly changed the ways in which people relate to one another. New tools for relating include everything from e-mail, Web sites, blogs, cell phones, and video sharing to online communities and social networks, such as Facebook, YouTube, and Twitter.

This changing communications environment also affects how companies and brands relate to customers. The new communications approaches let marketers create deeper customer involvement and a sense of community surrounding a brand—to make the brand a meaningful part of consumers' conversations and lives. "Becoming part of the conversation between consumers is infinitely more powerful than handing down information via traditional advertising," says one marketing expert. Says another, "People today want a voice and a role in their brand experiences. They want co-creation."[17]

However, at the same time that the new technologies create relationship-building opportunities for marketers, they also create challenges. They give consumers greater power and control. Today's consumers have more information about brands than ever before, and they have a wealth of platforms for airing and sharing their brand views with other consumers. Thus, the marketing world is now embracing not only customer relationship management, but also **customer-managed relationships**.

Customer-managed relationships
Marketing relationships in which customers, empowered by today's new digital technologies, interact with companies and with each other to shape their relationships with brands.

Greater consumer control means that, in building customer relationships, companies can no longer rely on marketing by *intrusion*. Instead, marketers must practice marketing by *attraction*—creating market offerings and messages that involve consumers rather than interrupt them. Hence, most marketers now augment their mass-media marketing efforts with a rich mix of direct marketing approaches that promote brand-consumer interaction.

For example, many brands are creating dialogues with consumers via their own or existing *online social networks*. To supplement their marketing campaigns, companies now routinely post their latest ads and made-for-the-Web videos on video-sharing sites. They join social networks. Or they launch their own blogs, online communities, or consumer-generated review systems, all with the aim of engaging customers on a more personal, interactive level.

Take Twitter, for example. Organizations ranging from Dell, JetBlue Airways, and Dunkin' Donuts to the Chicago Bulls, NASCAR, and the Los Angeles Fire Department have created Twitter pages and promotions. They use "tweets" to start conversations with Twitter's more than six million registered users, address customer service issues, research customer reactions, and drive traffic to relevant articles, Web sites, contests, videos, and other brand activities. For example, Dell monitors Twitter-based discussions and responds quickly to individual problems or questions. ● Tony Hsieh, CEO of the Zappos family of companies, who receives more than 1,000 customer tweets per day, says that Twitter lets him give customers "more depth into what we're like, and my own personality." Another marketer notes that companies can "use Twitter to get the fastest, most honest research any company ever heard—the good, bad, and ugly—and it doesn't cost a cent."[18]

● **Online social networks: Many brands are creating dialogues with consumers via their own or existing networks. For example, Tony Hsieh receives more than 1,000 customer tweets per day. Twitter lets him give customers "more depth into what we're like, and my own personality."**

Similarly, almost every company has something going on Facebook these days. Starbucks has more than six million Facebook "fans"; Coca-Cola has more than five million. Networks like Facebook can get consumers involved with and talking about a brand. For example, Honda's "Everybody Knows Somebody Who Loves a Honda" Facebook page let visitors upload photos of their cars or link up to owners of their favorite old Hondas worldwide. It asks people to help prove that "we all really can be connected through Honda love." The campaign netted about two million Facebook friends in less than two months, more than double previous fan levels.[19]

IKEA used a simple but inspired Facebook campaign to promote the opening of a new store in Malmo, Sweden. It opened a Facebook profile for the store's manager, Gordon Gustavsson. Then it uploaded pictures of IKEA showrooms to Gustavsson's Facebook photo album and announced that whoever was first to photo tag a product in the pictures with their name would win it. Thousands of customers rushed to tag items. Word spread quickly to friends, and customers were soon begging for more pictures. More than just looking at an ad with IKEA furniture in it, the Facebook promotion had people pouring over the pictures, examining products item by item.[20]

Most marketers are still learning how to use social media effectively. The problem is to find unobtrusive ways to enter consumers' social conversations with engaging and relevant brand messages. Simply posting a humorous video, creating a social network page, or hosting a blog isn't enough. Successful social network marketing means making relevant and genuine contributions to consumer conversations. "Nobody wants to be friends with a brand," says one online marketing executive. "Your job [as a brand] is to be part of other friends' conversations."[21]

Consumer-Generated Marketing. A growing part of the new customer dialogue is **consumer-generated marketing**, by which consumers themselves are playing a bigger role in shaping their own brand experiences and those of others. This might happen through uninvited consumer-to-consumer exchanges in blogs, video-sharing sites, and other digital forums. But increasingly, companies are *inviting* consumers to play a more active role in shaping products and brand messages.

Some companies ask consumers for new product ideas. For example, Coca-Cola's Vitaminwater brand recently set up a Facebook app to obtain consumer suggestions for a new flavor, promising to manufacture and sell the winner ("Vitaminwater was our idea; the next one will be yours."). The new flavor—Connect (black cherry-lime with vitamins and a kick of caffeine)—was a big hit. In the process, Vitaminwater doubled its Facebook fan base to more than one million.[22]

Other companies are inviting customers to play an active role in shaping ads. For example, PepsiCo, Southwest Airlines, MasterCard, Unilever, H.J. Heinz, and many other companies have run contests for consumer-generated commercials that have been aired on national television. For the past several years, PepsiCo's Doritos brand has held a "Crash the Super Bowl" contest in which it invites 30-second ads from consumers and runs the best ones during the game. The consumer-generated ads have been a huge success. Last year, consumers submitted nearly 4,000 entries. The winning fan-produced Doritos ad (called "Underdog") placed number two in the *USA Today* Ad Meter ratings, earning the creator a $600,000 cash prize from PepsiCo. The lowest-rated of the four consumer-made ads came in 17th out of 65 Super Bowl ads.[23]

However, harnessing consumer-generated content can be a time-consuming and costly process, and companies may find it difficult to glean even a little gold from all the garbage. ● For example, when Heinz invited consumers to submit homemade ads for its ketchup on its YouTube page, it ended up sifting through more than

Consumer-generated marketing
Brand exchanges created by consumers themselves—both invited and uninvited—by which consumers are playing an increasing role in shaping their own brand experiences and those of other consumers.

● Harnessing consumer-generated marketing: When H.J. Heinz invited consumers to submit homemade ads for its ketchup brand on YouTube, it received more than 8,000 entries—some were very good, but most were only so-so or even downright dreadful.

8,000 entries, of which it posted nearly 4,000. Some of the amateur ads were very good—entertaining and potentially effective. Most, however, were so-so at best, and others were downright dreadful. In one ad, a contestant chugged ketchup straight from the bottle. In another, the would-be filmmaker brushed his teeth, washed his hair, and shaved his face with Heinz's product.[24]

Consumer-generated marketing, whether invited by marketers or not, has become a significant marketing force. Through a profusion of consumer-generated videos, blogs, and Web sites, consumers are playing an increasing role in shaping their own brand experiences. Beyond creating brand conversations, customers are having an increasing say about everything from product design, usage, and packaging to pricing and distribution.

> **Author Comment** | Marketers can't create customer value and build customer relationships by themselves. They must work closely with other company departments and partners outside the firm.

Partner relationship management
Working closely with partners in other company departments and outside the company to jointly bring greater value to customers.

Partner Relationship Management

When it comes to creating customer value and building strong customer relationships, today's marketers know that they can't go it alone. They must work closely with a variety of marketing partners. In addition to being good at *customer relationship management*, marketers must also be good at **partner relationship management**. Major changes are occurring in how marketers partner with others inside and outside the company to jointly bring more value to customers.

Partners Inside the Company

Traditionally, marketers have been charged with understanding customers and representing customer needs to different company departments. The old thinking was that marketing is done only by marketing, sales, and customer-support people. However, in today's more connected world, every functional area can interact with customers, especially electronically. The new thinking is that—no matter what your job is in a company—you must understand marketing and be customer focused. David Packard, the late cofounder of HP, wisely said, "Marketing is far too important to be left only to the marketing department."[25]

Today, rather than letting each department go its own way, firms are linking all departments in the cause of creating customer value. Rather than assigning only sales and marketing people to customers, they are forming cross-functional customer teams. For example, P&G assigns customer development teams to each of its major retailer accounts. These teams—consisting of sales and marketing people, operations specialists, market and financial analysts, and others—coordinate the efforts of many P&G departments toward helping the retailer be more successful.

Marketing Partners Outside the Firm

Changes are also occurring in how marketers connect with their suppliers, channel partners, and even competitors. Most companies today are networked companies, relying heavily on partnerships with other firms.

Marketing channels consist of distributors, retailers, and others who connect the company to its buyers. The *supply chain* describes a longer channel, stretching from raw materials to components to final products that are carried to final buyers. For example, the supply chain for PCs consists of suppliers of computer chips and other components, the computer manufacturer, and the distributors, retailers, and others who sell the computers.

Through *supply chain management*, many companies today are strengthening their connections with partners all along the supply chain. They know that their fortunes rest not just on how well they perform. Success at building customer relationships also rests on how well their entire supply chain performs against competitors' supply chains. These companies don't just treat suppliers as vendors and distributors as customers. They treat both as partners in delivering customer value. On the one hand, for example, Toyota works closely with carefully selected suppliers to improve quality and operations efficiency. On the other hand, it works with its franchise dealers to provide top-grade sales and service support that will bring customers in the door and keep them coming back.

Author | Look back at Figure 1.1.
Comment | In the first four steps of
the marketing process, the company
creates value *for* target customers and
builds strong relationships with them.
If it does that well, it can capture value
from customers in return in the form
of loyal customers who buy and
continue to buy the company's brands.

Capturing Value from Customers (pp 20–22)

The first four steps in the marketing process outlined in Figure 1.1 involve building customer relationships by creating and delivering superior customer value. The final step involves capturing value in return in the form of current and future sales, market share, and profits. By creating superior customer value, the firm creates highly satisfied customers who stay loyal and buy more. This, in turn, means greater long-run returns for the firm. Here, we discuss the outcomes of creating customer value: customer loyalty and retention, share of market and share of customer, and customer equity.

Creating Customer Loyalty and Retention

Good customer relationship management creates customer delight. In turn, delighted customers remain loyal and talk favorably to others about the company and its products. Studies show big differences in the loyalty of customers who are less satisfied, somewhat satisfied, and completely satisfied. Even a slight drop from complete satisfaction can create an enormous drop in loyalty. Thus, the aim of customer relationship management is to create not only customer satisfaction but also customer delight.

The recent economic recession put strong pressures on customer loyalty. It created a new consumer frugality that will last well into the future. One recent study found that, even in an improved economy, 55 percent of consumers say they would rather get the best price than the best brand. Nearly two-thirds say they will now shop at a different store with lower prices even if it's less convenient. It's five times cheaper to keep an old customer than acquire a new one. Thus, companies today must shape their value propositions even more carefully and treat their profitable customers well.[26]

Losing a customer means losing more than a single sale. It means losing the entire stream of purchases that the customer would make over a lifetime of patronage. For example, here is a dramatic illustration of **customer lifetime value**:

Customer lifetime value
The value of the entire stream of purchases that the customer would make over a lifetime of patronage.

Stew Leonard, who operates a highly profitable four-store supermarket in Connecticut and New York, says he sees $50,000 flying out of his store every time he sees a sulking customer. Why? Because his average customer spends about $100 a week, shops 50 weeks a year, and remains in the area for about 10 years. If this customer has an unhappy experience and switches to another supermarket, Stew Leonard's has lost $50,000 in revenue. The loss can be much greater if the disappointed customer shares the bad experience with other customers and causes them to defect. To keep customers coming back, Stew Leonard's has created what the *New York Times* has dubbed the "Disneyland of Dairy Stores," complete with costumed characters, scheduled entertainment, a petting zoo, and animatronics throughout the store. From its humble beginnings as a small dairy store in 1969, Stew Leonard's has grown at an amazing pace. It's built 29 additions onto the original store, which now serves more than 300,000 customers each week. This legion of loyal shoppers is largely a result of the store's passionate approach to customer service. ● "Rule #1: The customer is always right. Rule #2: If the customer is ever wrong, re-read rule #1."[27]

Stew Leonard is not alone in assessing customer lifetime value. Lexus, for example, estimates that a single satisfied and loyal customer is worth more than $600,000 in lifetime sales. And the estimated lifetime value of a young mobile phone consumer is $26,000.[28] In fact, a company can lose money on a specific transaction but still benefit greatly from a long-term relationship. This means that companies must aim high in building customer relationships. Customer de-

● Customer lifetime value: To keep customers coming back, Stew Leonard's has created the "Disneyland of Dairy Stores." Rule #1—The customer is always right. Rule #2—If the customer is ever wrong, reread Rule #1.

light creates an emotional relationship with a brand, not just a rational preference. And that relationship keeps customers coming back.

Growing Share of Customer

Share of customer
The portion of the customer's purchasing that a company gets in its product categories.

Beyond simply retaining good customers to capture customer lifetime value, good customer relationship management can help marketers increase their **share of customer**—the share they get of the customer's purchasing in their product categories. Thus, banks want to increase "share of wallet." Supermarkets and restaurants want to get more "share of stomach." Car companies want to increase "share of garage," and airlines want greater "share of travel."

To increase share of customer, firms can offer greater variety to current customers. Or they can create programs to cross-sell and up-sell to market more products and services to existing customers. For example, Amazon.com is highly skilled at leveraging relationships with its 88 million customers to increase its share of each customer's purchases. Originally an online bookseller, Amazon.com now offers customers music, videos, gifts, toys, consumer electronics, office products, home improvement items, lawn and garden products, apparel and accessories, jewelry, tools, and even groceries. In addition, based on each customer's purchase history, previous product searches, and other data, the company recommends related products that might be of interest. This recommendation system influences up to 30 percent of all sales.[29] In these ways, Amazon.com captures a greater share of each customer's spending budget.

Building Customer Equity

We can now see the importance of not only acquiring customers but also keeping and growing them. One marketing consultant puts it this way: "The only value your company will ever create is the value that comes from customers—the ones you have now and the ones you will have in the future. Without customers, you don't have a business."[30] Customer relationship management takes a long-term view. Companies want not only to create profitable customers but also "own" them for life, earn a greater share of their purchases, and capture their customer lifetime value.

What Is Customer Equity?

Customer equity
The total combined customer lifetime values of all of the company's customers.

The ultimate aim of customer relationship management is to produce high *customer equity*.[31] **Customer equity** is the total combined customer lifetime values of all of the company's current and potential customers. As such, it's a measure of the future value of the company's customer base. Clearly, the more loyal the firm's profitable customers, the higher its customer equity. Customer equity may be a better measure of a firm's performance than current sales or market share. Whereas sales and market share reflect the past, customer equity suggests the future. ◉ Consider Cadillac:[32]

In the 1970s and 1980s, Cadillac had some of the most loyal customers in the industry. To an entire generation of car buyers, the name *Cadillac* defined American luxury. Cadillac's share of the luxury car market reached a whopping 51 percent in 1976. Based on market share and sales, the brand's future looked rosy. However, measures of customer equity would have painted a bleaker picture. Cadillac customers were getting older (average age 60) and average customer lifetime value was falling. Many Cadillac buyers were on their last cars. Thus, although Cadillac's market share was good, its customer equity was not. Compare this with BMW. Its more youthful and vigorous image didn't win BMW the early market share war. However, it did win BMW younger customers with

◉ Managing customer equity: To increase customer lifetime value and customer equity, Cadillac needs to come up with more stylish models and marketing that can attract younger buyers.

higher customer lifetime values. The result: In the years that followed, BMW's market share and profits soared while Cadillac's fortunes eroded badly.

In recent years, Cadillac has attempted to make the Caddy cool again by targeting a younger generation of consumers. Still, the average age of its buyers remains a less-than-youthful 62 (13 years older than typical BMW owners). Says one analyst, "no image remake can fully succeed until Cadillac comes up with more stylish models and marketing that can attract younger buyers. For now, the company's image will likely remain dinged as it continues churning out land yachts such as its DTS, which . . . appeals mainly to buyers in their 70s." It's a real "geezer-mobile." As a result, the brand's fortunes continue to fall; last year was its worst sales year since 1953. The moral: Marketers should care not just about current sales and market share. Customer lifetime value and customer equity are the name of the game.

Building the Right Relationships with the Right Customers

Companies should manage customer equity carefully. They should view customers as assets that must be managed and maximized. But not all customers, not even all loyal customers, are good investments. Surprisingly, some loyal customers can be unprofitable, and some disloyal customers can be profitable. Which customers should the company acquire and retain?

The company can classify customers according to their potential profitability and manage its relationships with them accordingly. One classification scheme defines four relationship groups based on potential profitability and projected loyalty: strangers, butterflies, true friends, and barnacles.[33] Each group requires a different relationship management strategy. For example, "strangers" show low potential profitability and little projected loyalty. There is little fit between the company's offerings and their needs. The relationship management strategy for these customers is simple: Don't invest anything in them.

"Butterflies" are potentially profitable but not loyal. There is a good fit between the company's offerings and their needs. However, like real butterflies, we can enjoy them for only a short while and then they're gone. An example is stock market investors who trade shares often and in large amounts but who enjoy hunting out the best deals without building a regular relationship with any single brokerage company. Efforts to convert butterflies into loyal customers are rarely successful. Instead, the company should enjoy the butterflies for the moment. It should create satisfying and profitable transactions with them, capturing as much of their business as possible in the short time during which they buy from the company. Then it should cease investing in them until the next time around.

"True friends" are both profitable and loyal. There is a strong fit between their needs and the company's offerings. The firm wants to make continuous relationship investments to delight these customers and nurture, retain, and grow them. It wants to turn true friends into "true believers," those who come back regularly and tell others about their good experiences with the company.

"Barnacles" are highly loyal but not very profitable. There is a limited fit between their needs and the company's offerings. An example is smaller bank customers who bank regularly but do not generate enough returns to cover the costs of maintaining their accounts. Like barnacles on the hull of a ship, they create drag. Barnacles are perhaps the most problematic customers. The company might be able to improve their profitability by selling them more, raising their fees, or reducing service to them. However, if they cannot be made profitable, they should be "fired."

The point here is an important one: Different types of customers require different relationship management strategies. The goal is to build the *right relationships* with the *right customers.*

Author | Marketing doesn't take **Comment** | place in a vacuum. Now that we've discussed the five steps in the marketing process, let's examine how the ever-changing marketplace affects both consumers and the marketers who serve them. We'll look more deeply into these and other marketing environment factors in Chapter 3.

The Changing Marketing Landscape (pp 22–29)

Every day, dramatic changes are occurring in the marketplace. Richard Love of HP observed, "The pace of change is so rapid that the ability to change has now become a competitive advantage." Yogi Berra, the legendary New York Yankees catcher and manager, summed it up more simply when he said, "The future ain't what it used to be." As the marketplace changes, so must those who serve it.

In this section, we examine the major trends and forces that are changing the marketing landscape and challenging marketing strategy. We look at five major developments: the uncertain economic environment, the digital age, rapid globalization, the call for more ethics and social responsibility, and the growth of not-for-profit marketing.

The Uncertain Economic Environment

Beginning in 2008, the United States and world economies experienced a stunning economic meltdown, unlike anything since the Great Depression of the 1930s. The stock market plunged, and trillions of dollars of market value simply evaporated. The financial crisis left shell-shocked consumers short of both money and confidence as they faced losses in income, a severe credit crunch, declining home values, and rising unemployment.

The so-called Great Recession caused many consumers to rethink their spending priorities and cut back on their buying. After a decade of overspending, "frugality has made a comeback," says one analyst. More than just a temporary change, the new consumer buying attitudes and spending behavior will likely remain for many years to come. "The 'new frugality,' born of the Great Recession, . . . is now becoming entrenched consumer behavior that is reshaping consumption patterns in ways that will persist even as the economy rebounds," says another analyst.[34] Even in its aftermath, consumers are now spending more carefully. (See Real Marketing 1.2.)

In response, companies in all industries—from discounters such as Target to luxury brands such as Lexus—have aligned their marketing strategies with the new economic realities. More than ever, marketers are emphasizing the *value* in their value propositions. They are focusing on value-for-the-money, practicality, and durability in their product offerings and marketing pitches. "Value is the magic word," says a P&G marketing executive. These days, "people are doing the math in their heads, and they're being much more thoughtful before making purchases. Now, we're going to be even more focused on helping consumers see value." For example, although it might cost a little more initially, P&G's Tide Total Care proclaims that the product "helps keep clothes like new even after 30 washes."[35]

Similarly, in the past, discount retailer Target focused on the "expect more" side of its "Expect More. Pay Less." value proposition. ◉ But that has now changed.[36]

For years, Target's carefully cultivated "upscale-discounter" image successfully differentiated it from Walmart's more hard-nosed "lowest price" position. But when the economy soured, many consumers believed that Target's trendier assortments and hip marketing also meant steeper prices, and Target's performance slipped relative to Walmart's. So Target shifted its focus more to the "pay less" half of the slogan. It's now making certain that its prices are in line with Walmart's and that customers are aware of it. Although still trendy, Target's ads feature explicit low-price and savings appeals. "We're . . . trying to define and find the right balance between 'Expect More. Pay Less.'" says Target's CEO.

◉ In tough economic times, companies must emphasize the *value* in their value propositions. Target is now focusing squarely on the "pay less" side of its "Expect More. Pay Less." positioning.

Even wealthier consumers have joined the trend toward frugality. Conspicuous free spending is no longer so fashionable. As a result, even luxury brands are stressing value. For years, Lexus has emphasized status and performance. For example, its pre-Christmas ads typically feature a loving spouse giving his or her significant other a new Lexus wrapped in a big red bow. Lexus is still running those ads, but it's also hedging its bets by running other ads with the tagline "lowest cost of ownership," referring to Lexus' decent fuel economy, durability, and resale value.

In adjusting to the new economy, companies were tempted to cut marketing budgets deeply and slash prices in an effort to coax cash-strapped customers into opening their wallets. However, although cutting costs and offering

Real Marketing 1.2

The New Era of Consumer Frugality

Frugality has made a comeback. Beaten down by the recent Great Recession, Americans are showing an enthusiasm for thriftiness not seen in decades. This behavioral shift isn't simply about spending less. The new frugality emphasizes stretching every dollar. It means bypassing the fashion mall for the discount chain store, buying secondhand clothes and furniture, packing a lunch instead of eating out, or trading down to store brands. Consumers are clipping more coupons and swiping their credit cards less. Says one analyst:

> A shift in behavior has taken place. Consumers across all income segments have responded to the economy by reining in spending, postponing big purchases, and trading down when possible. Above all else, they're seeking out the best value for their money. Marketers must take a different tack to reach these increasingly pragmatic consumers: Forego the flash and prove your products' worth.

Not that long ago, yoga teacher Gisele Sanders shopped at the Nordstrom in Portland, Oregon, and didn't think twice about dropping $30 for a bottle of Chianti to go with dinner. That was before the recession, when her husband, a real estate agent, began to feel the brunt of slowing home sales. Now, even with the improved economy, Sanders picks up grocery-store wine at $10 or less per bottle, shops for used clothes, and takes her mother's advice about turning down the thermostat during winter. "It's been a long time coming," she said. "We were so off the charts before."

Such frugality is likely to be more than a fad. "It is a whole reassessment of values," says a retailing consultant. "We had just been shopping until we drop, and consuming and buying it all, and replenishing before things wear out. People [have learned] again to say, 'No, not today.'" Even people who can afford to indulge themselves are doing so more sparingly and then bargain hunting to offset the big purchases.

When the recession hit, the housing bust, credit crunch, and stock-market plunge ate away at the retirement savings and confidence of consumers who for years operated on a buy-now, pay-later philosophy, chasing bigger homes, bigger cars, and better brands. The new economic realities have forced families to bring their spending in line with their incomes and rethink priorities. Notes a market analyst, "The recession has tempered rampant and excessive consumption, which has given way to more mindful choices." Keeping up with the Joneses and conspicuous consumption have taken a backseat to practical consumption and stretching buying dollars.

Even as the economy has recovered, it's difficult to predict how long the pullback will last, particularly among generations of consumers who have never seen such a sharp economic downturn. But experts agree that the impact of the recession will last well into the future. "The newfound thrifty consumer is not going anywhere," declares one business writer. "Frugality's in. Value's under scrutiny. There's a new consumer in town who's adapting to circumstances by spending less and scrutinizing more." Says another, "Americans will continue to pinch their pennies long into the post-recession era." A recent survey asked consumers whether they "intend to revert back to my prerecession buying habits" in several specific categories during the next year. In most categories, fewer than one in five consumers said they planned to do so.

But most consumers don't see the new frugality as such a bad thing. The survey also showed that 78 percent of people believed the recession has changed their spending habits for the better. In another survey, 79 percent of consumers agreed with the statement, "I feel a lot smarter now about the way I shop versus two years ago." According to a researcher, "They look at their old spending habits and are a bit embarrassed by their behavior. The new consumer is wiser and in more control, so while consumption may [not] be as carefree and fun as it was before, consumers seem to like their new outlook, mindfulness, and strength."

For example, in Maine, Sindi Card says her husband's job is now secure. However, because the couple has two sons in college in the rebounding but still uncertain economy, she fixed her broken 20-year-old clothes dryer herself. It was a stark change from the past, when she would have taken the old model to the dump and had a new one delivered. With help from an appliance-repair Web site, she saved hundreds of dollars. "We all need to find a way to live within our means," she said.

The new back-to-basics mentality applies to all kinds of purchases. Indeed, some of the behavior associated with the new frugality betrays an America having difficulty letting go of

The new consumer frugality: Today, marketers in all industries must clearly spell out their value propositions. Even diamond marketer De Beers has adjusted its long-standing "a diamond is forever" promise to these more frugal times.

expensive tastes. Donna Speigel has built a Cincinnati-area chain of upscale consignment shops called the Snooty Fox aimed at women who still have to have their Louis Vuitton and Ann Taylor products but want them at a fraction of the retail price. Her sales were up 17 percent last October. In the suburbs of Dallas, Kay Smith still drives a black Lexus but now passes by the high-end malls and heads to Walmart. "I think about everything I buy now," Ms. Smith says.

Still, the new frugality doesn't mean that consumers have resigned themselves to lives of deprivation. As the economy improves, they're starting to indulge in luxuries and bigger-ticket purchases again, just more selectively. "We're seeing an emergence in what we call 'conscious recklessness,' where consumers actually plan out frivolous or indulgent spending," says the researcher. It's like someone on a diet who saves up calories by eating prudently during the week and then lets loose on Friday night. But "people are more mindful now and aware of the consequences of their (and others') spending. So luxury is [again] on the 'to-do' list, but people are taking a more mindful approach to where, how, and on what they spend."

What does the new era of frugality mean to marketers? Whether it's for everyday products or expensive luxuries, marketers must clearly spell out their value propositions: what it is that makes their brands worth a customer's hard-earned money. "The saying has always been, 'Sell the sizzle, not the steak.' Well, I think there's been too much sizzle," says one luxury goods marketer. "Image alone doesn't sell anymore—consumers want to know what they're getting for their money."

Even diamond marketer De Beers has adjusted its long-standing "A diamond is forever" value proposition to these more frugal times. One ad headlined "Here's to Less," makes that next diamond purchase seem—what else—downright practical. "Our lives are filled with things. We're overwhelmed by possessions we own but do not treasure. Stuff we buy but never love. To be thrown away in weeks rather than passed down for generations. Perhaps we will be different now. Perhaps now is an opportunity to reassess what really matters. After all, if everything you ever bought her disappeared overnight, what would she truly miss? A diamond is forever."

Sources: Portions adapted from Dan Sewell, "New Frugality Emerges," *Washington Times*, December 1, 2008; with quotes, extracts, and other information from Noreen O'Leary, "Squeeze Play," *Adweek*, January 12, 2009, pp. 8–9; "Consumer 'New Frugality' May Be an Enduring Feature of Post-Recession Economy, Finds Booz & Company Survey," *Business Wire*, February 24, 2010; Piet Levy, "How to Reach the New Consumer," *Marketing News*, February 28, 2010, pp. 16–20; Mark Dolliver, "Will Traumatized Consumers Ever Recover?" *Adweek*, March 22, 2010, accessed at www.adweek.com; "Is Shopping Behavior Permanently Muted?" *USA Today* (*Magazine*), April 2010, pp. 3–4; and "Maybe Demand Isn't so Pent Up," *Adweek*, July 26, 2010, p. 19.

selected discounts can be important marketing tactics in a down economy, smart marketers understand that making cuts in the wrong places can damage long-term brand images and customer relationships. The challenge is to balance the brand's value proposition with the current times while also enhancing its long-term equity.

"A recession creates winners and losers just like a boom," notes one economist. "When a recession ends, when the road levels off and the world seems full of promise once more, your position in the competitive pack will depend on how skillfully you managed [during the tough times]."[37] Thus, rather than slashing prices, many marketers held the line on prices and instead explained why their brands are worth it. And rather than cutting their marketing budgets in the difficult times, companies such as Walmart, McDonald's, Hyundai, and General Mills maintained or actually increased their marketing spending. The goal in uncertain economic times is to build market share and strengthen customer relationships at the expense of competitors who cut back.

A troubled economy can present opportunities as well as threats. For example, the fact that 40 percent of consumers say they are eating out less poses threats for many full-service restaurants. However, it presents opportunities for fast-food marketers. For instance, during the recession, a Seattle McDonald's franchise operator took on Starbuck's in its hometown with billboards proclaiming "Large is the new grande" and "Four bucks is dumb." Playing on its cheap-eats value proposition, McDonald's worldwide sales grew steadily through the worst of the downturn, whereas Starbucks sales stuttered. The premier coffee chain was forced to shutter many unprofitable stores.[38]

Similarly, the trend toward saving money by eating at home plays into the hands of name-brand food makers, who have positioned their wares as convenient and—compared with a restaurant meal—inexpensive. Rather than lowering prices, many food manufacturers have instead pointed out the value of their products as compared to eating out. An ad for Francesco Rinaldi pasta sauce asserts, "Now you can feed a family of four for under $10." Kraft's DiGiorno pizza ads employ "DiGiornonomics," showing that the price of a DiGiorno pizza baked at home is half that of a delivery pizza.

The Digital Age

The recent technology boom has created a digital age. The explosive growth in computer, communications, information, and other digital technologies has had a major impact on the ways companies bring value to their customers. Now, more than ever before, we are all connected to each other and to information anywhere in the world. Where it once took days or weeks to receive news about important world events, we now learn about them as they are occurring via live satellite broadcasts and news Web sites. Where it once took weeks to correspond with others in distant places, they are now only moments away by cell phone, e-mail, or Web cam. For better or worse, technology has become an indispensable part of our lives:[39]

> Karl and Dorsey Gude of East Lansing, Michigan, can remember simpler mornings not too long ago. They sat together and chatted as they ate breakfast and read the newspaper and competed only with the television for the attention of their two teenage sons. That was so last century. Today, Karl wakes around 6:00 AM to check his work e-mail and his Facebook and Twitter accounts. The two boys, Cole and Erik, start each morning with text messages, video games, and Facebook. Dorsey cracks open her laptop right after breakfast. The Gudes' sons sleep with their phones next to their beds, so they start the day with text messages in place of alarm clocks. Karl, an instructor at Michigan State University, sends texts to his two sons to wake them up. "We use texting as an in-house intercom," he says. "I could just walk up stairs, but they always answer their texts." This is morning in the Internet age. After six to eight hours of network deprivation—also known as sleep—people are increasingly waking up and lunging for cell phones and laptops, sometimes even before swinging their legs to the floor and tending to more biologically current activities.

Internet
A vast public web of computer networks that connects users of all types all around the world to each other and to an amazingly large information repository.

The digital age has provided marketers with exciting new ways to learn about and track customers and create products and services tailored to individual customer needs. It's helping marketers communicate with customers in large groups or one-to-one. Through Web videoconferencing, marketing researchers at a company's headquarters in New York can look in on focus groups in Chicago or Paris without ever stepping onto a plane. With only a few clicks of a mouse button, a direct marketer can tap into online data services to learn anything from what car you drive to what you read to what flavor of ice cream you prefer. Or, using today's powerful computers, marketers can create their own detailed customer databases and use them to target individual customers with offers designed to meet their specific needs.

Digital technology has also brought a new wave of communication, advertising, and relationship building tools—ranging from online advertising, video-sharing tools, and cell phones to Web apps and online social networks. The digital shift means that marketers can no longer expect consumers to always seek them out. Nor can they always control conversations about their brands. The new digital world makes it easy for consumers to take marketing content that once lived only in advertising or on a brand Web site with them wherever they go and share it with friends. More than just add-ons to traditional marketing channels, the new digital media must be fully integrated into the marketer's customer-relationship-building efforts.

The most dramatic digital technology is the **Internet**. The number of Internet users worldwide now stands at more than 1.8 billion and will reach an estimated 3.4 billion by 2015. On a typical day, 58 percent of American adults check their e-mail, 50 percent use Google or another search engine to find information, 38 percent get the news, 27 percent keep in touch with friends on social-networking sites such as Facebook and LinkedIn, and 19 percent watch a video on a video-sharing site such as YouTube. And by 2020, many experts believe, the Internet will be accessed primarily via a mobile device operated by voice, touch, and even thought or "mind-controlled human-computer interaction."[40]

Whereas *Web 1.0* connected people with information, the next generation *Web 2.0* has connected people with people, employing a fast-growing set of new Web technologies such as blogs, social-networking sites, and video-sharing sites. ◉ *Web 3.0*, starting now, puts all these information and people connections together in ways that will make our Internet experience more relevant, useful, and enjoyable.[41]

In Web 3.0, small, fast, customizable Internet applications, accessed through multifunction mobile devices, "will bring you a virtual world you can carry in your pocket. We will

◉ Web 3.0—the third coming of the Web—"will bring you a virtual world you can carry in your pocket."

be carrying our amusements with us—best music collections, video collections, instant news access—all tailored to our preferences and perpetually updatable. And as this cooler stuff [evolves], we won't be connecting to this new Web so much as walking around inside it."[42] The interactive, community-building nature of these new Web technologies makes them ideal for relating with customers.

Online marketing is now the fastest-growing form of marketing. These days, it's hard to find a company that doesn't use the Web in a significant way. In addition to the click-only dot-coms, most traditional brick-and-mortar companies have now become "click-and-mortar" companies. They have ventured online to attract new customers and build stronger relationships with existing ones. Today, more than 75 percent of American online users use the Internet to shop.[43] Business-to-business (B-to-B) online commerce is also booming. It seems that almost every business has created shops on the Web.

Thus, the technology boom is providing exciting new opportunities for marketers. We will explore the impact of digital marketing technologies in future chapters, especially Chapter 17.

Rapid Globalization

As they are redefining their customer relationships, marketers are also taking a fresh look at the ways in which they relate with the broader world around them. In an increasingly smaller world, companies are now connected *globally* with their customers and marketing partners.

Today, almost every company, large or small, is touched in some way by global competition. A neighborhood florist buys its flowers from Mexican nurseries, and a large U.S. electronics manufacturer competes in its home markets with giant Korean rivals. A fledgling Internet retailer finds itself receiving orders from all over the world at the same time that an American consumer-goods producer introduces new products into emerging markets abroad.

American firms have been challenged at home by the skillful marketing of European and Asian multinationals. Companies such as Toyota, Nokia, Nestlé, and Samsung have often outperformed their U.S. competitors in American markets. Similarly, U.S. companies in a wide range of industries have developed truly global operations, making and selling their products worldwide. ◉ Quintessentially American McDonald's now serves 60 million customers daily in more than 32,000 local restaurants in 100 countries worldwide—65 percent of its corporate revenues come from outside the United States. Similarly, Nike markets in more than 180 countries, with non-U.S. sales accounting for 66 percent of its worldwide sales.[44] Today, companies are not only selling more of their locally produced goods in international markets but also buying more supplies and components abroad.

Thus, managers in countries around the world are increasingly taking a global, not just local, view of the company's industry, competitors, and opportunities. They are asking: What is global marketing? How does it differ from domestic marketing? How do global competitors and forces affect our business? To what extent should we "go global"? We will discuss the global marketplace in more detail in Chapter 19.

◉ **U.S. companies in a wide range of industries have developed truly global operations. Quintessentially American McDonald's captures 65 percent of its revenues from outside the United States.**

Sustainable Marketing—The Call for More Social Responsibility

Marketers are reexamining their relationships with social values and responsibilities and with the very Earth that sustains us. As the worldwide consumerism and environmentalism movements mature, today's marketers are being called to develop *sustainable marketing* practices. Corporate ethics and social responsibility have become hot topics for almost every business. And few companies can ignore the renewed and very demanding environmental movement. Every company action can affect customer relationships. Today's customers expect companies to deliver value in a socially and environmentally responsible way.

● Sustainable marketing: Patagonia believes in "using business to inspire solutions to the environmental crisis." It backs these words by pledging at least 1 percent of its sales or 10 percent of its profits, whichever is greater, to the protection of the natural environment.

The social-responsibility and environmental movements will place even stricter demands on companies in the future. Some companies resist these movements, budging only when forced by legislation or organized consumer outcries. More forward-looking companies, however, readily accept their responsibilities to the world around them. They view sustainable marketing as an opportunity to do well by doing good. They seek ways to profit by serving immediate needs and the best long-run interests of their customers and communities.

Some companies, such as Patagonia, Ben & Jerry's, Timberland, Method, and others, practice "caring capitalism," setting themselves apart by being civic minded and responsible. They build social responsibility and action into their company value and mission statements. ● For example, when it comes to environmental responsibility, outdoor gear marketer Patagonia is "committed to the core." "Those of us who work here share a strong commitment to protecting undomesticated lands and waters," says the company's Web site. "We believe in using business to inspire solutions to the environmental crisis." Patagonia backs these words with actions. Each year it pledges at least 1 percent of its sales or 10 percent of its profits, whichever is greater, to the protection of the natural environment.[45] We will revisit the topic of sustainable marketing in greater detail in Chapter 20.

The Growth of Not-for-Profit Marketing

In recent years, marketing also has become a major part of the strategies of many not-for-profit organizations, such as colleges, hospitals, museums, zoos, symphony orchestras, and even churches. The nation's not-for-profits face stiff competition for support and membership. Sound marketing can help them attract membership and support.[46] Consider the marketing efforts of the American Society for the Prevention of Cruelty to Animals (ASPCA):[47]

The ASPCA gets its funding from more than one million active supporters. However, like many not-for-profits, attracting new donors is tricky—that is, until singer-songwriter Sarah McLachlan came along and created what many in not-for-profit circles call "The Ad." ● Produced by a small 12-person Canadian firm, Eagle-Com, the two-minute television commercial features heart-breaking photographs of dogs and cats scrolling across the screen while McLachlan croons the haunting song "Angel" in the background (see the "The Ad" at www.youtube.com/watch?v=Iu_JqNdp2As). McLachlan appears only momentarily to ask viewers to share her support for the ASPCA. The heart-rending commercial has tugged at viewers' heartstrings and opened their wallets. This one ad attracted 200,000 new donors and raised roughly $30 million for the organization since it started running in early 2007. That makes it a landmark in nonprofit fund-raising, where such amounts are virtually unimaginable for a single commercial. The donations from the McLachlan commercial have enabled the ASPCA to buy prime-time slots on national networks, such as CNN, which in turn has generated more income. The ASPCA is now rolling out new McLachlan ads to further bolster its fund-raising efforts.

Government agencies have also shown an increased interest in marketing. For example, the U.S. military has a marketing plan to

● Not-for-profit marketing: A single two-minute TV commercial—"The Ad"—has attracted 200,000 new donors and raised roughly $30 million for the ASPCA since it started running in early 2007.

attract recruits to its different services, and various government agencies are now designing *social marketing campaigns* to encourage energy conservation and concern for the environment or discourage smoking, excessive drinking, and drug use. Even the once-stodgy U.S. Postal Service has developed innovative marketing to sell commemorative stamps, promote its priority mail services, and lift its image as a contemporary and competitive organization. In all, the U.S. government is the nation's 33rd largest advertiser, with an annual advertising budget of more than $1 billion.[48]

> **Author Comment** | Remember Figure 1.1 outlining the marketing process? Now, based on everything we've discussed in this chapter, we'll expand that figure to provide a road map for learning marketing throughout the remainder of this text.

So, What Is Marketing?
Pulling It All Together (pp 29–30)

At the start of this chapter, Figure 1.1 presented a simple model of the marketing process. Now that we've discussed all the steps in the process, ● **Figure 1.5** presents an expanded model that will help you pull it all together. What is marketing? Simply put, marketing is the process of building profitable customer relationships by creating value for customers and capturing value in return.

The first four steps of the marketing process focus on creating value for customers. The company first gains a full understanding of the marketplace by researching customer needs and managing marketing information. It then designs a customer-driven marketing strategy based on the answers to two simple questions. The first question is "What consumers will we serve?" (market segmentation and targeting). Good marketing companies know that they cannot serve all customers in every way. Instead, they need to focus their resources on the customers they can serve best and most profitably. The second marketing strategy question is "How can we best serve

> This expanded version of Figure 1.1 at the beginning of the chapter provides a good road map for the rest of the text. The underlying concept of the entire text is that marketing creates value *for* customers in order to capture value *from* customers in return.

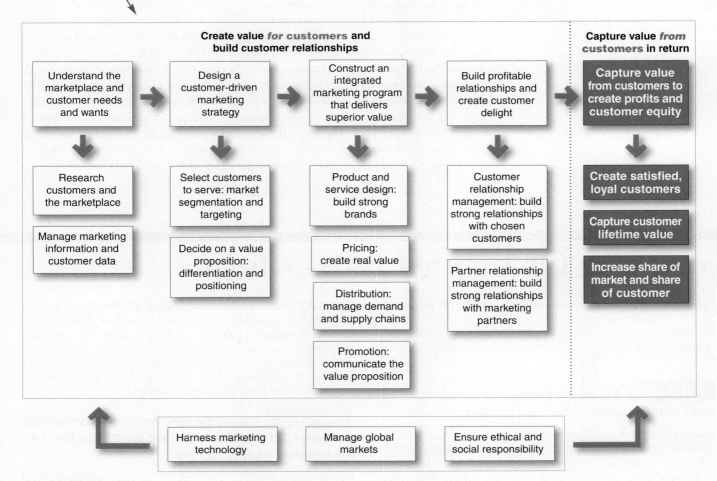

● **FIGURE | 1.5**
An Expanded Model of the Marketing Process

targeted customers?" (differentiation and positioning). Here, the marketer outlines a value proposition that spells out what values the company will deliver to win target customers.

With its marketing strategy chosen, the company now constructs an integrated marketing program—consisting of a blend of the four marketing mix elements—the four Ps—that transforms the marketing strategy into real value for customers. The company develops product offers and creates strong brand identities for them. It prices these offers to create real customer value and distributes the offers to make them available to target consumers. Finally, the company designs promotion programs that communicate the value proposition to target customers and persuade them to act on the market offering.

Perhaps the most important step in the marketing process involves building value-laden, profitable relationships with target customers. Throughout the process, marketers practice customer relationship management to create customer satisfaction and delight. In creating customer value and relationships, however, the company cannot go it alone. It must work closely with marketing partners both inside the company and throughout its marketing system. Thus, beyond practicing good customer relationship management, firms must also practice good partner relationship management.

The first four steps in the marketing process create value *for* customers. In the final step, the company reaps the rewards of its strong customer relationships by capturing value *from* customers. Delivering superior customer value creates highly satisfied customers who will buy more and buy again. This helps the company capture customer lifetime value and greater share of customer. The result is increased long-term customer equity for the firm.

Finally, in the face of today's changing marketing landscape, companies must take into account three additional factors. In building customer and partner relationships, they must harness marketing technology, take advantage of global opportunities, and ensure that they act in an ethical and socially responsible way.

Figure 1.5 provides a good road map to future chapters of this text. Chapters 1 and 2 introduce the marketing process, with a focus on building customer relationships and capturing value from customers. Chapters 3 through 6 address the first step of the marketing process—understanding the marketing environment, managing marketing information, and understanding consumer and business buyer behavior. In Chapter 7, we look more deeply into the two major marketing strategy decisions: selecting which customers to serve (segmentation and targeting) and determining a value proposition (differentiation and positioning). Chapters 8 through 17 discuss the marketing mix variables, one by one. Chapter 18 sums up customer-driven marketing strategy and creating competitive advantage in the marketplace. The final two chapters examine special marketing considerations: global marketing and sustainable marketing.

REVIEWING Objectives AND KEY Terms

Today's successful companies—whether large or small, for-profit or not-for-profit, domestic or global—share a strong customer focus and a heavy commitment to marketing. The goal of marketing is to build and manage customer relationships.

Objective 1 Define marketing and outline the steps in the marketing process. (pp 4–5)

Marketing is the process by which companies create value for customers and build strong customer relationships in order to capture value from customers in return.

The marketing process involves five steps. The first four steps create value *for* customers. First, marketers need to understand the marketplace and customer needs and wants. Next, marketers de-

sign a customer-driven marketing strategy with the goal of getting, keeping, and growing target customers. In the third step, marketers construct a marketing program that actually delivers superior value. All of these steps form the basis for the fourth step, building profitable customer relationships and creating customer delight. In the final step, the company reaps the rewards of strong customer relationships by capturing value *from* customers.

Objective 2 Explain the importance of understanding customers and the marketplace and identify the five core marketplace concepts. (pp 6–8)

Outstanding marketing companies go to great lengths to learn about and understand their customers' *needs*, *wants*, and *demands*. This understanding helps them to design want-satisfying market offerings and build value-laden customer relationships by which they can capture *customer lifetime value* and greater *share of customer*. The result is increased long-term *customer equity* for the firm.

The core marketplace concepts are needs, wants, and demands; *market offerings* (products, services, and experiences); value and satisfaction; exchange and relationships; and markets. Wants are the form taken by human needs when shaped by culture and individual personality. When backed by buying power, wants become demands. Companies address needs by putting forth a value proposition, a set of benefits that they promise to consumers to satisfy their needs. The value proposition is fulfilled through a market offering, which delivers customer value and satisfaction, resulting in long-term exchange relationships with customers.

Objective 3   Identify the key elements of a customer-driven marketing strategy and discuss the marketing management orientations that guide marketing strategy. (pp 8–12)

To design a winning marketing strategy, the company must first decide *whom* it will serve. It does this by dividing the market into segments of customers (*market segmentation*) and selecting which segments it will cultivate (*target marketing*). Next, the company must decide *how* it will serve targeted customers (how it will *differentiate and position* itself in the marketplace).

Marketing management can adopt one of five competing market orientations. The *production concept* holds that management's task is to improve production efficiency and bring down prices. The *product concept* holds that consumers favor products that offer the most in quality, performance, and innovative features; thus, little promotional effort is required. The *selling concept* holds that consumers will not buy enough of an organization's products unless it undertakes a large-scale selling and promotion effort. The *marketing concept* holds that achieving organizational goals depends on determining the needs and wants of target markets and delivering the desired satisfactions more effectively and efficiently than competitors do. The *societal marketing concept* holds that generating customer satisfaction *and* long-run societal well-being through sustainable marketing strategies keyed to both achieving the company's goals and fulfilling its responsibilities.

Objective 4   Discuss customer relationship management and identify strategies for creating value *for* customers and capturing value *from* customers in return. (pp 12–22)

Broadly defined, *customer relationship management* is the process of building and maintaining profitable customer relationships by delivering superior customer value and satisfaction. The aim of customer relationship management is to produce high *customer equity,* the total combined customer lifetime values of all of the company's customers. The key to building lasting relationships is the creation of superior *customer value* and *satisfaction*.

Companies want not only to acquire profitable customers but also build relationships that will keep them and grow "share of customer." Different types of customers require different customer relationship management strategies. The marketer's aim is to build the *right relationships* with the *right customers.* In return for creating value *for* targeted customers, the company captures value *from* customers in the form of profits and customer equity.

In building customer relationships, good marketers realize that they cannot go it alone. They must work closely with marketing partners inside and outside the company. In addition to being good at customer relationship management, they must also be good at *partner relationship management*.

Objective 5   Describe the major trends and forces that are changing the marketing landscape in this age of relationships. (pp 22–30)

Dramatic changes are occurring in the marketing arena. The recent Great Recession left many consumers short of both money and confidence, creating a new age of consumer frugality that will last well into the future. More than ever, marketers must now emphasize the *value* in their value propositions. The challenge is to balance a brand's value proposition with current times while also enhancing its long-term equity.

The boom in computer, telecommunications, information, transportation, and other technologies has created exciting new ways to learn about and relate to individual customers. It has also allowed new approaches by which marketers can target consumers more selectively and build closer, two-way customer relationships in the Web 3.0 era.

In an increasingly smaller world, many marketers are now connected *globally* with their customers and marketing partners. Today, almost every company, large or small, is touched in some way by global competition. Today's marketers are also reexamining their ethical and societal responsibilities. Marketers are being called to take greater responsibility for the social and environmental impact of their actions. Finally, in recent years, marketing also has become a major part of the strategies of many not-for-profit organizations, such as colleges, hospitals, museums, zoos, symphony orchestras, and even churches.

Pulling it all together, as discussed throughout the chapter, the major new developments in marketing can be summed up in a single word: *relationships*. Today, marketers of all kinds are taking advantage of new opportunities for building relationships with their customers, their marketing partners, and the world around them.

KEY Terms

OBJECTIVE 1

Marketing (p 5)

OBJECTIVE 2

Needs (p 6)
Wants (p 6)
Demands (p 6)
Market offerings (p 6)

Marketing myopia (p 7)
Exchange (p 7)
Market (p 7)

OBJECTIVE 3

Marketing management (p 8)
Production concept (p 9)
Product concept (p 9)

Selling concept (p 10)
Marketing concept (p 10)
Societal marketing concept (p 11)

OBJECTIVE 4

Customer relationship management (p 12)

Customer-perceived value (p 12)
Customer satisfaction (p 13)
Customer-managed relationships (p 17)
Consumer-generated marketing (p 18)

Partner relationship management (p 19)
Customer lifetime value (p 20)
Share of customer (p 21)

Customer equity (p 21)

OBJECTIVE 5
Internet (p 26)

PEARSON mymarketinglab

- Check your understanding of the concepts and key terms using the mypearsonmarketinglab study plan for this chapter.
- Apply the concepts in a business context using the simulation entitled **What Is Marketing?**

DISCUSSING & APPLYING THE Concepts

Discussing the Concepts

1. Define marketing and discuss how it is more than just "telling and selling." (AACSB: Communication; Reflective Thinking)

2. Marketing has been criticized because it "makes people buy things they don't really need." Refute or support this accusation. (AACSB: Communication; Reflective Thinking)

3. Discuss the two important questions a marketing manager must answer when designing a winning marketing strategy. How should a manager approach finding answers to these questions? (AACSB: Communication; Reflective Thinking)

4. What are the five different marketing management orientations? Which orientation do you believe Apple follows when marketing products such as the iPhone and iPad? (AACSB: Communication; Reflective Thinking)

5. Explain the difference between *share of customer* and *customer equity*. Why are these concepts important to marketers? (AACSB: Communication; Reflective Thinking)

6. Discuss trends impacting marketing and the implications of these trends on how marketers deliver value to customers. (AACSB: Communication)

Applying the Concepts

1. Talk to five people, varying in age from young adult to senior citizen, about their automobiles. Ask them what value means to them with regard to an automobile and how the manufacturer and dealer create such value. Write a brief report of what you learned about customer value. (AACSB: Communication; Reflective Thinking)

2. Select a retailer and calculate how much you are worth to that retailer if you continue to shop there for the rest of your life (your customer lifetime value). What factors should you consider when deriving an estimate of your lifetime value to a retailer? How can a retailer increase your lifetime value? (AACSB: Communication; Reflective Thinking; Analytic Reasoning)

3. Read Appendix 3 or go online to learn about careers in marketing. Interview someone who works in one of the marketing jobs described in the appendix and ask him or her the following questions:
   a. What does your job entail?
   b. How did you get to this point in your career? Is this what you thought you'd be doing when you grew up? What influenced you to get into this field?
   c. What education is necessary for this job?
   d. What advice can you give to college students?
   e. Add one additional question that you create.

Write a brief report of the responses to your questions and explain why you would or would not be interested in working in this field. (AACSB: Communication; Reflective Thinking)

FOCUS ON Technology

In only a few short years, *consumer-generated marketing* has increased exponentially. It's also known as *consumer-generated media* and *consumer-generated content*. More than 100 million Web sites contain user-generated content. You may be a contributor yourself if you've ever posted something on a blog; reviewed a product at Amazon.com; uploaded a video on YouTube; or sent a video from your mobile phone to a news Web site, such as CNN.com or FoxNews.com. This force has not gone unnoticed by marketers—and with good reason. Nielsen, the TV ratings giant, found that most consumers trust consumer opinions posted online. As a result, savvy marketers encourage consumers to generate content. For example, Coca-Cola has more than 3.5 million fans on Facebook, mothers can share information at Pampers Village (www.pampers.com), and Dorito's scored a touchdown with consumer-created advertising dur-

ing the past several Super Bowls. Apple even encourages iPhone users to develop applications for its device. However, consumer-generated marketing is not without problems—just search "I hate (insert company name)" in any search engine!

1. Find two examples (other than those discussed in the chapter) of marketer-supported, consumer-generated content and two examples of consumer-generated content that is not officially supported by the company whose product is involved. Provide the Web link to each and discuss how the information impacts your attitude toward the companies involved. (AACSB: Communication; Reflective Thinking; Technology)

2. Discuss the advantages and disadvantages of consumer-generated marketing. (AACSB: Communication; Reflective)

FOCUS ON Ethics

Sixty years ago, about 45 percent of Americans smoked cigarettes, but now the smoking rate is less than 20 percent. This decline results from acquired knowledge on the potential health dangers of smoking and marketing restrictions for this product. Although smoking rates are declining in most developed nations, however, more and more consumers in developing nations, such as Russia and China, are puffing away. Smoker rates in some countries run as high as 40 percent. Developing nations account for more than 70 percent of world tobacco consumption, and marketers are fueling this growth. Most of these nations do not have the restrictions prevalent in developed nations, such as advertising bans, warning labels, and distribution restrictions. Consequently, it is predicted that one billion people worldwide will die this century from smoking-related ailments.

1. Given the extreme health risks, should marketers stop selling cigarettes even though they are legal and demanded by consumers? Should cigarette marketers continue to use marketing tactics that are restricted in one country in other countries where they are not restricted? (AACSB: Communication; Ethical Reasoning)

2. Research the history of cigarette marketing in the United States. Are there any new restrictions with respect to marketing this product? (AACSB: Communication; Reflective Thinking)

MARKETING & THE Economy

Hershey

During uncertain economic times, there are still some things that today's consumers just aren't willing to give up—such as chocolate. But as with eating out and clothing purchases, they *are* trading down. That is just fine with Hershey, America's best-known chocolate maker. For years, riding the good times, premium chocolates grew faster than lower-priced confectionery products. Slow to jump on the premium bandwagon, Hershey lost market share to Mars Inc.'s Dove line. But as consumer frugality increased during the Great Recession, the sales of premium chocolate brands went flat. However, Hershey's sales, profits, and stock price increased as many consumers passed up higher-end goods in favor of Hershey's chocolate bars, Reese's Peanut Butter Cups, and Kit Kat wafers. Hershey seized the opportunity of this trend by running new ads that stressed their value. It also cut costs by paring back the varieties of products such as Hershey's Kisses. As supermarkets reduced the shelf space they allotted to premium chocolates, Hershey cashed in as consumers looked to affordable Hershey favorites to satisfy their cravings. After all, even on a tight budget, people need to indulge at least a little.

1. Is Hershey's resurgence based on a want or a need?

2. Evaluate the shift in chocolate sales based on benefits and costs that customers perceive.

3. What other products are harmed or helped by the new consumer frugality?

MARKETING BY THE Numbers

Marketing is expensive! A 30-second advertising spot during the 2010 Super Bowl cost $3 million, which doesn't include the $500,000 or more necessary to produce the commercial. Anheuser-Busch usually purchases multiple spots each year. Similarly, sponsoring one car during one NASCAR race costs $500,000. But Sprint, the sponsor of the popular Sprint Cup, pays much more than that. What marketer sponsors only one car for only one race? Do you want customers to order your product by phone? That will cost you $8–$13 per order. Do you want a sales representative calling on customers? That's about $100 per sales call, and that's if the rep doesn't have to get on an airplane and stay in a hotel, which can be very costly considering some companies have thousands of sales reps calling on thousands of customers. What about the $1 off coupon for Tropicana orange juice that you found in the Sunday newspaper? It costs Tropicana more than a $1 when you redeem it at the store. These are all examples of just one marketing element—promotion. Marketing costs also include the costs of product research and development (R&D), the costs of distributing products to buyers, and the costs of all the employees working in marketing.

1. Select a publically traded company and research how much the company spent on marketing activities in the most recent year of available data. What percentage of sales does marketing expenditures represent? Have these expenditures increased or decreased over the past five years? Write a brief report of your findings. (AACSB Communication; Analytic Reasoning)

2. Search the Internet for salary information regarding jobs in marketing. Use www.marketingsalaries.com/home/national_averages.htm?function=# or a similar Web site. What is the national average for five different jobs in marketing? How do the averages compare in different areas of the country? Write a brief report on your findings. (AACSB: Communication; Use of IT; Reflective Thinking)

VIDEO Case

Stew Leonard's

Stew Leonard's is a little-known grocery store chain based in Connecticut. It has only four stores. But its small number of locations doesn't begin to illustrate what customers experience when they visit what has been called the "Disneyland of dairy stores." Since opening its first dairy store in 1969, the company has been known for its customer-centric way of doing business. In fact, founder Stew Leonard's obsession with the concept of customer lifetime value made him determined to keep every customer who entered his store.

The video featuring Stew Leonard's shows how the retailer has delighted customers for more than 40 years. With singing animatronics farm animals, associates in costume, petting zoos, and free food and drink samples, this chain serves as many as 300,000 customers per store every week and has achieved the highest sales per square foot of any single store in the United States. After viewing the video, answer the following questions about the company.

1. What is Stew Leonard's value proposition?

2. How does Stew Leonard's build long-term customer relationships?

3. How has Stew Leonard's applied the concepts of customer equity and customer lifetime value?

COMPANY Case

JetBlue: Delighting Customers Through Happy Jetting

In 2007, JetBlue was a thriving young airline with a strong reputation for outstanding service. In fact, the low-fare airline referred to itself as a customer service company that just happened to fly planes. But on Valentine's Day 2007, JetBlue was hit by the perfect storm—literally—of events that led to an operational meltdown. One of the most severe storms of the decade covered JetBlue's main hub at New York's John F. Kennedy International Airport with a thick layer of snow and ice. Small JetBlue did not have the infrastructure to deal with such a crisis. The severity of the storm, coupled with a series of poor management decisions, left JetBlue passengers stranded in planes on the runway for up to 11 hours. Worse still, the ripple effect of the storm created major JetBlue flight disruptions for six more days.

Understandably, customers were livid. JetBlue's efforts to clean up the mess following the six-day Valentine's Day nightmare cost over $30 million dollars in overtime, flight refunds, vouchers for future travel, and other expenses. But the blow to the company's previously stellar customer-service reputation stung far more than the financial fallout. JetBlue became the butt of jokes by late night talk show hosts. Some industry observers even predicted that this would be the end of the seven-year-old airline.

But just three years later, the company is not only still flying, it is growing, profitable, and hotter than ever. During the recent economic downturn, even as most competing airlines were cutting routes, retiring aircraft, laying off employees, and losing money, JetBlue was adding planes, expanding into new cities, hiring thousands of new employees, and turning profits. Even more, JetBlue's customers adore the airline. For the fifth consecutive year (even including 2007), JetBlue has had the highest J.D. Power and Associates customer satisfaction score for the entire airline industry. Not only did JetBlue recover quickly from the Valentine's Day hiccup, it's now stronger than ever.

TRULY CUSTOMER FOCUSED

What's the secret to JetBlue's success? Quite simply, it's an obsession with making sure that every customer experience lives up to the company slogan, "Happy Jetting." Lots of companies say they focus on customers. But at JetBlue, customer well-being is ingrained in the culture.

From the beginning, JetBlue set out to provide features that would delight customers. For example, most air travelers expect to be squashed when flying coach. But JetBlue has configured its seats with three more inches of legroom than the average airline seat. That may not sound like much. But those three inches allow six-foot three-inch Arianne Cohen, author of *The Tall Book: A Celebration of Life from on High*, to stretch out and even cross her legs. If that's not enough, for as little as $10 per flight, travelers can reserve one of JetBlue's "Even More Legroom" seats, which offer even more space and a flatter recline position. Add the fact that every JetBlue seat is well padded and covered in leather, and you already have an air travel experience that rivals first-class accommodations (something JetBlue doesn't offer).

Food and beverage is another perk that JetBlue customers enjoy. The airline doesn't serve meals, but it offers the best selection of free beverages and snacks to be found at 30,000 feet. In addition to the standard soft drinks, juices, and salty snacks, JetBlue flyers enjoy Terra Blues chips, Immaculate Baking's Chocobillys cookies, and Dunkin' Donuts coffee. But it isn't just the selection; it's the fact that customers don't feel like they have to beg for a nibble. One customer describes snacking on JetBlue as an "open bar for snacks. They are constantly walking around offering it. I never feel thirsty. I never feel hungry. It's not 'Here, have a little sip,' and 'Good-bye, that's all you get.'"

Airlines often can't control flight delays, especially at busy airports like JFK. So JetBlue wants to be sure that customers will be entertained even in the event of a delay. That's why every seat has its own LCD entertainment system. Customers can watch any of 36 channels on DirectTV or listen to 100+ channels on Sirius XM Radio, free of charge. If that isn't enough, six bucks will buy a movie or your favorite television show. JetBlue rounds out the amenities with free Wi-Fi in terminals and free sending and receiving of e-mails and instant messages in the air.

Even JetBlue's main terminal, the new state-of-the-art T-5 terminal at JFK, is not the usual airline experience. With more security lanes than any terminal in the country, travelers scurry right through. High end dining (tapas, lobster tempura, and Kobe sliders, just to name a few options) can be found among the terminal's 22 restaurants. And its 25 retail stores are characteristic of the latest mall offerings. A children's play zone, comfortable lounge areas, work spaces, and piped in music from Sirius XM Radio make travelers hesitant to leave.

MORE THAN AMENITIES

Although the tangible amenities that JetBlue offers are likely to delight most travelers, CEO David Barger recognizes that these things are not nearly enough to provide a sustainable competitive advantage. "The hard product—airplanes, leather seats, satellite TVs, bricks and mortar—as long as you have a checkbook, they can be replicated," Barger tells a group of new hires in training. "It's the culture that can't be replicated. It's how we treat each other. Do we trust each other? Can we push back on each other? The human side of the equation is the most important part of what we're doing."

It's that culture that gives JetBlue customer service unlike that of any other airline. Taking care of customers starts as early as a customer's first encounter with a JetBlue call center. Many callers feel like they are talking to the lady next door. That's because, in all likelihood, they are. JetBlue's founder pioneered a reservation system that employs part-time reps working from home. Mary Driffill is one of 700 at-home reservations agents in Salt Lake City alone. She logs on to her computer and receives calls in her four-year-old daughter's bedroom, under the watchful eye of Raggedy Ann, Potbelly Bear, and Chewy, the family Pomeranian-Chihuahua mix. "It's the best job I've ever had," says Driffill. "Every day I talk to people who love the company as much as I do. That reminds me I'm part of this."

JetBlue employees are well acquainted with the company's core values: safety, integrity, caring, passion, and fun. If that sounds like an awful lot of warm fuzzies, it's intentional. But JetBlue hires the types of employees that fit these values. The values then provide the basis for what Robin Hayes, JetBlue's chief commercial officer, calls the company's S.O.C.I.A.L. currency program. In JetBlue's words:

Standing for something. JetBlue was formed with the idea of bringing humanity back to travel, and our engagement with our customers is central to that mission.

Operationalizing the brand. Whether it be in the airport, on the planes, on the phones, or online, the connection with our customers is a key factor in how we do business.

Conversing with customers, broadly. To be properly in touch with the community, it requires the ability to understand and react to the collective conversation that occurs.

Involving, immersing employees. Social media involvement requires understanding and involvement from all aspects and departments of the company.

Advocating the brand. For JetBlue, we understand the ability to market to a social community is dependent on our customers' willingness to hear and spread those marketing messages.

Listening. Waiving the carry-on bike fee . . . shows we quickly identify and adapt new policies based on feedback we receive through social media channels. It demonstrates our ability to listen and react holistically.

WHEN YOU LOVE YOUR CUSTOMERS, THEY LOVE YOU BACK

Customers who spread positive word-of-mouth are called many names—true friends, angels, apostles, evangelists. The religious overtones of such labels come from the idea that loyal customers are like true believers who share the good word like a missionary would. JetBlue has an unusually high ratio of such customers. Most airline customers are loyal because they have frequent flyer points. If not for those points, most couldn't care less with whom they fly. For most, flying is a generally unpleasant experience regardless of who operates the plane.

However, JetBlue customers are so enthralled with what the airline has to offer that they look forward to flying. And they want to keep in touch with the brand even when they aren't flying. JetBlue has 1.1 million followers on Twitter, more than any other company except Whole Foods Market and Zappos.com, two other customer service legends. Twitter even features JetBlue as a case study on smart corporate twittering. More broadly, by the metric of social currency (a fancy term for networks of customers spreading by word of mouth), JetBlue is the strongest U.S. brand, outperforming even Apple.

JetBlue's strong word of mouth has been fueled by the company's ability to delight customers.

> People love to talk about JetBlue because the experience is so unexpected. Most airline travel has a particular pattern: small seats, bad entertainment, and little (if any) food. JetBlue breaks this pattern. Leather seats, your own entertainment system with dozens of channels, and at least some choice of food. People can't stop talking about the experience because they have to express their surprise, especially given the "value" price. They are so used to airline travel being poor, late, or uncomfortable these days that cases where a company seems to care and provide good service seems noteworthy. Satisfaction itself is unexpected.

In ten short years, JetBlue has proven that an airline can deliver low fares, excellent service, and steady profits. It has shown that even in the airline business, a powerful brand can be built. Few other airlines have been able to write this story. If you're thinking Southwest Airlines, you'd be on target. In fact, JetBlue's founders modeled the airline after Southwest. JetBlue has often been called, "the Southwest of the Northeast." JetBlue's onboard crews even greet customers onboard with jokes, songs, and humorous versions of the safety routine, something Southwest has been known for since the 1970s. But where Southwest has made customers happy with no frills, JetBlue is arguably doing it all, including the frills.

Until last year, Southwest and JetBlue steered clear of each other. But then both airlines added a Boston-Baltimore route. Boston is a JetBlue stronghold; Baltimore is Southwest's biggest market. But with JetBlue's younger workforce and newer, more fuel-efficient planes, its cost per available seat mile is 8.88 cents, whereas it's 9.76 cents for Southwest. That has allowed JetBlue to do something that no other airline has done to Southwest; undercut it on price with $39 tickets that are $20 cheaper than Southwest's lowest fare. It's not clear yet how the battle of the low-fare, high-service airlines will play out. But it may well turn out that as JetBlue and Southwest cross paths on more routes, the losers will be the other airlines.

Questions for Discussion

1. Give examples of needs, wants, and demands that JetBlue customers demonstrate, differentiating these three concepts. What are the implications of each for JetBlue's practices?

2. Describe in detail all the facets of JetBlue's product. What is being exchanged in a JetBlue transaction?

3. Which of the five marketing management concepts best applies to JetBlue?

4. What value does JetBlue create for its customers?

5. Is JetBlue likely to continue being successful in building customer relationships? Why or why not?

Sources: Stuart Elliott, "JetBlue Asks Its Fliers to Keep Spreading the Word," *New York Times*, May 10, 2010, p. B7; Marc Gunther, "Nothing Blue about JetBlue," *Fortune*, September 14, 2009, p. 114; Chuck Salter, "Calling JetBlue," *Fast Company*, May 1, 2004, accessed at www.fastcompany.com/magazine/82/jetblue_agents.html; Kevin Randall, "Red, Hot, and Blue: The Hottest American Brand Is Not Apple," *Fast Company*, June 3, 2010, accessed at www.fastcompany.com/1656066/apple-jetblue-social-currency-twitter.

Company and Marketing
Strategy Partnering to Build Customer Relationships

Chapter Preview

In the first chapter, we explored the marketing process, the process by which companies create value for consumers in order to capture value from them in return. In this chapter, we dig deeper into steps two and three of that process: designing customer-driven marketing strategies and constructing marketing programs. First, we look at the organization's overall strategic planning, which guides marketing strategy and planning. Next, we discuss how, guided by the strategic plan, marketers partner closely with others inside and outside the firm to create value for customers. We then examine marketing strat-

egy and planning—how marketers choose target markets, position their market offerings, develop a marketing mix, and manage their marketing programs. Finally, we look at the important step of measuring and managing return on marketing investment (marketing ROI).

Let's begin by looking at Nike. Over the past several decades, Nike has built the Nike swoosh into one of the world's best-known brand symbols. Nike's outstanding success results from much more than just making and selling good sports gear. It's based on a customer-focused mission and strategy through which Nike creates valued brand experiences and deep brand community with its customers.

Nike's Mission: Creating Valued Brand Experiences and Deep Brand Community

The Nike swoosh—it's everywhere! Just for fun, try counting the number of swooshes whenever you pick up the sports pages, watch a pickup basketball game, or tune into a televised golf match. Through innovative marketing, Nike has built the ever-present swoosh into one of the best-known brand symbols on the planet.

Some 47 years ago, when young CPA Phil Knight and college track coach Bill Bowerman cofounded the company, Nike was a brash, young upstart in the athletic footwear industry. In 1964, the pair chipped in $500 apiece to start Blue Ribbon Sports. In 1970, Bowerman cooked up a new sneaker tread by stuffing a piece of rubber into his wife's waffle iron. The Waffle Trainer quickly became the nation's best-selling training shoe. In 1972, the company introduced its first Nike brand shoe, named after the Greek goddess of victory. And, in 1978, the company changed its name to Nike. By 1979, Nike had sprinted ahead of the competition, owning 50 percent of the U.S. running shoe market.

In the 1980s, Nike revolutionized sports marketing. To build its brand image and market share, Nike lavishly outspent its competitors on big-name endorsements, splashy promotional events, and big-budget, in-your-face "Just Do It" ads. Nike gave customers much more than just good athletic gear. Whereas competitors stressed technical performance, Nike built customer relationships. Beyond shoes, apparel, and equipment, Nike marketed a way of life, a genuine passion for sports, a just-do-it attitude. Customers didn't just *wear* their Nikes, they *experienced* them. As the company stated on its Web page, "Nike has always known the truth—it's not so much the shoes but where they take you."

Nike powered its way through the early 1990s, moving aggressively into a dozen new sports, including baseball, golf, skateboarding, wall climbing, bicycling, and hiking. The still-brash young company slapped its familiar swoosh logo on everything from sunglasses and soccer balls to batting gloves and golf clubs. It seemed that things couldn't be going any better.

In the late 1990s, however, Nike stumbled, and its sales slipped. As the company grew larger, its creative juices seemed to run a bit dry. Its ads began to look like just more of the same, and its ho-hum new sneaker designs collected dust on retailer shelves' as buyers seeking a new look switched to competing brands. Looking back, Nike's biggest obstacle may have been its own incredible success. As sales approached the $10 billion mark, the swoosh may have become too common to be cool. Instead of being *anti*establishment, Nike *was* the establishment, and its hip, once-hot relationship with customers cooled. Nike needed to rekindle its meaning to its customers.

To turn things around, Nike returned to its roots: new-product innovation and a focus on customer relationships. Its newly minted mission: Nike wants "to bring inspiration and innovation to every athlete* in the world (*if you have a body, you are an athlete.)" With its deep pockets, as in the past, Nike can outspend most competitors on marketing by a wide margin. But this time around, the sports marketer set out to create a new kind of customer relationship—a deeper, more involving one. Now, Nike no longer just talks *at* its customers through media ads and celebrity endorsers. Instead, it uses cutting-edge marketing tools to interact *with* customers to build brand experiences and deep brand community.

Nike still invests hundreds of millions of dollars each year on creative advertising. However, it now spends less than one-third of its $593 million annual promotion budget on television and other traditional media, down from 55 percent 10 years ago. These days, behind the bright lights, Nike has developed a host of innovative new relationship-building approaches.

Using community-oriented, digitally led, social-networking tools, Nike is now building communities of customers who talk not just with the company about the brand but with each other. "Nike's latest masterstroke is social networking, online and off," says one Nike watcher. Whether customers come to know Nike through ads, in-person events at a Niketown store, a local Nike running club, or at a one of the company's many community Web sites, more and more people are bonding closely with the Nike brand experience. Consider this example:

Twice a week, 30 or more people gather at a Nike store in Portland, Oregon, and go for an evening run. Afterward, the members of the Niketown running club chat in the store over refreshments. Nike's staff keeps track of their performances and hails members who have logged more than 100 miles. The event is a classic example of up-close-and-personal relationship building with core customers.

Nike augments such events with an online social network aimed at striking up meaningful and long-term interactions with even more runners. The Nike+ running Web site lets customers with iPod-linked Nike shoes monitor their performances—the distance, pace, time, and calories burned during their runs. Runners can upload and track their own performances over time, compare them with those of other runners, and even participate in local or worldwide challenges.

Talk about brand involvement. Nike+ can be the next best thing to your own personal trainer or jogging buddy. The Nike+ Web site offers a "Nike Coach" that provides advice and training routines to help you prepare for competitive races. When running, if you have earphones, at the end of every mile a friendly voice tells you how far you've gone and then counts down the final meters. If you hit the wall while running, the push of a button brings up a personally selected "power song" that gives you an extra boost and gets you going again. Back home again, after a quick upload of your running data, Nike+ charts and helps you analyze your run.

In four years, two million Nike+ members have logged more than 233 million miles on the site. Collectively, the Nike+ community has run the equivalent of 9,400 trips around the world or 490 journeys to the moon and back. Last October, a million runners competed

virtually in the second annual global "Human Race" 10K, posting their times on Nike+, comparing themselves with runners worldwide, and seeing how their cities or countries performed. The long-term goal is to have 15 percent of the world's 100 million runners using the system.

Thanks to efforts like Nike+, Nike has built a new kinship and sense of community with and between its customers. More than just something to buy, Nike products have once again become a part of customers' lives and times. As a result, the world's largest sportswear company is once again achieving outstanding results. Over the past five years, Nike's global sales and profits have surged nearly 40 percent. In the past three years, Nike's share of the U.S. running shoe market has grown from 48 percent to 61 percent. In 2008 and 2009, as the faltering economy had most sports apparel and footwear competitors gasping for breath, Nike raced ahead. It's global sales grew 14 and 3 percent, respectively. In troubled 2010, despite flat sales, Nike's profits shot ahead 28 percent. By contrast, at largest rival Adidas, sales fell 7 percent, and profits dropped by 68 percent.

In fact, Nike views uncertain economic times as "an incredible opportunity" to take advantage of its strong brand. As in sports competition, the strongest and best-prepared athlete has the best chance of winning. With deep customer relationships comes a powerful competitive advantage. And Nike is once again very close to its customers. As one writer notes, "Nike is blurring the line between brand and experience."[1]

> Nike creates deep brand community with its customers. For example, the Nike+ running system can be the next best thing to your own personal trainer or jogging buddy.

Nike's customer-focused mission and strategy have helped Nike to build strong customer relationships and a deep sense of brand community. As a result, while other sports gear companies are gasping for breath, Nike is sprinting ahead.

Like Nike, outstanding marketing organizations employ strongly customer-driven marketing strategies and programs that create customer value and relationships. These marketing strategies and programs, however, are guided by broader company-wide strategic plans, which must also be customer focused. Thus, to understand the role of marketing, we must first understand the organization's overall strategic planning process.

Author Comment | Company-wide strategic planning guides marketing strategy and planning. Like marketing strategy, the company's broad strategy must also be customer focused.

Company-Wide Strategic Planning: Defining Marketing's Role (pp 38–45)

Each company must find the game plan for long-run survival and growth that makes the most sense given its specific situation, opportunities, objectives, and resources. This is the focus of **strategic planning**—the process of developing and maintaining a strategic fit between the organization's goals and capabilities and its changing marketing opportunities.

Strategic planning
The process of developing and maintaining a strategic fit between the organization's goals and capabilities and its changing marketing opportunities.

Strategic planning sets the stage for the rest of planning in the firm. Companies usually prepare annual plans, long-range plans, and strategic plans. The annual and long-range plans deal with the company's current businesses and how to keep them going. In contrast, the strategic plan involves adapting the firm to take advantage of opportunities in its constantly changing environment.

At the corporate level, the company starts the strategic planning process by defining its overall purpose and mission (see ◉ **Figure 2.1**). This mission is then turned into detailed supporting objectives that guide the entire company. Next, headquarters decides what portfolio of businesses and products is best for the company and how much support to give each one. In turn, each business and product develops detailed marketing and other departmental plans that support the company-wide plan. Thus, marketing planning occurs at the business-unit, product, and market levels. It supports company strategic planning with more detailed plans for specific marketing opportunities.

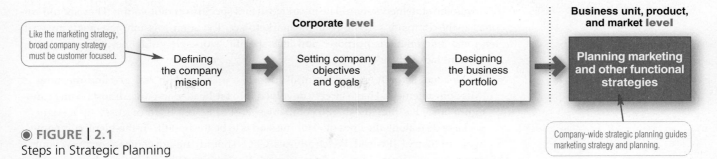

● **FIGURE | 2.1**
Steps in Strategic Planning

Defining a Market-Oriented Mission

An organization exists to accomplish something, and this purpose should be clearly stated. Forging a sound mission begins with the following questions: What *is* our business? Who is the customer? What do consumers value? What *should* our business be? These simple-sounding questions are among the most difficult the company will ever have to answer. Successful companies continuously raise these questions and answer them carefully and completely.

Many organizations develop formal mission statements that answer these questions. A **mission statement** is a statement of the organization's purpose—what it wants to accomplish in the larger environment. A clear mission statement acts as an "invisible hand" that guides people in the organization.

Some companies define their missions myopically in product or technology terms ("We make and sell furniture" or "We are a chemical-processing firm"). But mission statements should be *market oriented* and defined in terms of satisfying basic customer needs. Products and technologies eventually become outdated, but basic market needs may last forever. Under Armour's mission isn't just to make performance sports apparel; it's "to make all athletes better through passion, science, and the relentless pursuit of innovation." Likewise, Chipotle's mission isn't to sell burritos. Instead, the restaurant promises "Food with Integrity," highlighting its commitment to the immediate and long-term welfare of customers and the environment. Chipotle's serves only the very best natural, sustainable, local ingredients raised "with respect for the animals, the environment, and the farmers." ● **Table 2.1** provides several other examples of product-oriented versus market-oriented business definitions.[2]

Mission statement
A statement of the organization's purpose—what it wants to accomplish in the larger environment.

● **TABLE | 2.1**   Market-Oriented Business Definitions

Company	Product-Oriented Definition	Market-Oriented Definition
Charles Schwab	We are a brokerage firm.	We are the guardian of our customers' financial dreams.
Hulu	We are an online video service.	We help people find and enjoy the world's premium video content when, where, and how they want it—all for free.
General Mills	We make consumer food products.	We nourish lives by making them healthier, easier, and richer.
Home Depot	We sell tools and home repair and improvement items.	We empower consumers to achieve the homes of their dreams.
Nike	We sell athletic shoes and apparel.	We bring inspiration and innovation to every athlete* in the world. (*If you have a body, you are an athlete.)
Revlon	We make cosmetics.	We sell lifestyle and self-expression; success and status; memories, hopes, and dreams.
Ritz-Carlton Hotels & Resorts	We rent rooms.	We create the Ritz-Carlton experience—one that enlivens the senses, instills well-being, and fulfills even the unexpressed wishes and needs of our guests.
Walmart	We run discount stores.	We deliver low prices every day and give ordinary folks the chance to buy the same things as rich people. "Save Money. Live Better."

Mission statements should be meaningful and specific yet motivating. They should emphasize the company's strengths in the marketplace. Too often, mission statements are written for public relations purposes and lack specific, workable guidelines. Says marketing consultant Jack Welch:[3]

> Few leaders actually get the point of forging a mission with real grit and meaning. [Mission statements] have largely devolved into fat-headed jargon. Almost no one can figure out what they mean. [So companies] sort of ignore them or gussy up a vague package deal along the lines of: "our mission is to be the best fill-in-the-blank company in our industry." [Instead, Welch advises, CEOs should] make a choice about how your company will win. Don't mince words! Remember Nike's old mission, "Crush Reebok"? That's directionally correct. And Google's mission statement isn't something namby-pamby like "To be the world's best search engine." It's "To organize the world's information and make it universally accessible and useful." That's simultaneously inspirational, achievable, and completely graspable.

Finally, a company's mission should not be stated as making more sales or profits; profits are only a reward for creating value for customers. Instead, the mission should focus on customers and the customer experience the company seeks to create. Thus, McDonald's mission isn't "to be the world's best and most profitable quick-service restaurant"; it's "to be our customers' favorite place and way to eat." If McDonald's accomplishes this customer-focused mission, profits will follow (see Real Marketing 2.1).

Setting Company Objectives and Goals

The company needs to turn its mission into detailed supporting objectives for each level of management. Each manager should have objectives and be responsible for reaching them. For example, Kohler makes and markets familiar kitchen and bathroom fixtures—everything from bathtubs and toilets to kitchen sinks. But Kohler also offers a breadth of other products and services, including furniture, tile and stone, and even small engines and backup power systems. It also owns resorts and spas in the United States and Scotland. Kohler ties this diverse product portfolio together under the mission of "contributing to a higher level of gracious living for those who are touched by our products and services."

This broad mission leads to a hierarchy of objectives, including business objectives and marketing objectives. Kohler's overall objective is to build profitable customer relationships by developing efficient yet beautiful products that embrace the "essence of gracious living" mission. It does this by investing heavily in research and design. Research is expensive and must be funded through improved profit, so improving profits becomes another major objective for Kohler. Profits can be improved by increasing sales or reducing costs. Sales can be increased by improving the company's share of domestic and international markets. These goals then become the company's current marketing objectives.

Marketing strategies and programs must be developed to support these marketing objectives. To increase its market share, Kohler might increase its products' availability and promotion in existing markets and expand into new markets. For example, Kohler is boosting production capacity in India and China to better serve the Asian market.[4]

These are Kohler's broad marketing strategies. Each broad marketing strategy must then be defined in greater detail. For example, increasing the product's promotion may require more salespeople, advertising, and public relations efforts; if so, both requirements will need to be spelled out. In this way, the firm's mission is translated into a set of objectives for the current period.

Designing the Business Portfolio

Business portfolio
The collection of businesses and products that make up the company.

Guided by the company's mission statement and objectives, management now must plan its **business portfolio**—the collection of businesses and products that make up the company. The best business portfolio is the one that best fits the company's strengths and weaknesses to opportunities in the environment. Business portfolio planning involves two steps. First, the company must analyze its *current* business portfolio and determine which businesses should receive more, less, or no investment. Second, it must shape the *future* portfolio by developing strategies for growth and downsizing.

Real Marketing 2.1

McDonald's: On a Customer-Focused Mission

More than half a century ago, Ray Kroc, a 52-year-old salesman of milk-shake-mixing machines, set out on a mission to transform the way Americans eat. In 1955, Kroc discovered a string of seven restaurants owned by Richard and Maurice McDonald. He saw the McDonald brothers' fast-food concept as a perfect fit for America's increasingly on-the-go, time-squeezed, family-oriented lifestyles. Kroc bought the small chain for $2.7 million, and the rest is history.

From the start, Kroc preached a motto of QSCV—quality, service, cleanliness, and value. These goals became mainstays in McDonald's customer-focused mission statement. Applying these values, the company perfected the fast-food concept—delivering convenient, good-quality food at affordable prices.

McDonald's grew quickly to become the world's largest fast-feeder. The fast-food giant's more than 32,000 restaurants worldwide now serve 60 million customers each day, racking up system-wide sales of more than $79 billion annually. The Golden Arches are one of the world's most familiar symbols, and other than Santa Claus, no character in the world is more recognizable than Ronald McDonald.

In the mid-1990s, however, McDonald's fortunes began to turn. The company appeared to fall out of touch with both its mission and its customers. Americans were looking for fresher, better-tasting food and more contemporary atmospheres. They were also seeking healthier eating options. In a new age of health-conscious consumers and $5 lattes at Starbucks, McDonald's seemed a bit out of step with the times. One analyst sums it up this way:

McDonald's was struggling to find its identity amid a flurry of new competitors and changing consumer tastes. The company careened from one failed idea to another. It tried to keep pace by offering pizza, toasted deli sandwiches, and the Arch Deluxe, a heavily advertised new burger that flopped. It bought into nonburger franchises like Chipotle and Boston Market. It also tinkered with its menu, no longer toasting the buns, switching pickles, and changing the special sauce on Big Macs. None of these things worked. All the while, McDonald's continued opening new restaurants at a ferocious pace, as many as 2,000

per year. The new stores helped sales, but customer service and cleanliness declined because the company couldn't hire and train good workers fast enough. Meanwhile, McDonald's increasingly became a target for animal-rights activists, environmentalists, and nutritionists, who accused the chain of contributing to the nation's obesity epidemic with "super size" French fries and sodas as well as Happy Meals that lure kids with the reward of free toys.

Although McDonald's remained the world's most visited fast-food chain, the once-shiny Golden Arches lost some of their luster. Sales growth slumped, and its market share fell by more than 3 percent between 1997 and 2003. In 2002, the company posted its first-ever quarterly loss. In the face of changing customer value expectations, the company had lost sight of its fundamental value proposition. "We got distracted from the most important thing: hot, high-quality food at a great value at the speed and convenience of McDonald's," says current CEO Jim Skinner. The company and its mission needed to adapt.

In early 2003, a troubled McDonald's announced a turnaround plan—what it now calls its "Plan to Win." At the heart of this plan was a new mission statement that refocused the company on its customers. According to the analyst:

The company's mission was changed from "being the world's best quick-service restaurant" to "being our customers' favorite place and way to eat." The Plan to Win lays out where McDonald's wants to be and how it plans to get there, all centered on five basics of an exceptional customer experience: people,

products, place, price, and promotion. While the five Ps smack of corny corporate speak, company officials maintain that they have profoundly changed McDonald's direction and priorities. The plan, and the seemingly simple shift in mission, forced McDonald's and its employees to focus on quality, service, and the restaurant experience rather than simply providing the cheapest, most convenient option to customers. The Plan to Win—which barely fits on a single sheet of paper—is now treated as sacred inside the company.

Under the Plan to Win, McDonald's got back to the basic business of taking care of customers. The goal was to get "better, not just bigger." The company halted rapid expansion and instead poured money back into improving the food, the service, the atmosphere, and marketing at existing outlets. McDonald's redecorated its restaurants with clean, simple, more-modern interiors and

McDonald's new mission—"being our customers' favorite place and way to eat"—coupled with its Plan to Win, got the company back to the basics of creating exceptional customer experiences.

Continued on next page

amenities such as live plants, wireless Internet access, and flat-screen TVs showing cable news. Play areas in some new restaurants now feature video games and even stationary bicycles with video screens. To make the customer experience more convenient, McDonald's stores now open earlier to extend breakfast hours and stay open longer to serve late-night diners—more than one-third of McDonald's restaurants are now open 24 hours a day.

A reworked menu, crafted by Chef Daniel Coudreaut, a Culinary Institute of America graduate and former chef at the Four Seasons in Dallas, now provides more choice and variety, including healthier options, such as Chicken McNuggets made with white meat, a line of Snack Wraps, low-fat "milk jugs," apple slices, Premium Salads, and the Angus burger. Within only a year of introducing its Premium Salads, McDonald's became the world's largest salad seller. The company also launched a major multifaceted education campaign—themed "it's what i **eat** and what i **do** . . . i'm lovin'

it"—that underscores the important interplay between eating right and staying active.

McDonald's rediscovered dedication to customer value sparked a remarkable turnaround. Since announcing its Plan to Win, McDonald's sales have increased by more than 50 percent, and profits have more than quadrupled. In 2008, when the stock market lost one-third of its value—the worst loss since the Great Depression—McDonald's stock gained nearly 6 percent, making it one of only two companies in the Dow Jones Industrial Average whose share price rose during that year (the other was Walmart). Through 2010, as the economy and the restaurant industry as a whole continued to struggle,

McDonald's outperformed its competitors by a notable margin. Despite the tough times, McDonald's achieved a lofty 15.5 percent three-year compound annual total return to investors versus the S&P 500 average of −5.6 percent.

Thus, McDonald's now appears to have the right mission for the times. Now, once again, when you think McDonald's, you think value—whether it's a college student buying a sandwich for a buck or a working mother at the drive-through grabbing a breakfast latte that's a dollar cheaper than Starbucks. And that has customers and the company alike humming the chain's catchy jingle, "i'm lovin' it."

Sources: Extracts based on information found in Andrew Martin, "At McDonald's, the Happiest Meal Is Hot Profits," *New York Times*, January 11, 2009; Jeremy Adamy, "McDonald's Seeks Ways to Keep Sizzling," *Wall Street Journal*, March 10, 2009, p. A1; and John Cloud, "McDonald's Has a Chef?" *Time*, February 22, 2010, pp. 88–91. Financial and other information and facts from www.aboutmcdonalds.com/mcd/media_center.html/invest.html, accessed October 2010.

Analyzing the Current Business Portfolio

Portfolio analysis

The process by which management evaluates the products and businesses that make up the company.

The major activity in strategic planning is business **portfolio analysis**, whereby management evaluates the products and businesses that make up the company. The company will want to put strong resources into its more profitable businesses and phase down or drop its weaker ones.

Management's first step is to identify the key businesses that make up the company, called *strategic business units* (SBUs). An SBU can be a company division, a product line within a division, or sometimes a single product or brand. The company next assesses the attractiveness of its various SBUs and decides how much support each deserves. When designing a business portfolio, it's a good idea to add and support products and businesses that fit closely with the firm's core philosophy and competencies.

The purpose of strategic planning is to find ways in which the company can best use its strengths to take advantage of attractive opportunities in the environment. So most standard portfolio analysis methods evaluate SBUs on two important dimensions: the attractiveness of the SBU's market or industry and the strength of the SBU's position in that market or industry. The best-known portfolio-planning method was developed by the Boston Consulting Group, a leading management consulting firm.[5]

Growth-share matrix

A portfolio-planning method that evaluates a company's SBUs in terms of its market growth rate and relative market share.

The Boston Consulting Group Approach. Using the now-classic Boston Consulting Group (BCG) approach, a company classifies all its SBUs according to the **growth-share matrix**, as shown in ● **Figure 2.2**. On the vertical axis, *market growth rate* provides a measure of market attractiveness. On the horizontal axis, *relative market share* serves as a measure of company strength in the market. The growth-share matrix defines four types of SBUs:

1. *Stars.* Stars are high-growth, high-share businesses or products. They often need heavy investments to finance their rapid growth. Eventually their growth will slow down, and they will turn into cash cows.

2. *Cash Cows.* Cash cows are low-growth, high-share businesses or products. These established and successful SBUs need less investment to hold their market share. Thus, they

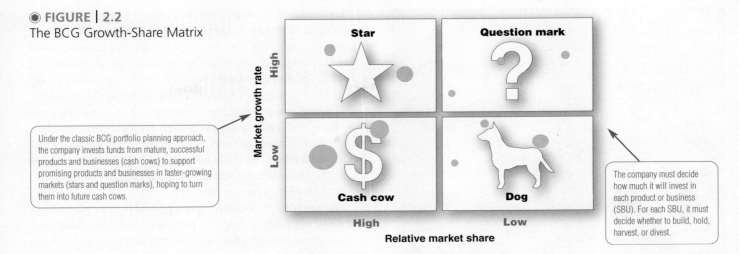

● FIGURE | 2.2
The BCG Growth-Share Matrix

Under the classic BCG portfolio planning approach, the company invests funds from mature, successful products and businesses (cash cows) to support promising products and businesses in faster-growing markets (stars and question marks), hoping to turn them into future cash cows.

The company must decide how much it will invest in each product or business (SBU). For each SBU, it must decide whether to build, hold, harvest, or divest.

produce a lot of the cash that the company uses to pay its bills and support other SBUs that need investment.

3. *Question Marks.* Question marks are low-share business units in high-growth markets. They require a lot of cash to hold their share, let alone increase it. Management has to think hard about which question marks it should try to build into stars and which should be phased out.

4. *Dogs.* Dogs are low-growth, low-share businesses and products. They may generate enough cash to maintain themselves but do not promise to be large sources of cash.

The 10 circles in the growth-share matrix represent the company's 10 current SBUs. The company has two stars, two cash cows, three question marks, and three dogs. The areas of the circles are proportional to the SBU's dollar sales. This company is in fair shape, although not in good shape. It wants to invest in the more promising question marks to make them stars and maintain the stars so that they will become cash cows as their markets mature. Fortunately, it has two good-sized cash cows. Income from these cash cows will help finance the company's question marks, stars, and dogs. The company should take some decisive action concerning its dogs and its question marks.

Once it has classified its SBUs, the company must determine what role each will play in the future. It can pursue one of four strategies for each SBU. It can invest more in the business unit to *build* its share. Or it can invest just enough to *hold* the SBU's share at the current level. It can *harvest* the SBU, milking its short-term cash flow regardless of the long-term effect. Finally, it can *divest* the SBU by selling it or phasing it out and using the resources elsewhere.

As time passes, SBUs change their positions in the growth-share matrix. Many SBUs start out as question marks and move into the star category if they succeed. They later become cash cows as market growth falls and then finally die off or turn into dogs toward the end of their life cycle. The company needs to add new products and units continuously so that some of them will become stars and, eventually, cash cows that will help finance other SBUs.

Problems with Matrix Approaches. The BCG and other formal methods revolutionized strategic planning. However, such centralized approaches have limitations: They can be difficult, time-consuming, and costly to implement. Management may find it difficult to define SBUs and measure market share and growth. In addition, these approaches focus on classifying *current* businesses but provide little advice for *future* planning.

Because of such problems, many companies have dropped formal matrix methods in favor of more customized approaches that better suit their specific situations. Moreover, unlike former strategic-planning efforts that rested mostly in the hands of senior managers at company headquarters, today's strategic planning has been decentralized. Increasingly, companies are placing responsibility for strategic planning in the hands of cross-functional teams of divisional managers who are close to their markets.

● Managing the business portfolio: Most people think of Disney as theme parks and wholesome family entertainment, but over the past two decades, it's become a sprawling collection of media and entertainment businesses that requires big doses of the famed "Disney Magic" to manage.

Product/market expansion grid
A portfolio-planning tool for identifying company growth opportunities through market penetration, market development, product development, or diversification.

Market penetration
Company growth by increasing sales of current products to current market segments without changing the product.

For example, consider The Walt Disney Company. ● Most people think of Disney as theme parks and wholesome family entertainment. But in the mid-1980s, Disney set up a powerful, centralized strategic planning group to guide its direction and growth. Over the next two decades, the strategic planning group turned The Walt Disney Company into a huge and diverse collection of media and entertainment businesses. The sprawling company grew to include everything from theme resorts and film studios (Walt Disney Pictures, Touchstone Pictures, Hollywood Pictures, and others) to media networks (ABC plus Disney Channel, ESPN, A&E, History Channel, and a half dozen others) to consumer products and a cruise line.

The newly transformed company proved hard to manage and performed unevenly. To improve performance, Disney disbanded the centralized strategic planning unit, decentralizing its functions to Disney division managers. As a result, Disney reclaimed its position at the head of the world's media conglomerates. And despite recently facing "the weakest economy in our lifetime," Disney's sound strategic management of its broad mix of businesses has helped it fare better than rival media companies.[6]

Developing Strategies for Growth and Downsizing

Beyond evaluating current businesses, designing the business portfolio involves finding businesses and products the company should consider in the future. Companies need growth if they are to compete more effectively, satisfy their stakeholders, and attract top talent. At the same time, a firm must be careful not to make growth itself an objective. The company's objective must be to manage "profitable growth."

Marketing has the main responsibility for achieving profitable growth for the company. Marketing needs to identify, evaluate, and select market opportunities and establish strategies for capturing them. One useful device for identifying growth opportunities is the **product/market expansion grid**, shown in ● **Figure 2.3**.[7] We apply it here to performance sports apparel maker Under Armour. Only 14 years ago, Under Armour introduced its innovative line of comfy, moisture-wicking shirts and shorts. Since then, it has grown rapidly in its performance-wear niche. Over just the past three years, even as retail sales slumped across the board in the down economy, Under Armour's sales more than doubled, and profits grew 22 percent. Looking forward, the company must look for new ways to keep growing.[8]

First, Under Armour might consider whether the company can achieve deeper **market penetration**—making more sales without changing its original product. It can spur growth

● FIGURE | 2.3
The Product/Market Expansion Grid

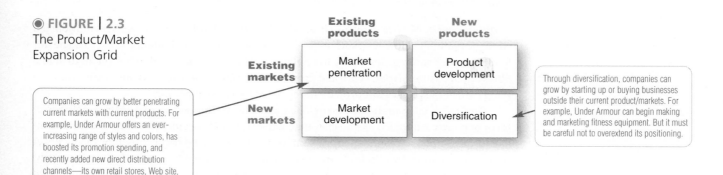

Companies can grow by better penetrating current markets with current products. For example, Under Armour offers an ever-increasing range of styles and colors, has boosted its promotion spending, and recently added new direct distribution channels—its own retail stores, Web site, and toll-free call center.

	Existing products	New products
Existing markets	Market penetration	Product development
New markets	Market development	Diversification

Through diversification, companies can grow by starting up or buying businesses outside their current product/markets. For example, Under Armour can begin making and marketing fitness equipment. But it must be careful not to overextend its positioning.

 **Growth: Under Armour has grown at a blistering rate under its multipronged growth strategy.**

Market development

Company growth by identifying and developing new market segments for current company products.

Product development

Company growth by offering modified or new products to current market segments.

Diversification

Company growth through starting up or acquiring businesses outside the company's current products and markets.

through marketing mix improvements—adjustments to its product design, advertising, pricing, and distribution efforts. For example, Under Armour offers an ever-increasing range of styles and colors in its original apparel lines. It recently boosted its promotion spending in an effort to drive home its "performance and authenticity" positioning. The company also added direct-to-consumer distribution channels, including its own retail stores, Web site, and toll-free call center. Direct-to-consumer sales grew almost 50 percent last year and now account for more than 15 percent of total revenues.

Second, Under Armour might consider possibilities for **market development**—identifying and developing new markets for its current products. Under Armour could review new *demographic markets.* For instance, the company recently stepped up its emphasis on women consumers and predicts that its women's apparel business will someday be larger than its men's apparel business. The Under Armour "Athletes Run" advertising campaign includes a 30-second "women's only" spot. Under Armour could also pursue new *geographical markets.* For example, the brand has announced its intentions to expand internationally.

Third, Under Armour could consider **product development**—offering modified or new products to current markets. In 2008, in an effort to transform itself from a niche player to a mainstream brand, Under Armour entered the $19 billion athletic footwear market with a line of cross-trainer shoes. Last year, it introduced high-performance running shoes. Although this puts the company into direct competition with sports heavyweights Nike and Adidas, it also offers promise for big growth.

Finally, Under Armour might consider **diversification**—starting up or buying businesses beyond its current products and markets. For example, it could move into nonperformance leisurewear or begin making and marketing Under Armour fitness equipment. When diversifying, companies must be careful not to overextend their brands' positioning.

Companies must not only develop strategies for growing their business portfolios but also strategies for *downsizing* them. There are many reasons that a firm might want to abandon products or markets. The firm may have grown too fast or entered areas where it lacks experience. This can occur when a firm enters too many international markets without the proper research or when a company introduces new products that do not offer superior customer value. The market environment might change, making some products or markets less profitable. For example, in difficult economic times, many firms prune out weaker, less-profitable products and markets to focus their more limited resources on the strongest ones. Finally, some products or business units simply age and die.

When a firm finds brands or businesses that are unprofitable or that no longer fit its overall strategy, it must carefully prune, harvest, or divest them. Weak businesses usually require a disproportionate amount of management attention. Managers should focus on promising growth opportunities, not fritter away energy trying to salvage fading ones.

Author Comment | Marketing alone can't create superior customer value. Under the company-wide strategic plan, marketers must work closely with other departments to form an effective internal company value chain and with other companies in the marketing system to create an overall external value delivery network that jointly serves customers.

Planning Marketing: Partnering to Build Customer Relationships (pp 45–47)

The company's strategic plan establishes what kinds of businesses the company will operate and its objectives for each. Then, within each business unit, more detailed planning takes place. The major functional departments in each unit—marketing, finance, accounting, purchasing, operations, information systems, human resources, and others—must work together to accomplish strategic objectives.

Marketing plays a key role in the company's strategic planning in several ways. First, marketing provides a guiding *philosophy*—the marketing concept—that suggests that company strategy should revolve around building profitable relationships with important consumer groups. Second, marketing provides *inputs* to strategic planners by helping to identify attractive market opportunities and assessing the firm's potential to take advantage of them. Finally, within individual business units, marketing designs *strategies* for reaching the unit's objectives. Once the unit's objectives are set, marketing's task is to help carry them out profitably.

Customer value is the key ingredient in the marketer's formula for success. However, as we noted in Chapter 1, marketers alone cannot produce superior value for customers. Although marketing plays a leading role, it can be only a partner in attracting, keeping, and growing customers. In addition to *customer relationship management*, marketers must also practice *partner relationship management*. They must work closely with partners in other company departments to form an effective internal *value chain* that serves customers. Moreover, they must partner effectively with other companies in the marketing system to form a competitively superior external *value delivery network*. We now take a closer look at the concepts of a company value chain and a value delivery network.

Partnering with Other Company Departments

Value chain

The series of internal departments that carry out value-creating activities to design, produce, market, deliver, and support a firm's products.

Each company department can be thought of as a link in the company's internal **value chain**.[9] That is, each department carries out value-creating activities to design, produce, market, deliver, and support the firm's products. The firm's success depends not only on how well each department performs its work but also on how well the various departments coordinate their activities.

For example, Walmart's goal is to create customer value and satisfaction by providing shoppers with the products they want at the lowest possible prices. Marketers at Walmart play an important role. They learn what customers need and stock the stores' shelves with the desired products at unbeatable low prices. They prepare advertising and merchandising programs and assist shoppers with customer service. Through these and other activities, Walmart's marketers help deliver value to customers.

However, the marketing department needs help from the company's other departments. Walmart's ability to offer the right products at low prices depends on the purchasing department's skill in developing the needed suppliers and buying from them at low cost. Walmart's information technology department must provide fast and accurate information about which products are selling in each store. And its operations people must provide effective, low-cost merchandise handling.

A company's value chain is only as strong as its weakest link. Success depends on how well each department performs its work of adding customer value and on how the company coordinates the activities of various departments. ◉ At Walmart, if purchasing can't obtain the lowest prices from suppliers, or if operations can't distribute merchandise at the lowest costs, then marketing can't deliver on its promise of unbeatable low prices.

Ideally, then, a company's different functions should work in harmony to produce value for consumers. But, in practice, departmental relations are full of conflicts and misunderstandings. The marketing department takes the consumer's point of view. But when marketing tries to develop customer satisfaction, it can cause other departments to do a poorer job *in their terms*. Marketing department actions can increase purchasing costs, disrupt production schedules, increase inventories, and create budget headaches. Thus, other departments may resist the marketing department's efforts.

◉ The value chain: Walmart's ability to help you "Save money. Live Better." by offering the right products at lower prices depends on the contributions of people in every department.

Yet marketers must find ways to get all departments to "think consumer" and develop a smoothly functioning value chain. One marketing expert puts it this way: "True market orientation does not mean becoming marketing-driven; it means that the entire company obsesses over creating value for the customer and views itself as a bundle of processes that profitably define, create, communicate, and deliver value to its target customers. . . . Everyone must do marketing regardless of function or department."[10] Thus, whether you're an accountant, an operations manager, a financial analyst, an IT specialist, or a human resources manager, you need to understand marketing and your role in creating customer value.

Partnering with Others in the Marketing System

In its quest to create customer value, the firm needs to look beyond its own internal value chain and into the value chains of its suppliers, distributors, and, ultimately, its customers. Consider McDonald's. People do not swarm to McDonald's only because they love the chain's hamburgers. Consumers flock to the McDonald's *system*, not only to its food products. Throughout the world, McDonald's finely tuned value delivery system delivers a high standard of QSCV—quality, service, cleanliness, and value. McDonald's is effective only to the extent that it successfully partners with its franchisees, suppliers, and others to jointly create "our customers' favorite place and way to eat."

Value delivery network
The network made up of the company, its suppliers, its distributors, and, ultimately, its customers who partner with each other to improve the performance of the entire system.

More companies today are partnering with other members of the supply chain—suppliers, distributors, and, ultimately, customers—to improve the performance of the customer **value delivery network**.  For example, cosmetics maker L'Oréal knows the importance of building close relationships with its extensive network of suppliers, who supply everything from polymers and fats to spray cans and packaging to production equipment and office supplies:[11]

L'Oréal is the world's largest cosmetics manufacturer, with 25 brands ranging from Maybelline and Kiehl's to Lancôme and Redken. The company's supplier network is crucial to its success. As a result, L'Oréal treats suppliers as respected partners. On the one hand, it expects a lot from suppliers in terms of design innovation, quality, and socially responsible actions. The company carefully screens new suppliers and regularly assesses the performance of current suppliers. On the other hand, L'Oréal works closely with suppliers to help them meet its exacting standards. Whereas some companies make unreasonable demands of their suppliers and "squeeze" them for short-term gains, L'Oréal builds long-term supplier relationships based on mutual benefit and growth. According to the company's supplier Web site, it treats suppliers with "fundamental respect for their business, their culture, their growth, and the individuals who work there. Each relationship is based on . . . shared efforts aimed at promoting growth and mutual profits that make it possible for suppliers to invest, innovate, and compete." As a result, more than 75 percent of L'Oréal's supplier-partners have been working with the company for 10 years or more and the majority of them for several decades. Says the company's head of purchasing, "The CEO wants to make L'Oréal a top performer and one of the world's most respected companies. Being respected also means being respected by our suppliers."

Increasingly in today's marketplace, competition no longer takes place between individual competitors. Rather, it takes place between the entire value delivery networks created by these competitors. Thus, Toyota's performance against Ford depends on the quality of Toyota's overall value delivery network versus Ford's. Even if Toyota makes the best cars, it might lose in the marketplace if Ford's dealer network provides more customer-satisfying sales and service.

L'ORÉAL
PARiS

● The value delivery system: L'Oréal builds long-term supplier relationships based on mutual benefit and growth. It "wants to make L'Oréal a top performer and one of the world's most respected companies. Being respected also means being respected by our suppliers."

Author | Now that we've set the
Comment | context in terms of
company-wide strategy, it's time to
discuss customer-driven marketing
strategies and programs.

Marketing Strategy and the Marketing Mix (pp 48–53)

The strategic plan defines the company's overall mission and objectives. Marketing's role is shown in ◉ **Figure 2.4**, which summarizes the major activities involved in managing a customer-driven marketing strategy and the marketing mix.

Consumers are in the center. The goal is to create value for customers and build profitable customer relationships. Next comes **marketing strategy**—the marketing logic by which the company hopes to create this customer value and achieve these profitable relationships. The company decides which customers it will serve (segmentation and targeting) and how (differentiation and positioning). It identifies the total market and then divides it into smaller segments, selects the most promising segments, and focuses on serving and satisfying the customers in these segments.

Guided by marketing strategy, the company designs an integrated *marketing mix* made up of factors under its control—product, price, place, and promotion (the four Ps). To find the best marketing strategy and mix, the company engages in marketing analysis, planning, implementation, and control. Through these activities, the company watches and adapts to the actors and forces in the marketing environment. We will now look briefly at each activity. In later chapters, we will discuss each one in more depth.

Marketing strategy
The marketing logic by which the company hopes to create customer value and achieve profitable customer relationships.

Customer-Driven Marketing Strategy

As emphasized throughout Chapter 1, to succeed in today's competitive marketplace, companies must be customer centered. They must win customers from competitors and then keep and grow them by delivering greater value. But before it can satisfy customers, a company must first understand customer needs and wants. Thus, sound marketing requires careful customer analysis.

Companies know that they cannot profitably serve all consumers in a given market—at least not all consumers in the same way. There are too many different kinds of consumers with too many different kinds of needs. Most companies are in a position to serve some segments better than others. Thus, each company must divide up the total market, choose the best segments, and design strategies for profitably serving chosen segments. This process involves *market segmentation*, *market targeting*, *differentiation*, and *positioning*.

◉ **FIGURE | 2.4**
Managing Marketing Strategies and the Marketing Mix

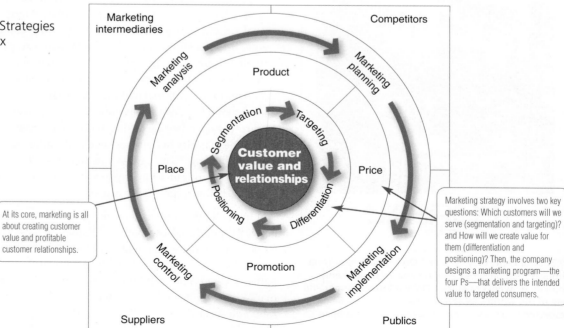

At its core, marketing is all about creating customer value and profitable customer relationships.

Marketing strategy involves two key questions: Which customers will we serve (segmentation and targeting)? and How will we create value for them (differentiation and positioning)? Then, the company designs a marketing program—the four Ps—that delivers the intended value to targeted consumers.

Market Segmentation

The market consists of many types of customers, products, and needs. The marketer must determine which segments offer the best opportunities. Consumers can be grouped and served in various ways based on geographic, demographic, psychographic, and behavioral factors. The process of dividing a market into distinct groups of buyers who have different needs, characteristics, or behaviors, and who might require separate products or marketing programs is called **market segmentation**.

Every market has segments, but not all ways of segmenting a market are equally useful. For example, Tylenol would gain little by distinguishing between low-income and high-income pain reliever users if both respond the same way to marketing efforts. A **market segment** consists of consumers who respond in a similar way to a given set of marketing efforts. In the car market, for example, consumers who want the biggest, most comfortable car regardless of price make up one market segment. Consumers who care mainly about price and operating economy make up another segment. It would be difficult to make one car model that was the first choice of consumers in both segments. Companies are wise to focus their efforts on meeting the distinct needs of individual market segments.

Market Targeting

After a company has defined its market segments, it can enter one or many of these segments. **Market targeting** involves evaluating each market segment's attractiveness and selecting one or more segments to enter. A company should target segments in which it can profitably generate the greatest customer value and sustain it over time.

A company with limited resources might decide to serve only one or a few special segments or market niches. Such nichers specialize in serving customer segments that major competitors overlook or ignore. For example, Ferrari sells only 1,500 of its very high-performance cars in the United States each year but at very high prices—from an eye-opening $229,500 for its Ferrari F430 F1 Spider convertible to an astonishing more than $2 million for its FXX super sports car, which can be driven only on race tracks (it usually sells 10 in the United States each year). Most nichers aren't quite so exotic. White Wave, the maker of Silk Soymilk, has found its niche as the nation's largest soymilk producer. And although Logitech is only a fraction the size of giant Microsoft, through skillful niching, it dominates the PC mouse market, with Microsoft as its runner up (see Real Marketing 2.2).

Alternatively, a company might choose to serve several related segments—perhaps those with different kinds of customers but with the same basic wants. Abercrombie & Fitch, for example, targets college students, teens, and kids with the same upscale, casual clothes and accessories in three different outlets: the original Abercrombie & Fitch, Hollister, and Abercrombie. Or a large company might decide to offer a complete range of products to serve all market segments. Large car companies such as Honda and Ford do this.

Most companies enter a new market by serving a single segment, and, if this proves successful, they add more segments. For example, Nike started with innovative running shoes for serious runners. Large companies eventually seek full market coverage. Nike now makes and sells a broad range of sports products for just about anyone and everyone, with the goal of "helping athletes at every level of ability reach their potential."[12] It has different products designed to meet the special needs of each segment it serves.

Market Differentiation and Positioning

After a company has decided which market segments to enter, it must decide how it will differentiate its market offering for each targeted segment and what positions it wants to occupy in those segments. A product's *position* is the place it occupies relative to competitors' products in consumers' minds. Marketers want to develop unique market positions for their products. If a product is perceived to be exactly like others on the market, consumers would have no reason to buy it.

Positioning is arranging for a product to occupy a clear, distinctive, and desirable place relative to competing products in the minds of target consumers. Marketers plan positions that distinguish their products from competing brands and give them the greatest advantage in their target markets.

Market segmentation
Dividing a market into distinct groups of buyers who have different needs, characteristics, or behaviors, and who might require separate products or marketing programs.

Market segment
A group of consumers who respond in a similar way to a given set of marketing efforts.

Market targeting
The process of evaluating each market segment's attractiveness and selecting one or more segments to enter.

Positioning
Arranging for a product to occupy a clear, distinctive, and desirable place relative to competing products in the minds of target consumers.

Real Marketing 2.2

Logitech: The Little Mouse That Roars

Among the big tech companies, market leader Microsoft is the king of the jungle. When giant Microsoft looms, even large competitors quake. But when it comes to dominating specific market niches, overall size isn't always the most important thing. For example, in its own corner of the high-tech jungle, Logitech International is the little mouse that roars. In its niches, small but mighty Logitech is the undisputed market leader.

Logitech focuses on what it calls "personal peripherals"—interface devices for PC navigation, Internet communications, home-entertainment systems, and gaming and wireless devices. Logitech's rapidly expanding product portfolio now includes everything from cordless mice and keyboards, gaming controllers, and remote controls to Webcams, PC speakers, headsets, notebook stands, and cooling pads. But it all started with computer mice.

Logitech makes every variation of mouse imaginable. Over the years, it has flooded the world with more than one billion computer mice of all varieties, mice for left- and right-handed people, wireless mice, travel mice, mini mice, 3-D mice, mice shaped like real mice for children, and even an "air mouse" that uses motion sensors to let you navigate your computer from a distance.

In the PC mouse market, Logitech competes head-on with Microsoft. At first glance, it looks like an unfair contest. With more than $58 billion in sales, Microsoft is nearly 30 times bigger than $2.2 billion Logitech. But when it comes to mice and other peripherals, Logitech has a depth of focus and knowledge that no other company in the world—including Microsoft—can match. Whereas mice and other interface devices are pretty much a sideline for software maker Microsoft—almost a distraction—they are the main attraction for Logitech. As a result, each new Logitech device is a true work of both art and science. Logitech's mice, for example, receive raves from designers, expert reviewers, and users alike.

A *BusinessWeek* analyst gives us a behind-the-scenes look at Logitech's deep design and development prowess:

One engineer, given the moniker "Teflon Tim" by amused colleagues, spent three months scouring the Far East to find just the right non-stick coatings and sound-deadening foam. Another spent hours taking apart wind-up toys. Others pored over the contours of luxury BMW motorcycles, searching for designs to crib. They were members of a most unusual team that spent thousands of hours during a two-year period on a single goal: to build a better mouse. The result: Logitech's revolutionary MX Revolution, the next-generation mouse that hit consumer electronics shelves like a flash of lightning. It represented the company's most ambitious attempt yet to refashion the lowly computer mouse into a kind of control center for a host of PC applications. The sheer scope of the secret mission—which crammed 420 components, including a tiny motor, into a palm-sized device that usually holds about 20—brought together nearly three dozen engineers, designers, and marketers from around the globe.

Part of Logitech's product-development strategy is defensive. Once content to design mice and other peripherals for PC makers to slap their own names on, Logitech over the past half-decade has increasingly focused on selling its branded add-on equipment directly to consumers. Nearly 90 percent of Logitech's annual sales now come from retail. That forces Logitech to deliver regular improvements and new devices to entice new shoppers and purchases.

"We think of mice as pretty simple," says one industry analyst, "but there's a pretty aggressive technology battle going on to prove what the mouse can do." One of Logitech's latest feats of cutting-edge wizardry is its MX Air, which promises to change the very definition of the computer mouse as we know it. More like an airborne remote control than a traditional mouse, you can surf the Web, play games, and control your home theater PC from up to 30 feet away. There's also a cool-factor at play. Wielding the MX Air is like holding a work of art.

And at Logitech, it's not just about mice anymore. Logitech now applies its cool-factor to create sleek, stylish, and functional devices that enhance not only your PC experience but also help you get the most out of everything from Internet navigation to all the new gadgets in today's digital home. For example, Logitech's family of Harmony advanced universal remote controls helps even technology challenged novices tame the complexities of their home-entertainment systems.

Breeding mice and other peripherals has been very good for nicher Logitech. For example, thanks to its dedication to creating the next best mouse, Logitech has captured a dominating 40 percent share of the world mouse market, with giant Microsoft as its runner-up. And although Logitech isn't nearly as big as Microsoft, pound for pound it's more profitable. Over the past seven years, despite tough economic times for the PC and consumer electronics industries, Logitech's sales and profits have more than doubled. Looking ahead, as Logitech forges forward in its personal peripherals niche, Logitech is well positioned to weather the recent economic storms and emerge stronger than ever.

"Our business is about the last inch between people and content and technology," explains Logitech CEO Guerrino De Luca. Nobody spans that last inch better than Logitech. The next time you navigate your PC, watch or listen to downloaded Web audio or video con-

Nichers: In its own corner of the high-tech jungle, Logitech is a little mouse that roars, with giant Microsoft as its runner-up.

tent, or pick up an entertainment-system re-mote, it's a pretty good bet that you'll have your hand on a Logitech device. It's also a good bet that you'll really like the way it works and feels. "The goal [is] passing the 'ooooh' test," says a Logitech project leader, "creating a visceral ex-perience that communicates both performance and luxury."

Sources: Lisa Johnston and John Laposky, "Logitech Intros Accessories, Ships Billion Mouse," *TWICE*, December 15, 2008, p. 84; Cliff Edwards, "Here Comes Mighty Mouse," *BusinessWeek*, September 4, 2006, p. 76; Cliff Edwards, "The Mouse That Soars," *BusinessWeek*, August 20, 2007, p. 22; Haig Simonian, "Logitech Warns of Gloom Ahead," FT.com, January 21, 2009, www.ft.com/cms/s/0/ba17c7e4-e75b-11dd-aef2-0000779fd2ac.html; "Logitech International S.A.," *Hoover's Company Records*, May 13, 2010, p. 42459; and annual reports and other information from http://ir.logitech.com/overview.cfm?cl=us.en and www.logitech.com, accessed October 2010.

BMW is "The ultimate driving machine." The Ford Escape promises "So much fun. So little fuel." At video site Hulu, you can "Watch Your Favorites. Anytime. Free." YouTube let's you "Broadcast Yourself." At McDonald's you'll be saying "i'm lovin' it," whereas at Burger King you can "Have it your way." Such deceptively simple statements form the backbone of a product's marketing strategy. ◉ For example, Burger King designs its entire worldwide integrated marketing campaign—from television and print commercials to its Web sites—around the "Have it your way" positioning.

In positioning its product(s), the company first identifies possible customer value differences that provide competitive advantages on which to build the position. The company can offer greater customer value by either charging lower prices than competi-tors or offering more benefits to justify higher prices. But if the company *promises* greater value, it must then *deliver* that greater value. Thus, effective posi-tioning begins with **differentiation**—actually *dif-ferentiating* the company's market offering so that it gives consumers more value. Once the company has chosen a desired position, it must take strong steps to deliver and communicate that position to target con-sumers. The company's entire marketing program should support the chosen positioning strategy.

◉ Positioning: Burger King builds its entire worldwide marketing campaign around its "Have it your way" positioning.

Developing an Integrated Marketing Mix

Differentiation
Actually differentiating the market offering to create superior customer value.

Marketing mix
The set of tactical marketing tools—product, price, place, and promotion—that the firm blends to produce the response it wants in the target market.

After determining its overall marketing strategy, the company is ready to begin planning the details of the marketing mix, one of the major concepts in modern marketing. The **marketing mix** is the set of tactical marketing tools that the firm blends to produce the re-sponse it wants in the target market. The marketing mix consists of everything the firm can do to influence the demand for its product. The many possibilities can be collected into four groups of variables—the four *P*s. Figure 2.5 shows the marketing tools under each *P*.

- *Product* means the goods-and-services combination the company offers to the target market. Thus, a Ford Escape consists of nuts and bolts, spark plugs, pistons, headlights, and thousands of other parts. Ford offers several Escape models and dozens of optional features. The car comes fully serviced and with a comprehensive warranty that is as much a part of the product as the tailpipe.

- *Price* is the amount of money customers must pay to obtain the product. Ford calculates suggested retail prices that its dealers might charge for each Escape. But Ford dealers rarely charge the full sticker price. Instead, they negotiate the price with each customer, offering discounts, trade-in allowances, and credit terms. These actions adjust prices for the current competitive and economic situations and bring them into line with the buyer's perception of the car's value.

- *Place* includes company activities that make the product available to target consumers. Ford partners with a large body of independently owned dealerships that sell the company's many different models. Ford selects its dealers carefully and strongly supports them. The dealers keep an inventory of Ford automobiles, demonstrate them to potential buyers, negotiate prices, close sales, and service the cars after the sale.

- *Promotion* means activities that communicate the merits of the product and persuade target customers to buy it. Ford spends more than $1.5 billion each year on U.S. advertising to tell consumers about the company and its many products.[13] Dealership salespeople assist potential buyers and persuade them that Ford is the best car for them. Ford and its dealers offer special promotions—sales, cash rebates, and low financing rates—as added purchase incentives.

An effective marketing program blends each marketing mix element into an integrated marketing program designed to achieve the company's marketing objectives by delivering value to consumers. The marketing mix constitutes the company's tactical tool kit for establishing strong positioning in target markets.

Some critics think that the four Ps may omit or underemphasize certain important activities. For example, they ask, "Where are services?" Just because they don't start with a *P* doesn't justify omitting them. The answer is that services, such as banking, airline, and retailing services, are products too. We might call them *service products*. "Where is packaging?" the critics might ask. Marketers would answer that they include packaging as one of many product decisions. All said, as ● **Figure 2.5** suggests, many marketing activities that might appear to be left out of the marketing mix are subsumed under one of the four Ps. The issue is not whether there should be four, six, or ten Ps so much as what framework is most helpful in designing integrated marketing programs.

There is another concern, however, that is valid. It holds that the four Ps concept takes the seller's view of the market, not the buyer's view. From the buyer's viewpoint,

● **FIGURE** | 2.5
The Four Ps of the Marketing Mix

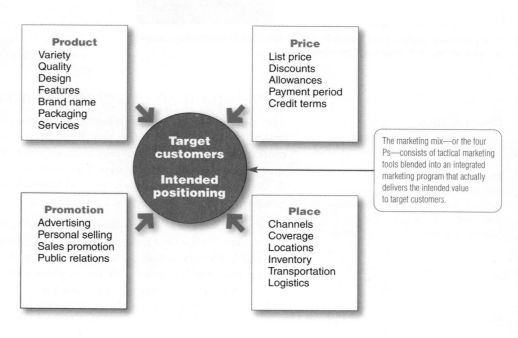

in this age of customer value and relationships, the four Ps might be better described as the four Cs:[14]

4Ps	4Cs
Product	Customer solution
Price	Customer cost
Place	Convenience
Promotion	Communication

Thus, whereas marketers see themselves as selling products, customers see themselves as buying value or solutions to their problems. And customers are interested in more than just the price; they are interested in the total costs of obtaining, using, and disposing of a product. Customers want the product and service to be as conveniently available as possible. Finally, they want two-way communication. Marketers would do well to think through the four Cs first and then build the four Ps on that platform.

> **Author Comment** | So far we've focused on the *marketing* in marketing management. Now, let's turn to the *management*.

Managing the Marketing Effort (pp 53–57)

In addition to being good at the *marketing* in marketing management, companies also need to pay attention to the *management*. Managing the marketing process requires the four marketing management functions shown in ● **Figure 2.6**—*analysis*, *planning*, *implementation*, and *control*. The company first develops company-wide strategic plans and then translates them into marketing and other plans for each division, product, and brand. Through implementation, the company turns the plans into actions. Control consists of measuring and evaluating the results of marketing activities and taking corrective action where needed. Finally, marketing analysis provides information and evaluations needed for all the other marketing activities.

Marketing Analysis

SWOT analysis
An overall evaluation of the company's strengths (S), weaknesses (W), opportunities (O), and threats (T).

Managing the marketing function begins with a complete analysis of the company's situation. The marketer should conduct a **SWOT analysis** (pronounced "swat" analysis), by which it evaluates the company's overall strengths (S), weaknesses (W), opportunities (O), and threats (T) (see ● **Figure 2.7**). Strengths include internal capabilities, resources, and positive situational factors that may help the company serve its customers and achieve its objectives. Weaknesses include internal limitations and negative situational factors that may interfere with the company's performance. Opportunities are favorable factors or trends in the external environment that the company may be able to exploit to

> We'll close the chapter by looking at how marketers manage those strategies and plans—how they implement marketing strategies and programs and evaluate the results.

● **FIGURE** | **2.6**
Managing Marketing: Analysis, Planning, Implementation, and Control

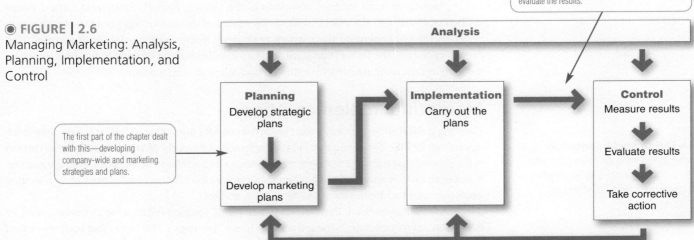

> The first part of the chapter dealt with this—developing company-wide and marketing strategies and plans.

● FIGURE | 2.7
SWOT Analysis: Strengths
(S), Weaknesses (W),
Opportunities (O), and
Threats (T)

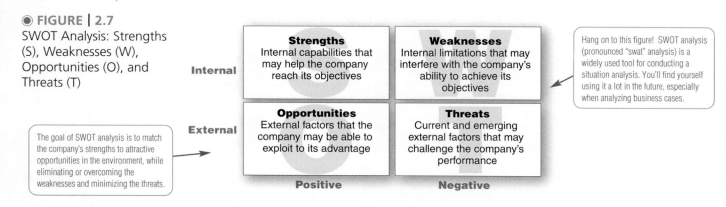

The goal of SWOT analysis is to match the company's strengths to attractive opportunities in the environment, while eliminating or overcoming the weaknesses and minimizing the threats.

Internal

External

| Strengths | Weaknesses |
Internal capabilities that may help the company reach its objectives | Internal limitations that may interfere with the company's ability to achieve its objectives |

| Opportunities | Threats |
External factors that the company may be able to exploit to its advantage | Current and emerging external factors that may challenge the company's performance |

Positive   **Negative**

Hang on to this figure! SWOT analysis (pronounced "swat" analysis) is a widely used tool for conducting a situation analysis. You'll find yourself using it a lot in the future, especially when analyzing business cases.

its advantage. And threats are unfavorable external factors or trends that may present challenges to performance.

The company should analyze its markets and marketing environment to find attractive opportunities and identify environmental threats. It should analyze company strengths and weaknesses as well as current and possible marketing actions to determine which opportunities it can best pursue. The goal is to match the company's strengths to attractive opportunities in the environment, while eliminating or overcoming the weaknesses and minimizing the threats. Marketing analysis provides inputs to each of the other marketing management functions. We discuss marketing analysis more fully in Chapter 3.

Marketing Planning

Through strategic planning, the company decides what it wants to do with each business unit. Marketing planning involves choosing marketing strategies that will help the company attain its overall strategic objectives. A detailed marketing plan is needed for each business, product, or brand. What does a marketing plan look like? Our discussion focuses on product or brand marketing plans.

● **Table 2.2** outlines the major sections of a typical product or brand marketing plan. (See Appendix 1 for a sample marketing plan.) The plan begins with an executive summary that quickly reviews major assessments, goals, and recommendations. The main section of the plan presents a detailed SWOT analysis of the current marketing situation as well as potential threats and opportunities. The plan next states major objectives for the brand and outlines the specifics of a marketing strategy for achieving them.

A *marketing strategy* consists of specific strategies for target markets, positioning, the marketing mix, and marketing expenditure levels. It outlines how the company intends to create value for target customers in order to capture value in return. In this section, the planner explains how each strategy responds to the threats, opportunities, and critical issues spelled out earlier in the plan. Additional sections of the marketing plan lay out an action program for implementing the marketing strategy along with the details of a supporting *marketing budget*. The last section outlines the controls that will be used to monitor progress, measure return on marketing investment, and take corrective action.

Marketing Implementation

Marketing implementation
Turning marketing strategies and plans into marketing actions to accomplish strategic marketing objectives.

Planning good strategies is only a start toward successful marketing. A brilliant marketing strategy counts for little if the company fails to implement it properly. **Marketing implementation** is the process that turns marketing *plans* into marketing *actions* to accomplish strategic marketing objectives. Whereas marketing planning addresses the *what* and *why* of marketing activities, implementation addresses the *who*, *where*, *when*, and *how*.

Many managers think that "doing things right" (implementation) is as important as, or even more important than, "doing the right things" (strategy). The fact is that both are critical to success, and companies can gain competitive advantages through effective implementation. One firm can have essentially the same strategy as another, yet win in the marketplace through

● TABLE | 2.2   Contents of a Marketing Plan

Section	Purpose
Executive summary	Presents a brief summary of the main goals and recommendations of the plan for management review, helping top management find the plan's major points quickly. A table of contents should follow the executive summary.
Current marketing situation	Describes the target market and a company's position in it, including information about the market, product performance, competition, and distribution. This section includes the following: • A *market description* that defines the market and major segments and then reviews customer needs and factors in the marketing environment that may affect customer purchasing. • A *product review* that shows sales, prices, and gross margins of the major products in the product line. • A review of *competition* that identifies major competitors and assesses their market positions and strategies for product quality, pricing, distribution, and promotion. • A review of *distribution* that evaluates recent sales trends and other developments in major distribution channels.
Threats and opportunities analysis	Assesses major threats and opportunities that the product might face, helping management to anticipate important positive or negative developments that might have an impact on the firm and its strategies.
Objectives and issues	States the marketing objectives that the company would like to attain during the plan's term and discusses key issues that will affect their attainment. For example, if the goal is to achieve a 15 percent market share, this section looks at how this goal might be achieved.
Marketing strategy	Outlines the broad marketing logic by which the business unit hopes to create customer value and relationships and the specifics of target markets, positioning, and marketing expenditure levels. How will the company create value for customers in order to capture value from customers in return? This section also outlines specific strategies for each marketing mix element and explains how each responds to the threats, opportunities, and critical issues spelled out earlier in the plan.
Action programs	Spells out how marketing strategies will be turned into specific action programs that answer the following questions: *What* will be done? *When* will it be done? *Who* will do it? *How* much will it cost?
Budgets	Details a supporting marketing budget that is essentially a projected profit-and-loss statement. It shows expected revenues (forecasted number of units sold and the average net price) and expected costs of production, distribution, and marketing. The difference is the projected profit. Once approved by higher management, the budget becomes the basis for materials buying, production scheduling, personnel planning, and marketing operations.
Controls	Outlines the control that will be used to monitor progress and allow higher management to review implementation results and spot products that are not meeting their goals. It includes measures of return on marketing investment.

faster or better execution. Still, implementation is difficult—it is often easier to think up good marketing strategies than it is to carry them out.

In an increasingly connected world, people at all levels of the marketing system must work together to implement marketing strategies and plans. At John Deere, for example, marketing implementation for the company's residential, commercial, agricultural, and industrial equipment requires day-to-day decisions and actions by thousands of people both inside and outside the organization. Marketing managers make decisions about target segments, branding, product development, pricing, promotion, and distribution. They talk with engineering about product design, with manufacturing about production and inventory levels, and with finance about funding and cash flows. They also connect with outside people, such as advertising agencies to plan ad campaigns and the news media to obtain publicity support. The sales force urges and supports John Deere dealers and large retailers like Lowe's in their efforts to convince residential, agricultural, and industrial customers that "Nothing Runs Like a Deere."

Marketing Department Organization

The company must design a marketing organization that can carry out marketing strategies and plans. If the company is very small, one person might do all the research, selling, advertising, customer service, and other marketing work. As the company expands, however, a marketing department emerges to plan and carry out marketing activities. In large companies,

● **Marketers must continually plan their analysis, implementation, and control activities.**

this department contains many specialists. It includes product and market managers, sales managers and salespeople, market researchers, advertising experts, and many other specialists.

To head up such large marketing organizations, many companies have now created a *chief marketing officer* (or CMO) position. This person heads up the company's entire marketing operation and represents marketing on the company's top management team. The CMO position puts marketing on equal footing with other C-level executives, such as the chief operating officer (COO) and the chief financial officer (CFO).[15]

Modern marketing departments can be arranged in several ways. The most common form of marketing organization is the *functional organization*. Under this organization, different marketing activities are headed by a functional specialist—a sales manager, an advertising manager, a marketing research manager, a customer service manager, or a new product manager. A company that sells across the country or internationally often uses a *geographic organization*. Its sales and marketing people are assigned to specific countries, regions, and districts. Geographic organization allows salespeople to settle into a territory, get to know their customers, and work with a minimum of travel time and cost. Companies with many very different products or brands often create a *product management organization*. Using this approach, a product manager develops and implements a complete strategy and marketing program for a specific product or brand.

For companies that sell one product line to many different types of markets and customers who have different needs and preferences, a *market* or *customer management organization* might be best. A market management organization is similar to the product management organization. Market managers are responsible for developing marketing strategies and plans for their specific markets or customers. This system's main advantage is that the company is organized around the needs of specific customer segments. Many companies develop special organizations to manage their relationships with large customers. For example, companies such as P&G and Stanley Black & Decker have created large teams, or even whole divisions, to serve large customers, such as Walmart, Target, Safeway, or Home Depot.

Large companies that produce many different products flowing into many different geographic and customer markets usually employ some *combination* of the functional, geographic, product, and market organization forms.

Marketing organization has become an increasingly important issue in recent years. More and more, companies are shifting their brand management focus toward *customer management*—moving away from managing only product or brand profitability and toward managing customer profitability and customer equity. They think of themselves not as managing portfolios of brands but as managing portfolios of customers. And rather than managing the fortunes or a brand, they see themselves as managing customer-brand experiences and relationships.

Marketing Control

Marketing control

Measuring and evaluating the results of marketing strategies and plans and taking corrective action to ensure that the objectives are achieved.

Because many surprises occur during the implementation of marketing plans, marketers must practice constant **marketing control**—evaluating the results of marketing strategies and plans and taking corrective action to ensure that the objectives are attained. Marketing control involves four steps. Management first sets specific marketing goals. It then measures its performance in the marketplace and evaluates the causes of any differences between expected and actual performance. Finally, management takes corrective action to close the gaps between goals and performance. This may require changing the action programs or even changing the goals.

Operating control involves checking ongoing performance against the annual plan and taking corrective action when necessary. Its purpose is to ensure that the company achieves the sales, profits, and other goals set out in its annual plan. It also involves determining the profitability of different products, territories, markets, and channels. *Strategic control* involves looking at whether the company's basic strategies are well matched to its opportunities. Marketing strategies and programs can quickly become outdated, and each company should periodically reassess its overall approach to the marketplace.

Author | Measuring return on **Comment** | marketing investment has become a major marketing emphasis. But it can be difficult. For example, a Super Bowl ad reaches more than 100 million consumers but may cost as much as $3 million for 30 seconds of airtime. How do you measure the specific return on such an investment in terms of sales, profits, and building customer relationships? We'll look at this question again in Chapter 15.

Measuring and Managing Return on Marketing Investment (pp 57–58)

Marketing managers must ensure that their marketing dollars are being well spent. In the past, many marketers spent freely on big, expensive marketing programs, often without thinking carefully about the financial returns on their spending. They believed that marketing produces intangible creative outcomes, which do not lend themselves readily to measures of productivity or return. But in today's more constrained economy, all that is changing:[16]

> For years, corporate marketers have walked into budget meetings like neighborhood junkies. They couldn't always justify how well they spent past handouts or what difference it all made. They just wanted more money—for flashy TV ads, for big-ticket events, for, you know, getting out the message and building up the brand. But those heady days of blind budget increases are fast being replaced with a new mantra: measurement and accountability. "Marketers have been pretty unaccountable for many years," notes one expert. "Now they are under big pressure to estimate their impact." Another analyst puts in more bluntly: "Marketing needs to stop fostering 'rock star' behavior and focus on rock-steady results."

According to a recent study, as finances have tightened, marketers see return on marketing investment as the second biggest issue after the economy. "Increasingly, it is important for marketers to be able to justify their expenses," says one marketer. For every brand and marketing program, says another, marketers need to ask themselves, "Do I have the right combination of strategy and tactics that will generate the most return in terms of share, revenue and/or profit objectives from my investment?"[17]

Return on marketing investment (or marketing ROI)
The net return from a marketing investment divided by the costs of the marketing investment.

In response, marketers are developing better measures of *marketing ROI*. **Return on marketing investment** (or **marketing ROI**) is the net return from a marketing investment divided by the costs of the marketing investment. It measures the profits generated by investments in marketing activities.

Marketing ROI can be difficult to measure. In measuring financial ROI, both the *R* and the *I* are uniformly measured in dollars. But there is, as of yet, no consistent definition of marketing ROI. "It's tough to measure, more so than for other business expenses," says one analyst. "You can imagine buying a piece of equipment . . . and then measuring the productivity gains that result from the purchase," he says. "But in marketing, benefits like advertising impact aren't easily put into dollar returns. It takes a leap of faith to come up with a number."[18]

A recent survey found that although two-thirds of companies have implemented return on marketing investment programs in recent years, only 22 percent of companies report making good progress in measuring marketing ROI. Another survey of chief financial officers reported that 93 percent of those surveyed are dissatisfied with their ability to measure marketing ROI. The major problem is figuring out what specific measures to use and obtaining good data on these measures.[19]

A company can assess marketing ROI in terms of standard marketing performance measures, such as brand awareness, sales, or market share. ● Many companies are assembling such measures into *marketing dashboards*—meaningful sets of marketing performance measures in a single display used to monitor strategic marketing performance. Just as automobile dashboards present drivers with details on how their cars are performing,

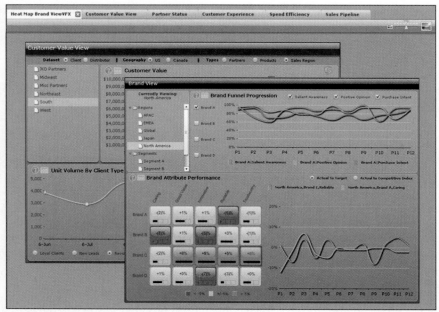

● Many companies are assembling marketing dashboards—meaningful sets of marketing performance measures in a single display used to set and adjust their marketing strategies.

the marketing dashboard gives marketers the detailed measures they need to assess and adjust their marketing strategies. For example, VF Corporation uses a marketing dashboard to track the performance of its 30 lifestyle apparel brands—including Wrangler, Lee, The North Face, Vans, Nautica, 7 For All Mankind, and others. VF's marketing dashboard tracks brand equity and trends, share of voice, market share, online sentiment, and marketing ROI in key markets worldwide, not only for VF brands but also for competing brands.[20]

Increasingly, however, beyond standard performance measures, marketers are using customer-centered measures of marketing impact, such as customer acquisition, customer retention, customer lifetime value, and customer equity. These measures capture not only current marketing performance but also future performance resulting from stronger customer relationships. ● **Figure 2.8** views marketing expenditures as investments that produce returns in the form of more profitable customer relationships.[21] Marketing investments result in improved customer value and satisfaction, which in turn increases customer attraction and retention. This increases individual customer lifetime values and the firm's overall customer equity. Increased customer equity, in relation to the cost of the marketing investments, determines return on marketing investment.

Regardless of how it's defined or measured, the marketing ROI concept is here to stay. "In good times and bad, whether or not marketers are ready for it, they're going to be asked to justify their spending with financial data," says one marketer. Adds another, marketers "have got to know how to count."[22]

● **FIGURE | 2.8**
Return on Marketing Investment
Source: Adapted from Roland T. Rust, Katherine N. Lemon, and Valerie A. Zeithaml, "Return on Marketing: Using Consumer Equity to Focus Marketing Strategy," *Journal of Marketing*, January 2004, p. 112.

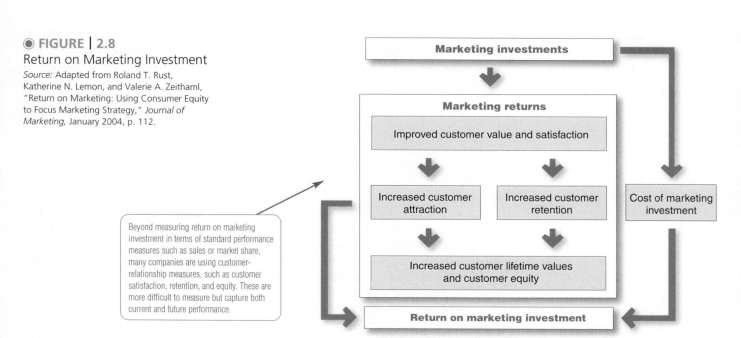

Beyond measuring return on marketing investment in terms of standard performance measures such as sales or market share, many companies are using customer-relationship measures, such as customer satisfaction, retention, and equity. These are more difficult to measure but capture both current and future performance.

REVIEWING Objectives AND KEY Terms

In Chapter 1, we defined *marketing* and outlined the steps in the marketing process. In this chapter, we examined company-wide strategic planning and marketing's role in the organization. Then we looked more deeply into marketing strategy and the marketing mix and reviewed the major marketing management functions. So you've now had a pretty good overview of the fundamentals of modern marketing.

Objective 1 Explain company-wide strategic planning and its four steps. (pp 38–40)

Strategic planning sets the stage for the rest of the company's planning. Marketing contributes to strategic planning, and the overall plan defines marketing's role in the company.

Strategic planning involves developing a strategy for long-run survival and growth. It consists of four steps: (1) defining the company's mission, (2) setting objectives and goals, (3) designing a business portfolio, and (4) developing functional plans. The company's *mission* should be market oriented, realistic, specific, motivating, and consistent with the market environment. The mission is then transformed into detailed *supporting goals and objectives*, which in turn guide decisions about the business portfolio. Then each business and product unit must develop *detailed marketing plans* in line with the company-wide plan.

Objective 2 Discuss how to design business portfolios and develop growth strategies. (pp 40–45)

Guided by the company's mission statement and objectives, management plans its *business portfolio*, or the collection of businesses and products that make up the company. The firm wants to produce a business portfolio that best fits its strengths and weaknesses to opportunities in the environment. To do this, it must analyze and adjust its *current* business portfolio and develop *growth* and *downsizing* strategies for adjusting the *future* portfolio. The company might use a formal portfolio-planning method. But many companies are now designing more-customized portfolio-planning approaches that better suit their unique situations.

Objective 3 Explain marketing's role in strategic planning and how marketing works with its partners to create and deliver customer value. (pp 45–47)

Under the strategic plan, the major functional departments—marketing, finance, accounting, purchasing, operations, information systems, human resources, and others—must work together to accomplish strategic objectives. Marketing plays a key role in the company's strategic planning by providing a *marketing concept philosophy* and *inputs* regarding attractive market opportunities.

Within individual business units, marketing designs *strategies* for reaching the unit's objectives and helps to carry them out profitably.

Marketers alone cannot produce superior value for customers. Marketers must practice *partner relationship management*, working closely with partners in other departments to form an effective *value chain* that serves the customer. And they must partner effectively with other companies in the marketing system to form a competitively superior *value delivery network*.

Objective 4 Describe the elements of a customer-driven marketing strategy and mix and the forces that influence it. (pp 48–53)

Customer value and relationships are at the center of marketing strategy and programs. Through market segmentation, targeting, differentiation, and positioning, the company divides the total market into smaller segments, selects segments it can best serve, and decides how it wants to bring value to target consumers in the selected segments. It then designs an *integrated marketing mix* to produce the response it wants in the target market. The marketing mix consists of product, price, place, and promotion decisions (the four Ps).

Objective 5 List the marketing management functions, including the elements of a marketing plan, and discuss the importance of measuring and managing return on marketing investment. (pp 53–58)

To find the best strategy and mix and to put them into action, the company engages in marketing analysis, planning, implementation, and control. The main components of a *marketing plan* are the executive summary, the current marketing situation, threats and opportunities, objectives and issues, marketing strategies, action programs, budgets, and controls. To plan good strategies is often easier than to carry them out. To be successful, companies must also be effective at *implementation*—turning marketing strategies into marketing actions.

Marketing departments can be organized in one or a combination of ways: *functional marketing organization, geographic organization, product management organization,* or *market management organization*. In this age of customer relationships, more and more companies are now changing their organizational focus from product or territory management to customer relationship management. Marketing organizations carry out *marketing control*, both operating control and strategic control.

Marketing managers must ensure that their marketing dollars are being well spent. In a tighter economy, today's marketers face growing pressures to show that they are adding value in line with their costs. In response, marketers are developing better measures of *return on marketing investment*. Increasingly, they are using customer-centered measures of marketing impact as a key input into their strategic decision making.

KEY Terms

OBJECTIVE 1

Strategic planning (p 38)
Mission statement (p 39)

OBJECTIVE 2

Business portfolio (p 40)
Portfolio analysis (p 42)
Growth-share matrix (p 42)
Product/market expansion grid (p 44)
Market penetration (p 44)
Market development (p 45)

Product development (p 45)
Diversification (p 45)

OBJECTIVE 3

Value chain (p 46)
Value delivery network (p 47)

OBJECTIVE 4

Marketing strategy (p 48)
Market segmentation (p 49)
Market segment (p 49)

Market targeting (p 49)
Positioning (p 49)
Differentiation (p 51)
Marketing mix (p 51)

OBJECTIVE 5

SWOT analysis (p 53)
Marketing implementation (p 54)
Marketing control (p 56)
Return on marketing investment (p 57)

PEARSON mymarketinglab

- Check your understanding of the concepts and key terms using the mypearsonmarketinglab study plan for this chapter.
- Apply the concepts in a business context using the simulations entitled **Strategic Marketing** and **The Marketing Mix.**

DISCUSSING & APPLYING THE Concepts

Discussing the Concepts

1. Explain what is meant by a *market-oriented* mission statement and discuss the characteristics of effective mission statements. (AACSB: Communication)

2. Define strategic planning and briefly describe the four steps that lead managers and a firm through the strategic planning process. Discuss the role marketing plays in this process. (AACSB: Communication)

3. Explain why it is important for all departments of an organization—marketing, accounting, finance, operations management, human resources, and so on—to "think consumer." Why is it important that even people who are not in marketing understand it? (AACSB: Communication)

4. Define *positioning* and explain how it is accomplished. Describe the positioning for the following brands: Wendy's, the Chevy Volt, Amazon.com, Twitter, and Coca-Cola. (AACSB: Communication; Reflective Thinking)

5. Define each of the four Ps. What insights might a firm gain by considering the four Cs rather than the four Ps? (AACSB: Communication; Reflective Thinking)

6. What is marketing ROI? Why is it difficult to measure? (AACSB: Communication; Reflective Thinking)

Applying the Concepts

1. In a small group, conduct a SWOT analysis, develop objectives, and create a marketing strategy for your school, a student organization you might be involved in, or a local business. (AACSB: Communication; Reflective Thinking)

2. Explain the role of a chief marketing officer. Summarize an article that describes the importance of this position, the characteristics of an effective officer, or any issues surrounding this position. (AACSB: Communication; Reflective Thinking)

3. Marketers are increasingly held accountable for demonstrating marketing success. Research the various marketing metrics, in addition to those described in the chapter and Appendix 2, used by marketers to measure marketing performance. Write a brief report of your findings. (AACSB: Communication; Reflective Thinking)

FOCUS ON Technology

Did you buy a Google Nexus One smartphone when it hit the market in early 2010? Didn't think so—few people did. That's why Google stopped selling them in the United States. The phone carried Google's brand and was powered by the Google Android operating system, which was found on other manufacturers' phones.

With the Nexus One, Google made several mistakes. First, in an effort to get products to market faster and make more money through direct sales, Google tried to change the way wireless phones are distributed. Rather than the typical carrier distribution

model (buying a phone through AT&T, Verizon Wireless, or another wireless provider), it used a Web-based sales model. The only way to buy a Nexus One was at Google's Web site. Looking back, notes one executive, Google would probably have sold more of the phones through the traditional carrier network. To make matters worse, Google invested little in advertising for the Nexus One. And it was ill-equipped to handle customer service queries, attempting at first to handle them through e-mail instead of offering dedicated customer-service support. Finally, analysts said the phone wasn't much better than other Android phones already on the market. No wonder the Nexus One failed. However, although Google discontinued the phone, its Android operating system remains strong, powering 27 percent of all U.S. smartphones, ahead of second place Apple's 23 percent.

1. Name and describe the four product and market expansion grid strategies and explain which strategy Google

implemented with the Nexus One. (AACSB: Communication; Reflective Thinking)

2. Discuss the marketing strategy and tactical mistakes Google made when introducing the Nexus One. (AACSB: Communication; Reflective Thinking)

FOCUS ON Ethics

With 64 percent of the women in the United States overweight or obese and less than half participating in regular physical activity, athletic shoe marketers saw an opportunity: "toning shoes." Marketers tout these shoes as revolutionary; you can tone your muscles, lose weight, and improve your posture just by wearing them and going about your daily business. The claims are based on shoemaker-sponsored studies, and the Podiatric Medical Association agrees that toning shoes have some health value. They purportedly perform their magic by destabilizing a person's gait, making leg muscles work harder. Consumers, particularly women, are buying it. Toning shoe sales reached an estimated $1.5 billion in 2010. Sketchers saw a 69 percent increase in sales due to its shoe that looks like a rocking chair on the bottom. Reebok expected toning shoe sales to increase tenfold to $10 million in 2010. Toning shoes accounted for 20 percent of the women's performance footwear category in 2009, with prices ranging from $80 to more than $200.

However, these shoes have their critics, who claim a shoe that comes with an instruction booklet and an educational DVD to ex-

plain proper usage should wave warning flags to consumers. Some doctors claim the shoes are dangerous, causing strained Achilles tendons or worse; one wearer broke her ankle while wearing them. A study by the American Council on Exercise found no benefit in toning shoes over regular walking or other exercise. Noticeably absent from the toning shoe feeding frenzy is Nike, which thinks it's all hype and is sticking to traditional performance athletic shoes. This leader in the women's shoe market, however, is losing market share to competitors.

1. Should these shoemakers capitalize on consumers who want to be fit without doing the work to achieve that goal? Do you think that basing claims on research sponsored by the company is ethical? Explain your reasoning. (AACSB: Communication; Ethical Reasoning)

2. Should Nike have entered this product category instead of giving up market share to competitors? Explain your reasoning. (AACSB: Communication; Ethical Reasoning)

MARKETING & THE Economy

Southwest Airlines

As more and more consumers cut back on spending, perhaps no industry has been hit harder than the airline industry. Even Southwest Airlines, which has posted profits in every one of its 37 years of operation, has felt the pinch. Although Southwest Airlines has suffered less than other airlines, recent passenger traffic has declined, driving down revenues in each of the last two years, which has also hit the company's profits and stock price.

So what's Southwest Airlines doing? For starters, it is expanding beyond the 70-plus cities it now serves and is beginning new flights to heavily trafficked airports. It is also attempting to sweeten the ride by boosting wine and coffee service and rolling out onboard Wi-Fi. But perhaps more important is what no-frills Southwest Air-

lines *isn't* doing—adding fees. Other airlines are generating millions of dollars in revenues by charging for basics, such as checking baggage, sitting in aisle seats, or using pillows. But Southwest Airlines insists that such fees are no way to grow an airline. Other attempts to jump-start demand include an ad campaign urging consumers to continue traveling despite the still-sluggish economy and a company-wide fare sale with one-way rates as low as $49. It hopes that these efforts will bring customers back and curb the revenue slide.

1. Consider every tactic that Southwest Airlines is employing to curtail slumping sales. Evaluate the degree to which each is effective at accomplishing its goal.

2. Are the company's efforts enough? Is it possible for Southwest Airlines to reverse the effects of a strong industry slump?

MARKETING BY THE Numbers

Appendix 2 discusses other marketing profitability metrics beyond the marketing ROI measure described in this chapter. On the next page are the profit-and-loss statements for two businesses. Review Appendix 2 and answer the following questions.

1. Calculate marketing return on sales and marketing ROI for both companies, as described in Appendix 2. (AACSB: Communication; Analytic Thinking)

2. Which company is doing better overall and with respect to marketing? Explain. (AACSB: Communication; Analytic Reasoning; Reflective Thinking)

Business A		
Net sales		$800,000,000
Cost of goods sold		375,000,000
Gross margin		$425,000,000
Marketing expenses		
Sales expenses	$70,000,000	
Promotion expenses	30,000,000	
		100,000,000
General and administrative expenses		
Marketing salaries and expenses	$10,000,000	
Indirect overhead	80,000,000	
		90,000,000
Net profit before income tax		$235,000,000

Business B		
Net sales		$900,000,000
Cost of goods sold		400,000,000
Gross margin		$500,000,000
Marketing expenses		
Sales expenses	$90,000,000	
Promotion expenses	50,000,000	
		140,000,000
General and administrative expenses		
Marketing salaries and expenses	$ 20,000,000	
Indirect overhead	100,000,000	
		120,000,000
Net profit before income tax		$240,000,000

VIDEO Case

Live Nation

Live Nation may not be a household name. But if you've been to a concert in the past few years, chances are you've purchased a Live Nation product. In fact, Live Nation has been the country's largest concert promoter for many years, promoting as many as 29,000 events annually. But through very savvy strategic planning, Live Nation is shaking up the structure of the music industry.

A recent $120 million deal with Madonna illustrates how this concert promoter is diving into other businesses as well. Under this deal, Live Nation will become Madonna's record label, concert promoter, ticket vendor, and merchandise agent. Similar deals have been reached with other performers such as Jay-Z and U2.

But contracting with artists is only part of the picture. Live Nation is partnering with other corporations as well. A venture with

Citi will expand its reach to potential customers through a leveraging of database technologies. Joining forces with ticket reseller powerhouses such as StubHub will give Live Nation a position in the thriving business of secondary ticket sales.

After viewing the video featuring Live Nation, answer the following questions about the role of strategic planning:

1. What is Live Nation's mission?

2. Based on the product/market expansion grid, provide support for the strategy that Live Nation is pursuing.

3. How does Live Nation's strategy provide better value for customers?

COMPANY Case

Trap-Ease America: The Big Cheese of Mousetraps

CONVENTIONAL WISDOM

One April morning, Martha House, president of Trap-Ease America, entered her office in Costa Mesa, California. She paused for a moment to contemplate the Ralph Waldo Emerson quote that she had framed and hung near her desk:

If a man [can] . . . make a better mousetrap than his neighbor . . . the world will make a beaten path to his door.

Perhaps, she mused, Emerson knew something that she didn't. She *had* the better mousetrap—Trap-Ease—but the world didn't seem all that excited about it.

The National Hardware Show Martha had just returned from the National Hardware Show in Chicago. Standing in the trade show display booth for long hours and answering the same questions hundreds of times had been tiring. Yet, all the hard work had paid off. Each year, National Hardware Show officials held a contest to select the best new product introduced at that year's show. The Trap-Ease had won the contest this year, beating out over 300 new products.

Such notoriety was not new for the Trap-Ease mousetrap, however. *People* magazine had run a feature article on the trap, and the trap had been the subject of numerous talk shows and articles in various popular press and trade publications.

Despite all of this attention, however, the expected demand for the trap had not materialized. Martha hoped that this award might stimulate increased interest and sales.

BACKGROUND

A group of investors had formed Trap-Ease America in January after it had obtained worldwide rights to market the innovative mousetrap. In return for marketing rights, the group agreed to pay the inventor and patent holder, a retired rancher, a royalty fee for each trap sold. The group then hired Martha to serve as president and to develop and manage the Trap-Ease America organization.

Trap-Ease America contracted with a plastics-manufacturing firm to produce the traps. The trap consisted of a square, plastic tube measuring about 6 inches long and 1-1/2 inches in diameter. The tube bent in the middle at a 30-degree angle, so that when the front part of the tube rested on a flat surface, the other end was elevated. The elevated end held a removable cap into which the user placed bait (cheese, dog food, or some other aromatic tidbit). The front end of the tube had a hinged door. When the trap was "open," this door rested on two narrow "stilts" attached to the two bottom corners of the door. (See Exhibit 1.)

The simple trap worked very efficiently. A mouse, smelling the bait, entered the tube through the open end. As it walked up the angled bottom toward the bait, its weight made the elevated end of the trap drop downward. This action elevated the open end, allowing the hinged door to swing closed, trapping the mouse. Small teeth on the ends of the stilts caught in a groove on the bottom of the trap, locking the door closed. The user could then dispose of the mouse while it was still alive, or the user could leave it alone for a few hours to suffocate in the trap.

Martha believed the trap had many advantages for the consumer when compared with traditional spring-loaded traps or poisons. Consumers could use it safely and easily with no risk of catching their fingers while loading it. It posed no injury or poisoning threat to children or pets. Furthermore, with Trap-Ease, consumers avoided the unpleasant "mess" they often encountered with the violent spring-loaded traps. The Trap-Ease created no "clean-up" problem. Finally, the user could reuse the trap or simply throw it away.

Martha's early research suggested that women were the best target market for the Trap-Ease. Men, it seemed, were more willing to buy and use the traditional, spring-loaded trap. The targeted women, however, did not like the traditional trap. These women often stayed at home and took care of their children. Thus, they wanted a means of dealing with the mouse problem that avoided the unpleasantness and risks that the standard trap created in the home.

To reach this target market, Martha decided to distribute Trap-Ease through national grocery, hardware, and drug chains such as Safeway, Kmart, Hechingers, and CB Drug. She sold the trap directly to these large retailers, avoiding any wholesalers or other middlemen.

The traps sold in packages of two, with a suggested retail price of $2.49. Although this price made the Trap-Ease about five to ten times more expensive than smaller, standard traps, consumers appeared to offer little initial price resistance. The manufacturing cost for the Trap-Ease, including freight and packaging costs, was about 31 cents per unit. The company paid an additional 8.2 cents per unit in royalty fees. Martha priced the traps to retailers at 99 cents per unit (two units to a package) and estimated that, after sales and volume discounts, Trap-Ease would produce net revenue from retailers of 75 cents per unit.

To promote the product, Martha had budgeted approximately $60,000 for the first year. She planned to use $50,000 of this amount for travel costs to visit trade shows and to make sales calls on retailers. She planned to use the remaining $10,000 for advertising. So far, however, because the mousetrap had generated so much publicity, she had not felt that she needed to do much advertising. Still, she had placed advertising in *Good Housekeeping* (after all, the trap had earned the *Good Housekeeping* Seal of Approval) and in other

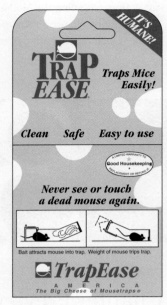

"home and shelter" magazines. Martha was the company's only salesperson, but she intended to hire more salespeople soon.

Martha had initially forecasted Trap-Ease's first-year sales at five million units. Through April, however, the company had only sold several hundred thousand units. Martha wondered if most new products got off to such a slow start, or if she was doing something wrong. She had detected some problems, although none seemed overly serious. For one, there had not been enough repeat buying. For another, she had noted that many of the retailers upon whom she called kept their sample mousetraps on their desks as conversation pieces—she wanted the traps to be used and demonstrated. Martha wondered if consumers were also buying the traps as novelties rather than as solutions to their mouse problems.

Martha knew that the investor group believed that Trap-Ease America had a "once-in-a-lifetime chance" with its innovative mousetrap, and she sensed the group's impatience with the company's progress so far. She had budgeted approximately $250,000 in administrative and fixed costs for the first year (not including marketing costs). To keep the investors happy, the company needed to sell enough traps to cover those costs and make a reasonable profit.

BACK TO THE DRAWING BOARD

In these first few months, Martha had learned that marketing a new product was not an easy task. Some customers were very demanding. For example, one national retailer had placed a large order with instructions that Trap-Ease America was to deliver the order to the loading dock at one of the retailer's warehouses between 1:00 and 3:00 p.m. on a specified day. When the truck delivering the order arrived after 3:00 p.m., the retailer had refused to accept the shipment. The retailer had told Martha it would be a year before she got another chance.

As Martha sat down at her desk, she realized she needed to rethink her marketing strategy. Perhaps she had missed something or made some mistake that was causing sales to be so slow. Glancing at the quotation again, she thought that perhaps she should send the picky retailer and other customers a copy of Emerson's famous quote.

Questions for Discussion

1. Martha and the Trap-Ease America investors believe they face a once-in-a-lifetime opportunity. What information do they need to evaluate this opportunity? How do you think the group would write its mission statement? How would *you* write it?

2. Has Martha identified the best target market for Trap-Ease? What other market segments might the firm target?

3. How has the company positioned the Trap-Ease for the chosen target market? Could it position the product in other ways?

4. Describe the current marketing mix for Trap-Ease. Do you see any problems with this mix?

5. Who is Trap-Ease America's competition?

6. How would you change Trap-Ease's marketing strategy? What kinds of control procedures would you establish for this strategy?

3 Analyzing the Marketing Environment

Chapter Preview

In Part 1, you learned about the basic concepts of marketing and the steps in the marketing process for building profitable relationships with targeted consumers. In Part 2, we'll look deeper into the first step of the marketing process—understanding the marketplace and customer needs and wants. In this chapter, you'll see that marketing operates in a complex and changing environment. Other actors in this environment—suppliers, intermediaries, customers, competitors, publics, and others—may work with or against the company. Major environmental forces—demographic, economic, natural, technological, political, and cultural—shape marketing opportunities, pose threats, and affect the company's ability to build customer relationships. To develop effective marketing strategies, you must first understand the environment in which marketing operates.

We start by looking at an American icon, Xerox. A half-century ago, this venerable old company harnessed changing technology to create a whole new industry—photocopying—and dominated that industry for decades. But did you know that, barely a decade ago, Xerox was on the verge of bankruptcy? Don't worry, the company is once again sound. But Xerox's harrowing experience provides a cautionary tale of what can happen when a company—even a dominant market leader—fails to adapt to its changing marketing environment.

Xerox: Adapting to the Turbulent Marketing Environment

Xerox introduced the first plain-paper office copier 50 years ago. In the decades that followed, the company that invented photocopying flat-out dominated the industry it had created. The name Xerox became almost generic for copying (as in "I'll Xerox this for you"). Through the years, Xerox fought off round after round of rivals to stay atop the fiercely competitive copier industry. In 1998, Xerox's profits were growing at 20 percent a year, and its stock price was soaring.

Then things went terribly wrong for Xerox. The legendary company's stock and fortunes took a stomach-churning dive. In only 18 months, Xerox lost some $38 billion in market value. By mid-2001, its stock price had plunged from almost $70 in 1999 to under $5. The once-dominant market leader found itself on the brink of bankruptcy. What happened? Blame it on change or—rather—on Xerox's failure to adapt to its rapidly changing marketing environment. The world was quickly going digital, but Xerox hadn't kept up.

In the new digital environment, Xerox customers no longer relied on the company's flagship products—stand-alone copiers—to share information and documents. Rather than pumping out and distributing stacks of black-and-white copies, they created digital documents and shared them electronically. Or they popped out copies on their nearby networked printer. On a broader level, while Xerox was busy perfecting copy machines, customers were looking for more sophisticated "document management solutions." They wanted systems that would let them scan documents in Frankfurt, weave them into colorful, customized showpieces in San Francisco, and print them on demand in London—even altering for American spelling.

As digital technology changed, so did Xerox's customers and competitors. Instead of selling copiers to equipment purchasing managers, Xerox found itself developing and selling document management systems to high-level information technology managers. Instead of competing head-on with copy machine competitors like Sharp, Canon, and Ricoh, Xerox was now squaring off against information technology companies like HP and IBM.

Xerox's large and long-respected sales force—made up of people in toner-stained shirts trained to sell and repair copy machines—simply wasn't equipped to deal effectively in the brave new world of digital document solutions. Xerox, the iconic "copier company," just wasn't cutting it in the new digital environment. Increasingly, Xerox found itself occupying the dusty and dying "copy machine" corner of the analog office.

Since those dark days on the brink, however, Xerox has rethought, redefined, and reinvented itself. The company has undergone a remarkable transformation. Xerox no longer defines itself as a "copier company." In fact, it doesn't even make stand-alone copiers anymore. Instead, Xerox bills itself as a leading global document-management and business-process technology and services enterprise. It wants to help companies and people "be smarter about their documents."

Documenting any communication used to mean committing it to paper, getting it down in black and white. Now communication is generally scanned, sent, searched, archived, merged, and personalized—often in color. It can move back and forth, many times, from physical to digital. So when we say our mission is to help people be smarter about their documents, it really means giving them a range of tools and techniques to capture, organize, facilitate, and enhance how they communicate. In any form. To an audience of one or many millions.

Ready For Real Business **xerox** ®

The Xerox transformation started with a new focus on the customer. Before developing new products, Xerox researchers held seemingly endless customer focus groups. Sophie Vandebroek, Xerox's chief technology officer, called this "dreaming with the customer." The goal, she argued, is "involving experts who know the technology with customers who know the pain points. . . . Ultimately innovation is about delighting the customer." The new Xerox believes that understanding customers is just as important as understanding technology.

As a result of this new thinking, Xerox now offers a broad portfolio of customer-focused products, software, and services that help its customers manage documents and information. Xerox has introduced more than 130 innovative new products in the past four years. It now offers digital products and systems ranging from network printers and multifunction devices to color printing and publishing systems, digital presses, and "book factories." It also offers an impressive array of print-management consulting and outsourcing services that help businesses develop online document archives, operate in-house print shops or mailrooms, analyze how employees can most efficiently share documents and knowledge, and build Web-based processes for personalizing direct mail, invoices, and brochures.

Thus, Xerox isn't an old, rusty copier company anymore. Thanks to a truly remarkable turnaround, Xerox is now on solid footing in today's digital world. Xerox's former chairman summed things up this way: "We have transformed Xerox into a business that connects closely with customers in a content-rich digital marketplace. We have expanded into new markets, created new businesses, acquired new capabilities, developed technologies that launched new industries—to ensure we make it easier, faster, and less costly for our customers to share information."

However, just as Xerox's turnaround seemed complete, yet another challenging environmental force arose—the Great Recession. The recession severely depressed Xerox's core printing and copying equipment and services business, and the company's sales and stock price tumbled once again. So in a major move to maintain its transition momentum, Xerox recently acquired Affiliated Computer Services (ACS), a $6.4 billion IT services company. With the ACS acquisition, Xerox can now help clients manage not only their document-related processes but also their even-faster growing IT processes. Xerox's newly expanded mission is to provide clients with the technologies and services they need to manage their documents, data, and work processes more efficiently and effectively. That leaves clients free to focus on what matters most—their real businesses.

Xerox knows that change and renewal are ongoing and never-ending. "The one thing that's predictable about business is that it's fundamentally unpredictable," says the company's most recent annual report. "Macroforces such as globalization, emerging technologies, and, most recently, depressed financial markets bring new challenges every day to businesses of all sizes." The message is clear. Even the most dominant companies can be vulnerable to the often turbulent and changing marketing environment. Companies that understand and adapt well to their environments can thrive. Those that don't risk their very survival.[1]

> Xerox isn't an old, fusty copier company anymore. It now provides a broad portfolio of digital print-management and IT-processing equipment and services that help customers be "Ready for Real Business."

> Xerox invented photocopying and for decades flat-out dominated the industry it had created. But Xerox's experience provides a cautionary tale of what can happen when a company—even a dominant market leader—fails to adapt to its changing marketing environment.

Marketing environment
The actors and forces outside marketing that affect marketing management's ability to build and maintain successful relationships with target customers.

Microenvironment
The actors close to the company that affect its ability to serve its customers—the company, suppliers, marketing intermediaries, customer markets, competitors, and publics.

Macroenvironment
The larger societal forces that affect the microenvironment—demographic, economic, natural, technological, political, and cultural forces.

Author Comment | The microenvironment includes all the actors close to the company that affect, positively or negatively, its ability to create value for and relationships with its customers.

A company's **marketing environment** consists of the actors and forces outside marketing that affect marketing management's ability to build and maintain successful relationships with target customers. Like Xerox, companies constantly watch and adapt to the changing environment.

More than any other group in the company, marketers must be environmental trend trackers and opportunity seekers. Although every manager in an organization should watch the outside environment, marketers have two special aptitudes. They have disciplined methods—marketing research and marketing intelligence—for collecting information about the marketing environment. They also spend more time in customer and competitor environments. By carefully studying the environment, marketers can adapt their strategies to meet new marketplace challenges and opportunities.

The marketing environment consists of a *microenvironment* and a *macroenvironment*. The **microenvironment** consists of the actors close to the company that affect its ability to serve its customers—the company, suppliers, marketing intermediaries, customer markets, competitors, and publics. The **macroenvironment** consists of the larger societal forces that affect the microenvironment—demographic, economic, natural, technological, political, and cultural forces. We look first at the company's microenvironment.

The Microenvironment (pp 66–69)

Marketing management's job is to build relationships with customers by creating customer value and satisfaction. However, marketing managers cannot do this alone. ● **Figure 3.1** shows the major actors in the marketer's microenvironment. Marketing success requires building relationships with other company departments, suppliers, marketing intermediaries, competitors, various publics, and customers, which combine to make up the company's value delivery network.

66

In creating value for customers, marketers must partner with other firms in the company's value delivery network. For example, Lexus can't create a high-quality ownership experience for its customers unless its suppliers provide quality parts and its dealers provide high sales and service quality.

Marketers must work in harmony with other company departments to create customer value and relationships. For example, Walmart's marketers can't promise us low prices unless its operations department delivers low costs.

Customers are the most important actors in the company's microenvironment. The aim of the entire value delivery system is to serve target customers and create strong relationships with them.

◉ **FIGURE | 3.1**
Actors in the Microenvironment

The Company

In designing marketing plans, marketing management takes other company groups into account—groups such as top management, finance, research and development (R&D), purchasing, operations, and accounting. All of these interrelated groups form the internal environment. Top management sets the company's mission, objectives, broad strategies, and policies. Marketing managers make decisions within the strategies and plans made by top management.

As we discussed in Chapter 2, marketing managers must work closely with other company departments. Other departments have an impact on the marketing department's plans and actions. And, under the marketing concept, all of these functions must "think consumer." According to a former Xerox CEO, to provide a great customer experience, Xerox must "find out what customers are facing—what their problems and opportunities are. Everyone at Xerox shares this responsibility. That includes people and departments that have not always been customer-facing, like finance, legal, and human resources."[2]

Suppliers

Suppliers form an important link in the company's overall customer value delivery network. They provide the resources needed by the company to produce its goods and services. Supplier problems can seriously affect marketing. Marketing managers must watch supply availability and costs. Supply shortages or delays, labor strikes, and other events can cost sales in the short run and damage customer satisfaction in the long run. Rising supply costs may force price increases that can harm the company's sales volume.

Most marketers today treat their suppliers as partners in creating and delivering customer value. For example, Toyota knows the importance of building close relationships with its suppliers. In fact, it even includes the phrase *achieve supplier satisfaction* in its mission statement.

Toyota's competitors often alienate suppliers through self-serving, heavy-handed dealings. According to one supplier, U.S. automakers "set annual cost-reduction targets [for the parts they buy]. To realize those targets, they'll do anything. [They've unleashed] a reign of terror, and it gets worse every year." By contrast, rather than bullying suppliers, Toyota partners with them and helps them meet its very high expectations. Toyota learns about their businesses, conducts joint improvement activities, helps train supplier employees, gives daily performance feedback, and actively seeks out supplier concerns. It even recognizes top performers with annual performance awards. High supplier satisfaction means that Toyota can rely on suppliers to help it improve its own quality, reduce costs, and quickly develop new products. Even after the recent massive recall following unanticipated acceleration problems with some Toyota models, the company didn't point blame at the accelerator part supplier. Instead, Toyota took blame for a faulty part design and even issued a statement supporting the "long-term and valued supplier." In all, creating satisfied suppliers helps Toyota produce lower-cost, higher-quality cars, which in turn results in more satisfied customers.[3]

Marketing Intermediaries

Marketing intermediaries
Firms that help the company to promote, sell, and distribute its goods to final buyers.

Marketing intermediaries help the company promote, sell, and distribute its products to final buyers. They include resellers, physical distribution firms, marketing services agencies, and financial intermediaries. *Resellers* are distribution channel firms that help the company find customers or make sales to them. These include wholesalers and retailers who buy and resell merchandise. Selecting and partnering with resellers is not easy. No longer do manufacturers have many small, independent resellers from which to choose. They now face large and growing reseller organizations, such as Walmart, Target, Home Depot, Costco, and Best Buy. These organizations frequently have enough power to dictate terms or even shut smaller manufacturers out of large markets.

Physical distribution firms help the company stock and move goods from their points of origin to their destinations. *Marketing services agencies* are the marketing research firms, advertising agencies, media firms, and marketing consulting firms that help the company target and promote its products to the right markets. *Financial intermediaries* include banks, credit companies, insurance companies, and other businesses that help finance transactions or insure against the risks associated with the buying and selling of goods.

Like suppliers, marketing intermediaries form an important component of the company's overall value delivery network. In its quest to create satisfying customer relationships, the company must do more than just optimize its own performance. It must partner effectively with marketing intermediaries to optimize the performance of the entire system.

Thus, today's marketers recognize the importance of working with their intermediaries as partners rather than simply as channels through which they sell their products. ● For example, when Coca-Cola signs on as the exclusive beverage provider for a fast-food chain, such as McDonald's, Wendy's, or Subway, it provides much more than just soft drinks. It also pledges powerful marketing support.[4]

Coca-Cola assigns cross-functional teams dedicated to understanding the finer points of each retail partner's business. It conducts a staggering amount of research on beverage consumers and shares these insights with its partners. It analyzes the demographics of U.S. zip code areas and helps partners determine which Coke brands are preferred in their areas. Coca-Cola has even studied the design of drive-through menu boards to better understand which layouts, fonts, letter sizes, colors, and visuals induce consumers to order more food and drink. Based on such insights, the Coca-Cola Food Service group develops marketing programs and merchandising tools that help its retail partners improve their beverage sales and profits. For example, Coca-Cola Food Service's Web site, www.CokeSolutions.com, provides retailers with a wealth of information, business solutions, and merchandising tips. "We know that you're passionate about delighting guests and enhancing their real experiences on every level," says Coca-Cola to its retail partners. "As your partner, we want to help in any way we can." Such intense partnering efforts have made Coca-Cola a runaway leader in the U.S. fountain soft-drink market.

● **Partnering with marketing intermediaries: Coca-Cola provides its retail partners with much more than just soft drinks. It also pledges powerful marketing support.**

Competitors

The marketing concept states that, to be successful, a company must provide greater customer value and satisfaction than its competitors do. Thus, marketers must do more than simply adapt to the needs of target consumers. They also must gain strategic advantage by positioning their offerings strongly against competitors' offerings in the minds of consumers.

No single competitive marketing strategy is best for all companies. Each firm should consider its own size and industry position compared to those of its competitors. Large firms with dominant positions in an industry can use certain strategies that smaller firms cannot afford. But being large is not enough. There are winning strategies for large firms, but there are also losing ones. And small firms can develop strategies that give them better rates of return than large firms enjoy.

Publics

Public
Any group that has an actual or potential interest in or impact on an organization's ability to achieve its objectives.

The company's marketing environment also includes various publics. A **public** is any group that has an actual or potential interest in or impact on an organization's ability to achieve its objectives. We can identify seven types of publics:

- *Financial publics.* This group influences the company's ability to obtain funds. Banks, investment analysts, and stockholders are the major financial publics.

- *Media publics.* This group carries news, features, and editorial opinion. It includes newspapers, magazines, television stations, and blogs and other Internet media.

- *Government publics.* Management must take government developments into account. Marketers must often consult the company's lawyers on issues of product safety, truth in advertising, and other matters.

- *Citizen-action publics.* A company's marketing decisions may be questioned by consumer organizations, environmental groups, minority groups, and others. Its public relations department can help it stay in touch with consumer and citizen groups.

- *Local publics.* This group includes neighborhood residents and community organizations. Large companies usually create departments and programs that deal with local community issues and provide community support. ⦿ For example, the P&G Tide Loads of Hope program recognizes the importance of community publics. It provides mobile laundromats and loads of clean laundry to families in disaster-stricken areas. P&G washes, dries, and folds clothes for these families for free because "we've learned [that] sometimes even the littlest things can make a difference."[5]

⦿ **Publics: P&G's Tide Loads of Hope program recognizes the importance of community publics. It washes, dries, and folds loads of clothes for families struck by local disasters.**

- *General public.* A company needs to be concerned about the general public's attitude toward its products and activities. The public's image of the company affects its buying.

- *Internal publics.* This group includes workers, managers, volunteers, and the board of directors. Large companies use newsletters and other means to inform and motivate their internal publics. When employees feel good about the companies they work for, this positive attitude spills over to the external publics.

A company can prepare marketing plans for these major publics as well as for its customer markets. Suppose the company wants a specific response from a particular public, such as goodwill, favorable word of mouth, or donations of time or money. The company would have to design an offer to this public that is attractive enough to produce the desired response.

Customers

As we've emphasized throughout, customers are the most important actors in the company's microenvironment. The aim of the entire value delivery network is to serve target customers and create strong relationships with them. The company might target any or all five types of customer markets. *Consumer markets* consist of individuals and households that buy goods and services for personal consumption. *Business markets* buy goods and services for further processing or use in their production processes, whereas *reseller markets* buy goods and services to resell at a profit. *Government markets* consist of government agencies that buy goods and services to produce public services or transfer the goods and services to others who need them. Finally, *international markets* consist of these buyers in other countries, including consumers, producers, resellers, and governments. Each market type has special characteristics that call for careful study by the seller.

Author | The macroenvironment
Comment | consists of broader forces that affect the actors in the microenvironment.

The Macroenvironment (pp 70–88)

The company and all of the other actors operate in a larger macroenvironment of forces that shape opportunities and pose threats to the company. ◉ **Figure 3.2** shows the six major forces in the company's macroenvironment. In the remaining sections of this chapter, we examine these forces and show how they affect marketing plans.

The Demographic Environment

Author | Changes in demographics
Comment | mean changes in markets, so they are very important to marketers. We first look at the biggest demographic trend—the changing age structure of the population.

Demography is the study of human populations in terms of size, density, location, age, gender, race, occupation, and other statistics. The demographic environment is of major interest to marketers because it involves people, and people make up markets. The world population is growing at an explosive rate. It now exceeds 6.8 billion people and is expected to grow to more than 8 billion by the year 2030.[6] The world's large and highly diverse population poses both opportunities and challenges.

Demography
The study of human populations in terms of size, density, location, age, gender, race, occupation, and other statistics.

Changes in the world demographic environment have major implications for business. For example, consider China. Thirty years ago, to curb its skyrocketing population, the Chinese government passed regulations limiting families to one child each. As a result, China's youth born after 1980—called "balinghou" or the "Me generation" by their elders—have been showered with attention and luxuries resulting in what's known as the "little emperor" or "little empress" syndrome. As many as six adults, two parents, and four doting grandparents may be indulging the whims of each only child—all 600 million of them (almost twice the entire U.S. population). Parents with only one child at home now spend about 40 percent of their income on their cherished child.[7]

China's Me generation, now ranging in age from newborns to their early 30s, is affecting markets for everything from children's products to financial services, cell phone services, and luxury goods. ◉ For example, Starbucks is targeting China's Me generation, positioning itself as new kind of informal but indulgent meeting place.[8]

China's one-child rule created a generation of people who have been pampered by parents and grandparents and have the means to make indulgent purchases. Instead of believing in traditional Chinese collective goals, these young people embrace individuality. "Their view of this world is very different," says the president of Starbucks Greater China. "They have never gone through the hardships of our generation." Starbucks is in sync with that, he says, given its customized drinks, personalized service, and original music compilations. "In the U.S., most of Starbucks' business is takeaway," says one analyst. "It is the opposite in China. [Young] people go to [Starbucks] as a destination and spend hours there. They like to be seen as chic and cosmopolitan."

◉ **Demographics and business: In China, Starbucks targets the "Me generation," positioning itself as a new kind of informal but indulgent meeting place.**

Thus, marketers keep a close eye on demographic trends and developments in their markets—both at home and abroad. They analyze changing age and family structures, geographic population shifts, educational characteristics, and population diversity. Here, we discuss the most important demographic trends in the United States.

The Changing Age Structure of the Population

The U.S. population is currently about 310 million and may reach almost 364 million by 2030.[9] The single most important demographic trend in the United States is the changing age structure of the population. The U.S. population contains several generational groups. Here, we discuss the three largest groups—the baby boomers, Generation X, and the Millennials—and their impact on today's marketing strategies.

Baby boomers
The 78 million people born during years following World War II and lasting until 1964.

The Baby Boomers. The post–World War II baby boom produced 78 million **baby boomers**, who were born between 1946 and 1964. Over the years, the baby boomers have

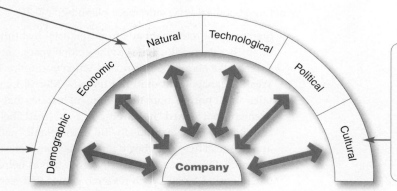

Concern for the natural environment has spawned a so-called green movement in industries ranging from PCs to diesel locomotives. For example, last year HP recovered and recycled 250 million pounds of electronics globally, equivalent to some 800 jumbo jets. The goal of many companies today is **environmental sustainability**—strategies and practices that the planet can support indefinitely.

Marketers also want to be socially responsible citizens in their markets and communities. For example, shoe brand TOMS was *founded* on a cause: "No complicated formulas. It's simple," says the company's founder. "You buy a pair of TOMS and I give a pair to a child on your behalf."

Changing demographics mean changes in markets, which in turn require changes in marketing strategies. For example, Merrill Lynch now targets aging baby boomers to help them overcome the hurdles to retirement planning.

● **FIGURE** | 3.2

Major Forces in the Company's Macroenvironment

been one of the most powerful forces shaping the marketing environment. The youngest boomers are now in their mid-forties; the oldest are in their sixties and approaching retirement. The maturing boomers are rethinking the purpose and value of their work, responsibilities, and relationships.

After years of prosperity, free spending, and saving little, the Great Recession hit many baby boomers hard, especially the preretirement boomers. A sharp decline in stock prices and home values ate into their nest eggs and retirement prospects. As a result, many boomers are now spending more carefully and planning to work longer. "You have a huge group of preretirement baby boomers, a huge number of people who are asking, 'Can I live off my savings and Social Security for the rest of my life?'" says one economist. "A whopping 70 percent of Americans currently age 45 to 74 plan to work during their retirement years . . . both for enjoyment and because they need the money," notes another.[10]

However, although some might be feeling the postrecession pinch, the baby boomers are still the wealthiest generation in U.S. history. Today's baby boomers account for about 25 percent of the U.S. population but hold 75 percent of the nation's financial assets and account for about 50 percent of total consumer spending. They spend about $2 trillion a year.[11] As they reach their peak earning and spending years, the boomers will continue to constitute a lucrative market for financial services, new housing and home remodeling, travel and entertainment, eating out, health and fitness products, and just about everything else.

It would be a mistake to think of the older boomers as phasing out or slowing down. Today's boomers think young no matter how old they are. One study showed that boomers, on average, see themselves 12 years younger than they actually are. And rather than viewing themselves as phasing out, they see themselves as entering new life phases. The more active boomers—sometimes called zoomers, or baby boomers with zip—have no intention of abandoning their youthful lifestyles as they age.[12]

"It is time to throw out the notion that the only things marketable to [the older boomers) are chiropractic mattresses, arthritis drugs, and [staid] cruises," says one marketer. "Boomers have sought the fountain of youth through all stages of life and have incorporated aspects of play and fun into everything from careers to cars."[13] Toyota recognizes these changing boomer life phases. Ads for its Toyota Highlander show empty-nest boomers and declare "For your newfound freedom." Similarly, Curves fitness centers targets boomer women. Curves' older regulars "want to be strong and fit," says one expert. "They just don't want to go into Gold's Gym and be surrounded by spandex-clad Barbie dolls."[14]

Perhaps no one is targeting the baby boomers more fervently than the financial services industry. Collectively, the baby boomers have earned $3.7 trillion, more than twice as much as members of the prior generation. They'll also be inheriting $7.2 trillion as their parents pass away. Thus, especially in the

● **Targeting Baby Boomers: Merrill Lynch's help2retire campaign aims to help boomers overcome the hurdles to retirement planning. It's not just about "the numbers" but also about "life goals."**

aftermath of the Great Recession, the boomers will need lots of money management help as they approach retirement. Merrill Lynch recently launched a marketing campaign aimed at helping boomers with retirement planning:[15]

Stereotypical retirement ads from financial institutions show attractive older couples on the beach enjoying their idyllic golden years. "In this industry, everybody [most always] talks about the future and when you retire," says the head of Merrill Lynch's Wealth Management unit. But the new Merrill Lynch retirement planning campaign talks about now—about the retirement hurdles that people face in getting ready for retirement. ● Themed "help2retire _____" (read "help2retire blank"), the campaign encourages 50-plus year olds to "fill in the blank" with aspects of their current working and financial lives that they'd like so they can focus on what matters most in retirement planning. Different ads suggest words such as help2retire Confusion, or Cold Feet, or Guesswork. Merrill Lynch research shows that recession-tempered boomers are cautiously optimistic about retirement but need help planning for it. Merrill wants to provide that help in the form of personalized financial advice. Merrill is approaching the topic from both a rational and an emotional standpoint. It's not just about "the numbers" but also about "life goals." Says the head of Merrill Lynch Wealth Management: "It's not just about aspiring to get a second home in a warm location [anymore]. It's about spending more time with your family and friends and relieving the anxiety around the guesswork that so many [boomers] are feeling."

Generation X
The 45 million people born between 1965 and 1976 in the "birth dearth" following the baby boom.

Generation X. The baby boom was followed by a "birth dearth," creating another generation of 49 million people born between 1965 and 1976. Author Douglas Coupland calls them **Generation X** because they lie in the shadow of the boomers and lack obvious distinguishing characteristics.

The Generation Xers are defined as much by their shared experiences as by their age. Increasing parental divorce rates and higher employment for their mothers made them the first generation of latchkey kids. Although they seek success, they are less materialistic; they prize experience, not acquisition. For many of the Gen Xers who are parents, family comes first—both children and their aging parents—and career second. From a marketing standpoint, the Gen Xers are a more skeptical bunch. They tend to research products before they consider a purchase, prefer quality to quantity, and tend to be less receptive to overt marketing pitches.

Once labeled as "the MTV generation" and viewed as body-piercing slackers who whined about "McJobs," the Gen Xers have grown up and are now taking over. They are increasingly displacing the lifestyles, culture, and values of the baby boomers. They are moving up in their careers, and many are proud homeowners with young, growing families. They are the most educated generation to date, and they possess hefty annual purchasing power. However, like the baby boomers, the Gen Xers now face growing economic pressures. Like almost everyone else these days, they are spending more carefully.[16]

Still, with so much potential, many brands and organizations are focusing on Gen Xers as a prime target segment. ● For example, the Virginia Tourism Corporation, the state's tourism arm, is now targeting Gen X families:[17]

Virginia's 40-year romance with the baby boomer generation is waning. The Virginia Tourism Corporation (VTC), best known for its enduring "Virginia is for Lovers" campaign, is now wooing a new audience: Generation X. They're younger and more adventuresome, and they spend more money on travel in Virginia. VTC research showed that Generation X households contribute about 45 percent of the $19.2 billion spent on travel in Virginia each year. Whereas most boomers

● Targeting Gen Xers: Virginia tourism now aims its well-known "Virginia is for Lovers" campaign at Gen X families, who want new experiences close to home. "Love: It's at the heart of every Virginia vacation."

are done or almost done with child rearing and lean toward more exotic travel locations farther from home, "the Generation Xers are new families who need new experiences close to home," says Alisa Bailey, CEO and president of VTC. "They want beaches, good places to relax, warm, friendly people. They love amusement and theme parks, and they want places that are good for what we call soft adventure, like canoeing, and hiking." Don't worry; the slogan won't change. "What *will* change," explains Bailey, "is our strategy toward the younger market. We will be showing more Gen X families in our marketing. It will be a more family-oriented campaign." VTC plans to use Facebook, Twitter, and blogs to help reach Generation X households.

Millennials (or Generation Y)
The 83 million children of the baby boomers, born between 1977 and 2000.

Millennials. Both the baby boomers and Gen Xers will one day be passing the reins to the **Millennials** (also called **Generation Y** or the echo boomers). Born between 1977 and 2000, these children of the baby boomers number 83 million, dwarfing the Gen Xers and larger even than the baby boomer segment. This group includes several age cohorts: *tweens* (ages 10–12), *teens* (13–18), and *young adults* (19–33). With total purchasing power of more than $733 billion, the Millennials are a huge and attractive market.[18]

One thing that all the Millennials have in common is their utter fluency and comfort with digital technology. They don't just embrace technology; it's a way of life. The Millennials were the first generation to grow up in a world filled with computers, cell phones, satellite TV, iPods, and online social networks. A recent study found that 91 percent of Millennials are on the Web, making up 32 percent of all U.S. Internet users. According to another study, 77 percent of Millennials frequent social-networking sites, and 71 percent use instant messaging. "All generations are comfortable with technology, but this is the generation that's been formed by technology," says a Yahoo! executive. For them, "it's not something separate. It's just something they do."[19]

Marketers of all kinds now target the Millennials segment, from automakers to political campaigns. The Millennials are bombarded with marketing messages coming at them from all directions. However, rather than having mass marketing messages pushed at them, they prefer to seek out information and engage in two-way brand conversations. Thus, reaching these message-saturated consumers effectively requires creative marketing approaches. ◉ Consider how the Barack Obama presidential campaign succeeded in reaching this group:[20]

"Barack Obama was the first presidential candidate to be marketed like a high-end consumer brand," observed a *Newsweek* reporter. His rising-sun logo echoes the one-world icons of PepsiCo, AT&T, and Apple. But what really set the Obama campaign apart was its immense appeal to Millennials, the country's youngest voters. The campaign's mastery of cutting-edge social media, such as the www.my.barackobama.com Web site, was optimized for Millennial appeal. For this generation, "the new pronoun is me, my," says a marketing expert. "Young people want to be in control of their relationship with a brand. They want to customize and personalize." The Obama campaign site allowed just that, with its use of tagging, discussion boards, photo uploads, and other interactive elements.

◉ Reaching Millennials: The Barack Obama presidential campaign's mastery of cutting-edge social media, such as www.my.barackobama.com, was optimized for Millennial appeal. It still is. You can connect with "Obama everywhere."

In addition, Obama enlisted eight million volunteers using social-networking sites, attracted two million friends on Facebook, and drew 90 million viewers to his video presentations on YouTube. On Election Day, the Obama team sent text messages to millions of young supporters. The Obama campaign didn't merely use young volunteers, as most campaigns do. It created a campaign specifically designed by and for today's tech-happy Millennial generation, using the communication tools young people rely on and trust. The result? Young people turned out at the polls in record numbers, with fully 66 percent favoring Obama, turning the tide his way in several key states.

Generational Marketing. Do marketers need to create separate products and marketing programs for each generation? Some experts warn that marketers need to be careful about turning off one generation each time they craft a product or message that appeals effectively to another. Others caution that each generation spans decades of time and many socioeconomic levels. For example, marketers often split the baby boomers into three smaller groups—leading-edge boomers, core boomers, and trailing-edge boomers—each with its own beliefs and behaviors. Similarly, they split the Millennials into tweens, teens, and young adults.

Thus, marketers need to form more precise age-specific segments within each group. More important, defining people by their birth date may be less effective than segmenting them by their lifestyle, life stage, or the common values they seek in the products they buy. We will discuss many other ways to segment markets in Chapter 7.

The Changing American Family

The traditional household consists of a husband, wife, and children (and sometimes grandparents). Yet, the once American ideal of the two-child, two-car suburban family has lately been losing some of its luster.

In the United States today, married couples with children represent only 22 percent of the nation's 117 million households, married couples without children represent 29 percent, and single parents are another 11 percent. A full 38 percent are nonfamily households—singles living alone or adults of one or both sexes living together.[21] More people are divorcing or separating, choosing not to marry, marrying later, or marrying without intending to have children. Marketers must increasingly consider the special needs of nontraditional households because they are now growing more rapidly than traditional households. Each group has distinctive needs and buying habits.

The number of working women has also increased greatly, growing from under 40 percent of the U.S. workforce in the late 1950s to 59 percent today. Both husband and wife work in 59 percent of all married-couple families. Meanwhile, more men are staying home with their children, managing the household while their wives go to work. According to the U.S. Census Bureau, the number of stay-at-home dads has risen 18 percent since 1994—some 158,000 fathers now stay at home.[22]

The significant number of women in the workforce has spawned the child day-care business and increased the consumption of career-oriented women's clothing, financial services, and convenience foods and services. Royal Caribbean targets time-crunched working moms with budget-friendly family vacations that are easy to plan and certain to wow the family. Royal Caribbean estimates that, although vacations are a joint decision, 80 percent of all trips are planned and booked by women—moms who are pressed for time, whether they work or not. "We want to make sure that you're the hero, that when your family comes on our ship, it's going to be a great experience for all of them," says a senior marketer at Royal Caribbean, "and that you, mom, who has done all the planning and scheduling, get to enjoy that vacation."[23]

Geographic Shifts in Population

This is a period of great migratory movements between and within countries. Americans, for example, are a mobile people, with about 15 percent of all U.S. residents moving each year. Over the past two decades, the U.S. population has shifted toward the Sunbelt states. The West and South have grown, whereas the Midwest and Northeast states have lost population.[24] Such population shifts interest marketers because people in different regions buy differently. For example, people in the Midwest buy more winter clothing than people in the Southeast.

Also, for more than a century, Americans have been moving from rural to metropolitan areas. In the 1950s, they made a massive exit from the cities to the suburbs. Today, the migration to the suburbs continues. And more and more Americans are moving to "micropolitan areas," small cities located beyond congested metropolitan areas, such as Bozeman, Montana; Natchez, Mississippi; and Torrington, Connecticut. Drawing refugees from rural and suburban America, these smaller micros offer many of the advantages of metro areas—jobs, restaurants, diversions, community organizations—but without the population crush, traffic jams, high crime rates, and high property taxes often associated with heavily urbanized areas.[25]

The shift in where people live has also caused a shift in where they work. For example, the migration toward micropolitan and suburban areas has resulted in a rapid increase

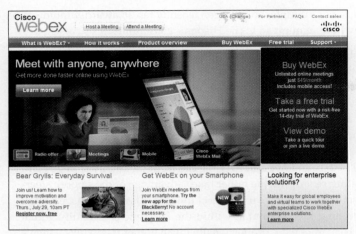

● Cisco targets the growing telecommuter market with WebEx, which lets people meet and collaborate online, no matter what their work location.

in the number of people who "telecommute"—work at home or in a remote office and conduct their business by phone, fax, modem, or the Internet. This trend, in turn, has created a booming SOHO (small office/home office) market. An increasing number of people are working from home with the help of electronic conveniences such as PCs, smartphones, and broadband Internet access. One recent study estimates that more than one-half of American businesses now support some kind of telecommuting program, and 5.9 million Americans work solely from home.[26]

Many marketers are actively courting the lucrative telecommuting market. ● For example, WebEx, the Web-conferencing division of Cisco, helps overcome the isolation that often accompanies telecommuting. With WebEx, people can meet and collaborate online via computer or smartphone, no matter what their work location. "All you need to run effective online meetings is a browser and a phone," says the company. With WebEx, people working anywhere can interact with other individuals or small groups to make presentations, exchange documents, and share desktops, complete with audio and full-motion video.[27]

A Better-Educated, More White-Collar, More Professional Population

The U.S. population is becoming better educated. For example, in 2007, 87 percent of the U.S. population over age 25 had completed high school, and 30 percent had completed college, compared with 69 percent and 17 percent, respectively, in 1980. Moreover, nearly two-thirds of high school graduates now enroll in college within 12 months of graduating.[28] The rising number of educated people will increase the demand for quality products, books, travel, computers, and Internet services.

The workforce also is becoming more white collar. Between 1983 and 2007, the proportion of managers and professionals in the workforce increased from 23 percent to more than 36 percent. Job growth is now strongest for professional workers and weakest for manufacturing workers. Between 2008 and 2018, the number of professional workers is expected to increase 17 percent, while manufacturing workers are expected to decline more than 24 percent.[29]

Increasing Diversity

Countries vary in their ethnic and racial makeup. At one extreme is Japan, where almost everyone is Japanese. At the other extreme is the United States, with people from virtually all nations. The United States has often been called a melting pot, where diverse groups from many nations and cultures have melted into a single, more homogenous whole. Instead, the United States seems to have become more of a "salad bowl" in which various groups have mixed together but have maintained their diversity by retaining and valuing important ethnic and cultural differences.

Marketers now face increasingly diverse markets, both at home and abroad as their operations become more international in scope. The U.S. population is about 63 percent white, with Hispanics at about 16 percent and African Americans at about 13.6 percent. The U.S. Asian American population now totals about 4.9 percent of the population, with the remaining 2.5 percent being American Indian, Eskimo, Aleut, or people of two or more races. Moreover, more than 34 million people living in the United States—more than 12 percent of the population—were born in another country. The nation's ethnic populations are expected to explode in coming decades. By 2050, Hispanics are expected to be an estimated 24 percent of the population, African Americans will hold steady at about 13 percent, and Asians will almost double to 9 percent.[30]

Most large companies, from P&G, Walmart, Allstate, and Bank of America to Levi Strauss and Volkswagen, now target specially designed products, ads, and promotions to one or more of these groups. For example, Volkswagen recently ran an award-winning campaign to introduce its new Routan minivan to the Hispanic community:[31]

> Research in core markets with Hispanic minivan prospects showed that, contrary to the happy serenity competitors' campaigns show, chaos rules inside a minivan on family outings. So Volkswagen built a Spanish-language campaign to show how it's Routan minivan could help Hispanic families in "managing mayhem." The campaign tells the story of the Routan as a comfortable, multifeature vehicle engineered with the whole family in mind. In a spot called "Spill," one kid spills a bottle of water on her brother, who strips off his wet clothes and stows them in a storage compartment. In "Frog," a frog escapes from its shoe box and hops all over the car, from the roomy storage compartment to the soft leather seats, until the father takes advantage of the smooth steering and suspension to quickly stop the car and eject the frog. The mayhem campaign created a unique positioning for the Routan within the Hispanic community. Initial sales of the minivan to Hispanics were proportionally much higher than Volkswagen's overall Hispanic sales (which account for almost 10 percent total U.S. VW sales). Volkswagen later extended the campaign in English to non-Hispanic markets as well.

Diversity goes beyond ethnic heritage. For example, many major companies explicitly target gay and lesbian consumers. According to one estimate, the 6–7 percent of U.S. adults who identify themselves as lesbian, gay, bisexual, and transgender (LGBT) have buying power of $712 billion. A Simmons Research study of readers of the National Gay Newspaper Guild's 12 publications found that, compared to the average American, LGBT respondents are 12 times more likely to be in professional jobs, almost twice as likely to own a vacation home, eight times more likely to own a notebook computer, and twice as likely to own individual stocks. More than two-thirds have graduated from college, and 21 percent hold a master's degree.[32]

As a result of TV shows like *Modern Family*, *Ugly Betty*, and *The Ellen DeGeneres Show* and Oscar-winning movies like *Brokeback Mountain* and *Milk*, the LGBT community has increasingly emerged into the public eye. A number of media now provide companies with access to this market. For example, Planet Out Inc., a leading global media and entertainment company that exclusively serves the LGBT community, offers several successful magazines (*Out*, the *Advocate*, *Out Traveler*) and Web sites (Gay.com and PlanetOut.com). And media giant Viacom's MTV Networks introduced LOGO, a cable television network aimed at gays and lesbians and their friends and family. LOGO is now available in 33 million U.S. households. More than 100 mainstream marketers have advertised on LOGO, including Ameriprise Financial, Anheuser-Busch, Continental Airlines, Dell, Levi Strauss, eBay, J&J, Orbitz, Sears, Sony, and Subaru.

Companies in a wide range of industries are now targeting the LGBT community with gay-specific marketing efforts. For example, American Airlines has a dedicated LGBT sales team, sponsors gay community events, and offers a special gay-oriented Web site (www.aa .com/rainbow) that features travel deals, an e-newsletter, podcasts, and a gay events calendar. The airline's focus on gay consumers has earned it double-digit revenue growth from the LGBT community each year for more than a decade.[33]

Another attractive diversity segment is the nearly 60 million U.S. adults with disabilities—a market larger than African Americans or Hispanics—representing more than $200 billion in annual spending power. Most individuals with disabilities are active consumers. For example, one study found that more than two-thirds of adults with disabilities had traveled at least once for business or pleasure during the preceding two years. Thirty-one percent had booked at least one flight, more than half had stayed in hotels, and 20 percent had rented a car. More than 75 percent of people with disabilities dine out at least once a week.[34]

How are companies trying to reach consumers with disabilities? Many marketers now recognize that the worlds of people with disabilities and those without disabilities are one in

● **Targeting consumers with disabilities: Samsung features people with disabilities in its mainstream advertising and signs endorsement deals with Paralympic athletes.**

the same. Marketers such as McDonald's, Verizon Wireless, Nike, Samsung, and Honda have featured people with disabilities in their mainstream advertising. ◉ For instance, Samsung and Nike sign endorsement deals with Paralympic athletes and feature them in advertising.

Other companies use specially targeted media to reach this attractive segment. The Web site www.Disaboom.com reaches people with disabilities through social-networking features akin to Facebook combined with relevant information, everything from medical news to career advice, dating resources, and travel tips. Several large marketers, including J&J, Netflix, Avis, GM, and Ford advertise on Disaboom.com. Ford uses the site to highlight its Mobility Motoring Program. Among other things, the program provides $1,000 allowances for new car buyers to defray costs of adding adaptive equipment, such as wheelchair or scooter lifts, pedal extensions, and steering wheel knobs. Marketing on Disaboom.com has "been a new concept for us and we are pleased with the performance so far," says Ford's mobility motoring manager.[35]

As the population in the United States grows more diverse, successful marketers will continue to diversify their marketing programs to take advantage of opportunities in fast-growing segments.

Economic environment
Economic factors that affect consumer purchasing power and spending patterns.

> **Author Comment** | The economic environment can offer both opportunities and threats. For example, facing a still-uncertain economy, luxury car maker Infiniti now promises to "make luxury affordable."

The Economic Environment

Markets require buying power as well as people. The **economic environment** consists of economic factors that affect consumer purchasing power and spending patterns. Marketers must pay close attention to major trends and consumer spending patterns both across and within their world markets.

Nations vary greatly in their levels and distribution of income. Some countries have *industrial economies*, which constitute rich markets for many different kinds of goods. At the other extreme are *subsistence economies*; they consume most of their own agricultural and industrial output and offer few market opportunities. In between are *developing economies* that can offer outstanding marketing opportunities for the right kinds of products.

now you can.

Can you imagine a car within the reach of all?

Can you fit your family into the smallest of cars? Without a squeeze?

Can you feel the safety of a big car? In a car nearly half its size?

Can you find more miles in your every litre? Almost as much, as a two wheeler?

Can you make a difference to the environment? By hurting it the least?

Can you imagine a car that will change the world? Again.

nano

TATA MOTORS

◉ **Economic environment: To capture India's growing middle class, Tata Motors introduced the small, affordable Tata Nano. "Can you imagine a car within the reach of all?" asks this advertisement. "Now you can."**

Consider India with its population of more than 1.1 billion people. In the past, only India's elite could afford to buy a car. In fact, only one in seven Indians now owns one. But recent dramatic changes in India's economy have produced a growing middle class and rapidly rising incomes. Now, to meet the new demand, European, North American, and Asian automakers are introducing smaller, more-affordable vehicles in India. But they'll have to find a way to compete with India's Tata Motors, which markets the least expensive car ever in the world, the Tata Nano. Dubbed "the people's car," the Nano sells for just over 100,000 rupees (about US$2,500). It can seat four passengers, gets 50 miles per gallon, and travels at a top speed of 60 miles per hour. The ultralow-cost car is designed to be India's Model T—the car that puts the developing nation on wheels. ◉ "Can you imagine a car within the reach of all?" asks a Nano advertisement. "Now you can," comes the answer. Tata hopes to sell one million of these vehicles per year.[36]

Changes in Consumer Spending

Economic factors can have a dramatic effect on consumer spending and buying behavior. For example, until fairly recently, American consumers spent freely, fueled by income growth, a boom in the stock market, rapid increases in housing values, and other economic good fortunes. They bought and bought, seemingly without caution, amassing record levels of debt. However, the free spending and high expectations of those days were dashed by the Great Recession. Says one economist, "For a generation that . . . substituted rising home equity and stock prices for personal savings, the . . . economic meltdown [was] psychologically wrenching after a quarter century of unquestioned prosperity."[37]

As a result, as discussed in Chapter 1, consumers have now adopted a back-to-basics frugality in their lifestyles and spending patterns that will likely persist for years to come. They are buying less and looking for greater value in the things that they do buy. In turn, *value marketing* has become the watchword for many marketers. Marketers in all industries are looking for ways to offer today's more financially cautious buyers greater value—just the right combination of product quality and good service at a fair price.

You'd expect value pitches from the makers of everyday products. For example, alongside milk mustache ads featuring glamorous celebrities, such as Brooke Shields and Beyoncé Knowles, you now see one featuring celebrity financial advisor Suze Orman, telling consumers how to "Milk your budget." And discounter Kohl's offers "style and savings inspiration." However, these days, even luxury-brand marketers are emphasizing good value. For instance, upscale car brand Infiniti now promises to "make luxury affordable."

Income Distribution

Marketers should pay attention to *income distribution* as well as income levels. Over the past several decades, the rich have grown richer, the middle class has shrunk, and the poor have remained poor. The top 5 percent of American earners get more than 21 percent of the country's adjusted gross income, and the top 20 percent of earners capture 49 percent of all income. In contrast, the bottom 40 percent of American earners get just 13 percent of the total income.[38]

This distribution of income has created a tiered market. Many companies—such as Nordstrom and Neiman Marcus—aggressively target the affluent. Others—such as Dollar General and Family Dollar—target those with more modest means. In fact, dollar stores are now the fastest-growing retailers in the nation. Still other companies tailor their marketing offers across a range of markets, from the affluent to the less affluent. For example, outfitter L.L.Bean, long known for timeless, affordable apparel and accessories, recently broadened its appeal by introducing an upscale Signature Collection. Shaped by designer Alex Carleton, the new line competes with the more fashion-forward wares of J.Crew and Ralph Lauren's Rugby line. The collection—everything from chinos to evening wear and the Bean's Heritage Tote—hints of L.L.Bean's Maine roots but has an edgier look and feel and, of course, higher prices. The Heritage Tote, for example, sells for $189.[39]

Changes in major economic variables, such as income, cost of living, interest rates, and savings and borrowing patterns have a large impact on the marketplace. Companies watch these variables by using economic forecasting. Businesses do not have to be wiped out by an economic downturn or caught short in a boom. With adequate warning, they can take advantage of changes in the economic environment.

Author Comment | Today's enlightened companies are developing *environmentally sustainable* strategies in an effort to create a world economy that the planet can support indefinitely.

The Natural Environment

The **natural environment** involves the natural resources that are needed as inputs by marketers or that are affected by marketing activities. Environmental concerns have grown steadily over the past three decades. In many cities around the world, air and water pollution have reached dangerous levels. World concern continues to mount about the possibilities of global warming, and many environmentalists fear that we soon will be buried in our own trash.

Marketers should be aware of several trends in the natural environment. The first involves growing shortages of raw materials. Air and water may seem to be infinite resources, but some groups see long-run dangers. Air pollution chokes many of the world's large cities, and water shortages are already a big problem in some parts of the United States and the world. By 2030, more than one in three of the world's population will not have enough water to drink.[40] Renewable resources, such as forests and food, also have to be used wisely. Nonrenewable resources, such as oil, coal, and various minerals, pose a serious problem. Firms making products that require these scarce resources face large cost increases, even if the materials remain available.

A second environmental trend is *increased pollution*. Industry will almost always damage the quality of the natural environment. Consider the disposal of chemical and nuclear

Natural environment
Natural resources that are needed as inputs by marketers or that are affected by marketing activities.

wastes; the dangerous mercury levels in the ocean; the quantity of chemical pollutants in the soil and food supply; and the littering of the environment with nonbiodegradable bottles, plastics, and other packaging materials.

A third trend is *increased government intervention* in natural resource management. The governments of different countries vary in their concern and efforts to promote a clean environment. Some, such as the German government, vigorously pursue environmental quality. Others, especially many poorer nations, do little about pollution, largely because they lack the needed funds or political will. Even richer nations lack the vast funds and political accord needed to mount a worldwide environmental effort. The general hope is that companies around the world will accept more social responsibility and that less expensive devices can be found to control and reduce pollution.

In the United States, the Environmental Protection Agency (EPA) was created in 1970 to create and enforce pollution standards and conduct pollution research. In the future, companies doing business in the United States can expect continued strong controls from government and pressure groups. Instead of opposing regulation, marketers should help develop solutions to the material and energy problems facing the world.

Concern for the natural environment has spawned the so-called green movement. Today, enlightened companies go beyond what government regulations dictate. They are developing strategies and practices that support **environmental sustainability**—an effort to create a world economy that the planet can support indefinitely. They are responding to consumer demands with more environmentally responsible products.

For example, GE is using its "ecomagination" to create products for a better world—cleaner aircraft engines, cleaner locomotives, cleaner fuel technologies. Taken together, for instance, all the GE Energy wind turbines in the world could produce enough power for 2.4 million U.S. homes. And in 2005, GE launched its Evolution series locomotives, diesel engines that cut fuel consumption by 5 percent and emissions by 40 percent compared to locomotives built just a year earlier. Up next is a triumph of sheer coolness: a GE hybrid diesel-electric locomotive that, just like a Prius, captures energy from braking and will reduce fuel consumption by 15 percent and emissions by as much as 50 percent compared to most locomotives in use today.[41]

Other companies are developing recyclable or biodegradable packaging, recycled materials and components, better pollution controls, and more energy-efficient operations. For example, PepsiCo—which owns brands ranging from Frito-Lay and Pepsi to Quaker, Gatorade, and Tropicana—is working to dramatically reduce its environmental footprint.

PepsiCo markets hundreds of products that are grown, produced, and consumed worldwide. Making and distributing these products requires water, electricity, and fuel. In 2007, the company set as its goal to reduce water consumption by 20 percent, electricity consumption by 20 percent, and fuel consumption by 25 percent per unit of production by 2015. It's already well on its way to meeting these goals. ◉ For example, a solar-panel field now generates power for three-quarters of the heat used in Frito-Lay's Modesto, California, SunChips plant and SunChips themselves come in the world's first 100 percent combustible package. A wind turbine now supplies more than two-thirds of the power at PepsiCo's beverage plant in Mamandur, India. On the packaging front, PepsiCo recently introduced new half-liter bottles of its Lipton iced tea, Tropicana juice, Aquafina FlavorSplash, and Aquafina Alive beverages that contain 20 percent less plastic than the original packaging. Aquafina has trimmed the amount of plastic used in its bottles by 35 percent since 2002, saving 50 million pounds of plastic annually.[42]

Companies today are looking to do more than just good deeds. More and more, they are recognizing the link between a healthy ecology and a healthy economy. They are learning that environmentally responsible actions can also be good business.

Environmental sustainability
Developing strategies and practices that create a world economy that the planet can support indefinitely.

◉ Environmental sustainability: PepsiCo is working to reduce its environmental footprint. For example, solar power now provides three-quarters of the heat used in Frito-Lay's Modesto, California, SunChips plant and SunChips themselves come in the world's first 100 percent compostable package.

Author | Technological advances
Comment | are perhaps the most dramatic forces affecting today's marketing strategies. Just think about the tremendous impact of the Web—which emerged in the mid-1990s—on marketing. You'll see examples of the fast-growing world of online marketing throughout every chapter, and we'll discuss it in detail in Chapter 17.

The Technological Environment

The **technological environment** is perhaps the most dramatic force now shaping our destiny. Technology has released such wonders as antibiotics, robotic surgery, miniaturized electronics, smartphones, and the Internet. It also has released such horrors as nuclear missiles, chemical weapons, and assault rifles. It has released such mixed blessings as the automobile, television, and credit cards. Our attitude toward technology depends on whether we are more impressed with its wonders or its blunders.

New technologies can offer exciting opportunities for marketers. For example, what would you think about having tiny little transmitters implanted in all the products you buy, which would allow tracking of the products from their point of production through use and disposal? On the one hand, it would provide many advantages to both buyers and sellers. On the other hand, it could be a bit scary. Either way, it's already happening:

> Envision a world in which every product contains a tiny transmitter, loaded with information. As you stroll through supermarket aisles, shelf sensors detect your selections and beam ads to your shopping cart screen, offering special deals on related products. As your cart fills, scanners detect that you might be buying for a dinner party; the screen suggests a wine to go with the meal you've planned. When you leave the store, exit scanners total up your purchases and automatically charge them to your credit card. At home, readers track what goes into and out of your pantry, updating your shopping list when stocks run low. For Sunday dinner, you pop a Butterball turkey into your "smart oven," which follows instructions from an embedded chip and cooks the bird to perfection. Seem far-fetched? Not really. In fact, it might soon become a reality, thanks to radio-frequency identification (RFID) transmitters that can be embedded in the products you buy.

Many firms are already using RFID technology to track products through various points in the distribution channel. For example, Walmart has strongly encouraged suppliers shipping products to its distribution centers to apply RFID tags to their pallets. So far, more than 600 Walmart suppliers are doing so. And clothing retailer American Apparel uses RFID to manage inventory in many of its retail stores. ● Every stocked item carries an RFID tag, which is scanned at the receiving docks as the item goes into inventory. American Apparel puts only one of each item on the store floor at a time. When the item is sold, a point-of-sale RFID reader alerts the inventory system and prompts employees to bring a replacement onto the floor. Another RFID reader located between the stockroom and the store floor checks to see that this was done. In all, the system creates inventory efficiencies and ensures that the right items are always on the sales floor. As a result, American Apparel stores with RFID systems average 14 percent higher sales but 15 percent lower stockroom inventories than other stores. And the chain's RFID stores require 20–30 percent fewer staff because employees don't have to spend five or more hours a day doing manual inventory checks.[43]

The technological environment changes rapidly. Think of all of today's common products that were not available 100 years ago—or even 30 years ago. Abraham Lincoln did not know about automobiles, airplanes, radios, or the electric light. Woodrow Wilson did not know about television, aerosol cans, automatic dishwashers, air conditioners, antibiotics, or computers. Franklin Delano Roosevelt did not know about xerography, synthetic detergents, birth control pills, jet engines, or earth satellites. John F. Kennedy did not know about PCs, cell phones, the Internet, or Google.

New technologies create new markets and opportunities. However, every new technology replaces an older technology. Transistors hurt the vacuum-tube industry, CDs hurt phonograph records, and digital photography hurt the film business. When old industries fought or ignored new technologies, their businesses declined. Thus, marketers should watch the technological environment

Technological environment
Forces that create new technologies, creating new product and market opportunities.

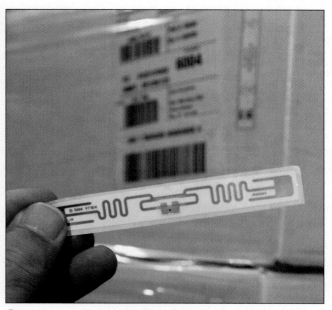
● **Technological environment: American Apparel uses RFID to track and manage inventory in many of its retail stores.**

closely. Companies that do not keep up will soon find their products outdated. And they will miss new product and market opportunities.

The United States leads the world in R&D spending. Total U.S. R&D spending reached an estimated $389 billion last year. The federal government was the largest R&D spender at about $114 billion.[44] Scientists today are researching a wide range of promising new products and services, ranging from practical solar energy, electric cars, and paint-on computer and entertainment video displays to powerful computers that you can wear or fold into your pocket to go-anywhere concentrators that produce drinkable water from the air.

Today's research usually is carried out by research teams rather than by lone inventors like Thomas Edison or Alexander Graham Bell. Many companies are adding marketing people to R&D teams to try to obtain a stronger marketing orientation. Scientists also speculate on fantasy products, such as flying cars and space colonies. The challenge in each case is not only technical but also commercial—to make *practical, affordable* versions of these products.

As products and technology become more complex, the public needs to know that these are safe. Thus, government agencies investigate and ban potentially unsafe products. In the United States, the Food and Drug Administration (FDA) has created complex regulations for testing new drugs. The Consumer Product Safety Commission (CPSC) establishes safety standards for consumer products and penalizes companies that fail to meet them. Such regulations have resulted in much higher research costs and longer times between new product ideas and their introduction. Marketers should be aware of these regulations when applying new technologies and developing new products.

The Political and Social Environment

Marketing decisions are strongly affected by developments in the political environment. The **political environment** consists of laws, government agencies, and pressure groups that influence or limit various organizations and individuals in a given society.

Legislation Regulating Business

Even the most liberal advocates of free-market economies agree that the system works best with at least some regulation. Well-conceived regulation can encourage competition and ensure fair markets for goods and services. Thus, governments develop *public policy* to guide commerce—sets of laws and regulations that limit business for the good of society as a whole. Almost every marketing activity is subject to a wide range of laws and regulations.

Increasing Legislation. Legislation affecting business around the world has increased steadily over the years. The United States has many laws covering issues such as competition, fair trade practices, environmental protection, product safety, truth in advertising, consumer privacy, packaging and labeling, pricing, and other important areas (see ◉ **Table 3.1**). The European Commission has been active in establishing a new framework of laws covering competitive behavior, product standards, product liability, and commercial transactions for the nations of the European Union.

Understanding the public policy implications of a particular marketing activity is not a simple matter. For example, in the United States, there are many laws created at the national, state, and local levels, and these regulations often overlap. Aspirins sold in Dallas are governed by both federal labeling laws and Texas state advertising laws. Moreover, regulations are constantly changing; what was allowed last year may now be prohibited, and what was prohibited may now be allowed. Marketers must work hard to keep up with changes in regulations and their interpretations.

Business legislation has been enacted for a number of reasons. The first is to *protect companies* from each other. Although business executives may praise competition, they sometimes try to neutralize it when it threatens them. So laws are passed to define and prevent unfair competition. In the United States, such laws are enforced by the FTC and the Antitrust Division of the Attorney General's office.

The second purpose of government regulation is to *protect consumers* from unfair business practices. Some firms, if left alone, would make shoddy products, invade consumer privacy, mislead consumers in their advertising, and deceive consumers through their

---

Author Comment | Even the most liberal free-market advocates agree that the system works best with at least some regulation. But beyond regulation, most companies *want* to be socially responsible. If you look at almost any company's Web site, you'll find long lists of good deeds and environmentally responsible actions. For example, check out the Nike Responsibility page (www.nikebiz.com/responsibility/). We'll dig deeper into marketing and social responsibility in Chapter 20.

Political environment

Laws, government agencies, and pressure groups that influence and limit various organizations and individuals in a given society.

⊙ **TABLE | 3.1** Major U.S. Legislation Affecting Marketing

Legislation	Purpose
Sherman Antitrust Act (1890)	Prohibits monopolies and activities (price fixing, predatory pricing) that restrain trade or competition in interstate commerce.
Federal Food and Drug Act (1906)	Created the Food and Drug Administration (FDA). It forbids the manufacture or sale of adulterated or fraudulently labeled foods and drugs.
Clayton Act (1914)	Supplements the Sherman Act by prohibiting certain types of price discrimination, exclusive dealing, and tying clauses (which require a dealer to take additional products in a seller's line).
Federal Trade Commission Act (1914)	Established the Federal Trade Commission (FTC), which monitors and remedies unfair trade methods.
Robinson-Patman Act (1936)	Amends the Clayton Act to define price discrimination as unlawful. Empowers the FTC to establish limits on quantity discounts, forbid some brokerage allowances, and prohibit promotional allowances except when made available on proportionately equal terms.
Wheeler-Lea Act (1938)	Makes deceptive, misleading, and unfair practices illegal regardless of injury to competition. Places advertising of food and drugs under FTC jurisdiction.
Lanham Trademark Act (1946)	Protects and regulates distinctive brand names and trademarks.
National Traffic and Safety Act (1958)	Provides for the creation of compulsory safety standards for automobiles and tires.
Fair Packaging and Labeling Act (1966)	Provides for the regulation of packaging and the labeling of consumer goods. Requires that manufacturers state what the package contains, who made it, and how much it contains.
Child Protection Act (1966)	Bans the sale of hazardous toys and articles. Sets standards for child resistant packaging.
Federal Cigarette Labeling and Advertising Act (1967)	Requires that cigarette packages contain the following statement: "Warning: The Surgeon General Has Determined That Cigarette Smoking Is Dangerous to Your Health."
National Environmental Policy Act (1969)	Establishes a national policy on the environment. The 1970 Reorganization Plan established the Environmental Protection Agency (EPA).
Consumer Product Safety Act (1972)	Established the Consumer Product Safety Commission and authorizes it to set safety standards for consumer products as well as exact penalties for failing to uphold those standards.
Magnuson-Moss Warranty Act (1975)	Authorizes the FTC to determine rules and regulations for consumer warranties and provides consumer access to redress, such as the class action suit.
Children's Television Act (1990)	Limits the number of commercials aired during children's programs.
Nutrition Labeling and Education Act (1990)	Requires that food product labels provide detailed nutritional information.
Telephone Consumer Protection Act (1991)	Establishes procedures to avoid unwanted telephone solicitations. Limits marketers' use of automatic telephone dialing systems and artificial or prerecorded voices.
Americans with Disabilities Act (1991)	Makes discrimination against people with disabilities illegal in public accommodations, transportation, and telecommunications.
Children's Online Privacy Protection Act (2000)	Prohibits Web sites or online services operators from collecting personal information from children without obtaining consent from a parent and allowing parents to review information collected from their children.
Do-Not-Call Implementation Act (2003)	Authorizes the FTC to collect fees from sellers and telemarketers for the implementation and enforcement of a National Do-Not-Call Registry.
CAN-SPAM Act (2003)	Regulates the distribution and content of unsolicited commercial e-mail.
Financial Reform Law (2010)	Creates the Bureau of Consumer Financial Protection, which writes and enforces rules for the marketing of financial products to consumers. It is also responsible for enforcement of the Truth-in-Lending Act, the Home Mortgage Disclosure Act, and other laws designed to protect consumers.

packaging and pricing. Unfair business practices have been defined and are enforced by various agencies.

The third purpose of government regulation is to *protect the interests of society* against unrestrained business behavior. Profitable business activity does not always create a better quality of life. Regulation arises to ensure that firms take responsibility for the social costs of their production or products.

Changing Government Agency Enforcement. International marketers will encounter dozens, or even hundreds, of agencies set up to enforce trade policies and regulations. In the

United States, Congress has established federal regulatory agencies, such as the FTC, the FDA, the Federal Communications Commission, the Federal Energy Regulatory Commission, the Federal Aviation Administration, the Consumer Product Safety Commission, the Environmental Protection Agency, and hundreds of others. Because such government agencies have some discretion in enforcing the laws, they can have a major impact on a company's marketing performance.

New laws and their enforcement will continue to increase. Business executives must watch these developments when planning their products and marketing programs. Marketers need to know about the major laws protecting competition, consumers, and society. They need to understand these laws at the local, state, national, and international levels.

Increased Emphasis on Ethics and Socially Responsible Actions

Written regulations cannot possibly cover all potential marketing abuses, and existing laws are often difficult to enforce. However, beyond written laws and regulations, business is also governed by social codes and rules of professional ethics.

Socially Responsible Behavior. Enlightened companies encourage their managers to look beyond what the regulatory system allows and simply "do the right thing." These socially responsible firms actively seek out ways to protect the long-run interests of their consumers and the environment.

The recent rash of business scandals and increased concerns about the environment have created fresh interest in the issues of ethics and social responsibility. Almost every aspect of marketing involves such issues. Unfortunately, because these issues usually involve conflicting interests, well-meaning people can honestly disagree about the right course of action in a given situation. Thus, many industrial and professional trade associations have suggested codes of ethics. And more companies are now developing policies, guidelines, and other responses to complex social responsibility issues.

The boom in Internet marketing has created a new set of social and ethical issues. Critics worry most about online privacy issues. There has been an explosion in the amount of personal digital data available. Users, themselves, supply some of it. They voluntarily place highly private information on social-networking sites, such as Facebook or LinkedIn, or on genealogy sites that are easily searched by anyone with a computer or a smartphone.

However, much of the information is systematically developed by businesses seeking to learn more about their customers, often without consumers realizing that they are under the microscope. Legitimate businesses plant cookies on consumers' PCs and collect, analyze, and share digital data from every move consumers make at their Web sites. Critics are concerned that companies may now know *too* much and might use digital data to take unfair advantage of consumers. Although most companies fully disclose their Internet privacy policies and most work to use data to benefit their customers, abuses do occur. As a result, consumer advocates and policymakers are taking action to protect consumer privacy. In Chapter 20, we discuss these and other societal marketing issues in greater depth.

Cause-Related Marketing. To exercise their social responsibility and build more positive images, many companies are now linking themselves to worthwhile causes. These days, every product seems to be tied to some cause. Buy a pink mixer from KitchenAid and support breast cancer research. Purchase a special edition bottle of Dawn dishwashing detergent, and P&G will donate a dollar to help rescue and rehabilitate wildlife affected by oil spills. Go to Staples' DoSomething101 Web site or Facebook page and fill a virtual backpack with essential school supplies needed by school children living in poverty. Pay for these purchases with the right charge card and you can support a local cultural arts group or help fight heart disease.

In fact, some companies are founded entirely on cause-related missions. Under the concept of "value-led business" or "caring capitalism," their mission is to use business to make the world a better place. For example, TOMS Shoes was founded as a for-profit company—it wants to make money selling shoes. But the company has an equally important not-for-profit mission—putting shoes on the feet of needy children around the world. For every pair of shoes you buy from TOMS, the company will give another pair to a child in need on your behalf (see Real Marketing 3.1).

Real Marketing **3.1**

TOMS Shoes: "*Be* the Change You Want to See in the World"

If the world were a village of 1,000 people, 140 of the 1,000 would be illiterate, 200 would be malnourished, 230 would drink polluted water, 250 would have no shelter, 330 would have no electricity, and 400 would have no shoes. In 2006, these stark facts, especially the last one, struck Blake Mycoskie up close and personally as he visited Argentina to learn how to play polo, practice his tango, and do some community service work. While there, the sight of barefooted children, too poor to have shoes, stunned him.

So in May 2006, Mycoskie launched TOMS Shoes with $300,000 of his own money. The founding concept was this: For every pair of TOMS shoes that customers bought, the company would donate another pair of shoes to a child in need around the world. Mycoskie had previously started five successful strictly for-profit businesses. "But I was ready to do something more meaningful," says Mycoskie. "I always knew I wanted to help others. Now, it was time to do something that wasn't just for profit." Mycoskie remembered Mahatma Gandhi's saying: "*Be* the change you want to see in the world."

"Doing good" is an important part of TOMS' mission. But so is "doing well"—the company is very much a for-profit venture. However, at TOMS Shoes, the two missions go hand in hand. Beyond being socially admirable, the buy-one-give-one-away concept is also a good business proposition. In addition to scratching Mycoskie's itch to help people, "the timing was perfect for the American consumer, too," he says. "With the rise of social and eco-consciousness and the economy in a downturn, people were looking for innovative and affordable ways to make the world a better place."

With all these "do good" and "do well" goals swirling in his head, Mycoskie returned home from his Argentina trip, hired an intern, and set about making 250 pairs of shoes in the loft of his Santa Monica, California, home. Stuffing the shoes into three duffel bags, he made the fledgling company's first "Shoe Drop" tour, returning to the Argentine village

and giving one pair of shoes to each child. Mycoskie arrived back home to find an article about his project on the front page of the *Los Angeles Times* Calendar section. TOMS had been in business for only two weeks, but by that very afternoon, he had orders for 2,200 pairs of shoes on his Web site.

By October 2006, TOMS had sold 10,000 pairs of shoes. True to the company's one-for-one promise, Mycoskie undertook a second TOMS Shoe Drop tour. Consistent with his new title, "Chief Shoe Giver of TOMS Shoes," he led 15 employees and volunteers back to Argentina, where they went from school to school, village to village and gave away another 10,000 pairs of shoes.

"We don't just drop the shoes off, as the name might imply," says Mycoskie. "We place the shoes on each child's feet so that we can establish a connection, which is such an important part of our brand. We want to give the children the feeling of love, and warmth, and experience. But *we* also get those feelings as we give the shoes."

The one-for-one idea caught fire. As word spread about TOMS, a not-for-profit organization called "Friends of TOMS" formed to "create avenues for individuals to volunteer and experience [the TOMS] mission," participate in Shoe Drops, and "perform good works in their own communities and their own lives." *Vogue* magazine and other major publications ran stories on the company's philosophy and good works. In November 2007, 40 TOMS employees and volunteers embarked on the third Shoe Drop, travelling to South Africa to place shoes on the feet of 50,000 more children.

Next, TOMS Shoes turned its attention to Ethiopia, where 11 million people are at risk

for podoconiosis, a disease often caused by silica in volcanic soils. Children's bare feet absorb the silica, which can cause elephantitis, severe swelling of the legs and feet. The disease progresses until surgery is required. The simple preventive cure? Shoes. As part of the Christmas season in 2008, TOMS offered gift card packages, which included a certificate for a pair of shoes and a DVD telling the TOMS story. The goal was to give 30,000 pairs of shoes to Ethiopian children in 30 days.

TOMS has also focused on needy children in the United States, stepping in to help children whose families were still recovering from natural disasters, such as Hurricane Katrina in Louisiana. Also in the United States, TOMS started a grassroots marketing movement called "TOMS Vagabonds." These traveling groups of TOMS disciples hit the road in vans full of TOMS shoes and help to organize events on college and school campuses and in communities all around the country. The Vagabonds' goal is to raise awareness about TOMS, sell shoes, and inspire more people to get involved with the company's movement. The Vagabonds chronicle their travels on TOMS' Facebook page (www.facebook.com/TOMSVagabonds), blog (www.tomsshoesblog.com), and Twitter site (http://twitter.com/tomsshoes).

By mid-2010, TOMS had provided more than 600,000 pairs of shoes to children in need around the world, selling their counterparts at roughly $55 each. That rings up to $33

Cause-related marketing: TOMS pledges: "No complicated formulas, it's simple . . . you buy a pair of TOMS and we give a pair to a child on your behalf." Here, TOMs founder and CEO Blake Mycoskie gives out shoes in Argentina."

million worth of shoes. Retailers such as Nordstroms, Urban Outfitters, and even Whole Foods Market are now offering TOMS in more than 400 U.S. outlets. In fact, Whole Foods Market is the company's biggest customer.

TOMS' rapid growth is the result of purchases by caring customers who then tell the TOMS story to their friends. Whereas the typical shoe company spends about 20 percent of sales on traditional advertising and promotion, TOMS hasn't spent a single dollar on it. It hasn't had to. "Ultimately, it is our customers who drive our success," says Mycoskie. "Giving not only makes you feel good, but it actually is a very good business strategy, especially in this day and age. Your customers become your marketers."

Moreover, as TOMS' success shows, consumers like to feel good. A recent global study found that 71 percent of consumers said that despite the recession they had given just as much time and money to causes they deemed worthy. Fifty-five percent of respondents also indicated they would pay more for a brand if it supported a good cause.

TOMS Shoes is a great example of cause-related marketing—of "doing well by doing good." Mycoskie hopes that his company will inspire people to think differently about business. "My thinking was that TOMS would show that entrepreneurs no longer had to choose between earning money or making a difference in the world," he says. "Business and charity or public service don't have to be mutually exclusive. In fact, when they come together, they can be very powerful."

Sources: Quotes and other information from Tamara Schweitzer, "The Way I Work," *Inc.*, June 2010, pp. 112–116; Stacy Perman, "Making a Do-Gooder's Business Model Work," *BusinessWeek*, January 26, 2009, accessed at www .businessweek.com/smallbiz/content/jan2009/sb20090123_264702.htm; Blake Mycoskie, "Shoes for a Better Tomorrow," presentation made March 13, 2009, accessed at www.clintonschoolspeakers.com/lecture/view/toms-shoes-better-tomorrow; Michael Bush, "Consumers Continue to Stand by Their Causes During Downturn," *Advertising Age*, November 17, 2008, p. 4; Jessica Sambora, "How TOMS Shoes Founder Blake Mycoskie Got Started," *Fortune*, March 16, 2010, accessed at http://money.cnn.com/2010/03/16/smallbusiness/toms_shoes_blake_mycoskie.fortune/ index.htm; Christina Binkley, "Style—On Style: Charity Gives Shoe Brand Extra Shine," *Wall Street Journal*, April 1, 2010, p. D7; and information found at www.toms.com and http://friendsoftoms.org, accessed November 2010.

⊙ Cause-related marketing: The Pepsi Refresh Project is awarding $20 million in grants to fund hundreds of worthwhile ideas by individuals and communities that will "refresh the world."

Cause-related marketing has become a primary form of corporate giving. It lets companies "do well by doing good" by linking purchases of the company's products or services with fund-raising for worthwhile causes or charitable organizations. Companies now sponsor dozens of cause-related marketing campaigns each year. Many are backed by large budgets and a full complement of marketing activities. ⊙ For example, PepsiCo's year-long Pepsi Refresh Project is awarding $20 million in grants to fund hundreds of worthwhile ideas by individuals and communities that will "refresh the world." "What do you care about?" asks one Pepsi Refresh ad. "Maybe it's green spaces. Or educational comics. Maybe it's teaching kids to rock out." PepsiCo is spending millions of dollars on a full-blown multimedia campaign promoting the cause-related marketing program.[45]

Cause-related marketing has stirred some controversy. Critics worry that cause-related marketing is more a strategy for selling than a strategy for giving—that "cause-related" marketing is really "cause-exploitative" marketing. Thus, companies using cause-related marketing might find themselves walking a fine line between increased sales and an improved image and facing charges of exploitation.

However, if handled well, cause-related marketing can greatly benefit both the company and the cause. The company gains an effective marketing tool while building a more positive public image. The charitable organization or cause gains greater visibility and important new sources of funding and support. Spending on cause-related marketing in the United States skyrocketed from only $120 million in 1990 to more than $1.6 billion in 2010.[46]

Cultural environment
Institutions and other forces that affect
society's basic values, perceptions,
preferences, and behaviors.

The Cultural Environment

The **cultural environment** consists of institutions and other forces that affect a society's basic values, perceptions, preferences, and behaviors. People grow up in a particular society that shapes their basic beliefs and values. They absorb a worldview that defines their relationships with others. The following cultural characteristics can affect marketing decision making.

The Persistence of Cultural Values

People in a given society hold many beliefs and values. Their core beliefs and values have a high degree of persistence. For example, most Americans believe in individual freedom, hard work, getting married, and achievement and success. These beliefs shape more specific attitudes and behaviors found in everyday life. *Core* beliefs and values are passed on from parents to children and are reinforced by schools, churches, business, and government.

Secondary beliefs and values are more open to change. Believing in marriage is a core belief; believing that people should get married early in life is a secondary belief. Marketers have some chance of changing secondary values but little chance of changing core values. For example, family-planning marketers could argue more effectively that people should get married later than not getting married at all.

Shifts in Secondary Cultural Values

Although core values are fairly persistent, cultural swings do take place. Consider the impact of popular music groups, movie personalities, and other celebrities on young people's hairstyling and clothing norms. Marketers want to predict cultural shifts to spot new opportunities or threats. Several firms offer "futures" forecasts in this connection. For example, the Yankelovich Monitor has tracked consumer value trends for years. Its annual State of the Consumer report analyzes and interprets the forces that shape consumers' lifestyles and their marketplace interactions. The major cultural values of a society are expressed in people's views of themselves and others, as well as in their views of organizations, society, nature, and the universe.

People's Views of Themselves. People vary in their emphasis on serving themselves versus serving others. Some people seek personal pleasure, wanting fun, change, and escape. Others seek self-realization through religion, recreation, or the avid pursuit of careers or other life goals. Some people see themselves as sharers and joiners; others see themselves as individualists. People use products, brands, and services as a means of self-expression, and they buy products and services that match their views of themselves.

Marketers can target their products and services based on such self-views. For example, TOMS Shoes appeals to people who see themselves as part of the broader world community. In contrast, Kenneth Cole shoes appeal to fashion individualists. ◉ In its ads, the company declares, "We all walk in different shoes," asserting that Kenneth Cole represents "25 years of nonuniform thinking."

People's Views of Others. In past decades, observers have noted several shifts in people's attitudes toward others. Recently, for example, many trend trackers have seen a new wave of "cocooning" or "nesting." Due in part to the uncertain economy, people are going out less with others and are staying home more. One observer calls it "Cocooning 2.0," in which people are "newly intent on the

WE ALL WALK IN DIFFERENT SHOES.

THEO KOGAN.
SINGER, ACTOR,
ENTREPRENEUR
AND FEMINIST.

KENNETHCOLE
.COM
25 YEARS OF
NON-UNIFORM
THINKING.

◉ **People's self-views: In its ads, Kenneth Cole targets fashion individualists. "25 years of nonuniform thinking."**

simple pleasures of hearth and home." Says another, "The instability of the economy . . . creates uncertainty for consumers, and this uncertainty tends to make them focus more on being home and finding ways to save money. It's a return to more traditional values, like home-cooked meals."[47]

For example, the weaker economy of the past few years and increased nesting have given a boost to home appliances, such as high-end coffee makers and big-screen TVs. Consumer electronics chain Best Buy even ran an ad that cast the purchase of a 60-inch flat-screen HDTV not as self-indulgence but as an act of loving sacrifice and a practical alternative to other forms of entertainment.[48]

In the ad, after a man sells his football season tickets to pay for the wedding, his grateful bride surprises him with a huge set so he can still watch the big game. A kindly salesman sums it up this way: "Another love story at Best Buy with a 60-inch TV in the middle." Says a Samsung marketer, "People still have to live their lives. [They] may not spring for that 61-inch [TV], but they may get a 42-inch HDTV because they're home and they're with their families and they'll spend $5 on a movie rental, versus $40 for the theater and $80 for dinner."

People's Views of Organizations. People vary in their attitudes toward corporations, government agencies, trade unions, universities, and other organizations. By and large, people are willing to work for major organizations and expect them, in turn, to carry out society's work.

The past two decades have seen a sharp decrease in confidence in and loyalty toward America's business and political organizations and institutions. In the workplace, there has been an overall decline in organizational loyalty. Waves of company downsizings bred cynicism and distrust. In just the last decade, rounds of layoffs resulting from the recent recession, major corporate scandals, the financial meltdown triggered by Wall Street bankers' greed and incompetence, and other unsettling activities have resulted in a further loss of confidence in big business. Many people today see work not as a source of satisfaction but as a required chore to earn money to enjoy their nonwork hours. This trend suggests that organizations need to find new ways to win consumer and employee confidence.

People's Views of Society. People vary in their attitudes toward their society—patriots defend it, reformers want to change it, and malcontents want to leave it. People's orientation to their society influences their consumption patterns and attitudes toward the marketplace. American patriotism has been increasing gradually for the past two decades. It surged, however, following the September 11, 2001, terrorist attacks and the Iraq war. For example, the summer following the start of the Iraq war saw a surge of pumped-up Americans visiting U.S. historic sites, ranging from the Washington D.C. monuments, Mount Rushmore, the Gettysburg battlefield, and the *USS Constitution* ("Old Ironsides") to Pearl Harbor and the Alamo. Following these peak periods, patriotism in the United States still remains high. A recent global survey on "national pride" found Americans tied for number one among the 17 democracies polled.[49]

Marketers respond with patriotic products and promotions, offering everything from floral bouquets to clothing with patriotic themes. Although most of these marketing efforts are tasteful and well received, waving the red, white, and blue can prove tricky. Except in cases where companies tie product sales to charitable contributions, such flag-waving promotions can be viewed as attempts to cash in on triumph or tragedy. Marketers must take care when responding to such strong national emotions.

People's Views of Nature. People vary in their attitudes toward the natural world—some feel ruled by it, others feel in harmony with it, and still others seek to master it. A long-term trend has been people's growing mastery over nature through technology and the belief that nature is bountiful. More recently, however, people have recognized that nature is finite and fragile; it can be destroyed or spoiled by human activities.

This renewed love of things natural has created a 63-million-person "lifestyles of health and sustainability" (LOHAS) market, consumers who seek out everything from natural, organic, and nutritional products to fuel-efficient cars and alternative medicine. This segment spends nearly $300 billion annually on such products. In the green building market alone, consumers spent $100 billion in 2008 on items such as certified homes, solar systems, and Energy Star appliances.[50]

Food producers have also found fast-growing markets for natural and organic products. ⦿ Consider Earthbound Farm, a company that grows and sells organic produce. It started in 1984 as a 2.5-acre raspberry farm in California's Carmel Valley. Founders Drew and Myra Goodman wanted to do the right thing by farming the land organically and producing food they would feel good about serving to their family, friends, and neighbors. Today, Earthbound Farm has grown to become the world's largest producer of organic vegetables, with 35,000 crop acres, annual sales of $450 million, and products available in 75 percent of America's supermarkets.[51]

In total, the U.S. organic food market generated nearly $27 billion in sales last year, more than doubling over the past five years. Niche marketers, such as Whole Foods Market, have sprung up to serve this market, and traditional food chains, such as Kroger and Safeway, have added separate natural and organic food sections. Even pet owners are joining the movement as they become more aware of what goes into Fido's food. Almost every major pet food brand now offers several types of natural foods.[52]

People's Views of the Universe. Finally, people vary in their beliefs about the origin of the universe and their place in it. Although most Americans practice religion, religious conviction and practice have been dropping off gradually through the years. According to a recent poll, 16 percent of Americans now say they are not affiliated with any particular faith, almost double the percentage of 18 years earlier. Among Americans ages 18-29, 25 percent say they are not currently affiliated with any particular religion.[53]

However, the fact that people are dropping out of organized religion doesn't mean that they are abandoning their faith. Some futurists have noted a renewed interest in spirituality, perhaps as a part of a broader search for a new inner purpose. People have been moving away from materialism and dog-eat-dog ambition to seek more permanent values—family, community, earth, faith—and a more certain grasp of right and wrong. "We are becoming a nation of spiritually anchored people who are not traditionally religious," says one expert.[54] This changing spiritualism affects consumers in everything from the television shows they watch and the books they read to the products and services they buy.

⦿ Riding the trend towards all things natural, Earthbound Farm has grown to become the world's largest producer of organic salads, fruits, and vegetables, with products in 75 percent of America's supermarkets.

Responding to the Marketing Environment (pp 89–91)

Someone once observed, "There are three kinds of companies: those who make things happen, those who watch things happen, and those who wonder what's happened." Many companies view the marketing environment as an uncontrollable element to which they must react and adapt. They passively accept the marketing environment and do not try to change it. They analyze environmental forces and design strategies that will help the company avoid the threats and take advantage of the opportunities the environment provides.

Other companies take a *proactive* stance toward the marketing environment. "Instead of letting the environment define their strategy," advises one marketing expert, "craft a strategy that defines your environment."[55] Rather than assuming that strategic options are bounded by the current environment, these firms develop strategies to change the environment. "Business history . . . reveals plenty of cases in which firms' strategies shape industry structure," says the expert, "from Ford's Model T to Nintendo's Wii."

Even more, rather than simply watching and reacting to environmental events, these firms take aggressive actions to affect the publics and forces in their marketing environment. Such companies hire lobbyists to influence legislation affecting their industries and stage media events to gain favorable press coverage. They run "advertorials" (ads expressing editorial points of view) to shape public opinion. They press lawsuits and file complaints with regulators to keep competitors in line, and they form contractual agreements to better control their distribution channels.

By taking action, companies can often overcome seemingly uncontrollable environmental events. For example, whereas some companies view the seemingly ceaseless online rumor mill as something over which they have no control, others work proactively to prevent or counter negative word of mouth. Kraft foods did this when its Oscar Mayer brand fell victim to a potentially damaging e-mail hoax:[56]

> The bogus e-mail, allegedly penned by a Sgt. Howard C. Wright, claimed that Marines in Iraq had written Oscar Mayer saying how much they liked its hot dogs and requested that the company send some to the troops there. According to the e-mail, Oscar Mayer refused, saying that it supported neither the war nor anyone in it. The soldier called on all patriotic Americans to forward the e-mail to friends and boycott Oscar Mayer and its products.
>
> As the e-mail circulated widely, rather than waiting and hoping that consumers would see through the hoax, Kraft responded vigorously with its own e-mails, blog entries, and a "Rumor and Hoaxes" Web page. It explained that Kraft and Oscar Mayer do, in fact, strongly support American troops, both in Iraq and at home. It works with the military to ensure that Kraft products are available wherever in the world troops are stationed. On the home front, Kraft explained, Oscar Mayer Weinermobiles visit about half of all major U.S. military bases each year, about 70 total. The offending e-mail turned out to be a nearly verbatim copy of a 2004 chain e-mail circulated against Starbucks, signed by the same fictitious soldier but with "Oscar Mayer" and "hot dog" substituted for "Starbucks" and "coffee." Kraft's proactive counter campaign quickly squelched the rumor, and Oscar Mayer remains America's favorite hot dog.

Marketing management cannot always control environmental forces. In many cases, it must settle for simply watching and reacting to the environment. For example, a company would have little success trying to influence geographic population shifts, the economic environment, or major cultural values. But whenever possible, smart marketing managers will take a *proactive* rather than *reactive* approach to the marketing environment (see Real Marketing 3.2).

Real Marketing 3.2

YourCompanySucks.com

Marketers have hailed the Internet as the great new relational medium. Companies use the Web to engage customers, gain insights into their needs, and create customer community. In turn, Web-empowered consumers share their brand experiences with companies and with each other. All of this back-and-forth helps both the company and its customers. But sometimes, the dialog can get nasty. Consider the following examples:

MSN Money columnist Scott Burns accuses Home Depot of being a "consistent abuser" of customers' time. Within hours, MSN's servers are caving under the weight of 14,000 blistering e-mails and posts from angry Home Depot customers who storm the MSN comment room, taking the company to task for pretty much everything. It is the biggest response in MSN Money's history.

Blogger Jeff Jarvis posts a series of irate messages to his BuzzMachine blog about the many failings of his Dell computer and his struggles with Dell's customer support. The post quickly draws national attention, and an open letter posted by Jarvis to Dell founder Michael Dell becomes the third most linked-to post on the blogosphere the day after it appears. Jarvis's headline—Dell Hell—becomes shorthand for the ability of a lone blogger to deliver a body blow to an unsuspecting business.

Systems engineer Michael Whitford wakes up one morning to find that his favorite-ever laptop, an Apple MacBook, still under warranty, has "decided not to work." Whitford takes the machine to his local Apple store, where the counter person obligingly sends it off for repairs. However, Whitford later gets a call from an Apple Care representative, who claims that the laptop has "spill damage" not covered by the warranty and says that repairs will cost him $774. "I did not spill anything on my laptop," declares Whitford. "Too bad," says the Apple rep, and the MacBook is returned unrepaired. But that's not the end of the story—far from it. A short time later, Whitford posts a video on YouTube (www.youtube.com/watch?v=hHbrQqrgVgg). In the video, a seemingly rational Whitford calmly selects among a golf club, an ax, and a sword before finally deciding on a sledgehammer as his weapon of choice for bashing his nonfunctioning MacBook to smithereens. More than 520,000 people have viewed the smashup on YouTube, and the video has been passed along on countless blogs and other Web sites.

Extreme events? Not anymore. The Internet has turned the traditional power relationship between businesses and consumers upside-down. In the good old days, disgruntled consumers could do little more than bellow at a company service rep or shout out their complaints from a street corner. Now, armed with only a PC or a smartphone and a broadband connection, they can take it public, airing their gripes to millions on blogs, chats, online social networks, or even hate sites devoted exclusively to their least favorite corporations.

"I hate" and "sucks" sites are becoming almost commonplace. These sites target some highly respected companies with some highly *dis*respectful labels: PayPalSucks.com (aka No-PayPal); WalMart-blows.com; Mac-Sucks.com, Microsucks.com; AmexSux.com (American Express); IHateStarbucks.com; DeltaREALLYsucks.com; and UnitedPackageSmashers.com (UPS), to name only a few. "Sucks" videos on YouTube and other video sites also abound. For example, a search of "Apple sucks" on YouTube turns up 4,660 videos; a similar search for Microsoft finds 4,820 videos. An "Apple sucks" search on Facebook links to 540 groups.

Some of these sites, videos, and other Web attacks air legitimate complaints that should be addressed. Others, however, are little more than anonymous, vindictive slurs that unfairly ransack brands and corporate reputations. Some of the attacks are only a passing nuisance; others can draw serious attention and create real headaches.

How should companies react to online attacks? The real quandary for targeted companies is figuring out how far they can go to protect their images without fueling the already raging fire. One point on which all experts seem to agree: Don't try to retaliate in kind. "It's rarely a good idea to lob bombs at the fire starters," says one analyst. "Preemption, engagement, and diplomacy are saner tools."

Some companies have tried to silence the critics through lawsuits, but few have succeeded. The courts have tended to regard such criticism as opinion and, therefore, protected speech. Given the difficulties of trying to sue consumer online criticisms out of existence, some companies have tried other strategies. For example, most big companies now routinely buy up Web addresses for their firm names preceded by the words "I hate" or followed by "sucks.com." But this approach is easily thwarted, as Walmart learned when it registered ihatewalmart.com, only to find that someone else then registered ireallyhatewalmart.com.

In general, attempts to block, counterattack, or shut down consumer attacks may be shortsighted. Such criticisms are often based

Today, armed only with a PC and a broadband connection, the little guy can take it public against corporate America. By listening and proactively responding to such seemingly uncontrollable environmental events, companies can prevent the negatives from spiraling out of control or even turn them into positives.

on real consumer concerns and unresolved anger. Hence, the best strategy might be to proactively monitor these sites and respond to the concerns they express. "The most obvious thing to do is talk to the customer and try to deal with the problem, instead of putting your fingers in your ears," advises one consultant.

For example, Home Depot CEO Francis Blake drew praise when he heeded the criticisms expressed in the MSN Money onslaught and responded positively. Blake posted a heartfelt letter in which he thanked critic Scott Burns, apologized to angry customers, and promised to make things better. And within a month of the YouTube video, Apple fessed up to its misdeeds and replaced Michael Whitford's laptop. "I'm very happy now," says Whitford. "Apple has regained my loyalty. I guess I finally got their attention."

Many companies have now created teams of specialists that monitor Web conversations and engage disgruntled consumers. In the years since the Dell Hell incident, Dell has set up a 40-member "communities and conversation team," which does outreach on Twitter and communicates with bloggers. The social media team at Southwest Airlines "includes a chief Twitter officer who tracks Twitter comments and monitors Facebook groups, an online representative who checks facts and interacts with bloggers, and another person

who takes charge of the company's presence on sites such as YouTube, Flickr, and LinkedIn. So if someone posts a complaint in cyberspace, the company can respond in a personal way."

Thus, by listening and proactively responding to seemingly uncontrollable events in the environment, companies can prevent the negatives from spiraling out of control or even turn them into positives. Who knows? With the right responses, Walmart-blows.com might even become Walmart-rules.com. Then again, probably not.

Sources: Quotes, excerpts, and other information from Todd Wasserman, "Tell Your Customers to Crowdsource This," *Brandweek*, October 19, 2009, p. 26; Michelle Conlin, "Web Attack," *BusinessWeek*, April 16, 2007, pp. 54–56; Jena McGregor, "Consumer Vigilantes," *BusinessWeek*, March 3, 2008, p. 38; Christopher L. Marting and Nathan Bennett, "Corporate Reputation; What to Do About Online Attacks," *Wall Street Journal*, March 10, 2008, p. R6; Carolyn Y. Johnson, *Boston Globe*, July 7, 2008, p. B6; and "Corporate Hate Sites," New Media Institute, www.newmedia.org/articles/corporate-hate-sites—nmi-white-paper.html, accessed August 2010.

REVIEWING Objectives AND KEY Terms

In this chapter and the next three chapters, you'll examine the environments of marketing and how companies analyze these environments to better understand the marketplace and consumers. Companies must constantly watch and manage the *marketing environment* to seek opportunities and ward off threats. The marketing environment consists of all the actors and forces influencing the company's ability to transact business effectively with its target market.

Objective 1 Describe the environmental forces that affect the company's ability to serve its customers. (pp 66–70)

The company's *microenvironment* consists of actors close to the company that combine to form its value delivery network or that affect its ability to serve its customers. It includes the company's *internal environment*—its several departments and management levels—as it influences marketing decision making. *Marketing channel firms*—suppliers and marketing intermediaries, including resellers, physical distribution firms, marketing services agencies, and financial intermediaries—cooperate to create customer value. *Competitors* vie with the company in an effort to serve customers better. Various *publics* have an actual or potential interest in or impact on the company's ability to meet its objectives. Finally, five types of customer *markets* include consumer, business, reseller, government, and international markets.

The *macroenvironment* consists of larger societal forces that affect the entire microenvironment. The six forces making up the company's macroenvironment include demographic, economic,

natural, technological, political/social, and cultural forces. These forces shape opportunities and pose threats to the company.

Objective 2 Explain how changes in the demographic and economic environments affect marketing decisions. (pp 70–78)

Demography is the study of the characteristics of human populations. Today's *demographic environment* shows a changing age structure, shifting family profiles, geographic population shifts, a better-educated and more white-collar population, and increasing diversity. The *economic environment* consists of factors that affect buying power and patterns. The economic environment is characterized by more frugal consumers who are seeking greater value—the right combination of good quality and service at a fair price. The distribution of income also is shifting. The rich have grown richer, the middle class has shrunk, and the poor have remained poor, leading to a two-tiered market.

Objective 3 Identify the major trends in the firm's natural and technological environments. (pp 78–81)

The *natural environment* shows three major trends: shortages of certain raw materials, higher pollution levels, and more government intervention in natural resource management. Environmental concerns create marketing opportunities for alert companies. The *technological environment* creates both opportunities and challenges. Companies that fail to keep up with technological change will miss out on new product and marketing opportunities.

Objective 4 **Explain the key changes in the political and cultural environments.** (pp 81–88)

The *political environment* consists of laws, agencies, and groups that influence or limit marketing actions. The political environment has undergone three changes that affect marketing worldwide: increasing legislation regulating business, strong government agency enforcement, and greater emphasis on ethics and socially responsible actions. The *cultural environment* consists of institutions and forces that affect a society's values, perceptions, preferences, and behaviors. The environment shows trends toward "cocooning," a lessening trust of institutions, increasing patriotism, greater appreciation for nature, a changing spiritualism, and the search for more meaningful and enduring values.

Objective 5 **Discuss how companies can react to the marketing environment.** (pp 89–91)

Companies can passively accept the marketing environment as an uncontrollable element to which they must adapt, avoiding threats and taking advantage of opportunities as they arise. Or they can take a *proactive* stance, working to change the environment rather than simply reacting to it. Whenever possible, companies should try to be proactive rather than reactive.

KEY Terms

OBJECTIVE 1

Marketing environment (p 66)
Microenvironment (p 66)
Macroenvironment (p 66)
Marketing intermediaries (p 68)
Public (p 69)

OBJECTIVE 2

Demography (p 70)
Baby boomers (p 70)
Generation X (p 72)
Millennials (Generation Y) (p 73)
Economic environment (p 77)

OBJECTIVE 3

Natural environment (p 78)
Environmental sustainability (p 79)
Technological environment (p 80)

OBJECTIVE 4

Political environment (p 81)
Cultural environment (p 86)

PEARSON
mymarketinglab

- Check your understanding of the concepts and key terms using the mypearsonmarketinglab study plan for this chapter.
- Apply the concepts in a business context using the simulation entitled **The Marketing Environment**.

DISCUSSING & APPLYING THE Concepts

Discussing the Concepts

1. Describe the elements of a company's marketing environment and why marketers play a critical role in tracking environmental trends and spotting opportunities. (AACSB: Communication; Reflective Thinking)

2. List some of the demographic trends of interest to marketers in the United States and discuss whether these trends pose opportunities or threats for marketers. (AACSB: Communication; Reflective Thinking)

3. Discuss current trends in the economic environment that marketers must be aware of and provide examples of company responses to each trend. (AACSB: Communication; Reflective Thinking)

4. Discuss trends in the natural environment that marketers must be aware of and provide examples of company responses to them. (AACSB: Communication)

5. Compare and contrast core beliefs/values and secondary beliefs/values. Provide an example of each and discuss the potential impact marketers have on each. (AACSB: Communication; Reflective Thinking)

6. Explain how companies can take a proactive stance toward the marketing environment. (AACSB: Communication)

Applying the Concepts

1. China and India are emerging markets that will have a significant impact on the world in coming years. The term *Chindia* is used to describe the growing power of these two countries. In a small group, research demographic and economic trends related to Chindia's power and its impact on marketers in the United States. Write a brief report, supporting your discussion of these trends with statistics. (AACSB: Communication; Reflective Thinking)

2. In a small group, search the Internet for U.S. population distribution maps and create a PowerPoint presentation illustrating factors such as geographical population shifts, languages spoken, age distributions, and ancestry. Discuss the demographic implications for marketers. (AACSB: Communication; Use of IT; Diversity)

3. Various federal agencies impact marketing activities. Research each agency listed below, discuss the elements of marketing that are impacted by that agency, and present a recent marketing case or issue on which each agency has focused. (AACSB: Communication; Reflective Thinking)
   a. Federal Trade Commission (www.ftc.gov)
   b. Food and Drug Administration (www.fda.gov)
   c. Consumer Product Safety Commission (www.cpsc.gov)

FOCUS ON Technology

If you really want to identify the zeitgeist, or "spirit of the times," look at the top Web sites visited, the top videos watched on YouTube, the top songs downloaded, or the top Twitter feeds. Trend spotters such as Faith Popcorn and Tom Peters have been mainstays for marketers trying to understand cultural trends, but the Internet is now the new crystal ball for anyone wanting to predict where society is going in real time. The World Mind Network provides a clearinghouse of links to "top" lists at www.thetopeverything.net. In just a few minutes a day, you, too, can be up on what's hot in today's culture.

1. Visit www.thetopeverything.net and review the Web sites identified. What can you learn about culture and cultural trends from these sources? Write a brief report on your conclusions. (AACSB: Communication; Use of IT; Reflective Thinking)

2. Do you think these sources accurately reflect cultural trends? Identify other Web sites that might be useful in learning about cultural trends. (AACSB: Communication; Use of IT; Reflective Thinking)

FOCUS ON Ethics

You've probably heard of some specific heart procedures, such as angioplasty and stents, that are routinely performed on adults. But such heart procedures, devices, and related medications are not available for infants and children, despite the fact that almost 40,000 children are born in the United States each year with heart defects that often require repair. This is a life or death situation for many young patients, yet doctors must improvise by using devices designed and tested on adults. For instance, doctors use an adult kidney balloon in an infant's heart because it is the appropriate size for a newborn's aortic valve. However, this device is not approved for the procedure. Why are specific devices and medicines developed for the multibillion-dollar cardiovascular market not also designed for children's health care? It's a matter of economics; this segment of young consumers is just too small. One lead-ing cardiologist attributed the discrepancy to a "profitability gap" between the children's market and the much more profitable adult market for treating heart disease. Although this might make good economic sense for companies, it is little comfort to the parents of these small patients.

1. Discuss the environmental forces acting on medical device and pharmaceutical companies that are preventing them from meeting the needs of the infant and child market segment. Is it wrong for these companies to not address the needs of this segment? (AACSB: Communication; Reflective Thinking; Ethical Reasoning)

2. Suggest some solutions to this problem. (AACSB: Communication; Reflective Thinking)

MARKETING & THE Economy

Netflix

Although the recent down economy has taken its toll on the retail industry as a whole, the stars are still shining on Netflix. Business has been so good that Netflix met its most recent new subscriber goal weeks before the deadline. In early 2009, Netflix surpassed 10 million subscribers—a remarkable feat. Eighteen months later, that number had grown by 50 percent to 15 million subscribers. Clearly, all these new customers are good for the company's financials. Customers are signing up for the same reasons they always have—the convenience of renting movies without leaving home, a selection of more than 100,000 DVD titles, and low monthly fees. But the company's current good fortunes may also be the result of consumers looking for less expensive means of entertainment. They may even be the result of consumers escaping the gloom of financial losses and economic bad news. Whatever the case, Netflix appears to have a product that thrives in bad times as well as in good.

1. Visit www.netflix.com. After browsing the Web site and becoming more familiar with the company's offerings, assess the macroenvironmental trends that have led to Netflix's success in recent years.

2. Which trends do you think have contributed most to Netflix's current growth following recent economic woes?

MARKETING BY THE Numbers

Many marketing decisions boil down to numbers. An important question is this: What is the market sales potential in a given segment? If the sales potential in a market is not large enough to warrant pursing that market, then companies will not offer products and services to that market, even though a need may exist. Consider the market segment of infants and children discussed above in Focus on Ethics. Certainly there is a need for medical products to save children's lives. Still, companies are not pursuing this market.

1. Using the chain ratio method described in Appendix 2, estimate the market sales potential for heart catheterization products to meet the needs of the infant and child segment. Assume that of the 40,000 children with heart defects each year, 60 percent will benefit from these types of products and only 50 percent of their families have the financial resources to obtain such treatment. Also assume the average price for a device is $1,000. (AACSB: Communication; Analytical Reasoning)

2. Research the medical devices market and compare the market potential you estimated to the sales of various devices. Are companies justified in not pursuing the infant and child segment? (AACSB: Communication; Reflective Thinking)

VIDEO Case

TOMS Shoes

"Get involved: Changing a life begins with a single step." This sounds like a mandate from a nonprofit volunteer organization. But in fact, this is the motto of a for-profit shoe company located in Santa Monica, California. In 2006, Tom Mycoskie founded TOMS Shoes because he wanted to do something different. He wanted to run a company that would make a profit while at the same time helping the needy of the world.

Specifically, for every pair of shoes that TOMS sells, it gives a pair of shoes to a needy child somewhere in the world. So far, the company has given away tens of thousands of pairs of shoes and is on track to give away hundreds of thousands. Can TOMS succeed and thrive based on this idealistic concept? That all depends on how TOMS executes its strategy within the constantly changing marketing environment.

After viewing the video featuring TOMS Shoes, answer the following questions about the marketing environment:

1. What trends in the marketing environment have contributed to the success of TOMS Shoes?

2. Did TOMS Shoes first scan the marketing environment in creating its strategy, or did it create its strategy and fit the strategy to the environment? Does this matter?

3. Is TOMS' strategy more about serving needy children or about creating value for customers? Explain.

COMPANY Case

Target: From "Expect More" to "Pay Less"

When you hear the term *discount retail*, two names that usually come to mind: Walmart and Target. The two have been compared so much that the press rarely covers one without at least mentioning the other. The reasons for the comparison are fairly obvious. These corporations are two of the largest discount retailers in the United States. Category for category, they offer very similar merchandise. They tend to build their stores in close proximity to one another, even facing each other across major boulevards.

But even with such strong similarities, ask consumers if there's a difference between the two, and they won't even hesitate. Walmart is all about low prices; Target is about style and fashion. The "cheap chic" label applied by consumers and the media over the years perfectly captures the long-standing company positioning: "Expect More. Pay Less." With its numerous designer product lines, Target has been so successful with its brand positioning that for a number of years it has slowly chipped away at Walmart's massive market share. Granted, the difference in the scale for the two companies has always been huge. Walmart's most recent annual revenues of $408 billion are more than six times those of Target. But for many years, Target's business grew at a much faster pace than Walmart's.

In fact, as Walmart's same-store sales began to lag in the mid-2000s, the world's largest retailer unabashedly attempted to become more like Target. It spruced up its store environment, added more fashionable clothing and housewares, and stocked organic and gourmet products in its grocery aisles. Walmart even experimented with luxury brands. After 19 years of promoting the slogan, "Always Low Prices. Always." Walmart replaced it with the very Target-esque tagline, "Save Money. Live Better." None of those efforts seemed to speed up Walmart's revenue growth or slow down Target's.

But oh what a difference a year or two can make. As the global recession began to tighten its grip on the world's retailers in 2008, the dynamics between the two retail giants reversed almost overnight. As unemployment rose and consumers began pinching their pennies, Walmart's familiar price "rollbacks" resonated with consumers, while Target's image of slightly better stuff for slightly higher prices did not. Target's well-cultivated "upscale discount" image was turning away customers who believed that its fashionable products and trendy advertising meant steeper prices. By mid-2008, Target had experienced three straight quarters of flat same-store sales growth and a slight dip in store traffic. At the same time, Walmart was defying the economic slowdown, posting quarterly increases in same-store sales of close to 5 percent along with substantial jumps in profits.

SAME SLOGAN, DIFFERENT EMPHASIS

In fall 2008, Target acknowledged the slide and announced its intentions to do something about it. Target CEO Gregg Steinhafel succinctly summarized the company's new strategy: "The customer is very cash strapped right now. And in some ways, our greatest strength has become somewhat of a challenge. So, we're still trying to define and find the right balance between 'Expect More. Pay Less.' The current environment means that the focus is squarely on the 'Pay Less' side of it."

In outlining Target's new strategy, company executives made it clear that Walmart was the new focus. Target would make certain that its prices were in line with Walmart's. Future promotions would communicate the "pay less" message to consumers, while also highlighting the fact that Target is every bit the convenient one-stop shopping destination as its larger rival.

The new communications program included massive changes to in-store signage. Instead of in-store images and messages highlighting trendy fashion, store visitors were greeted with large signs boasting price points and value messages. Similarly, weekly newspaper circulars featured strong value headlines, fewer products, and clearly labeled price points. In fact, Target's ads began looking very much like those of Walmart or even Kmart. Further recognizing the consumer trend toward thriftiness, Target increased the emphasis on its own store brands of food and home goods.

While making the shift toward "Pay Less," Target was careful to reassure customers that it would not compromise the "Expect More" part of its brand. Target has always been known for having more designer partnerships than any other retailer. From the Michael Graves line of housewares to Isaac Mizrahi's clothing line, Target boasts more than a dozen product lines created exclusively for Target by famous designers. Kathryn Tesija, Target's executive vice president of merchandising, assured customers that not only would Target continue those relationships but also add several new designer partnerships in the apparel and beauty categories.

MOUNTING PRESSURE

Although Steinhafel's "Pay Less" strategy was aggressive, Target's financials were slow to respond. In fact, things initially got worse with sales at one point dropping by 10 percent from the previous year. Target's profits suffered even more. It didn't help matters that Walmart bucked the recessionary retail trend by posting revenue increases. When confronted with this fact, Steinhafel responded that consumers held perceptions that Target's value proposition was not as strong as that of its biggest rival. He urged investors to be patient, that its value message would take time to resonate with consumers. Given that Walmart had a decades-long lead in building its cost structure as a formative competitive advantage, Steinhafel couldn't stress that point enough.

While Target continued to struggle with this turn-around challenge, it received a new threat in the form of one of its largest investors. Activist shareholder William Ackman, whose company had invested $2 billion in Target only to lose 85 percent of it, was holding the retailer's feet to the fire. Ackman openly chided Target for failing to deal effectively with the economic downturn. He charged that Target's board of directors lacked needed experience and sought to take control of five of the board's seats. "Target is not Gucci," he said in a letter to investors. "It should be a business that does well, even in tough economic times."

Making the changes that Ackman and others were calling for was exactly what Steinhafel was trying to do. Steinhafel refused to give up on his strategy. Instead, he intensified Target's "Pay Less" emphasis. In addition to aggressive newspaper advertising, Target unveiled a new set of television spots. Each ad played to a catchy tune with a reassuring voice singing, "This is a brand new day. And it's getting better every single day." Ads showed ordinary people consuming commonly purchased retail products but with a unique twist.

In one ad, a couple was shown drinking coffee in what appeared to be a fancy coffee house with the caption, "The new coffee spot." But the camera pulled back to reveal that the couple was sitting in their own kitchen, with a coffee pot on the stove. The caption confirmed: "Espresso maker, $24.99." In another segment of the ad headlined "The new salon trip," a glamorous woman with flowing red hair appeared to be in an upscale salon. The camera angle then shifted to show her in her own modest bathroom, revealing a small bottle sitting on the sink with the caption, "Hair color, $8.49." Every ad repeated this same theme multiple times, with takes such as "The new car wash," "The new movie night," and "The new gym."

In addition to the new promotional efforts, Target made two significant operational changes. First, it began converting a corner of its department stores into mini-grocery stores carrying a narrow selection of 90 percent of the food categories found in full-size grocery stores, including fresh produce. One shopper's reaction was just what Target was hoping for. A Wisconsin housewife and mother of two stopped by her local Target to buy deodorant and laundry detergent before heading to the local grocery store. But as she worked her way through the fresh-food aisles, she found everything on her list. "I'm done," she said, as she grabbed a 99-cent green pepper. "I just saved myself a trip."

While the mini-grocery test stores showed promising results, groceries also represented a low-margin expansion. Walmart was seeing most of its gains in higher margin discretionary goods like bedding, traditionally Target's stronghold. But in a second operational change, Target surprised many analysts by unveiling a new package for its main store brand . . . one without the familiar Target bulls-eye! That is, the packages discard the bull's-eye, replacing it with big, colorful, upward-pointing arrows on a white background, with the new brand name, "up & up."

Continuing to address the trend of higher store brand sales, Tesija stated, "We believe that it will stand out on the shelf, and it is so distinctive that we'll get new guests that will want to try it that maybe didn't even notice the Target brand before." Up & up products are priced about 30 percent lower than comparable name brand products. Target began promoting the store brand in its circulars and planned to expand the total number of products under the label from 730 to 800. While initial results showed an increase in store brand sales for products with the new design, it is unclear just how many of those sales came at the expense of name brand products.

SIGNS OF LIFE

Target's journey over the past few years demonstrates that changing the direction of a large corporation is like trying to reverse a moving freight train. Things have to slow down before they can go the other way. But after 18 months of aggressive change, it appears that consumers may have finally gotten the message. During the first half of 2010, sales rose by as much as 5 percent with profits up a whopping 54 percent. Both spending per visit and the number of store visits increased. All this could be attributed to the fact that the effects of the recession were starting to loosen up and consumer confidence was stabilizing. But in a sign that Target's efforts were truly paying off, Walmart's sales growth was slowing during this same period and even showing signs of decline. Customer perceptions of Target's value were indeed on the rise.

Steinhafel made it very clear that the new signs of life at Target were being met with cautious optimism. "Clearly the economy and consumer sentiment have improved since their weakest point in 2009," said the Target CEO. "But we believe that both are still somewhat unstable and fragile and will likely continue to experience occasional setbacks as the year progresses." Steinhafel's comments reflected an understanding that even as the economy showed signs of recovery, research indicated that consumers everywhere were adopting a newfound sense of frugality and monetary responsibility.

Target's "Pay Less" strategy has continued forward without wavering. Pricing seems to have found the sweet spot as Steinhafel announced that few adjustments are needed. Ads continue to emphasize low prices on everyday items. And the expansion of groceries and store brands has continued. In fact, for 2010, Target planned just 10 store openings, the lowest in its history. "It will be a long time before we approach the development pace of several years ago," said Doug Scovanner, Target's chief financial officer. Instead, Target is putting its money into remodeling existing stores to better accommodate the shifts in inventory.

Some Wall Street analysts have expressed concern that Target's recent value strategy may weaken the brand as customers lose sight of the distinctive features that set it apart from Walmart. But the words of one shopper are a good indication that Target may still be retaining the "Expect More" part of its image, despite having emphasized "Pay Less." "Target is a nice place to go. Walmart may have good prices, but I would rather tell my friends that I came back from shopping at Target."

Questions for Discussion

1. What microenvironmental factors have affected Target's performance over the past few years?

2. What macroenvironmental factors have affected Target's performance during that period?

3. By focusing on the "Pay Less" part of its slogan, has Target pursued the best strategy? Why or why not?

4. What alternative strategy might Target have followed in responding to the first signs of declining revenues and profits?

5. Given Target's current situation, what recommendations would you make to Steinhafel for his company's future?

Sources: Karen Talley, "Target Profit Rises on Strong Sales, Improved Credit-Card Operations," *Wall Street Journal*, May 20, 2010, accessed at http://online.wsj.com; John Kell and Karen Talley, "Target's Profit Rises 54% on Higher Sales, Improved Margins," *Wall Street Journal*, February 24, 2010, accessed at http://online.wsj.com; Natalie Zmuda, "Target to Put More Focus on Value," *Advertising Age*, August 19, 2008, accessed at http://adage.com; Ann Zimmerman, "Target Believes a Rebound Recipe Is in Grocery Aisle," *Wall Street Journal*, May 12, 2009, p. B1; Nicole Maestri, "Target Revamps Its Target Brand as 'Up & Up,'" *Reuters*, May 19, 2009, accessed at www.reuters.com; Nicole Maestri, "Target, BJ's Wholesale Results Beat the Street," *Reuters*, May 20, 2009, accessed at www.reuters.com.

4 Managing Marketing Information to Gain Customer Insights

Chapter Preview

In this chapter, we continue our exploration of how marketers gain insights into consumers and the marketplace. We look at how companies develop and manage information about important marketplace elements: customers, competitors, products, and marketing programs. To succeed in today's marketplace, companies must know how to turn mountains of marketing information into fresh customer insights that will help them deliver greater value to customers.

Let's start with a good story about marketing research and customer insights in action at P&G, one of the world's largest and most respected marketing companies. P&G makes and markets a who's who list of consumer megabrands, including the likes of Tide, Crest, Bounty, Charmin, Puffs, Pampers, Pringles, Gillette, Dawn, Ivory, Febreze, Swiffer, Olay, Cover Girl, Pantene, Scope, NyQuil, Duracell, and dozens more. The company's stated purpose is to provide products that "improve the lives of the world's consumers." P&G's brands really do create value for consumers by solving their problems. But to build meaningful relationships with customers, you first have to understand them and how they connect with your brand. That's where marketing research comes in.

P&G: Deep Customer Insights Yield Meaningful Customer Relationships

Creating customer value. Building meaningful customer relationships. All this sounds pretty lofty, especially for a company like P&G, which sells seemingly mundane, low-involvement consumer products such as detergents, shampoos, toothpastes, fabric softeners, toilet paper, and disposable diapers. Can you really develop a meaningful relationship between customers and a laundry detergent? For P&G, the resounding answer is yes. But first you have to get to know your customers well—really well.

More than 60 years ago, P&G's Tide revolutionized the industry as the first detergent to use synthetic compounds rather than soap chemicals for cleaning clothes. Tide really does get clothes clean. For decades, Tide's marketers have positioned the brand on superior functional performance, with hard-hitting ads showing before-and-after cleaning comparisons. But as it turns out, to consumers, Tide means a lot more than just getting grass stains out of that old pair of jeans.

So for several years, P&G has been on a consumer research mission: to unearth and cultivate the deep connections that customers have with its products. Under this mandate, a few years back, the Tide marketing team decided that it needed a new message for the brand. Tide's brand share, although large, had been stagnant for several years. Also, as a result of its hard-hitting functional advertising, consumers saw the Tide brand as arrogant, self-absorbed, and very male. The brand needed to recapture the hearts and minds of its core female consumers.

The Tide team set out to gain a deeper understanding of the emotional connections that women have with their laundry. Rather than just conducting the usual focus groups and marketing research surveys, however, marketing executives and strategists from P&G and its longtime ad agency, Saatchi & Saatchi, conducted research at a deeper level. They engaged in a two-week consumer immersion in which they tagged along with women in Kansas City, Missouri, and Charlotte, North Carolina, as they worked, shopped, and ran errands. The team also sat in on discussions to hear women talk about what's important to them.

"We got to an incredibly deep and personal level," says a Tide marketing executive. "We wanted to understand the role of laundry in their life." But "one of the great things," adds a Saatchi strategist about the research effort, "is we didn't talk [to consumers] about their laundry habits [and practices]. We talked about their lives, what their needs were, how they felt as women. And we got a lot of rich stuff that we hadn't tapped into before."

> P&G, one of the world's most respected marketing companies, knows that to build meaningful relationships with customers, you must first understand them and how they connect with your brand. That's the role of marketing research.

The immersion research produced some remarkable consumer insights. The Tide marketers learned that, although Tide and laundry aren't the most important things in customers' lives, women are very emotional about their clothing. For example, "there was the joy a plus-size, divorced woman described when she got a whistle from her boyfriend while wearing her "foolproof (sexiest) outfit." According to one P&G account: "Day-to-day fabrics in women's lives hold meaning and touch them in many ways. Women like taking care of their clothes and fabrics because they are filled with emotions, stories, feelings, and memories. The fabrics in their lives (anything from jeans to sheets) allow them to express their personalities, their multidimensions as women, their attitudes."

The marketing research impacted everything the brand did moving forward. Tide, the marketers decided, can do more than solve women's laundry problems. It can make a difference in something they truly care about—the fabrics that touch their lives. Based on these insights, P&G and Saatchi developed an award-winning advertising campaign, built around the theme "Tide knows fabrics best." Rather than the mostly heartless demonstrations and side-by-side comparisons of past Tide advertising, the new campaign employed rich visual imagery and meaningful emotional connections.

The initial "Tide knows fabrics best" ads had just the right mix of emotional connections and soft sell. In one television commercial, a pregnant woman dribbled ice cream on the one last shirt that still fit. It's Tide with Bleach to the rescue, so that "your clothes can outlast your cravings." Another ad showed touching scenes of a woman first holding a baby and then cuddling romantically with her husband, all to the tune of "Be My Baby." Tide with Febreze, said the ad, can mean "the difference between smelling like a mom and smelling like a woman." In all, the "Tide knows fabrics best" campaign showed women that Tide really does make a difference in fabrics that touch their lives.

The most recent incarnation of the Tide campaign—"Style Is an Option. Clean Is Not."—connects Tide's cleaning prowess with powerful emotions such as style and self-expression. Linking laundry to style and self-expression isn't really that big a leap. "In watching consumers use [their detergent], many of them talked about how it maintained their clothes in the same way that shampoo and conditioner nurtured one's hair," says a Tide assistant brand manager. In the "Style Is an Option. Clean Is Not" campaign, "Tide celebrates the expression of personal style and helps to give people . . . a sense of pride and dignity when they walk out the door knowing that what they wear is clean," says another Tide marketer. It links Tide and cleaning "to something that is really important to people: our clothes, and the way we look."

So . . . back to the original question: *Can* you develop a relationship with a laundry detergent brand? Insights gained from P&G's deep-immersion consumer research showed that

YOU MAKE IT WORK. WE'LL KEEP IT CLEAN. STYLE IS AN OPTION. **CLEAN IS NOT.** Tide

The Tide marketing teams' deep immersion research with consumers revealed some important insights. The most recent Tide campaign connects Tide's cleaning prowess with powerful emotions such as style and self-expression.

such relationships aren't just possible—they're inevitable. The key is to really understand the true nature of the relationship and shape it by creating real value for customers. Such an understanding comes from marketing research, not only on a company's products and marketing programs but also on core customer needs and brand experiences.

No brand is more successful at creating customer relationships than Tide. Incredibly, P&G's flagship brand captures a more than 40 percent share of the cluttered and competitive laundry detergent market. That's right, more than 40 percent and growing—including a 7 percent increase in the year following the start of the "Tide knows fabrics best" campaign.[1]

As the P&G Tide story highlights, good products and marketing programs begin with good customer information. Companies also need an abundance of information on competitors, resellers, and other actors and marketplace forces. But more than just gathering information, marketers must *use* the information to gain powerful *customer and market insights*.

Author Comment | Marketing information by itself has little value. The value is in the *customer insights* gained from the information and how these insights are used to make better marketing decisions.

Marketing Information and Customer Insights (pp 98–100)

To create value for customers and build meaningful relationships with them, marketers must first gain fresh, deep insights into what customers need and want. Companies use such customer insights to develop competitive advantage. "In today's hypercompetitive world," states a marketing expert, "the race for competitive advantage is really a race for customer and market insights." Such insights come from good marketing information.[2]

Consider Apple's phenomenally successful iPod. ◉ The iPod wasn't the first digital music player, but Apple was the first to get it right. Apple's research uncovered a key insight about how people want to consume digital music—they want to take all their music with them, but they want personal music players to be unobtrusive. This insight led to two key design goals: make it as small as a deck of cards and build it to hold 1,000 songs. Add a dash of Apple's design and usability magic to this insight, and you have a recipe for a blockbuster. Apple's expanded iPod and iPod Touch lines now capture more than a 75 percent market share. And they've spawned other Apple blockbusters such as the iPhone and the iPad.

Although customer and market insights are important for building customer value and relationships, these insights can be very difficult to obtain. Customer needs and buying motives are often anything but obvious—consumers themselves usually can't tell you exactly what they need and why they buy. To gain good customer insights, marketers must effectively manage marketing information from a wide range of sources.

Today's marketers have ready access to plenty of marketing information. With the recent explosion of information technologies, companies

◉ Key customer insights, plus a dash of Apple's design and usability magic, have made the iPod a blockbuster. It now captures a more than 75 percent market share and has spawned other Apple blockbusters such as the iPhone and the iPad.

can now generate information in great quantities. Moreover, consumers themselves are now generating tons of "bottom-up" marketing information.

Not long ago, the only way a consumer could communicate with an organization was by mailing a handwritten letter. Then came the call center, followed by e-mail, text messaging, instant messaging and, indirectly, blogging, Facebook, Twitter, and so on. Each one has contributed to a growing tidal wave of "bottom-up" information that individuals volunteer to each other and to organizations. Organizations able to . . . elicit and use such [volunteered information] will be able to gain much richer, more timely customer insights at lower cost.[3]

Far from lacking information, most marketing managers are overloaded with data and often overwhelmed by it. For example, when a company such as Pepsi monitors online discussions about its brands by searching key words in tweets, blogs, posts, and other sources, its servers take in a stunning six million public conversations a day, more than two billion a year.[4] That's far more information than any manager can digest.

Despite this data glut, marketers frequently complain that they lack enough information of the right kind. They don't need *more* information; they need *better* information. And they need to make better *use* of the information they already have.

The real value of marketing research and marketing information lies in how it is used—in the **customer insights** that it provides. Based on such thinking, many companies are now restructuring their marketing research and information functions. They are creating "customer insights teams," headed by a vice president of customer insights and composed of representatives from all of the firm's functional areas. For example, the head of marketing research at Kraft Foods is called the director of consumer insights and strategy. At Unilever, marketing research is done by the Consumer and Market Insight division, which helps brand teams harness information and turn it into customer insights.

Customer insights groups collect customer and market information from a wide variety of sources, ranging from traditional marketing research studies to mingling with and observing consumers to monitoring consumer online conversations about the company and its products. Then they *use* this information to develop important customer insights from which the company can create more value for its customers.

Thus, companies must design effective marketing information systems that give managers the right information, in the right form, at the right time and help them to use this information to create customer value and stronger customer relationships. A **marketing information system (MIS)** consists of people and procedures for assessing information needs, developing the needed information, and helping decision makers use the information to generate and validate actionable customer and market insights.

Figure 4.1 shows that the MIS begins and ends with information users—marketing managers, internal and external partners, and others who need marketing information.

Customer insights
Fresh understandings of customers and the marketplace derived from marketing information that become the basis for creating customer value and relationships.

Marketing information system (MIS)
People and procedures for assessing information needs, developing the needed information, and helping decision makers to use the information to generate and validate actionable customer and market insights.

FIGURE | 4.1
The Marketing Information System

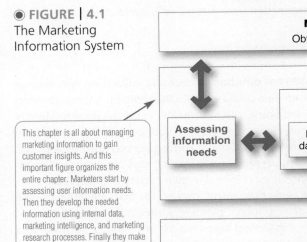

This chapter is all about managing marketing information to gain customer insights. And this important figure organizes the entire chapter. Marketers start by assessing user information needs. Then they develop the needed information using internal data, marketing intelligence, and marketing research processes. Finally they make the information available to users in the right form at the right time.

Marketing managers and other information users
Obtaining customer and market insights from marketing information

Marketing information system

Developing needed information

Assessing information needs — Internal databases — Marketing intelligence — Marketing research — Analyzing and using information

Marketing environment

Target markets — Marketing channels — Competitors — Publics — Macroenvironment forces

First, it interacts with these information users to *assess information needs*. Next, it interacts with the marketing environment to *develop needed information* through internal company databases, marketing intelligence activities, and marketing research. Finally, the MIS helps users to analyze and use the information to develop customer insights, make marketing decisions, and manage customer relationships.

> **Author Comment** | The marketing information system begins and ends with users—assessing their information needs and then delivering information that meets those needs.

Assessing Marketing Information Needs (p 100)

The marketing information system primarily serves the company's marketing and other managers. However, it may also provide information to external partners, such as suppliers, resellers, or marketing services agencies. For example, Walmart's RetailLink system gives key suppliers access to information on everything from customers' buying patterns and store inventory levels to how many items they've sold in which stores in the past 24 hours.[5]

A good MIS balances the information users would *like* to have against what they really *need* and what is *feasible* to offer. The company begins by interviewing managers to find out what information they would like. Some managers will ask for whatever information they can get without thinking carefully about what they really need. Too much information can be as harmful as too little.

Other managers may omit things they ought to know, or they may not know to ask for some types of information they should have. For example, managers might need to know about surges in favorable or unfavorable consumer discussions about their brands on blogs or online social networks. Because they do not know about these discussions, they do not think to ask about them. The MIS must monitor the marketing environment to provide decision makers with information they should have to better understand customers and make key marketing decisions.

Sometimes the company cannot provide the needed information, either because it is not available or because of MIS limitations. For example, a brand manager might want to know how competitors will change their advertising budgets next year and how these changes will affect industry market shares. The information on planned budgets probably is not available. Even if it is, the company's MIS may not be advanced enough to forecast resulting changes in market shares.

Finally, the costs of obtaining, analyzing, storing, and delivering information can quickly mount. The company must decide whether the value of insights gained from additional information is worth the costs of providing it, and both value and cost are often hard to assess.

> **Author Comment** | The problem isn't *finding* information; the world is bursting with information from a glut of sources. The real challenge is to find the *right* information—from inside and outside sources—and turn it into customer insights.

Developing Marketing Information (pp 100–102)

Marketers can obtain the needed information from *internal data*, *marketing intelligence*, and *marketing research*.

Internal Data

Internal databases
Electronic collections of consumer and market information obtained from data sources within the company network.

Many companies build extensive **internal databases**, electronic collections of consumer and market information obtained from data sources within the company's network. Marketing managers can readily access and work with information in the database to identify marketing opportunities and problems, plan programs, and evaluate performance. Internal data can provide strong competitive advantage. "Locked within your own records is a huge, largely untapped asset that no [competitor] can hope to match," says one analyst. Companies are "sitting on a gold mine of unrealized potential in their current customer base."[6]

Information in the database can come from many sources. The marketing department furnishes information on customer demographics, psychographics, sales transactions, and Web site visits. The customer service department keeps records of customer satisfaction or service problems. The accounting department prepares financial statements and keeps detailed records of sales, costs, and cash flows. Operations reports on production schedules, shipments, and inventories. The sales force reports on reseller reactions and competitor ac-

 **Internal data: Barneys has found a wealth of actionable customer insights by analyzing online customers' browsing and buying behavior at its Web site.**

tivities, and marketing channel partners provide data on point-of-sale transactions. Harnessing such information can provide powerful customer insights and competitive advantage.

For example, consider upscale retailer ⊙ Barneys, which has found a wealth of information contained in online customers' browsing and buying data:[7]

> A glance at any spam folder is proof positive that most online retailers haven't yet refined their customer tracking. To wit: My spam box currently features Petco.com advertisements for kitty litter (I'm a dog person), a Staples.com ad for Windows software (I'm a Mac girl), and four ads for Viagra (enough said). But the e-mails from Barneys.com are different. Barneys knows that I like jewelry and yoga. My most recent Barneys e-mail read, "Love it! Jennifer Meyer Ohm Necklace." I do love it. How does Barneys know? It sorts through the data left by millions of anonymous people clicking around its site and predicts who's likely to buy which products, when, and at what price.

> Digging deep into such data provides a wealth of actionable insights into customer buying patterns. Barney's can target customers based on their overall habits, such as "fashionistas" who buy risky new designer products, "bottom feeders" who always buy sale items, or cosmetics zealots. "We even know when you're gonna run out of shampoo, so we might as well send you an e-mail," says Barneys director of Internet marketing. Rather than feeling spied on, customers are thrilled because the message is relevant. Barneys is now considering expanding such analysis to its stores—tracking products as well as customers—to marry its in-store and online marketing efforts.

Internal databases usually can be accessed more quickly and cheaply than other information sources, but they also present some problems. Because internal information is often collected for other purposes, it may be incomplete or in the wrong form for making marketing decisions. Data also ages quickly; keeping the database current requires a major effort. Finally, managing the mountains of information that a large company produces requires highly sophisticated equipment and techniques.

Competitive Marketing Intelligence

Competitive marketing intelligence
The systematic collection and analysis of publicly available information about consumers, competitors, and developments in the marketing environment.

Competitive marketing intelligence is the systematic collection and analysis of publicly available information about consumers, competitors, and developments in the marketplace. The goal of competitive marketing intelligence is to improve strategic decision making by understanding the consumer environment, assessing and tracking competitors' actions, and providing early warnings of opportunities and threats.

Marketing intelligence gathering has grown dramatically as more and more companies are now busily eavesdropping on the marketplace and snooping on their competitors. Techniques range from monitoring Internet buzz or observing consumers firsthand to quizzing the company's own employees, benchmarking competitors' products, researching the Internet, lurking around industry trade shows, and even rooting through rivals' trash bins.

Good marketing intelligence can help marketers gain insights into how consumers talk about and connect with their brands. Many companies send out teams of trained observers to mix and mingle with customers as they use and talk about the company's products. Other companies routinely monitor consumers' online chatter with the help of monitoring services such as Nielsen Online or Radian6. For example, ⊙ Radian6 helps companies to keep track of almost any relevant online conversation:[8]

> Social media make it easier than ever for people to share—to have conversations and express their opinions, needs, ideas, and complaints. And they're doing it with millions of

Who's talking about your brand?

Social media makes it easier than ever for people to share. To have conversations and express their opinions, needs, ideas, complaints. And they're doing it with millions of blogs, tweets, videos, and comments.

But as a business, how do you pinpoint all the conversations happening about your brand? Radian6 gives you a complete platform to listen, share, learn, and engage – both inside your company, and with your customers across the entire social web.

Your brand is defined by the sum of all conversations.
Listen and join the dialogue with Radian6.

radian⁶

● **Many companies routinely monitor consumers' online conversations with the help of monitoring services and platforms such as Radian6.**

blogs, tweets, videos, and comments daily. Marketers face the difficult task of sifting through all the noise to find the gems about their brands. Radian6 gives companies a Web-based platform that lets them listen to, share with, learn from, and engage customers across the entire social Web. Radian6's Web dashboard provides for real-time monitoring of consumer mentions of the company, its brands, relevant issues, and competitors on millions of blog posts, viral videos, reviews in forums, sharing of photos, and twitter updates. For example, lifestyle retailer PacSun uses Radian6 to track important trends and better respond to customers in the online space. Microsoft uses Radian6 to monitor what's being said online about the company and its products and respond to problems after purchase.

Companies also need to actively monitor competitors' activities. Firms use competitive marketing intelligence to gain early warnings of competitor moves and strategies, new-product launches, new or changing markets, and potential competitive strengths and weaknesses. Much competitor intelligence can be collected from people inside the company—executives, engineers and scientists, purchasing agents, and the sales force. The company can also obtain important intelligence information from suppliers, resellers, and key customers. And it can get good information by observing competitors and monitoring their published information.

Competitors often reveal intelligence information through their annual reports, business publications, trade show exhibits, press releases, advertisements, and Web pages. The Internet has become an invaluable source for competitive intelligence. Using Internet search engines, marketers can search specific competitor names, events, or trends and see what turns up. And tracking consumer conversations about competing brands is often as revealing as tracking conversations about the company's own brands. Moreover, most competitors now place volumes of information on their Web sites, providing details of interest to customers, partners, suppliers, investors, or franchisees. This can provide a wealth of useful information about competitors' strategies, markets, new products, facilities, and other happenings.

Intelligence seekers can also pore through any of thousands of online databases. Some are free. For example, the U.S. Security and Exchange Commission's database provides a huge stockpile of financial information on public competitors, and the U.S. Patent Office and Trademark database reveals patents that competitors have filed. For a fee, companies can also subscribe to any of the more than 3,000 online databases and information search services, such as Hoover's, LexisNexis, and Dun & Bradstreet. Today's marketers have an almost overwhelming amount of competitor information only a few keystrokes away.

The intelligence game goes both ways. Facing determined competitive marketing intelligence efforts by competitors, most companies are now taking steps to protect their own information. The growing use of marketing intelligence also raises a number of ethical issues. Although the preceding techniques are legal, others may involve questionable ethics. Clearly, companies should take advantage of publicly available information. However, they should not stoop to snoop. With all the legitimate intelligence sources now available, a company does not need to break the law or accepted codes of ethics to get good intelligence.

Author | Whereas marketing
Comment | intelligence involves
actively scanning the general
marketing environment, marketing
research involves more focused studies
to gain customer insights relating to
specific marketing decisions.

Marketing Research (pp 103–119)

In addition to marketing intelligence information about general consumer, competitor, and marketplace happenings, marketers often need formal studies that provide customer and market insights for specific marketing situations and decisions. For example, Budweiser wants to know what appeals will be most effective in its Super Bowl advertising. Google wants to know how Web searchers will react to a proposed redesign of its site. Or Samsung wants to know how many and what kinds of people will buy its next-generation, ultrathin televisions. In such situations, marketing intelligence will not provide the detailed information needed. Managers will need marketing research.

Marketing research is the systematic design, collection, analysis, and reporting of data relevant to a specific marketing situation facing an organization. Companies use marketing research in a wide variety of situations. For example, marketing research gives marketers insights into customer motivations, purchase behavior, and satisfaction. It can help them to assess market potential and market share or measure the effectiveness of pricing, product, distribution, and promotion activities.

Some large companies have their own research departments that work with marketing managers on marketing research projects. This is how P&G, GE, and many other corporate giants handle marketing research. In addition, these companies—like their smaller counterparts—frequently hire outside research specialists to consult with management on specific marketing problems and conduct marketing research studies. Sometimes firms simply purchase data collected by outside firms to aid in their decision making.

The marketing research process has four steps (see ◉ **Figure 4.2**): defining the problem and research objectives, developing the research plan, implementing the research plan, and interpreting and reporting the findings.

Marketing research
The systematic design, collection, analysis, and reporting of data relevant to a specific marketing situation facing an organization.

Defining the Problem and Research Objectives

Marketing managers and researchers must work closely together to define the problem and agree on research objectives. The manager best understands the decision for which information is needed; the researcher best understands marketing research and how to obtain the information. Defining the problem and research objectives is often the hardest step in the research process. The manager may know that something is wrong, without knowing the specific causes.

After the problem has been defined carefully, the manager and the researcher must set the research objectives. A marketing research project might have one of three types of objectives. The objective of **exploratory research** is to gather preliminary information that will help define the problem and suggest hypotheses. The objective of **descriptive research** is to describe things, such as the market potential for a product or the demographics and attitudes of consumers who buy the product. The objective of **causal research** is to test hypotheses about cause-and-effect relationships. For example, would a 10 percent decrease in tuition at a private college result in an enrollment increase sufficient to offset the reduced tuition? Managers often start with exploratory research and later follow with descriptive or causal research.

The statement of the problem and research objectives guides the entire research process. The manager and the researcher should put the statement in writing to be certain that they agree on the purpose and expected results of the research.

Exploratory research
Marketing research to gather preliminary information that will help define problems and suggest hypotheses.

Descriptive research
Marketing research to better describe marketing problems, situations, or markets, such as the market potential for a product or the demographics and attitudes of consumers.

Causal research
Marketing research to test hypotheses about cause-and-effect relationships.

This first step is probably the most difficult but also the most important one. It guides the entire research process. It's frustrating to reach the end of an expensive research project only to learn that you've addressed the wrong problem!

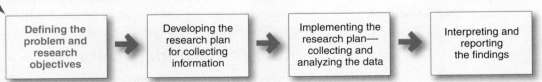

◉ **FIGURE | 4.2**
The Marketing Research Process

Developing the Research Plan

Once the research problem and objectives have been defined, researchers must determine the exact information needed, develop a plan for gathering it efficiently, and present the plan to management. The research plan outlines sources of existing data and spells out the specific research approaches, contact methods, sampling plans, and instruments that researchers will use to gather new data.

● **A decision by Red Bull to add a line of enhanced waters to its already successful mix of energy and cola drinks would call for marketing research that provides lots of specific information.**

Research objectives must be translated into specific information needs. ● For example, suppose that Red Bull wants to conduct research on how consumers would react to a proposed new vitamin-enhanced water drink in several flavors sold under the Red Bull name. Red Bull currently dominates the worldwide energy drink market. However, in an effort to expand beyond its energy drink niche, the company recently introduced Red Bull Cola ("Why not?" asks the company; it's strong and natural, just like the original Red Bull energy drink). A new line of enhanced waters—akin to Glacéau's VitaminWater—might help Red Bull leverage its strong brand position even further. The proposed research might call for the following specific information:

- The demographic, economic, and lifestyle characteristics of current Red Bull customers. (Do current customers also consume enhanced-water products? Are such products consistent with their lifestyles? Or would Red Bull need to target a new segment of consumers?)

- The characteristics and usage patterns of the broader population of enhanced-water users: What do they need and expect from such products, where do they buy them, when and how do they use them, and what existing brands and price points are most popular? (The new Red Bull product would need strong, relevant positioning in the crowded enhanced-water market.)

- Retailer reactions to the proposed new product line: Would they stock and support it? Where would they display it? (Failure to get retailer support would hurt sales of the new drink.)

- Forecasts of sales of both the new and current Red Bull products. (Will the new enhanced waters create new sales or simply take sales away from current Red Bull products? Will the new product increase Red Bull's overall profits?)

Red Bull's marketers will need these and many other types of information to decide whether and how to introduce the new product.

The research plan should be presented in a *written proposal*. A written proposal is especially important when the research project is large and complex or when an outside firm carries it out. The proposal should cover the management problems addressed, the research objectives, the information to be obtained, and how the results will help management decision making. The proposal also should include estimated research costs.

To meet the manager's information needs, the research plan can call for gathering secondary data, primary data, or both. **Secondary data** consist of information that already exists somewhere, having been collected for another purpose. **Primary data** consist of information collected for the specific purpose at hand.

Secondary data
Information that already exists somewhere, having been collected for another purpose.

Primary data
Information collected for the specific purpose at hand.

Gathering Secondary Data

Researchers usually start by gathering secondary data. The company's internal database provides a good starting point. However, the company can also tap into a wide assortment of external information sources, including commercial data services and government sources (see ● **Table 4.1**).

● TABLE | 4.1 Selected External Information Sources

Business Data

The Nielsen Company (http://nielsen.com) provides point-of-sale scanner data on sales, market share, and retail prices; data on household purchasing; and data on television audiences.

Experian Consumer Research (Simmons) (http://smrb.com) provides detailed analysis of consumer patterns in 400 product categories in selected markets.

Symphony IRI Group (www.symphonyiri.com) provides supermarket scanner data for tracking grocery product movement and new product purchasing data.

IMS Health (www.imshealth.com) tracks drug sales, monitors the performance of pharmaceutical sales representatives, and offers pharmaceutical market forecasts.

Arbitron (http://arbitron.com) provides local market and Internet radio audience and advertising expenditure information, among other media and ad spending data.

J.D. Power and Associates (www.jdpower.com) provides information from independent consumer surveys of product and service quality, customer satisfaction, and buyer behavior.

Dun & Bradstreet (http://dnb.com) maintains a database containing information on more than 50 million individual companies around the globe.

comScore (http://comscore.com) provides consumer behavior information and geodemographic analysis of Internet and digital media users around the world.

Thomson Dialog (www.dialog.com) offers access to more than 900 databases containing publications, reports, newsletters, and directories covering dozens of industries.

LexisNexis (www.lexisnexis.com) features articles from business, consumer, and marketing publications plus tracking of firms, industries, trends, and promotion techniques.

Factiva (http://factiva.com) specializes in in-depth financial, historical, and operational information on public and private companies.

Hoover's, Inc. (http://hoovers.com) provides business descriptions, financial overviews, and news about major companies around the world.

CNN (www.cnn.com) reports U.S. and global news and covers the markets and news-making companies in detail.

Government Data

Securities and Exchange Commission Edgar database (http://sec.gov/edgar.shtml) provides financial data on U.S. public corporations.

Small Business Administration (http://sba.gov) features information and links for small business owners.

Federal Trade Commission (http://ftc.gov) shows regulations and decisions related to consumer protection and antitrust laws.

Stat-USA (http://stat-usa.gov), a Department of Commerce site, highlights statistics on U.S. business and international trade.

U.S. Census (www.census.gov) provides detailed statistics and trends about the U.S. population.

U.S. Patent and Trademark Office (www.uspto.gov) allows searches to determine who has filed for trademarks and patents.

Internet Data

ClickZ (www.clickz.com) brings together a wealth of information about the Internet and its users, from consumers to e-commerce.

Interactive Advertising Bureau (www.iab.net) covers statistics about advertising on the Internet.

Forrester.com (www.forrester.com/rb/research) monitors Web traffic and ranks the most popular sites.

Companies can buy secondary data reports from outside suppliers. For example, Nielsen sells shopper insight data from a consumer panel of more than 260,000 households in 27 countries worldwide, with measures of trial and repeat purchasing, brand loyalty, and buyer demographics. Experian Consumer Research (Simmons) sells information consumer panel data on more than 8,000 brands in 450 product categories, including detailed consumer profiles that assess everything from the products consumers buy and the brands they prefer to their lifestyles, attitudes, and media preferences. The

MONITOR service by Yankelovich sells information on important social and lifestyle trends. These and other firms supply high-quality data to suit a wide variety of marketing information needs.[9]

Commercial online databases
Collections of information available from online commercial sources or accessible via the Internet.

Using **commercial online databases**, marketing researchers can conduct their own searches of secondary data sources. General database services such as Dialog, ProQuest, and LexisNexis put an incredible wealth of information at the keyboards of marketing decision makers. Beyond commercial Web sites offering information for a fee, almost every industry association, government agency, business publication, and news medium offers free information to those tenacious enough to find their Web sites. There are so many Web sites offering data that finding the right ones can become an almost overwhelming task.

Internet search engines can be a big help in locating relevant secondary information sources. However, they can also be very frustrating and inefficient. For example, a Red Bull marketer Googling "enhanced water products" would come up with some 200,000 hits! Still, well-structured, well-designed Web searches can be a good starting point to any marketing research project.

Secondary data can usually be obtained more quickly and at a lower cost than primary data. Also, secondary sources can sometimes provide data an individual company cannot collect on its own—information that either is not directly available or would be too expensive to collect. For example, it would be too expensive for Red Bull's marketers to conduct a continuing retail store audit to find out about the market shares, prices, and displays of competitors' brands. But it can buy the InfoScan service from SymphonyIRI Group, which provides this information based on scanner and other data from 34,000 retail stores in markets around the nation.[10]

Secondary data can also present problems. The needed information may not exist; researchers can rarely obtain all the data they need from secondary sources. For example, Red Bull will not find existing information about consumer reactions about a new enhanced-water line that it has not yet placed on the market. Even when data can be found, the information might not be very usable. The researcher must evaluate secondary information carefully to make certain it is *relevant* (fits research project needs), *accurate* (reliably collected and reported), *current* (up-to-date enough for current decisions), and *impartial* (objectively collected and reported).

Primary Data Collection

Secondary data provide a good starting point for research and often help to define research problems and objectives. In most cases, however, the company must also collect primary data. Just as researchers must carefully evaluate the quality of secondary information, they also must take great care when collecting primary data. They need to make sure that it will be relevant, accurate, current, and unbiased. ◉ **Table 4.2** shows that designing a plan for primary data collection calls for a number of decisions on *research approaches*, *contact methods*, the *sampling plan*, and *research instruments*.

◉ **TABLE | 4.2** Planning Primary Data Collection

Research Approaches	Contact Methods	Sampling Plan	Research Instruments
Observation	Mail	Sampling unit	Questionnaire
Survey	Telephone	Sample size	Mechanical instruments
Experiment	Personal	Sampling procedure	
	Online		

Research Approaches

Research approaches for gathering primary data include observation, surveys, and experiments. We discuss each one in turn.

Observational research
Gathering primary data by observing relevant people, actions, and situations.

Observational Research. **Observational research** involves gathering primary data by observing relevant people, actions, and situations. For example, Family Dollar might evaluate possible new store locations by checking traffic patterns, neighborhood conditions, and the location of competing discount retail stores.

Researchers often observe consumer behavior to glean customer insights they can't obtain by simply asking customers questions. For instance, Fisher-Price has established an observation lab in which it can observe the reactions of little tots to new toys. The Fisher-Price Play Lab is a sunny, toy-strewn space where lucky kids get to test Fisher-Price prototypes, under the watchful eyes of designers who hope to learn what will get them worked up into a new-toy frenzy. Similarly, in its research labs, using high-tech cameras and other equipment, Gillette observes men and women shaving and uses the insights to design new razors and shaving products.

Marketers not only observe what consumers do but also observe what consumers are saying. As discussed earlier, marketers now routinely listen in on consumer conversations on blogs, social networks, and Web sites. Observing such naturally occurring feedback can provide inputs that simply can't be gained through more structure and formal research approaches.

Observational research can obtain information that people are unwilling or unable to provide. In contrast, some things simply cannot be observed, such as feelings, attitudes, motives, or private behavior. Long-term or infrequent behavior is also difficult to observe. Finally, observations can be very difficult to interpret. Because of these limitations, researchers often use observation along with other data collection methods.

Ethnographic research
A form of observational research that involves sending trained observers to watch and interact with consumers in their "natural environments."

A wide range of companies now use **ethnographic research**. Ethnographic research involves sending observers to watch and interact with consumers in their "natural environments." The observers might be trained anthropologists and psychologists or company researchers and managers (see Real Marketing 4.1). Consider this example:[11]

● **Ethnographic research: Kraft Canada sent out its president (above center) and other high-level executives to observe actual family life in diverse Canadian homes. Videos of their experiences helped marketers and others across the company to understand the role of Kraft's brands in people's lives.**

● Kraft Canada recently sent its president and other high-level Kraft executives to observe actual family life in a dozen diverse Canadian homes. "We went out with the purpose of understanding the Canadian family, what's going on in their homes, particularly the kitchen," says Kraft Canada's vice president of consumer insights and strategy. After viewing hours of video of all 12 families visited, the consumer insights group found some unifying themes across Kraft's diverse markets. It learned that almost all families faced the same "mad rush to have something ready to feed the family, a hectic-ness, last-minute decisions, the need to balance the child's needs and different food needs." Kraft shared a compilation of the videos with marketing and sales teams, who used it as a basis for brainstorming sessions, and even put the video on an internal Web site for Kraft's 4,500 employees across Canada to view. The experience

Real Marketing 4.1

Ethnographic Research:
Watching What Consumers *Really* Do

A girl walks into a bar and says to the bartender, "Give me a Diet Coke and a clear sight line to those guys drinking Miller Lite in the corner." If you're waiting for a punch line, this is no joke. The "girl" in this situation is Emma Gilding, corporate ethnographer at ad agency Ogilvy & Mather. In this case, her job is to hang out in bars around the country and watch groups of guys knocking back beers with their friends. No kidding. This is honest-to-goodness, cutting-edge marketing research—ethnography style.

As a videographer filmed the action, Gilding kept tabs on how close the guys stood to one another. She eavesdropped on stories and observed how the mantle was passed from one speaker to another, as in a tribe around a campfire. Back at the office, a team of trained anthropologists and psychologists pored over more than 70 hours of footage from five similar nights in bars from San Diego to Philadelphia. One key insight: Miller is favored by groups of drinkers, while its main competitor, Bud Lite, is a beer that sells to individuals. The result was a hilarious series of ads that cut from a Miller Lite drinker's weird experiences in the world—getting caught in the subway taking money from a blind musician's guitar case or hitching a ride in the desert with a deranged trucker—to shots of him regaling friends with tales over a brew. The Miller Lite ads got high marks from audiences for their entertainment value and emotional resonance.

Today's marketers face many difficult questions: What do customers *really* think about a product and what do they say about it to their friends? How do they *really* use it? Will they tell you? *Can* they tell you? All too often, traditional research simply can't provide accurate answers. To get deeper insights, many companies use ethnographic research, watching and interacting with consumers in their "natural environments."

Ethnographers are looking for "consumer truth." In surveys and interviews, customers may state (and fully believe) certain preferences and behaviors, when the reality is actually quite different. Ethnography provides an insider's tour of the customer's world, helping marketers get at what consumers *really* do

rather than what they *say* they do. "That might mean catching a heart-disease patient scarfing down a meatball sub and a cream soup while extolling the virtues of healthy eating," observes one ethnographer, "or a diabetic vigorously salting his sausage and eggs after explaining how he refuses jelly for his toast."

By entering the customer's world, ethnographers can scrutinize how customers think and feel as it relates to their products. Here's another example:

Kelly Peña, also known as "the kid whisperer," was digging through a 12-year-old boy's dresser drawer one recent afternoon. Her undercover mission: to unearth what makes him tick and help the Walt Disney Company reassert itself as a cultural force among boys. Peña, a Disney researcher, zeroed in on a ratty rock 'n' roll T-shirt. Black Sabbath? "Wearing it makes me feel like I'm going to an R-rated movie," said Dean, the shy redheaded boy under scrutiny. Jackpot! Peña and her team of anthropologists have spent 18 months peering inside the heads of incommunicative boys in

search of just that kind of psychological nugget.

Disney is relying on Peña's insights to create new entertainment for boys 6 to 14, who account for $50 billion a year in spending worldwide. With the exception of "Cars," Disney—home to more girl-focused fare such as the "Princesses" merchandising line; "Hannah Montana," and "Pixie Hollow"—has been notably weak on hit entertainment for boys. Peña's research is sometimes conducted in groups; sometimes it involves going shopping with a teenage boy and his mother. Walking through Dean's house, Peña looked for unspoken clues about his likes and dislikes. "What's on the back shelves that he hasn't quite gotten rid of will be telling," she said beforehand. "What's on his walls? How does he interact with his siblings?" One big takeaway from the two-hour visit: Although Dean was trying to sound grown-up and nonchalant in his answers, he still had a lot of little kid in him. He had dinosaur sheets and stuffed animals at the bottom of his bed. "I think he's trying to push a lot of boundaries for the first time," Peña said later.

Children can already see the results of Peña's scrutiny on Disney XD, a new cable channel and Web site. It's no accident, for instance, that the central character on "Aaron Stone" is a mediocre basketball player. Peña told producers that boys identify with protagonists who try hard to grow. "Winning isn't nearly as important to boys as Hollywood thinks," she said.

Ethnographic research: **To better understand the challenges faced by elderly shoppers, this Kimberly-Clark executive tries to shop while wearing vision-impairment glasses and bulky gloves that simulate arthritis.**

Ethnographic research often yields the kinds of intimate details that just don't emerge from traditional focus groups and surveys. For example, focus groups told the Best Western hotel chain that it's men who decide when to stop for the night and where to stay. But videotapes of couples on cross-country journeys showed it was usually the women. And observation can often uncover problems that customers don't even know they have. By videotaping consumers in the shower, plumbing fixture maker Moen uncovered safety risks that consumers didn't recognize—such as the habit some women have of shaving their legs while holding on to one unit's temperature control. Moen would find it almost impossible to discover such design flaws simply by asking questions.

Experiencing first-hand what customers experience can also provide powerful insights. To that end, consumer products giant Kimberly-Clark even runs a program that puts executives from retail chains such as Walgreens, Rite Aid, and Family Dollar directly into their customers' shoes—literally. The executives shop in their own stores with glasses that blur their vision, unpopped popcorn in their shoes, and bulky rubber gloves on their hands. It's all part of an exercise designed to help marketers understand the physical challenges faced by elderly shoppers, who will represent 20 percent of the total U.S. population by 2030.

The vision-blurring glasses simulate common vision ailments such as cataracts, macular degeneration, and glaucoma. Unpopped popcorn in shoes gives a feel for what it's like to walk with aching joints. And the bulky gloves simulate the limitations to manual dexterity brought on by arthritis. Participants come back from these experiences bursting with ideas for elderly friendly store changes, such as bigger typefaces and more eye-friendly colors on packaging and fliers, new store lighting and clearer signage, and instant call buttons near heavy merchandise such as bottled water and laundry detergent.

Thus, more and more, marketing researchers are getting up close and personal with consumers—watching them closely as they act and interact in natural settings or stepping in to feel first-hand what they feel. "Knowing the individual consumer on an intimate basis has become a necessity," says one research consultant, "and ethnography is the intimate connection to the consumer."

Sources: Adapted excerpts and other information from Brooks Barnes, "Disney Expert Uses Science to Draw Boy Viewers," *New York Times*, April 14, 2009, p. A1; Linda Tischler, "Every Move You Make," *Fast Company*, April 2004, pp. 73–75; and Ellen Byron, "Seeing Store Shelves Through Senior Eyes," *Wall Street Journal*, September 14, 2009, p. B1.

of "living with customers" helped Kraft's marketers and others understand how the company's brands help customers by providing more convenient products that reduce the stress of getting meals on the table.

Beyond conducting ethnographic research in physical consumer environments, many companies now routinely conduct "Webnography" research—observing consumers in a natural context on the Internet. Observing people as they interact online can provide useful insights into both online and off-line buying motives and behavior.[12]

Observational and ethnographic research often yields the kinds of details that just don't emerge from traditional research questionnaires or focus groups. Whereas traditional quantitative research approaches seek to test known hypotheses and obtain answers to well-defined product or strategy questions, observational research can generate fresh customer and market insights. "The beauty of ethnography," says a research expert, is that it "allows companies to zero in on their customers' unarticulated desires." Agrees another researcher, "Classic market research doesn't go far enough. It can't grasp what people can't imagine or articulate. Think of the Henry Ford quote: 'If I had asked people what they wanted, they would have said faster horses.'"[13]

Survey research

Gathering primary data by asking people questions about their knowledge, attitudes, preferences, and buying behavior.

Survey Research. **Survey research**, the most widely used method for primary data collection, is the approach best suited for gathering descriptive information. A company that wants to know about people's knowledge, attitudes, preferences, or buying behavior can often find out by asking them directly.

The major advantage of survey research is its flexibility; it can be used to obtain many different kinds of information in many different situations. Surveys addressing almost any marketing question or decision can be conducted by phone or mail, in person, or on the Web.

However, survey research also presents some problems. Sometimes people are unable to answer survey questions because they cannot remember or have never thought about what they do and why. People may be unwilling to respond to unknown interviewers or about things they consider private. Respondents may answer survey questions even when they do not know the answer just to appear smarter or more informed. Or they may try to help the interviewer by giving pleasing answers. Finally, busy people may not take the time, or they might resent the intrusion into their privacy.

Experimental research
Gathering primary data by selecting matched groups of subjects, giving them different treatments, controlling related factors, and checking for differences in group responses.

Experimental Research. Whereas observation is best suited for exploratory research and surveys for descriptive research, **experimental research** is best suited for gathering causal information. Experiments involve selecting matched groups of subjects, giving them different treatments, controlling unrelated factors, and checking for differences in group responses. Thus, experimental research tries to explain cause-and-effect relationships.

For example, before adding a new sandwich to its menu, McDonald's might use experiments to test the effects on sales of two different prices it might charge. It could introduce the new sandwich at one price in one city and at another price in another city. If the cities are similar, and if all other marketing efforts for the sandwich are the same, then differences in sales in the two cities could be related to the price charged.

Contact Methods

Information can be collected by mail, telephone, personal interview, or online. ● **Table 4.3** shows the strengths and weaknesses of each contact method.

Mail, Telephone, and Personal Interviewing. *Mail questionnaires* can be used to collect large amounts of information at a low cost per respondent. Respondents may give more honest answers to more personal questions on a mail questionnaire than to an unknown interviewer in person or over the phone. Also, no interviewer is involved to bias respondents' answers.

However, mail questionnaires are not very flexible; all respondents answer the same questions in a fixed order. Mail surveys usually take longer to complete, and the response rate—the number of people returning completed questionnaires—is often very low. Finally, the researcher often has little control over the mail questionnaire sample. Even with a good mailing list, it is hard to control *whom* at a particular address fills out the questionnaire. As a result of the shortcomings, more and more marketers are now shifting to faster, more flexible, and lower cost e-mail and online surveys.

Telephone interviewing is one of the best methods for gathering information quickly, and it provides greater flexibility than mail questionnaires. Interviewers can explain difficult questions and, depending on the answers they receive, skip some questions or probe on others. Response rates tend to be higher than with mail questionnaires, and interviewers can ask to speak to respondents with the desired characteristics or even by name.

However, with telephone interviewing, the cost per respondent is higher than with mail or online questionnaires. Also, people may not want to discuss personal questions with an interviewer. The method introduces interviewer bias—the way interviewers talk, how they ask questions, and other differences that may affect respondents' answers. Finally, in this age of do-not-call lists and promotion-harassed consumers, potential survey respondents are increasingly hanging up on telephone interviewers rather than talking with them.

Personal interviewing takes two forms: individual interviewing and group interviewing. *Individual interviewing* involves talking with people in their homes or offices, on the street, or

● **TABLE | 4.3** Strengths and Weaknesses of Contact Methods

	Mail	**Telephone**	**Personal**	**Online**
Flexibility	Poor	Good	Excellent	Good
Quantity of data that can be collected	Good	Fair	Excellent	Good
Control of interviewer effects	Excellent	Fair	Poor	Fair
Control of sample	Fair	Excellent	Good	Excellent
Speed of data collection	Poor	Excellent	Good	Excellent
Response rate	Poor	Poor	Good	Good
Cost	Good	Fair	Poor	Excellent

Source: Based on Donald S. Tull and Del I. Hawkins, *Marketing Research: Measurement and Method,* 7th ed. (New York: Macmillan Publishing Company, 1993). Adapted with permission of the authors.

in shopping malls. Such interviewing is flexible. Trained interviewers can guide interviews, explain difficult questions, and explore issues as the situation requires. They can show subjects actual products, advertisements, or packages and observe reactions and behavior. However, individual personal interviews may cost three to four times as much as telephone interviews.

Group interviewing consists of inviting six to ten people to meet with a trained moderator to talk about a product, service, or organization. Participants normally are paid a small sum for attending. The moderator encourages free and easy discussion, hoping that group interactions will bring out actual feelings and thoughts. At the same time, the moderator "focuses" the discussion—hence the name **focus group interviewing**.

Researchers and marketers watch the focus group discussions from behind one-way glass and record comments in writing or on video for later study. Today, focus group researchers can even use videoconferencing and Internet technology to connect marketers in distant locations with live focus group action. Using cameras and two-way sound systems, marketing executives in a far-off boardroom can look in and listen, using remote controls to zoom in on faces and pan the focus group at will.

Along with observational research, focus group interviewing has become one of the major qualitative marketing research tools for gaining fresh insights into consumer thoughts and feelings. However, focus group studies present some challenges. They usually employ small samples to keep time and costs down, and it may be hard to generalize from the results. Moreover, consumers in focus groups are not always open and honest about their real feelings, behavior, and intentions in front of other people.

Thus, although focus groups are still widely used, many researchers are tinkering with focus group design. For example, some companies prefer "immersion groups"—small groups of consumers who interact directly and informally with product designers without a focus group moderator present. Still other researchers are changing the environments in which they conduct focus groups. To help consumers relax and to elicit more authentic responses, they use settings that are more comfortable and more relevant to the products being researched. For example, to get a better understanding of how women shave their legs, ● Schick Canada and ad agency F.E.M. created "Slow Sip" sessions designed to be like a simple get-together with girlfriends.

In these Slow Sip sessions, participants gathered together at a local café to sip coffee or tea and munch on snacks. The structure was loose, and the congenial setting helped the women open up and share personal shaving and moisturizing stories on a subject that might have been sensitive in a more formal setting. The Slow Sip sessions produced a number of new customer insights. For example, researchers discovered that the message for their Schick Quattro for Women razor—that Quattro has four-blade technology—was too technical. Women don't care about the engineering behind a razor; they care about shaving results. So Schick Canada repositioned the Quattro as offering a smooth, long-lasting shave. As a side benefit, participants enjoyed the sessions so much that they wanted to stick around for more. They became a kind of ongoing advisory board for Schick's marketers and "brand ambassadors" for Schick's products.[14]

Thus, in recent years, many companies have been moving away from traditional, more formal and numbers-oriented research approaches and contact methods. Instead, they are employing more new ways of listening to consumers that don't involve traditional questionnaire formats. "Long known for crunching numbers and being statistical gatekeepers of the marketing industry," says one marketer, "market researchers need to shift their focus toward listening and developing ideas better on the front end and away

Focus group interviewing
Personal interviewing that involves inviting six to ten people to gather for a few hours with a trained interviewer to talk about a product, service, or organization. The interviewer "focuses" the group discussion on important issues.

● **New focus group environments: To create a more congenial setting in which women could open up and share personal shaving and moisturizing stories, Schick sponsored "Slow Sip" sessions in local cafes.**

from 'feeding the metrics monster.'" Beyond conducting surveys and tracking brand metrics, "researchers need to employ softer skills."[15]

Online marketing research

Collecting primary data online through Internet surveys, online focus groups, Web-based experiments, or tracking consumers' online behavior.

Online Marketing Research. The growth of the Internet has had a dramatic impact on the conduct of marketing research. Increasingly, researchers are collecting primary data through **online marketing research**: Internet surveys, online panels, experiments, and online focus groups. By one estimate, U.S. online research spending reached an estimated $4.45 billion last year and is growing at 15–20 percent per year.[16]

Online research can take many forms. A company can use the Web as a survey medium: It can include a questionnaire on its Web site and offer incentives for completing it. It can use e-mail, Web links, or Web pop-ups to invite people to answer questions. It can create online panels that provide regular feedback or conduct live discussions or online focus groups.

Beyond surveys, researchers can conduct experiments on the Web. They can experiment with different prices, headlines, or product features on different Web sites or at different times to learn the relative effectiveness of their offers. Or they can set up virtual shopping environments and use them to test new products and marketing programs. Finally, a company can learn about the behavior of online customers by following their click streams as they visit the Web site and move to other sites.

The Internet is especially well suited to *quantitative* research—conducting marketing surveys and collecting data. Close to three-quarters of all Americans now have access to the Web, making it a fertile channel for reaching a broad cross section of consumers. As response rates for traditional survey approaches decline and costs increase, the Web is quickly replacing mail and the telephone as the dominant data collection methodology. Online research now accounts for about 50 percent of all survey research done in the United States.[17]

Web-based survey research offers some real advantages over traditional phone, mail, and personal interviewing approaches. The most obvious advantages are speed and low costs. By going online, researchers can quickly and easily distribute Internet surveys to thousands of respondents simultaneously via e-mail or by posting them on selected Web sites. Responses can be almost instantaneous, and because respondents themselves enter the information, researchers can tabulate, review, and share research data as they arrive.

Online research usually costs much less than research conducted through mail, phone, or personal interviews. Using the Internet eliminates most of the postage, phone, interviewer, and data-handling costs associated with the other approaches. As a result, Internet surveys typically cost 15–20 percent less than mail surveys and 30 percent less than phone surveys. Moreover, sample size has little impact on costs. Once the questionnaire is set up, there's little difference in cost between 10 respondents and 10,000 respondents on the Web.

Thus, online research is well within the reach of almost any business, large or small. In fact, with the Internet, what was once the domain of research experts is now available to almost any would-be researcher. ● Even smaller, less sophisticated researchers can use online survey services such as Zoomerang (www.zoomerang.com) and SurveyMonkey (www.surveymonkey.com) to create, publish, and distribute their own custom surveys in minutes.

Beyond their speed and cost advantages, Web-based surveys also tend to be more interactive and engaging, easier to complete, and less intrusive than traditional phone or mail surveys. As a result, they usually garner higher response rates. The Internet is an excellent medium for reaching the hard-to-reach—for example, the often-elusive teen, single, affluent, and well-educated audiences. It's also good for reaching

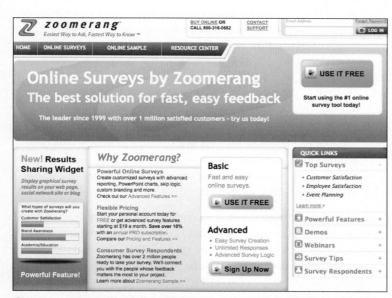

● **Online research: Thanks to survey services such as Zoomerang, almost any business, large or small, can create, publish, and distribute its own custom surveys in minutes.**

working mothers and other people who lead busy lives. Such people are well represented online, and they can respond in their own space and at their own convenience.

Just as marketing researchers have rushed to use the Internet for quantitative surveys and data collection, they are now also adopting *qualitative* Web-based research approaches, such as online depth interviews, focus groups, blogs, and social networks. The Internet can provide a fast, low-cost way to gain qualitative customer insights.

A primary qualitative Web-based research approach is **online focus groups**. Such focus groups offer many advantages over traditional focus groups. Participants can log in from anywhere; all they need is a laptop and a Web connection. Thus, the Internet works well for bringing together people from different parts of the country or world, especially those in higher-income groups who can't spare the time to travel to a central site. Also, researchers can conduct and monitor online focus groups from just about anywhere, eliminating travel, lodging, and facility costs. Finally, although online focus groups require some advance scheduling, results are almost immediate.

Online focus groups can take any of several formats. Most occur in real time, in the form of online chat room discussions in which participants and a moderator sit around a virtual table exchanging comments. Alternatively, researchers might set up an online message board on which respondents interact over the course of several days or a few weeks. Participants log in daily and comment on focus group topics.

Although low in cost and easy to administer, online focus groups can lack the real-world dynamics of more personal approaches. To overcome these shortcomings, some researchers are now adding real-time audio and video to their online focus groups. For example, online research firm Channel M2 "puts the human touch back into online research" by assembling focus group participants in people-friendly "virtual interview rooms."[18]

> Participants are recruited using traditional methods and then sent a Web camera so that both their verbal and nonverbal reactions can be recorded. Participants receive instructions via e-mail, including a link to the Channel M2 online interviewing room and a toll-free teleconference number to call. At the appointed time, when they click on the link and phone in, participants sign on and see the Channel M2 interview room, complete with live video of the other participants, text chat, screen or slide sharing, and a whiteboard. Once the focus group is underway, questions and answers occur in "real time" in a remarkably lively setting. Participants comment spontaneously—verbally, via text messaging, or both. Researchers can "sit in" on the focus group from anywhere, seeing and hearing every respondent. Or they can review a recorded version at a later date.

Although the use of online marketing research is growing rapidly, both quantitative and qualitative Web-based research does have some drawbacks. One major problem is controlling who's in the online sample. Without seeing respondents, it's difficult to know who they really are. To overcome such sample and context problems, many online research firms use opt-in communities and respondent panels. For example, Zoomerang offers an online consumer and business panel profiled on more than 500 attributes.[19] Alternatively, many companies are now developing their own custom social networks and using them to gain customer inputs and insights. ● Consider adidas:[20]

> When adidas developed a Facebook fan page, it quickly attracted 2 million users. Ditto for its pages on Twitter and YouTube. But monitoring and analyzing postings by two million members in public online communities isn't realistic, so the sporting goods giant created its own private online community called adidas

Online focus groups
Gathering a small group of people online with a trained moderator to chat about a product, service, or organization and gain qualitative insights about consumer attitudes and behavior.

● Online customer social networks—such as Adidas Insiders—can help companies gain customer inputs and insights. Adidas Insiders are surprisingly willing—and even anxious—to be involved.

Insiders, inviting only the most active users on its public pages to join. Through online conversations with and among adidas Insiders, company marketers can quickly gather real-time consumer feedback about brand perceptions, product ideas, and marketing campaigns. Adidas Insiders are surprisingly willing—and even anxious—to be involved. "It's a great help to [us] spending time with consumers that love the brand as much as we do," says adidas's director of digital media.

Testing strategies and concepts with the Insiders group provides fast and actionable customer insights for adidas's product marketing teams. "We're able to play with colors and materials and get instant feedback from these fans, which allows us to be more efficient in development and go-to-market planning," says the adidas marketing executive. "We've even asked about things like voiceovers for videos and received surprising feedback that's caused us to alter creative."

Thus, in recent years, the Internet has become an important new tool for conducting research and developing customer insights. But today's marketing researchers are going even further on the Web—well beyond structured online surveys, focus groups, and Web communities. Increasingly, they are listening to and watching consumers by actively mining the rich veins of unsolicited, unstructured, "bottom up" customer information already coursing around the Web. This might be as simple as scanning customer reviews and comments on the company's brand site or shopping sites such as Amazon.com or BestBuy.com. Or it might mean using sophisticated Web-analysis tools to deeply analyze mountains of consumer comments and messages found in blogs or on social networking sites, such as Facebook or Twitter. Listening to and watching consumers online can provide valuable insights into what consumers are saying or feeling about brands. As one information expert puts it, "The Web knows what you want."[21] (See Real Marketing 4.2.)

Perhaps the most explosive issue facing online researchers concerns consumer privacy. Some critics fear that unethical researchers will use the e-mail addresses and confidential responses gathered through surveys to sell products after the research is completed. They are concerned about the use of technologies that collect personal information online without the respondents' consent. Failure to address such privacy issues could result in angry, less-cooperative consumers and increased government intervention. Despite these concerns, most industry insiders predict continued healthy growth for online marketing research.[22]

Sampling Plan

Sample
A segment of the population selected for marketing research to represent the population as a whole.

Marketing researchers usually draw conclusions about large groups of consumers by studying a small sample of the total consumer population. A **sample** is a segment of the population selected for marketing research to represent the population as a whole. Ideally, the sample should be representative so that the researcher can make accurate estimates of the thoughts and behaviors of the larger population.

Designing the sample requires three decisions. First, *who* is to be studied (what *sampling unit*)? The answer to this question is not always obvious. For example, to learn about the decision-making process for a family automobile purchase, should the subject be the husband, the wife, other family members, dealership salespeople, or all of these? Second, *how many* people should be included (what *sample size*)? Large samples give more reliable results than small samples. However, larger samples usually cost more, and it is not necessary to sample the entire target market or even a large portion to get reliable results.

Finally, *how* should the people in the sample be *chosen* (what *sampling procedure*)? ⦿ **Table 4.4** describes different kinds of samples. Using *probability samples*, each population member has a known chance of being included in the sample, and researchers can calculate confidence limits for sampling error. But when probability sampling costs too much or takes too much time, marketing researchers often take *nonprobability samples*, even though their sampling error cannot be measured. These varied ways of drawing samples have different costs and time limitations as well as different accuracy and statistical properties. Which method is best depends on the needs of the research project.

Real Marketing 4.2

Listening Online:
The Web Knows What You Want

"Are your ears burning?" asks an online marketing analyst. "Someone's surely talking about you [on the Web], and it might be worth your while to listen in." Thanks to the burgeoning world of blogs, social networks, and other Internet forums, marketers now have near-real-time access to a flood of online consumer information. It's all there for the digging—praise, criticism, recommendations, actions—revealed in what consumers are saying and doing as they ply the Internet. Forward-looking marketers are now mining valuable customer insights from this rich new vein of unprompted, "bottom-up" information.

Whereas traditional marketing research provides insights into the "logical, representative, structured aspect of our consumers," says Kristin Bush, senior manager of consumer and market knowledge at P&G, online listening "provides much more of the intensity, much more of the . . . context and the passion, and more of the spontaneity that consumers are truly giving you [when they offer up their opinions] unsolicited."

Listening online might involve something as simple as scanning customer reviews on the company's brand site or on popular shopping sites such as Amazon.com or Best Buy.com. Such reviews are plentiful, address specific products, and provide unvarnished customer reactions. Amazon.com alone features detailed customer reviews on everything it sells, and its customers rely heavily on these reviews when making purchases. If customers in the market for a company's brands are reading and reacting to such reviews, so should the company's marketers.

Many companies are now adding customer review sections to their own brand Web sites. "Sure, it's scary to let consumers say what they will about your products on your home turf," says an analyst. "But both the positive and negative feedback provides hints to what you're doing well and where improvement is needed." Negative reviews can provide early warning of product issues or consumer misunderstandings that need to be quickly addressed.

At a deeper level, marketers now employ sophisticated Web-analysis tools to listen in on and mine nuggets from the churning mass of consumer comments and conversations in blogs, in news articles, in online forums, and on social networking sites such as Facebook or Twitter. But beyond monitoring what customers are *saying* about them online, companies are also watching what customers are *doing* online. Marketers scrutinize consumer Web-browsing behavior in precise detail and use the resulting insights to personalize shopping experiences. Consider this example:

A shopper at the retail site FigLeaves.com takes a close look at a silky pair of women's slippers. Next, a recommendation appears for a man's bathrobe. This could seem terribly wrong—unless, of course, it turns out to be precisely what she wanted. Why the bathrobe? Analysis of FigLeaves.com site behavior data—from mouse clicks to search queries—shows that certain types of female shoppers at certain times of the week are likely to be shopping for men. What a given customer sees at the site might also depend on other behaviors. For example, shoppers who seem pressed for time (say, shopping from work and clicking rapidly from screen to screen) might see more simplified pages with a direct path to the shopping cart and checkout. Alternatively, more leisurely shoppers (say, those shopping from home or on weekends and browsing product reviews) might receive pages with more features, video clips, and comparison information. The goal of such analysis is to teach Web sites "something close to the savvy of a flesh-and-blood sales clerk," says a Web-analytics expert. "In the first five minutes in a store, the sales guy is observing a customer's body language and tone of voice. We have to teach machines to pick up on those same insights from movements online."

More broadly, information about what consumers do while trolling the vast expanse of the Internet—what searches they make, the sites they visit, what they buy—is pure gold to marketers. And today's marketers are busy mining that gold.

On the Internet today, everybody knows who you are. In fact, legions of Internet companies also know your gender, your age, the neighborhood you live in, that you like pickup trucks, and that you spent, say, three hours and 43 seconds on a Web site for pet lovers on

Online listening, behavioral targeting, social targeting—wherever you go on the Internet, marketers are looking over your shoulder to mine consumer insights. Is it smart marketing or just "a little bit creepy"?

Continued on next page

a rainy day in January. All that data streams through myriad computer networks, where it's sorted, cataloged, analyzed, and then used to deliver ads aimed squarely at you, potentially anywhere you travel on the Web. It's called *behavioral targeting*—tracking consumers' online behavior and using it to target ads to them. So, for example, if you place a cell phone in your Amazon.com shopping cart but don't buy it, you might expect to see some ads for that very type of phone the next time you visit your favorite ESPN site to catch up on the latest sports scores.

That's amazing enough, but the newest wave of Web analytics and targeting take online eavesdropping even further—from *behavioral* targeting to *social* targeting. Whereas behavioral targeting tracks consumer movements across Web sites, social targeting also mines individual online social connections.

"It's getting back to the old adage that birds of a feather flock together," says a social targeting expert. Research shows that consumers shop a lot like their friends and are five times more likely to respond to ads from brands friends use. So identifying and targeting friends of current prospects makes sense. Social targeting links customer data to social interaction data from social networking sites. In effect, it matches a prospect with his or her closest connections and targets them as well.

This can stretch a marketing campaign that would have reached one million prospects into one that reaches eight million or ten million prospects, most of them new.

Online listening. Behavioral targeting. Social targeting. All of these are great for marketers as they work to mine customer insights from the massive amounts of consumer information swirling around the Web. The biggest question? You've probably already guessed it. As marketers get more adept at trolling blogs, social networks, and other Web domains, what happens to consumer privacy? Yup, that's the downside. At what point does sophisticated Web research cross the line into consumer stalking? Proponents claim that behavioral and social targeting benefit more than abuse consumers by feeding back ads and products that are more relevant to their interests. But to many consumers and public advocates, following consumers online and stalking them with ads feels more than just a little creepy. Behavioral targeting, for example, has already been the subject of congressional and regulatory hearings.

Despite such concerns, however, online listening will continue to grow. And, with appropriate safeguards, it promises benefits for both companies and customers. Tapping into online conversations and behavior lets companies "get the unprompted voice of the consumer, the real sentiments, the real values, and the real points of view that they have of our products and services," says P&G's Bush. "Companies that figure out how to listen and respond . . . in a meaningful, valuable way are going to win in the marketplace." After all, knowing what customers really want is an essential first step in creating customer value. And, as one online information expert puts it, "The Web knows what you want."

Sources: Adapted excerpts, quotes, and other information from Stephen Baker, "The Web Knows What You Want," *BusinessWeek*, July 27, 2009, p. 48; Brian Morrissey, "Connect the Thoughts," *Adweek*, June 29, 2009, pp. 10–11; Paul Sloan, "The Quest for the Perfect Online Ad," *Business 2.0*, March 2007, p. 88; Abbey Klaassen, "Forget Twitter; Your Best Marketing Tool Is the Humble Product Review," *Advertising Age*, June 29, 2009, pp. 1, 17; David Wiesenfeld, Kristin Bush, and Ronjan Sikdar, "Listen Up: Online Yields New Research Pathway," *Nielsen Consumer Insights*, August 2009, http://en-us.nielsen.com/; and Elizabeth A. Sullivan, "10 Minutes with Kristin Bush," *Marketing News*, September 30, 2009, pp. 26–28.

⊙ TABLE | 4.4   Types of Samples

Probability Sample

Simple random sample	Every member of the population has a known and equal chance of selection.
Stratified random sample	The population is divided into mutually exclusive groups (such as age groups), and random samples are drawn from each group.
Cluster (area) sample	The population is divided into mutually exclusive groups (such as blocks), and the researcher draws a sample of the groups to interview.

Nonprobability Sample

Convenience sample	The researcher selects the easiest population members from which to obtain information.
Judgment sample	The researcher uses his or her judgment to select population members who are good prospects for accurate information.
Quota sample	The researcher finds and interviews a prescribed number of people in each of several categories.

Research Instruments

In collecting primary data, marketing researchers have a choice of two main research instruments: the *questionnaire* and *mechanical devices*.

Questionnaires. The questionnaire is by far the most common instrument, whether administered in person, by phone, by e-mail, or online. Questionnaires are very flexible—there are many ways to ask questions. Closed-end questions include all the possible answers, and subjects make choices among them. Examples include multiple-choice questions and scale questions. Open-end questions allow respondents to answer in their own words. In a survey of airline users, Southwest Airlines might simply ask, "What is your opinion of Southwest Airlines?" Or it might ask people to complete a sentence: "When I choose an airline, the most important consideration is. . . ." These and other kinds of open-end questions often reveal more than closed-end questions because they do not limit respondents' answers.

Open-end questions are especially useful in exploratory research, when the researcher is trying to find out *what* people think but is not measuring *how many* people think in a certain way. Closed-end questions, on the other hand, provide answers that are easier to interpret and tabulate.

Researchers should also use care in the *wording* and *ordering* of questions. They should use simple, direct, and unbiased wording. Questions should be arranged in a logical order. The first question should create interest if possible, and difficult or personal questions should be asked last so that respondents do not become defensive.

⦿ **Mechanical instruments: To find out what ads work and why, Disney researchers have developed an array of devices to track eye movement, monitor heart rates, and measure other physical responses.**

Mechanical Instruments. Although questionnaires are the most common research instrument, researchers also use mechanical instruments to monitor consumer behavior. Nielsen Media Research attaches people meters to television sets, cable boxes, and satellite systems in selected homes to record who watches which programs. Retailers use checkout scanners to record shoppers' purchases.

Other mechanical devices measure subjects' physical responses. ⦿ For example, consider Disney Media Networks' new consumer research lab in Austin, Texas:[23]

A technician in a black lab coat gazed at the short, middle-aged man seated inside Disney's secretive new research facility, his face shrouded with eye-tracking goggles. "Read ESPN.com on that BlackBerry," she told him soothingly, like a nurse about to draw blood. "And have fun," she added, leaving the room. In reality, the man's appetite for sports news was not of interest. (The site was a fake version anyway.) Rather, the technician and her fellow researchers from Disney Media Networks—which includes ABC, ESPN, and other networks—were eager to know how the man responded to ads of varying size. How small could the banners become and still draw his attention? A squadron of Disney executives scrutinized the data as it flowed in real time onto television monitors in an adjacent room. "He's not even looking at the banner now," said one researcher. The man clicked to another page. "There we go, that one's drawing his attention." The tools are advanced: In addition to tracking eye movement, the research team uses heart-rate monitors, skin temperature readings, and facial expressions (probes are attached to facial muscles) to gauge reactions. The goal: to learn what works and what does not in the high-stakes game of new media advertising.

Still other researchers are applying "neuromarketing," measuring brain activity to learn how consumers feel and respond. Marketing scientists using MRI scans and EEG devices have learned that tracking brain electrical activity and blood flow can provide companies with insights into what turns consumers on and off regarding their brands and marketing. "Companies have always aimed for the customers heart, but the head may make a better target," suggests one neuromarketer. "Neuromarketing is reaching consumers where the action is: the brain."[24]

Companies ranging from Hyundai and PepsiCo to Google and Microsoft now hire neuromarketing research companies such as NeuroFocus and EmSense to help figure out what people are really thinking.[25]

Thirty men and women are studying a sporty silver test model of a next-generation Hyundai. The 15 men and 15 women are asked to stare at specific parts of the vehicle, including the bumper, the windshield, and the tires. Electrode-studded caps on their heads capture the electrical activity in their brains as they view the car for an hour. That brain-wave information is recorded in a hard drive each person wears on a belt. Hyundai believes that their brain activity will show preferences that could lead to purchasing decisions. "We want to know what consumers think about a car before we start manufacturing thousands of them," says Hyundai America's manager of brand strategy. He expects the carmaker will tweak the exterior based on the EEG reports, which track activity in all parts of the brain.

Similarly, PepsiCo's Frito-Lay unit uses neuromarketing to test commercials, product designs, and packaging. Recent EEG tests showed that, compared with shiny packages showing pictures of potato chips, matte beige bags showing potatoes and other healthy ingredients trigger less activity in an area of the brain associated with feelings of guilt. Needless to say, Frito-Lay quickly switched away from the shiny packaging. And eBay's PayPal began pitching its online payment service as "fast" after brain-wave research showed that speed turns consumers on more than security and safety, earlier themes used in eBay ad campaigns.

Although neuromarketing techniques can measure consumer involvement and emotional responses second by second, such brain responses can be difficult to interpret. Thus, neuromarketing is usually used in combination with other research approaches to gain a more complete picture of what goes on inside consumers' heads.

Implementing the Research Plan

The researcher next puts the marketing research plan into action. This involves collecting, processing, and analyzing the information. Data collection can be carried out by the company's marketing research staff or outside firms. Researchers should watch closely to make sure that the plan is implemented correctly. They must guard against problems with interacting with respondents, with the quality of participants' response, and with interviewers who make mistakes or take shortcuts.

Researchers must also process and analyze the collected data to isolate important information and insight. They need to check data for accuracy and completeness and code it for analysis. The researchers then tabulate the results and compute statistical measures.

Interpreting and Reporting the Findings

The market researcher must now interpret the findings, draw conclusions, and report them to management. The researcher should not try to overwhelm managers with numbers and fancy statistical techniques. Rather, the researcher should present important findings and insights that are useful in the major decisions faced by management.

However, interpretation should not be left only to researchers. They are often experts in research design and statistics, but the marketing manager knows more about the problem and the decisions that must be made. The best research means little if the manager blindly accepts faulty interpretations from the researcher. Similarly, managers may be biased; they might tend to accept research results that show what they expected and reject those that they did not expect or hope for. In many cases, findings can be interpreted in different ways, and discussions between researchers and managers will help point to the best interpretations. Thus, managers and researchers must work together closely when interpreting research results, and both must share responsibility for the research process and resulting decisions.

Analyzing and Using Marketing Information (pp 119–121)

Information gathered in internal databases and through competitive marketing intelligence and marketing research usually requires additional analysis. Managers may need help applying the information to gain customer and market insights that will improve their marketing decisions. This help may include advanced statistical analysis to learn more about the relationships within a set of data. Information analysis might also involve the application of analytical models that will help marketers make better decisions.

Once the information has been processed and analyzed, it must be made available to the right decision makers at the right time. In the following sections, we look deeper into analyzing and using marketing information.

Customer Relationship Management

> **Author Comment** We've talked generally about managing customer relationships throughout the book. But here, "customer relationship management" (CRM) has a much narrower data-management meaning. It refers to capturing and using customer data from all sources to manage customer interactions and build customer relationships.

The question of how best to analyze and use individual customer data presents special problems. Most companies are awash in information about their customers. In fact, smart companies capture information at every possible customer *touch point*. These touch points include customer purchases, sales force contacts, service and support calls, Web site visits, satisfaction surveys, credit and payment interactions, market research studies—every contact between a customer and a company.

Unfortunately, this information is usually scattered widely across the organization. It is buried deep in the separate databases and records of different company departments. To overcome such problems, many companies are now turning to **customer relationship management (CRM)** to manage detailed information about individual customers and carefully manage customer touch points to maximize customer loyalty.

CRM first burst onto the scene in the early 2000s. Many companies rushed in, implementing overly ambitious CRM programs that produced disappointing results and many failures. More recently, however, companies are moving ahead more cautiously and implementing CRM systems that really work. Last year, companies worldwide spent $7.8 billion on CRM systems from companies such as Oracle, Microsoft, Salesforce.com, and SAS, up 14.2 percent from the previous year. By 2012, they will spend an estimated $13.3 billion on CRM systems.[26]

CRM consists of sophisticated software and analytical tools that integrate customer information from all sources, analyze it in depth, and apply the results to build stronger customer relationships. CRM integrates everything that a company's sales, service, and marketing teams know about individual customers, providing a 360-degree view of the customer relationship.

CRM analysts develop *data warehouses* and use sophisticated *data mining* techniques to unearth the riches hidden in customer data. A data warehouse is a company-wide electronic database of finely detailed customer information that needs to be sifted through for gems. The purpose of a data warehouse is not only to gather information but also pull it together into a central, accessible location. Then, once the data warehouse brings the data together, the company uses high-powered data mining techniques to sift through the mounds of data and dig out interesting findings about customers.

These findings often lead to marketing opportunities. For example, Walmart's huge database provides deep insights for marketing decisions. A few years ago, as Hurricane Ivan roared toward the Florida coast, reports one observer, the giant retailer "knew exactly what to rush onto the shelves of stores in the hurricane's path—strawberry Pop Tarts. By

Customer relationship management (CRM)
Managing detailed information about individual customers and carefully managing customer touch points to maximize customer loyalty.

● Grocery chain Kroger works with data mining firm Dunnhumby to dig deeply into data obtained from customer loyalty cards. It uses the customer insights gained for everything from targeting coupons to locating and stocking its stores.

mining years of sales data from just prior to other hurricanes, [Walmart] figured out that shoppers would stock up on Pop Tarts—which don't require refrigeration or cooking."[27]

● Grocery chain Kroger works with the data mining firm Dunnhumby, which it co-owns with successful London-based retailer Tesco, to dig deeply into data obtained from customer loyalty cards. It uses the customer insights gained for everything from targeting coupons to locating and stocking its stores:[28]

Lisa Williams has never liked sorting through coupons, and she no longer has to at Kroger grocery stores. Every few weeks, a personalized assortment of coupons arrives from Kroger in Williams' Elizabethtown, Kentucky, mailbox for items she usually loads into her cart: Capri Sun drinks for her two children, Reynolds Wrap foil, Hellmann's mayonnaise. While Kroger is building loyalty—with 95 percent of a recent mailing tailored to specific households—Williams is saving money without searching through dozens of pages of coupons. Although the recent recession revived penny-pinching, Americans are still redeeming only 1 percent to 3 percent of paper coupons. In contrast, Kroger says as many as *half* the coupons it sends to regular customers do get used.

Kroger digs deep into the reams of information from its more than 55 million shopper cards and uses the resulting insights, augmented with customer interviews, to guide strategies for tailored promotions, pricing, placement, and even stocking variations from store to store. Such personalization creates more value for customers and makes them feel more appreciated. In turn, Kroger's ability to turn data into insights builds customer loyalty and drives profitable sales. Says Kroger's CEO, "This level of personalization is a direct link to our customers that no other U.S. grocery retailer can [match]."

By using CRM to understand customers better, companies can provide higher levels of customer service and develop deeper customer relationships. They can use CRM to pinpoint high-value customers, target them more effectively, cross-sell the company's products, and create offers tailored to specific customer requirements.

CRM benefits don't come without costs or risk, either in collecting the original customer data or in maintaining and mining it. The most common CRM mistake is to view CRM as a technology and software solution only. Yet technology alone cannot build profitable customer relationships. Companies can improve customer relationships by simply installing some new software. Instead, CRM is just one part of an effective overall *customer relationship management strategy*. "There's lots of talk about CRM and these days it usually has to do with a software solution," says one analyst. But marketers should start by adhering to "some basic tenets of actual customer relationship management—and *then* empower them with high-tech solutions."[29] They should focus first on the *R*; it's the *relationship* that CRM is all about.

Distributing and Using Marketing Information

Marketing information has no value until it is used to gain customer insights and make better marketing decisions. Thus, the marketing information system must make the information readily available to managers and others who need it. In some cases, this means providing managers with regular performance reports, intelligence updates, and reports on the results of research studies.

But marketing managers may also need nonroutine information for special situations and on-the-spot decisions. For example, a sales manager having trouble with a large customer may want a summary of the account's sales and profitability over the past year. Or a retail store manager who has run out of a best-selling product may want to know the current inventory levels in the chain's other stores. These days, therefore, information distribution involves entering information into databases and making it available in a timely, user-friendly way.

Many firms use a company *intranet* and internal CRM systems to facilitate this process. The internal information systems provide ready access to research information, customer contact information, reports, shared work documents, contact information for employees and other stakeholders, and more. For example, the CRM system at phone and online gift retailer 1-800-Flowers gives customer-facing employees real-time access to customer information. When a repeat customer calls, the system immediately calls up data on previous transactions and other contacts, helping reps make the customer's experience easier and more relevant. For instance, "if a customer usually buys tulips for his wife, we [talk about] our newest and best tulip selections," says the company's vice president of customer knowledge management. "No one else in the business is able to connect customer information with real-time transaction data the way we can."[30]

In addition, companies are increasingly allowing key customers and value-network members to access account, product, and other data on demand through *extranets*. Suppliers, customers, resellers, and select other network members may access a company's extranet to update their accounts, arrange purchases, and check orders against inventories to improve customer service. ⬤ For example, Penske Truck Leasing's extranet site, MyFleetAtPenske.com, lets Penske customers access all the data about their fleets in one spot and provides an array of tools and applications designed to help fleet managers manage their Penske accounts and maximize efficiency.[31]

⬤ **Extranets:** Penske Truck Leasing's extranet site, MyFleetAtPenske.com, lets Penske customers access all of the data about their fleets in one spot and provides tools to help fleet managers manage their Penske accounts and maximize efficiency.

Thanks to modern technology, today's marketing managers can gain direct access to the information system at any time and from virtually any location. They can tap into the system while working at a home office, from a hotel room, or from the local Starbucks through a wireless network—anyplace where they can turn on a laptop or BlackBerry. Such systems allow managers to get the information they need directly and quickly and tailor it to their own needs.

> **Author Comment** | We finish this chapter by examining three special marketing information topics.

Other Marketing Information Considerations (pp 121–126)

This section discusses marketing information in two special contexts: marketing research in small businesses and nonprofit organizations and international marketing research. Finally, we look at public policy and ethics issues in marketing research.

Marketing Research in Small Businesses and Nonprofit Organizations

Just like larger firms, small organizations need market information and the customer and market insights that it can provide. Managers of small businesses and nonprofit organizations often think that marketing research can be done only by experts in large companies with big research budgets. True, large-scale research studies are beyond the budgets of most

● **Before opening Bibbentuckers dry cleaner, owner Robert Byerley conducted research to gain insights into what customers wanted. First on the list: quality.**

small businesses. However, many of the marketing research techniques discussed in this chapter also can be used by smaller organizations in a less formal manner and at little or no expense. ● Consider how one small-business owner conducted market research on a shoestring before even opening his doors:[32]

After a string of bad experiences with his local dry cleaner, Robert Byerley decided to open his own dry-cleaning business. But before jumping in, he conducted plenty of market research. He needed a key customer insight: How would he make his business stand out from the others? To start, Byerley spent an entire week in the library and online, researching the dry-cleaning industry. To get input from potential customers, using a marketing firm, Byerley held focus groups on the store's name, look, and brochure. He also took clothes to the 15 best competing cleaners in town and had focus group members critique their work. Based on his research, he made a list of features for his new business. First on his list: quality. His business would stand behind everything it did. Not on the list: cheap prices. Creating the perfect dry-cleaning establishment simply didn't fit with a discount operation.

With his research complete, Byerley opened Bibbentuckers, a high-end dry cleaner positioned on high-quality service and convenience. It featured a banklike drive-through area with curbside delivery. A computerized bar code system read customer cleaning preferences and tracked clothes all the way through the cleaning process. Byerley added other differentiators, such as decorative awnings, TV screens, and refreshments (even "candy for the kids and a doggy treat for your best friend"). "I wanted a place . . . that paired five-star service and quality with an establishment that didn't look like a dry cleaner," he says. The market research yielded results. Today, Bibbentuckers is a thriving six-store operation.

"Too [few] small-business owners have a . . . marketing mind-set," says a small-business consultant. "You have to think like Procter & Gamble. What would they do before launching a new product? They would find out who their customer is and who their competition is."[33]

Thus, small businesses and not-for-profit organizations can obtain good marketing insights through observation or informal surveys using small convenience samples. Also, many associations, local media, and government agencies provide special help to small organizations. For example, the U.S. Small Business Administration offers dozens of free publications and a Web site (www.sba.gov) that give advice on topics ranging from starting, financing, and expanding a small business to ordering business cards. Other excellent Web resources for small businesses include the U.S. Census Bureau (www.census.gov) and the Bureau of Economic Analysis (www.bea.gov). Finally, small businesses can collect a considerable amount of information at very little cost online. They can scour competitor and customer Web sites and use Internet search engines to research specific companies and issues.

In summary, secondary data collection, observation, surveys, and experiments can all be used effectively by small organizations with small budgets. However, although these informal research methods are less complex and less costly, they still must be conducted with care. Managers must think carefully about the objectives of the research, formulate questions in advance, recognize the biases introduced by smaller samples and less skilled researchers, and conduct the research systematically.[34]

International Marketing Research

International marketing research has grown tremendously over the past decade. International researchers follow the same steps as domestic researchers, from defining the research problem and developing a research plan to interpreting and reporting the results. However, these researchers often face more and different problems. Whereas domestic researchers deal with fairly homogeneous markets within a single country, international researchers deal with diverse markets in many different countries. These markets often vary greatly in their levels of economic development, cultures and customs, and buying patterns.

In many foreign markets, the international researcher may have a difficult time finding good secondary data. Whereas U.S. marketing researchers can obtain reliable secondary data from dozens of domestic research services, many countries have almost no research services at all. Some of the largest international research services do operate in many countries. ● For example, The Nielsen Company (the world's largest marketing research company) has offices in more than 100 countries, from Schaumburg, Illinois, to Hong Kong to Nicosia, Cyprus.[35] However, most research firms operate in only a relative handful of countries only. Thus, even when secondary information is available, it usually must be obtained from many different sources on a country-by-country basis, making the information difficult to combine or compare.

Because of the scarcity of good secondary data, international researchers often must collect their own primary data. For example, they may find it difficult simply to develop good samples. U.S. researchers can use current telephone directories, e-mail lists, census tract data, and any of several sources of socioeconomic data to construct samples. However, such information is largely lacking in many countries.

Once the sample is drawn, the U.S. researcher usually can reach most respondents easily by telephone, by mail, on the Internet, or in person. Reaching respondents is often not so easy in other parts of the world. Researchers in Mexico cannot rely on telephone, Internet, and mail data collection; most data collection is

● **Some of the largest research services firms have large international organizations. The Nielsen Company has offices in more than 100 countries.**

door to door and concentrated in three or four of the largest cities. In some countries, few people have phones or personal computers. For example, whereas there are 74 Internet users per 100 people in the United States, there are only 21 Internet users per 100 people in Mexico. In Kenya, the numbers drop to 8 Internet users per 100 people. In some countries, the postal system is notoriously unreliable. In Brazil, for instance, an estimated 30 percent of the mail is never delivered. In many developing countries, poor roads and transportation systems make certain areas hard to reach, making personal interviews difficult and expensive.[36]

Cultural differences from country to country cause additional problems for international researchers. Language is the most obvious obstacle. For example, questionnaires must be prepared in one language and then translated into the languages of each country researched. Responses then must be translated back into the original language for analysis and interpretation. This adds to research costs and increases the risks of error.

Translating a questionnaire from one language to another is anything but easy. Many idioms, phrases, and statements mean different things in different cultures. For example, a Danish executive noted, "Check this out by having a different translator put back into English what you've translated from English. You'll get the shock of your life. I remember [an example in which] 'out of sight, out of mind' had become 'invisible things are insane.'"[37]

Consumers in different countries also vary in their attitudes toward marketing research. People in one country may be very willing to respond; in other countries, nonresponse can be a major problem. Customs in some countries may prohibit people from talking with strangers. In certain cultures, research questions often are considered too personal. For example, in many Muslim countries, mixed-gender focus groups are taboo, as is videotaping female-only focus groups. Even when respondents are *willing* to respond, they may not be *able* to because of high functional illiteracy rates.

Despite these problems, as global marketing grows, global companies have little choice but to conduct such international marketing research. Although the costs and problems associated with international research may be high, the costs of not doing it—in terms of missed opportunities and mistakes—might be even higher. Once recognized, many of the problems associated with international marketing research can be overcome or avoided.

Public Policy and Ethics in Marketing Research

Most marketing research benefits both the sponsoring company and its consumers. Through marketing research, companies gain insights into consumers' needs, resulting in more satisfying products and services and stronger customer relationships. However, the misuse of marketing research can also harm or annoy consumers. Two major public policy and ethics issues in marketing research are intrusions on consumer privacy and the misuse of research findings.

Intrusions on Consumer Privacy

Many consumers feel positive about marketing research and believe that it serves a useful purpose. Some actually enjoy being interviewed and giving their opinions. However, others strongly resent or even mistrust marketing research. They don't like being interrupted by researchers. They worry that marketers are building huge databases full of personal information about customers. Or they fear that researchers might use sophisticated techniques to probe our deepest feelings, peek over our shoulders as we shop, or eavesdrop on our conversations and then use this knowledge to manipulate our buying.

There are no easy answers when it comes to marketing research and privacy. For example, is it a good or bad thing that marketers track and analyze consumers' Web clicks and target ads to individuals based on their browsing and social networking behavior? Similarly, should we applaud or resent companies that monitor consumer discussions on YouTube, Facebook, Twitter, or other public social networks in an effort to be more responsive? For example, Dell uses Radian6 to routinely track social media conversations and often responds quickly. Someone commenting about Dell on a popular blog might be surprised by a response from a Dell representative within only a few hours. Dell views such monitoring as an opportunity to engage consumers in helpful two-way conversations. However, some disconcerted consumers might see it as an intrusion on their privacy.

Consumers may also have been taken in by previous "research surveys" that actually turned out to be attempts to sell them something. Still other consumers confuse legitimate marketing research studies with promotional efforts and say "no" before the interviewer can even begin. Most, however, simply resent the intrusion. They dislike mail, telephone, or Web surveys that are too long or too personal or that interrupt them at inconvenient times.

Increasing consumer resentment has become a major problem for the marketing research industry, leading to lower survey response rates in recent years. Just as companies face the challenge of unearthing valuable but potentially sensitive consumer data while also maintaining consumer trust, consumers wrestle with the trade-offs between personalization and privacy. Although many consumers willingly exchange personal information for free services, easy credit, discounts, upgrades, and all sorts of rewards, they also worry about the growth in online identity theft.

A study by TRUSTe, an organization that monitors the privacy practices of Web sites, found that more than 90 percent of respondents view online privacy as a "really" or "somewhat" important issue. More than 75 percent agreed with the statement, "The Internet is not well regulated, and naïve users can easily be taken advantage of." And 66 percent of Americans do not want marketers to track their online behavior and tailor advertisements to their interests. So it's no surprise that they are now less than willing to reveal personal information on Web sites.[38]

The marketing research industry is considering several options for responding to this problem. One example is the Marketing Research Association's "Your Opinion Counts" and "Respondent Bill of Rights" initiatives to educate consumers about the benefits of marketing research and distinguish it from telephone selling and database building. The industry also has considered adopting broad standards, perhaps based on the International Chamber of Commerce's International Code of Marketing and Social Research Practice. This code outlines researchers' responsibilities to respondents and the general public. For example, it says that researchers should make their names and addresses available to participants. It also bans companies from representing activities such as database compilation or sales and promotional pitches as research.[39]

Most major companies—including IBM, Facebook, Citigroup, American Express, and Microsoft—have now appointed a chief privacy officer (CPO), whose job is to safeguard the privacy of consumers who do business with the company. IBM's CPO claims that her job requires "multidisciplinary thinking and attitude." She needs to get all company departments, from technology, legal, and accounting to marketing and communications working together to safeguard customer privacy.[40]

In the end, if researchers provide value in exchange for information, customers will gladly provide it. For example, Amazon.com's customers do not mind if the firm builds a database of products they buy as a way to provide future product recommendations. This saves time and provides value. Similarly, Bizrate users gladly complete surveys rating online seller sites because they can view the overall ratings of others when making purchase decisions. The best approach is for researchers to ask only for the information they need, use it responsibly to provide customer value, and avoid sharing information without the customer's permission.

Misuse of Research Findings

Research studies can be powerful persuasion tools; companies often use study results as claims in their advertising and promotion. Today, however, many research studies appear to be little more than vehicles for pitching the sponsor's products. In fact, in some cases, the research surveys appear to have been designed just to produce the intended effect. Few advertisers openly rig their research designs or blatantly misrepresent the findings; most abuses tend to be more subtle "stretches." ⊙ Consider the following example:

Based on a scientific study, the Kellogg Company recently proclaimed in ads and on packaging for Frosted Mini-Wheats that the cereal was "clinically shown to improve kids attentiveness by nearly 20%." When challenged by the Federal Trade Commission, however, the claims turned out to be a substantial stretch of the study results. Fine print at the bottom of the box revealed the following: "Based upon independent clinical research, kids who ate Kellogg's Frosted Mini-Wheats cereal for breakfast had up to 18 percent better attentiveness three hours after breakfast than kids who ate no breakfast." That is, as one critic noted, "Frosted Mini-Wheats are (up to) 18 percent better than starving." Moreover, according to the FTC complaint, the clinical study referred to by Kellogg actually showed that children who ate the cereal for breakfast *averaged* just under 11 percent better in attentiveness than children who ate no breakfast, and that only about one in nine improved by 20 percent or more. Kellogg

⊙ Misuse of research findings: The Federal Trade Commission recently challenged research-based advertising and packaging claims that Kellogg's Frosted Mini-Wheats were "clinically shown to improve kids attentiveness by nearly 20%."

settled with the FTC, agreeing to refrain from making unsubstantiated health claims about Frosted Mini-Wheats or other products and from misrepresenting the results of scientific tests.[41]

Recognizing that surveys can be abused, several associations—including the American Marketing Association, the Marketing Research Association, and the Council of American Survey Research Organizations (CASRO)—have developed codes of research ethics and standards of conduct. For example, the CASRO Code of Standards and Ethics for Survey Research outlines researcher responsibilities to respondents, including confidentiality, privacy, and avoidance of harassment. It also outlines major responsibilities in reporting results to clients and the public.[42]

In the end, however, unethical or inappropriate actions cannot simply be regulated away. Each company must accept responsibility for policing the conduct and reporting of its own marketing research to protect consumers' best interests and its own.

REVIEWING Objectives AND KEY Terms

To create value for customers and build meaningful relationships with them, marketers must first gain fresh, deep insights into what customers need and want. Such insights come from good marketing information. As a result of the recent explosion of marketing technology, companies can now obtain great quantities of information, sometimes even too much. The challenge is to transform today's vast volume of consumer information into actionable customer and market insights.

Objective 1 Explain the importance of information in gaining insights about the marketplace and customers. (pp 98–100)

The marketing process starts with a complete understanding of the marketplace and consumer needs and wants. Thus, the company needs sound information to produce superior value and satisfaction for its customers. The company also requires information on competitors, resellers, and other actors and forces in the marketplace. Increasingly, marketers are viewing information not only as an input for making better decisions but also as an important strategic asset and marketing tool.

Objective 2 Define the marketing information system and discuss its parts. (pp 100–102)

The *marketing information system* (*MIS*) consists of people and procedures for assessing information needs, developing the needed information, and helping decision makers use the information to generate and validate actionable customer and market insights. A well-designed information system begins and ends with users.

The MIS first *assesses information needs*. The MIS primarily serves the company's marketing and other managers, but it may also provide information to external partners. Then the MIS *develops information* from internal databases, marketing intelligence activities, and marketing research. *Internal databases* provide information on the company's own operations and departments. Such data can be obtained quickly and cheaply but often needs to be adapted for marketing decisions. *Marketing intelligence* activities supply everyday information about develop-

ments in the external marketing environment. *Market research* consists of collecting information relevant to a specific marketing problem faced by the company. Lastly, the MIS helps users analyze and use the information to develop customer insights, make marketing decisions, and manage customer relationships.

Objective 3 Outline the steps in the marketing research process. (pp 103–119)

The first step in the marketing research process involves *defining the problem and setting the research objectives*, which may be exploratory, descriptive, or causal research. The second step consists of *developing a research plan* for collecting data from primary and secondary sources. The third step calls for *implementing the marketing research plan* by gathering, processing, and analyzing the information. The fourth step consists of *interpreting and reporting the findings*. Additional information analysis helps marketing managers apply the information and provides them with sophisticated statistical procedures and models from which to develop more rigorous findings.

Both *internal* and *external* secondary data sources often provide information more quickly and at a lower cost than primary data sources, and they can sometimes yield information that a company cannot collect by itself. However, needed information might not exist in secondary sources. Researchers must also evaluate secondary information to ensure that it is *relevant, accurate, current*, and *impartial*.

Primary research must also be evaluated for these features. Each primary data collection method—*observational, survey*, and *experimental*—has its own advantages and disadvantages. Similarly, each of the various research contact methods—mail, telephone, personal interview, and online—also has its own advantages and drawbacks.

Objective 4 Explain how companies analyze and use marketing information. (pp 119–121)

Information gathered in internal databases and through marketing intelligence and marketing research usually requires more analysis. To analyze individual customer data, many companies have now acquired or developed special software and analysis techniques—called *customer relationship management (CRM)*—that integrate, analyze, and apply the mountains of individual customer data contained in their databases.

Marketing information has no value until it is used to make better marketing decisions. Thus, the MIS must make the information available to managers and others who make marketing decisions or deal with customers. In some cases, this means providing regular reports and updates; in other cases, it means making non-routine information available for special situations and on-the-spot decisions. Many firms use company intranets and extranets to facilitate this process. Thanks to modern technology, today's marketing managers can gain direct access to marketing information at any time and from virtually any location.

Objective 5 **Discuss the special issues some marketing researchers face, including public policy and ethics issues.** (pp 121–126)

Some marketers face special marketing research situations, such as those conducting research in small business, not-for-profit, or international situations. Marketing research can be conducted effectively by small businesses and nonprofit organizations with limited budgets. International marketing researchers follow the same steps as domestic researchers but often face more and different problems. All organizations need to act responsibly to major public policy and ethical issues surrounding marketing research, including issues of intrusions on consumer privacy and misuse of research findings.

KEY Terms

OBJECTIVE 1

Customer insights (p 99)
Marketing information system (MIS) (p 99)

OBJECTIVE 2

Internal databases (p 100)
Competitive marketing intelligence (p 101)

OBJECTIVE 3

Marketing research (p 103)
Exploratory research (p 103)
Descriptive research (p 103)
Causal research (p 103)
Secondary data (p 104)
Primary data (p 104)
Commercial online databases (p 106)
Observational research (p 107)
Ethnographic research (p 107)

Survey research (p 109)
Experimental research (p 110)
Focus group interviewing (p 111)
Online marketing research (p 112)
Online focus groups (p 113)
Sample (p 114)

OBJECTIVE 4

Customer relationship management (CRM; p 119)

PEARSON mymarketinglab

- Check your understanding of the concepts and key terms using the mypearsonmarketinglab study plan for this chapter.
- Apply the concepts in a business context using the simulation entitled **Marketing Research**.

DISCUSSING & APPLYING THE Concepts

Discussing the Concepts

1. Discuss the real value of marketing research and marketing information and how that value is attained. (AACSB: Communication)

2. Discuss the sources of internal data and the advantages and disadvantages associated with this data. (AACSB: Communication)

3. Explain the role of secondary data in gaining customer insights. Where do marketers obtain secondary data, and what are the potential problems in using such data? (AACSB: Communication)

4. What are the advantages of Web-based survey research over traditional survey research? (AACSB: Communication)

5. Compare open-ended and closed-ended questions. When and for what is each type of question useful in marketing research? (AACSB: Communication; Reflective Thinking)

6. What are the similarities and differences when conducting research in another country versus the domestic market? (AACSB: Communication)

Applying the Concepts

1. Perform an Internet search on "social media monitoring" to find companies that specialize in monitoring social media. Discuss two of these companies. Then find two more sites that allow free monitoring and describe how marketers can use these to monitor their brands. Write a brief report on your findings. (AACSB: Communication; Use of IT; Reflective Thinking)

2. Summarize an article describing a marketing research study. Describe how the data were collected. Is the research objective exploratory, descriptive, or causal? Explain your conclusions. (AACSB: Communication; Reflective Thinking)

3. Focus groups are commonly used during exploratory research. A focus group interview entails gathering a group of people to discuss a specific topic. In a small group, research how to conduct a focus group interview and then conduct one with six to ten other students to learn what services your university could offer to better meet student needs. Assign one person in your group to be the moderator while the others observe and interpret the responses from the focus group participants. Present a report of what you learned from this research. (AACSB: Communication; Reflective Thinking)

FOCUS ON Technology

Picture yourself with wires hooked up to your head or entering a magnetic tube that can see inside your brain. You must be undergoing some medical test, right? Think again—it's marketing research! Marketing research is becoming more like science fiction with a new field called neuromarketing, which uses technologies such as magnetic resonance imaging (MRI) to peer into consumers' brains in an attempt to understand cognitive and affective responses to marketing stimuli. One company, Thinkingcraft, uses a methodology called "neurographix" to help marketers develop messages that fit the way customers think. The Omnicon advertising agency uses "neuroplanning" to determine the appropriate media mix for a client. One study found that consumers preferred Pepsi over Coke in blind taste tests but preferred Coke when

they could see the names of the brands tasted. Different areas of the brain were activated when they knew the brand compared to when they did not, suggesting that what marketers make us believe is more persuasive than what our own taste buds tell us.

1. Learn more about neuromarketing and discuss another example of its application. (AACSB: Communication; Technology)

2. Critics have raised concerns over the usefulness and ethics of this type of marketing research. Discuss both sides of the debate surrounding this methodology. (AACSB: Communication; Ethical Reasoning)

FOCUS ON Ethics

Marketing information helps develop insights into the needs of customers, and gathering competitive intelligence (CI) data supplies part of this information. CI has blossomed into a full-fledged industry, with most major companies establishing CI units. But not all CI gathering is ethical or legal—even at venerable P&G. In 1943, a P&G employee bribed a Lever Brothers (now Unilever) employee to obtain bars of Swan soap, which was then under development, to improve its Ivory brand. P&G settled the case by paying Unilever almost $6 million (about $60 million in today's dollars) for patent infringement—a small price to pay given the market success of Ivory. In 2001, P&G once again paid a $10 million settlement to Unilever for a case that involved a contractor rummaging through a trash dumpster outside Unilever's office, an infraction that was actually reported by P&G itself. More recently, the U.S. Attorney General's office halted a corporate espionage lawsuit be-

tween Starwood Hotels and Hilton Hotels because it is already pursuing criminal charges against Hilton and two executives it hired away from Starwood. The U.S. Secret Service estimates that employees commit 75 percent of intellectual property theft. The threat is not just internal, though. The FBI is tracking approximately 20 countries actively spying on U.S. companies.

1. Find another example of corporate espionage and write a brief report on it. Did the guilty party pay restitution or serve prison time? Discuss what punishments, if any, should be levied in cases of corporate espionage. (AACSB: Communication; Ethical Reasoning)

2. How can businesses protect themselves from corporate espionage? (AACSB: Communication; Reflective Thinking)

MARKETING & THE Economy

Harrah's Entertainment

Over the past decade, Harrah's Entertainment has honed its CRM skills to become bigger and more profitable than any other company in the gaming industry. The foundation of its success is Total Rewards, a loyalty program that collects a mother lode of customer information and mines it to identify important customers and meet their specific needs through a personalized experience. But in recent times, Harrah's has seen its flow of customers slow to a trickle. Not only are customers visiting less often, but the normally $50 gamer is now playing only $25. As a result, Harrah's revenues have slid for the past two years in a row. Harrah's isn't alone; the rest of the industry is also suffering as more people save their money or

spend it on necessities rather than entertainment. Harrah's CRM efforts have always focused on delighting every customer. The company claims that customer spending increases 24 percent with a happy experience. But even Harrah's uncanny ability to predict which customers will be motivated by show tickets, room upgrades, or free chips has not made Harrah's immune to the woes of an economic downturn.

1. Is the dip in Harrah's business unavoidable given recent economic troubles or can Harrah's find new ways to connect with customers? What would you recommend?

2. In difficult economic times, is it responsible for Harrah's to try to get people to spend more money on gambling?

MARKETING BY THE Numbers

Have you ever been disappointed because a television network cancelled one of your favorite television shows because of "low ratings"? The network didn't ask your opinion, did it? It probably didn't ask any of your friends, either. That's because estimates of television audience sizes are based on research done by the Nielsen Company, which uses a sample of 9,000 households out of the more than 113 million households in the United States to determine national ratings for television programs. That doesn't seem like enough, does it? As it turns out, statistically, it's significantly more than enough.

1. Go to http://www.surveysystem.com/sscalc.htm to determine the appropriate sample size for a population of 113 million households. Assuming a confidence interval of 5, how large should the sample of households be if desiring a 95 percent confidence level? How large for a 99 percent confidence level? Briefly explain what is meant by *confidence interval* and *confidence level*. (AACSB: Communication; Use of IT; Analytical Reasoning)

2. What sample sizes are necessary at population sizes of 1 billion, 10,000, and 100 with a confidence interval of 5 and a 95 percent confidence level? Explain the effect population size has on sample size. (AACSB: Communication; Use of IT; Analytical Reasoning)

VIDEO Case

Radian6

As more and more consumers converse through digital media, companies are struggling to figure out how to "listen in" on the conversations. Traditional marketing research methods can't sift through the seemingly infinite number of words flying around cyberspace at any given moment. But one company is helping marketers get a handle on "word-of-Web" communication. Radian6 specializes in monitoring social media, tracking Web sites ranging from Facebook to Flickr. Radian6's unique software opens a door to an entirely different kind of research. Instead of using questionnaires, interviews, or focus groups, Radian6 scans online social media for whatever combination of keywords a marketer might specify. This gives companies valuable insights into what consumers are saying about their products and brands.

After viewing the video featuring Radian6, answer the following questions.

1. What benefits does Radian6 provide to marketers over more traditional market research methods? What shortcomings?

2. Classify Radian6's software with respect to research approaches, contact methods, sampling plan, and research instruments.

3. How is Radian6 helping companies develop stronger relationships with customers?

COMPANY Case

Harrah's Entertainment:
Hitting the CRM Jackpot

Joseph, a 30-something New Yorker, recently went on a weekend trip to Atlantic City, New Jersey, where he hoped to stay at one of his favorite Harrah's resorts and enjoy some gaming and entertainment. Unfortunately for Joseph, he picked a weekend when all the hotels were booked solid. But after swiping his Harrah's Total Rewards card to play the tables, the pit boss came by and directed him to the front desk. He was told that a room had become available, and he could stay in it for a reduced rate of $100 a night. When he checked out two nights later, Joseph was told that all the room charges were on the house.

Was this sudden vacancy a case of lady luck smiling down on an Atlantic City visitor? Or was it a case of a company that knows what managing customer relationships truly means? If you ask any of Harrah's Total Rewards program members, they will tell you without hesitation that it's the latter. "They are very good at upgrading or in some cases finding a room in a full hotel," Joseph reported later. "And I always liked the fact that no matter where I gambled, Atlantic City, Vegas, Kansas City, or New Orleans, or which of their hotels I gambled in, I was always able to use my [Total Rewards card]."

Harrah's customers like Joseph aren't the only ones praising its customer-relationship management (CRM) capabilities. In fact, Harrah's program is considered by CRM experts to set the gold standard. With the Total Rewards program at the center of its business and marketing strategies, Harrah's Entertainment has the ability to gather data, convert that data into customer insights, and use those insights to serve up a customer experience like no other.

GATHERING DATA

One thing that makes Total Rewards so effective is that Harrah's has a customer relationship culture that starts at the top with president and CEO Gary Loveman. In 1998, Loveman joined the company and turned its existing loyalty program into Total Rewards. The program worked well from the start. But through smart investments and a continued focus, Harrah's has hit the CRM jackpot.

The mechanics of the program go something like this: Total Rewards members receive points based on the amount they spend at Harrah's facilities. They can then redeem the points for a variety of perks, such as cash, food, merchandise, rooms, and hotel show tickets.

The simplicity of Total Rewards gains power in volume and flexibility. Through numerous acquisitions over the past decade, Harrah's has grown to more than 50 properties under several brands across the United States, including Harrah's, Caesars, Bally's, Planet Hollywood, the Flamingo, and Showboat. Total Rewards members swipe their card every time they spend a dime at one of these properties: checking into 1 of 40,000 hotel rooms, playing 1 of 60,000 slot machines, eating at 1 of 390 restaurants, picking up a gift at 1 of 240 retail shops, or playing golf at 1 of its 7 golf courses. Over 80 percent of Harrah's customers—40 million in all—use a Total Rewards card. That's roughly one out of six adults in the United States. That's a big pile of data points. Added to this, Harrah's regularly surveys samples of its customers to gain even more details.

CUSTOMER INSIGHTS

Analyzing all this information gives Harrah's detailed insights into its casino operations. For example, "visualization software" can generate a dynamic "heat map" of a casino floor, with machines glowing red when at peak activity and then turning blue and then white as the action moves elsewhere. More importantly, Harrah's uses every customer interaction to learn something new about individuals—their characteristics and behaviors, such as who they are, how often they visit, how long they stay, and how much they gamble and entertain. "We know if you like gold . . . chardonnay, down pillows; if you like your room close to the elevator, which properties you visit, what games you play, and which offers you redeemed," says David Norton, Harrah's chief marketing officer.

From its Total Rewards data, Harrah's has learned that 26 percent of its customers produce 82 percent of revenues. And these best customers aren't the "high-rollers" that have long been focus of the industry. Rather, they are ordinary folks from all walks of life—middle-aged and retired teachers, assembly line workers, and even bankers and doctors who have discretionary income and time. Harrah's "low-roller" strategy is based on the discovery that these customers might just visit casinos for an evening rather than staying overnight at the hotel. And they are more likely to play the slots than the tables. What motivates them? It's mostly the intense anticipation and excitement of gambling itself.

Kris Hart, vice president of brand management for Harrah's, reports on a survey of 14,000 Total Rewards members.

> We did a lot of psychographic segmenting—looking at what were the drivers of people's behavior. Were they coming because of the location? Were they coming because there were incented to do so with a piece of direct mail? Were they coming because they have an affinity for a loyalty program? And that allowed us to look at segments that clumped around certain drivers . . . and it enabled us to construct our brands and messaging . . . in a way that would capitalize on those drivers.

CUSTOMER EXPERIENCE

Using such insights, Harrah's focuses its marketing and service development strategies on the needs of its best customers. For example, the company's advertising reflects the feeling of exuberance that target customers seek. Harrah's sends out over 250 million pieces of direct mail and almost 100 million e-mails to its members every year. A good customer can receive as many as 150 pieces of mail in a given year from one or all of its properties. From the customer's perspective, that might sound like a nightmare. But Harrah's has tested customer sentiment on receiving multiple mailings from multiple locations, and they actually like it. The reason is that the information that any given customer receives is relevant to them, not annoying. That's why Harrah's has a higher-than-average direct mail response rate.

Harrah's is certainly concerned about metrics, such as response rates, click-through rates, revenue, and customer profitability. But Harrah's program is one of the best because it places emphasis on knowing how all the outcomes are linked. And because Harrah's CRM culture extends from the IT department to front line employees, the gaming giant has an uncanny ability to translate all its data into an exceptional customer experience.

Marilyn Winn, the president of three Las Vegas resorts, lives and breathes Harrah's CRM culture. "My job is to make money for Harrah's Entertainment by creating a great climate for customers and employees." She focuses on what goes on inside her properties. She spot-checks details on casino floors and in gift shops. She attends weekly employee rallies that are not only a party but also a communications tool. Winn points out how Harrah's motivates its employees to do their best. "Every week, we survey our customers. Customer service is very specific at Harrah's, systematic." Based on customer service scores, employees have their own system for accumulating points and redeeming them for a wide variety of rewards, from iPads to pool equipment. "Every property has the goal to improve service. This is just one way we do it. We also use mystery shoppers to verify we are getting the service we want and we train our employees to our standards."

Harrah's combines its service culture with the brain center of Total Rewards. After a day's gaming, Harrah's knows which customers should be rewarded with free show tickets, dinner vouchers, or room upgrades. In fact, Harrah's processes customer information in real time, from the moment customers swipe their rewards cards, creating the ideal link between data and the customer experience. Harrah's chief information officer calls this "operational CRM." Based on up-to-the-minute customer information, "the hotel clerk can see your history and determine whether you should get a room upgrade, based on booking levels in the hotel at that time and on your past level of play. A person might walk up to you while you're playing and offer you $5 to play more slots, or a free meal, or perhaps wish you a happy birthday."

Harrah's is constantly improving its technology so that it can better understand its customers and deliver a more fine-tuned experience. Most recently, Total Rewards gained the ability to track and reward nongaming spending. This is good for people who don't view themselves as big gamblers. "We wanted to make it relevant to them as well because they could spend a couple of hundred dollars on a room, the spa, food, and shows and not be treated any better than a $50-a-day customer," Norton said. This demonstrates the "total" part of Total Rewards. It isn't a program about getting people into casinos. It's a program designed to maximize the customer experience, regardless of what that experience includes.

HITTING TWENTY-ONE

Harrah's CRM efforts have paid off in spades. The company has found that happy customers are much more loyal. Whereas customer spending decreases by 10 percent based on an unhappy casino experience, it increases by 24 percent with a happy experience. And Harrah's Total Rewards customers appear to be a happier bunch. Compared with nonmembers, member customers visit the company's casinos more frequently, stay longer, and spend more of their gambling and entertainment dollars in Harrah's rather than in rival casinos. Since setting up Total Rewards, Harrah's has seen its share of customers' average annual gambling budgets rise 20 percent, and revenue from customers gambling at Harrah's rather than their "home casino" has risen 18 percent.

Although Harrah's and the entire gaming industry were hit hard by the Great Recession, things are turning back around. Through its acquisitions and the success of its Total Rewards program, Harrah's is the biggest in its industry, with over $10 billion in revenue last year. Loveman calls Total Rewards "the vertebrae of our business," and says "it touches, in some form or fashion, 85 percent of our revenue." He says that Harrah's "customer-loyalty strategy [and] relationship-marketing . . . are constantly bringing us closer to our customers so we better understand their preferences, and from that understanding we are able to improve the entertainment experiences we offer." Companies everywhere covet the title "The world's greatest." In the gaming industry, Harrah's Entertainment rightly claims that title.

Questions for Discussion

1. Briefly discuss Harrah's marketing information system, using Figure 4.1 as a guide.

2. Describe the relationship between Harrah's marketing information system and Harrah's managers and employees.

3. Why does Harrah's system work so well compared to MIS efforts by other companies?

4. To what extent is Harrah's in danger of a competitor copying its system?

Sources: Richard Abowitz, "The Movable Buffet," *Los Angeles Times*, May 23, 2010, p. D12; Michael Bush, "Why Harrah's Loyalty Effort Is Industry's Gold Standard," *Advertising Age*, October 5, 2009, p. 8; Megan McIlroy, "Why Harrah's Opted to Roll Dice on $5 Billion Merger with Caesars," *Advertising Age*, October 15, 2007, p. 18; Daniel Lyons, "Too Much Information," *Forbes*, December 13, 2004, p. 110; John Kell, "Harrah's Loss Widens on Debt-Payment Costs," *Wall Street Journal*, April 27, 2010.

5 Consumer Markets and Consumer Buyer Behavior

Chapter Preview

In the previous chapter, you studied how marketers obtain, analyze, and use information to develop customer insights and assess marketing programs. In this chapter and the next, we continue with a closer look at the most important element of the marketplace—customers. The aim of marketing is to affect how customers think and act. To affect the *whats*, *whens*, and *hows* of buyer behavior, marketers must first understand the *whys*. In this chapter, we look at *final consumer* buying influences and processes. In the next chapter, we'll study the buyer behavior of *business customers*. You'll see that understanding buyer behavior is an essential but very difficult task.

To get a better sense of the importance of understanding consumer behavior, we begin by first looking at Apple. What makes Apple users so fanatically loyal? Just what is it that makes them buy a Mac computer, an iPod, an iPhone, an iPad, or all of these? Partly, it's the way the equipment works. But at the core, customers buy from Apple because the brand itself is a part of their own self-expression and lifestyle. It's a part of what the loyal Apple customer is.

Apple: The Keeper of All Things Cool

Few brands engender such intense loyalty as that found in the hearts of core Apple buyers. Whether they own a Mac computer, an iPod, an iPhone, or an iPad, Apple devotees are granitelike in their devotion to the brand. At one end are the quietly satisfied Mac users, folks who own a Mac and use it for e-mailing, browsing, and social networking. At the other extreme, however, are the Mac zealots—the so-called MacHeads or Macolytes. The *Urban Dictionary* defines a Macolyte as "one who is fanatically devoted to Apple products," as in "He's a Macolyte; don't even *think* of mentioning Microsoft within earshot."

The chances are good that you know one of these Mac-Heads. Maybe you *are* one. They're the diehards who buy all the latest Apple products and accessories to maximize their Mac lives. They virtually live in the local Apple store. Some have even been known to buy two iPhones—one for themselves and the other just to take apart, to see what it looks like on the inside, and maybe, just to marvel at Apple's ingenious ability to cram so much into a tight little elegant package.

There's at least a little MacHead in every Apple customer. Mac enthusiasts see Apple founder Steve Jobs as the Walt Disney of technology. Say the word *Apple* in front of Mac fans, and they'll go into rhapsodies about the superiority of the brand. Some MacHeads even tattoo the Apple logo on their bodies. According to one industry observer, a Mac or iPhone comes "not just as a machine in a box, it [comes] with a whole community" of fellow believers.

What is it that makes Apple buyers so loyal? Why do they buy a Mac instead of an HP or a Dell, or an iPhone instead of brands from Nokia, LG, or Motorola? Ask the true believers, and they'll tell you simply that Apple's products work better and do more or are simpler to use. But Apple buyer behavior has much deeper roots. Apple puts top priority on understanding its customers and what makes them tick deep down. It knows that, to Apple buyers, a Mac computer or an iPhone is much more than just a piece of electronics equipment. It's a part of the buyer's own self-expression and lifestyle—a part of what each person is. When you own a Mac, you are anything but mainstream. You're an independent thinker, an innovator, and ahead of the crowd.

Apple plays to these deep-seated customer buying needs and motives in everything it makes and sells. By one account:

Apple is the epitome of cool—a company that has gained a cultlike following because it somehow manages to breathe new life into every category it touches. From sleek laptops to the even sleeker iPhone, Apple products are imaginative, irreverent, pleasing to the eye, and fun to use. Apple has shown "a marketing and creative genius with a rare ability to get inside the imaginations

> **Thanks to Apple's deep understanding of consumer behavior, the Apple brand engenders an intense loyalty in the hearts of core Apple customers. This consumer love affair with Apple has produced stunning sales and profit results.**

of consumers and understand what will captivate them," says one analyst. Apple has been "obsessed with the Apple user's experience."

Apple's obsession with understanding customers and deepening their Apple experience shows in everything the company does. For example, a visit to an Apple retail store is a lot more than a simple shopping trip. Apple stores are very seductive places. The store design is clean, simple, and just oozing with style—much like an iPod or iPhone. The stores invite shoppers to stay a while, use the equipment, and soak up all of the exciting new technology:

It was two o'clock in the morning but in the subterranean retailing mecca in Midtown Manhattan, otherwise known as the Apple store, it might as well have been midafternoon. Late one night shortly before Christmas, parents pushed strollers, and tourists straight off the plane mingled with nocturnal New Yorkers, clicking through iPod playlists, cruising the Internet on Macs, and touch-padding their way around iPhones. And through the night, cheerful sales staff stayed busy, ringing up customers at the main checkout counter and on handheld devices in an uninterrupted stream of brick-and-mortar commerce.

Not only has the company made many of its stores feel like gathering places, but the bright lights and equally bright acoustics create a buzz that makes customers feel more like they are at an event than a retail store. Apple stores encourage a lot of purchasing, to be sure. But they also encourage lingering, with dozens of fully functioning computers, iPods, and iPhones for visitors to try—for hours on end. The policy has even given some stores, especially those in urban neighborhoods, the feel of a community center. You don't visit an Apple store; you experience it.

Apple's keen understanding of customers and their needs helped the brand to build a core segment of enthusiastic disciples. The most recent American Consumer Satisfaction Index gave Apple a market-leading customer-satisfaction score of 84, a full 10 points above the rest of the pack in the personal computer industry. Another survey showed that Apple commands the strongest repurchase intent of any personal computer brand: 81 percent of households with an Apple as their primary home personal computer plan to repurchase an Apple.

In turn, the consumer love affair with Apple has produced stunning sales and profit results. In the past five years, despite the worst economic conditions since the Great Depression, Apple sales have nearly tripled to a record $36.5 billion, while earnings soared more than fourfold. The company was worth only $5 billion in 2000; it's worth about $170 billion today. Apple captures more than 30 percent of the U.S. cell phone market with the iPhone and more than 73 percent of the MP3 market with the iPod and iTunes. Last year alone, it sold more than 20 million iPhones and 54 million iPods. Apple now claims a 9 percent share of the U.S. personal computer market—third behind HP and Dell. But it dominates the high-end, accounting for an amazing 90 percent of dollars spent on computers costing more than $1,000.

"To say Apple is hot just doesn't do the company justice," concludes one Apple watcher. "Apple is smoking, searing, blisteringly hot, not to mention hip, with a side order of funky. Gadget geeks around the world have crowned Apple the keeper of all things cool." Just ask your Macolyte friends. In fact—they've probably already brought it up.[1]

Apple plays to deep-seated customer buying needs in everything it makes and sells. The company has gained a cultlike following because it somehow manages to breathe new life into every category it touches.

Consumer buyer behavior
The buying behavior of final consumers—individuals and households that buy goods and services for personal consumption.

Consumer market
All the individuals and households that buy or acquire goods and services for personal consumption.

The Apple example shows that factors at many levels affect consumer buying behavior. Buying behavior is never simple, yet understanding it is an essential task of marketing management. **Consumer buyer behavior** refers to the buying behavior of final consumers—individuals and households that buy goods and services for personal consumption. All of these final consumers combine to make up the **consumer market**. The American consumer market consists of more than 308 million people who consume more than $10 trillion worth of goods and services each year, making it one of the most attractive consumer markets in the world. The world consumer market consists of more than 6.8 billion people who annually consume an estimated $70 trillion worth of goods and services.[2]

Objective 1 **Define the consumer market and construct a simple model of consumer buyer behavior.**

Objective 2 **Name the four major factors that influence consumer buyer behavior.**

Objective 3 **List and define the major types of buying decision behavior and the stages in the buyer decision process.**

Objective 4 **Describe the adoption and diffusion process for new products.**

Consumers around the world vary tremendously in age, income, education level, and tastes. They also buy an incredible variety of goods and services. How these diverse consumers relate with each other and with other elements of the world around them impacts their choices among various products, services, and companies. Here we examine the fascinating array of factors that affect consumer behavior.

Author Comment | Despite the simple-looking model in Figure 5.1, understanding the *whys* of buying behavior is very difficult. Says one expert, "the mind is a whirling, swirling, jumbled mass of neurons bouncing around. . . ."

Model of Consumer Behavior (pp 134–135)

Consumers make many buying decisions every day, and the buying decision is the focal point of the marketer's effort. Most large companies research consumer buying decisions in great detail to answer questions about what consumers buy, where they buy, how and how much they buy, when they buy, and why they buy. Marketers can study actual consumer purchases to find out what they buy, where, and how much. But learning about the *whys* of consumer buying behavior is not so easy—the answers are often locked deep within the consumer's mind.

Often, consumers themselves don't know exactly what influences their purchases. "The human mind doesn't work in a linear way," says one marketing expert. "The idea that the mind is a computer with storage compartments where brands or logos or recognizable packages are stored in clearly marked folders that can be accessed by cleverly written ads or commercials simply doesn't exist. Instead, the mind is a whirling, swirling, jumbled mass of neurons bouncing around, colliding and continuously creating new concepts and thoughts and relationships inside every single person's brain all over the world."[3]

The central question for marketers is as follows: How do consumers respond to various marketing efforts the company might use? The starting point is the stimulus-response model of buyer behavior shown in ◉ **Figure 5.1**. This figure shows that marketing and other stimuli enter the consumer's "black box" and produce certain responses. Marketers must figure out what is in the buyer's black box.

Marketing stimuli consist of the four Ps: product, price, place, and promotion. Other stimuli include major forces and events in the buyer's environment: economic, technological, political, and cultural. All these inputs enter the buyer's black box, where they are turned into a set of buyer responses: the buyer's brand and company relationship behavior and what he or she buys, when, where, and how often.

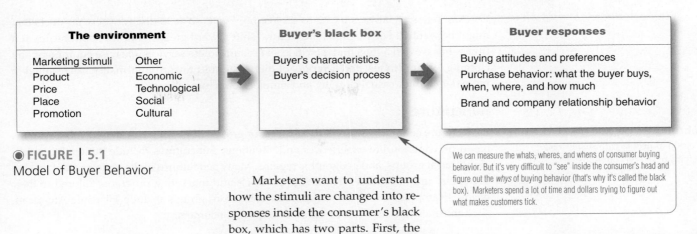

● FIGURE | 5.1
Model of Buyer Behavior

We can measure the whats, wheres, and whens of consumer buying behavior. But it's very difficult to "see" inside the consumer's head and figure out the *whys* of buying behavior (that's why it's called the black box). Marketers spend a lot of time and dollars trying to figure out what makes customers tick.

Marketers want to understand how the stimuli are changed into responses inside the consumer's black box, which has two parts. First, the buyer's characteristics influence how he or she perceives and reacts to the stimuli. Second, the buyer's decision process itself affects his or her behavior. We look first at buyer characteristics as they affect buyer behavior and then discuss the buyer decision process.

> **Author Comment** | Many levels of factors affect our buying behavior—from broad cultural and social influences to motivations, beliefs, and attitudes lying deep within us. For example, why *did* you buy *that* specific cell phone?

Characteristics Affecting Consumer Behavior (pp 135–150)

Consumer purchases are influenced strongly by cultural, social, personal, and psychological characteristics, as shown in ● **Figure 5.2**. For the most part, marketers cannot control such factors, but they must take them into account.

Cultural Factors

Cultural factors exert a broad and deep influence on consumer behavior. Marketers need to understand the role played by the buyer's *culture, subculture*, and *social class*.

Culture

Culture
The set of basic values, perceptions, wants, and behaviors learned by a member of society from family and other important institutions.

Culture is the most basic cause of a person's wants and behavior. Human behavior is largely learned. Growing up in a society, a child learns basic values, perceptions, wants, and behaviors from his or her family and other important institutions. A child in the United States normally learns or is exposed to the following values: achievement and success, individualism, freedom, hard work, activity and involvement, efficiency and practicality, material comfort, youthfulness, and fitness and health. Every group or society has a culture, and cultural influences on buying behavior may vary greatly from country to country. A failure to adjust to these differences can result in ineffective marketing or embarrassing mistakes.

● FIGURE | 5.2
Factors Influencing
Consumer Behavior

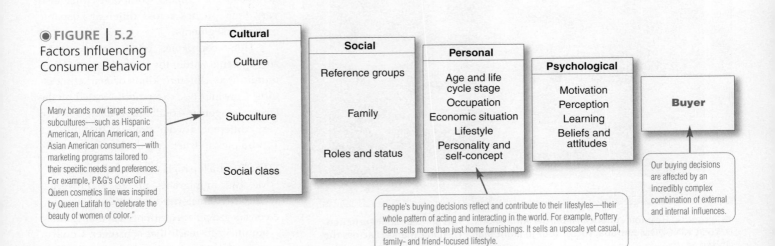

Many brands now target specific subcultures—such as Hispanic American, African American, and Asian American consumers—with marketing programs tailored to their specific needs and preferences. For example, P&G's CoverGirl Queen cosmetics line was inspired by Queen Latifah to "celebrate the beauty of women of color."

People's buying decisions reflect and contribute to their lifestyles—their whole pattern of acting and interacting in the world. For example, Pottery Barn sells more than just home furnishings. It sells an upscale yet casual, family- and friend-focused lifestyle.

Our buying decisions are affected by an incredibly complex combination of external and internal influences.

Marketers are always trying to spot *cultural shifts* so as to discover new products that might be wanted. For example, the cultural shift toward greater concern about health and fitness has created a huge industry for health-and-fitness services, exercise equipment and clothing, organic foods, and a variety of diets. The shift toward informality has resulted in more demand for casual clothing and simpler home furnishings.

Subculture

Subculture
A group of people with shared value systems based on common life experiences and situations.

Each culture contains smaller **subcultures**, or groups of people with shared value systems based on common life experiences and situations. Subcultures include nationalities, religions, racial groups, and geographic regions. Many subcultures make up important market segments, and marketers often design products and marketing programs tailored to their needs. Examples of four such important subculture groups include Hispanic American, African American, Asian American, and mature consumers.

Hispanic American Consumers. The nation's nearly 50 million Hispanic consumers have an annual buying power of more than $950 billion, a figure that will grow to an estimated $1.4 trillion by 2013. Hispanic consumer spending has grown at more than twice the rate of general-market spending over the past four years.[4]

Although Hispanic consumers share many characteristics and behaviors with the mainstream buying pubic, there are also distinct differences. They tend to be deeply family oriented and make shopping a family affair; children have a big say in what brands they buy. Perhaps more important, Hispanic consumers, particularly first-generation immigrants, are very brand loyal, and they favor brands and sellers who show special interest in them.

Companies such as P&G, AT&T, Verizon, McDonald's, Toyota, Walmart, Burger King, and many others have developed special targeting efforts for this large consumer group. For example, Walmart converted two existing stores in Phoenix and Houston to serve local Hispanic consumers under the name Supermercado de Walmart. ● And Burger King sponsors an annual FÚTBOL KINGDOM national soccer tour in eight major Hispanic markets across the United States. The family-oriented tour treats visitors to innovative street-level soccer events for all ages and skill levels, including skills challenges such as Domina como Rey (ball control), Los Reyes del Balon (speed), and Mata Penales (blocking ability). The BK FÚTBOLADORES soccer team puts on exhibitions featuring head-to-head demonstrations. It's a "one-of-a-kind experience that has been incredibly successful with Hispanics around the United States," says Burger King's director of multicultural marketing.[5]

Even within the Hispanic market, there exist many distinct subsegments based on nationality, age, income, and other factors. For example, a company's product or message may be more relevant to one nationality over another, such as Mexicans, Costa Ricans, Argentineans, or Cubans. Companies must also vary their pitches across different Hispanic economic segments.

Thus, companies often target specific subsegments within the larger Hispanic community with different kinds of marketing efforts. Consider two campaigns created by the Hispanic agency Conill Advertising for two very different Toyota brands: the full-size Tundra pickup truck and the Lexus.[6]

The Tundra is a high-volume seller among Mexican immigrants in the Southwest who are characterized as *Jefes*, local heroes considered pillars of strength in their communities. To reach that consumer, Conill devised a campaign that catered to *El Jefe's*

● Targeting Hispanic Americans: Burger King sponsors an annual family-oriented FÚTBOL KINGDOM national soccer tour in eight major Hispanic markets across the United States.

penchant for the national Mexican sport of *charreadas* (Mexican-style rodeos). The pitch: The Tundra is as tough as the guy who gets behind the wheel.

Conill's campaign for Lexus couldn't be more different. For Lexus, the agency targeted the luxury market in Miami, reaching out to affluent Hispanic Americans who appreciate refinement, art, and culture with a campaign that centered on art and design. The result was a brightly displayed Lexus print campaign placed in local Hispanic lifestyle magazines that helped move Lexus from the fourth-ranked player in the Miami luxury car market to market leader in only 18 months.

African American Consumers. With an annual buying power of $913 billion, estimated to reach $1.2 trillion by 2013, the nation's 42 million African American consumers also attract much marketing attention. The U.S. black population is growing in affluence and sophistication. Although more price conscious than other segments, blacks are also strongly motivated by quality and selection. Brands are important. So is shopping. Black consumers seem to enjoy shopping more than other groups, even for something as mundane as groceries.[7]

In recent years, many companies have developed special products, appeals, and marketing programs for African American consumers. For example, P&G's roots run deep in this market. P&G has long been the leader in African American advertising, spending nearly twice as much as the second-place spender. It has a long history of using black spokespeople in its ads, beginning in 1969 with entertainer Bill Cosby endorsing Crest. Today, you'll see Angela Bassett promoting the benefits of Olay body lotion for black skin, Derek Jeter discussing the virtues of Gillette razors and deodorant, and ● Queen Latifah in commercials promoting a CoverGirl line for women of color.[8] In addition to traditional product marketing efforts, P&G also supports a broader "My Black Is Beautiful" movement.[9]

Created by a group of African American women at P&G, the campaign aims "to ignite and support a sustained national conversation by, for, and about black women." P&G discovered that black women spend, on average, three times more than the general market on beauty products. Yet, 71 percent of black women feel they're portrayed worse than other women in media and advertising. Supported by brands such as Crest, Pantene Pro-V Relaxed & Natural, CoverGirl Queen Collection, and Olay Definity, the goals of the My Black Is Beautiful movement are to make all black girls and women feel beautiful regardless of skin tone or origin and, of course, to forge a closer relationship between P&G brands and African American consumers in the process. With P&G as the main sponsor, My Black Is Beautiful includes traditional television programming and Webisodes featuring interviews, vignettes, and style tips focusing on African American beauty.

Asian American Consumers. Asian Americans are the most affluent U.S. demographic segment. They now number nearly 15 million and wield more than $500 billion in annual spending power, expected to reach $750 billion in 2013. They are the second-fastest-growing population subsegment after Hispanic Americans. And like Hispanic Americans, they are a diverse group. Chinese Americans constitute the largest group, followed by Filipinos, Asian Indians, Vietnamese, Korean Americans, and Japanese Americans. Asian consumers may be the most tech-savvy segment; more than 90 percent of Asian Americans go online regularly and are most comfortable with Internet technologies such as online banking.[10]

As a group, Asian consumers shop frequently and are the most brand conscious of all the ethnic groups. They can be fiercely brand loyal. As a result, many firms are now targeting the Asian American market, companies like State Farm, McDonald's, Verizon, Toyota, and Walmart. For example, among its many other Asian American targeting efforts, McDonald's has built a special Web site for this segment (www.myinspirasian.com), offered in both English and Asian languages. The fun and involving, community-oriented site highlights how McDonald's is working with and serving the Asian American community.

State Farm has also developed comprehensive advertising, marketing, and public relations campaigns that have helped it to gain significant brand equity and market share among Asian American consumers. It even recast its familiar "Like a good neighbor, State Farm is there," tagline so that it would retain the spirit of the original line but better resonate

● P&G's roots run deep in targeting African American consumers. For example, its Cover Girl Queen Latifah line is specially formulated "to celebrate the beauty of women of color."

 Targeting Asian Americans: State Farm has developed comprehensive advertising, marketing, and public relations campaigns that have helped it to gain significant brand equity among Asian American consumers.

with each Asian American market. ● For example, the Chinese version translates back into English as "With a good neighbor, you are reassured every day." But State Farm's commitment to the Asian American community goes well beyond just slogans. "Being a good neighbor today means investing in tomorrow's leaders," says State Farm's vice president of multicultural business development. Over the years, State Farm has invested in "providing leadership opportunities for [Asian American] youth, teen auto-safety programs, youth and college education-excellence opportunities, financial education for all age groups, and community development."[11]

Mature Consumers. As the U.S. population ages, mature consumers are becoming a very attractive market. By 2015, when all the baby boomers will be 50-plus, people ages 50 to 75 will account for 40 percent of adult consumers. By 2030, adults ages 65 and older will represent nearly 20 percent of the population. And these mature consumer segments boast the most expendable cash. The 50-plus consumer segment now accounts for nearly 50 percent of all consumer spending, more than any current or previous generation. They have 2.5 times the discretionary buying power of those ages 18 to 34. As one marketing executive puts it, they have "assets, not allowances." Despite some financial setbacks resulting from the recent economic crisis, mature consumers remain an attractive market for companies in all industries, from pharmaceuticals, furniture, groceries, beauty products, and clothing to consumer electronics, travel and entertainment, and financial services.[12]

For decades, many marketers stereotyped mature consumers as doddering, impoverished shut-ins who are less willing to change brands. One problem: Brand managers and advertising copywriters tend to be younger. "Ask them to do an ad targeting the 50-plus demographic," bemoans one marketer, "and they'll default to a gray-haired senior living on a beach trailed by an aging golden retriever." For example, in a recent survey, advertising professionals regarded the term *over the hill* as meaning people over 57. In contrast, baby boomer respondents related the term to people over age 75.[13]

As a group, however, mature consumers are anything but "stuck in their ways." To the contrary, a recent AARP study showed that older consumers for products such as stereos, computers, and mobile phones are more willing to shop around and switch brands than their younger counterparts. For example, notes one expert, "some 25 percent of Apple's iPhones—the epitome of cool, cutting-edge product—have been bought by people over 50."[14]

And in reality, people whose ages would seem to place them squarely in the "old" category usually don't act old or see themselves that way. Thanks to advances in longevity, people are redefining what the mature life stage means. "They're having a second middle-age before becoming elderly," says a generational marketing expert. Marketers need to appeal to these consumers in a vibrant but authentic way.[15]

Today's mature consumers create an attractive market for convenience services. For example, Home Depot and Lowe's now target older consumers who are less enthusiastic about do-it-yourself chores than with "do-it-for-me" handyman services. And their desire to be active and look as young as they feel makes more-mature consumers good candidates for cosmetics and personal care products, health foods, fitness products, and other items that combat the effects of aging. The best strategy is to appeal to their active, multidimensional lives. ● For example, a recent Jeep ad in the *AARP magazine* features a mature consumer who's nowhere near "elderly," at least in her own view. "I know you're only as old as you feel, and I *still* feel 30. I can text, but I prefer to talk. I'll do a bake sale and hit a few trails, too. The grandkids say I'm 'really cool now,' but what they don't know is, I always was." The ad concludes: "I live. I ride. I am. Jeep."

i know you're only
as old as you feel
and i *still* feel 30
i can text but i prefer to talk
i'll do a bake sale
and hit a few trails too
the grandkids say i'm
'really cool now'
but what they don't know is,
i always was.

i live. i ride. i am. **Jeep**

Here's an exclusive offer
for AARP full members.
Get an additional
$750 CASH ALLOWANCE
on a 2010 Jeep Compass.

Visit your dealership and
show your AARP membership
card to receive this offer.
Offer ends 5/31/10.

Only one $750 AARP cash allowance offer can be
applied to the retail purchase or lease of an eligible
vehicle and only one allowance per eligible customer.
See your dealer for details. Must take retail delivery
by 5/31/10. Program Number: 39CA2. Jeep is a
registered trademark of Chrysler Group LLC.

Targeting mature consumers: In this AARP magazine ad, Jeep targets the mature consumers who see themselves as anything but elderly. "The grandkids say I'm 'really cool now,' but what they don't know is, I always was."

Social class
Relatively permanent and ordered divisions in a society whose members share similar values, interests, and behaviors.

Group
Two or more people who interact to accomplish individual or mutual goals.

Opinion leader
A person within a reference group who, because of special skills, knowledge, personality, or other characteristics, exerts social influence on others.

Social Class

Almost every society has some form of social class structure. **Social classes** are society's relatively permanent and ordered divisions whose members share similar values, interests, and behaviors. Social scientists have identified the seven American social classes shown in ◉ **Figure 5.3**.

Social class is not determined by a single factor, such as income, but is measured as a combination of occupation, income, education, wealth, and other variables. In some social systems, members of different classes are reared for certain roles and cannot change their social positions. In the United States, however, the lines between social classes are not fixed and rigid; people can move to a higher social class or drop into a lower one.

Marketers are interested in social class because people within a given social class tend to exhibit similar buying behavior. Social classes show distinct product and brand preferences in areas such as clothing, home furnishings, leisure activity, and automobiles.

Social Factors

A consumer's behavior also is influenced by social factors, such as the consumer's *small groups*, *family*, and *social roles* and *status*.

Groups and Social Networks

Many small **groups** influence a person's behavior. Groups that have a direct influence and to which a person belongs are called membership groups. In contrast, reference groups serve as direct (face-to-face) or indirect points of comparison or reference in forming a person's attitudes or behavior. People often are influenced by reference groups to which they do not belong. For example, an aspirational group is one to which the individual wishes to belong, as when a young basketball player hopes to someday emulate basketball star LeBron James and play in the National Basketball Association (NBA).

Marketers try to identify the reference groups of their target markets. Reference groups expose a person to new behaviors and lifestyles, influence the person's attitudes and self-concept, and create pressures to conform that may affect the person's product and brand choices. The importance of group influence varies across products and brands. It tends to be strongest when the product is visible to others whom the buyer respects.

Word-of-Mouth Influence and Buzz Marketing. Word-of-mouth influence can have a powerful impact on consumer buying behavior. The personal words and recommendations of trusted friends, associates, and other consumers tend to be more credible than those coming from commercial sources, such as advertisements or salespeople. Most word-of-mouth influence happens naturally: Consumers start chatting about a brand they use or feel strongly about one way or the other. Often, however, rather than leaving it to chance, marketers can help to create positive conversations about their brands.

Marketers of brands subjected to strong group influence must figure out how to reach **opinion leaders**—people within a reference group who, because of special skills, knowledge, personality, or other characteristics, exert social influence on others. Some experts call this group *the influentials* or *leading adopters*. When these influentials talk, consumers listen. Marketers try to identify opinion leaders for their products and direct marketing efforts toward them.

Buzz marketing involves enlisting or even creating opinion leaders to serve as "brand ambassadors" who spread the word about a company's products. Many companies now create

◉ **FIGURE** | **5.3**
The Major American
Social Classes

Wealth

Education

Occupation

Income

America's social classes show distinct brand preferences. Social class is not determined by a single factor but by a combination of all of these factors.

Upper Class
Upper Uppers (1 percent): The social elite who live on inherited wealth. They give large sums to charity, own more than one home, and send their children to the finest schools.

Lower Uppers (2 percent): Americans who have earned high income or wealth through exceptional ability. They are active in social and civic affairs and buy expensive homes, educations, and cars.

Middle Class
Upper Middles (12 percent): Professionals, independent businesspersons, and corporate managers who possess neither family status nor unusual wealth. They believe in education, are joiners and highly civic minded, and want the "better things in life."

Middle Class (32 percent): Average-pay white- and blue-collar workers who live on "the better side of town." They buy popular products to keep up with trends. Better living means owning a nice home in a nice neighborhood with good schools.

Working Class
Working Class (38 percent): Those who lead a "working-class lifestyle," whatever their income, school background, or job. They depend heavily on relatives for economic and emotional support, advice on purchases, and assistance in times of trouble.

Lower Class
Upper Lowers (9 percent): The working poor. Although their living standard is just above poverty, they strive toward a higher class. However, they often lack education and are poorly paid for unskilled work.

Lower Lowers (7 percent): Visibly poor, often poorly educated unskilled laborers. They are often out of work, and some depend on public assistance. They tend to live a day-to-day existence.

brand ambassador programs in an attempt to turn influential but everyday customers into brand evangelists. A recent study found that such programs can increase the effectiveness of word-of-mouth marketing efforts by as much as 50 percent.[16] ◉ For example, JetBlue's CrewBlue program employs real customers to create buzz on college campuses.[17]

Over the past few years, the JetBlue CrewBlue program has recruited a small army of college student ambassadors—all loyal JetBlue lovers. CrewBlue representatives advise JetBlue on its campus marketing efforts, talk up the brand to other students, and help organize campus events, such as JetBlue's BlueDay. Held each fall on 21 campuses, the highly successful event urges students to wear outlandish blue costumes (and, on occasion, blue skin and hair). Students with the best costumes are each given a pair of free airline tickets.

The CrewBlue ambassadors are crucial to the success of JetBlue's campus marketing efforts: "Students know what kinds of activities are important to other kids, what we should say to them in our marketing, and how we should say it," says a JetBlue marketing executive. You might think that such brand ambassadors would be perceived as hucksters—or, worse, as annoying evangelists

◉ **Brand ambassadors: JetBlue's CrewBlue program employs real customers to create buzz on college campuses.**

best avoided. Not so, says the executive. "Our brand ambassadors are seen by their college friends as entrepreneurial, creative people." What they aren't, he adds, are the super-cool people on campus who are typically thought of as influentials. The best ambassadors, says the executive, are "friendly, everyday brand loyalists who love to talk to people."

Online Social Networks. Over the past few years, a new type of social interaction has exploded onto the scene—online social networking. **Online social networks** are online communities where people socialize or exchange information and opinions. Social networking media range from blogs (Gizmodo) and message boards (Craigslist) to social networking Web sites (Facebook and Twitter) and virtual worlds (Second Life). This new form of consumer-to-consumer and business-to-consumer dialog has big implications for marketers.

Online social networks
Online social communities—blogs, social networking Web sites, or even virtual worlds—where people socialize or exchange information and opinions.

Marketers are working to harness the power of these new social networks and other "word-of-Web" opportunities to promote their products and build closer customer relationships. Instead of throwing more one-way commercial messages at consumers, they hope to use the Internet and social networks to *interact* with consumers and become a part of their conversations and lives (see Real Marketing 5.1).

For example, brands ranging from Burger King and American Greetings to the Chicago Bulls are tweeting on Twitter. Jeep connects with customers via a community page that links to photos on Flickr, the company's Facebook and MySpace pages, and a list of enthusiast groups. Southwest Airlines employees share stories with each other and customers on the company's "Nuts about Southwest" blog. And during the 2010 winter Olympics, VISA launched a "Go World" microsite featuring athlete videos, photos, and widgets that tied into nets like Facebook. VISA customized the campaign for global markets, featuring a different set of athletes for Canada and Russia.[18]

Other companies regularly post ads or custom videos on video-sharing sites such as YouTube. For example, Toyota developed two YouTube channels to market its Corolla. One of these channels, Sketchies 11, hosted a competition offering cash and prizes worth $40,000 for the best user-generated comedy sketches. The most-watched video received some 900,000 views. Similarly, small Blendtec has developed a kind of cult following for its flood of "Will It Blend?" videos, in which the seemingly indestructible Blendtec Total Blender grinds everything from a hockey puck and a golf club to an iPhone and iPad into dust. The low-cost, simple idea led to a fivefold increase in Blendtec's sales.[19]

But marketers must be careful when tapping into online social networks. Results are difficult to measure and control. Ultimately, the users control the content, so social network marketing attempts can easily backfire. We will dig deeper into online social networks as a marketing tool in Chapter 17.

● **Using online social networks: Blendtec has developed a kind of cult following for its flood of "Will It Blend?" videos on YouTube, resulting in a fivefold increase in Blendtec's sales.**

Family

Family members can strongly influence buyer behavior. The family is the most important consumer buying organization in society, and it has been researched extensively. Marketers are interested in the roles and influence of the husband, wife, and children on the purchase of different products and services.

Husband-wife involvement varies widely by product category and by stage in the buying process. Buying roles change with evolving consumer lifestyles. In the United States, the wife traditionally has been the main purchasing agent for the family in the areas of food, household products, and clothing. But with 70 percent of women holding jobs outside the

Real Marketing 5.1

Word of Web: Harnessing the Power of Online Social Influence

People love talking with others about things that make them happy—including their favorite products and brands. Say you really like JetBlue Airways—they fly with flair and get you there at an affordable price. Or you just plain love your new Sony GPS camera—it's too cool to keep to yourself. In the old days, you'd have chatted up these brands with a few friends and family members. But these days, thanks to online technology, anyone can share brand experiences with thousands, even millions, of other consumers via the Web.

In response, marketers are now feverishly working to harness today's newfound technologies and get people talking about and interacting with their brands online. Whether it's creating online brand ambassadors, tapping into existing online influentials and social networks, or developing conversation-provoking events and videos, the Web is awash with marketer attempts to create brand conversations and involvement online.

A company can start by creating its own online brand evangelists. For example, Sony used online brand ambassadors to jump-start the launch of its new GPS camera, a high-tech device that lets you record the exact location of every picture you take and later map them out online using Google Maps. The company selected 25 customers who like to travel, take pictures, and blog; gave them a camera; and taught them how to use it. Then it encouraged the ambassadors to show the camera to friends, associates, and anyone else who asked; hand out discount coupons; and blog weekly about their travel and picture-taking adventures on a dedicated Sony microsite and a host of social networking sites.

Similarly, Coca-Cola recently launched Expedition 206, which dispatched three "Happiness Ambassadors"—chosen in an online vote—on a 365-day journey across the 206 countries where Coca-Cola products are sold. Their mission was to document "what makes people happy" around the world and share their experiences with consumers worldwide through blogs, tweets, videos, and pictures posted on Facebook, Twitter, YouTube, Flickr, and an official Expedition 206 Web site. Fans following the adventure served as "virtual travel agents," suggesting places the Happiness Ambassadors might go and what they might do. The ambassadors generated lots of online buzz, all within the context of Coca-Cola's broader "Open Happiness" marketing campaign. The idea was to create brand-related conversations, not immediate sales. "It's not about having the Coca-Cola brand first and foremost," said a Coca-Cola social media marketer. "It's about telling the story that involves . . . what Coca-Cola is about, optimism and joy."

Beyond creating their own brand ambassadors, companies looking to harness the Web's social power can work with the army of self-made influencers already plying today's Internet—independent bloggers. The blogosphere has exploded onto the scene in recent years. Two-thirds of all U.S. Internet users now read blogs regularly and nearly one-third write one. Believe it or not, there are almost as many people making a living as bloggers as there are lawyers. No matter what the interest area, there are probably hundreds of bloggers covering it. Moreover, research shows that 90 percent of bloggers post about their favorite and least favorite brands.

As a result, most companies try to form relationships with influential bloggers. For example, Panasonic recruited five big-name tech bloggers to travel to a recent consumer electronics show and share their impressions, including Panasonic product reviews, with their readers via blog posts, Twitter updates, and YouTube videos. Although Panasonic paid the bloggers' travel and event expenses and loaned them digital camcorders and cameras, it had—and wanted—no say in what the bloggers posted. And the bloggers freely and fully disclosed Panasonic's sponsorship. Still, the resulting "sponsored conversations" let Panasonic tap into the groundswell of Internet buzz surrounding the show. "When you give [bloggers] equipment and they love it, just like any other consumer they'll evangelize it," says a Panasonic spokesperson.

The key is to find bloggers who have strong networks of relevant readers, a credible voice, and a good fit with the brand. For example, companies ranging from P&G and Johnson & Johnson to Walmart work closely with influential "mommy bloggers." And you'll no doubt cross paths with the likes of climbers blogging for North Face, bikers blogging for Harley-Davidson, and shoppers blogging for Whole Foods Market or Trader Joe's.

Perhaps the best way to generate brand conversations and social involvement on the Web is simply to do something conversation worthy—to actually involve people with the brand online. Pepsi's Mountain Dew brand

Harnessing online influence: Mountain Dew runs "DEWmocracy" campaigns that invite avid Mountain Dew customers to participate at all levels in launching a new Mountain Dew flavor.

runs "DEWmocracy" campaigns that invite avid Mountain Dew customers to participate at all levels in launching a new Mountain Dew flavor, from choosing and naming the flavor to designing the can to submitting and selecting TV commercials and even picking an ad agency and media. Presented through a dedicated Web site, as well as Facebook, Twitter, Flickr, and other public network pages, DEWmocracy has been a perfect forum for getting youthful, socially savvy Dew drinkers talking with each other and the company about the brand. For example, Mountain Dew's Facebook fan page grew five-fold at the launch of the latest DEWmocracy campaign.

Ironically, one of the simplest means of capturing social influence through the Web is one of the oldest—produce a good ad that gets people talking. But in this day and age, both the ads and the media have changed. Almost every brand, large and small, is now creating innovative brand-sponsored videos, posting them online, and hoping they'll go viral. The videos range from traditional 60-second

ads to intricate 10- or 12-minute film shorts. Last year's ten most innovative viral videos, as rated by social media guide Mashable.com, included everything from a very creative three-minute ad for a small Charlotte, North Carolina, ad agency to longer videos from giants such as Samsung and Volkswagen. Such videos can create lots of attention and talk. One five-minute action video for Inspired Bicycles garnered 15 million rapt views, while a 12-minute love story for Schweppes drew nearly four million views and critical acclaim.

So, whether through online ambassadors, bloggers, social networks, or talked-about videos and events, companies are finding innovative ways to tap social influence online. Called word-of-Web, it's growing fast as *the* place to be—for both consumers and marketers. Last year, the time consumers spent on social networking sites nearly tripled; marketer spending at those sites nearly kept pace. "Social [media] is one of the key trends driving business," says a social marketing executive. "It's more than pure marketing. It's about fast connections with customers and building an ongoing relationship."

Sources: Elisabeth A. Sullivan, "Blog Savvy," *Marketing News*, November 15, 2009, p. 8; Mark Penn, "America's Newest Profession: Bloggers for Hire," *Wall Street Journal*, April 21, 2009, www.wsj.com; Emily Fredrix, "Coca-Cola Sends 3 Bloggers Around the World," *Forbes*, October 21, 2009, accessed at www.forbes.com; Ellen McGirt, "Mr. Social: Ashton Kutcher Plans to Be the Next New-Media Mogul," *Fast Company*, December 1, 2009, accessed at www.fastcompany.com; Lisa Lacy, "Nielsen: Social Ad Spending Up Sharply," September 25, 2009, www.clickz .com/3635095/print; Josh Warner, "The Ten Most Viral Videos of 2009," December 7, 2009, accessed at www .mashable.com, December 7, 2009; Natalie Zmuda, "Why Mountain Dew Let Skater Dudes Take Control of Its Marketing," *Advertising Age*, February 22, 2010, p. 30; Laurie Sullivan, "Mountain Dew Fans Crowdsourced Ad Media Buys," *MediaPost News*, May 24, 2010, accessed at www.mediapost.com; and information from www .expedition206.com/e206_ambassadors.aspx and www.youtube.com/watch?v=MhAmMosaG7Y, accessed March 2010.

home and the willingness of husbands to do more of the family's purchasing, all this is changing. A recent study found that 65 percent of men grocery shop regularly and prepare at least one meal a week for others in the household. At the same time, women now influence 65 percent of all new car purchases, 91 percent of new home purchases, and 92 percent of vacation purchases. In all, women make almost 85 percent of all family purchases and control some 73 percent of all household spending. Says one analyst, "today's woman is . . . the designated chief operating officer of the home."[20]

Such changes suggest that marketers in industries that have sold their products to only men or only women are now courting the opposite sex. For example, today women account for 50 percent of all technology purchases. ⦿ So consumer electronics companies are increasingly designing products that are easier to use and more appealing to female buyers:[21]

Consumer electronics engineers and designers are bringing a more feminine sensibility to products historically shaped by masculine tastes, habits, and requirements. Designs are more "feminine and softer," rather than masculine and angular. But many of the new touches are more subtle, like the wider spacing of the keys on a Sony netbook computer. It accommodates the longer fingernails that women tend to have. Some of the latest cell phones made by LG Electronics have the cameras' automatic focus calibrated to arms' length. The company observed that young women are fond of taking pictures of themselves with a friend. Men, not so much. Nikon and Olympus recently introduced lines of lighter, more compact, and easy-to-use digital, single-lens reflex cameras that were designed with women in mind because they tend to be a family's primary keeper of memories.

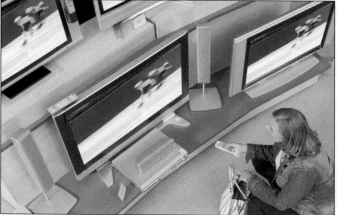

● **Family buying:** Family buying roles are changing. For example, 65 percent of men grocery shop regularly while women influence 50 percent of all new technology purchases. Technology companies are redesigning their products accordingly.

However, marketers must be careful to avoid insensitive stereotypes. For example, last year Dell launched the Della Web site, geared toward women. The Web site emphasized colors, computer accessories, and tips for counting calories and finding recipes. Many women consumers were offended, describing the site as "slick but disconcerting" and "condescending." On the flip side, one stay-at-home dad and blogger ("Rebel Dad") took diaper brand Pampers to task for sending him its annual Mother's Day e-mail, with the friendly and personalized greeting: "Happy Mother's Day, Brian!" Said Rebel Dad in a letter to Pampers, "Every year, you blanket me (and, presumably tens of thousands of other dads) with a sweet reminder that one [you] still assume that every person who wants diaper coupons is a woman. That's dumb."[22]

Children may also have a strong influence on family buying decisions. The nation's 36 million children ages 8 to 12 wield an estimated $30 billion in disposable income. They also influence an additional $150 billion that their families spend on them in areas such as food, clothing, entertainment, and personal care items. One study found that kids significantly influence family decisions about everything from where they take vacations to what cars and cell phones they buy.[23]

For example, to encourage families to take their children out to eat again following the recent recession, casual restaurants reached out to children with everything from sophisticated children's menus and special deals to a wealth of kid-focused activities. At Applebee's, children eat free on Mondays with the purchase of an adult entrée. Carrabba's Italian Grill gives children a ball of dough, pepperoni slices, and cheese so they can make their own pizzas at the table, which are then cooked in the kitchen. And at Roy's Restaurants, as soon as children are seated, the Roy's server learns their names (and addresses them by name throughout the meal). "We want them to get excited and happy immediately," says a Roy's executive. Other kids perks at Roy's include portable DVD players with movies and headphones on request and sundaes with kids' names written in chocolate. "They love seeing their name in chocolate," says a Roy's executive. Roy's big-hearted commitment to children's happiness is a no-brainer. Happy children equal happy parents.[24]

Roles and Status

A person belongs to many groups—family, clubs, organizations, online communities. The person's position in each group can be defined in terms of both role and status. A *role* consists of the activities people are expected to perform according to the people around them. Each role carries a status reflecting the general esteem given to it by society.

People usually choose products appropriate to their roles and status. Consider the various roles a working mother plays. In her company, she plays the role of a brand manager; in her family, she plays the role of wife and mother; at her favorite sporting events, she plays the role of avid fan. As a brand manager, she will buy the kind of clothing that reflects her role and status in her company.

Personal Factors

A buyer's decisions also are influenced by personal characteristics such as the buyer's *age and life-cycle stage, occupation, economic situation, lifestyle,* and *personality and self-concept.*

Age and Life-Cycle Stage

People change the goods and services they buy over their lifetimes. Tastes in food, clothes, furniture, and recreation are often age related. Buying is also shaped by the stage of the family life cycle—the stages through which families might pass as they mature over time. Life-stage changes usually result from demographics and life-changing events—marriage, having children, purchasing a home, divorce, children going to college, changes in personal income, moving out of the house, and retirement. Marketers often define their target markets in terms of life-cycle stage and develop appropriate products and marketing plans for each stage.

● Life-stage segmentation: PersonicX's 21 life-stage groupings let marketers see customers as they really are and target them precisely. "People aren't just a parent or only a doctor or simply a scuba diver. They are all of these things."

● Consumer information giant Acxiom's PersonicX life-stage segmentation system places U.S. households into one of 70 consumer segments and 21 life-stage groups, based on specific consumer behavior and demographic characteristics. PersonicX includes life-stage groups with names such as *Beginnings*, *Taking Hold*, *Cash & Careers*, *Jumbo Families*, *Transition Blues*, *Our Turn*, *Golden Years*, and *Active Elders*. For example, the *Taking Hold* group consists of young, energetic, well-funded couples and young families who are busy with their careers, social lives, and interests, especially fitness and active recreation. *Transition Blues* are blue-collar, less-educated, mid-income consumers who are transitioning to stable lives and talking about marriage and children.

"Consumers experience many life-stage changes during their lifetimes," says Acxiom. "As their life stages change, so do their behaviors and purchasing preferences. Marketers who are armed with the data to understand the timing and makeup of life-stage changes among their customers will have a distinct advantage over their competitors."[25]

In line with today's tougher economic times, Acxiom has also developed a set of economic life-stage segments, including groups such as *Squeaking By*, *Eye on Essentials*, *Tight with a Purpose*, *It's My Life*, *Full Speed Ahead*, and *Potential Rebounders*. The *Potential Rebounders* are those more likely to loosen up on spending sooner. This group appears more likely than other segments to use online research before purchasing electronics, appliances, home decor, and jewelry. Thus, home improvement retailers appealing to this segment should have a strong online presence, providing pricing, features and benefits, and product availability.

Occupation

A person's occupation affects the goods and services bought. Blue-collar workers tend to buy more rugged work clothes, whereas executives buy more business suits. Marketers try to identify the occupational groups that have an above-average interest in their products and services. A company can even specialize in making products needed by a given occupational group.

For example, Carhartt makes rugged, durable, no-nonsense work clothes—what it calls "original equipment for the American worker. From coats to jackets, bibs to overalls . . . if the apparel carries the name Carhartt, the performance will be legendary." Its Web site carries real-life testimonials of hard-working Carhartt customers. One electrician, battling the cold in Canada's arctic region, reports wearing Carhartt's lined Arctic bib overalls, Arctic jacket, and other clothing for more than two years without a single "popped button, ripped pocket seam, or stuck zipper." And a railroadman in northern New York, who's spent years walking rough railroad beds, climbing around trains, and switching cars in conditions ranging from extreme heat to frigid cold, calls his trusty brown Carhartt jacket part of his "survival gear—like a bulletproof vest is to a policeman."[26]

Economic Situation

A person's economic situation will affect his or her store and product choices. Marketers watch trends in personal income, savings, and interest rates. Following the recent recession, most companies have taken steps to redesign, reposition, and reprice their products. For example, at Target, to counter the effects of the recession, "cheap has taken over chic." The discount retailer unveiled "The Great Save," a nationwide event featuring low prices on a variety of products. "The Great Save is a way for Target to offer our guests exceptional deals on everyday essentials—a treasure-hunt experience with a variety of exciting designer brands," says a Target marketing vice president. "This event is a fresh approach to meeting our guests' evolving needs [by letting them] save even more at Target." Says another Target marketer, "Our [tagline] is 'Expect more. Pay less.' [These days,] we're putting more emphasis on the pay less promise."[27]

Lifestyle

Lifestyle
A person's pattern of living as expressed in his or her activities, interests, and opinions.

People coming from the same subculture, social class, and occupation may have quite different lifestyles. **Lifestyle** is a person's pattern of living as expressed in his or her psychographics. It involves measuring consumers' major AIO dimensions—activities (work, hobbies, shopping, sports, social events), interests (food, fashion, family, recreation), and opinions (about themselves, social issues, business, products). Lifestyle captures something more than the person's social class or personality. It profiles a person's whole pattern of acting and interacting in the world.

When used carefully, the lifestyle concept can help marketers understand changing consumer values and how they affect buying behavior. Consumers don't just buy products; they buy the values and lifestyles those products represent. ⦿ For example, Triumph doesn't just sell motorcycles; it sells an independent, "Go your own way" lifestyle. And lifestyle shoemaker Merrell says "Let's Get Outside." Says one marketer, "People's product choices are becoming more and more like value choices. It's not, 'I like this water, the way it tastes.' It's 'I feel like this car, or this show, is more reflective of who I am.'"[28]

For example, retailer Anthropologie, with its whimsical, French flea market store atmosphere, sells a bohemian-chic lifestyle to which its young women customers aspire:

⦿ Lifestyle: Triumph doesn't just sell motorcycles; it sells an independent, "Go your own way" lifestyle.

In downtown San Francisco, which is teeming with both high-end and cheap chic outlets, Anthropologie is a mecca. It evokes hole-in-the-wall antique stores, Parisian boutiques, flea markets, and Grandma's kitchen in one fell swoop. It's a lifestyle emporium that you want to move into, or at least have a small piece of, even if it's just a lacquered light switch cover or retro tea towel. When customers enter an Anthropologie, they immediately leave behind the sterile mall or not-so-sterile street and are transported into another lifestyle. In freestanding stores, Anthropologie's expressive exteriors also reflect local lifestyles. In Burlingame, California, the Anthropologie store is reminiscent of the northern California coast with concrete and wood. In Albuquerque, New Mexico, located in a lifestyle center, the store features painted reclaimed wood to emulate surrounding rock, soil, and mesas of the area. Down South in Huntsville, Alabama, Anthropologie went for a lush, green design that features planting boxes with seasonal plants. As a result, even when retail sales in general have slumped, Anthropologie's sales have continued to grow.[29]

Personality and Self-Concept

Personality
The unique psychological characteristics that distinguish a person or group.

Each person's distinct personality influences his or her buying behavior. **Personality** refers to the unique psychological characteristics that distinguish a person or group. Personality is usually described in terms of traits such as self-confidence, dominance, sociability, autonomy, defensiveness, adaptability, and aggressiveness. Personality can be useful in analyzing consumer behavior for certain product or brand choices.

The idea is that brands also have personalities, and consumers are likely to choose brands with personalities that match their own. A *brand personality* is the specific mix of human traits that may be attributed to a particular brand. One researcher identified five brand personality traits: *sincerity* (down-to-earth, honest, wholesome, and cheerful); *excitement* (daring, spirited, imaginative, and up-to-date); *competence* (reliable, intelligent, and successful); *sophistication* (upper class and charming); and *ruggedness* (outdoorsy and tough).[30]

Most well-known brands are strongly associated with one particular trait: Jeep with "ruggedness," Apple with "excitement," CNN with "competence," and Dove with "sincerity." Hence, these brands will attract persons who are high on the same personality traits.

Many marketers use a concept related to personality—a person's *self-concept* (also called *self-image*). The idea is that people's possessions contribute to and reflect their identities—that is, "we are what we have." Thus, to understand consumer behavior, marketers must first understand the relationship between consumer self-concept and possessions.

Apple applied these concepts in its long-running "Get a Mac" ad series that characterized two people as computers: one guy played the part of an Apple Mac, and the other played a personal computer (PC). The two had very different personalities and self-concepts. "Hello, I'm a Mac," said the guy on the right, who was younger and dressed in jeans. "And I'm a PC," said the one on the left, who was wearing dweeby glasses and a jacket and tie. The two men discussed the relative advantages of Macs versus PCs, with the Mac coming out on top. The ads presented the Mac brand personality as young, laid back, and cool. The PC was portrayed as buttoned down, corporate, and a bit dorky. The message? If you saw yourself as young and with it, you needed a Mac.[31]

Psychological Factors

A person's buying choices are further influenced by four major psychological factors: *motivation*, *perception*, *learning*, and *beliefs and attitudes*.

Motivation

Motive (drive)
A need that is sufficiently pressing to direct the person to seek satisfaction of the need.

A person has many needs at any given time. Some are biological, arising from states of tension such as hunger, thirst, or discomfort. Others are psychological, arising from the need for recognition, esteem, or belonging. A need becomes a motive when it is aroused to a sufficient level of intensity. A **motive** (or **drive**) is a need that is sufficiently pressing to direct the person to seek satisfaction. Psychologists have developed theories of human motivation. Two of the most popular—the theories of Sigmund Freud and Abraham Maslow—have quite different meanings for consumer analysis and marketing.

Sigmund Freud assumed that people are largely unconscious about the real psychological forces shaping their behavior. He saw the person as growing up and repressing many urges. These urges are never eliminated or under perfect control; they emerge in dreams, in slips of the tongue, in neurotic and obsessive behavior, or, ultimately, in psychoses.

Freud's theory suggests that a person's buying decisions are affected by subconscious motives that even the buyer may not fully understand. ● Thus, an aging baby boomer who buys a sporty BMW Z4 Roadster convertible might explain that he simply likes the feel of the wind in his thinning hair. At a deeper level, he may be trying to impress others with his success. At a still deeper level, he may be buying the car to feel young and independent again.

The term *motivation research* refers to qualitative research designed to probe consumers' hidden, subconscious motivations. Consumers often don't know or can't describe why they act as they do. Thus, motivation researchers use a variety of

● Motivation: an aging baby boomer who buys a sporty convertible might explain that he simply likes the feel of the wind in his thinning hair. At a deeper level, he may be buying the car to feel young and independent again.

probing techniques to uncover underlying emotions and attitudes toward brands and buying situations.

Many companies employ teams of psychologists, anthropologists, and other social scientists to carry out motivation research. One ad agency routinely conducts one-on-one, therapy-like interviews to delve into the inner workings of consumers. Another company asks consumers to describe their favorite brands as animals or cars (say, Cadillacs versus Chevrolets) to assess the prestige associated with various brands. Still others rely on hypnosis, dream therapy, or soft lights and mood music to plumb the murky depths of consumer psyches.

Such projective techniques seem pretty goofy, and some marketers dismiss such motivation research as mumbo jumbo. But many marketers use such touchy-feely approaches, now sometimes called *interpretive consumer research*, to dig deeper into consumer psyches and develop better marketing strategies.

Abraham Maslow sought to explain why people are driven by particular needs at particular times. Why does one person spend a lot of time and energy on personal safety and another on gaining the esteem of others? Maslow's answer is that human needs are arranged in a hierarchy, as shown in ⦿ **Figure 5.4**, from the most pressing at the bottom to the least pressing at the top.[32] They include *physiological* needs, *safety* needs, *social* needs, *esteem* needs, and *self-actualization* needs.

A person tries to satisfy the most important need first. When that need is satisfied, it will stop being a motivator, and the person will then try to satisfy the next most important need. For example, starving people (physiological need) will not take an interest in the latest happenings in the art world (self-actualization needs) nor in how they are seen or esteemed by others (social or esteem needs) nor even in whether they are breathing clean air (safety needs). But as each important need is satisfied, the next most important need will come into play.

Perception

A motivated person is ready to act. How the person acts is influenced by his or her own perception of the situation. All of us learn by the flow of information through our five senses: sight, hearing, smell, touch, and taste. However, each of us receives, organizes, and interprets this sensory information in an individual way. **Perception** is the process by which people select, organize, and interpret information to form a meaningful picture of the world.

People can form different perceptions of the same stimulus because of three perceptual processes: selective attention, selective distortion, and selective retention. People are exposed to a great amount of stimuli every day. For example, people are exposed to an estimated 3,000 to 5,000 ad messages every day. It is impossible for a person to pay attention to all these stimuli. *Selective attention*—the tendency for people to screen out most of the infor-

Perception
The process by which people select, organize, and interpret information to form a meaningful picture of the world.

⦿ **FIGURE** | 5.4
Maslow's Hierarchy of Needs

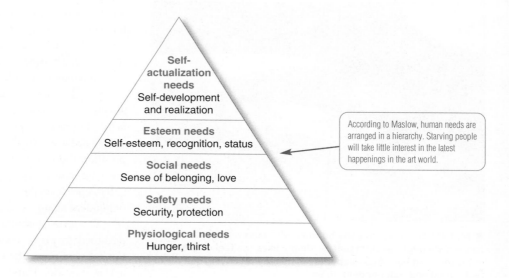

Self-actualization needs
Self-development and realization

Esteem needs
Self-esteem, recognition, status

Social needs
Sense of belonging, love

Safety needs
Security, protection

Physiological needs
Hunger, thirst

According to Maslow, human needs are arranged in a hierarchy. Starving people will take little interest in the latest happenings in the art world.

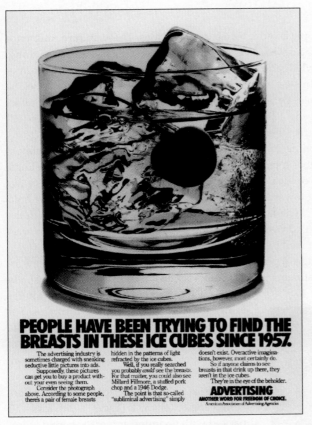

PEOPLE HAVE BEEN TRYING TO FIND THE BREASTS IN THESE ICE CUBES SINCE 1957.

The advertising industry is sometimes charged with sneaking seductive little pictures into ads.

Supposedly, these pictures can get you to buy a product without your even seeing them.

Consider the photograph above. According to some people, there's a pair of female breasts

hidden in the patterns of light refracted by the ice cubes.

Well, if you really searched you probably *could* see the breasts. For that matter, you could also see Millard Fillmore, a stuffed pork chop and a 1946 Dodge.

The point is that so-called "subliminal advertising" simply

doesn't exist. Overactive imaginations, however, most certainly do.

So if anyone claims to see breasts in that drink up there, they aren't in the ice cubes.

They're in the eye of the beholder.

ADVERTISING

ANOTHER WORD FOR FREEDOM OF CHOICE.

American Association of Advertising Agencies

● **This classic ad from the American Association of Advertising Agencies pokes fun at subliminal advertising. "So-called 'subliminal advertising' simply doesn't exist," says the ad. "Overactive imaginations, however, most certainly do."**

mation to which they are exposed—means that marketers must work especially hard to attract the consumer's attention.[33]

Even noticed stimuli do not always come across in the intended way. Each person fits incoming information into an existing mind-set. *Selective distortion* describes the tendency of people to interpret information in a way that will support what they already believe. People also will forget much of what they learn. They tend to retain information that supports their attitudes and beliefs. *Selective retention* means that consumers are likely to remember good points made about a brand they favor and forget good points made about competing brands. Because of selective attention, distortion, and retention, marketers must work hard to get their messages through.

Interestingly, although most marketers worry about whether their offers will be perceived at all, some consumers worry that they will be affected by marketing messages without even knowing it—through *subliminal advertising*. More than 50 years ago, a researcher announced that he had flashed the phrases "Eat popcorn" and "Drink Coca-Cola" on a screen in a New Jersey movie theater every five seconds for 1/300th of a second. He reported that although viewers did not consciously recognize these messages, they absorbed them subconsciously and bought 58 percent more popcorn and 18 percent more Coke. Suddenly advertisers and consumer-protection groups became intensely interested in subliminal perception. Although the researcher later admitted to making up the data, the issue has not died. Some consumers still fear that they are being manipulated by subliminal messages.

Numerous studies by psychologists and consumer researchers have found little or no link between subliminal messages and consumer behavior. Recent brain wave studies have found that in certain circumstances, our brains may register subliminal messages. ● However, it appears that subliminal advertising simply doesn't have the power attributed to it by its critics. Scoffs one industry insider, "Just between us, most [advertisers] have difficulty getting a 2 percent increase in sales with the help of $50 million in media and *extremely liminal* images of sex, money, power, and other [motivators] of human emotion. The very idea of [us] as puppeteers, cruelly pulling the strings of consumer marionettes, is almost too much to bear."[34]

Learning

Learning
Changes in an individual's behavior arising from experience.

When people act, they learn. **Learning** describes changes in an individual's behavior arising from experience. Learning theorists say that most human behavior is learned. Learning occurs through the interplay of drives, stimuli, cues, responses, and reinforcement.

A *drive* is a strong internal stimulus that calls for action. A drive becomes a motive when it is directed toward a particular *stimulus object*. For example, a person's drive for self-actualization might motivate him or her to look into buying a camera. The consumer's response to the idea of buying a camera is conditioned by the surrounding cues. *Cues* are minor stimuli that determine when, where, and how the person responds. For example, the person might spot several camera brands in a shop window, hear of a special sale price, or discuss cameras with a friend. These are all cues that might influence a consumer's *response* to his or her interest in buying the product.

Suppose the consumer buys a Nikon camera. If the experience is rewarding, the consumer will probably use the camera more and more, and his or her response will be *reinforced*. Then the next time he or she shops for a camera, or for binoculars or some similar product, the probability is greater that he or she will buy a Nikon product. The practical significance of learning theory for marketers is that they can build up demand for a product by associating it with strong drives, using motivating cues, and providing positive reinforcement.

Beliefs and Attitudes

Belief
A descriptive thought that a person holds about something.

Through doing and learning, people acquire beliefs and attitudes. These, in turn, influence their buying behavior. A **belief** is a descriptive thought that a person has about something. Beliefs may be based on real knowledge, opinion, or faith and may or may not carry an emotional charge. Marketers are interested in the beliefs that people formulate about specific products and services because these beliefs make up product and brand images that affect buying behavior. If some of the beliefs are wrong and prevent purchase, the marketer will want to launch a campaign to correct them.

People have attitudes regarding religion, politics, clothes, music, food, and almost everything else. **Attitude** describes a person's relatively consistent evaluations, feelings, and tendencies toward an object or idea. Attitudes put people into a frame of mind of liking or disliking things, of moving toward or away from them. Our camera buyer may hold attitudes such as "Buy the best," "The Japanese make the best electronics products in the world," and "Creativity and self-expression are among the most important things in life." If so, the Nikon camera would fit well into the consumer's existing attitudes.

Attitude
A person's consistently favorable or unfavorable evaluations, feelings, and tendencies toward an object or idea.

Attitudes are difficult to change. A person's attitudes fit into a pattern; changing one attitude may require difficult adjustments in many others. Thus, a company should usually try to fit its products into existing attitudes rather than attempt to change attitudes. For example, today's beverage marketers now cater to people's new attitudes about health and well-being with drinks that do a lot more than just taste good or quench your thirst. Pepsi's SoBe brand, for example, offers "Lifewater," "elixirs" (juices), and teas—all packed with vitamins, minerals, herbal ingredients, and antioxidants but without artificial preservatives, sweeteners, or colors. SoBe promises drinks that are good tasting (with flavors like YumBerry Pomegranate Purify, Nirvana Mango Melon, and Tsunami Orange Cream) but are also good for you. By matching today's attitudes about life and healthful living, the SoBe brand has become a leader in the New Age beverage category.

Beliefs and attitudes: By matching today's attitudes about life and healthful living, the SoBe brand has become a leader in the New Age beverage category.

We can now appreciate the many forces acting on consumer behavior. The consumer's choice results from the complex interplay of cultural, social, personal, and psychological factors.

Author Comment | Some purchases are simple and routine, even habitual. Others are far more complex—involving extensive information gathering and evaluation—and are subject to sometimes subtle influences. For example, think of all that goes into a new car buying decision.

Types of Buying Decision Behavior (pp 150–152)

Buying behavior differs greatly for a tube of toothpaste, an iPhone, financial services, and a new car. More complex decisions usually involve more buying participants and more buyer deliberation. **Figure 5.5** shows the types of consumer buying behavior based on the degree of buyer involvement and the degree of differences among brands.

Complex Buying Behavior

Complex buying behavior
Consumer buying behavior in situations characterized by high consumer involvement in a purchase and significant perceived differences among brands.

Consumers undertake **complex buying behavior** when they are highly involved in a purchase and perceive significant differences among brands. Consumers may be highly involved when the product is expensive, risky, purchased infrequently, and highly self-expressive. Typically, the consumer has much to learn about the product category. For example, a PC buyer may not know what attributes to consider. Many product features carry no real meaning: a "3.2GHz Intel Core i7 processor," "WUXGA active matrix screen," or "8GB dual-channel DDR2 SDRAM memory."

This buyer will pass through a learning process, first developing beliefs about the product, then attitudes, and then making a thoughtful purchase choice. Marketers of high-involvement products must understand the information-gathering and evaluation behavior of high-involvement consumers. They need to help buyers learn about product-class attributes and their relative importance. They need to differentiate their brand's features, perhaps by describing the brand's benefits using print media with long copy. They must motivate store salespeople and the buyer's acquaintances to influence the final brand choice.

Dissonance-Reducing Buying Behavior

Dissonance-reducing buying behavior occurs when consumers are highly involved with an expensive, infrequent, or risky purchase but see little difference among brands. For example, consumers buying carpeting may face a high-involvement decision because carpeting is expensive and self-expressive. Yet buyers may consider most carpet brands in a given price range to be the same. In this case, because perceived brand differences are not large, buyers may shop around to learn what is available but buy relatively quickly. They may respond primarily to a good price or purchase convenience.

After the purchase, consumers might experience *postpurchase dissonance* (after-sale discomfort) when they notice certain disadvantages of the purchased carpet brand or hear favorable things about brands not purchased. To counter such dissonance, the marketer's after-sale communications should provide evidence and support to help consumers feel good about their brand choices.

Habitual Buying Behavior

Habitual buying behavior occurs under conditions of low-consumer involvement and little significant brand difference. For example, take table salt. Consumers have little involvement in this product category—they simply go to the store and reach for a brand. If they keep reaching for the same brand, it is out of habit rather than strong brand loyalty. Consumers appear to have low involvement with most low-cost, frequently purchased products.

In such cases, consumer behavior does not pass through the usual belief-attitude-behavior sequence. Consumers do not search extensively for information about the brands, evaluate brand characteristics, and make weighty decisions about which brands to buy. Instead, they passively receive information as they watch television or read magazines. Ad repetition creates *brand familiarity* rather than *brand conviction*. Consumers do not form strong attitudes toward a brand; they select the brand because it is familiar. Because they are not highly involved with the product, consumers may not evaluate the choice, even after purchase. Thus, the buying process involves brand beliefs formed by passive learning, followed by purchase behavior, which may or may not be followed by evaluation.

Because buyers are not highly committed to any brands, marketers of low-involvement products with few brand differences often use price and sales promotions to promote buying. Alternatively, they can add product features or enhancements to differentiate their

---

Dissonance-reducing buying behavior
Consumer buying behavior in situations characterized by high involvement but few perceived differences among brands.

Habitual buying behavior
Consumer buying behavior in situations characterized by low-consumer involvement and few significantly perceived brand differences.

⊙ FIGURE | 5.5
Four Types of Buying Behavior
Source: Adapted from Henry Assael, *Consumer Behavior and Marketing Action* (Boston: Kent Publishing Company, 1987), p. 87. Used with permission of the author.

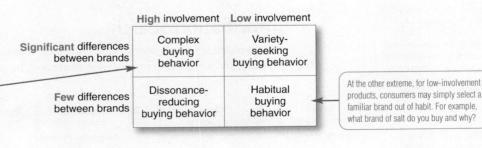

Buying behavior varies greatly for different types of products. For example, someone buying an expensive new PC might undertake a full information-gathering and brand evaluation process.

	High involvement	**Low** involvement
Significant differences between brands	Complex buying behavior	Variety-seeking buying behavior
Few differences between brands	Dissonance-reducing buying behavior	Habitual buying behavior

At the other extreme, for low-involvement products, consumers may simply select a familiar brand out of habit. For example, what brand of salt do you buy and why?

brands from the rest of the pack and raise involvement. For example, to set its brand apart, Charmin toilet tissue offers Ultrastrong, Ultrasoft, and Freshmate (wet) versions that are so absorbent that you can "soften your bottom line" by using four times less than value brands. Charmin also raises brand involvement by sponsoring a "Sit or Squat" Web site and cell phone app that helps travelers who "Gotta go on the go!" find and rate clean public restrooms.

Variety-Seeking Buying Behavior

Variety-seeking buying behavior
Consumer buying behavior in situations characterized by low consumer involvement but significant perceived brand differences.

Consumers undertake **variety-seeking buying behavior** in situations characterized by low consumer involvement but significant perceived brand differences. In such cases, consumers often do a lot of brand switching. For example, when buying cookies, a consumer may hold some beliefs, choose a cookie brand without much evaluation, and then evaluate that brand during consumption. But the next time, the consumer might pick another brand out of boredom or simply to try something different. Brand switching occurs for the sake of variety rather than because of dissatisfaction.

In such product categories, the marketing strategy may differ for the market leader and minor brands. The market leader will try to encourage habitual buying behavior by dominating shelf space, keeping shelves fully stocked, and running frequent reminder advertising. Challenger firms will encourage variety seeking by offering lower prices, special deals, coupons, free samples, and advertising that presents reasons for trying something new.

> **Author Comment** | The actual purchase decision is part of a much larger buying process—starting with need recognition through how you feel after making the purchase. Marketers want to be involved throughout the entire buyer decision process.

The Buyer Decision Process (pp 152–156)

Now that we have looked at the influences that affect buyers, we are ready to look at how consumers make buying decisions. ● **Figure 5.6** shows that the buyer decision process consists of five stages: *need recognition, information search, evaluation of alternatives, purchase decision,* and *postpurchase behavior.* Clearly, the buying process starts long before the actual purchase and continues long after. Marketers need to focus on the entire buying process rather than on the purchase decision only.

Figure 5.6 suggests that consumers pass through all five stages with every purchase. But in more routine purchases, consumers often skip or reverse some of these stages. A woman buying her regular brand of toothpaste would recognize the need and go right to the purchase decision, skipping information search and evaluation. However, we use the model in Figure 5.6 because it shows all the considerations that arise when a consumer faces a new and complex purchase situation.

Need Recognition

Need recognition
The first stage of the buyer decision process, in which the consumer recognizes a problem or need.

The buying process starts with **need recognition**—the buyer recognizes a problem or need. The need can be triggered by *internal stimuli* when one of the person's normal needs—for example, hunger or thirst—rises to a level high enough to become a drive. A need can also be triggered by *external stimuli.* ● For example, an advertisement or a discussion with a friend might get you thinking about buying a new car. At this stage, the marketer should research consumers to find out what kinds of needs or problems arise, what brought them about, and how they led the consumer to this particular product.

Information Search

> The buying process starts long before the actual purchase and continues long after. In fact, it might result in a decision *not* to buy. Therefore, marketers must focus on the entire buying process, not just the purchase decision.

An interested consumer may or may not search for more information. If the consumer's drive is strong and a satisfying product is near at hand, he or she is likely to buy it then. If not, the

Need recognition → Information search → Evaluation of alternatives → Purchase decision → Postpurchase behavior

● **FIGURE | 5.6**
Buyer Decision Process

Some relationships are meant to be.

Pure dark chocolate.
Light exquisite cookie.
Made for each other.
And for you.
MILANO.

PEPPERIDGE FARM

GOOD IS IN THE DETAILS.

pepperidgefarm.com

Milano

● **Need recognition can be triggered by advertising: Is it time for a snack?**

Information search

The stage of the buyer decision process in which the consumer is aroused to search for more information; the consumer may simply have heightened attention or may go into an active information search.

Alternative evaluation

The stage of the buyer decision process in which the consumer uses information to evaluate alternative brands in the choice set.

consumer may store the need in memory or undertake an **information search** related to the need. For example, once you've decided you need a new car, at the least, you will probably pay more attention to car ads, cars owned by friends, and car conversations. Or you may actively search the Web, talk with friends, and gather information in other ways.

Consumers can obtain information from any of several sources. These include *personal sources* (family, friends, neighbors, acquaintances), *commercial sources* (advertising, salespeople, dealer Web sites, packaging, displays), *public sources* (mass media, consumer rating organizations, Internet searches), and *experiential sources* (handling, examining, using the product). The relative influence of these information sources varies with the product and the buyer.

Generally, the consumer receives the most information about a product from commercial sources—those controlled by the marketer. The most effective sources, however, tend to be personal. Commercial sources normally *inform* the buyer, but personal sources *legitimize* or *evaluate* products for the buyer. For example, a recent study found that word of mouth is the biggest influence in people's electronics (43.7 percent) and apparel (33.6 percent) purchases. As one marketer states, "It's rare that an advertising campaign can be as effective as a neighbor leaning over the fence and saying, 'This is a wonderful product.'" Increasingly, that "fence" is a digital one. Another recent study revealed that consumers find sources of user-generated content—discussion forums, blogs, online review sites, and social networking sites—three times more influential when making a purchase decision than conventional marketing methods such as TV advertising.[35]

As more information is obtained, the consumer's awareness and knowledge of the available brands and features increase. In your car information search, you may learn about the several brands available. The information might also help you to drop certain brands from consideration. A company must design its marketing mix to make prospects aware of and knowledgeable about its brand. It should carefully identify consumers' sources of information and the importance of each source.

Evaluation of Alternatives

We have seen how consumers use information to arrive at a set of final brand choices. How does the consumer choose among alternative brands? Marketers need to know about **alternative evaluation**, that is, how the consumer processes information to arrive at brand choices. Unfortunately, consumers do not use a simple and single evaluation process in all buying situations. Instead, several evaluation processes are at work.

The consumer arrives at attitudes toward different brands through some evaluation procedure. How consumers go about evaluating purchase alternatives depends on the individual consumer and the specific buying situation. In some cases, consumers use careful calculations and logical thinking. At other times, the same consumers do little or no evaluating; instead they buy on impulse and rely on intuition. Sometimes consumers make buying decisions on their own; sometimes they turn to friends, online reviews, or salespeople for buying advice.

Suppose you've narrowed your car choices to three brands. And suppose that you are primarily interested in four attributes—styling, operating economy, warranty, and price. By this time, you've probably formed beliefs about how each brand rates on each attribute. Clearly, if one car rated best on all the attributes, the marketer could predict that you would choose it. However, the brands will no doubt vary in appeal. You might base your buying decision on only one attribute, and your choice would be easy to predict. If you wanted styling above everything else, you would buy the car that you think has the best styling. But most buyers consider several attributes, each with different importance. If the marketer knew the importance that you assigned to each attribute, he or she could predict your car choice more reliably.

Marketers should study buyers to find out how they actually evaluate brand alternatives. If marketers know what evaluative processes go on, they can take steps to influence the buyer's decision.

Purchase Decision

Purchase decision
The buyer's decision about which brand to purchase.

In the evaluation stage, the consumer ranks brands and forms purchase intentions. Generally, the consumer's **purchase decision** will be to buy the most preferred brand, but two factors can come between the purchase *intention* and the purchase *decision*. The first factor is the attitudes *of others*. If someone important to you thinks that you should buy the lowest-priced car, then the chances of you buying a more expensive car are reduced.

The second factor is *unexpected situational factors*. The consumer may form a purchase intention based on factors such as expected income, expected price, and expected product benefits. However, unexpected events may change the purchase intention. For example, the economy might take a turn for the worse, a close competitor might drop its price, or a friend might report being disappointed in your preferred car. Thus, preferences and even purchase intentions do not always result in actual purchase choice.

Postpurchase Behavior

Postpurchase behavior
The stage of the buyer decision process in which consumers take further action after purchase based on their satisfaction or dissatisfaction with a purchase.

The marketer's job does not end when the product is bought. After purchasing the product, the consumer will either be satisfied or dissatisfied and will engage in **postpurchase behavior** of interest to the marketer. What determines whether the buyer is satisfied or dissatisfied with a purchase? The answer lies in the relationship between the *consumer's expectations* and the product's *perceived performance*. If the product falls short of expectations, the consumer is disappointed; if it meets expectations, the consumer is satisfied; if it exceeds expectations, the consumer is delighted. The larger the gap between expectations and performance, the greater the consumer's dissatisfaction. This suggests that sellers should promise only what their brands can deliver so that buyers are satisfied.

Cognitive dissonance
Buyer discomfort caused by postpurchase conflict.

Almost all major purchases, however, result in **cognitive dissonance**, or discomfort caused by postpurchase conflict. After the purchase, consumers are satisfied with the benefits of the chosen brand and are glad to avoid the drawbacks of the brands not bought. However, every purchase involves compromise. So consumers feel uneasy about acquiring the drawbacks of the chosen brand and about losing the benefits of the brands not purchased. Thus, consumers feel at least some postpurchase dissonance for every purchase.[36]

Why is it so important to satisfy the customer? Customer satisfaction is a key to building profitable relationships with consumers—to keeping and growing consumers and reaping their customer lifetime value. Satisfied customers buy a product again, talk favorably to others about the product, pay less attention to competing brands and advertising, and buy other products from the company. Many marketers go beyond merely *meeting* the expectations of customers—they aim to *delight* the customer (see Real Marketing 5.2).

A dissatisfied consumer responds differently. Bad word of mouth often travels farther and faster than good word of mouth. It can quickly damage consumer attitudes about a company and its products. But companies cannot simply rely on dissatisfied customers to volunteer their complaints when they are dissatisfied. Most unhappy customers never tell the company about their problems. Therefore, a company should measure customer satisfaction regularly. It should set up systems that *encourage* customers to complain. In this way, the company can learn how well it is doing and how it can improve.

By studying the overall buyer decision process, marketers may be able to find ways to help consumers move through it. For example, if consumers are not buying a new product because they do not perceive a need for it, marketing might launch advertising messages that trigger the need and show how the product solves customers' problems. If customers know about the product but are not buying because they hold unfavorable attitudes toward it, marketers must find ways to change either the product or consumer perceptions.

Lexus: Delighting Customers after the Sale to Keep Them Coming Back

Close your eyes for a minute and picture a typical car dealership. Not impressed? Talk to a friend who owns a Lexus, and you'll no doubt get a very different picture. The typical Lexus dealership is, well, anything but typical. And some Lexus dealers will go to almost any length to take care of customers and keep them coming back. Consider the following examples:

Jordan Case has big plans for the ongoing expansion of his business. He's already put in wireless Internet access. He's adding a café. And he's installing a putting green for customers who want to hone their golf skills while waiting for service. Case isn't the manager of a swank hotel or restaurant. He's the president of Park Place Lexus, an auto dealership with two locations in the Dallas area, and he takes pride that his dealership is, well, the antidealership. In addition to the café, putting green, and Internet access, customer perks include free car washes and portable DVD players with movies loaned to waiting service clients. Park Place Lexus's passion for customer service even earned it a Malcolm Baldrige National Quality Award, a business-excellence honor bestowed by the U.S. government, making it the first automotive dealership ever in the award's history to win the award. "Buying a car doesn't rank up there with the top five things you like to do," Case says. "So we try to make the experience different."

For many people, a trip to the auto dealer means the mind-numbing hour or two in a plastic chair with some tattered magazines and stale coffee. But JM Lexus in Margate, Florida, features four massage chairs, in addition to its Starbucks coffee shop, two putting greens, two customer lounges, and a library. At another gleaming glass-and-stone Lexus dealership north of Miami, "guests," as Lexus calls its customers, leave their cars with a valet and are then guided by a concierge to a European-style coffee bar offering complimentary espresso, cappuccino, and a selection of pastries prepared by a chef trained in Rome. "We have customers checking into world-class hotels," says a dealership executive. "They shop on Fifth Avenue and they expect a certain kind of experience."

Lexus knows that good marketing doesn't end with making a sale. Keeping customers happy *after* the sale is the key to building lasting relationships. Dealers across the country have a common goal: to delight customers and keep them coming back. Lexus believes that if you "delight the customer, and continue to delight the customer, you will have a customer for life." And Lexus understands just how valuable a customer can be; it estimates that the average lifetime value of a Lexus customer is $600,000.

Despite the amenities, few Lexus customers spend much time hanging around the dealership. Lexus knows that the best dealership visit is the one that you never make. So it builds customer-pleasing cars to start with—high-quality cars that need little servicing. In its "Lexus Covenant," the company vows that it will make "the finest cars ever built." In survey after industry survey, Lexus rates at or near the top in quality. Lexus has topped the list in seven of the last nine annual J.D. Power and Associates Initial Quality Study ratings.

Still, when a car does need servicing, Lexus goes out of its way to make it easy and painless. Most dealers will even pick up the car and then return it when the maintenance is finished. And the car comes back spotless, thanks to a complimentary cleaning to remove bugs and road grime from the exterior and smudges from the leather interior. You might even be surprised to find that they've touched up a door ding to help restore the car to its fresh-from-the-factory luster. "My wife will never buy another car except a Lexus," says one satisfied Lexus owner. "They come to our house, pick up the car, do an oil change, [spiff it up,] and bring it back. She's sold for life." And when a customer does bring a car in, Lexus repairs it right the first time, on time. Dealers know that their well-heeled customers have money, "but what they don't have is time."

According to its Web site, from the very start, Lexus set out to "revolutionize the automotive experience with a passionate commitment to the finest products, supported by dealers who create the most satisfying ownership experience the world has ever seen. We vow to value the customer as an important individual. To do things right the first time. And to always exceed expectations." Jordan Case of Park Place Lexus fully embraces this philosophy: "You've got to do it right, on time, and make people feel like they are the only one in the room." Proclaims the Lexus Covenant, "Lexus will treat each customer as we would a guest in our own home."

At Lexus, exceeding customer expectations sometimes means fulfilling even seemingly

To delight customers and keep them coming back, the Lexus Covenant promises that its dealers will "treat each customer as we would a guest in our home" and "go to any lengths to serve them better."

Continued on next page

outrageous customer requests. Dave Wilson, owner of several Lexus dealerships in Southern California, tells of a letter he once received from an angry Lexus owner who spent $374 to repair her car at his dealership. She'd owned four prior Lexus vehicles without a single problem. She said in her letter that she resented paying to fix her current one. Turns out, she thought they were maintenance free—as in get in and drive . . . and drive and drive. "She didn't think she had to do anything to her Lexus," says Wilson. "She had 60,000 miles on it, and never had the oil changed." Wilson sent back her $374.

By all accounts, Lexus has lived up to its ambitious customer-satisfaction promise. It has created what appear to be the world's most satisfied car owners. Lexus regularly tops not just the industry quality ratings but also customer-satisfaction ratings in both the United States and globally. Last year, Lexus once again ranked number one in the American Customer Satisfaction Index, which measures customer satisfaction with the overall ownership experience. Customer satisfaction translates into sales and customer loyalty. Lexus is the nation's number-one selling luxury car.

Once a Lexus customer, always a Lexus customer. Just ask someone who owns one. "I'm telling you, this is class, buddy," says customer Barry Speak while reclining in a vibrating massage chair at the Palm Beach Lexus store. An owner of a late-model Lexus LS sedan, Speak says there is no doubt he will come to the Palm Beach store for a new vehicle in a year or two. "My wife and I are going to be fighting over who gets to take the car in now," he says over the chair's hum. "You're not kidding!" Jane Speak chimes in from the store's other massage chair. A Lexus executive puts it simply: "Lexus consistently delivers an exceptional ownership experience."

Sources: Adapted examples, quotes, and other information from "Lexus and Prius Star for Toyota," *Birmingham Mail*, June 19, 2009, p. 44; Mac Gordon, "He Runs the Largest Lexus Store," *Ward's Dealer Business*, February 2008, p. 64; Neil E. Boudette, "Luxury Car Sellers Put on the Ritz," *Wall Street Journal*, December 18, 2007, p. B1; Julia Chang, "At Your Service," *Sales & Marketing Management*, June 2006, pp. 42–43; Steve Finlay, "At Least She Put Fuel in It," *Ward's Dealer Business*, August 1, 2003, http://wardsdealer.com/ar/auto_least_she_put/ Michael Harley; "Lexus Leads, Hyundai Improves, While Infinity Drops in J.D. Power 2009 Initial Quality Study," June 22, 2009, accessed at www .autoblog.com; "Automobiles & Light Vehicles," American Customer Satisfaction Index," www.theacsi.org, accessed March 2010; and "Lexus Covenant," www.lexus.com/about/corporate/covenant.html, accessed December 2010.

Author Comment | Here we look at some special considerations in *new-product* buying decisions.

The Buyer Decision Process for New Products (pp 156–158)

We have looked at the stages buyers go through in trying to satisfy a need. Buyers may pass quickly or slowly through these stages, and some of the stages may even be reversed. Much depends on the nature of the buyer, the product, and the buying situation.

We now look at how buyers approach the purchase of new products. A **new product** is a good, service, or idea that is perceived by some potential customers as new. It may have been around for a while, but our interest is in how consumers learn about products for the first time and make decisions on whether to adopt them. We define the **adoption process** as "the mental process through which an individual passes from first learning about an innovation to final adoption," and *adoption* as the decision by an individual to become a regular user of the product.[37]

New product
A good, service, or idea that is perceived by some potential customers as new.

Adoption process
The mental process through which an individual passes from first hearing about an innovation to final adoption.

Stages in the Adoption Process

Consumers go through five stages in the process of adopting a new product:

Awareness: The consumer becomes aware of the new product but lacks information about it.

Interest: The consumer seeks information about the new product.

Evaluation: The consumer considers whether trying the new product makes sense.

Trial: The consumer tries the new product on a small scale to improve his or her estimate of its value.

Adoption: The consumer decides to make full and regular use of the new product.

This model suggests that the new-product marketer should think about how to help consumers move through these stages. ◉ For example, during the recent recession, Hyundai developed a unique way to help customers get past evaluation and make a positive purchase decision about a new vehicle.

Hyundai discovered many potential customers were interested in buying new cars but couldn't get past the evaluation stage of the buying process. Consumers worried that

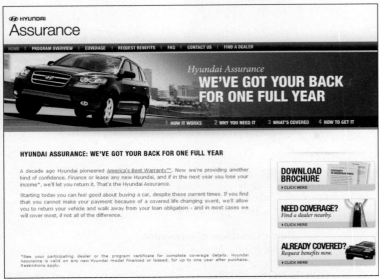

● **The adoption process: To help potential customers get past concerns about the uncertain economy, Hyundai offered an Assurance Program protecting customers against lost jobs and incomes.**

they might buy a car and then lose their jobs and subsequently their new cars and their good credit ratings. To help buyers over this hurdle, the carmaker offered the Hyundai Assurance Program, which promised to let buyers who financed or leased a new Hyundai vehicle return their vehicles at no cost and with no harm to their credit rating if they lost their jobs or incomes within a year. The Assurance Program, combined with a 10-year powertrain warranty and a five-year, 24-hour roadside assistance program, all at no extra charge, made the buying decision much easier for customers concerned about the future economy. Sales of the Hyundai Sonata surged 85 percent in the month following the start of the Assurance campaign, and the brand's market share grew at an industry-leading pace during the following year. Hyundai continued the program on its 2010 models, and other carmakers soon followed with their own assurance plans.[38]

Individual Differences in Innovativeness

People differ greatly in their readiness to try new products. In each product area, there are "consumption pioneers" and early adopters. Other individuals adopt new products much later. People can be classified into the adopter categories shown in ● **Figure 5.7.** As shown by the black curve, after a slow start, an increasing number of people adopt the new product. The number of adopters reaches a peak and then drops off as fewer nonadopters remain. As successive groups of consumers adopt the innovation (the red curve), it eventually reaches its saturation level. Innovators are defined as the first 2.5 percent of buyers to adopt a new idea (those beyond two standard deviations from mean adoption time); the early adopters are the next 13.5 percent (between one and two standard deviations); and so forth.

The five adopter groups have differing values. *Innovators* are venturesome—they try new ideas at some risk. *Early adopters* are guided by respect—they are opinion leaders in their communities and adopt new ideas early but carefully. The *early majority* is deliberate—although they rarely are leaders, they adopt new ideas before the average person. The *late majority* is skeptical—they adopt an innovation only after a majority of people have tried it. Finally, *laggards* are tradition bound—they are suspicious of changes and adopt the innovation only when it has become something of a tradition itself.

This adopter classification suggests that an innovating firm should research the characteristics of innovators and early adopters in their product categories and direct marketing efforts toward them.

Influence of Product Characteristics on Rate of Adoption

The characteristics of the new product affect its rate of adoption. Some products catch on almost overnight; for example, both the iPod and iPhone flew off retailers' shelves at an astounding rate from the day they were first introduced. Others take a longer time to gain acceptance. For example, the first HDTVs were introduced in the United States in the 1990s, but the percentage of U.S. households owning a high definition set stood at only 28 percent by 2007 and 62 percent by 2010.[39]

Five characteristics are especially important in influencing an innovation's rate of adoption. For example, consider the characteristics of HDTV in relation to the rate of adoption:

Relative advantage: The degree to which the innovation appears superior to existing products. HDTV offers substantially improved picture quality. This speeded up its rate of adoption.

Part Two

● FIGURE | 5.7

Adopter Categorization on the
Basis of Relative Time of
Adoption of Innovations

Source: Based on figures found at
http://en.wikipedia.org/wiki/Everett_Rogers,
October 2010; and Everett M. Rogers, *Diffusion
of Innovations*, 5th ed. (New York: Simon &
Shuster, 2003), p. 281.

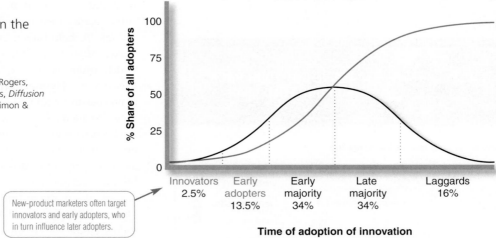

New-product marketers often target innovators and early adopters, who in turn influence later adopters.

Compatibility: The degree to which the innovation fits the values and experiences of potential consumers. HDTV, for example, is highly compatible with the lifestyles of the TV-watching public. However, in the early years, HDTV was not yet compatible with programming and broadcasting systems, which slowed adoption. Now, as more and more high definition programs and channels have become available, the rate of HDTV adoption has increased rapidly.

Complexity: The degree to which the innovation is difficult to understand or use. HDTVs are not very complex. Therefore, as more programming has become available and prices have fallen, the rate of HDTV adoption is increasing faster than that of more complex innovations.

Divisibility: The degree to which the innovation may be tried on a limited basis. Early HDTVs and HD cable and satellite systems were very expensive, which slowed the rate of adoption. As prices fall, adoption rates increase.

Communicability: The degree to which the results of using the innovation can be observed or described to others. Because HDTV lends itself to demonstration and description, its use will spread faster among consumers.

Other characteristics influence the rate of adoption, such as initial and ongoing costs, risk and uncertainty, and social approval. The new-product marketer must research all these factors when developing the new product and its marketing program.

REVIEWING Objectives AND KEY Terms

The American consumer market consists of more than 310 million people who consume more than $10 trillion worth of goods and services each year, making it one of the most attractive consumer markets in the world. The world consumer market consists of more than 6.8 billion people. Consumers around the world vary greatly in terms of cultural, social, personal, and psychological makeup. Understanding how these differences affect *consumer buying behavior* is one of the biggest challenges marketers face.

Objective 1 Define the consumer market
and construct a simple model of consumer
buyer behavior. (pp 134–135)

The *consumer market* consists of all the individuals and households who buy or acquire goods and services for personal con-

sumption. The simplest model of consumer buyer behavior is the stimulus-response model. According to this model, marketing stimuli (the four Ps) and other major forces (economic, technological, political, cultural) enter the consumer's "black box" and produce certain responses. Once in the black box, these inputs produce observable buyer responses, such as product choice, brand choice, purchase timing, and purchase amount.

Objective 2 Name the four major factors that
influence consumer buyer behavior. (pp 135–150)

Consumer buyer behavior is influenced by four key sets of buyer characteristics: cultural, social, personal, and psychological. Although many of these factors cannot be influenced by the marketer, they can be useful in identifying interested buyers and shaping products and appeals to serve consumer needs better. *Culture* is the most basic determinant of a person's wants and behavior. *Subcultures* are "cultures within cultures" that have distinct values and lifestyles and can be based on anything from age to ethnicity. Many companies focused their marketing programs on the special needs of certain cultural and subcultural segments.

Social factors also influence a buyer's behavior. A person's *reference groups*—family, friends, social networks, professional associations—strongly affect product and brand choices. The buyer's age, life-cycle stage, occupation, economic circumstances, personality, and other *personal characteristics* influence his or her buying decisions. Consumer *lifestyles*—the whole pattern of acting and interacting in the world—are also an important influence on purchase decisions. Finally, consumer buying behavior is influenced by four major *psychological factors*: motivation, perception, learning, and beliefs and attitudes. Each of these factors provides a different perspective for understanding the workings of the buyer's black box.

Objective 3 List and define the major types of buying decision behavior and the stages in the buyer decision process. (pp 150–156)

Buying behavior may vary greatly across different types of products and buying decisions. Consumers undertake *complex buying behavior* when they are highly involved in a purchase and perceive significant differences among brands. *Dissonance-reducing behavior* occurs when consumers are highly involved but see little difference among brands. *Habitual buying behavior* occurs under conditions of low involvement and little significant brand difference. In situations characterized by low involvement but significant perceived brand differences, consumers engage in *variety-seeking buying behavior*.

When making a purchase, the buyer goes through a decision process consisting of *need recognition*, *information search*, *evaluation of alternatives*, *purchase decision*, and *postpurchase behavior*. The marketer's job is to understand the buyer's behavior at each stage and the influences that are operating. During *need recognition*, the consumer recognizes a problem or need that could be satisfied by a product or service in the market. Once the need is recognized, the consumer is aroused to seek more information and moves into the *information search* stage. With information in hand, the consumer proceeds to *alternative evaluation*, during which the information is used to evaluate brands in the choice set. From there, the consumer makes a *purchase decision* and actually buys the product. In the final stage of the buyer decision process, *postpurchase behavior*, the consumer takes action based on satisfaction or dissatisfaction.

Objective 4 Describe the adoption and diffusion process for new products. (pp 156–158)

The product *adoption process* is made up of five stages: awareness, interest, evaluation, trial, and adoption. New-product marketers must think about how to help consumers move through these stages. With regard to the *diffusion process* for new products, consumers respond at different rates, depending on consumer and product characteristics. Consumers may be innovators, early adopters, early majority, late majority, or laggards. Each group may require different marketing approaches. Marketers often try to bring their new products to the attention of potential early adopters, especially those who are opinion leaders. Finally, several characteristics influence the rate of adoption: relative advantage, compatibility, complexity, divisibility, and communicability.

KEY Terms

OBJECTIVE 1

Consumer buyer behavior (p 133)
Consumer market (p 133)

OBJECTIVE 2

Culture (p 135)
Subculture (p 136)
Social class (p 139)
Group (p 139)
Opinion leader (p 139)
Online social networks (p 141)
Lifestyle (p 146)

Personality (p 146)
Motive (drive) (p 147)
Perception (p 148)
Learning (p 149)
Belief (p 150)
Attitude (p 150)

OBJECTIVE 3

Complex buying behavior (p 150)
Dissonance-reducing buying behavior (p 151)
Habitual buying behavior (p 151)

Variety-seeking buying behavior (p 152)
Need recognition (p 152)
Information search (p 153)
Alternative evaluation (p 153)
Purchase decision (p 154)
Postpurchase behavior (p 154)
Cognitive dissonance (p 154)

OBJECTIVE 4

New product (p 156)
Adoption process (p 156)

PEARSON mymarketinglab

- Check your understanding of the concepts and key terms using the mypearsonmarketinglab study plan for this chapter.
- Apply the concepts in a business context using the simulation entitled **Consumer Behavior.**

DISCUSSING & APPLYING THE Concepts

Discussing the Concepts

1. How do consumers respond to various marketing efforts the company might use? Which buyer characteristics that affect buyer behavior influence you most when making a clothing purchase decision? Are these the same characteristics that

would influence you when making a computer purchase? Explain. (AACSB: Communication; Reflective Thinking)

2. What is an opinion leader? Describe how marketers attempt to use opinion leaders to help sell their products. (AACSB: Communication; Reflective Thinking)

3. Name and describe the types of consumer buying behavior. Which one would most likely be involved in the purchase of a mobile phone purchase? For choosing a frozen dinner? (AACSB: Communication; Reflective Thinking)

4. Explain the stages of the consumer buyer decision process and describe how you or your family went through this process to make a recent purchase. (AACSB: Communication; Reflective Thinking)

5. Name and describe the adopter categories and explain how a marketer of three-dimensional televisions can use this knowledge in its market targeting decision. (AACSB: Communication; Reflective Thinking)

Applying the Concepts

1. Marketers often target consumers before, during, or after a trigger event, an event in one's life that triggers change. For example, after having a child, new parents have an increased need for baby furniture, clothes, diapers, car seats, and lots of other baby-related goods. Consumers who never paid attention to marketing efforts for certain products may now be focused on ones related to their life change. In a small group, discuss other trigger events that may provide opportunities to target the right buyer at the right time. (AACSB: Communication; Reflective Thinking)

2. Hemopure is a human blood substitute derived from cattle blood. OPK Biotech still has this product in clinical trials, but the company has received FDA approval for a similar product, Oxyglobin, in the veterinary market. Visit http://opkbiotech .com/ to learn about Hemopure. Then explain how the product characteristics of relative advantage, compatibility, complexity, divisibility, and communicability will influence the rate of adoption of this product once FDA approval is attained. (AACSB: Communication; Reflective Thinking)

3. Go to the Strategic Business Insights Web site and complete the VALS survey at www.strategicbusinessinsights.com/vals/ presurvey.shtml. What does VALS measure, and what is your VALS type? Does it adequately describe you? On what dimensions are the VALS types based? How can marketers use this tool to better understand consumers? (AACSB: Communication; Use of IT; Reflective Thinking)

FOCUS ON Technology

Have you noticed that some of your Facebook friends like certain advertisements? Marketers know what Facebook users like and are using that knowledge to influence users' friends. "Social context ads" are based on data collected on the likes and friends of Facebook users. When you click on an ad indicating that you like it, you also give Facebook permission to share that preference with all your friends. Marketers like this feature because it appears as though you are endorsing the brand to your friends. Nike bought ads on users' homepages in twenty countries prior to the World Cup, and Ford uses Facebook's social context ads to promote the Explorer. Although most ads on Facebook cost as little as $1 per click for marketers, the total cost for a social context ad can be as much as $100,000.

1. Which factors are marketers advertising on Facebook using to influence consumers? Would you be influenced by an ad if you saw that your friends liked it? (AACSB: Communication; Use of IT; Reflective Thinking)

2. How would you feel about Facebook using your name in these types of ads? (AACSB: Communication; Reflective Thinking)

FOCUS ON Ethics

Vitaminwater—sounds healthy, right? Although Vitaminwater has vitamins, it also has thirty-three grams—that's two heaping tablespoons—of sugar, making it not much better than a soda. Vitaminwater, owned by Coca-Cola, has been under fire from the Center for Science in the Public Interest (CSPI), a consumer-advocacy group that fights for safer, more nutritious foods. The CSPI filed a class-action lawsuit against Coca-Cola, claiming names for Vitaminwater flavors such as "endurance peach mango" and "focus kiwi strawberry" are misleading for two reasons: (1) The drinks contain zero to one percent juice, and (2) words like *endurance*, *focus*, *defense*, *rescue*, and *energy* imply health benefits. Coca-Cola's defense was that reasonable consumers would not be misled into believing that Vitaminwater is healthy for them.

1. Debate whether or not Coca-Cola is deliberately trying to deceive consumers into believing that Vitaminwater is a healthy alternative to soda. Which psychological factor is most affected by the product name and ad claims and might influence consumers to purchase this product? (AACSB: Communication; Ethical Reasoning)

2. Find two other examples of brands that use names, words, colors, package shapes, or other elements to convey potentially deceptive meanings to consumers. (AACSB: Communication; Reflective Thinking)

MARKETING & THE Economy

AutoZone

Detroit is suffering and everyone knows it. New car sales were down by 21 percent for 2009 handing the industry its worst performance in nearly 30 years. But Detroit's loss has been AutoZone's gain. The do-it-yourself car part retailer's sales and profits have been running counter to those of the retail world as a whole. One reason is that AutoZone's traditional customers have been tackling more complicated do-it-yourself car repair jobs and visiting stores more frequently. But the retail auto parts giant has also seen a notable increase in customers with incomes over $100,000 a year, people who typically never so much as pop the hoods of their own cars.

In the more frugal economy, all types of drivers are now looking to save money by doing their own repairs and maintenance. And as people keep their cars longer, the older cars need more re-pairs. AutoZone has seen this day coming, long ago scrapping its grungy, industrial-store format for one that's more colorful, brightly lit, and filled with super-friendly sales clerks. Soccer moms are now as comfortable getting "into the Zone" as NASCAR fans. Believing that, even in an economic recovery, America's spendthrift habits have now become a thing of the past, that's the way AutoZone planned it.

1. Consider the auto parts buyer decision process. How has this process changed for new AutoZone customers. How has the economy influenced this change?

2. Visit www.autozone.com. Does it appear that the company is trying to help the newer, less-knowledgeable customer? Based on your observations, what recommendations would you make to AutoZone?

MARKETING BY THE Numbers

One way consumers can evaluate alternatives is to identify important attributes and assess how purchase alternatives perform on those attributes. Consider the purchase of a notebook computer. Each attribute, such as memory, is given a weight to reflect its level of importance to that consumer. Then the consumer evaluates each alternative on each attribute. For example, in the table, memory (weighted at 0.5) is the most important computer purchase attribute for this consumer. The consumer believes that Brand C performs best on memory, rating it 7 (higher ratings indicate higher performance). Brand B rates worst on this attribute (rating of 3). Size and price are the consumer's next most important attributes. Warranty is least important.

A score can be calculated for each brand by multiplying the importance weight for each attribute by the brand's score on that attribute. These weighted scores are then summed to determine the score for that brand. For example, $Score_{Brand\ A} = (0.2 \times 4) + (0.5 \times 6) + (0.1 \times 5) + (0.2 \times 4) = 0.8 + 3.0 + 0.5 + 0.8 = 5.1$. This consumer will select the brand with the highest score.

Attributes	Importance Weight (e)	Alternative Brands A	B	C
Size	0.2	4	6	2
Memory	0.5	6	3	7
Warranty	0.1	5	5	4
Price	0.2	4	6	7

1. Calculate the scores for brands B and C. Which brand would this consumer likely choose? (AACSB: Communication; Analytic Reasoning)

2. Which brand is this consumer least likely to purchase? Discuss two ways the marketer of this brand can enhance consumer attitudes toward purchasing its brand. (AACSB: Communication; Reflective Thinking; Analytic Reasoning)

VIDEO Case

RADIAN6

Social networking has had a huge impact on society. And for marketers, online social communications are changing the way that consumers make purchase decisions. Radian6 specializes in monitoring social media. It tracks a wide array of Web sites at which consumers might "chat" about companies, brands, and general market offerings. Companies such as Dell and Microsoft obtain valuable insights about what consumers are saying about their products and about what factors or events are generating the discussions. But more importantly, companies are gaining a stronger understanding of how consumer online conversations are affecting purchase decisions. In this manner. Radian6 is on the cutting edge of getting a grip on the ever-expanding scope of social networking and "word-of-Web" communication.

After viewing the video featuring Radian6, answer the following questions.

1. What cultural factors have led to the explosion of social networking?

2. How has Radian6 changed the way companies understand opinion leaders and marketing?

3. How is Radian6 helping companies gain insights into the buying decision process?

COMPANY Case

Porsche: Guarding the Old While Bringing in the New

Porsche (pronounced *Porsh*-uh) is a unique company. It has always been a niche brand that makes cars for a small and distinctive segment of automobile buyers. In 2009, Porsche sold only 27,717 cars in the five models it sells in the United States. Honda sold about 10 times that many Accords alone. But Porsche owners are as rare as their vehicles. For that reason, top managers at Porsche spend a great deal of time thinking about customers. They want to know who their customers are, what they think, and how they feel. They want to know why they buy a Porsche rather then a Jaguar, a Ferrari, or a big Mercedes coupe. These are challenging questions to answer; even Porsche owners themselves don't know exactly what motivates their buying. But given Porsche's low volume and the increasingly fragmented auto market, it is imperative that management understands its customers and what gets their motors running.

THE PROFILE OF A PORSCHE OWNER

Porsche was founded in 1931 by Ferdinand Porsche, the man credited for designing the original Volkswagen Beetle—Adolf Hitler's "people's car" and one of the most successful car designs of all time. For most of its first two decades, the company built Volkswagen Beetles for German citizens and tanks and Beetles for the military. As Porsche AG began to sell cars under its own nameplate in the 1950s and 1960s, a few constants developed. The company sold very few models, creating an image of exclusivity. Those models had a rounded, bubble shape that had its roots in the original Beetle but evolved into something more Porsche-like with the world famous 356 and 911 models. Finally, Porsche's automobiles featured air-cooled four- and six-cylinder "boxer" motors (cylinders in an opposed configuration) in the rear of the car. This gave the cars a unique and often dangerous characteristic—a tendency for the rear end to swing out when cornering hard. That's one of the reasons that Porsche owners were drawn to them. They were challenging to drive, which kept most people away.

Since its early days, Porsche has appealed to a very narrow segment of financially successful people. These are achievers who see themselves as entrepreneurial, even if they work for a corporation. They set very high goals for themselves and then work doggedly to meet them. And they expect no less from the clothes they wear, the restaurants they go to, or the cars they drive. These individuals see themselves not as a part of the regular world but as exceptions to it. They buy Porsches because the car mirrors their self-image; it stands for the things owners like to see in themselves and their lives.

Most of us buy what Porsche executives call utility vehicles. That is, we buy cars primarily to go to work, transport children, and run errands. Because we use our cars to accomplish these daily tasks, we base buying decisions on features such as price, size, fuel economy, and other practical considerations. But Porsche is more than a utility car. Its owners see it as a car to be enjoyed, not just used. Most Porsche buyers are not moved by information

but by feelings. A Porsche is like a piece of clothing—something the owner "wears" and is seen in. They develop a personal relationship with their cars, one that has more to do with the way the car sounds, vibrates, and feels, rather than the how many cup holders it has or how much cargo it can hold in the trunk. They admire their Porsche because it is a competent performance machine without being flashy or phony.

People buy Porsches because they enjoy driving. If all they needed was something to get them from point A to point B, they could find something much less expensive. And while many Porsche owners are car enthusiasts, some of them are not. One successful businesswoman and owner of a high-end Porsche said, "When I drive this car to the high school to pick up my daughter, I end up with five youngsters in the car. If I drive any other car, I can't even find her; she doesn't want to come home."

FROM NICHE TO NUMEROUS

For its first few decades, Porsche AG lived by the philosophy of Ferry Porsche, Ferdinand's son. Ferry created the Porsche 356 because no one else made a car like he wanted. "We did no market research, we had no sales forecasts, no return-on-investment calculations. None of that. I very simply built my dream car and figured that there would be other people who share that dream." So, really, Porsche AG from the beginning was very much like its customers: an achiever that set out to make the very best.

But as the years rolled on, Porsche management became concerned with a significant issue: Were there enough Porsche buyers to keep the company afloat? Granted, the company never had illusions of churning out the numbers of a Chevrolet or a Toyota. But to fund innovation, even a niche manufacturer has to grow a little. And Porsche began to worry that the quirky nature of the people who buy Porsches might just run out on them.

This led Porsche to extend its brand outside the box. In the early 1970s, Porsche introduced the 914, a square-ish, mid-engine, two-seater that was much cheaper than the 911. This meant that a different class of people could afford a Porsche. It was no surprise that the 914 became Porsche's top selling model. By the late 1970s, Porsche replaced the 914 with a hatchback coupe that had something no other regular Porsche model had ever had: an engine in the front. At less than $20,000, more than $10,000 less than the 911, the 924 and later 944 models were once again Porsche's pitch to affordability. At one point, Porsche increased its sales goal by nearly 50 percent to 60,000 cars a year.

Although these cars were in many respects sales successes, the Porsche faithful cried foul. They considered these entry-level models to be cheap and underperforming. Most loyalists never really accepted these models as "real" Porsches. In fact, they were not at all happy that they had to share their brand with a customer who didn't fit the Porsche owner profile. They were turned off by what they saw as a corporate strategy that had focused on *mass* over *class* marketing. This tarnished image was compounded by the fact that Nissan, Toyota, BMW, and other car manufacturers had ramped up high-end sports car offerings, creating some fierce competition. In fact, both the Datsun 280-ZX and the Toyota Supra were not only cheaper than Porsche's 944 but also faster. A struggling economy threw more sand in Porsche's tank. By 1990, Porsche sales had plummeted, and the company flirted with bankruptcy.

RETURN TO ITS ROOTS?

But Porsche wasn't going down without a fight. It quickly recognized the error of its ways and halted production of the entry-level models. It rebuilt its damaged image by revamping its higher-end model lines with more race-bred technology. In an effort to regain rapport with customers, Porsche once again targeted the high end of the market in both price and performance. It set modest sales goals and decided that moderate growth with higher margins would be more profitable in the long term. Thus, the company set out to make one less Porsche than the public demanded. According to one executive, "We're not looking for volume; we're searching for exclusivity."

Porsche's efforts had the desired effect. By the late 1990s, the brand was once again favored by the same type of achiever who had so deeply loved the car for decades. The cars were once again exclusive. And the company was once again profitable. But by the early 2000s, Porsche management was again asking itself a familiar question: To have a sustainable future, could Porsche rely on only the Porsche faithful? According to then CEO Wendelin Wiedeking, "For Porsche to remain independent, it can't be dependent on the most fickle segment in the market. We don't want to become just a marketing department of some giant. We have to make sure we're profitable enough to pay for future development ourselves."

So in 2002, Porsche did the unthinkable. It became one of the last car companies to jump into the insatiable sport utility vehicle (SUV) market. At roughly 5,000 pounds, the new Porsche Cayenne was heavier than anything that Porsche had ever made, with the exception of some prototype tanks it made during WWII. Once again, the new model featured an engine up front. And it was the first Porsche to ever be equipped with seatbelts for five. As news spread about the car's development, howls could be heard from Porsche's customer base.

But this time, Porsche did not seem too concerned that the loyalists would be put off. Could it be that the company had already forgotten what happened the last time it deviated from the mold? After driving one of the first Cayenne's off the assembly line, one journalist stated, "A day at the wheel of the 444 horsepower Cayenne Turbo leaves two overwhelming impressions. First, the Cayenne doesn't behave or feel like an SUV, and second, it drives like a Porsche." This was no entry-level car. Porsche had created a two-and-a-half ton beast that could accelerate to 60 miles per hour in just over five seconds, corner like it was on rails, and hit 165 miles per hour, all while coddling five adults in sumptuous leather seats with almost no wind noise from the outside world. On top of that, it could keep up with a Land Rover when the pavement ended. Indeed, Porsche had created the Porsche of SUVs.

Last year, Porsche upped the ante one more time. It unveiled another large vehicle. But this time, it was a low-slung, five-door luxury sedan. The Porsche faithful and the automotive press again gasped in disbelief. But by the time the Panamera hit the pavement, Porsche had proven once again that Porsche customers could have their cake and eat it to. The Panamera is almost as big as the Cayenne but can move four adults down the road at speeds of up to 188 miles per hour and accelerate from a standstill to 60 miles per hour in four seconds flat.

Although some Porsche traditionalists would never be caught dead driving a front engine Porsche that has more than two doors, Porsche insists that two trends will sustain these new models. First, a category of Porsche buyers has moved into life stages that have them facing inescapable needs; they need to haul more people and stuff. This not only applies to certain regular Porsche buyers, but Porsche is again seeing buyers enter its dealerships that otherwise wouldn't have. Only this time, the price points of the new vehicles are drawing only the well heeled, allowing Porsche to maintain its exclusivity. These buyers also seem to fit the achiever profile of regular Porsche buyers.

The second trend is the growth of emerging economies. Whereas the United States has long been the world's biggest consumer of Porsches, the company expects China to become its biggest customer before too long. Twenty years ago, the United States accounted for about 50 percent of Porsche's worldwide sales. Now, it accounts for only about 26 percent. In China, many people who can afford to buy a car as expensive as a Porsche also hire a chauffeur. The Cayenne and the Panamera are perfect for those who want to be driven around in style but who may also want to make a quick getaway if necessary.

The most recent economic downturn has brought down the sales of just about every maker of premium automobiles. When times are tough, buying a car like a Porsche is the ultimate deferrable purchase. But as this downturn turns back up, Porsche is better poised than it has ever been to meet the needs of its customer base. It is also in better shape than ever to maintain its brand image with the Porsche faithful and with others as well. Sure, understanding Porsche buyers is still a difficult task. But a former CEO of Porsche summed it up this way: "If you really want to understand our customers, you have to understand the phrase, 'If I were going to be a car, I'd be a Porsche.'"

Questions for Discussion

1. Analyze the buyer decision process of a traditional Porsche customer.

2. Contrast the traditional Porsche customer decision process to the decision process for a Cayenne or a Panamera customer.

3. Which concepts from the chapter explain why Porsche sold so many lower-priced models in the 1970s and 1980s?

4. Explain how both positive and negative attitudes toward a brand like Porsche develop. How might Porsche change consumer attitudes toward the brand?

5. What role does the Porsche brand play in the self-concept of its buyers?

Sources: Christoph Rauwald, "Porsche Raises Outlook," *Wall Street Journal*, June 18, 2010, accessed at http://online.wsj.com/article/SB10001424052748704122904575314062459444270.htm; Jonathan Welsh, "Porsche Relies Increasingly on Sales in China," *Wall Street Journal*, April 2, 2010, accessed at http://blogs.wsj.com/drivers-seat/2010/04/02/porsche-relies-increasingly-on-sales-in-china/; David Gumpert, "Porsche on Nichemanship," *Harvard Business Review*, March/April 1986, pp. 98–106; Peter Robinson, "Porsche Cayenne—Driving Impression," *Car and Driver*, January 2003, accessed at www.caranddriver.com; Jens Meiners, "2010 Porsche Panamera S/4S/Turbo—First Drive Review," *Car and Driver*, June 2009, accessed at www.caranddriver.com.

6 Business Markets and Business Buyer Behavior

Chapter Preview

In the previous chapter, you studied *final consumer* buying behavior and factors that influence it. In this chapter, we'll do the same for *business customers*—those that buy goods and services for use in producing their own products and services or for resale to others. As when selling to final buyers, firms marketing to business customers must build profitable relationships with business customers by creating superior customer value.

We begin by looking at another American icon—Boeing. Business-to-business marketing is a way of life at Boeing. All of the aerospace giant's more than $60 billion of annual revenues come from large organizational buyers—commercial airlines, air-freight carriers, and government and military buyers. Selling airplanes to large organizational buyers is a lot different from selling cars or cameras to final consumers. And the stakes are significantly higher.

Boeing: Selling to Businesses—The Stakes Are Much, Much Higher

Most times, buying a new car is an involved and time-consuming process. Before committing to spend $15,000 or more, you spend lots of time searching the Internet for information, watching car ads, talking with friends or salespeople to get their advice, and visiting dealer lots to check out competing models and take test drives. New cars are expensive, and you expect to live with your decision for several years. So you want to get it right.

Now assume that you are a member of the aircraft purchasing team at All Nippon Airways (ANA), Japan's second-largest airline. Your team is charged with making recommendations for the purchase of 50 new airplanes for the company's fleet, at a total cost of more than $5 billion. All of a sudden, by comparison, your new car purchase decision looks pretty simple. The difference, of course, is that new airplanes aren't lined up in dealership showrooms. You can't go down to the lot to kick the tires and test-fly a new plane. And there are a lot more dollars at stake.

In this case, before shelling out more than $150 million per plane, ANA's high-level buying team completed an arduous evaluation of its own needs and available aircraft offerings. You can just imagine the research, evaluation, and debate that went into making such a multibillion dollar buying decision. ANA finally announced that it would buy 50 Boeing 787 Dreamliners. More recently, the company announced that it would also buy five Boeing 777s and five 767s, worth another $2 billion.

Those are mind-blowing figures by almost any standard—$5 billion; $2 billion. But it's kind of business as usual for Boeing. "The word *big* does not begin to describe Boeing," says one analyst. As the world's commercial aviation leader, Boeing's 12,000 planes dominate the skies. Its small but popular 737 is the workhorse for many airlines, and its giant, two-level 747 was the world's first jumbo jet. Boeing military aircraft include massive cargo planes and tankers, Chinook and other helicopters, and the F-22, the nation's newest, fastest, and most-expensive military fighter. Boeing even operates the space shuttle and the international space station, and it is working on the next generation of space vehicles to replace NASA's shuttle fleet.

At a general level, selling commercial aircraft to large business customers is like selling cars to final consumers. It requires a deep-down understanding of customer needs and a customer-driven marketing strategy that delivers superior customer value. But that's where the similarities end. Boeing sells to only a relatively small number of very large buyers worldwide. It has only three major commercial airline competitors: Airbus, Lockheed Martin, and Northrup Grumman. And buying a batch of jetliners involves dozens or even hundreds of decision makers from all levels of the buying organization, and layer upon layer of subtle and not-so-subtle buying influences. Moreover, whereas it might be disappointing when a car buyer chooses a competing brand, losing a single sale to a large business customer can cost Boeing billions of dollars in lost business.

It takes more than fast talk and a warm smile to sell expensive high-tech aircraft. Before any sale, a team of Boeing company specialists—sales and design engineers, financial analysts, planners, and others—dedicates itself to becoming an expert on the airline customer. They find out where the airline wants to grow, when it will be replacing planes, and its financial situation. They run Boeing and competing planes through exhaustive analysis, simulating the airline's routes, cost per seat, and other factors to show that Boeing's planes are more effective and efficient. The selling process is nerve-rackingly slow—it can take two or three years from the first marketing presentation to the day the sale is announced.

Moreover, each sale is just part of a bigger buyer-seller interaction. Boeing's real challenge is to win buyers' business by building day-in, day-out, year-in, year-out customer partnerships based on superior products and close collaboration—before *and* after the sale. When a customer buys an airplane, it also places its trust in a future working relationship with Boeing. "When you buy an airplane, it's like getting married," says a Boeing executive. "It is a long-term relationship."

ANA's decision to buy from Boeing was based in part on the qualities of Boeing's futuristic, yet-to-be-produced 787 Dreamliner aircraft. Just as important, however, was the strong, long-running relationship between ANA and Boeing. When ANA placed that huge order, the Dreamliner was still in the design stage. Not a single plane had yet been built or tested. That took a whole lot of trust on ANA's part.

However, that was more than five years ago, and ANA is still waiting for delivery of the first plane. In fact, events surrounding the development of the 787 highlight the scale and complexities of business-to-business selling, for both the buyer and the seller. Boeing announced its plans for this radical new midsized, wide-body commercial airplane in 2004. Fifty percent of the 787's fuselage consists of one piece of lightweight carbon fiber—eliminating 40,000–50,000 individual fasteners and 1,500 aluminum sheets compared with a traditional design. That puts the 787 in a design class with the stealth bomber. Add innovative new jet engines and other weight-saving innovations, and the 787 will be the lightest, most fuel-efficient passenger jet on the market. The 787's interior will also feature many enhanced passenger comforts: a 60 percent quieter ride, more leg room, cleaner air, and higher cabin pressure and humidity to reduce passenger fatigue on long trips.

Sounds great? Commercial airlines around the world thought so too. ANA jumped onboard first with its April 2004 order for 50 planes. Fifty-five other companies quickly followed, ballooning Boeing's 787 orders to 895 planes and making it the fastest-selling

new commercial aircraft in history. Boeing promised delivery of the first 787s by mid-2008, promising that it would deliver 109 planes the first year. To meet that target, the company developed an innovative but very complex manufacturing process.

However, problems plagued the new manufacturing process from the start, causing a numbing two-year delay. The first 787 Dreamliner didn't complete its maiden, three-hour test flight until December 2009, and Boeing pushed back delivery of the first 787s to ANA to the end of 2010 or even later.

The long delays caused substantial problems for both customers and Boeing and put long-established customer relationships to a real test. Some airlines cancelled their orders, and Boeing paid out an estimated $2.5 billion in penalties and concessions. But most customers stayed the course. In a nod to its faith in Boeing and the 787 Dreamliner, ANA remained a patient partner and even added five more planes to its order. At the same time, however, ANA demanded that Boeing provide a detailed plan for avoiding more surprises and a realistic estimate of when ANA would get its first airplane.

Boeing learned a long list of customer relationship lessons from the delays. In business-to-business partnerships, as in any relationship, trust must be earned anew every day. Says Boeing's president, "We really disappointed our customers. . . . The past three years have been tough for our partners. [But] we are developing closer bonds—it's like climbing a mountain together." In the end, meeting the revised schedules and delivering planes to customers will be a must in repairing strained relationships. Says one Boeing watcher, "good relationships and reputations are built on outstanding performance, not delayed promises."[1]

> Selling airplanes to large organizational buyers is a lot different from selling cars or cameras to final consumers. And the stakes are much, much higher.

> To succeed in its business-to-business markets, Boeing must build day-in, day-out, year-in, year-out customer partnerships based on superior products, close collaboration, and trust. "When you buy an airplane, it's like getting married," says a Boeing executive. "It is a long-term relationship."

Like Boeing, in one way or another, most large companies sell to other organizations. Companies such as Boeing, DuPont, IBM, Caterpillar, and countless other firms sell *most* of their products to other businesses. Even large consumer-products companies, which make products used by final consumers, must first sell their products to other businesses. For example, General Mills makes many familiar consumer brands—Big G cereals (Cheerios, Wheaties, Trix, Chex), baking products (Pillsbury, Betty Crocker, Gold Medal flour), snacks (Nature Valley, Pop Secret, Chex Mix), Yoplait yogurt, Häagen-Dazs ice cream, and others. But to sell these products to consumers, General Mills must first sell them to its wholesaler and retailer customers, who in turn serve the consumer market.

Business buyer behavior refers to the buying behavior of the organizations that buy goods and services for use in the production of other products and services that are sold, rented, or supplied to others. It also includes the behavior of retailing and wholesaling firms that acquire goods to resell or rent them to others at a profit. In the **business buying process**, business buyers determine which products and services their organizations need to purchase and then find, evaluate, and choose among alternative suppliers and brands. *Business-to-business (B-to-B) marketers* must do their best to understand business markets and business buyer behavior. Then, like businesses that sell to final buyers, they must build profitable relationships with business customers by creating superior customer value.

Business buyer behavior

The buying behavior of organizations that buy goods and services for use in the production of other products and services that are sold, rented, or supplied to others.

Business buying process

The decision process by which business buyers determine which products and services their organizations need to purchase and then find, evaluate, and choose among alternative suppliers and brands.

Author | Business markets operate
Comment | "behind the scenes" to most consumers. Most of the things you buy involve many sets of business purchases before you ever see them.

Business Markets (pp 166–170)

The business market is *huge*. In fact, business markets involve far more dollars and items than do consumer markets. For example, think about the large number of business transactions involved in the production and sale of a single set of Goodyear tires. Various suppliers sell Goodyear the rubber, steel, equipment, and other goods that it needs to produce tires. Goodyear then sells the finished tires to retailers, who in turn sell them to consumers. Thus, many sets of *business* purchases were made for only one set of *consumer* purchases. In addition, Goodyear sells tires as original equipment to manufacturers that install them on new vehicles and as replacement tires to companies that maintain their own fleets of company cars, trucks, buses, or other vehicles.

⦿ TABLE | 6.1   Characteristics of Business Markets

Market Structure and Demand

Business markets contain *fewer but larger buyers*.

Business buyer demand is *derived* from final consumer demand.

Demand in many business markets is *more inelastic*—not affected as much in the short run by price changes.

Demand in business markets *fluctuates more* and more quickly.

Nature of the Buying Unit

Business purchases involve *more buyers*.

Business buying involves a *more professional purchasing effort*.

Types of Decisions and the Decision Process

Business buyers usually face *more complex buying decisions*.

The business buying process is *more formalized*.

In business buying, buyers and sellers work more closely together and build close long-term *relationships*.

In some ways, business markets are similar to consumer markets. Both involve people who assume buying roles and make purchase decisions to satisfy needs. However, business markets differ in many ways from consumer markets. The main differences, shown in ⦿ **Table 6.1**, are in *market structure and demand*, the *nature of the buying unit*, and the *types of decisions and the decision process* involved.

Market Structure and Demand

The business marketer normally deals with *far fewer but far larger buyers* than the consumer marketer does. Even in large business markets, a few buyers often account for most of the purchasing. For example, when Goodyear sells replacement tires to final consumers, its potential market includes the owners of the millions of cars currently in use around the world. But Goodyear's fate in the business market depends on getting orders from one of only a handful of large automakers. Similarly, Black & Decker sells its power tools and outdoor equipment to tens of millions of consumers worldwide. However, it must sell these products through three huge retail customers—Home Depot, Lowe's, and Walmart—which combined account for more than half its sales.

Derived demand
Business demand that ultimately comes from (derives from) the demand for consumer goods.

Further, business demand is **derived demand**—it ultimately comes from (derives from) the demand for consumer goods. HP and Dell buy Intel microprocessor chips to operate the computers they manufacture. If consumer demand for computers drops, so will the demand for microprocessors. Therefore, B-to-B marketers sometimes promote their products directly to final consumers to increase business demand. For example, W. L. Gore & Associates promotes its Gore-Tex fabrics directly to final consumers.

You can't buy anything directly from Gore, but increased demand for Gore-Tex fabrics boosts the demand for outdoor apparel and other brands made from them. So Gore advertises to consumers to educate them on the benefits of the Gore-Tex brand in the products they buy. It also markets brands containing Gore-Tex—from Arc'teryx, Marmot, and The North Face to Burton and L.L. Bean—directly to consumers on its own Web site (www.gore-tex.com/remote/Satellite/home). To deepen its relationship with outdoor enthusiasts further, Gore even sponsors an "Experience More" online community in which members can share experiences and videos, connect with

● **Derived demand:** You can't buy anything directly from Gore, but to increase demand for Gore-Tex fabrics, the company markets directly to the buyers of outdoor apparel and other brands made from them. Both Gore and its partner brands win.

outdoor experts, and catch exclusive gear offers from partner brands. As a result of these and other marketing efforts, consumers around the world have learned to look for the familiar Gore-Tex brand label, and both Gore and its partner brands win. ● No matter what brand of apparel or footwear you buy, says the label, if it's made with Gore-Tex fabric, it's "guaranteed to keep you dry."

Many business markets have *inelastic demand*; that is, the total demand for many business products is not much affected by price changes, especially in the short run. A drop in the price of leather will not cause shoe manufacturers to buy much more leather unless it results in lower shoe prices that, in turn, will increase the consumer demand for shoes.

Finally, business markets have more *fluctuating demand*. The demand for many business goods and services tends to change more—and more quickly—than the demand for consumer goods and services does. A small percentage increase in consumer demand can cause large increases in business demand. Sometimes a rise of only 10 percent in consumer demand can cause as much as a 200 percent rise in business demand during the next period.

Nature of the Buying Unit

Compared with consumer purchases, a business purchase usually involves *more decision participants* and a *more professional purchasing effort*. Often, business buying is done by trained purchasing agents who spend their working lives learning how to buy better. The more complex the purchase, the more likely it is that several people will participate in the decision-making process. Buying committees composed of technical experts and top management are common in the buying of major goods. Beyond this, B-to-B marketers now face a new breed of higher-level, better-trained supply managers. Therefore, companies must have well-trained marketers and salespeople to deal with these well-trained buyers.

Types of Decisions and the Decision Process

Business buyers usually face *more complex* buying decisions than do consumer buyers. Business purchases often involve large sums of money, complex technical and economic considerations, and interactions among many people at many levels of the buyer's organization. Because the purchases are more complex, business buyers may take longer to make their decisions. The business buying process also tends to be *more formalized* than the consumer buying process. Large business purchases usually call for detailed product specifications, written purchase orders, careful supplier searches, and formal approval.

Finally, in the business buying process, the buyer and seller are often much *more dependent* on each other. B-to-B marketers may roll up their sleeves and work closely with their customers during all stages of the buying process—from helping customers define problems, to finding solutions, to supporting after-sale operation. They often customize their offerings to individual customer needs.

In the short run, sales go to suppliers who meet buyers' immediate product and service needs. In the long run, however, business-to-business marketers keep a customer's sales and create customer value by meeting current needs *and* by partnering with customers to help them solve their problems. For example, Dow Plastics doesn't just sell commodity plastics *to* its industrial customers; it works *with* these customers to help them succeed in their own markets. "We believe in a simple concept," says the company. "If you win, we win." (See Real Marketing 6.1.)

In recent years, relationships between customers and suppliers have been changing from downright adversarial to close and chummy. In fact, many customer companies are

Real Marketing 6.1

Dow Plastics: "If You Win, We Win"

When you pick up your cell phone to text a friend or hop into your car to head for the mall, you probably don't think much about the plastics that make those state-of-the-art products possible. But at Dow Plastics, thinking about how plastics can make our lives better is at the very core of its business strategy. What makes that noteworthy is that Dow doesn't sell its products to you and me. Instead, it sells mountains of raw materials to its business customers—such as Nokia and BMW—who in turn sell their products final users. But Dow Plastics understands that its own success depends heavily on how successfully its business customers use Dow plastic polymers and resins in satisfying final consumer needs. It's not just selling commodity plastics; it's helping the businesses that buy its plastics to be heroes with their own customers.

To get a better perspective on this strategy, let's go back a few years. In the late 1980s, Dow Chemical realigned its dozen or so widely varied plastics businesses into a single subsidiary, called Dow Plastics. One of the first things Dow had to do was to decide how to position its new division competitively. Initial research showed that Dow Plastics rated a distant third in customer preference behind industry leaders DuPont and GE Plastics. The research also revealed, however, that customers were unhappy with the service—or lack thereof—that they received from all three suppliers. "Vendors peddled resins as a commodity," said the head of Dow Plastics' advertising agency. "They competed on price and delivered on time but gave no service."

These findings led to a positioning strategy that went far beyond simply selling good products and delivering them on time. Dow Plastics set out to build deeper relationships with business customers. The organization wasn't just selling products and services; it was partnering with customers to help them win with their own final consumers. Said the agency executive, "Whether they're using Dow's plastics to make bags for Safeway or for complex [automotive] applications, we had to help them succeed in their markets." This new

thinking was summed up in the positioning statement, "We don't succeed unless you do."

This new philosophy got Dow out of selling plastics and into selling customer success. The problems of Dow's organizational customers became more than just engineering challenges. Dow's business customers sell to somebody else, so the company now faced new challenges of marketing to and helping satisfy customers' customers.

Over the past two decades, the customer success philosophy has come to permeate everything Dow Plastics does. Dow Plastics doesn't just sell *to* its business customers; it works *with* them to grow and succeed together. Now, whenever Dow Plastics people encounter a new product or market, the first question they always ask is, "How does this fit with 'We don't succeed unless you do'?"

For example, carmaker BMW sells to some of the world's most demanding customers. BMW owners want high performance, but they also want reasonable prices and fuel economy. Thus, to help deliver more value to its customers, BMW looks for two important attributes in every vehicle component: cost savings and weight reduction. Lower costs mean more palatable prices for car buyers, and weight reduction yields customer benefits

such as improved fuel economy, increased acceleration, and better handling and braking.

So when BMW and its electronic parts supplier Tyco needed an advanced electronics box for the engine compartment of BMW's latest 7 Series models, they looked for something that would not only meet complex performance specifications but also be cost efficient and lightweight. Enter Dow Plastics. Working together, the Dow-Tyco team developed a lightweight plastic box that yields "exceptional dimensional stability, low warpage, low weight, and improved hydrolysis resistance," all at a surprisingly economical cost. That might sound like gibberish to you, but it's sweet music to companies like Tyco and BMW. In the final analysis, of course, the folks at Dow Plastics care most about how such parts will help BMW succeed with car buyers. The more cars BMW sells to final buyers, the more plastics Dow sells to Tyco and BMW. Through such innovations, Dow Plastics has helped BMW give customers a full-sized 5,100-pound sedan that hits 60 miles per hour from a standstill in 4.4 seconds, blasts through corners like a go-cart, and still gets decent gas mileage.

Selling customer success has turned Dow Plastics into a world-leading supplier of plastic resins and material science innovations. Plastics now account for about half of Dow Chemical's $57 billion in annual revenues. Dow Plastics doesn't come up with winning solutions for customers by simply dipping into its current product portfolio. It works closely with customers in every stage of product development and production,

Dow Plastics isn't just selling commodity plastics; it's helping the businesses that buy its plastics to be heroes with their own customers. "We believe in a simple concept . . . if you win, we win."

Continued on next page

from material selection through final part testing. Dow Plastics considers itself a partner, not just a supplier. As the company summarizes on its Web site:

Think of Dow as the team behind your team. Dow Plastics' greatest asset, and the one that can make the biggest difference to your busi-

ness, is our people. Knowledgeable, flexible, and committed to your success, our team puts all our resources together to provide you with

competitive edge. We believe in a simple concept . . . if you win, we win.

Sources: For historical background, see Nancy Arnott, "Getting the Picture: The Grand Design—We Don't Succeed Unless You Do," *Sales & Marketing Management*, June 1994, pp. 74–76. Current quotes and other information from http://plastics.dow.com/ and www.omnexus.com/sf/dow/?id=plastics, accessed March 2010.

Supplier development
Systematic development of networks of supplier-partners to ensure an appropriate and dependable supply of products and materials for use in making products or reselling them to others.

now practicing **supplier development**, systematically developing networks of supplier-partners to ensure an appropriate and dependable supply of products and materials that they will use in making their own products or resell to others. For example, Walmart doesn't have a "Purchasing Department"; it has a "Supplier Development Department." ● And giant Swedish furniture retailer IKEA doesn't just buy from its suppliers; it involves them deeply in the customer value-creation process.

IKEA, the world's largest furniture retailer, is the quintessential global cult brand. Customers from Beijing to Moscow to Middletown, Ohio, flock to the $32 billion Scandinavian retailer's more than 300 huge stores in 38 countries, drawn by IKEA's trendy but simple and practical furniture at affordable prices. But IKEA's biggest obstacle to growth isn't opening new stores and attracting customers. Rather, it's finding enough of the right kinds of *suppliers* to help design and produce the billions of dollars of affordable goods that customers will carry out of its stores. IKEA currently relies on some 1,220 suppliers in 55 countries to stock its shelves. IKEA can't just rely on spot suppliers who might be available when needed. Instead, it has systematically developed a robust network of supplier-partners that reliably provide the more than 9,500 items it stocks. IKEA's designers start with a basic customer value proposition. Then they find and work closely with key suppliers to bring that proposition to market. Thus, IKEA does more than just buy from suppliers; it also involves them deeply in the process of designing and making stylish but affordable products to keep IKEA's customers coming back.[2]

● **Giant Scandinavian furniture retailer IKEA doesn't just buy from its suppliers. It involves them deeply in the process of designing and making stylish but affordable furniture that keeps customers coming back.**

Author | Comment | Business buying decisions can range from routine to incredibly complex, involving only a few or very many decision makers and buying influences.

Business Buyer Behavior (pp 170–176)

At the most basic level, marketers want to know how business buyers will respond to various marketing stimuli. ● **Figure 6.1** shows a model of business buyer behavior. In this model, marketing and other stimuli affect the buying organization and produce certain buyer responses. These stimuli enter the organization and are turned into buyer responses. To design good marketing strategies, marketers must understand what happens within the organization to turn stimuli into purchase responses.

Within the organization, buying activity consists of two major parts: the buying center, composed of all the people involved in the buying decision, and the buying decision

● FIGURE | 6.1
A Model of Business Buyer
Behavior

● FIGURE | 6.1
A Model of Business Buyer
Behavior

In some ways, business markets are similar to consumer markets—this model looks a lot like the model of consumer buyer behavior presented in Figure 5.1. But there are some major differences, especially in the nature of the buying unit, the types of decisions made, and the decision process.

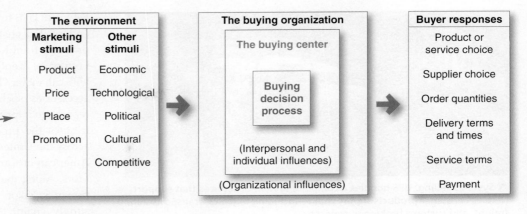

The environment		The buying organization	Buyer responses
Marketing stimuli	**Other stimuli**	**The buying center**	Product or service choice
Product	Economic	**Buying decision process**	Supplier choice
Price	Technological		Order quantities
Place	Political		Delivery terms and times
Promotion	Cultural	(Interpersonal and individual influences)	Service terms
	Competitive	(Organizational influences)	Payment

process. The model shows that the buying center and the buying decision process are influenced by internal organizational, interpersonal, and individual factors as well as external environmental factors.

The model in Figure 6.1 suggests four questions about business buyer behavior: What buying decisions do business buyers make? Who participates in the buying process? What are the major influences on buyers? How do business buyers make their buying decisions?

Major Type of Buying Situations

There are three major types of buying situations.[3] In a **straight rebuy**, the buyer reorders something without any modifications. It is usually handled on a routine basis by the purchasing department. To keep the business, "in" suppliers try to maintain product and service quality. "Out" suppliers try to find new ways to add value or exploit dissatisfaction so that the buyer will consider them.

In a **modified rebuy**, the buyer wants to modify product specifications, prices, terms, or suppliers. The in suppliers may become nervous and feel pressured to put their best foot forward to protect an account. Out suppliers may see the modified rebuy situation as an opportunity to make a better offer and gain new business.

A company buying a product or service for the first time faces a **new task** situation. In such cases, the greater the cost or risk, the larger the number of decision participants and the greater the company's efforts to collect information. The new task situation is the marketer's greatest opportunity and challenge. The marketer not only tries to reach as many key buying influences as possible but also provides help and information. The buyer makes the fewest decisions in the straight rebuy and the most in the new task decision.

Many business buyers prefer to buy a complete solution to a problem from a single seller rather than separate products and services from several suppliers and putting them together. The sale often goes to the firm that provides the most complete *system* for meeting the customer's needs and solving its problems. Such **systems selling** (or **solutions selling**) is often a key business marketing strategy for winning and holding accounts.

Thus, transportation and logistics giant UPS does more than just ship packages for its business customers; it develops entire solutions to customers' transportation and logistics problems. ● For example, UPS bundles a complete system of services that support Nikon's consumer products supply chain—including logistics, transportation, freight, and customs brokerage services—into one smooth-running system.[4]

When Nikon entered the digital camera market, it decided that it needed an entirely new distribution strategy as well. So it asked transportation and logistics giant UPS to design a complete system for moving its entire electronics product line from its Asian factories to retail stores throughout the United States, Latin America, and the Caribbean. Now products leave Nikon's Asian manufacturing centers and arrive on American retailers' shelves in as few as two days, with UPS handling everything in

Straight rebuy
A business buying situation in which the buyer routinely reorders something without any modifications.

Modified rebuy
A business buying situation in which the buyer wants to modify product specifications, prices, terms, or suppliers.

New task
A business buying situation in which the buyer purchases a product or service for the first time.

Systems selling (or solutions selling)
Buying a packaged solution to a problem from a single seller, thus avoiding all the separate decisions involved in a complex buying situation.

○ **Systems selling: UPS bundles a complete system of services that support Nikon's consumer products supply chain—including logistics, transportation, freight, and customs brokerage services.**

between. UPS first manages air and ocean freight and related customs brokerage to bring Nikon products from Korea, Japan, and Indonesia to its Louisville, Kentucky, operations center. There, UPS can either "kit" the Nikon merchandise with accessories such as batteries and chargers or repackage it for in-store display. Finally, UPS distributes the products to thousands of retailers across the United States or exports them to Latin American or Caribbean retail outlets and distributors. Along the way, UPS tracks the goods and provides Nikon with a "snapshot" of the entire supply chain, letting Nikon keep retailers informed of delivery times and adjust them as needed.

Participants in the Business Buying Process

Buying center

All the individuals and units that play a role in the purchase decision-making process.

Who does the buying of the trillions of dollars' worth of goods and services needed by business organizations? The decision-making unit of a buying organization is called its **buying center**—all the individuals and units that play a role in the business purchase decision-making process. This group includes the actual users of the product or service, those who make the buying decision, those who influence the buying decision, those who do the actual buying, and those who control buying information.

The buying center includes all members of the organization who play any of five roles in the purchase decision process.[5]

Users

Members of the buying organization who will actually use the purchased product or service.

- **Users** are members of the organization who will use the product or service. In many cases, users initiate the buying proposal and help define product specifications.

Influencers

People in an organization's buying center who affect the buying decision; they often help define specifications and also provide information for evaluating alternatives.

- **Influencers** often help define specifications and also provide information for evaluating alternatives. Technical personnel are particularly important influencers.

- **Buyers** have formal authority to select the supplier and arrange terms of purchase. Buyers may help shape product specifications, but their major role is in selecting vendors and negotiating. In more complex purchases, buyers might include high-level officers participating in the negotiations.

Buyers

People in an organization's buying center who make an actual purchase.

- **Deciders** have formal or informal power to select or approve the final suppliers. In routine buying, the buyers are often the deciders, or at least the approvers.

Deciders

People in an organization's buying center who have formal or informal power to select or approve the final suppliers.

- **Gatekeepers** control the flow of information to others. For example, purchasing agents often have authority to prevent salespersons from seeing users or deciders. Other gatekeepers include technical personnel and even personal secretaries.

Gatekeepers

People in an organization's buying center who control the flow of information to others.

The buying center is not a fixed and formally identified unit within the buying organization. It is a set of buying roles assumed by different people for different purchases. Within the organization, the size and makeup of the buying center will vary for different products and for different buying situations. For some routine purchases, one person—say, a purchasing agent—may assume all the buying center roles and serve as the only person involved in the buying decision. For more complex purchases, the buying center may include 20 or 30 people from different levels and departments in the organization.

The buying center concept presents a major marketing challenge. The business marketer must learn who participates in the decision, each participant's relative influence, and what evaluation criteria each decision participant uses. This can be difficult.

For instance, the medical products and services group of Cardinal Health sells disposable surgical gowns to hospitals. It identifies the hospital personnel involved in this buying decision as the vice president of purchasing, the operating room administrator, and the surgeons. ○ Each participant plays a different role. The vice president of purchasing analyzes whether the hospital should buy disposable gowns or reusable gowns. If analysis favors dis-

● **Buying center: Cardinal Health deals with a wide range of buying influences, from purchasing executives and hospital administrators to the surgeons who actually use its products.**

posable gowns, then the operating room administrator compares competing products and prices and makes a choice. This administrator considers the gowns' absorbency, antiseptic quality, design, and cost and normally buys the brand that meets the requirements at the lowest cost. Finally, surgeons affect the decision later by reporting their satisfaction or dissatisfaction with the purchased brand.

The buying center usually includes some obvious participants who are involved formally in the buying decision. For example, the decision to buy a corporate jet will probably involve the company's CEO, the chief pilot, a purchasing agent, some legal staff, a member of top management, and others formally charged with the buying decision. It may also involve less obvious, informal participants, some of whom may actually make or strongly affect the buying decision. Sometimes, even the people in the buying center are not aware of all the buying participants. For example, the decision about which corporate jet to buy may actually

be made by a corporate board member who has an interest in flying and who knows a lot about airplanes. This board member may work behind the scenes to sway the decision. Many business buying decisions result from the complex interactions of ever-changing buying center participants.

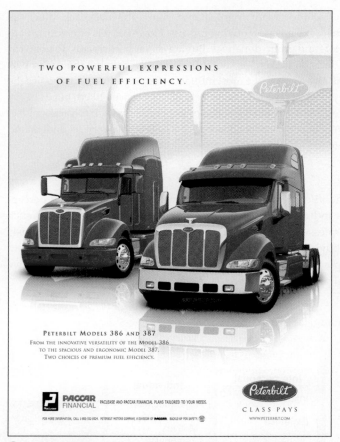

● **Emotions play an important role in business buying: This Peterbilt advertisement stresses performance factors such as fuel efficiency. But it also stresses more emotional factors, such as the raw beauty of Peterbilt trucks and the pride of owning and driving one. "Class Pays."**

Major Influences on Business Buyers

Business buyers are subject to many influences when they make their buying decisions. Some marketers assume that the major influences are economic. They think buyers will favor the supplier who offers the lowest price or the best product or the most service. They concentrate on offering strong economic benefits to buyers. Such economic factors are very important to most buyers, especially in a rough economy. However, business buyers actually respond to both economic and personal factors. Far from being cold, calculating, and impersonal, business buyers are human and social as well. They react to both reason and emotion.

Today, most B-to-B marketers recognize that emotion plays an important role in business buying decisions. For example, you might expect that an advertisement promoting large trucks to corporate fleet buyers or independent owner-operators would stress objective technical, performance, and economic factors. ● For instance, befitting today's tougher economic times, premium heavy-duty truck maker Peterbilt does stress performance—its dealers and Web site provide plenty of information about factors such as maneuverability, productivity, reliability, comfort, and fuel efficiency. But Peterbilt ads appeal to buyers' emotions as well. They show the raw beauty of the trucks, and the Peterbilt slogan—"Class Pays"—suggests that owning a Peterbilt truck is a matter of pride as well as superior performance. Says the company, "Peterbilt . . . the class of the industry. On highways, construction sites, city streets, logging roads—everywhere customers earn their living—Peterbilt's red oval is a familiar symbol of performance, reliability, and pride."[6]

When suppliers' offers are very similar, business buyers have little basis for strictly rational choices. Because they can meet organizational goals with any supplier, buyers can allow personal factors to play a larger role in their decisions. However, when competing products differ greatly, business buyers are more accountable for their choices and tend to pay more attention to economic factors. ● **Figure 6.2** lists various groups of influences on business buyers—environmental, organizational, interpersonal, and individual.

Environmental Factors

Business buyers are heavily influenced by factors in the current and expected *economic environment*, such as the level of primary demand, the economic outlook, and the cost of money. Another environmental factor is the *supply* of key materials. Many companies now are more willing to buy and hold larger inventories of scarce materials to ensure adequate supply. Business buyers also are affected by technological, political, and competitive developments in the environment. Finally, *culture and customs* can strongly influence business buyer reactions to the marketer's behavior and strategies, especially in the international marketing environment (see Real Marketing 6.2). The business buyer must watch these factors, determine how they will affect the buyer, and try to turn these challenges into opportunities.

Organizational Factors

Each buying organization has its own objectives, strategies, structure, systems, and procedures, and the business marketer must understand these factors well. Questions such as these arise: How many people are involved in the buying decision? Who are they? What are their evaluative criteria? What are the company's policies and limits on its buyers?

Interpersonal Factors

The buying center usually includes many participants who influence each other, so *interpersonal factors* also influence the business buying process. However, it is often difficult to assess such interpersonal factors and group dynamics. Buying center participants do not wear tags that label them as "key decision maker" or "not influential." Nor do buying center participants with the highest rank always have the most influence. Participants may influence the buying decision because they control rewards and punishments, are well liked, have special expertise, or have a special relationship with other important participants. Interpersonal factors are often very subtle. Whenever possible, business marketers must try to understand these factors and design strategies that take them into account.

Individual Factors

Each participant in the business buying decision process brings in personal motives, perceptions, and preferences. These individual factors are affected by personal characteristics such as age, income, education, professional identification, personality, and attitudes toward risk. Also, buyers have different buying styles. Some may be technical types who make in-depth analyses of competitive proposals before choosing a supplier. Other buyers may be intuitive negotiators who are adept at pitting the sellers against one another for the best deal.

● **FIGURE | 6.2**
Major Influences on
Business Buyer Behavior

Like consumer buying decisions in Figure 5.2, business buying decisions are affected by an incredibly complex combination of environmental, interpersonal, and individual influences, but with an extra layer of organizational factors thrown into the mix.

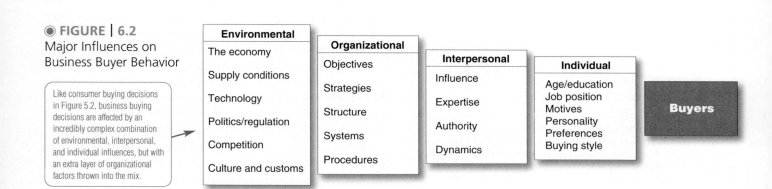

Real Marketing 6.2

International Marketing Manners:
When in Rome, Do as the Romans Do

Picture this: Consolidated Amalgamation, Inc., thinks it's time that the rest of the world enjoyed the same fine products it has offered American consumers for two generations. It dispatches Vice President Harry E. Slicksmile to Europe, Africa, and Asia to explore the territory. Mr. Slicksmile stops first in London, where he makes short work of some bankers—he rings them up on the phone. He handles Parisians with similar ease: After securing a table at La Tour d'Argent, he greets his luncheon guest, the director of an industrial engineering firm, with the words, "Just call me Harry, Jacques."

In Germany, Mr. Slicksmile is a powerhouse. Whisking through a lavish, state-of-the-art marketing presentation, complete with flip PowerPoints and videos, he shows 'em that this Georgia boy *knows* how to make a buck. Heading on to Milan, Harry strikes up a conversation with the Japanese businessman sitting next to him on the plane. He flips his card onto the guy's tray and, when the two say good-bye, shakes hands warmly and clasps the man's right arm. Later, for his appointment with the owner of an Italian packaging design firm, our hero wears his comfy corduroy sport coat, khaki pants, and Timberland hikers. Everybody knows Italians are zany and laid back.

Mr. Slicksmile next swings through Saudi Arabia, where he coolly presents a potential client with a multimillion-dollar proposal in a classy pigskin binder. At his next stop in Beijing, China, he talks business over lunch with a group of Chinese executives. After completing the meal, he drops his chopsticks into his bowl of rice and presents each guest with an elegant Tiffany clock as a reminder of his visit. Then, at his final stop in Phuket, Thailand, Mr. Slicksmile quickly dives into his business proposal before lunch is served.

A great tour, sure to generate a pile of orders, right? Wrong. Six months later, Consolidated Amalgamation has nothing to show for the trip but a stack of bills. Abroad, they weren't wild about Harry.

This hypothetical case has been exaggerated for emphasis. Americans are seldom such

dolts. But experts say success in international business has a lot to do with knowing the territory and its people. By learning English and extending themselves in other ways, the world's business leaders have met Americans more than halfway. In contrast, Americans too often do little except assume that others will march to their music. "We want things to be 'American' when we travel. Fast. Convenient. Easy. So we become 'ugly Americans' by demanding that others change," says one American world trade expert. "I think more business would be done if we tried harder."

Poor Harry tried, all right, but in all the wrong ways. The British do not, as a rule, make deals over the phone as much as Americans do. It's not so much a "cultural" difference as a difference in approach. A proper Frenchman neither likes instant familiarity—questions about family, church, or alma mater—nor refers to strangers by their first names. "That poor fellow, Jacques, probably wouldn't show anything, but he'd recoil. He'd

not be pleased," explains an expert on French business practices.

Harry's flashy presentation would likely have been a flop with the Germans, who dislike overstatement and showiness. And when he grabbed his new Japanese acquaintance by the arm, the executive probably considered him disrespectful and presumptuous. Japan, like many Asian countries, is a "no-contact culture" in which even shaking hands is a strange experience. Harry made matters worse by tossing his business card. Japanese people revere the business card as an extension of self and as an indicator of rank. They do not *hand* it to people; they *present* it—with both hands. In addition, the Japanese are sticklers about rank. Unlike Americans, they don't heap praise on subordinates in a room; they will praise only the highest-ranking official present.

Hapless Harry also goofed when he assumed that Italians are like Hollywood's stereotypes of them. The flair for design and style that has characterized Italian culture for centuries is embodied in the businesspeople of Milan and Rome. They dress beautifully and admire flair, but they blanch at garishness or impropriety in others' attire.

To the Saudi Arabians, the pigskin binder would have been considered vile. An American salesperson who actually presented such a binder was unceremoniously tossed out, and his company was blacklisted from working

American companies must help their managers understand international customers and customs. For example, Japanese people revere the business card as an extension of self: They do not hand it out to people; they present it.

Continued on next page

with Saudi businesses. In China, Harry's casually dropping his chopsticks could have been misinterpreted as an act of aggression. Stabbing chopsticks into a bowl of rice and leaving them signifies death to the Chinese. The clocks Harry offered as gifts might have confirmed such dark intentions. To "give a clock" in Chinese sounds the same as "seeing someone off to his end." And in Thailand, it's considered inappropriate to speak about business matters until after the meal is served and eaten.

Thus, to compete successfully in global markets, or even to deal effectively with international firms in their home markets, companies must help their managers to understand the needs, customs, and cultures of international business buyers. "When doing business in a foreign country and a foreign culture—particularly a non-Western culture—assume nothing," advises an international business specialist. "Take nothing for granted. Turn every stone. Ask every question. Dig into every detail. Because cultures really are different, and those differences can have a major impact." So the old advice is still good advice: When in Rome, do as the Romans do.

Sources: Portions adapted from Susan Harte, "When in Rome, You Should Learn to Do What the Romans Do," *The Atlanta Journal-Constitution*, January 22, 1990, pp. D1, D6. Additional information and examples can be found in Gary Stroller, "Doing Business Abroad? Simple Faux Pas Can Sink You," *USA Today*, August 24, 2007, p. 1B; Roger E. Axtell, *Essential Do's and Taboos* (New York: Wiley, 2007); Janette S. Martin and Lillian H. Cheney, *Global Business Etiquette* (Santa Barbara, CA: Praeger Publishers, 2008); and www.executiveplanet.com, accessed August 2010.

The Business Buying Process

◉ **Figure 6.3** lists the eight stages of the business buying process.[7] Buyers who face a new task buying situation usually go through all stages of the buying process. Buyers making modified or straight rebuys may skip some of the stages. We will examine these steps for the typical new task buying situation.

Problem Recognition

The buying process begins when someone in the company recognizes a problem or need that can be met by acquiring a specific product or service. **Problem recognition** can result from internal or external stimuli. Internally, the company may decide to launch a new product that requires new production equipment and materials. Or a machine may break down and need new parts. Perhaps a purchasing manager is unhappy with a current supplier's product quality, service, or prices. Externally, the buyer may get some new ideas at a trade show, see an ad, or receive a call from a salesperson who offers a better product or a lower price.

In fact, in their advertising, business marketers often alert customers to potential problems and then show how their products and services provide solutions. ◉ For example, an award-winning ad from Makino Engineering Services, a leading maker of advanced machining tools, highlights a daunting customer problem: hard-to-machine parts. In the ad, the powerful visual shows a machined part that looks like a scary monster, complete with fangs. The ad's headline then offers the solution: "Our application engineers love the scary parts." The ad goes on to reassure customers that Makino can help them with their most difficult-to-machine parts and urges, "Don't be afraid of the part."

General Need Description

Having recognized a need, the buyer next prepares a **general need description** that describes the characteristics and quantity of the needed item. For standard items, this process

Problem recognition
The first stage of the business buying process in which someone in the company recognizes a problem or need that can be met by acquiring a good or a service.

General need description
The stage in the business buying process in which a buyer describes the general characteristics and quantity of a needed item.

◉ **FIGURE | 6.3**
Stages of the Business Buying Process

Buyers facing new, complex buying decisions usually go through all of these stages. Those making rebuys often skip some of the stages. Either way, the business buying process is usually much more complicated than this simple flow diagram suggests.

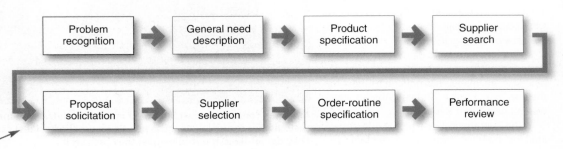

presents few problems. For complex items, however, the buyer may need to work with others—engineers, users, consultants—to define the item. The team may want to rank the importance of reliability, durability, price, and other attributes desired in the item. In this phase, the alert business marketer can help the buyers define their needs and provide information about the value of different product characteristics.

Product Specification

The buying organization next develops the item's technical **product specifications**, often with the help of a value analysis engineering team. *Product value analysis* is an approach to cost reduction in which components are studied carefully to determine if they can be redesigned, standardized, or made by less costly methods of production. The team decides on the best product characteristics and specifies them accordingly. Sellers, too, can use value analysis as a tool to help secure a new account. By showing buyers a better way to make an object, outside sellers can turn straight rebuy situations into new task situations that give them a chance to obtain new business.

Supplier Search

The buyer now conducts a **supplier search** to find the best vendors. The buyer can compile a small list of qualified suppliers by reviewing trade directories, doing computer searches, or phoning other companies for recommendations. Today, more and more companies are turning to the Internet to find suppliers. For marketers, this has leveled the playing field—the Internet gives smaller suppliers many of the same advantages as larger competitors.

The newer the buying task, and the more complex and costly the item, the greater the amount of time the buyer will spend searching for suppliers. The supplier's task is to get listed in major directories and build a good reputation in the marketplace. Salespeople should watch for companies in the process of searching for suppliers and make certain that their firm is considered.

Proposal Solicitation

In the **proposal solicitation** stage of the business buying process, the buyer invites qualified suppliers to submit proposals. In response, some suppliers will send only a catalog or a salesperson. However, when the item is complex or expensive, the buyer will usually require detailed written proposals or formal presentations from each potential supplier.

Business marketers must be skilled in researching, writing, and presenting proposals in response to buyer proposal solicitations. Proposals should be marketing documents, not just technical documents. Presentations should inspire confidence and make the marketer's company stand out from the competition.

Supplier Selection

The members of the buying center now review the proposals and select a supplier or suppliers. During **supplier selection**, the buying center often will draw up a list of the desired supplier attributes and their relative importance. Such attributes include product and service quality, reputation, on-time delivery, ethical corporate behavior, honest communication, and competitive prices. The members of the buying center will rate suppliers against these attributes and identify the best suppliers.

Buyers may attempt to negotiate with preferred suppliers for better prices and terms before making the final selections. In the end, they may select a single supplier or a few suppliers. Many buyers prefer multiple sources of supplies to avoid being totally dependent on one supplier and allow comparisons of prices and performance of several suppliers over

● Problem recognition: Machine tools maker Makino uses ads like this one to alert customers to problems and reassure them that Makino can help find solutions. "Our applications engineers love the scary parts."

Product specification
The stage of the business buying process in which the buying organization decides on and specifies the best technical product characteristics for a needed item.

Supplier search
The stage of the business buying process in which the buyer tries to find the best vendors.

Proposal solicitation
The stage of the business buying process in which the buyer invites qualified suppliers to submit proposals.

Supplier selection
The stage of the business buying process in which the buyer reviews proposals and selects a supplier or suppliers.

time. Today's supplier development managers want to develop a full network of supplier-partners that can help the company bring more value to its customers.

Order-Routine Specification

Order-routine specification
The stage of the business buying process in which the buyer writes the final order with the chosen supplier(s), listing the technical specifications, quantity needed, expected time of delivery, return policies, and warranties.

The buyer now prepares an **order-routine specification**. It includes the final order with the chosen supplier or suppliers and lists items such as technical specifications, quantity needed, expected delivery time, return policies, and warranties. In the case of maintenance, repair, and operating items, buyers may use blanket contracts rather than periodic purchase orders. A blanket contract creates a long-term relationship in which the supplier promises to resupply the buyer as needed at agreed prices for a set time period.

Many large buyers now practice *vendor-managed inventory*, in which they turn over ordering and inventory responsibilities to their suppliers. Under such systems, buyers share sales and inventory information directly with key suppliers. The suppliers then monitor inventories and replenish stock automatically as needed. For example, most major suppliers to large retailers such as Walmart, Target, Home Depot, and Lowe's assume vendor-managed inventory responsibilities.

Performance Review

Performance review
The stage of the business buying process in which the buyer assesses the performance of the supplier and decides to continue, modify, or drop the arrangement.

In this stage, the buyer reviews supplier performance. The buyer may contact users and ask them to rate their satisfaction. The **performance review** may lead the buyer to continue, modify, or drop the arrangement. The seller's job is to monitor the same factors used by the buyer to make sure that the seller is giving the expected satisfaction.

In all, the eight-stage buying-process model shown in Figure 6.3 provides a simple view of the business buying as it might occur in a new task buying situation. However, the actual process is usually much more complex. In the modified rebuy or straight rebuy situation, some of these stages would be compressed or bypassed. Each organization buys in its own way, and each buying situation has unique requirements.

Different buying center participants may be involved at different stages of the process. Although certain buying-process steps usually do occur, buyers do not always follow them in the same order, and they may add other steps. Often, buyers will repeat certain stages of the process. Finally, a customer relationship might involve many different types of purchases ongoing at a given time, all in different stages of the buying process. The seller must manage the total *customer relationship*, not just individual purchases.

E-Procurement: Buying on the Internet

E-procurement
Purchasing through electronic connections between buyers and sellers—usually online.

Advances in information technology have changed the face of the B-to-B marketing process. Electronic purchasing, often called **e-procurement**, has grown rapidly in recent years. Virtually unknown a decade and a half ago, online purchasing is standard procedure for most companies today. E-procurement gives buyers access to new suppliers, lowers purchasing costs, and hastens order processing and delivery. In turn, business marketers can connect with customers online to share marketing information, sell products and services, provide customer support services, and maintain ongoing customer relationships.

Companies can do e-procurement in any of several ways. They can conduct *reverse auctions*, in which they put their purchasing requests online and invite suppliers to bid for the business. Or they can engage in online *trading exchanges*, through which companies work collectively to facilitate the trading process. Companies also can conduct e-procurement by setting up their own *company buying sites*. For example, GE operates a company trading site on which it posts its buying needs and invites bids, negotiates terms, and places orders. Or companies can create *extranet links* with key suppliers. For instance, they can create direct procurement accounts with suppliers such as Dell or Office Depot, through which company buyers can purchase equipment, materials, and supplies directly.

B-to-B marketers can help customers who wish to purchase online by creating well-designed, easy-to-use Web sites. ● For example, *BtoB* magazine rated the site of Cisco

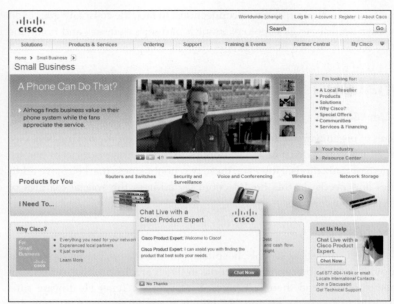

● **Online buying: The Cisco Systems site helps customers who want to purchase online by providing deep access to information about thousands of products and services. The site can also personalize the online experience for users and connect them with appropriate Cisco partner resellers.**

Systems—a market leader in Web networking hardware, software, and services—as one of its "10 great B-to-B Web sites":[8]

To spur growth, Cisco Systems recently stepped up its focus on the small and midsize business (SMB) segment. Its award-winning new SMB-specific Web site is simple, action-oriented, and engaging but gives SMB buyers deep access. At the most basic level, customers can find and download information about thousands of Cisco products and services. Digging deeper, the site is loaded with useful video content—everything from testimonials to "how to" videos to informational and educational on-demand Webcasts.

Cisco's SMB site gets customers interacting with both the company and its partner resellers. For example, its live click-to-chat feature puts users in immediate touch with Cisco product experts. WebEx Web-conferencing software connects potential SMB customers with appropriate Cisco partner resellers, letting them share Web pages, PowerPoints, and other documents in a collaborative online space. Finally, the Cisco SMB site can actually personalize the online experience for users. For example, if it detects that someone from the legal industry is paying attention to wireless content, it might put together relevant pieces of content to create a page for that visitor. Such personalization really pays off. Customers visiting personalized pages stay two times longer than other visitors and go much deeper into the site.

Business-to-business e-procurement yields many benefits. First, it shaves transaction costs and results in more efficient purchasing for both buyers and suppliers. E-procurement reduces the time between order and delivery. And a Web-powered purchasing program eliminates the paperwork associated with traditional requisition and ordering procedures and helps an organization keep better track of all purchases. Finally, beyond the cost and time savings, e-procurement frees purchasing people from a lot of drudgery and paperwork. In turn, it frees them to focus on more-strategic issues, such as finding better supply sources and working with suppliers to reduce costs and develop new products.

To demonstrate these advantages, consider Kodak. When it remodeled its headquarters facilities in Rochester, New York, it used e-procurement only. From demolition to restoration, the massive project involved managing more than 1,600 contract bids from 150 contractors. Throughout the project, e-procurement reduced paperwork and speeded up review and award times. In the end, the project was completed on time, and Kodak estimates that using e-procurement saved 15 percent on purchasing-process costs (including $186,000 on photocopying expenses alone).[9]

The rapidly expanding use of e-procurement, however, also presents some problems. For example, at the same time that the Web makes it possible for suppliers and customers to share business data and even collaborate on product design, it can also erode decades-old customer-supplier relationships. Many buyers now use the power of the Web to pit suppliers against one another and search out better deals, products, and turnaround times on a purchase-by-purchase basis.

E-procurement can also create potential security disasters. Although e-mail and home banking transactions can be protected through basic encryption, the secure environment that businesses need to carry out confidential interactions is sometimes still lacking. Companies are spending millions for research on defensive strategies to keep hackers at bay. Cisco Systems, for example, specifies the types of routers, firewalls, and security procedures that its partners must use to safeguard extranet connections. In fact, the company goes even further; it sends its own security engineers to examine a partner's defenses and holds the partner liable for any security breach that originates from its computers.

Author | These two nonbusiness
Comment | organizational markets
provide attractive opportunities for
many companies. Because of their
unique nature, we give them special
attention here.

Institutional and Government Markets (pp 180–182)

So far, our discussion of organizational buying has focused largely on the buying behavior of business buyers. Much of this discussion also applies to the buying practices of institutional and government organizations. However, these two nonbusiness markets have additional characteristics and needs. In this final section, we address the special features of institutional and government markets.

Institutional Markets

Institutional market

Schools, hospitals, nursing homes, prisons, and other institutions that provide goods and services to people in their care.

The **institutional market** consists of schools, hospitals, nursing homes, prisons, and other institutions that provide goods and services to people in their care. Institutions differ from one another in their sponsors and their objectives. For example, Tenet Healthcare runs 49 for-profit hospitals in 12 states, generating $8.7 billion in annual revenues. By contrast, the Shriners Hospitals for Children is a nonprofit organization with 22 hospitals that provide free specialized healthcare for children, whereas the government-run Veterans Affairs Medical Centers located across the country provide special services to veterans.[10] Each institution has different buying needs and resources.

Institutional markets can be huge. Consider the massive and expanding U.S. prisons economy:

> One in every 31 adults, or 7.3 million Americans, is in prison, on parole, or on probation, at a cost to the states of $47 billion a year. Criminal correction spending is outpacing budget growth in education, transportation, and public assistance. U.S. prisons, which hold 1.5 million adults, spend on average $29,000 per year per prisoner. The ultimate captive market, it translates into plenty of work for companies looking to break into the prison market. "Our core business touches so many things—security, medicine, education, food service, maintenance, technology—that it presents a unique opportunity for any number of vendors to do business with us," says an executive at Corrections Corporation of America, the largest private prison operator in the country.[11]

Many institutional markets are characterized by low budgets and captive patrons. For example, hospital patients have little choice but to eat whatever food the hospital supplies. A hospital purchasing agent has to decide on the quality of food to buy for patients. Because the food is provided as a part of a total service package, the buying objective is not profit. Nor is strict cost minimization the goal—patients receiving poor-quality food will complain to others and damage the hospital's reputation. Thus, the hospital purchasing agent must search for institutional-food vendors whose quality meets or exceeds a certain minimum standard and whose prices are low.

Many marketers set up separate divisions to meet the special characteristics and needs of institutional buyers. ◉ For example, the General Mills Foodservice unit produces, packages, prices, and markets its broad assortment of cereals, cookies, snacks, and other products to better serve the specific food service requirements of hospitals, schools, hotels, and other institutional markets.[12]

◉ **General Mills Foodservice produces, packages, prices, and markets its broad assortment of foods to better serve the specific food service requirements of various institutional markets.**

Government Markets

Government market

Governmental units—federal, state, and local—that purchase or rent goods and services for carrying out the main functions of government.

The **government market** offers large opportunities for many companies, both big and small. In most countries, government organizations are major buyers of goods and services. In the United States alone, federal, state, and local governments contain more than 82,000 buying units that purchase more than $1 trillion in goods and services each year.[13] Government buying and business buying are similar in many ways. But there are also differences that must be understood by companies that wish to sell products and services to governments. To succeed in the government market, sellers must locate key decision makers, identify the factors that affect buyer behavior, and understand the buying decision process.

Government organizations typically require suppliers to submit bids, and normally they award the contract to the lowest bidder. In some cases, a governmental unit will make allowances for the supplier's superior quality or reputation for completing contracts on time. Governments will also buy on a negotiated contract basis, primarily in the case of complex projects involving major R&D costs and risks, and in cases where there is little competition.

Government organizations tend to favor domestic suppliers over foreign suppliers. A major complaint of multinationals operating in Europe is that each country shows favoritism toward its nationals in spite of superior offers that are made by foreign firms. The European Economic Commission is gradually removing this bias.

Like consumer and business buyers, government buyers are affected by environmental, organizational, interpersonal, and individual factors. One unique thing about government buying is that it is carefully watched by outside publics, ranging from Congress to a variety of private groups interested in how the government spends taxpayers' money. Because their spending decisions are subject to public review, government organizations require considerable paperwork from suppliers, who often complain about excessive paperwork, bureaucracy, regulations, decision-making delays, and frequent shifts in procurement personnel.

Given all the red tape, why would any firm want to do business with the U.S. government? The reasons are quite simple: The U.S. government is the world's largest buyer of products and services—more than $425 billion worth each year—and its checks don't bounce. For example, last year, the federal government spent a whopping $73 billion on information technology alone. The Transportation Security Administration spent approximately $700 million just for electronic baggage screening technology.[14]

Most governments provide would-be suppliers with detailed guides describing how to sell to the government. For example, the U.S. Small Business Administration provides on its Web site detailed advice for small businesses seeking government contracting opportunities (www.sba.gov/contractingopportunities/index.html). And the U.S. Commerce Department's Web site is loaded with information and advice on international trade opportunities (www.commerce.gov/about-commerce/grants-contracting-trade-opportunities).

In several major cities, the General Services Administration operates *Business Service Centers* with staffs to provide a complete education on the way government agencies buy, the steps that suppliers should follow, and the procurement opportunities available. Various trade magazines and associations provide information on how to reach schools, hospitals, highway departments, and other government agencies. And almost all of these government organizations and associations maintain Internet sites offering up-to-date information and advice.

Still, suppliers have to master the system and find ways to cut through the red tape, especially for large government purchases. Consider Envisage Technologies, a small software development company that specializes in Internet-based training applications and human resource management platforms. All of its contracts fall in the government sector; 65 percent are with the federal government. Envisage uses the General Services Administration's Web site to gain access to smaller procurements, often receiving responses within 14 days. However, it puts the most sweat into seeking large, highly coveted contracts. A comprehensive bid proposal for one of these contracts can easily run from 600 to 700 pages because of federal paperwork requirements. And the company's president estimates that to prepare a single bid proposal, the firm has spent as many as 5,000 man-hours over the course of a few years.[15]

Noneconomic criteria also play a growing role in government buying. Government buyers are asked to favor depressed business firms and areas; small business firms; minority-owned firms; and business firms that avoid race, gender, or age discrimination. Sellers need to keep these factors in mind when deciding to seek government business.

Many companies that sell to the government have not been very marketing oriented for a number of reasons. Total government spending is determined by elected officials rather than by any marketing effort to develop this market. Government buying has emphasized price, making suppliers invest their effort in technology to bring costs down. When the product's characteristics are specified carefully, product differentiation is not a marketing factor. Nor do advertising or personal selling matter much in winning bids on an open-bid basis.

Several companies, however, have established separate government marketing departments, including GE, Kodak, and Goodyear. These companies anticipate government needs and projects, participate in the product specification phase, gather competitive intelligence, prepare bids carefully, and produce stronger communications to describe and enhance their companies' reputations.

Other companies have established customized marketing programs for government buyers. For example, Dell has specific business units tailored to meet the needs of federal as well as state and local government buyers. Dell offers its customers tailor-made Premier Dell.com Web pages that include special pricing, online purchasing, and service and support for each city, state, and federal government entity.

During the past decade, a great deal of the government's buying has gone online. ◉ The Federal Business Opportunities Web site (www.fbo.gov) provides a single point of entry through which commercial vendors and government buyers can post, search, monitor, and retrieve opportunities solicited by the entire federal contracting community. The three federal agencies that act as purchasing agents for the rest of government have also launched Web sites supporting online government purchasing activity. The General Services Administration, which influences more than one-quarter of the federal government's total procurement dollars, has set up a GSA Advantage! Web site (www.gsaadvantage.gov). The Defense Logistics Agency offers an Internet Bid Board System (www.dibbs.bsm.dla.mil/) for purchases by America's military services. And the Department of Veterans Affairs facilitates e-procurement through its VA Advantage! Web site (https://VAadvantage.gsa.gov).

Such sites allow authorized defense and civilian agencies to buy everything from office supplies, food, and information technology equipment to construction services through online purchasing. The General Services Administration, the Defense Logistics Agency, and Department of Veterans Affairs not only sell stocked merchandise through their Web sites but also create direct links between buyers and contract suppliers. For example, the branch of the Defense Logistics Agency that sells 160,000 types of medical supplies to military forces transmits orders directly to vendors such as Bristol-Myers Squibb. Such Internet systems promise to eliminate much of the hassle sometimes found in dealing with government purchasing.[16]

◉ Government markets: The U.S. government is the world's largest buyer of products and services; and its checks don't bounce. The Federal Business Opportunities Web site (www.fbo.gov) provides a single point of entry to the entire federal contracting community.

REVIEWING Objectives AND KEY Terms

Business markets and consumer markets are alike in some key ways. For example, both include people in buying roles who make purchase decisions to satisfy needs. But business markets also differ in many ways from consumer markets. For one thing, the business market is *huge*, far larger than the consumer market. Within the United States alone, the business market includes organizations that annually purchase trillions of dollars' worth of goods and services.

Objective 1 Define the business market and explain how business markets differ from consumer markets. (pp 166–170)

The *business market* comprises all organizations that buy goods and services for use in the production of other products and services or for the purpose of reselling or renting them to others at a profit. As compared to consumer markets, business markets usually have fewer but larger buyers. Business demand is derived demand, which tends to be more inelastic and fluctuating than consumer demand. The business buying decision usually involves more, and more professional, buyers. Business buyers usually face more complex buying decisions, and the buying process tends to be more formalized. Finally, business buyers and sellers are often more dependent on each other.

Objective 2 Identify the major factors that influence business buyer behavior. (pp 170–176)

Business buyers make decisions that vary with the three types of *buying situations*: straight rebuys, modified rebuys, and new tasks. The decision-making unit of a buying organization—the *buying center*—can consist of many different persons playing many different roles. The business marketer needs to know the following: Who are the major buying center participants? In what decisions do they exercise influence and to what degree? What evaluation criteria does each decision participant use? The business marketer also needs to understand the major environmental, organizational, interpersonal, and individual influences on the buying process.

Objective 3 List and define the steps in the business buying decision process. (pp 176–180)

The *business buying decision process* itself can be quite involved, with eight basic stages: problem recognition, general need description, product specification, supplier search, proposal solicitation, supplier selection, order-routine specification, and performance review. Buyers who face a new task buying situation usually go through all stages of the buying process. Buyers making modified or straight rebuys may skip some of the stages. Companies must manage the overall customer relationship, which often includes many different buying decisions in various stages of the buying decision process.

Recent advances in information technology have given birth to "e-procurement," by which business buyers are purchasing all kinds of products and services online. The Internet gives business buyers access to new suppliers, lowers purchasing costs, and hastens order processing and delivery. However, e-procurement can also erode customer-supplier relationships and create potential security problems. Still, business marketers are increasingly connecting with customers online to share marketing information, sell products and services, provide customer support services, and maintain ongoing customer relationships.

Objective 4 Compare the institutional and government markets and explain how institutional and government buyers make their buying decisions. (pp 180–182)

The *institutional market* consists of schools, hospitals, prisons, and other institutions that provide goods and services to people in their care. These markets are characterized by low budgets and captive patrons. The *government market*, which is vast, consists of government units—federal, state, and local—that purchase or rent goods and services for carrying out the main functions of government.

Government buyers purchase products and services for defense, education, public welfare, and other public needs. Government buying practices are highly specialized and specified, with open bidding or negotiated contracts characterizing most of the buying. Government buyers operate under the watchful eye of the U.S. Congress and many private watchdog groups. Hence, they tend to require more forms and signatures and respond more slowly and deliberately when placing orders.

KEY Terms

OBJECTIVE 1

Business buyer behavior (p 166)
Business buying process (p 166)
Derived demand (p 167)
Supplier development (p 170)

OBJECTIVE 2

Straight rebuy (p 171)
Modified rebuy (p 171)
New task (p 171)
Systems selling (or solutions selling) (p 171)

Buying center (p 172)
Users (p 172)
Influencers (p 172)
Buyers (p 172)
Deciders (p 172)
Gatekeepers (p 172)

OBJECTIVE 3

Problem recognition (p 176)
General need description (p 176)
Product specification (p 177)

Supplier search (p 177)
Proposal solicitation (p 177)
Supplier selection (p 177)
Order-routine specification (p 178)
Performance review (p 178)
E-procurement (p 178)

OBJECTIVE 4

Institutional market (p 180)
Government market (p 181)

DISCUSSING & APPLYING THE Concepts

Discussing the Concepts

1. Explain how the business market differs from the consumer market for a product such as automobiles. (AACSB: Communication; Reflective Thinking)

2. Name and describe the three types of business buying situations. (AACSB: Communication)

3. In a buying center purchasing process, which buying center participant is most likely to make each of the following statements? (AACSB: Communication; Reflective Thinking)

- "This bonding agent better be good because I have to put this product together."
- "I specified this bonding agent on another job, and it worked for them."
- "Without an appointment, no sales rep gets in to see Ms. Johnson."
- "Okay, it's a deal; we'll buy it."
- "I'll place the order first thing tomorrow."

4. List the major influences on business buyer behavior. Why is it important for the B-to-B marketer to understand these major influences? (AACSB: Communication; Reflective Thinking)

5. Name and briefly describe the stages of the business buying process. (AACSB: Communication)

6. Describe how electronic purchasing has changed the B-to-B marketing process and discuss the advantages and disadvantages of electronic purchasing. (AACSB: Communication)

Applying the Concepts

1. Business buying occurs worldwide, so marketers need to be aware of cultural factors influencing business customers. In a small group, select a country and develop a multimedia presentation on proper business etiquette and manners, including appropriate appearance, behavior, and communication. Include a map showing the location of the country as well as a description of the country in terms of its demographics, culture, and economic history. (AACSB: Communication; Multicultural and Diversity; Use of IT)

2. Interview a businessperson to learn how purchases are made in his or her organization. Ask this person to describe a recent straight rebuy, a modified rebuy, and a new task buying situation of which he or she is aware. (If necessary, define these terms for the businessperson.) Did the buying process differ for different types of products or purchase situations? Ask the businessperson to explain his or her role in a recent purchase and discuss the factors that influenced the decision. Write a brief report of your interview, applying the concepts you learned in this chapter regarding business buyer behavior. (AACSB: Communication; Reflective Thinking)

3. The North American Industry Classification System (NAICS) codes classify businesses by production processes, providing a common classification system for North America and better compatibility with the International Standard Industrial Classification system. This six-digit number (in some cases, seven or ten digits) is useful for understanding business markets. Visit www.naics.com and learn what the six digits of the NAICS code represent. What industry is represented by the NAICS code 448210? How many businesses comprise this code? How can marketers use NAICS codes to better deliver customer satisfaction and value? (AACSB: Communication; Reflective Thinking; Use of IT)

FOCUS ON Technology

How would you like to sell to a customer that spends billions of dollars per year on contractors? If so, you need to learn how to crack the federal government market. The federal government purchases goods ranging from toilet paper to aircraft carriers and services from janitorial supplies to high-tech IT. This is a lucrative market—especially during economic downturns. Companies such as Dataguise, a database security solutions company, and Kearney & Company, an accounting firm, focus their marketing solely on this market. How do businesses—big and small—find out about opportunities in this market? One way is to search the government's Web site for opportunities. A great deal of the government's buying is now done online.

1. Go to the Federal Business Opportunities Web site (https://www.fbo.gov) and watch the general overview

demonstration video for vendors. After watching the video, conduct a search for opportunities using tips you learned in the video. Are there many opportunities in your geographic area? Write a brief report describing the usefulness of this Web site for businesses desiring to sell to the government market. (AACSB: Communication; Use of IT; Reflective Thinking)

2. Visit the Web sites of other government buying resources listed in the chapter to learn more about them. Write a brief report explaining how small businesses can use these resources. (AACSB: Communication; Use of IT; Reflective Thinking)

FOCUS ON Ethics

Pharmaceutical companies give physicians money and other promotional benefits when marketing their products; some receive hundreds of thousands of dollars. J&J, Pfizer, GSK, and other drug manufacturers are now disclosing payments to physicians, medical centers, and academic institutions. In the second half of 2009, Pfizer paid $35 million to 4,500 doctors and academic medical centers, and GSK reported paying $14.6 in the second quarter of 2009. In total, the drug industry spends about $20 billion per year marketing to health professionals. These payments are in the form of gifts, food, trips, speaking fees, drug samples, and educational programs. The companies are providing this information voluntarily now. However, because of the "sunshine provisions" of the Health Care Reform Act, pharmaceutical companies will be re-quired by law beginning in 2013 to publicly disclose cumulative payments to health-care providers totaling $100 or more per year.

1. What type of demand exists for pharmaceutical and medical device products? Discuss the roles doctors play in the business buying process for medical equipment used in a hospital and why companies market so heavily to them. (AACSB: Communication; Reflective Thinking)

2. Should the promotional relationships between doctors and drug and medical device companies be allowed? Discuss the pros and cons of this practice. Will a disclosure of this relationship influence your decision regarding which doctor to visit? (AACSB: Communication; Reflective Thinking; Ethical Reasoning)

MARKETING & THE Economy

Caterpillar

Caterpillar had been on a growth tear for 15 years. As the largest and most geographically diverse heavy equipment maker, it was best positioned to weather a slow economy. And although Caterpillar did okay throughout 2008 while the recent economic crisis remained largely centered in the United States, it took a blow once the recession spread worldwide and institutions everywhere just stopped building things. For Caterpillar, annual revenue toppled 37 percent in 2009 (from $51 billion to $32 billion), while profits spiraled downward 75 percent. Caterpillar responded by dramatically cutting costs. It has also rolled out promotional incentives similar to those offered by automotive manufacturers in order to spark sales. By mid-2010, as some important economic sectors began to recover, Caterpillar's sales and profits also rebounded. But like most other companies, Caterpillar is still waiting for a slower-than-expected economic turnaround to materialize.

1. Given the nature of the demand for its products, is there anything that Caterpillar could do to maintain or increase revenues in a down economy?

2. As a corporation that fuels the economy to some extent, is there anything that Caterpillar could do to facilitate a global economic recovery?

MARKETING BY THE Numbers

B-to-B marketing relies heavily on sales reps. Salespeople do more than just sell products and services; they manage relationships with customers to deliver value to both the customer and their companies. Thus, for many companies, sales reps visit customers several times per year—often for hours at a time. Sales managers must ensure that their companies have enough salespeople to adequately deliver value to customers.

1. Refer to appendix 2 to determine the number of salespeople a company needs if it has 3,000 customers who need to be called on 10 times per year. Each sales call lasts approximately 2.5 hours, and each sales rep has approximately 1,250 hours per year to devote to customers per year. (AACSB: Communication; Analytical Reasoning)

2. If each sales rep earns a salary of $60,000 per year, what sales are necessary to break even on the sales force costs if the company has a contribution margin of 40 percent? What effect will adding each additional sales representative have on the break-even sales? (AACSB: Communication; Analytical Reasoning)

VIDEO Case

EATON

With nearly 60,000 employees doing business in 125 countries and sales last year of more than $11 billion, Eaton is one of the world's largest suppliers of diversified industrial goods. Eaton's products make cars more peppy, 18-wheelers safer to drive, and airliners more fuel efficient. So why haven't you heard of the company? Because Eaton sells its products not to end consumers but to other businesses.

At Eaton, B-to-B marketing means working closely with customers to develop a better product. So the company partners with its sophisticated, knowledgeable clients to create total solutions that meet their needs. Along the way, Eaton maps the decision-making process to better understand the concerns and interests of decision makers. In the end, Eaton's success depends on its ability to provide high-quality, dependable customer service and product support.

Through service and support, Eaton develops a clear understanding of consumer needs and builds stronger relationships with clients.

After viewing the video featuring Eaton, answer the following questions about business markets and business buyer behavior:

1. What is Eaton's value proposition?

2. Who are Eaton's customers? Describe Eaton's customer relationships.

3. Discuss the different ways that Eaton provides value beyond that which companies can provide for themselves.

COMPANY Case

Cisco Systems: Solving Business Problems Through Collaboration

Perhaps you've heard of Cisco Systems. It's the company that runs those catchy "Human Network" ads. It also produces those familiar Linksys wireless Internet routers and owns Pure Digital Technologies, the company that makes the trendy Flip video cameras. But most of what Cisco sells is not for regular consumers like you and me. Cisco is a tried and true B-to-B company. In fact, it earned honors as *BtoB* magazine's 2009 "marketer of the year."

Three-quarters of Cisco's sales are in routers, switches, and advanced network technologies—the things that keep data moving around cyberspace 24/7. But over the past decade, in addition to all that hardware, Cisco has pioneered the next generation of Internet networking tools, from cybersecurity to set-top boxes to videoconferencing.

But this story is about much more than just a tech giant that makes equipment and software that companies need to run their Internet and intranet activities. It's about a forward-thinking firm that has transitioned from a manufacturer to a leadership consultancy. To make that happen, Cisco has perfected one major concept that seems to drive both its own business and its interactions with customer organizations—collaboration. Cisco is all about collaborating with its clients in order to help those clients better collaborate employees, suppliers, partners, and customers.

COLLABORATION WITHIN AND WITHOUT

John Chambers became the CEO of Cisco in 1995, when annual revenues were a mere $1.2 billion. He successfully directed the growth of Cisco as a hardware provider. But following the dot-com bust in 2000, he knew the world was a different place. In response, he engineered a massive, radical, and often bumpy reorganization of the company. Chambers turned Cisco inside out, creating a culture of 63,000 employees that truly thrives on collaboration. As such, Cisco is the perfect laboratory for developing and using the collaboration tools that it subsequently sells to external clients. Cisco not only manufactures the hardware and software that makes collaboration possible but also is the foremost expert on how to use it. All this collaboration has helped Cisco's business explode, hitting $36 billion last year.

Cisco's advertising campaign, "Human Network Effect," illustrates the company's philosophy. The campaign highlights the benefits that come to organizations that use their people networks more effectively. According to Susan Bostrom, Cisco's chief marketing officer, the pragmatic campaign helps customers understand how Cisco's technologies can save them money, bring products to market faster, and even have an impact on the environment. At the same time it has communicated why customers need Cisco's products and services, the campaign has helped Cisco become the 14th most valuable brand in the world.

Chambers tells the story of how Cisco began its transition from hardware into services. "Our customers literally pulled us kicking and screaming into providing consultancy," says Chambers. Some years ago, the CEO of financial services company USAA asked Chambers to help the company figure out what to do with the Internet. Chambers replied that Cisco wasn't in the Web consulting business. But when USAA committed to giving all its networking business to Cisco if it would take the job, Chambers proclaimed, "We are in that business!" Now Cisco has both the products and the knowledge to help other companies succeed on the Internet. Cisco itself is the best model of how to use its products to network and collaborate on the Web, so who better to help other companies do it?

A turning point for Chambers in further understanding the impact that Cisco can have on clients was the major earthquake in China in 2008.

> Tae Yoo, a 19-year Cisco veteran, supervises the company's social-responsibility efforts and sits on the China strategy board and the emerging-countries council. "I had always been a believer in collaboration," she says, but after the earthquake, "I saw it really happen. Our local team immediately mobilized, checking in with employees, customers, and [nongovernmental organization] NGO partners. The council got people on the phone, on [video conference], to give us a complete assessment of what was happening locally. We connected West China Hospital to a specialized trauma center in Maryland via the network." High-level medical centers from the other side of the world were able to weigh in on diagnostics remotely. Cisco employees were on the ground helping rural areas recover and rebuild homes and schools. Within 14 days, Yoo continues, "I walked over to the China board with a complete plan and $45 million to fund it." That number ultimately grew to more than $100 million. "Our business is growing 30 percent year over year there," Chambers says, adding that Cisco has committed to investing $16 billion in public-private partnerships in China. "No one has the reach and trust that we do. No one could offer the help that we could."

COLLABORATION BENEFITS

Cisco management knows that number one on most CEO's lists is to break down the communication barriers between a company and its customers, suppliers, and partners. According to Jim Grubb, Chambers' long-time product-demo sidekick, "If we can accelerate the productivity of scientists who are working on the next solar technology because we're hooking them together, we're doing a great thing for the world." Doing a great thing for the world—while at the same time selling a ton of routers and switches.

But while routers and switches still account for most of Cisco's business, the really interesting stuff is far more cutting edge. Consider Cisco's involvement in what it calls the Smart+Connected Communities initiative. Perhaps the best example of a smart and connected community is New Songdo City in South Korea, a city the size of downtown Boston being built from scratch on a man-made island in the Yellow Sea. Cisco was hired as the technology partner for this venture and is teaming up with the construction company, architects, 3M, and United Technologies as partners in the instant-city business.

Cisco's involvement goes way beyond installing routers, switches, and citywide Wi-Fi. The networking giant is wiring every square inch of the city with electronic synapses. Through trunk lines under the streets, filaments will branch out through every wall and fixture like a nervous system. Cisco is intent on having this city run on information, with its control room playing the part of New Songdo's brain stem.

Not content to simply sell the hardware, Cisco will sell and operate services layered on top of its hardware. Imagine a city where every home and office is wired to Cisco's TelePresence videoconferencing screens. Engineers will listen, learn, and release new Cisco-branded services for modest monthly fees. Cisco intends to bundle urban necessities—water, power, traffic, communications, and entertainment—into a single, Internet-enabled utility. This isn't just big brother stuff. This Cisco system will allow New Songdo to reach new heights in environmental sustainability and efficiency. Because of these efficiencies, the cost for such services to residents will be cheaper as well.

The smart cities business is an emerging industry with a $30 billion potential. Gale International, the construction company behind New Songdo, believes that China alone could use 500 such cities, each with a capacity for one million residents. It already has established the goal to build 20 of them.

Smart cities make one of Cisco's other businesses all the more relevant. Studies show that telecommuting produces enormous benefits for companies, communities, and employees. For example, telecommuters have higher job satisfaction. For that reason, they are more productive, giving back as much as 60 percent of their commuting time to the company. There is even evidence that people like working from home so much that they would be willing to work for less pay. An overwhelming majority of telecommuters produce work in a more timely manner with better quality. Their ability to communicate with coworkers is at least as good and in many cases better than when they work in the office. With products like Cisco Virtual Office and Cisco's expertise in running it, for example, Sun Microsystems saved $68 million. It also reduced carbon emissions by 29,000 metric tons.

Cisco has also recently unveiled a set of Web-based communication products that enhance organizations' collaborative activities. Cisco says this is all about making business more people-centric than document-centric. Along with a cloud-based mail system, WebEx Mail, Cisco Show and Share "helps organizations create and manage highly secure video communities to share ideas and expertise, optimize global video collaboration, and personalize the connection between customers, employees, and students with user-generated content." Also on its way is what Cisco calls the Enterprise Collaboration Platform, a cross between a corporate directory and Facebook. These products allow the free-flow of information to increase exponentially over existing products because they exist behind an organization's firewall with no filters, lawyers, or security issues to get in the way.

Cisco's client list and product portfolio are expansive, and these examples represent just the tip of an iceberg that is growing bigger and bigger all the time. As Bostrom points out, Cisco's own products and services are helping the company itself to become even more efficient at managing the purchase process. "I don't think I had realized how powerful the Web could be in taking a customer through the purchase journey. We can get data on an hourly basis, find out right away what's working and not working, and evolve our Web capabilities to meet those customers' expectations." Through its customer consultancy efforts, Cisco can share these insights and experiences to help customers do the same. That's a powerful selling proposition.

A BRIGHT FUTURE

This year, Cisco's financial performance is down. But Chambers thinks that's only a blip in the grand scheme of things. He points out that Cisco has emerged from every economic downturn of the past two decades stronger and more flexible. During this downturn, Cisco moved quickly, seizing every opportunity to snatch up businesses and develop new products. During the 2000s, Cisco acquired 48 venture-backed companies. But last year alone, the company announced an astounding 61 new technologies, all focused on helping customers through and with collaboration. With these resources—and $35 billion in cash that it has stowed away—Cisco is now expanding into 30 different markets, each with the potential to produce $1 billion a year in revenue. Moving forward, the company has committed to adding 20 percent more new businesses annually. And because Cisco enters a new market only when it's confident that it can gain a 40 percent share, the chance of failure is far below normal.

The collaboration market is estimated at $35 billion, a figure that will grow substantially in years to come. Because Cisco is the leader in this emerging industry, analysts have no problem accepting John Chambers' long-term goal of 12–17 percent revenue growth per year. Cisco has demonstrated that it has the product portfolio and the leadership structure necessary to pull it off. One thing is for sure. Cisco is no longer just a plumber, providing the gizmos and gadgets necessary to make the Web go around. It is a networking leader, a core competency that will certainly make it a force to be reckoned with for years to come.

Questions for Discussion

1. Discuss the nature of the market structure and the demand for Cisco's products.

2. Given the industries in which Cisco competes, what are the implications for the major types of buying situations?

3. What specific customer benefits will likely result from the Cisco products mentioned in the case?

4. Discuss the customer buying process for one of Cisco's products. Discuss the selling process. In what ways do these processes differ from those found in buying and selling a broadband router for home use?

5. Is the relationship between Cisco's own collaborative culture and the products and services it sells something that could work for all companies? Consider this issue for a consumer products company like P&G.

Sources: Ellen McGirt, "How Cisco's CEO John Chambers Is Turning the Tech Giant Socialist," *Fast Company*, November 25, 2008, accessed at www.fastcompany.com; Anya Kamenetz, "Cisco Systems," *Fast Company*, March, 2010, p. 72; Greg Lindsay, "Cisco's Big Bet on New Songdo: Creating Cities from Scratch," *Fast Company*, February 1, 2010, accessed at www.fastcompany.com; Ariel Schwartz, "Cisco Says Telecommuting Save Money, and the World," *Fast Company*, June 26, 2009, accessed at www.fastcompany.com; "Susan Bostrom, Exec VP-CMO, Cisco Systems," *BtoB*, October 26, 2009, accessed online at www.btobonline.com.

Customer-Driven Marketing Strategy
Creating Value for Target Customers

Chapter Preview

So far, you've learned what marketing is and about the importance of understanding consumers and the marketplace environment. With that as background, you're now ready to delve deeper into marketing strategy and tactics. This chapter looks further into key customer-driven marketing strategy decisions: dividing up markets into meaningful customer groups (*segmentation*), choosing which customer groups to serve (*targeting*), creating market offerings that best serve targeted customers (*differentiation*), and positioning the offer-

ings in the minds of consumers (*positioning*). The chapters that follow explore the tactical marketing tools—the four Ps—by which marketers bring these strategies to life.

To start our discussion of the ins and outs of segmentation, targeting, differentiation, and positioning, let's look at Best Buy, the nation's largest consumer electronics retailer. Best Buy knows that it can't make all its customers happy all the time. Instead, it has segmented its market carefully and concentrates on serving its best customers better.

Best Buy: Embracing the Angels and Ditching the Demons

There's no such thing as a bad customer. Right? And the more customers, the merrier. Makes sense, right? After all, more customers mean more money in the till. As it turns out, however, that's often not so. These days, many marketers are discovering a new truth: Some customers can be way, way wrong for the company—as in unprofitable. And trying to serve any and all customers can mean serving none of them well. Instead, companies need to make certain that they are serving the *right* customers and serving them in the *right* way. They need to decide who their best potential customers are—and who they aren't.

Few companies do that better than Best Buy, the nation's leading consumer electronics retailer. Six years ago, Best Buy embarked on a "customer-centricity" segmentation strategy, by which it set out to identify its best customers and win their loyalty by serving them better. At the same time, it identified less attractive customers and began to send them packing—off to Walmart or some other competitor.

Best Buy began in 1966 as a small Minnesota home and car stereo chain. It has since blossomed into a profitable $45 billion mega retailer, with 1,023 U.S. stores and another 2,835 stores worldwide. Today's Best Buy stores are huge, warehouselike emporiums featuring a treasure trove of goods—from consumer electronics, home office equipment, and appliances to software, CDs, and DVDs—all at low discount prices. A decade ago, however, Best Buy saw an influx of new competitors encroaching on its profitable consumer electronics turf. On one side was Walmart, the world's largest retailer and now number two in store sales of consumer electronics. On the other side was a fast-

growing cadre of online and direct retailers, ranging from computer maker Dell to Web giant Amazon.com.

To better differentiate itself in this more crowded marketplace, Best Buy needed to stake out its own turf—to identify its best customers and serve them in ways that no discount or online competitor could. Rather than trying to make all customers happy all the time, Best Buy needed to segment its market, narrow its targeting, and sharpen its positioning. The answer: customer centricity.

The customer-centricity strategy draws on the research of consultant Larry Selden, a Columbia University emeritus business professor. Selden argues that a company should see itself as a portfolio of *customers*, not product lines. His research identified two basic types of customers: angels and demons. Angel customers are profitable, whereas demon customers may actually cost a company more to serve than it makes from them. In fact, Selden claims, serving the demons often wipes out the profits earned by serving the angels.

Following this logic, Best Buy assigned a task force to analyze its customers' purchasing habits. Sure enough, the analysts found both angels and demons. The angels included the 20 percent of Best Buy customers who produced the bulk of its profits. They snapped up HDTVs, portable electronics, and newly released DVDs without waiting for markdowns or rebates. In contrast, the demons formed an "underground of bargain-hungry shoppers intent on wringing every nickel of savings out of the big retailer. They loaded up on loss leaders . . . then flipped the goods at a profit on eBay. They slapped down rock-bottom price quotes from Web sites and demanded that Best Buy make good on its lowest-price pledge." According to a senior Best Buy executive, these demon customers could account for up to 100 million of Best Buy's 500 million customer visits each year. "They can wreak enormous economic havoc," he says.

Further segmentation analysis revealed that the angels fell into eight groups of typical Best Buy shoppers, such as "Barrys," high-income men; "Jills," suburban moms; "Buzzes," male technology enthusiasts; "Rays," young family men on a budget; or "Charlies and Helens," empty nesters with money to spend. Each group has unique needs and spending habits. Take "Ray." He's "no ordinary customer," notes one analyst. "He loves Best Buy, [he's] a hardcore 'techno-tainment' enthusiast, and he's the company's 'bread-and-butter,' accounting for over 20 percent of [the retailer's] sales." And although "Helen" is "by no means a Best Buy regular, she is rediscovering 'me time' and is open to being sold technology that will keep her connected to her community."

Based on these segmentation findings, Best Buy set out to embrace the angels and ditch the demons. To attract the angels, the retailer began stocking more merchandise and offering better service to them. For example, it set up digital photo centers and the "Geek Squad," which offers one-on-one in-store or at-home assistance to high-value buyers. It established a Reward Zone loyalty program, in which regular customers can earn points toward discounts on future purchases. To discourage the demons, Best Buy removed them from its marketing lists, reduced the promotions and other sales tactics that tended to attract them, and installed a 15 percent restocking fee.

In line with its customer-centricity approach, Best Buy then combed through customer databases and began remodeling each store to align its product and service mix to reflect the store's make-up of core customer segments. At customer-centric stores, sales clerks now receive hours of training in identifying desirable customers according to their shopping preferences and behavior.

At one store targeting upper-income Barrys, blue-shirted sales clerks prowl the DVD aisles looking for promising candidates. The goal is to steer them into the store's Magnolia Home Theater Center, a store within a store that features premium home-theater systems and knowledgeable, no-pressure home-theater consultants. Unlike the usual television sections at Best Buy stores, the center has easy chairs, a leather couch, and a basket of popcorn to mimic the media rooms popular with home-theater fans. At stores popular with young Buzzes, Best Buy has created videogame areas with leather chairs and game players hooked to mammoth, plasma-screen televisions. The games are conveniently stacked outside the playing area, and the glitzy new TVs are a short stroll away.

How is Best Buy's customer-centricity strategy working? Very well. Early customer-centricity stores clobbered Best Buy's traditional stores, with many posting sales gains more than triple those of stores with conventional formats. Since rolling out the new strategy six years ago, Best Buy's overall sales (and profits) have more than doubled. And despite the recently gloomy economy, which has seen competitors such as Circuit City, Tiger Direct, and CompUSA biting the dust or undergoing major restructuring, Best Buy has seen profit growth year after year. Revenue grew nearly 13 percent last year. And according to a recent survey, Best Buy is rated as the preferred place to shop for consumer electronics by 40 percent of U.S. shoppers, with Walmart a distant second at 14 percent.

"We started this [customer-centricity] journey by learning how to see the differences in the desires of our customers, and then learning how to meet them," says former CEO Brad Anderson. Customer-centricity means "listening to understand how customers are going to deploy the stuff they buy from us and use it to enrich their lives, . . . rather than worrying about selling the product." Best Buy wants to focus on customers' individual wants and needs—to become "that trusted advisor capable of helping customers use technology the way they dreamed," says Anderson. "That unlocks enormous horizons of growth opportunities for us."[1]

At Best Buy, customer-centricity means listening to target customers and helping them use technology the way they dreamed. "We're about people. People just like you. We really mean it. Really."

> Best Buy's "customer-centricity" strategy serves its best customer segments better while sending less attractive customers packing. The result: Sales are jumping despite the recently gloomy economy.

Companies today recognize that they cannot appeal to all buyers in the marketplace—or at least not to all buyers in the same way. Buyers are too numerous, widely scattered, and varied in their needs and buying practices. Moreover, the companies themselves vary widely in their abilities to serve different segments of the market. Instead, like Best Buy, a company must identify the parts of the market that it can serve best and most profitably. It must design customer-driven marketing strategies that build the right relationships with the right customers.

Thus, most companies have moved away from mass marketing and toward *target marketing:* identifying market segments, selecting one or more of them, and developing products and marketing programs tailored to each. Instead of scattering their marketing efforts (the "shotgun" approach), firms are focusing on the buyers who have greater interest in the values they create best (the "rifle" approach).

● **Figure 7.1** shows the four major steps in designing a customer-driven marketing strategy. In the first two steps, the company selects the customers that it will serve. **Market segmentation** involves dividing a market into smaller segments of buyers with distinct needs, characteristics, or behaviors that might require separate marketing strategies or mixes. The company identifies different ways to segment the market and develops profiles of the resulting market segments. **Market targeting** (or **targeting**) consists of evaluating each market segment's attractiveness and selecting one or more market segments to enter.

In the final two steps, the company decides on a value proposition—how it will create value for target customers. **Differentiation** involves actually differentiating the firm's market offering to create superior customer value. **Positioning** consists of arranging for a market offering to occupy a clear, distinctive, and desirable place relative to competing products in the minds of target consumers. We discuss each of these steps in turn.

Market segmentation
Dividing a market into smaller segments with distinct needs, characteristics, or behavior that might require separate marketing strategies or mixes.

Market targeting (targeting)
The process of evaluating each market segment's attractiveness and selecting one or more segments to enter.

Differentiation
Differentiating the market offering to create superior customer value.

Positioning
Arranging for a market offering to occupy a clear, distinctive, and desirable place relative to competing products in the minds of target consumers.

Author Comment | Market segmentation addresses the first simple-sounding marketing question: What customers will we serve?

Market Segmentation (pp 190–200)

Buyers in any market differ in their wants, resources, locations, buying attitudes, and buying practices. Through market segmentation, companies divide large, heterogeneous markets into smaller segments that can be reached more efficiently and effectively with products and services that match their unique needs. In this section, we discuss four important segmentation topics: segmenting consumer markets, segmenting business markets, segmenting international markets, and the requirements for effective segmentation.

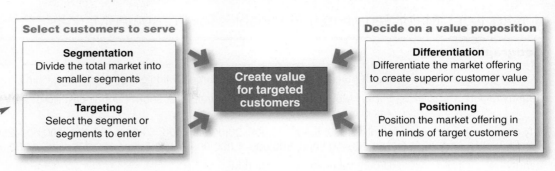

⦿ **FIGURE | 7.1**
Designing a Customer-
Driven Marketing Strategy

In concept, marketing boils down to two questions: (1) Which customers will we serve? and (2) How will we serve them? Of course, the tough part is coming up with good answers to these simple-sounding yet difficult questions. The goal is to create more value for the customers we serve than competitors do.

Segmenting Consumer Markets

There is no single way to segment a market. A marketer has to try different segmentation variables, alone and in combination, to find the best way to view market structure. ⦿ **Table 7.1** outlines the major variables that might be used in segmenting consumer markets. Here we look at the major *geographic, demographic, psychographic,* and *behavioral* variables.

Geographic Segmentation

Geographic segmentation
Dividing a market into different geographical units, such as nations, states, regions, counties, cities, or even neighborhoods.

Demographic segmentation
Dividing the market into segments based on variables such as age, gender, family size, family life cycle, income, occupation, education, religion, race, generation, and nationality.

Age and life-cycle segmentation
Dividing a market into different age and life-cycle groups.

Geographic segmentation calls for dividing the market into different geographical units, such as nations, regions, states, counties, cities, or even neighborhoods. A company may decide to operate in one or a few geographical areas or operate in all areas but pay attention to geographical differences in needs and wants.

Many companies today are localizing their products, advertising, promotion, and sales efforts to fit the needs of individual regions, cities, and even neighborhoods. For example, Walmart operates virtually everywhere but has developed special formats tailored to specific types of geographic locations. In strongly Hispanic neighborhoods in Texas and Arizona, Walmart is now testing Hispanic-focused Supermercado de Walmart stores, which feature layouts, signage, product assortment, and bilingual staff to make them more relevant to local Hispanic customers. In markets where full-size superstores are impractical, Walmart has opened supermarket-style Marketside grocery stores. Marketside stores are one-third the size of Walmart's other small-store format, ⦿ Neighborhood Market supermarkets, and one-tenth the size of one of its supercenters.[2]

Similarly, Citibank offers different mixes of branch banking services depending on neighborhood demographics. And Baskin-Robbins practices what it calls "three-mile marketing," emphasizing local events and promotions close to each local store location.[3]

Demographic Segmentation

Demographic segmentation divides the market into segments based on variables such as age, gender, family size, family life cycle, income, occupation, education, religion, race, generation, and nationality. Demographic factors are the most popular bases for segmenting customer groups. One reason is that consumer needs, wants, and usage rates often vary closely with demographic variables. Another is that demographic variables are easier to measure than most other types of variables. Even when marketers first define segments using other bases, such as benefits sought or behavior, they must know a segment's demographic characteristics to assess the size of the target market and reach it efficiently.

Age and Life-Cycle Stage. Consumer needs and wants change with age. Some companies use **age and life-cycle segmentation**, offering different products or using different marketing approaches for different age and life-cycle groups. For example, for children,

⦿ **Geographic segmentation: Walmart has developed special formats tailored to specific types of geographic locations, from Hispanic-focused Supermercado de Walmart stores to smaller Marketside and Neighborhood Market supermarkets.**

⦿ TABLE | 7.1   Major Segmentation Variables for Consumer Markets

Geographic

World region or country	North America, Canada, Western Europe, Middle East, Pacific Rim, China, India, Brazil
Country region	Pacific, Mountain, West North Central, West South Central, East North Central, East South Central, South Atlantic, Middle Atlantic, New England
City or metro size	Under 5,000; 5,000–20,000; 20,000–50,000; 50,000–100,000; 100,000–250,000; 250,000–500,000; 500,000–1,000,000; 1,000,000–4,000,000; over 4,000,000
Density	Urban, suburban, exurban, rural
Climate	Northern, southern

Demographic

Age	Under 6, 6–11, 12–19, 20–34, 35–49, 50–64, 65 and over
Gender	Male, female
Family size	1–2, 3–4, 5 or more
Family life cycle	Young, single; married, no children; married with children; single parents; unmarried couples; older, married, no children under 18; older, single; other
Income	Under $20,000; $20,000–$30,000; $30,000–$50,000; $50,000–$100,000; $100,000–$250,000; over $250,000
Occupation	Professional and technical; managers, officials, and proprietors; clerical; sales; craftspeople; supervisors; farmers; students; homemakers; unemployed; retired
Education	Primary school or less; some high school; high school graduate; some college; college graduate, advanced degree
Religion	Catholic, Protestant, Jewish, Muslim, Hindu, other
Race	Asian, Hispanic, Black, White
Generation	Baby boomer, Generation X, Millennial
Nationality	North American, South American, British, French, German, Russian, Japanese

Psychographic

Social class	Lower lowers, upper lowers, working class, middle class, upper middles, lower uppers, upper uppers
Lifestyle	Achievers, strivers, survivors
Personality	Compulsive, outgoing, authoritarian, ambitious

Behavioral

Occasions	Regular occasion; special occasion; holiday; seasonal
Benefits	Quality, service, economy, convenience, speed
User status	Nonuser, ex-user, potential user, first-time user, regular user
User rates	Light user, medium user, heavy user
Loyalty status	None, medium, strong, absolute
Readiness stage	Unaware, aware, informed, interested, desirous, intending to buy
Attitude toward product	Enthusiastic, positive, indifferent, negative, hostile

Oscar Mayer offers Lunchables, full of fun, kid-appealing finger food. For older generations, it markets Deli Creations, "with all the warmth, flavor, and fresh-baked taste you look forward to—in a microwave minute without having to go out."

Other companies focus on the specific age of life-stage groups. ⦿ For example, although consumers in all age segments love Disney cruises, Disney Cruise Lines focuses primarily on families with children, large and small. Most of its destinations and shipboard activities are

Life-stage segmentation: Disney Cruise Lines targets primarily families with children, large and small. Most of its destinations and shipboard activities are designed with parents and their children in mind.

designed with parents and their children in mind. On board, Disney provides trained counselors who help younger kids join in hands-on activities, teen-only spaces for older children, and family-time or individual-time options for parents and other adults. It's difficult to find a Disney Cruise Lines ad or Web page that doesn't feature a family full of smiling faces. In contrast, Viking River Cruises, the deluxe smaller-boat cruise line that offers tours along the world's great rivers, primarily targets older-adult couples and singles. You won't find a single child in a Viking ad or Web page.

Marketers must be careful to guard against stereotypes when using age and life-cycle segmentation. Although some 80-year-olds fit the doddering stereotypes, others play tennis. Similarly, whereas some 40-year-old couples are sending their children off to college, others are just beginning new families. Thus, age is often a poor predictor of a person's life cycle, health, work or family status, needs, and buying power. Companies marketing to mature consumers usually employ positive images and appeals. For example, one Carnival Cruise Lines ad for its Fun Ships features an older boomer and child riding waterslides, stating "fun has no age limit."

Gender segmentation

Dividing a market into different segments based on gender.

Gender. **Gender segmentation** has long been used in clothing, cosmetics, toiletries, and magazines. For example, P&G was among the first with Secret, a brand specially formulated for a woman's chemistry, packaged and advertised to reinforce the female image. More recently, many mostly women's cosmetics makers have begun marketing men's lines. For example, Nivea markets Nivea for Men, a product line for men ranging from its 3-in-1 Active3 body wash, shampoo, and shaving cream combination to a revitalizing eye cream. According to a Nivea marketer, Active3 appeals to the male mind-set of, "I wanted to be fast, convenient, and economical. I wanted to fit with these times." It's "What Men Want."[4]

A neglected gender segment can offer new opportunities in markets ranging from consumer electronics to motorcycles. For example, Harley-Davidson has traditionally targeted its product design and marketing to a bread-and-butter market of males between 35 and 55 years old. Women were more often just along for the ride—but no longer:[5]

Women are now among the fastest growing customer segments in the motorcycle business. The number of female Harley-Davidson owners has tripled in the past 20 years, and female buyers now account for 12 percent of new Harley-Davidson purchases. So the company is boosting its efforts to move more women from the back of the bike onto the rider's seat. Rather than indulging in female stereotypes, however, Harley-Davidson is appealing to "strong, independent women who enjoy taking on a challenge and a feeling of adventure," says the company's women's outreach manager. A recent ad sports this headline: "Not pictured: the weaker sex." A women's Web microsite encourages women to share inspirational riding stories with one another. And to kick off Women Riders Month, Harley-Davidson recently hosted special riding events designed to "celebrate the millions of women who have already grabbed life by the handlebars."

In marketing to women, Harley-Davidson is staying true to its tough, road-tested image. "I don't think we're going to see any pink [Harley-Davidson motorcycles] on the road," says an analyst. And "they don't have to add bigger mirrors so women can do their cosmetics. . . . They want to sell Harleys to women, and they want to sell them to women who want to ride a *Harley*."

Harley-Davidson has boosted its efforts to move women from the back of the bike onto the rider's seat.

Income segmentation
Dividing a market into different income segments.

Income. The marketers of products and services such as automobiles, clothing, cosmetics, financial services, and travel have long used **income segmentation**. Many companies target affluent consumers with luxury goods and convenience services. For example, luxury hotels provide special packages to attract affluent travelers. The Four Seasons Miami recently offered a Five Diamond package that included a two-carat Graff diamond eternity band (or another diamond piece designed to your specifications) and a stay in the presidential suite with a bottle of 1990 Dom Pérignon Oenothéque champagne, caviar for two, and an 80-minute in-suite couples massage using a lotion infused with real ground diamonds. The price tag: "From $50,000."[6]

Other marketers use high-touch marketing programs to court the well-to-do. Consider these examples:[7]

> Seadream Yacht Club, a small-ship luxury cruise line, calls select guests after every cruise and offers to have the CEO fly out to their home and host, at Seadream's expense, a brunch or reception for a dozen of the couple's best friends. The cruisers tell the story of their cruise. Seadream offers a great rate to their guests and sells several cruises at $1,000 per person per night—not to mention the friends of the couple telling their friends. This has been so successful for Seadream that it has abandoned most traditional advertising. Similarly, when Steinway sells a Steinway grand piano, it offers to host a social event for buyers in their homes, including having a Steinway artist perform. Such highly personal marketing creates a community of "brand evangelists" who tell the story to prospective affluent buyers and friends—precisely the right target group.

However, not all companies that use income segmentation target the affluent. For example, many retailers—such as the Dollar General, Family Dollar, and Dollar Tree store chains—successfully target low- and middle-income groups. The core market for such stores is represented by families with incomes under $30,000. When Family Dollar real-estate experts scout locations for new stores, they look for lower-middle-class neighborhoods where people wear less-expensive shoes and drive old cars that drip a lot of oil. With their low-income strategies, dollar stores are now the fastest-growing retailers in the nation.

The recent troubled economy has provided challenges for marketers targeting all income groups. Consumers at all income levels—including affluent consumers—are cutting back on their spending and seeking greater value from their purchases. In many cases, luxury marketers targeting high-income consumers have been hardest hit. Even consumers who can still afford to buy luxuries appear to be pushing the pause button. "It's conspicuous *non*consumption," says one economist. "The wealthy still have the wealth, [but] it's the image you project in a bad economy of driving a nice car when your friends or colleagues may be losing their businesses."[8]

Psychographic Segmentation

Psychographic segmentation
Dividing a market into different segments based on social class, lifestyle, or personality characteristics.

Psychographic segmentation divides buyers into different segments based on social class, lifestyle, or personality characteristics. People in the same demographic group can have very different psychographic characteristics.

In chapter 5, we discussed how the products people buy reflect their *lifestyles*. As a result, marketers often segment their markets by consumer lifestyles and base their marketing strategies on lifestyle appeals. For example, car-sharing nicher Zipcar rents cars by the hour or the day. But it doesn't see itself as a car-rental company. Instead it sees itself as enhancing its customers urban lifestyles and targets accordingly. "It's not about cars," says Zipcar's CEO, "it's about urban life." (See Real Marketing 7.1.)

Marketers also use *personality* variables to segment markets. For example, cruise lines target adventure seekers. Royal Caribbean appeals to high-energy couples and families by providing hundreds of activities, such as rock wall climbing and ice skating. Its commercials urge travelers to "declare your independence and become a citizen of our nation—Royal Caribbean, The Nation of Why Not." By contrast, the Regent Seven Seas Cruise Line targets more serene

Real Marketing 7.1

Zipcar: "It's Not about Cars; It's about Urban Life"

Imagine a world in which no one owns a car. Cars would still exist, but rather than owning cars, people would just share them. Sounds crazy, right? But Scott Griffith, CEO of Zipcar, the world's largest car-share company, paints a picture of just such an imaginary world. And he has 325,000 passionate customers, or "Zipsters" as they are called, who will back him up.

Zipcar specializes in renting out cars by the hour or day. The service isn't for everyone—it doesn't try to be. Instead, it zeros in on narrowly defined lifestyle segments, people who live or work in densely populated neighborhoods in New York City, Boston, Atlanta, San Francisco, London, or one of the more than a dozen big cities in which Zipcar operates (or on more than 100 college campuses across North America). For these customers, owning a car (or a second or third car) is difficult, costly, and environmentally irresponsible. Interestingly, Zipcar doesn't see itself as a car-rental company. Instead, it's selling a lifestyle. "It's not about cars," says CEO Griffith, "it's about urban life. We're creating a lifestyle brand that happens to have a lot of cars."

Initially, Zipcar targeted mostly trendy, young, well-educated, environmentally conscious urbanites. But, gradually, the Zipster profile is broadening, becoming more mature and mainstream. However, Zipsters share a number of common urban lifestyle traits. For starters, the lifestyle is rooted in environmental consciousness. In fact, at first, Zipcar focused almost exclusively on the benefits of reduced traffic congestion and carbon emissions. It targeted green-minded customers with promotional pitches such as "We ♥ Earth" and "Imagine a world with a million fewer cars on the road." Zipcar's vibrant green logo reflects this save-the-Earth philosophy. And Zipcar really does deliver on its environmental promises. Studies show that every shared Zipcar takes up to 20 cars off the road and cuts emissions by up to 50 percent per user. On average, Zipsters travel 44 percent fewer miles than when they owned a car.

But if Zipcar was going to grow, it needed to move beyond just being green. "It is an important part of the brand," says Griffith, but "I don't think people are going to use Zipcar [just] because it's green." So the company has broadened its appeals to include other urban lifestyle benefits. One of those benefits is convenience. Owning a car in a densely populated urban area can be a real hassle. Zipcar lets customers focus on driving, not on the complexities of car ownership. It gives them "Wheels when you want them," in four easy steps: "Join. Reserve. Unlock. Drive."

To join, you pay a $50 annual fee and receive your personal Zipcard, which unlocks any of thousands of cars in urban areas around the world. Then, when you need a car, reserve one—minutes or months in advance—online, by phone, or using an iPhone app. You can choose the car you want, when and where you want it, and drive it for as little as $7 an hour, including gas, insurance, and free miles. When you're ready, walk to the car, hold your Zipcard to the windshield to unlock the doors, and you're good to go. When done, you drop the car off at the same parking spot; Zipcar worries about the maintenance and cleaning.

Zipcar not only eliminates the hassle of urban car ownership but also saves money. By living with less, the average Zipster saves $600 a month on car payments, insurance, gas, maintenance, and other car ownership expenses.

Zipcar's operating system is carefully aligned with its tight urban lifestyle targeting. For starters, Zipcar "pods" (a dozen or so vehicles located in a given neighborhood) are stocked with over 50 different models that trendy urbanites love. The vehicles are both hip and fuel efficient: Toyota Priuses, Honda CRVs, MINIs, Volvo S60s, BMW 328s, Toyota Tacomas, Toyota Siennas, Subaru Outbacks, and others. And Zipcar is now eyeing plug-in hybrids and full electric vehicles. Each car has a

personality—a name and profile created by a Zipster. For example, Prius Ping "jogs in the morning; doesn't say much," whereas Civic Carlos "teaches yoga; loves to kayak." Such personal touches make it feel like you're borrowing the car from a friend, rather than being assigned whatever piece of metal happens to be available.

Zipcar's promotion tactics also focus tightly on its narrowly defined urban segments. The company targets urbanites within a 10-minute walk of its car pods—no easy task. "Even with today's highly targeted Web, it's hard to target at that hyper-local level," says Griffith. "So our street teams do it block by block, zip code by zip code." Thus, in addition to local Web ads and transit advertising, Zipcar reps are beating the streets in true guerilla fashion.

For example, in San Francisco, passersby got to swing a sledgehammer at an SUV, while on Harvard's campus, students tried to guess how many frozen IKEA meatballs were stuffed inside a MINI. In Washington, D.C., Zipcar street teams planted a couch on a busy sidewalk with the sign "You need a Zipcar to move this." And the company has launched several "Low-Car Diet" events, in which it asks urban residents to give up their cars and blog about

Geographic segmentation: Car-sharing service Zipcar focuses only on densely populated areas, positioning itself as a low-cost alternative to urban car ownership. As it has grown, Zipcar has expanded its targeting to include a different type of urban dweller: businesses and other organizations.

Continued on next page

it. Zipcar partnered with a bike company to give away a free bike to a lucky dieter in each of the 69 cities where Zipcars can be found. Surveyed dieters reported saving 67 percent on vehicle costs compared to operating their own cars. Nearly half of them also said that they lost weight.

As Zipcar has taken off, it has expanded its targeting to include a different type of urban dweller: businesses and other organizations. Companies such as Google now encourage employees to be environmentally conscious by commuting via a company shuttle and then using Zipcars for both business and personal use during the day. Other companies are turning to Zipcar as an alternative to black sedans, long taxi rides, and congested parking lots. Government agencies are getting into the game as well. The city of Washington, D.C., now saves more than $1 million a year using Zipcar. Fleet manager Ralph Burns says that it's such a no-brainer, and he has departments lining up. "Agencies putting their budgets together for next year are calling me up and saying, 'Ralph, I've got 25 cars I want to get rid of!'"

Zipcar's lifestyle targeting fosters a tight-knit sense of customer community. Zipsters are as fanatically loyal as the hardcore fans of Harley-Davidson or Apple, brands that have been nurturing customer relationships for decades. Loyal Zipsters serve as neighborhood brand ambassadors; 30 percent of new members join up at the recommendation of existing customers. "When I meet another Zipcar member at a party or something, I feel like we have something in common," says one Brooklyn Zipster. "It's like we're both making intelligent choices about our lives."

How is Zipcar's urban lifestyle targeting working? By all accounts, the young car-sharing nicher has the pedal to the metal, and its tires are smoking. In just the past six years, Zipcar's annual revenues have rocketed 65-fold, from $2 million to $130 million, and it's looking to hit $1 billion in revenues within the next few years. Last year alone, Zipcar boosted its membership by more than 40 percent.

Zipcar's rapid growth has sounded alarms at the traditional car-rental giants. Enterprise, Hertz, Avis, and Thrifty now have their own car-sharing operations. Even U-Haul is getting into the act. These veteran companies have deep pockets and large fleets. But Zipcar has a 10-year head start, cozy relationships in targeted neighborhoods, and an urban hipster creed that corporate giants like Hertz will have trouble matching. To Zipsters, Hertz rents cars, but Zipcar is part of their hectic urban lives.

Sources: Kunur Patel, "Zipcar: An America's Hottest Brands Case Study," *Advertising Age*, November 16, 2009, p. 16; Paul Keegan, "Zipcar: The Best New Idea in Business," *Fortune*, August 27, 2009, accessed at www.fortune .com; Elizabeth Olson, "Car Sharing Reinvents the Company Wheels," *New York Times*, May 7, 2009, p. F2; Stephanie Clifford, "How Fast Can This Thing Go, Anyway?" *Inc*, March 2008, accessed at www.inc.com; and www.zipcar.com, accessed October 2010.

● **Occasion segmentation: M&Ms runs special ads and packaging for holidays and events such as Easter.**

and cerebral adventurers, mature couples seeking a more elegant ambiance and exotic destinations, such as the Orient. Regent invites them to come along as "luxury goes exploring."[9]

Behavioral Segmentation

Behavioral segmentation divides buyers into segments based on their knowledge, attitudes, uses, or responses to a product. Many marketers believe that behavior variables are the best starting point for building market segments.

Occasions. Buyers can be grouped according to occasions when they get the idea to buy, actually make their purchase, or use the purchased item. **Occasion segmentation** can help firms build up product usage. For example, most consumers drink orange juice in the morning, but orange growers have promoted drinking orange juice as a cool, healthful refresher at other times of the day. By contrast, Coca-Cola's "Good Morning" campaign attempts to increase Diet Coke consumption by promoting the soft drink as an early morning pick-me-up.

Some holidays, such as Mother's Day and Father's Day, were originally promoted partly to increase the sale of candy, flowers, cards, and other gifts. And many marketers prepare special offers and ads for holiday occasions. ● For example, M&Ms runs ads throughout the year but prepares special ads and packaging for holidays and events such as Christmas, Easter, and the Super Bowl.

Benefits Sought. A powerful form of segmentation is grouping buyers according to the different *benefits* that they seek from a prod-

Behavioral segmentation
Dividing a market into segments based on consumer knowledge, attitudes, uses, or responses to a product.

Occasion segmentation
Dividing the market into segments according to occasions when buyers get the idea to buy, actually make their purchase, or use the purchased item.

Benefit segmentation
Dividing the market into segments according to the different benefits that consumers seek from the product.

uct. **Benefit segmentation** requires finding the major benefits people look for in a product class, the kinds of people who look for each benefit, and the major brands that deliver each benefit.

Champion athletic wear segments its markets according to benefits that different consumers seek from their activewear. For example, "Fit and Polish" consumers seek a balance between function and style—they exercise for results but want to look good doing it. "Serious Sports Competitors" exercise heavily and live in and love their activewear—they seek performance and function. By contrast, "Value-Seeking Moms" have low sports interest and low activewear involvement—they buy for the family and seek durability and value. Thus, each segment seeks a different mix of benefits. Champion must target the benefit segment or segments that it can serve best and most profitably, using appeals that match each segment's benefit preferences.

User Status. Markets can be segmented into nonusers, ex-users, potential users, first-time users, and regular users of a product. Marketers want to reinforce and retain regular users, attract targeted nonusers, and reinvigorate relationships with ex-users.

Included in the potential user group are consumers facing life-stage changes—such as newlyweds and new parents—who can be turned into heavy users. For example, upscale kitchen and cookware retailer Williams-Sonoma actively targets newly engaged couples.

Eight-page Williams-Sonoma inserts in bridal magazines show a young couple strolling through a park or talking intimately in the kitchen over a glass of wine. The bride-to-be asks, "Now that I've found love, what else do I need?" Pictures of Williams-Sonoma knife sets, toasters, glassware, and pots and pans provide some strong clues. The retailer also offers a bridal registry, of course, but it takes its registry a step further. Through a program called "The Store Is Yours," it opens its stores after hours, by appointment, exclusively for individual couples to visit and make their wish lists. This segment is very important to Williams-Sonoma. About half the people who register are new to the brand, and they'll be buying a lot of kitchen and cookware in the future.[10]

Usage Rate. Markets can also be segmented into light, medium, and heavy product users. Heavy users are often a small percentage of the market but account for a high percentage of total consumption. For example, Burger King targets what it calls "Super Fans," young (ages 18 to 34), Whopper-wolfing males and females who make up 18 percent of the chain's customers but account for almost half of all customer visits. They eat at Burger King an average of 13 times a month. Burger King targets these Super Fans openly with ads that exalt monster burgers containing meat, cheese, and more meat and cheese that can turn "innies into outies."[11]

Loyalty Status. A market can also be segmented by consumer loyalty. Consumers can be loyal to brands (Tide), stores (Target), and companies (Apple). Buyers can be divided into groups according to their degree of loyalty.

Some consumers are completely loyal—they buy one brand all the time. For example, as we discussed in the previous chapter, ⦿ Apple has an almost cultlike following of loyal users. Other consumers are somewhat loyal—they are loyal to two or three brands of a given product or favor one brand while sometimes buying others. Still other buyers show no loyalty to any brand—they either want something different each time they buy, or they buy whatever's on sale.

A company can learn a lot by analyzing loyalty patterns in its market. It should start by studying its own loyal customers. For example, by studying Mac fanatics, Apple can better pinpoint its target market and develop marketing appeals. By studying its less-loyal buyers, the company can detect which brands are most competitive with its own. By looking at customers who are shifting away from its brand, the company can learn about its marketing weaknesses.

⦿ Consumer loyalty: "Mac fanatics"—fanatically loyal Apple users—helped keep Apple afloat during the lean years, and they are now at the forefront of Apple's burgeoning iPod, iTunes, and iPhone empire.

Using Multiple Segmentation Bases

Marketers rarely limit their segmentation analysis to only one or a few variables only. Rather, they often use multiple segmentation bases in an effort to identify smaller, better-defined target groups. Thus, a bank may not only identify a group of wealthy, retired adults but also, within that group, distinguish several segments based on their current income, assets, savings and risk preferences, housing, and lifestyles.

Several business information services—such as Nielsen, Acxiom, and Experian—provide multivariable segmentation systems that merge geographic, demographic, lifestyle, and behavioral data to help companies segment their markets down to zip codes, neighborhoods, and even households. One of the leading segmentation systems is the PRIZM system by Nielsen. PRIZM classifies every American household based on a host of demographic factors—such as age, educational level, income, occupation, family composition, ethnicity, and housing—and behavioral and lifestyle factors—such as purchases, free-time activities, and media preferences.

PRIZM classifies U.S. households into 66 demographically and behaviorally distinct segments, organized into 14 different social groups. ● PRIZM segments carry such exotic names as "Kids & Cul-de-Sacs," "Gray Power," "Bohemian Mix," "Mayberry-ville," "Shotguns & Pickups," "Old Glories," "Multi-Culti Mosaic," "Big City Blues," and "Bright Lites L'il City." The colorful names help to bring the clusters to life.[12]

PRIZM and other such systems can help marketers segment people and locations into marketable groups of like-minded consumers. Each cluster has its own pattern of likes, dislikes, lifestyles, and purchase behaviors. For example, "Winner's Circle" neighborhoods, part of the Elite Suburbs social group, are suburban areas populated by well-off couples, between the ages of 35 and 54, with large families in new-money neighborhoods. People in this segment are more likely to own a Mercedes GL Class, go jogging, shop at Neiman Marcus, and read *The Wall Street Journal*. In contrast, the "Bedrock America" segment, part of the Rustic Living social group, is populated by young, economically challenged families in small, isolated towns located throughout the nation's heartland. People in this segment are more likely to eat at Hardee's, buy a used vehicle, and read *Parents Magazine*.

Such segmentation provides a powerful tool for marketers of all kinds. It can help companies identify and better understand key customer segments, target them more efficiently, and tailor market offerings and messages to their specific needs.

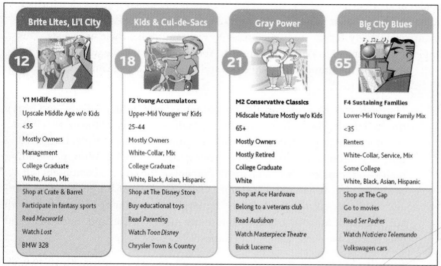

● Using Nielsen's PRIZM system, marketers can paint a surprisingly precise picture of who you are and what you might buy. PRIZM segments carry such exotic names as "Brite Lites, L'il City," "Kids & Cul-de-Sacs," "Gray Power," and "Big City Blues."

Segmenting Business Markets

Consumer and business marketers use many of the same variables to segment their markets. Business buyers can be segmented geographically, demographically (industry, company size), or by benefits sought, user status, usage rate, and loyalty status. Yet, business marketers also use some additional variables, such as customer *operating characteristics*, *purchasing approaches*, *situational factors*, and *personal characteristics*.

Almost every company serves at least some business markets. For example, American Express targets businesses in three segments: merchants, corporations, and small businesses. It has developed distinct marketing programs for each segment. In the merchants segment, American Express focuses on convincing new merchants to accept the card and managing relationships with those that already do. For larger corporate customers, the company offers a corporate card program, which includes extensive employee expense and travel management services. It also offers this segment a wide range of asset management, retirement planning, and financial education services.

Finally, for small business customers, American Express has created OPEN: The Small Business Network, a system of small business cards and financial services. It includes credit cards and lines of credit, special usage rewards, financial monitoring and spending report features, and 24/7 customized financial support services. "OPEN is how we serve small business," says American Express.[13]

Many companies establish separate systems for dealing with larger or multiple-location customers. For example, Steelcase, a major producer of office furniture, first divides customers into seven segments, including biosciences, higher education, U.S. and Canadian governments, state and local governments, healthcare, professional services, and retail banking. Next, company salespeople work with independent Steelcase dealers to handle smaller, local, or regional Steelcase customers in each segment. But many national, multiple-location customers, such as ExxonMobil or IBM, have special needs that may reach beyond the scope of individual dealers. So Steelcase uses national account managers to help its dealer networks handle national accounts.

Within a given target industry and customer size, the company can segment by purchase approaches and criteria. As in consumer segmentation, many marketers believe that *buying behavior* and *benefits* provide the best basis for segmenting business markets.

Segmenting International Markets

Few companies have either the resources or the will to operate in all, or even most, of the countries that dot the globe. Although some large companies, such as Coca-Cola or Sony, sell products in more than 200 countries, most international firms focus on a smaller set. Operating in many countries presents new challenges. Different countries, even those that are close together, can vary greatly in their economic, cultural, and political makeup. Thus, just as they do within their domestic markets, international firms need to group their world markets into segments with distinct buying needs and behaviors.

Companies can segment international markets using one or a combination of several variables. They can segment by *geographic location*, grouping countries by regions such as Western Europe, the Pacific Rim, the Middle East, or Africa. Geographic segmentation assumes that nations close to one another will have many common traits and behaviors. Although this is often the case, there are many exceptions. For example, although the United States and Canada have much in common, both differ culturally and economically from neighboring Mexico. Even within a region, consumers can differ widely. For example, some U.S. marketers lump all Central and South American countries together. However, the Dominican Republic is no more like Brazil than Italy is like Sweden. Many Central and South Americans don't even speak Spanish, including 200 million Portuguese-speaking Brazilians and the millions in other countries who speak a variety of Indian dialects.

World markets can also be segmented on the basis of *economic factors*. Countries might be grouped by population income levels or by their overall level of economic development. A country's economic structure shapes its population's product and service needs and, therefore, the marketing opportunities it offers. For example, many companies are now targeting the BRIC countries—Brazil, Russia, India, and China—which are fast-growing developing economies with rapidly increasing buying power.

Countries can also be segmented by *political and legal factors* such as the type and stability of government, receptivity to foreign firms, monetary regulations, and amount of bureaucracy. *Cultural factors* can also be used, grouping markets according to common languages, religions, values and attitudes, customs, and behavioral patterns.

● Intermarket segmentation: Coca-Cola targets the world's teens—core consumers of its soft drinks—no matter where they live.

Segmenting international markets based on geographic, economic, political, cultural, and other factors presumes that segments should consist of clusters of countries. However, as new communications technologies, such as satellite TV and the Internet, connect consumers around the world, marketers can define and reach segments of like-minded consumers no matter where in the world they are. Using **intermarket segmentation** (also called **cross-market segmentation**), they form segments of consumers who have similar needs and buying behaviors even though they are located in different countries. For example, Lexus targets the world's well-to-do—the "global elite" segment—regardless of their country. ● Coca-Cola creates special programs to target teens, core consumers of its soft drinks the world over. And Swedish furniture giant IKEA targets the aspiring global middle class—it sells good-quality furniture that ordinary people worldwide can afford.

Intermarket segmentation (cross-market segmentation)
Forming segments of consumers who have similar needs and buying behavior even though they are located in different countries.

Requirements for Effective Segmentation

Clearly, there are many ways to segment a market, but not all segmentations are effective. For example, buyers of table salt could be divided into blond and brunette customers. But hair color obviously does not affect the purchase of salt. Furthermore, if all salt buyers bought the same amount of salt each month, believed that all salt is the same, and wanted to pay the same price, the company would not benefit from segmenting this market.

To be useful, market segments must be

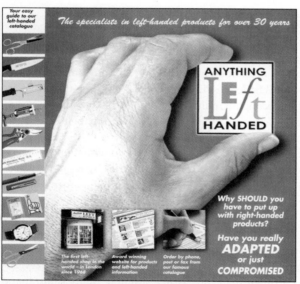

● The "leftie" segment can be hard to identify and measure. As a result, few companies tailor their offers to left-handers. However, some nichers such as Anything Left-Handed in the United Kingdom target this segment.

- *Measurable:* The size, purchasing power, and profiles of the segments can be measured. Certain segmentation variables are difficult to measure. ● For example, there are approximately 30.5 million left-handed people in the United States, which is nearly the entire population of Canada. Yet few products are targeted toward this left-handed segment. The major problem may be that the segment is hard to identify and measure. There are no data on the demographics of lefties, and the U.S. Census Bureau does not keep track of left-handedness in its surveys. Private data companies keep reams of statistics on other demographic segments but not on left-handers.

- *Accessible:* The market segments can be effectively reached and served. Suppose a fragrance company finds that heavy users of its brand are single men and women who stay out late and socialize a lot. Unless this group lives or shops at certain places and is exposed to certain media, its members will be difficult to reach.

- *Substantial:* The market segments are large or profitable enough to serve. A segment should be the largest possible homogeneous group worth pursuing with a tailored marketing program. It would not pay, for example, for an automobile manufacturer to develop cars especially for people whose height is greater than seven feet.

- *Differentiable:* The segments are conceptually distinguishable and respond differently to different marketing mix elements and programs. If men and women respond similarly to marketing efforts for soft drinks, they do not constitute separate segments.

- *Actionable:* Effective programs can be designed for attracting and serving the segments. For example, although one small airline identified seven market segments, its staff was too small to develop separate marketing programs for each segment.

Author Comment | After dividing the market into segments, it's time to answer that first seemingly simple marketing strategy question we raised in Figure 7.1: Which customers will the company serve?

Market Targeting (pp 200–207)

Market segmentation reveals the firm's market segment opportunities. The firm now has to evaluate the various segments and decide how many and which segments it can serve best. We now look at how companies evaluate and select target segments.

Evaluating Market Segments

In evaluating different market segments, a firm must look at three factors: segment size and growth, segment structural attractiveness, and company objectives and resources. The company must first collect and analyze data on current segment sales, growth rates, and the expected profitability for various segments. It will be interested in segments that have the right size and growth characteristics.

But "right size and growth" is a relative matter. The largest, fastest-growing segments are not always the most attractive ones for every company. Smaller companies may lack the skills and resources needed to serve larger segments. Or they may find these segments too competitive. Such companies may target segments that are smaller and less attractive, in an absolute sense, but that are potentially more profitable for them.

The company also needs to examine major structural factors that affect long-run segment attractiveness.[14] For example, a segment is less attractive if it already contains many strong and aggressive *competitors*. The existence of many actual or potential *substitute products* may limit prices and the profits that can be earned in a segment. The relative *power of buyers* also affects segment attractiveness. Buyers with strong bargaining power relative to sellers will try to force prices down, demand more services, and set competitors against one another—all at the expense of seller profitability. Finally, a segment may be less attractive if it contains *powerful suppliers* who can control prices or reduce the quality or quantity of ordered goods and services.

Even if a segment has the right size and growth and is structurally attractive, the company must consider its own objectives and resources. Some attractive segments can be dismissed quickly because they do not mesh with the company's long-run objectives. Or the company may lack the skills and resources needed to succeed in an attractive segment. For example, given the current economic conditions, the economy segment of the automobile market is large and growing. But given its objectives and resources, it would make little sense for luxury-performance carmaker BMW to enter this segment. A company should enter only segments in which it can create superior customer value and gain advantages over its competitors.

Selecting Target Market Segments

After evaluating different segments, the company must decide which and how many segments it will target. A **target market** consists of a set of buyers who share common needs or characteristics that the company decides to serve. Market targeting can be carried out at several different levels. ◉ **Figure 7.2** shows that companies can target very broadly (undifferentiated marketing), very narrowly (micromarketing), or somewhere in between (differentiated or concentrated marketing).

Undifferentiated Marketing

Using an **undifferentiated marketing** (or **mass marketing**) strategy, a firm might decide to ignore market segment differences and target the whole market with one offer. Such a strategy focuses on what is *common* in the needs of consumers rather than on what is *different*. The company designs a product and a marketing program that will appeal to the largest number of buyers.

Target market
A set of buyers sharing common needs or characteristics that the company decides to serve.

Undifferentiated (mass) marketing
A market-coverage strategy in which a firm decides to ignore market segment differences and go after the whole market with one offer.

> This figure covers a broad range of targeting strategies, from mass marketing (virtually no targeting) to individual marketing (customizing products and programs to individual customers). An example of individual marketing: At myMMs.com you can order a batch of M&Ms with your face and personal message printed on each little candy.

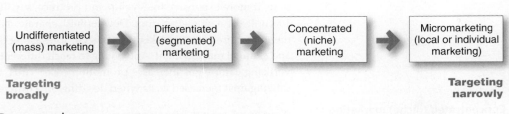

| Undifferentiated (mass) marketing | → | Differentiated (segmented) marketing | → | Concentrated (niche) marketing | → | Micromarketing (local or individual marketing) |

Targeting broadly   **Targeting narrowly**

◉ **FIGURE | 7.2**
Market Targeting Strategies

As noted earlier in the chapter, most modern marketers have strong doubts about this strategy. Difficulties arise in developing a product or brand that will satisfy all consumers. Moreover, mass marketers often have trouble competing with more-focused firms that do a better job of satisfying the needs of specific segments and niches.

Differentiated Marketing

Differentiated (segmented) marketing

A market-coverage strategy in which a firm decides to target several market segments and designs separate offers for each.

Using a **differentiated marketing** (or **segmented marketing**) strategy, a firm decides to target several market segments and designs separate offers for each. Toyota Corporation produces several different brands of cars—from Scion to Toyota to Lexus—each targeting its own segments of car buyers. P&G markets six different laundry detergent brands in the United States, which compete with each other on supermarket shelves. ◉ And VF Corporation offers a closet full of more than thirty premium lifestyle brands, which "fit the lives of consumers the world over" in well-defined segments—"from commuters to cowboys, surfers to soccer moms, sports fans to rock bands."[15]

VF is the nation's number-one jeans maker, with brands such as Lee, Riders, Rustler, and Wrangler. But jeans are not the only focus for VF. The company's brands are carefully separated into five major segments—Jeanswear, Imagewear (workwear), Outdoor, Sportswear, and Contemporary Brands. The North Face, part of the Outdoor unit, offers top-of-the-line gear and apparel for diehard outdoor enthusiasts, especially those who prefer cold weather activities. From the Sportswear unit, Nautica focuses on people who enjoy high-end casual apparel inspired by sailing and the sea. Vans began as a skate shoemaker, and Reef features surf-inspired footwear and apparel. In the Contemporary Brands unit, Lucy features upscale active-wear, whereas 7 for All Mankind supplies premium denim and accessories sold in boutiques and high-end department stores such as Saks and Nordstrom. At the other end of the spectrum, Sentinel, part of the Image-wear unit, markets uniforms for security officers. No matter who you are, says the company, "We fit your life."

◉ Differentiated marketing: VF Corporation offers a closet full of over 30 premium lifestyle brands, each of which "taps into consumer aspirations to fashion, status, and well-being" in a well-defined segment.

By offering product and marketing variations to segments, companies hope for higher sales and a stronger position within each market segment. Developing a stronger position within several segments creates more total sales than undifferentiated marketing across all segments. VF Corporation's combined brands give it a much greater, more stable market share than any single brand could. The four Jeanswear brands alone account for one-fourth of all jeans sold in the United States. Similarly, P&G's multiple detergent brands capture four times the market share of its nearest rival.

But differentiated marketing also increases the costs of doing business. A firm usually finds it more expensive to develop and produce, say, 10 units of 10 different products than 100 units of a single product. Developing separate marketing plans for the separate segments requires extra marketing research, forecasting, sales analysis, promotion planning, and channel management. And trying to reach different market segments with different advertising campaigns increases promotion costs. Thus, the company must weigh increased sales against increased costs when deciding on a differentiated marketing strategy.

Concentrated Marketing

Concentrated (niche) marketing

A market-coverage strategy in which a firm goes after a large share of one or a few segments or niches.

Using a **concentrated marketing** (or **niche marketing**) strategy, instead of going after a small share of a large market, a firm goes after a large share of one or a few smaller segments or niches. For example, Whole Foods Market has about 285 stores and $8 billion in sales, compared with goliaths such as Kroger (more than 3,600 stores and sales of $76 billion) and Walmart (8,400 stores and sales of $408 billion).[16] Yet, over the past five years, the smaller, more upscale retailer has grown faster and more profitably than either of its giant rivals. Whole Foods thrives by catering to affluent customers who the Walmarts of the world can't serve well, offering them "organic, natural, and gourmet foods, all swaddled in Earth Day politics." In fact, a typical Whole Foods customer is more likely to boycott the local Walmart than to shop at it.

Through concentrated marketing, the firm achieves a strong market position because of its greater knowledge of consumer needs in the niches it serves and the special reputation it acquires. It can market more *effectively* by fine-tuning its products, prices, and programs to the needs of carefully defined segments. It can also market more *efficiently*, targeting its products or services, channels, and communications programs toward only consumers that it can serve best and most profitably.

Whereas segments are fairly large and normally attract several competitors, niches are smaller and may attract only one or a few competitors. Niching lets smaller companies focus their limited resources on serving niches that may be unimportant to or overlooked by larger competitors. Many companies start as nichers to get a foothold against larger, more-resourceful competitors and then grow into broader competitors. For example, Southwest Airlines began by serving intrastate, no-frills commuters in Texas but is now one of the nation's largest airlines. And Enterprise Rent-A-Car began by building a network of neighborhood offices rather competing with Hertz and Avis in airport locations. Enterprise is now the nation's largest car rental company.

In contrast, as markets change, some megamarketers develop niche products to create sales growth. For example, in recent years, as consumers have grown more health conscious, the demand for carbonated soft drinks has declined, and the market for energy drinks and juices has grown. Carbonated soft drink sales fell 3 percent last year; energy drink sales rose 11 percent. To meet this shifting demand, mainstream cola marketers PepsiCo and Coca-Cola have both developed or acquired their own niche products. PepsiCo developed Amp energy drink and purchased the SoBe and Izze brands of enhanced waters and juices. Similarly, Coca-Cola developed Vault and acquired the Vitaminwater and Odwalla brands. Says Pepsi-Cola North America's chief marketing officer, "The era of the mass brand has been over for a long time."[17]

Today, the low cost of setting up shop on the Internet makes it even more profitable to serve seemingly miniscule niches. Small businesses, in particular, are realizing riches from serving small niches on the Web. Consider Etsy:

● Etsy is "an online marketplace for buying and selling all things handmade"—from hand-knit leg warmers to Conan O'Brien cufflinks. Sometimes referred to as eBay's funky little sister, the Etsy online crafts fair site was launched five years ago by three New York University grads. The site makes money three ways: a 20-cent listing fee for every item, a 3.5 percent sales fee on every transaction, and an internal advertising system that sells ad space to Etsy sellers who want to promote their items. A far cry from the old-fashioned street-corner flea market, thanks to the reach and power of the Web, Etsy now counts 5 million members and 5.7 million listings in 150 countries. Last year alone, Etsy more than doubled its gross sales to $180 million. And Etsy is more than an e-commerce site; it's a thriving community. For example, it sponsors actual and virtual meet-ups

● **Concentrated marketing: Thanks to the reach and power of the Web, online nicher Etsy—sometimes referred to as eBay's funky little sister— is thriving.**

organized by location (from Syracuse to Saskatchewan and Singapore), medium (papier-mâché, mosaic), and interest area (Chainmaillers Guild, Lizards, and Lollipops). Etsy's main goal? According to former CEO Maria Thomas, it's "to help people make a living by doing what they love and making things."[18]

Concentrated marketing can be highly profitable. At the same time, it involves higher-than-normal risks. Companies that rely on one or a few segments for all of their business will suffer greatly if the segment turns sour. Or larger competitors may decide to enter the same segment with greater resources. For these reasons, many companies prefer to diversify in several market segments.

Micromarketing

Differentiated and concentrated marketers tailor their offers and marketing programs to meet the needs of various market segments and niches. At the same time, however, they do not customize their offers to each individual customer. **Micromarketing** is the practice of tailoring products and marketing programs to suit the tastes of specific individuals and locations. Rather than seeing a customer in every individual, micromarketers see the individual in every customer. Micromarketing includes local marketing and individual marketing.

Local Marketing. **Local marketing** involves tailoring brands and promotions to the needs and wants of local customer groups—cities, neighborhoods, and even specific stores. For example, Walmart customizes its merchandise store by store to meet the needs of local shoppers. The retailer's store designers create each new store's format according to neighborhood characteristics—stores near office parks, for instance, contain prominent islands featuring ready-made meals for busy workers. By using a wealth of customer data on daily sales in every store, Walmart tailors individual store merchandise with similar precision. For example, it uses more than 200 finely tuned planograms (shelf plans) to match soup assortments to each store's demand patterns.[19]

Advances in communications technology have given rise to a new high-tech version of location-based marketing. ◉ For example, retailers have long been intrigued by the promise of cell phones, which live in people's pockets and send signals about shoppers' locations. The idea is to send people ads tailored to their location, like a coupon for cappuccino when passing a Starbucks. That idea is fast becoming a reality. Consider The North Face, an outdoor apparel and gear retailer:[20]

> The North Face is trying a new tactic: sending people text messages as soon as they get near one of its stores. The new marketing campaign first singles out customers depending on where they are, as gleaned from their phone's GPS signal or location data provided by a phone carrier. It uses "geo-fencing," which draws half-mile-wide virtual perimeters around selected store locations. When someone steps into a geo-fenced area, The North Face sends a text message to consumers who have opted in. Within each geo-fence, it can personalize messages to local weather and other factors.
>
> For now, The North Face sends texts about promotions, like a free water bottle with a purchase or seasonal merchandise arrivals. A text message might say, for example, "TNF: The new spring running apparel has hit the stores! Check it out @ TNF Downtown Seattle." But that's just for starters. Eventually, the company plans to send branded texts when people arrive at a hiking trail or mountain to alert them about weather conditions or logistics for a ski competition, for example. It also created an iPhone app called The North Face Snow Report that provides local snow conditions and trail maps. The store doesn't want to be intrusive, says the vice president of marketing. For brand fans who opt in, "We are bringing something to the table," he says, something that "connects to a person's passions"—locally.

Local marketing has some drawbacks. It can drive up manufacturing and marketing costs by reducing the economies of scale. It can also create logistics problems as

Micromarketing
Tailoring products and marketing programs to the needs and wants of specific individuals and local customer segments; It includes *local marketing* and *individual marketing*.

Local marketing
Tailoring brands and promotions to the needs and wants of local customer segments—cities, neighborhoods, and even specific stores.

◉ Local marketing: The North Face uses "geo-fencing" to send localized text messages to consumers who get near one of its stores.

companies try to meet the varied requirements of different regional and local markets. Further, a brand's overall image might be diluted if the product and message vary too much in different localities.

Still, as companies face increasingly fragmented markets, and as new supporting technologies develop, the advantages of local marketing often outweigh the drawbacks. Local marketing helps a company to market more effectively in the face of pronounced regional and local differences in demographics and lifestyles.

Individual marketing

Tailoring products and marketing programs to the needs and preferences of individual customers—also called *one-to-one marketing*, *customized marketing*, and *markets-of-one marketing*.

Individual Marketing. In the extreme, micromarketing becomes **individual marketing**—tailoring products and marketing programs to the needs and preferences of individual customers. Individual marketing has also been labeled *one-to-one marketing*, *mass customization*, and *markets-of-one marketing*.

The widespread use of mass marketing has obscured the fact that for centuries consumers were served as individuals: The tailor custom-made a suit, the cobbler designed shoes for an individual, and the cabinetmaker made furniture to order. Today, however, new technologies are permitting many companies to return to customized marketing. More detailed databases, robotic production and flexible manufacturing, and interactive communication media such as cell phones and the Internet have combined to foster "mass customization." *Mass customization* is the process through which firms interact one-to-one with masses of customers to design products and services tailor-made to individual needs.

Dell, HP, and Apple create custom-configured computers. Hockey-stick maker Branches Hockey lets customers choose from more than two dozen options—including stick length, blade patterns, and blade curve—and turns out a customized stick in five days. Visitors to Nike's Nike ID Web site can personalize their sneakers by choosing from hundreds of colors and putting an embroidered word or phrase on the tongue. At www.myMMs.com, you can upload your photo and order a batch of M&Ms with your face and a personal message printed on each little piece of candy.

Marketers are also finding new ways to personalize promotional messages. ● For example, plasma screens placed in shopping malls around the country can now analyze shoppers' faces and place ads based on an individual shopper's gender, age, or ethnicity:[21]

> If you watch an ad on a video screen in a mall, health club, or grocery store, there is a growing chance that the ad is also watching you. Small cameras can now be embedded in or around the screen, tracking who looks at the screen and for how long. With surprising accuracy, the system can determine the viewer's gender, approximate age range, and, in some cases, ethnicity—and change the ads accordingly. That could mean razor ads for men, cosmetics ads for women, and videogame ads for teens. Or a video screen might show a motorcycle ad for a group of men but switch to a minivan ad when women and children join them. "This is proactive merchandising," says a media executive. "You're targeting people with smart ads."

Business-to-business marketers are also finding new ways to customize their offerings. For example, John Deere manufactures seeding equipment that can be configured in more than two million versions to individual customer specifications. The seeders are produced one at a time, in any sequence, on a single production line. Mass customization provides a way to stand out against competitors.

Unlike mass production, which eliminates the need for human interaction, one-to-one marketing has made relationships with customers more important than ever. Just as mass production was the marketing principle of the twentieth century, interactive marketing is becoming a marketing principle for the twenty-first century. The world appears to be coming full circle—from the good old days when customers were treated as individuals to mass marketing when nobody knew your name and then back again.

● **Individual marketing: Video screens in malls and stores can now determine who's watching them and change the ads accordingly.**

Choosing a Targeting Strategy

Companies need to consider many factors when choosing a market-targeting strategy. Which strategy is best depends on the company's resources. When the firm's resources are limited, concentrated marketing makes the most sense. The best strategy also depends on the degree of product variability. Undifferentiated marketing is more suited for uniform products, such as grapefruit or steel. Products that can vary in design, such as cameras and cars, are more suited to differentiation or concentration. The product's life-cycle stage also must be considered. When a firm introduces a new product, it may be practical to launch one version only, and undifferentiated marketing or concentrated marketing may make the most sense. In the mature stage of the product life cycle (PLC), however, differentiated marketing often makes more sense.

Another factor is *market variability*. If most buyers have the same tastes, buy the same amounts, and react the same way to marketing efforts, undifferentiated marketing is appropriate. Finally, *competitors' marketing strategies* are important. When competitors use differentiated or concentrated marketing, undifferentiated marketing can be suicidal. Conversely, when competitors use undifferentiated marketing, a firm can gain an advantage by using differentiated or concentrated marketing, focusing on the needs of buyers in specific segments.

Socially Responsible Target Marketing

Smart targeting helps companies become more efficient and effective by focusing on the segments that they can satisfy best and most profitably. Targeting also benefits consumers—companies serve specific groups of consumers with offers carefully tailored to their needs. However, target marketing sometimes generates controversy and concern. The biggest issues usually involve the targeting of vulnerable or disadvantaged consumers with controversial or potentially harmful products.

For example, over the years, marketers in a wide range of industries—from cereal, soft drinks, and fast food to toys and fashion—have been heavily criticized for their marketing efforts directed toward children. Critics worry that premium offers and high-powered advertising appeals presented through the mouths of lovable animated characters will overwhelm children's defenses.

Other problems arise when the marketing of adult products spills over into the children's segment—intentionally or unintentionally. ◉ For example, Victoria's Secret targets its highly successful Pink line of young, hip, and sexy clothing to young women from 18 to 30 years old. However, critics charge that Pink is now all the rage among girls as young as 11 years old. Responding to Victoria's Secret's designs and marketing messages, tweens are flocking into stores and buying Pink, with or without their mothers. More broadly, critics worry that marketers of everything from lingerie and cosmetics to Barbie dolls are directly or indirectly targeting young girls with provocative products, promoting a premature focus on sex and appearance.[22]

◉ **Socially responsible targeting: Victoria's Secret targets its Pink line of young, hip, and sexy clothing to young women from 18 to 30 years old. However, critics charge that Pink is now all the rage among girls as young as 11 years old.**

Ten-year-old girls can slide their low-cut jeans over "eye-candy" panties. French maid costumes, garter belt included, are available in preteen sizes. Barbie now comes in a "bling-bling" style, replete with halter top and go-go boots. And it's not unusual for girls under 12 years old to sing, "Don't cha wish your girlfriend was hot like me?" American girls, say experts, are increasingly being fed a cultural catnip of products and images that promote looking and acting sexy. "The message we're telling our girls is a simple one," laments one reporter about the Victoria's Secret Pink line. "You'll have a great life if people find you sexually attractive. Grown women struggle enough with this ridiculous standard. Do we really need to start worrying about it at 11?"

To encourage responsible advertising, the Children's Advertising Review Unit, the advertising industry's self-regulatory agency, has published extensive children's advertising guidelines that recognize the special needs of child audiences. Still, critics feel that more should been done. Some have even called for a complete ban on advertising to children.

Cigarette, beer, and fast-food marketers have also generated controversy in recent years by their attempts to target inner-city minority consumers. For example, McDonald's and other chains have drawn criticism for pitching their high-fat, salt-laden fare to low-income, urban residents who are much more likely than suburbanites to be heavy consumers. Similarly, big banks and mortgage lenders have been criticized for targeting consumers in poor urban areas with attractive adjustable rate home mortgages that they can't really afford.

The growth of the Internet and other carefully targeted direct media has raised fresh concerns about potential targeting abuses. The Internet allows more precise targeting, letting the makers of questionable products or deceptive advertisers zero in on the most vulnerable audiences. Unscrupulous marketers can now send tailor-made, deceptive messages by e-mail directly to millions of unsuspecting consumers. For example, the FBI's Internet Crime Complaint Center Web site alone received more than 336,000 complaints last year.[23]

Not all attempts to target children, minorities, or other special segments draw such criticism. In fact, most provide benefits to targeted consumers. For example, Pantene markets Relaxed and Natural hair products to women of color. Samsung markets the Jitterbug, an easy-to-use phone, directly to seniors who need a simpler cell phone that is bigger and has a louder speaker. And Colgate makes a large selection of toothbrush shapes and toothpaste flavors for children—from Colgate SpongeBob SquarePants Mild Bubble Fruit toothpaste to Colgate Dora the Explorer character toothbrushes. Such products help make tooth brushing more fun and get children to brush longer and more often.

Thus, in target marketing, the issue is not really *who* is targeted but rather *how* and for *what*. Controversies arise when marketers attempt to profit at the expense of targeted segments—when they unfairly target vulnerable segments or target them with questionable products or tactics. Socially responsible marketing calls for segmentation and targeting that serve not just the interests of the company but also the interests of those targeted.

Author Comment | At the same time that the company is answering the first simple-sounding question (Which customers will we serve?), it must be asking the second question (How will we serve them?). For example, The Ritz-Carlton serves the top 5 percent of corporate and leisure travelers. Its parallel value proposition is "The Ritz-Carlton Experience"—one that "enlivens the senses, instills a sense of well-being, and fulfills even the unexpressed wishes and needs of our guests."

Differentiation and Positioning (pp 207–215)

Beyond deciding which segments of the market it will target, the company must decide on a *value proposition*—how it will create differentiated value for targeted segments and what positions it wants to occupy in those segments. A **product's position** is the way the product is *defined by consumers* on important attributes—the place the product occupies in consumers' minds relative to competing products. Products are made in factories, but brands happen in the minds of consumers.

Tide is positioned as a powerful, all-purpose family detergent; Ivory is positioned as the gentle detergent for fine washables and baby clothes. At IHOP, you "Come hungry. Leave happy."; at Olive Garden, "When You're Here, You're Family"; and Chili's wants you to "Pepper in Some Fun." In the automobile market, the Nissan Versa and Honda Fit are positioned on economy, Mercedes and Cadillac on luxury, and Porsche and BMW on performance. And Toyota positions its fuel-efficient, hybrid Prius as a high-tech solution to the energy shortage: "Harmony between man, nature, and machine."

Product position

The way the product is defined by consumers on important attributes—the place the product occupies in consumers' minds relative to competing products.

Consumers are overloaded with information about products and services. They cannot reevaluate products every time they make a buying decision. To simplify the buying process, consumers organize products, services, and companies into categories and "position" them in their minds. A product's position is the complex set of perceptions, impressions, and feelings that consumers have for the product compared with competing products.

Consumers position products with or without the help of marketers. But marketers do not want to leave their products' positions to chance. They must *plan* positions that will give their products the greatest advantage in selected target markets, and they must design marketing mixes to create these planned positions.

Positioning Maps

In planning their differentiation and positioning strategies, marketers often prepare *perceptual positioning maps* that show consumer perceptions of their brands versus competing products on important buying dimensions. ◉ **Figure 7.3** shows a positioning map for the U.S. large luxury sport utility vehicle (SUV) market.[24] The position of each circle on the map indicates the brand's perceived positioning on two dimensions: price and orientation (luxury versus performance). The size of each circle indicates the brand's relative market share.

Thus, customers view the market-leading Cadillac Escalade as a moderately priced, large, luxury SUV with a balance of luxury and performance. The Escalade is positioned on urban luxury, and, in its case, "performance" probably means power and safety performance. You'll find no mention of off-road adventuring in an Escalade ad.

By contrast, the Range Rover and the Land Cruiser are positioned on luxury with nuances of off-road performance. For example, the Toyota Land Cruiser began in 1951 as a four-wheel drive, Jeeplike vehicle designed to conquer the world's most grueling terrains and climates. In recent years, the Land Cruiser has retained this adventure and performance positioning but with luxury added. Its Web site brags of "legendary off-road capability," with off-road technologies such as downhill assist control and kinetic dynamic suspension systems. "In some parts of the world, it's an essential." Despite its ruggedness, however, the company notes that "its available Bluetooth hands-free technology, DVD entertainment, and a sumptuous interior have softened its edges."

Choosing a Differentiation and Positioning Strategy

Some firms find it easy to choose a differentiation and positioning strategy. For example, a firm well known for quality in certain segments will go for this position in a new segment if there are enough buyers seeking quality. But in many cases, two or more firms will go after the same position. Then each will have to find other ways to set itself apart. Each firm must differentiate its offer by building a unique bundle of benefits that appeals to a substantial group within the segment.

Above all else, a brand's positioning must serve the needs and preferences of well-defined target markets. For example, although both Dunkin' Donuts and Starbucks are coffee shops, they offer very different product assortments and store atmospheres. Yet each succeeds because it creates just the right value proposition for its unique mix of customers. (See Real Marketing 7.2.)

The differentiation and positioning task consists of three steps: identifying a set of differentiating competitive advantages on which to build a position, choosing the right competitive advantages, and selecting an overall positioning strategy. The company must then effectively communicate and deliver the chosen position to the market.

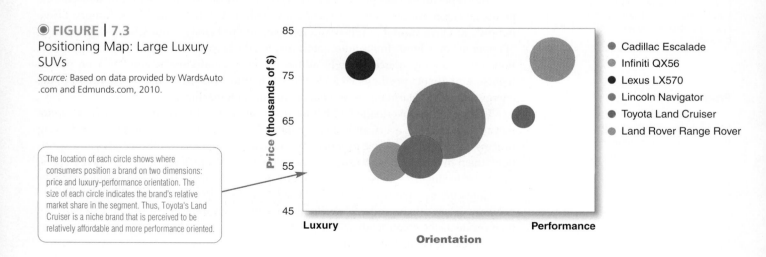

◉ **FIGURE** | **7.3**
Positioning Map: Large Luxury SUVs
Source: Based on data provided by WardsAuto.com and Edmunds.com, 2010.

The location of each circle shows where consumers position a brand on two dimensions: price and luxury-performance orientation. The size of each circle indicates the brand's relative market share in the segment. Thus, Toyota's Land Cruiser is a niche brand that is perceived to be relatively affordable and more performance oriented.

● Cadillac Escalade
● Infiniti QX56
● Lexus LX570
● Lincoln Navigator
● Toyota Land Cruiser
● Land Rover Range Rover

Real Marketing 7.2

Dunkin' Donuts:
Positioning for the Average Joe

A few years ago, Dunkin' Donuts paid dozens of faithful customers in Phoenix, Chicago, and Charlotte, North Carolina, $100 a week to buy coffee at Starbucks instead. At the same time, the no-frills coffee chain paid Starbucks customers to make the opposite switch. When it later debriefed the two groups, Dunkin' says it found them so polarized that company researchers dubbed them "tribes," each of whom loathed the very things that made the other tribe loyal to their coffee shop. Dunkin' fans viewed Starbucks as pretentious and trendy, whereas Starbucks loyalists saw Dunkin' as plain and unoriginal. "I don't get it," one Dunkin' regular told researchers after visiting Starbucks. "If I want to sit on a couch, I stay at home."

Dunkin' Donuts has ambitious plans to expand into a national coffee powerhouse, on par with Starbucks, the nation's largest coffee chain. But the research confirmed a simple fact: Dunkin' is not Starbucks. In fact, it doesn't want to be. To succeed, Dunkin' must have its own clear vision of just which customers it wants to serve (what *segments* and *targeting* strategy) and how (what *positioning* or *value proposition*). Dunkin' and Starbucks target very different customers, who want very different things from their favorite coffee shops. Starbucks is strongly positioned as a sort of high-brow "third place"—outside the home and office—featuring couches, eclectic music, wireless Internet access, and art-splashed walls. Dunkin' has a decidedly more low-brow, "everyman" kind of positioning.

Dunkin' Donuts built itself on serving simple fare at a reasonable price to working-class customers. But recently, to broaden its appeal and fuel expansion, the chain has been moving upscale—a bit but not too far. It's spiffing up its more than 6,500 stores in 34 states and adding new menu items, such as lattes and flatbread sandwiches. Dunkin' has made dozens of store-redesign decisions, big and small, ranging from where to put the espresso machines to how much of its signature pink and orange color scheme to retain and where to display its fresh baked goods. However, as it inches upscale, it's being careful not to alien-

ate its traditional customer base. There are no couches in the remodeled stores. And Dunkin' renamed a new hot sandwich a "stuffed melt" after customers complained that calling it a "panini" was too fancy; it then dropped it altogether when faithful customers thought it was too messy. "We're walking [a fine] line," says the chain's vice president of consumer insights. "The thing about the Dunkin' tribe is, they see through the hype."

Dunkin' Donuts' research showed that although loyal customers want nicer stores, they were bewildered and turned off by the atmosphere at Starbucks. They groused that crowds of laptop users made it difficult to find a seat. They didn't like Starbucks' "tall," "grande," and "venti" lingo for small, medium, and large coffees. And they couldn't understand why anyone would pay so much for a cup of coffee. "It was almost as though they were a group of Martians talking about a group of

Earthlings," says an executive from Dunkin's ad agency. The Starbucks customers that Dunkin' paid to switch were equally uneasy in Dunkin' shops. "The Starbucks people couldn't bear that they weren't special anymore," says the ad executive.

Such opposing opinions aren't surprising, given the differences in the two stores' customers. Dunkin's customers include more middle-income blue- and white-collar workers across all age, race, and income demographics. By contrast, Starbucks targets a higher-income, more professional group. But Dunkin' researchers concluded that it was more the ideal, rather than income, that set the two tribes apart: Dunkin's tribe members want to be part of a crowd, whereas members of the Starbucks tribe want to stand out as individuals. "You could open a Dunkin' Donuts right next to Starbucks and get two completely different types of consumers," says one retailing expert.

Over the past several years, each targeting its own tribe of customers, both Dunkin' Donuts and Starbucks have grown rapidly, riding the wave of America's growing thirst for coffee. However, the recent recession has highlighted differences in the positioning strategies of the two chains. Dunkin' Donuts

Differentiation and positioning: Starbucks is strongly positioned as a sort of high-brow "third place"; Dunkin' Donuts has a decidedly more low-brow, "everyman" kind of positioning. Dunkin's "not going after the Starbucks coffee snob"; it's "going after the average Joe."

Continued on next page

has found itself well-positioned for tougher economic times; Starbucks not so much so. Paying a premium price for the "Starbucks Experience" doesn't sell as well in bad times as in good. When the economy drooped, many cash-strapped Starbucks customers cut back or switched to less expensive brands. After years of sizzling growth, Starbucks sales fell for the first time ever in 2009, down 6 percent for the year.

In contrast, Dunkin' Donuts' positioning seemed to resonate strongly with customers during hard times. Even as competition grew in the superheated coffee category, with everyone from McDonald's to 7-Eleven offering their own premium blends, Dunkin's 2009 sales grew by 2.5 percent. While Starbucks was closing stores, Dunkin' opened 200 new ones. And the company is aggressively expanding menu options, adding everything from personal pizzas and flatbread sandwiches to smoothies and gourmet cookies. Befitting its positioning, Dunkin' now offers a ninety-nine-cent breakfast wrap, proclaiming "Breakfast NOT Brokefast."

In refreshing its positioning, whatever else happens, Dunkin' Donuts plans to stay true to the needs and preferences of the Dunkin' tribe. Dunkin' is "not going after the Starbucks coffee snob," says one analyst, it's "going after the average Joe." So far so good. For four years running, Dunkin' Donuts has ranked number one in the coffee category in a leading customer loyalty survey, ahead of number-two Starbucks. According to the survey, Dunkin' Donuts was the top brand for consistently meeting or exceeding customer expectations with respect to taste, quality, and customer service. And on BrandIndex's buzz rating, the overall buzz score of Dunkin' Donuts is double that of McDonald's and triple that of Starbucks.

Dunkin' Donuts' positioning and value proposition are pretty well summed up in its popular ad slogan "America Runs on Dunkin'," and its latest campaign iteration—"You Kin' Do It." Dunkin' Donuts ads show ordinary Americans relying on the chain to get them through their day, especially in a tighter economic environment:

The "You Kin' Do It" campaign encapsulates the spirit of Dunkin' Donuts and the brands' understanding of what everyday folks need to keep themselves and the country running. "The 'You Kin' Do It' campaign shines the spotlight on the accomplishments of hard-working Americans," says a Dunkin' Donuts marketing executive, "while reinforcing that Dunkin' Donuts will continue to fuel their busy day and provide a bit of happiness without blowing the lid off their budget." The campaign cheers on everyday people who keep America running by reminding them that they can take on any task, even during challenging times. With a big, steaming cup of Dunkin' Donuts coffee, you kin' make it through the workday, you kin' shovel the snow out of that driveway, you kin' finish that paperwork. America runs on Dunkin'—it's where everyday people get things done every day.

Sources: Quotes, extracts, and other information from "Dunkin' Donuts New Advertising Offers a Rallying Cry for 2009: 'You Kin' Do It'," *PR Newswire*, January 5, 2009; Janet Adamy, "Battle Brewing: Dunkin' Donuts Tries to Go Upscale, But Not Too Far," *Wall Street Journal*, April 8, 2006, p. A1; Emily Bryson York, "Dunkin' Looks to New Executives to Keep Up Buzz," *Advertising Age*, November 2, 2009, p. 6; Eric Zeitoun, "Yes You 'Kin': New Dunkin' Spots Prove That Coffee Is the Great Enabler," *Adweek*, February 23, 2009, p. 11; "Dunkin' Donuts One in Customer Loyalty for Fourth Straight Year," February 16, 2010, http://news.dunkindonuts.com/article_display.cfm?article_id=1082; Thomas Grillo, "At 60, It's Still Time to Make the Donuts," *Boston Herald*, February 19, 2010, www.bostonherald.com; and www.starbucks.com and www.dunkindonuts.com, accessed October 2010.

Identifying Possible Value Differences and Competitive Advantages

Competitive advantage

An advantage over competitors gained by offering greater customer value, either by having lower prices or providing more benefits that justify higher prices.

To build profitable relationships with target customers, marketers must understand customer needs better than competitors do and deliver more customer value. To the extent that a company can differentiate and position itself as providing superior customer value, it gains **competitive advantage**.

But solid positions cannot be built on empty promises. If a company positions its product as *offering* the best quality and service, it must actually differentiate the product so that it *delivers* the promised quality and service. Companies must do much more than simply shout out their positions with slogans and taglines. They must first *live* the slogan. For example, when Staples' research revealed that it should differentiate itself on the basis of "an easier shopping experience," the office supply retailer held back its "Staples: That was easy" marketing campaign for more than a year. First, it remade its stores to actually deliver the promised positioning.[25]

A few years ago, things weren't so easy for Staples—or for its customers. The ratio of customer complaints to compliments was running a dreadful eight to one at Staples stores. Weeks of focus groups produced an answer: Customers wanted an easier shopping experience. That simple revelation has resulted in one of the most successful marketing campaigns in recent history, built around the now-familiar "Staples: That was easy" tagline. But Staples' positioning turnaround took a lot more than simply bombarding customers with a new slogan. Before it could promise customers a simplified shopping experience, Staples had to actually deliver one. First, it had to *live* the slogan.

So, for more than a year, Staples worked to revamp the customer experience. It remodeled its stores, streamlined its inventory, retrained employees, and even simplified customer communications. Only when all of the customer-experience pieces were in place did Staples begin communicating its new positioning to customers. The "Staples: That was easy" repositioning campaign has met with striking success, helping to make Staples the runaway leader in office retail. No doubt about it, clever marketing helped. But marketing promises count for little if they are not backed by the reality of the customer experience.

To find points of differentiation, marketers must think through the customer's entire experience with the company's product or service. An alert company can find ways to differentiate itself at every customer contact point. In what specific ways can a company differentiate itself or its market offer? It can differentiate along the lines of *product*, *services*, *channels*, *people*, or *image*.

Through *product differentiation*, brands can be differentiated on features, performance, or style and design. Thus, Bose positions its speakers on their striking design and sound characteristics. By gaining the approval of the American Heart Association as an approach to a healthy lifestyle, Subway differentiates itself as the healthy fast-food choice. And Seventh Generation, a maker of household cleaning and laundry supplies, paper products, diapers and wipes, differentiates itself not so much by how its products perform but by the fact that its products are greener. Seventh Generation products are "protecting planet home."

Beyond differentiating its physical product, a firm can also differentiate the services that accompany the product. Some companies gain *services differentiation* through speedy, convenient, or careful delivery. For example, First Convenience Bank of Texas offers "Real Hours for Real People"; it is open seven days a week, including evenings. Others differentiate their service based on high-quality customer care. In an age where customer satisfaction with airline service is in constant decline, Singapore Airlines sets itself apart through extraordinary customer care and the grace of its flight attendants. "Everyone expects excellence from us," says the international airline. "[So even] in the smallest details of flight, we rise to each occasion and deliver the Singapore Airlines experience."[26]

Firms that practice *channel differentiation* gain competitive advantage through the way they design their channel's coverage, expertise, and performance. Amazon.com and GEICO set themselves apart with their smooth-functioning direct channels. Companies can also gain a strong competitive advantage through *people differentiation*—hiring and training better people than their competitors do. Disney World people are known to be friendly and upbeat. People differentiation requires that a company select its customer-contact people carefully and train them well. For example, Disney trains its theme park people thoroughly to ensure that they are competent, courteous, and friendly—from the hotel check-in agents, to the monorail drivers, to the ride attendants, to the people who sweep Main Street USA. Each employee is carefully trained to understand customers and to "make people happy."

Even when competing offers look the same, buyers may perceive a difference based on company or brand *image differentiation*. A company or brand image should convey a product's distinctive benefits and positioning. Developing a strong and distinctive image calls for creativity and hard work. A company cannot develop an image in the public's mind overnight by using only a few ads. If The Ritz-Carlton means quality, this image must be supported by everything the company says and does.

Symbols, such as the McDonald's golden arches, the red Travelers umbrella, the Nike swoosh, or Apple's "bite mark" logo, can provide strong company or brand recognition and image differentiation. The company might build a brand around a famous person, as Nike did with its Michael Jordan, Kobe Bryant, and LeBron James basketball shoe and apparel collections. Some companies even become associated with colors, such as Coca-Cola (red), IBM (blue), or UPS (brown). The chosen symbols, characters, and other image elements must be communicated through advertising that conveys the company's or brand's personality.

Choosing the Right Competitive Advantages

Suppose a company is fortunate enough to discover several potential differentiations that provide competitive advantages. It now must choose the ones on which it will build its positioning strategy. It must decide how many differences to promote and which ones.

How Many Differences to Promote. Many marketers think that companies should aggressively promote only one benefit to the target market. Advertising executive Rosser Reeves, for example, said a company should develop a *unique selling proposition* (USP) for each brand and stick to it. Each brand should pick an attribute and tout itself as "number one" on that attribute. Buyers tend to remember number one better, especially in this over-communicated society. Thus, Walmart promotes its unbeatable low prices, and Burger King promotes personal choice—"have it your way."

Other marketers think that companies should position themselves on more than one differentiator. This may be necessary if two or more firms are claiming to be best on the same attribute. Today, in a time when the mass market is fragmenting into many small segments, companies and brands are trying to broaden their positioning strategies to appeal to more segments.  For example, whereas most laundry products marketers offer separate products for cleaning, softening, and reducing static cling, Henkel's Purex brand recently introduced a product that offers all three benefits in a single sheet: Purex Complete 3-in-1 Laundry Sheets. "Cleans. Softens. Removes static. If only it could fold," says one ad. Clearly, many buyers want these multiple benefits. The challenge is to convince them that one brand can do it all. However, as companies increase the number of claims for their brands, they risk disbelief and a loss of clear positioning.

⊙ **Purex Complete 3-in-1 Laundry Sheets are positioned on multiple benefits. The challenge is to convince customers that one brand can do it all.**

Which Differences to Promote. Not all brand differences are meaningful or worthwhile; not every difference makes a good differentiator. Each difference has the potential to create company costs as well as customer benefits. A difference is worth establishing to the extent that it satisfies the following criteria:

- *Important:* The difference delivers a highly valued benefit to target buyers.
- *Distinctive:* Competitors do not offer the difference, or the company can offer it in a more distinctive way.
- *Superior:* The difference is superior to other ways that customers might obtain the same benefit.
- *Communicable:* The difference is communicable and visible to buyers.
- *Preemptive:* Competitors cannot easily copy the difference.
- *Affordable:* Buyers can afford to pay for the difference.
- *Profitable:* The company can introduce the difference profitably.

Many companies have introduced differentiations that failed one or more of these tests. When the Westin Stamford Hotel in Singapore once advertised that it is the world's tallest hotel, it was a distinction that was not important to most tourists; in fact, it turned many off. Polaroid's Polarvision, which produced instantly developed home movies, bombed too. Although Polarvision was distinctive and even preemptive, it was inferior to another way of capturing motion, namely, camcorders.

Thus, choosing competitive advantages on which to position a product or service can be difficult, yet such choices may be crucial to success. Choosing the right differentiators can help a brand stand out from the pack of competitors. For example, when carmaker Nissan introduced its novel little Cube, it didn't position the car only on attributes shared with competing models, such as affordability and customization. It positioned it as a "mobile device" that fits today's digital lifestyles.

Selecting an Overall Positioning Strategy

Value proposition

The full positioning of a brand—the full mix of benefits on which it is positioned.

The full positioning of a brand is called the brand's **value proposition**—the full mix of benefits on which a brand is differentiated and positioned. It is the answer to the customer's

● FIGURE | 7.4
Possible Value Propositions

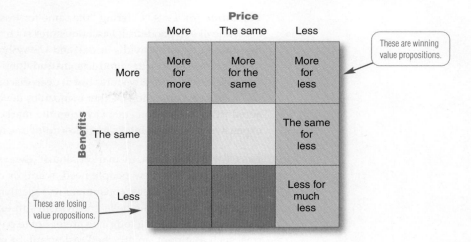

● FIGURE | 7.4
Possible Value Propositions

question "Why should I buy your brand?" Volvo's value proposition hinges on safety but also includes reliability, roominess, and styling, all for a price that is higher than average but seems fair for this mix of benefits.

● **Figure 7.4** shows possible value propositions on which a company might position its products. In the figure, the five green cells represent winning value propositions—differentiation and positioning that gives the company competitive advantage. The red cells, however, represent losing value propositions. The center yellow cell represents at best a marginal proposition. In the following sections, we discuss the five winning value propositions on which companies can position their products: more for more, more for the same, the same for less, less for much less, and more for less.

More for More. "More-for-more" positioning involves providing the most upscale product or service and charging a higher price to cover the higher costs. Four Seasons hotels, Rolex watches, Mercedes automobiles, SubZero appliances—each claims superior quality, craftsmanship, durability, performance, or style and charges a price to match. Not only is the market offering high in quality, but it also gives prestige to the buyer. It symbolizes status and a loftier lifestyle. Often, the price difference exceeds the actual increment in quality.

Sellers offering "only the best" can be found in every product and service category, from hotels, restaurants, food, and fashion to cars and household appliances. Consumers are sometimes surprised, even delighted, when a new competitor enters a category with an unusually high-priced brand. Starbucks coffee entered as a very expensive brand in a commodity category. When Apple premiered its iPhone, it offered higher-quality features than a traditional cell phone with a hefty price tag to match.

In general, companies should be on the lookout for opportunities to introduce a "more-for-more" brand in any underdeveloped product or service category. Yet "more-for-more" brands can be vulnerable. They often invite imitators who claim the same quality but at a lower price. For example, Starbucks now faces "gourmet" coffee competitors ranging from Dunkin' Donuts to McDonald's. Also, luxury goods that sell well during good times may be at risk during economic downturns when buyers become more cautious in their spending. The recent gloomy economy hit premium brands, such as Starbucks, the hardest.

More for the Same. Companies can attack a competitor's more-for-more positioning by introducing a brand offering comparable quality at a lower price. For example, Toyota introduced its Lexus line with a "more-for-the-same" value proposition versus Mercedes and BMW. Its first headline read: "Perhaps the first time in history that trading a $72,000 car for a $36,000 car could be considered trading up." It communicated the high quality of its new Lexus through rave reviews in car magazines and a widely distributed videotape showing side-by-side comparisons of Lexus and Mercedes automobiles. It published surveys showing that Lexus dealers were providing customers with better sales and service experiences than were Mercedes dealerships. Many Mercedes owners switched to Lexus, and the Lexus repurchase rate has been 60 percent, twice the industry average.

The Same for Less. Offering "the same for less" can be a powerful value proposition—everyone likes a good deal. Discount stores such as Walmart and "category killers" such as Best Buy, PetSmart, David's Bridal, and DSW Shoes use this positioning. They don't claim to offer different or better products. Instead, they offer many of the same brands as department stores and specialty stores but at deep discounts based on superior purchasing power and lower-cost operations. Other companies develop imitative but lower-priced brands in an effort to lure customers away from the market leader. For example, AMD makes less-expensive versions of Intel's market-leading microprocessor chips.

Less for Much Less. A market almost always exists for products that offer less and therefore cost less. Few people need, want, or can afford "the very best" in everything they buy. In many cases, consumers will gladly settle for less than optimal performance or give up some of the bells and whistles in exchange for a lower price. For example, many travelers seeking lodgings prefer not to pay for what they consider unnecessary extras, such as a pool, an attached restaurant, or mints on the pillow. Hotel chains such as Ramada Limited, Holiday Inn Express, and Motel 6 suspend some of these amenities and charge less accordingly.

"Less-for-much-less" positioning involves meeting consumers' lower performance or quality requirements at a much lower price. For example, Family Dollar and Dollar General stores offer more affordable goods at very low prices. Sam's Club and Costco warehouse stores offer less merchandise selection and consistency and much lower levels of service; as a result, they charge rock-bottom prices. ⊚ Southwest Airlines, the nation's most consistently profitable air carrier, also practices less-for-much-less positioning.

⊚ **Less for much less positioning: Southwest has positioned itself firmly as the no-frills, low-price airline. But no frills doesn't mean drudgery; Southwest's cheerful employees—like those here—go out of their way to amuse, surprise, or somehow entertain passengers.**

From the start, Southwest Airlines has positioned itself firmly as *the* no-frills, low-price airline. Southwest's passengers have learned to fly without the amenities. For example, the airline provides no meals—just pretzels. It offers no first-class section, only three-across seating in all of its planes. And there's no such thing as a reserved seat on a Southwest flight. Why, then, do so many passengers love Southwest? Perhaps most importantly, Southwest excels at the basics of getting passengers where they want to go on time and with their luggage. Beyond the basics, however, Southwest offers low prices, with no extra charges for checked baggage, aisle seats, or other services. No frills and low prices, however, don't mean drudgery. Southwest's cheerful employees go out of their way to amuse, surprise, or somehow entertain passengers. One analyst sums up Southwest's less-for-much-less positioning this way: "It is not luxurious, but it's cheap and it's fun."

More for Less. Of course, the winning value proposition would be to offer "more for less." Many companies claim to do this. And, in the short run, some companies can actually achieve such lofty positions. For example, when it first opened for business, Home Depot had arguably the best product selection, the best service, *and* the lowest prices compared to local hardware stores and other home improvement chains.

Yet in the long run, companies will find it very difficult to sustain such best-of-both positioning. Offering more usually costs more, making it difficult to deliver on the "for-less" promise. Companies that try to deliver both may lose out to more focused competitors. For example, facing determined competition from Lowe's stores, Home Depot must now decide whether it wants to compete primarily on superior service or on lower prices.

All said, each brand must adopt a positioning strategy designed to serve the needs and wants of its target markets. "More for more" will draw one target market, "less for much less" will draw another, and so on. Thus, in any market, there is usually room for many different companies, each successfully occupying different positions. The important thing is

It's your space. Cube mobile device™ lets you personalize with over 40 different colorful accessories. Go ahead and edit your shag dash topper, 20-color interior illumination, ripple hooks and interior appliques. Then upgrade your storage capacity with front-door bungees and a utility pouch. Your undos and redos are limitless. Visit NissanUSA.com. **cube mobile device™** starting at **$13,990:**

Look Closer: Text "nissancube" to 44144 for music and goodies.

*As shown $16,910 for Nissan cube® 1.8 SL with Preferred Package and accessories. Starting at MSRP for Nissan cube® 1.8 with manual transmission. Prices are MSRP excluding tax, title, license, destination charge and options. Dealer sets actual price. Limited availability in dealer stock. Available through dealer order. Available May 2009. Standard text message and data fees apply. Not all prepaid phones are supported. ©2009 Nissan North America, Inc.

SHIFT_the way you move

◉ **Points of difference: Sometimes marketers put a brand in a surprisingly different category. Nissan positions its smallish, funky looking Cube not as a car but as a personal mobile device.**

Positioning statement
A statement that summarizes company or brand positioning. It takes this form: *To (target segment and need) our (brand) is (concept) that (point of difference).*

that each company must develop its own winning positioning strategy, one that makes it special to its target consumers.

Developing a Positioning Statement

Company and brand positioning should be summed up in a **positioning statement**. The statement should follow the form: To (target segment and need) our (brand) is (concept) that (point of difference).[27] Here is an example: "To busy, mobile professionals who need to always be in the loop, the BlackBerry is a wireless connectivity solution that gives you an easier, more reliable way to stay connected to data, people, and resources while on the go."

Note that the positioning statement first states the product's membership in a category (wireless connectivity solution) and then shows its point of difference from other members of the category (easier, more reliable connections to data, people, and resources). Placing a brand in a specific category suggests similarities that it might share with other products in the category. But the case for the brand's superiority is made on its points of difference.

Sometimes marketers put a brand in a surprisingly different category before indicating the points of difference. For example, when Nissan recently introduced its smallish, funky looking city car—the Cube—in the United States, it looked for a way to differentiate the brand in a market already crammed full of small-car models. ◉ So Nissan positioned the Cube not as a small *car* but as a personal *mobile device*—something that enhances young target customers' individual, mobile, connected lifestyles. Already hugely popular in Japan, the Nissan Cube was introduced in the United States as a device designed "to bring young people together—like every mobile device they have." It's "a part of a fun, busy life that can be . . . personalized as easily as a cell phone ring or a Web page." Such out-of-category positioning helps make the Cube distinctive.[28]

Communicating and Delivering the Chosen Position

Once it has chosen a position, the company must take strong steps to deliver and communicate the desired position to its target consumers. All the company's marketing mix efforts must support the positioning strategy.

Positioning the company calls for concrete action, not just talk. If the company decides to build a position on better quality and service, it must first *deliver* that position. Designing the marketing mix—product, price, place, and promotion—involves working out the tactical details of the positioning strategy. Thus, a firm that seizes on a more-for-more position knows that it must produce high-quality products, charge a high price, distribute through high-quality dealers, and advertise in high-quality media. It must hire and train more service people, find retailers who have a good reputation for service, and develop sales and advertising messages that broadcast its superior service. This is the only way to build a consistent and believable more-for-more position.

Companies often find it easier to come up with a good positioning strategy than to implement it. Establishing a position or changing one usually takes a long time. In contrast, positions that have taken years to build can quickly be lost. Once a company has built the desired position, it must take care to maintain the position through consistent performance and communication. It must closely monitor and adapt the position over time to match changes in consumer needs and competitors' strategies. However, the company should avoid abrupt changes that might confuse consumers. Instead, a product's position should evolve gradually as it adapts to the ever-changing marketing environment.

REVIEWING Objectives AND KEY Terms

In this chapter, you learned about the major elements of a customer-driven marketing strategy: segmentation, targeting, differentiation, and positioning. Marketers know that they cannot appeal to all buyers in their markets, or at least not to all buyers in the same way. Therefore, most companies today practice *target marketing*—identifying market segments, selecting one or more of them, and developing products and marketing mixes tailored to each.

Objective 1 Define the major steps in designing a customer-driven marketing strategy: market segmentation, targeting, differentiation, and positioning. (p 190)

A customer-driven marketing strategy begins with selecting which customers to serve and determining a value proposition that best serves the targeted customers. It consists of four steps. *Market segmentation* is the act of dividing a market into distinct segments of buyers with different needs, characteristics, or behaviors who might require separate products or marketing mixes. Once the groups have been identified, *market targeting* evaluates each market segment's attractiveness and selects one or more segments to serve. Market targeting consists of designing strategies to build the *right relationships* with the *right customers*. *Differentiation* involves actually differentiating the market offering to create superior customer value. *Positioning* consists of positioning the market offering in the minds of target customers.

Objective 2 List and discuss the major bases for segmenting consumer and business markets. (pp 190–200)

There is no single way to segment a market. Therefore, the marketer tries different variables to see which give the best segmentation opportunities. For consumer marketing, the major segmentation variables are geographic, demographic, psychographic, and behavioral. In *geographic segmentation*, the market is divided into different geographical units, such as nations, regions, states, counties, cities, or even neighborhoods. In *demographic segmentation*, the market is divided into groups based on demographic variables, including age, gender, family size, family life cycle, income, occupation, education, religion, race, generation, and nationality. In *psychographic segmentation*, the market is divided into different groups based on social class, lifestyle, or personality characteristics. In *behavioral segmentation*, the market is divided into groups based on consumers' knowledge, attitudes, uses, or responses to a product.

Business marketers use many of the same variables to segment their markets. But business markets also can be segmented by business *demographics* (industry, company size), *operating characteristics*, *purchasing approaches*, *situational factors*, and *personal characteristics*. The effectiveness of the segmentation analysis depends on finding segments that are *measurable*, *accessible*, *substantial*, *differentiable*, and *actionable*.

Objective 3 Explain how companies identify attractive market segments and choose a market-targeting strategy. (pp 200–207)

To target the best market segments, the company first evaluates each segment's size and growth characteristics, structural attractiveness, and compatibility with company objectives and resources. It then chooses one of four market-targeting strategies—ranging from very broad to very narrow targeting. The seller can ignore segment differences and target broadly using *undifferentiated* (or *mass*) *marketing*. This involves mass producing, mass distributing, and mass promoting about the same product in about the same way to all consumers. Or the seller can adopt *differentiated marketing*—developing different market offers for several segments. *Concentrated marketing* (or *niche marketing*) involves focusing on one or a few market segments only. Finally, *micromarketing* is the practice of tailoring products and marketing programs to suit the tastes of specific individuals and locations. Micromarketing includes *local marketing* and *individual marketing*. Which targeting strategy is best depends on company resources, product variability, the PLC stage, market variability, and competitive marketing strategies.

Objective 4 Discuss how companies differentiate and position their products for maximum competitive advantage. (pp 207–215)

Once a company has decided which segments to enter, it must decide on its *differentiation and positioning strategy*. The differentiation and positioning task consists of three steps: identifying a set of possible differentiations that create competitive advantage, choosing advantages on which to build a position, and selecting an overall positioning strategy.

The brand's full positioning is called its *value proposition*—the full mix of benefits on which the brand is positioned. In general, companies can choose from one of five winning value propositions on which to position their products: more for more, more for the same, the same for less, less for much less, or more for less. Company and brand positioning are summarized in positioning statements that state the target segment and need, the positioning concept, and specific points of difference. The company must then effectively communicate and deliver the chosen position to the market.

KEY Terms

OBJECTIVE 1

Market segmentation (p 190)
Market targeting (targeting) (p 190)
Differentiation (p 190)
Positioning (p 190)

OBJECTIVE 2

Geographic segmentation (p 191)
Demographic segmentation (p 191)
Age and life-cycle segmentation (p 191)
Gender segmentation (p 193)
Income segmentation (p 194)

Psychographic segmentation (p 194)
Behavioral segmentation (p 196)
Occasion segmentation (p 196)
Benefit segmentation (p 197)
Intermarket segmentation (p 200)

OBJECTIVE 3

Target market (p 201)
Undifferentiated (mass) marketing (p 201)
Differentiated (segmented) marketing (p 202)

Concentrated (niche) marketing (p 202)
Micromarketing (p 204)
Local marketing (p 204)
Individual marketing (p 205)

OBJECTIVE 4

Product position (p 207)
Competitive advantage (p 210)
Value proposition (p 212)
Positioning statement (p 215)

PEARSON mymarketinglab

- Check your understanding of the concepts and key terms using the mypearsonmarketinglab study plan for this chapter.
- Apply the concepts in a business context using the simulation entitled **Segmentation, Targeting, Positioning.**

DISCUSSING & APPLYING THE Concepts

Discussing the Concepts

1. Briefly describe the four major steps in designing a customer-driven marketing strategy. (AACSB: Communication)

2. Name and describe the four major sets of variables that might be used in segmenting consumer markets. Which segmenting variables does Starbucks use? (AACSB: Communication; Reflective Thinking)

3. Discuss the factors marketers consider when choosing a targeting strategy. (AACSB: Communication)

4. Explain how micromarketing differs from differentiated and concentrated marketing and discuss the two types of micromarketing. (AACSB: Communication)

5. Explain how a company differentiates its products from competitors' products. (AACSB: Communication)

6. Name and define the five winning value propositions described in the chapter. Which value proposition describes Walmart? Neiman Marcus? Explain your answers. (AACSB: Communication; Reflective Thinking)

Applying the Concepts

1. In a small group, visit a grocery store and examine the brands of breakfast cereal. Using the bases for segmenting consumer markets, identify the segmentation variables a specific brand appears to be using. Summarize the segmentation and targeting strategy for each brand. Identify brands with similar positioning strategies. (AACSB: Communication; Reflective Thinking)

2. Assume you work at a regional state university whose traditional target market, high school students within your region, is shrinking. This segment is projected to decrease over the next ten years. Recommend other potential market segments and discuss the criteria you should consider to ensure that the identified segments are useful. (AACSB: Communication; Reflective Thinking)

3. Form a small group and create an idea for a new business. Using the steps described in the chapter, develop a customer-driven marketing strategy. Describe your strategy and conclude with a positioning statement for your business. (AACSB: Communication; Reflective Thinking)

FOCUS ON Technology

Most companies want customers to be heavy users of its products or services. When it comes to the Internet and wireless broadband services, however, that's not necessarily the case. Internet providers, such as Comcast, may block or slow down Internet traffic for some heavy users, such as those who watch a lot of videos on YouTube. In 2009, the Federal Communications Commission (FCC) banned Comcast from blocking video file sharing; this ban was overturned in 2010 by a court ruling that the FCC does not have authority to enforce its "network neutrality" rules. Google, once a champion for unfettered Internet access for all, is changing its tune now that it can profit from favoring some customers over others in the burgeoning wireless broadband arena. Google

and Verizon have teamed up to lobby for laws that allow them to favor some Web services over others.

1. Research the concept of net neutrality and write a report on the pros and cons of this principle from the viewpoint of businesses providing Internet and wireless broadband services. (AACSB: Communication; Reflective Thinking)

2. What effect does very heavy usage by some customers have on other customers of broadband services? What are marketers of these services doing to counter the effect of heavy users? (AACSB: Communication; Reflective Thinking)

FOCUS ON Ethics

The obesity rate among children in the United States is 17 percent—triple what it was 30 years ago. Who's to blame? One study reported that 76 percent of parents thought food advertising is a major contributor to childhood obesity but also found that over 80 percent blamed parents, not marketers. Yet, the federal government is homing its sights on marketers. Reminiscent of the 1970s when the FTC proposed banning advertising to children, a provision in the American Recovery and Reinvention Act of 2009 created an Interagency Working Group (IWG) on Food Marketing to Children. Although most regulations regarding marketing to children are limited to children ages 12 and younger, the current IWG guidelines include children up to 17 years old and propose restrictions on food marketing targeted to children. With $1.6 billion spent on food

marketing and promotions targeted to children—$745 million of that on television—more than just marketers will be affected by marketing restrictions to this market segment.

1. Are marketers to blame for increasing obesity rates among children? Should the government ban the advertising of food products to children ages 17 and younger? Discuss the consequences of imposing such a ban. (AACSB: Communication; Ethical Reasoning)

2. What actions have food marketers taken to stem the threat of a ban on marketing to children? (AACSB: Communication; Reflective Thinking)

MARKETING & THE Economy

Vanilla Bikes

Portland-based Vanilla Bicycles sells hand-built bikes with price tags ranging from $4,000 to $12,000. But last year, after only nine years in business, owner Sacha White stopped taking orders—not because business had dried up but because he had a five-year waiting list. White and his crew of three make only 40 to 50 bikes each year. Frames are made from exotic metals, are welded with silver alloy, and weigh as little as 30 ounces. No two Vanilla bikes are the same. Each is custom fitted to the client and features intricate metal carvings and an artisan paint job. Amazingly, almost all of these high-end bicycles are sold to middle-class customers. Still, orders did not ebb during the recent economic downturn. In fact,

Vanilla could have ramped up production significantly during the heart of the recession and still sold everything it made. However, White claims that ramping up would compromise the special nature of what customers consider works of art. Vanilla bikes are so special that when Portland bike couriers describe something as cool, they routinely say, "That's soooo Vanilla."

1. Based on the segmentation variables discussed in the chapter, construct a profile for Vanilla Bicycle's probable target market.

2. Given that most luxury products suffer in an economic downturn, why has Vanilla still succeeded?

MARKETING BY THE Numbers

When you think of hybrid or electric automobiles, you probably think don't think of the sports car. But the Fisker Karma is about to shatter that stereotype. It's been called the hybrid with sex appeal and is often compared to a Mercedes-Benz roadster. In the increasingly crowded field of new-generation electric vehicles, Fisker

Automotive wants to carve out a niche as a high-performance eco-car with lots of style. The Fisker Karma goes from 0 to 60 miles per hour in six seconds, can go up to 125 miles per hour, and can travel 50 miles on electric power and 300 miles on combined electric and gasoline power. All this performance and style does not come cheap; prices range from $87,900 to $106,000. Before bringing it to market, however, the company needs to identify its target market and estimate the market potential in this segment.

1. Identify an appropriate market segment for this product. Discuss variables the company should consider when estimating the potential number of buyers for the high-performance Fisker Karma sports car. (AACSB: Communication; Reflective Thinking)

2. Using the chain ratio method described in Appendix 2, estimate the market potential for the Fisker Karma sports car. Search the Internet for reasonable numbers to represent the factors you identified in the previous question. Assume each buyer will purchase only one automobile and that the average price of automobiles in this market is $100,000. (AACSB: Communication; Use of IT; Analytical Reasoning)

VIDEO Case

Meredith

The Meredith Corporation has developed an expertise in building customer relationships through segmentation, targeting, and positioning. Amazingly, however, it has done this by focusing on only half of the population—the female half. Meredith has developed the largest database of any U.S. media company and uses that database to meet the specific needs and desires of women.

Meredith is known for leading titles such as *Better Homes and Gardens, Family Circle,* and *Ladies' Home Journal.* But that list has grown to a portfolio of 14 magazines and more than 200 special interest publications. Through these magazines alone, Meredith regularly reaches about 30 million readers. By focusing on core categories of home, family, and personal development, Meredith

has developed a product mix designed to meet various needs of women. This creates multiple touch points as individual women engage with more than one magazine, as well as with specialty books and Web sites.

After viewing the video featuring Meredith, answer the following questions about segmenting, targeting, and positioning:

1. On what main variables has Meredith focused in segmenting its markets?

2. Which target marketing strategy best describes Meredith's efforts? Support your choice.

3. How does Meredith use its variety of products to build relationships with the right customers?

COMPANY Case

Starbucks: Just Who Is the Starbucks Customer?

By now, you should be familiar with the Starbucks story. After a trip to Italy in the early 1980s, Howard Schultz was inspired to transform Starbucks—then just a handful of coffee shops in Seattle—into a chain of European-style coffeehouses. His vision wasn't based on selling only gourmet coffees, espressos, and lattes, however. He wanted to provide customers with what he called a "third place"— a place away from home and work. As CEO of Starbucks, Schultz developed what became known as the *Starbucks Experience*, built around great coffee, personal service, and an inviting ambiance.

WHAT GOES UP . . .

It wasn't long before Starbucks became a household word—a powerhouse premium brand in a category that previously consisted of only cheaper commodity products. In 20 years time, Schultz grew the company to almost 17,000 stores in dozens of countries. From 1995 to 2005, Starbucks added U.S. stores at an annual rate of 27 percent, far faster than the 17 percent annual growth of McDonald's in its heyday. At one point, Starbucks opened over 3,300 locations in a single year—an average of 9 per day. In one stretch of crowded Manhattan, a person could get their caffeine fix at any of five Starbucks outlets in less than a block and a half. In fact, cramming so many stores so close together caused one satirical publication to run this headline: "A New Starbucks Opens in the Restroom of Existing Starbucks."

For many years, new store growth was what kept Starbucks percolating. As it grew, company sales and profits rose like steam

from a mug of hot java. Growth routinely averaged 20 percent or more each year. And Starbucks made investors happy with a 25 percent annual increase in the value of its stock for more than a decade. Schultz confidently predicted that there was no end in sight for the Starbucks boom. Just a few years ago, he announced his intentions to open 10,000 new stores in just four years and then push Starbucks to 40,000 stores.

But not long after Schultz shocked Wall Street and the industry with his projections, Starbucks' steam engine of growth started to slow. Then it started running in reverse. By the end of 2008, the 20 percent annual growth had dropped to 10 percent, with existing-store sales *decreasing* by 3 percent. Total company profits dropped by a scalding 53 percent for the year. And for a second year in a row, Starbucks' stock value dropped by 50 percent to around $10 a share.

The weakened economy certainly played a role. But for years, many industry observers had worried that the company was growing too fast. Revenue and traffic at Starbucks began slowing more than a year before anyone uttered the word *recession.* In a sign of recognizing a problem, Schultz cut back on the number of new store openings. Then he did what had previously seemed unthinkable. In 2008, he announced store closures—first 600, then 300 more. In fact, as Starbucks trimmed its 2009 forecast for new store openings to 310, it projected a *decrease* in its number of outlets for the first time ever.

THE EVOLUTION OF THE STARBUCKS CUSTOMER

There was no shortage of armchair CEOs willing to give their opinions as to what had gone wrong that led to Starbucks' fall from perpetual growth. One issue often mentioned was that Starbucks had developed an identity crisis with respect to its target customer. In its early years, the Starbucks customer profile was clearly defined. The typical customer was wealthier, better educated, and more professional than the average American. The customer was far more likely to be female than male, predominately Caucasian, and between the ages of 24 and 44. It was this customer who fell in love with the *Starbucks Experience*. She was very loyal, often visiting a store every day or even more than once a day. She loved the fact that the barista greeted her by name when she came in and chatted with her while making her custom coffee drink, not caring if it took awhile. She lounged on the comfy furniture, enjoying the perfect mix of music that always seemed to fit her mood. She met friends or just hung out by herself reading a good book.

But the more Starbucks grew, the more the *Starbucks Experience* began to change. With more stores, the place wasn't quite so special. As each location filled with more customers, baristas had more names to put with faces. As the menu expanded with more options, the number of combinations for coffee drinks grew into the hundreds, leaving baristas less time to chat with customers. As the atmosphere in each store turned to "hustle and bustle," it became a less attractive place to hang out.

With all these changes, Starbucks progressively appealed less to the traditional customer and more to a new customer. This customer shift was inevitable; there simply were not enough traditional customers around to fuel the kind of growth that Schultz sought. The new breed of customer was less affluent, less educated, and less professional. Not only was Starbucks drawing in different customers in places where stores already existed, but it was also putting stores in different neighborhoods, cities, and countries.

As the customer profile evolved, the *Starbucks Experience* grew to mean something different. To the new breed of customer, it meant good coffee on the run. It was a place to meet and then move on. The more accessible Starbucks was, the better. Speed of service was more important than a barista who wanted to talk current events. This new customer came in much less frequently than the traditional customer, as seldom as once a month. As a sign of just how much this shift in customer was affecting its business, by 2007, 80 percent of all Starbucks coffee purchased was consumed outside the store.

SOUL SEARCHING

When Starbucks' growth first started tapering off, the executives took notice. In a now famous memo to management, Schultz lamented that "in order to achieve the growth, development, and scale necessary to go from less than 1,000 stores to 15,000 stores and beyond, [Starbucks had made decisions that may] have led to the watering down of the Starbucks experience. Stores no longer have the soul of the past and reflect a chain of stores versus the warm feeling of a neighborhood store."

Starbucks management believed that efforts to recapture that soul would get the company back on track. At first, however, Starbucks was caught between the conflicting goals of reestablishing its image as the provider of a holistic experience and offering better value to the cash-strapped consumer. Starbucks set out to put some water on the fire and get some of its customers back. It added labor hours and time-saving automated machines to stores. It focused on the quality of its coffee with a Coffee Master training program for its baristas and a new line of ultrapremium whole-bean coffees. It even tried free Wi-Fi service and sold its own music.

But none of these actions seemed to address the core problem: Although Starbucks still charged a premium price, it was no longer a special place. As the recession tightened its grip and more people cut back on discretionary purchases, the problem grew worse. Compounding the problem was an increase in competition. For

years, if you wanted a latte, Starbucks was about the only option. Not only were Dunkin' Donuts and McDonald's selling premium coffee drinks to the masses, but just about every mini-mart in the country boasted about the quality of its coffee. All of these competitors had prices considerably lower than those of Starbucks, which made the most well-known coffee bar much less justifiable to the "grab and go" crowd. As much as Schultz denied being in direct competition with the lower-status coffee pourers, many critics seemed to be thinking the same thing: Starbucks had shifted from a warm and intimate coffeehouse to little more than a filling station, battling fast-food outlets for some of the same customer dollars.

"VALUE" TO THE RESCUE?

Throughout 2009, Schultz continued to direct activities aimed at increasing growth. Starbucks launched a campaign designed to educate consumers that Starbucks really wasn't as expensive as they thought it was. That was followed by something Schultz held back for as long as possible: price reductions. "Breakfast pairings"—coffee cake, oatmeal, and an egg sandwich—soon followed.

All these tactics helped. By the end of 2009, Starbucks was regaining ground. With same-store sales up 4 percent and profits up 24 percent for the year, Starbucks' stock price doubled versus the previous year. But Schultz made it clear that he was just getting started. "What a difference a year makes. We're going to radically reframe Starbucks growth strategy." He outlined a three-pronged growth strategy to illustrate that Starbucks might have a grip on defining segments of coffee customers after all. In searching for Starbucks' roots and re-creating the Starbucks store experience, Schultz also aimed to reach customers outside the store.

The first prong of the new strategy centers on Via, an instant coffee that Starbucks introduced last year. It is available in single-serve packets at all Starbucks stores and in grocery stores at $1 each or $9.95 for 12 packs. Via lets Starbucks promote a genuine cup of Starbucks coffee for under a buck. Promotions for the new instant have made it clear that Starbucks isn't moving downscale; instant coffee is moving upscale. At a New York taste testing, Schultz told a group of analysts, journalists, and retailers that he was ready for the critics who say, "This is desperate, this is a Hail Mary pass, this is off-brand for Starbucks. We are going to reinvent the category. This is not your mother's instant coffee."

Via is off to a good start, having surpassed company expectations. In fact, Via accounted for more than half of the 4 percent increase in Starbucks' 2009 same-store sales. According to Annie Young-Scrivner, global chief marketing officer for Starbucks, half of all Via serving occasions are at home, 25 percent are in the office, and 25 percent are "on the go." Many Via customers aren't just out for a cheap coffee fix. (You can mix up a cup of Folger's for about 25 cents.) They are people who want premium coffee but are in situations where they don't have access to a store or brewing their own. An ad campaign supporting Via is the first concerted advertising push aimed at grocery customers, who are now accessible through 37,000 retail locations.

The second prong of Starbucks strategy also focuses on the grocery business but through ground-flavored coffees. According to NPD Group, four out of five cups of coffee are consumed at home. Starbucks has a very small share of that market. Via will certainly help. But aiming more directly at the "brew it at home" customer, Starbucks is partnering with Kraft to launch flavored coffees you can brew yourself. Sixty percent of bagged coffee buyers are either drinking flavored coffee or adding flavored creamer. Seventy-five percent of those customers said they would buy a flavored product at the grocery store if Starbucks made one. So after more than two years of testing, this substantial segment of grocery-store buying customers can now get Starbucks Natural Fusions in vanilla, caramel, and cinnamon.

The third prong of Starbucks strategy is its ace in the hole—Seattle's Best Coffee. Starbucks purchased the brand back in 2003 but is just now doing something with it. Rebranding efforts have given Seattle's Best a new look and tagline, "Great Coffee Everywhere." As with Via and Natural Fusions, and now with Seattle's Best, Starbucks is going after customers who don't normally buy Starbucks coffee. It is placing Seattle's Best where Starbuck's customers aren't—in vending machines, coffee carts, fast-food restaurants (Burger King and Subway, among others), theatres, and convenience stores. These are places that Starbucks has avoided for fear of eroding its upscale image. With prices ranging from $1 to just over $2, Seattle's Best also reaches customers who perceive Starbucks as too expensive. Gap has Old Navy. BMW has Mini. Now, Seattle's Best allows Starbucks to go head-to-head with competitors like McDonald's without putting the Starbucks name in the same sentence as downscale competitors.

Michelle Gass, Seattle's Best president, clearly defines the difference versus Starbucks: "Starbucks is a destination coffee experience and an active choice made by the customer. Seattle's Best will instead be brought to the consumer when they make other retail choices." Gass is going to make sure that she has as many of those other retail choices covered as possible. She is taking the brand from 3,000 points of distribution in 2009 to more than 30,000 by the end of 2010.

The three-pronged strategy provides three good reasons to believe that Starbucks growth story will return, even without opening nine stores per day. As icing on the coffee cake, only one-fifth of Starbucks' sales come from outside the United States. The company sees huge potential growth abroad. But perhaps the greatest strength in Starbucks' new strategy is that it will allow the company to go after new customer segments while also restoring the essence of the *Starbucks Experience*.

Questions for Discussion

1. Using the full spectrum of segmentation variables, describe how Starbucks initially segmented and targeted the coffee market.

2. What changed first—the Starbucks customer or the *Starbucks Experience*? Explain your response by discussing the principles of market targeting.

3. Based on the segmentation variables, how is Starbucks now segmenting and targeting the coffee market?

4. Will Starbucks ever return to the revenue and profit growth that it once enjoyed? Why or why not?

Sources: Beth Kowitt, "Can Starbucks Still Be Seattle's Best If It Grows By Hyping Seattle's Best?" *Fortune*, May 25, 2010, accessed at http://money .cnn.com/2010/05/25/news/companies/starbucks_seattles_best.fortune/ index.htm; Emily Bryson York, "Why You Are Not Drinking Nearly Enough Starbucks," *Advertising Age*, May 17, 2010, p. 1; Dan Mitchell, "Starbucks Faces Existential Crisis In Downturn," *Washington Post*, March 22, 2009, p. G01; Bruce Horovitz, "Starbucks Perks Up with First Dividend," *USA Today*, March 25, 2010, p. 1B.

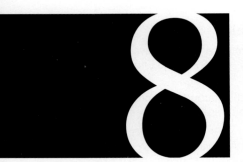

8 Products, Services, and Brands
Building Customer Value

Chapter Preview

After examining customer-driven marketing strategy, we now take a deeper look at the marketing mix: the tactical tools that marketers use to implement their strategies and deliver superior customer value. In this and the next chapter, we'll study how companies develop and manage products and brands. Then, in the chapters that follow, we'll look at pricing, distribution, and marketing communication tools. The product is usually the first and most basic marketing consideration. We start with a seemingly simple question: What *is* a product? As it turns out, the answer is not so simple.

Before starting into the chapter, let's look at an interesting brand story. Marketing is all about building brands that connect deeply with customers. So, when you think about top brands, which ones pop up first? Perhaps traditional megabrands such as Coca-Cola, Nike, or McDonald's come to mind. Or maybe a trendy tech brand such as Google or Facebook. But if we asked you to focus on sports entertainment, you'd probably name ESPN. When it comes to your life and sports, ESPN probably has it covered.

The ESPN Brand: Every Sport Possible—Now

When you think of ESPN, you probably don't think of it as a "brand." You think of it as a cable TV network, a magazine, or perhaps a Web site. ESPN is all of those things. But more than that, ESPN is a brand experience—a meaningful part of customers' lives that goes well beyond the cable networks, publications, and other entities it comprises. To consumers, ESPN is synonymous with sports entertainment, inexorably linked with their sports memories, realities, and anticipations.

In 1979, entrepreneur Bill Rasmussen took a daring leap and founded the round-the-clock sports network ESPN (Entertainment and Sports Programming Network). Two years later, George Bodenheimer took a job in ESPN's mailroom. The rest, as they say, is history. Despite many early skeptics, Bodenheimer (who rose through the ranks to become ESPN's energetic president in 1998) currently presides over a multibillion dollar sports empire.

Today, ESPN is as much recognized and revered as iconic megabrands like Coca-Cola, Nike, or Google. No matter who you are, chances are good that ESPN has touched you in some meaningful way. Perhaps you're a *SportsCenter* junkie who just has to watch ESPN every day to keep up with all the sports news and scores. Or perhaps you're one of the more than five million fans in March who post their brackets for the NCAA men's basketball tournament. Or perhaps you rely on ESPN Radio for up-to-the-minute scores and knowledgeable sports talk while at work or in your car. No matter what the sport or where, ESPN seems to be everywhere at once.

Here's a brief summary of the incredible variety of entities tied together under the ESPN brand:

Television: From its original groundbreaking cable network—which now serves 98 million households—the ESPN brand has sprouted six additional networks—ESPN2, ESPN Classic, ESPNEWS, ESPNU, ESPN Deportes (Spanish language), and ESPN International (46 international networks around the world serving fans in more than 200 countries on every continent). ESPN also produces the sports programming on ABC, dubbed ESPN on ABC, and is the home of the NBA Finals, NASCAR, college football, college basketball, World Cup Soccer, the Indy 500, the Little League World Series, and more.

One of the pioneers in high-definition TV broadcasting, ESPN last year outbid the major broadcast networks to capture the rights to air college football's Bowl Championship Series (BCS) beginning in 2011. Paying a reported $500 million for those rights, ESPN settled a decade-long argument over whether cable TV had the mass appeal necessary to support major sports events.

Radio: Sports radio is thriving, and ESPN operates the largest sports radio network, with 750 U.S. affiliates and more than 350 full-time stations plus Spanish-language ESPN Deportes in major markets. Overseas, ESPN has radio and syndicated radio programs in 11 countries.

> The ever-expanding ESPN brand is as much recognized and revered as iconic megabrands like Coca-Cola, Nike, or Google. When it comes to your life and sports, chances are good that ESPN plays a meaningful role.

Digital: ESPN.com is one of the world's leading sports Web sites. And ESPNRadio.com is the most listened-to online sports destination, with 35 original podcasts each week. ESPN360.com—a broadband sports network available at no cost to fans who receive their high-speed Internet connection from an affiliated service provider—delivers more than 3,500 live sporting events each year. It also provides on-demand video from ESPN's other networks plus exclusive content and video games. ESPN also delivers mobile sports content via all the major U.S. wireless providers—including real-time scores, stats, late-breaking news, video-on-demand, and even live TV. ESPN recently extended the brand further through an agreement with YouTube, featuring an ESPN channel of ad-supported short-form sports content and highlights.

Publishing: When ESPN first published *ESPN The Magazine* in 1998, critics gave it little chance against the mighty *Sports Illustrated* (SI). Yet, with its bold look, bright colors, and unconventional format, the ESPN publication now serves more than 2 million subscribers and growing, as compared with SI's stagnant 3.3 million subscribers. ESPN also publishes books through its ESPN Books division, including 10 new titles last year.

As if all this weren't enough, ESPN also manages events, including the X Games, the Winter X Games, ESPN Outdoors (featuring the Bassmaster Classic), the Skins Games, the Jimmy V Classic, and several football bowl games. It also develops ESPN-branded consumer products and services, including CDs, DVDs, video games, and even golf schools. If reading all this makes you hungry, you may be near an ESPN Zone, which includes a sports-themed restaurant, interactive games, and sports-related merchandise sales.

You'll now find ESPN content in airports and on planes, in health clubs, and even in gas stations. "Now you're not going to be bored when you fill up your tank. It gives new meaning to pulling into a full-service station," says Bodenheimer. "I've been on flights where people are watching our content and don't want to get off the flight."

Sports fans around the world love their ESPN. This fan affinity for the brand, in turn, makes it attractive to marketers as a vehicle for reaching their customers. Advertisers recently ranked ESPN number one for the sixth consecutive year for having appealing audience demographics, providing creative marketing and promotion opportunities, and having a positive brand image and an appealing programming environment. The combination of per-subscriber-based revenue from cable affiliates plus revenues from advertisers who buy time on its networks gives ESPN the financial muscle to compete with the traditional broadcast networks for sports programming.

Thus, no matter what your sport or where you are, the ESPN brand probably plays a prominent part in the action. To fans around the world, ESPN means sports. Tech savvy, creative, and often irreverent, the well-managed, ever-extending brand continues to build meaningful customer experiences and relationships. If it has to do with your life and sports—large or small—ESPN covers it for you, anywhere you are, 24/7.

Bodenheimer notes that ESPN's flagship show, *SportsCenter*, is locally produced in 13 locales and eight languages around the globe. "The sun never sets on *SportsCenter*," he boasts. Perhaps the company should rename ESPN to stand for Every Sport Possible—Now.[1]

> ESPN is more than just cable networks, publications, and other media. To consumers, ESPN is synonymous with sports entertainment, inexorably linked with consumers' sports memories, realities, and anticipations.

As the ESPN example shows, in their quest to create customer relationships, marketers must build and manage products and brands that connect with customers. This chapter begins with a deceptively simple question: *What is a product?* After addressing this question, we look at ways to classify products in consumer and business markets. Then we discuss the important decisions that marketers make regarding individual products, product lines, and product mixes. Next, we examine the characteristics and marketing requirements of a special form of product—services. Finally, we look into the critically important issue of how marketers build and manage product and service brands.

What Is a Product? (pp 224–229)

Author Comment | As you'll see, this is a deceptively simple question with a very complex answer. For example, think back to our opening ESPN story. What is the ESPN "product"?

We define a **product** as anything that can be offered to a market for attention, acquisition, use, or consumption that might satisfy a want or need. Products include more than just tangible objects, such as cars, computers, or cell phones. Broadly defined, "products" also include services, events, persons, places, organizations, ideas, or a mixture of these. Throughout this text, we use the term *product* broadly to include any or all of these entities. Thus, an Apple iPhone, a Toyota Camry, and a Caffé Mocha at Starbucks are products. But so are a trip to Las Vegas, E*Trade online investment services, and advice from your family doctor.

Because of their importance in the world economy, we give special attention to services. **Services** are a form of product that consists of activities, benefits, or satisfactions offered for sale that are essentially intangible and do not result in the ownership of anything. Examples include banking, hotel services, airline travel, retail, wireless communication, and home-repair services. We will look at services more closely later in this chapter.

Product
Anything that can be offered to a market for attention, acquisition, use, or consumption that might satisfy a want or need.

Service
An activity, benefit, or satisfaction offered for sale that is essentially intangible and does not result in the ownership of anything.

Products, Services, and Experiences

Products are a key element in the overall *market offering*. Marketing-mix planning begins with building an offering that brings value to target customers. This offering becomes the basis on which the company builds profitable customer relationships.

A company's market offering often includes both tangible goods and services. At one extreme, the market offer may consist of a *pure tangible good*, such as soap, toothpaste, or salt; no services accompany the product. At the other extreme are *pure services*, for which the market offer consists primarily of a service. Examples include a doctor's exam or financial services. Between these two extremes, however, many goods-and-services combinations are possible.

Today, as products and services become more commoditized, many companies are moving to a new level in creating value for their customers. To differentiate their offers, beyond simply making products and delivering services, they are creating and managing customer *experiences* with their brands or company.

Experiences have always been an important part of marketing for some companies. Disney has long manufactured dreams and memories through its movies and theme parks. And Nike has long declared, "It's not so much the shoes but where they take you." Today, however, all kinds of firms are recasting their traditional goods and services to create ex-

● Creating customer experiences: The Olive Garden sells more than just Italian food. It serves up an idealized Italian family meal experience. "When you're here, you're family."

periences. ● For example, the Olive Garden knows that it's selling more than just Italian food; it's selling a complete dining experience.[2]

A decade ago, Olive Garden's menu had grown stale, and sales were declining. Research showed that "people missed the emotional comfort and connectivity that comes with family," says Drew Madsen, president and COO of parent company Darden Restaurants. So the Olive Garden set out to recraft its guest dining experience, under the tagline "When you're here, you're family." To actually deliver that guest experience, the Olive Garden began tying everything it did to an idealized Italian family meal. For example, it designed new restaurants to suggest Italian farmhouses, with a large family-style table, modeled on one in a Florentine trattoria. In partnership with Italians, the Olive Garden even founded the Culinary Institute of Tuscany (CIT) in an 11th-century Tuscan village.

Through CIT, hundreds of Olive Garden chefs and restaurant team members have traveled to Italy to gain inspiration and learn the secrets of authentic Italian foods "that you'll enjoy sharing with your friends and family." More than 10 times a year, the company sends restaurant team members, many of whom have never set foot in Italy, to spend a week at CIT, where local experts expose them to everything from how olive oil gets pressed to how to layer flavors in Bolognese. Back home, such inspiring employee experiences translate into an authentic guest experience that's rare for a casual dining restaurant. "People come to a restaurant for both physical and emotional nourishment," says Madsen. "The physical is the food; and the emotional is how you feel when you leave." The now highly successful Olive Garden chain delivers on both.

Companies that market experiences realize that customers are really buying much more than just products and services. They are buying what those offers will *do* for them. A recent BMW ad puts it this way: "We realized a long time ago that what you make people feel is just as important as what you make." "A brand, product, or service is more than just a physical thing. Humans that connect with the brand add meaning and value to it," says one marketing executive. "Successfully managing the customer experience is the ultimate goal," adds another.[3]

Levels of Product and Services

Product planners need to think about products and services on three levels (see ● **Figure 8.1**). Each level adds more customer value. The most basic level is the *core customer value*, which addresses the question *What is the buyer really buying?* When designing products, marketers must first define the core, problem-solving benefits or services that consumers seek. A woman buying lipstick buys more than lip color. Charles Revson of Revlon saw this early: "In the factory, we make cosmetics; in the store, we sell hope." ● And people who buy a BlackBerry smartphone are buying more than a cell phone, an e-mail device, or a personal organizer. They are buying freedom and on-the-go connectivity to people and resources.

At the second level, product planners must turn the core benefit into an *actual product*. They need to develop product and service features, design, a quality level, a brand name, and packaging. For example, the BlackBerry is an actual product. Its name, parts, styling, features, packaging, and other attributes have all been carefully combined to deliver the core customer value of staying connected.

● Core, actual, and augmented product: People who buy a BlackBerry device are buying more than a cell phone, an e-mail device, or an organizer. They are buying freedom and on-the-go connectivity to people and resources.

◉ **FIGURE | 8.1**
Three Levels of Product

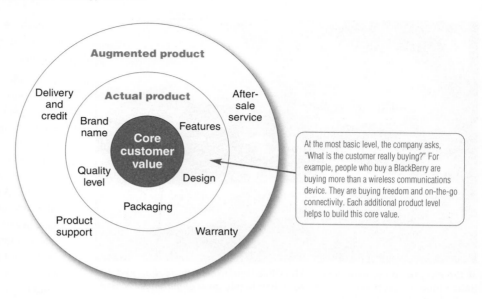

At the most basic level, the company asks, "What is the customer really buying?" For example, people who buy a BlackBerry are buying more than a wireless communications device. They are buying freedom and on-the-go connectivity. Each additional product level helps to build this core value.

Finally, product planners must build an *augmented product* around the core benefit and actual product by offering additional consumer services and benefits. The BlackBerry is more than just a communications device. It provides consumers with a complete solution to mobile connectivity problems. Thus, when consumers buy a BlackBerry, the company and its dealers also might give buyers a warranty on parts and workmanship, instructions on how to use the device, quick repair services when needed, and a toll-free telephone number and Web site to use if they have problems or questions.

Consumers see products as complex bundles of benefits that satisfy their needs. When developing products, marketers first must identify the *core customer value* that consumers seek from the product. They must then design the *actual* product and find ways to *augment* it to create this customer value and the most satisfying customer experience.

Product and Service Classifications

Products and services fall into two broad classes based on the types of consumers that use them: *consumer products* and *industrial products*. Broadly defined, products also include other marketable entities such as experiences, organizations, persons, places, and ideas.

Consumer Products

Consumer product

A product bought by final consumers for personal consumption.

Convenience product

A consumer product that customers usually buy frequently, immediately, and with minimal comparison and buying effort.

Shopping product

A consumer product that the customer, in the process of selecting and purchasing, usually compares on such attributes as suitability, quality, price, and style.

Specialty product

A consumer product with unique characteristics or brand identification for which a significant group of buyers is willing to make a special purchase effort.

Consumer products are products and services bought by final consumers for personal consumption. Marketers usually classify these products and services further based on how consumers go about buying them. Consumer products include *convenience products*, *shopping products*, *specialty products*, and *unsought products*. These products differ in the ways consumers buy them and, therefore, in how they are marketed (see ◉ **Table 8.1**).

Convenience products are consumer products and services that customers usually buy frequently, immediately, and with minimal comparison and buying effort. Examples include laundry detergent, candy, magazines, and fast food. Convenience products are usually low priced, and marketers place them in many locations to make them readily available when customers need or want them.

Shopping products are less frequently purchased consumer products and services that customers compare carefully on suitability, quality, price, and style. When buying shopping products and services, consumers spend much time and effort in gathering information and making comparisons. Examples include furniture, clothing, used cars, major appliances, and hotel and airline services. Shopping products marketers usually distribute their products through fewer outlets but provide deeper sales support to help customers in their comparison efforts.

Specialty products are consumer products and services with unique characteristics or brand identification for which a significant group of buyers is willing to make a special pur-

● **TABLE | 8.1** Marketing Considerations for Consumer Products

Marketing Considerations	Type of Consumer Product			
	Convenience	**Shopping**	**Specialty**	**Unsought**
Customer buying behavior	Frequent purchase; little planning, little comparison or shopping effort; low customer involvement	Less frequent purchase; much planning and shopping effort; comparison of brands on price, quality, and style	Strong brand preference and loyalty; special purchase effort; little comparison of brands; low price sensitivity	Little product awareness; knowledge (or, if aware, little or even negative interest)
Price	Low price	Higher price	High price	Varies
Distribution	Widespread distribution; convenient locations	Selective distribution in fewer outlets	Exclusive distribution in only one or a few outlets per market area	Varies
Promotion	Mass promotion by the producer	Advertising and personal selling by both the producer and resellers	More carefully targeted promotion by both the producer and resellers	Aggressive advertising and personal selling by the producer and resellers
Examples	Toothpaste, magazines, and laundry detergent	Major appliances, televisions, furniture, and clothing	Luxury goods, such as Rolex watches or fine crystal	Life insurance and Red Cross blood donations

chase effort. Examples include specific brands of cars, high-priced photographic equipment, designer clothes, and the services of medical or legal specialists. A Lamborghini automobile, for example, is a specialty product because buyers are usually willing to travel great distances to buy one. Buyers normally do not compare specialty products. They invest only the time needed to reach dealers carrying the wanted products.

Unsought products are consumer products that the consumer either does not know about or knows about but does not normally consider buying. Most major new innovations are unsought until the consumer becomes aware of them through advertising. Classic examples of known but unsought products and services are life insurance, preplanned funeral services, and blood donations to the Red Cross. By their very nature, unsought products require a lot of advertising, personal selling, and other marketing efforts.

Industrial Products

Unsought product
A consumer product that the consumer either does not know about or knows about but does not normally consider buying.

Industrial product
A product bought by individuals and organizations for further processing or for use in conducting a business.

Industrial products are those purchased for further processing or for use in conducting a business. Thus, the distinction between a consumer product and an industrial product is based on the *purpose* for which the product is purchased. If a consumer buys a lawn mower for use around home, the lawn mower is a consumer product. If the same consumer buys the same lawn mower for use in a landscaping business, the lawn mower is an industrial product.

The three groups of industrial products and services include materials and parts, capital items, and supplies and services. *Materials and parts* include raw materials and manufactured materials and parts. Raw materials consist of farm products (wheat, cotton, livestock, fruits, vegetables) and natural products (fish, lumber, crude petroleum, iron ore). Manufactured materials and parts consist of component materials (iron, yarn, cement, wires) and component parts (small motors, tires, castings). Most manufactured materials and parts are sold directly to industrial users. Price and service are the major marketing factors; branding and advertising tend to be less important.

Capital items are industrial products that aid in the buyer's production or operations, including installations and accessory equipment. Installations consist of major purchases such as buildings (factories, offices) and fixed equipment (generators, drill presses, large computer systems, elevators). Accessory equipment includes portable factory equipment and tools (hand tools, lift trucks) and office equipment (computers, fax machines, desks). They have a shorter life than installations and simply aid in the production process.

The final group of industrial products is *supplies and services*. Supplies include operating supplies (lubricants, coal, paper, pencils) and repair and maintenance items (paint, nails, brooms). Supplies are the convenience products of the industrial field because they are usually purchased with a minimum of effort or comparison. Business services include maintenance and repair services (window cleaning, computer repair) and business advisory services (legal, management consulting, advertising). Such services are usually supplied under contract.

Organizations, Persons, Places, and Ideas

In addition to tangible products and services, marketers have broadened the concept of a product to include other market offerings: organizations, persons, places, and ideas.

Organizations often carry out activities to "sell" the organization itself. *Organization marketing* consists of activities undertaken to create, maintain, or change the attitudes and behavior of target consumers toward an organization. Both profit and not-for-profit organizations practice organization marketing. Business firms sponsor public relations or *corporate image advertising* campaigns to market themselves and polish their images. For example, food, agriculture, and industrial products giant Cargill markets itself to the public as a company that works closely with its business customers—from farmers and fisherman to fast-food restaurants and furniture manufacturers—to help bring the world everything from heart-healthy milk and trans fat–free french fries to furniture and bedding foam created from renewable resources. It says in its ads, "This is how Cargill works with customers: "collaborate > create > succeed." Similarly, not-for-profit organizations, such as churches, colleges, charities, museums, and performing arts groups, market their organizations to raise funds and attract members or patrons.

People can also be thought of as products. *Person marketing* consists of activities undertaken to create, maintain, or change attitudes or behavior toward particular people. People ranging from presidents, entertainers, and sports figures to professionals such as doctors, lawyers, and architects use person marketing to build their reputations. And businesses, charities, and other organizations use well-known personalities to help sell their products or causes. For example, Nike is represented by well-known athletes such as Kobe Bryant, Serena Williams, and hundreds of others around the globe in sports ranging from tennis and basketball to ice hockey and cricket. At the other extreme, Taylor Guitar markets a Baby Taylor model named after country pop superstar Taylor Swift, and Fender offers a John Mayer Stratocaster.

The skillful use of marketing can turn a person's name into a powerhouse brand. Carefully managed and well-known names, including Oprah Winfrey, Martha Stewart, and Donald Trump, now adorn everything from sports apparel, housewares, and magazines to book clubs and casinos. Such well-known names hold substantial branding power. ◉ Consider the chefs on the Food Network. These days it's hard to shop for kitchen products without bumping into goods endorsed by these culinary all-stars:[4]

In an age when its chefs approximate rock stars, the Food Network is the ultimate launching ground for their endorsed products. Every chef offers a library of cookbooks, but it goes far beyond that. Fans can cook just like their favorite Food Network guru by purchasing accessories to outfit their kitchens and a variety of essential signature flavors to stock their pantries. For example, Emeril Lagasse's

◉ **Person marketing: Food Network chefs like Rachael Ray and Bobby Flay now approximate rock stars. Each offers a slew of cook books, endorsed brands, and signature lines of cookware and condiments.**

name peppers products such as his own spices (Bam!!) and a line of cookware from All-Clad. Giada De Laurentiis has her own spread of goods to create the perfect everyday Italian meal—from cheese graters to pasta—available only at Target. "Good Eats" and "Iron Chef" host Alton Brown is a spokesperson for Welch's and GE Appliances and has his own line of Shun knives. And Rachael Ray is a one-woman marketing phenomenon. Beyond her Food Network shows, she landed her own daytime talk show; endorses a litany of orange-colored cookware, bakeware, and cutlery; has her own brand of dog food called Nutrish; and brands her own EVOO (extra virgin olive oil, for those not familiar with Rayisms).

Place marketing involves activities undertaken to create, maintain, or change attitudes or behavior toward particular places. Cities, states, regions, and even entire nations compete to attract tourists, new residents, conventions, and company offices and factories. New York State advertises "I ❤ NY, and California urges you to "Find yourself here." Tourism Ireland, the agency responsible for marketing Irish tourism to the rest of the world, invites travelers to "Go where Ireland takes you." The agency works with the travel trade, media, and other partners in key world markets, such as the United States, Canada, Australia, and a dozen European countries. At its Discover Ireland Web site, Tourism Ireland offers information about the country and its attractions, a travel planner, special vacation offers, lists of tour operators, and much more information that makes it easier to say "yes" to visiting Ireland.[5]

Ideas can also be marketed. In one sense, all marketing is the marketing of an idea, whether it is the general idea of brushing your teeth or the specific idea that Crest toothpastes create "healthy, beautiful smiles for life." Here, however, we narrow our focus to the marketing of *social ideas*. This area has been called **social marketing**, defined by the Social Marketing Institute (SMI) as the use of commercial marketing concepts and tools in programs designed to bring about social change.[6]

Social marketing programs include public health campaigns to reduce smoking, drug abuse, and obesity. Other social marketing efforts include environmental campaigns to promote wilderness protection, clean air, and conservation. Still others address issues such as family planning, human rights, and racial equality. The Ad Council of America (www.adcouncil.org) has developed dozens of social advertising campaigns, involving issues ranging from preventive health, education, and personal safety to environmental preservation.

But social marketing involves much more than just advertising—the SMI encourages the use of a broad range of marketing tools. "Social marketing goes well beyond the promotional '*P*' of the marketing mix to include every other element to achieve its social change objectives," says the SMI's executive director.[7]

Social marketing
The use of commercial marketing concepts and tools in programs designed to influence individuals' behavior to improve their well-being and that of society.

Author | Now that we've answered
Comment | the "What is a product?"
question, we dig into the specific
decisions that companies must make
when designing and marketing
products and services.

Product and Service Decisions (pp 229–236)

Marketers make product and service decisions at three levels: individual product decisions, product line decisions, and product mix decisions. We discuss each in turn.

Individual Product and Service Decisions

Don't forget Figure 8.1! The focus
of all of these decisions is to create
core customer value.

● **Figure 8.2** shows the important decisions in the development and marketing of individual products and services. We will focus on decisions about *product attributes, branding, packaging, labeling,* and *product support services*.

● FIGURE | 8.2
Individual Product Decisions

| Product attributes | Branding | Packaging | Labeling | Product support services |

Product and Service Attributes

Developing a product or service involves defining the benefits that it will offer. These benefits are communicated and delivered by product attributes such as *quality*, *features*, and *style and design*.

Product quality

The characteristics of a product or service that bear on its ability to satisfy stated or implied customer needs.

Product Quality. **Product quality** is one of the marketer's major positioning tools. Quality has a direct impact on product or service performance; thus, it is closely linked to customer value and satisfaction. In the narrowest sense, quality can be defined as "freedom from defects." But most customer-centered companies go beyond this narrow definition. Instead, they define quality in terms of creating customer value and satisfaction. The American Society for Quality defines quality as the characteristics of a product or service that bear on its ability to satisfy stated or implied customer needs. Similarly, Siemens defines quality this way: "Quality is when our customers come back and our products don't."[8]

Total quality management (TQM) is an approach in which all of the company's people are involved in constantly improving the quality of products, services, and business processes. For most top companies, customer-driven quality has become a way of doing business. Today, companies are taking a "return on quality" approach, viewing quality as an investment and holding quality efforts accountable for bottom-line results.

Product quality has two dimensions: level and consistency. In developing a product, the marketer must first choose a *quality level* that will support the product's positioning. Here, product quality means *performance quality*—the ability of a product to perform its functions. For example, a Rolls-Royce provides higher performance quality than a Chevrolet: It has a smoother ride, provides more luxury and "creature comforts," and lasts longer. Companies rarely try to offer the highest possible performance quality level; few customers want or can afford the high levels of quality offered in products such as a Rolls-Royce automobile, a Viking range, or a Rolex watch. Instead, companies choose a quality level that matches target market needs and the quality levels of competing products.

Beyond quality level, high quality also can mean high levels of quality consistency. Here, product quality means *conformance quality*—freedom from defects and *consistency* in delivering a targeted level of performance. All companies should strive for high levels of conformance quality. In this sense, a Chevrolet can have just as much quality as a Rolls-Royce. Although a Chevy doesn't perform at the same level as a Rolls-Royce, it can deliver as consistently the quality that customers pay for and expect.

Product Features. A product can be offered with varying features. A stripped-down model, one without any extras, is the starting point. The company can create higher-level models by adding more features. Features are a competitive tool for differentiating the company's product from competitors' products. Being the first producer to introduce a valued new feature is one of the most effective ways to compete.

How can a company identify new features and decide which ones to add to its product? It should periodically survey buyers who have used the product and ask these questions: How do you like the product? Which specific features of the product do you like most? Which features could we add to improve the product? The answers to these questions provide the company with a rich list of feature ideas. The company can then assess each feature's *value* to customers versus its *cost* to the company. Features that customers value highly in relation to costs should be added.

Product Style and Design. Another way to add customer value is through distinctive *product style and design*. Design is a larger concept than style. *Style* simply describes the appearance of a product. Styles can be eye catching or yawn producing. A sensational style may grab attention and produce pleasing aesthetics, but it does not necessarily make the product *perform* better. Unlike style, *design* is more than skin deep—it goes to the very heart of a product. Good design contributes to a product's usefulness as well as to its looks.

Good design doesn't start with brainstorming new ideas and making prototypes. Design begins with observing customers and developing a deep understanding of their needs. More than simply creating product or service attributes, it involves shaping the customer's

We've remodeled the most important parts of your kitchen.

We've remodeled the peeler. We've remodeled the garlic press, the can opener and the wooden spoon. And we didn't stop there. Any kitchen tools that weren't comfortable or easy to use were fair game. The idea isn't to make the old tools obsolete, it's to make them better. If we can't make them better, we don't make them at all. Pick up OXO Good Grips and you'll feel what we mean. They're easy to hold, easy to use and easy to love. In fact, they might just change the way you feel about your kitchen.

OXO **GOOD GRIPS**

For information call 1-800-545-4411

● **Product design: OXO focuses on the desired end-user experience and then translates its pie-cutter-in-the-sky notions into eminently usable gadgets.**

product-use experience. Product designers should think less about product attributes and technical specifications and more about how customers will use and benefit from the product. ● Consider OXO's outstanding design philosophy and process:[9]

OXO's uniquely designed kitchen and gardening gadgets look pretty cool. But to OXO, good design means a lot more than good looks. It means that OXO tools work— *really* work—for anyone and everyone. "OXO is practically the definition of 'good experience,'" notes one observer. For OXO, design means a salad spinner that can be used with one hand; tools with pressure-absorbing, nonslip handles that make them more efficient; or a watering can with a spout that rotates back toward the body, allowing for easier filling and storing. Ever since it came out with its supereffective Good Grips vegetable peeler in 1990, OXO has been known for clever designs that make everyday living easier. Its eye-catching, super-useful houseware designs have even been featured in museum exhibitions, and OXO is now extending its design touch to office supplies, medical devices, and baby products.

Much of OXO's design inspiration comes directly from users. "Every product that we make starts with . . . watching how people use things," says Alex Lee, OXO's president. "Those are the gems—when you pull out a latent problem." For example, after watching people struggle with the traditional Pyrex measuring cup, OXO discovered a critical flaw: You can't tell how full it is without lifting it up to eye level. The resulting OXO measuring cups have markings down the *inside* that can be read from above, big enough to read without glasses. Thus, OXO begins with a desired end-user experience and then translates pie-cutter-in-the-sky notions into eminently usable gadgets.

Branding

Perhaps the most distinctive skill of professional marketers is their ability to build and manage brands. A **brand** is a name, term, sign, symbol, or design, or a combination of these, that identifies the maker or seller of a product or service. Consumers view a brand as an important part of a product, and branding can add value to a product. Customers attach meanings to brands and develop brand relationships. Brands have meaning well beyond a product's physical attributes. For example, consider Coca-Cola:[10]

In an interesting taste test of Coca-Cola versus Pepsi, 67 subjects were connected to brain-wave-monitoring machines while they consumed both products. When the soft drinks were unmarked, consumer preferences were split down the middle. But when the brands were identified, subjects choose Coke over Pepsi by a margin of 75 percent to 25 percent. When drinking the identified Coke brand, the brain areas that lit up most were those associated with cognitive control and memory—a place where culture concepts are stored. That didn't happen as much when drinking Pepsi. Why? According to one brand strategist, it's because of Coca-Cola's long-established brand imagery—the almost 100-year-old contour bottle and cursive font and its association with iconic images ranging from Mean Joe Greene and the Polar Bears to Santa Claus. Pepsi's imagery isn't quite as deeply rooted. Although people might associate Pepsi with a hot celebrity or the "Pepsi generation" appeal, they probably don't link it to the strong and emotional American icons associated with Coke. The conclusion? Plain and simple: Consumer preference isn't based on taste alone. Coke's iconic brand appears to make a difference.

Brand
A name, term, sign, symbol, design, or a combination of these, that identifies the products or services of one seller or group of sellers and differentiates them from those of competitors.

Branding has become so strong that today hardly anything goes unbranded. Salt is packaged in branded containers, common nuts and bolts are packaged with a distributor's label, and automobile parts—spark plugs, tires, filters—bear brand names that differ from those of the automakers. Even fruits, vegetables, dairy products, and poultry are branded—Sunkist oranges, Dole Classic iceberg salads, Horizon Organic milk, and Perdue chickens.

Branding helps buyers in many ways. Brand names help consumers identify products that might benefit them. Brands also say something about product quality and consistency—buyers who always buy the same brand know that they will get the same features, benefits, and quality each time they buy. Branding also gives the seller several advantages. The brand name becomes the basis on which a whole story can be built about a product's special qualities. The seller's brand name and trademark provide legal protection for unique product features that otherwise might be copied by competitors. And branding helps the seller to segment markets. For example, Toyota Motor Corporation can offer the major Lexus, Toyota, and Scion brands, each with numerous subbrands—such as Camry, Corolla, Prius, Matrix, Yaris, Tundra, Land Cruiser, and others—not just one general product for all consumers.

Building and managing brands are perhaps the marketer's most important tasks. We will discuss branding strategy in more detail later in the chapter.

Packaging

Packaging involves designing and producing the container or wrapper for a product. Traditionally, the primary function of the package was to hold and protect the product. In recent times, however, numerous factors have made packaging an important marketing tool as well. Increased competition and clutter on retail store shelves means that packages must now perform many sales tasks—from attracting attention, to describing the product, to making the sale.

Companies are realizing the power of good packaging to create immediate consumer recognition of a brand. For example, an average supermarket stocks 47,000 items; the average Walmart supercenter carries 142,000 items. The typical shopper passes by some 300 items per minute, and from 40 percent to 70 percent of all purchase decisions are made in stores. In this highly competitive environment, the package may be the seller's last and best chance to influence buyers. Thus, for many companies, the package itself has become an important promotional medium.[11]

Poorly designed packages can cause headaches for consumers and lost sales for the company. Think about all those hard-to-open packages, such as DVD cases sealed with impossibly sticky labels, packaging with finger-splitting wire twist-ties, or sealed plastic clamshell containers that take the equivalent of the fire department's Jaws of Life to open. ● Such packaging causes what Amazon.com calls "'wrap rage'—the frustration we feel when trying to free a product from a nearly impenetrable package." Amazon.com recently launched a multiyear initiative to alleviate wrap rage. It's working with companies such as Fisher-Price, Mattel, Microsoft, and others to create "frustration-free packaging"—smaller, easy-to-open recyclable packages that use less packaging material and no frustrating plastic clamshells or wire ties. These new packages not only reduce customer frustration, but they also cut down on packaging waste and energy usage. "It will take many years," says the company, "but our vision is to offer our entire catalog of products in frustration-free packaging."[12]

Innovative packaging can give a company an advantage over competitors and boost sales. Sometimes even seemingly small packaging improvements can make a big difference. For example, Heinz revolutionized the 170-year-old condiments industry by inverting the good old ketchup bottle, letting customers quickly squeeze out even the last bit of ketchup. At the same time, it adopted a "fridge-door-fit" shape that not only slots into shelves more easily but also has a cap that is simpler for children to open. In the four months following the introduction of the new package, sales jumped 12 percent. Even more, the new package does double duty as a promotional tool. Says a packaging analyst, "When consumers see the Heinz logo on the fridge door every time they open it, it's taking marketing inside homes."[13]

Packaging
The activities of designing and producing the container or wrapper for a product.

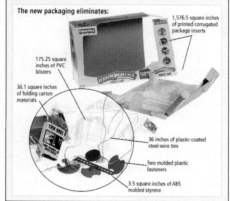

● **Better packaging: Amazon.com recently launched a multiyear initiative to create "frustration-free packaging" and eliminate "wrap rage." Its goal is to eventually offer its entire catalog of products in frustration-free packaging.**

In recent years, product safety has also become a major packaging concern. We have all learned to deal with hard-to-open "childproof" packaging. After the rash of product tampering scares in the 1980s, most drug producers and food makers now put their products in tamper-resistant packages. In making packaging decisions, the company also must heed growing environmental concerns. Fortunately, many companies have gone "green" by reducing their packaging and using environmentally responsible packaging materials.

Labeling

Labels range from simple tags attached to products to complex graphics that are part of the packaging. They perform several functions. At the very least, the label *identifies* the product or brand, such as the name Sunkist stamped on oranges. The label might also *describe* several things about the product—who made it, where it was made, when it was made, its contents, how it is to be used, and how to use it safely. Finally, the label might help to *promote* the brand, support its positioning, and connect with customers. For many companies, labels have become an important element in broader marketing campaigns.

Labels and brand logos can support the brand's positioning and add personality to the brand. For example, many companies are now redesigning their brand and company logos to make them more approachable, upbeat, and engaging. "The boxy, monochromatic look is out, and soft fonts, lots of colors, and natural imagery is in," says one analyst. For instance, Kraft recently replaced its blocky red, white, and blue hexagon logo with a lowercase, multifont, multicolor one that includes a colorful starburst and the company's new slogan, "Make today delicious." Similarly, Walmart swapped its blocky, single-color logo for one that has two colors and a sun icon. ◉ And Pepsi's recently updated packaging sports a new, more uplifting smiling logo. "It feels like the same Pepsi we know and love," says a brand expert, "but it's more adventurous, more youthful, with a bit more personality to it." It presents a "spirit of optimism and youth," says a Pepsi marketer.[14]

◉ Labeling and logos can enhance a brand's positioning and personality: Pepsi's new logo is "more adventurous, more youthful, with a bit more personality to it." It presents a "spirit of optimism and youth."

Along with the positives, labeling also raises concerns. There has been a long history of legal concerns about packaging and labels. The Federal Trade Commission Act of 1914 held that false, misleading, or deceptive labels or packages constitute unfair competition. Labels can mislead customers, fail to describe important ingredients, or fail to include needed safety warnings. As a result, several federal and state laws regulate labeling. The most prominent is the Fair Packaging and Labeling Act of 1966, which set mandatory labeling requirements, encouraged voluntary industry packaging standards, and allowed federal agencies to set packaging regulations in specific industries.

Labeling has been affected in recent times by *unit pricing* (stating the price per unit of standard measure), *open dating* (stating the expected shelf life of the product), and *nutritional labeling* (stating the nutritional values in the product). The Nutritional Labeling and Educational Act of 1990 requires sellers to provide detailed nutritional information on food products, and recent sweeping actions by the Food and Drug Administration (FDA) regulate the use of health-related terms such as *low fat*, *light*, and *high fiber*. Sellers must ensure that their labels contain all the required information.

Product Support Services

Customer service is another element of product strategy. A company's offer usually includes some support services, which can be a minor part or a major part of the total offering. Later in this chapter, we will discuss services as products in themselves. Here, we discuss services that augment actual products.

⦿ Nordstrom thrives on stories about its after-sale service. Nordstrom wants to "Take care of customers, no matter what it takes," before, during, and after the sale.

Product line
A group of products that are closely related because they function in a similar manner, are sold to the same customer groups, are marketed through the same types of outlets, or fall within given price ranges.

Support services are an important part of the customer's overall brand experience. ⦿ For example, upscale department store retailer Nordstrom knows that good marketing doesn't stop with making the sale. Keeping customers happy *after* the sale is the key to building lasting relationships. Nordstrom's motto: "Take care of customers, no matter what it takes," before, during, and after the sale.[15]

Nordstrom thrives on stories about its after-sale service heroics, such as employees dropping off orders at customer's homes or warming up cars while customers spend a little more time shopping. In one case, a sales clerk reportedly gave a customer a refund on a tire—Nordstrom doesn't carry tires, but the store prides itself on a no-questions-asked return policy. In another case, a Nordstrom sales clerk stopped a customer in the store and asked if the shoes she was wearing had been bought there. When a customer said yes, the clerk insisted on replacing them on the spot, saying that they hadn't worn as well as they should. There's even a story about a man whose wife, a loyal Nordstrom customer, died with her Nordstrom account $1,000 in arrears. Not only did Nordstrom settle the account, but it also sent flowers to the funeral. Such service heroics keep Nordstrom customers coming back again and again.

The first step in designing support services is to survey customers periodically to assess the value of current services and obtain ideas for new ones. Once the company has assessed the quality of various support services to customers, it can take steps to fix problems and add new services that will both delight customers and yield profits to the company.

Many companies are now using a sophisticated mix of phone, e-mail, fax, Internet, and interactive voice and data technologies to provide support services that were not possible before. For example, HP offers a complete set of sales and after-sale services. It promises "HP Total Care—expert help for every stage of your computer's life. From choosing it, to configuring it, to protecting it, to tuning it up—all the way to recycling it." Customers can click on the HP Total Care service portal that offers online resources for HP products and 24/7 tech support, which can be accessed via e-mail, instant online chat, and telephone.[16]

Product Line Decisions

Beyond decisions about individual products and services, product strategy also calls for building a product line. A **product line** is a group of products that are closely related because they function in a similar manner, are sold to the same customer groups, are marketed through the same types of outlets, or fall within given price ranges. For example, Nike produces several lines of athletic shoes and apparel, and Marriott offers several lines of hotels.

The major product line decision involves *product line length*—the number of items in the product line. The line is too short if the manager can increase profits by adding items; the line is too long if the manager can increase profits by dropping items. Managers need to analyze their product lines periodically to assess each item's sales and profits and understand how each item contributes to the line's overall performance.

Product line length is influenced by company objectives and resources. For example, one objective might be to allow for upselling. Thus BMW wants to move customers up from its 1-series models to 3-, 5-, 6-, and 7-series models. Another objective might be to allow cross-selling: HP sells printers as well as cartridges. Still another objective might be to protect against economic swings: Gap runs several clothing-store chains (Gap, Old Navy, and Banana Republic) covering different price points.

A company can expand its product line in two ways: by *line filling* or *line stretching*. *Product line filling* involves adding more items within the present range of the line. There are several reasons for product line filling: reaching for extra profits, satisfying dealers, using excess capacity, being the leading full-line company, and plugging holes to keep out competitors. However, line filling is overdone if it results in cannibalization and customer confusion. The company should ensure that new items are noticeably different from existing ones.

Product line stretching occurs when a company lengthens its product line beyond its current range. The company can stretch its line downward, upward, or both ways. Companies located at the upper end of the market can stretch their lines *downward*. A company may stretch downward to plug a market hole that otherwise would attract a new competitor or respond to a competitor's attack on the upper end. Or it may add low-end products because it finds faster growth taking place in the low-end segments. Honda stretched downward for all these reasons by adding its thrifty little Honda Fit to its line. The Fit, economical to drive and priced in the $14,000 to $15,000 range, met increasing consumer demands for more frugal cars and preempted competitors in the new-generation minicar segment.

Companies can also stretch their product lines *upward*. Sometimes, companies stretch upward to add prestige to their current products. Or they may be attracted by a faster growth rate or higher margins at the higher end. For example, some years ago, each of the leading Japanese auto companies introduced an upmarket automobile: Honda launched Acura; Toyota launched Lexus; and Nissan launched Infiniti. They used entirely new names rather than their own names.

Companies in the middle range of the market may decide to stretch their lines in *both directions*. Marriott did this with its hotel product line. ◉ Along with regular Marriott hotels, it added eight new branded hotel lines to serve both the upper and lower ends of the market. For example, Renaissance Hotels & Resorts aims to attract and please top executives; Fairfield Inn by Marriott, vacationers and business travelers on a tight travel budget; and Courtyard by Marriott, salespeople and other "road warriors."[17] The major risk with this strategy is that some travelers will trade down after finding that the lower-price hotels in the Marriott chain give them pretty much everything they want. However, Marriott would rather capture its customers who move downward than lose them to competitors.

◉ **Product line stretching: Marriott offers a full line of hotel brands—each aimed at a different target market.**

Product Mix Decisions

Product mix (or product portfolio)
The set of all product lines and items that a particular seller offers for sale.

An organization with several product lines has a product mix. A **product mix** (or **product portfolio**) consists of all the product lines and items that a particular seller offers for sale. Colgate's product mix consists of four major product lines: oral care, personal care, home care, and pet nutrition. Each product line consists of several sublines.[18] For example, the home care line consists of dishwashing, fabric conditioning, and household cleaning products. Each line and subline has many individual items. Altogether, Colgate's product mix includes hundreds of items.

A company's product mix has four important dimensions: width, length, depth, and consistency. Product mix *width* refers to the number of different product lines the company carries. For example, the "Colgate World of Care" includes a fairly contained product mix, consisting of personal and home care products that you can "trust to care for yourself, your home, and the ones you love." By contrast, GE manufactures as many as 250,000 items across a broad range of categories, from light bulbs to jet engines and diesel locomotives.

Product mix *length* refers to the total number of items a company carries within its product lines. Colgate typically carries many brands within each line. For example, its personal care line includes Softsoap liquid soaps and body washes, Irish Spring bar soaps, Speed Stick deodorant, and Skin Bracer and Afta aftershaves.

Product mix *depth* refers to the number of versions offered for each product in the line. Colgate toothpastes come in 16 varieties, ranging from Colgate Total, Colgate Max Fresh, Colgate Sensitive, Colgate Cavity Protection, and Colgate Tartar Protection to Ultra-brite, Colgate Sparkling White, Colgate Luminous, and Colgate Kids Toothpastes. Each variety comes in its own special forms and formulations. For example, you can buy Colgate Total in regular, mint stripe gel, or whitening liquid.

Finally, the *consistency* of the product mix refers to how closely related the various product lines are in end use, production requirements, distribution channels, or some other way. Colgate product lines are consistent insofar as they are consumer products and go through the same distribution channels. The lines are less consistent insofar as they perform different functions for buyers.

These product mix dimensions provide the handles for defining the company's product strategy. The company can increase its business in four ways. (1) It can add new product lines, widening its product mix. In this way, its new lines build on the company's reputation in its other lines. (2) The company can lengthen its existing product lines to become a more full-line company. (3) It can add more versions of each product and thus deepen its product mix. (4) The company can pursue more product line consistency—or less—depending on whether it wants to have a strong reputation in a single field or in several fields.

In the face of recent economic difficulties, many companies have streamlined their product mixes to pare out marginally performing lines and models and sharpen their value propositions. Others have bolstered their product mixes by adding more affordable options. Because of the economy, "consumers are talking about reassessing their favorite brands . . . if they think they can get a better value with the same price," says a marketing consultant. As consumers rethink their brand preferences and priorities, marketers must do the same. They need to align their product mixes with changing customer needs and profitably create better value for customers.[19]

Author Comment │ As noted at the start of this chapter, services are "products," too—intangible ones. So all the product topics we've discussed so far apply to services as well as to physical products. However, in this section, we focus on the special characteristics and marketing needs that set services apart.

Services Marketing (pp 236–243)

Services have grown dramatically in recent years. Services now account for close to 80 percent of the U.S. gross domestic product (GDP). And the service industry is growing. By 2014, it is estimated that nearly four out of five jobs in the United States will be in service industries. Services are growing even faster in the world economy, making up 64 percent of the gross world product.[20]

Service industries vary greatly. *Governments* offer services through courts, employment services, hospitals, military services, police and fire departments, the postal service, and schools. *Private not-for-profit organizations* offer services through museums, charities, churches, colleges, foundations, and hospitals. A large number of *business organizations* offer services—airlines, banks, hotels, insurance companies, consulting firms, medical and legal practices, entertainment and telecommunications companies, real-estate firms, retailers, and others.

The Nature and Characteristics of a Service

A company must consider four special service characteristics when designing marketing programs: intangibility, inseparability, variability, and perishability (see ● **Figure 8.3**).

Service intangibility
Services cannot be seen, tasted, felt, heard, or smelled before they are bought.

Service intangibility means that services cannot be seen, tasted, felt, heard, or smelled before they are bought. For example, people undergoing cosmetic surgery cannot see the result before the purchase. Airline passengers have nothing but a ticket and a promise that they and their luggage will arrive safely at the intended destination, hopefully at the same time. To reduce uncertainty, buyers look for "signals" of service quality. They draw conclusions about quality from the place, people, price, equipment, and communications that they can see.

Therefore, the service provider's task is to make the service tangible in one or more ways and send the right signals about quality. One analyst calls this *evidence management*,

● FIGURE | 8.3
Four Service Characteristics

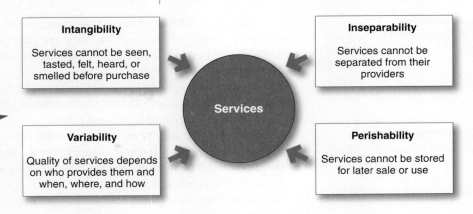

Although services are "products" in a general sense, they have special characteristics and marketing needs. The biggest differences come from the fact that services are essentially intangible and that they are created through direct interactions with customers. Think about your experiences with an airline versus Nike or Apple.

Intangibility
Services cannot be seen, tasted, felt, heard, or smelled before purchase

Inseparability
Services cannot be separated from their providers

Services

Variability
Quality of services depends on who provides them and when, where, and how

Perishability
Services cannot be stored for later sale or use

in which the service organization presents its customers with organized, honest evidence of its capabilities. The Mayo Clinic practices good evidence management:[21]

> When it comes to hospitals, it's very hard for the average patient to judge the quality of the "product." You can't try it on, you can't return it if you don't like it, and you need an advanced degree to understand it. And so, when we're considering a medical facility, most of us unconsciously turn into detectives, looking for evidence of competence, caring, and integrity. The Mayo Clinic doesn't leave that evidence to chance. By carefully managing a set of visual and experiential clues, both inside and outside the clinic, the Mayo Clinic offers patients and their families concrete evidence of its strengths and values.

> Inside, staff is trained to act in a way that clearly signals Mayo Clinic's patient-first focus. "My doctor calls me at home to check on how I am doing," marvels one patient. "She wants to work with what is best for my schedule." The clinic's physical facilities also send the right signals. They've been carefully designed to offer a place of refuge, convey caring and respect, and signal competence. Looking for external confirmation? Go online and hear directly from those who've been to the clinic or work there. The Mayo Clinic now uses social networking—everything from blogs to Facebook and YouTube—to enhance the patient experience. ● For example, on the Sharing Mayo Clinic blog (http://sharing.mayoclinic.org), patients and their families retell their Mayo experiences, and Mayo employees offer behind-the-scenes views. The result? Exceptionally positive word of mouth and abiding customer loyalty have allowed the Mayo Clinic to build what is arguably the most powerful brand in health care with very little advertising. "The quality of the [patient] experience is key," says Dr. Thoraf Sundt, a heart surgeon and chair of Mayo's marketing committee.

Service inseparability
Services are produced and consumed at the same time and cannot be separated from their providers.

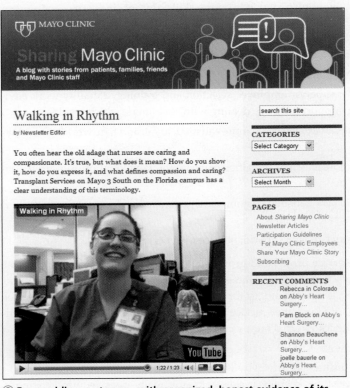

● By providing customers with organized, honest evidence of its capabilities, the Mayo Clinic has built one of the most powerful brands in healthcare. Its Sharing Mayo Clinic blog lets you hear directly from those who have been to the clinic or work there.

Physical goods are produced, then stored, later sold, and still later consumed. In contrast, services are first sold and then produced and consumed at the same time. In services marketing, the service provider is the product. **Service inseparability** means that services cannot be separated from their providers, whether the providers are people or machines. If a service employee provides the service, then the employee becomes a part of the service. Because the customer is also present as the service is produced, *provider-customer interaction* is a special feature of services marketing. Both the provider and the customer affect the service outcome.

Service variability
The quality of services may vary greatly depending on who provides them and when, where, and how.

Service variability means that the quality of services depends on who provides them as well as when, where, and how they are provided. For example, some hotels—say, Marriott—have reputations for providing better service than others. Still, within a given Marriott hotel, one registration-counter employee may be cheerful and efficient, whereas another standing just a few feet away may be unpleasant and slow. Even the quality of a single Marriott employee's service varies according to his or her energy and frame of mind at the time of each customer encounter.

Service perishability
Services cannot be stored for later sale or use.

Service perishability means that services cannot be stored for later sale or use. Some doctors charge patients for missed appointments because the service value existed only at that point and disappeared when the patient did not show up. The perishability of services is not a problem when demand is steady. However, when demand fluctuates, service firms often have difficult problems. For example, because of rush-hour demand, public transportation companies have to own much more equipment than they would if demand were even throughout the day. Thus, service firms often design strategies for producing a better match between demand and supply. Hotels and resorts charge lower prices in the off-season to attract more guests. And restaurants hire part-time employees to serve during peak periods.

Marketing Strategies for Service Firms

Just like manufacturing businesses, good service firms use marketing to position themselves strongly in chosen target markets. JetBlue promises "Happy Jetting"; Target says "Expect more. Pay less." At Hampton, "We love having you here." And St. Jude Children's Hospital it is "Finding cures. Saving children." These and other service firms establish their positions through traditional marketing mix activities. However, because services differ from tangible products, they often require additional marketing approaches.

The Service Profit Chain

In a service business, the customer and the front-line service employee *interact* to create the service. Effective interaction, in turn, depends on the skills of front-line service employees and on the support processes backing these employees. Thus, successful service companies focus their attention on *both* their customers and their employees. They understand the **service profit chain**, which links service firm profits with employee and customer satisfaction. This chain consists of five links:[22]

Service profit chain
The chain that links service firm profits with employee and customer satisfaction.

- *Internal service quality:* superior employee selection and training, a quality work environment, and strong support for those dealing with customers, which results in . . .
- *Satisfied and productive service employees:* more satisfied, loyal, and hardworking employees, which results in . . .
- *Greater service value:* more effective and efficient customer value creation and service delivery, which results in . . .
- *Satisfied and loyal customers:* satisfied customers who remain loyal, repeat purchase, and refer other customers, which results in . . .
- *Healthy service profits and growth:* superior service firm performance.

Therefore, reaching service profits and growth goals begins with taking care of those who take care of customers. Four Seasons Hotels and Resorts, a chain legendary for its outstanding customer service, is also legendary for its motivated and satisfied employees (see Real Marketing 8.1). Similarly, customer-service all-star Zappos.com, the online shoe, clothing, and accessories retailer, knows that happy customers begin with happy, dedicated, and energetic employees:[23]

Most of Zappos.com's business is driven by word-of-mouth and customer interactions with company employees. So keeping *customers* happy really does require keeping *employees* happy. Zappos.com, Inc., starts by recruiting the right people and training them thoroughly in customer-service basics. Then the Zappos family culture takes over, a culture that emphasizes "a satisfying and fulfilling job . . . and a career you can be proud of. Work hard. Play hard. All the time!" It's a great place to work. The online retailer

Real Marketing 8.1

The Four Seasons: Taking Care of Those Who Take Care of Customers

At a Four Seasons hotel, every guest is a somebody. Other exclusive resorts pamper their guests, but the Four Seasons has perfected the art of high-touch, carefully crafted service. Guests paying $1,000 or more a night expect to have their minds read, and this luxury hotel doesn't disappoint. Its mission is to perfect the travel experience through the highest standards of hospitality. "From elegant surroundings of the finest quality, to caring, highly personalized 24-hour service," says the company, "Four Seasons embodies a true home away from home for those who know and appreciate the best."

As a result, the Four Seasons has a cultlike customer clientele. As one Four Seasons Maui guest recently told a manager, "If there's a heaven, I hope it's run by Four Seasons." But what makes the Four Seasons so special? It's really no secret. Just ask anyone who works there. From the CEO to the doorman, they'll tell you: It's the Four Seasons staff. "What you see from the public point of view is a reflection of our people—they are the heart and soul of what makes this company succeed," says Isadore Sharp, the founder and CEO of the Four Seasons. "When we say people are our most important asset—it's not just talk." Just as it does for customers, the Four Seasons respects and pampers its employees. It knows that happy, satisfied employees make for happy, satisfied customers.

The Four Seasons customer-service legacy is deeply rooted in the company's culture, which in turn is grounded in the Golden Rule. "In all of our interactions with our guests, customers, business associates, and colleagues, we seek to deal with others as we would have them deal with us," says Sharp. "Personal service is not something you can dictate as a policy," he adds. "How you treat your employees is a reflection of how you expect them to treat customers."

The Four Seasons brings this culture to life by hiring the best people, orienting them carefully, instilling in them a sense of pride, and motivating them by recognizing and rewarding outstanding service deeds. It all starts with hiring the right people—those who fit the Four Seasons culture. "Every job applicant, whether hoping to fold laundry or teach yoga, goes through at least four interviews," notes one reporter. "We look for employees who share that Golden Rule—people who, by nature, believe in treating others as they would have them treat us," says Sharp.

Once on board, all new employees receive three months of training, including improvisation exercises that help them to fully understand customer needs and behavior. At the Four Seasons, the training never stops. But even more important are the people themselves and the culture under which they work. "I can teach anyone to be a waiter," says Sharp. "But you can't change an ingrained poor attitude. We look for people who say, 'I'd be proud to be a doorman.'" And the most important cultural guideline, restates Sharp, is "the Golden Rule: Do unto others. . . . That's not a gimmick." As a result, Four Seasons employees know what good service is and are highly motivated to give it.

Most importantly, once it has the right people in place, the Four Seasons treats them as it would its most important guests. According to the reporter:

Compared with the competition, Four Seasons salaries are in the 75th to 90th percentile, with generous retirement and profit sharing plans. All employees—for example, seamstresses, valets, the ski concierge, and the general manager—eat together regularly, free, in the hotel cafeteria. It may not have white linen or a wine list, but the food and camaraderie are good. Another killer perk for all employees: free rooms. After six months, any staffer can stay three nights free per year at any Four Seasons hotel or resort. That number increases to six nights after a year and steadily thereafter. Although the benefit may cost a few thousand dollars a year per employee, the returns seem invaluable. The room stays make employees feel as important and pampered as the guests they serve. Says employee Kanoe Braun, a burly pool attendant at the Four Seasons Maui, "I've been to the one in Bali. That was by far my favorite. You walk in, and they say, 'How are you, Mr. Braun?' and you say, 'Yeah, I'm somebody!'" Adds another Four Season staffer, "You're never treated like just an employee. You're a guest. You come back from those trips on fire. You want to do so much for the guests."

The service-profit chain: Happy employees make for happy customers. At the Four Seasons, employees feel as important and pampered as the guests.

Continued on next page

As a result, the Four Seasons staff loves the hotel just as much as customers do. Although guests can check out anytime they like, employees never want to leave. The annual turnover for full-time employees is only 18 percent, half the industry average. The Four Seasons has been included on *Fortune* magazine's list of 100 Best Companies to Work For every year since the list began in 1998. And that's the biggest secret to the Four Seasons'

success. Just as the service profit chain suggests, taking good care of customers begins

with taking good care of those who take care of customers.

Sources: Extract adapted from Jeffrey M. O'Brien, "A Perfect Season," *Fortune*, January 22, 2008, pp. 62–66. Other quotes and information from Michael B. Baker, "Four Seasons Tops Ritz-Carlton in Deluxe Photo-Finish," *Business Travel News*, March 23, 2009, p, 10: Sean Drakes, "Keeping the Brand Sacred," *Black Enterprise*, April 2009, p. 47; "100 Best Companies to Work For," *Fortune*, February 8, 2010, p. 55; and http://jobs.fourseasons .com/Pages/Home.aspx and www.fourseasons.com/about_us/, accessed November 2010.

● **The service profit chain: Zappos.com knows that happy customers begin with happy, dedicated, and "perpetually chipper" employees.**

Internal marketing
Orienting and motivating customer-contact employees and supporting service people to work as a team to provide customer satisfaction.

Interactive marketing
Training service employees in the fine art of interacting with customers to satisfy their needs.

creates a relaxed, fun-loving, and close-knit family atmosphere, complete with free meals, full benefits, profit sharing, a nap room, and even a full-time life coach. ● The result is what one observer calls "1,550 perpetually chipper employees." Every year, the company publishes a "culture book," filled with unedited, often gushy testimonials from Zapponians about what it's like to work there. "Oh my gosh," says one employee, "this is my home away from home. . . . It's changed my life. . . . Our culture is the best reason to work here." Says another, "the most surprising thing about coming to work here is that there are no limits. So pretty much anything you are passionate about is possible." And about what are Zapponians most passionate? The Zappos family's No. 1 core value: "Creating WOW through service."

Thus, service marketing requires more than just traditional external marketing using the four Ps. ● **Figure 8.4** shows that service marketing also requires *internal marketing* and *interactive marketing*. **Internal marketing** means that the service firm must orient and motivate its customer-contact employees and supporting service people to work as a *team* to provide customer satisfaction. Marketers must get everyone in the organization to be customer centered. In fact, internal marketing must *precede* external marketing. For example, Four Seasons Hotels and Resorts starts by hiring the right people and carefully orienting and inspiring them to give unparalleled customer service.

Interactive marketing means that service quality depends heavily on the quality of the buyer-seller interaction during the service encounter. In product marketing, product quality often depends little on how the product is obtained. But in services marketing, service quality depends on both the service deliverer and the quality of delivery. Service marketers, therefore, have to master interactive marketing skills. Thus, Four Seasons selects only people with an innate "passion to serve" and instructs them carefully in the fine art of interacting with customers to satisfy their every need. All new hires complete a three-month training regimen, including improvisation exercises to help them improve their customer-interaction skills.

In today's marketplace, companies must know how to deliver interactions that are not only "high touch" but also "high tech." For example, customers can log onto the Charles Schwab Web site and access account information, investment research, real-time quotes, after-hours trading, and the Schwab learning center. They can also participate in live online events and chat online with customer-service representatives. Customers seeking more personal interactions can contact service representatives by phone or visit a local Schwab

● FIGURE | 8.4
Three Types of Service Marketing

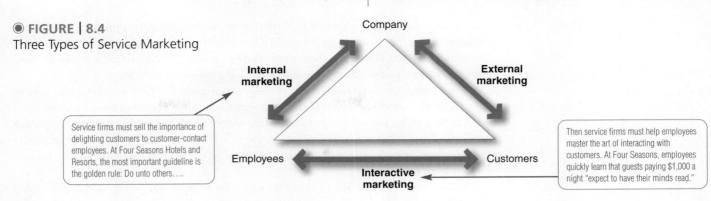

Company

Internal marketing

External marketing

Service firms must sell the importance of delighting customers to customer-contact employees. At Four Seasons Hotels and Resorts, the most important guideline is the golden rule: Do unto others....

Then service firms must help employees master the art of interacting with customers. At Four Seasons, employees quickly learn that guests paying $1,000 a night "expect to have their minds read."

Employees

Customers

Interactive marketing

branch office to "talk with Chuck." Thus, Schwab has mastered interactive marketing at all three levels—calls, clicks, *and* personal visits.

Today, as competition and costs increase, and as productivity and quality decrease, more service marketing sophistication is needed. Service companies face three major marketing tasks: They want to increase their *service differentiation, service quality,* and *service productivity.*

Managing Service Differentiation

In these days of intense price competition, service marketers often complain about the difficulty of differentiating their services from those of competitors. To the extent that customers view the services of different providers as similar, they care less about the provider than the price.

The solution to price competition is to develop a differentiated offer, delivery, and image. The *offer* can include innovative features that set one company's offer apart from competitors' offers. Some hotels offer no-wait kiosk registration, car-rental, banking, and business-center services in their lobbies and free high-speed Internet connections in their rooms. Some retailers differentiate themselves by offerings that take you well beyond the products they stock. ● For example, PetSmart isn't your average pet shop. Most locations offer training, grooming salons, veterinarian services, and even a "PetsHotel with a Doggie Day Camp," making it your one-stop shop for all your pet's needs.

Service companies can differentiate their service *delivery* by having more able and reliable customer-contact people, developing a superior physical environment in which the service product is delivered, or designing a superior delivery process. For example, many grocery chains now offer online shopping and home delivery as a better way to shop than having to drive, park, wait in line, and tote groceries home. And most banks allow you to access your account information from almost anywhere—from the ATM to your cell phone.

Finally, service companies also can work on differentiating their *images* through symbols and branding. Aflac adopted the duck as its symbol in its advertising—even as stuffed animals, golf club covers, and free ring tones and screensavers. The well-known Aflac duck helped make the big but previously unknown insurance company memorable and approachable. Other well-known service symbols include Merrill Lynch's bull, MGM's lion, McDonald's golden arches, Allstate's "good hands," and the Travelers red umbrella.

Managing Service Quality

A service firm can differentiate itself by delivering consistently higher quality than its competitors provide. Like manufacturers before them, most service industries have now joined the customer-driven quality movement. And like product marketers, service providers need to identify what target customers expect in regard to service quality.

● **Service differentiation: PetSmart differentiates itself by offering services that go well beyond the products it stocks. It even offers a PetsHotel with a Doggie Day Camp.**

Unfortunately, service quality is harder to define and judge than product quality. For instance, it is harder to agree on the quality of a haircut than on the quality of a hair dryer. Customer retention is perhaps the best measure of quality; a service firm's ability to hang onto its customers depends on how consistently it delivers value to them.

Top service companies set high service-quality standards. They watch service performance closely, both their own and that of competitors. They do not settle for merely good service; they strive for 100 percent defect-free service. A 98 percent performance standard may sound good, but using this standard, the U.S. Postal Service would lose or misdirect 560,000 pieces of mail each hour, and U.S. pharmacists would misfill more than 1.4 million prescriptions each week.[24]

Unlike product manufacturers who can adjust their machinery and inputs until everything is perfect, service quality will always vary, depending on the interactions between employees and customers. As hard as they may try, even the best companies will have an occasional late delivery, burned steak, or grumpy employee. However, good *service recovery* can turn angry customers into loyal ones. In fact, good recovery can win more customer purchasing and loyalty than if things had gone well in the first place. Consider this example:[25]

Bob Emig was flying home from St. Louis on Southwest Airlines when an all-too-familiar travel nightmare began to unfold. After his airplane backed away from the gate, he and his fellow passengers were told that the plane would need to be de-iced. When the aircraft was ready to fly two and a half hours later, the pilot had reached the hour limit set by the Federal Aviation Administration, and a new pilot was required. By that time, the plane had to be de-iced again. Five hours after the scheduled departure time, Emig's flight was finally ready for takeoff. A customer-service disaster, right? Not if you hear Emig tell it. Throughout the wait, the pilot walked the aisles, answering questions and offering constant updates. Flight attendants, who Emig says "really seemed like they cared," kept up with the news on connecting flights. And within a couple of days of arriving home, Emig received a letter of apology from Southwest that included two free round-trip ticket vouchers.

● Service recovery: Southwest created a high-level group—headed by Fred Taylor, senior manager of proactive customer service communications—that carefully coordinates responses to major flight disruptions, turning wronged customers into even more loyal ones.

Unusual? Not at all. It's the standard service-recovery procedure for Southwest Airlines. ● Years ago, Southwest created a high-level group—headed by a senior manager of proactive customer service communications—that carefully coordinates information sent to all frontline reps in the event of major flight disruptions. It also sends out letters, and in many cases flight vouchers, to customers caught up in flight delays or cancellations, customer bumping incidents, baggage problems, or other travel messes—even those beyond Southwest's control. Thanks to such caring service recovery, Southwest doesn't just appease wronged customers like Bob Emig; it turns them into even more loyal customers.

Managing Service Productivity

With their costs rising rapidly, service firms are under great pressure to increase service productivity. They can do so in several ways. They can train current employees better or hire new ones who will work harder or more skillfully. Or they can increase the quantity of their service by giving up some quality. The provider can "industrialize the service" by adding equipment and standardizing production, as in McDonald's assembly-line approach to fast-food retailing. Finally, a service provider can harness the power of technology. Although we often think of technology's power to save time and costs in manufacturing companies, it also has great—and often untapped—potential to make service workers more productive.

However, companies must avoid pushing productivity so hard that doing so reduces quality. Attempts to industrialize a service or cut costs can make a service company more efficient in the short run. But that can also reduce its longer-run ability to innovate, maintain service quality, or respond to consumer needs and desires. For example, some airlines have learned this lesson the hard way as they attempt to economize in the face of rising costs. They stopped offering even the little things for free—such as in-flight snacks—and began charging extra for everything from curbside luggage check-in to aisle seats. The result is a plane full of resentful customers who avoid the airline whenever they can. In their attempts to improve productivity, these airlines mangled customer service.

Thus, in attempting to improve service productivity, companies must be mindful of how they create and deliver customer value. In short, they should be careful not to take the "service" out of service.

Branding Strategy: Building Strong Brands (pp 243–252)

> **Author Comment** | A brand represents everything that a product or service *means* to consumers. As such, brands are valuable assets to a company. For example, when you hear someone say "Coca-Cola," what do you think, feel, or remember? What about "Target"? Or "Google"?

Some analysts see brands as *the* major enduring asset of a company, outlasting the company's specific products and facilities. John Stewart, former CEO of Quaker Oats, once said, "If this business were split up, I would give you the land and bricks and mortar, and I would keep the brands and trademarks, and I would fare better than you." A former CEO of McDonald's declared, "If every asset we own, every building, and every piece of equipment were destroyed in a terrible natural disaster, we would be able to borrow all the money to replace it very quickly because of the value of our brand. . . . The brand is more valuable than the totality of all these assets."[26]

Thus, brands are powerful assets that must be carefully developed and managed. In this section, we examine the key strategies for building and managing product and service brands.

Brand Equity

Brands are more than just names and symbols. They are a key element in the company's relationships with consumers. Brands represent consumers' perceptions and feelings about a product and its performance—everything that the product or the service *means* to consumers. In the final analysis, brands exist in the heads of consumers. As one well-respected marketer once said, "Products are created in the factory, but brands are created in the mind." Adds Jason Kilar, CEO of the online video service Hulu, "A brand is what people say about you when you're not in the room."[27]

Brand equity
The differential effect that knowing the brand name has on customer response to the product or its marketing.

A powerful brand has high *brand equity*. **Brand equity** is the differential effect that knowing the brand name has on customer response to the product and its marketing. It's a measure of the brand's ability to capture consumer preference and loyalty. A brand has positive brand equity when consumers react more favorably to it than to a generic or unbranded version of the same product. It has negative brand equity if consumers react less favorably than to an unbranded version.

Brands vary in the amount of power and value they hold in the marketplace. Some brands—such as Coca-Cola, Nike, Disney, GE, McDonald's, Harley-Davidson, and others—become larger-than-life icons that maintain their power in the market for years, even generations. Other brands create fresh consumer excitement and loyalty, brands such as Google, YouTube, Apple, eBay, Twitter, and Wikipedia. These brands win in the marketplace not simply because they deliver unique benefits or reliable service. Rather, they succeed because they forge deep connections with customers.

Ad agency Young & Rubicam's Brand Asset Valuator measures brand strength along four consumer perception dimensions: *differentiation* (what makes the brand stand out), *relevance* (how consumers feel it meets their needs), *knowledge* (how much consumers know about the brand), and *esteem* (how highly consumers regard and respect the brand). Brands with strong brand equity rate high on all four dimensions. The brand must be distinct, or consumers will have no reason to choose it over other brands. But the fact that a brand is highly differentiated doesn't necessarily mean that consumers will buy it. The brand must stand out in ways that are relevant to consumers' needs. But even a differentiated, relevant brand is far from a shoe-in. Before consumers will respond to the brand, they must first know about and understand it. And that familiarity must lead to a strong, positive consumer-brand connection.[28]

● **Consumers sometimes bond very closely with specific brands. Perhaps the ultimate expression of brand devotion is tattooing the brand on your body.**

Thus, positive brand equity derives from consumer feelings about and connections with a brand. Consumers sometimes bond *very* closely with specific brands. ● As perhaps the ultimate expression of brand devotion, a surprising number of people—and not just Harley-Davidson fans—have their favorite brand tattooed on their bodies.

A brand with high brand equity is a very valuable asset. *Brand valuation* is the process of estimating the total financial value of a brand. Measuring such value is difficult. However, according to one estimate, the brand value of Google is a whopping $100 billion, with Microsoft at $76 billion and Coca-Cola at $67 billion. Other brands rating among the world's most valuable include IBM, McDonald's, Apple, China Mobile, GE, Walmart, and Nokia.[29]

High brand equity provides a company with many competitive advantages. A powerful brand enjoys a high level of consumer brand awareness and loyalty. Because consumers expect stores to carry the particular brand, the company has more leverage in bargaining with resellers. Because a brand name carries high credibility, the company can more easily launch line and brand extensions. A powerful brand offers the company some defense against fierce price competition.

Above all, however, a powerful brand forms the basis for building strong and profitable customer relationships. The fundamental asset underlying brand equity is *customer equity*— the value of customer relationships that the brand creates. A powerful brand is important, but what it really represents is a profitable set of loyal customers. The proper focus of marketing is building customer equity, with brand management serving as a major marketing tool. Companies need to think of themselves not as portfolios of products but as portfolios of customers.

Building Strong Brands

Branding poses challenging decisions to the marketer. ● **Figure 8.5** shows that the major brand strategy decisions involve *brand positioning, brand name selection, brand sponsorship,* and *brand development.*

Brand Positioning

Marketers need to position their brands clearly in target customers' minds. They can position brands at any of three levels.[30] At the lowest level, they can position the brand on *product attributes.* For example, P&G invented the disposable diaper category with its Pampers brand. Early Pampers marketing focused on attributes such as fluid absorption, fit, and disposability. In general, however, attributes are the least desirable level for brand positioning. Competitors can easily copy attributes. More importantly, customers are not interested in attributes as such; they are interested in what the attributes will do for them.

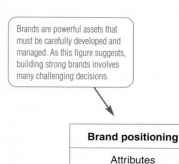

Brands are powerful assets that must be carefully developed and managed. As this figure suggests, building strong brands involves many challenging decisions.

Brand positioning	**Brand name selection**	**Brand sponsorship**	**Brand development**
Attributes Benefits Beliefs and values	Selection Protection	Manufacturer's brand Private brand Licensing Co-branding	Line extensions Brand extensions Multibrands New brands

● **FIGURE | 8.5**
Major Brand Strategy Decisions

THE DINING CAR

HAPPINESS LOVES COMPANY

The warm and lively Dining car. Where you can meet new friends over a delicious meal, and savor every moment. It's just one of the many exciting destinations aboard an Amtrak® train.

1-800-USA-RAIL · AMTRAK.COM   *AMTRAK Enjoy the journey.*℠

● **Brand positioning: Amtrak goes beyond attributes and benefits, engaging customers on a deeper level. In the "warm and lively dining room . . . you can meet new friends over a delicious meal, and savor every moment. Enjoy the journey."**

A brand can be better positioned by associating its name with a desirable *benefit*. Thus, Pampers can go beyond technical product attributes and talk about the resulting containment and skin-health benefits from dryness. "There are fewer wet bottoms in the world because of us," says Jim Stengel, P&G's former global marketing officer. Some successful brands positioned on benefits are FedEx (guaranteed on-time delivery), Nike (performance), Lexus (quality), and Walmart (low prices).

The strongest brands go beyond attribute or benefit positioning. They are positioned on strong *beliefs and values*. These brands pack an emotional wallop. Brands such as Godiva, Apple, Victoria's Secret, and Trader Joe's rely less on a product's tangible attributes and more on creating surprise, passion, and excitement surrounding a brand. ● Even a seemingly mundane brand such as Amtrak can be positioned this way. Recent Amtrak ads suggest that an Amtrak train ride does more than just get you from point A to point B. In a "spacious and peaceful coach car . . . you can gaze at a pristine landscape onboard a greener alternative to cars and planes." In "the warm and lively dining car . . . you can meet new friends over a delicious meal, and savor every moment." Don't just ride a train, says Amtrak. "Enjoy the Journey."

Successful brands engage customers on a deep, emotional level. According to Stengel, "marketing inspires life, and life inspires marketing." Thus, P&G knows that, to parents, Pampers mean much more than just containment and dryness:[31]

In the past, we often thought of P&G's brands in terms of functional benefits. But when we began listening very closely to customers, they told us Pampers meant much more to them: Pampers are more about parent-child relationships and total baby care. So we started to say, "We want to be a brand experience; we want to be there to help support parents and babies as they grow and develop." In the initial days people thought we were nuts. How can a diaper help a baby's development? But babies wear diapers 24/7 for almost three years. It actually reorients R&D to ask a question like "How can we help babies sleep better?" Why are we concerned about babies sleeping better? Because sleep is important to brain development. It helps relationship skills. Thinking like that, we're able to help improve life for our consumers. The equity of great brands has to be something that a consumer finds inspirational and the organization finds inspirational. You know, our baby care business didn't start growing aggressively until we changed Pampers from being about dryness to helping mom with her baby's development.

When positioning a brand, the marketer should establish a mission for the brand and a vision of what the brand must be and do. A brand is the company's promise to deliver a specific set of features, benefits, services, and experiences consistently to buyers. The brand promise must be simple and honest. Motel 6, for example, offers clean rooms, low prices, and good service but does not promise expensive furnishings or large bathrooms. In contrast, The Ritz-Carlton offers luxurious rooms and a truly memorable experience but does not promise low prices.

Brand Name Selection

A good name can add greatly to a product's success. However, finding the best brand name is a difficult task. It begins with a careful review of the product and its benefits, the target market, and proposed marketing strategies. After that, naming a brand becomes part science, part art, and a measure of instinct.

Desirable qualities for a brand name include the following: (1) It should suggest something about the product's benefits and qualities. Examples: Beautyrest, Acuvue, Breathe

Right, Food Saver. (2) It should be easy to pronounce, recognize, and remember: Tide, Jelly Belly, iPod, JetBlue. (3) The brand name should be distinctive: Panera, Uggs. (4) It should be extendable; Amazon.com began as an online bookseller but chose a name that would allow expansion into other categories. (5) The name should translate easily into foreign languages. Before changing its name to Exxon, Standard Oil of New Jersey rejected the name Enco, which it learned meant a stalled engine when pronounced in Japanese. (6) It should be capable of registration and legal protection. A brand name cannot be registered if it infringes on existing brand names.

Choosing a new brand name is hard work. After a decade of choosing quirky names (Yahoo!, Google) or trademark-proof made-up names (Novartis, Aventis, Accenture), today's style is to build brands around names that have real meaning. For example, names like Silk (soy milk), Method (home products), Smartwater (beverages), and Blackboard (school software) are simple and make intuitive sense. But with trademark applications soaring, *available* new names can be hard to find. Try it yourself. Pick a product and see if you can come up with a better name for it. How about Moonshot? Tickle? Vanilla? Treehugger? Simplicity? Google them and you'll find that they're already taken.

Once chosen, the brand name must be protected. Many firms try to build a brand name that will eventually become identified with the product category. Brand names such as Kleenex, Levi's, JELL-O, BAND-AID, Scotch Tape, Formica, and Ziploc have succeeded in this way. However, their very success may threaten the company's rights to the name. Many originally protected brand names—such as cellophane, aspirin, nylon, kerosene, linoleum, yo-yo, trampoline, escalator, thermos, and shredded wheat—are now generic names that any seller can use. To protect their brands, marketers present them carefully using the word *brand* and the registered trademark symbol, as in "BAND-AID® Brand Adhesive Bandages." Even the long-standing "I am stuck on BAND-AID and BAND-AID's stuck on me" jingle has now become "I am stuck on BAND-AID *brand* and BAND-AID's stuck on me."

Brand Sponsorship

A manufacturer has four sponsorship options. The product may be launched as a *national brand* (or *manufacturer's brand*), as when Sony and Kellogg sell their output under their own brand names (Sony Bravia HDTV or Kellogg's Frosted Flakes). Or the manufacturer may sell to resellers who give the product a *private brand* (also called a *store brand* or *distributor brand*). Although most manufacturers create their own brand names, others market *licensed brands*. Finally, two companies can join forces and *co-brand* a product. We discuss each of these options in turn.

National Brands versus Store Brands. National brands (or manufacturers' brands) have long dominated the retail scene. In recent times, however, an increasing number of retailers and wholesalers have created their own **store brands** (or **private brands**). Although store brands have been gaining strength for more than a decade, recent tougher economic times have created a store-brand boom. Studies show that consumers are buying more private brands, and most don't plan to return to name brands anytime soon. "Bad times are good times for private labels," says a brand expert. "As consumers become more price-conscious, they also become less brand-conscious."[32] (See Real Marketing 8.2.)

In fact, store brands are growing much faster than national brands. In all, private label goods account for more than 22 percent of all unit sales. Since 2008, unit sales of private label goods have grown at more than twice the rate of national brands. Private-label apparel, such as Hollister, The Limited, Arizona Jean Company (JCPenney), and Xhilaration (Target), captures a 40 percent share of all U.S. apparel sales.[33]

Many large retailers skillfully market a deep assortment of store-brand merchandise. For example, Kroger, the nation's largest grocery retailer, stocks some 14,000 store brand items under its own Private Selection, Banner, and Value brands. Store brands now account for more than 27 percent of Kroger's dollar sales and more than one-third of all its unit sales. At the other end of the grocery spectrum, upscale Whole Foods Market offers an array of store brand products under its 365 Everyday Value brand, from organic Canadian maple syrup and frozen chicken Caesar pizza to chewy children's multivitamins and organic whole wheat pasta.[34]

Store brand (or private brand)
A brand created and owned by a reseller of a product or service.

Real Marketing 8.2

Bad Times Are Good Times for Store Brands. But What's a National Brand to Do?

Over the past six months, Elizabeth O'Herron has banished nearly all brand names from her household. So long Pampers, Hefty, and Birds Eye. Instead, the pantry is stocked with cheaper imitations of the same goods: Walmart diapers, BJ's garbage bags, and Stop & Shop's frozen veggies. At the local Walmart, she stocks up on store's Great Value brand; at Kroger it's Private Selection or Kroger Value products. "I'm not loyal to any grocery store or any brand," says O'Herron. "I'm loyal to savings."

These days, more and more consumers are joining O'Herron's way of thinking. In the aftermath of the recent recession, as shoppers look to stretch their dollars, the popularity of store brands has soared. From trying cheaper laundry detergents to slipping on a more affordable pair of jeans, Americans are changing their spending habits to save money. "Bad times are good times for private labels," says one analyst. "As consumers become more price-conscious, they also become less brand-conscious."

It seems that almost every retailer now carries its own store brands. Walmart's private brands account for a whopping 40 percent of its sales: brands such as Great Value food products; Sam's Choice beverages; Equate pharmacy, health, and beauty products; White Cloud brand toilet tissue and diapers; Simple Elegance laundry products; and Canopy outdoor home products. Its private label brands alone generate nearly twice the sales of all P&G brands combined, and Great Value is the nation's largest single food brand. At the other end of the spectrum, even upscale retailer Saks Fifth Avenue carries its own clothing line, which features $98 men's ties, $200 halter tops, and $250 cotton dress shirts.

Once known as "generic" or "no-name" brands, today's store brands are shedding their image as cheap knockoffs of national brands. Store brands now offer much greater selection, and they are rapidly achieving name-brand quality. In fact, retailers such as Target and Trader Joe's are out-innovating many of their national-brand competitors. Rather than simply creating low-end generic brands that offer a low-price alternative to national brands, retailers are now moving toward higher-end private brands that boost both a store's revenues and its image.

As store-brand selection and quality have improved, and as the recent recession put the brakes on spending, consumers have shown an ever-increasing openness to store brands. Some 50 percent of U.S. consumers now purchase store brands "all the time" as part of their regular shopping behavior, up from just 12 percent in the early 1990s. And in a recent 23-country survey, 89 percent of consumers agreed that store brands are "the same as or better than" national brands when it comes to "providing a good value for the money." Eighty percent agreed that store brands are as good or better at "offering products that I trust."

Some retail strategists predict that the slowdown in consumer spending could last for years. The new consumer frugality could "lead to a 'downturn generation' that learns to scrimp and save permanently, including buying more private-label," says one strategist.

Just ask shopper Lisa Dean, whose shopping cart last week was filled with store-brand goods—milk, eggs, tomato sauce, tortilla chips, and trash bags, to name a few. "Once I started trying store brands, and the quality, taste, and price was right, I have continued to purchase store brands and try new things," she says. She estimates that she is saving at least 30 percent on groceries. Will she return to her old favorite brands in an improved economy? No way. "This is absolutely a permanent switch," says Dean.

Does the surge in store brands spell doom for name-brand products? Not likely. But what should national-brand marketers do to thwart the growing competition from store brands? For starters, they need to sharpen their value propositions in these more frugal times.

So far, many national brands have been fighting back with a variety of value pitches. P&G rolled out campaigns for Pantene and Gillette,

The popularity of store brands has soared recently. Walmart's store brands account for a whopping 40 percent of its sales, and its Great Value brand is the nation's largest single food brand.

Continued on next page

among others, that stress the brand's bang for one's buck. Pantene positions itself as an affordable salon alternative. And Gillette Fusion claims that its pricey razor blades deliver "high-performance" shaves for "as little as a dollar a week." According to one P&G rep, that claim is meant to address an outdated notion about the brand. "Guys have consistently told us that they think our blades are costly, so reframing the true expense for them makes good sense." Faced with tighter-fisted consumers, other national brands have reacted by significantly repositioning themselves. For example, Unilever has integrated a value message into its campaign for Ragú. One print ad reads, "With Ragú and a pound of pasta, you can feed a family of four for less than four dollars. The perfect meal when your family is growing and the economy is shrinking."

Although such value pitches might work for now, long-term national-brand success requires continued investment in product innovation and brand marketing. In these lean times and beyond, rather than cheapening their products or lowering their prices, national brands need to distinguish themselves through superior customer value. For example, the Ragú value positioning emphasizes affordable quality rather than low prices.

When asked whether, in a weak economy, consumers aren't more concerned about lower prices (via store brands) than brand purpose (via national brands), marketing consultant and former P&G global marketing chief Jim Stengel replied:

> I don't think it's an either/or. I think great brands have a strong sense of their meaning, their ideals, their mission—and their ideas represent a tremendous value to consumers. I think great brands have to tell their stories. They have to do great things . . . [bringing] joy, help, and service to people by making them laugh, giving them an idea, or solving a problem. If they do that, [more than survive in down times,] national brands will thrive.

So, even when the economic pendulum swings downward, national-brand marketers must remain true to their brand stories. "You can have a value proposition that accentuates good value, but you don't want to walk away from the core proposition of the brand," says one marketing executive. "That's the only thing you have to protect yourself" from private labels in the long run. Even some die-hard store-brand buyers prove this important point.

Kalixt Smith has recently given up national brands for bread, milk, toilet paper, and dish detergent, saving up to $50 a month on groceries for her family of four. She's even gone to great lengths to hide some of the changes from her family. "I resorted to buying things like store-brand ketchup, hot sauce, BBQ sauce, and syrup in bulk or large containers and reusing the containers from Heinz, Frank's Red Hot, Kraft, and Mrs. Butterworth's to mask the switch," says Smith. "My kids do not seem to notice the difference." But there're some store-brand items she can't sneak under the family radar, including attempted replacements for Honey Nut Cheerios and Velveeta Shells & Cheese. And, to her surprise, Spam. It turns out that there is no tasty substitute for Spam, at least not for her brood. Thus, despite her tighter spending, Smith still finds many national brands well worth the higher price.

Sources: Excerpts adapted from Jenn Abelson, "Seeking Savings, Some Ditch Brand Loyalty," *Boston Globe*, January 29, 2010; Elaine Wong, "Foods OK, But Some Can't Stomach More Increases," *Brandweek*, January 5, 2009, p. 7; and Elaine Wong, "Stengel: Private Label, Digital Change Game," *Brandweek*, April 13, 2009, pp. 7, 37. Also see Sarah Skidmore, "Walmart Revamping Own Brand," *Cincinnati Enquirer*, March 17, 2009, http://news.cincinnati.com/article/20090317/BIZ/903170336/-1/TODAY; Mark Dolliver, "Consumers Praise Store Brands," *Adweek*, April 8, 2010, www.adweek.com; and http://walmartstores.com/Video/?id=1305, accessed November 2010.

In the so-called *battle of the brands* between national and private brands, retailers have many advantages. They control what products they stock, where they go on the shelf, what prices they charge, and which ones they will feature in local circulars. Retailers often price their store brands lower than comparable national brands, thereby appealing to the budget-conscious shopper in all of us. Although store brands can be hard to establish and costly to stock and promote, they also yield higher profit margins for the reseller. And they give resellers exclusive products that cannot be bought from competitors, resulting in greater store traffic and loyalty. Fast-growing retailer Trader Joe's, which carries 80 percent store brands, began creating its own brands so that "we could put our destiny in our own hands," says the company's president.[35]

To compete with store brands, national brands must sharpen their value propositions, especially in these lean economic times. In the long run, however, leading brand marketers must invest in R&D to bring out new brands, new features, and continuous quality improvements. They must design strong advertising programs to maintain high awareness and preference. And they must find ways to "partner" with major distributors in a search for distribution economies and improved joint performance.

Licensing. Most manufacturers take years and spend millions to create their own brand names. However, some companies license names or symbols previously created by other manufacturers, names of well-known celebrities, or characters from popular movies and books. For a fee, any of these can provide an instant and proven brand name.

Apparel and accessories sellers pay large royalties to adorn their products—from blouses to ties and linens to luggage—with the names or initials of well-known fashion innovators such as Calvin Klein, Tommy Hilfiger, Gucci, or Armani. Sellers of children's products attach an almost endless list of character names to clothing, toys, school supplies, linens, dolls, lunch boxes, cereals, and other items. Licensed character names range from classics such as Sesame Street, Disney, Star Wars, the Muppets, Scooby Doo, Hello Kitty, and Dr. Seuss characters to the more recent Dora the Explorer; Go, Diego, Go!; Little Einsteins; and Hannah Montana. And currently a number of top-selling retail toys are products based on television shows and movies.

⦿ **Licensing: Nickelodeon has developed a stable full of hugely popular characters, such as SpongeBob SquarePants, that generate billions of dollars of retail sales each year.**

Name and character licensing has grown rapidly in recent years. Annual retail sales of licensed products worldwide have grown from only $4 billion in 1977 to $55 billion in 1987 and more than $192 billion today. Licensing can be a highly profitable business for many companies. For example, Disney, the world's biggest licensor, reported more than $30 billion in worldwide merchandise sales last year. ⦿ And Nickelodeon has developed a stable full of hugely popular characters, such as Dora the Explorer; Go, Diego, Go!; iCarly; and SpongeBob SquarePants. SpongeBob alone has generated more than $8 billion in sales and licensing fees over the past decade. "When it comes to licensing its brands for consumer products, Nickelodeon has proved that it has the Midas touch," states a brand licensing expert.[36]

Co-branding
The practice of using the established brand names of two different companies on the same product.

Co-branding. **Co-branding** occurs when two established brand names of different companies are used on the same product. Co-branding offers many advantages. Because each brand dominates in a different category, the combined brands create broader consumer appeal and greater brand equity. For example, high-end shaving products brand The Art of Shaving partnered with mainstream marketer Gillette to create the Fusion Chrome Collection, featuring a $150 power razor billed as "the world's most technologically advanced razor." Through the partnership, The Art of Shaving gains access to Gillette's broader market; Gillette, in turn, adds high-end luster to its shaving products line.

Co-branding can take advantage of the complementary strengths of two brands. For example, the Tim Hortons coffee chain is establishing co-branded Tim Hortons–Cold Stone Creamery shops. Tim Hortons is strong in the morning and midday periods, with coffee and baked goods, soups, and sandwiches. By contrast, Cold Stone Creamery's ice cream snacks are strongest in the afternoon and evening, which are Tim Hortons's nonpeak periods. The co-branded locations offer customers a reason to visit morning, noon, and night.[37]

Co-branding also allows a company to expand its existing brand into a category it might otherwise have difficulty entering alone. For example, Nike and Apple co-branded the Nike+iPod Sport Kit, which lets runners link their Nike shoes with their iPods to track and enhance running performance in real time. "Your iPod Nano [or iPod Touch] becomes your coach. Your personal trainer. Your favorite workout companion." The Nike+iPod arrangement gives Apple a presence in the sports and fitness market. At the same time, it helps Nike bring new value to its customers.[38]

Co-branding can also have limitations. Such relationships usually involve complex legal contracts and licenses. Co-branding partners must carefully coordinate their advertising, sales promotion, and other marketing efforts. Finally, when co-branding, each partner must trust that the other will take good care of its brand. If something damages the reputation of one brand, it can tarnish the co-brand as well.

Brand Development

A company has four choices when it comes to developing brands (see ⦿ **Figure 8.6**). It can introduce *line extensions*, *brand extensions*, *multibrands*, or *new brands*.

● FIGURE | 8.6
Brand Development Strategies

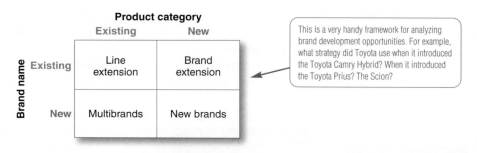

This is a very handy framework for analyzing brand development opportunities. For example, what strategy did Toyota use when it introduced the Toyota Camry Hybrid? When it introduced the Toyota Prius? The Scion?

Product category

	Existing	New
Existing	Line extension	Brand extension
New	Multibrands	New brands

(Brand name on vertical axis)

Line extension

Extending an existing brand name to new forms, colors, sizes, ingredients, or flavors of an existing product category.

Line Extensions. **Line extensions** occur when a company extends existing brand names to new forms, colors, sizes, ingredients, or flavors of an existing product category. Thus, the Cheerios line of cereals includes Honey Nut, Frosted, Yogurt Burst, MultiGrain, Banana Nut, Yogurt Burst, and several other variations.

A company might introduce line extensions as a low-cost, low-risk way to introduce new products. Or it might want to meet consumer desires for variety, use excess capacity, or simply command more shelf space from resellers. However, line extensions involve some risks. An overextended brand name might lose some of its specific meaning. Or heavily extended brands can cause consumer confusion or frustration.

Want a Coke? Okay, but what kind? You can pick from some 20 different varieties. In no-calorie versions alone, Coca-Cola offers two subbrands: Diet Coke and Coke Zero. Throw in flavored and no-caffeine versions—caffeine-free Diet Coke, cherry Diet Coke, black cherry vanilla Diet Coke, Diet Coke with lemon, Diet Coke with lime, vanilla Coke Zero, cherry Coke Zero—and you come up with a head-spinning ten diet colas from Coca-Cola. And that doesn't count Diet Coke with Splenda, Diet Coke Plus (with vitamins B3, B6, and B12 plus minerals zinc and magnesium). Each subbrand has its own marketing spin. But really, are we talking about choices here or just plain confusion? I mean, can you really tell the difference?

Another risk is that sales of an extension may come at the expense of other items in the line. For example, how much would yet another Diet Coke extension steal from Coca-Cola's own lines versus Pepsi's? A line extension works best when it takes sales away from competing brands, not when it "cannibalizes" the company's other items.

Brand extension

Extending an existing brand name to new product categories.

Brand Extensions. A **brand extension** extends a current brand name to new or modified products in a new category. For example, Kellogg's has extended its Special K cereal brand into a full line of cereals plus lines of crackers, fruit crisps, snack and nutrition bars, breakfast shakes, protein waters, and other health and nutrition products. Victorinox extended its venerable Swiss Army brand from multitool knives to products ranging from cutlery and ballpoint pens to watches, luggage, and apparel. And P&G has leveraged the strength of its Mr. Clean household cleaner brand to launch several new lines: cleaning pads (Magic Eraser), bathroom cleaning tools (Magic Reach), and home auto cleaning kits (Mr. Clean AutoDry). ● It even launched Mr. Clean–branded car washes.

A brand extension gives a new product instant recognition and faster acceptance. It also saves the high advertising costs usually required to build a new brand name. At the same time, a brand extension strategy involves some risk. The extension may confuse the image of the main brand. Brand extensions such as Cheetos lip balm, Heinz pet food, and Life Savers gum met early deaths. And if a brand extension fails, it may harm consumer attitudes toward other products carrying the same brand name. Furthermore, a brand name may not

● Brand extensions: P&G has leveraged the strength of its Mr. Clean brand to launch new lines, including Mr. Clean–branded car washes.

be appropriate to a particular new product, even if it is well made and satisfying—would you consider flying on Hooters Air or wearing an Evian water-filled padded bra (both failed).

Each year, a survey by brand consultancy TippingSprung rates the year's best and worst brand extensions. The most recent poll gave a strong thumbs-up to extensions such as Coppertone sunglasses, Mr. Clean car washes, Zagat physician ratings, and Thin Mint Cookie Blizzard (Girl Scout–inspired treat at Dairy Queen, which sold 10 million in only one month). Among the worst extensions—those that least fit the brand's core values—were Burger King men's apparel, Playboy energy drink, Allstate Green insurance, and Kellogg's hip-hop streetwear. "Marketers have come to learn that the potential harm inflicted on the brand can more than offset short-term revenue opportunities," says TippingSprung co-founder Robert Sprung. "But that doesn't seem to stop many from launching extensions that in retrospect seem questionable or even ludicrous." Thus, companies that are tempted to transfer a brand name must research how well the brand's associations fit the new product.[39]

Multibrands. Companies often market many different brands in a given product category. For example, in the United States, P&G sells six brands of laundry detergent (Tide, Cheer, Gain, Era, Dreft, and Ivory), five brands of shampoo (Pantene, Head & Shoulders, Aussie, Herbal Essences, and Infusium 23); and four brands of dishwashing detergent (Dawn, Ivory, Joy, and Cascade). *Multibranding* offers a way to establish different features that appeal to different customer segments, lock up more reseller shelf space, and capture a larger market share. For example, P&G's six laundry detergent brands combined capture a whopping 62 percent of the U.S. laundry detergent market.

A major drawback of multibranding is that each brand might obtain only a small market share, and none may be very profitable. The company may end up spreading its resources over many brands instead of building a few brands to a highly profitable level. These companies should reduce the number of brands they sell in a given category and set up tighter screening procedures for new brands. This happened to GM, which in recent years has cut numerous brands from its portfolio, including Saturn, Oldsmobile, Pontiac, Hummer, and Saab.

New Brands. A company might believe that the power of its existing brand name is waning, so a new brand name is needed. Or it may create a new brand name when it enters a new product category for which none of its current brand names are appropriate. For example, Toyota created the separate Scion brand, targeted toward millennial consumers.

As with multibranding, offering too many new brands can result in a company spreading its resources too thin. And in some industries, such as consumer packaged goods, consumers and retailers have become concerned that there are already too many brands, with too few differences between them. Thus, P&G, Frito-Lay, Kraft, and other large consumer-product marketers are now pursuing *megabrand* strategies—weeding out weaker or slower-growing brands and focusing their marketing dollars on brands that can achieve the number-one or number-two market share positions with good growth prospects in their categories.

Managing Brands

Companies must manage their brands carefully. First, the brand's positioning must be continuously communicated to consumers. Major brand marketers often spend huge amounts on advertising to create brand awareness and build preference and loyalty. For example, Verizon spends more than $3.7 billion annually to promote its brand. McDonald's spends more than $1.2 billion.[40]

Such advertising campaigns can help create name recognition, brand knowledge, and perhaps even some brand preference. However, the fact is that brands are not maintained by advertising but by customers' *brand experiences*. Today, customers come to know a brand through a wide range of contacts and touch points. These include advertising but also personal experience with the brand, word of mouth, company Web pages, and many others. The company must put as much care into managing these touch points as it does into producing its ads. "Managing each customer's experience is perhaps the most important

● Managing brands requires managing "touch points." Says a former Disney executive: "A brand is a living entity, and it is enriched or undermined cumulatively over time, the product of a thousand small gestures."

ingredient in building [brand] loyalty," states one branding expert. "Every memorable interaction . . . must be completed with excellence and . . . must reinforce your brand essence." ● A former Disney top executive agrees: "A brand is a living entity, and it is enriched or undermined cumulatively over time, the product of a thousand small gestures."[41]

The brand's positioning will not take hold fully unless everyone in the company lives the brand. Therefore the company needs to train its people to be customer centered. Even better, the company should carry on internal brand building to help employees understand and be enthusiastic about the brand promise. Many companies go even further by training and encouraging their distributors and dealers to serve their customers well.

Finally, companies need to periodically audit their brands' strengths and weaknesses.[42] They should ask: Does our brand excel at delivering benefits that consumers truly value? Is the brand properly positioned? Do all of our consumer touch points support the brand's positioning? Do the brand's managers understand what the brand means to consumers? Does the brand receive proper, sustained support? The brand audit may turn up brands that need more support, brands that need to be dropped, or brands that must be rebranded or repositioned because of changing customer preferences or new competitors.

REVIEWING Objectives AND KEY Terms

A product is more than a simple set of tangible features. Each product or service offered to customers can be viewed on three levels. The *core customer value* consists of the core problem-solving benefits that consumers seek when they buy a product. The *actual product* exists around the core and includes the quality level, features, design, brand name, and packaging. The *augmented product* is the actual product plus the various services and benefits offered with it, such as a warranty, free delivery, installation, and maintenance.

Objective 1 Define *product* and the major classifications of products and services. (pp 224–229)

Broadly defined, a *product* is anything that can be offered to a market for attention, acquisition, use, or consumption that might satisfy a want or need. Products include physical objects but also services, events, persons, places, organizations, or ideas, or mixtures of these entities. *Services* are products that consist of activities, benefits, or satisfactions offered for sale that are essentially intangible, such as banking, hotel, tax preparation, and home-repair services.

Products and services fall into two broad classes based on the types of consumers that use them. *Consumer products*—those bought by final consumers—are usually classified according to consumer shopping habits (convenience products, shopping products, specialty products, and unsought products). *Industrial products*—purchased for further processing or for use in conducting a business—include materials and parts, capital items, and supplies and services. Other marketable entities—such as organizations, persons, places, and ideas—can also be thought of as products.

Objective 2 Describe the decisions companies make regarding their individual products and services, product lines, and product mixes. (pp 229–236)

Individual product decisions involve product attributes, branding, packaging, labeling, and product support services. *Product attribute* decisions involve product quality, features, and style and design. *Branding* decisions include selecting a brand name and developing a brand strategy. *Packaging* provides many key benefits, such as protection, economy, convenience, and promotion. Package decisions often include designing *labels*, which identify, describe, and possibly promote the product. Companies also develop *product support services* that enhance customer service and satisfaction and safeguard against competitors.

Most companies produce a product line rather than a single product. A *product line* is a group of products that are related in function, customer-purchase needs, or distribution channels. All product lines and items offered to customers by a particular seller make up the *product mix*. The mix can be described by four dimensions: width, length, depth, and consistency. These dimensions are the tools for developing the company's product strategy.

Objective 3 Identify the four characteristics that affect the marketing of services and the additional marketing considerations that services require. (pp 236–243)

Services are characterized by four key characteristics: they are *intangible*, *inseparable*, *variable*, and *perishable*. Each characteristic poses problems and marketing requirements. Marketers work to find ways to make the service more tangible, increase the productivity of providers who are inseparable from their products, standardize quality in the face of variability, and improve demand movements and supply capacities in the face of service perishability.

Good service companies focus attention on *both* customers and employees. They understand the *service profit chain*, which links service firm profits with employee and customer satisfaction. Services marketing strategy calls not only for external marketing but also for *internal marketing* to motivate employees and *interactive marketing* to create service delivery skills among service providers. To succeed, service marketers must create *competitive differentiation*, offer high *service quality*, and find ways to increase *service productivity*.

Objective 4 Discuss branding strategy—the decisions companies make in building and managing their brands. (pp 243–252)

Some analysts see brands as *the* major enduring asset of a company. Brands are more than just names and symbols; they embody everything that the product or the service *means* to consumers. *Brand equity* is the positive differential effect that knowing the brand name has on customer response to the product or the service. A brand with strong brand equity is a very valuable asset.

In building brands, companies need to make decisions about brand positioning, brand name selection, brand sponsorship, and brand development. The most powerful *brand positioning* builds around strong consumer beliefs and values. *Brand name selection* involves finding the best brand name based on a careful review of product benefits, the target market, and proposed marketing strategies. A manufacturer has four *brand sponsorship* options: it can launch a *national brand* (or manufacturer's brand), sell to resellers who use a *private brand*, market *licensed brands*, or join forces with another company to *co-brand* a product. A company also has four choices when it comes to developing brands. It can introduce *line extensions*, *brand extensions*, *multibrands*, or *new brands*.

Companies must build and manage their brands carefully. The brand's positioning must be continuously communicated to consumers. Advertising can help. However, brands are not maintained by advertising but by customers' *brand experiences*. Customers come to know a brand through a wide range of contacts and interactions. The company must put as much care into managing these touch points as it does into producing its ads. Companies must periodically audit their brands' strengths and weaknesses.

KEY Terms

OBJECTIVE 1

Product (p 224)
Service (p 224)
Consumer product (p 226)
Convenience product (p 226)
Shopping product (p 226)
Specialty product (p 226)
Unsought product (p 227)
Industrial product (p 227)
Social marketing (p 229)

OBJECTIVE 2

Product quality (p 230)
Brand (p 231)
Packaging (p 232)
Product line (p 234)
Product mix (product portfolio) (p 235)

OBJECTIVE 3

Service intangibility (p 236)
Service inseparability (p 237)
Service variability (p 238)

Service perishability (p 238)
Service profit chain (p 238)
Internal marketing (p 240)
Interactive marketing (p 240)

OBJECTIVE 4

Brand equity (p 243)
Store brand (private brand) (p 246)
Co-branding (p 249)
Line extension (p 250)
Brand extension (p 250)

PEARSON mymarketinglab

- Check your understanding of the concepts and key terms using the mypearsonmarketinglab study plan for this chapter.
- Apply the concepts in a business context using the simulation entitled **Service Marketing.**

DISCUSSING & APPLYING THE Concepts

Discussing the Concepts

1. Define *product* and the three levels of product. (AACSB: Communication)

2. Compare and contrast industrial products and consumer products. (AACSB: Communication; Reflective Thinking)

3. Explain the importance of product quality and discuss how marketers use quality to create customer value. (AACSB: Communication)

4. Compare and contrast the four brand sponsorship options available to a manufacturer and give an example of each. (AACSB: Communication; Reflective Thinking)

5. Discuss the brand development strategies marketers use to develop brands. Give an example of each strategy. (AACSB: Communication; Reflective Thinking)

6. Describe the four characteristics of services that marketers must consider when designing marketing programs. According to these characteristics, how do the services offered by a massage therapist differ from those offered by a grocery store? (AACSB: Communication, Reflective Thinking)

Applying the Concepts

1. What do Betty Crocker, Pillsbury, Cheerios, and Hamburger Helper have in common? They are all familiar brands that are part of the General Mills product mix. Visit the General Mills Web site (www.generalmills.com) and examine its list of brands. Name and define the four dimensions of a company's product mix and describe General Mills' product mix on these dimensions. (AACSB: Communication; Reflective Thinking; Use of IT)

2. Branding is not just for products and services; states are getting in on the action, too, as you learned from reading about *place marketing* in the chapter. One of the most recent examples of state branding comes from Michigan with its "Pure Michigan" campaign, resulting in millions of dollars of tourism revenue. Other famous place branding campaigns include "Virginia is for Lovers," "Florida—the Sunshine State," and "What Happens in Vegas Stays in Vegas." In a small group, develop a brand identity proposal for your state.

Present your idea to the rest of the class and explain the meaning you are trying to convey. (AACSB: Communication; Reflective Thinking)

3. A product's package is often considered a "silent salesperson." It is the last marketing effort before consumers make a selection in the store. One model that is used to evaluate a product's package is the view model: visibility, information, emotion, and workability. Visibility refers to the package's ability to stand out among competing products on the store shelf. Information is the type and amount of information included on the package. Some packages try to simulate an emotional response to influence buyers. Finally, all product packages perform the basic function of protecting and dispensing the product. Select two competing brands in a product category and evaluate each brand's packaging on these dimensions. Which brand's packaging is superior? Suggest ways to improve the other brand's packaging. (AACSB: Communication; Reflective Thinking)

FOCUS ON Technology

Who would pay $330,000 for a virtual space station? Or $100,000 for an asteroid space resort? How about $99,000 for a virtual bank license? Players of Entropia Universe, a massively multiplayer online game (MMOG), did. Those players are making money, and so are the game developers. There's a new business model—called "freemium"—driving the economics of these games. Under this model, users play for free but can purchase virtual goods with real money. Worldwide sales of virtual goods were $2.2 billion in 2009 and are predicted to reach $6 billion by 2013. Most virtual goods are inexpensive—costing about $1—such as the tractor you can buy in *Farmerville* or a weapon in *World of*

Warcraft. That doesn't seem like much, but when you consider that Zynga's *Frontierville* had five million players within one month of launch, we're talking real money!

1. How would you classify virtual goods—a tangible good, an experience, or a service? Discuss the technological factors enabling the growth of virtual goods. (AACSB: Communication; Reflective Thinking)

2. How do players purchase virtual goods? Identify three virtual currencies and their value in U.S. dollars. (AACSB: Communication; Reflective Thinking)

FOCUS ON Ethics

"Meet us before you need us"—that's the motto of a cemetery in Denver. Facing decreasing demand as more Americans choose cremation, cemeteries across the country are marketing to the living in hopes they will become customers in the future. Although funeral homes and cemeteries have long urged customers to prepurchase funeral services before they are needed, it's the new marketing that is drawing criticism. Some activities are low-key, such as poetry workshops, art shows, and nature walks, but some are downright lively. One cemetery staged a fireworks show and sky divers. Other festivities include concerts, outdoor movies, and clowns. Cemetery directors pine for the old days when, more than

a century ago, cemeteries were a place for social gatherings where families visited and picnicked near a loved one's grave. Although many of the new activities are staged in the evening, some occur during the day, so directors must use discretion to avoid interrupting a funeral.

1. What types of products are burial plots and prepurchased funeral services? Explain. (AACSB: Communication; Reflective Thinking)

2. Are these marketing activities appropriate for this product? (AACSB: Communication; Ethical Reasoning)

MARKETING & THE Economy

Batteries Plus

A retail store that sells only batteries? That might sound like a sure-fire product flop in any economy. But weak economic conditions during and following the Great Recession have given a major jolt to Batteries Plus, the nation's first and largest all-battery franchise operation. Same-store sales are up a whopping 20 percent year-over-year. What is the secret to this chain's success? Demand for its products and services comes from products that retain high

consumption patterns regardless of economic conditions. Specifically, no matter what the economy, people and businesses alike still use laptops, mp3 players, digital cameras, cell phones, camcorders, and even vehicles. And all these necessary items need battery power. In fact, as people hold onto their devices longer instead of replacing them, that's all the better for Batteries Plus. As older batteries lose their ability to hold a charge, consumers head to Batteries Plus for replacements. This dynamic has made Batteries Plus one of the top franchise opportunities in the United States. People may cut back on luxuries, but the demand for batteries is here to stay.

1. Based on derived demand principles—as in the nature of demand for Batteries Plus's market offering—what other businesses should do well in a weak economy?

2. If Batteries Plus does nothing, it still does well in an economic downturn. What recommendations would you make to Batteries Plus to take even better advantage of such conditions and position itself for an economic upturn?

MARKETING BY THE Numbers

What is a brand's worth? It depends on who is measuring it. For example, in 2009, Google was valued to be worth $100 billion by one brand valuation company but only $32 billion by another. Although this variation is extreme, it is not uncommon to find valuations of the same brand differing by $20 to $30 billion. Interbrand and BrandZ publish global brand value rankings each year, but a comparison of these two companies' 2009 ranking reveals an overlap of only six of the top ten brands.

1. Compare and contrast the methodologies used by Interbrand (www.interbrand.com) and BrandZ (www.brandz.com) to determine brand value. Explain why there is a discrepancy in the rankings from these two companies. (AACSB: Communication; Reflective Thinking; Analytical Reasoning)

2. In 2008, BrandZ ranked Toyota the number one brand of automobiles, valuing the brand at more than $35 billion. In 2010, however, it valued the Toyota brand under $22 billion. Discuss some of the reasons for the drop in Toyota's brand value. (AACSB: Communication; Reflective Thinking)

VIDEO Case

General Mills—GoGurt
General Mills makes a lot of food. As the sixth largest food company in the world, it sold almost $15 billion worth of packaged food last year. In the United States alone, General Mills markets more than 100 leading brands, such as Cheerios, Betty Crocker, Pillsbury, and Green Giant. With all this experience in managing brands, it has an advantage when it comes to building equity in brands.

Such is the case of GoGurt. The GoGurt video illustrates how General Mills virtually created the category of portable yogurt. But as competitive pressures mounted and dipped into GoGurt's market share, the brand faced many challenges. GoGurt managers needed to apply many branding and brand management concepts to turn GoGurt around and reestablish it as the dominant market leader. After viewing the video featuring GoGurt, answer the following questions about the company.

1. GoGurt is the pioneer brand in its category. Is that an advantage or a disadvantage?

2. Discuss brand equity as it relates to GoGurt.

3. How did the managers of GoGurt apply principles of branding to confront the challenges that the brand faced?

COMPANY Case

Las Vegas: What's Not Happening in Vegas

When you hear someone mention Las Vegas, what comes to mind? Sin City? Wholesome entertainment for the entire family? An indulgent luxury vacation? Or perhaps a value-oriented reward for hard-working Americans? If you answered "all of the above," you wouldn't necessarily be wrong. The truth: All of these have been characteristics associated with Las Vegas over the years. In recent times, the Las Vegas Convention and Visitors Authority (LVCVA) fielded several national ad campaigns. Tourism is Vegas's biggest industry, and the LVCVA is charged with maintaining the city's brand image and keeping visitors coming to one of the world's most famous cities.

Although the positioning of the Vegas brand has changed from time to time, the town will probably never entirely lose the "Sin City" label. That title was born when Las Vegas was young—an anything-goes gambling town full of smoke-filled casinos, bawdy all-girl revues, all-you-can-eat buffets, Elvis impersonators, and no-wait weddings on the Vegas Strip. This was the Vegas epitomized by the Rat Pack, when Frank Sinatra, Dean Martin, Sammy Davis Jr., and the rest of the crew appeared nightly on stage to standing-room-only crowds at the Sands Hotel. Sinatra was even known for referring to anywhere that wasn't Las Vegas as "dullsville."

But as the 1990s rolled around, many Las Vegas officials felt that the town needed to broaden its target audience. So they set out to appeal to—of all things—families. Some of the biggest casinos on the Las Vegas Strip built roller coasters and other thrill rides, world-class water parks, and family-friendly shows like Treasure Island's live-action swashbuckler spectacle, visible to everyone passing by on the street. Although this strategy seemed effective for a brief time, marketers came to realize that the family image just didn't sync well with the classic vices that were still alive and well in Vegas.

As the LVCVA started to consider its options, the terrorist attacks of September 11, 2001, dealt Las Vegas tourism one of its worst blows ever. Declining tourism led to 15,000 lost jobs. The LVCVA decided that it was time to unabashedly proclaim that Las Vegas was a destination for adults. That didn't just mean a return to the classic vices. The LVCVA engineered an image of Vegas as a luxury destination oozing with excess and indulgence. The theme parks were replaced by five-star resorts, high-rise condos, expansive shopping malls filled with the world's top luxury brands, and restaurants bearing the names of world-renowned chefs. A new breed of expensive stage shows for adult audiences replaced family-friendly entertainment. This change of strategy worked. Even as Las Vegas struggled through economic recovery in the post 9-11 world, visitors returned in record numbers.

However, to Rossi Ralenkotter, CEO of the LVCVA, it soon became apparent that the town was much more than just an assortment of facilities and amenities. "We talked to old customers and new customers to determine the essence of the brand of Las Vegas," he said. The LVCVA found that to the nearly 40 million who flocked to the city each year, Vegas is an emotional connection—a total brand experience.

And just what *is* the "Las Vegas experience"? Research showed that when people come to Las Vegas, they're a little naughtier—a little less inhibited. They stay out longer, eat more, do some gambling, and spend more on shopping and dining. "We found that [the Las Vegas experience] centered on adult freedom," says Ralenkotter. "People could stay up all night and do things they wouldn't normally do in their own towns."

Based on these customer insights, the LVCVA coined the now-familiar catchphrase—"Only Vegas: What happens here, stays here." The phrase captured the essence of the Las Vegas experience—that it's okay to be a little naughty in Vegas. That simple phrase became the centerpiece of what is now deemed one of the most successful tourism campaigns in history. The campaign transformed Las Vegas's image from the down-and-dirty "Sin City" to the enticing and luxurious "Only Vegas."

The $75 million ad campaign showed the naughty nature of people once they arrive in Las Vegas. In one ad, a woman spontaneously married a visibly younger man in a Las Vegas wedding chapel. Then, ignoring his ardent pleas, she kissed him goodbye and pulled herself away, insisting that she had to get back to her business convention. In another ad, an outgoing young woman is shown introducing herself to various men, each time giving a different name. In a third ad, a sexy woman hops into a limo, flirts with the driver, and emerges from the car at the airport for her trip home as a conservative business woman. At the end of each ad was the simple reminder, "What happens here, stays here."

The LVCVA continued investing heavily in the bold and provocative campaign and in a variation on the theme, "Your Vegas is showing." All the while, Las Vegas experienced its biggest growth boom in history. Hotel occupancy rates hovered at an incredible 90 percent, visitors came in ever-increasing numbers, and there was seemingly no end to the construction of lavish new luxury properties. To top it off, Las Vegas was dubbed the number two hottest brand by respected brand consultancy Landor Associates, right behind Google. It seemed that the LVCVA had found the magic formula and that Vegas had found its true identity. With everything going so well, what could possibly go wrong?

Then in 2008, Las Vegas suffered another one-two punch. First, the worst recession since the Great Depression had consumers scaling back on unnecessary expenses. Second, in the wake of government bailouts and a collapsing financial industry, company CEOs and executives everywhere came under scrutiny

for lavish expenses. Suddenly, Las Vegas' carefully nurtured, naughty, indulgent image, made even prudent, serious company conferences held there look bad. It didn't help matters when President Obama delivered a statement that Las Vegas' mayor, Oscar Goodman, perceived as the straw that broke the camel's back. Obama scolded Wall Street executives by saying, "You can't get corporate jets; you can't go take a trip to Las Vegas or go down to the Super Bowl on the taxpayer's dime." As a result of the new economic realities, both leisure travel and the convention industry—two staples in Las Vegas' success—took a big hit.

As a result, 2008 and 2009 were some of the worst years ever for Las Vegas. For 2009, the total number of visitors dropped to 36.4 million, 7 percent less than the 2007 peak of 39.1 million. This translated into a 24 percent decrease in convention attendance, a 22 percent drop in room occupancy, and a 10 percent decline in gambling revenues. "People aren't coming in the numbers they used to, and those that are bet on the cheaper tables" said Steven Kent, an analyst for Goldman Sachs. Nevada's unemployment rate climbed to one of the highest in the United States. The Las Vegas hospitality industry responded by chopping prices. Rooms on the Las Vegas Strip could be had as cheaply as $25 a night. Gourmet meals were touted for half price. The town was practically begging for visitors.

After years of successfully pedaling Vegas naughtiness as the primary selling point, the LVCVA realized it had to make a shift. So in the midst of the economic carnage, with so much to offer and great deals to be had, it focused on the value and affordability of a Vegas vacation. A new ad campaign, "Vegas Bound," urged hard-working Americans to take a well-deserved break in Las Vegas to recharge their batteries before returning return home to brave the tough economy. A series of Vegas Bound ads and online mini-documentaries showed average Americans in high-end nightclubs, spas, and restaurants. One grinning 81-year-old woman was even shown giving a thumbs-up after an indoor skydiving session.

"We had to think how we should address our customers during this financial crisis when they're reluctant to make big financial commitments," said Ralenkotter at the start of the campaign. "We're appealing to Americans saying, 'You're working hard. It's OK to take a break.'" The campaign didn't eliminate glamour and luxury. Rather, it repackaged these traits in an "affordable" and "well-deserved" wrapper.

But after so many years of hearing about Las Vegas as a guilt-free adult playground, no matter what the ad campaign said, consumers had a hard time seeing Vegas as prudent. Research showed that even in a painful recession, consumers still saw Vegas for what it was: a place they could go to for simple pleasures not available at home. It took the LVCVA only five months to pull the plug on "Vegas Bound" and resurrect "What happens here, stays here." In a near 180-degree flip, Ralenkotter said, "We feel it is time to get back to our brand messaging."

Although there is rarely a magic bullet in a situation like the one Las Vegas faced, the LVCVA's return to its core brand message seems to be working. As 2010 unfolded, the number of visitors was up. The LVCVA projected a 3 percent growth in visitors for the year to 37.5 million. "I think there's pent-up demand," said Cathy Tull, senior vice president of marketing for the authority. "People want to travel, they want to escape, and Vegas works very well for that."

Just as the needle started to budge, MGM Resorts International opened the most ambitious project Las Vegas had ever seen. In fact, its $8.5 billion CityCenter was said to be the largest privately funded construction project in U.S. history. A pedestrian-friendly resort, CityCenter was designed as a small city in and of itself with four luxury hotels, two residential condo towers, and a 500,000-square-foot high-end shopping and dining center.

Adding 6,000 rooms and 12,000 jobs to the Las Vegas Strip has met with mixed reactions. Some speculate that this game-changing property will put an exclamation point on Las Vegas' image and provide additional oomph in a time of crisis. "History has shown that new properties increase visitation across the board," said Ralenkotter. But others see the introduction of such a large property as hazardous to recovery. "Will it cannibalize other properties?" asked Tony Henthorne, professor and chair of tourism and convention administration at the University of Nevada at Las Vegas. "Probably so, within a short-term period."

But even as such major signs of life are sprouting up along the Las Vegas Strip, there's an air of caution. Jim Murren, CEO for MGM believes his company is not yet out of the woods. When asked if he thought CityCenter was in the clear, he responded emphatically. "Absolutely not. We're not declaring victory at all. We are a year or two away from even having a chance to consider that." That is probably the best attitude to take. After all, the Las Vegas Monorail just filed for bankruptcy. Two other major projects that were expected to boost the Vegas economy have been shelved. Cheap (i.e., inexpensive) rooms are still available on the Las Vegas Strip. And although tourist visits are on the rise, even if Las Vegas makes its projections for 2010, it will still be down from its 2007 peak.

Las Vegas has certainly had its share of ups and downs. Times may be brightening now. But the city will face many challenges in the months and years to come. Goldman analyst Kent expresses confidence in the brand. "For the long-term, we believe in Vegas and its ability to transform itself and attract more customers." R&R Partners, the ad agency handling the Las Vegas marketing campaigns, made an important discovery that supports Kent's point of view. It found through its research that, especially during hard economic times, people wanted to know that the same Vegas they've known and loved is still there.

Questions for Discussion

1. Given all the changes in the branding strategy for Las Vegas over the years, has the Vegas brand had a consistent meaning to consumers? Is this a benefit or a detriment to the city as it moves forward?

2. What is Las Vegas selling? What are visitors really buying? Discuss these questions in terms of the core benefit, actual product, and augmented product levels.

3. Will the most recent efforts by the LVCVA continue to work? Why or why not?

4. What recommendations would you make to LVCVA managers for Las Vegas' future?

Sources: Jeff Delong, "After a Down Year, Vegas Hoping for a Rebound," *USA Today*, May 21, 2010, p. 2A; Nancy Trejos, "Las Vegas Bets the Future on a Game-Changing New Hotel Complex," *Washington Post*, January 31, 2010, p. F01; Tamara Audi, "Vegas Plans a New Push to Attract More People," *Wall Street Journal*, January 7, 2008, p. B2; John King, "Luck Running Low in Las Vegas—Will It Turn Around," *CNN.com*, May 22, 2009, accessed at www.cnn.com; Tamara Audi, "Vegas Tries Luck with Old Slogan," *Wall Street Journal*, May 13, 2009, p. B5; Damon Hodge, "Tourism Chief Aims to Continue Vegas' Hot Streak," *Travel Weekly*, February 12, 2007, p. 64; and Tamara Audi, "Las Vegas Touts Its Affordability," *Wall Street Journal*, February 4, 2009, p. B5.

9 New Product Development and Product Life-Cycle Strategies

Chapter Preview

In the previous chapter, you learned how marketers manage and develop products and brands. In this chapter, we examine two additional product topics: developing new products and managing products through their life cycles. New products are the lifeblood of an organization. However, new-product development is risky, and many new products fail. So, the first part of this chapter lays out a process for finding and growing successful new products. Once introduced, marketers want their products to enjoy long and happy lives. In the second part of this chapter, you'll see that every product passes through several life-cycle stages, and each stage poses new challenges requir-

ing different marketing strategies and tactics. Finally, we wrap up our product discussion by looking at two additional considerations: social responsibility in product decisions and international product and services marketing.

For openers, consider Google, one of the world's most innovative companies. Google seems to come up with an almost unending flow of knock-your-eye-out new technologies and services. If it has to do with finding, refining, or using information, there's probably an innovative Google solution for it. At Google, innovation isn't just a process; it's in the very spirit of the place.

Google: New-Product Innovation at the Speed of Light

Google is wildly innovative. It recently topped *Fast Company* magazine's list of the world's most innovative companies, and it regularly ranks among everyone else's top two or three innovators. Google is also spectacularly successful. Despite formidable competition from giants like Microsoft and Yahoo!, Google's share in its core business—online search—stands at a decisive 66 percent, 2.5 times the combined market shares of its two closest competitors. The company also captures 86 percent of the mobile-search market and 60 percent of all search-related advertising revenues.

But Google has grown to become much more than just an Internet search and advertising company. Google's mission is "to organize the world's information and make it universally accessible and useful." In Google's view, information is a kind of natural resource—one to be mined and refined and universally distributed. That idea unifies what would otherwise appear to be a widely diverse set of Google projects, such as mapping the world, searching the Web on a cell phone screen, or even providing for the early detection of flu epidemics. If it has to do with harnessing and using information, Google's got it covered in some innovative way.

Google knows how to innovate. At many companies, new-product development is a cautious, step-by-step affair that might take a year or two to unfold. In contrast, Google's free-wheeling new-product development process moves at the speed of light. The nimble innovator implements major new services in less time than it takes competitors to refine and approve an initial idea. For example, a Google senior project manager de-

scribes the lightning-quick development of iGoogle, Google's customizable home page:

> It was clear to Google that there were two groups [of Google users]: people who loved the site's clean, classic look and people who wanted tons of information there—e-mail, news, local weather. [For those who wanted a fuller home page,] iGoogle started out with me and three engineers. I was 22, and I thought, "This is awesome." Six weeks later, we launched the first version in May. The happiness metrics were good, there was healthy growth, and by September, we had [iGoogle fully operational with] a link on Google.com.

Such fast-paced innovation would boggle the minds of product developers at most other companies, but at Google it is standard operating procedure. "That's what we do," says Google's vice president for search products and user experience. "The hardest part about indoctrinating people into our culture is when engineers show me a prototype

> **Google's famously chaotic innovation process has unleashed a seemingly unending flurry of diverse new products. But at Google, innovation is more than a process. It's part of the company's DNA. "Where does innovation happen at Google? It happens everywhere."**

and I'm like, 'Great, let's go!' They'll say, 'Oh, no, it's not ready.' I tell them, 'The Googly thing is to launch it early on Google Labs [a site where users can try out experimental Google applications] and then to iterate, learning what the market wants—and making it great.'" Adds a Google engineering manager, "We set an operational tempo: When in doubt, do something. If you have two paths and you're not sure which is right, take the fastest path."

According to Google CEO Eric Schmidt, when it comes to new-product development at Google, there are no two-year plans. The company's new-product planning looks ahead only four to five months. Schmidt says that he would rather see projects fail quickly than see a carefully planned, long drawn-out project fail.

Google's famously chaotic innovation process has unleashed a seemingly unending flurry of diverse products, ranging from an e-mail service (Gmail), a blog search engine (Google Blog Search), an online payment service (Google Checkout), and a photo sharing service (Google Picasa) to a universal platform for mobile-phone applications (Google Android), a cloud-friendly Web browser (Chrome), projects for mapping and exploring the world (Google Maps and Google Earth), and even an early-warning system for flu outbreaks in your area (FluTrends). Google claims that FluTrends has identified outbreaks two weeks sooner than has the U.S. Centers for Disease Control and Prevention.

Google is open to new-product ideas from about any source. What ties it all together is the company's passion for helping people find and use information. Innovation is the responsibility of every Google employee. Google engineers are encouraged to spend 20 percent of their time developing their own new-product ideas. And all new Google ideas are quickly tested in beta form by the ultimate judges—those who will use them. According to one observer:

> Any time you cram some 20,000 of the world's smartest people into one company, you can expect to grow a garden of unrelated ideas. Especially when you give some of those geniuses one workday a week—Google's famous "20 percent time"—to work on whatever projects fan their passions. And especially when you create Google Labs

(www.googlelabs.com), a Web site where the public can kick the tires on half-baked Google creations. Some Labs projects go on to become real Google services, and others are quietly snuffed out.

In the end, at Google, innovation is more than a process—it's part of the company's DNA. "Where does innovation happen at Google? It happens everywhere," says a Google research scientist.

Talk to Googlers at various levels and departments, and one powerful theme emerges: Whether they're designing search engines for the blind or preparing meals for their colleagues, these people feel that their work can change the world. The marvel of Google is its ability to continue to instill a sense of creative fearlessness and ambition in its employees. Prospective hires are often asked, "If you could change the world using Google's resources, what would you build?" But here, this isn't a goofy or even theoretical question: Google wants to know because thinking—and building—on that scale is what Google does. This, after all, is the company that wants to make available online every page of every book ever published. Smaller-gauge ideas die of disinterest. When it comes to innovation, Google *is* different. But the difference isn't tangible. It's in the air—in the spirit of the place.[1]

> Google is spectacularly successful and wildly innovative. Ask the people who work there, and they'll tell you that innovation is more than just a process; it's in the air, in the spirit of the place.

As the Google story suggests, companies that excel at developing and managing new products reap big rewards. Every product seems to go through a life cycle: it is born, goes through several phases, and eventually dies as newer products come along that create new or greater value for customers.

This product life cycle presents two major challenges: First, because all products eventually decline, a firm must be good at developing new products to replace aging ones (the challenge of *new-product development*). Second, a firm must be good at adapting its marketing strategies in the face of changing tastes, technologies, and competition as products pass through stages (the challenge of *product life-cycle strategies*). We first look at the problem of finding and developing new products and then at the problem of managing them successfully over their life cycles.

> **Author Comment** | New products are the lifeblood of a company. As old products mature and fade away, companies must develop new ones to take their place. For example, only eight years after it unveiled its first iPod, 51 percent of Apple's revenues come from iPods, iPhones, and iTunes.

New-Product Development Strategy (pp 260–261)

A firm can obtain new products in two ways. One is through *acquisition*—by buying a whole company, a patent, or a license to produce someone else's product. The other is through the firm's own **new-product development** efforts. By *new products* we mean original products, product improvements, product modifications, and new brands that the firm develops through its own R&D efforts. In this chapter, we concentrate on new-product development.

New-product development
The development of original products, product improvements, product modifications, and new brands through the firm's own product development efforts.

New products are important—to both customers and the marketers who serve them. For customers, they bring new solutions and variety to their lives. For companies, new products are a key source of growth. Even in a down economy, companies must continue to innovate. New products provide new ways to connect with customers as they adapt their buying to changing economic times. Bad times are "when winners and losers get created," says former Xerox CEO Anne Mulcahy. "The ability to reinforce great marketing and great brand is extraordinarily important." John Hayes, CEO of American Express, agrees: "The world will pass you by if you are not constantly innovating."[2]

Yet innovation can be very expensive and very risky. New products face tough odds. According to one estimate, 80 percent of all new products fail or dramatically underperform. Each year, companies lose an estimated $20 billion to $30 billion on failed food products alone.[3]

Why do so many new products fail? There are several reasons. Although an idea may be good, the company may overestimate market size. The actual product may be poorly designed. Or it might be incorrectly positioned, launched at the wrong time, priced too high, or poorly advertised. A high-level executive might push a favorite idea despite poor marketing research findings. Sometimes the costs of product development are higher than expected, and sometimes competitors fight back harder than expected. However, the reasons behind some new-product failures seem pretty obvious. Try the following on for size:[4]

Strolling the aisles of GfK's NewProductWorks collection is like finding yourself in a new-product history museum. ● Many of the more than 110,000 products on display

● Visiting GfK's NewProductWorks Showcase and Learning Center is like finding yourself in some nightmare version of a supermarket. Each product failure represents squandered dollars and hopes.

were quite successful. Others, however, were abject flops. Behind each flop are squandered dollars and hopes and the classic question, "What were they thinking?" Some products failed because they simply didn't bring value to customers—for example, Look of Buttermilk Shampoo, Cucumber antiperspirant spray, or Premier smokeless cigarettes. *Smokeless* cigarettes? What were they thinking? Other companies failed because they attached trusted brand names to something totally out of character. Can you imagine swallowing Ben-Gay aspirin? Or how about Gerber Singles food for adults (perhaps the tasty pureed sweet-and-sour pork or chicken Madeira)? Other misbegotten attempts to stretch a good name include Cracker Jack cereal, Exxon fruit punch, Smucker's premium ketchup, Fruit of the Loom laundry detergent, and Harley-Davidson cake-decorating kits. Really, what were they thinking?

Author | Comment Companies can't just hope that they'll stumble across good new products. Instead, they must develop a systematic new-product development process.

The New-Product Development Process (pp 261–269)

Companies face a problem: They must develop new products, but the odds weigh heavily against success. To create successful new products, a company must understand its consumers, markets, and competitors and develop products that deliver superior value to customers. It must carry out strong new-product planning and set up a systematic, customer-driven *new-product development process* for finding and growing new products. ● **Figure 9.1** shows the eight major steps in this process.

Idea Generation

Idea generation
The systematic search for new-product ideas.

New-product development starts with **idea generation**—the systematic search for new-product ideas. A company typically generates hundreds of ideas, even thousands, to find a few good ones. Major sources of new-product ideas include internal sources and external sources such as customers, competitors, distributors and suppliers, and others.

Internal Idea Sources

Using *internal sources*, the company can find new ideas through formal R&D. However, in one survey, 750 global CEOs reported that only 14 percent of their innovation ideas came from traditional R&D. Instead, 41 percent came from employees, and 36 percent came from customers.[5]

New-product development starts with good new-product ideas—*lots* of them. For example, Cisco's recent I-Prize "crowdsourcing" challenge attracted 1,200 ideas from 2,500 innovators in 104 countries.

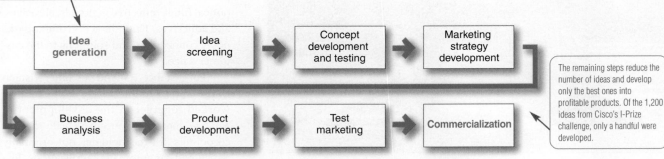

The remaining steps reduce the number of ideas and develop only the best ones into profitable products. Of the 1,200 ideas from Cisco's I-Prize challenge, only a handful were developed.

● **FIGURE | 9.1**
Major Stages in New-Product Development

Thus, beyond its internal R&D process, companies can pick the brains of its employees—from executives to scientists, engineers, and manufacturing staff to salespeople. Many companies have developed successful "intrapreneurial" programs that encourage employees to envision and develop new-product ideas. For example, the Internet networking company Cisco makes it everybody's business to come up with great ideas. It set up an internal wiki called Idea Zone or I-Zone, through which any Cisco employee can propose an idea for a new product or comment on or modify someone else's proposed idea. Since its inception, I-Zone has generated hundreds of ideas, leading to the formation of four new Cisco business units.[6]

External Idea Sources

Companies can also obtain good new-product ideas from any of a number of external sources. For example, *distributors and suppliers* can contribute ideas. Distributors are close to the market and can pass along information about consumer problems and new-product possibilities. Suppliers can tell the company about new concepts, techniques, and materials that can be used to develop new products. *Competitors* are another important source. Companies watch competitors' ads to get clues about their new products. They buy competing new products, take them apart to see how they work, analyze their sales, and decide whether they should bring out a new product of their own. Other idea sources include trade magazines, shows, and seminars; government agencies; advertising agencies; marketing research firms; university and commercial laboratories; and inventors.

Perhaps the most important source of new-product ideas are *customers* themselves. The company can analyze customer questions and complaints to find new products that better solve consumer problems. Or it can invite customers to share suggestions and ideas. For example, Starbucks sponsors My Starbucks Idea, a Web site that invites customers to share, discuss, and vote on new product and service ideas. "You know better than anyone else what you want from Starbucks," says the site. "So tell us. What's your Starbucks idea? Revolutionary or simple—we want to hear it."[7]

To harness customer new-product input, 3M has opened nearly two dozen customer innovation centers throughout the world, including sites in the United States, Brazil, Germany, India, China, and Russia. ● The innovation centers not only generate plenty of customer-driven new-product ideas but also help 3M establish productive, long-term customer relationships.[8]

Typically located near company research facilities, the innovation centers engage 3M's corporate customers directly in the innovation process. The idea behind the centers is to gain a richer understanding of customer needs and link these needs to 3M technologies. In a typical customer visit, a customer team meets with 3M marketing and technology experts who pepper them with open-ended questions. Next, together, the customer and 3M teams visit the "World of Innovation" showroom, where they are exposed to more than 40 3M technology platforms—core technologies in areas like optical films, reflective materials, abrasives, and adhesives. This interaction often sparks novel connections and solutions to the customer's needs.

For instance, 3M and customer Visteon Corporation, an automotive supplier, have worked together in the development of a next-generation concept vehicle that incorporates 3M technologies not originally developed for automated applications. Visteon's visit to an innovation center led to the idea of using 3M's 3D technology for navi-

● **Customer-driven new-product ideas: At 3M innovation centers, customer teams meet with 3M marketing and technology experts to spark novel solutions to customer problems.**

gation displays, Thinsulate materials to reduce noise, and optical films to hide functional elements of the dashboard unless the driver wants them displayed.

Crowdsourcing

More broadly, many companies are now developing *crowdsourcing* or *open-innovation* new-product idea programs. **Crowdsourcing** throws the innovation doors wide open, inviting broad communities of people—customers, employees, independent scientists and researchers, and even the public at large—into the new-product innovation process. The idea, says one analyst, is that when it comes to helping to improve "your products, services, Web site, or marketing efforts . . . two heads—or 2,000 or 20,000—are better than one."[9]

For example, when Netflix wanted to improve the accuracy of its Cinematch online recommendation system, which makes movie recommendations to customers based on their ratings of other movies they've rented, it launched a crowdsourcing effort called Netflix Prize.[10]

Crowdsourcing
Inviting broad communities of people—customers, employees, independent scientists and researchers, and even the public at large—into the new-product innovation process.

● **Crowdsourcing: When Netflix wanted ideas for improving the accuracy of its Cinematch online recommendation system, it decided to "open it up to the world," promising a $1 million prize for the best solution.**

It was a quest that Netflix scientists and mathematicians have been working on for about a decade. Rather than hiring even more computer scientists to work on the project, Netflix decided to open it up to the world. "We'd like to think that we have smart people bumping around the building, but we don't have anything compared to the worldwide intelligentsia," says Netflix vice president Steve Swasey. ● The company created a Web site, NetflixPrize.com, which issued an open challenge and promised a $1 million prize to whomever submitted the best solution for improving the accuracy of the Cinematch by at least 10 percent. Nearly three years and more than 51,000 participants later, Netflix awarded the prize to BellKors Pragmatic Chaos, a seven-member superteam consisting of engineers, statisticians, and researchers from the United States, Austria, Canada, and Israel. "It was a very innovative way to generate more ideas," says Swasey. "If you think about it, 51,000 scientists" devoted their intelligence, creativity, and man-hours to the project, all for only $1 million.

Similarly, Dell's IdeaStorm Web site asks consumers or anyone else for insights on how to improve the company's product offering. Users post suggestions, the community votes, and the most popular ideas rise to the top. Since its launch in 2007, the site has received more than 13,000 ideas and 713,000 votes.[11]

Crowdsourcing network InnoCentive puts its corporate clients ("seekers") in touch with its global network of more than 200,000 scientists ("solvers"). The seeker companies post "challenges," and solvers can earn up to $1 million for providing solutions. For example, P&G wanted to create a dishwashing detergent smart enough to reveal when just the right amount of soap has been added to a sink full of dirty dishes. After seeing the problem posted on InnoCentive, an Italian chemist working from her home laboratory solved the problem by creating a new kind of dye that turns dishwater blue when a certain amount of soap is added. Her reward: $30,000. P&G estimates that more than 50 percent of its new-product innovations today have elements that originated outside the company, up from 15 percent in 2000.[12]

Crowdsourcing can produce a flood of innovative ideas. In fact, opening the floodgates to anyone and everyone can overwhelm the company with ideas—some good and some bad. "Even a small crowdsourcing event can generate a few hundred ideas. If I told you next year you're going to get 20,000 ideas from your customers, how would you process that?" For example, when Cisco Systems sponsored an open-innovation effort called I-Prize, soliciting ideas from external sources, it received more than 1,200 distinct ideas from more than 2,500 innovators from 104 countries. "The evaluation process was far more labor-intensive than we'd anticipated," says Cisco's chief technology officer. It required "significant investments of time, energy, patience, and imagination . . . to discern the gems hidden within rough stones." In the end, a team of six Cisco people worked full-time for three months to carve 40 semifinalists from more than 1,200 ideas.[13]

Truly innovative companies don't rely only on one source or another for new-product ideas. Instead, according to one expert, they create "extensive networks for capturing inspiration from every possible source, from employees at every walk of the company to customers to other innovators and myriad points beyond."[14]

Idea Screening

Idea screening
Screening new-product ideas to spot good ideas and drop poor ones as soon as possible.

The purpose of idea generation is to create a large number of ideas. The purpose of the succeeding stages is to *reduce* that number. The first idea-reducing stage is **idea screening**, which helps spot good ideas and drop poor ones as soon as possible. Product development costs rise greatly in later stages, so the company wants to go ahead only with those product ideas that will turn into profitable products.

Many companies require their executives to write up new-product ideas in a standard format that can be reviewed by a new-product committee. The write-up describes the product or the service, the proposed customer value proposition, the target market, and the competition. It makes some rough estimates of market size, product price, development time and costs, manufacturing costs, and rate of return. The committee then evaluates the idea against a set of general criteria.

One marketing expert proposes an R-W-W ("real, win, worth doing") new-product screening framework that asks three questions. First, *Is it real?* Is there a real need and desire for the product and will customers buy it? Is there a clear product concept and will such a product satisfy the market? Second, *Can we win?* Does the product offer a sustainable competitive advantage? Does the company have the resources to make such a product a success? Finally, *Is it worth doing?* Does the product fit the company's overall growth strategy? Does it offer sufficient profit potential? The company should be able to answer yes to all three R-W-W questions before developing the new-product idea further.[15]

Concept Development and Testing

Product concept
A detailed version of the new-product idea stated in meaningful consumer terms.

An attractive idea must be developed into a **product concept**. It is important to distinguish between a product idea, a product concept, and a product image. A *product idea* is an idea for a possible product that the company can see itself offering to the market. A *product concept* is a detailed version of the idea stated in meaningful consumer terms. A *product image* is the way consumers perceive an actual or potential product.

Concept Development

Suppose a car manufacturer has developed a practical battery-powered, all-electric car. ⦿ Its initial prototype is a sleek, sporty roadster convertible that sells for more than $100,000.[16] However, in the near future, it plans to introduce more-affordable, mass-market versions that will compete with today's hybrid cars. This 100 percent electric car will accelerate from zero to sixty miles per hour in 5.6 seconds, travel more than 300 miles on a single charge, recharge in 45 minutes from a normal 120-volt electrical outlet, and cost about one penny per mile to power.

⦿ **This is Tesla's initial all-electric roadster. Later, more-affordable mass-market models will travel more than 300 miles on a single charge, recharge in 45 minutes from a normal 120-volt electrical outlet, and cost about one penny per mile to power.**

Looking ahead, the marketer's task is to develop this new product into alternative product concepts, find out how attractive each concept is to customers, and choose the best one. It might create the following product concepts for this electric car:

- *Concept 1:* An affordably priced midsize car designed as a second family car to be used around town for running errands and visiting friends.
- *Concept 2:* A mid-priced sporty compact appealing to young singles and couples.
- *Concept 3:* A "green" car appealing to environmentally conscious people who want practical, low-polluting transportation.
- *Concept 4:* A high-end midsize utility vehicle appealing to those who love the space SUVs provide but lament the poor gas mileage.

Concept Testing

Concept testing

Testing new-product concepts with a group of target consumers to find out if the concepts have strong consumer appeal.

Concept testing calls for testing new-product concepts with groups of target consumers. The concepts may be presented to consumers symbolically or physically. Here, in more detail, is concept 3:

An efficient, fun-to-drive, battery-powered compact car that seats four. This 100 percent electric wonder provides practical and reliable transportation with no pollution. It goes more than 300 miles on a single charge and costs pennies per mile to operate. It's a sensible, responsible alternative to today's pollution-producing gas-guzzlers. Its fully equipped price is $25,000.

Many firms routinely test new-product concepts with consumers before attempting to turn them into actual new products. For some concept tests, a word or picture description might be sufficient. However, a more concrete and physical presentation of the concept will increase the reliability of the concept test. After being exposed to the concept, consumers then may be asked to react to it by answering questions similar to those in ◉ **Table 9.1**.

The answers to such questions will help the company decide which concept has the strongest appeal. For example, the last question asks about the consumer's intention to buy. Suppose 2 percent of consumers say they "definitely" would buy, and another 5 percent say "probably." The company could project these figures to the full population in this target group to estimate sales volume. Even then, the estimate is uncertain because people do not always carry out their stated intentions.

Marketing Strategy Development

Marketing strategy development

Designing an initial marketing strategy for a new product based on the product concept.

Suppose the carmaker finds that concept 3 for the electric car tests best. The next step is **marketing strategy development**, designing an initial marketing strategy for introducing this car to the market.

The *marketing strategy statement* consists of three parts. The first part describes the target market; the planned value proposition; and the sales, market share, and profit goals for the first few years. Thus:

The target market is younger, well-educated, moderate- to high-income individuals, couples, or small families seeking practical, environmentally responsible transportation.

◉ **TABLE | 9.1** Questions for Battery-Powered Electric Car Concept Test

1. Do you understand the concept of a battery-powered electric car?
2. Do you believe the claims about the car's performance?
3. What are the major benefits of the battery-powered electric car compared with a conventional car?
4. What are its advantages compared with a gas-electric hybrid car?
5. What improvements in the car's features would you suggest?
6. For what uses would you prefer a battery-powered electric car to a conventional car?
7. What would be a reasonable price to charge for the car?
8. Who would be involved in your decision to buy such a car? Who would drive it?
9. Would you buy such a car (definitely, probably, probably not, definitely not)?

The car will be positioned as more fun to drive and less polluting than today's internal combustion engine or hybrid cars. The company will aim to sell 50,000 cars in the first year, at a loss of not more than $15 million. In the second year, the company will aim for sales of 90,000 cars and a profit of $25 million.

The second part of the marketing strategy statement outlines the product's planned price, distribution, and marketing budget for the first year:

The battery-powered electric car will be offered in three colors—red, white, and blue—and will have a full set of accessories as standard features. It will sell at a retail price of $25,000, with 15 percent off the list price to dealers. Dealers who sell more than 10 cars per month will get an additional discount of 5 percent on each car sold that month. A marketing budget of $50 million will be split 50–50 between a national media campaign and local event marketing. Advertising and the Web site will emphasize the car's fun spirit and low emissions. During the first year, $100,000 will be spent on marketing research to find out who is buying the car and what their satisfaction levels are.

The third part of the marketing strategy statement describes the planned long-run sales, profit goals, and marketing mix strategy:

We intend to capture a 3 percent long-run share of the total auto market and realize an after-tax return on investment of 15 percent. To achieve this, product quality will start high and be improved over time. Price will be raised in the second and third years if competition and the economy permit. The total marketing budget will be raised each year by about 10 percent. Marketing research will be reduced to $60,000 per year after the first year.

Business Analysis

Once management has decided on its product concept and marketing strategy, it can evaluate the business attractiveness of the proposal. **Business analysis** involves a review of the sales, costs, and profit projections for a new product to find out whether they satisfy the company's objectives. If they do, the product can move to the product development stage.

To estimate sales, the company might look at the sales history of similar products and conduct market surveys. It can then estimate minimum and maximum sales to assess the range of risk. After preparing the sales forecast, management can estimate the expected costs and profits for the product, including marketing, R&D, operations, accounting, and finance costs. The company then uses the sales and costs figures to analyze the new product's financial attractiveness.

Business analysis
A review of the sales, costs, and profit projections for a new product to find out whether these factors satisfy the company's objectives.

Product development
Developing the product concept into a physical product to ensure that the product idea can be turned into a workable market offering.

Product Development

For many new-product concepts, a product may exist only as a word description, a drawing, or perhaps a crude mock-up. If the product concept passes the business test, it moves into **product development**. Here, R&D or engineering develops the product concept into a physical product. The product development step, however, now calls for a huge jump in investment. It will show whether the product idea can be turned into a workable product.

The R&D department will develop and test one or more physical versions of the product concept. R&D hopes to design a prototype that will satisfy and excite consumers and that can be produced quickly and at budgeted costs. Developing a successful prototype can take days, weeks, months, or even years depending on the product and prototype methods.

Often, products undergo rigorous tests to make sure that they perform safely and effectively, or that consumers will find value in them. Companies can do their own product testing or outsource testing to other firms that specialize in testing.

● **Product testing:** HP signs up consumers to evaluate prototype imaging and printing products in their homes and offices to gain insights about their entire "out-of-box experience."

Marketers often involve actual customers in product testing. ◉ For example, HP signs up consumers to evaluate prototype imaging and printing products in their homes and offices. Participants work with prerelease products for periods ranging from a few days to eight weeks and share their experiences about how the products perform in an actual use environment. The product-testing program gives HP a chance to interact with customers and gain insights about their entire "out-of-box experience," from product setup and operation to system compatibility. HP personnel might even visit participants' homes to directly observe installation and first usage of the product.[17]

A new product must have the required functional features and also convey the intended psychological characteristics. The battery-powered electric car, for example, should strike consumers as being well built, comfortable, and safe. Management must learn what makes consumers decide that a car is well built. To some consumers, this means that the car has "solid-sounding" doors. To others, it means that the car is able to withstand heavy impact in crash tests. Consumer tests are conducted in which consumers test-drive the car and rate its attributes.

Test Marketing

Test marketing
The stage of new-product development in which the product and its proposed marketing program are tested in realistic market settings.

If the product passes both the concept test and the product test, the next step is **test marketing**, the stage at which the product and its proposed marketing program are introduced into realistic market settings. Test marketing gives the marketer experience with marketing a product before going to the great expense of full introduction. It lets the company test the product and its entire marketing program—targeting and positioning strategy, advertising, distribution, pricing, branding and packaging, and budget levels.

The amount of test marketing needed varies with each new product. Test marketing costs can be high, and it takes time that may allow competitors to gain advantages. When the costs of developing and introducing the product are low, or when management is already confident about the new product, the company may do little or no test marketing. In fact, test marketing by consumer-goods firms has been declining in recent years. Companies often do not test-market simple line extensions or copies of successful competitor products.

However, when introducing a new product requires a big investment, when the risks are high, or when management is not sure of the product or its marketing program, a company may do a lot of test marketing. ◉ For instance, KFC conducted more than three years of product and market testing before rolling out its major new Kentucky Grilled Chicken product. The fast-food chain built its legacy on serving crispy, seasoned fried chicken but hopes that the new product will lure back health-conscious consumers who dropped fried chicken from their diets. "This is transformational for our brand," says KFC's chief food innovation officer. Given the importance of the decision, "You might say, 'what took you so long,'" says the chain's president. "I've asked that question a couple of times myself. The answer is we had to get it right."[18]

ARE YOU UNTHINKING WHAT I'M UNTHINKING?

NEW Kentucky Grilled Chicken

TASTE THE UNFRIED SIDE OF KFC.
www.unthinkfc.com

◉ **Test marketing: KFC test marketed its new Kentucky Grilled Chicken product for three years before rolling it out nationally. Says the chain's president, "We had to get it right."**

As an alternative to extensive and costly standard test markets, companies can use controlled test markets or simulated test markets. In *controlled test markets*, such as SymphonyIRI's BehaviorScan, new products and tactics are tested among controlled groups of customers and stores. In each BehaviorScan market, SymphonyIRI maintains a panel of shoppers who report all of their purchases by showing an identification card at checkout in participating stores. Within test stores, SymphonyIRI controls such factors as shelf placement, price, and in-store promotions for the products being tested. SymphonyIRI also measures TV viewing in each panel household and sends special commercials to panel member television sets to test their affect on shopping decisions.[19]

By combining information on each consumer's purchases with consumer demographic and TV viewing information, BehaviorScan can provide store-by-store, week-by-week reports on the sales of tested products and the impact of in-store and in-home marketing efforts. Such controlled test markets usually cost much less than standard test markets and can provide accurate forecasts in as little as 12 to 24 weeks.

Companies can also test new products using *simulated test markets*, in which researchers measure consumer responses to new products and marketing tactics in laboratory stores or simulated shopping environments. Many marketers are now using new online simulated marketing technologies to reduce the costs of test marketing and speed up the process. For example, Frito-Lay worked with the research firm Decision Insight to create an online virtual convenience store in which to test new products and marketing ideas.[20]

Decision Insight's SimuShop online shopping environment lets Frito-Lay's marketers test shopper reactions to different extensions, shelf placements, pricing, and packaging of its Lay's, Doritos, Cheetos, and Fritos brands in a variety of store setups without investing huge amounts of time and money on actual in-store research in different locations. Recruited shoppers visit the online store, browse realistic virtual shelves featuring Frito-Lay's and competing products, click on individual products to view them in more detail, and select products to put in their carts. When the shopping is done, selected customers are questioned in one-on-one, on-screen interviews about why they chose the products they did. Watching the entire decision process unfold gives Frito-Lay marketers reams of information about what would happen in the real world. With 200-some bags of Frito-Lay products sitting on a typical store shelf, the company doesn't have the luxury of test marketing in actual market settings. "For us, that can only really be done virtually," says a Frito-Lay marketer. The SimuShop tests produce a 90 percent or better correlation to real shopper behavior when compared with later real-world data.

Rather than just simulating the shopping environment, P&G recently launched an actual online store that will serve as a "learning lab" by which the company can test new products and marketing concepts. The online store lets P&G quickly do real-time testing of marketing tactics—such as e-coupons, cross-selling efforts, and advertising—and learn how they affect consumer buying. The online store probably won't boost the company's revenues or profits much. Says an analyst, P&G is "more interested in the data [it will produce] about shoppers and what works for them: [new products,] product pairings, environmentally friendly pitches, and packaging options." Says an executive associated with P&G's eStore, "We're creating this giant sandbox for the brands to play in."[21]

Commercialization

Test marketing gives management the information needed to make a final decision about whether to launch the new product. If the company goes ahead with **commercialization**—introducing the new product into the market—it will face high costs. The company may need to build or rent a manufacturing facility. And, in the case of a major new consumer product, it may spend hundreds of millions of dollars for advertising, sales promotion, and other marketing efforts in the first year. For example, to introduce its McCafé coffee in the United States, McDonald's spent $100 million on an advertising blitz that spanned TV, print, radio, outdoor, the Internet, events, public relations, and sampling. Similarly, Verizon spent $100 million to introduce the Droid smart phone, and Microsoft spent $100 million or more on marketing to introduce its Bing search engine.[22]

The company launching a new product must first decide on introduction *timing*. If the carmaker's new battery-powered electric car will eat into the sales of its other cars, the introduction may be delayed. If the car can be improved further, or if the economy is down, the company may wait until the following year to launch it. However, if competitors are ready to introduce their own battery-powered models, the company may push to introduce its car sooner.

Next, the company must decide *where* to launch the new product—in a single location, a region, the national market, or the international market. Few companies have the confi-

Commercialization
Introducing a new product into the market.

dence, capital, and capacity to launch new products into full national or international distribution from the get-go. Instead, they develop a planned *market rollout* over time. For example, when Miller introduced Miller Chill, a lighter Mexican-style lager flavored with lime and salt, it started in selected southwestern states, such as Arizona, New Mexico, and Texas, supported by local TV commercials. Based on strong sales in these initial markets, the company then rolled out Miller Chill nationally, supported by $35 million worth of TV commercials and print ads. Finally, based on the brand's U.S. success, Miller rolled out Miller Chill internationally, starting in Australia.[23]

Some companies, however, may quickly introduce new models into the full national market. Companies with international distribution systems may introduce new products through swift global rollouts. Microsoft did this with its Windows 7 operating system, using a mammoth advertising blitz to launch the operating system simultaneously in more than 30 markets worldwide.

> **Author Comment** | Above all else, new-product development must focus on creating customer value. Says P&G's CEO about the company's new-product development: "We've figured out how to keep the consumer at the center of all our decisions. As a result, we don't go far wrong."

Managing New-Product Development (pp 269–273)

The new-product development process shown in Figure 9.1 highlights the important activities needed to find, develop, and introduce new products. However, new-product development involves more than just going through a set of steps. Companies must take a holistic approach to managing this process. Successful new-product development requires a customer-centered, team-based, and systematic effort.

Customer-Centered New-Product Development

Above all else, new-product development must be customer centered. When looking for and developing new products, companies often rely too heavily on technical research in their R&D laboratories. But like everything else in marketing, successful new-product development begins with a thorough understanding of what consumers need and value. **Customer-centered new-product development** focuses on finding new ways to solve customer problems and create more customer-satisfying experiences.

Customer-centered new-product development

New-product development that focuses on finding new ways to solve customer problems and create more customer-satisfying experiences.

One study found that the most successful new products are ones that are differentiated, solve major customer problems, and offer a compelling customer value proposition. Another study showed that companies that directly engage their customers in the new-product innovation process had twice the return on assets and triple the growth in operating income of firms that did not. Thus, customer involvement has a positive effect on the new-product development process and product success.[24]

For example, whereas the consumer package goods industry's new-product success rate is only about 15–20 percent, P&G's success rate is over 50 percent. According to former P&G CEO A. G. Lafley, the most important factor in this success is understanding what consumers want. In the past, says Lafley, P&G tried to push new products down to consumers rather than first understanding their needs. But now, P&G employs an immersion process it calls "Living It," in which researchers go so far as to live with shoppers for several days at a time to envision product ideas based directly on consumer needs. P&Gers also hang out in stores for similar insights, a process they call "Working It." And at its Connect + Develop crowdsourcing site, P&G urges customers to submit their own ideas and suggestions for new products and services, current product design, and packaging. "We figured out how to keep the consumer at the center of all our decisions," says Lafley. "As a result, we don't go far wrong."[25]

For products ranging from consumer package goods to financial services, today's innovative companies get out of the research lab and mingle with customers in the search for new customer value. For example, when PNC Bank sought new digital services that would connect with high-tech millennial consumers, it started by observing these consumers in their day-to-day lives:[26]

For three months, researchers and designers followed about 30 young consumers on their daily living paths and quizzed them on how they use their money, where they kept it, what they thought about it, and which mobile and online banking programs they used. Next, PNC Bank set up discussion groups composed of both consumers and company employees, who jointly brainstormed hundreds of ideas and then whittled them down to a few core ones. The result was PNC Bank's successful real-time money management widget/smartphone app called Virtual Wallet. The digital tool combines three accounts—spend, grow, and reserve—into one high-definition deal. A Calendar feature provides daily-to-monthly monitoring of every bill and payment. The Money Bar slider lets young customers move money quickly between their spend and save accounts. The savings component offers a feature called "Punch the Pig," a fun, customizable widget that lets users click to transfer cash instantly into a high-yield savings account. And a "Danger Days" feature automatically warns of potential overspending. In all, based on in-depth consumer insights, PNC Bank's Virtual Wallet puts real-time money management at the fingertips of the millennial generation.

Thus, customer-centered new-product development begins and ends with understanding customers and involving them in the process. (See Real Marketing 9.1 for another great example.) Successful innovation boils down to finding fresh ways to meet customer needs.

Team-Based New-Product Development

Good new-product development also requires a total-company, cross-functional effort. Some companies organize their new-product development process into the orderly sequence of steps shown in Figure 9.1, starting with idea generation and ending with commercialization. Under this *sequential product development* approach, one company department works individually to complete its stage of the process before passing the new product along to the next department and stage. This orderly, step-by-step process can help bring control to complex and risky projects. But it can also be dangerously slow. In fast-changing, highly competitive markets, such slow-but-sure product development can result in product failures, lost sales and profits, and crumbling market positions.

Team-based new-product development

An approach to developing new products in which various company departments work closely together, overlapping the steps in the product development process to save time and increase effectiveness.

To get their new products to market more quickly, many companies use a **team-based new-product development** approach. Under this approach, company departments work closely together in cross-functional teams, overlapping the steps in the product development process to save time and increase effectiveness. Instead of passing the new product from department to department, the company assembles a team of people from various departments that stays with the new product from start to finish. Such teams usually include people from the marketing, finance, design, manufacturing, and legal departments and even supplier and customer companies. In the sequential process, a bottleneck at one phase can seriously slow an entire project. In the team-based approach, if one area hits snags, it works to resolve them while the team moves on.

The team-based approach does have some limitations, however. For example, it sometimes creates more organizational tension and confusion than the more orderly sequential approach. However, in rapidly changing industries facing increasingly shorter PLCs, the rewards of fast and flexible product development far exceed the risks. Companies that combine a customer-centered approach with team-based new-product development gain a big competitive edge by getting the right new products to market faster.

Systematic New-Product Development

Finally, the new-product development process should be holistic and systematic rather than compartmentalized and haphazard. Otherwise, few new ideas will surface, and many good ideas will sputter and die. To avoid these problems, a company can install an *innovation management system* to collect, review, evaluate, and manage new-product ideas.

The company can appoint a respected senior person to be the company's innovation manager. It can set up Web-based idea management software and encourage all company stakeholders—employees, suppliers, distributors, dealers—to become involved in finding and developing new products. It can assign a cross-functional innovation management committee to evaluate proposed new-product ideas and help bring good ideas to market. It can create recognition programs to reward those who contribute the best ideas.

The innovation management system approach yields two favorable outcomes. First, it helps create an innovation-oriented company culture. It shows that top management

Real Marketing 9.1

LEGO Group: Building Customer Relationships, Brick by Brick

Classic LEGO plastic bricks have been fixtures in homes around the world for more than 60 years. A mind-blowing 400 billion LEGO bricks now populate the planet, enough to build a tower to the moon ten times over. In fact, the Danish-based LEGO Group (TLG) now sells seven LEGO sets every second in 130 countries, making it the world's fifth-largest toymaker.

But only six years ago, TLG was near bankruptcy. Sales were sagging, and the company was losing money at a rate of $300 million a year. The problem: The classic toy company had fallen out of touch with its customers. As a result, its products had fallen out of touch with the times. In the age of the Internet, videogames, iPods, and high-tech playthings, traditional toys such as LEGO bricks had been pushed to the back of the closet. So in 2004, the company set out to rebuild its aging product line-brick by brick.

The LEGO product makeover, however, didn't start with engineers working in design labs. First, TLG had to reconnect with customers. So it started by listening to customers, understanding them, and including them in the new-product development process. Then it used the insights it gained to develop new generations of more relevant products. Rather than simply pushing the same old construction sets out *to* customers, TLG worked *with* customers to co-create new products and concepts.

To get to know its customers better, for instance, LEGO conducted up-close-and-personal ethnographic studies—hanging out with and observing children ages seven to nine on their home turf. "We thought we understood our consumers, the children of the world," says a LEGO Group marketer, but it turns out that "we didn't know them as well as we thought." The ethnographic research produced a lot of "Aha! moments" that shattered many of the brand's long-held traditions.

For example, TLG had long held fast to a "keep it simple" mantra. From the beginning, it offered only basic play sets—bricks, building bases, beams, doors, windows, wheels, and slanting roof tiles—with few or no instructions. The philosophy was that giving children unstructured building sets would stimulate their imaginations and foster creativity. But that concept just wasn't cutting it in the modern world. Today's children get bored easily, and in today's fast-moving environment, they are exposed to many more characters and themes.

In response, TLG shifted toward more-specialized, more-structured products. It now churns out some 7,000 unique building pieces each year, which support a seemingly endless assortment of themed product lines and specific building projects. So instead of just buying a set of basic square LEGO bricks and building a house or a car, children can now buy specialized kits to construct anything from a realistic fire engine to a city police helicopter to a working robot. And the LEGO brick lineup is refreshed regularly; 60 percent of the core LEGO product assortment changes every year.

To add desired variety and familiarity, TLG now builds plays sets around popular movie and TV themes and characters. It offers an ever-changing assortment of licensed lines based on everything from *Indiana Jones* and *Star Wars* to *Toy Story*. About 60 percent of U.S. LEGO sales are now linked to licenses, more than double that of five years ago. In fact, it's getting harder and harder to find a set of basic LEGO blocks.

TLG's more thematic and structured play sets have given a big boost to sales, but not everyone is thrilled. One industry observer notes, "What LEGO loses is what makes it so special. When you have a less-structured, less-themed set, kids [can] start from scratch. When you have kids playing out Indiana Jones, they're playing out Hollywood's imagination, not their own." But TLG doesn't see this shift as a compromise of values, and most customers agree. For example, one father of two

At LEGO, new-product development begins with listening to customers and including them in the design process. The LEGO Design by Me site lets customers download 3D design software, create a LEGO toy, and then order the kit to build it.

Continued on next page

recognizes that LEGO toys have changed since he was a boy, but he thinks that they have retained their innocence. "The most exotic thing I could build when I was a kid was an ambulance," he says. "Now [my kids] can build the Death Star." The fact that "the pieces and the sets are a lot cooler than they were 30 years ago," means that they lure kids away from less imaginative pastimes. "Instead of watching TV or playing computer games, the kids are building something, and [we] build stuff together."

Of course, kids aren't the only ones playing with LEGO bricks. The classic brick sets have a huge fan base of adults that never got over the toys of their youth. TLG estimates that it has as many as 250,000 active AFOLs (adult fans of LEGO) around the globe who spend large sums on LEGO products. These adults maintain thousands of LEGO fan sites and blogs, flock to conventions with names such as BrickFest, and compete with each other to construct "the Biggest LEGO Train Layout Ever (3,343 feet; it ran through an entire LEGO cityscape) or beat the Fastest Time to Build the LEGO Imperial Star Destroyer (3,104 pieces; five builders maximum and no presorting allowed; record: 1 hour 42 minutes 43 seconds)."

In developing new products, TLG actively taps into the AFOL community. It has created a roster of customer ambassadors who provide regular input, and it even invites customers to participate directly in the product-development process. For example, it invited 250 LEGO train-set enthusiasts to visit its New York office to assess new designs. The result was the LEGO Santa Fe Super Chief set, which sold out the first 10,000 units in less than two weeks with virtually no additional marketing. Similarly, TLG used customer co-creation to develop its most popular product ever, LEGO MINDSTORMS:

> The LEGO MINDSTORMS build-it-yourself robot was initially an internal effort in partnership with MIT. Within three weeks of its introduction, however, more than 1,000 intrigued customers formed their own Web community to outdo each other in making it better. TLG quickly embraced the co-creation idea. The next generation of LEGO MINDSTORMS featured user-defined parts. Then, LEGO made customer co-creation official by creating the MINDSTORMS Development Program (MDP), through which it selected the most avid MINDSTORMS fans—100 pioneers, inventors, and innovators from across the globe—to play with LEGO MINDSTORMS and create innovative new features and applications. The MDP fans share their ideas with other customers and invite feedback.

Listening to adult customers has also led to the development of the LEGO Design by Me site, which lets customers download 3D design software, create a LEGO toy, and then order the kit to build it. And TLG recently launched LEGO Universe, an MMOG (massively multiplayer online game) in which adults and children alike can act out roles from LEGO sets and build toys from virtual blocks.

Thanks to customer-centered new-product development, TLG is now thriving. In the past five years, even as the overall toy market has declined in a weakened economy and as competitors such as Mattel and Hasbro have struggled, LEGO's sales have soared 66 percent, and its profits have jumped tenfold. "Kids [including the adult variety] are ruthless," says a senior LEGO executive. "If they don't like the product, then at the end of the day . . . all the rest of it won't make any difference. What counts, all that counts, is that you're at the top of kids' wish lists." Thanks to all that listening and customer involvement, that's where the LEGO Group is again."

Sources: "LEGO Grows by Listening to Customers," *Advertising Age*, November 9, 2009, p. 15; Nelson D. Schwartz, "Beyond the Blocks," *New York Times*, September 6, 2009, p. BU1; Jon Henley, "Toy Story," *Guardian*, March 26, 2009, p. F4; Kevin O'Donnell, "Where Do the Best Ideas Come From? The Unlikeliest Sources," *Advertising Age*, July 14, 2008, p. 15; Lewis Borg Cardona, "LEGO Learns a Lesson," *Change Agent*, June 2008, http://www.synovate.com/changeagent/index.php/site/full_story/lego_learns_a_lesson/; and www.lego.com/eng/info/ and http://mindstorms.lego.com/en-us/community/default.aspx, accessed September 2010.

supports, encourages, and rewards innovation. Second, it will yield a larger number of new-product ideas, among which will be found some especially good ones. The good new ideas will be more systematically developed, producing more new-product successes. No longer will good ideas wither for the lack of a sounding board or a senior product advocate.

Thus, new-product success requires more than simply thinking up a few good ideas, turning them into products, and finding customers for them. It requires a holistic approach for finding new ways to create valued customer experiences, from generating and screening new-product ideas to creating and rolling out want-satisfying products to customers.

More than this, successful new-product development requires a whole-company commitment. At companies known for their new-product prowess, such as Google, Apple, IDEO, 3M, P&G, and GE, the entire culture encourages, supports, and rewards innovation.

New-Product Development in Turbulent Times

When tough economic times hit, or when a company faces financial difficulties, management may be tempted to reduce spending on new-product development. However, such thinking is usually shortsighted. By cutting back on new products, the company may make itself less competitive during or after the downturn. In fact, tough times might call for even greater new-product development, as the company struggles to better align its market offerings with changing consumer needs and tastes. In difficult times, innovation more often helps than hurts in making the company more competitive and positioning it better for the future. Summarizes one analyst:[27]

> Innovation is a messy process—hard to measure and hard to manage. When revenues and earnings decline, executives often conclude that their innovation efforts just aren't worth it. Better to focus on the tried and true than to risk money on untested ideas. The contrary view, of course, is that innovation is both a vaccine against market downturns and an elixir that rejuvenates growth. In today's economy, for example, imagine how much better off General Motors might have fared if it had matched the pace of innovation set by Honda or Toyota. Imagine how much worse off Apple would be had it not—in the midst of previously very difficult times for the company—created the iPod, iTunes, and iPhone.

Thus, rain or shine, good times or bad, a company must continue to innovate and develop new products if it wants to grow and prosper. "The good news is . . . downturns are times of turbulence [but] are also times of incredible opportunity," says one marketing consultant. "Your competitors may be hunkering down, giving you more opportunities." Another analyst notes that P&G launched two of its most successful (and highest-priced) new products, Swiffer and White Strips, during recessions.[28]

Author | A company's products are
Comment | born, grow, mature, and
then decline, just as living things do. To remain vital, the firm must continually develop new products and manage them effectively through their life cycles.

Product life cycle (PLC)

The course of a product's sales and profits over its lifetime. It involves five distinct stages: product development, introduction, growth, maturity, and decline.

Product Life-Cycle Strategies (pp 273–279)

After launching the new product, management wants that product to enjoy a long and happy life. Although it does not expect that product to sell forever, the company wants to earn a decent profit to cover all the effort and risk that went into launching it. Management is aware that each product will have a life cycle, although its exact shape and length is not known in advance.

● **Figure 9.2** shows a typical **product life cycle (PLC)**, the course that a product's sales and profits take over its lifetime. The PLC has five distinct stages:

1. *Product development* begins when the company finds and develops a new-product idea. During product development, sales are zero, and the company's investment costs mount.

2. *Introduction* is a period of slow sales growth as the product is introduced in the market. Profits are nonexistent in this stage because of the heavy expenses of product introduction.

3. *Growth* is a period of rapid market acceptance and increasing profits.

4. *Maturity* is a period of slowdown in sales growth because the product has achieved acceptance by most potential buyers. Profits level off or decline because of increased marketing outlays to defend the product against competition.

5. *Decline* is the period when sales fall off and profits drop.

Not all products follow all five stages of the PLC. Some products are introduced and die quickly; others stay in the mature stage for a long, long time. Some enter the decline stage

● **FIGURE | 9.2**
Sales and Profits over the Product's Life from Inception to Decline

Some products die quickly; others stay in the mature stage for a long, long time. For example, TABASCO sauce has been around for more than 140 years. Even then, to keep the product young, the company has added a full line of flavors (such as Sweet & Spicy and Chipotle) and a kitchen cabinet full of new TABASCO products (such as spicy beans, a chili mix, and jalapeno nacho slices).

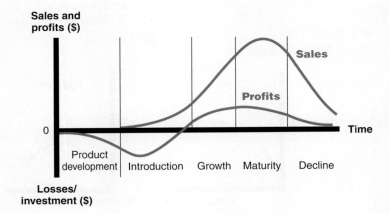

● **Product life cycle: Some products die quickly; others stay in the mature stage for a long, long time. TABASCO® sauce is "over 140 years old and yet still able to totally whup your butt!"**

Style
A basic and distinctive mode of expression.

Fashion
A currently accepted or popular style in a given field.

Fad
A temporary period of unusually high sales driven by consumer enthusiasm and immediate product or brand popularity.

and are then cycled back into the growth stage through strong promotion or repositioning. It seems that a well-managed brand could live forever. Venerable brands like Coca-Cola, Gillette, Budweiser, Guinness, American Express, Wells Fargo, Kikkoman, and TABASCO sauce, for instance, are still going strong after more than 100 years. Guinness beer recently celebrated its 250th anniversary; ● and TABASCO sauce brags that it's "over 140 years old and still able to totally whup your butt!"

The PLC concept can describe a *product class* (gasoline-powered automobiles), a *product form* (SUVs), or a *brand* (the Ford Escape). The PLC concept applies differently in each case. Product classes have the longest life cycles; the sales of many product classes stay in the mature stage for a long time. Product forms, in contrast, tend to have the standard PLC shape. Product forms such as "dial telephones" and "VHS tapes" passed through a regular history of introduction, rapid growth, maturity, and decline.

A specific brand's life cycle can change quickly because of changing competitive attacks and responses. For example, although laundry soaps (product class) and powdered detergents (product form) have enjoyed fairly long life cycles, the life cycles of specific brands have tended to be much shorter. Today's leading brands of powdered laundry soap are Tide and Cheer; the leading brands almost 100 years ago were Fels-Naptha, Octagon, and Kirkman.

The PLC concept also can be applied to what are known as styles, fashions, and fads. Their special life cycles are shown in ● **Figure 9.3**. A **style** is a basic and distinctive mode of expression. For example, styles appear in homes (colonial, ranch, transitional), clothing (formal, casual), and art (realist, surrealist, abstract). Once a style is invented, it may last for generations, passing in and out of vogue. A style has a cycle showing several periods of renewed interest.

A **fashion** is a currently accepted or popular style in a given field. For example, the more formal "business attire" look of corporate dress of the 1980s and 1990s gave way to the "business casual" look of the 2000s. Fashions tend to grow slowly, remain popular for a while, and then decline slowly.

Fads are temporary periods of unusually high sales driven by consumer enthusiasm and immediate product or brand popularity.[29] A fad may be part of an otherwise normal life cycle, as in the case of recent surges in the sales of poker chips and accessories. Or the fad may comprise a brand's or product's entire life cycle. "Pet rocks" are a classic example. Upon hearing his friends complain about how expensive it was to care for their dogs, advertising copywriter Gary Dahl joked about his pet rock. He soon wrote a spoof of a dog-training manual for it, titled "The Care and Training of Your Pet Rock." Soon Dahl was selling some 1.5 million ordinary beach pebbles at $4 a pop. Yet the fad, which broke one October, had sunk like a stone by the next February. Dahl's advice to those who want to succeed with a fad: "Enjoy it while it lasts." Other examples of fads include the Rubik's Cube and low-carb diets.[30]

Marketers can apply the PLC concept as a useful framework for describing how products and markets work. And when used carefully, the PLC concept can help in developing good marketing strategies for its different stages. But using the PLC concept for forecasting

● **FIGURE | 9.3**
Styles, Fashions, and Fads

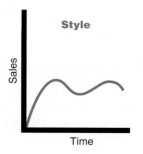

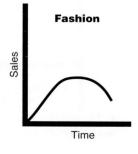

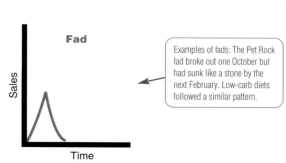

Examples of fads: The Pet Rock fad broke out one October but had sunk like a stone by the next February. Low-carb diets followed a similar pattern.

product performance or developing marketing strategies presents some practical problems. For example, in practice, it is difficult to forecast the sales level at each PLC stage, the length of each stage, and the shape of the PLC curve. Using the PLC concept to develop marketing strategy also can be difficult because strategy is both a cause and a result of the PLC. The product's current PLC position suggests the best marketing strategies, and the resulting marketing strategies affect product performance in later stages.

Moreover, marketers should not blindly push products through the traditional PLC stages. Instead, marketers often defy the "rules" of the life cycle and position or reposition their products in unexpected ways. By doing this, they can rescue mature or declining products and return them to the growth phase of the life cycle. Or they can leapfrog obstacles to slow consumer acceptance and propel new products forward into the growth phase.

The moral of the product life cycle is that companies must continually innovate or else they risk extinction. No matter how successful its current product lineup, a company must skillfully manage the life cycles of existing products for future success. And to grow, it must develop a steady stream of new products that bring new value to customers (see Real Marketing 9.2).

We looked at the product-development stage of the PLC in the first part of this chapter. We now look at strategies for each of the other life-cycle stages.

Introduction Stage

Introduction stage
The PLC stage in which a new product is first distributed and made available for purchase.

The **introduction stage** starts when a new product is first launched. Introduction takes time, and sales growth is apt to be slow. Well-known products such as frozen foods and HDTVs lingered for many years before they entered a stage of more rapid growth.

In this stage, as compared to other stages, profits are negative or low because of the low sales and high distribution and promotion expenses. Much money is needed to attract distributors and build their inventories. Promotion spending is relatively high to inform consumers of the new product and get them to try it. Because the market is not generally ready for product refinements at this stage, the company and its few competitors produce basic versions of the product. These firms focus their selling on those buyers who are the most ready to buy.

A company, especially the *market pioneer*, must choose a launch strategy that is consistent with the intended product positioning. It should realize that the initial strategy is just the first step in a grander marketing plan for the product's entire life cycle. If the pioneer chooses its launch strategy to make a "killing," it may be sacrificing long-run revenue for the sake of short-run gain. As the pioneer moves through later stages of the life cycle, it must continuously formulate new pricing, promotion, and other marketing strategies. It has the best chance of building and retaining market leadership if it plays its cards correctly from the start.

Growth Stage

Growth stage
The PLC stage in which a product's sales start climbing quickly.

If the new product satisfies the market, it will enter a **growth stage**, in which sales will start climbing quickly. The early adopters will continue to buy, and later buyers will start following their lead, especially if they hear favorable word of mouth. Attracted by the opportunities for profit, new competitors will enter the market. They will introduce new product features, and the market will expand. The increase in competitors leads to an increase in the number of distribution outlets, and sales jump just to build reseller inventories. Prices remain where they are or decrease only slightly. Companies keep their promotion spending at the same or a slightly higher level. Educating the market remains a goal, but now the company must also meet the competition.

Profits increase during the growth stage as promotion costs are spread over a large volume and as unit manufacturing costs decrease. The firm uses several strategies to sustain rapid market growth as long as possible. It improves product quality and adds new product features and models. It enters new market segments and new distribution channels. It shifts some advertising from building product awareness to building product conviction and purchase, and it lowers prices at the right time to attract more buyers.

Real Marketing 9.2

Kraft: Lots of Good Old Products; Too Few Good New Ones?

Kraft makes and markets an incredible portfolio of known and trusted brands, including eleven $1 billion brands and another 70 that top $100 million in sales. Beyond the Kraft label of cheeses, snacks, dips, and dressings, its megabrands include the likes of Oscar Mayer, Post cereals, Maxwell House coffee, JELL-O, Cool Whip, Kool-Aid, A1 sauce, Velveeta, Planters, Miracle Whip, Light 'n Lively, Grey Poupon, Capri Sun, Cadbury, and Nabisco (Oreo, Chips Ahoy!, Triscuit, SnackWells, and a whole lot more). If you search America's pantries, you'll find at least one Kraft product in 199 of every 200 households.

However, despite its long list of familiar brands, five years ago, Kraft wasn't doing very well. Its sales and profits had stagnated, and its stock price had flatlined. The problem? Kraft did a poor job of managing the product life cycle. Although it had a slew of good *old* products, it had far too few good *new* products.

Many of Kraft's venerable old brands—such as Maxwell House, Velveeta, and JELL-O—were showing their age. Other brands were extended about as far as they could go—for instance, Kraft markets more than 20 varieties of Oreos, from the original sandwich cookies, Oreo Double Stuf, Oreo Double Double Stuf, Chocolate-Covered Oreos, and Double Delight Chocolate Mint'n Crème Oreos to Oreo Mini Bites, Oreo Snack Cakes, and even Oreo ice cream cones. How much pop could yet one more variety provide?

Over the years, competitors such as P&G had invested dollars and energy in their mature or declining brands, such as Mr. Clean and Old Spice, moving them back into the growth stage of the PLC. In contrast, Kraft focused on costcutting, leaving its mature brands to wither. Whereas rival P&G developed a constant stream of really new products, even inventing all new product categories with products such as Swiffer and Febreze, Kraft was slow to innovate. And while P&G was intensely customer focused, bringing innovative new solutions to its customers, Kraft slowly lost touch with its customers.

In 2006, however, under the leadership of new CEO Irene Rosenfeld, Kraft laid out an ambitious turnaround plan to restore sales and profit growth. For starters, it announced that it would make heavy investments to reconnect with customers and improve product quality. "We're going to connect with the consumer wherever she is," said Rosenfeld. "On the quality side, [we need to] shift from 'good enough' to 'truly delicious,' turning brands that [our] consumers have lived with for years into brands they can't live without." Most importantly, Kraft pronounced that it would invest heavily in innovation and new-product development.

Kraft began its new-product development efforts not in test kitchens but by visiting consumers' homes to see the world through customers' eyes rather than through a company's lens. We want to take our products "in a new direction that's more consistent with the reality of consumers' lives today," declared Rosenfeld. We need "customer-focused innovation!" Kraft discovered the simple truth about the way customers live their lives today: They want high-quality but convenient and healthy foods. "Wouldn't it be a whole lot easier if you could have restaurant-quality food at home for a fraction of the cost?" asked Rosenfeld.

The team also realized that Kraft already had all the fixings it needed to complete this mission. It needed only to reframe its offerings in ways that fit customers' changing lifestyles. For example, Kraft developed the highly successful "Deli Creations" brand—a build-your-own premium sandwich kit that includes bread, Oscar Mayer meats, Kraft cheeses, and condiments such as A1 steak sauce and Grey Poupon mustard. Customers can quickly assemble the sandwiches, pop them into the microwave for one minute, and wrap their mouths around a hot, restaurant-style sandwich. In a similar fashion, Kraft rolled out "Fresh Creations" salads, complete with Oscar Mayer meat, Kraft cheese, Good Season's salad dressing, and Planter's nuts, a move that took its product portfolio into a whole new section of the grocery store, the produce section.

Dozens of other new products ranged from higher-quality Oscar Mayer Deli Fresh cold cuts and an entirely rejuvenated line of Kraft salad dressings with no artificial preservatives to Kraft Bagel-Fuls handheld breakfast sandwiches, Cakesters snack cakes, healthy LiveActive products with probiotic cultures and prebiotic fiber, and Oscar Mayer Fast Franks prepackaged microwavable stadium-style hotdogs.

Kraft even invested to reinvigorate some of its old brands. For example, it added four bold new flavors to the Grey Poupon brand, a name that had retained 70 percent consumer awareness even without much investment. The new flavors were supported by a fresh version of the old and much-liked Grey Poupon "Pardon me" ad campaign. Kraft also infused new life into existing brands such as Knudsen and Breakstone by co-marketing them with the LiveActive health brand.

To support its new-product lineup, Kraft also boosted marketing expenditures and refreshed the look and feel of its packaging and advertising. The once old-school marketer now sports a revamped Web site, a splashy Food & Family e-magazine, and e-mail newsletters. Kraft even offers a much-lauded iPhone app—iFood Assistant—that serves up simple recipes anytime anywhere, complete with shopping lists and a food store locator.

Thus, it appears, Kraft is back—or at least heading in the right direction. Although profits

Managing the PLC: Despite its long list of familiar old brands, until recently, Kraft had far too few good new products. It's now emphasizing new-product innovation. "Welcome to the new Kraft."

still languished, sales grew 27 percent in the first two years under the turnaround plan. Kraft also sweetened its top line with the recent acquisition of confectionary giant Cadbury, making it the world's second-largest food company. Although the weak economy has dented recent sales growth, Rosenfeld is optimistic. "Our brands are getting stronger every day," she says. "Our insights about consumers are deeper and richer than ever before. And our new product pipeline is flowing with exciting ideas. I'm pleased to tell you, the new Kraft is taking shape."

Kraft has learned that a company can't just sit back, basking in the glory of today's successful brands. Continued success requires skillful management of the PLC. But Kraft still has a long way to go. For example, in the shadow of the recent recession, Kraft appears to have

taken "a less risky approach to new products," observes one analyst, "introducing modified versions of existing products rather than wholly new ones." Rosenfeld admits as much: "You will see lots of new products—they are the lifeblood of our business—but you will see them in the context of platforms and ideas that have already been proven in the marketplace."

Only time will tell whether playing it safe in a sour economy is a smart strategy, especially

when some competitors are moving ahead more aggressively. "There is a tendency to crawl into a foxhole and wait for the barrage of competition to end," says the analyst. "But it's unfortunate that they are missing a chance to grab more market share." Rosenfeld counsels patience. "This is not *Extreme Makeover: Home Edition* that'll get fixed in 60 minutes," she says. "We've [still] got some fundamental work to do."

Sources: Quotes and other information from David Sterrett, "Kraft Holds Off on New Products," *Crain's Chicago Business*, March 2, 2009, p. 3; John Schmeltzer, "Foodmaker Whips Up Plan for a Comeback," *Chicago Tribune*, February 21, 2007, p. 1; Michael Arndt, "It Just Got Hotter in Kraft's Kitchen," *BusinessWeek*, February 12, 2007, p. 36; Emily Bryson York, "Behind Kraft's Marketing Makeover: From New Ad Agencies to New Attitude," *Advertising Age*, February 8, 2010, p. 10; and annual reports and other information from www.kraft.com, accessed September 2010.

In the growth stage, the firm faces a trade-off between high market share and high current profit. By spending a lot of money on product improvement, promotion, and distribution, the company can capture a dominant position. In doing so, however, it gives up maximum current profit, which it hopes to make up in the next stage.

Maturity Stage

Maturity stage
The PLC stage in which a product's sales growth slows or levels off.

At some point, a product's sales growth will slow down, and it will enter the **maturity stage**. This maturity stage normally lasts longer than the previous stages, and it poses strong challenges to marketing management. Most products are in the maturity stage of the life cycle, and therefore most of marketing management deals with the mature product.

The slowdown in sales growth results in many producers with many products to sell. In turn, this overcapacity leads to greater competition. Competitors begin marking down prices, increasing their advertising and sales promotions, and upping their product development budgets to find better versions of the product. These steps lead to a drop in profit. Some of the weaker competitors start dropping out, and the industry eventually contains only well-established competitors.

Although many products in the mature stage appear to remain unchanged for long periods, most successful ones are actually evolving to meet changing consumer needs. Product managers should do more than simply ride along with or defend their mature products—a good offense is the best defense. They should consider modifying the market, product, and marketing mix.

In *modifying the market*, the company tries to increase consumption by finding new users and new market segments for its brands. For example, mature 101-year old card maker American Greetings is now reaching younger consumers through social-networking widgets and instant-messaging channels.[31]

Women buy 80 percent of the greeting cards in the United States, and their median age is 47—not exactly the Facebook crowd. To younger buyers in this digital age, a snail-mail card is as antiquated as getting a $5 birthday check from grandma. ⦿ So to make its brand more youthful, American Greetings' fast-growing digital division, AG Interactive (AGI), created Kiwee.com, a repository for emoticons, video winks, postcards, graphics, widgets, and glitter text for all the major social-networking sites and instant-messaging services. A 47-year-old housewife may not be interested in the winking-turd emoticon that her 15-year-old son adores, but "we sell emotions," says AGI's chief technology

● **Modifying the market: 101-year old cardmaker American Greetings is reaching out to younger consumers through social-networking widgets and instant-messaging channels.**

officer. "Even younger people need help saying better what they want to say." Kiwee.com content is now being downloaded millions of times per day, signaling American Greetings' adjustment to a segment where paper cards are passé. Young people may not send paper anymore, but being remembered is universal.

The manager may also look for ways to increase usage among present customers. For example, Glad Products Company helps customers find new uses for its Press'n Seal wrap, the plastic wrap that creates a Tupperware-like seal. As more and more customers contacted the company about alternative uses for the product, Glad set up a special "1000s of Uses. What's Yours?" Web site (www.1000uses.com) at which customers can swap usage tips. Suggested uses for Press'n Seal range from protecting a computer keyboard from dirt and spills and keeping garden seeds fresh to use by soccer moms sitting on damp benches while watching their tykes play. "We just roll out the Glad Press'n Seal over the long benches," says the mom who shared the tip, "and everyone's bottom stays nice and dry."[32]

The company might also try *modifying the product*—changing characteristics such as quality, features, style, or packaging to attract new users and inspire more usage. It can improve the product's styling and attractiveness. It might improve the product's quality and performance—its durability, reliability, speed, and taste. Thus, makers of consumer food and household products introduce new flavors, colors, scents, ingredients, or packages to enhance performance and revitalize consumer buying. For example, TABASCO pepper sauce may have been around for more than 140 years, but to keep the brand young, the company has added a full line of flavors (such as Garlic, Sweet & Spicy, and Chipotle) and a kitchen cabinet full of new products under the TABASCO name (such as steak sauces, spicy beans, a chili mix, salsas, jalapeno nacho slices, and even spicy chocolate and a TABASCO lollipop).

Finally, the company can try *modifying the marketing mix*—improving sales by changing one or more marketing mix elements. The company can offer new or improved services to buyers. It can cut prices to attract new users and competitors' customers. It can launch a better advertising campaign or use aggressive sales promotions—trade deals, cents-off, premiums, and contests. In addition to pricing and promotion, the company can also move into new marketing channels to help serve new users.

Decline Stage

The sales of most product forms and brands eventually dip. The decline may be slow, as in the cases of stamps and oatmeal cereal, or rapid, as in the cases of cassette and VHS tapes. Sales may plunge to zero, or they may drop to a low level where they continue for many years. This is the **decline stage**.

Decline stage
The PLC stage in which a product's sales decline.

Sales decline for many reasons, including technological advances, shifts in consumer tastes, and increased competition. As sales and profits decline, some firms withdraw from the market. Those remaining may prune their product offerings. They may drop smaller market segments and marginal trade channels, or they may cut the promotion budget and reduce their prices further.

Carrying a weak product can be very costly to a firm, and not just in profit terms. There are many hidden costs. A weak product may take up too much of management's time. It often requires frequent price and inventory adjustments. It requires advertising and salesforce attention that might be better used to make "healthy" products more profitable. A product's failing reputation can cause customer concerns about the company and its other products. The biggest cost may well lie in the future. Keeping weak products delays the search for replacements, creates a lopsided product mix, hurts current profits, and weakens the company's foothold on the future.

For these reasons, companies need to pay more attention to their aging products. A firm's first task is to identify those products in the decline stage by regularly reviewing sales, market shares, costs, and profit trends. Then management must decide whether to maintain, harvest, or drop each of these declining products.

Management may decide to *maintain* its brand, repositioning or reinvigorating it in hopes of moving it back into the growth stage of the PLC. P&G has done this with several brands, including Mr. Clean and Old Spice. Management may decide to *harvest* the product, which means reducing various costs (plant and equipment, maintenance, R&D, advertising, sales force), hoping that sales hold up. If successful, harvesting will increase the company's profits in the short run.

Finally, management may decide to *drop* the product from its line. It can sell it to another firm or simply liquidate it at salvage value. In recent years, P&G has sold off several lesser or declining brands, such as Folgers coffee, Crisco oil, Comet cleanser, Sure deodorant, Duncan Hines cake mixes, and Jif peanut butter. If the company plans to find a buyer, it will not want to run down the product through harvesting.

Table 9.2 summarizes the key characteristics of each stage of the PLC. The table also lists the marketing objectives and strategies for each stage.[33]

TABLE | 9.2 Summary of Product Life-Cycle Characteristics, Objectives, and Strategies

	Introduction	**Growth**	**Maturity**	**Decline**
Characteristics				
Sales	Low sales	Rapidly rising sales	Peak sales	Declining sales
Costs	High cost per customer	Average cost per customer	Low cost per customer	Low cost per customer
Profits	Negative	Rising profits	High profits	Declining profits
Customers	Innovators	Early adopters	Middle majority	Laggards
Competitors	Few	Growing number	Stable number beginning to decline	Declining number
Marketing Objectives				
	Create product awareness and trial	Maximize market share	Maximize profit while defending market share	Reduce expenditure and milk the brand
Strategies				
Product	Offer a basic product	Offer product extensions, service, warranty	Diversify brand and models	Phase out weak items
Price	Use cost-plus	Price to penetrate market	Price to match or beat competitors	Cut price
Distribution	Build selective distribution	Build intensive distribution	Build more intensive distribution	Go selective: phase out unprofitable outlets
Advertising	Build product awareness among early adopters and dealers	Build awareness and interest in the mass market	Stress brand differences and benefits	Reduce to level needed to retain hard-core loyals
Sales Promotion	Use heavy sales promotion to entice trial	Reduce to take advantage of heavy consumer demand	Increase to encourage brand switching	Reduce to minimal level

Source: Philip Kotler and Kevin Lane Keller, *Marketing Management*, 13th ed. (Upper Saddle River, NJ: Prentice Hall, 2009), p. 288. © 2009. Printed and Electronically reproduced by permission of Pearson Education, Inc., Upper Saddle River, New Jersey.

Author Comment | Let's look at just a few more product topics, including regulatory and social responsibility issues and the special challenges of marketing products internationally.

Additional Product and Service Considerations (pp 280–282)

We wrap up our discussion of products and services with two additional considerations: social responsibility in product decisions and issues of international product and services marketing.

Product Decisions and Social Responsibility

Marketers should carefully consider public policy issues and regulations regarding acquiring or dropping products, patent protection, product quality and safety, and product warranties.

Regarding new products, the government may prevent companies from adding products through acquisitions if the effect threatens to lessen competition. Companies dropping products must be aware that they have legal obligations, written or implied, to their suppliers, dealers, and customers who have a stake in the dropped product. Companies must also obey U.S. patent laws when developing new products. A company cannot make its product illegally similar to another company's established product.

Manufacturers must comply with specific laws regarding product quality and safety. The Federal Food, Drug, and Cosmetic Act protects consumers from unsafe and adulterated food, drugs, and cosmetics. Various acts provide for the inspection of sanitary conditions in the meat- and poultry-processing industries. Safety legislation has been passed to regulate fabrics, chemical substances, automobiles, toys, and drugs and poisons. The Consumer Product Safety Act of 1972 established the Consumer Product Safety Commission, which has the authority to ban or seize potentially harmful products and set severe penalties for violation of the law.

If consumers have been injured by a product with a defective design, they can sue manufacturers or dealers. A recent survey of manufacturing companies found that product liability was the second-largest litigation concern, behind only labor and employment matters. Product liability suits are now occurring in federal courts at the rate of over 20,000 per year. Although manufacturers are found at fault in only 6 percent of all product liability cases, when they are found guilty, the median jury award is $1.5 million, and individual awards can run into the tens or even hundreds of millions of dollars. Class-action suits can run into the billions. For example, after it recalled some nine million vehicles due to problems with sudden acceleration, Toyota faced at least 234 class-action lawsuits that could end up costing the company $6 billion or more.[34]

This litigation phenomenon has resulted in huge increases in product liability insurance premiums, causing big problems in some industries. Some companies pass these higher rates along to consumers by raising prices. Others are forced to discontinue high-risk product lines. Some companies are now appointing "product stewards," whose job is to protect consumers from harm and the company from liability by proactively ferreting out potential product problems.

Many manufacturers offer written product warranties to convince customers of their products' quality. To protect consumers, Congress passed the Magnuson-Moss Warranty Act in 1975. The act requires that full warranties meet certain minimum standards, including repair "within a reasonable time and without charge" or a replacement or full refund if the product does not work "after a reasonable number of attempts" at repair. Otherwise, the company must make it clear that it is offering only a limited warranty. The law has led several manufacturers to switch from full to limited warranties and others to drop warranties altogether.

International Product and Services Marketing

International product and services marketers face special challenges. First they must figure out what products and services to introduce and in which countries. Then they must decide how much to standardize or adapt their products and services for world markets.

おばあちゃんの字みると、
なんだか、ほっとするよ。

キット、サクラよ。

言葉みたいで、声みたいで、顔みたい
キットメール 発売中
郵便局と KK は、受験生を応援します。

● **The Nestlé Kit Kat chocolate bar in Japan benefits from the coincidental similarity between the bar's name and the Japanese phrase *kitto katsu*, which roughly translates to "You will surely win!" The brand's innovative "May cherries blossom" campaign has turned the Kit Kat bar and logo into national good luck charms.**

On the one hand, companies would like to standardize their offerings. Standardization helps a company develop a consistent worldwide image. It also lowers the product design, manufacturing, and marketing costs of offering a large variety of products. On the other hand, markets and consumers around the world differ widely. Companies must usually respond to these differences by adapting their product offerings. For example, Nestlé sells a variety of very popular Kit Kat flavors in Japan that might make the average Western chocolate-lover's stomach turn, such as green tea, red bean, and red wine. Beyond taste, Kit Kat's strong following in Japan may also be the result of some unintended cultural factors:[35]

In recent years, Kit Kat—the world's number two chocolate bar behind Snickers—has become very popular in Japan. Some of this popularity, no doubt, derives from the fact that the notoriously sweet-toothed Japanese love the bar's taste. ● But part of the bar's appeal may also be attributed to the coincidental similarity between its name and the Japanese phrase *kitto katsu*, which roughly translates in Japanese as "You will surely win!" Spotting this opportunity, marketers for Nestlé Japan developed an innovative *Juken* (college entrance exam) Kit Kat campaign. The multimedia campaign positions the Kit Kat bar and logo as good luck charms during the highly stressful university entrance exam season. Nestlé even developed a cherry flavored Kit Kat bar in packaging containing the message "May cherries blossom," wishing students luck in achieving their dreams. And it partnered with Japan's postal service to create "Kit Kat Mail," a postcardlike product sold at the post office that could be mailed to students as an edible good-luck charm. The campaign has been such a hit in Japan that it has led to a nationwide social movement to cheer up students for *Juken*. Kit Kat has also become an even broader national good luck charm. For example, a large flag featuring the Kit Kat logo and the phrase *Kitto Katsu!* has been used by fans of professional football team Jubilo IWATA, which is sponsored by Nestlé Japan.

Packaging also presents new challenges for international marketers. Packaging issues can be subtle. For example, names, labels, and colors may not translate easily from one country to another. A firm using yellow flowers in its logo might fare well in the United States but meet with disaster in Mexico, where a yellow flower symbolizes death or disrespect. Similarly, although Nature's Gift might be an appealing name for gourmet mushrooms in America, it would be deadly in Germany, where *gift* means poison. Packaging may also need to be tailored to meet the physical characteristics of consumers in various parts of the world. For instance, soft drinks are sold in smaller cans in Japan to better fit the smaller Japanese hand. Thus, although product and package standardization can produce benefits, companies must usually adapt their offerings to the unique needs of specific international markets.

Service marketers also face special challenges when going global. Some service industries have a long history of international operations. For example, the commercial banking industry was one of the first to grow internationally. Banks had to provide global services to meet the foreign exchange and credit needs of their home country clients wanting to sell overseas. In recent years, many banks have become truly global. Germany's Deutsche Bank, for example, serves more than 13 million customers through 1,981 branches in 72 countries. For its clients around the world who wish to grow globally, Deutsche Bank can raise money not only in Frankfurt but also in Zurich, London, Paris, Tokyo, and Moscow.[36]

Professional and business services industries, such as accounting, management consulting, and advertising, have also globalized. The international growth of these firms followed the globalization of the client companies they serve. For example, as more clients employ worldwide marketing and advertising strategies, advertising agencies have responded by globalizing their own operations. McCann Worldgroup, a large U.S.-based advertising and marketing services agency, operates in more than 130 countries. It serves international clients such as Coca-Cola, GM, ExxonMobil, Microsoft, MasterCard, Johnson & Johnson, and Unilever in markets ranging from the United States and Canada to Korea and Kazakhstan. Moreover, McCann Worldgroup is one company in the Interpublic Group of Companies, an immense, worldwide network of advertising and marketing services companies.[37]

Retailers are among the latest service businesses to go global. As their home markets become saturated, American retailers such as Walmart, Office Depot, and Saks Fifth Avenue are expanding into faster-growing markets abroad. For example, since 1991, Walmart has entered 15 countries; its international division's sales grew more than 9 percent last year, skyrocketing to more than $98.6 billion. Foreign retailers are making similar moves. Asian shoppers can now buy American products in French-owned Carrefour stores. Carrefour, the world's second-largest retailer behind Walmart, now operates more than 15,000 stores in more than 30 countries. It is the leading retailer in Europe, Brazil, and Argentina and the largest foreign retailer in China.[38]

The trend toward growth of global service companies will continue, especially in banking, airlines, telecommunications, and professional services. Today, service firms are no longer simply following their manufacturing customers. Instead, they are taking the lead in international expansion.

REVIEWING Objectives AND KEY Terms

A company's current products face limited life spans and must be replaced by newer products. But new products can fail—the risks of innovation are as great as the rewards. The key to successful innovation lies in a customer focus, total-company effort, strong planning, and a systematic *new-product development* process.

Objective 1 Explain how companies find and develop new-product ideas. (pp 260–261)

Companies find and develop new-product ideas from a variety of sources. Many new-product ideas stem from *internal sources*. Companies conduct formal R&D. Or they pick the brains of their employees, urging them to think up and develop new-product ideas. Other ideas come from *external sources*. Companies track *competitors'* offerings and obtain ideas from *distributors and suppliers* who are close to the market and can pass along information about consumer problems and new-product possibilities.

Perhaps the most important source of new-product ideas are customers themselves. Companies observe customers, invite their ideas and suggestions, or even involve customers in the new-product development process. Many companies are now developing *crowdsourcing* or *open-innovation* new-product idea programs, which invite broad communities of people—customers,

employees, independent scientists and researchers, and even the general public—into the new-product innovation process. Truly innovative companies do not rely only on one source or another for new-product ideas.

Objective 2 List and define the steps in the new-product development process and the major considerations in managing this process. (pp 261–273)

The new-product development process consists of eight sequential stages. The process starts with *idea generation*. Next comes *idea screening*, which reduces the number of ideas based on the company's own criteria. Ideas that pass the screening stage continue through *product concept development*, in which a detailed version of the new-product idea is stated in meaningful consumer terms. In the next stage, *concept testing*, new-product concepts are tested with a group of target consumers to determine whether the concepts have strong consumer appeal. Strong concepts proceed to *marketing strategy development*, in which an initial marketing strategy for the new product is developed from the product concept. In the *business-analysis* stage, a review of the sales, costs, and profit projections for a new product is conducted to determine whether the new product is likely to satisfy the company's objectives. With positive results here, the ideas become more concrete through *product development* and *test marketing* and finally are launched during *commercialization*.

New-product development involves more than just going through a set of steps. Companies must take a systematic, holistic approach to managing this process. Successful new-product development requires a customer-centered, team-based, systematic effort.

comes a *maturity stage* in which the product's sales growth slows down and profits stabilize. Finally, the product enters a *decline stage* in which sales and profits dwindle. The company's task during this stage is to recognize the decline and decide whether it should maintain, harvest, or drop the product. The different stages of the PLC require different marketing strategies and tactics.

Objective 3   Describe the stages of the product life cycle (PLC) and how marketing strategies change during the PLC. (pp 273–279)

Each product has a *life cycle* marked by a changing set of problems and opportunities. The sales of the typical product follow an S-shaped curve made up of five stages. The cycle begins with the *product development stage* in which the company finds and develops a new-product idea. The *introduction stage* is marked by slow growth and low profits as the product is distributed to the market. If successful, the product enters a *growth stage*, which offers rapid sales growth and increasing profits. Next

Objective 4   Discuss two additional product issues: socially responsible product decisions and international product and services marketing. (pp 280–282)

Marketers must consider two additional product issues. The first is *social responsibility*. This includes public policy issues and regulations involving acquiring or dropping products, patent protection, product quality and safety, and product warranties. The second involves the special challenges facing international product and services marketers. International marketers must decide how much to standardize or adapt their offerings for world markets.

KEY Terms

OBJECTIVE 1
New-product development (p 260)

OBJECTIVE 2
Idea generation (p 261)
Crowdsourcing (p 263)
Idea screening (p 264)
Product concept (p 264)
Concept testing (p 265)

Marketing strategy development (p 265)
Business analysis (p 266)
Product development (p 266)
Test marketing (p 267)
Commercialization (p 268)
Customer-centered new-product development (p 269)
Team-based new-product development (p 270)

OBJECTIVE 3
Product life cycle (PLC; p 273)
Style (p 274)
Fashion (p 274)
Fad (p 274)
Introduction stage (p 275)
Growth stage (p 275)
Maturity stage (p 277)
Decline stage (p 278)

mymarketinglab

- Check your understanding of the concepts and key terms using the mypearsonmarketinglab study plan for this chapter.
- Apply the concepts in a business context using the simulation entitled **Product Life Cycle**.

DISCUSSING & APPLYING THE Concepts

Discussing the Concepts

1. Name and describe the major steps in developing a new product. (AACSB: Communication)

2. Define *crowdsourcing* and describe an example not already presented in the chapter. (AACSB: Communication; Reflective Thinking)

3. Compare and contrast the terms *product idea, product concept*, and *product image*. (AACSB: Communication)

4. Explain why successful new product development requires a customer-centered, team-based, and systematic effort. (AACSB: Communication)

5. Why do products enter the decline stage of the product life cycle? Discuss marketers' options at this stage. (AACSB: Communication)

6. Discuss the special challenges facing international product and service marketers. (AACSB: Communication)

Applying the Concepts

1. Visit http://creatingminds.org/tools/tools_ideation.htm to learn about idea generation techniques. Form a small group and have each group member explain a different technique to the rest of the group. Apply one or more of the techniques to generate four new product ideas. Present your ideas to the rest of the class and explain the techniques your group applied to generate the ideas. (AACSB: Communication; Use of IT; Reflective Thinking)

2. Coca-Cola has sustained success in the maturity stage of the product life cycle for many years. Visit Coca-Cola's Web site (www.thecoca-colacompany.com/heritage/ourheritage.html)

and discuss how Coca-Cola has evolved over the years. Identify ways that Coca-Cola can continue to evolve to meet changing consumer needs and wants. (AACSB: Communication; Use of IT; Reflective Thinking)

3. To acquire new products, many companies purchase other firms or buy individual brands from other companies. For

example, Disney purchased Marvel Entertainment and its portfolio of more than 5,000 characters, such as Spider-Man and Captain America. Discuss two other examples of companies acquiring new products through this means. (AACSB: Communication; Reflective Thinking)

FOCUS ON Technology

Technology is speeding up new product development while also reducing its costs. What formerly took months and cost millions of dollars can now be done in seconds and for pennies. Because technology is making new product testing easy and accessible to just about any employee, from the chief executive officer to maintenance personnel, predictions are for a groundbreaking change in corporate cultures surrounding new product development—much like the Google culture described at the beginning of this chapter. An employee may come up with a great idea and test it—all in a single day. This new environment may present some challenges, however. One is that managers must be prepared to give up control and empower employees. Another is "scaling," which

means companies must be able to scale or implement new ideas rapidly and efficiently.

1. What skills would you need to function in this type of work environment? (AACSB: Communication; Reflective Thinking)

2. As described at the beginning of this chapter, Google is already ahead of this curve. Visit Google Labs (www .googlelabs.com) to learn about new products that are still in the testing stage—what Google calls the "playground stage." Briefly discuss two of the experiments and explain why Google hosts a site such as Google Labs. (AACSB: Communication; Reflective Thinking; Use of IT)

FOCUS ON Ethics

There is usually lots of publicity surrounding the launch of a new Apple product. The iPhone 4 was no exception. Unfortunately, much of it was negative, with some critics even labeling the introduction "antenna-gate." Within days of the product's release, reports surfaced of reduced signal strength and dropped calls. The problem resulted from the sleeker, slimmer phone's antenna, consisting of a metal band around the side of the phone. Apple's response was that all smartphones have signal problems, users should hold the phone differently, and users should purchase a case for about $30 to fix the problem. It turns out that Apple engineers knew of this issue a year before the product was launched, but Steve Jobs, CEO of Apple Inc., liked the design and opted to go ahead with it. The controversy even caught the ear of a U.S. senator, who urged Jobs to fix the problem at no cost to consumers. Contrary to typical industry practice, AT&T, the exclusive service provider for Apple's phones, was allowed to test only a dis-

guised phone for a very limited time without touching it, so the problem was not discovered during testing. Apple later announced that all purchasers would receive a free case and reimbursed users who had already purchased one. This controversy didn't hurt sales, though; Apple sold three million of the new phones in just three weeks and could not keep up with demand.

1. Should Apple have released the iPhone 4 when engineers were aware of the antenna problem? Discuss the pros and cons of further testing before launching the product. (AACSB: Communication; Ethical Reasoning; Reflective Thinking)

2. Did Apple handle the situation effectively? Did Apple's iPhone lose brand equity from this controversy? (AACSB: Communication; Ethical Reasoning; Reflective Thinking)

MARKETING & THE Economy

Coach, Inc.

As consumer shopping patterns began to shift during a slowing economy in late 2007, executives at Coach, Inc., were paying attention. Through ongoing research, they determined that a new "normal" was emerging—one in which more frugal consumers shopped less and spent less when they did shop. At that time, the average price of a Coach handbag was about $330. Coach knew it had to become more innovative, relevant, and value oriented without cheapening the brand's image. Coach's managers went to work to find new sources of materials, renegotiate terms with suppliers, and develop new products. As the result of a yearlong

effort, Coach unveiled a new line of products called "Poppy." With the average price of a Poppy handbag at $260, the line is designed to be more affordable without compromising the brand's image. Unlike most luxury brands, Coach's revenue has maintained moderate but steady growth over the past four years. And although profit growth wavered somewhat, the company has remained in the black. Perhaps that's why during the most recent 18 months, its stock price is up 167 percent. Coach really does seem to understand the new "normal."

1. Explain how a $260 purse can be viewed as a good value in the context of the Coach brand.

2. Is Coach safe or will the new "normal" still catch up with the company's financial performance?

3. What suggestions would you make to Coach management for future product development?

MARKETING BY THE Numbers

Apple introduced the iPhone 4 in 2010 but still continued to offer the iPhone 3G. The 16GB base version of the iPhone 4 was priced at $199, with unit variable costs equal to $187. The iPhone 3G's price had decreased to $99 by the time the iPhone 4 was introduced, and its unit variable costs were $65.

1. Refer to Appendix 2 and calculate the incremental contribution realized by adding the new iPhone 4 if sales during the first six months of launch were five million units. However, the company also estimated that 30 percent of

iPhone 4 sales came from customers who would have purchased the iPhone 3G but instead purchased the base model of the iPhone 4. (AACSB: Communication; Analytic Reasoning)

2. Apple also offered a 32GB version of the iPhone 4 at $299. Variable costs for that version were $250. Besides its higher price, explain why Apple would encourage customers to purchase the 32GB over the 16GB version. (AACSB: Communication; Analytic Reasoning; Reflective Reasoning)

VIDEO Case

General Mills—FiberOne
General Mills has been mass marketing food since 1860. Today, it sells over $15 billion worth of packaged food each year in over 100 countries. In the United States alone, General Mills markets over 100 leading brands, such as Cheerios, Betty Crocker, Pillsbury, and Green Giant. With all this experience, General Mills certainly has an advantage when it comes to introducing and managing products.

Not many years ago, FiberOne was a little-known brand without much of a footprint. The FiberOne video illustrates how General Mills grew the brand's annual sales from $35 million to more than $500 million in just five years. This growth came primarily from creating and managing new products. FiberOne was originally a

line of food bars. But the FiberOne brand name is now found on numerous products, including toaster pastries, bread, yogurt, cold cereal, and even cottage cheese. After viewing the video featuring FiberOne, answer the following questions about the company.

1. Most new products fail. Why has General Mills had success with so many new product introductions in the FiberOne line?

2. Give an example of a FiberOne product in each phase of the product life cycle. Give evidence to support your decisions.

3. For each product identified in question 2, identify one strategy that General Mills is employing for each product that is appropriate for its life-cycle phase.

COMPANY Case

Samsung: From Gallop to Run

In the world of consumer electronics, copycat brands are a dime a dozen. These are the brands consumers turn to if they don't want to pay the price for the high-end market leaders. So if consumers want a top-tier television, they'll probably look at one from Sony or LG. If they want something cheaper that's probably not quite as good, they'll look at brands such as Insignia, Dynex, or Vizio.

But what about Samsung? Believe it or not, Samsung Electronics was a maker of cheap consumer electronic knock-offs from the time it started making calculators and black-and-white TVs in 1969 through the mid 1990s. Today, however, Samsung is the world's largest television manufacturer and offers the most cutting-edge models around.

Putting the brand in context, Samsung Electronics is part of the world's largest conglomerate, South Korea's Samsung Group. Founded in 1938, the huge Samsung Group also owns the world's second largest shipbuilder, a major global construction company, and the largest life insurance company in Korea. The conglomerate is so big that it accounts for 25 percent of all corporate prof-

its in South Korea, well ahead of the number two Hyundai-Kia Automotive Group at 6.4 percent. Under the direction of Lee Kun-hee, CEO and chairman, the third son of founder Lee Byung-Chull, Samsung Electronics has made major strides.

THE NEW MANAGEMENT STRATEGY
In 1993, Lee unveiled what he called "new management," a top-to-bottom strategy for the entire company. As part of Lee's new management, he took Samsung Electronics in a very ambitious new direction. The goal: He wanted Samsung to become a premier brand that would dethrone Sony as the biggest consumer electronics firm in the world. Instead of being a copycat, Samsung was to become a cutting-edge product leader. The company hired a new crop of fresh, young designers who unleashed a torrent of new products—not humdrum, me-too products, but sleek, bold, and beautiful products targeting high-end users. Samsung called them "lifestyle works of art." Every new product had to pass the "Wow!" test: If it didn't get a "Wow!" reaction during market testing, it went straight back to the design studio.

As part of Samsung's revamped strategy and positioning, along with developing stylish and innovative new products, the company altered distribution to match. It abandoned low-end distributors like Walmart and Kmart, choosing to build strong relationships with specialty retailers like Best Buy and Circuit City. "We're not el cheapo anymore," said one Samsung designer.

In less that two decades, Samsung Electronics has achieved its lofty goals—and much more. In 2009, the company rang up revenues of $117 billion with profits of $8.3 billion. Compare that to Sony at $77 billion in revenues and a net loss of almost $1 billion. Interbrand crowned Samsung as the world's fastest growing brand over one five-year period. Most recently, Samsung hit number 17 on Interbrand's list of most valuable global brands as Sony fell to number 29.

Samsung is now by far the largest consumer electronics company in the world and has been since 2005. It's the world's largest TV manufacturer and the second-largest cell phone producer. Samsung competes strongly in the markets for DVD players, home theaters, digital cameras and camcorders, home appliances, and laser printers. But more than just making finished consumer products, Samsung Electronics is also the world's largest technology electronic components company. It makes a sizable share of LCD and LED panels, mobile displays, and telecommunications components used in other company's products. It's also the world's largest manufacturer of flash memory.

WORKS OF ART

Samsung has become more than just big. It has also achieved its goal to become a producer of state-of-the-art products. In fact, both *Fast Company* and *BusinessWeek* recently placed Samsung high on their lists of most innovative companies. As evidence of its design prowess, Samsung took home eight prizes at the International Design Excellence Awards (IDEA), where entries are judged based on appearance, functionality, and the thinking behind each one. Design darling Apple took home only seven awards.

Consider some of this year's winners. A Samsung "Touch of Color" Blu-ray DVD player featuring a hint of red tone blended naturally into a piano black frame had the judges ogling. Comments indicated that, with color and appearance that changed in different lighting, the DVD player looked like a work of art made of glass. Samsung's Luxia LED TV series also packed "wow" appeal. With specs that exceed anything on the market, a 55-inch model is a mere one-inch thick and weighs just 49 pounds. Samsung's EcoFit monitors feature a transparent stand that give the appearance of floating in the air. The Samsung YP-S2 Pebble is part MP3 player, part fashion item. Designed to conjure up images of nature with its pebble shape and stunning colors, it can be worn around the neck and sports five tactile keys that make it simple enough for grandma to use. And the Samsung Kiwi mini notebook PC is a 10-inch laptop that is high-tech, convenient, cute, and familiar all at once. These and the other Samsung winners at last year's IDEA awards earned Samsung the designation of "a company that's hitting its design stride."

Samsung is moving many of its product categories forward. For example, as the cell phone industry moves from "dumbphones" to smartphones, Samsung aims to double its market share of the higher-end market from 5 to 10 percent. With the release of its latest high-tech communication phone, the Galaxy S, Samsung no doubt has a shot. One industry analyst says, "Samsung may easily meet [its] target as the handset market is sharply transferring to smartphones and the hardware features of the Galaxy S are pretty competitive in the market." Running on Google's new Android operating system, the phone features a four-inch screen, an e-book reader, a five-megapixel camera, and a high-definition video recorder and player. But perhaps the best thing going for it is the fact that it will not be tied exclusively to any single carrier, as are many of the top smartphones. More than 100 mobile operators around the world will offer the Galaxy S.

MABULJUNGJE

Lee was recently named the top CEO of the Decade by *Fortune Korea*. True to that title, he has just recently announced that the "new management" is now old news. After 17 years of remarkable success, Lee admitted that the world's largest technology firm's current main products may likely become obsolete within the next 10 years. That forward thinking has him again in reform mode. He has dubbed Samsung's newest strategy "mabuljungje," a Chinese axiom that means "horse that does not stop." In a memo to Samsung employees, Lee said, "The 'new management' doctrine for the past 17 years helped catapult the company into being one of the world's best electronics makers. Now is not a time to be complacent but a time to run."

As with any truly forward thinking, innovative company, Samsung doesn't claim to know what will replace today's products as they become obsolete. Rather, it is investing heavily to ensure that it is the company that develops them. Samsung recently unveiled a $23 billion investment plan—its biggest to date. That amount is three times the one that Samsung discarded only months earlier. It's also bigger than the combined investment budgets of Intel, IBM, and Sony. Much of this year's budget is earmarked for capital expenditures, new equipment, and plants to ensure that Samsung stays ahead of the game. The rest is for R&D. At a groundbreaking ceremony for a new chip plant outside of Seoul, Lee announced that despite Samsung's past success, the company risked losing market share if it did not completely overhaul its business model.

According to Timothy Baxter, president of Samsung Electronics America, as a major pillar of mabuljungje, Samsung will capitalize on interactivity—as in mobile phones with TVs and TVs with the Internet. Samsung's future will bring many products that will talk to each other. At a recent expo, Baxter stared at a pair of aces displayed on his Samsung Omnia II mobile phone. After tapping a few phone buttons, up popped a poker table on a Samsung big-screen TV with a pile of cards held by his opponent—a poker buddy in another city. "There's no reason these phones can't interact with the TV," Baxter said, indicating that if he has his way, Texas Hold 'em is just the first in a series of such synergistic exchanges.

But such advances in product interactivity go beyond just presenting consumers with flashy hardware features. They will take Samsung into a competition for consumer eyeballs with companies such as Apple. Samsung knows that it cannot thrive in the long term by merely offering sharper colors or better sound quality. Pricing power comes only from unique features or control over content. Samsung is putting plenty into discovering the unique features. But its investment strategy will also position Samsung as somewhat of a broker between advertisers and the devices that carry the ads. Although Samsung is now hush-hush about its plans, it has announced its intention to unveil a tablet computer and an app store similar to Apple's that will give Samsung control over that content. Samsung sees apps as the advertising vehicle of the future.

In its favor, Samsung has access to a piece of the puzzle that Apple doesn't—big screens. Thus, as its small devices interact with its Web-enabled TVs, Samsung could bring in lots of ad dollars from companies eager to pitch their products on screens 25 times the size of an iPhone's. If successful, Samsung will pose a threat to not only Apple but also cable companies. That's because the type of network that Samsung has planned will also make it a data collector, privy to insight about the kinds of applications its TV owners like so that it could help suggest what ads they should receive.

Questions for Discussion

1. How was Samsung able to go from copycat brand to product leader?

2. Is Samsung's product development process customer centered? Team based? Systematic?

3. Based on the PLC, what challenges does Samsung face in managing its high-tech products?

4. Will Samsung likely achieve its goals in markets where it does not dominate, such as smartphones? Why or why not?

Sources: Mark Borden, "The World's 50 Most Innovative Companies: #36: Samsung," *Fast Company*, February 17, 2010, p. 90; Shinhye Kang, "Samsung Aims to Double Its Smartphone Market Share," *Bloomberg's BusinessWeek*, June 21, 2010, accessed at www.businessweek.com/news/2010-06-21/samsung-aims-to-double-its-smartphone-market-share-update1-.html; Laurie Burkitt, "Samsung Courts Consumers, Marketers," *Forbes*, June 7, 2010, accessed at www.forbes.com/global/2010/0607/marketing-apps-consumer-electronics-apple-samsungs-big-spend.html; Choi He-suk, "Samsung Renews Resolve to Reform," *Korea Herald*, June 8, 2010, accessed online at www.koreaherald.com.

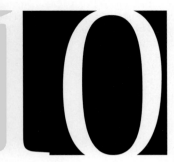

Pricing Understanding
and **Capturing Customer Value**

Chapter Preview

We now look at the second major marketing mix tool—pricing. If effective product development, promotion, and distribution sow the seeds of business success, effective pricing is the harvest. Firms successful at creating customer value with the other marketing mix activities must still capture some of this value in the prices they earn. In this chapter, we discuss the importance of pricing, dig into three major pricing strategies, and look at internal and external considerations that affect pricing decisions. In the next chapter, we examine some additional pricing considerations and approaches.

For openers, let's examine the importance of pricing in online retailing. In case you haven't noticed, there's a war going on—between Walmart, by far the world's largest retailer, and Amazon.com, the world's largest online merchant. The weapon of choice? Prices. Only time will tell who will win on the Web. But for now, the two retailers, especially Walmart, seem determined to fight it out on price.

Amazon vs. Walmart: Fighting It Out Online on Price

Walmart to Amazon: "Let's Rumble" read the headline. Ali had Frazier. Coke has Pepsi. The Yankees have the White Sox. Now Walmart, the mightiest retail giant in history may have met its own worthy adversary: Amazon.com. In what is emerging as one of the main storylines of the post-recession shopping scene, the two heavyweight retailers are waging a war. The weapon of choice? Prices—not surprising given the two combatants' long-held low-cost positions.

The price war between Walmart and Amazon.com began prior to the past holiday season, with skirmishes over online prices for new books and DVDs. It then escalated quickly to video game consoles, mobile phones, and even toys. At stake: the fortunes of not only the two companies but also whole industries whose products they sell, both online and in retail stores. Price can be a potent strategic weapon, but it can also be a double-edged sword.

Amazon.com, its seems, wants to be the "Walmart of the Web"—our digital general store—and it's well on its way to achieving that goal. Although Walmart's overall sales total an incredible $405 billion a year, 20 times Amazon's $20 billion annually, Amazon.com's online sales are 12 times greater than Walmart's online sales. Moreover, Amazon attracts more than 70 million unique U.S. visitors to its Web site monthly, double Walmart's number. One analyst estimates that more than one-half of all U.S. consumers who look online for retail items start their search at Amazon.com.

Why does this worry Walmart? After all, online sales account for only 4–5 percent of its overall U.S. retail sales. Walmart captures most of its business by offering affordable prices to Middle Americans in its more than 4,000 brick-and-mortar stores. By comparison, according to one analyst, Amazon.com sells mostly to "affluent urbanites who would rather click with their mouse than push around a cart."

But this battle isn't about now; it's about the future. Although still a small market by Walmart's standards, within the next decade, online sales will soar to an estimated 15 percent of total U.S. retail sales. And, increasingly, Amazon.com owns the online space. In the third quarter of last year, whereas overall retail sales plunged 4 percent in the struggling economy and e-commerce sales were flat, Amazon.com's sales skyrocketed 24 percent. Even more importantly, Amazon.com's electronics and general merchandise sales, which compete directly with much of the selection found in Walmart stores, zoomed 44 percent.

Amazon has shown a relentless ambition to offer more of almost everything on the Web. It started by selling only books online, but now it sells everything from books, movies, and musicals to consumer electronics, home and garden products, clothing, jewelry, toys, tools, and even groceries. It keeps expanding into new lines—last year it added separate hubs for outdoor and sporting goods and cell phones. Then, it purchased online shoe retailer Zappos.com. It's even beefing up its private-label selection, adding new lines of Amazon-branded goods. If Amazon.com's expansion continues and online sales spurt as predicted, the Web seller will eat further and further into Walmart's bread-and-butter store sales.

But Walmart isn't about to let that happen. Instead, it's taking the battle to Amazon.com's home territory—the Web. Through aggressive pricing, it is now fighting for every dollar consumers spend online. Walmart fired the first shot before last year's holiday shopping season. It announced that it would take online preorders for 10 soon-to-be-released hardback books—all projected best sellers by authors such as John Grisham, Stephen King, Barbara Kingsolver, and James Patterson—at an unprecedented low price of just $10 each. (Actually, the new hardcover prices matched the $9.99 price that Amazon was already charging for e-book versions of bestsellers, downloaded to its Kindle or other readers, but Walmart does not sell e-books.) To take it a step further, Walmart also cut prices by 50 percent on 200 other best sellers, undercutting Amazon's prices. When Amazon quickly announced that it would match Walmart's $10 price on the 10 best sellers, the price war was on. Walmart dropped its price to $9.00, Amazon.com did likewise, and Walmart lowered its prices yet again, to $8.98.

These low book prices represented a 59–74 percent reduction off the list price, much more than the 30–40 percent reduction you might expect in traditional retail bookstores such as Barnes & Noble or Borders. In fact, Walmart and Amazon.com discounted these best sellers below costs—as so-called "loss-leaders"—to lure shoppers to their Web sites in hopes that they would buy other, more profitable items.

The book price war is having an impact beyond the two primary combatants—it's causing collateral damage across the entire book industry. "When your product is treated as a loss leader, it lowers its perceived value," says one publishing executive. In the long run, that's not great for either the companies that publish the books or the retailers who sell them. Price carries messages about customer value, notes another publisher. Companies want to be careful about the messages they send. And it's not just books. If you compare prices at Walmart.com and Amazon.com, you'll find the price battle raging across a broad range of product categories.

Who will win the online battle for the hearts and dollars of online buyers? Certainly, low prices will be an important factor. And when it comes to low prices, Walmart appears to have the upper hand. With its huge size, it can negotiate better terms with its suppliers. And by combining its online and off-line operations, it can provide some unique services, such as free and convenient delivery and returns of Web orders to stores (Walmart's site gives you three buying op-

tions: online, in-store, and site-to-store). Walmart is even experimenting with drive-through windows where shoppers can pick up their Internet orders. But Amazon.com also has advantages, including a highly recognizable online brand, a sophisticated distribution network built specifically for Web shopping, an unparalleled online customer shopping experience, and fast and free shipping with Amazon Prime. And, of course, Amazon.com is no stranger to low prices.

In the long run, however, reckless price cutting will likely do more damage than good to both Walmart and Amazon.com. Price wars can turn whole product categories into unattractive, low-margin commodities (think DVDs, for example). And buying online is about much more than just getting the best prices, even in today's economy. In the end, winning online consumers will require offering not only the lowest prices but also the best customer value in terms of price *and* product selection, speed, convenience, and overall shopping experience.

For now, the two retailers, especially Walmart, seem determined to fight it out on price. Amazon.com's CEO, Jeff Bezos, has long maintained that there's plenty of room for all competitors in the big world of retailing. However, Paul Vazquez, president and CEO of Walmart.com, says that it's "only a matter of time" before Walmart dominates Web shopping. Pricing, he thinks, will be key. "Our company is based on low prices," says Vazquez, laying down the challenge. "Even in books, we kept going until we were the low-priced leader. And we will do that in every category we need to. Our company is based on low prices." Offering the low price "is in our DNA."[1]

> Only time will tell who will win on the Web, Walmart or Amazon.com. But for now, the two retail giants, especially Walmart, seem determined to fight it out on price.

> **Walmart, the world's largest retailer, and Amazon.com, the world's largest online merchant, are at war over the hearts and dollars of online shoppers. The weapon of choice? Prices. However, although price can be a potent strategic weapon, it can also be a double-edged sword.**

Companies today face a fierce and fast-changing pricing environment. Value-seeking customers have put increased pricing pressure on many companies. Thanks to recent economic woes, the pricing power of the Internet, and value-driven retailers such as Walmart, today's more frugal consumers are pursuing spend-less strategies. In response, it seems that almost every company is looking for ways to cut prices.

Yet, cutting prices is often not the best answer. Reducing prices unnecessarily can lead to lost profits and damaging price wars. It can cheapen a brand by signaling to customers that price is more important than the customer value a brand delivers. ⦿ Instead, no matter what the state of the economy, companies should sell value, not price. In some cases, that means selling lesser products at rock-bottom prices. But in most cases, it means persuading customers that paying a higher price for the company's brand is justified by the greater value they gain.[2]

⦿ **Pricing: No matter what the state of the economy, companies should sell value, not price.**

What Is a Price? (p 290)

In the narrowest sense, **price** is the amount of money charged for a product or a service. More broadly, price is the sum of all the values that customers give up to gain the benefits of having or using a product or service. Historically, price has been the major factor affecting buyer choice. In recent decades, nonprice factors have gained increasing importance. However, price still remains one of the most important elements that determines a firm's market share and profitability.

Price is the only element in the marketing mix that produces revenue; all other elements represent costs. Price is also one of the most flexible marketing mix elements. Unlike product features and channel commitments, prices can be changed quickly. At the same time, pricing is the number-one problem facing many marketing executives, and many companies do not handle pricing well. Some managers view pricing as a big headache, preferring instead to focus on other marketing mix elements. However, smart managers treat pricing as a key strategic tool for creating and capturing customer value. Prices have a direct impact on a firm's bottom line. A small percentage improvement in price can generate a large percentage increase in profitability. More importantly, as part of a company's overall value proposition, price plays a key role in creating customer value and building customer relationships. "Instead of running away from pricing," says an expert, "savvy marketers are embracing it."[3]

Price
The amount of money charged for a product or service; the sum of the values that customers exchange for the benefits of having or using the product or service.

290

Author | Comment Setting the right price is one of the marketer's most difficult tasks. A host of factors come into play. But finding and implementing the right price strategy is critical to success.

Major Pricing Strategies (pp 291–300)

The price the company charges will fall somewhere between one that is too high to produce any demand and one that is too low to produce a profit. ● **Figure 10.1** summarizes the major considerations in setting price. Customer perceptions of the product's value set the ceiling for prices. If customers perceive that the product's price is greater than its value, they will not buy the product. Product costs set the floor for prices. If the company prices the product below its costs, the company's profits will suffer. In setting its price between these two extremes, the company must consider several internal and external factors, including competitors' strategies and prices, the overall marketing strategy and mix, and the nature of the market and demand.

Figure 10.1 suggests three major pricing strategies: customer value-based pricing, cost-based pricing, and competition-based pricing.

Author | Comment Like everything else in marketing, good pricing starts with *customers* and their perceptions of value.

Customer Value-Based Pricing

In the end, the customer will decide whether a product's price is right. Pricing decisions, like other marketing mix decisions, must start with customer value. When customers buy a product, they exchange something of value (the price) to get something of value (the benefits of having or using the product). Effective, customer-oriented pricing involves understanding how much value consumers place on the benefits they receive from the product and setting a price that captures this value.

Customer value-based pricing
Setting price based on buyers' perceptions of value rather than on the seller's cost.

Customer value-based pricing uses buyers' perceptions of value, not the seller's cost, as the key to pricing. Value-based pricing means that the marketer cannot design a product and marketing program and then set the price. Price is considered along with all other marketing mix variables *before* the marketing program is set.

● **Figure 10.2** compares value-based pricing with cost-based pricing. Although costs are an important consideration in setting prices, cost-based pricing is often product driven. The company designs what it considers to be a good product, adds up the costs of making the product, and sets a price that covers costs plus a target profit. Marketing must then convince buyers that the product's value at that price justifies its purchase. If the price turns out to be too high, the company must settle for lower markups or lower sales, both resulting in disappointing profits.

Value-based pricing reverses this process. The company first assesses customer needs and value perceptions. It then sets its target price based on customer perceptions of value. The targeted value and price drive decisions about what costs can be incurred and the resulting product design. As a result, pricing begins with analyzing consumer needs and value perceptions, and the price is set to match perceived value.

It's important to remember that "good value" is not the same as "low price." For example, a Steinway piano—any Steinway piano—costs a lot. But to those who own one, a Steinway is a great value:[4]

A Steinway grand piano typically runs anywhere from $40,000 to $165,000. The most popular model sells for around $72,000. But ask anyone who owns a Steinway grand piano, and they'll tell you that, when it comes to Steinway, price is nothing; the Steinway experience is everything. Steinway makes very high quality pianos; handcrafting

● **FIGURE | 10.1**
Considerations in Setting Price

If customers perceive that a product's price is greater than its value, they won't buy it. If the company prices a product below its costs, profits will suffer. Between the two extremes, the "right" pricing strategy is one that delivers both value to the customer and profits to the company.

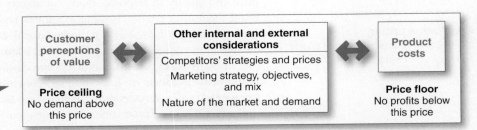

Customer perceptions of value
Price ceiling
No demand above this price

Other internal and external considerations
Competitors' strategies and prices
Marketing strategy, objectives, and mix
Nature of the market and demand

Product costs
Price floor
No profits below this price

⦿ **FIGURE | 10.2**
Value-Based Pricing Versus
Cost-Based Pricing

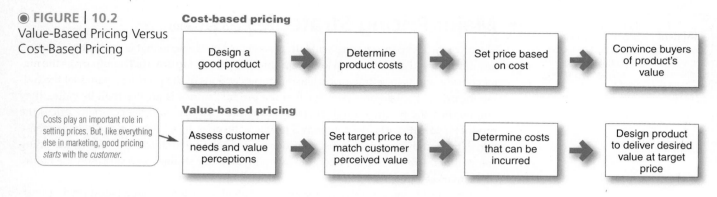

Cost-based pricing

Design a good product → Determine product costs → Set price based on cost → Convince buyers of product's value

Value-based pricing

Costs play an important role in setting prices. But, like everything else in marketing, good pricing starts with the customer.

Assess customer needs and value perceptions → Set target price to match customer perceived value → Determine costs that can be incurred → Design product to deliver desired value at target price

each Steinway requires up to one full year. But, more importantly, owners get the Steinway mystique. The Steinway name evokes images of classical concert stages and the celebrities and performers who've owned and played Steinway pianos across more than 155 years.

But Steinways aren't just for world-class pianists and the wealthy. Ninety-nine percent of all Steinway buyers are amateurs who perform only in their dens. ⦿ To such customers, whatever a Steinway costs, it's a small price to pay for the value of owning one. "A Steinway takes you places you've never been," says an ad. As one Steinway owner puts it, "My friendship with the Steinway piano is one of the most important and beautiful things in my life." Who can put a price on such feelings?

Companies often find it hard to measure the value customers will attach to its product. For example, calculating the cost of ingredients in a meal at a fancy restaurant is relatively easy. But assigning value to other satisfactions such as taste, environment, relaxation, conversation, and status is very hard. Such value is subjective; it varies both for different consumers and different situations.

Still, consumers will use these perceived values to evaluate a product's price, so the company must work to measure them. Sometimes, companies ask consumers how much they would pay for a basic product and for each benefit added to the offer. Or a company might conduct experiments to test the perceived value of different product offers. According to an old Russian proverb, there are two fools in every market—one who asks too much and one who asks too little. If the seller charges more than the buyers' perceived value, the company's sales will suffer. If the seller charges less, its products sell very well, but they produce less revenue than they would if they were priced at the level of perceived value.

We now examine two types of value-based pricing: *good-value pricing* and *value-added pricing*.

⦿ **Perceived value: A Steinway piano—any Steinway piano—costs a lot. But to those who own one, a Steinway is a great value. "A Steinway takes you places you've never been."**

Good-Value Pricing

Good-value pricing
Offering the right combination of quality and good service at a fair price.

Recent economic events have caused a fundamental shift in consumer attitudes toward price and quality. In response, many companies have changed their pricing approaches to bring them in line with changing economic conditions and consumer price perceptions. More and more, marketers have adopted **good-value pricing** strategies—offering the right combination of quality and good service at a fair price.

In many cases, this has involved introducing less-expensive versions of established, brand-name products. To meet tougher economic times and more frugal consumer spending habits, fast-food restaurants such as Taco Bell and McDonald's offer value meals and dollar menu items. Armani offers the less-expensive, more-casual Armani Exchange fashion line. Alberto-Culver's TRESemmé hair care line promises "A salon look and feel at a frac-

● **Good-value pricing: Ryanair appears to have found a radical new pricing solution, one that customers are sure to love: Make flying free!**

tion of the price." And every car company now offers small, inexpensive models better suited to the strapped consumer's budget.

In other cases, good-value pricing has involved redesigning existing brands to offer more quality for a given price or the same quality for less. Some companies even succeed by offering less value but at rock-bottom prices. ● For example, passengers flying the low-cost European airline Ryanair won't get much in the way of free amenities, but they'll like the airline's unbelievably low prices.[5]

Ireland's Ryanair, Europe's most profitable airline over the past decade, appears to have found a radical pricing solution: Make flying *free*! Before long, Ryanair promises, more than half of its passengers will pay nothing for their tickets. Remarkably, the airline already offers virtually free fares to one-fourth of its customers. What's its secret? Ryanair's frugal cost structure makes even the most cost-conscious competitor look like a reckless spender. In addition, however, Ryanair charges for virtually everything except the seat itself, from baggage check-in to seat-back advertising space. Once in the air, flight attendants hawk everything from scratch-card games to perfume and digital cameras to their captive audience. After arriving at some out-of-the-way airport, Ryanair will sell you a bus or train ticket into town. The airline even gets commissions from sales of Hertz rental cars, hotel rooms, ski packages, and travel insurance. Despite Ryanair's sometimes pushy efforts to extract more revenue from each traveler, customers aren't complaining. Most of the additional purchases are discretionary, and you just can't beat those outrageously low prices.

An important type of good-value pricing at the retail level is *everyday low pricing* (*EDLP*). EDLP involves charging a constant, everyday low price with few or no temporary price discounts. Retailers such as Costco and the furniture seller Room & Board practice EDLP. The king of EDLP is Walmart, which practically defined the concept. Except for a few sale items every month, Walmart promises everyday low prices on everything it sells. In contrast, *high-low pricing* involves charging higher prices on an everyday basis but running frequent promotions to lower prices temporarily on selected items. Department stores such as Kohl's and Macy's practice high-low pricing by having frequent sales days, early-bird savings, and bonus earnings for store credit-card holders.

Value-added pricing
Attaching value-added features and services to differentiate a company's offers and charging higher prices.

● **Value-added pricing: Rather than dropping prices for its venerable Stag umbrella brand to match cheaper imports, Currims successfully launched umbrellas with funky designs, cool colors, and value-added features and sold them at even higher prices.**

Value-Added Pricing

Value-based pricing doesn't mean simply charging what customers want to pay or setting low prices to meet competition. Instead, many companies adopt **value-added pricing** strategies. Rather than cutting prices to match competitors, they attach value-added features and services to differentiate their offers and thus support higher prices. For example, at a time when competing restaurants lowered their prices and screamed "value" in a difficult economy, fast-casual chain Panera Bread has prospered by adding value and charging accordingly (see Real Marketing 10.1). ● Also consider this example:

The monsoon season in Mumbai, India, is three months of near-nonstop rain. For 147 years, most Mumbaikars protected themselves with a Stag umbrella from venerable Ebrahim Currim & Sons. Like Ford's Model T, the basic Stag was sturdy, affordable, and of any color, as long as it was black. By the end of the twentieth century,

Real Marketing 10.1

Panera Bread Company:
It's Not about Low Prices

In the restaurant business these days, "value" typically means one thing—"cheap." When the economy dipped, so did fast-food restaurant prices, fare, and tactics. Now, casual restaurants are offering a seemingly endless hodgepodge of value meals, dollar items, budget sandwiches, and rapid-fire promotional deals that scream "value, value, value." But one everyday eatery— Panera Bread—understands that, even in uncertain economic times, low prices often aren't the best value. Instead, at Panera, value means wholesome food and fresh-baked bread, served in a warm and inviting environment, even if you have to pay a little more for it. Ronald Shaich, CEO of Panera, sums up this value-added concept perfectly. "Give people something of value and they'll happily pay for it," he says.

Shaich realized more than 25 years ago that people wanted something between fast food and casual dining. He perfected the "fast-casual" dining formula and opened Panera (Spanish for "bread basket"). Today, the bakery-café segment, which Shaich practically created, is the fastest growing sector in the fast-casual market. And Panera does bakery-café better than anyone else. In fact, Panera's $1.4 billion in sales more than doubles the combined sales of its next four competitors.

Why is Panera Bread so successful? Unlike so many competitors in the post-recession era, Panera isn't about having the lowest prices. Instead, it's about the *value* you get for what you pay, and what you get is a full-value dining experience.

At Panera, it all starts with the food, which centers around fresh-baked bread. When customers walk through the door, the first thing they see are massive displays of bread, all hand-formed and baked on-site. Bakers pass out warm bread samples to customers throughout the day. All new employees get "dough training," and even employee meetings start with the staff breaking bread together—literally. Bread is so central to Panera's DNA that the company's R&D team will scrap new dishes if the bread feels like an afterthought.

Of course, the food at Panera goes well beyond bread. Fresh bagels, pastries, egg soufflés, soups, salads, sandwiches and pani-

nis, and coffee drinks and smoothies give customers full meal options any time of day. Menu items brim with upscale ingredients such as Gorgonzola cheese, fresh basil, chipotle mayonnaise, and applewood-smoked bacon (the kind you'd find at the Four Seasons, not Wendy's). In all, Panera's target audience is more Food Network than fast food. "We hit a chord with people who understand and respond to food," says Scott Davis, chief concept officer. Our profile is "closer to what you'd find in a bistro than a fast-food joint." And to all that good food, Panera adds first-rate customer service. According to one research firm, Panera Bread continually stands in the top 10 of restaurant chains for overall service excellence. Last year, Panera rated among *BusinessWeek's* top 25 "Customer Service Champs."

But good fast-casual food and outstanding service are only part of Panera's value-

added proposition. Perhaps even more important is the Panera experience—one so inviting that people don't want to leave. Comfortable booths, leather sofas and chairs, warm lighting, a fireplace, and free Wi-Fi all beg customers to relax and stay awhile. In fact, the local Panera has become a kind of community gathering spot. At any given moment, you'll find a diverse group of customers hanging out together for a variety of reasons. One recent sample included a bride-to-be chatting with her wedding photographer, two businesspeople with laptops, a teacher grading papers, a church group engaged in Bible study, and a baker's dozen of couples and families just enjoying each others' company. Shaich knows that, although the food's important, what he's really selling is an inviting place to be. "In many ways," he says, "we're renting space to people, and the food is the price of admission."

Rather than cutting back on value and lowering prices in difficult times, Panera is looking for ways to add even more value. Freshness remains a driving force. Shaich has improved the freshness of lettuce by cutting the time from field to plate in half and using only the hearts of romaine. Store ovens now produce warm bread throughout the day, rather than just in the wee hours of the morning. And the chain's development labs are test-

Panera Bread understands that, even in uncertain economic times, low prices often aren't the best value. Says Panera CEO Ronald Shaich, "Give people something of value and they'll happily pay for it."

ing a new grill that churns out paninis in half the time. "This is the time to increase the food experience, when the customer least expects it," Shaich insists.

Panera's strategy of adding value and charging accordingly has paid off handsomely, through good economic times and bad. At a time when most chains, including those that are slashing their prices, are struggling and closing stores, Panera is flourishing. Over the past five years, its sales have more than tripled, and profits have more than doubled, including six straight quarters of double-digit profit gains through the heart of the recent recession. This year, Panera plans to add 100 new stores to its current portfolio of 1,500 cafés.

"Most of the world seems to be focused on the Americans who are unemployed,"

says Shaich. "We're focused on the 90 percent that are still employed." Although everyone wants value, he insists, not everyone wants it in the form of a value meal. Anne Skrodzki, a 28-year-old Chicago attorney, agrees. She recently spent $9.72 at Panera on a chicken Caesar salad and frozen lemonade. "I think it's a pretty good value. The portions are generous. The food is high quality . . . I've also gotten used to coming here for the free Wi-Fi."

The Panera Web site spells out the chain's valued-added positioning this way: "We are Panera. We are bakers of bread. We are fresh from the oven. We are a symbol of warmth and welcome. We are a simple pleasure, honest and genuine. We are a life story told over dinner. We are a long lunch with an old friend. We are your weekday morning ritual. We are the kindest gesture of neighbors. We are home. We are family. We are friends." Low prices? Not even on the radar.

Sources: Kate Rockwood, "Rising Dough: Why Panera Bread Is on a Roll," *Fast Company*, October 2009, pp. 69–70; Emily Bryson York, "Panera: An America's Hottest Brands Case Study," *Advertising Age*, November 16, 2009, p. 16; Julie Jargon, "Slicing the Bread But Not the Prices," *Wall Street Journal*, August 18, 2009, p. B1; Bruce Horovitz, "Panera Bakes a Recipe for Success," *USA Today*, July 23, 2009, accessed at www.usatoday.com; and www.panerabread.com, accessed September 2010.

however, the Stag was threatened by cheaper imports from China. Stag responded by dropping prices and scrimping on quality. It was a bad move: For the first time since the 1940s, the brand began losing money.

Finally, however, Stag came to its senses. It abandoned the price war and started innovating. It launched designer umbrellas in funky designs and cool colors. Teenagers and young adults lapped them up. It then launched umbrellas with a built-in high-power flashlight for those who walk unlit roads at night and models with prerecorded tunes for music lovers. For women who walk secluded streets after dark, there's Stag's Bodyguard model, armed with glare lights, emergency blinkers, and an alarm. Customers willingly pay up to a 100 percent premium for the new products. Under the new value-added strategy, the Stag brand has now returned to profitability. Come the monsoon season in June, the grand old black Stags still reappear on the streets of Mumbai—but now priced 15 percent higher than the imports.[6]

The Stag example illustrates once again that customers are motivated not by price but by what they get for what they pay. "If consumers thought the best deal was simply a question of money saved, we'd all be shopping in one big discount store," says one pricing expert. "Customers want value and are willing to pay for it. Savvy marketers price their products accordingly."[7]

Cost-based pricing

Setting prices based on the costs for producing, distributing, and selling the product plus a fair rate of return for effort and risk.

Author Comment | Costs set the floor for price, but the goal isn't always to *minimize* costs. In fact, many firms invest in higher costs so that they can claim higher prices and margins (think about Steinway pianos). The key is to manage the *spread* between costs and prices—how much the company makes for the customer value it delivers.

Cost-Based Pricing

Whereas customer-value perceptions set the price ceiling, costs set the floor for the price that the company can charge. **Cost-based pricing** involves setting prices based on the costs for producing, distributing, and selling the product plus a fair rate of return for its effort and risk. A company's costs may be an important element in its pricing strategy.

Some companies, such as Ryanair and Walmart, work to become the "low-cost producers" in their industries. Companies with lower costs can set lower prices that result in smaller margins but greater sales and profits. However, other companies—such as Apple, BMW, and Steinway—intentionally pay higher costs so that they can claim higher prices and margins. For example, it costs more to make a "handcrafted" Steinway piano than a Yamaha production model. But the higher costs result in higher quality, justifying that eye-popping $72,000 price. The key is to manage the spread between costs and prices—how much the company makes for the customer value it delivers.

Fixed costs (overhead)
Costs that do not vary with production or sales level.

Variable costs
Costs that vary directly with the level of production.

Total costs
The sum of the fixed and variable costs for any given level of production.

Types of Costs

A company's costs take two forms: fixed and variable. **Fixed costs** (also known as **overhead**) are costs that do not vary with production or sales level. For example, a company must pay each month's bills for rent, heat, interest, and executive salaries—whatever the company's output. **Variable costs** vary directly with the level of production. Each PC produced by HP involves a cost of computer chips, wires, plastic, packaging, and other inputs. Although these costs tend to be the same for each unit produced, they are called variable costs because the total varies with the number of units produced. **Total costs** are the sum of the fixed and variable costs for any given level of production. Management wants to charge a price that will at least cover the total production costs at a given level of production.

The company must watch its costs carefully. If it costs the company more than its competitors to produce and sell a similar product, the company will need to charge a higher price or make less profit, putting it at a competitive disadvantage.

Costs at Different Levels of Production

To price wisely, management needs to know how its costs vary with different levels of production. For example, suppose Texas Instruments (TI) built a plant to produce 1,000 calculators per day. ● **Figure 10.3A** shows the typical short-run average cost curve (SRAC). It shows that the cost per calculator is high if TI's factory produces only a few per day. But as production moves up to 1,000 calculators per day, the average cost per unit decreases. This is because fixed costs are spread over more units, with each one bearing a smaller share of the fixed cost. TI can try to produce more than 1,000 calculators per day, but average costs will increase because the plant becomes inefficient. Workers have to wait for machines, the machines break down more often, and workers get in each other's way.

If TI believed it could sell 2,000 calculators a day, it should consider building a larger plant. The plant would use more efficient machinery and work arrangements. Also, the unit cost of producing 2,000 calculators per day would be lower than the unit cost of producing 1,000 units per day, as shown in the long-run average cost (LRAC) curve (Figure 10.3B). In fact, a 3,000-capacity plant would be even more efficient, according to Figure 10.3B. But a 4,000-daily production plant would be less efficient because of increasing diseconomies of scale—too many workers to manage, paperwork slowing things down, and so on. Figure 10.3B shows that a 3,000-daily production plant is the best size to build if demand is strong enough to support this level of production.

Costs as a Function of Production Experience

Suppose TI runs a plant that produces 3,000 calculators per day. As TI gains experience in producing calculators, it learns how to do it better. Workers learn shortcuts and become more familiar with their equipment. With practice, the work becomes better organized, and TI finds better equipment and production processes. With higher volume, TI becomes more efficient and gains economies of scale. As a result, the average cost tends to decrease with accumulated production experience. This is shown in ● **Figure 10.4**.[8] Thus, the average cost of producing the first 100,000 calculators is $10 per calculator. When the company has produced the first 200,000 calculators, the average cost has fallen to $8.50. After its accumu-

● FIGURE | 10.3
Cost per Unit at Different Levels of Production per Period

What's the point of all the cost curves in this and the next few figures? Costs are an important factor in setting price, and companies must understand them well!

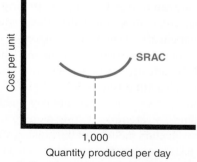

A. Cost behavior in a fixed-size plant

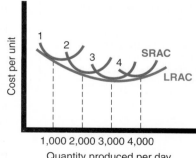

B. Cost behavior over different-size plants

FIGURE | 10.4
Cost per Unit as a Function
of Accumulated Production:
The Experience Curve

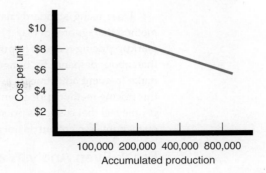

FIGURE | 10.4
Cost per Unit as a Function
of Accumulated Production:
The Experience Curve

Experience curve (learning curve)
The drop in the average per-unit
production cost that comes with
accumulated production experience.

lated production experience doubles again to 400,000, the average cost is $7. This drop in the average cost with accumulated production experience is called the **experience curve** (or the **learning curve**).

If a downward-sloping experience curve exists, this is highly significant for the company. Not only will the company's unit production cost fall, but it will fall faster if the company makes and sells more during a given time period. But the market has to stand ready to buy the higher output. And to take advantage of the experience curve, TI must get a large market share early in the product's life cycle. This suggests the following pricing strategy: TI should price its calculators low; its sales will then increase, and its costs will decrease through gaining more experience, and then it can lower its prices further.

Some companies have built successful strategies around the experience curve. However, a single-minded focus on reducing costs and exploiting the experience curve will not always work. Experience-curve pricing carries some major risks. The aggressive pricing might give the product a cheap image. The strategy also assumes that competitors are weak and not willing to fight it out by meeting the company's price cuts. Finally, while the company is building volume under one technology, a competitor may find a lower-cost technology that lets it start at prices lower than those of the market leader, who still operates on the old experience curve.

Cost-Plus Pricing

Cost-plus pricing (markup pricing)
Adding a standard markup to the cost of
the product.

The simplest pricing method is **cost-plus pricing** (or **markup pricing**)—adding a standard markup to the cost of the product. Construction companies, for example, submit job bids by estimating the total project cost and adding a standard markup for profit. Lawyers, accountants, and other professionals typically price by adding a standard markup to their costs. Some sellers tell their customers they will charge cost plus a specified markup; for example, aerospace companies often price this way to the government.

To illustrate markup pricing, suppose a toaster manufacturer had the following costs and expected sales:

Variable cost	$10
Fixed costs	$300,000
Expected unit sales	50,000

Then the manufacturer's cost per toaster is given by the following:

$$\text{unit cost} = \text{variable cost} + \frac{\text{fixed costs}}{\text{unit sales}} = \$10 + \frac{\$300,000}{50,000} = \$16$$

Now suppose the manufacturer wants to earn a 20 percent markup on sales. The manufacturer's markup price is given by the following:[9]

$$\text{markup price} = \frac{\text{unit cost}}{(1 - \text{desired return on sales})} = \frac{\$16}{1 - .2} = \$20$$

The manufacturer would charge dealers $20 per toaster and make a profit of $4 per unit. The dealers, in turn, will mark up the toaster. If dealers want to earn 50 percent on the sales price, they will mark up the toaster to $40 ($20 + 50% of $40). This number is equivalent to a *markup on cost* of 100 percent ($20/$20).

Does using standard markups to set prices make sense? Generally, no. Any pricing method that ignores demand and competitor prices is not likely to lead to the best price. Still, markup pricing remains popular for many reasons. First, sellers are more certain about costs than about demand. By tying the price to cost, sellers simplify pricing; they do not need to make frequent adjustments as demand changes. Second, when all firms in the industry use this pricing method, prices tend to be similar, so price competition is minimized. Third, many people feel that cost-plus pricing is fairer to both buyers and sellers. Sellers earn a fair return on their investment but do not take advantage of buyers when buyers' demand becomes great.

Break-Even Analysis and Target Profit Pricing

Break-even pricing (target return pricing)

Setting price to break even on the costs of making and marketing a product or setting price to make a target return.

Another cost-oriented pricing approach is **break-even pricing** (or a variation called **target return pricing**). The firm tries to determine the price at which it will break even or make the target return it is seeking.

Target return pricing uses the concept of a *break-even chart*, which shows the total cost and total revenue expected at different sales volume levels. ◉ **Figure 10.5** shows a break-even chart for the toaster manufacturer discussed here. Fixed costs are $300,000 regardless of sales volume. Variable costs are added to fixed costs to form total costs, which rise with volume. The total revenue curve starts at zero and rises with each unit sold. The slope of the total revenue curve reflects the price of $20 per unit.

The total revenue and total cost curves cross at 30,000 units. This is the *break-even volume*. At $20, the company must sell at least 30,000 units to break even, that is, for total revenue to cover total cost. Break-even volume can be calculated using the following formula:

$$\text{break-even volume} = \frac{\text{fixed cost}}{\text{price} - \text{variable cost}} = \frac{\$300{,}000}{\$20 - \$10} = 30{,}000$$

If the company wants to make a profit, it must sell more than 30,000 units at $20 each. Suppose the toaster manufacturer has invested $1,000,000 in the business and wants to set a price to earn a 20 percent return, or $200,000. In that case, it must sell at least 50,000 units at $20 each. If the company charges a higher price, it will not need to sell as many toasters to achieve its target return. But the market may not buy even this lower volume at the higher price. Much depends on price elasticity and competitors' prices.

The manufacturer should consider different prices and estimate break-even volumes, probable demand, and profits for each. This is done in ◉ **Table 10.1**. The table shows that as price increases, the break-even volume drops (column 2). But as price increases, the demand for toasters also decreases (column 3). At the $14 price, because the manufacturer clears only $4 per toaster ($14 less $10 in variable costs), it must sell a very high volume to break even. Even though the low price attracts many buyers, demand still falls below the high break-even point, and the manufacturer loses money. At the other extreme, with a $22 price, the manufacturer clears $12 per toaster and must sell only 25,000 units to break

◉ **FIGURE | 10.5**
Break-Even Chart for Determining Target-Return Price and Break-Even Volume

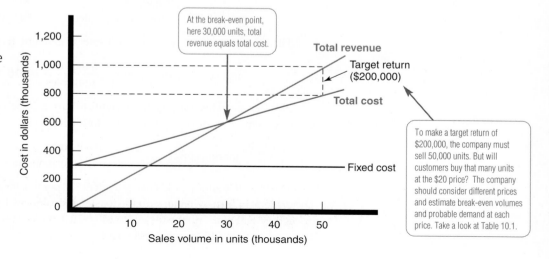

At the break-even point, here 30,000 units, total revenue equals total cost.

Total revenue

Target return ($200,000)

Total cost

Fixed cost

To make a target return of $200,000, the company must sell 50,000 units. But will customers buy that many units at the $20 price? The company should consider different prices and estimate break-even volumes and probable demand at each price. Take a look at Table 10.1.

⊙ TABLE | 10.1   Break-Even Volume and Profits at Different Prices

Price	Unit Demand Needed to Break Even	Expected Unit Demand at Given Price	Total Revenue (1) × (3)	Total Costs*	Profit (4) – (5)
$14	75,000	71,000	$994,000	$1,010,000	−$16,000
16	50,000	67,000	1,072,000	970,000	102,000
18	37,500	60,000	1,080,000	900,000	180,000
20	30,000	42,000	840,000	720,000	120,000
22	25,000	23,000	506,000	530,000	−$24,000

*Assumes fixed costs of $300,000 and constant unit variable costs of $10.

even. But at this high price, consumers buy too few toasters, and profits are negative. The table shows that a price of $18 yields the highest profits. Note that none of the prices produce the manufacturer's target return of $200,000. To achieve this return, the manufacturer will have to search for ways to lower the fixed or variable costs, thus lowering the break-even volume.

Author Comment | In setting prices, the company must also consider competitors' prices. No matter what price it charges—high, low, or in-between—the company must be certain to give customers superior value for that price.

Competition-based pricing

Setting prices based on competitors' strategies, prices, costs, and market offerings.

Competition-Based Pricing

Competition-based pricing involves setting prices based on competitors' strategies, costs, prices, and market offerings. Consumers will base their judgments of a product's value on the prices that competitors charge for similar products.

In assessing competitors' pricing strategies, the company should ask several questions. First, how does the company's market offering compare with competitors' offerings in terms of customer value? If consumers perceive that the company's product or service provides greater value, the company can charge a higher price. If consumers perceive less value relative to competing products, the company must either charge a lower price or change customer perceptions to justify a higher price.

Next, how strong are current competitors, and what are their current pricing strategies? If the company faces a host of smaller competitors charging high prices relative to the value they deliver, it might charge lower prices to drive weaker competitors from the market. If the market is dominated by larger, low-price competitors, the company may decide to target unserved market niches with value-added products at higher prices.

For example, ⊙ Annie Bloom's Books, an independent bookseller in Portland, Oregon, isn't likely to win a price war against Amazon.com or Barnes & Noble—it doesn't even try. Instead, the shop relies on its personal approach, cozy atmosphere, and friendly and knowledgeable staff to turn local book lovers into loyal patrons, even if they have to pay a little more. Customers writing on a consumer review Web site recently gave Annie Bloom's five-star ratings, supported by the kinds of comments you likely wouldn't see for Barnes & Noble:[10]

Annie Bloom's is not the biggest bookstore, nor the most convenient to park at, nor are the prices incredibly discounted, nor is the bathroom easy to find . . . however, [i]t is one of the friendliest bookstores in town. It is just big enough for a solid hour of browsing. And it has a talented, smart, and long-term staff with incredible taste. . . . You'll find common best sellers here, but you'll also find all those cool books you heard about on NPR or in Vanity Fair that you never see featured at Barnes & Noble. [It's a] bookstore for the book crowd. . . . Good customer service here! Also, be nice to the cat. PS: [It] has a kid's play area in the back.

⊙ **Pricing against larger, low-price competitors:** Independent bookstore Annie Bloom's Books isn't likely to win a price war against Amazon.com or Barnes & Noble. Instead, it relies on outstanding customer service and a cozy atmosphere to turn booklovers into loyal customers.

What principle should guide decisions about what price to charge relative to those of competitors? The answer is simple in concept but often difficult in practice: No matter what price you charge—high, low, or in-between—be certain to give customers superior value for that price.

Author
Comment | Now that we've looked at the three general pricing approaches—value-, cost-, and competitor-based pricing—let's dig into some of the many other factors that affect pricing decisions.

Other Internal and External Considerations Affecting Price Decisions (pp 300–306)

Beyond customer value perceptions, costs, and competitor strategies, the company must consider several additional internal and external factors. Internal factors affecting pricing include the company's overall marketing strategy, objectives, and marketing mix, as well as other organizational considerations. External factors include the nature of the market and demand and other environmental factors.

Overall Marketing Strategy, Objectives, and Mix

Price is only one element of the company's broader marketing strategy. Thus, before setting price, the company must decide on its overall marketing strategy for the product or service. If the company has selected its target market and positioning carefully, then its marketing mix strategy, including price, will be fairly straightforward. For example, when Honda developed its Acura brand to compete with European luxury-performance cars in the higher-income segment, this required charging a high price. In contrast, when it introduced the Honda Fit model—billed as "a pint-sized fuel miser with feisty giddy up"—this positioning required charging a low price. Thus, pricing strategy is largely determined by decisions on market positioning.

Pricing may play an important role in helping to accomplish company objectives at many levels. A firm can set prices to attract new customers or profitably retain existing ones. It can set prices low to prevent competition from entering the market or set prices at competitors' levels to stabilize the market. It can price to keep the loyalty and support of resellers or avoid government intervention. Prices can be reduced temporarily to create excitement for a brand. Or one product may be priced to help the sales of other products in the company's line.

Price is only one of the marketing mix tools that a company uses to achieve its marketing objectives. Price decisions must be coordinated with product design, distribution, and promotion decisions to form a consistent and effective integrated marketing program. Decisions made for other marketing mix variables may affect pricing decisions. For example, a decision to position the product on high-performance quality will mean that the seller must charge a higher price to cover higher costs. And producers whose resellers are expected to support and promote their products may have to build larger reseller margins into their prices.

Companies often position their products on price and then tailor other marketing mix decisions to the prices they want to charge. Here, price is a crucial product-positioning factor that defines the product's market, competition, and design. Many firms support such price-positioning strategies with a technique called **target costing**. Target costing reverses the usual process of first designing a new product, determining its cost, and then asking, "Can we sell it for that?" Instead, it starts with an ideal selling price based on customer-value considerations and then targets costs that will ensure that the price is met. For example, when Honda set out to design the Fit, it began with a $13,950 starting price point and an operating efficiency of 33 miles per gallon firmly in mind. It then designed a stylish, peppy little car with costs that allowed it to give target customers those values.

Target costing
Pricing that starts with an ideal selling price and then targets costs that will ensure that the price is met.

Other companies deemphasize price and use other marketing mix tools to create *nonprice* positions. Often, the best strategy is not to charge the lowest price but rather differentiate the marketing offer to make it worth a higher price. For example, Bang & Olufsen (B&O)—known for its cutting-edge consumer electronics—builds more value into its products and charges sky-high prices. A B&O 50-inch BeoVision 4 HDTV will cost you $7,500; a 65-inch model runs $13,500, and a 103-inch model goes for $93,050. A complete B&O entertainment system? Well, you don't really want to know the price. But target customers recognize B&O's very high quality and are willing to pay more to get it.

● **Positioning on high price: Titus features its lofty prices in its advertising— "suggested retail price: $7,750.00."**

Some marketers even position their products on *high* prices, featuring high prices as part of their product's allure. For example, Grand Marnier offers a $225 bottle of Cuvée du Cent Cinquantenaire that's marketed with the tagline "Hard to find, impossible to pronounce, and prohibitively expensive." And Titus Cycles, a premium bicycle manufacturer, features its high prices in its advertising. ● One ad humorously shows a man giving his girlfriend a "cubic zirconia" engagement ring so that he can purchase a Titus Vuelo for himself. "Suggested retail price: $7,750.00."

Thus, marketers must consider the total marketing strategy and mix when setting prices. But again, even when featuring price, marketers need to remember that customers rarely buy on price alone. Instead, they seek products that give them the best value in terms of benefits received for the prices paid.

Organizational Considerations

Management must decide who within the organization should set prices. Companies handle pricing in a variety of ways. In small companies, prices are often set by top management rather than by the marketing or sales departments. In large companies, pricing is typically handled by divisional or product line managers. In industrial markets, salespeople may be allowed to negotiate with customers within certain price ranges. Even so, top management sets the pricing objectives and policies, and it often approves the prices proposed by lower-level management or salespeople.

In industries in which pricing is a key factor (airlines, aerospace, steel, railroads, oil companies), companies often have pricing departments to set the best prices or help others in setting them. These departments report to the marketing department or top management. Others who have an influence on pricing include sales managers, production managers, finance managers, and accountants.

The Market and Demand

As noted earlier, good pricing starts with an understanding of how customers' perceptions of value affect the prices they are willing to pay. Both consumer and industrial buyers balance the price of a product or service against the benefits of owning it. Thus, before setting prices, the marketer must understand the relationship between price and demand for the company's product. In this section, we take a deeper look at the price-demand relationship and how it varies for different types of markets. We then discuss methods for analyzing the price-demand relationship.

Pricing in Different Types of Markets

The seller's pricing freedom varies with different types of markets. Economists recognize four types of markets, each presenting a different pricing challenge.

Under *pure competition*, the market consists of many buyers and sellers trading in a uniform commodity, such as wheat, copper, or financial securities. No single buyer or seller has much effect on the going market price. In a purely competitive market, marketing research, product development, pricing, advertising, and sales promotion play little or no role. Thus, sellers in these markets do not spend much time on marketing strategy.

Under *monopolistic competition*, the market consists of many buyers and sellers who trade over a range of prices rather than a single market price. A range of prices occurs because sellers can differentiate their offers to buyers. Sellers try to develop differentiated offers for different customer segments and, in addition to price, freely use branding, advertising, and personal selling to set their offers apart. Thus, Toyota sets its Prius brand apart through strong branding and advertising, reducing the impact of price. It advertises that the third generation Prius takes you from "zero to sixty in 70% fewer emissions." Because there are many competitors in such markets, each firm is less affected by competitors' pricing strategies than in oligopolistic markets.

Under *oligopolistic competition*, the market consists of a few sellers who are highly sensitive to each other's pricing and marketing strategies. Because there are few sellers, each seller is alert and responsive to competitors' pricing strategies and moves.

In a *pure monopoly*, the market consists of one seller. The seller may be a government monopoly (the U.S. Postal Service), a private regulated monopoly (a power company), or a private nonregulated monopoly (DuPont when it introduced nylon). Pricing is handled differently in each case.

Analyzing the Price-Demand Relationship

Demand curve
A curve that shows the number of units the market will buy in a given time period, at different prices that might be charged.

Each price the company might charge will lead to a different level of demand. The relationship between the price charged and the resulting demand level is shown in the **demand curve** in ● **Figure 10.6**. The demand curve shows the number of units the market will buy in a given time period at different prices that might be charged. In the normal case, demand and price are inversely related—that is, the higher the price, the lower the demand. Thus, the company would sell less if it raised its price from P_1 to P_2. In short, consumers with limited budgets probably will buy less of something if its price is too high.

Understanding a brand's price-demand curve is crucial to good pricing decisions. ConAgra Foods learned this lesson when pricing its Banquet frozen dinners.[11]

ConAgra found out the hard way about the perils of pushing up the price of a Banquet frozen dinner. When it tried to recoup high commodity costs by hiking the list price last year, many retailers began charging up to $1.25 a meal. The response from shoppers used to paying $1? The cold shoulder. The resulting sales drop forced ConAgra to peddle excess dinners to discounters and contributed to a 40 percent drop in the company's stock price for the year. ● It turns out that "the key component for Banquet dinners—the key attribute—is you've got to be at $1," says ConAgra's CEO Gary Rodkin. "Everything else pales in comparison to that." The price is now back to a buck a dinner. To make money at that price, ConAgra is doing a better job of managing costs. It tossed out pricey items such as barbecued chicken and country-fried pork in favor of grilled meat patties and rice and beans. It also shrank portion sizes while swapping in cheaper ingredients, such as mashed potatoes for brownies. Consumers are responding well to the brand's efforts to keep prices down. Where else can you find dinner for $1?

● The price-demand curve: When ConAgra raised prices on its Banquet frozen dinners, sales fell sharply. "The key component . . . is you've got to be at $1," says CEO Gary Rodkin, pictured above. "Everything else pales in comparison to that."

Most companies try to measure their demand curves by estimating demand at different prices. The type of market makes a difference. In a monopoly, the demand curve shows the total market demand resulting from different prices. If the company faces competition, its demand at different prices will depend on whether competitors' prices stay constant or change with the company's own prices.

Price Elasticity of Demand

Consider the two demand curves in Figure 10.6. In Figure 10.6A, a price increase from P_1 to P_2 leads to a relatively small drop in demand from Q_1 to Q_2. In Figure 10.6B, however, the same price increase leads to a large drop in demand from Q'_1 to Q'_2. If demand hardly

● FIGURE | 10.6
Demand Curves

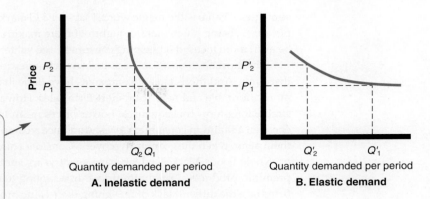

A. Inelastic demand

B. Elastic demand

Price and demand are related—no big surprise there. Usually, higher prices result in lower demand. But in the case of some prestige goods, the relationship might be reversed. A higher price signals higher quality and status, resulting in more demand, not less.

Price elasticity

A measure of the sensitivity of demand to changes in price.

changes with a small change in price, we say the demand is *inelastic*. If demand changes greatly, we say the demand is *elastic*. The **price elasticity** of demand is given by the following formula:

$$\text{price elasticity of demand} = \frac{\text{\% change in quantity demanded}}{\text{\% change in price}}$$

Suppose demand falls by 10 percent when a seller raises its price by 2 percent. The price elasticity of demand is therefore −5 (the minus sign confirms the inverse relation between price and demand), and demand is elastic. If demand falls by 2 percent with a 2 percent increase in price, then elasticity is −1. In this case, the seller's total revenue stays the same: The seller sells fewer items but at a higher price that preserves the same total revenue. If demand falls by 1 percent when price is increased by 2 percent, then elasticity is $-\frac{1}{2}$, and demand is inelastic. The less elastic the demand, the more it pays for the seller to raise the price.

What determines the price elasticity of demand? Buyers are less price sensitive when the product they are buying is unique or when it is high in quality, prestige, or exclusiveness; substitute products are hard to find or when they cannot easily compare the quality of substitutes; and the total expenditure for a product is low relative to their income or when the cost is shared by another party.[12]

If demand is elastic rather than inelastic, sellers will consider lowering their prices. A lower price will produce more total revenue. This practice makes sense as long as the extra costs of producing and selling more do not exceed the extra revenue. At the same time, most firms want to avoid pricing that turns their products into commodities. In recent years, forces such as dips in the economy, deregulation, and the instant price comparisons afforded by the Internet and other technologies have increased consumer price sensitivity, turning products ranging from telephones and computers to new automobiles into commodities in some consumers' eyes.

Marketers need to work harder than ever to differentiate their offerings when a dozen competitors are selling virtually the same product at a comparable or lower price. More than ever, companies need to understand the price sensitivity of their customers and the trade-offs people are willing to make between price and product characteristics.

The Economy

Economic conditions can have a strong impact on the firm's pricing strategies. Economic factors such as a boom or recession, inflation, and interest rates affect pricing decisions because they affect consumer spending, consumer perceptions of the product's price and value, and the company's costs of producing and selling a product.

In the aftermath of the recent Great Recession, consumers have rethought the price-value equation. Many consumers have tightened their belts and become more value conscious. In the new, more-frugal economy, bemoans one marketer, "The frill is gone." Even more, consumers will likely continue their thrifty ways well beyond any economic recovery. As a result, many marketers have increased their emphasis on value-for-the-money pricing strategies. "Value is the magic word," says a P&G marketer. "In these economic times, people are . . . being much more thoughtful before making purchases. . . . Now, we're going to be even more focused on helping consumers see value."[13]

The most obvious response to the new economic realities is to cut prices and offer deep discounts. And thousands of companies have done just that. Lower prices make products more affordable and help spur short-term sales. However, such price cuts can have undesirable long-term consequences. Lower prices mean lower margins. Deep discounts may cheapen a brand in consumers' eyes. And once a company cuts prices, it's difficult to raise them again when the economy recovers. Consider companies such as Starbucks, Tiffany's, or Whole Foods Market, which have spent years successfully positioning themselves on premium products at premium prices. In adapting to the new pricing environment, such firms face the difficult task of realigning their value propositions while staying true to their longer-term "more-for-more" positioning (see Real Marketing 10.2).

Rather than cutting prices, many companies are instead shifting their marketing focus to more affordable items in their product mixes. ⦿ For example, whereas its previous promotions emphasized high-end products and pricey concepts such as creating dream kitchens, Home Depot's more recent advertising pushes items like potting soil and hand tools under the tagline: "More saving. More doing. That's the power of Home Depot." Other companies are holding prices but redefining the "value" in their value propositions. For instance, Unilever has repositioned its higher-end Bertolli frozen meals as an eat-at-home brand that's more affordable than eating out. And Kraft's Velveeta cheese ads tell shoppers to "forget the cheddar, Velveeta is better," claiming that a package of Velveeta is "twice the size of cheddar, for the same price."[14]

Remember, even in tough economic times, consumers do not buy based on prices alone. They balance the price they pay against the value they receive. For example, according to a recent survey, despite selling its shoes for as much as $150 a pair, Nike commands the highest consumer loyalty of any brand in the footwear segment.[15] Customers perceive the value of Nike's products and the Nike ownership experience to be well worth the price. Thus, no matter what price they charge—low or high— companies need to offer great *value for the money*.

⦿ Pricing and the economy: Rather than just cutting prices, Home Depot shifted its marketing focus to more affordable items and projects under the tagline: "More saving. More doing."

Other External Factors

Beyond the market and the economy, the company must consider several other factors in its external environment when setting prices. It must know what impact its prices will have on other parties in its environment. How will *resellers* react to various prices? The company should set prices that give resellers a fair profit, encourage their support, and help them to sell the product effectively. The *government* is another important external influence on pricing decisions. Finally, *social concerns* may need to be taken into account. In setting prices, a company's short-term sales, market share, and profit goals may need to be tempered by broader societal considerations. We will examine public policy issues in pricing at the end of Chapter 11.

Real Marketing 10.2

Whole Foods Market: Price and Value in a Troubled Economy

Only a few years ago, consumers were flush with cash, and Whole Foods Market was thriving. The upscale grocery retailer was a model "more-for-more" marketer, offering premium value at premium prices. Under its motto, "Whole Foods, Whole People, Whole Planet," it served up a gourmet assortment of high-quality grocery items, including a strong mix of natural and organic foods and health products. Its upscale, health-conscious customers were willing and able to pay higher prices for the extra value they got. Over the previous two decades, Whole Foods Market's sales had soared, and its stock price had grown at an eye-popping compounded annual rate of 25 percent, peaking at almost $80 a share.

Then came the Great Recession of 2008. People in all walks of life began rethinking the price-value equation and looking for ways to save. They asked tough questions, such as "I love the wonderful foods and smells in my Whole Foods Market, but is it worth the extra 30 percent versus shopping at Walmart?" All of a sudden, Whole Foods Market's seemingly perfect premium marketing strategy looked less like a plum and more like a bruised organic banana. Even relatively affluent customers were cutting back and spending less. For the first time in its history, the company faced declines in same-store sales, and its stock price plunged to a shocking low of close to $8. "The company had long touted its premium food offerings in its marketing, and that branding [was] now actually hurting them," observed a retail analyst. Some customers even amended the company's motto, making it "Whole Foods, Whole Paycheck."

Hit hard by the economic downturn, Whole Foods Market faced difficult questions. Should it hold the line on the premium positioning that had won it so much success in the past? Or should it cut prices and reposition itself to fit the leaner times? On the one hand, it could simply batten down the hatches and wait for the economic storm to pass. But a wait-and-see strategy made little sense; the newfound consumer frugality probably will last for years to come. At the other extreme, Whole Foods could reshuffle its product as-

sortment, cut prices, and reposition downward to fit the new times. But that strategy would sacrifice most of what had made the upscale grocer unique over the years.

So Whole Foods Market decided to stick with its core up-market positioning but subtly realign its value proposition to better meet the needs of recession-rattled customers. It set out to downplay the gourmet element of its positioning while playing up the real value of the healthy but exciting food it offers. First, rather than dropping its everyday prices across the board, Whole Foods lowered prices on many basic items that customers demand most and bolstered these savings by offering significant sales on selected other items. It also started emphasizing its private-label brand, 365 Everyday Value.

Next, Whole Foods Market launched a new marketing program aimed at tempering the chain's high-price reputation, reconnecting with customers, and convincing them that Whole Foods Market was, in fact, an afford-

able place to shop. To help consumers see the value, it beefed up its communications about private-label and sale items using newsletters, coupons, and its Web site. It assigned workers to serve as "value tour guides" to escort shoppers around stores pointing out value items. New ads featured headlines such as "No wallets were harmed in the buying of our 365 Everyday Value products," and "Sticker shock, but in a good way."

But the new marketing efforts did more than simply promote more affordable merchandise. They worked to convince shoppers that Whole Foods Market's regular products and prices offer good value as well—that when it comes to quality food, price isn't everything. As one tour guide notes, wherever you go, you'll have to pay a premium for organic food. "Value means getting a good exchange for your money." Such conversations helped to shift customers' eyes off of price and back to value.

To strengthen customer relationships further in tighter times, Whole Foods Market also boosted its social media presence. It set up a Facebook page and dozens of Twitter accounts to address specific value and other topics related to every product category and every store. Videos on its Whole Tube YouTube channel advised customers to "waste not, want not." At the official Whole Foods Market

When the economy dipped, rather than cutting everyday prices, Whole Foods set out to convince shoppers that it was, in fact, an affordable place to shop. It even assigned workers to serve as "value tour guides," like the one above, to escort shoppers around stores pointing out value items.

Continued on next page

blog—The Whole Story—customers learned about and exchanged views on organic and natural food, recipes, and other topics. Interestingly, customer conversations on this blog tended to focus more heavily on the "what you get" from Whole Foods Market than the "what you pay." Customers more interested in the value side of the price-value equation could log onto The Whole Deal, an official blog that offers coupons, deals, budget-friendly recipes, and other things that help you make "wiser choices for your budget, the Earth, and your fellow Earthlings." Whole Foods also offered iPhone and iPod apps, providing more than 2,000 recipes using Whole Foods Market natural and organic products and highlighting meals that feed a family of four for less than $15.

How is the Whole Foods Market value realignment working out? So far, so good. By late 2010, the chain appeared to have regained its footing. Same-store sales and profits were growing once again, and its stock

price had recovered to over $45 a share. Regarding the move to value offerings, says Whole Foods Market's COO, "We did it early, we did it strong, and we've done it consistently." Customers now "give us credit for being more competitive and for meeting their needs in these times, and now they can see the better deals, the better pricing, the better choices."

Most important, however, Whole Foods Market has managed to realign its value proposition in a way that preserves all the things that have made it special to its customers through the years. In all, things aren't really much different inside a local Whole Foods Market these days. There are more sale items, and the private-label 365 Everyday Value brand is more prominently presented, but customers can still find the same alluring assortment of high-quality, flavorful, and natural foods wrapped in Whole Foods, Whole People, Whole Planet values. Thanks to the subtle shifts in its value strategy, however, customers might just appreciate the value side of the Whole Foods Market formula a little bit more.

Sources: Quotes and other information from Mike Duff, "Whole Foods Dropping Prices to Raise Its Prospects," *R&FF Retailer*, November 2009, p. 14; "Whole Foods Market Reports First Quarter Results," February 16, 2010, www.wholefoodsmarket.com/company/pdfs/Q110financial.pdf; Elliot Zwiebach, "Whole Foods 'Bullish' as Trends Improve," *Supermarket News*, August 10, 2009, p. 1; David Kesmodel, "Whole Foods Net Falls 31% in Slow Economy," *Wall Street Journal*, August 6, 2008, p. B1; Stuart Elliott, "With Shoppers Pinching Pennies, Some Big Retailers Get the Message," *New York Times*, April 13, 2009, p. B6; "Whole Web," *Progressive Grocer*, June 19, 2009, accessed at http://progressivegrocer.com; and information from http://blog.wholefoodsmarket.com, www.wholefoodsmarket.com/products/wholedeal/index.php, and www.wholefoodsmarket.com, accessed November 2010.

REVIEWING Objectives AND KEY Terms

Companies today face a fierce and fast-changing pricing environment. Firms successful at creating customer value with the other marketing mix activities must still capture some of this value in the prices they earn. This chapter examined the importance of pricing, general pricing strategies, and the internal and external considerations that affect pricing decisions.

marketing mix. It is the only marketing mix element that produces revenue; all other elements represent costs. More importantly, as a part of a company's overall value proposition, price plays a key role in creating customer value and building customer relationships. Smart managers treat pricing as a key strategic tool for creating and capturing customer value.

Objective 1 Answer the question "What is a price?" and discuss the importance of pricing in today's fast-changing environment. (p 290)

Price can be defined narrowly as the amount of money charged for a product or service. Or it can be defined more broadly as the sum of the values that consumers exchange for the benefits of having and using the product or service. The pricing challenge is to find the price that will let the company make a fair profit by getting paid for the customer value it creates.

Despite the increased role of nonprice factors in the modern marketing process, price remains an important element in the

Objective 2 Identify the three major pricing strategies and discuss the importance of understanding customer-value perceptions, company costs, and competitor strategies when setting prices. (pp 291–300)

Companies can choose from three major pricing strategies: customer value-based pricing, cost-based pricing, and competition-based pricing. *Customer value-based pricing* uses buyers' perceptions of value as the basis for setting price. Good pricing begins with a complete understanding of the value that a product or service creates for customers and setting a price that captures that value. Customer perceptions of the product's value set the ceiling for prices. If customers perceive that a product's price is greater than its value, they will not buy the product.

Companies can pursue either of two types of value-based pricing. *Good-value pricing* involves offering just the right combination of quality and good service at a fair price. EDLP is an example of this strategy. *Value-added pricing* involves attaching value-added features and services to differentiate the company's offers and support charging higher prices.

Cost-based pricing involves setting prices based on the costs for producing, distributing, and selling products plus a fair rate of return for effort and risk. Company and product costs are an important consideration in setting prices. Whereas customer value perceptions set the price ceiling, costs set the floor for pricing. However, cost-based pricing is product driven rather than customer driven. The company designs what it considers to be a good product and sets a price that covers costs plus a target profit. If the price turns out to be too high, the company must settle for lower markups or lower sales, both resulting in disappointing profits. If the company prices the product below its costs, its profits will also suffer. Cost-based pricing approaches include *cost-plus pricing* and *break-even pricing* (or target profit pricing).

Competition-based pricing involves setting prices based on competitors' strategies, costs, prices, and market offerings. Consumers base their judgments of a product's value on the prices that competitors charge for similar products. If consumers perceive that the company's product or service provides greater value, the company can charge a higher price. If consumers perceive less value relative to competing products, the company must either charge a lower price or change customer perceptions to justify a higher price.

Objective 3 **Identify and define the other important internal and external factors affecting a firm's pricing decisions.** (pp 300–306)

Other *internal* factors that influence pricing decisions include the company's overall marketing strategy, objectives, and marketing mix, as well as organizational considerations. Price is only one element of the company's broader marketing strategy. If the company has selected its target market and positioning carefully, then its marketing mix strategy, including price, will be fairly straightforward. Some companies position their products on price and then tailor other marketing mix decisions to the prices they want to charge. Other companies deemphasize price and use other marketing mix tools to create *nonprice* positions.

Other *external* pricing considerations include the nature of the market and demand and environmental factors such as the economy, reseller needs, and government actions. The seller's pricing freedom varies with different types of markets. Ultimately, the customer decides whether the company has set the right price. The customer weighs price against the perceived values of using the product: If the price exceeds the sum of the values, consumers will not buy. So the company must understand concepts such as demand curves (the price-demand relationship) and price elasticity (consumer sensitivity to prices).

Economic conditions can also have a major impact on pricing decisions. The Great Recession caused consumers to rethink the price-value equation. Marketers have responded by increasing their emphasis on value-for-the-money pricing strategies. Even in tough economic times, however, consumers do not buy based on prices alone. Thus, no matter what price they charge—low or high—companies need to offer superior value for the money.

KEY Terms

OBJECTIVE 1

Price (p 290)

OBJECTIVE 2

Customer value-based pricing (p 291)
Good-value pricing (p 292)
Value-added pricing (p 293)

OBJECTIVE 3

Cost-based pricing (p 295)
Fixed costs (overhead; p 296)
Variable costs (p 296)
Total costs (p 296)
Experience curve (learning curve; p 297)

Cost-plus pricing (markup pricing; p 297)
Break-even pricing (target return pricing; p 298)
Competition-based pricing (p 299)
Target costing (p 300)
Demand curve (p 302)
Price elasticity (p 303)

PEARSON mymarketinglab

- Check your understanding of the concepts and key terms using the mypearsonmarketinglab study plan for this chapter.
- Apply the concepts in a business context using the simulation entitled **Pricing**.

DISCUSSING & APPLYING THE Concepts

Discussing the Concepts

1. What factors must marketers consider when setting prices? (AACSB: Communication).

2. Name and describe the two types of value-based pricing methods. (AACSB: Communication)

3. Describe the types of cost-based pricing and the methods of implementing each. (AACSB: Communication)

4. What is *target costing* and how is it different from the usual process of setting prices? (AACSB: Communication)

5. Discuss the impact of the economy on a company's pricing strategies. (AACSB: Communication)

6. Name and describe the four types of markets recognized by economists and discuss the pricing challenges posed by each. (AACSB: Communication)

Applying the Concepts

1. In a small group, discuss your perceptions of value and how much you are willing to pay for the following products: automobiles, frozen dinners, jeans, and athletic shoes. Are there differences among members of your group? Explain why those differences exist. Discuss some examples of brands of these products that are positioned to deliver different value to consumers. (AACSB: Communication; Reflective Thinking)

2. Find estimates of price elasticity for a variety of consumer goods and services. Explain what price elasticities of 0.5 and 2.4 mean. (*Note*: These are absolute values, as price elasticity is usually negative.) (AACSB: Communication; Reflective Thinking)

3. In a small group, determine the costs associated with offering an online MBA degree in addition to a traditional MBA degree at a university. Which costs are fixed and which are variable? Determine the tuition (that is, price) to charge for a three-credit course in this degree program. Which pricing method is your group using to determine the price? (AACSB: Communication; Reflective Thinking)

FOCUS ON Technology

Would you shop around for the best price on a medical procedure? Most patients do not know the price of a medical procedure, and many might not care because they think insurance will cover it. But that is not always the case. Many patients are paying out of their own pockets for their health care. However, health-care costs and doctors' prices are now more transparent thanks to the Internet. Several Web sites arm patients with cost information, and others allow them to make price comparisons in their areas. They might even get a coupon for a price reduction from a participating provider.

1. Go to www.outofpocket.com/OOP/Default.aspx to determine the average cost for a colonoscopy. Using a source such as www.newchoicehealth.com, determine the cost for a colonoscopy in your city and in a nearby city. What is the most and least expensive in each city? Are prices comparable to the national average? Why are there differences or similarities in the range of prices for the two cities? (AACSB: Communication; Use of IT; Reflective Thinking)

2. Health-care providers offer price deals through these types of Web sites. Debate the likelihood of consumers taking advantage of Internet price discounts for medical care. (AACSB: Communication; Reflective Thinking)

FOCUS ON Ethics

In airline pricing, $5 here and $10 there; it all starts to add up. Airlines are nickel-and-diming flyers right and left, except that there are more zeros after the fives and tens! Add-on fees contributed more than $5 billion in airline revenue in 2009. Change your flight—that will cost upward of $150. Check a bag—add another $10 to $25 and perhaps $50 for a second bag if traveling overseas. Spirit Airlines even charges for carry-on bags! Taking a pet along? That's another $50 to $100. Hungry? $10 or more, please. For $10 to $30, you can jump to the front of the check-in and se-curity lines and board before other passengers. These fees are in addition to all the other taxes and fees imposed on flyers. A recent Government Accountability Office report, however, raises concerns over the disclosure of fees. Airlines are required to disclose only check-bag fees, making it harder for consumers to compare total costs when booking flights.

1. Go to www.delta.com and determine what it would cost to fly Delta Airlines from Atlanta to Denver for a one-week

roundtrip next month. What additional fees would you have to pay to change your flight, check one bag, bring your dog with you, and eat lunch while flying? (AACSB: Communication; Reflective Thinking)

2. How easy was it to determine the total cost of your flight? Should airlines be required to disclose all fees through an easier method? (AACSB: Communication; Ethical Reasoning)

MARKETING & THE Economy

Colgate-Palmolive

As the uncertain economy has made people more aware of their spending, many companies have slashed prices on their products and services. Still other companies successfully held prices steady, selling as much or more than they did before the economic bottom fell out. But Colgate-Palmolive is one of the fortunate few that has actually been able to *increase* prices during this more frugal era and reap benefits from doing so. Think about it—how grim would your budget have to get before you'd stop brushing your teeth or taking a shower? Economic conditions have relatively little impact on people's basic personal care habits, and brand preferences are deeply ingrained for these necessities. Based on an

accurate evaluation of customer buying habits, Colgate-Palmolive raised prices by an average of 7.5 percent without experiencing any dip in sales. Higher prices and stable volumes equal—cha-ching— higher profits. Indeed, Colgate-Palmolive saw its profits rise by 20 percent in 2008 and 17 percent in 2009, during the heart of the recent recession. It seems as though looking and smelling clean might just be recession-proof concepts.

1. Does the success of Colgate-Palmolive's price increases have anything to do with the economy?

2. In the longer term, as the economy recovers, what should Colgate-Palmolive anticipate in the wake of its price increases?

MARKETING BY THE Numbers

One external factor that manufacturers must consider when setting prices is reseller margins. Manufacturers do not have the final say concerning the price to consumers; retailers do. So manufacturers must start with their suggested retail prices and work back, subtracting out the markups required by resellers that sell the product to consumers. Once that is considered, manufacturers know at what price to sell their products to resellers, and they can determine what volume they must sell to break even at that price and cost combination. To answer the following questions, refer to Appendix 2.

1. A consumer purchases a computer for $800 from a retailer. If the retailer's markup is 30 percent and the wholesaler's

markup is 10 percent, both based on their respective selling prices, at what price does the manufacturer sell the product to the wholesaler? (AACSB: Communication; Analytical Reasoning)

2. If the unit variable cost for each computer is $350 and the manufacturer has fixed costs totaling $2 million, how many computers must this manufacturer sell to break even? How many must it sell to realize a profit of $50 million? (AACSB: Communication; Analytical Reasoning)

VIDEO Case

IKEA

Lots of companies have idealistic missions. But IKEA's vision, "To create a better everyday life for the many people," seems somewhat implausible. How can a company that makes furniture improve everyday life for the masses? Interestingly, the most important part of that strategy is price. For every product that it designs, from leather sofas to plastic mugs, IKEA starts with a target price. The target price is one that's deemed affordable, making the product accessible to the masses.

Only then does IKEA begin the grueling process of creating a high-quality, stylish, and innovative product that can be delivered to the customer for that target price. As IKEA points out, anyone can make high-quality goods for a high price or poor-quality goods for a low price. The real challenge is making high-quality

products at a low price. To do so requires a relentless focus on costs combined with a thirst for innovation. That has been IKEA's quest for more than 65 years.

After viewing the video featuring IKEA, answer the following questions about the company's pricing strategy:

1. What is IKEA's promise of value?

2. Referring to the Klippan sofa, illustrate how IKEA delivers its promise of value to consumers.

3. Based on the concepts from the text, does IKEA employ a value-based pricing approach or a cost-based pricing approach? Support your answer.

COMPANY Case

Southwest Airlines: Balancing the Price-Value Equation

It's the same plane going to the same place at exactly the same time. But these days, not all airline passengers are equal. Nor do they all pay equally. In fact, a person on any given flight has likely paid a different price for his or her ticket than the people on either side of them. No matter where they sit, however, all passengers seem to have one thing in common: Almost nobody's happy with what they get for what they pay. Tempers are flaring over rising air travel prices coupled with fewer amenities and less attentive customer service. Industry-wide, satisfaction ratings dropped last year for the third year in a row. Something is just not right with the airline price-value equation.

Most of us probably have had experiences like those of Doug Fesler, an executive at a medical research group in Washington, D.C.

He wasn't expecting much in the way of amenities on his American Airlines flight to Honolulu. In fact, knowing the airline no longer served free meals, he had packed his own lunch for the second leg of his flight from Dallas to Honolulu. But he said he was shocked at the lack of basic services and the overall condition of the cabin. On that flight, the audio for the movie was broken. The light that indicated when the bathroom was occupied was squirrelly, causing confusion and, in some cases, embarrassingly long waits for passengers in need of the lavatory. And though food was available for purchase, the quantity of food was depleted before the flight attendants could serve the entire cabin, leaving some fellow passengers looking longingly at the snack he had packed.

His return flight was just as disappointing. This time the audio for the movie worked—but only in Spanish—and his seat refused to stay in the upright position. "I was just appalled," said Fesler. "You pay $500 or $600 for a seat, and you expect it to be functional." He said he has considered refusing to fly airlines with such poor service but added that "if you did that with every airline that made you mad, you'd never get anywhere in this country."

Certainly, these aren't the best of times for airlines. The long recession has had the dual effect of decreasing revenues while increasing costs. This has made it more difficult to maintain aircraft and provide the niceties that customers have come to expect.

In the midst of the turmoil, however, one airline in particular seems to be flying high. Southwest Airlines is setting records for customer loads and profitability. This isn't just a recent phenomenon for the most famous low-fare airline. Since it started flying in 1972, Southwest Airlines has never lost money, something no other U.S. airline can claim. And for 2009, Southwest was the only airline to carry more passengers than it did the year before. What's its secret? In short, it has been able to provide airline service that maximizes value by giving customers great benefits for the price paid.

THE SOUTHWEST FORMULA

From its humble beginnings, the airline has been known for a few things that truly classify it as a "no-frills" airline. For starters, it does not assign seats. Rather, passengers board on a first-come,

first-served basis, a procedure that customers prefer by a two-to-one ratio. It doesn't serve meals on any flights, only basic snacks. It flies only 737 narrow-body planes and doesn't have a first-class section. And it doesn't provide electronic entertainment, relying instead on humorous flight attendants to entertain passengers.

From the beginning, its main draw has been low prices. It has communicated very effectively to customers that the lack of amenities allows it to charge some of the lowest fares in the industry. In fact, this has long been a competitive advantage for Southwest. As the airline expanded into city after city, other airlines were forced to drop their fares to compete. That overall lowering of fares in markets that Southwest enters has become widely known as the "Southwest effect."

But during the mid-2000s, Southwest's cost advantage over other airlines narrowed considerably. The bigger carriers in the industry cut costs tremendously as fuel and labor costs rose. New low-fare carriers gained strength. Competition became leaner and better able to match Southwest's prices.

But Southwest didn't put all its eggs in the price basket. For years, it focused on providing the types of benefits that truly matter to air travel patrons. Gary Kelly, CEO since 2004, summarizes these benefits:

Ultimately, our industry is a customer-service business, and we have the best people to provide special customer service. Clearly, as the differences between air carriers narrow with respect to fares, we must execute in order to differentiate ourselves. But that's our core advantage. Since the U.S. Department of Transportation began collecting and publishing operating statistics, we've excelled at on-time performance, baggage handling, fewest complaints, and fewest canceled flights. Besides, we're still the low-cost producer and the low-fare leader in the U.S. We have no intention of conceding that position.

HOW TO INCREASE PROFITS

As the effects of the global recession tightened its grip on the travel industry, many major carriers struggled to find ways to cut costs and increase revenue. Northwest discovered that it could save $2 million a year by cutting pretzels from its coach seating. American dropped $30 million a year by eliminating free meal service on longer flights. In fact, in a move that extinguished any hope of hot meals returning to coach, the airline removed the rear galleys from its MD-80 aircraft and replaced them with four seats, an addition worth another $34 million a year. Eliminating pillows was good for another million. The cutting of such amenities has made some traditional airlines even lower on frills than "no-frills" Southwest. After all, you can still get free snacks and a pillow on its flights. "I actually have more respect for Southwest Airlines in this area," says one experienced traveler. "They've never pretended to have more than they do."

But the most common—and perhaps annoying—new practice is the addition of baggage fees. Almost every airline now charges a fee of $15 to $35 for the first checked bag, even more for the second bag, and as much $125 if you have to check a third bag. And that's only for the departing trip! Customers pay the same fees on the return. And Spirit Airlines recently announced the unthinkable. It will soon begin charging customers between $30 and $45 to stow carry-on bags in the overhead bin.

On this matter, Southwest has taken a stand. In a nationwide ad campaign, it communicated to customers that "bags fly free." In fact, it is the only U.S. carrier that does not charge for checking luggage. Despite criticism that Southwest has faced for not taking advantage of the revenue stream from charging for bags, the airline has chosen to side with customers. "At Southwest, we try to give you more, while all our competitors are taking away," said Kelly.

Kelly couldn't be happier with the results of this campaign. He doesn't see it as a missed opportunity for revenue. In fact, he quickly points out that Southwest is the only airline that has actually gained customers. "We're beating the pants off everybody in terms of our revenue production. We have fewer seats offered every day, and we're carrying more passengers. We're defying gravity." Kelly claims that Southwest has gained about $1 billion in revenue this past year by taking market share from its rivals.

Although he is quick to point out that it is difficult to determine just how much of that revenue increase is due to its "bags-fly-free" campaign, Kelly thinks that this policy is the biggest factor in its current financial success. "We can't prove to you it is the source of the (market share) shift, but what we can prove is the awareness," Kelly said. "The ad campaign has been very powerful. It has definitely penetrated the American traveler's consciousness. They definitely know that we don't charge for bags." Kelly believes that the airline's increase in revenues from its higher load factors dwarfs what it could have collected in bag fees.

A STRONG VALUE EQUATION

In addition to charging fees for checking bags, airlines are continually searching for ways to squeeze any dollar they can from customers. Some airlines charge a fee if you want to sit in an aisle or window seat. There are now booking fees, fees for checking in online or at the airport, and fuel surcharges. One airline even hinted that it might begin charging customers to use the onboard lavatory. All these new ways to make money make it difficult for customers to easily determine the actual price of a ticket. They also

don't seem to be working as USAirways, Continental, United, Delta, and American combined lost almost $4 billion in 2009.

If Southwest was beginning to lose its low fare advantage, it is now evident that the airline has found a new way to compete on price. By not adding new fees, it is driving home the message that it is once again the cheaper choice. Combined with the fact that it has not cut services, customers are eager to board its planes. The tried and true method of increasing customer benefits while decreasing costs is working better than ever for Southwest. And if Kelly has his way, it will continue to assert its competitive strength for years to come.

Questions for Discussion

1. What benefits do airline customers seek when they buy air travel tickets? Has Southwest done a better job than competitors of meeting the needs of these air travelers? In what ways?

2. How has Southwest executed value-based pricing?

3. What are the benefits and risks to airlines of cutting costs? What impact are these factors now having on airline pricing and profitability?

4. Does the airline's current strategy truly differentiate it from its competitors? Is the strategy sustainable?

5. What marketing recommendations, including pricing recommendations, would you make to Southwest as it moves into the next decade?

Sources: Dan Reed, "Southwest: 'Bags Fly Free' Pays Off," *USA Today*, May 20, 2010, p. 1B; Susan Warren, "Keeping Ahead of the Pack," *Wall Street Journal*, December 19, 2005, p. B1; Michelle Higgins, "Class Conflict," *New York Times*, November 25, 2007, p. 5.1; Cheryl Hall, "Southwest's Chief Is Flying High," *Los Angeles Times*, May 3, 2010, p. A19; William Pack, "Southwest Airlines Is Expecting a Better 2011," *San Antonio Express-News*, April 8, 2010, p. 2C.

Part 1: Defining Marketing and the Marketing Process (Chapters 1–2)
Part 2: Understanding the Marketplace and Consumers (Chapters 3–6)
Part 3: Designing a Customer-Driven Strategy and Mix (Chapters 7–17)
Part 4: Extending Marketing (Chapters 18–20)

11 Pricing Strategies

Chapter Preview

In the previous chapter, you learned that price is an important marketing mix tool for both creating and capturing customer value. You explored the three main pricing strategies—customer value-based, cost-based, and competition-based pricing—and the many internal and external factors that affect a firm's pricing decisions. In this chapter, we'll look at some additional pricing considerations: new-product pricing, product mix pricing, price adjustments, and initiating and reacting to prices changes. We close the chapter with a discussion of public policy and pricing.

For openers, we look at Trader Joe's, whose unique price and value strategy has made it one of the nation's fastest-growing, most popular food stores. Trader Joe's understands that success comes not only from what products you offer customers or the prices you charge. It comes from offering the combination of products and prices that produces the greatest customer *value*—what customers get for the prices they pay.

Trader Joe's: A Special Twist on the Price-Value Equation— Cheap Gourmet

As they prepared to open the new Trader Joe's store in Chapel Hill, North Carolina, manager Greg Fort (the "captain") and his Hawaiian-shirt-clad employees (the "crew") scurried about, stocking shelves, hanging plastic lobsters, and posting hand-painted signs in preparation for the expected tidal wave of 5,000 customers who would descend on the store on opening day. A veteran of two other store openings, Fort knew that customers would soon be lined up 10 deep at checkouts with carts full of Trader Joe's exclusive $2.99 Charles Shaw wine—aka "Two-Buck Chuck"—and an assortment of other exclusive gourmet products at impossibly low prices. Fort also knew that he would have to spend time explaining Trader Joe's prices to new customers. "These are our everyday prices, not grand-opening specials," he'd tell them. "There's no need to buy a year's worth in one visit!"

Trader Joe's isn't really a gourmet food store. Then again, it's not a discount food store either. It's actually a bit of both. One of America's hottest retailers, Trader Joe's has put its own special twist on the food price-value equation—call it "cheap gourmet." It offers gourmet-caliber, one-of-a-kind products at bargain prices, all served up in a festive, vacation-like atmosphere that makes shopping fun. "When you look at food retailers, there is the low end, the big middle, and then there is the cool edge—that's Trader Joe's," says one food marketing expert. Whatever you call it, Trader Joe's inventive price-value positioning has earned it an almost cultlike following of devoted customers who love what they get from Trader Joe's for the prices they pay.

Trader Joe's describes itself as an "island paradise" where "value, adventure, and tasty treasures are discovered, every day." Shoppers bustle and buzz amid cedar-plank-lined walls and fake palm trees as a ship's bell rings out occasionally at checkout, alerting them to special announcements. Unfailingly helpful and cheery associates in aloha shirts chat with customers about everything from the weather to menu suggestions for dinner parties. Customers don't just shop at Trader Joe's; they experience it.

Shelves bristle with an eclectic assortment of gourmet-quality grocery items. Trader Joe's stocks only a limited assortment of about 2,000 specialty products (compared with the 45,000 items found in an average Safeway). However, the assortment is uniquely Trader Joe's, including special concoctions of gourmet packaged foods and sauces, ready-to-eat soups, fresh and frozen entrees, snacks, and desserts—all free of artificial colors, flavors, and preservatives. Trader Joe's is a gourmet foodie's delight, featuring everything from wasabi peas, organic strawberry lemonade, dark-chocolate-dipped spiced dry mango, and fair trade coffees to chile lime chicken burgers and triple-ginger ginger snaps. "Where else can you find Soy & Flax Cereal clusters, Gin-

> Trader Joe's understands that success comes not only from what products you offer customers or the prices you charge. It comes from offering the combination of products and prices that produces the greatest customer value.

ger Cats Cookies, and Jalapeño Blue Corn Bread Mix?" asks one shopper.

Another thing that makes Trader Joe's products so special is that you simply can't get them anywhere else. More than 80 percent of the store's brands are private label goods, sold exclusively by Trader Joe's. If asked, almost any customer can tick off a ready list of Trader Joe's favorites that they just can't live without—a list that quickly grows. "People get hooked on something and they keep coming back for it. That's how it starts," says a Trader Joe's store captain. "They end up filling up their baskets, then entire carts. That's the most common complaint that we hear. They came in for one or two things, and ended up with a whole cart full of stuff."

A special store atmosphere, exclusive gourmet products, helpful and attentive associates—this all sounds like a recipe for high prices. Not so at Trader Joe's. Whereas upscale competitors such as Whole Foods Market charge upscale prices to match their wares ("Whole Foods, Whole Paycheck"), Trader Joe's amazes customers with its relatively frugal prices. The prices aren't all that low in absolute terms, but they're a real bargain compared with what you'd pay for the same quality and coolness elsewhere. "At Trader Joe's, we're as much about value as we are about great food," says the company. "So you can afford to be adventurous without breaking the bank."

How does Trader Joe's keep its gourmet prices so low? It all starts with lean operations and a near-fanatical focus on saving money. To keep costs down, Trader Joe's typically locates its stores in low-rent, out-of-the-way locations, such as suburban strip malls. Its small store size and limited product assortment results in reduced facilities and inventory costs. Trader Joe's stores save money by eliminating large produce sections and expensive on-site bakery, butcher, deli, and seafood shops. And for its private label brands, Trader Joe's buys directly from suppliers and negotiates hard on price. "We buy in huge quantities straight from our distributors, which cuts out the middle man and lets us offer the lowest possible prices," says the store manager.

Finally, the frugal retailer saves money by spending almost nothing on advertising. Trader Joe's unique combination of quirky products and low prices produces so much word-of-mouth promotion that the company doesn't really need to advertise. The closest thing to an official promotion is the company's Web site or a newsletter mailed out to people who opt in to receive it. Trader Joe's most potent promotional

weapon is its army of faithful followers. Trader Joe's customers have even started their own fan Web site, www.traderjoesfan.com, where they discuss new products and stores, trade recipes, and swap their favorite Trader Joe's stories.

Thus, finding the right price-value formula has made Trader Joe's one of the nation's fastest-growing and most popular food stores. Its more than 350 stores in 25 states now reap annual sales of more than $8 billion, up more than 77 percent in just the previous four years. Trader Joe's stores pull in an amazing $1,780 per square foot, more than twice the supermarket industry average. *Consumer Reports* recently ranked Trader Joe's, along with Wegmans, as the best supermarket chain in the nation.

It's all about value and price—what you get for what you pay. Just ask Trader Joe's regular Chrissi Wright, found early one morning browsing her local Trader Joe's in Bend, Oregon.

Trader Joe's unique price-value strategy has earned it an almost cultlike following of devoted customers who love what they get for the prices they pay.

Chrissi expects she'll leave Trader Joe's with eight bottles of the popular Charles Shaw wine priced at $2.99 each tucked under her arms. "I love Trader Joe's because they let me eat like a yuppie without taking all my money," says Wright. "Their products are gourmet, often environmentally conscientious and beautiful . . . and, of course, there's Two-Buck Chuck—possibly the greatest innovation of our time."[1]

As we learned in the previous chapter, pricing decisions are subject to a complex array of company, environmental, and competitive forces. To make things even more complex, a company does not set a single price but rather a *pricing structure* that covers different items in its line. This pricing structure changes over time as products move through their life cycles. The company adjusts its prices to reflect changes in costs and demand and account for variations in buyers and situations. As the competitive environment changes, the company considers when to initiate price changes and when to respond to them.

This chapter examines additional pricing approaches used in special pricing situations and adjusting prices to meet changing situations. We then look at *new-product pricing* for products in the introductory stage of the product life cycle, *product mix pricing* for related products in the product mix, *price adjustment tactics* that account for customer differences and changing situations, and strategies for initiating and responding to *price changes.*[2]

New-Product Pricing Strategies (pp 314–315)

Author Comment | Pricing new products can be especially challenging. Just think about all the things you need to consider in pricing a new cell phone, say the first Apple iPhone. Even more, you need to start thinking about the price—along with many other marketing considerations—at the very beginning of the design process.

Pricing strategies usually change as the product passes through its life cycle. The introductory stage is especially challenging. Companies bringing out a new product face the challenge of setting prices for the first time. They can choose between two broad strategies: *market-skimming pricing* and *market-penetration pricing*.

Market-Skimming Pricing

Market-skimming pricing (price skimming)
Setting a high price for a new product to skim maximum revenues layer by layer from the segments willing to pay the high price; the company makes fewer but more profitable sales.

Many companies that invent new products set high initial prices to "skim" revenues layer by layer from the market. Apple frequently uses this strategy, called **market-skimming pricing** (or **price skimming**). When Apple first introduced the iPhone, its initial price was as much as $599 per phone. The phones were purchased only by customers who really wanted the sleek new gadget and could afford to pay a high price for it. Six months later, Apple dropped the price to $399 for an 8GB model and $499 for the 16GB model to attract new buyers. Within a year, it dropped prices again to $199 and $299, respectively, and you can now buy an 8GB model for $99. In this way, Apple skimmed the maximum amount of revenue from the various segments of the market.

Market skimming makes sense only under certain conditions. First, the product's quality and image must support its higher price, and enough buyers must want the product at that price. Second, the costs of producing a smaller volume cannot be so high that they cancel the advantage of charging more. Finally, competitors should not be able to enter the market easily and undercut the high price.

Market-Penetration Pricing

Market-penetration pricing
Setting a low price for a new product to attract a large number of buyers and a large market share.

Rather than setting a high initial price to skim off small but profitable market segments, some companies use **market-penetration pricing**. Companies set a low initial price to *penetrate* the market quickly and deeply—to attract a large number of buyers quickly and

● **Penetration pricing: To lure famously frugal Chinese customers, IKEA slashed its prices. The strategy worked. Weekend crowds at its cavernous Beijing store are so big that employees need to use megaphones to keep them in control.**

win a large market share. The high sales volume results in falling costs, allowing companies to cut their prices even further. ● For example, the giant Swedish retailer IKEA used penetration pricing to boost its success in the Chinese market:[3]

> When IKEA first opened stores in China in 2002, people crowded in but not to buy home furnishings. Instead, they came to take advantage of the freebies— air conditioning, clean toilets, and even decorating ideas. Chinese consumers are famously frugal. When it came time to actually buy, they shopped instead at local stores just down the street that offered knockoffs of IKEA's designs at a fraction of the price. So to lure the finicky Chinese customers, IKEA slashed its prices in China to the lowest in the world, the opposite approach of many Western retailers there. By increasingly stocking its Chinese stores with China-made products, the retailer pushed prices on some items as low as 70 percent below prices in IKEA's outlets outside China. The penetration pricing strategy worked. IKEA now captures a 43 percent market share of China's fast-growing home wares market alone, and the sales of its seven mammoth Chinese stores surged 25 percent last year. The cavernous Beijing store draws nearly six million visitors annually. Weekend crowds are so big that employees need to use megaphones to keep them in control.

Several conditions must be met for this low-price strategy to work. First, the market must be highly price sensitive so that a low price produces more market growth. Second, production and distribution costs must decrease as sales volume increases. Finally, the low price must help keep out the competition, and the penetration pricer must maintain its low-price position. Otherwise, the price advantage may be only temporary.

Author Comment | Most individual products are part of a broader product mix and must be priced accordingly. For example, Gillette prices its Fusion razors low. But once you buy the razor, you're a captive customer for its higher-margin replacement cartridges.

Product Mix Pricing Strategies (pp 315–319)

The strategy for setting a product's price often has to be changed when the product is part of a product mix. In this case, the firm looks for a set of prices that maximizes its profits on the total product mix. Pricing is difficult because the various products have related demand and costs and face different degrees of competition. We now take a closer look at the five product mix pricing situations summarized in ● **Table 11.1**: *product line pricing*, *optional product pricing*, *captive product pricing*, *by-product pricing*, and *product bundle pricing*.

Product Line Pricing

Companies usually develop product lines rather than single products. For example, Rossignol offers seven different collections of alpine skis of all designs and sizes, at prices that range from $150 for its junior skis, such as Fun Girl, to more than $1,100 for a pair from its Radical racing collection. It also offers lines of Nordic and backcountry skis, snowboards, and ski-related apparel. In **product line pricing**, management must determine the price steps to set between the various products in a line.

The price steps should take into account cost differences between products in the line. More importantly, they should account for differences in customer perceptions of the value of different features. For example, Quicken offers an entire line of financial management software, including Starter, Deluxe, Premier, Home & Business, and Rental Property versions priced at $29.99, $59.99, $89.99, $99.99, and $149.99, respectively. Although it costs Quicken no more to produce the CD containing the Premier version than the CD containing the Starter version, many buyers happily pay more to obtain additional Premier features, such as financial-planning and investment-monitoring tools. Quicken's task is to establish perceived value differences that support the price differences.

Product line pricing

Setting the price steps between various products in a product line based on cost differences between the products, customer evaluations of different features, and competitors' prices.

⊙ **TABLE | 11.1**   Product Mix Pricing

Pricing Situation	Description
Product line pricing	Setting prices across an entire product line
Optional product pricing	Pricing optional or accessory products sold with the main product
Captive product pricing	Pricing products that must be used with the main product
By-product pricing	Pricing low-value by-products to get rid of them
Product bundle pricing	Pricing bundles of products sold together

Optional Product Pricing

Optional product pricing
The pricing of optional or accessory products along with a main product.

Many companies use **optional product pricing**—offering to sell optional or accessory products along with the main product. For example, a car buyer may choose to order a global positioning system (GPS) and Bluetooth wireless communication. Refrigerators come with optional ice makers. And when you order a new PC, you can select from a bewildering array of processors, hard drives, docking systems, software options, and service plans. Pricing these options is a sticky problem. Companies must decide which items to include in the base price and which to offer as options.

Captive Product Pricing

Captive product pricing
Setting a price for products that must be used along with a main product, such as blades for a razor and games for a videogame console.

By-product pricing
Setting a price for by-products to make the main product's price more competitive.

Companies that make products that must be used along with a main product are using **captive product pricing**. Examples of captive products are razor blade cartridges, videogames, and printer cartridges. Producers of the main products (razors, videogame consoles, and printers) often price them low and set high markups on the supplies. For example, when Sony first introduced its PS3 videogame console, priced at $499 and $599 for the regular and premium versions, it lost as much as $306 per unit sold. Sony hoped to recoup the losses through the sales of more lucrative PS3 games.

However, companies that use captive product pricing must be careful. Finding the right balance between the main product and captive product prices can be tricky. For example, despite industry-leading PS3 videogame sales, Sony has yet to earn back its losses on the PS3 console. Even more, consumers trapped into buying expensive captive products may come to resent the brand that ensnared them. This happened in the inkjet printer and cartridges industry (see Real Marketing 11.1).[4]

In the case of services, captive product pricing is called *two-part pricing*. The price of the service is broken into a *fixed fee* plus a *variable usage rate*. ⊙ Thus, at Six Flags and other amusement parks, you pay a daily ticket or season pass charge plus additional fees for food and other in-park features.

⊙ Captive-product pricing: At Six Flags, you pay a daily ticket or season pass charge plus additional fees for food and other in-park features.

By-Product Pricing

Producing products and services often generates by-products. If the by-products have no value and if getting rid of them is costly, this will affect pricing of the main product. Using **by-product pricing**, the company seeks a market for these by-products to help offset the costs of disposing of them and help make the price of the main product more competitive.

Real Marketing 11.1

Kodak: A Whole New Concept in Printer Pricing and Economics

HP, Epson, Canon, and Lexmark have long dominated the $50 billion printer industry with a maddening "razor-and-blades" pricing strategy (as in give away the razor and then make your profits on the blades). They sell printers at little or no profit. But once you own the printer, you're stuck buying their grossly overpriced, high-margin replacement ink cartridges.

For example, you can pick up a nifty little HP multifunction inkjet printer for only $69.99. But the HP tricolor inkjet cartridge that goes with it costs $28.99. And a 100-count pack of HP four-by-six-inch photo paper costs another $22.99. The price per ounce of inkjet printer ink can exceed the per-ounce price of an expensive perfume, premium champagne, or even caviar. By one estimate, if you bought a gallon of the stuff at those prices, it would cost you a horrifying $4,731.

The big manufacturers have seemed content with this captive product pricing strategy. In fact, they pull in four times more revenues from ink cartridges and paper than from the printers themselves. Customers don't like being held hostage and having to pay through the nose for ink and paper—some are outraged by it. But what can they do? Only HP cartridges work with HP printers. Buying another brand isn't the answer, either—all of the manufacturers pursue the same pricing strategy.

Enter Kodak—with a unique solution. Kodak recently introduced its first line of printers—EasyShare All-in-One printers—with a revolutionary pricing strategy that has turned the entire inkjet printer industry upside-down. In a twist on typical industry practice, Kodak sells its printers at premium prices with no discounts and then sells the ink cartridges for less. EasyShare printers sell for $129.99 to $299.99, depending on features, about $50 higher than comparable printers sold by competitors. However, EasyShare black and color ink cartridges go for just $9.99 and $14.99, respectively, about half the prevailing competitor prices. It's a whole new concept in printer pricing and economics.

To make the strategy work, Kodak first had to create a new kind of inkjet printer. It de-veloped an innovative technology that uses tiny nozzles to squirt pigment ink drops that are just a few atoms in size. EasyShare printers take about 55 seconds to produce a four-by-six-inch print, longer than some competitive printers that do it in 32 seconds. But the resulting photos take up to 90 years to fade versus dye-based inks that can begin to fade in as little as a year.

Moreover, Kodak found a way to contain all the printing electronics within the EasyShare printer itself, whereas rivals include some of the electronics in the cartridges. This lets Kodak charge less for the cartridges. As a result, according to one independent lab study, Kodak's new printers "whomped" rival's printers in price per printout. The study showed that consumers using an EasyShare printer can save on average of $110 a year based on printing four pages per day compared to using a competitor's printer.

Thus, Kodak had the right printer and the right ink prices. Now, all it had to do was to reeducate consumers about printer pricing—about the benefits of paying more up front to reduce long-run printing costs. To do this, Kodak launched a "Think Ink" marketing campaign, built around the visual image "ThINK," with the first two letters in black and the last three in gold. The campaign asked this pivotal question: "Is it smarter to save money on a printer or save money on ink? (Hint: You only buy the printer once.)"

The ThINK campaign began with online viral efforts, centered on a series of popular "Inkisit" videos, featuring two dorky guys, Nathan and Max, who love to print photos but who don't like the ink's high cost. In the videos, posted on YouTube and an entertaining Kodak microsite, they asked enthusiastically, "Have you ever thought about what life would be like if ink was cheaper?" Then came the bread-and-butter "ThINK" media campaign, targeting budget-conscious consumers who want to print at home but have limited this activity because of high ink costs.

THE WORLD'S MOST EXPENSIVE LIQUID ISN'T FOUND IN THE MIDDLE EAST. IT'S FOUND IN YOUR INKJET PRINTER.

SWITCH TO A **KODAK ESP** ALL-IN-ONE PRINTER AND STOP OVERPAYING FOR INK.

Kodak

PRINT & PROSPER

FIND OUT HOW MUCH YOU OVERPAY FOR INK AT PRINT AND PROSPER.COM

Kodak's revolutionary pricing sells printers at full prices but ink cartridges for less. At Kodak's Print & Prosper Web site, you can even calculate how much you're overpaying for ink with your current printer.

Continued on next page

The ThINK campaign tackled the very difficult task of shifting consumer value perceptions away from initial printer prices and toward prices per print. "Our strategy," said a Kodak marketing executive, "is to crystallize for consumers that they're not only buying a printer today but also buying into three to four years of ink purchases." The campaign sent shockwaves through the inkjet printer industry and its "razor-and-blades" pricing mentality.

Kodak's most recent ad campaign rants that "Last year, America paid $5 billion too much for inkjet printer ink." And the Kodak "Print & Prosper" Web site proclaims that Kodak printers use only "fairly priced ink." The site even provides an "overpayment calculator," which lets visitors calculate how much they are overpaying for ink with their current printer versus a Kodak EasyShare printer. "When buying a printer, it's easy to be se-

duced by low prices and cheap bundles," says the site. "Some people end up paying more for ink than they do for their printer. Switch to Kodak, and you can print more and pay less."

It's still too soon to tell whether Kodak's revolutionary pricing strategy is working, but the early results are promising. The company exceeded its sales forecasts and sold 780,000 EasyShare printers in its first year. Last year, p. C1, while competitors' sales plunged nearly 24 percent, Kodak's sales of printers and sup-

plies jumped 44 percent. Competitors are now scrambling to introduce their own lower-priced cartridges and longer lasting inks.

As one observer concludes, Kodak "Has its priorities straight: Great-looking photos that last a lifetime," with affordable per-print prices in the bargain. "It makes a world-rocking point about the razor-blades model that's lined the coffers of the inkjet industry for years. If you're mad as hell, you don't have to take it anymore."

Sources: Quotes and other information from Beth Snyder Bulik, "Kodak Develops New Model: Inexpensive Printer, Cheap Ink," *Advertising Age*, March 12, 2007, p. 4; David Pogue, "Paying More for Printer, But Less for Ink," *New York Times*, May 17, 2007, p. C1; "Consumer Launch Campaign of the Year 2008," *PRweek*, March 10, 2008, p. S11; Stuart Elliott, "Are You Fed Up? This Ad's for You," *News and Observer* (Raleigh), May 15, 2009, p. 1; Greg Tarr, "Kodak Targets Value Items," *TWICE*, September 10, 2009, p. 4; "Eastman Kodak Company: Kodak Works with FTC to Enhance Messaging on Inkjet Savings Claim," *Economics Week*, January 8, 2010, p. 12; and www.kodak.com/global/mul/consumer/print/en_ca/index.html, accessed November 2010.

◉ By-product pricing: "There's green and money to be made in animal poop!" exclaims Dan Corum, the Woodland Zoo's enthusiastic compost and recycling coordinator (also known as the prince of poo, the emperor of excrement, the GM of BM, or just plain Dr. Doo).

The by-products themselves can even turn out to be profitable—turning trash into cash. ◉ For example, Seattle's Woodland Park Zoo has learned that one of its major by-products—animal poo—can be an excellent source of extra revenue.[5]

"What happens to all that poo at the zoo?" asks a recent video about the Woodland Park Zoo. Not long ago, the answer was that it had to be hauled away to the landfill at a cost of about $60,000 a year. But now, the zoo carefully collects all that poo, turns it into compost, and sells it under its Zoo Doo and Bedspread brands, pitched as "the most exotic and highly prized compost in the Pacific Northwest, composed of exotic species feces contributed by the zoo's non-primate herbivores." Customers can buy these coveted compost products by the bucket at the zoo's store. The zoo also sponsors annual FecalFests, where lucky lottery winners can buy the processed poo by the trash can or truck full. "There's green *and* money to be made in animal poop!" exclaims Dan Corum, the Woodland Zoo's enthusiastic compost and recycling coordinator (also known as the prince of poo, the emperor of excrement, the GM of BM, or just plain Dr. Doo). Selling Zoo Doo keeps it out of the landfill, so it's good for the planet. It's also good for the zoo, saving disposal costs and generating $15,000 to $20,000 in annual sales.

Product Bundle Pricing

Product bundle pricing
Combining several products and offering the bundle at a reduced price.

Using **product bundle pricing**, sellers often combine several products and offer the bundle at a reduced price. For example, fast-food restaurants bundle a burger, fries, and a soft drink at a "combo" price. Bath & Body Works offers "three-fer" deals on its soaps and lotions (such as three antibacterial soaps for $10). And Comcast, Time Warner, Verizon, and other telecommunications companies bundle TV service, phone service, and high-speed Internet connections at a low combined price. Price bundling can promote the sales of products consumers might not otherwise buy, but the combined price must be low enough to get them to buy the bundle.

Price Adjustment Strategies (pp 319–325)

Author Comment | Setting the base price for a product is only the start. The company must then adjust the price to account for customer and situational differences. When was the last time you paid the full suggested retail price for something?

Companies usually adjust their basic prices to account for various customer differences and changing situations. Here we examine the seven price adjustment strategies summarized in ◉ **Table 11.2**: *discount and allowance pricing*, *segmented pricing*, *psychological pricing*, *promotional pricing*, *geographical pricing*, *dynamic pricing*, and *international pricing*.

Discount and Allowance Pricing

Discount

A straight reduction in price on purchases during a stated period of time or of larger quantities.

Most companies adjust their basic price to reward customers for certain responses, such as the early payment of bills, volume purchases, and off-season buying. These price adjustments—called *discounts* and *allowances*—can take many forms.

The many forms of **discounts** include a *cash discount*, a price reduction to buyers who pay their bills promptly. A typical example is "2/10, net 30," which means that although payment is due within 30 days, the buyer can deduct 2 percent if the bill is paid within 10 days. A *quantity discount* is a price reduction to buyers who buy large volumes. A seller offers a *functional discount* (also called a *trade discount*) to trade-channel members who perform certain functions, such as selling, storing, and record keeping. A *seasonal discount* is a price reduction to buyers who buy merchandise or services out of season.

Allowance

Promotional money paid by manufacturers to retailers in return for an agreement to feature the manufacturer's products in some way.

Allowances are another type of reduction from the list price. For example, *trade-in allowances* are price reductions given for turning in an old item when buying a new one. Trade-in allowances are most common in the automobile industry but are also given for other durable goods. *Promotional allowances* are payments or price reductions to reward dealers for participating in advertising and sales support programs.

Segmented Pricing

Segmented pricing

Selling a product or service at two or more prices, where the difference in prices is not based on differences in costs.

Companies will often adjust their basic prices to allow for differences in customers, products, and locations. In **segmented pricing**, the company sells a product or service at two or more prices, even though the difference in prices is not based on differences in costs.

◉ **TABLE | 11.2** Price Adjustments

Strategy	Description
Discount and allowance pricing	Reducing prices to reward customer responses such as paying early or promoting the product
Segmented pricing	Adjusting prices to allow for differences in customers, products, or locations
Psychological pricing	Adjusting prices for psychological effect
Promotional pricing	Temporarily reducing prices to increase short-run sales
Geographical pricing	Adjusting prices to account for the geographic location of customers
Dynamic pricing	Adjusting prices continually to meet the characteristics and needs of individual customers and situations
International pricing	Adjusting prices for international markets

● **Product-form pricing:** Evian water in a one-liter bottle might cost you 5 cents an ounce at your local supermarket, whereas the same water might run $2.28 an ounce when sold in five-ounce aerosol cans as Evian Brumisateur Mineral Water Spray moisturizer.

Segmented pricing takes several forms. Under *customer-segment* pricing, different customers pay different prices for the same product or service. Museums and movie theaters, for example, may charge a lower admission for students and senior citizens. Under *product-form pricing*, different versions of the product are priced differently but not according to differences in their costs. ● For instance, a one-liter bottle (about 34 ounces) of Evian mineral water may cost $1.59 at your local supermarket. But a five-ounce aerosol can of Evian Brumisateur Mineral Water Spray sells for a suggested retail price of $11.39 at beauty boutiques and spas. The water is all from the same source in the French Alps, and the aerosol packaging costs little more than the plastic bottles. Yet you pay about 5 cents an ounce for one form and $2.28 an ounce for the other.

Using *location-based pricing*, a company charges different prices for different locations, even though the cost of offering each location is the same. For instance, state universities charge higher tuition for out-of-state students, and theaters vary their seat prices because of audience preferences for certain locations. Tickets for a Saturday night performance of Green Day's *American Idiot* on Broadway start at $32 for a seat in the rear balcony, whereas orchestra center seats go for $252. Finally, using *time-based pricing*, a firm varies its price by the season, the month, the day, and even the hour. Movie theaters charge matinee pricing during the daytime. Resorts give weekend and seasonal discounts.

For segmented pricing to be an effective strategy, certain conditions must exist. The market must be segmentable, and segments must show different degrees of demand. The costs of segmenting and reaching the market cannot exceed the extra revenue obtained from the price difference. Of course, the segmented pricing must also be legal.

Most importantly, segmented prices should reflect real differences in customers' perceived value. Consumers in higher price tiers must feel that they're getting their extra money's worth for the higher prices paid. By the same token, companies must be careful not to treat customers in lower price tiers as second-class citizens. Otherwise, in the long run, the practice will lead to customer resentment and ill will. For example, in recent years, the airlines have incurred the wrath of frustrated customers at both ends of the airplane. Passengers paying full fare for business or first class seats often feel that they are being gouged. At the same time, passengers in lower-priced coach seats feel that they're being ignored or treated poorly.

Psychological Pricing

Price says something about the product. For example, many consumers use price to judge quality. A $100 bottle of perfume may contain only $3 worth of scent, but some people are willing to pay the $100 because this price indicates something special.

Psychological pricing

Pricing that considers the psychology of prices, not simply the economics; the price says something about the product.

In using **psychological pricing**, sellers consider the psychology of prices, not simply the economics. For example, consumers usually perceive higher-priced products as having higher quality. When they can judge the quality of a product by examining it or by calling on past experience with it, they use price less to judge quality. But when they cannot judge quality because they lack the information or skill, price becomes an important quality signal. For example, who's the better lawyer, one who charges $50 per hour or one who charges $500 per hour? You'd have to do a lot of digging into the respective lawyers' credentials to answer this question objectively; even then, you might not be able to judge accurately. Most of us would simply assume that the higher-priced lawyer is better.

Reference prices

Prices that buyers carry in their minds and refer to when they look at a given product.

Another aspect of psychological pricing is **reference prices**—prices that buyers carry in their minds and refer to when looking at a given product. The reference price might be formed by noting current prices, remembering past prices, or assessing the buying situation. Sellers can influence or use these consumers' reference prices when setting price. For example, a grocery retailer might place its store brand of bran flakes and raisins cereal priced at

Psychological pricing: What do the prices marked on this tag suggest about the product and buying situation?

$1.89 next to Kellogg's Raisin Bran priced at $3.20. Or a company might offer more expensive models that don't sell very well to make their less expensive but still-high-priced models look more affordable by comparison:[6]

> In the midst of the recent recession, Ralph Lauren was selling a "Ricky" alligator bag for $14,000, making its Tiffin Bag a steal at just $2,595. And Williams-Sonoma once offered a fancy bread maker for $279. Then it added a $429 model. The costly model flopped, but sales of the cheaper one doubled.

For most purchases, consumers don't have all the skill or information they need to figure out whether they are paying a good price. They don't have the time, ability, or inclination to research different brands or stores, compare prices, and get the best deals. ● Instead, they may rely on certain cues that signal whether a price is high or low. Interestingly, such pricing cues are often provided by sellers, in the form of sales signs, price-matching guarantees, loss-leader pricing, and other helpful hints.[7]

Even small differences in price can signal product differences. For example, in a recent study, people were asked how likely they were to choose among LASIK eye surgery providers based only on the prices they charged: $299 or $300. The actual price difference was only $1, but the study found that the psychological difference was much greater. Preference ratings for the providers charging $300 were much higher. Subjects perceived the $299 price as significantly less, but it also raised stronger concerns about quality and risk.[8] Some psychologists even argue that each digit has symbolic and visual qualities that should be considered in pricing. Thus, eight is round and even and creates a soothing effect, whereas seven is angular and creates a jarring effect.

Promotional Pricing

Promotional pricing

Temporarily pricing products below the list price, and sometimes even below cost, to increase short-run sales.

With **promotional pricing**, companies will temporarily price their products below list price and sometimes even below cost to create buying excitement and urgency. Promotional pricing takes several forms. A seller may simply offer *discounts* from normal prices to increase sales and reduce inventories. Sellers also use *special-event pricing* in certain seasons to draw more customers. Thus, large-screen TVs and other consumer electronics are promotionally priced in November and December to attract holiday shoppers into the stores.

Manufacturers sometimes offer *cash rebates* to consumers who buy the product from dealers within a specified time; the manufacturer sends the rebate directly to the customer. Rebates have been popular with automakers and producers of cell phones and small appliances, but they are also used with consumer packaged goods. Some manufacturers offer *low-interest financing*, *longer warranties*, or *free maintenance* to reduce the consumer's "price." This practice has become another favorite of the auto industry.

Promotional pricing, however, can have adverse effects. Used too frequently and copied by competitors, price promotions can create "deal-prone" customers who wait until brands go on sale before buying them. Or, constantly reduced prices can erode a brand's value in the eyes of customers. Marketers sometimes become addicted to promotional pricing, especially in difficult economic times. They use price promotions as a quick fix instead of sweating through the difficult process of developing effective longer-term strategies for building their brands. But companies must be careful to balance short-term sales incentives against long-term brand building. One analyst advises:[9]

> When times are tough, there's a tendency to panic. One of the first and most prevalent tactics that many companies try is an aggressive price cut. Price trumps all. At least, that's how it feels these days. 20% off. 30% off. 50% off. Buy one, get one free. Whatever it is you're selling, you're offering it at a discount just to get customers in the door. But aggressive pricing strategies can be risky business. Companies should be very wary of risking their brands' perceived quality by resorting to deep and frequent price cuts. Some discounting is unavoidable in a tough economy, and consumers have come

● **Promotional pricing: Companies offer promotional prices to create buying excitement and urgency.**

to expect it. But marketers have to find ways to shore up their brand identity and brand equity during times of discount mayhem.

● The point is that promotional pricing can be an effective means of generating sales for some companies in certain circumstances. But it can be damaging for other companies or if taken as a steady diet.

Geographical Pricing

A company also must decide how to price its products for customers located in different parts of the United States or the world. Should the company risk losing the business of more-distant customers by charging them higher prices to cover the higher shipping costs? Or should the company charge all customers the same prices regardless of location? We will look at five **geographical pricing** strategies for the following hypothetical situation:

The Peerless Paper Company is located in Atlanta, Georgia, and sells paper products to customers all over the United States. The cost of freight is high and affects the companies from whom customers buy their paper. Peerless wants to establish a geographical pricing policy. It is trying to determine how to price a $10,000 order to three specific customers: Customer A (Atlanta), Customer B (Bloomington, Indiana), and Customer C (Compton, California).

Geographical pricing

Setting prices for customers located in different parts of the country or world.

FOB-origin pricing

A geographical pricing strategy in which goods are placed free on board a carrier; the customer pays the freight from the factory to the destination.

Uniform-delivered pricing

A geographical pricing strategy in which the company charges the same price plus freight to all customers, regardless of their location.

Zone pricing

A geographical pricing strategy in which the company sets up two or more zones. All customers within a zone pay the same total price; the more distant the zone, the higher the price.

Basing-point pricing

A geographical pricing strategy in which the seller designates some city as a basing point and charges all customers the freight cost from that city to the customer.

One option is for Peerless to ask each customer to pay the shipping cost from the Atlanta factory to the customer's location. All three customers would pay the same factory price of $10,000, with Customer A paying, say, $100 for shipping; Customer B, $150; and Customer C, $250. Called **FOB-origin pricing**, this practice means that the goods are placed *free on board* (hence, *FOB*) a carrier. At that point the title and responsibility pass to the customer, who pays the freight from the factory to the destination. Because each customer picks up its own cost, supporters of FOB pricing feel that this is the fairest way to assess freight charges. The disadvantage, however, is that Peerless will be a high-cost firm to distant customers.

Uniform-delivered pricing is the opposite of FOB pricing. Here, the company charges the same price plus freight to all customers, regardless of their location. The freight charge is set at the average freight cost. Suppose this is $150. Uniform-delivered pricing therefore results in a higher charge to the Atlanta customer (who pays $150 freight instead of $100) and a lower charge to the Compton customer (who pays $150 instead of $250). Although the Atlanta customer would prefer to buy paper from another local paper company that uses FOB-origin pricing, Peerless has a better chance of winning over the California customer.

Zone pricing falls between FOB-origin pricing and uniform-delivered pricing. The company sets up two or more zones. All customers within a given zone pay a single total price; the more distant the zone, the higher the price. For example, Peerless might set up an East Zone and charge $100 freight to all customers in this zone, a Midwest Zone in which it charges $150, and a West Zone in which it charges $250. In this way, the customers within a given price zone receive no price advantage from the company. For example, customers in Atlanta and Boston pay the same total price to Peerless. The complaint, however, is that the Atlanta customer is paying part of the Boston customer's freight cost.

Using **basing-point pricing**, the seller selects a given city as a "basing point" and charges all customers the freight cost from that city to the customer location, regardless of the city from which the goods are actually shipped. For example, Peerless might set Chicago as the basing point and charge all customers $10,000 plus the freight from Chicago to their locations. This means that an Atlanta customer pays the freight cost from Chicago to Atlanta, even though the goods may be shipped from Atlanta. If all sellers used the same basing-point city, delivered prices would be the same for all customers, and price competition would be eliminated.

Finally, the seller who is anxious to do business with a certain customer or geographical area might use **freight-absorption pricing**. Using this strategy, the seller absorbs all or part of the actual freight charges to get the desired business. The seller might reason that if it can get more business, its average costs will decrease and more than compensate for its extra freight cost. Freight-absorption pricing is used for market penetration and to hold on to increasingly competitive markets.

Dynamic Pricing

Throughout most of history, prices were set by negotiation between buyers and sellers. *Fixed price* policies—setting one price for all buyers—is a relatively modern idea that arose with the development of large-scale retailing at the end of the nineteenth century. Today, most prices are set this way. However, some companies are now reversing the fixed pricing trend. They are using **dynamic pricing**—adjusting prices continually to meet the characteristics and needs of individual customers and situations.

For example, think about how the Internet has affected pricing. From the mostly fixed pricing practices of the past century, the Internet seems to be taking us back into a new age of fluid pricing. The flexibility of the Internet allows Web sellers to instantly and constantly adjust prices on a wide range of goods based on demand dynamics (sometimes called *real-time pricing*). ● In other cases, customers control pricing by bidding on auction sites such as eBay or negotiating on sites such as Priceline. Still other companies customize their offers based on the characteristics and behaviors of specific customers:[10]

It's an offer you can't resist: fly Alaska Airlines to Honolulu for $200 round trip. But what you might not know is that the offer was designed especially for you. Alaska Airlines has introduced a system that creates unique prices and ads for people as they surf the Internet. The system identifies consumers by their computers, using a small piece of code known as a cookie. It then combines detailed data from several sources to paint a picture of who's sitting on the other side of the screen. When the person clicks on an ad, the system quickly analyzes the data to assess how price-sensitive customers seem to be. Then, in an instant, one customer gets an offer for a flight from Seattle to Portland for $99 and another is quoted $109. Or someone who had visited Alaska Airlines' site frequently but then abruptly stopped visiting might be greeted with the $200 Hawaii offer. "I guarantee you there are a lot of people who will say yes to that," says Marston Gould, director of customer relationship management and online marketing for Alaska Airlines.

● **Dynamic pricing: The Internet seems to be taking us back into a new age of fluid pricing. At Priceline.com, you can "name your own price."**

Dynamic pricing offers many advantages for marketers. For example, Internet sellers such as Amazon.com can mine their databases to gauge a specific shopper's desires, measure his or her means, instantaneously tailor products to fit that shopper's behavior, and price products accordingly. Catalog retailers such as L.L.Bean or Spiegel can change prices

Freight-absorption pricing
A geographical pricing strategy in which the seller absorbs all or part of the freight charges to get the desired business.

Dynamic pricing
Adjusting prices continually to meet the characteristics and needs of individual customers and situations.

on the fly according to changes in demand or costs, changing prices for specific items on a day-by-day or even hour-by-hour basis. And many direct marketers monitor inventories, costs, and demand at any given moment and adjust prices instantly.

Consumers also benefit from the Internet and dynamic pricing. A wealth of price comparison sites—such as Yahoo! Shopping, Bizrate.com, NexTag.com, Epinions.com, PriceGrabber.com, mySimon.com, and PriceScan.com—offer instant product and price comparisons from thousands of vendors. Epinions.com, for instance, lets shoppers browse by category or search for specific products and brands. It then searches the Web and reports back links to sellers offering the best prices along with customer reviews. In addition to simply finding the best product and the vendor with the best price for that product, customers armed with price information can often negotiate lower prices.

In addition, consumers can negotiate prices at online auction sites and exchanges. Suddenly the centuries-old art of haggling is back in vogue. Want to sell that antique pickle jar that's been collecting dust for generations? Post it on eBay, the world's biggest online flea market. Want to name your own price for a hotel room or rental car? Visit Priceline.com or another reverse auction site. Want to bid on a ticket to a Coldplay show? Check out Ticketmaster.com, which now offers an online auction service for concert tickets.

Dynamic pricing makes sense in many contexts; it adjusts prices according to market forces, and it often works to the benefit of the customer. But marketers need to be careful not to use dynamic pricing to take advantage of certain customer groups, damaging important customer relationships.

International Pricing

Companies that market their products internationally must decide what prices to charge in the different countries in which they operate. In some cases, a company can set a uniform worldwide price. For example, Boeing sells its jetliners at about the same price everywhere, whether in the United States, Europe, or a third-world country. However, most companies adjust their prices to reflect local market conditions and cost considerations.

The price that a company should charge in a specific country depends on many factors, including economic conditions, competitive situations, laws and regulations, and the development of the wholesaling and retailing system. Consumer perceptions and preferences also may vary from country to country, calling for different prices. Or the company may have different marketing objectives in various world markets, which require changes in pricing strategy. For example, Samsung might introduce a new product into mature markets in highly developed countries with the goal of quickly gaining mass-market share—this would call for a penetration-pricing strategy. In contrast, it might enter a less-developed market by targeting smaller, less price-sensitive segments; in this case, market-skimming pricing makes sense.

Costs play an important role in setting international prices. Travelers abroad are often surprised to find that goods that are relatively inexpensive at home may carry outrageously higher price tags in other countries. A pair of Levi's selling for $30 in the United States might go for $63 in Tokyo and $88 in Paris. A McDonald's Big Mac selling for a modest $3.57 in the United States might cost $5.29 in Norway, and an Oral-B toothbrush selling for $2.49 at home may cost $10 in China. Conversely, a Gucci handbag going for only $140 in Milan, Italy, might fetch $240 in the United States. In some cases, such *price escalation* may result from differences in selling strategies or market conditions. In most instances, however, it is simply a result of the higher costs of selling in another country—the additional costs of operations, product modifications, shipping and insurance, import tariffs and taxes, exchange-rate fluctuations, and physical distribution.

● **International pricing: To lower prices in developing countries, Unilever developed smaller, more affordable packages that put the company's premier brands within the reach of the cash-strapped customers.**

Price has become a key element in the international marketing strategies of companies attempting to enter emerging markets, such as China, India, and Brazil. ● Consider Unilever's pricing strategy for developing countries:

> There used to be one way to sell a product in developing markets, if you bothered to sell there at all: Slap on a local label and market at premium prices to the elite. Unilever—the maker of such brands as Dove, Lipton, and Vaseline—changed that. Instead, it built a following among the world's poorest consumers by shrinking packages to set a price even consumers living on $2 a day could afford. The strategy was forged about 25 years ago when Unilever's Indian subsidiary found its products out of reach for millions of Indians. To lower the price while making a profit, Unilever developed single-use packets for everything from shampoo to laundry detergent, costing just pennies a pack. The small, affordable packages put the company's premier brands within reach of the world's poor. Today, Unilever continues to woo cash-strapped customers with great success. For example, its approachable pricing helps explain why Unilever now captures 70 percent of the Brazil detergent market.[11]

Thus, international pricing presents some special problems and complexities. We discuss international pricing issues in more detail in Chapter 19.

Author Comment | When and how should a company change its price? What if costs rise, putting the squeeze on profits? What if the economy sags and customers become more price-sensitive? Or what if a major competitor raises or drops its prices? As Figure 11.1 suggests, companies face many price-changing options.

Price Changes (pp 325–328)

After developing their pricing structures and strategies, companies often face situations in which they must initiate price changes or respond to price changes by competitors.

Initiating Price Changes

In some cases, the company may find it desirable to initiate either a price cut or a price increase. In both cases, it must anticipate possible buyer and competitor reactions.

Initiating Price Cuts

Several situations may lead a firm to consider cutting its price. One such circumstance is excess capacity. Another is falling demand in the face of strong price competition or a weakened economy. In such cases, the firm may aggressively cut prices to boost sales and market share. But as the airline, fast-food, automobile, and other industries have learned in recent years, cutting prices in an industry loaded with excess capacity may lead to price wars as competitors try to hold onto market share.

A company may also cut prices in a drive to dominate the market through lower costs. Either the company starts with lower costs than its competitors, or it cuts prices in the hope of gaining market share that will further cut costs through larger volume. Lenovo uses an aggressive low-cost, low-price strategy to increase its share of the PC market in developing countries.

Initiating Price Increases

A successful price increase can greatly improve profits. For example, if the company's profit margin is 3 percent of sales, a 1 percent price increase will boost profits by 33 percent if the sales volume is unaffected. A major factor in price increases is cost inflation. Rising costs squeeze profit margins and lead companies to pass cost increases along to customers. Another factor leading to price increases is overdemand: When a company cannot supply all that its customers need, it may raise its prices, ration products to customers, or both. Consider today's worldwide oil and gas industry.

When raising prices, the company must avoid being perceived as a *price gouger*. ● For example, when gasoline prices rise rapidly, angry customers often accuse the major oil companies of enriching themselves at the expense of consumers.

● Initiating price increases: When gasoline prices rise rapidly, angry consumers often accuse the major oil companies of enriching themselves by gouging customers.

Customers have long memories, and they will eventually turn away from companies or even whole industries that they perceive as charging excessive prices. In the extreme, claims of price gouging may even bring about increased government regulation.

There are some techniques for avoiding these problems. One is to maintain a sense of fairness surrounding any price increase. Price increases should be supported by company communications telling customers why prices are being raised.

Wherever possible, the company should consider ways to meet higher costs or demand without raising prices. For example, it can consider more cost-effective ways to produce or distribute its products. It can shrink the product or substitute less-expensive ingredients instead of raising the price, as ConAgra did in an effort to hold its Banquet frozen dinner prices at $1. Or it can "unbundle" its market offering, removing features, packaging, or services and separately pricing elements that were formerly part of the offer.

Buyer Reactions to Price Changes

Customers do not always interpret price changes in a straightforward way. A price *increase*, which would normally lower sales, may have some positive meanings for buyers. For example, what would you think if Rolex *raised* the price of its latest watch model? On the one hand, you might think that the watch is even more exclusive or better made. On the other hand, you might think that Rolex is simply being greedy by charging what the traffic will bear.

Similarly, consumers may view a price *cut* in several ways. For example, what would you think if Rolex were to suddenly cut its prices? You might think that you are getting a better deal on an exclusive product. More likely, however, you'd think that quality had been reduced, and the brand's luxury image might be tarnished.

A brand's price and image are often closely linked. A price change, especially a drop in price, can adversely affect how consumers view the brand. ● Tiffany found this out when it attempted to broaden its appeal by offering a line of more affordable jewelry:[12]

● Price changes: A brand's price and image are often closely linked, and a change in price can adversely affect how consumers view the brand. Tiffany found this out when it attempted to broaden its appeal by offering a line of more affordable jewelry.

> Tiffany is all about luxury and the cachet of its blue boxes. However, in the late 1990s, the high-end jeweler responded to the "affordable luxuries" craze with a new "Return to Tiffany" line of less expensive silver jewelry. The "Return to Tiffany" silver charm bracelet quickly became a must-have item, as teens jammed Tiffany's hushed stores clamoring for the $110 silver bauble. Sales skyrocketed. But despite this early success, the bracelet fad appeared to alienate the firm's older, wealthier, and more conservative clientele, damaging Tiffany's reputation for luxury. So, in 2002, the firm began reemphasizing its pricier jewelry collections. Although high-end jewelry has once again replaced silver as Tiffany's fastest growing business, the company has yet to fully regain its exclusivity. Say's one well-heeled customer: "You used to aspire to be able to buy something at Tiffany, but now it's not that special anymore."

Competitor Reactions to Price Changes

A firm considering a price change must worry about the reactions of its competitors as well as those of its customers. Competitors are most likely to react when the number of firms involved is small, when the product is uniform, and when the buyers are well informed about products and prices.

How can the firm anticipate the likely reactions of its competitors? The problem is complex because, like the customer, the competitor can interpret a company price cut in many ways. It might think the company is trying to grab a larger market share or that it's doing poorly and trying to boost its sales. Or it might think that the company wants the whole industry to cut prices to increase total demand.

The company must guess each competitor's likely reaction. If all competitors behave alike, this amounts to analyzing only a typical competitor. In contrast, if the competitors do not behave alike—perhaps because of differences in size, market shares, or policies—then separate analyses are necessary. However, if some competitors will match the price change, there is good reason to expect that the rest will also match it.

Responding to Price Changes

Here we reverse the question and ask how a firm should respond to a price change by a competitor. The firm needs to consider several issues: Why did the competitor change the price? Is the price change temporary or permanent? What will happen to the company's market share and profits if it does not respond? Are other competitors going to respond? Besides these issues, the company must also consider its own situation and strategy and possible customer reactions to price changes.

● **Figure 11.1** shows the ways a company might assess and respond to a competitor's price cut. Suppose the company learns that a competitor has cut its price and decides that this price cut is likely to harm its sales and profits. It might simply decide to hold its current price and profit margin. The company might believe that it will not lose too much market share, or that it would lose too much profit if it reduced its own price. Or it might decide that it should wait and respond when it has more information on the effects of the competitor's price change. However, waiting too long to act might let the competitor get stronger and more confident as its sales increase.

If the company decides that effective action can and should be taken, it might make any of four responses. First, it could *reduce its price* to match the competitor's price. It may decide that the market is price sensitive and that it would lose too much market share to the lower-priced competitor. Cutting the price will reduce the company's profits in the short run. Some companies might also reduce their product quality, services, and marketing communications to retain profit margins, but this will ultimately hurt long-run market share. The company should try to maintain its quality as it cuts prices.

Alternatively, the company might maintain its price but *raise the perceived value* of its offer. It could improve its communications, stressing the relative value of its product over that of the lower-price competitor. The firm may find it cheaper to maintain price and spend money to improve its perceived value than to cut price and operate at a lower margin. Or, the company might *improve* quality *and increase price*, moving its brand into a higher price-value position. The higher quality creates greater customer value, which justifies the higher price. In turn, the higher price preserves the company's higher margins.

● **FIGURE | 11.1**
Assessing and Responding
to Competitor Price Changes

When a competitor cuts prices, a company's first reaction may be to drop its prices as well. But that is often the wrong response. Instead, the firm may want to emphasize the "value" side of the price-value equation.

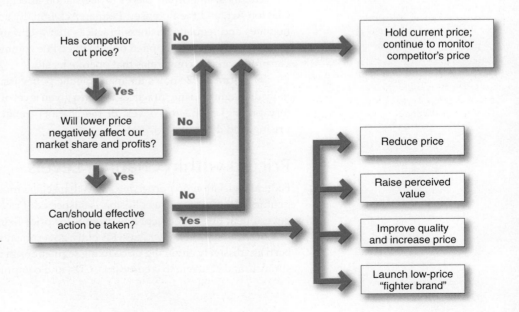

● **Fighter brands:** To compete with budget bus lines, Greyhound rolled out BoltBus, which offers lots of amenities at low prices that today's budget-conscious intercity commuters find very appealing.

Finally, the company might *launch a low-price "fighter brand"*—adding a lower-price item to the line or creating a separate lower-price brand. This is necessary if the particular market segment being lost is price sensitive and will not respond to arguments of higher quality. Thus, to compete with a growing number of budget bus services, rather than dropping its own fares on select, highly competitive routes, Greyhound Lines rolled out the BoltBus fighter brand, which provides service between New York City and other cities in the northeastern United States. ● BoltBus offers amenities such as Wi-Fi, reserved seating, a clean bathroom, and extra legroom, all at low fares that today's budget-conscious intercity commuters find very appealing. For example, the one-way BoltBus fare from New York City to Washington, DC, runs just $16 to $20, compared to the regular $31 to $58 Greyhound fare.[13]

To counter store brands and other low-price entrants in a weakened economy, P&G turned a number of its brands into fighter brands. Luvs disposable diapers give parents "premium leakage protection for less than pricier brands." And P&G offers popular budget-priced basic versions of several of its major brands. For example, Charmin Basic is "the quality toilet tissue at a price you'll love," and Bounty Basic is "practical, not pricey." Tide Basic gives you "Big Value. Basic Clean." at a 20 percent lower price. However, companies must use caution when introducing fighter brands. Such brands can tarnish the image of the main brand. And although they may attract budget buyers away from lower-priced rivals, they can also take business away from the firm's higher-margin brands.[14]

Author Comment | Pricing decisions are often constrained by social and legal issues. For example, think about the pharmaceuticals industry. Are rapidly rising prescription prices justified? Or are the drug companies unfairly lining their pockets by gouging consumers who have few alternatives? Should the government step in?

Public Policy and Marketing (pp 328–332)

Price competition is a core element of our free-market economy. In setting prices, companies usually are not free to charge whatever prices they wish. Many federal, state, and even local laws govern the rules of fair play in pricing. In addition, companies must consider broader societal pricing concerns. In setting their prices, for example, pharmaceutical firms must balance their development costs and profit objectives against the sometimes life-and-death needs of drug consumers (see Real Marketing 11.2).

The most important pieces of legislation affecting pricing are the Sherman Act, the Clayton Act, and the Robinson-Patman Act, initially adopted to curb the formation of monopolies and regulate business practices that might unfairly restrain trade. Because these federal statutes can be applied only to interstate commerce, some states have adopted similar provisions for companies that operate locally.

● **Figure 11.2** shows the major public policy issues in pricing. These include potentially damaging pricing practices within a given level of the channel (price-fixing and predatory pricing) and across levels of the channel (retail price maintenance, discriminatory pricing, and deceptive pricing).[15]

Pricing within Channel Levels

Federal legislation on *price-fixing* states that sellers must set prices without talking to competitors. Otherwise, price collusion is suspected. Price-fixing is illegal per se—that is, the government does not accept any excuses for price-fixing. Companies found guilty of such practices can receive heavy fines. Recently, governments at the state and national levels have been aggressively enforcing price-fixing regulations in industries ranging from gasoline, insurance, and concrete to credit cards, CDs, and computer chips.

Real Marketing 11.2

GlaxoSmithKline:
No Easy Answers in Pharmaceutical Pricing

The U.S. pharmaceutical industry has historically been one of the nation's most profitable industries. Annual revenues have grown at a growth rate that few industries can match. As the world's second-largest pharmaceutical company, GlaxoSmithKline (GSK) has played a large role in the industry's success. It produces a medicine cabinet full of well-known prescription drugs that combat infections, depression, adverse skin conditions, asthma, heart and circulatory disease, and cancer. It also makes dozens of familiar over-the-counter remedies, from Contac, Panadol, Nicorette, Aquafresh, and Sensodyne to Tagamet and Tums.

GSK is doing very well in a high-performing industry. In most situations, we applaud companies for such strong performance. However, when it comes to pharmaceutical firms, critics claim, healthy sales and profits may not be so healthy for consumers. Learning that companies like GSK are reaping big profits leaves a bad taste in the mouths of many consumers. It's like learning that the oil companies are profiting when gas prices rocket upward. Although most consumers appreciate the steady stream of beneficial drugs produced by pharmaceutical companies, they worry that the industry's huge success may be coming at their own expense—literally.

Americans spend more than $300 billion a year on prescription medications, nearly half of worldwide spending. Prescription prices have risen rapidly over the years, and healthcare costs continue to jump. Last year, while many other industries were cutting prices and many recession-weary consumers struggled just to make ends meet, the pharmaceutical industry raised wholesale prices for brandname prescription drugs by 9 percent in the United States, adding up to $10 billion to its revenues.

The critics claim that competitive forces don't operate well in the pharmaceutical market, allowing GSK and other companies to charge excessive prices. Unlike purchases of other consumer products, drug purchases cannot be postponed. And consumers don't usually shop for the best deals on medicines; they

simply take what the doctor orders. Because physicians who write the prescriptions don't pay for the medicines they recommend, they have little incentive to be price conscious. Finally, because of patents and Food and Drug Administration (FDA) approvals, few competing brands exist to force lower prices, and existing brands don't go on sale.

The critics claim that these market factors leave pharmaceutical companies free to practice monopoly pricing, resulting in unfair practices and price gouging. To add insult to injury, the critics say, drug companies pour more than $4 billion a year into direct-to-consumer advertising and another $18 billion into sampling. These marketing efforts dictate higher prices at the same time that they build demand for more expensive remedies. Thus, the severest critics say, GSK and the other big drug companies may be profiting unfairly—even at the expense of human life—by promoting and pricing products beyond the reach of many people who need them.

But there's another side to the drug-pricing issue. Industry proponents point out that, over the years, the drug companies have developed a steady stream of medicines that transform people's lives. Developing such new drugs is a risky and expensive endeavor, involving legions of scientists, expensive technology, and years of effort with no certainty of success. The pharmaceutical industry invests nearly $50 billion a year in R&D; GSK alone invested $5 billion last year. GSK now has 134 drug projects under development. On average, each new drug takes 12–15 years to develop and typically costs $850 million. Seventy percent of new drugs never generate enough revenue to recover the cost of development. Although the prices of prescription drugs seem high, they're needed to fund the development of important future drugs. Additionally, a publically held company like GSK has a bona fide responsibility to return a profit to shareholders.

A recent GSK ad notes that it took 15 years to complete all the tests and find the exact right compound for a new heart medicine, at a cost of more than the price of a space shuttle mission. Profits from the heart drug will help to fund critical research on diseases such as multiple sclerosis and Alzheimer's. The ad concludes: "Inventing new medicines isn't easy, but it's worth it. . . . Today's medicines finance tomorrow's miracles."

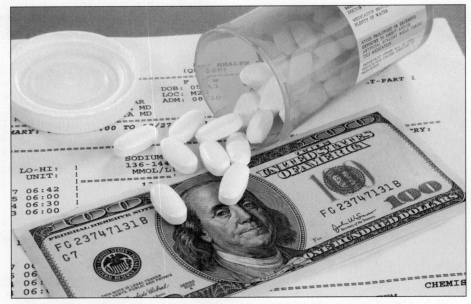

Responsible pricing: Most consumers understand that they'll have to pay the price for beneficial drugs. They just want to be treated fairly in the process.

Continued on next page

As for all that expensive prescription drug advertising, the industry argues that the ads have strong information value: They help educate people about treatments and encourage them to get help for conditions of which they might not otherwise have been aware.

And so the controversy continues. As drug prices climb, GSK and the industry are facing pressures from the federal government, insurance companies, managed-care providers, and advocacy groups to exercise restraint in setting prices. Rather than waiting for tougher legislation on prices—or simply because it's the right thing to do—GSK has undertaken several initiatives to make drugs available to those who need but can't afford them.

For example, internationally, GSK employs tiered-pricing—selling its medicines in different countries at varying prices based on the ability to pay in each country. People in the poorest countries pay the least, typically one-fifth or less the price in industrialized countries. GSK sells its malaria vaccine, sold almost exclusively in developing countries, at little or no profit to keep prices as low as possible. The company also reinvests 20 percent of the

profits from selling drugs in lesser-developed countries (LDCs) to strengthen healthcare infrastructure in those countries. And GSK regularly donates free medicines in response to disaster relief efforts around the globe. "I want GSK to be a very successful company but not at the expense of leaving the population of Africa behind," says GSK's CEO.

Tiered pricing is an admirable solution, but it's fraught with challenges. For one thing, it requires that consumers in industrialized countries foot the massive bill for medications to LDCs—for example, 80 percent of GSK's vaccines go to LDCs. Tiered pricing also overlooks the fact that there are many poor people in even the wealthiest countries who can't afford to pay for prescription drugs. That's why

in the United States and other developed countries, GSK sponsors patient assistance programs and discount cards that provide prescription medicines to low-income, uninsured patients free or at minimal cost.

In all, pharmaceuticals pricing is no easy issue. For GSK, it's more than a matter of sales and profits. In setting prices, short-term financial goals must be tempered by broader societal considerations. GSK's heartfelt mission is "to improve the quality of human life by enabling people to do more, feel better, and live longer." Accomplishing this mission won't come cheap. Most consumers understand that. One way or another, they know, they'll have to pay the price. All they really ask is that they be treated fairly in the process.

Sources: Linda A. Johnson, "Drugmakers Boost Consumer Ad Spending 2 Percent in '09," March 2, 2010, http://abcnews.go.com/Business/wireStory?id=10024145; Andrew Jack, "GSK Gives Price Pledge on Malaria Vaccine," *Financial Times*, January 21, 2010, accessed at www.ft.com; Duff Wilson, "Drug Makers Raise Prices in Face of Health Care Reform," *New York Times*, November 15, 2009; Congressional Budget Office "Promotional Spending for Prescription Drugs," *Economic and Budget Issue Brief*, December 2, 2009; "Drug Company Reaches out to Poor," *Financial Chronicle*, February 10, 2010, www.mydigitalfc.com/news/drug-company-reaches-out-poor-589; and information from www.gsk.com, accessed November 2010.

Sellers are also prohibited from using *predatory pricing*—selling below cost with the intention of punishing a competitor or gaining higher long-run profits by putting competitors out of business. This protects small sellers from larger ones who might sell items below cost temporarily or in a specific locale to drive them out of business. The biggest problem is determining just what constitutes predatory pricing behavior. Selling below cost to unload ex-

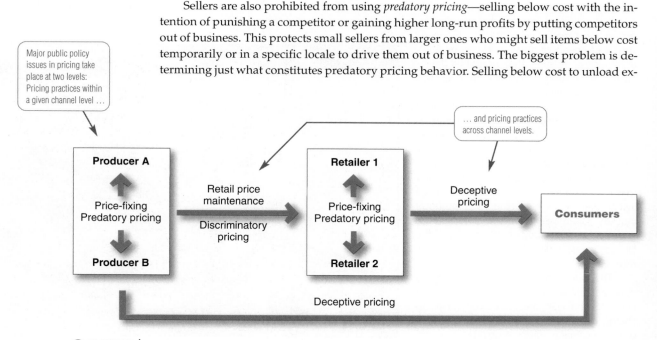

● **FIGURE** | 11.2

Public Policy Issues in Pricing

Source: Based on Dhruv Grewal and Larry D. Compeau, "Pricing and Public Policy: A Research Agenda and Overview of the Special Issue," *Journal of Public Policy and Marketing*, Spring 1999, pp. 3–10.

● Predatory pricing: Some critics charge that the big-box stores like Best Buy price CDs as loss leaders to drive music competitors out of business. But is it predatory pricing or just plain good marketing?

cess inventory is not considered predatory; selling below cost to drive out competitors is. Thus, the same action may or may not be predatory depending on intent, and intent can be very difficult to determine or prove.

In recent years, several large and powerful companies have been accused of predatory pricing. However, turning an accusation into a lawsuit can be difficult. ● For example, many music retailers have accused Walmart and Best Buy of predatory CD pricing. Since 2007 alone, CD sales have plummeted almost 20 percent each year, putting music-only retailers such as Tower Records, Musicland, and a megamall full of small mom-and-pop music shops out of business. Many industry experts attribute slumping CD sales to new music distribution strategies—mainly digital downloads. Others, however, blame the big-box stores for pricing CDs as loss leaders to drive competitors out of business. Low CD prices don't hurt Walmart; it derives less than 2 percent of its sales from CDs, and low-priced CDs pull customers into stores, where they buy other products. Such pricing tactics, however, cut deeply into the profits of music retailers. Still, no predatory pricing charges have ever been filed against Walmart or Best Buy. It would be extremely difficult to prove that such loss-leader CD pricing is purposefully predatory as opposed to just plain good marketing.[16]

Pricing Across Channel Levels

The Robinson-Patman Act seeks to prevent unfair *price discrimination* by ensuring that sellers offer the same price terms to customers at a given level of trade. For example, every retailer is entitled to the same price terms from a given manufacturer, whether the retailer is Sears or your local bicycle shop. However, price discrimination is allowed if the seller can prove that its costs are different when selling to different retailers—for example, that it costs less per unit to sell a large volume of bicycles to Sears than to sell a few bicycles to the local dealer.

The seller can also discriminate in its pricing if the seller manufactures different qualities of the same product for different retailers. The seller has to prove that these differences are proportional. Price differentials may also be used to "match competition" in "good faith," provided the price discrimination is temporary, localized, and defensive rather than offensive.

Laws also prohibit *retail (or resale) price maintenance*; a manufacturer cannot require dealers to charge a specified retail price for its product. Although the seller can propose a manufacturer's *suggested* retail price to dealers, it cannot refuse to sell to a dealer that takes independent pricing action nor can it punish the dealer by shipping late or denying advertising allowances. For example, the Florida attorney general's office investigated Nike for allegedly fixing the retail price of its shoes and clothing. It was concerned that Nike might be withholding items from retailers who were not selling its most expensive shoes at prices the company considered suitable.

Deceptive pricing occurs when a seller states prices or price savings that mislead consumers or are not actually available to consumers. This might involve bogus reference or comparison prices, as when a retailer sets artificially high "regular" prices and then announces "sale" prices close to its previous everyday prices. For example, Overstock.com recently came under scrutiny for inaccurately listing manufacturer's suggested retail prices, often quoting them higher than the actual price. Such comparison pricing is widespread.

Comparison pricing claims are legal if they are truthful. However, the FTC's *Guides Against Deceptive Pricing* warns sellers not to advertise a price reduction unless it is a savings from the usual retail price, "factory" or "wholesale" prices unless such prices are what they are claimed to be, and comparable value prices on imperfect goods.[17]

Other deceptive pricing issues include *scanner fraud* and price confusion. The widespread use of scanner-based computer checkouts has led to increasing complaints of retailers overcharging their customers. Most of these overcharges result from poor management—from a failure to enter current or sale prices into the system. Other cases, however, involve intentional overcharges.

Many federal and state statutes regulate against deceptive pricing practices. For example, the Automobile Information Disclosure Act requires automakers to attach a statement on new vehicle windows stating the manufacturer's suggested retail price, the prices of optional equipment, and the dealer's transportation charges. However, reputable sellers go beyond what is required by law. Treating customers fairly and making certain that they fully understand prices and pricing terms is an important part of building strong and lasting customer relationships.

REVIEWING Objectives AND KEY Terms

In this chapter, we examined some additional pricing considerations—new-product pricing, product mix pricing, price adjustments, and initiating and reacting to prices changes. A company sets not a single price but rather a *pricing structure* that covers its entire mix of products. This pricing structure changes over time as products move through their life cycles. The company adjusts product prices to reflect changes in costs and demand and account for variations in buyers and situations. As the competitive environment changes, the company considers when to initiate price changes and when to respond to them.

Objective 1 Describe the major strategies for pricing new products. (pp 314–315)

Pricing is a dynamic process, and pricing strategies usually change as the product passes through its life cycle. The introductory stage—setting prices for the first time—is especially challenging. The company can decide on one of several strategies for pricing innovative new products: It can use *market-skimming pricing* by initially setting high prices to "skim" the maximum amount of revenue from various segments of the market. Or it can use *market-penetrating pricing* by setting a low initial price to penetrate the market deeply and win a large market share. Several conditions must be set for either new-product pricing strategy to work.

Objective 2 Explain how companies find a set of prices that maximizes the profits from the total product mix. (pp 315–319)

When the product is part of a product mix, the firm searches for a set of prices that will maximize the profits from the total mix. In *product line pricing*, the company determines the price steps for the entire product line it offers. In addition, the company must set prices for *optional products* (optional or accessory products included with the main product), *captive products* (products that are required for using the main product), *by-products* (waste or residual products produced when making the main product), and *product bundles* (combinations of products at a reduced price).

Objective 3 Discuss how companies adjust their prices to take into account different types of customers and situations. (pp 319–325)

Companies apply a variety of *price adjustment strategies* to account for differences in consumer segments and situations. One is *discount and allowance pricing*, whereby the company establishes cash, quantity, functional, or seasonal discounts, or varying types of allowances. A second strategy is *segmented pricing*, where the company sells a product at two or more prices to accommodate different customers, product forms, locations, or times. Sometimes companies consider more than economics in their pricing decisions, using *psychological pricing* to better communicate a product's intended position. In *promotional pricing*, a company offers discounts or temporarily sells a product below list price as a special event, sometimes even selling below cost as a loss leader. Another approach is *geographical pricing*, whereby the company decides how to price to distant customers, choosing from such alternatives as *FOB-origin pricing*, *uniform-delivered pricing*, *zone pricing*, *basing-point pricing*, and *freight-absorption pricing*. Finally, *international pricing* means that the company adjusts its price to meet different conditions and expectations in different world markets.

Objective 4 Discuss the key issues related to initiating and responding to price changes. (pp 325–328)

When a firm considers initiating a *price change*, it must consider customers' and competitors' reactions. There are different implications to *initiating price cuts* and *initiating price increases*. Buyer reactions to price changes are influenced by the meaning customers see in the price change. Competitors' reactions flow from a set reaction policy or a fresh analysis of each situation.

There are also many factors to consider in responding to a competitor's price changes. The company that faces a price change initiated by a competitor must try to understand the competitor's intent as well as the likely duration and impact of the change. If a swift reaction is desirable, the firm should preplan its reactions to different possible price actions by competitors. When facing a competitor's price change, the company might sit tight, reduce its own price, raise perceived quality, improve quality and raise price, or launch a fighting brand.

Overview the social and legal issues that affect pricing decisions. (pp 328–332)

Many federal, state, and even local laws govern the rules of fair pricing. Also, companies must consider broader societal pricing con-

cerns. The major public policy issues in pricing include potentially damaging pricing practices *within* a given level of the channel, such as price-fixing and predatory pricing. They also include pricing practices *across* channel levels, such as retail price maintenance, discriminatory pricing, and deceptive pricing. Although many federal and state statutes regulate pricing practices, reputable sellers go beyond what is required by law. Treating customers fairly is an important part of building strong and lasting customer relationships.

KEY Terms

OBJECTIVE 1

Market-skimming pricing (p 314)
Market-penetration pricing (p 314)

OBJECTIVE 2

Product line pricing (p 315)
Optional product pricing (p 316)
Captive product pricing (p 316)
By-product pricing (p 316)
Product bundle pricing (p 318)

OBJECTIVE 3

Discount (p 319)
Allowance (p 319)
Segmented pricing (p 319)
Psychological pricing (p 320)
Reference prices (p 320)
Promotional pricing (p 321)
Geographical pricing (p 322)

FOB-origin pricing (p 322)
Uniform-delivered pricing (p 322)
Zone pricing (p 322)
Basing-point pricing (p 322)
Freight-absorption pricing (p 323)
Dynamic pricing (p 323)

PEARSON
mymarketinglab

- Check your understanding of the concepts and key terms using the mypearsonmarketinglab study plan for this chapter.
- Apply the concepts in a business context using the simulation entitled **Pricing Strategies.**

DISCUSSING & APPLYING THE Concepts

Discussing the Concepts

1. Compare and contrast market-skimming and market-penetration pricing strategies and discuss the conditions under which each is appropriate. (AACSB: Communication; Reflective Thinking)

2. Name and briefly describe the five product mix pricing decisions. (AACSB: Communication)

3. Explain how discounts and allowances differ from promotional pricing. (AACSB: Communication; Reflective Thinking)

4. Compare and contrast the geographic pricing strategies that companies use for customers located in different parts of the country or the world. Which strategy is best? (AACSB: Communication; Reflective Thinking)

5. What factors influence the prices a company charges in different countries? (AACSB: Communication)

6. Why would a company consider increasing its price? What precautions must be taken to avoid being perceived as a price gouger? (AACSB: Communication)

Applying the Concepts

1. Identify three price-comparison shopping Web sites and shop for a specific model of a digital camera on all three sites. Compare the price ranges given at each site. Based on your search, determine a fair price for the camera. (AACSB: Communication; Use of IT)

2. Convert U.S.$1.00 to the currencies of five other countries. (You can do this at www.xe.com.) What implications do currency exchange rates hold for setting prices in other countries? (AACSB: Communication; Use of IT; Reflective Thinking)

3. One psychological pricing tactic is just-below pricing. It is also called "9-ending" pricing because prices usually end in the number 9 (or 99). In a small group, have each member select five different products and visit a store to find the price of those items. Is there a variation among the items and stores with regard to 9-ending pricing? Why do marketers use this pricing tactic? (AACSB: Communication; Reflective Thinking)

FOCUS ON Technology

The Internet is great for selling products and services. But don't make a pricing mistake online! Intercontinental Hotels mistakenly priced rooms at one of its four-star hotels near Venice, Italy, for 1 euro per night instead of the actual price of 150 euros per night. Internet users booked 1,400 nights before the mistake was realized. Intercontinental Hotels honored the reservations at a cost of 90,000 euros to the company. In Taiwan, an eight-hour online pricing snafu on Dell's Web site created tremendous problems for the company, such as 40,000 orders for a laptop computer priced at about one-fourth the intended price. Unlike Intercontinental Hotels, however, Dell refused to honor the erroneous price and of-fered a discount instead. The Taiwanese government disagreed, ordered Dell to honor orders for erroneously priced products, and fined the company.

1. Find two other examples of online pricing mistakes. How did the companies handle the problems resulting from the pricing errors? (AACSB: Communication; Reflective Thinking)

2. Research ways in which marketers protect against the consequences of online pricing errors and write a brief report summarizing what you learn. (AACSB: Communication; Reflective Thinking)

FOCUS ON Ethics

You'd think that the farther you fly, the more expensive your airfare would be. According to U.S. Department of Transportation data, however, that's not the case. For example, the average cost of a 280-mile flight from Boston to Philadelphia was $342, which is $1.22 per mile. A 2,602-mile flight from Boston to Long Beach, California, cost $169, or $0.06 per mile! That's the average cost; fliers sitting next to each other likely paid different prices. Many factors influence the pricing of airfares; distance has minor impact, even though two major expenses—fuel and labor—increase the longer the flight. In this example, one factor might be that the Boston-Philadelphia route averages 484 passengers per day, while the Boston–Long Beach route averages only 330 passengers per day. Airlines claim they are just charging what the market will bear.

1. Should airlines be required to charge standard prices based on distance and equal airfares for passengers seated in the same class (such as coach or business class) on the same flight? What will likely happen to prices if the government requires airlines to base fares only on distance and passenger class? (AACSB: Communication; Ethical Reasoning; Reflective Thinking)

2. What factors account for the variation in airfares? Should airlines be permitted to get as much as they can for a seat? (AACSB: Communication; Reflective Thinking)

MARKETING & THE Economy

Pizza Hut

Restaurants of all kinds have scrambled to keep customers coming in during recent difficult economic times. Pizza Hut is in an unusual spot. It isn't exactly fast food, but it isn't quite full-service fare either. Pizza Hut has never been perceived as being on the low end of pizza prices. As the economy sagged, all these factors cooled down business for the red-roofed purveyor of pies. So Pizza Hut did what many companies did. It cut prices. At first, it shocked the pizza category with its "$10 any" promotion—any pizza, any size, any crust, any toppings, for just $10.

Customers really responded to the limited time offer. But as soon as the price deal ended, Pizza Hut's incremental promotional revenues disappeared. So the company has made more perma-nent adjustments to the new frugality reality. To increase customer loyalty, it has introduced everyday low prices. Most medium pizzas cost $8, most large pizzas cost $10, and most specialty pizzas cost $12; these price cuts represent up to 50 percent reductions from previous pricing. Under this new pricing, Pizza Hut expects that revenues will increase significantly. But the new pricing mechanism will require some time before it proves itself.

1. What are the implications of Pizza Hut's big price cuts for its brand image?

2. Can customer loyalty be generated through low prices?

3. Can Pizza Hut sustain such dramatically lower prices and still remain profitable?

MARKETING BY THE Numbers

The recently weak economy caused many consumers to switch to lower-priced products. Although P&G had sales of $77 billion in 2009, many of its relatively expensive brands, such as Tide detergent and Secret deodorant, were stranded on store shelves. So, in 2010, P&G did the unthinkable: It slashed prices on many of its products, such as batteries (13.3 percent), liquid laundry detergents (5.1 percent), shampoos (5.4 percent), and conditioners (6.6 percent). The price cuts come at a cost, however, and sales must increase considerably just to break even or make the price cuts profitable.

1. P&G's average contribution margin before the price cuts was 20 percent. Refer to Appendix 2 and calculate the new contribution margin if prices are reduced 10 percent. (AACSB: Communication; Analytical Reasoning)

2. What level of total sales must P&G capture at the new price levels to maintain the same level of total contribution before the price reduction (that is, total contribution = $15.4 billion, which is 20 percent of $77 billion in sales)? (AACSB: Communication; Analytic Reasoning)

VIDEO Case

Smashburger

Hamburgers are America's favorite food. Consumers spend more than $100 billion on beef sandwiches every year. Despite America's infatuation with burgers, however, there is considerable dissatisfaction with hamburger quality and value among consumers. Many customers are not happy with what is available at market-leading fast-food outlets. They want a better burger, and they won't hesitate to pay a higher price to get one. Enter Smashburger. Started just a few years ago in Denver, Colorado, Smashburger is now a rapidly expanding chain of more than 100 stores in 17 states. And all this growth occurred during a severe economic downturn despite Smashburger's average lunch check of $8. Many customers pay as much as $10 or $12 for a burger, fries,

and shake. The Smashburger video shows how this small start-up has pulled off a seemingly impossible challenge. After viewing the video, answer the following questions.

1. Describe customer dissatisfaction with fast-food hamburger options. Why do people continue to consume burgers if they are not satisfied?

2. What effect does Smashburger's premium price have on consumer perceptions? How did a restaurant with a premium-priced product and little track record take off during a recession?

3. Is Smashburger's success based on novelty alone or will it continue to succeed?

COMPANY Case

Payless ShoeSource:
Paying Less for Fashion

When you think of New York's Fifth Avenue, what retailers come to mind? Tiffany? Gucci? Armani? One name that probably *doesn't* come to mind is Payless. But for the past few years, Payless ShoeSource has been operating one of its low-priced shoe stores on the famed avenue of luxury retailing. In fact, Payless is now well on its way to placing stores in more than 100 higher-end malls around the country.

Although the discount shoe peddler still focuses on selling inexpensive shoes to the masses, Payless is moving upscale. It's on a mission to "democratize fashion"—to make truly fashionable products more accessible by applying its cost-effective model to a product portfolio infused with well-known brand labels and some of the hottest high-end designers in the business. Sound like a hair-brained scheme? You might change your mind after hearing the whole story.

Founded in 1956 in Topeka, Kansas, Payless grew rapidly based on what was then a revolutionary idea: selling shoes in a self-service environment. Fifty years later, it had become the largest shoe retailer in the Western Hemisphere, with over 4,500 stores in all 50 states and throughout the Americas. Targeting budget-minded families, Payless was serving up more than 150 million pairs of shoes each year, approximately one in every ten pairs of shoes purchased in America.

While all seemed rosy for the choose-it-yourself shoe store, by 2005, Payless was losing market share and closing stores. The retail landscape had changed, and giant discount one-stop shops like Walmart, Target, and Kohl's had become the vendors of choice for budget conscious shopper's buying shoes. Said one industry in-

sider, "You can no longer produce the same boring shoes year after year and hope that price alone will get customers to your door." With thrift as its only positioning point, Payless had lost its edge.

AN IMAGE OVERHAUL

To reverse its sliding market share, Payless had to engineer a completely new strategy. To get things started, it hired a new CEO, Matt Rubel, who came with extensive experience with high-end brands like Cole Haan and J.Crew. Rubel knew that Payless would have to design shoes that *Sex and the City*'s Carrie Bradshaw would drool over but at prices that Roseanne could afford. It had to change its image from the dusty dungeon of cheap footwear into the fun, hip merchant of fashion. "We have the ability to make shoes at the most affordable prices anywhere in the world, and we want to marry that with the greatest creativity," said Rubel. The overall objective of Rubel's strategy was to not only give the brand image a makeover but also position Payless in such a way that a slight price increase would seem like a bargain.

Rubel wasted no time in making big changes. The strategic plan that he drafted was based on four major components.

Expanding the Brand Portfolio. Rubel implemented a "House of Brands" strategy, shifting the product line from one consisting almost entirely of store brands to one dominated by well-known national brands. Payless now sells shoes under numerous brand names that it either owns or licenses, including Airwalk, Champion, Dexter, Dunkman (endorsed by Shaquille O'Neal), American Eagle, Hello Kitty, Star Wars, and various Disney brands. Rubel also acquired the Stride Rite chain and all its associated brands, including Keds, Sperry Top-Sider, Tommy Hilfiger, and Saucony. To organize the new corporate structure and keep track of all the brands,

Rubel created a holding company (Collective Brands) as an umbrella over Payless, Stride Rite, and all the licensing activities for the company's brands.

The Payless Design Team. To develop products that would resonate better with consumers, Payless stepped up its emphasis on fashion. The Payless Design Team, an in-house design group, dedicated itself to developing original footwear and accessory designs to keep new styles on target with changing fashion trends. Top designers from Kenneth Cole and Michael Kors were hired as full-time employees to head the new team.

Designer Collections. In perhaps the biggest move to raise the caché of the brand, Rubel started what he called "Designer Collections." Aiming for the highest levels of haute couture, Payless has forged relationships with three top New York-based designers—Lela Rose, Stacey Bendet, and Christian Siriano. The three are designing everything from pumps to boots to handbags under the brands Lela Rose, alice + olivia, and Christian Siriano. A fourth designer, Isabel Toledo, will soon have products on Payless shelves. Toledo was an underground designer until Michelle Obama chose to wear some of her creations on the day her husband was inaugurated president of the United States.

After signing its first designer, Payless did something very out of character for a discount brand. It took its designs to the runway of New York's Fashion Week, the invitation-only event where designers debut fall fashions for the industry. In another first, Payless began running full-page ads in *Elle*, *Vogue*, and *W*, featuring the tagline, "Look Again."

The benefits of such alliances are plentiful. The designers get tremendous exposure, a large customer base, and the power and budget of a mass retailer. Payless gets brand caché, almost certain to transform its outdated image. And consumers get runway styles they can afford.

Fun Inspiring Store Formats. To reflect the new image and communicate change to consumers, Payless redesigned its logo for the first time in 20 years. It then launched new "Fashion Lab" and "Hot Zone" store formats. Both were a drastic improvement, making the stores more open, light, and airy, with a more satisfying consumer experience built around style and design rather than price. Of the new store atmosphere, Rubel said, "It makes the $12 shoe look like a $20 shoe." Rubel hopes that the new formats will not only attract more customers but also entice customers to pay a little bit more than they have in the past. All the new stores now have one of the two new formats, and old stores are being progressively remodeled.

STROKE OF GENIUS?
OR DESTINED FOR FAILURE?

Can the "luxury-meets-low-price" strategy work? Or will this go down as a disaster of two drastically different worlds that collided, crashed, and burned? "There's nothing cool about shopping at Payless," says skeptic Marian Salzman, a trends forecaster at a major ad firm. "It gets the cash-strapped working girl." But Rubel refutes this view, quickly pointing out that its shoppers have median household incomes that are higher than those of both Walmart and Target. "All we've done is bring Payless into the 21st century. We're . . . speaking with greater clarity to who our customer already is."

Maxine Clark, former president of Payless and now chief executive officer of Build-A-Bear Workshop, also recognizes the potential of the new strategy. "The customer who wants to buy Prada will not

come to Payless. But this will energize the old customers who they lost and attract new ones." Mardi Larson, head of public relations, claims that the trendy new image is perfect for existing customers. "We target the 24-year-old demographic, because women in their 40s who shop for their family are nostalgic about that time in their lives, while [at the same time] teenagers aspire to that age group."

But what about that potential new customer? Does this risky venture into high-fashion stand a chance of appealing to those who have never crossed the threshold of a Payless store? Rubel admits going after new customers. The "cheap chic" approach is attempting to lure 20-to-30-year-old women who are looking for something trendy. Given that such fashion-conscious females buy 50 percent more shoes than most current customers, going after new customers make sense.

Perhaps Lela Rose's Fashion Week experience best illustrates why Payless might just succeed in attracting this previously out-of-reach customer:

> When actresses Sophia Bush (*One Tree Hill*) and Brittany Snow (*Hairspray*) landed backstage in Lela Rose's showroom at New York Fashion Week, they swooned over the designer's new shoe collection that was about to debut on the runway. Rose, best known for $1,500 frocks, happily handed pairs of navy peep-toe pumps and polka-dot round-toe pumps over to the young celebs, who would soon be flaunting them on the sidelines of the catwalk. "Did they know they were Payless shoes?" says Rose, who's now designing her fifth exclusive line for the discounter. "Absolutely. They didn't care. They looked cute to them and that's all that mattered."

Additionally, Payless is not the first to try this new direction. In fact, co-branded designer lines for discount retailers date back decades. But in recent years, the trend is proliferating. Karl Lagerfeld has designed for Britain's H&M, Vera Wang has teamed up with Kohl's, Ralph Lauren has put store brands on JCPenney's shelves, and Todd Oldham has stepped out with Old Navy, to name just a few.

Although many ventures such as these *have* failed miserably, some have been wildly successful. Lela Rose claims that she would never have considered her arrangement with Payless if it hadn't been for the success of Target's alliance with Isaac Mizrahi. Mizrahi's couture career was pretty much on the rocks. Then he started designing preppy cashmere sweaters, cheerful jersey dresses, and trendy trench coats for Target, all priced at under $40. With the low-rent strategy, Mizrahi became more popular and famous than ever. After that, he once again had high-end retailers knocking on his door. Since Mizrahi's successful entry to the mainstream, more than two dozen designers have cobranded with mass retailers.

PAYING LESS OR PAYING MORE?

There's more in it for Payless than just making the brand more attractive to both old and new customers. The company is looking to move its average price point up a notch or two. Whereas "higher price" is a relative term when most of a store's product line is priced below $15, higher margins are higher margins. Rubel has suggested that, in many cases, price increases may be as little as $0.50 per pair of shoes. But the expansion of its brand portfolio to include famous labels will certainly give Payless greater pricing flexibility. And the designer collections will allow for some of the highest priced products that have ever graced its shelves—think $25 for pumps and up to $45 for boots. Whereas that is a substantial price increase from average, it's a bargain for fashion-conscious consumers.

Yet just as Rubel's strategy began to gain steam, so did the worst global recession since the Great Depression. Like retailers everywhere, Payless took a hit. But while many retailers suffered catastrophic losses, existing store sales at Payless fared much better. And after profits sunk briefly to a loss of $60 million in 2008, Payless posted a net profit of $88 million for 2009. Payless recently opened its first stores in the Eastern Hemisphere in Saudi Arabia, Kuwait, and the United Arab Emirates. Russia is next on its agenda.

With the expansion, wholesaling, and licensing activities of Rubel's plan, Payless is poised to return to a growth trajectory. Low production costs continue to provide a competitive advantage that will boost profits. And in good times as well as bad, Payless has struck a formula for value that customers love. It remains confident that its strategy to democratize fashion will produce great results, regardless of future economic conditions.

Questions for Discussion

1. Which of the different product mix pricing strategies discussed in the text applies best to Payless's new strategy? Discuss this in detail.

2. How do concepts such as psychological pricing and reference pricing apply to the Payless strategy? In what ways does the strategy deviate from these concepts?

3. Discuss the benefits and risks of the new strategy for both Payless and the designers with whom it partners. Which of these two stands to lose the most?

4. Consider the scale on which Payless operates. How much of a price increase does Payless need to achieve to make this venture worthwhile?

Sources: Sigal Ratner-Arias, "Payless Snags Top Designer," *The Spectator*, April 13, 2010, p. G9; Jonathan Birchall, "Payless Moves into Russia," *Financial Times*, September 2, 2009, p. 19; Gene Marcial, "The Shine on Collective's Shoes," *BusinessWeek*, April 13, 2009, p. 61; Danielle Sacks, "The Fast 50 Companies," *Fast Company*, March, 2008, p. 112; Maria Puente, "Top Designers Go Down-Market," *USA Today*, September 26, 2007, p. 11B; Bruce Horovitz, "Payless Is Determined to Put a Fashionably Shod Foot Forward," *USA Today*, July 28, 2006, p. 1B; Nicole Zerillo, "Payless Launches 'I Love Shoes,'" *PR Week*, March 10, 2008, p. 3; www.payless.com, accessed July 2010.

12 Marketing Channels
Delivering Customer Value

Chapter Preview

We now arrive at the third marketing mix tool—distribution. Firms rarely work alone in creating value for customers and building profitable customer relationships. Instead, most are only a single link in a larger supply chain and marketing channel. As such, an individual firm's success depends not only on how well *it* performs but also on how well its *entire marketing channel* competes with competitors' channels. To be good at customer relationship management, a company must also be good at partner relationship management. The first part of this chapter explores the nature of marketing channels and the marketer's channel design and management decisions. We then examine physical distribution—or logistics—an area that is growing dramatically in importance and sophistication. In the next chapter, we'll look more closely at two major channel intermediaries: retailers and wholesalers.

We start by looking at a company whose groundbreaking, customer-centered distribution strategy took it to the top of its industry.

Enterprise: Leaving Car Rental Competitors in the Rear View Mirror

Quick, which rental car company is number one? Chances are good that you said Hertz. Okay, who's number two? That must be Avis, you say. After all, for years Avis's advertising said, "We're #2, so we try harder!" But if you said Hertz or Avis, you're about to be surprised. By any measure—most revenues, employees, transactions, or number of vehicles—the number-one rental-car company in the world is Enterprise Holdings, which owns and operates the Enterprise Rent-A-Car, Alamo Rent A Car, and National Car Rental brands. Even more, this is no recent development. Enterprise left number-two Hertz in its rearview mirror in the late 1990s and has never looked back.

What may have fooled you is that the Hertz brand was for a long time number one in airport car rentals. However, with all of its combined brands and markets, Enterprise Holdings now captures 53 percent of the total rental car market with Hertz a distant second at 16 percent.[1] What's more, by all estimates, the privately owned Enterprise is much more profitable as well.

How did Enterprise become such a powerful industry leader? The company might argue that it was through better prices or better marketing. But what contributed most to Enterprise taking the lead was an industry-changing, customer-driven distribution strategy. While competitors such as Hertz and Avis focused on serving travelers at airports, Enterprise developed a new distribution doorway to a large and untapped segment. It opened off-airport, neighborhood locations that provided short-term car-replacement rentals for people whose cars were wrecked, stolen, or being serviced or for people who simply wanted a different car for a short trip or a special occasion.

It all started more than half a century ago when Enterprise founder Jack Taylor discovered an unmet customer need. He was working at a St. Louis auto dealership, and customers often asked him where they could get a replacement car when theirs was in the shop for repairs or body work. To meet this need, Taylor opened a car-leasing business. But rather than compete head-on with the likes of Hertz and Avis serving travelers at airports, Taylor located his rental offices in center-city and neighborhood areas, closer to his target customers. These locations also gave Taylor a cost advantage: Property rents were lower, and he didn't have to pay airport taxes and fees.

This groundbreaking distribution strategy worked, and the business grew quickly. As the Taylor family opened multiple locations in St. Louis and other cities, they renamed the business Enterprise Rent-A-Car after the U.S. Navy aircraft carrier on which Jack Taylor had served as a naval aviator. Enterprise continued to focus steadfastly on what it called the "home city" market, primarily serving customers who'd been in wrecks or whose cars were being serviced. Enterprise branch managers developed strong relationships with local

> Thanks to an industry-changing, customer-driven distribution strategy, Enterprise left number-two Hertz in its rearview mirror more than a decade ago and has never looked back.

auto insurance adjusters, dealership sales and service personnel, and body shops and service garages, making Enterprise a popular neighborhood rental car provider.

Customers in the home city market had special needs. Often, they were at the scene of a wreck or at a repair shop and had no way to get to an Enterprise office to pick up a rental car. So the company came up with another game-changing idea—picking customers up wherever they happen to be and bringing them back to the rental office. Hence, the tagline: "Pick Enterprise. We'll Pick You Up," which remains the Enterprise Rent-A-Car brand's main value proposition to this day.

By the late 1980s, Enterprise had a large nationwide network of company-owned, off-airport locations. From this strong base, in the mid-1990s Enterprise began expanding its distribution system by directly challenging Hertz and Avis in the on-airport market. A decade later, it had set up operations in 240 airports in North America and Europe. Then, in late 2007, the Taylor family purchased the Vanguard Car Rental Group, which owned the National and Alamo brands. National focused on the corporate-negotiated airport market, while Alamo served primarily the leisure traveler airport market.

With the Vanguard acquisition, Enterprise Holdings now captures a more than 31 percent share of the airport market, putting it ahead of Avis Budget Group and Hertz. That, combined with its share of the off-airport market, makes Enterprise Holdings the runaway leader in overall car rentals. It now operates 7,600 locations in the United States and four other countries.

Another secret to Enterprise's success is its passion for creating customer satisfaction. To measure satisfaction, Enterprise developed what it calls its ESQi (Enterprise Service Quality index). The company calls some two million customers a year and asks a simple question: "Were you completely satisfied with the service?" Enterprise managers don't get promoted unless they keep customers *completely* satisfied. It's as simple as that. If customer feedback is bad, "we call it going to ESQi jail," says an Enterprise human resources manager. "Until the numbers start to improve, you're going nowhere." As a result, for six years running, customers have rated the Enterprise Rent-A-Car brand number one in the annual J.D. Power U.S. Car Rental Satisfaction Study.

Looking ahead, rather than resting on its laurels, Enterprise Rent-A-Car continues to seek better ways to keep customers happy by getting cars where people want them. The enterprising company has now motored into yet another inno-

vative distribution venue—"car sharing" and hourly rentals—called WeCar. This operation parks automobiles at convenient locations on college campuses and in densely populated urban areas, where residents often don't own cars and where business commuters would like to have occasional car access. Enterprise is also targeting businesses that want to have WeCar vehicles available in their parking lots for commuting employees to use. WeCar members pay $35 for an annual membership fee, depending on the location. They can then rent conveniently located, fuel-efficient cars (mostly Toyota Prius hybrids) for $10 per hour or $60 to $75 for the day; the rate includes gas and a 200-mile allotment. Renting a WeCar vehicle is a simple get-in-and-go operation. Just pass your member key fob over a sensor to unlock the car, open the glove box, and enter a PIN to release the car key.

Thus, Enterprise Holdings continues to move ahead aggressively with its winning distribution strategy. Says Andy Taylor, founder Jack's son and now long-time CEO, "We own the high ground in this business and we aren't going to give it up. As the dynamics of our industry continue to evolve, it's clear to us that the future belongs to the service providers who offer the broadest array of services for anyone who needs or wants to rent a car." The company intends to make cars available wherever, whenever, and however customers want them.[2]

While competitors Hertz and Avis focused on serving travelers at airports, Enterprise Rent-A-Car opened off-airport, neighborhood locations that provided short-term car-replacement rentals for people whose cars were wrecked, stolen, or being serviced.

As the Enterprise story shows, good distribution strategies can contribute strongly to customer value and create competitive advantage for a firm. But firms cannot bring value to customers by themselves. Instead, they must work closely with other firms in a larger value delivery network.

Author Comment | These are pretty hefty terms for a really simple concept: A company can't go it alone in creating customer value. It must work within an entire network of partners to accomplish this task. Individual companies and brands don't compete; their entire value delivery networks do.

Supply Chains and the Value Delivery Network (pp 340–341)

Producing a product or service and making it available to buyers requires building relationships not only with customers but also with key suppliers and resellers in the company's *supply chain*. This supply chain consists of upstream and downstream partners. Upstream from the company is the set of firms that supply the raw materials, components, parts, information, finances, and expertise needed to create a product or service. Marketers, however, have traditionally focused on the downstream side of the supply chain—on the *marketing channels* (or *distribution channels*) that look toward the customer. Downstream marketing channel partners, such as wholesalers and retailers, form a vital connection between the firm and its customers.

The term *supply chain* may be too limited—it takes a *make-and-sell* view of the business. It suggests that raw materials, productive inputs, and factory capacity should serve as the starting point for market planning. A better term would be *demand chain* because it suggests a *sense-and-respond* view of the market. Under this view, planning starts by identifying the needs of target customers, to which the company responds by organizing a chain of resources and activities with the goal of creating customer value.

Yet, even a demand chain view of a business may be too limited because it takes a step-by-step, linear view of purchase-production-consumption activities. With the advent of the Internet and other technologies, however, companies are now forming more numerous and complex relationships with other firms. For example, Ford manages many supply chains—think about all the parts it takes to create a vehicle, from radios to catalytic converters to tires to transistors. Ford also sponsors or transacts on many B-to-B Web sites and online pur-

Value delivery network: In making and marketing just one of its many models—say, the Ford Escape hybrid—Ford manages a huge network of people within Ford plus thousand of suppliers and dealers outside the company who work together to give final customers "the most fuel-efficient SUV on the market."

Value delivery network

A network composed of the company, suppliers, distributors, and, ultimately, customers who "partner" with each other to improve the performance of the entire system in delivering customer value.

chasing exchanges as needs arise. Like Ford, most large companies today are engaged in building and managing a complex, continuously evolving *value delivery network*.

As defined in Chapter 2, a **value delivery network** is made up of the company, suppliers, distributors, and, ultimately, customers who "partner" with each other to improve the performance of the entire system. ◉ For example, in making and marketing just one of its many models—say the Ford Escape hybrid—Ford manages a huge network of people within Ford plus thousand of suppliers and dealers outside the company who work together effectively to give final customers "the most fuel-efficient SUV on the market."

This chapter focuses on marketing channels—on the downstream side of the value delivery network. We examine four major questions concerning marketing channels: What is the nature of marketing channels and why are they important? How do channel firms interact and organize to do the work of the channel? What problems do companies face in designing and managing their channels? What role do physical distribution and supply chain management play in attracting and satisfying customers? In Chapter 13, we will look at marketing channel issues from the viewpoint of retailers and wholesalers.

Author Comment | In this section, we look at the downstream side of the value delivery network—the marketing channel organizations that connect the company and its customers. To understand their value, imagine life without retailers—say, without grocery stores or department stores.

The Nature and Importance of Marketing Channels (pp 341–344)

Few producers sell their goods directly to final users. Instead, most use intermediaries to bring their products to market. They try to forge a **marketing channel** (or **distribution channel**)—a set of interdependent organizations that help make a product or service available for use or consumption by the consumer or business user.

Marketing channel (or distribution channel)

A set of interdependent organizations that help make a product or service available for use or consumption by the consumer or business user.

A company's channel decisions directly affect every other marketing decision. Pricing depends on whether the company works with national discount chains, uses high-quality specialty stores, or sells directly to consumers via the Web. The firm's sales force and communications decisions depend on how much persuasion, training, motivation, and support its channel partners need. Whether a company develops or acquires certain new products may depend on how well those products fit the capabilities of its channel members. For example, Kodak initially sold its EasyShare printers only in Best Buy stores because of the retailer's on-the-floor sales staff and their ability to educate buyers on the economics of paying a higher initial printer price but lower long-term ink costs.

Companies often pay too little attention to their distribution channels—sometimes with damaging results. In contrast, many companies have used imaginative distribution systems to gain a competitive advantage. Enterprise revolutionized the car-rental business by setting up off-airport rental offices. Apple turned the retail music business on its head by selling music for the iPod via the Internet on iTunes. And FedEx's creative and imposing distribution system made it a leader in express delivery.

Distribution channel decisions often involve long-term commitments to other firms. For example, companies such as Ford, McDonald's, or HP can easily change their advertising, pricing, or promotion programs. They can scrap old products and introduce new ones as market tastes demand. But when they set up distribution channels through contracts with franchisees, independent dealers, or large retailers, they cannot readily replace these channels with company-owned stores or Web sites if the conditions change. Therefore, management must design its channels carefully, with an eye on both tomorrow's likely selling environment and today's.

How Channel Members Add Value

Why do producers give some of the selling job to channel partners? After all, doing so means giving up some control over how and to whom they sell their products. Producers use intermediaries because they create greater efficiency in making goods available to target markets. Through their contacts, experience, specialization, and scale of operation, intermediaries usually offer the firm more than it can achieve on its own.

◉ **Figure 12.1** shows how using intermediaries can provide economies. Figure 12.1A shows three manufacturers, each using direct marketing to reach three customers. This system requires nine different contacts. Figure 12.1B shows the three manufacturers working through one distributor, which contacts the three customers. This system requires only six contacts. In this way, intermediaries reduce the amount of work that must be done by both producers and consumers.

From the economic system's point of view, the role of marketing intermediaries is to transform the assortments of products made by producers into the assortments wanted by consumers. Producers make narrow assortments of products in large quantities, but consumers want broad assortments of products in small quantities. Marketing channel members buy large quantities from many producers and break them down into the smaller quantities and broader assortments desired by consumers.

For example, Unilever makes millions of bars of Lever 2000 hand soap each week, but you want to buy only a few bars at a time. So big food, drug, and discount retailers, such as Kroger, Walgreens, and Target, buy Lever 2000 by the truckload and stock it on their stores' shelves. In turn, you can buy a single bar of Lever 2000, along with a shopping cart full of small quantities of toothpaste, shampoo, and other related products as you need them. Thus, intermediaries play an important role in matching supply and demand.

In making products and services available to consumers, channel members add value by bridging the major time, place, and possession gaps that separate goods and services from those who use them. Members of the marketing channel perform many key functions. Some help to complete transactions:

- *Information:* Gathering and distributing marketing research and intelligence information about actors and forces in the marketing environment needed for planning and aiding exchange.
- *Promotion:* Developing and spreading persuasive communications about an offer.
- *Contact:* Finding and communicating with prospective buyers.
- *Matching:* Shaping and fitting the offer to the buyer's needs, including activities such as manufacturing, grading, assembling, and packaging.

◉ **FIGURE | 12.1**
How Adding a Distributor Reduces the Number of Channel Transactions

Marketing channel intermediaries make buying a lot easier for consumers. Again, think about life without grocery retailers. How would you go about buying that 12-pack of Coke or any of the hundreds of other items that you now routinely drop into your shopping cart?

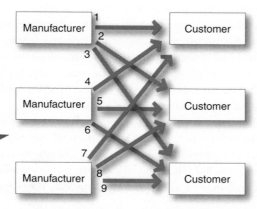

A. Number of contacts without a distributor
M × C = 3 × 3 = 9

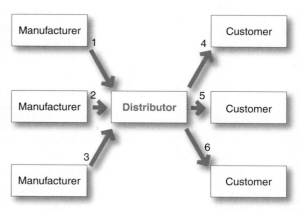

B. Number of contacts with a distributor
M + C = 3 + 3 = 6

- *Negotiation:* Reaching an agreement on price and other terms of the offer so that ownership or possession can be transferred.

Others help to fulfill the completed transactions:

- *Physical distribution:* Transporting and storing goods.
- *Financing:* Acquiring and using funds to cover the costs of the channel work.
- *Risk taking:* Assuming the risks of carrying out the channel work.

The question is not *whether* these functions need to be performed—they must be—but rather *who* will perform them. To the extent that the manufacturer performs these functions, its costs go up, and, therefore, its prices must be higher. When some of these functions are shifted to intermediaries, the producer's costs and prices may be lower, but the intermediaries must charge more to cover the costs of their work. In dividing the work of the channel, the various functions should be assigned to the channel members who can add the most value for the cost.

Number of Channel Levels

Companies can design their distribution channels to make products and services available to customers in different ways. Each layer of marketing intermediaries that performs some work in bringing the product and its ownership closer to the final buyer is a **channel level**. Because both the producer and the final consumer perform some work, they are part of every channel.

The *number of intermediary levels* indicates the *length* of a channel. ◉ **Figure 12.2A** shows several consumer distribution channels of different lengths. Channel 1, called a **direct marketing channel**, has no intermediary levels; the company sells directly to consumers. For example, Mary Kay Cosmetics and Amway sell their products door-to-door, through home and office sales parties, and on the Internet; GEICO sells insurance direct via the telephone and the Internet. The remaining channels in Figure 12.2A are **indirect marketing channels**, containing one or more intermediaries.

Channel level
A layer of intermediaries that performs some work in bringing the product and its ownership closer to the final buyer.

Direct marketing channel
A marketing channel that has no intermediary levels.

Indirect marketing channel
Channel containing one or more intermediary levels.

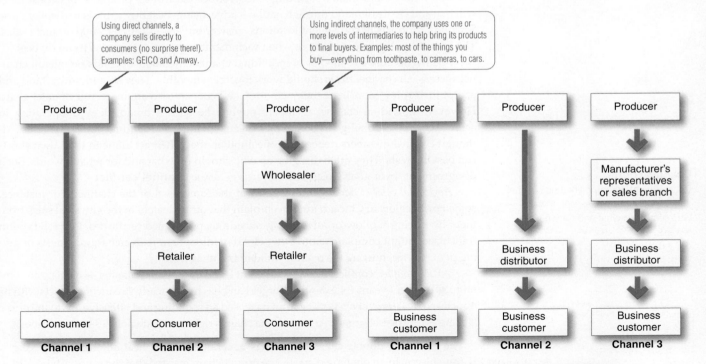

◉ FIGURE | 12.2
Consumer and Business Marketing Channels

Figure 12.2B shows some common business distribution channels. The business marketer can use its own sales force to sell directly to business customers. Or it can sell to various types of intermediaries, who in turn sell to these customers. Consumer and business marketing channels with even more levels can sometimes be found, but these are less common. From the producer's point of view, a greater number of levels means less control and greater channel complexity. Moreover, all the institutions in the channel are connected by several types of *flows*. These include the *physical flow* of products, the *flow of ownership*, the *payment flow*, the *information flow*, and the *promotion flow*. These flows can make even channels with only one or a few levels very complex.

Channel Behavior and Organization (pp 344–351)

Distribution channels are more than simple collections of firms tied together by various flows. They are complex behavioral systems in which people and companies interact to accomplish individual, company, and channel goals. Some channel systems consist of only informal interactions among loosely organized firms. Others consist of formal interactions guided by strong organizational structures. Moreover, channel systems do not stand still; new types of intermediaries emerge, and whole new channel systems evolve. Here we look at channel behavior and how members organize to do the work of the channel.

Channel Behavior

A marketing channel consists of firms that have partnered for their common good. Each channel member depends on the others. For example, a Ford dealer depends on Ford to design cars that meet customer needs. In turn, Ford depends on the dealer to attract customers, persuade them to buy Ford cars, and service the cars after the sale. Each Ford dealer also depends on other dealers to provide good sales and service that will uphold the brand's reputation. In fact, the success of individual Ford dealers depends on how well the entire Ford marketing channel competes with the channels of other auto manufacturers.

Each channel member plays a specialized role in the channel. For example, the role of consumer electronics maker Samsung is to produce electronics products that consumers will like and create demand through national advertising. Best Buy's role is to display these Samsung products in convenient locations, answer buyers' questions, and complete sales. The channel will be most effective when each member assumes the tasks it can do best.

Ideally, because the success of individual channel members depends on overall channel success, all channel firms should work together smoothly. They should understand and accept their roles, coordinate their activities, and cooperate to attain overall channel goals. However, individual channel members rarely take such a broad view. Cooperating to achieve overall channel goals sometimes means giving up individual company goals. Although channel members depend on one another, they often act alone in their own short-run best interests. They often disagree on who should do what and for what rewards. Such disagreements over goals, roles, and rewards generate **channel conflict**.

Horizontal conflict occurs among firms at the same level of the channel. For instance, some Ford dealers in Chicago might complain that other dealers in the city steal sales from them by pricing too low or advertising outside their assigned territories. Or Holiday Inn franchisees might complain about other Holiday Inn operators overcharging guests or giving poor service, hurting the overall Holiday Inn image.

Vertical conflict, conflicts between different levels of the same channel, is even more common. ⬤ In recent years, for example, Burger King has had a steady stream of conflicts with its franchised dealers over everything from increased ad spending and offensive ads to the prices it charges for cheeseburgers. At issue is the chain's right to dictate policies to franchisees.[3]

The price of a double cheeseburger has generated a lot of heat among Burger King franchisees. In an ongoing dispute, the burger chain insisted that the sandwich be sold for no more than $1—in line with other items on its "Value Menu." Burger King saw the value price as key to competing effectively in the current economic environment. But the company's franchisees claimed that they would lose money at that price. To re-

Author Comment | Channels are made up of more than just boxes and arrows on paper. They are behavioral systems made up of real companies and people who interact to accomplish their individual and collective goals. Like groups of people, sometimes they work well together and sometimes they don't.

Channel conflict
Disagreement among marketing channel members on goals, roles, and rewards—who should do what and for what rewards.

In recent years, Burger King has had a steady stream of conflicts with its franchised dealers over everything from advertising content to the price of its cheeseburgers.

solve the dispute, angry franchisees filed a lawsuit (only one of several over the years) asserting that Burger King's franchise agreements don't allow it to dictate prices. (The company had won a separate case in 2008 requiring franchisees to offer the Value Menu, which is core to its efforts to attract price-conscious consumers.) After months of public wrangling, Burger King finally let franchisees have it their way. It introduced a $1 double-patty burger with just one slice of cheese, instead of two, cutting the cost of ingredients. The regular quarter-pound double cheeseburger with two pieces of cheese remained on the Value Menu but was priced at $1.19.

Some conflict in the channel takes the form of healthy competition. Such competition can be good for the channel; without it, the channel could become passive and noninnovative. For example, Burger King's conflict with its franchisees might represent normal give-and-take over the respective rights of the channel partners. But severe or prolonged conflict can disrupt channel effectiveness and cause lasting harm to channel relationships. Burger King should manage the channel conflict carefully to keep it from getting out of hand.

Vertical Marketing Systems

For the channel as a whole to perform well, each channel member's role must be specified, and channel conflict must be managed. The channel will perform better if it includes a firm, agency, or mechanism that provides leadership and has the power to assign roles and manage conflict.

Historically, *conventional distribution channels* have lacked such leadership and power, often resulting in damaging conflict and poor performance. One of the biggest channel developments over the years has been the emergence of *vertical marketing systems* that provide channel leadership. ◉ **Figure 12.3** contrasts the two types of channel arrangements.

A **conventional distribution channel** consists of one or more independent producers, wholesalers, and retailers. Each is a separate business seeking to maximize its own profits, perhaps even at the expense of the system as a whole. No channel member has much control over the other members, and no formal means exists for assigning roles and resolving channel conflict.

In contrast, a **vertical marketing system (VMS)** consists of producers, wholesalers, and retailers acting as a unified system. One channel member owns the others, has contracts with them, or wields so much power that they must all cooperate. The VMS can be dominated by the producer, the wholesaler, or the retailer.

We look now at three major types of VMSs: *corporate*, *contractual*, and *administered*. Each uses a different means for setting up leadership and power in the channel.

Corporate VMS

A **corporate VMS** integrates successive stages of production and distribution under single ownership. Coordination and conflict management are attained through regular organizational channels. For example, the grocery giant Kroger owns and operates 40 manufacturing plants—18 dairies, 10 deli and bakery plants, five grocery product plants, three beverage plants, two meat plants, and two cheese plants—that crank out 40 percent of the more than 14,000 private label items found on its store shelves. Little-known Italian eyewear maker Luxottica produces many famous eyewear brands—including its own Ray-Ban and Oakley brands and licensed brands such as Burberry, Chanel, Polo Ralph Lauren, Dolce&Gabbana, Donna Karan, Prada, Versace, and Bulgari. It then sells these brands through some of the

Conventional distribution channel
A channel consisting of one or more independent producers, wholesalers, and retailers, each a separate business seeking to maximize its own profits, even at the expense of profits for the system as a whole.

Vertical marketing system (VMS)
A distribution channel structure in which producers, wholesalers, and retailers act as a unified system. One channel member owns the others, has contracts with them, or has so much power that they all cooperate.

Corporate VMS
A vertical marketing system that combines successive stages of production and distribution under single ownership—channel leadership is established through common ownership.

⦿ **FIGURE | 12.3**

Comparison of Conventional Distribution Channel with Vertical Marketing System

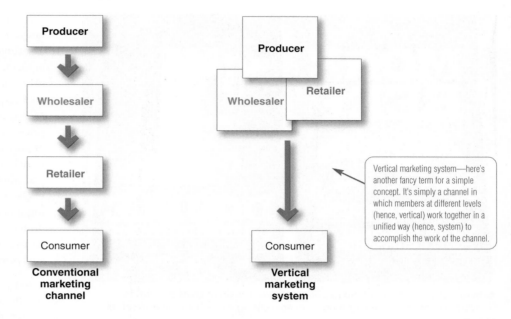

Vertical marketing system—here's another fancy term for a simple concept. It's simply a channel in which members at different levels (hence, vertical) work together in a unified way (hence, system) to accomplish the work of the channel.

Contractual VMS

A vertical marketing system in which independent firms at different levels of production and distribution join together through contracts.

Franchise organization

A contractual vertical marketing system in which a channel member, called a franchisor, links several stages in the production-distribution process.

world's largest optical chains—LensCrafters, Pearle Vision, and Sunglass Hut—that it also owns.[4] Controlling the entire distribution chain has turned Spanish clothing chain Zara into the world's fastest-growing fashion retailer (see Real Marketing 12.1).

Contractual VMS

A **contractual VMS** consists of independent firms at different levels of production and distribution who join together through contracts to obtain more economies or sales impact than each could achieve alone. Channel members coordinate their activities and manage conflict through contractual agreements.

The **franchise organization** is the most common type of contractual relationship. A channel member called a *franchisor* links several stages in the production-distribution process. In the United States alone, some 1,500 franchise businesses and 883,000 franchise outlets account for more than $844 billion of economic output. Industry analysts estimate that a new franchise outlet opens somewhere in the United States every eight minutes and that about one out of every 12 retail business outlets is a franchised business.[5] ⦿ Almost every kind of business has been franchised—from motels and fast-food restaurants to dental centers and dating services, from wedding consultants and maid services to fitness centers and funeral homes.

There are three types of franchises. The first type is the *manufacturer-sponsored retailer franchise system*—for example, Ford and its network of independent franchised dealers. The second type is the *manufacturer-sponsored wholesaler franchise system*—Coca-Cola licenses bottlers (wholesalers) in various markets who buy Coca-Cola syrup concentrate and then bottle and sell the finished product to retailers in local markets. The third type is the *service-firm-sponsored retailer franchise system*—for example, Burger King and its nearly 10,500 franchisee-operated restaurants around the world. Other examples can be found in everything from auto rentals (Hertz, Avis), apparel retailers (The Athlete's Foot, Plato's Closet), and motels (Holiday Inn, Ramada Inn) to real estate (Century 21) and personal services (Great Clips, Mr. Handyman, Molly Maid).

The fact that most consumers cannot tell the difference between contractual and corporate VMSs shows how successfully

⦿ Franchising systems: Almost every kind of business has been franchised—from motels and fast-food restaurants to dating services and cleaning and handyman companies.

Real Marketing 12.1

Zara: Fast Fashions—*Really* Fast

Fashion retailer Zara is on a tear. It sells "cheap chic"—stylish designs that resemble those of big-name fashion houses but at moderate prices. Zara is the prototype for a new breed of "fast-fashion" retailers, companies that recognize and respond to the latest fashion trends quickly and nimbly. While competing retailers are still working out their designs, Zara has already put the latest fashion into its stores and is moving on to the next big thing.

Zara has attracted a near cultlike clientele in recent years. Following the recent economic slide, even upscale shoppers are swarming to buy Zara's stylish but affordable offerings. Thanks to Zara's torrid growth, the sales, profits, and store presence of its parent company, Spain-based Inditex, have more than quadrupled since 2000. Despite the poor economy, Inditex opened 450 stores last year, while other big retailers such as Gap closed stores. Despite the poor economy, Inditex's sales grew 9 percent last year. By comparison, Gap's sales *fell*. As a result, Inditex has now sprinted past Gap to become the world's largest clothing retailer. Inditex's 4,670 stores in 74 countries sewed up $14.9 billion in sales last year.

Zara clearly sells the right goods for these times. But its amazing success comes not just from *what* it sells. Perhaps more important, success comes from how and how fast Zara's cutting-edge distribution system *delivers* what it sells to eagerly awaiting customers. Zara delivers fast fashion—*really* fast fashion. Through vertical integration, Zara controls all phases of the fashion process, from design and manufacturing to distribution through its own managed stores. The company's integrated supply system makes Zara faster, more flexible, and more efficient than international competitors such as Gap, Benetton, and H&M. Zara can take a new fashion concept through design, manufacturing, and store-shelf placement in as little as two weeks, whereas competitors often take six months or more. And the resulting low costs let Zara offer the very latest midmarket chic at downmarket prices.

The whole process starts with input about what consumers want. Zara store managers act as trend spotters. They patrol store aisles using handheld computers, reporting in real time what's selling and what's not selling. They talk with customers to learn what they're looking for but not yet finding. At the same time, Zara trend seekers roam fashion shows in Paris and concerts in Tokyo, looking for young people who might be wearing something new or different. Then they're on the phone to company headquarters in tiny La Coruña, Spain, reporting on what they've seen and heard. Back home, based on this and other feedback, the company's team of 300 designers, 200 specifically for Zara, conjures up a prolific flow of hot new fashions.

Once the designers have done their work, production begins. But rather than relying on a hodgepodge of slow-moving suppliers in Asia, as most competitors do, Zara makes 40 percent of its own fabrics and produces more than half of its own clothes. Even farmed-out manufacturing goes primarily to local contractors. Almost all clothes sold in Zara's stores worldwide are made quickly and efficiently at or near company headquarters in a remote corner of northwest Spain.

Finished goods then feed into Zara's modern distribution centers, which ship them immediately and directly to stores around the world, saving time, eliminating the need for warehouses, and keeping inventories low. The highly automated centers can sort, pack, label, and allocate up to 80,000 items per hour.

Again, the key word describing Zara's distribution system is *fast*. The time between receiving an order at the distribution center to the delivery of goods to a store averages 24 hours for European stores and a maximum of 48 hours for American or Asian stores. Zara stores receive small shipments of new merchandise two to three times each week, compared with competing chains' outlets, which get large shipments seasonally, usually just four to six times per year.

Speedy design and distribution allows Zara to introduce a copious supply of new fashions—some 30,000 items last year, compared with a competitor average of less than 10,000. The combination of a large number of new fashions delivered in frequent small batches gives Zara stores a continually updated merchandise mix that brings customers back more often. Zara customers visit the store an average of 17 times per year, compared to less than five customer visits at competing stores. Fast turnover also results in less outdated and discounted merchandise. Because Zara makes what consumers already want or are now wearing, it doesn't have to guess what will be hot six months in the future.

In all, Zara's carefully integrated design and distribution process gives the fast-moving retailer a tremendous competitive advantage.

Controlling the entire distribution chain makes Zara more flexible and more efficient—a virtual blur compared with its competitors. It can take a new line from design to production to worldwide distribution in its own stores in less than a month (versus an industry average of nine months).

Continued on next page

Its turbocharged system gets out the goods customers what, when they want them—perhaps even before:

A few summers ago, Zara managed to latch onto one of the season's hottest trends in just four weeks. The process started when trend spotters spread the word back to headquarters: White eyelet—cotton with tiny holes in it—was set to become white-hot. A quick telephone survey of Zara store managers confirmed that the fabric could be a winner, so in-house designers got down to work. They zapped patterns electronically to Zara's factory across the street, and the fabric was cut. Local subcontractors stitched white-eyelet V-neck belted dresses—think Jackie Kennedy, circa 1960—and finished them in less than a week. The $129 dresses were inspected, tagged, and transported through a tunnel under the street to a distribution center. From there, they were quickly dispatched to Zara stores from New York to Tokyo—where they were flying off the racks just two days later.

Sources: Emilie Marsh, "Zara Helps Lift Inditex 4th-Qtr Net," *WWD*, March 18, 2010, p. 11; Cecilie Rohwedder, "Zara Grows as Retail Rivals Struggle," *Wall Street Journal*, March 26, 2009, p. B1; Kerry Capell, "Fashion Conquistador," *BusinessWeek*, September 4, 2006, pp. 38–39; Rohwedder, "Turbocharged Supply Chain May Speed Zara Past Gap as Top Clothing Retailer," *Globe and Mail*, March 26, 2009, p. B12; www.gap.com, accessed April 2010; and information from the Inditex Press Dossier, www.inditex.com/en/press/information/press_kit, accessed October 2010.

Administered VMS
A vertical marketing system that coordinates successive stages of production and distribution through the size and power of one of the parties.

Horizontal marketing system
A channel arrangement in which two or more companies at one level join together to follow a new marketing opportunity.

Multichannel distribution system
A distribution system in which a single firm sets up two or more marketing channels to reach one or more customer segments.

the contractual organizations compete with corporate chains. Chapter 13 presents a fuller discussion of the various contractual VMSs.

Administered VMS

In an **administered VMS**, leadership is assumed not through common ownership or contractual ties but through the size and power of one or a few dominant channel members. Manufacturers of a top brand can obtain strong trade cooperation and support from resellers. For example, GE, P&G, and Kraft can command unusual cooperation from resellers regarding displays, shelf space, promotions, and price policies. In turn, large retailers such as Walmart, Home Depot, and Barnes & Noble can exert strong influence on the many manufacturers that supply the products they sell.

Horizontal Marketing Systems

Another channel development is the **horizontal marketing system**, in which two or more companies at one level join together to follow a new marketing opportunity. By working together, companies can combine their financial, production, or marketing resources to accomplish more than any one company could alone.

Companies might join forces with competitors or noncompetitors. They might work with each other on a temporary or permanent basis, or they may create a separate company. ◉ For example, McDonald's places "express" versions of its restaurants in Walmart stores. McDonald's benefits from Walmart's heavy store traffic, and Walmart keeps hungry shoppers from needing to go elsewhere to eat.

Competitors Microsoft and Yahoo! have joined forces to create a horizontal Internet search alliance. For the next decade, Microsoft's Bing will be the search engine on Yahoo! Web sites, serving up the same search results listings available directly through Bing. In turn, Yahoo! will focus on creating a richer search experience by integrating strong Yahoo! content and providing tools to tailor the Yahoo! user experience. Although they haven't been able to do it individually, together Microsoft and Yahoo! might become a strong challenger to search leader Google.[6]

◉ Horizontal marketing channels: McDonald's places "express" versions of its restaurants in Walmart stores. McDonald's benefits from Walmart's heavy store traffic, and Walmart keeps hungry shoppers from needing to go elsewhere to eat.

Multichannel Distribution Systems

In the past, many companies used a single channel to sell to a single market or market segment. Today, with the proliferation of customer segments and channel possibilities, more and more companies have adopted **multichannel distribution systems**. Such multichannel marketing occurs when a single firm sets up two or more marketing channels to reach one or more customer segments. The use of multichannel systems has increased greatly in recent years.

● **Figure 12.4** shows a multichannel marketing system. In the figure, the producer sells directly to consumer segment 1 using catalogs, telemarketing, and the Internet and reaches consumer segment 2 through retailers. It sells indirectly to business segment 1 through distributors and dealers and to business segment 2 through its own sales force.

These days, almost every large company and many small ones distribute through multiple channels. ● For example, John Deere sells its familiar green and yellow lawn and garden tractors, mowers, and outdoor power products to consumers and commercial users through several channels, including John Deere retailers, Lowe's home improvement stores, and online. It sells and services its tractors, combines, planters, and other agricultural equipment through its premium John Deere dealer network. And it sells large construction and forestry equipment through selected large, full-service John Deere dealers and their sales forces.

Multichannel distribution systems offer many advantages to companies facing large and complex markets. With each new channel, the company expands its sales and market coverage and gains opportunities to tailor its products and services to the specific needs of diverse customer segments. But such multichannel systems are harder to control, and they generate conflict as more channels compete for customers and sales. For example, when John Deere began selling selected consumer products through Lowe's home improvement stores, many of its dealers complained loudly. To avoid such conflicts in its Internet marketing channels, the company routes all of its Web site sales to John Deere dealers.

● **Multichannel distribution: John Deere sells its familiar green and yellow lawn and garden equipment to consumers and commercial users through several channels, including Lowe's home improvement stores and online. It sells its agricultural equipment through the premium John Deere dealer network.**

● **FIGURE | 12.4**
Multichannel Distribution System

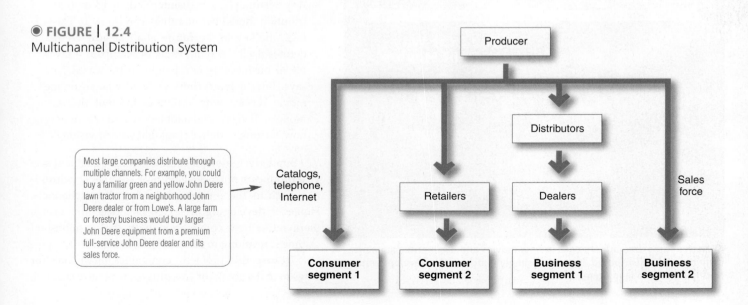

Most large companies distribute through multiple channels. For example, you could buy a familiar green and yellow John Deere lawn tractor from a neighborhood John Deere dealer or from Lowe's. A large farm or forestry business would buy larger John Deere equipment from a premium full-service John Deere dealer and its sales force.

Producer

Distributors

Catalogs, telephone, Internet

Retailers

Dealers

Sales force

Consumer segment 1

Consumer segment 2

Business segment 1

Business segment 2

Changing Channel Organization

Disintermediation

The cutting out of marketing channel intermediaries by product or service producers or the displacement of traditional resellers by radical new types of intermediaries.

Changes in technology and the explosive growth of direct and online marketing are having a profound impact on the nature and design of marketing channels. One major trend is toward **disintermediation**—a big term with a clear message and important consequences. Disintermediation occurs when product or service producers cut out intermediaries and go directly to final buyers or when radically new types of channel intermediaries displace traditional ones.

Thus, in many industries, traditional intermediaries are dropping by the wayside. For example, Southwest, JetBlue, and other airlines sell tickets directly to final buyers, cutting travel agents from their marketing channels altogether. In other cases, new forms of resellers are displacing traditional intermediaries. For example, online marketers have taken business from traditional brick-and-mortar retailers. Consumers can buy hotel rooms and airline tickets from Expedia.com and Travelocity.com; electronics from Sonystyle.com; clothes and accessories from Bluefly.com; and books, videos, toys, jewelry, sports, consumer electronics, home and garden items, and almost anything else from Amazon.com—all without ever stepping into a traditional retail store. Online music download services such as iTunes and Amazon.com are threatening the very existence of traditional music-store retailers. In fact, once-dominant music retailers such as Tower Records have declared bankruptcy and closed their doors for good.

Disintermediation presents both opportunities and problems for producers and resellers. Channel innovators who find new ways to add value in the channel can sweep aside traditional resellers and reap the rewards. In turn, traditional intermediaries must continue to innovate to avoid being swept aside. For example, when Netflix pioneered online video rentals, it sent traditional brick-and-mortar video stores such as Blockbuster reeling. To meet the threat, Blockbuster developed its own online DVD rental service, but it was too little too late. In late 2010, Blockbuster declared Chapter 11 bankruptcy and closed hundreds of stores. Now, both Netflix and a reorganized Blockbuster face disintermediation threats from an even hotter channel—digital video downloads and video on demand. ◉ But instead of simply watching digital video distribution developments, Netflix intends to lead them:[7]

> Netflix has already added a "Watch Instantly" feature to its Web site that allows subscribers to instantly stream near-DVD quality video for a growing list of movie titles and TV programs. And it recently announced that it will soon let users stream movies to selected cell phones. "Our intention," says Netflix founder and CEO Reed Hastings, "is to get [our Watch Instantly] service to every Internet-connected screen, from cell phones to laptops to Wi-Fi-enabled plasma screens." In this way, Netflix plans to disintermediate its own distribution model before others can do it. To Hastings, the key to the future is all in how Netflix defines itself. "If [you] think of Netflix as a DVD rental business, [you're] right to be scared," he says. But "if [you] think of Netflix as an online movie service with multiple different delivery models, then [you're] a lot less scared. We're only now starting to deliver [on] that second vision."

◉ Netflix faces dramatic changes in how movies and other entertainment content will be distributed. Instead of simply watching the developments, Netflix intends to lead them.

Similarly, to remain competitive, product and service producers must develop new channel opportunities, such as the Internet and other direct channels. However, developing these new channels often brings them into direct competition with their established channels, resulting in conflict.

To ease this problem, companies often look for ways to make going direct a plus for the entire channel.

For example, guitar and amp maker Fender knows that many customers would prefer to buy its guitars, amps, and accessories online. But selling directly through its Web site would create conflicts with retail partners, from large chains such as Guitar Center, Sam Ash, and Best Buy to small shops scattered throughout the world, such as the Musician's Junkyard in Windsor, Vermont, or Freddy for Music in Amman, Jordan. So Fender's Web site provides detailed information about the company's products, but you can't buy a new Fender Stratocaster or Acoustasonic guitar there. Instead, the Fender Web site refers you to resellers' Web sites and stores. Thus, Fender's direct marketing helps both the company and its channel partners.

> **Author** | Like everything else in **Comment** | marketing, good channel design begins with analyzing customer needs. Remember, marketing channels are really *customer-value delivery networks*.

Channel Design Decisions (pp 351–354)

We now look at several channel decisions manufacturers face. In designing marketing channels, manufacturers struggle between what is ideal and what is practical. A new firm with limited capital usually starts by selling in a limited market area. Deciding on the best channels might not be a problem: The problem might simply be how to convince one or a few good intermediaries to handle the line.

If successful, the new firm can branch out to new markets through existing intermediaries. In smaller markets, the firm might sell directly to retailers; in larger markets, it might sell through distributors. In one part of the country, it might grant exclusive franchises; in another, it might sell through all available outlets. Then it might add a Web store that sells directly to hard-to-reach customers. In this way, channel systems often evolve to meet market opportunities and conditions.

For maximum effectiveness, however, channel analysis and decision making should be more purposeful. **Marketing channel design** calls for analyzing consumer needs, setting channel objectives, identifying major channel alternatives, and evaluating those alternatives.

Marketing channel design
Designing effective marketing channels by analyzing customer needs, setting channel objectives, identifying major channel alternatives, and evaluating those alternatives.

Analyzing Consumer Needs

As noted previously, marketing channels are part of the overall *customer-value delivery network*. Each channel member and level adds value for the customer. Thus, designing the marketing channel starts with finding out what target consumers want from the channel. Do consumers want to buy from nearby locations or are they willing to travel to more distant and centralized locations? Would customers rather buy in person, by phone, or online? Do they value breadth of assortment or do they prefer specialization? Do consumers want many add-on services (delivery, installation, repairs), or will they obtain these services elsewhere? The faster the delivery, the greater the assortment provided, and the more add-on services supplied, the greater the channel's service level.

Providing the fastest delivery, the greatest assortment, and the most services may not be possible or practical. The company and its channel members may not have the resources or skills needed to provide all the desired services. Also, providing higher levels of service results in higher costs for the channel and higher prices for consumers. ◉ For example, your local hardware store probably provides more personalized service, a more convenient location, and less shopping hassle than the nearest huge Home Depot or Lowe's store. But it may also charge higher prices. The company must balance consumer needs not only against the feasibility and costs of meeting these needs but also against customer price preferences. The success of discount retailing shows that consumers will often accept lower service levels in exchange for lower prices.

◉ **Meeting customers' channel service needs: Your local hardware store probably provides more personalized service, a more convenient location, and less shopping hassle than a huge Home Depot or Lowe's store. But it may also charge higher prices.**

Setting Channel Objectives

Companies should state their marketing channel objectives in terms of targeted levels of customer service. Usually, a company can identify several segments wanting different levels of service. The company should decide which segments to serve and the best channels to use in each case. In each segment, the company wants to minimize the total channel cost of meeting customer-service requirements.

The company's channel objectives are also influenced by the nature of the company, its products, its marketing intermediaries, its competitors, and the environment. For example, the company's size and financial situation determine which marketing functions it can handle itself and which it must give to intermediaries. Companies selling perishable products may require more direct marketing to avoid delays and too much handling.

In some cases, a company may want to compete in or near the same outlets that carry competitors' products. For example, Maytag wants its appliances displayed alongside competing brands to facilitate comparison shopping. In other cases, companies may avoid the channels used by competitors. Mary Kay Cosmetics, for example, sells directly to consumers through its corps of more than two million independent beauty consultants in more than 35 markets worldwide rather than going head-to-head with other cosmetics makers for scarce positions in retail stores.[8] GEICO primarily markets auto and homeowner's insurance directly to consumers via the telephone and the Internet rather than through agents.

Finally, environmental factors such as economic conditions and legal constraints may affect channel objectives and design. For example, in a depressed economy, producers want to distribute their goods in the most economical way, using shorter channels and dropping unneeded services that add to the final price of the goods.

Identifying Major Alternatives

When the company has defined its channel objectives, it should next identify its major channel alternatives in terms of the *types* of intermediaries, the *number* of intermediaries, and the *responsibilities* of each channel member.

Types of Intermediaries

A firm should identify the types of channel members available to carry out its channel work. Most companies face many channel member choices. For example, until recently, Dell sold directly to final consumers and business buyers only through its sophisticated phone and Internet marketing channel. It also sold directly to large corporate, institutional, and government buyers using its direct sales force. However, to reach more consumers and match competitors such as HP, Dell now sells indirectly through retailers such as Best Buy, Staples, and Walmart. It also sells indirectly through value-added resellers, independent distributors and dealers who develop computer systems and applications tailored to the special needs of small- and medium-sized business customers.

Using many types of resellers in a channel provides both benefits and drawbacks. For example, by selling through retailers and value-added resellers in addition to its own direct channels, Dell can reach more and different kinds of buyers. However, the new channels will be more difficult to manage and control. And the direct and indirect channels will compete with each other for many of the same customers, causing potential conflict. In fact, Dell often finds itself "stuck in the middle," with its direct sales reps complaining about competition from retail stores, while its value-added resellers complain that the direct sales reps are undercutting their business.

Number of Marketing Intermediaries

Companies must also determine the number of channel members to use at each level. Three strategies are available: intensive distribution, exclusive distribution, and selective distribution. Producers of convenience products and common raw materials typically seek **intensive distribution**—a strategy in which they stock their products in as many outlets

Intensive distribution
Stocking the product in as many outlets as possible.

● Exclusive distribution: Luxury carmakers such as Bentley sell exclusively through a limited number of retailers. Such limited distribution enhances a car's image and generates stronger retailer support.

Exclusive distribution
Giving a limited number of dealers the exclusive right to distribute the company's products in their territories.

Selective distribution
The use of more than one but fewer than all the intermediaries who are willing to carry the company's products.

as possible. These products must be available where and when consumers want them. For example, toothpaste, candy, and other similar items are sold in millions of outlets to provide maximum brand exposure and consumer convenience. Kraft, Coca-Cola, Kimberly-Clark, and other consumer-goods companies distribute their products in this way.

By contrast, some producers purposely limit the number of intermediaries handling their products. The extreme form of this practice is **exclusive distribution**, in which the producer gives only a limited number of dealers the exclusive right to distribute its products in their territories. Exclusive distribution is often found in the distribution of luxury brands. ● For example, exclusive Bentley automobiles are typically sold by only a handful of authorized dealers in any given market area. By granting exclusive distribution, Bentley gains stronger dealer selling support and more control over dealer prices, promotion, and services. Exclusive distribution also enhances the brand's image and allows for higher markups.

Between intensive and exclusive distribution lies **selective distribution**—the use of more than one but fewer than all the intermediaries who are willing to carry a company's products. Most television, furniture, and home appliance brands are distributed in this manner. For example, Whirlpool and GE sell their major appliances through dealer networks and selected large retailers. By using selective distribution, they can develop good working relationships with selected channel members and expect a better-than-average selling effort. Selective distribution gives producers good market coverage with more control and less cost than does intensive distribution.

Responsibilities of Channel Members

The producer and the intermediaries need to agree on the terms and responsibilities of each channel member. They should agree on price policies, conditions of sale, territory rights, and the specific services to be performed by each party. The producer should establish a list price and a fair set of discounts for the intermediaries. It must define each channel member's territory, and it should be careful about where it places new resellers.

Mutual services and duties need to be spelled out carefully, especially in franchise and exclusive distribution channels. For example, McDonald's provides franchisees with promotional support, a record-keeping system, training at Hamburger University, and general management assistance. In turn, franchisees must meet company standards for physical facilities and food quality, cooperate with new promotion programs, provide requested information, and buy specified food products.

Evaluating the Major Alternatives

Suppose a company has identified several channel alternatives and wants to select the one that will best satisfy its long-run objectives. Each alternative should be evaluated against economic, control, and adaptability criteria.

Using *economic criteria*, a company compares the likely sales, costs, and profitability of different channel alternatives. What will be the investment required by each channel alternative, and what returns will result? The company must also consider *control issues*. Using intermediaries usually means giving them some control over the marketing of the product, and some intermediaries take more control than others. Other things being equal, the company prefers to keep as much control as possible. Finally, the company must apply *adaptability criteria*. Channels often involve long-term commitments, yet the company wants to keep the channel flexible so that it can adapt to environmental changes. Thus, to be considered, a channel involving long-term commitments should be greatly superior on economic and control grounds.

Designing International Distribution Channels

International marketers face many additional complexities in designing their channels. Each country has its own unique distribution system that has evolved over time and changes very slowly. These channel systems can vary widely from country to country. Thus, global marketers must usually adapt their channel strategies to the existing structures within each country.

In some markets, the distribution system is complex and hard to penetrate, consisting of many layers and large numbers of intermediaries. For example, many Western companies find Japan's distribution system difficult to navigate. It's steeped in tradition and very complex, with many distributors touching one product before it makes it to the store shelf.

At the other extreme, distribution systems in developing countries may be scattered, inefficient, or altogether lacking. For example, China and India are huge markets—each with a population well over one billion people. However, because of inadequate distribution systems, most companies can profitably access only a small portion of the population located in each country's most affluent cities. "China is a very decentralized market," notes a China trade expert. "[It's] made up of two dozen distinct markets sprawling across 2,000 cities. Each has its own culture. . . . It's like operating in an asteroid belt." China's distribution system is so fragmented that logistics costs to wrap, bundle, load, unload, sort, reload, and transport goods amount to more than 22 percent of the nation's GDP, far higher than in most other countries. (U.S. logistics costs account for just over 10 percent of the nation's GDP.) After years of effort, even Walmart executives admit that they have been unable to assemble an efficient supply chain in China.[9]

⦿ **International channel complexities: When the Chinese government banned door-to-door selling, Avon had to abandon its traditional direct marketing approach and sell through retail shops.**

Sometimes customs or government regulation can greatly restrict how a company distributes products in global markets. ⦿ For example, an inefficient distribution structure wasn't the cause of problems for Avon in China; the cause was restrictive government regulation. Fearing the growth of multilevel marketing schemes, the Chinese government banned door-to-door selling altogether in 1998, forcing Avon to abandon its traditional direct marketing approach and sell through retail shops. In 2006, the Chinese government gave Avon and other direct sellers permission to sell door-to-door again, but that permission is tangled in a web of restrictions. Fortunately for Avon, its earlier focus on store sales is helping it weather the restrictions better than most other direct sellers. In fact, through a combination of direct and retail sales, Avon's sales in China are now booming.[10]

International marketers face a wide range of channel alternatives. Designing efficient and effective channel systems between and within various country markets poses a difficult challenge. We discuss international distribution decisions further in Chapter 19.

Author | Now it's time to **Comment** | implement the chosen channel design and work with selected channel members to manage and motivate them.

Channel Management Decisions (pp 354–356)

Once the company has reviewed its channel alternatives and determined the best channel design, it must implement and manage the chosen channel. **Marketing channel management** calls for selecting, managing, and motivating individual channel members and evaluating their performance over time.

Selecting Channel Members

Marketing channel management
Selecting, managing, and motivating individual channel members and evaluating their performance over time.

Producers vary in their ability to attract qualified marketing intermediaries. Some producers have no trouble signing up channel members. For example, when Toyota first introduced its Lexus line in the United States, it had no trouble attracting new dealers. In fact, it had to turn down many would-be resellers.

At the other extreme are producers who have to work hard to line up enough qualified intermediaries. For example, when Timex first tried to sell its inexpensive watches through regular jewelry stores, most jewelry stores refused to carry them. The company then managed to get its watches into mass-merchandise outlets. This turned out to be a wise decision because of the rapid growth of mass merchandising.

Even established brands may have difficulty gaining and keeping desired distribution, especially when dealing with powerful resellers. For example, in an effort to streamline its product assortment, Walmart recently removed Glad and Hefty food storage bags from its shelves. It now carries only Ziploc and its own Great Value store brand (produced by the makers of Hefty). Walmart's decision was a real blow to the Glad and Hefty brands, which captured one-third or more of their sales through the giant retailer.[11]

When selecting intermediaries, the company should determine what characteristics distinguish the better ones. It will want to evaluate each channel member's years in business, other lines carried, growth and profit record, cooperativeness, and reputation. If the intermediaries are sales agents, the company will want to evaluate the number and character of other lines carried and the size and quality of the sales force. If the intermediary is a retail store that wants exclusive or selective distribution, the company will want to evaluate the store's customers, location, and future growth potential.

Managing and Motivating Channel Members

Once selected, channel members must be continuously managed and motivated to do their best. The company must sell not only *through* the intermediaries but also *to* and *with* them. Most companies see their intermediaries as first-line customers and partners. They practice strong *partner relationship management (PRM)* to forge long-term partnerships with channel members. This creates a value delivery system that meets the needs of both the company *and* its marketing partners.

In managing its channels, a company must convince distributors that they can succeed better by working together as a part of a cohesive value delivery system. Thus, P&G works closely with Target to create superior value for final consumers. The two jointly plan merchandising goals and strategies, inventory levels, and advertising and promotion programs.

Similarly, heavy-equipment manufacturer Caterpillar and its worldwide network of independent dealers work in close harmony to find better ways to bring value to customers.[12]

One-hundred-year-old Caterpillar produces innovative, high-quality products. Yet the most important reason for Caterpillar's dominance is its distribution network of 220 outstanding independent dealers worldwide. Caterpillar and its dealers work as partners. According to a former Caterpillar CEO: "After the product leaves our door, the dealers take over. They are the ones on the front line. They're the ones who live with the product for its lifetime. They're the ones customers see." ◉ When a big piece of Caterpillar equipment breaks down, customers know that they can count on Caterpillar and its outstanding dealer network for support. Dealers play a vital role in almost every aspect of Caterpillar's operations, from product design and delivery to product service and support.

Caterpillar really knows its dealers and cares about their success. It closely monitors each dealership's sales, market position, service capability, and financial situation. When it sees a problem, it jumps in to help. In addition to more formal business ties, Caterpillar forms close personal ties with dealers in a kind of family relationship. Caterpillar and its dealers feel a deep pride in what they are accomplishing together. As the former CEO puts it, "There's a camaraderie among our dealers around the world that really makes it more than just a financial arrangement. They feel that what

● Caterpillar works closely with its worldwide network of independent dealers to find better ways to bring value to customers. When a big piece of CAT equipment breaks down, customers know they can count on Caterpillar and its outstanding dealer network for support.

they're doing is good for the world because they are part of an organization that makes, sells, and tends to the machines that make the world work."

As a result of its partnership with dealers, Caterpillar dominates the world's markets for heavy construction, mining, and logging equipment. Its familiar yellow tractors, crawlers, loaders, bulldozers, and trucks capture some 40 percent of the worldwide heavy-equipment business, twice that of number-two Komatsu.

Many companies are now installing integrated high-tech PRM systems to coordinate their whole-channel marketing efforts. Just as they use CRM software systems to help manage relationships with important customers, companies can now use PRM and supply chain management (SCM) software to help recruit, train, organize, manage, motivate, and evaluate relationships with channel partners.

Evaluating Channel Members

The company must regularly check channel member performance against standards such as sales quotas, average inventory levels, customer delivery time, treatment of damaged and lost goods, cooperation in company promotion and training programs, and services to the customer. The company should recognize and reward intermediaries who are performing well and adding good value for consumers. Those who are performing poorly should be assisted or, as a last resort, replaced.

Finally, companies need to be sensitive to their channel partners. Those who treat their partners poorly risk not only losing their support but also causing some legal problems. The next section describes various rights and duties pertaining to companies and other channel members.

Public Policy and Distribution Decisions (pp 356–357)

For the most part, companies are legally free to develop whatever channel arrangements suit them. In fact, the laws affecting channels seek to prevent the exclusionary tactics of some companies that might keep another company from using a desired channel. Most channel law deals with the mutual rights and duties of channel members once they have formed a relationship.

Many producers and wholesalers like to develop exclusive channels for their products. When the seller allows only certain outlets to carry its products, this strategy is called *exclusive distribution*. When the seller requires that these dealers not handle competitors' products, its strategy is called *exclusive dealing*. Both parties can benefit from exclusive arrangements: The seller obtains more loyal and dependable outlets, and the dealers obtain a steady source of supply and stronger seller support. But exclusive arrangements also exclude other producers from selling to these dealers. This situation brings exclusive dealing contracts under the scope of the Clayton Act of 1914. They are legal as long as they do not substantially lessen competition or tend to create a monopoly and as long as both parties enter into the agreement voluntarily.

Exclusive dealing often includes *exclusive territorial agreements*. The producer may agree not to sell to other dealers in a given area, or the buyer may agree to sell only in its own territory. The first practice is normal under franchise systems as a way to increase dealer enthusiasm and commitment. It is also perfectly legal—a seller has no legal obligation to sell through more outlets than it wishes. The second practice, whereby the producer tries to keep a dealer from selling outside its territory, has become a major legal issue.

Producers of a strong brand sometimes sell it to dealers only if the dealers will take some or all the rest of the line. This is called full-line forcing. Such *tying agreements* are not necessarily illegal, but they violate the Clayton Act if they tend to lessen competition substantially. The practice may prevent consumers from freely choosing among competing suppliers of these other brands.

Finally, producers are free to select their dealers, but their right to terminate dealers is somewhat restricted. In general, sellers can drop dealers "for cause." However, they cannot drop dealers if, for example, the dealers refuse to cooperate in a doubtful legal arrangement, such as exclusive dealing or tying agreements.

<table>
<tr><td>

Author | Marketers used to call this
Comment | plain old "physical distribution." But as these titles suggest, the topic has grown in importance, complexity, and sophistication.

</td></tr>
</table>

Marketing Logistics and Supply Chain Management (pp 357–365)

In today's global marketplace, selling a product is sometimes easier than getting it to customers. Companies must decide on the best way to store, handle, and move their products and services so that they are available to customers in the right assortments, at the right time, and in the right place. Logistics effectiveness has a major impact on both customer satisfaction and company costs. Here we consider the nature and importance of logistics management in the supply chain, the goals of the logistics system, major logistics functions, and the need for integrated supply chain management.

Nature and Importance of Marketing Logistics

To some managers, marketing logistics means only trucks and warehouses. But modern logistics is much more than this. **Marketing logistics**—also called **physical distribution**—involves planning, implementing, and controlling the physical flow of goods, services, and related information from points of origin to points of consumption to meet customer requirements at a profit. In short, it involves getting the right product to the right customer in the right place at the right time.

In the past, physical distribution planners typically started with products at the plant and then tried to find low-cost solutions to get them to customers. However, today's marketers prefer *customer-centered* logistics thinking, which starts with the marketplace and works backward to the factory or even to sources of supply. Marketing logistics involves not only *outbound distribution* (moving products from the factory to resellers and ultimately to customers) but also *inbound distribution* (moving products and materials from suppliers to the factory) and *reverse distribution* (moving broken, unwanted, or excess products returned by consumers or resellers). That is, it involves entire **supply chain management**—managing upstream and downstream value-added flows of materials, final goods, and related information among suppliers, the company, resellers, and final consumers, as shown in ● **Figure 12.5**.

Marketing logistics (or physical distribution)
Planning, implementing, and controlling the physical flow of materials, final goods, and related information from points of origin to points of consumption to meet customer requirements at a profit.

Supply chain management
Managing upstream and downstream value-added flows of materials, final goods, and related information among suppliers, the company, resellers, and final consumers.

● FIGURE | 12.5
Supply Chain Management

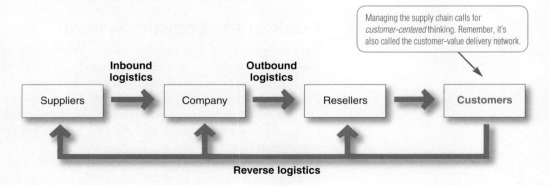

Managing the supply chain calls for *customer-centered* thinking. Remember, it's also called the customer-value delivery network.

Inbound logistics · Outbound logistics

Suppliers → Company → Resellers → Customers

Reverse logistics

● Logistics: American companies spent $1.3 trillion last year—about 10 percent of the U.S. GDP—to wrap, bundle, load, unload, sort, reload, and transport goods.

The logistics manager's task is to coordinate the activities of suppliers, purchasing agents, marketers, channel members, and customers. These activities include forecasting, information systems, purchasing, production planning, order processing, inventory, warehousing, and transportation planning.

Companies today are placing greater emphasis on logistics for several reasons. First, companies can gain a powerful competitive advantage by using improved logistics to give customers better service or lower prices. Second, improved logistics can yield tremendous cost savings to both a company and its customers. As much as 20 percent of an average product's price is accounted for by shipping and transport alone. This far exceeds the cost of advertising and many other marketing costs. ● American companies spent $1.3 trillion last year—about 10 percent of GDP—to wrap, bundle, load, unload, sort, reload, and transport goods. That's more than the national GDPs of all but 12 countries worldwide. Even more, as fuel and other costs rise, so do logistics costs. For example, the cost of shipping one 40-foot container from Shanghai to the United States rose from $3,000 in 2000 to more than $8,000 last year.[13]

Shaving off even a small fraction of logistics costs can mean substantial savings. For example, Walmart recently undertook a program of logistics improvements through more efficient sourcing, better inventory management, and greater supply chain productivity that will reduce supply chain costs by 5–15 percent over the next five years—that's a whopping $4 billion to $12 billion.[14]

Third, the explosion in product variety has created a need for improved logistics management. For example, in 1911 the typical A&P grocery store carried only 270 items. The store manager could keep track of this inventory on about 10 pages of notebook paper stuffed in a shirt pocket. Today, the average A&P carries a bewildering stock of more than 25,000 items. A Walmart Supercenter store carries more than 100,000 products, 30,000 of which are grocery products.[15] Ordering, shipping, stocking, and controlling such a variety of products presents a sizable logistics challenge.

Improvements in information technology have also created opportunities for major gains in distribution efficiency. Today's companies are using sophisticated supply chain management software, Web-based logistics systems, point-of-sale scanners, RFID tags, satellite tracking, and electronic transfer of order and payment data. Such technology lets them quickly and efficiently manage the flow of goods, information, and finances through the supply chain.

Finally, more than almost any other marketing function, logistics affects the environment and a firm's environmental sustainability efforts. Transportation, warehousing, packaging, and other logistics functions are typically the biggest supply chain contributors to the company's environmental footprint. At the same time, they also provide one of the most fertile areas for cost savings. So developing a *green supply chain* is not only environmentally responsible but can also be profitable. "Sustainability shouldn't be about Washington jamming green stuff down your throat," says one supply chain expert. "This is a lot about money, about reducing costs."[16] (See Real Marketing 12.2.)

Goals of the Logistics System

Some companies state their logistics objective as providing maximum customer service at the least cost. Unfortunately, as nice as this sounds, no logistics system can *both* maximize customer service *and* minimize distribution costs. Maximum customer service implies rapid delivery, large inventories, flexible assortments, liberal returns policies, and other services—all of which raise distribution costs. In contrast, minimum distribution costs imply slower delivery, smaller inventories, and larger shipping lots—which represent a lower level of overall customer service.

The goal of marketing logistics should be to provide a *targeted* level of customer service at the least cost. A company must first research the importance of various distribution services to

Real Marketing 12.2

Greening the Supply Chain:
It's the Right Thing to Do—And It's Profitable, Too

You may remember the old song in which Kermit the Frog laments, "it's not easy bein' green." That's often as true for company supply chains as it is for the Muppet. Greening up a company's channels often takes substantial commitment, ingenuity, and investment. Although challenging, however, today's supply channels are getting ever greener.

Companies have many reasons for reducing the environmental impact of their supply chains. For one thing, in the not too distant future, if companies don't green up voluntarily, a host of "green laws" and sustainability regulations enacted around the world will require them to do so. For another, many large customers—from HP to Walmart to the federal government—are demanding it. "Environmental sustainability is fast becoming a critical element in supplier selection and performance evaluation," says a channels expert. Supply chain managers "need to begin thinking green, and quickly, or they chance risking relationships with prime customers." Perhaps even more important than *having* to do it, designing more environmentally responsible supply chains is simply the *right* thing to do. It's one more way that companies can contribute to saving our world for future generations.

But that's all pretty heady stuff. As it turns out, companies have a more immediate and practical reason for turning their supply chains green. Not only are green channels good for the world, they're also good for the company's bottom line. Companies green their supply chains through greater efficiency, and greater efficiency means lower costs and higher profits. This cost-savings side of environmental responsibility makes good sense. The very logistics activities that create the biggest environmental footprint—such as transportation, warehousing, and packaging—are also the ones that account for a lion's share of logistics costs, especially in an age of scarce resources and soaring energy prices. Although it may require an up-front investment, it doesn't cost more to green up channels. In the long run, it usually costs less.

Here are a few examples of how creating greener supply chains can benefit both the environment and the company's bottom line:

- Stonyfield Farm, the world's largest yogurt maker, recently set up a small, dedicated truck fleet to make regional deliveries in New England and replaced its national less-than-truckload distribution network with a regional multistop truckload system. As a result, Stonyfield now moves more product in fewer trucks, cutting in half the number of miles traveled. The changes produced a 40 percent reduction in transportation-related carbon dioxide emissions; they also knocked an eye-popping 8 percent off Stonyfield's shipping expenses. Says Stonyfield's director of logistics, "We're surprised. We understand that environmental responsibility can be profitable. We expected some savings, but not really in this range."

- Consumer package goods maker SC Johnson made a seemingly simple but smart—and profitable—change in the way it packs its trucks. Under the old system, a load of its Ziploc products filled a truck trailer before reaching the maximum weight limit. In contrast, a load of Windex glass cleaner hit the maximum weight before the trailer was full. By strategically mixing the two products, SC Johnson found it could send the same amount of products with 2,098 fewer shipments, while burning 168,000 fewer

gallons of diesel fuel and eliminating 1,882 tons of greenhouse gasses. Says the company's director of environmental issues, "Loading a truck may seem simple, but making sure that a truck is truly full is a science. Consistently hitting a trailer's maximum weight provided a huge opportunity to reduce our energy consumption, cut our greenhouse gas emissions, and save money [in the bargain]."

- Con-way, a $4.2 billion freight transportation company, made the simple decision to lower the maximum speed of its truck fleet from 65 miles per hour to 62 miles per hour. This small three-mile-per-hour change produced a savings of six million gallons of fuel per year and an emissions reduction equivalent to taking 12,000 to 15,000 cars off the road. Similarly, grocery retailer Safeway switched its fleet of 1,000 trucks to run on cleaner-burning biodiesel fuel. This change will reduce annual carbon dioxide emissions by 75 million pounds—equivalent to taking another 7,500 cars off the road.

- Walmart is perhaps the world's biggest green-channels champion. Among dozens of other major initiatives (see Real Marketing 20.1), the giant retailer is now installing more efficient engines and tires, hybrid drive systems, and other technologies in its fleet of 7,000 trucks in an effort to reduce carbon dioxide emissions and increase efficiency 25 percent by 2012. Walmart is also pressuring its throng of suppliers to clean up their environmental acts. For example, it recently set a goal to reduce supplier packaging by 5 percent. Given Walmart's size, even small changes make a substantial impact. For instance, it convinced P&G to produce Charmin toilet paper in more-shippable compact

Con-way made the simple decision to lower the maximum speed of its truck fleet by 3 miles per hour, which produced a savings of 6 million gallons of fuel per year and emissions reductions equivalent to taking 12,000 to 15,000 cars off of the road.

Continued on next page

rolls: a six-pack of Charmin Mega Roll contains as much paper as a regular pack of 24 rolls. This change alone saves 89.5 million cardboard rolls and 360,000 pounds of plastic wrapping a year. Logistics-wise, it also allows Walmart to ship 42 percent more units on its trucks, saving about 54,000 gallons of fuel. More broadly, Walmart estimates that the reduced supplier-packaging initiative will produce savings of $3.4 billion and prevent 667,000 metric tons of carbon dioxide emissions, equivalent to removing 213,000 trucks from the road.

So when it comes to supply chains, Kermit might be right—it's not easy bein' green. But it's now more necessary than ever, and it can pay big returns. It's a challenging area, says one supply chain expert, "but if you look at it from a pure profit-and-loss perspective, it's also a rich one." Another expert concludes, "It's now easier than ever to build a green supply chain without going into the red, while actually saving cash along the way."

Sources: Quotes, examples, and other information from Bill Mongelluzzo, "Supply Chain Expert Sees Profits in Sustainability," *Journal of Commerce*, March 11, 2010; Connie Robbins Gentry, "Green Means Go," *Chain Store Age*, March 2009, p. 47; Daniel P. Bearth, "Finding Profit in Green Logistics," *Transport Topics*, January 21, 2008, p. S4; Dan R. Robinson and Shannon Wilcox, "The Greening of the Supply Chain," *Logistics Management*, October 2008; William Hoffman, "Supplying Sustainability," *Traffic World*, April 7, 2008; "Supply Chain Standard: Going Green without Going into the Red," *Logistics Manager*, March 2009, p. 22; and "Supply Chain Standard: Take the Green Route Out of the Red," *Logistics Manager*, May 2009, p. 28.

customers and then set desired service levels for each segment. The objective is to maximize *profits*, not sales. Therefore, the company must weigh the benefits of providing higher levels of service against the costs. Some companies offer less service than their competitors and charge a lower price. Other companies offer more service and charge higher prices to cover higher costs.

Major Logistics Functions

Given a set of logistics objectives, the company is ready to design a logistics system that will minimize the cost of attaining these objectives. The major logistics functions include *warehousing, inventory management, transportation,* and *logistics information management.*

Warehousing

Production and consumption cycles rarely match, so most companies must store their goods while they wait to be sold. For example, Snapper, Toro, and other lawn mower manufacturers run their factories all year long and store up products for the heavy spring and summer buying seasons. The storage function overcomes differences in needed quantities and timing, ensuring that products are available when customers are ready to buy them.

A company must decide on *how many* and *what types* of warehouses it needs and *where* they will be located. The company might use either *storage warehouses* or *distribution centers*. Storage warehouses store goods for moderate to long periods. **Distribution centers** are designed to move goods rather than just store them. They are large and highly automated warehouses designed to receive goods from various plants and suppliers, take orders, fill them efficiently, and deliver goods to customers as quickly as possible.

For example, Walmart operates a network of 147 huge distribution centers. A single center, serving the daily needs of 75–100 Walmart stores, typically contains some one million square feet of space (about 20 football fields) under a single roof. At a typical center, laser scanners route as many as 190,000 cases of goods per day along five miles of conveyer belts, and the center's 500 to 1,000 workers load or unload some 500 trucks daily. Walmart's Monroe, Georgia, distribution center contains a 127,000-square-foot freezer (that's about 2.5 football fields) that can hold 10,000 pallets—room enough for 58 million Popsicles.[17]

Like almost everything else these days, warehousing has seen dramatic changes in technology in recent years. Outdated materials-handling methods are steadily being replaced by newer, computer-controlled systems requiring few employees. Computers and scanners read orders and direct lift trucks, electric hoists, or robots to gather goods, move them to

Distribution center
A large, highly automated warehouse designed to receive goods from various plants and suppliers, take orders, fill them efficiently, and deliver goods to customers as quickly as possible.

● **High-tech distribution centers: Staples employs a team of super-retrievers—in day-glo orange—to keep its warehouse humming.**

loading docks, and issue invoices. For example, office supplies retailer Staples now employs "a team of super-retrievers—in day-glo orange—that keep its warehouse humming":[18]

Imagine a team of employees that works 16 hours a day, seven days a week. They never call in sick or show up late because they never leave the building. They demand no benefits, require no health insurance, and receive no paychecks. And they never complain. Sounds like a bunch of robots, huh? ● They are, in fact, robots—and they're dramatically changing the way Staples delivers notepads, pens, and paper clips to its customers. Every day, Staples' huge Chambersburg, Pennsylvania, distribution center receives thousands of customer orders, each containing a wide range of office supply items. Having people run around a warehouse looking for those items is expensive, especially when the company has promised to delight customers by delivering orders the next day.

Enter the robots. On the distribution center floor, the 150 robots resemble a well-trained breed of working dogs, say, golden retrievers. When orders come in, a centralized computer tells the robots where to find racks with the appropriate items. The robots retrieve the racks and carry them to picking stations, then wait patiently as humans pull the correct products and place them in boxes. When orders are filled, the robots neatly park the racks back among the rest. The robots pretty much take care of themselves. When they run low on power, they head to battery-charging terminals, or, as warehouse personnel say, "They get themselves a drink of water." The robots now run 50 percent of the Chambersburg facility, where average daily output is up 60 percent since they arrived on the scene.

Inventory Management

Inventory management also affects customer satisfaction. Here, managers must maintain the delicate balance between carrying too little inventory and carrying too much. With too little stock, the firm risks not having products when customers want to buy. To remedy this, the firm may need costly emergency shipments or production. Carrying too much inventory results in higher-than-necessary inventory-carrying costs and stock obsolescence. Thus, in managing inventory, firms must balance the costs of carrying larger inventories against resulting sales and profits.

Many companies have greatly reduced their inventories and related costs through *just-in-time* logistics systems. With such systems, producers and retailers carry only small inventories of parts or merchandise, often enough for only a few days of operations. New stock arrives exactly when needed, rather than being stored in inventory until being used. Just-in-time systems require accurate forecasting along with fast, frequent, and flexible delivery so that new supplies will be available when needed. However, these systems result in substantial savings in inventory-carrying and handling costs.

Marketers are always looking for new ways to make inventory management more efficient. In the not-too-distant future, handling inventory might even become fully automated. For example, in Chapter 3 we discussed RFID or "smart tag" technology, by which small transmitter chips are embedded in or placed on products and packaging on everything from flowers and razors to tires. "Smart" products could make the entire supply chain—which accounts for nearly 75 percent of a product's cost—intelligent and automated.

Companies using RFID would know, at any time, exactly where a product is located physically within the supply chain. "Smart shelves" would not only tell them when it's time to reorder but also place the order automatically with their suppliers. Such exciting new information technology applications will revolutionize distribution as we know it. Many large and resourceful marketing companies, such as Walmart, P&G, Kraft, IBM, HP, and Best Buy, are investing heavily to make the full use of RFID technology a reality.[19]

Transportation

The choice of transportation carriers affects the pricing of products, delivery performance, and the condition of goods when they arrive—all of which will affect customer satisfaction. In shipping goods to its warehouses, dealers, and customers, the company can choose among five main transportation modes: truck, rail, water, pipeline, and air, along with an alternative mode for digital products—the Internet.

If you rely on it,

wear it,

consume it,

or depend on it,

Trucks Bring It.

Trucks are essential to deliver everything America needs.
Eighty-two percent of U.S. communities depend solely on truck transport for their goods and commodities. Simply put, trucks move America safely, efficiently and on time.

Good stuff.

TRUCKS BRING IT

www.TrucksBringIt.com

● Truck transportation: **More than 80 percent of American communities depend solely on the trucking industry for the delivery of their goods. "Good stuff. Trucks bring it."**

Trucks have increased their share of transportation steadily and now account for more than 68 percent of total freight tonnage in the United States. U.S. trucks travel more than 431 billion miles a year—more than double the distance traveled 25 years ago—carrying 10.2 billion tons of freight. ● According to the American Trucking Association, 80 percent of U.S. communities depend solely on trucks for their goods and commodities. Trucks are highly flexible in their routing and time schedules, and they can usually offer faster service than railroads. They are efficient for short hauls of high-value merchandise. Trucking firms have evolved in recent years to become full-service providers of global transportation services. For example, large trucking firms now offer everything from satellite tracking, Web-based shipment management, and logistics planning software to cross-border shipping operations.[20]

Railroads account for 37 percent of the total cargo ton-miles moved. They are one of the most cost-effective modes for shipping large amounts of bulk products—coal, sand, minerals, and farm and forest products—over long distances. In recent years, railroads have increased their customer services by designing new equipment to handle special categories of goods, providing flatcars for carrying truck trailers by rail (piggyback), and providing in-transit services such as the diversion of shipped goods to other destinations en route and the processing of goods en route.

Water carriers, which account for about 5 percent of the cargo ton-miles, transport large amounts of goods by ships and barges on U.S. coastal and inland waterways. Although the cost of water transportation is very low for shipping bulky, low-value, nonperishable products such as sand, coal, grain, oil, and metallic ores, water transportation is the slowest mode and may be affected by the weather. *Pipelines*, which account for about 1 percent of the cargo ton-miles, are a specialized means of shipping petroleum, natural gas, and chemicals from sources to markets. Most pipelines are used by their owners to ship their own products.

Although *air* carriers transport less than 1 percent of the cargo ton-miles of the nation's goods, they are an important transportation mode. Airfreight rates are much higher than rail or truck rates, but airfreight is ideal when speed is needed or distant markets have to be reached. Among the most frequently airfreighted products are perishables (fresh fish, cut flowers) and high-value, low-bulk items (technical instruments, jewelry). Companies find that airfreight also reduces inventory levels, packaging costs, and the number of warehouses needed.

The *Internet* carries digital products from producer to customer via satellite, cable, or phone wire. Software firms, the media, music and video companies, and education all make use of the Internet to transport digital products. Although these firms primarily use traditional transportation to distribute DVDs, newspapers, and more, the Internet holds the potential for lower product distribution costs. Whereas planes, trucks, and trains move freight and packages, digital technology moves information bits.

Shippers also use **intermodal transportation**—combining two or more modes of transportation. The total cargo ton-miles moved via multiple modes is 14 percent. *Piggyback*

Intermodal transportation
Combining two or more modes of transportation.

describes the use of rail and trucks; *fishyback*, water and trucks; *trainship*, water and rail; and *airtruck*, air and trucks. Combining modes provides advantages that no single mode can deliver. Each combination offers advantages to the shipper. For example, not only is piggyback cheaper than trucking alone, but it also provides flexibility and convenience.

In choosing a transportation mode for a product, shippers must balance many considerations: speed, dependability, availability, cost, and others. Thus, if a shipper needs speed, air and truck are the prime choices. If the goal is low cost, then water or rail might be best.

Logistics Information Management

Companies manage their supply chains through information. Channel partners often link up to share information and make better joint logistics decisions. From a logistics perspective, flows of information, such as customer transactions, billing, shipment and inventory levels, and even customer data, are closely linked to channel performance. Companies need simple, accessible, fast, and accurate processes for capturing, processing, and sharing channel information.

Information can be shared and managed in many ways, but most sharing takes place through traditional or Internet-based *electronic data interchange* (*EDI*), the computerized exchange of data between organizations, which primarily is transmitted via the Internet. Walmart, for example, requires EDI links with its more than 90,000 suppliers. If new suppliers don't have EDI capability, Walmart will work with them to find and implement the needed software. "EDI has proven to be the most efficient way of conducting business with our product suppliers," says Walmart. "This system of exchanging information . . . allows us to improve customer service, lower expenses, and increase productivity."[21]

In some cases, suppliers might actually be asked to generate orders and arrange deliveries for their customers. Many large retailers—such as Walmart and Home Depot—work closely with major suppliers such as P&G or Black & Decker to set up *vendor-managed inventory* (VMI) systems or *continuous inventory replenishment* systems. Using VMI, the customer shares real-time data on sales and current inventory levels with the supplier. The supplier then takes full responsibility for managing inventories and deliveries. Some retailers even go so far as to shift inventory and delivery costs to the supplier. Such systems require close cooperation between the buyer and seller.

Integrated Logistics Management

Integrated logistics management
The logistics concept that emphasizes teamwork—both inside the company and among all the marketing channel organizations—to maximize the performance of the entire distribution system.

Today, more and more companies are adopting the concept of **integrated logistics management**. This concept recognizes that providing better customer service and trimming distribution costs require *teamwork*, both inside the company and among all the marketing channel organizations. Inside, the company's various departments must work closely together to maximize its own logistics performance. Outside, the company must integrate its logistics system with those of its suppliers and customers to maximize the performance of the entire distribution network.

Cross-Functional Teamwork Inside the Company

Most companies assign responsibility for various logistics activities to many different departments—marketing, sales, finance, operations, and purchasing. Too often, each function tries to optimize its own logistics performance without regard for the activities of the other functions. However, transportation, inventory, warehousing, and information management activities interact, often in an inverse way. Lower inventory levels reduce inventory-carrying costs. But they may also reduce customer service and increase costs from stockouts, back orders, special production runs, and costly fast-freight shipments. Because distribution activities involve strong trade-offs, decisions by different functions must be coordinated to achieve better overall logistics performance.

The goal of integrated supply chain management is to harmonize all of the company's logistics decisions. Close working relationships among departments can be achieved in several ways. Some companies have created permanent logistics committees composed of managers responsible for different physical distribution activities. Companies can also create

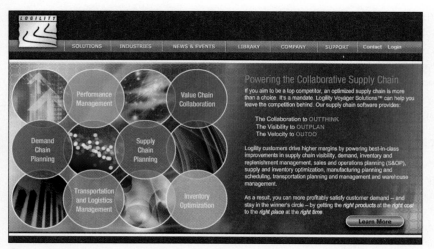

 Integrated logistics management: Many companies now employ sophisticated, systemwide supply chain management software, which is available from companies such as Logility.

supply chain manager positions that link the logistics activities of functional areas. For example, P&G has created product supply managers who manage all the supply chain activities for each product category. Many companies have a vice president of logistics with cross-functional authority.

Finally, companies can employ sophisticated, systemwide supply chain management software, now available from a wide range of software enterprises large and small, from SAP and Oracle to Infor and ⊙ Logility. The worldwide market for supply chain management software topped $6.6 billion last year and will reach an estimated $11.6 billion by 2013.[22] The important thing is that the company must coordinate its logistics and marketing activities to create high market satisfaction at a reasonable cost.

Building Logistics Partnerships

Companies must do more than improve their own logistics. They must also work with other channel partners to improve whole-channel distribution. The members of a marketing channel are linked closely in creating customer value and building customer relationships. One company's distribution system is another company's supply system. The success of each channel member depends on the performance of the entire supply chain. For example, IKEA can create its stylish but affordable furniture and deliver the "IKEA lifestyle" only if its entire supply chain—consisting of thousands of merchandise designers and suppliers, transport companies, warehouses, and service providers—operates at maximum efficiency and customer-focused effectiveness.

Smart companies coordinate their logistics strategies and forge strong partnerships with suppliers and customers to improve customer service and reduce channel costs. Many companies have created *cross-functional, cross-company teams*. For example, P&G has a team of more than 200 people working in Bentonville, Arkansas, home of Walmart. The P&Gers work jointly with their counterparts at Walmart to find ways to squeeze costs out of their distribution system. Working together benefits not only P&G and Walmart but also their shared, final consumers.

Other companies partner through *shared projects*. For example, many large retailers conduct joint in-store programs with suppliers. Home Depot allows key suppliers to use its stores as a testing ground for new merchandising programs. The suppliers spend time at Home Depot stores watching how their product sells and how customers relate to it. They then create programs specially tailored to Home Depot and its customers. Clearly, both the supplier and the customer benefit from such partnerships. The point is that all supply chain members must work together in the cause of bringing value to final consumers.

Third-Party Logistics

Most big companies love to make and sell their products. But many loathe the associated logistics "grunt work." They detest the bundling, loading, unloading, sorting, storing, reloading, transporting, customs clearing, and tracking required to supply their factories and get products to their customers. They hate it so much that a growing number of firms now outsource some or all of their logistics to **third-party logistics (3PL) providers**. Here's an example:[23]

Third-party logistics (3PL) provider
An independent logistics provider that performs any or all of the functions required to get a client's product to market.

Whirlpool's ultimate goal is to create loyal customers who continue to buy its brands over their lifetimes. One key loyalty factor is good repair service, which in turn depends on fast and reliable parts distribution. Only a few years ago, however, Whirlpool's replacement parts distribution system was fragmented and ineffective,

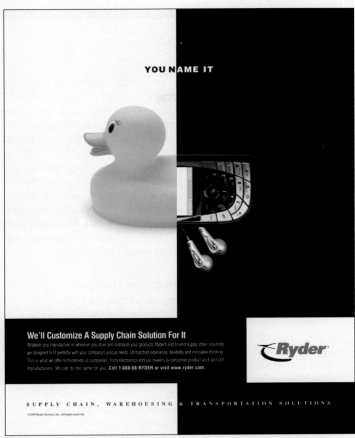

YOU NAME IT

We'll Customize A Supply Chain Solution For It

Whatever you manufacture or wherever you store and distribute your products, Ryder's end-to-end supply chain solutions are designed to fit perfectly with your company's unique needs. Unmatched experience, flexibility and innovative thinking. This is what we offer to hundreds of companies, from electronics and car makers to consumer product and aircraft manufacturers. We can do the same for you. **Call 1-888-88-RYDER or visit www.ryder.com.**

≈ **Ryder**

SUPPLY CHAIN, WAREHOUSING & TRANSPORTATION SOLUTIONS

©2009 Ryder System, Inc. All rights reserved.

◉ **Third-party logistics (3PL):** Companies such as Ryder help clients tighten up sluggish, overstuffed supply chains, slash inventories, and get products to customers more quickly and reliably.

often causing frustrating customer service delays. "Whirlpool is the world's largest manufacturer and marketer of appliances, but we're not necessarily experts in parts warehousing and distribution," says Whirlpool's national director of parts operations. So to help fix the problem, ◉ Whirlpool turned the entire job over to 3PL provider Ryder, which quickly streamlined Whirlpool's service parts distribution system. Ryder now provides order fulfillment and worldwide distribution of Whirlpool's service parts across six continents to hundreds of customers that include, in addition to end consumers, the Sears service network, authorized repair centers, and independent parts distributors that in turn ship parts out to a network of service companies and technicians. "Through our partnership with Ryder, we are now operating at our highest service level ever," says the Whirlpool executive. "We've . . . dramatically reduced [our parts distribution] costs. Our order cycle time has improved, and our customers are getting their parts more quickly."

The 3PL providers—companies such as Ryder, UPS Supply Chain Solutions, Penske Logistics, BAX Global, DHL Logistics, and FedEx Logistics—help clients tighten up sluggish, overstuffed supply chains, slash inventories, and get products to customers more quickly and reliably. According to a survey of chief logistics executives at *Fortune 500* companies, 82 percent of these companies use 3PL (also called *outsourced logistics* or *contract logistics*) services. In all, North American shippers spend 47 percent of their logistics budget on outsourced logistics; European and Asian shippers spend more than 62 percent. In just the past 10 years, the revenues for 3PL companies in the United States has more than doubled in size to $105 billion and is expected to grow 7 percent annually.[24]

Companies use third-party logistics providers for several reasons. First, because getting the product to market is their main focus, these providers can often do it more efficiently and at lower cost. Outsourcing typically results in 15–30 percent in cost savings. Second, outsourcing logistics frees a company to focus more intensely on its core business. Finally, integrated logistics companies understand increasingly complex logistics environments.

3PL partners can be especially helpful to companies attempting to expand their global market coverage. For example, companies distributing their products across Europe face a bewildering array of environmental restrictions that affect logistics, including packaging standards, truck size and weight limits, and noise and emissions pollution controls. By outsourcing its logistics, a company can gain a complete pan-European distribution system without incurring the costs, delays, and risks associated with setting up its own system.

REVIEWING Objectives AND KEY Terms

Some companies pay too little attention to their distribution channels, but others have used imaginative distribution systems to gain competitive advantage. A company's channel decisions directly affect every other marketing decision. Management must make channel decisions carefully, incorporating today's needs with tomorrow's likely selling environment.

Objective 1 **Explain why companies use marketing channels and discuss the functions these channels perform. (pp 340–341)**

In creating customer value, a company can't go it alone. It must work within an entire network of partners—a value delivery network—to accomplish this task. Individual companies and brands don't compete, their entire value delivery networks do.

Most producers use intermediaries to bring their products to market. They forge a *marketing channel* (or *distribution channel*)—a set of interdependent organizations involved in the process of making a product or service available for use or consumption by the consumer or business user. Through their contacts, experience, specialization, and scale of operation, intermediaries usually offer the firm more than it can achieve on its own.

Marketing channels perform many key functions. Some help *complete* transactions by gathering and distributing *information* needed for planning and aiding exchange, developing and spreading persuasive *communications* about an offer, performing *contact* work (finding and communicating with prospective buyers), *matching* (shaping and fitting the offer to the buyer's needs), and entering into *negotiation* to reach an agreement on price and other terms of the offer so that ownership can be transferred. Other functions help to *fulfill* the completed transactions by offering *physical distribution* (transporting and storing goods), *financing* (acquiring and using funds to cover the costs of the channel work, and *risk taking* (assuming the risks of carrying out the channel work.

Objective 2 **Discuss how channel members interact and how they organize to perform the work of the channel. (pp 344–351)**

The channel will be most effective when each member assumes the tasks it can do best. Ideally, because the success of individual channel members depends on overall channel success, all channel firms should work together smoothly. They should understand and accept their roles, coordinate their goals and activities, and cooperate to attain overall channel goals. By cooperating, they can more effectively sense, serve, and satisfy the target market.

In a large company, the formal organization structure assigns roles and provides needed leadership. But in a distribution channel composed of independent firms, leadership and power are not formally set. Traditionally, distribution channels have lacked the leadership needed to assign roles and manage conflict. In recent years, however, new types of channel organizations have appeared that provide stronger leadership and improved performance.

Objective 3 **Identify the major channel alternatives open to a company. (pp 351–354)**

Channel alternatives vary from direct selling to using one, two, three, or more intermediary *channel levels*. Marketing channels face continuous and sometimes dramatic change. Three of the most important trends are the growth of *vertical*, *horizontal*, and *multichannel marketing systems*. These trends affect channel cooperation, conflict, and competition.

Channel design begins with assessing customer channel service needs and company channel objectives and constraints. The company then identifies the major channel alternatives in terms of the *types* of intermediaries, the *number* of intermediaries, and the *channel responsibilities* of each. Each channel alternative must be evaluated according to economic, control, and adaptive criteria. *Channel management* calls for selecting qualified intermediaries and motivating them. Individual channel members must be evaluated regularly.

Objective 4 **Explain how companies select, motivate, and evaluate channel members. (pp 354–357)**

Producers vary in their ability to attract qualified marketing intermediaries. Some producers have no trouble signing up channel members. Others have to work hard to line up enough qualified intermediaries. When selecting intermediaries, the company should evaluate each channel member's qualifications and select those that best fit its channel objectives.

Once selected, channel members must be continuously motivated to do their best. The company must sell not only *through* the intermediaries but also *with* them. It should forge strong partnerships with channel members to create a marketing system that meets the needs of both the manufacturer *and* the partners.

Objective 5 **Discuss the nature and importance of marketing logistics and integrated supply chain management. (pp 357–365)**

Marketing logistics (or *physical distribution*) is an area of potentially high cost savings and improved customer satisfaction. Marketing logistics addresses not only *outbound distribution* but also *inbound distribution* and *reverse distribution*. That is, it involves the entire *supply chain management*—managing value-added flows between suppliers, the company, resellers, and final users. No logistics system can both maximize customer service and minimize distribution costs. Instead, the goal of logistics management is to provide a *targeted* level of service at the least cost. The major logistics functions include *warehousing*, *inventory management*, *transportation*, and *logistics information management*.

The *integrated supply chain management concept* recognizes that improved logistics requires teamwork in the form of close working relationships across functional areas inside the company and across various organizations in the supply chain. Companies can achieve logistics harmony among functions by creating cross-functional logistics teams, integrative supply manager positions, and senior-level logistics executives with cross-functional authority. Channel partnerships can take the form of cross-company teams, shared projects, and information-sharing systems. Today, some companies are outsourcing their logistics functions to third-party logistics (3PL) providers to save costs, increase efficiency, and gain faster and more effective access to global markets.

KEY Terms

OBJECTIVE 1

Value delivery network (p 341)
Marketing channel (distribution channel; p 341)
Channel level (p 343)
Direct marketing channel (p 343)
Indirect marketing channel (p 343)

OBJECTIVE 2

Channel conflict (p 344)
Conventional distribution channel (p 345)
Vertical marketing system (VMS; p 345)
Corporate VMS (p 345)
Contractual VMS (p 346)

Franchise organization (p 346)
Administered VMS (p 348)
Horizontal marketing system (p 348)
Multichannel distribution system (p 349)
Disintermediation (p 350)

OBJECTIVE 3

Marketing channel design (p 351)
Intensive distribution (p 352)
Exclusive distribution (p 353)
Selective distribution (p 353)

OBJECTIVE 4

Marketing channel management (p 354)

OBJECTIVE 5

Marketing logistics (physical distribution; p 357)
Supply chain management (p 357)
Distribution center (p 360)
Intermodal transportation (p 362)
Integrated logistics management (p 363)
Third-party logistics (3PL) provider (p 364)

PEARSON
mymarketinglab™

- Check your understanding of the concepts and key terms using the mypearsonmarketinglab study plan for this chapter.
- Apply the concepts in a business context using the simulation entitled **Supply Chain**.

DISCUSSING & APPLYING THE Concepts

Discussing the Issues

1. Describe the key functions performed by marketing channel members. (AACSB: Communication)

2. Compare and contrast direct and indirect marketing channels and discuss the types of *flows* in a distribution channel. (AACSB: Communication)

3. What is a franchise organization? Discuss the types of franchise organizations and give an example of each. (AACSB: Communication; Reflective Thinking)

4. Describe the three strategies available regarding the number of intermediaries and discuss the types of products for which each is appropriate. (AACSB: Communication; Reflective Thinking)

5. Discuss the complexities international marketers face when designing channels in other countries. (AACSB: Communication)

6. List and briefly describe the major logistics functions. Give an example of a decision a logistics manager would make for each major function. (AACSB: Communication; Reflective Thinking)

Applying the Concepts

1. In a small group, debate whether or not the Internet will result in disintermediation of the following retail stores: (1) video rental stores, (2) music stores, and (3) clothing stores. (AACSB: Communication; Reflective Thinking)

2. Consumer packaged goods manufacturers typically distribute products to retailers through wholesalers. However, Walmart deals directly with manufacturers, many having offices in Bentonville, Arkansas, and catering just to Walmart. Discuss the consequences of manufacturers, such as Kraft and P&G, distributing products directly to one or more large retailers while distributing the same products indirectly to smaller retailers through wholesalers. (AACSB: Communication; Reflective Thinking)

3. Visit http://www.youtube.com/watch?v=eob532iEpqk and watch the "The Future Market" video. What impact will RFID tags have on each major logistical function? What are the biggest current obstacles in adopting this technology? (AACSB: Communication; Use of IT; Reflective Thinking)

FOCUS ON Technology

Brewing craft beer is both an art and a science, and Sonia Collin, a Belgian researcher, is trying to devise a way for this highly perishable beer to have a longer shelf life. If successful, brewers can ship more beer longer distances. Hoping to boost exports of homegrown products, the Belgian government is investing $7 million for research, with $1.7 million of that allocated to Ms. Collins' research. A $250,000 tasting machine in her laboratory identifies the chemical compounds in a sample of beer, which allowed researchers to recommend using organic ingredients, adjusting the oxygen and yeast levels, and reducing the time the beer is at high temperatures in the brewing process. Although pasteurization and bottling methods allow giants such as Heineken and

Anheuser to export their brews, aficionados prefer the more delicate flavor of craft beers. But craft brews don't travel well—time and sunlight are its worst enemies—so they are limited to local distribution. Most craft beers lose flavor in less than three months.

1. Describe the channel of distribution for a craft beer from Belgium to your city or town. How many channel levels will be involved? (AACSB: Communication; Reflective Thinking)

2. Discuss the options facing Belgian craft brewers desiring to sell their products in the United States if researchers cannot discover a way to sufficiently extend the shelf life of craft beers. (AACSB: Communication; Reflective Thinking)

FOCUS ON Ethics

Tension is escalating between apparel retailers and suppliers during the economic recovery. Retailers previously placed orders almost a year in advance, and suppliers produced high volumes cheaply. Now many retailers are placing small initial orders, and if styles take off with consumers, they quickly reorder—a tactic known as "chasing." Teen retailer Aeropostale has been buying conservatively and chasing for items that are hot with buyers. Appropriate inventory levels in the apparel industry have always been difficult to predict, but it appears that retailers are pushing this worry back to suppliers.

1. Discuss the concerns of suppliers (i.e., garment makers) and retailers in the apparel channel of distribution. Is it fair that retailers should expect suppliers to respond so quickly? Is it fair that suppliers should demand long lead times? (AACSB: Communication; Ethical Reasoning; Reflective Thinking)

2. What type of channel conflict does this represent? Are there any benefits from this conflict? (AACSB: Communication; Reflective Thinking)

MARKETING & THE Economy

Expedia.com

When the travel business takes a hit, so do travel intermediaries. As individuals and businesses have cut back their travel budgets over the past few years, travel Web sites in general faced financial difficulties. With Priceline.com returning to its "name your own price" roots, competition is becoming tougher than ever. Even Expedia, the market leader, has had to drastically reformulate its strategy to survive. To keep customers from bypassing travel sites and booking directly with airlines, Expedia permanently eliminated its $10 booking fee. Most recently, it has engaged in a new branding campaign called "Where you book matters," which targets frequent leisure travelers and seeks to earn their loyalty. Compared to Priceline's singular focus on price, Expedia is aiming higher up on the food chain.

It wants to establish itself as the generic place to shop for all things travel, highlighting its full range of services. In a market driven by frugality, this approach might seem risky. But as travel now shows signs of renewed life, Expedia might be turning things around quicker than the rest. Its recent U.S. bookings are up 20 percent, compared to a 16 percent increase for Priceline.

1. As an intermediary, does Expedia have power to spur demand when the travel industry suffers?
2. Is Expedia taking the right approach with its branding and promotional strategy?
3. If the economy doesn't recover as quickly as hoped, will Expedia be in good shape?

MARKETING BY THE Numbers

Consumers typically buy products such as toiletries, food, and clothing from retailers rather than directly from the manufacturer. Likewise, retailers buy from wholesalers. Resellers perform functions for the manufacturer and the consumer and mark up the price to reflect that value. Refer to Appendix 2 to answer the following questions.

1. If a manufacturer sells its laundry detergent to a wholesaler for $2.50, at what price will the wholesaler sell it to a retailer

if the wholesaler wants a 15 percent margin based on the selling price? (AACSB: Communication; Analytical Reasoning)

2. If a retailer wants a 20 percent margin based on the selling price, at what price will the retailer sell the product to consumers? (AACSB: Communication; Analytical Reasoning)

VIDEO Case

Progressive

Progressive has attained top-tier status in the insurance industry by focusing on innovation. Progressive was the first company to offer drive-in claims services, installment payment of premiums, and 24/7 customer service. But some of Progressive's most innovative moves involve its channels of distribution. Whereas most insurance companies distribute their products to consumers via intermediary agents or direct-to-consumer methods, Progressive was one of the first companies to recognize the value in doing both. In the late 1980s, it augmented its agency distribution with a direct 800-number channel.

In 1995, Progressive moved into the future by becoming the first major insurer in the world to launch a Web site. In 1997, customers could buy auto insurance policies online in real time. To-

day, at Progressive's Web site, customers can do everything from managing their own account information to reporting claims directly. Progressive even offers one-stop concierge claim service.

After viewing the Progressive video, answer the following questions about marketing channels:

1. Apply the concept of the supply chain to Progressive.
2. Using the model of consumer and business channels found in the chapter, sketch out as many channels for Progressive as you can. How does each of these channels meet distinct customer needs?
3. Discuss the various ways that Progressive has had an impact on the insurance industry.

COMPANY Case

Netflix: Disintermediator or Disintermediated?

Baseball great Yogi Berra, known more for his mangled phrasing than for his baseball prowess, once said, "The future ain't what it used to be." For Netflix, the world's largest online movie-rental ser-

vice, no matter how you say it, figuring out the future is challenging and a bit scary. Netflix faces dramatic changes in how movies and other entertainment content will be distributed. So, will Netflix be among the disintermediat*ors* or among the disintermediat*ed*?

Less than a decade ago, if you wanted to watch a movie in the comfort of your own home, your only choice was to roust yourself out of your recliner and trot down to the local Blockbuster or other neighborhood movie-rental store. Blockbuster is still the world's largest store-rental chain with over 9,000 stores in 25 countries and $4.1 billion in annual sales. But its revenues have been flat or in decline for the past few years. To make matters worse, it has lost money in all but one of the last 13 years—over $550 million in 2009 alone! Blockbuster's stock price has plummeted to a mere $0.28 a share while the company teeters on the brink of bankruptcy. This riches-to-rags story underscores the fact that the old model for distributing movies is simply not working anymore.

One thing about the future is certain. The business of distributing home video is full of disruption and confusion. Things are really changing, and the dust is far from settling. HBO offers its classic subscription service as well as its new premium service, HBO On Demand. Then there's Redbox, the Coinstar Company that rents DVDs for a dollar a day through vending machines in more than 25,000 convenience stores, supermarkets, and fast-food restaurants. That's from a company that no one had even heard of just a few years ago. Adding even more chaos to the mix, Hulu leads the army of start-ups and veterans that show full-length movies, TV shows, and clips for free, as long as you're willing to watch some ads.

THE NETFLIX REVOLUTION

But amid the chaos, Netflix has carved out its own successful niche. Netflix CEO Reed Hastings remains focused on a well-defined strategy with unwavering commitment. That strategy outlines not only what Netflix will do but also what it won't do. The company won't distribute content in brick-and-mortar stores, through vending machines, as pay-per-view, or in an ad-supported format. "Commercial-free subscription is where we can compete. It's our best shot."

Netflix is demonstrating how its model can flexibly reach millions of viewers through various channels. In the late 1990s, Netflix pioneered a new way to rent movies—via the Web and direct mail. For a monthly subscription fee, members could create a movie wish list online. The company would then send out a set of DVDs from that list via the USPS. One of Netflix's main selling points was that members could keep the DVDs as long as they wanted. When they were done with them, they simply returned the DVDs in the mail with a prepaid return envelope. Netflix then automatically sent the next set of DVDs from the member's list.

The Netflix DVD-by-mail model was quickly favored by hundreds of thousands of viewers, then by millions. It's easy to see why. As Netflix's clever ad campaign has been pointing out, there is no hassle or cost from those trips to the video store. There is no worry about late fees. The selection from more than 100,000 DVD titles dwarfs anything that a brick-and-mortar store could hold. Finding rare, old, documentary, or independent films is easy. And the cost of renting—set by members based on how many DVDs they can check out at one time—is always the same and as little as $5 a month.

NOTHING LASTS FOREVER

As much as this Netflix model revolutionized the movie rental business, Hastings quickly points out that it will not last forever. In fact, he predicts that the Netflix core business model will be in decline in as little as three years. What Netflix has in store offers a rare case of how a company manages a still-hot business as it watches the clock tick down. Rather than clinging to an entrenched business model, Netflix is determined to out-innovate its competitors. In fact, in a true sign of forward thinking, Hastings avoided naming the company something catchy like "Movies-by-Mail" when he founded it. He knew that such branding would be far too limiting to allow dynamic change.

Netflix's innovation really took off just a little more than three years ago when it launched Instant Watch, a feature that allowed members to stream videos instantly via their computers as part of their monthly membership fee. At first, the selection was slim—only a few thousand movies available for streaming—and the quality wasn't all that great. But Netflix has been hard at work expanding its library of streaming videos. That library now stands at more than 17,000 films and TV shows and is growing rapidly. And with technology advancements, viewers can watch movies in beautiful high-definition, full-screen splendor.

As media touchpoints exploded, Hastings knew that Netflix's growth would be limited if it streamed only to computers and laptops. So Hastings assembled a team to develop a prototype set-top box that would access the Web through a viewer's broadband connection, allowing members to stream movies remotely to their TVs from the comfort of their couches. Barry McCarthy, Netflix's chief financial officer, recalls that Hastings was so infatuated with the plan that it could be described only as "Apple lust." But just as Netflix neared a public unveiling of the set-top box, Netflix executives had an epiphany. "Are we out of our [minds]?" McCarthy recalls thinking. "We don't even know what we don't know about this business." The Netflix-only set-top box is now available, but Netflix turned it over to Roku, a small electronics company.

At that critical turning point, Hastings and his team realized that they had to move into other distribution points. They decided that it made much more sense to partner with experts who already market popular devices. Netflix moved quickly. Now, every xBox, PlayStation, and Wii has become a home theatre, allowing members full access to Netflix's streaming library. The same access can be had through Blu-ray DVD players and TiVo DVRs.

Hastings also sees a future with Web-enabled TVs. He believes that in five to ten years, viewers will interact with the big screen in the same way they now interact with the small screen. "We'll be calling up movies and channels and Web sites with a click of a button or just a spoken word: 'Wizard of Oz.' Or 'ESPN.' Or 'Netflix.'" In small measure, it's already happening. Instant Watch is available on TVs from Sony, LG, and Vizio. Netflix's streaming service is available only through U.S.-based Web addresses for now. But with a projected 500 million Web-connected devices worldwide by 2013, Netflix plans to expand internationally.

Along with TVs, DVD players, and gaming platforms, Netflix is also moving into mobile devices. It now offers an Instant Watch app for Windows Phone 7 and Apple's iPad and iPhone. Other mobile platforms will follow soon, including Google's Android.

FOCUS ON THE CUSTOMER

As Blockbuster's financial performance has plummeted, Netflix's has skyrocketed. With more than 12 million members and 2.5 billion movie views under its belt, annual revenue has increased 70 percent in the past three years to $1.7 billion. Profits have climbed 130 percent. And in less than two years, Netflix stock has risen from $20 a share to $118. That's a return on investment of more than 500 percent for those savvy enough to have bought in at the right time. Such performance is even more amazing when you consider that it happened in the midst of a global economic meltdown. "We were growing at 25 percent when the economy was growing. We're growing at 25 percent now," says Hastings.

Hastings has no intention of slowing down. And it isn't just about distribution points. The dynamic Hastings is on a crusade to improve the viewing experience of its members. "For most people, they watch one or two movies a week. Only maybe once a month do they get a movie that's like, 'Wow. I loved that movie!'

It really is a hard problem to figure out which ones to watch with your valuable time. We're trying to get it to where every other movie that you watch from Netflix is 'Wow. I loved that movie!' As we get closer to achieving that, we increase human happiness with movies."

Netflix has its work cut out for it. The various delivery models being pursued by its competitors and the complexities of dealing with content producers don't make it any easier. But with unlimited DVDs by mail and unlimited instant streaming to computers, TVs, and other Web-enabled devices for a flat $8.99 a month, the future looks bright for Netflix.

Questions for Discussion

1. As completely as possible, sketch the value chain for Netflix from the production of content to viewer.

2. How do horizontal and vertical conflict impact Netflix?

3. How does Netflix add value for customers through distribution functions?

4. What threats does Netflix face in the future?

5. Will Netflix be successful in the long term? Why or why not?

Sources: Patricia Sellers, "Netflix CEO Focuses on the Future," *Fortune*, July 22, 2009, accessed at http://postcards.blogs.fortune.cnn.com/2009/07/22/netflix-ceo-focuses-on-the-future/; Chuck Salter, "The World's 50 Most Innovative Companies: #12 Netflix," *Fast Company*, February 17, 2010, p. 68; Nick Wingfield, "Netflix Boss Plots Life after the DVD," *Wall Street Journal*, June 23, 2009, p. A1; Beth Snyder Bulik, "How Netflix Stays Ahead of Shifting Consumer Behavior," *Advertising Age*, February 22, 2010, p. 28.

13 Retailing and Wholesaling

Chapter Preview

In the previous chapter, you learned the basics of delivering customer value through good distribution channel design and management. Now, we'll look more deeply into the two major intermediary channel functions: retailing and wholesaling. You already know something about retailing—retailers of all shapes and sizes serve you everyday. However, you probably know much less about the hoard of wholesalers that work behind the scenes. In this chapter, we examine the characteristics of different kinds of retailers and wholesalers, the marketing decisions they make, and trends for the future.

When it comes to retailers, you have to start with Walmart. This megaretailer's phenomenal success has resulted from an unrelenting focus on bringing value to its customers. Day in and day out, Walmart lives up to its promise: "Save money. Live better." That focus on customer value has made Walmart not only the world's largest *retailer* but also the world's largest *company*.

Walmart: The World's Largest *Retailer*—the World's Largest *Company*

Walmart is almost unimaginably big. It's the world's largest retailer—the world's largest company. It rang up an incredible $408 billion in sales last year—1.7 times the sales of competitors Costco, Target, Sears/Kmart, Macy's, JCPenney, and Kohl's *combined*.

Walmart is the number-one seller in several categories of consumer products, including groceries, clothing, toys, CDs, and pet care products. It sells more than twice as many groceries as Kroger, the leading grocery-only food retailer, and its clothing and shoe sales alone last year exceeded the total revenues of Macy's Inc., parent of both Macy's and Bloomingdale's department stores. Incredibly, Walmart sells 30 percent of the disposable diapers purchased in the United States each year, 30 percent of the hair care products, 30 percent of all health and beauty products, 26 percent of the toothpaste, and 20 percent of the pet food. On average, worldwide, Walmart serves customers more than 200 million times per week.

It's also hard to fathom Walmart's impact on the U.S. economy. It's the nation's largest employer—one out of every 220 men, women, and children in the United States is a Walmart associate. Its sales of $1.52 billion on a single day in 2003 exceeded the GDPs of 26 countries. According to one study, Walmart was responsible for about 25 percent of the nation's astonishing productivity gains in the 1990s. Another study found that—through its own low prices and impact on competitors' prices—Walmart saves the average American household $2,500 each year, equivalent to more than six months worth of groceries for the average family.

What's behind this spectacular success? First and foremost, Walmart is passionately dedicated to its long-time, low-price value proposition and what its low prices mean to customers: "Save money. Live better." Its mission is to "lower the world's cost of living." To accomplish this mission, Walmart offers a broad selection of carefully selected goods at "unbeatable low prices." No other retailer has come nearly so close to mastering the concepts of everyday low prices and one-stop shopping. As one analyst put it, "The company gospel . . . is relatively simple: Be an agent for customers—find out what they want and sell it to them for the lowest possible price." Says Walmart's president and CEO, "We're obsessed with delivering value to customers."

How does Walmart make money with such low prices? Walmart is a lean, mean, distribution machine—it has the lowest cost structure in the industry. Low costs let the giant retailer charge lower prices but still reap higher profits. Lower prices attract more shoppers, producing more sales, making the company more efficient, and enabling it to lower prices even more.

Walmart's low costs result in part from superior management and more sophisticated tech-

> Day in and day out, giant Walmart lives up to its promise: "Save money. Live better." Its obsession with customer value has made Walmart not only the world's largest *retailer* but also the world's largest *company*.

nology. Its Bentonville, Arkansas, headquarters contains a computer communications system that the U.S. Department of Defense would envy, giving managers around the country instant access to sales and operating information. And its huge, fully automated distribution centers employ the latest technology to supply stores efficiently.

Walmart also keeps costs down through good old "tough buying." The company is known for the calculated way it wrings low prices from suppliers. "Don't expect a greeter and don't expect friendly," said one supplier's sales executive after a visit to Walmart's buying offices. "Once you are ushered into one of the spartan little buyers' rooms, expect a steely eye across the table and be prepared to cut your price. They are very, very focused people, and they use their buying power more forcefully than anyone else in America."

Some critics argue that Walmart squeezes its suppliers too hard, driving some out of business. Walmart proponents counter, however, that it is simply acting in its customers' interests by forcing suppliers to be more efficient. And most suppliers seem to agree that although Walmart is tough, it's honest and straightforward in its dealings.

Despite its incredible success over the past four decades, mighty Walmart faces some weighty challenges ahead. Having grown so big, the maturing giant is having difficulty maintaining the exploding growth rates of its youth. To reignite growth, Walmart is pushing into new, faster-growing product and service lines, including organic foods, store brands, in-store health clinics, and consumer financial services. It's also pushing its expansion into international markets and online sales. Still, growth remains a daunting task. Think about this: To grow just 7 percent next year, Walmart will have to add nearly $30 billion in new sales. That's a sales *increase* equivalent to the *total* sales of Coca-Cola, DuPont, or more than 1.5 Nikes. That's a lot of growth.

Recently, to refresh its positioning relative to younger, hipper competitors such as Target, Walmart has been giving itself a modest image face-lift. For example, it's spruced up its stores with a cleaner, brighter, more open look and less clutter to make them more shopper-friendly, like Target. It's added some new,

higher-quality merchandise: Many urban Walmarts now carry a slew of higher-end consumer electronics products, from Sony plasma televisions to Dell and Toshiba laptops to Apple iPods. The retailer has also dressed up its apparel racks with more-stylish fashion lines. Finally, Walmart has dropped its old, hard-sell "rollback prices" advertising in favor of softer, more refined lifestyle ads that better support its "Save money. Live better." slogan.

But don't expect Walmart to try to out-Target Target. In fact, given the recently troubled retail economy, Target has moved more toward Walmart than the other way around. During and following the recent recession, Walmart found itself strongly positioned to serve today's thriftier consumers. By contrast, the more stylish Target was forced to drop its prices and margins to avoid losing market share to Walmart. And whereas other retailers' sales suffered in hard times, Walmart's continued to grow.

So even as it brushes up its image, in no way will Walmart ever give up its core low price value proposition. After all, Walmart is and always will be a discount store. "I don't think Walmart's . . . ever going to be edgy," says a Walmart marketer. "I don't think that fits our brand. Our brand is about saving people money" so that they can live better.[1]

At Walmart, the company promises, you'll "Save money. Live better." Says Walmart's CEO, "We're obsessed with delivering value to customers."

The Walmart story sets the stage for examining the fast-changing world of today's resellers. This chapter looks at *retailing* and *wholesaling*. In the first section, we look at the nature and importance of retailing, the major types of store and nonstore retailers, the decisions retailers make, and the future of retailing. In the second section, we discuss these same topics as they apply to wholesalers.

Author Comment	You already know a lot about retailers. You deal with them every day—store retailers, service retailers, online retailers, and others.

Retailing

All the activities involved in selling goods or services directly to final consumers for their personal, nonbusiness use.

Retailer

A business whose sales come *primarily* from retailing.

Retailing (pp 374–394)

What is retailing? We all know that Costco, Home Depot, Macy's, Best Buy, and Target are retailers, but so are Avon representatives, Amazon.com, the local Hampton Inn, and a doctor seeing patients. **Retailing** includes all the activities involved in selling products or services directly to final consumers for their personal, nonbusiness use. Many institutions—manufacturers, wholesalers, and retailers—do retailing. But most retailing is done by **retailers**, businesses whose sales come *primarily* from retailing.

Retailing plays a very important role in most marketing channels. Each year, retailers account for more than $4.1 trillion of sales to final consumers. They connect brands to consumers in what marketing agency OgilvyAction, calls "the last mile"—the final stop in the consumer's path to purchase. It's the "distance a consumer travels between an attitude and an action," explains OgilvyAction's CEO. Some 40 percent of all consumer decisions are made in or near the store. Thus, retailers "reach consumers at key moments of truth, ultimately [influencing] their actions at the point of purchase."[2]

In fact, many marketers are now embracing the concept of **shopper marketing**, using in-store promotions and advertising to extend brand equity to "the last mile" and encourage favorable in-store purchase decisions. ⬤ Shopper marketing recognizes that the retail store itself is an important marketing medium. Thus, marketing must drive shoppers to action at the store level. For example, P&G follows a "store back" concept, in which all marketing ideas need to be effective at the store-shelf level and work back from there. "We are now brand-building from the eyes of the consumer toward us," says a P&G executive.[3]

Point-of-sale marketing inside a large retail store chain can produce the same kinds of numbers as advertising on a hit TV show. For example, whereas 21 million people watch an average episode of *Dancing with the Stars*, even bigger crowds attack the aisles of large retailers. Costco, Walgreens, Safeway, and Kroger attract 20 million, 30 million, 44 million, and 68 million weekly shoppers, respectively. Another 150 million people pass through the automatic doors of Walmart stores across America each week. What's more, unlike TV advertising's remote impact, point-of-sale promotions hit consumers when they are actually making purchase decisions.[4]

⬤ Shopper marketing: Connecting with customers in "the last mile"—all marketing ideas need to be effective at the store-shelf level and work back from there.

Shopper marketing
Using in-store promotions and advertising to extend brand equity to "the last mile" and encourage favorable in-store purchase decisions.

Shopper marketing involves focusing the entire marketing process—from product and brand development to logistics, promotion, and merchandising—toward turning shoppers into buyers at the point of sale. Of course, every well-designed marketing effort focuses on customer buying behavior. But the concept of shopper marketing suggests that these efforts should be coordinated around the shopping process itself. "By starting with the store and working backward, you design an integrated program that make sense to the consumer."[5]

Although most retailing is done in retail stores, in recent years *nonstore retailing* has been growing much faster than store retailing. Nonstore retailing includes selling to final consumers via the Internet, direct mail, catalogs, the telephone, and other direct-selling approaches. We discuss such direct-marketing approaches in detail in Chapter 17. In this chapter, we focus on store retailing.

Types of Retailers

Retail stores come in all shapes and sizes—from your local hairstyling salon or family-owned restaurant to national specialty chain retailers such as REI or Williams-Sonoma to megadiscounters such as Costco or Walmart. The most important types of retail stores are described in ⦾ **Table 13.1** and discussed in the following sections. They can be classified in terms of several characteristics, including the *amount of service* they offer, the breadth and depth of their *product lines*, the *relative prices* they charge, and how they are *organized*.

⦿ **TABLE | 13.1** Major Store Retailer Types

Type	Description	Examples
Specialty store	A store that carries a narrow product line with a deep assortment, such as apparel stores, sporting-goods stores, furniture stores, florists, and bookstores. A clothing store would be a *single-line* store, a men's clothing store would be a *limited-line* store, and a men's custom-shirt store would be a *superspecialty* store.	REI, Radio Shack, Williams-Sonoma
Department store	A store that carries several product lines—typically clothing, home furnishings, and household goods—with each line operated as a separate department managed by specialist buyers or merchandisers.	Macy's, Sears, Neiman Marcus
Supermarket	A relatively large, low-cost, low-margin, high-volume, self-service operation designed to serve the consumer's total needs for grocery and household products.	Kroger, Safeway, Supervalu, Publix
Convenience store	A relatively small store located near residential areas, open long hours seven days a week, and carrying a limited line of high-turnover convenience products at slightly higher prices.	7-Eleven, Stop-N-Go, Circle K, Sheetz
Discount store	A store that carries standard merchandise sold at lower prices with lower margins and higher volumes.	Walmart, Target, Kohl's
Off-price retailer	A store that sells merchandise bought at less-than-regular wholesale prices and sold at less than retail: often leftover goods, overruns, and irregulars obtained at reduced prices from manufacturers or other retailers. These include *factory outlets* owned and operated by manufacturers; *independent off-price retailers* owned and run by entrepreneurs or by divisions of larger retail corporations; and *warehouse (or wholesale) clubs* selling a limited selection of brand-name groceries, appliances, clothing, and other goods at deep discounts to consumers who pay membership fees.	Mikasa (factory outlet); TJ Maxx (independent off-price retailer); Costco, Sam's Club, BJ's Wholesale Club (warehouse clubs)
Superstore	A very large store traditionally aimed at meeting consumers' total needs for routinely purchased food and nonfood items. This category includes *supercenters*, combined supermarket and discount stores, and *category killers*, which carry a deep assortment in a particular category and have a knowledgeable staff.	Walmart Supercenter, SuperTarget, Meijer (discount stores); Best Buy, PetSmart, Staples, Barnes & Noble (category killers)

Amount of Service

Different types of customers and products require different amounts of service. To meet these varying service needs, retailers may offer one of three service levels: self-service, limited service, and full service.

Self-service retailers serve customers who are willing to perform their own "locate-compare-select" process to save time or money. Self-service is the basis of all discount operations and is typically used by retailers selling convenience goods (such as supermarkets) and nationally branded, fast-moving shopping goods (such as Target or Kohl's). *Limited-service retailers*, such as Sears or JCPenney, provide more sales assistance because they carry more shopping goods about which customers need information. Their increased operating costs result in higher prices.

In *full-service retailers*, such as high-end specialty stores (for example, Tiffany or Williams-Sonoma) and first-class department stores (such as Nordstrom or Neiman Marcus), salespeople assist customers in every phase of the shopping process. Full-service stores usually carry more specialty goods for which customers need or want assistance or advice. They provide more services resulting in much higher operating costs, which are passed along to customers as higher prices.

Product Line

Specialty store
A retail store that carries a narrow product line with a deep assortment within that line.

Retailers can also be classified by the length and breadth of their product assortments. Some retailers, such as **specialty stores**, carry narrow product lines with deep assortments within those lines. Today, specialty stores are flourishing. The increasing use of market segmentation, market targeting, and product specialization has resulted in a greater need for stores that focus on specific products and segments.

Department store
A retail organization that carries a wide variety of product lines—each line is operated as a separate department managed by specialist buyers or merchandisers.

In contrast, **department stores** carry a wide variety of product lines. In recent years, department stores have been squeezed between more focused and flexible specialty stores on the one hand and more efficient, lower-priced discounters on the other. In response, many have added promotional pricing to meet the discount threat. Others have stepped up the use of store brands and single-brand "designer shops" to compete with specialty stores. Still others are trying catalog, telephone, and Web selling. Service remains the key differentiating factor. Retailers such as Nordstrom, Saks, Neiman Marcus, and other high-end department stores are doing well by emphasizing exclusive merchandise and high-quality service.

Supermarket
A large, low-cost, low-margin, high-volume, self-service store that carries a wide variety of grocery and household products.

Supermarkets are the most frequently shopped type of retail store. Today, however, they are facing slow sales growth because of slower population growth and an increase in competition from discount supercenters (Walmart) on the one hand and specialty food stores (Whole Foods Market, Trader Joe's) on the other. Supermarkets also have been hit hard by the rapid growth of out-of-home eating over the past two decades. In fact, supermarkets' share of the groceries and consumables market plunged from 89 percent in 1989 to less than 50 percent in 2008.[6] Thus, many traditional supermarkets are facing hard times.

In the battle for "share of stomachs," some supermarkets have moved upscale, providing improved store environments and higher-quality food offerings, such as from-scratch bakeries, gourmet deli counters, natural foods, and fresh seafood departments. Others, however, are attempting to compete head-on with food discounters such as Costco and Walmart, the nation's largest grocery seller, by cutting costs, establishing more-efficient operations, and lowering prices. For example, Kroger, the nation's largest grocery-only retailer has done this successfully:

> Despite the recently sagging economy, while other grocery chains have suffered, Kroger's sales have grown steadily. The chain's seven-year-old strategy of cutting costs and lowering prices has put Kroger in the right position for the times. The food seller's price reductions have been just one part of a four-pronged strategy called "Customer First," by which Kroger seeks to continually improve its response to shopper needs through its prices, products, people, and the shopping experience it creates in its stores. The Customer First effort began at a time when most other traditional supermarkets were trying to distinguish themselves from discount food retailers by emphasizing

● Thanks to customer-focused pricing, despite a sagging economy, leading grocery-only retailer Kroger's sales and market share gains have been the best in the industry. Kroger gives you "more value for the way you live."

Convenience store

A small store, located near a residential area, that is open long hours seven days a week and carries a limited line of high-turnover convenience goods.

higher-level service, quality, and selection. But instead of trying to maintain higher prices, Kroger recognized lower prices as an important part of the changing food-buying experience. Guided by a detailed analysis of customer sales data, it made substantial costs and price cuts, beginning with the most price-sensitive products and categories and then expanding to include additional items each year. To help cost-conscious customers further, Kroger also boosted its private-label offerings. It now offers more than 11,000 private-label items, which account for more than 27 percent of its overall sales. ● Thanks to customer-focused pricing, Kroger's recent sales and market-share gains have been the best in the supermarket industry. The food retailer is now well positioned to take advantage of better economic days ahead.[7]

Convenience stores are small stores that carry a limited line of high-turnover convenience goods. After several years of stagnant sales, convenience stores are now experiencing healthy growth. Last year, U.S. convenience stores posted sales of $624 billion, an 8 percent increase over the previous year. About 75 percent of overall convenience store revenues come from sales of gasoline; a majority of in-store sales are from tobacco products (33 percent) and beer and other beverages (24 percent).[8]

In recent years, convenience store chains have tried to expand beyond their primary market of young, blue-collar men, redesigning their stores to attract female shoppers. They are shedding the image of a "truck stop" where men go to buy beer, cigarettes, or shriveled hot-dogs on a roller grill and are instead offering freshly prepared foods and cleaner, safer, more-upscale environments. ● For example, consider Sheetz, widely recognized as one of the nation's top convenience stores. Driven by its Total Customer Focus mission and the motto "Feel the Love," Sheetz aims to provide "convenience without compromise while being more than just a convenience store. It's our devotion to your satisfaction that makes the difference."[9]

Whether it's for road warriors, construction workers, or soccer moms, Sheetz offers "a mecca for people on the go"—fast, friendly service and quality products in clean and convenient locations. "We really care about our customers," says the company. "If you need to refuel your car or refresh your body, . . . Sheetz has what you need, when you need it. And, we're here 24/7/365." Sheetz certainly isn't your run-of-the-mill convenience store operation. Stores offer up a menu of made-to-order cold and toasted subs, sandwiches, and salads, along with hot fries, onion rings, chicken fingers, and burgers—all ordered through touch-screen terminals. Locations feature Sheetz Bros. Coffeez, a full-service espresso bar staffed by a trained barista. Frozen fruit smoothies round out the menu. To help make paying easier, Sheetz was the first chain in the nation to install system-wide MasterCard PayPass, allowing customers to quickly tap their credit cards and go. Sheetz also partnered with M&T Bank to offer ATM services at any Sheetz without a surcharge. Some analysts say that Sheetz aims to become the Walmart of convenience stores, and it just might get there. The average Sheetz store is nearly twice the size of the average 7-Eleven. And although the privately held company

● Convenience stores: Sheetz positions itself as more than just a convenience store. Driven by its Total Customer Focus mission and the motto "Feel the Love," Sheetz aims to provide "convenience without compromise."

now operates in only six states, it generates sales of more than $3.7 billion. President and CEO Stan Sheetz was recently named by *Chain Store Age* on its list of the top 25 people who have completely changed the way the world does business.

Superstore

A store much larger than a regular supermarket that offers a large assortment of routinely purchased food products, nonfood items, and services.

Superstores are much larger than regular supermarkets and offer a large assortment of routinely purchased food products, nonfood items, and services. Walmart, Target, Meijer, and other discount retailers offer *supercenters*, very large combination food and discount stores. Whereas a traditional grocery store brings in about $333,000 a week in sales, a supercenter brings in about $1.5 million a week. Walmart, which opened its first supercenter in 1988, now has more than 2,750 supercenters worldwide and is opening new ones at a rate of about 140 per year.[10]

Recent years have also seen the explosive growth of superstores that are actually giant specialty stores, the so-called **category killers** (e.g., Best Buy, Home Depot, and PetSmart). They feature stores the size of airplane hangars that carry a very deep assortment of a particular line with a knowledgeable staff. Category killers are prevalent in a wide range of categories, including electronics, home-improvement products, books, baby gear, toys, linens and towels, party goods, sporting goods, and even pet supplies.

Category killer

A giant specialty store that carries a very deep assortment of a particular line and is staffed by knowledgeable employees.

Service retailer

A retailer whose product line is actually a service, including hotels, airlines, banks, colleges, and many others.

Finally, for many retailers, the product line is actually a service. **Service retailers** include hotels and motels, banks, airlines, colleges, hospitals, movie theaters, tennis clubs, bowling alleys, restaurants, repair services, hair salons, and dry cleaners. Service retailers in the United States are growing faster than product retailers.

Relative Prices

Retailers can also be classified according to the prices they charge (see Table 13.1). Most retailers charge regular prices and offer normal-quality goods and customer service. Others offer higher-quality goods and service at higher prices. Retailers that feature low prices are discount stores and "off-price" retailers.

Discount store

A retail operation that sells standard merchandise at lower prices by accepting lower margins and selling at higher volume.

Discount Stores. A **discount store** (e.g., Target, Kmart, and Walmart) sells standard merchandise at lower prices by accepting lower margins and selling higher volume. The early discount stores cut expenses by offering few services and operating in warehouselike facilities in low-rent, heavily traveled districts.

Today's discounters have improved their store environments and increased their services, while at the same time keeping prices low through lean, efficient operations. Leading "big-box" discounters, such as Walmart, Costco, and Target, now dominate the retail scene. However, even "small-box" discounters are thriving in the current economic environment. For example, dollar stores are now today's fastest-growing retail format. Dollar General, the nation's largest small-box discount retailer, makes a powerful value promise for the times: "Save time. Save money. Every day." (See Real Marketing 13.1.)

Off-price retailer

A retailer that buys at less-than-regular wholesale prices and sells at less than retail. Examples are factory outlets, independents, and warehouse clubs.

Off-Price Retailers. As the major discount stores traded up, a new wave of **off-price retailers** moved in to fill the ultralow-price, high-volume gap. Ordinary discounters buy at regular wholesale prices and accept lower margins to keep prices down. In contrast, off-price retailers buy at less-than-regular wholesale prices and charge consumers less than retail. Off-price retailers can be found in all areas, from food, clothing, and electronics to no-frills banking and discount brokerages.

Independent off-price retailer

An off-price retailer that is either independently owned and run or is a division of a larger retail corporation.

The three main types of off-price retailers are *independents*, *factory outlets*, and *warehouse clubs*. **Independent off-price retailers** either are independently owned and run or are divisions of larger retail corporations. Although many off-price operations are run by smaller independents, most large off-price retailer operations are owned by bigger retail chains. Examples include store retailers such as TJ Maxx and Marshalls, owned by TJX Companies, and Web sellers such as Overstock.com.

Factory outlet

An off-price retailing operation that is owned and operated by a manufacturer and normally carries the manufacturer's surplus, discontinued, or irregular goods.

Factory outlets—manufacturer-owned and operated stores by firms such as J. Crew, Gap, Levi Strauss, and others—sometimes group together in *factory outlet malls* and *value-retail centers*, where dozens of outlet stores offer prices as much as 50 percent below retail on a wide range of mostly surplus, discounted, or irregular goods. Whereas outlet malls consist primarily of manufacturers' outlets, value-retail centers combine manufacturers' outlets

Real Marketing 13.1

Dollar General:
Today's Hottest Retailing Format

"Save time. Save money. Every day." Given today's economics, that sounds like a winning proposition. In fact, it's the slogan of discount retailer Dollar General—and it *is* a winning proposition. "Dollar stores" and other hard discounters are today's hottest retailing format, and Dollar General is the nation's leading dollar store.

Whereas the Walmarts, Costcos, and Targets of the world are "big-box" discounters, Dollar General and the other dollar stores are "small-box" discounters. They are still only a relatively small threat to their bigger rivals; the combined annual sales of all dollar stores amount to only about 15 percent of Walmart's annual sales. But they are by far the fastest-growing threat. In the recent down economy, as the big-box discounters have struggled, the dollar stores have spurted, rapidly adding new stores, customers, and sales. "Nowhere in the retail world are we seeing more growth than from the dollar store sector," says a retailing analyst.

For example, Dollar General's cash registers are really ringing these days. Over the past 40 years, the retailer's sales have grown from $40 million to nearly $12 billion—an average growth rate of 14 percent a year. During the past two years, even as the economy withered and competitors' sales suffered, Dollar General's same-store sales grew more than 9 percent each year. The company now operates 8,800 stores in 35 states, and it plans to open 600 new stores this year and overhaul another 500. It plans eventually to grow to more than 12,000 stores (about equivalent to the number of McDonald's restaurants nationwide and more than 20 times the number of Target stores).

What's the story behind Dollar General's success? If you haven't been in a dollar store lately, you might be surprised at what you'd find. Back in the day, dollar stores sold mostly odd-lot assortments of novelties, factory overruns, closeouts, and outdated merchandise—most priced at $1. Not anymore. "Dollar stores have come a long way, baby," says another retailing analyst. "The Great Recession accelerated the iconic American chains' transformation from purveyors of kitschy $1 trinkets to discounters in a position to lure shoppers from

the likes of supermarkets, drugstores, and Walmart stores." Dollar General now sells a carefully selected assortment of mostly brand-name items. More than two-thirds of its sales come from groceries and household goods. And it isn't really a "dollar store" anymore. Only 25 percent of its merchandise is now priced at a dollar or less.

Dollar General's "Save time. Save money. Every day." slogan isn't just for show. It's a carefully crafted statement of the store's value promise. The company sums up its positioning this way: "Our goal is to provide our customers a better life, and we think our customers are best served when we keep it real and keep it simple. We make shopping for everyday needs simpler and hassle-free by offering a carefully edited assortment of the most popular brands at low everyday prices in small, convenient locations."

Dollar General saves customers time by keeping things simple. Its carefully edited product assortment includes only about 12,000 core items (compared with 47,000 items in an average supermarket or 142,000 items in a Walmart supercenter). But Dollar General still stocks your favorite sizes and many of your favorite quality brands, such as Coca-Cola, Bounty, Palmolive, Hefty, Kraft, Folgers, and Betty Crocker. Dollar General has even added brands such as Hanes underwear, L'Oreal cosmetics, and Rexall vitamins and herbal supplements.

Keeping it simple also means smaller stores. Dollar General stores average about 7,100 square feet in size—you could fit more than 25 Dollar General stores inside the average Walmart supercenter. And most stores are located in convenient strip malls. That means customers can usually park right in front of a store. Once inside, they encounter fewer aisles to navigate, fewer goods to consider, and smaller crowds to

out-wrangle than in big-box stores. All that adds up to a quick trip. The average Dollar General customer is in and out of the store in less than 10 minutes. Although Dollar General is experimenting with larger format stores that carry produce, meat, and baked goods, those Super Dollar Generals are still much, much smaller and more manageable than a Walmart supercenter.

As for the "save money" part of the value promise, Dollar General's prices on the brand-name products it carries are an estimated 20–40 percent lower than grocery store prices and are roughly in line with those of the big-name discount stores. There are also plenty of savings to be had on dollar items and the increasing selection of Dollar General private-label merchandise. Finally, Dollar General gets a boost from customer perceptions of its dollar store format. Even though only about 25 percent of its goods are priced at $1 or less, almost anything in the store can be had for less than $10. That lends assurance that not only draws customers in but also allows them to shop a little more freely than they would elsewhere.

Keeping things simple for consumers also benefits the company's bottom line. Smaller stores are less expensive to operate, and locating them in smaller markets and less glamorous neighborhoods keeps real estate costs down as well. Dollar General's cost per square foot is as low as one-tenth that of supermarkets. Cheaper stores have also allowed Dollar General to build more of them. In fact, Dollar General now has more stores in the United States than any other discounter.

Discounter Dollar General, the nation's largest small-box discount retailer, makes a powerful value promise for the times: "Save time. Save money. Every day."

Continued on next page

Dollar General's product mix strategy also contributes to its financial performance. Although it carries top brands, it leans toward brands that are not market leaders. Customers are more likely to encounter Gain than Tide. Stores don't stock products in all sizes, just the ones that sell the best. Finally, Dollar General's merchandise buyers focus on getting the best deals possible at any given time. This opportunistic buying might mean Heinz ketchup one month and Hunts the next. Such practices contribute to lower costs and higher margins.

The recently sagging economy gave Dollar General and other dollar stores a real boost as consumers looked for ways to cut their spending. Not only is Dollar General attracting more sales from existing customers, it's also attracting new higher-income customers. A recent survey showed that 65 percent of consumers with incomes under $50,000 had shopped at a dollar store in the past three months. However, 47 percent of households with incomes over $100,000 had done so as well. Although its core customers are still those who make less than $40,000 a year, Dollar General's fastest-growth segment is those earning more than $75,000 a year.

Put it all together, and things are sizzling right now at the nation's largest small-box discount retailer. Dollar General has the right value proposition for the times. But what will happen to Dollar General and its fellow dollar stores as economic conditions improve? Will newly acquired customers abandon them and return to their previous shopping haunts?

Dollar General doesn't think so. Dollar stores seem to do as well in good times as in bad. The format had already been growing at a healthy rate before the economy soured. And customers who recently switched over show no signs of relapsing into their old, free-spending ways. We "see signs of a new consumerism," says Dollar General's CEO, as people shift where they shop, switch to lower-cost brands, and stay generally more frugal. And company research shows that 97 percent of new customers plan to continue shopping at Dollar General even if the economy improves, the same percentage as old customers. Low prices and convenience, it seems, will not soon go out of style.

Sources: Mary Ellen Lloyd, "Dollar General Profit Rises 6.5%," *Wall Street Journal*, March 31, 2010; Suzanne Kapner, "The Mighty Dollar," *Fortune*, April 15, 2009, accessed at http://money.cnn.com/2009/04/14/news/companies/kapner_dollar.fortune/index.htm; Jack Neff, "Stuck-in-the-Middle Walmart Starts to Lose Share," *Advertising Age*, March 8, 2010, pp. 1, 23; Kelly Evans, "Dollar General Flexing Its Discount Muscle," *Wall Street Journal*, March 31, 2010, accessed at www.wsj.com; and information from www.dollargeneral.com, accessed November 2010.

with off-price retail stores and department store clearance outlets. Factory outlet malls have become one of the hottest growth areas in retailing.

The malls in general are now moving upscale—and even dropping "factory" from their descriptions. A growing number of outlet malls now feature luxury brands such as Coach, Polo Ralph Lauren, Dolce&Gabbana, Giorgio Armani, Burberry, and Versace. As consumers become more value-minded, even upper-end retailers are accelerating their factory outlet strategies, placing more emphasis on outlets such as Nordstrom Rack, Neiman Marcus Last Call, Bloomingdale's Outlets, and Saks Off 5th. Many companies now regard outlets not simply as a way of disposing of problem merchandise but as an additional way of gaining business for fresh merchandise.

The combination of highbrow brands and lowbrow prices found at outlets provides powerful shopper appeal, especially in a tighter economy:[11]

> Faced with unprecedented sales declines at full-price stores, a growing group of high-end retailers and luxury brands are building more factory outlets, where sales have fared much better. It is a strategy that would likely have backfired during the 1980s recession when outlets were bare-bones boxes built in the middle of nowhere and designers routinely cut out labels before selling them to off-price retailers to protect their brand's cachet. "These days, customers are saying they want a brand, customer service, *and* a deal," says the president of Saks's Off 5th outlet division.
>
> What else explains the host of weekday afternoon shoppers recently standing elbow to elbow inside a Coach factory store, as word of an unadvertised sale spread around one outdoor mall? Two clerks directed traffic at the door. Another walked in and out of the stock room armed with fresh handbags and wallets. Three cashiers rang up sales as customers stood in line. Shopper Joan Nichols scored a $458 violet leather satchel from Coach's Parker collection for $145. Her 19-year-old daughter bought a $468 cream Coach logo handbag for $130. Their savings: about 70 percent each. "If [spending's tight]," Nichols said, "it's not apparent here."

Warehouse clubs (or *wholesale clubs* or *membership warehouses*), such as Costco, Sam's Club, and BJ's, operate in huge, drafty, warehouselike facilities and offer few frills. However, they offer ultralow prices and surprise deals on selected branded merchandise. Warehouse

Warehouse club
An off-price retailer that sells a limited selection of brand name grocery items, appliances, clothing, and a hodgepodge of other goods at deep discounts to members who pay annual membership fees.

clubs have grown rapidly in recent years. These retailers appeal not only to low-income consumers seeking bargains on bare-bones products but also all kinds of customers shopping for a wide range of goods, from necessities to extravagances.

Consider Costco, now the nation's third-largest retailer, behind only Walmart and Kroger. Low price is an important part of Costco's equation, but what really sets Costco apart is the products it carries and the sense of urgency that it builds into the Costco shopper's store experience.[12]

⦿ **Warehouse clubs: Costco is a retail treasure hunt, where one's shopping cart could contain a $50,000 diamond ring resting on top of a vat of mayonnaise.**

Costco brings flair to an otherwise dreary setting. Alongside the gallon jars of peanut butter and 2,250-count packs of Q-Tips, Costco offers an ever-changing assortment of high-quality products—even luxuries—all at tantalizingly low margins. ⦿ As one industry analyst puts it, "Costco is a retail treasure hunt, where one's shopping cart could contain a $50,000 diamond ring resting on top of a vat of mayonnaise." It's the place where high-end products meet deep-discount prices. In just one year, Costco sold 91 million hot dog and soda combinations (still only $1.50 as they have been for more than 25 years). At the same time, it sold more than 96,000 carats of diamonds at up to $100,000 per item. It's the nation's biggest baster of poultry (77,000 rotisserie chickens a day at $4.99) but also the country's biggest seller of fine wines (including the likes of a Chateau Cheval Blanc Premier Grand Cru Classe at $1,750 a bottle). It once even offered a Pablo Picasso drawing at Costco.com for only $129,999.99!

Each Costco store is a theater of retail that creates buying urgency and excitement for customers. Mixed in with its regular stock of staples, Costco features a glittering, constantly shifting array of one-time specials, such as discounted Prada bags, Calloway golf clubs, or Kenneth Cole bags—deals you just won't find anywhere else. In fact, of the 4,000 items that Costco carries, 1,000 are designated as "treasure items" (Costco's words). The changing assortment and great prices keep people coming back, wallets in hand. There was a time when only the great, unwashed masses shopped at off-price retailers, but Costco has changed all that. Even people who don't have to pinch pennies shop there.

Organizational Approach

Although many retail stores are independently owned, others band together under some form of corporate or contractual organization. The major types of retail organizations—*corporate chains*, *voluntary chains*, *retailer cooperatives*, and *franchise organizations* are described in ⦿ **Table 13.2**.

Chain stores
Two or more outlets that are commonly owned and controlled.

Chain stores are two or more outlets that are commonly owned and controlled. They have many advantages over independents. Their size allows them to buy in large quantities at lower prices and gain promotional economies. They can hire specialists to deal with areas such as pricing, promotion, merchandising, inventory control, and sales forecasting.

The great success of corporate chains caused many independents to band together in one of two forms of contractual associations. One is the *voluntary chain*—a wholesaler-sponsored group of independent retailers that engages in group buying and common merchandising. Examples include the Independent Grocers Alliance (IGA), Western Auto, and Do-It Best. The other type of contractual association is the *retailer cooperative*—a group of independent retailers that bands together to set up a jointly owned, central wholesale operation and conduct joint merchandising and promotion efforts. Examples are Associated Grocers and Ace Hardware. These organizations give independents the buying and promotion economies they need to meet the prices of corporate chains.

Franchise
A contractual association between a manufacturer, wholesaler, or service organization (a franchisor) and independent businesspeople (franchisees) who buy the right to own and operate one or more units in the franchise system.

Another form of contractual retail organization is a **franchise**. The main difference between franchise organizations and other contractual systems (voluntary chains and retail

● **TABLE | 13.2** Major Types of Retail Organizations

Type	Description	Examples
Corporate chain store	Two or more outlets that are commonly owned and controlled. Corporate chains appear in all types of retailing, but they are strongest in department stores, discount stores, food stores, drug stores, and restaurants.	Sears (department stores), Target (discount stores), Kroger (grocery stores), CVS (drugstores)
Voluntary chain	Wholesaler-sponsored group of independent retailers engaged in group buying and merchandising.	Independent Grocers Alliance (IGA), Do-It Best (hardware), Western Auto, True Value
Retailer cooperative	Group of independent retailers who jointly establish a central buying organization and conduct joint promotion efforts.	Associated Grocers (groceries), Ace Hardware (hardware)
Franchise organization	Contractual association between a franchisor (a manufacturer, wholesaler, or service organization) and franchisees (independent businesspeople who buy the right to own and operate one or more units in the franchise system).	McDonald's, Subway, Pizza Hut, Jiffy Lube, Meineke Mufflers, 7-Eleven

cooperatives) is that franchise systems are normally based on some unique product or service; a method of doing business; or the trade name, goodwill, or patent that the franchisor has developed. Franchising has been prominent in fast-food restaurants, motels, health and fitness centers, auto sales and service, and real estate.

But franchising covers a lot more than just burger joints and fitness centers. Franchises have sprung up to meet just about any need. For example, Mad Science Group franchisees put on science programs for schools, scout troops, and birthday parties. And Mr. Handyman provides repair services for homeowners, while Merry Maids tidies up their houses.

Once considered upstarts among independent businesses, franchises now command 40 percent of all retail sales in the United States. ● These days, it's nearly impossible to stroll down a city block or drive on a city street without seeing a McDonald's, Subway, Jiffy Lube, or Holiday Inn. One of the best-known and most successful franchisers, McDonald's, now has 32,000 stores in 118 countries, including almost 14,000 in the United States. It serves 58 million customers a day and racks up more than $54 billion in annual systemwide sales. Nearly 80 percent of McDonald's restaurants worldwide are owned and operated by franchisees. Gaining fast is Subway, one of the fastest-growing franchises, with more than 32,000 shops in 91 countries, including more than 23,000 in the United States.[13]

Retailer Marketing Decisions

Retailers are always searching for new marketing strategies to attract and hold customers. In the past, retailers attracted customers with unique product assortments and more or better services. Today, retail assortments and services are looking more and more alike. Many national-brand manufacturers, in their drive for volume, have placed their brands almost

● **Franchising: These days, it's nearly impossible to stroll down a city block or drive on a suburban street without seeing a McDonald's, Jiffy Lube, Subway, or Holiday Inn.**

everywhere. You can find most consumer brands not only in department stores but also in mass-merchandise discount stores, off-price discount stores, and all over the Web. Thus, it's now more difficult for any one retailer to offer exclusive merchandise.

Service differentiation among retailers has also eroded. Many department stores have trimmed their services, whereas discounters have increased theirs. Customers have become smarter and more price sensitive. They see no reason to pay more for identical brands, especially when service differences are shrinking. For all these reasons, many retailers today are rethinking their marketing strategies.

As shown in ◉ **Figure 13.1**, retailers face major marketing decisions about *segmentation and targeting*, *store differentiation and positioning*, and the *retail marketing mix*.

Segmentation, Targeting, Differentiation, and Positioning Decisions

Retailers must first segment and define their target markets and then decide how they will differentiate and position themselves in these markets. Should the store focus on upscale, midscale, or downscale shoppers? Do target shoppers want variety, depth of assortment, convenience, or low prices? Until they define and profile their markets, retailers cannot make consistent decisions about product assortment, services, pricing, advertising, store décor, or any of the other decisions that must support their positions.

Too many retailers, even big ones, fail to clearly define their target markets and positions. For example, what market does the clothing chain Gap target? What is its value proposition and positioning? If you're having trouble answering those questions, you're not alone—so is Gap's management.[14]

Gap was founded in San Francisco in 1969 by Doris and Don Fisher with the intent to "make it easier to find a pair of jeans." By its heyday in the late 1980s and early 1990s, Gap was solidly positioned on the then-fashionable preppy look. But as its core customers aged and moved on, Gap stores didn't. In the past five years, as the chain has struggled unsuccessfully to define new positioning that works with today's younger shoppers, Gap store sales have slipped more than 22 percent. Says one industry expert, "Gap is in danger of death by a thousand cuts. Abercrombie & Fitch does the authentic preppy look. Uniqlo sells staples such as cashmere [sweaters] and scarves for a penny apiece. Primark, Topshop, and Zara offer access to high-end fashion cheaply, so what is left?" Agrees another expert, "Right now, Gap could be anything. It hasn't got a story." The answer? Gap needs to "define who the brand's core customers are and be exceptional to them; make distinctive and desirable clothes; and be noticed."

In contrast, successful retailers define their target markets well and position themselves strongly. For example, Walmart positions itself strongly on low prices and what those always

◉ **FIGURE** | **13.1**
Retailer Marketing Strategy

Retail strategy	Retail marketing mix
Retail segmentation and targeting	Product and service assortment
Store differentiation and positioning	Retail prices
	Promotion
	Distribution (location)

Create value for targeted retail customers

As with other types of marketers, the name of the game for retailers is to find the customer-driven marketing strategy and mix that will let them create value for customers and capture value in return. Remember Trader Joe's "cheap gourmet" value proposition? And Olive Garden's "When you're here, you're family"?

● Retail targeting and positioning: Whole Foods Market succeeds by positioning itself strongly away from Walmart and other discounters. A devoted Whole Foods Market customer is more likely to boycott the local Walmart than to shop at it.

low prices mean to its customers. It promises that customers will "Save money. Live better."

But if giant Walmart owns the low-price position, how can other retailers hope to compete? Again, the answer is good targeting and positioning. For example, Whole Foods Market has fewer than 300 stores and slightly more than $8 billion in sales versus Walmart's more than 8,400 stores worldwide and sales of $408 billion.[15] How does this small grocery chain compete with Walmart? It doesn't—at least not directly. ● Whole Foods Market succeeds by carefully positioning itself *away* from Walmart (remember the Whole Foods Market story in Chapter 10?). It targets a select group of upscale customers and offers them "organic, natural, and gourmet foods, all swaddled in Earth Day politics." In fact, a devoted Whole Foods Market customer is more likely to boycott the local Walmart than to shop at it.

Whole Foods Market can't match Walmart's massive economies of scale, incredible volume purchasing power, ultraefficient logistics, wide selection, and hard-to-beat prices. But then again, it doesn't even try. By positioning itself strongly away from Walmart and other discounters, Whole Foods Market has grown rapidly over the past two decades and is now more than holding its own, even in tighter economic times.

Product Assortment and Services Decision

Retailers must decide on three major product variables: product assortment, services mix, and store atmosphere.

The retailer's product assortment should differentiate the retailer while matching target shoppers' expectations. One strategy is to offer merchandise that no other competitor carries, such as store brands or national brands on which it holds exclusives. For example, Saks gets exclusive rights to carry a well-known designer's labels. It also offers its own private-label lines—the Saks Fifth Avenue Signature, Classic, and Sport collections. At JCPenney, private-label and exclusive brands account for 52 percent of its sales.[16]

Another strategy is to feature blockbuster merchandising events. Bloomingdale's is known for running spectacular shows featuring goods from a certain country, such as India or China. Or the retailer can offer surprise merchandise, as when Costco offers surprise assortments of seconds, overstocks, and closeouts. Finally, the retailer can differentiate itself by offering a highly targeted product assortment: Lane Bryant carries plus-size clothing; Brookstone offers an unusual assortment of gadgets and gifts; and BatteryDepot.com offers about every imaginable kind of replacement battery.

The *services mix* can also help set one retailer apart from another. For example, some retailers invite customers to ask questions or consult service representatives in person or via phone or keyboard. Nordstrom promises to "take care of the customer, no matter what it takes." Home Depot offers a diverse mix of services to do-it-yourselfers, from "how-to" classes and "do-it-herself" and kid workshops to a proprietary credit card.

The *store's atmosphere* is another important element in the reseller's product arsenal. Retailers want to create a unique store experience, one that suits the target market and moves customers to buy. Many retailers practice "experiential retailing." ● For example, at several REI stores, consumers can get hands-on experience with merchandise before buying it via the store's mountain bike test trail, gear-testing stations, a huge rock climbing wall, or an in-store simulated rain shower. Similarly, outdoor goods retailer Cabela's stores are as much natural history museums for outdoor enthusiasts as they are retail outlets (see Real Marketing 13.2).

● Experiential retailing: At this REI store, consumers can get hands-on experience with merchandise via the store's mountain bike test trail, gear-testing stations, a huge rock climbing wall, or an in-store simulated rain shower.

Real Marketing 13.2

Cabela's: Creating a Sense of Wonder for People Who Hate to Shop

At first glance, outdoor-products retailer Cabela's seems to break all the rules of retailing. First, it locates its stores in tiny, off-the-beaten-path locations—places like Sidney, Nebraska; Prairie du Chien, Wisconsin; Dundee, Michigan; Owatonna, Minnesota; and Gonzales, Louisiana. Then, to make matters worse, it targets customers who hate to shop! The typical Cabela's customer is a reclusive male outdoorsman who yearns for the great outdoors, someone who detests jostling crowds and shopping.

So how do you explain Cabela's success? Over the past decade, Cabela's has evolved from a mail-order catalog business into a popular $2.6 billion multichannel retailer. Despite Cabela's often remote locations, customers flock to its 31 superstores to buy hunting, fishing, and outdoor gear. A typical Cabela's store draws 4.4 million customers a year—an average of 40,000 customers on a Saturday and 50,000–100,000 on a holiday weekend. Half of Cabela's customers drive 100 miles or more to get there, and many travel up to 350 miles. Schools even send busloads of kids.

Cabela's isn't just a store chain; it's a name with star power. According to reporters' accounts:

> When a store opened in Scottsdale, Arizona, two news helicopters hovered overhead as if covering some celebrity wedding. In other cities, customers pitched tents and camped out to be the first in the store. Some 3,500 eager customers showed up for the recent opening of a new Billings, Montana, location. Most arrived three or more hours early, and it took nearly 20 minutes for the crowd, pouring constantly through the door shoulder-to-shoulder, to get in the store. Cars with license plates from all over the state were parked in the lot. One Canadian couple even drove down from Alberta just to see the store.

In fact, Cabela's stores have become tourist destinations. Its store in Michigan is the state's largest tourist attraction, drawing more than 6 million people a year. The Minnesota store trails only the Mall of America in the number of annual visitors. And the Cabela's in Sidney, Nebraska, a town of only 6,200 people

located 150 miles from the nearest major city (Denver), attracts 1.2 million visitors a year, making it Nebraska's second-largest tourist attraction behind the Omaha Zoo. In all, Cabela's captures an astonishing 37 cents of every retail dollar spent by hunters.

Just what is it that attracts these hordes of otherwise reluctant shoppers to Cabela's remote stores? Part of the answer lies in all the stuff the stores sell. Cabela's huge superstores (as much as 1.5 times larger than a typical Walmart supercenter) house a vast assortment of quality merchandise at reasonable prices. Cabela's competes on price with discounters but carries a selection that's six to ten times deeper—more than 200,000 kinds of items for hunting, fishing, boating, camping, and archery.

Cabela's also sells lines of branded clothing and gifts that appeal to customers' wives and children, making it a popular stop for the whole family. And to top things off, Cabela's offers first-class service. It staffs its departments with a generous supply of employees, all of whom must pass a 100-question test on the products they sell. For customers who stop by during hunting trips, Cabela's even offers the use of outdoor kennels and corrals to house their hunting dogs or horses while they shop. Hunters with rifles are welcomed.

But deep product assortments and good service don't explain the huge crowds that show up at Cabela's. The retailer's real magic lies in the *experiences* it creates for those who visit. "This is more than a place to go get fishhooks," says a Cabela's spokesperson. "The Cabelas"—Nebraska brothers Dick and Jim—"wanted to create a sense of wonder." Mission accomplished! In each of its stores, Cabela's has created what amounts to a natural history theme park for outdoor enthusiasts.

Take the store near Fort Worth, Texas, for example. Dominating the center of the store is Conservation Mountain, a two-story mountain replica with two waterfalls and cascading streams. The mountain is divided into four ecosystems and five bioregions: a Texas prairie, an Alaskan habitat, an Arctic icecap, an American woodland, and an Alpine mountaintop. Each bioregion is populated by lifelike, museum-quality taxidermy animals in action poses—everything from prairie dogs, deer, elk, and caribou to brown bears, polar bears, musk oxen, and mountain goats.

Elsewhere in the store, Cabela's has created an African diorama, complete with African animals depicted in their natural habitats—an

Store atmosphere: Cabela's real magic lies in the experiences it creates for those who visit. **"This is more than a place to go get fishhooks . . . we wanted to create a sense of wonder."**

Continued on next page

elephant, a rhinoceros, a Cape buffalo, and lions downing their prey. Other store attractions include a trophy deer museum and three walk-through aquariums, where visitors can view trophy-quality freshwater fish and learn to identify them. Getting hungry? Drop by the Mesquite Grill café for an elk, ostrich, or wild boar sandwich—no Big Macs here! The nearby General Store offers old-fashioned candy and snacks.

Cabela's spares no expense in developing this sportsman's paradise. A stuffed polar bear can cost up to $10,000. The Fort Worth store presents 800 such animals, right down to a Texas rattlesnake. Cabela's even created a new executive post—the taxidermy purchasing specialist—a person who seeks out stuffed animals and mounts them in authentic scenes—two grizzly bears locked in battle, a leopard leaping for a monkey—even the droppings are real. "The muscle tone of the animal, the eyes, the posture—everything must be just right," says the executive. The taxidermy collection at Cabela's Fort Worth store is twice as large as the one at the Fort Worth Museum of Science and History. Cabela's shoppers typically spend

an hour or more touring the wildlife displays before they start shopping.

So, if you scratch a little deeper, you will find that far from breaking the rules, Cabela's is doing all the right things. It's creating total experiences that delight the senses as well as the wallets of carefully targeted customers. Put it all together and you've got a powerful magnet for outdoorsmen and their families. Just ask one of the millions of anything-but-reluctant Cabela's customers:

> Mike and Jolene Lande brought their four-year-old son, Isaiah, to the Billings, Montana, grand opening just to browse. Jolene says she's been to six other Cabela's stores; it's a family tradition to stop at them while on road trips. "It's just awesome in there," says Mike.

"I'll do just about anything to avoid shopping," says John Brown, a small-business owner in Cheyenne, Wyoming. In 35 years of marriage, his wife says she's persuaded him to go shopping only twice. Yet one day last month he invited her to drive 100 miles with him for a day of shopping at Cabela's. "I'm like a kid in a candy store here," he said, dropping a new tackle box into his cart.

The trick is appealing to the family member who is usually the most reluctant to shop—Dad. One recent morning, Lara Miller was trying to round up her husband and three kids, as their morning trip to Cabela's stretched into the afternoon. Mrs. Miller—normally the only family member who likes to shop—now was the one most ready to leave. "We haven't had breakfast yet," she moaned. Her husband, Darren Miller, a farmer in Jerome, Idaho, said, "I love this place."

Sources: Extracts, quotes, and other information from "Cabela's Has Lived up to Its Hype," *McClatchy-Tribune Business News,* March 31, 2010; Zach Benoit, "New Cabela's Packs Them In," *McClatchy-Tribune Business News,* May 15, 2009; Heather Landy, "Plenty in Store," *McClatchy-Tribune Business News,* May 22, 2005, p. 1; Kevin Helliker, "Hunter Gatherer: Rare Retailer Scores by Targeting Men Who Hate to Shop," *Wall Street Journal,* December 17, 2002, p. A1; Bud Kennedy, "Bud Kennedy Column," *Fort Worth Star-Telegram,* May 26, 2005, p. 1; "Bargain Hunting," *Fortune,* November 24, 2008, p. 16; Jan Falstad, "Outdoor Retailer Adds New Dynamic to Local Marketplace," *McClatchy-Tribune Business News,* May 10, 2009; and information from www.cabelas.com, accessed October 2010.

Today's successful retailers carefully orchestrate virtually every aspect of the consumer store experience. The next time you step into a retail store—whether it sells consumer electronics, hardware, or high fashion—stop and carefully consider your surroundings. Think about the store's layout and displays. Listen to the background sounds. Smell the smells. Chances are good that everything in the store, from the layout and lighting to the music and even the smells, has been carefully orchestrated to help shape the customer's shopping experience—and open their wallets. At a Sony Style store, for instance, the environment is designed to encourage touch, from the silk wallpaper to the smooth maple wood cabinets, to the etched-glass countertops. Products are displayed like museum pieces and are set up to be touched and tried.

Perhaps the hottest store environment frontier these days is scent—that's right, the way the store smells. Most large retailers are developing "signature scents" that you smell only in their stores:[17]

Luxury shirtmaker Thomas Pink pipes the smell of clean, pressed shirts into its stores—its signature "line-dried linen" scent. Bloomingdale's uses different essences in different departments: the soft scent of baby powder in the baby store, coconut in the swimsuit area, lilacs in intimate apparel, and sugar cookies and evergreen scent during the holiday season. At a Sony Style store, the subtle fragrance of vanilla and mandarin orange—designed exclusively for Sony—wafts down on shoppers, relaxing them and helping them believe that this is a very nice place to be. Such scents can increase customer "dwell times" and, in turn, buying. Says the founder of ScentAir, a company that produces such scents, "Developing a signature fragrance is much like [developing] a message in print or radio: What do you want to communicate to consumers and how often?"

Such "experiential retailing" confirms that retail stores are much more than simply assortments of goods. They are environments to be experienced by the people who shop in them. Store atmospheres offer a powerful tool by which retailers can differentiate their stores from those of competitors.

In fact, retail establishments sometimes become small communities in themselves—places where people get together. These places include coffee shops and cafés, shopping malls, bookstores, children's play spaces, superstores, and urban greenmarkets. For example, today's bookstores have become part bookstore, part library, part living room, and part coffeehouse. On an early evening at your local Barnes & Noble, for example, you'll likely find backpack-toting high school students doing homework with friends in the coffee bar. Nearby, retirees sit in cushy chairs thumbing through travel or gardening books while parents read aloud to their children. Barnes & Noble sells more than just books; it sells comfort, relaxation, and community.

Price Decision

A retailer's price policy must fit its target market and positioning, product and service assortment, the competition, and economic factors. All retailers would like to charge high markups and achieve high volume, but the two seldom go together. Most retailers seek *either* high markups on lower volume (most specialty stores) *or* low markups on higher volume (mass merchandisers and discount stores).

● A retailer's price policy must fit its targeting and positioning. Bergdorf Goodman caters to the upper crust with prices to match.

Thus, 110-year-old Bergdorf Goodman caters to the upper crust by selling apparel, shoes, and jewelry created by designers such as Chanel, Prada, and Hermes. ● The up-market retailer pampers its customers with services such as a personal shopper and in-store showings of the upcoming season's trends with cocktails and hors d'oeuvres. By contrast, T.J. Maxx sells brand-name clothing at discount prices aimed at the Middle Americans. Stocking new products each week, the discounter provides a treasure hunt for bargain shoppers.

Retailers must also decide on the extent to which they will use sales and other price promotions. Some retailers use no price promotions at all, competing instead on product and service quality rather than on price. For example, it's difficult to imagine Bergdorf Goodman holding a two-for-the-price-of-one sale on Chanel handbags, even in a down economy. Other retailers—such as Walmart, Costco, and Family Dollar—practice *everyday low pricing (EDLP)*, charging constant, everyday low prices with few sales or discounts.

Still other retailers practice *"high-low" pricing*—charging higher prices on an everyday basis, coupled with frequent sales and other price promotions to increase store traffic, create a low-price image, or attract customers who will buy other goods at full prices. The recent economic downturn caused a rash of high-low pricing, as retailers poured on price cuts and promotions to coax bargain-hunting customers into their stores. Which pricing strategy is best depends on the retailer's overall marketing strategy, the pricing approaches of its competitors, and the economic environment.

Promotion Decision

Retailers use any or all of the five promotion tools—advertising, personal selling, sales promotion, public relations (PR), and direct marketing—to reach consumers. They advertise in newspapers and magazines and on the radio, television, and the Internet. Advertising may be supported by newspaper inserts and catalogs. Store salespeople greet customers, meet their needs, and build relationships. Sales promotions may include in-store demonstrations, displays, sales, and loyalty programs. PR activities, such as store openings, special events, newsletters and blogs, store magazines, and public service activities, are always available to retailers. Most retailers have also created Web sites, offering customers information and other features and selling merchandise directly.

Place Decision

Retailers often point to three critical factors in retailing success: *location, location,* and *location*! It's very important that retailers select locations that are accessible to the target market in areas that are consistent with the retailer's positioning. For example, Apple locates its stores in high-end malls and trendy shopping districts—such as the "Magnificent Mile" on Chicago's Michigan Avenue or Fifth Avenue in Manhattan—not low-rent strip malls on the edge of town. By contrast, Trader Joe's places its stores in low-rent, out-of-the-way locations to keep costs down and support its "cheap gourmet" positioning. Small retailers may have to settle for whatever locations they can find or afford. Large retailers, however, usually employ specialists who use advanced methods to select store locations.

Most stores today cluster together to increase their customer pulling power and give consumers the convenience of one-stop shopping. *Central business districts* were the main form of retail cluster until the 1950s. Every large city and town had a central business district with department stores, specialty stores, banks, and movie theaters. When people began to move to the suburbs, however, these central business districts, with their traffic, parking, and crime problems, began to lose business. In recent years, many cities have joined with merchants to revive downtown shopping areas, generally with only mixed success.

Shopping center

A group of retail businesses built on a site that is planned, developed, owned, and managed as a unit.

A **shopping center** is a group of retail businesses built on a site that is planned, developed, owned, and managed as a unit. A *regional shopping center*, or *regional shopping mall*, the largest and most dramatic shopping center, has from 50 to more than 100 stores, including 2 or more full-line department stores. It is like a covered mini downtown and attracts customers from a wide area. A *community shopping center* contains between 15 and 50 retail stores. It normally contains a branch of a department store or variety store, a supermarket, specialty stores, professional offices, and sometimes a bank. Most shopping centers are *neighborhood shopping centers* or *strip malls* that generally contain between 5 and 15 stores. They are close and convenient for consumers. They usually contain a supermarket, perhaps a discount store, and several service stores—dry cleaner, drugstore, video-rental store, hardware store, local restaurant, or other stores.[18]

With more than 100,000 shopping centers in the United States, many experts suggest that the country is now "overmalled." During the 1990s, shopping center space grew at about twice the rate of population growth. However, more recently, several factors have caused hard times for the nation's shopping malls. First, consumer spending cutbacks following the recession have forced many retailers—small and large—out of business, increasing mall vacancy rates. Second, shopping centers face increased competition—everything from the rapid growth of online shopping to ever-growing sales by megaretailers such as Walmart and Costco. As a result, increased numbers of traditional shopping centers are going under.

Although some traditional shopping centers are dying, other types of centers are still being constructed. The current trend is toward the so-called power centers. *Power centers* are huge unenclosed shopping centers consisting of a long strip of retail stores, including large, freestanding anchors such as Walmart, Home Depot, Costco, Best Buy, Michaels, PetSmart, and OfficeMax. Each store has its own entrance with parking directly in front for shoppers who wish to visit only one store. Power centers have increased rapidly over the past few years and challenge traditional indoor malls.

In contrast, *lifestyle centers* are smaller, open-air malls with upscale stores, convenient locations, and nonretail activities, such as a playground, skating rink, hotel, dining establishments, and a movie theater. They are usually located near affluent residential neighborhoods and cater to the retail needs of consumers in their areas. "Think of lifestyle centers as part Main Street and part Fifth Avenue," comments an industry observer. In fact, the original power center and lifestyle center concepts are now morphing into hybrid lifestyle-power centers. "The idea is to combine the hominess and community of an old-time village square with the cachet of fashionable urban stores; the smell and feel of a neighborhood park with the brute convenience of a strip center." ◉ In all, today's centers are more about "creating places to be rather than just places to buy."[19]

◉ Shopping centers: The current trend is toward large "power centers" on the one hand and smaller "lifestyle centers" on the other—or a hybrid version of the two called a lifestyle-power center. In all, today's centers are more about "creating places to be rather than just places to buy."

Retailing Trends and Developments

Retailers operate in a harsh and fast-changing environment, which offers threats as well as opportunities. For example, the industry suffers from chronic overcapacity, resulting in fierce competition for customer dollars, especially in tough economic times. Consumer demographics, lifestyles, and spending patterns are changing rapidly, as are retailing technologies. To be successful, retailers need to choose target segments carefully and position themselves strongly. They need to take the following retailing developments into account as they plan and execute their competitive strategies.

A Slowed Economy and Tighter Consumer Spending

Following many years of good economic times for retailers, the recent recession turned many retailers' fortunes from boom to bust. According to one observer:[20]

It was great to be in retailing during the past 15 years. Inflated home values, freely available credit, and low interest rates fueled unprecedented levels of consumer spending. Retailers responded by aggressively adding new stores, launching new concepts, building an online presence, and expanding internationally. While the U.S. economy grew 5 percent annually from 1996 to 2006, . . . the retail sector grew at more than double that rate—an eye-popping 12 percent. Revenues rose sharply, profits ballooned, and share prices soared. But that's all gone now. [Since the recent recession,] same-store sales . . . have dropped by double digits for many chains, store closures have accelerated, store openings are slowed, and shareholder-value destruction has been massive.

Some retailers actually benefit from a down economy. For example, as consumers cut back and look for ways to spend less on what they buy, big discounters such as Walmart scoop up new business from bargain-hungry shoppers. Similarly, lower-priced fast-food chains, such as McDonald's, have taken business from their pricier eat-out competitors.

For most retailers, however, a sluggish economy means tough times. Several large and familiar retailers have recently declared bankruptcy or closed their doors completely—including household names such as Linens 'n Things, Circuit City, KB Toys, and Sharper Image, to name a few. Other retailers, from Macy's and Home Depot to Starbucks, have laid off employees, cut their costs, and offered deep price discounts and promotions aimed at luring cash-strapped customers back into their stores.

Beyond costcutting and price promotions, many retailers have also added new value pitches to their positioning. For example, Home Depot replaced its older "You can do it. We can help." theme with a thriftier one: "More saving. More doing." ● Similarly, Whole Foods Market kicked up the promotion of its 365 Everyday Value private-label brand with ads sporting headlines such as "Sticker shock, but in a good way" and "No wallets were harmed in the buying of our 365 Everyday Value products." And following significant declines in same-store sales caused by the recent recession, Target, for the first time in its history, introduced TV ads featuring price messages. "Our [tagline] is 'Expect more. Pay less.'" a Target marketer said. "We're putting more emphasis on the pay less promise."[21]

When reacting to economic difficulties, retailers must be careful that their short-run actions don't damage their long-run images and positions. Drastic price discounting is "a sign of panic," says a retail strategist. "Anyone can sell product by dropping their prices, but it does not breed loyalty."[22] Instead of relying on costcutting and price reductions, retailers should focus on building greater customer value within their long-term store positioning strategies. For example, although it might make sense in the short run to move toward the "pay less" part of Target's positioning, in the long run, Target cannot afford to abandon the quality and sharp

● **New value pitches from retailers: Even upscale Whole Foods Market has promoted its private-label brand, 365 Everyday Value, with headlines such as "Sticker shock, but in a good way."**

design that differentiate it from Walmart and other discounters. As the economy recovers, Target will likely reassert its "Target-ness" by moving back toward the "expect more" side of its value equation.[23]

New Retail Forms, Shortening Retail Life Cycles, and Retail Convergence

New retail forms continue to emerge to meet new situations and consumer needs, but the life cycle of new retail forms is getting shorter. Department stores took about 100 years to reach the mature stage of the life cycle; more recent forms, such as warehouse stores, reached maturity in about 10 years. In such an environment, seemingly solid retail positions can crumble quickly. Of the top 10 discount retailers in 1962 (the year that Walmart and Kmart began), not one exists today. Even the most successful retailers can't sit back with a winning formula. To remain successful, they must keep adapting.

Wheel-of-retailing concept
A concept that states that new types of retailers usually begin as low-margin, low-price, low-status operations but later evolve into higher-priced, higher-service operations, eventually becoming like the conventional retailers they replaced.

Many retailing innovations are partially explained by the **wheel-of-retailing concept**. According to this concept, many new types of retailing forms begin as low-margin, low-price, and low-status operations. They challenge established retailers that have become "fat" by letting their costs and margins increase. The new retailers' success leads them to upgrade their facilities and offer more services. In turn, their costs increase, forcing them to increase their prices. Eventually, the new retailers become like the conventional retailers they replaced. The cycle begins again when still newer types of retailers evolve with lower costs and prices. The wheel-of-retailing concept seems to explain the initial success and later troubles of department stores, supermarkets, and discount stores and the recent success of off-price retailers.

● Retail convergence: Microwave ovens at RitzCamera.com? You bet.

Although new retail forms are always emerging, today's forms appear to be converging. Increasingly, different types of retailers now sell the same products at the same prices to the same consumers. For example, you can buy brand-name home appliances at department stores, discount stores, home improvement stores, off-price retailers, electronics superstores, and a slew of Web sites that all compete for the same customers. ● So if you can't find the microwave oven you want at Sears, step across the street and find one for a better price at Lowe's or Best Buy—or just order one online from Amazon.com or even RitzCamera.com. This merging of consumers, products, prices, and retailers is called *retail convergence*. Such convergence means greater competition for retailers and greater difficulty in differentiating the product assortments of different types of retailers.

The Rise of Megaretailers

The rise of huge mass merchandisers and specialty superstores, the formation of vertical marketing systems, and a rash of retail mergers and acquisitions have created a core of superpower megaretailers. Through their superior information systems and buying power, these giant retailers can offer better merchandise selections, good service, and strong price savings to consumers. As a result, they grow even larger by squeezing out their smaller, weaker competitors.

The megaretailers have shifted the balance of power between retailers and producers. A small handful of retailers now control access to enormous numbers of consumers, giving them the upper hand in their dealings with manufacturers. For example, you may never have heard of specialty coatings and sealants manufacturer RPM International, but you've probably used one or more of its many familiar do-it-yourself brands—such as Rust-Oleum paints, Plastic Wood and Dap fillers, Mohawk and Watco finishes, and Testors hobby cements and paints—all of which you can buy at your local Home Depot store. Home Depot is a very important customer to RPM, accounting for a significant share of its consumer sales. However, Home Depot's sales of $66 billion are close to 20 times RPM's sales of $3.4 billion. As a result, the giant retailer can, and often does, use this power to wring concessions from RPM and thousands of other smaller suppliers.[24]

Growth of Nonstore Retailing

Most of us still make most of our purchases the old-fashioned way: We go to the store, find what we want, wait patiently in line to plunk down our cash or credit card, and bring home the goods. However, consumers now have a broad array of nonstore alternatives, including mail order, phone, and online shopping. Americans are increasingly avoiding the hassles and crowds at malls by doing more of their shopping by phone or computer. As we'll discuss in Chapter 17, direct and online marketing are currently the fastest-growing forms of marketing.

Today, thanks to advanced technologies, easier-to-use and enticing Web sites, improved online service, and the increasing sophistication of search technologies, online retailing is thriving. In fact, although it currently accounts for less than 4 percent of total U.S. retail sales, online buying is growing at a much brisker pace than retail buying as a whole. Despite a flagging economy, or perhaps because of it, last year's U.S. online retail sales reached an estimated $134 billion.[25]

Retailer online sites also influence a large amount of in-store buying. Here are some surprising statistics: 80 percent of shoppers research products online before going to a store to make a purchase; 62 percent say that they spend at least 30 minutes online every week to help them decide whether and what to buy.[26] So it's no longer a matter of customers deciding to shop in the store *or* shop online. Increasingly, customers are merging store and online outlets into a single shopping process. ⦿ In fact, the Internet has spawned a whole new breed of shopper and way of shopping:[27]

⦿ The Internet has spawned a whole new breed of shopper—people who just can't buy anything unless they first look it up online and get the lowdown.

Many people just can't buy anything unless they first look it up online and get the lowdown. In a recent survey, 78 percent of shoppers said that ads no longer have enough information. So many buyers search online for virtually everything. Window shoppers have become "Windows shoppers." A whopping 92 percent said they had more confidence in information they sought online than anything coming from a salesclerk or other source. As a result, shoppers are devoting time and energy to ferreting out detailed information before they buy. Whether it's cars, homes, PCs, or medical care, nearly four in five shoppers say they gather information on their own from the Web before buying. "Do-it-yourself doctors" (that is, info-seeking patients) show up at their doctor's office with the Web-derived diagnosis in hand and a list of the medicines they need prescribed. Customers appear at the car dealership with the wholesale price and the model already picked out. Now this trend is spreading down the product chain. In the survey, 24 percent of shoppers said they are even doing online research before buying shampoo. And they have questions: How does this shampoo work on different hair types, thicknesses, and colors? Are the bottles recyclable? Has the product been tested on animals?

All types of retailers now employ direct and online channels. The online sales of large brick-and-mortar retailers, such as Walmart, Sears, Staples, and Best Buy, are increasing rapidly. Several large online-only retailers—Amazon.com, Zappos.com, online travel companies such as Travelocity.com and Expedia.com, and others—are now making it big on the Web. At the other extreme, hordes of niche marketers are using the Internet to reach new markets and expand their sales.

Still, much of the anticipated growth in online sales will go to multichannel retailers—the click-and-brick marketers who can successfully merge the virtual and physical worlds.

In a recent ranking of the top 500 online retail sites, 58 percent were multichannel retailers.[28] For example, Macy's beefed-up Web site complements its more than 800 Macy's stores around the country. Although many Macy's customers make purchases online, the site offers a range of features designed to build loyalty to Macy's and pull customers into stores. Like many retailers, Macy's has discovered that its best customers shop both online and offline. "When our customers shop [both] online and in stores they spend 20 percent more in stores than the average in-store shopper, and 60 percent more online than the average online shopper at Macys.com," says the chairman of Macys.com. But the Web site aims to do more than just sell products online. "We see Macys.com as far more than a selling site. We see it as the online hub of the Macy's brand."[29]

Growing Importance of Retail Technology

Retail technologies have become critically important as competitive tools. Progressive retailers are using advanced IT and software systems to produce better forecasts, control inventory costs, interact electronically with suppliers, send information between stores, and even sell to customers within stores. They have adopted sophisticated systems for checkout scanning, RFID inventory tracking, merchandise handling, information sharing, and interacting with customers.

Perhaps the most startling advances in retail technology concern the ways in which retailers are connecting with consumers. Today's customers have gotten used to the speed and convenience of buying online and to the control that the Internet gives them over the buying process. The Web lets consumers shop when they like and where they like, with instant access to gobs of information about competing products and prices. No real-world store can do all that.

Increasingly, however, retailers are attempting to meet these new consumer expectations by bringing Web-style technologies into their stores. Many retailers now routinely use technologies ranging from touch-screen kiosks, mobile handheld shopping assistants, and customer-loyalty cards to self-scanning checkout systems and in-store access to store inventory databases. ● Consider the supermarket chain Stop & Shop:[30]

> To engage shoppers as they roll their carts down the aisles, speed up checkout, and generally improve the shopping experience, Stop & Shop provides customers with mobile handheld Scan It scanners. Shoppers retrieve a scanner by swiping their loyalty card and then use it to scan and bag products as they shop. The device keeps a running total of purchases. As customers wend their way through the aisles, based on each customer's shopping history and current selections, the Scan It scanners call out sale prices and issue electronic coupons. Customers can even use the scanners to place deli orders while they shop elsewhere in the store. When customers arrive at the deli counter, their order is waiting for them. When done, shoppers pay and go quickly at a dedicated self-checkout lane. The Scan It scanners now process about 10 percent of all Stop & Shop store sales. The new technology not only makes shopping faster and more convenient for customers but also reduces store operating costs.

● Retail technology: Stop & Shop uses technology to make shopping faster and more convenient for its customers.

Green Retailing

Today's retailers are increasingly adopting environmentally sustainable practices. They are greening up their stores and operations, promoting more environmentally responsible products, launching programs to help customers be more responsible, and working with channel partners to reduce their environmental impact.

● McDonald's Golden Arches are now going green. Its new eco-friendly restaurants are designed from the bottom up with a whole new eco-attitude.

At the most basic level, most large retailers are making their stores more environmentally friendly through sustainable building design, construction, and operations. For example, new Safeway stores employ extensive recycling and compost programs, wind energy and solar panels for power, and regionally sourced sustainable building materials. ● Similarly, McDonald's Golden Arches are now going green. Its new eco-friendly restaurants are designed from the bottom up with a whole new eco-attitude.[31]

A new "green" McDonald's in Cary, North Carolina, is built and furnished mostly with reclaimed building materials. The parking lot is made with permeable pavers, which absorb and clean storm water and filter it back into the water table. Exterior and interior lighting uses energy-efficient LEDs, which consume as much as 78 percent less energy and last 10 to 20 times longer than traditional lighting. The restaurant is landscaped with hearty, drought-resistant native plants, which require less water. Then, what little water they do need comes from rainwater channeled from the roof and condensation from the super–high-efficiency HVAC system. Inside the restaurant, solartube skylights bring in natural light and reduce energy use. A sophisticated lighting system adjusts indoor illumination based on light entering through the skylights. The dining room is filled with materials made from recycled content (recycled floor tiles, for example, and counters made from recycled glass and concrete), and paints and cleaning chemicals were chosen for their low environmental impact. Other green features include high-efficiency kitchen equipment and water-saving, low-flow faucets and toilets. The restaurant even offers electric vehicle charging stations for customers.

Retailers are also greening up their product assortments. For example, JCPenney's Simply Green designation identifies store-brand products that are organic, renewable, or made from recycled content. "Every product with the Simply Green designation helps the environment heal, little by little," says the company. Similarly, Safeway offers its own Bright Green line of home care products, featuring cleaning and laundry soaps made with biodegradable and naturally derived ingredients, energy-efficient light bulbs, and paper products made from 100 percent recycled content. Such products can both boost sales and lift the retailer's image as a responsible company. "More than ever, our consumers are aware of the choices and behaviors that affect the world around us," says a Safeway marketing executive. "We want to simplify 'choosing green.'"[32]

Many retailers have also launched programs that help consumers make more environmentally responsible decisions. Staples' EcoEasy program helps customers identify green products sold in its stores and makes it easy to recycle printer cartridges, cell phones, computers, and other office technology products. Staples recycles some 30 million printer cartridges and four million pounds of electronic waste each year. Similarly, Best Buy's "Greener Together" program helps customers select more energy-efficient new products and recycle old ones.[33]

Finally, many large retailers are joining forces with suppliers and distributors to create more sustainable products, packaging, and distribution systems. For example, Amazon.com works closely with the producers of many of the products it sells to reduce and simplify their packaging. And beyond its own substantial sustainability initiatives, Walmart wields its huge buying power to urge its army of suppliers to improve their environmental impact and practices. The retailer has even developed a worldwide Sustainable Product Index, by which it rates suppliers. It plans to translate the index into a simple rating for consumers to help them make more sustainable buying choices.

Green retailing yields both top and bottom line benefits. Sustainable practices lift a retailer's top line by attracting consumers looking to support environmentally friendly sellers and products. They also help the bottom line by reducing costs. For example, Amazon.com's reduced-packaging efforts increase customer convenience and eliminate "wrap rage" while at the same time save packaging costs. And an earth-friendly McDonald's restaurant not only appeals to customers and helps save the planet but costs less to operate. "Green retailing has recently become another legitimate differentiator in the [retail] brand equation, and it creates significant quick-hit ROI opportunities, as well," concludes a retail analyst.[34]

Global Expansion of Major Retailers

Retailers with unique formats and strong brand positioning are increasingly moving into other countries. Many are expanding internationally to escape mature and saturated home markets. Over the years, some giant U.S. retailers, such as McDonald's, have become globally prominent as a result of their marketing prowess. Others, such as Walmart, are rapidly establishing a global presence. Walmart, which now operates more than 4,000 stores in 14 countries abroad, sees exciting global potential. Its international division alone last year racked up sales of more than $100 billion, over 50 percent more than rival Target's *total* sales of $63 billion.[35]

However, most U.S retailers are still significantly behind Europe and Asia when it comes to global expansion. Ten of the world's top 20 retailers are U.S. companies; only four of these retailers have established stores outside North America (Walmart, Home Depot, Sears, and Costco). Of the 10 non-U.S. retailers in the world's top 20, seven have stores in at least 10 countries. Among foreign retailers that have gone global are France's Carrefour and Auchan chains, Germany's Metro and Aldi chains, and Britain's Tesco.[36]

French discount retailer Carrefour, the world's second-largest retailer after Walmart, has embarked on an aggressive mission to extend its role as a leading international retailer:

The Carrefour Group has an interest in more than 15,400 stores in over 30 countries in Europe, Asia, and the Americas, including over 1,000 hypermarkets (supercenters). It leads Europe in supermarkets and the world in hypermarkets. Carrefour is outpacing Walmart in several emerging markets, including South America, China, and the Pacific Rim. It's the leading retailer in Brazil and Argentina, where it operates more than 1,000 stores, compared to Walmart's 477 units in those two countries. Carrefour is the largest foreign retailer in China, where it operates more than 443 stores versus Walmart's 279. In short, although Walmart has more than three times Carrefour's overall sales, Carrefour is forging ahead of Walmart in most markets outside North America. The only question: Can the French retailer hold its lead? Although no one retailer can safely claim to be in the same league with Walmart as an overall retail presence, Carrefour stands a better chance than most to hold its own in global retailing.[37]

Wholesaling

All the activities involved in selling goods and services to those buying for resale or business use.

Wholesaler

A firm engaged *primarily* in wholesaling activities.

Wholesaling (pp 394–400)

Wholesaling includes all the activities involved in selling goods and services to those buying for resale or business use. Firms engaged *primarily* in wholesaling activities are called **wholesalers**.

Wholesalers buy mostly from producers and sell mostly to retailers, industrial consumers, and other wholesalers. As a result, many of the nation's largest and most important wholesalers are largely unknown to final consumers. ● For example, you may never have heard of Grainger, even though it's very well known and much valued by its more than 1.8 million business and institutional customers across North America, India, China, and Panama.[38]

Grainger may be the biggest market leader you've never heard of. It's a $6 billion business that offers 1 million maintenance, repair, and operating (MRO) products to more than 2 million customers. Through its branch network, service centers, sales

Author Comment | Whereas retailers primarily sell goods and services directly to final consumers for personal use, wholesalers sell primarily to those buying for resale or business use. Because wholesalers operate behind the scenes, they are largely unknown to final consumers. But they are very important to their business customers.

Wholesaling: Many of the nation's largest and most important wholesalers—like Grainger—are largely unknown to final consumers. But they are very well known and much valued by the business customers they serve.

reps, catalog, and Web site, Grainger links customers with the supplies they need to keep their facilities running smoothly—everything from light bulbs, cleaners, and display cases to nuts and bolts, motors, valves, power tools, test equipment, and safety supplies. Grainger's 600 branches, 22 strategically located distribution centers, more than 18,000 employees, and innovative Web sites handle more than 115,000 transactions a day, and 98 percent of orders ship within 24 hours. Grainger's customers include organizations ranging from factories, garages, and grocers to schools and military bases. Customers include notables such as Abbott Laboratories, General Motors, Campbell's Soup, American Airlines, and the U.S. Postal Service.

Grainger operates on a simple value proposition: to make it easier and less costly for customers to find and buy MRO supplies. It starts by acting as a one-stop shop for products needed to maintain facilities. On a broader level, it builds lasting relationships with customers by helping them find *solutions* to their overall MRO problems. Acting as consultants, Grainger sales reps help buyers with everything from improving their supply chain management to reducing inventories and streamlining warehousing operations. So, how come you've never heard of Grainger? Perhaps it's because the company operates in the not-so-glamorous world of MRO supplies, which are important to every business but not so important to consumers. More likely, it's because Grainger is a wholesaler. And like most wholesalers, it operates behind the scenes, selling mostly to other businesses.

Why are wholesalers important to sellers? For example, why would a producer use wholesalers rather than selling directly to retailers or consumers? Simply put, wholesalers add value by performing one or more of the following channel functions:

- *Selling and promoting:* Wholesalers' sales forces help manufacturers reach many small customers at a low cost. The wholesaler has more contacts and is often more trusted by the buyer than the distant manufacturer.

- *Buying and assortment building:* Wholesalers can select items and build assortments needed by their customers, thereby saving much work.

- *Bulk breaking:* Wholesalers save their customers money by buying in carload lots and breaking bulk (breaking large lots into small quantities).

- *Warehousing:* Wholesalers hold inventories, thereby reducing the inventory costs and risks of suppliers and customers.

- *Transportation:* Wholesalers can provide quicker delivery to buyers because they are closer to buyers than are producers.

- *Financing:* Wholesalers finance their customers by giving credit, and they finance their suppliers by ordering early and paying bills on time.

- *Risk bearing:* Wholesalers absorb risk by taking title and bearing the cost of theft, damage, spoilage, and obsolescence.

- *Market information:* Wholesalers give information to suppliers and customers about competitors, new products, and price developments.

- *Management services and advice:* Wholesalers often help retailers train their salesclerks, improve store layouts and displays, and set up accounting and inventory control systems.

Merchant wholesaler
An independently owned wholesale business that takes title to the merchandise it handles.

Broker
A wholesaler who does not take title to goods and whose function is to bring buyers and sellers together and assist in negotiation.

Agent
A wholesaler who represents buyers or sellers on a relatively permanent basis, performs only a few functions, and does not take title to goods.

Manufacturers' sales branches and offices
Wholesaling by sellers or buyers themselves rather than through independent wholesalers.

Types of Wholesalers

Wholesalers fall into three major groups (see ● **Table 13.3**): *merchant wholesalers, agents and brokers*, and *manufacturers' sales branches and offices*. **Merchant wholesalers** are the largest single group of wholesalers, accounting for roughly 50 percent of all wholesaling. Merchant wholesalers include two broad types: full-service wholesalers and limited-service wholesalers. *Full-service wholesalers* provide a full set of services, whereas the various *limited-service wholesalers* offer fewer services to their suppliers and customers. The different types of limited-service wholesalers perform varied specialized functions in the distribution channel.

Brokers and *agents* differ from merchant wholesalers in two ways: They do not take title to goods, and they perform only a few functions. Like merchant wholesalers, they generally specialize by product line or customer type. A **broker** brings buyers and sellers together and assists in negotiation. **Agents** represent buyers or sellers on a more permanent basis. *Manufacturers' agents* (also called *manufacturers' representatives*) are the most common type of agent wholesaler. The third major type of wholesaling is that done in **manufacturers' sales branches and offices** by sellers or buyers themselves rather than through independent wholesalers.

Wholesaler Marketing Decisions

Wholesalers now face growing competitive pressures, more-demanding customers, new technologies, and more direct-buying programs on the part of large industrial, institutional, and retail buyers. As a result, they have taken a fresh look at their marketing strategies. As with retailers, their marketing decisions include choices of segmentation and targeting, differentiation and positioning, and the marketing mix—product and service assortments, price, promotion, and distribution (see ● **Figure 13.2**).

Segmentation, Targeting, Differentiation, and Positioning Decisions

Like retailers, wholesalers must segment and define their target markets and differentiate and position themselves effectively—they cannot serve everyone. They can choose a target group by size of customer (large retailers only), type of customer (convenience stores only), the need for service (customers who need credit), or other factors. Within the target group, they can identify the more profitable customers, design stronger offers, and build better relationships with them. They can propose automatic reordering systems, establish management-training and advisory systems, or even sponsor a voluntary chain. They can discourage less-profitable customers by requiring larger orders or adding service charges to smaller ones.

Marketing Mix Decisions

Like retailers, wholesalers must decide on product and service assortments, prices, promotion, and place. Wholesalers add customer value though the *products and services* they offer. They are often under great pressure to carry a full line and stock enough for immediate delivery. But this practice can damage profits. Wholesalers today are cutting down on the number of lines they carry, choosing to carry only the more-profitable ones. They are also rethinking which services count most in building strong customer relationships and which should be dropped or paid for by the customer. The key is to find the mix of services most valued by their target customers.

Price is also an important wholesaler decision. Wholesalers usually mark up the cost of goods by a standard percentage—say, 20 percent. Expenses may run 17 percent of the gross margin, leaving a profit margin of 3 percent. In grocery wholesaling, the average profit margin is often less than 2 percent. Wholesalers are trying new pricing approaches. The recent economic downturn put heavy pressure on wholesalers to cut their costs and prices. As their retail and industrial customers face sales and margin declines, these customers turn to wholesalers looking for lower prices. Wholesalers may cut their margins on some lines to keep important customers. They may ask suppliers for special price breaks, when they can turn them into an increase in the supplier's sales.

⊙ **TABLE | 13.3**   Major Types of Wholesalers

Type	Description
Merchant wholesalers	Independently owned businesses that take title to all merchandise handled. There are *full-service wholesalers* and *limited-service wholesalers*.
Full-service wholesalers	Provide a full line of services: carrying stock, maintaining a sales force, offering credit, making deliveries, and providing management assistance. Full-service wholesalers include wholesale merchants and industrial distributors.
Wholesale merchants	Sell primarily to retailers and provides a full range of services. *General merchandise wholesalers* carry several merchandise lines, whereas *general line wholesalers* carry one or two lines in great depth. *Specialty wholesalers* specialize in carrying only part of a line.
Industrial distributors	Sell to manufacturers rather than to retailers. Provide several services, such as carrying stock, offering credit, and providing delivery. May carry a broad range of merchandise, a general line, or a specialty line.
Limited-service wholesalers	Offer fewer services than full-service wholesalers. Limited-service wholesalers are of several types:
Cash-and-carry wholesalers	Carry a limited line of fast-moving goods and sell to small retailers for cash. Normally do not deliver.
Truck wholesalers (or truck jobbers)	Perform primarily a selling and delivery function. Carry a limited line of semiperishable merchandise (such as milk, bread, snack foods), which is sold for cash as deliveries are made to supermarkets, small groceries, hospitals, restaurants, factory cafeterias, and hotels.
Drop shippers	Do not carry inventory or handle the product. On receiving an order, drop shippers select a manufacturer, who then ships the merchandise directly to the customer. Drop shippers operate in bulk industries, such as coal, lumber, and heavy equipment.
Rack jobbers	Serve grocery and drug retailers, mostly in nonfood items. Rack jobbers send delivery trucks to stores, where the delivery people set up toys, paperbacks, hardware items, health and beauty aids, or other items. Rack jobbers price the goods, keep them fresh, set up point-of-purchase displays, and keep inventory records.
Producers' cooperatives	Farmer-owned members that assemble farm produce for sale in local markets. Producers' cooperatives often attempt to improve product quality and promote a co-op brand name, such as Sun-Maid raisins, Sunkist oranges, or Diamond walnuts.
Mail-order or Web wholesalers	Send catalogs to or maintain Web sites for retail, industrial, and institutional customers featuring jewelry, cosmetics, specialty foods, and other small items. Its primary customers are businesses in small outlying areas.
Brokers and agents	Do not take title to goods. Main function is to facilitate buying and selling, for which they earn a commission on the selling price. Generally specialize by product line or customer type.
Brokers	Bring buyers and sellers together and assist in negotiation. Brokers are paid by the party who hired the broker and do not carry inventory, get involved in financing, or assume risk. Examples include food brokers, real estate brokers, insurance brokers, and security brokers.
Agents	Represent either buyers or sellers on a more permanent basis than brokers do. There are four types:
Manufacturers' agents	Represent two or more manufacturers of complementary lines. Often used in such lines as apparel, furniture, and electrical goods. A manufacturer's agent is hired by small manufacturers who cannot afford their own field sales forces and by large manufacturers who use agents to open new territories or cover territories that cannot support full-time salespeople.
Selling agents	Have contractual authority to sell a manufacturer's entire output. The selling agent serves as a sales department and has significant influence over prices, terms, and conditions of sale. Found in product areas such as textiles, industrial machinery and equipment, coal and coke, chemicals, and metals.
Purchasing agents	Generally have a long-term relationship with buyers and make purchases for them, often receiving, inspecting, warehousing, and shipping the merchandise to buyers. Purchasing agents help clients obtain the best goods and prices available.

(continued)

● TABLE | 13.3   Major Types of Wholesalers—*continued*

Type	Description
Commission merchants	Take physical possession of products and negotiate sales. Used most often in agricultural marketing by farmers who do not want to sell their own output. Takes a truckload of commodities to a central market, sells it for the best price, deducts a commission and expenses, and remits the balance to the producers.
Manufacturers' and retailers' branches and offices	Wholesaling operations conducted by sellers or buyers themselves rather than through independent wholesalers. Separate branches and offices can be dedicated to either sales or purchasing.
Sales branches and offices	Set up by manufacturers to improve inventory control, selling, and promotion. *Sales branches* carry inventory and are found in industries such as lumber and automotive equipment and parts. *Sales offices* do not carry inventory and are most prominent in the dry goods and notions industries.
Purchasing officers	Perform a role similar to that of brokers or agents but are part of the buyer's organization. Many retailers set up purchasing offices in major market centers, such as New York and Chicago.

Although *promotion* can be critical to wholesaler success, most wholesalers are not promotion minded. They use largely scattered and unplanned trade advertising, sales promotion, personal selling, and PR. Many are behind the times in personal selling; they still see selling as a single salesperson talking to a single customer instead of as a team effort to sell, build, and service major accounts. Wholesalers also need to adopt some of the nonpersonal promotion techniques used by retailers. They need to develop an overall promotion strategy and make greater use of supplier promotion materials and programs.

Finally, *distribution* (location) is important. Wholesalers must choose their locations, facilities, and Web locations carefully. There was a time when wholesalers could locate in low-rent, low-tax areas and invest little money in their buildings, equipment, and systems. Today, however, as technology zooms forward, such behavior results in outdated systems for material handling, order processing, and delivery.

Instead, today's large and progressive wholesalers have reacted to rising costs by investing in automated warehouses and IT systems. Orders are fed from the retailer's information system directly into the wholesaler's, and the items are picked up by mechanical devices and automatically taken to a shipping platform where they are assembled. Most

● FIGURE | 13.2
Wholesaler Marketing Strategy

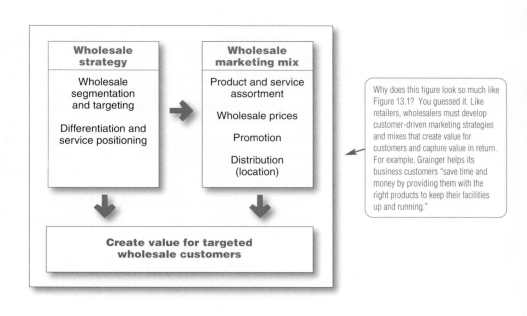

large wholesalers use technology to carry out accounting, billing, inventory control, and forecasting. Modern wholesalers are adapting their services to the needs of target customers and finding cost-reducing methods of doing business. They are also transacting more business online. For example, e-commerce is Grainger's fastest growing sales channel. Online purchasing now accounts for 24 percent of the wholesaler's U.S. sales.[39]

Trends in Wholesaling

Today's wholesalers face considerable challenges. The industry remains vulnerable to one of its most enduring trends—the need for ever-greater efficiency. Recent economic conditions have led to demands for even lower prices and the winnowing out of suppliers who are not adding value based on cost and quality. Progressive wholesalers constantly watch for better ways to meet the changing needs of their suppliers and target customers. They recognize that their only reason for existence comes from adding value by increasing the efficiency and effectiveness of the entire marketing channel.

As with other types of marketers, the goal is to build value-adding customer relationships. For example, Grainger succeeds by making life easier and more efficient for the commercial and institutional buyers and sellers it serves:

> Beyond making it easier for customers to find the products they need, Grainger also helps them streamline their acquisition processes. For most companies, acquiring MRO supplies is a very costly process. In fact, 40 percent of the cost of MRO supplies stems from the purchase process, including finding a supplier, negotiating the best deal, placing the order, receiving the order, and paying the invoice. Grainger constantly seeks ways to reduce the costs associated with MRO supplies acquisition, both internally and externally. One company found that working with Grainger cut MRO requisition time by more than 60 percent, and lead times went from days to hours. Its supply chain dropped from 12,000 suppliers to 560—significantly reducing expenses. Similarly, a large timber and paper-products company has come to appreciate Grainger's selection and streamlined ordering process. It orders two-thirds of its supplies from Grainger's Web site at an annual acquisition cost of only $300,000. By comparison, for the remainder of its needs, this company deals with more than 1,300 small distributors at an acquisition cost of $2.4 million each year—eight times the cost of dealing with Grainger for over half the volume. The company is now looking for ways to buy all of its MRO supplies from Grainger. As one Grainger branch manager puts it, "If we don't save [customers] time and money every time they come [to us], they won't come back."[40]

McKesson, a diversified healthcare services provider and the nation's leading wholesaler of pharmaceuticals, health and beauty care, home health care, and medical supply and equipment products, provides another example of progressive, value-adding wholesaling. To survive, especially in a harsh economic environment, McKesson has to be more cost effective than manufacturers' sales branches. Thus, the company has built efficient automated warehouses, established direct computer links with drug manufacturers, and created extensive online supply management and accounts receivable systems for customers. It offers retail pharmacists a wide range of online resources, including supply-management assistance, catalog searches, real-time order tracking, and an account-management system. It has also created solutions such as automated pharmaceutical-dispensing machines that assist pharmacists by reducing costs and improving accuracy. ◉ Retailers can even use the McKesson systems to maintain prescription histories and medical profiles on their customers.

McKesson's medical-surgical supply and equipment customers receive a rich assortment of online solutions and supply management tools, including an online order management system and real-time information on products and pricing, inventory availability, and order status. According to McKesson, it

◉ Pharmaceuticals wholesaler McKesson helps its retail pharmacist customers be more efficient by offering a wide range of online resources. Retail pharmacists can even use the McKesson system to maintain medical profiles on their customers.

adds value in the channel by providing "supply, information, and health care management products and services designed to reduce costs and improve quality across healthcare."[41]

The distinction between large retailers and large wholesalers continues to blur. Many retailers now operate formats such as wholesale clubs and supercenters that perform many wholesale functions. In return, many large wholesalers are setting up their own retailing operations. For example, until recently, SuperValu was classified as a food wholesaler, with a majority of its business derived from supplying grocery products to independent grocery retailers. However, over the past decade, SuperValu has started or acquired several retail food chains of its own—including Albertsons, Jewel-Osco, Save-A-Lot, Cub Foods, Acme, and others—to become the nation's third-largest food retailer (behind Walmart and Kroger). Thus, even though it remains the country's largest food wholesaler, SuperValu is now classified as a retailer because 75 percent of its $44 billion in sales come from retailing.[42]

Wholesalers will continue to increase the services they provide to retailers—retail pricing, cooperative advertising, marketing and management information reports, accounting services, online transactions, and others. Both the recently sluggish economy and the demand for increased services have put the squeeze on wholesaler profits. Wholesalers who do not find efficient ways to deliver value to their customers will soon drop by the wayside. However, the increased use of computerized, automated, and Web-based systems will help wholesalers contain the costs of ordering, shipping, and inventory holding, thus boosting their productivity.

Finally, facing slow growth in their domestic markets and such developments as the North American Free Trade Agreement (NAFTA), many large wholesalers are now going global. For example, McKesson now derives almost 8 percent of its revenues from Canadian and other international operations. Its Information Solutions group operates widely throughout North America, the United Kingdom, and other European countries.[43]

REVIEWING Objectives AND KEY Terms

Retailing and wholesaling consist of many organizations bringing goods and services from the point of production to the point of use. In this chapter, we examined the nature and importance of retailing, the major types of retailers, the decisions retailers make, and the future of retailing. We then examined these same topics for wholesalers.

Objective 1 Explain the role of retailers in the distribution channel and describe the major types of retailers. (pp 374–382)

Retailing includes all the activities involved in selling goods or services directly to final consumers for their personal, nonbusiness use. Retail stores come in all shapes and sizes, and new retail types keep emerging. Store retailers can be classified by the *amount of service* they provide (self-service, limited service, or full service), *product line sold* (specialty stores, department stores, supermarkets, convenience stores, superstores, and service businesses), and *relative prices* (discount stores and off-price retailers). Today, many retailers are banding together in corporate and contractual *retail organizations* (corporate chains, voluntary chains, retailer cooperatives, and franchise organizations).

Objective 2 Describe the major retailer marketing decisions. (pp 382–388)

Retailers are always searching for new marketing strategies to attract and hold customers. They face major marketing decisions about segmentation and targeting, store differentiation and positioning, and the retail marketing mix.

Retailers must first segment and define their target markets and then decide how they will differentiate and position themselves in these markets. Those that try to offer "something for everyone" end up satisfying no market well. In contrast, successful retailers define their target markets well and position themselves strongly.

Guided by strong targeting and positioning, retailers must decide on a retail marketing mix—product and services assortment, price, promotion, and place. Retail stores are much more than simply an assortment of goods. Beyond the products and services they offer, today's successful retailers carefully orchestrate virtually every aspect of the consumer store experience. A retailer's price policy must fit its target market and positioning, products and services assortment, and competition. Retailers use any or all of the five promotion tools—advertising, personal selling, sales promotion, PR, and direct marketing—to reach consumers. Finally, it's very important that retailers select locations that are accessible to the target market in areas that are consistent with the retailer's positioning.

Objective 3 Discuss the major trends and developments in retailing. (pp 389–394)

Retailers operate in a harsh and fast-changing environment, which offers threats as well as opportunities. Following years of good economic times for retailers, the recent recession turned many retailers' fortunes from boom to bust. New retail forms continue to emerge. At the same time, however, different types of retailers are increasingly serving similar customers with the same products and prices (retail convergence), making differentiation more difficult.

Other trends in retailing include the rise of megaretailers, the rapid growth of nonstore retailing, the growing importance of retail technology, a surge in green retailing, and the global expansion of major retailers.

Objective 4 — Explain the major types of wholesalers and their marketing decisions.
(pp 394–400)

Wholesaling includes all the activities involved in selling goods or services to those who are buying for the purpose of resale or business use. Wholesalers fall into three groups. First, *merchant wholesalers* take possession of the goods. They include *full-service wholesalers* (wholesale merchants and industrial distributors) and *limited-service wholesalers* (cash-and-carry wholesalers, truck wholesalers, drop shippers, rack jobbers, producers' cooperatives,

and mail-order wholesalers). Second, *brokers* and *agents* do not take possession of the goods but are paid a commission for aiding buying and selling. Finally, *manufacturers' sales branches and offices* are wholesaling operations conducted by nonwholesalers to bypass the wholesalers.

Like retailers, wholesalers must target carefully and position themselves strongly. And, like retailers, wholesalers must decide on product and service assortments, prices, promotion, and place. Progressive wholesalers constantly watch for better ways to meet the changing needs of their suppliers and target customers. They recognize that, in the long run, their only reason for existence comes from adding value by increasing the efficiency and effectiveness of the entire marketing channel. As with other types of marketers, the goal is to build value-adding customer relationships.

KEY Terms

OBJECTIVE 1

Retailing (p 374)
Retailer (p 374)
Shopper marketing (p 374)
Specialty store (p 376)
Department store (p 376)
Supermarket (p 376)
Convenience store (p 377)
Superstore (p 378)
Category killer (p 378)

Service retailer (p 378)
Discount store (p 378)
Off-price retailer (p 378)
Independent off-price retailer (p 378)
Factory outlet (p 378)
Warehouse club (p 380)
Chain stores (p 381)
Franchise (p 381)

OBJECTIVE 2

Shopping center (p 388)

OBJECTIVE 3

Wheel-of-retailing concept (p 390)

OBJECTIVE 4

Wholesaling (p 394)
Wholesaler (p 394)
Merchant wholesaler (p 396)
Broker (p 396)
Agent (p 396)
Manufacturers' sales branches and offices (p 396)

mymarketinglab

- Check your understanding of the concepts and key terms using the mypearsonmarketinglab study plan for this chapter.
- Apply the concepts in a business context using the simulation entitled **Retailing/Wholesaling**.

DISCUSSING & APPLYING THE Concepts

Discussing the Concepts

1. Discuss how retailers and wholesalers add value to the marketing system. Explain why marketers are embracing the concept of *shopper marketing*. (AACSB: Communication; Reflective Thinking)

2. Discuss the factors used to classify retail establishments and list the types within each classification. (AASCB: Communication)

3. List and briefly discuss the trends impacting the future of retailing. (AACSB: Communication)

4. Suppose you are a manufacturer's agent for three lines of complementary women's apparel. Discuss the types of marketing mix decisions you will make. (AACSB: Communication; Reflective Thinking)

5. Discuss the different organizational approaches for retailers and provide an example of each. (AACSB: Communication; Reflective Thinking)

6. What is retail convergence? Has it helped or harmed small retailers? (AACSB: Communication; Reflective Thinking)

Applying the Concepts

1. The atmosphere in a retail store is carefully crafted to influence shoppers. Select a retailer with both a physical store and an online store. Describe the elements of the physical store's atmosphere, such as coloring, lighting, music, scents, and décor. What image is the store's atmosphere projecting? Is the atmosphere appropriate given the store's merchandise assortment and target market? Which elements of the physical store's atmosphere are in the online store's atmosphere? Does the retailer integrate the physical store's atmosphere with its online presence? Explain. (AACSB: Communication; Use of IT; Reflective Thinking)

2. Shop for a product of your choice on Amazon.com. Do consumer reviews influence your perception of a product or brand offered? Consumers participating in the Amazon Vine

Program submit many of the product reviews found on Amazon.com. Learn about this program and discuss whether or not a review from a consumer in this program is more useful than a review from a consumer not in this program. (AACSB: Communication; Use of IT; Reflective Thinking)

3. Determining the target market and the positioning for a retail store are very important marketing decisions. In a small

group, develop the concept for a new retail store. Who is the target market for your store? How is your store positioned? What retail atmospherics will enhance this positioning effectively to attract and satisfy your target market? (AACSB: Communication; Reflective Thinking)

FOCUS ON Technology

"Mirror, mirror on the wall, who's the fairest of them all?" This is no fairy tale feature anymore and can be found online or at a retailer near you. EZFace, a virtual mirror using augmented reality, is changing the cosmetics aisle in some Walmart stores. A shopper stands in front of the magical mirror, swipes the bar code of the cosmetic she is interested in, and virtually tries it on without opening the package. No more regrets about buying the wrong shade of lipstick! Self-service retailers are interested in this technology because it can reduce damaged inventory from consumers opening a package and then not buying it. This is just one of the interactive digital technologies that retailers are experimenting with; keep an eye out for many more!

1. Visit www.ezface.com or www.ray-ban.com/usa/science/virtual-mirror and use the virtual mirror to try on makeup or sunglasses. Does this technology help you select an appropriate product for your face? (AACSB: Communication; Use of IT; Reflective Thinking)

2. Find other examples of how retailers are using digital technologies, such as digital signage and mobile technologies, to better serve customers. (AACSB: Communication; Use of IT; Reflective Thinking)

FOCUS ON Ethics

In the United States, paying for purchases with a credit card is old news. That's not so in much of Asia. The United States leads the world in credit cards per capita—2.01, which is much higher than many Asian countries, such as China with 0.15 cards per capita or India with 0.02. But that's changing dramatically. Between 2004 and 2009, Asian card transactions grew 158 percent, approaching one-fourth of the global transaction volume. Asian governments are encouraging this growth because it stimulates the economy and brings in more tax revenue. Retailers embrace it because consumers spend more when using cards as compared to cash. This trend is not without critics, however, given the historical aversion to debt exhibited by Asians.

1. What are the ethical implications of encouraging electronic payment methods compared to cash payments in Asian countries? (AACSB: Communication; Ethical Reasoning; Reflective Thinking)

2. Most stores have eliminated layaway options for customers and encourage credit purchases. Should retailers encourage customers to rely heavily on credit? (AACSB: Communication; Reflective Thinking)

MARKETING & THE Economy

Walmart

In tough economic times, low-price leaders generally do well. They keep existing customers and gain new ones who are trading down. That was the case for Walmart throughout most of the recent economic downturn. But more recently, Walmart has seen a changing dynamic. By late 2010, traffic and same-store sales at U.S. stores had been declining for a year. This is puzzling, especially given that the retailer had been aggressively discounting its already low prices during that period. There are two possible reasons for Walmart's declining numbers. First, Walmart's core shoppers have lower average incomes than typical Target shoppers and have felt little relief from the economic recovery. Already at the

ends of their budgets, they are not ready to increase spending, even when something enticing goes on sale. Second, better-off customers who traded down to Walmart are now feeling more relaxed about spending. But rather than spending at Walmart, those customers are returning to other stores they frequented prior to the economic downturn. With a bleak forecast for job growth, Walmart's revenue trend is not expected to change anytime soon.

1. Are there any other options for Walmart other than waiting out the recovering economy?

2. What needs to change in the external environment before Walmart sees stronger growth?

MARKETING BY THE Numbers

Retailers need merchandise to make sales. In fact, a retailer's inventory is its biggest asset. The cost of goods sold greatly impacts a retailer's gross profit margin. Moreover, not stocking enough merchandise can result in lost sales, whereas carrying too much inventory increases costs and lowers margins. Both circumstances reduce profits. One measure of a reseller's inventory management effectiveness is its *stockturn rate* (also called *inventory turnover rate* for manufacturers). The key to success in retailing is realizing a large volume of sales on as little inventory as possible while maintaining enough stock to meet customer demands. Refer to Appendix 2 to answer the following questions.

1. Calculate the gross margin percentage of a retailer with annual sales of $5,000,000 and cost of goods sold of $2,000,000. (AACSB: Analytical Reasoning)

2. Determine the stockturn rate if this retailer carries an average inventory at a cost of $750,000, with a cost of goods sold of $2,000,000. If this company's stockturn rate was 3.5 last year, is the stockturn rate you just calculated better or worse? Explain. (AACSB: Communication; Analytical Reasoning)

VIDEO Case

Zappos.com

These days, online retailers are a dime a dozen. But in less than 10 years, Zappos.com has become a billion dollar company. How did it hit the dot-com jackpot? By providing some of the best service available anywhere. Zappos customers are showered with such perks as free shipping both ways, surprise upgrades to overnight service, a 365-day return policy, and a call center that is always open. Customers are also delighted by employees who are empowered to spontaneously hand out rewards based on unique needs. It's no surprise that Zappos.com has an almost cult-like following of repeat customers.

After viewing the video featuring Zappos.com, answer the following questions.

1. How has Zappos.com differentiated itself from other retailers through each element of the retail marketing mix?

2. What is the relationship between how Zappos.com treats its employees and how it treats its customers?

3. Why did Amazon.com buy Zappos.com, given that it already sells what Zappos.com sells?

COMPANY Case

Tesco Fresh & Easy:
Another British Invasion

One beautiful autumn morning in Ontario, California, a long line of people waited anxiously with shopping carts. The occasion? The grand opening of a Fresh & Easy Neighborhood Market. This was big news for a community starving for decent retail outlets. "The residents have been screaming for this," said Mayor Paul Leon. "For years residents have been asking for more choices in the south Ontario area," a growing suburb populated formerly by more cows than people.

INTRODUCING TESCO

What is Fresh & Easy? To answer that question, let's step back and look at the company behind the new Fresh & Easy grocery chain—Tesco. You may not have heard of Tesco, but it's one of the world's hottest retailers. The first Tesco opened its doors in London in 1919, selling surplus groceries. In the decades that followed, it developed into a traditional grocery store chain and one of the biggest in the United Kingdom, selling 15 percent of the country's groceries.

But in 1997, new CEO Terry Leahy performed a truly amazing feat. Under Leahy's direction, Tesco became the third largest retailer

in the world, trailing only Walmart and France's Carrefour. In just 13 years, Leahy opened more than 4,000 stores, bringing Tesco's current total to over 4,800. Under Leahy's leadership, Tesco grew from selling mostly groceries to becoming a major force in general merchandise. The mega-retailer's portfolio now includes Walmart-style supercenters, full-sized supermarkets, Walgreen's-style stores, and even nonfood discount stores. With 94 million total square feet of retail space, the company employs 472,000 people. During Leahy's tenure, Tesco's UK market share doubled to 30 percent as it expanded from 6 to 14 countries, gaining a presence in the emerging economies of Asia, the Middle East, and Eastern Europe. Revenue soared to $93 billion for 2010 while profits hit $4.7 billion, figures that both grew even during the Great Recession.

With everything going its way, Leahy surprisingly announced his retirement in the summer of 2010 at the age of 55. "My work here is done," he claimed. The accolades came pouring in. "He must surely be written up as one of Britain's greatest businessmen," proclaimed analyst Darren Shirley. "The way that the Tesco brand has been developed, extended, and enhanced by geography and category has been a textbook exercise." In addition to expanding the company, Leahy was known for bringing the business of grocery and discount retailing closer to the shopper with the Tesco Clubcard, an incentive-based loyalty program.

SIZING UP THE U.S. MARKET

With Tesco's resources and momentum, it was only a matter of time before it made a move to crack the U.S. market. In 2007, Tesco made that move with a fat $2-billion commitment and a goal of 1,000 U.S. stores in the first five years. In the years leading up to Tesco's 2007 debut, the U.S. economy was still riding high. Housing developments were spreading like wildfire, and all those new homes and people needed retailers to feed them. As far as Tesco was concerned, it couldn't have picked a better time.

But Tesco also knew that it would face heavily entrenched competition. Walmart dominated the retail landscape. But other entrenched U.S. chains, such as Kroger, Safeway, and SuperValue, all had strong market shares. Then there were the countless regional chains that provided the allure of supporting local and state economies.

Tesco spent lots of time, effort, and money researching the U.S. markets and making decisions on what approach it would take. It examined 20 years worth of data. But it didn't just rely on numbers. "We went into people's houses, talked to them about food and food shopping," said Simon Uwins, Tesco's marketing director. "We went into their kitchens and poked around pantries." In this manner, Tesco videotaped and monitored every habit of American families.

Tesco's research led to some important conclusions. For starters, it chose to focus its United States rollout on California, spilling over into Arizona and Nevada. One of the biggest reasons was that Walmart actually had a minimal presence in California, a state with a GDP big enough to make it the eighth largest country in the world. Despite Walmart's dominance, the mega-retailer had opened only 22 grocery-selling supercenters in the Golden state, compared to 279 in Texas.

Big box stores become a dominant force in the United States. Aside from Walmart Supercenters, the success of retailers such as Best Buy, Bed Bath & Beyond, and Home Depot suggested that growth in just about every category was dominated by superstores. But Tesco decided that, for maximum impact, it would buck this trend and differentiate itself from existing superstore choices. Tim Mason, CEO of Fresh & Easy, discusses insights that helped Tesco reach that conclusion.

> Probably the most surprising thing to me was the number of different stores that an American family uses to shop. They shop in up to 20 different stores—many more than the equivalent [family] would in the UK. They will use different types of shops for their food, for their cleaning products, and for their personal care products. What I discovered is that you just can't get everything that you want in one place. The main retail brands in Britain have much higher levels of loyalty and genuinely do fulfill the notion of a one-stop shop. That's less of the case here. People will wait for flyers and coupons and indeed, people who have time but not money will actually take their shopping list and walk to two or three big players and then decide what to buy.

INTRODUCING FRESH & EASY

With that, Tesco decided to not even try the one-stop supercenter approach. Instead, Fresh & Easy was designed from the beginning as a smaller neighborhood style store positioned between convenience stores and full-sized supermarkets. Tesco calls this an "express" mini-supermarket. The average size of a Fresh & Easy Neighborhood Market is 15,000 square feet. Compare that to a full-sized supermarket at 50,000 to 60,000 square feet or a Walmart Supercenter that reaches up to 260,000 square feet.

With the smaller size, a Fresh & Easy clearly can't carry everything. The chain focuses on fresh, prepared, and ready-to-eat foods with a bit of an emphasis on gourmet—think bags of pomegranates, rose-gold apples, watercress, Japanese shrimp dumplings, and Indian samosas. The stores carry a big selection of store-labeled products with a good balance of premium brands. If you're thinking Trader Joe's, that's exactly the comparison that is often made.

Fresh & Easy promises "big box discounts without the big box." In another Web site headline, Tesco takes a direct shot at Whole Foods Market. "Wholesome food, not whole paycheck." With this combination of benefits, store openings often play out like the one in Ontario. Customers are greeted by a brightly painted storefront and a green logo in lowercase letters. Inside, cheerful employees in green shirts move about a bright, clean store with wide uncluttered aisles. Every food item in Fresh & Easy, even produce, has an expiration date. The stores tout another distinguishing feature—no cashiers. Instead, shoppers are met at a self-checkout aisle by an animated female avatar that guides them through the process.

Fresh & Easy is betting on another strong point of differentiation. The green logo and shirts are intentional. Fresh & Easy has positioned itself as a chain with "sustainability" in its DNA. All stores are designed with energy-efficient lighting and refrigerators. Most of the meats, vegetables, and other fresh foods arrive in reusable plastic containers rather than disposable cardboard. Some stores offer reserved parking for hybrids. And one California Fresh & Easy store has even received the coveted seal of approval from the Leadership in Energy and Environmental Design. The company's Southern California distribution center hosts the largest solar roof array in the state. And all products reach stores in hybrid electric-diesel semitrailers. Fresh & Easy even plans to roll out carbon labels, a simple calculation of the amount of greenhouse gases emitted from an item's production, distribution, use, and disposal.

NOT QUITE A HIT

This kind of venture seems like a no-brainer; one that can't fail. In fact, many predicted that Fresh & Easy would be a category killer. But initial results have given Tesco cause for concern. For starters, the first Fresh & Easy store openings coincided with the beginning of the subprime-mortgage crisis. California, Arizona, and Nevada were among the states hardest hit. As foreclosures multiplied, houses sat vacant in the very developments where Fresh & Easy stores were expected to make a big splash.

Fresh & Easy may also have missed the mark on meeting consumer needs. One observer stated harshly, "It's as if the place purports to solve all kinds of vexing marketing 'problems' while failing to address the most basic real world problem. Namely, why would anyone even want to come here to begin with?" After her initial visit to a Fresh & Easy, one Trader Joe's loyalist said, "I'm sure the food here is tasty. But we are going to have to find more useful things if we are going to shop here much." To compound this problem, initial perceptions of everyday low prices left a lot to be desired.

Tesco claims to be responsive to customer feedback. Indeed, it moved quickly to make some changes after the feedback it received from its first store openings. It hit pricing harder with reductions and increased the use of coupons, including regular coupons for $5 off a $20 shopping bill. And it put higher shelves in stores to add 1,000 new products without taking any items away.

Although Tesco asserts that it is exceeding sales targets, it also slowed its rate of store openings. Whereas it had initially planned to open 100 new stores in the first year and then increase that rate, after three years there are now just over 150 Fresh & Easy stores. Given the high sunk cost of its distribution system, Tesco needs bigger store numbers to defray that expense across more stores. Indeed, the U.S. arm of Tesco lost $260 million on $550 million in sales this year.

Many analysts now speculate as to what will happen with Fresh & Easy as the economy shows signs of improvement. Leahy predicts that by the time he steps down in March 2011, the economy will have seen a "strong recovery." But many economists and analysts aren't so optimistic about what the future holds for the grocery business. Dave McCarthy, a Citigroup managing director and former Tesco employee, provides cautionary advice for Tesco. "The sector is heading for its most difficult time in many years. Opening programs are doubling, industry like-for-likes are currently negative, and discretionary income is falling. And there's uncertainty on how Tesco will deal with the changing industry environment. It will be interesting to see if [Tesco] maintains long-term commitment to the United States if it continues to drain profits."

Questions for Discussion

1. Describe Fresh & Easy according to the different types of retailers discussed in the chapter.

2. As a retail brand, assess the Fresh & Easy retail strategy with respect to segmentation, targeting, differentiation, and positioning.

3. Evaluate Tesco's research efforts for the U.S. market. Did this research help or hurt?

4. Will Fresh & Easy succeed or fail in the long term? Support your answer.

5. What recommendations would you make to Tesco for Fresh & Easy?

Sources: Simon Zekaria, "Leahy's Work Not Yet Done," *Wall Street Journal*, June 8, 2010, accessed at www.wsj.com; Paul Sonne, "Tesco's CEO-to-Be Unfolds Map for Global Expansion," *Wall Street Journal*, June 9, 2010, p. B1; Judie Lannon, "Every Little Bit Helps: Fresh & Easy Brings 21st Century Retailing to the US," *Market Leader*, Autumn 2007, accessed at www.marketing-society.org.uk; Jeffrey Ball, "Tesco to Launch U.S. 'Green' Grocer," *Wall Street Journal*, September 24, 2009, p. B4; Matthew Boyle and Michael V. Copeland, "Tesco Reinvents the 7-Eleven," *Fortune*, November 9, 2007, p. 34; Liset Marquez, "Customers Line Up at South Ontario Fresh and Easy," *Inland Valley Daily Bulletin*, December 2, 2009, accessed at www.dailybulletin.com.

14 Communicating Customer Value Integrated Marketing Communications Strategy

Chapter Preview

In this and the next four chapters, we'll examine the last of the marketing mix tools—promotion. Companies must do more than just create customer value; they must also use promotion to clearly and persuasively communicate that value. Promotion is not a single tool but, rather, a mix of several tools. Under the concept of integrated marketing communications, the company must carefully coordinate these promotion tools to deliver a clear, consistent, and compelling message about its organization and its brands.

We begin by introducing the various promotion mix tools. Next, we examine the rapidly changing communications environment and the need for integrated marketing communications. Finally, we discuss the steps in developing marketing communications and the promotion budgeting process. In the next three chapters, we'll present the specific marketing communications tools.

Let's start by looking at a good integrated marketing communications campaign—the "Häagen-Dazs loves honey bees" campaign. From TV and print ads and an engaging Web site to public affairs and grassroots community events, the campaign employs a rich mix of promotional elements that work harmoniously to communicate Häagen-Dazs' unique message and positioning.

Häagen-Dazs: A Beautifully Integrated Marketing Communications Campaign

Häagen-Dazs is one of today's top-selling super premium ice cream brands. But only a few years ago, the brand teetered on the verge of commodity status. A glut of top ice cream brands had turned to beating each other up on price in an increasingly frugal marketplace. Häagen-Dazs needed to find a way to strengthen its emotional connection to consumers—to stand out from the crowd of competing brands. "We needed a socially relevant idea . . . linked to the brand's core essence," says Katty Pien, brand director for Häagen-Dazs.

In response, the brand launched its "Häagen-Dazs loves honey bees" campaign. The campaign centered on an issue that's important to both the brand and its customers—a mysterious colony-collapse disorder threatening the U.S. honey bee population. Honey bees pollinate one-third of all the natural products we eat and up to 40 percent of the natural flavors used in Häagen-Dazs ice cream. Yet, the nation's honey bee populations are disappearing at an alarming rate. The "HD loves HB" message is a natural one for the brand. "We want to keep these little heroes buzzing," says the company.

Perhaps even more important than the "help the honey bees" message itself is the way that Häagen-Dazs communicates that message. More than just running a few ads and a Web site,

Häagen-Dazs has created a full-fledged, beautifully integrated marketing communications campaign, using a wide range of media and PR elements that work harmoniously for the cause. At the heart of the campaign is a Web site, www .helpthehoneybees.com, a kind of honey bee central where customers can learn about the problem and find out how they can help.

The campaign began with creative broadcast and print ads that were designed to drive traffic to the Web site. The first TV ad was a beautifully staged mini-opera that poignantly outlined the plight of the honey bee. "Honey bees are dying, and we rely on them for many of our natural ingredients," said the ad. "Help us save them." An early print ad introduced Häagen-Dazs' Vanilla Honey Bee flavor ice cream and implored, "Honey, please don't go. Nature needs honey bees. We all do." A more

The beautifully integrated "Häagen-Dazs loves honey bees" marketing communications campaign has helped make Häagen-Dazs more than just another premium ice cream brand. It's now "a brand with a heart and a soul."

recent ad, printed in *Newsweek* on a recycled linen sheet embedded with actual flower seeds, invites readers to "Plant this page. Save a bee." and then visit www.helpthehoneybees .com to learn about other things they can do.

Once at the Web site, which is carefully integrated with other campaign elements, the emotional connections really blossom. With the sounds of birds chirping and bees buzzing, the site greets visitors with the headline "Imagine a world without honey bees" and explains the colony-collapse disorder problem. "Get involved," the site suggests. "Donate now! Buy a carton, save a bee. Plant a bee-friendly garden." At the site, visitors can read more about the bee crisis and what Häagen-Dazs is doing, tap into a news feed called *The Buzz*, turn on Bee TV, purchase Bee-Ts with phrases like "Long live the queen" and "Bee a hero," create their own animated honey bee and "Bee-mail" it to friends, or make a direct donation to support honey bee research.

At the grass roots level, to create even more bee buzz, Häagen-Dazs hands out samples of Vanilla Honey Bee ice cream and wildflower seeds at local farmers markets across the country. It sponsors projects and fund-raisers by local community groups and schools. It also donates a portion of the sales of all bee-dependent flavors (including all of the proceeds from Vanilla Honey Bee) to fund pollination and colony-collapse disorder research at two major universities.

From the start, the "HD loves HB" communications campaign has been a resounding success. Initially, Häagen-Dazs wanted to achieve 125 million media impressions within a year. "We were blown away to see that we reached that goal in the first two weeks," says Pien. Moreover, the campaign helped boost Häagen-Dazs' sales by 16 percent during a recessionary year. And brand advocacy among consumers for Häagen-Dazs hit 69 percent, the highest among nineteen brands tracked in one study.

Beyond traditional advertising media and the www .helpthehoneybee.com Web site, the "HD loves HB" campaign has begun integrating social networking into the communications mix. For example, during a recent one-week period, Häagen-Dazs used Twitter's social-cause portal, TwitCause, to encourage people to spread the message, donating $1 per tweet to honey bee research. The brand has also leveraged the substantial public affairs potential of the honey bee crisis by lobbying Congress. The public affairs campaign included a Capitol Hill ice cream social, media outreach efforts, and even testimony by Pien before Congress to save the honey bee. The burst of media attention from the public affairs efforts added new momentum. "We originally thought this was one small part of the integrated campaign," says Pien. "But it has breathed new life into our consumer campaign."

Thus, the "Häagen-Dazs loves honey bees" integrated marketing campaign uses a rich, well-coordinated blend of communications elements to successfully deliver Häagen-Dazs' unique message and positioning. Only a few years ago, Häagen-Dazs was just a brand of ice cream. But now, thanks to the "HD loves HB" campaign, the premium ice cream brand also stands out as one of the nation's premium social marketers. It's "a brand with a heart and a soul," says Pien. "We're not only raising brand awareness," she says, "but making a difference in the world."[1]

The HD loves HB integrated marketing communications campaign uses a rich, well-coordinated blend of promotion elements to successfully deliver Häagen-Dazs' unique message.

Building good customer relationships calls for more than just developing a good product, pricing it attractively, and making it available to target customers. Companies must also *communicate* their value propositions to customers, and what they communicate should not be left to chance. All communications must be planned and blended into carefully integrated programs. Just as good communication is important in building and maintaining any kind of relationship, it is a crucial element in a company's efforts to build profitable customer relationships.

Author Comment | The promotion mix is the marketer's bag of tools for communicating with customers and other stakeholders. To deliver a clear and compelling message, each tool must be carefully coordinated under the concept of *integrated marketing communications*.

The Promotion Mix (p 408)

A company's total **promotion mix**—also called its **marketing communications mix**—consists of the specific blend of advertising, public relations, personal selling, sales promotion, and direct-marketing tools that the company uses to persuasively communicate customer value and build customer relationships. The five major promotion tools are defined as follows:[2]

- *Advertising:* Any paid form of nonpersonal presentation and promotion of ideas, goods, or services by an identified sponsor.
- *Sales promotion:* Short-term incentives to encourage the purchase or sale of a product or service.
- *Personal selling:* Personal presentation by the firm's sales force for the purpose of making sales and building customer relationships.
- *Public relations:* Building good relations with the company's various publics by obtaining favorable publicity, building up a good corporate image, and handling or heading off unfavorable rumors, stories, and events.
- *Direct marketing:* Direct connections with carefully targeted individual consumers to both obtain an immediate response and cultivate lasting customer relationships.

Each category involves specific promotional tools used to communicate with customers. For example, **advertising** includes broadcast, print, Internet, outdoor, and other forms. **Sales promotion** includes discounts, coupons, displays, and demonstrations. **Personal selling** includes sales presentations, trade shows, and incentive programs. **Public relations (PR)** includes press releases, sponsorships, special events, and Web pages. And **direct marketing** includes catalogs, telephone marketing, kiosks, the Internet, mobile marketing, and more.

At the same time, marketing communication goes beyond these specific promotion tools. The product's design, its price, the shape and color of its package, and the stores that sell it *all* communicate something to buyers. Thus, although the promotion mix is the company's primary communications activity, the entire marketing mix—promotion *and* product, price, and place—must be coordinated for greatest impact.

Promotion mix (or marketing communications mix)
The specific blend of promotion tools that the company uses to persuasively communicate customer value and build customer relationships.

Advertising
Any paid form of nonpersonal presentation and promotion of ideas, goods, or services by an identified sponsor.

Sales promotion
Short-term incentives to encourage the purchase or sale of a product or service.

Personal selling
Personal presentation by the firm's sales force for the purpose of making sales and building customer relationships.

Public relations (PR)
Building good relations with the company's various publics by obtaining favorable publicity, building up a good corporate image, and handling or heading off unfavorable rumors, stories, and events.

Author | This is a really hot
Comment | marketing topic these
days. Perhaps no other area of
marketing is changing so quickly and
profoundly as marketing
communications.

Direct marketing
Direct connections with carefully targeted
individual consumers to both obtain an
immediate response and cultivate lasting
customer relationships.

Integrated Marketing Communications (pp 409–414)

In past decades, marketers perfected the art of mass marketing: selling highly standardized products to masses of customers. In the process, they developed effective mass-media communications techniques to support these strategies. Large companies now routinely invest millions or even billions of dollars in television, magazine, or other mass-media advertising, reaching tens of millions of customers with a single ad. Today, however, marketing managers face some new marketing communications realities. Perhaps no other area of marketing is changing so profoundly as marketing communications, creating both exciting and anxious times for marketing communicators.

The New Marketing Communications Model

Several major factors are changing the face of today's marketing communications. First, *consumers* are changing. In this digital, wireless age, they are better informed and more communications empowered. Rather than relying on marketer-supplied information, they can use the Internet and other technologies to find information on their own. They can connect more easily with other consumers to exchange brand-related information or even create their own marketing messages.

Second, *marketing strategies* are changing. As mass markets have fragmented, marketers are shifting away from mass marketing. More and more, they are developing focused marketing programs designed to build closer relationships with customers in more narrowly defined micromarkets.

Finally, sweeping advances in *communications technology* are causing remarkable changes in the ways in which companies and customers communicate with each other. The digital age has spawned a host of new information and communication tools—from smartphones and iPods to satellite and cable television systems to the many faces of the Internet (e-mail, social networks, blogs, brand Web sites, and so much more). These explosive developments have had a dramatic impact on marketing communications. Just as mass marketing once gave rise to a new generation of mass-media communications, the new digital media have given birth to a new marketing communications model.

Although television, magazines, newspapers, and other mass media remain very important, their dominance is declining. In their place, advertisers are now adding a broad selection of more-specialized and highly targeted media to reach smaller customer segments with more-personalized, interactive messages. The new media range from specialty cable television channels and made-for-the-Web videos to Internet catalogs, e-mail, blogs, cell phone content, and online social networks. In all, companies are doing less *broadcasting* and more *narrowcasting*.

Some advertising industry experts even predict that the old mass-media communications model will soon be obsolete. Mass media costs are rising, audiences are shrinking, ad clutter is increasing, and viewers are gaining control of message exposure through technologies such as video streaming or DVRs that let them skip past disruptive television commercials. As a result, they suggest, marketers are shifting ever-larger portions of their marketing budgets away from old-media mainstays such as 30-second TV commercials and glossy magazine ads to digital and other new-age media. For example, one study forecasts that whereas TV advertising spending will grow by only 4 percent per year over the next five years, ad spending on the Internet and other digital media will surge by 17 percent a year.[3]

When Kimberly-Clark recently launched its Huggies Pure & Natural line of diapers, for instance, it skipped national TV advertising altogether—something once unthinkable in the consumer products industry. Instead, it targeted new and expectant mothers through mommy blogs, Web sites, print and online ads, e-mail, in-store promotions, and in-hospital TV programming. ⬤ Similarly, when Microsoft recently relaunched its Zune Pass online music service, it used 30-second spots but placed them online only, allowing more precise targeting. By using ads on many smaller sites, Zune Pass reached as many of its targeted

● The new marketing communications model: In relaunching Zune Pass, Microsoft used 30-second spots but placed them online only, reaching as many target consumers but at half the cost of traditional media.

young, male consumers as it did using national TV ads the previous year but in a more relevant way and at half the cost.[4]

In the new marketing communications world, rather than old approaches that interrupt customers and force-feed them mass messages, new media formats let marketers reach smaller groups of consumers in more interactive, engaging ways. For example, think about television viewing these days. Consumers can now watch their favorite programs on just about anything with a screen—on televisions but also laptops, cell phones, or iPods. And they can choose to watch programs whenever and wherever they wish, often with or without commercials. Increasingly, some programs, ads, and videos are being produced only for Internet viewing.

Despite the shift toward new digital media, however, traditional mass media still capture a lion's share of the promotion budgets of most major marketing firms, a fact that probably won't change quickly. For example, P&G, a leading proponent of digital media, still spends a lion's share of its huge advertising budget on mass media. Although P&G's digital outlay more than doubled last year, digital still accounts for only about 5 percent of the company's total advertising spending.[5]

At a broader level, although some may question the future of the 30-second TV spot, it's still very much in use today. Last year, more than 48 percent of U.S. advertising dollars was spent on network, spot, and cable television commercials versus 7.8 percent on Internet advertising. Some 99 percent of video watching in the United States is still done via traditional TV, and average viewership is up 20 percent from 10 years ago. So, says one media expert, "Traditional TV [is] still king."[6]

Thus, rather than the old media model rapidly collapsing, most industry insiders see a more gradual blending of new and traditional media. The new marketing communications model will consist of a shifting mix of both traditional mass media and a wide array of exciting, new, more-targeted, and more-personalized media. The challenge is to bridge the "media divide" that too often separates traditional creative and media approaches from new interactive and digital ones. Many advertisers and ad agencies are now grappling with this transition (see Real Marketing 14.1). In the end, however, regardless of whether it's traditional or digital, the key is to find the mix of media that best communicates the brand message and enhances the customer's brand experience.

The Need for Integrated Marketing Communications

The shift toward a richer mix of media and communication approaches poses a problem for marketers. Consumers today are bombarded by commercial messages from a broad range of sources. But consumers don't distinguish between message sources the way marketers do. In the consumer's mind, messages from different media and promotional approaches all become part of a single message about the company. Conflicting messages from these different sources can result in confused company images, brand positions, and customer relationships.

All too often, companies fail to integrate their various communications channels. The result is a hodgepodge of communications to consumers. Mass-media advertisements say one thing, while an in-store promotion sends a different signal, and company sales literature creates still another message. And the company's Web site, e-mails, Facebook page, or videos posted on YouTube say something altogether different.

The problem is that these communications often come from different parts of the company. Advertising messages are planned and implemented by the advertising department or an ad agency. Personal selling communications are developed by sales management. Other company specialists are responsible for PR, sales promotion events, Internet or social network efforts, and other forms of marketing communications. However, whereas these

Real Marketing 14.1

The Shifting Advertising Universe:
SoBe It!

SoBe made a big splash in the 2008 Super Bowl with a big-budget, 60-second commercial produced by the Arnell Group, an old-line Madison Avenue creative ad agency. The ad extravaganza featured supermodel Naomi Campbell and a full troupe of SoBe lizards, energized by colorful droplets of the brand's new enhanced water, LifeWater. The computer-generated graphics were stunning, the colors alluring, and Naomi Campbell was, well, Naomi Campbell. However, although the ad drew attention, it was not a viewer favorite. It just didn't connect with consumers.

Not to be denied, for the 2009 Super Bowl, SoBe and parent company PepsiCo assigned the Arnell Group to create an even more elaborate (and even more expensive) commercial, a 3D spectacular featuring pro football players in white tutus performing a ballet, directed by a SoBe lizard. Once the athletes and lizards got a taste of SoBe Life-Water, a DJ cranked up the music, and the dance switched to hip-hop. Once again, although the ad generated a ton of awareness, it simply didn't deliver much in the way of consumer-brand engagement. As one journalist stated bluntly: "The SoBe spots [were] among the biggest wastes of money in Super Bowl history."

Finally the wiser, SoBe ran no ads during the 2010 Super Bowl. In fact, in a move that sent shivers down the spines of many old-line Madison Avenue agencies, SoBe abandoned its traditional big-media, "TV-first," advertising approach altogether and adopted a more bottom-up, digital, new-media approach. It fired the Arnell Group, replacing the big creative agency with a team of smaller digital, PR, and promotion shops. "The passionate fans weren't saying things we thought they should be saying," says Angelique Krembs, SoBe's marketing director. "Going forward, we needed to get engagement. That's why we evolved our approach."

SoBe's new advertising model turns the old approach upside down. Instead of starting with mass-market TV and print advertising, SoBe now aims first to hook its 18-to-29-year-old target audience with more focused and involving digital and interactive media. "We're not tied to the old methods," says Krembs. "The key to success is we're not starting with 'Here is our TV plan, and here's what we're going to create for it.' As opposed to creating advertising, we're creating content," and then figuring out where to put it to engage customers in the most effective way. In a reverse of past thinking, Krembs notes, SoBe's first choice going forward would be to have content appear online first and then moved to traditional TV. That kind of thinking spells trouble for traditional Madison Avenue creative agencies, which cut their teeth on developing creative ads for big-budget, mostly television and print campaigns.

SoBe's new advertising approach reflects a broader industry trend. In today's splintering advertising universe, in which there are more new places than ever to stick ads—online, on cell phones, in all places digital and interactive—advertisers and traditional ad agencies alike are scrambling to stay relevant. Says one agency CEO:

TV viewers are using DVRs to blast through the very commercials that are [the traditional agency's] bread and butter. Marketers are stampeding online, where [these traditional agencies] lack the tools and talent to compete. Digital boutiques are proliferating, staffed with tech vets and Gen Y video artists dedicated to making ads for video-sharing and social-networking sites and whatever comes after them.

For decades, the traditional creative agencies ruled the roost. They were about coming up with strategic Big Ideas that would connect brands emotionally with millions of consumers through large-scale mass-media campaigns. But today, the Small Idea is on the rise. Increasingly, like SoBe, marketers are adding a host of new digital and interactive media—Web sites, viral video, blogs, social networks—that let them target individuals or small communities of consumers rather than the masses.

In this shifting advertising universe, traditional creative agencies, such as the Arnell Group, often find themselves outmaneuvered by smaller, more nimble and specialized digital, interactive, and media agencies. However, these smaller digital shops lack experience in leading accounts and driving brand strategy. The competition is fierce, with traditional agencies struggling to become more digital and digital agencies struggling to become more traditional. "We in the ad business are faced with the question of who is going to lead this new world," says an industry analyst. "Will it be digitized traditional agencies or the new breed of digital agencies with big ambitions? Every day we see evidence of the contest afoot. The outcome, however, is far from clear."

Rather than starting with mass-market TV and print ads, SoBe's new bottom-up advertising approach now begins with more engaging and interactive online content.

Continued on next page

At SoBe, however, things seem clear enough. The brand's latest campaign involves no traditional agencies. Rather, SoBe's brand team includes Firstborn, a digital shop, as the lead agency, which partners with PR agency Weber Shandwick and promotional agency TracyLocke. Under the old approach, the SoBe brand team would have developed a "creative brief" that outlined the brand and advertising strategy and then let the Arnell Group take the lead in creating the advertising (usually a traditional television-plus-print campaign). Under the new approach, the SoBe brand team and the three agencies work jointly in an ongoing process to create and distribute engaging message content, often starting with digital and interactive venues. "The process might seem more chaotic," says Krembs, "but there's more opportunity to improve, because you keep 'workshoping' it. It's not, 'Here's [a brief,] go out and make it.'"

One of the SoBe team's first efforts illustrates the new approach. The team created two new TV spots using footage first shot at a SoBe print-ad shoot. The footage featured *Twilight* star Ashley Greene and was part of *Sports Illustrated*'s famed swimsuit issue. SoBe first used the footage online and then in a PR effort. Only then did it repurpose the material into TV ads.

By creating ads from material that has debuted interactively online, SoBe can see what resonates most with customers and avoid expensive missteps, such as its previous Super Bowl ads. "We're creating production efficiencies, but it's more of a strategic decision to let consumers react to different things out there and then reuse [successful content] in a different way," says the president of Firstborn. Krembs agrees: "By the time we get to TV, we should be referencing something that's culturally relevant."

Consumer relevance and interaction seem to be the key to the new approach. For example, go to the SoBe Web site and you'll see customer testimonials from real on-the-street tastings of SoBe flavors or even a "Join the Debate" feature inviting consumers to vote for the next SoBe flavor.

Interestingly, SoBe's shifting communication strategy comes at a time when the brand is doing extremely well. With its LifeWater efforts, its share of the enhanced water category nearly doubled to 10.7 percent. That's only about one-third the share of Coca-Cola's Vitaminwater, but it represents tremendous growth. Last year, with the launch of a zero-calorie line, SoBe posted a 68 percent rise in volume. So the new advertising approach evolved not to meet a crisis but as a forward-thinking effort to adjust to the new advertising environment.

Thus, for advertisers and their agencies, as oft-misspoken baseball legend Yogi Berra once said, "The future ain't what it used to be." In the fast-changing advertising universe, SoBe and other brands are scrambling to master the new digital and interactive technologies and merge them effectively with traditional approaches. In turn, the shift in advertising thinking is spurring traditional creative agencies to add digital know-how at the same time that the new digital agencies are trying to build brand-stewardship skills. For advertisers and agencies alike, the message is clear. Says the agency CEO, "We've got to reinvent and transform the way we work."

Sources: Quotes, extracts, and other information from Ken Wheaton, "Is Pepsi's Pass on Super Bowl an Offensive or Defensive Move?" *Advertising Age*, January 4, 2010, p. 12; Tony Quin, "Race to Relevance: Why the Winners Will Come from Both Sides," *Brandweek*, March 15, 2010, p. 14; Burt Helm, "Struggles of a Mad Man," *BusinessWeek*, December 3, 2007, pp. 44–49; Bob Garfield, "Ed McMahon's Bad Ad Steals the Super Bowl," *Advertising Age*, February 2, 2009, accessed at http://adage.com/article?article_id=134248; and Natalie Zmuda, "SoBe Ditches Creative Agency in New Marketing Approach," *Advertising Age*, April 14, 2010, accessed at http://adage.com/agencynews/article?article_id=143303.

Integrated marketing communications (IMC)
Carefully integrating and coordinating the company's many communications channels to deliver a clear, consistent, and compelling message about the organization and its products.

companies have separated their communications tools, customers don't. Mixed communications from these sources result in blurred brand perceptions by consumers.

Today, more companies are adopting the concept of **integrated marketing communications (IMC)**. Under this concept, as illustrated in ⊙ **Figure 14.1**, the company carefully integrates its many communications channels to deliver a clear, consistent, and compelling message about the organization and its brands.

Integrated marketing communications calls for recognizing all touchpoints where the customer may encounter the company and its brands. Each *brand contact* will deliver a message—whether good, bad, or indifferent. The company's goal should be to deliver a consistent and positive message to each contact. IMC leads to a total marketing communications strategy aimed at building strong customer relationships by showing how the company and its products can help customers solve their problems.

Integrated marketing communications ties together all of the company's messages and images. Its television and print ads have the same message, look, and feel as its e-mail and personal selling communications. And its PR materials project the same image as its Web site or social network presence. Often, different media play unique roles in attracting, informing, and persuading consumers; these roles must be carefully coordinated under the overall marketing communications plan.

A great example of the power of a well-integrated marketing communications effort is the "Häagen-Dazs loves honey bees" campaign discussed at the start of this chapter. Another is Burger King's now-classic, award-winning, Whopper Freakout campaign:[7]

● **FIGURE** | **14.1**
Integrated Marketing
Communications

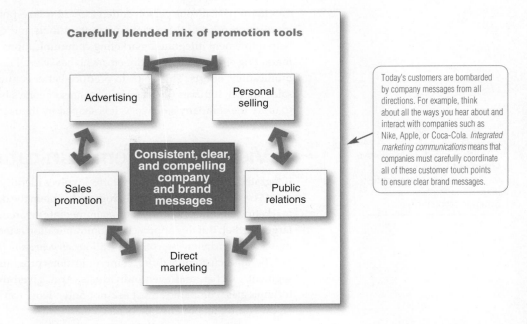

Carefully blended mix of promotion tools

Advertising

Personal selling

Consistent, clear, and compelling company and brand messages

Sales promotion

Public relations

Direct marketing

Today's customers are bombarded by company messages from all directions. For example, think about all the ways you hear about and interact with companies such as Nike, Apple, or Coca-Cola. *Integrated marketing communications* means that companies must carefully coordinate all of these customer touch points to ensure clear brand messages.

● **Integrated marketing communications: Burger King's richly integrated, multipronged Whopper Freakout campaign, which employed a carefully coordinated mix of everything from TV and radio ads to rich media ad banners and a Freakout Web site, boosted store traffic and Whopper sales by 29 percent.**

To celebrate the 50th anniversary of the iconic Whopper, Burger King launched a campaign to show what would happen if it suddenly removed the sandwich from its menu "forever." It dropped the Whopper in selected restaurants and used hidden cameras to capture the real-time reactions of stricken customers. It then shared the results in a carefully integrated, multipronged promotional campaign. The campaign began with coordinated TV, print, and radio spots announcing that "We stopped selling the Whopper for one day to see what would happen. . . . What happened was, people freaked!" The ads drove consumers to www.whopperfreakout.com, which featured a video documentary outlining the entire experiment. ● The documentary was also uploaded to YouTube. At the Web site, visitors could view Freakout ads showing the disbelieving, often angry reactions of a dozen or more customers. Burger King also promoted the campaign through rich media ad banners on several other popular Web sites. Customers themselves extended the campaign with spoofs and parodies posted on YouTube. The richly integrated Whopper Freakout campaign was a smashing success. The ads became the most recalled campaign in Burger King's history, and the whopperfreakout.com Web site received 4 million views in only the first three months. In all, the IMC campaign drove store traffic and sales of the Whopper up a whopping 29 percent.

In the past, no one person or department was responsible for thinking through the communication roles of the various promotion tools and coordinating the promotion mix. To help implement integrated marketing communications, some companies have appointed a marketing communications director who has overall responsibility for the company's communications efforts. This helps to produce better communications consistency and greater sales impact. It places the responsibility in someone's hands—where none existed before—to unify the company's image as it is shaped by thousands of company activities.

> **Author Comment** | To develop effective marketing communications, you must first understand the general communication process.

A View of the Communication Process (pp 414–415)

Integrated marketing communications involves identifying the target audience and shaping a well-coordinated promotional program to obtain the desired audience response. Too often, marketing communications focus on immediate awareness, image, or preference goals in the target market. But this approach to communication is too shortsighted. Today, marketers are moving toward viewing communications as *managing the customer relationship over time*.

Because customers differ, communications programs need to be developed for specific segments, niches, and even individuals. And, given the new interactive communications technologies, companies must ask not only "How can we reach our customers?" but also "How can we let our customers reach us?"

Thus, the communications process should start with an audit of all the potential touch-points that target customers may have with the company and its brands. For example, someone purchasing a new cell phone plan may talk to others, see television ads, read articles and ads in newspapers and magazines, visit various Web sites for prices and reviews, and check out plans at Best Buy, Walmart, or a wireless provider's kiosk or store at the mall. The marketer needs to assess what influence each communication experience will have at different stages of the buying process. This understanding helps marketers allocate their communication dollars more efficiently and effectively.

To communicate effectively, marketers need to understand how communication works. Communication involves the nine elements shown in ◉ **Figure 14.2**. Two of these elements are the major parties in a communication—the *sender* and the *receiver*. Another two are the major communication tools—the *message* and the *media*. Four more are major communication functions—*encoding*, *decoding*, *response*, and *feedback*. The last element is *noise* in the system. Definitions of these elements follow and are applied to a McDonald's "i'm lovin' it" television commercial.

◉ **FIGURE | 14.2**
Elements in the Communication Process

There is a lot going on in this figure! For example, apply this model to McDonald's. To create great adertising—such as its long-running "i'm lovin' it" campaign—McDonald's must thoroughly understand its customers and how communication works.

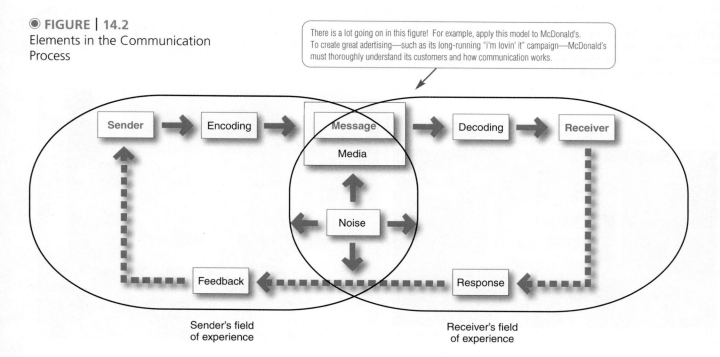

- *Sender:* The *party sending the message* to another party—here, McDonald's.
- *Encoding:* The process of *putting thought into symbolic form*—for example, McDonald's ad agency assembles words, sounds, and illustrations into a TV advertisement that will convey the intended message.
- *Message:* The *set of symbols* that the sender transmits—the actual McDonald's ad.
- *Media:* The *communication channels* through which the message moves from the sender to the receiver—in this case, television and the specific television programs that McDonald's selects.
- *Decoding:* The process by which the receiver *assigns meaning to the symbols* encoded by the sender—a consumer watches the McDonald's commercial and interprets the words and images it contains.
- *Receiver:* The *party receiving the message* sent by another party—the customer who watches the McDonald's ad.
- *Response:* The *reactions of the receiver* after being exposed to the message—any of hundreds of possible responses, such as the consumer likes McDonald's better, is more likely to eat at McDonald's next time, hums the "i'm lovin' it" jingle, or does nothing.
- *Feedback:* The part of the *receiver's response communicated back to the sender*—McDonald's research shows that consumers are either struck by and remember the ad or they write or call McDonald's, praising or criticizing the ad or its products.
- *Noise:* The *unplanned static or distortion* during the communication process, which results in the receiver getting a different message than the one the sender sent—the consumer is distracted while watching the commercial and misses its key points.

For a message to be effective, the sender's encoding process must mesh with the receiver's decoding process. The best messages consist of words and other symbols that are familiar to the receiver. The more the sender's field of experience overlaps with that of the receiver, the more effective the message is likely to be. Marketing communicators may not always *share* their customer's field of experience. For example, an advertising copywriter from one socioeconomic level might create ads for customers from another level—say, wealthy business owners. However, to communicate effectively, the marketing communicator must *understand* the customer's field of experience.

This model points out several key factors in good communication. Senders need to know what audiences they wish to reach and what responses they want. They must be good at encoding messages that take into account how the target audience decodes them. They must send messages through media that reach target audiences, and they must develop feedback channels so that they can assess an audience's response to the message.

> **Author Comment** | Now that we understand how communication works, it's time to turn all of those promotion mix elements into an actual marketing communications program.

Steps in Developing Effective Marketing Communication (pp 415–422)

We now examine the steps in developing an effective integrated communications and promotion program. Marketers must do the following: Identify the target audience, determine the communication objectives, design a message, choose the media through which to send the message, select the message source, and collect feedback.

Identifying the Target Audience

A marketing communicator starts with a clear target audience in mind. The audience may be current users or potential buyers, those who make the buying decision or those who influence it. The audience may be individuals, groups, special publics, or the general public. The target audience will heavily affect the communicator's decisions on *what* will be said, *how* it will be said, *when* it will be said, *where* it will be said, and *who* will say it.

Determining the Communication Objectives

Once the target audience has been defined, marketers must determine the desired response. Of course, in many cases, they will seek a *purchase* response. But purchase may result only after a lengthy consumer decision-making process. The marketing communicator needs to know where the target audience now stands and to what stage it needs to be moved. The target audience may be in any of six **buyer-readiness stages**, the stages consumers normally pass through on their way to making a purchase. These stages include *awareness*, *knowledge*, *liking*, *preference*, *conviction*, and *purchase* (see ● **Figure 14.3**).

Buyer-readiness stages
The stages consumers normally pass through on their way to a purchase, including awareness, knowledge, liking, preference, conviction, and, finally, the actual purchase.

The marketing communicator's target market may be totally unaware of the product, know only its name, or know only a few things about it. Thus, the communicator must first build *awareness* and *knowledge*. ● For example, Kia used its biggest-ever marketing campaign—centered around last year's Super Bowl—to introduce its redesigned 2011 Sorento CUV.[8]

● Moving customers through the buyer-readiness stages: Kia used its biggest-ever marketing campaign—centered around a major Super Bowl commercial—to create awareness and knowledge of its redesigned Sorento SUV.

To build early interest and excitement, Kia first ran 15-second teaser ads weeks prior to the game. The commercials featured life-sized versions of Nick Jr.'s *Yo Gabba Gabba* character Muno and In My Own Dream Studio's Sock Monkey character, Mr. X, Teddy Bear, and Robot partying in Las Vegas to the neo soul tune "How You Like Me Now?" by the British Indie rock band The Heavy. The teaser ads never showed or even mentioned the Sorento but closed by inviting viewers to "See us in the third quarter of the Big Game. Kia. The Power to Surprise." The new Sorento was then unveiled in a full one-minute commercial aired during the Super Bowl, which featured the unlikely characters visiting various Vegas venues. In the end, it was all a dream; the toys were back to normal, resting next to a child in the backseat of a new Sorento. The commercial ended with rapid-fire screens reviewing the benefits of the redesigned CUV—technology, built in the United States, fuel efficiency, prices starting at $29K—all wrapped up in the slogan "A departure from the expected."

Assuming that target consumers *know* about the product, how do they *feel* about it? Once potential buyers knew about the redesigned Sorento, Kia's marketers wanted to move them through successively stronger stages of feelings toward the new model. These stages include *liking* (feeling favorable about the CUV), *preference* (preferring the Sorento to other CUVs), and *conviction* (believing that the Sorento is the best vehicle for them).

Kia marketers used a combination of the promotion mix tools to create positive feelings and conviction. The initial commercials helped build anticipation and an emotional brand connection. Print and digital ads illustrated the Sorento's design and features. Press releases and other PR activities helped keep the buzz going about the product. A packed Web site informed potential buyers about technical specifications, features and options, safety ratings, and prices. And dealer salespeople told buyers about options, value for the price, and after-sale service.

A goal of marketing in general, and of marketing communications in particular, is to move target customers through the buying process. Once again, it all starts with understanding customer needs and wants.

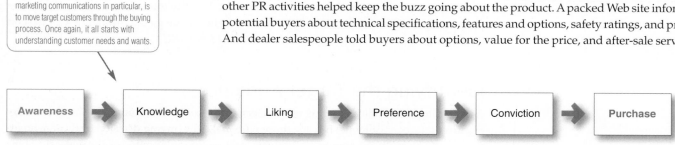

● **FIGURE | 14.3**
Buyer-Readiness Stages

Finally, some members of the target market might be convinced about the product but not quite get around to making the *purchase*. Potential Sorento buyers might have decided to wait for more information or for the economy to improve. The communicator must lead these consumers to take the final step. Actions might include offering special promotional prices, rebates, or premiums. Dealers might call, write, or e-mail selected customers, inviting them to visit the showroom. The Sorento Web site even offers a $25 gift card for simply signing up for a test drive at a local Kia dealership.

Of course, marketing communications alone could not create positive feelings and purchases for the Sorento. The vehicle itself must provide superior value for the customer. In fact, outstanding marketing communications can actually speed the demise of a poor product. The more quickly potential buyers learn about the poor product, the more quickly they become aware of its faults. Thus, good marketing communications call for "good deeds followed by good words."

Designing a Message

Having defined the desired audience response, the communicator then turns to developing an effective message. Ideally, the message should get *attention*, hold *interest*, arouse *desire*, and obtain *action* (a framework known as the *AIDA model*). In practice, few messages take the consumer all the way from awareness to purchase, but the AIDA framework suggests the desirable qualities of a good message.

When putting the message together, the marketing communicator must decide what to say (*message content*) and how to say it (*message structure* and *format*).

Message Content

The marketer has to figure out an appeal or theme that will produce the desired response. There are three types of appeals: rational, emotional, and moral. *Rational appeals* relate to the audience's self-interest. They show that the product will produce the desired benefits. Examples are messages showing a product's quality, economy, value, or performance. Thus, in one ad, Quaker states, "You love it. And it *loves* your heart. Quaker Instant Oatmeal. A warm, yummy way to help lower your cholesterol." And a Weight Watchers' ad states this simple fact: "The diet secret to end all diet secrets is that there is no diet secret."

Emotional appeals attempt to stir up either negative or positive emotions that can motivate purchase. Communicators may use emotional appeals ranging from love, joy, and humor to fear and guilt. Advocates of emotional messages claim that they attract more attention and create more belief in the sponsor and the brand. The idea is that consumers often feel before they think, and persuasion is emotional in nature. Thus, Michelin sells tires using mild fear appeals, showing families riding in cars and telling parents "Michelin: Because so much is riding on your tires." And the Diamond Trading Company runs emotional ads showing men surprising the women they love with diamond jewelry. Concludes one commercial, "With every waking moment love grows. A diamond is forever."

Moral appeals are directed to an audience's sense of what is "right" and "proper." They are often used to urge people to support social causes, such as a cleaner environment or aid to the disadvantaged. ● For example, the United Way's Live United campaign urges people to give back to their communities—to "Live United. Make a difference. Help create opportunities for everyone in your community." An EarthShare ad

● Ad message content: United Way uses moral appeals—urging people to "Live United. Make a difference. Help create opportunities for everyone in your community."

urges environmental involvement by reminding people that "We live in the house we all build. Every decision we make has consequences. . . . We choose the world we live in, so make the right choices. . . ."

These days, it seems as if every company is using humor in its advertising, from consumer product firms such as Anheuser-Busch to the scholarly *American Heritage Dictionary*. For example, nine of the top 10 most popular ads in *USA Today*'s ad meter consumer rankings of last year's Super Bowl ads used humor. Properly used, humor can capture attention, make people feel good, and give a brand personality. However, advertisers must be careful when using humor. Used poorly, it can detract from comprehension, wear out its welcome fast, overshadow the product, and even irritate consumers.

Message Structure

Marketers must also decide how to handle three message structure issues. The first is whether to draw a conclusion or leave it to the audience. Research suggests that, in many cases, rather than drawing a conclusion, the advertiser is better off asking questions and letting buyers come to their own conclusions.

The second message structure issue is whether to present the strongest arguments first or last. Presenting them first gets strong attention but may lead to an anticlimactic ending.

The third message structure issue is whether to present a one-sided argument (mentioning only the product's strengths) or a two-sided argument (touting the product's strengths while also admitting its shortcomings). Usually, a one-sided argument is more effective in sales presentations—except when audiences are highly educated or likely to hear opposing claims or when the communicator has a negative association to overcome. In this spirit, Heinz ran the message "Heinz Ketchup is slow good," and Listerine ran the message "Listerine tastes bad twice a day." In such cases, two-sided messages can enhance an advertiser's credibility and make buyers more resistant to competitor attacks.

Message Format

The marketing communicator also needs a strong *format* for the message. In a print ad, the communicator has to decide on the headline, copy, illustration, and colors. ◉ To attract attention, advertisers can use novelty and contrast; eye-catching pictures and headlines; distinctive formats; message size and position; and color, shape, and movement. If the message is to be carried over the radio, the communicator has to choose words, sounds, and voices. The "sound" of an ad promoting banking services should be different from one promoting an iPod.

If the message is to be carried on television or in person, then all these elements plus body language must be planned. Presenters plan every detail—facial expressions, gestures, dress, posture, and hairstyles. If the message is carried on the product or its package, the communicator must watch texture, scent, color, size, and shape. For example, color alone can enhance message recognition for a brand. One study suggests that color increases brand recognition by up to 80 percent—think about Target (red), McDonald's (yellow and red), John Deere (green and yellow), IBM (blue); or UPS (brown). Thus, in designing effective marketing communications, marketers must consider color and other seemingly unimportant details carefully.[9]

Choosing Media

The communicator must now select the *channels of communication*. There are two broad types of communication channels: *personal* and *nonpersonal*.

◉ **Message format: To attract attention, advertisers can use novelty and contrast, eye-catching pictures and headlines, or distinctive formats, as in this PEDIGREE ad.**

DOGGIE DENTURES
Because brushing is just too hard.

Or, there's DENTASTIX.
The treat that's clinically proven to reduce up to 80% of tartar buildup.
Dogsrule.com

Personal Communication Channels

Personal communication channels

Channels through which two or more people communicate directly with each other, including face to face, on the phone, via mail or e-mail, or even through an Internet "chat."

In **personal communication channels**, two or more people communicate directly with each other. They might communicate face to face, on the phone, via mail or e-mail, or even through an Internet "chat." Personal communication channels are effective because they allow for personal addressing and feedback.

Some personal communication channels are controlled directly by the company. For example, company salespeople contact business buyers. But other personal communications about the product may reach buyers through channels not directly controlled by the company. These channels might include independent experts—consumer advocates, online buying guides, and others—making statements to buyers. Or they might be neighbors, friends, family members, and associates talking to target buyers. This last channel, **word-of-mouth influence**, has considerable effect in many product areas.

Word-of-mouth influence

Personal communications about a product between target buyers and neighbors, friends, family members, and associates.

Personal influence carries great weight for products that are expensive, risky, or highly visible. Consider the power of simple customer reviews on Amazon.com:[10]

> It doesn't matter how loud or often you tell consumers your "truth," few today are buying a big-ticket item before they know what existing users have to say about the product. This is a low-trust world. That's why "recommendation by a relative or friend" comes out on top in just about every survey of purchasing influences. One study found that 90 percent of customers trust recommendations from people they know and 70 percent trust consumer opinions posted online, whereas the trust in ads runs from a high of about 62 percent to less than 24 percent, depending on the medium. Customer reviews are also a major reason for Amazon's success in growing sales per customer. Who hasn't made an Amazon purchase based on another customer's review or the "Customers who bought this also bought . . ." section? And it explains what a recent Shop.org survey found—that 96 percent of retailers find ratings and reviews to be an effective tactic in lifting online sales.

Buzz marketing

Cultivating opinion leaders and getting them to spread information about a product or service to others in their communities.

Companies can take steps to put personal communication channels to work for them. For example, as we discussed in Chapter 5, they can create *opinion leaders* for their brands—people whose opinions are sought by others—by supplying influencers with the product on attractive terms or by educating them so that they can inform others. **Buzz marketing** involves cultivating opinion leaders and getting them to spread information about a product or service to others in their communities.

Nonpersonal communication channels

Media that carry messages without personal contact or feedback, including major media, atmospheres, and events.

P&G has created a huge word-of-mouth marketing arm—Vocalpoint—consisting of 500,000 moms. ● Vocalpoint recruits "connectors"—natural-born buzzers with vast networks of friends and a gift for gab. They create buzz not only for P&G brands but also for those of other client companies as well. P&G recently used the Vocalpoint network in the launch of its new Crest Weekly Clean teeth cleaning paste. P&G didn't pay the moms or coach them on what to say. It simply educated the Vocalpointers about the product, armed them with free samples and coupons for friends, and then asked them to share their "honest opinions with us and with other real women." In turn, the Vocalpoint moms created hundreds of thousands of personal recommendations for the new product.[11]

Nonpersonal Communication Channels

Nonpersonal communication channels are media that carry messages without personal contact or feedback. They include major media, atmospheres, and events. Major *media* include print media (newspapers, magazines, direct-mail), broadcast media (television, radio), display media (billboards, signs, posters), and online media (e-mail, company Web sites, and online social and

● **Buzz marketing: The Vocalpoint marketing arm of P&G has enlisted an army of buzzers to create word-of-mouth for P&G and other company brands.**

sharing networks). *Atmospheres* are designed environments that create or reinforce the buyer's leanings toward buying a product. Thus, lawyers' offices and banks are designed to communicate confidence and other qualities that might be valued by clients. *Events* are staged occurrences that communicate messages to target audiences. For example, PR departments arrange grand openings, shows and exhibits, public tours, and other events.

Nonpersonal communication affects buyers directly. In addition, using mass media often affects buyers indirectly by causing more personal communication. For example, communications might first flow from television, magazines, and other mass media to opinion leaders and then from these opinion leaders to others. Thus, opinion leaders step between the mass media and their audiences and carry messages to people who are less exposed to media. Interestingly, marketers often use nonpersonal communications channels to replace or stimulate personal communications by embedding consumer endorsements or word-of-mouth testimonials in their ads and other promotions.

Selecting the Message Source

In either personal or nonpersonal communication, the message's impact also depends on how the target audience views the communicator. Messages delivered by highly credible sources are more persuasive. Thus, many food companies promote to doctors, dentists, and other health-care providers to motivate these professionals to recommend specific food products to their patients. And marketers hire celebrity endorsers—well-known athletes, actors, musicians, and even cartoon characters— to deliver their messages. Sarah Jessica Parker speaks for Garnier and Keith Richards endorses Louis Vuitton.[12] ⦿ A host of NBA superstars lend their images to brands such as Nike, McDonald's, and Coca-Cola.

But companies must be careful when selecting celebrities to represent their brands. Picking the wrong spokesperson can result in embarrassment and a tarnished image. For example, the Kellogg Company dismissed Olympic swimmer Michael Phelps after he was caught on video smoking marijuana. And more than a dozen big brands faced embarrassment when golfer Tiger Woods' personal problems were publically exposed, tarnishing his previously pristine image. Gatorade, AT&T, and Accenture abruptly ended their associations with Woods; Nike, Gillette, EA Sports, and others stayed with the troubled golf superstar in hopes that the public would forgive his indiscretions. "Arranged marriages between brands and celebrities are inherently risky," notes one expert. "Ninety-nine percent of celebrities do a strong job for their brand partners," says another, "and 1 percent goes off the rails."[13] (See Real Marketing 14.2.)

⦿ Celebrity endorsers: LeBron James, Kobe Bryant, and a host of other NBA superstars lend their images to Nike brands.

Collecting Feedback

After sending the message, the communicator must research its effect on the target audience. This involves asking the target audience members whether they remember the message, how many times they saw it, what points they recall, how they felt about the message, and their past and present attitudes toward the product and company. The communicator would also like to measure behavior resulting from the message—how many people bought the product, talked to others about it, or visited the store.

Feedback on marketing communications may suggest changes in the promotion program or in the product offer itself. For example, Macy's uses television and newspaper advertising to inform area consumers about its stores, services, and merchandising events.

Real Marketing 14.2

Celebrity Endorsers:
The Good, the Bad, and the Ugly

Companies often invest large amounts of money, time, and other resources to nurture celebrities as spokespersons for their brands. Sometimes, they even build entire product lines and positions around well-known superstars—for example, Nike's Air Jordan line or Accenture's long-running but since abandoned "Go on. Be a Tiger." corporate campaign. Linking up with a major celebrity can add substantial interest and appeal to a brand. However, as the spectacular 2009 tumble of pitchman extraordinaire Tiger Woods demonstrated, such partnerships can also create difficulties. Endorsers are people, and people often make poor choices. When a scandal strikes, brand-celebrity relationships can sour quickly.

Tiger Woods wasn't the first celebrity pitchman to fall from grace. But the Tiger tale may be the best recent example of the good, the bad, and the ugly of celebrity endorsement deals. First, the good: In 1996, just after going pro, the 21-year-old Woods signed deals with Nike, Accenture, GM, Titleist, and American Express. Four years later, Nike renegotiated Woods' contract, signing him to a 5-year, $105 million agreement, one of its biggest ever. Many questioned Nike's investment—golf was only a niche sport, and Nike had little presence in golf apparel and equipment. But less than a decade later, few would question the genius of Nike's deal with Tiger. Nike is now one of the fastest growing brands in golf. And Wood's incredible performance on the links not only boosted the Nike brand but also grew the entire sport.

Along the way, Tiger Woods became an official endorser for more than a dozen big brands, including Nike, Accenture, Gatorade, Buick, Gillette, AT&T, EA Sports, and Tag Heuer. In 2009, at age 34, Woods earned more than $100 million in endorsement income and became the first athlete ever to make more than $1 billion dollars in career earnings. Estimates were that Woods' lifetime endorsement earnings would top $6 billion. He was considered by many as the world's most marketable athlete, the perfect picture of a winner—good looking, clean-cut, scandal-free, and the epitome of discipline and focus—both on and off the course.

No company capitalized more on Tiger's image than Nike. With its contract, Nike purchased nearly every aspect of the golf star's public persona. Anywhere and everywhere that Woods appears, even in ads for other brands, the Nike Swoosh is plainly visible somewhere on his person. As one branding expert notes, "Tiger is so closely associated with Nike that whether you see [other] brands or not, you think of Nike."

But then came the bad and the ugly. In late 2009, following a bizarre late-night auto collision with a tree, a shocked public learned that the squeaky-clean Woods had been living a lie, in the form of years of extramarital affairs with more than a dozen women. As news of Woods' indiscretions and marital problems spread, Tiger went silent and took a hiatus from golf. Fans didn't react well to his infidelities. Woods' appeal ranking on the Davie Brown Index, the standard gauge of a celebrity's ability to influence consumers, dropped from 11th to 2,258th, placing him alongside the likes of sensationalist reporter Geraldo Rivera, quirky television talk-show host Kathy Lee Gifford, and exercise guru Richard Simmons. "We have never seen an athlete's score drop like this," said a Davie Brown executive.

Stunned sponsors reacted quickly to limit the damage to their own images. Three major sponsors—Gatorade, Accenture, and AT&T—dropped Woods altogether, costing him more than $25 million in endorsement contracts. Other sponsors, such as Gillette and Tag Heuer, distanced themselves but took a wait-and-see approach. Only Nike and EA Sports stood by Woods, stating that they would retain and support the golf superstar as he worked through his personal problems.

Whatever a given sponsor's decision, it was not an easy one. "Those companies have already made a significant investment in Tiger," says the president of a sports PR firm. "You walk away now, you lose that investment. And do you have a strategy to replace Tiger, another ad campaign ready to go?" There's also a risk of backlash. Celebrities often become so strongly linked to a brand that dropping them might do more damage than the celebrity's errant behaviors.

The wait-and-see approach might make more sense—lay low and keep an eye on consumer attitudes. History has shown that the public can be very forgiving. Take the case of NBA superstar Kobe Bryant, another major Nike endorser. In 2003, a Colorado hotel concierge accused Bryant of sexual assault. Bryant admitted to having an extramarital

Celebrity endorsers can be risky: Tag Heuer and a dozen other big brands faced embarrassment when golfer Tiger Woods' personal problems were publicly exposed, tarnishing his previously pristine image.

Continued on next page

sexual encounter with the woman but denied the assault. The charges against Bryant were eventually dropped. So were endorsement contracts with McDonald's, Nutella, and Sprite. But as it has with Woods, Nike stood by Bryant. Nike was rewarded for that loyalty as Bryant's on-court performance and subsequent Boy Scout–like personal behavior overpowered the memories of his scandalous past. "Kobe is bigger than ever," notes one sports marketer. "Success makes people forget," concludes another.

By staying with Woods, Nike is betting that the golfer's image will be rehabilitated. Tiger Woods seems almost too big to fail. His participation in the 2010 Masters tournament—his first public appearance after the scandal—seemed to bear this out. Wood's presence at the tournament resulted in a 47 percent increase in television viewer ratings and almost doubled Web traffic to sports sites over the

previous year, suggesting that the public is eager for him to play and succeed. Companies that kept Woods as an endorser reaped a windfall of exposure.

As long as he keeps his nose clean and plays well, Woods will probably regain most of his endorsement potential. Says Peter Moore, president of EA Sports, "Regardless of what's going on in his personal life, when you talk tennis, you talk Roger Federer, and if you talk cycling, you talk Lance Armstrong, and when you talk golf, boy, you'd better be talking Tiger Woods."

More broadly, despite the difficulties, celebrity endorsements are bigger than ever. "Life goes on," concludes one observer. "Right or wrong, people have short-term memories. Meanwhile, brands need to compete, grow awareness, increase market share. That's what celebrity deals can do." Although we live in "a media-saturated society where paparazzi, flip cams, cell phones, and bloggers are ready to catch stars bathed in an unflattering light, there's a thriving market for these matchups. It's clear we live in a celebrity-crazed culture. Advertisers will never abandon them."

Sources: Extracts, quotes, and other information from T. L. Stanley, "Dancing with the Stars," *Brandweek*, March 8, 2010, pp. 10–12; Robert Klara, "I'm with a Celebrity, Get Me Out of Here!" *Brandweek*, March 8, 2010, p. 13; Yukari Iwatani Kane, "EA Firmly Committed to Tiger Woods," *Wall Street Journal*, January 22, 2010, accessed at www.wsj.com; Diane Pucin, "And Now, for a Short Commercial Break," *Los Angeles Times*, December 10, 2009, p. C1; Ben Klayman, "Woods' Financial Losses May Be Short Lived," *Reuters*, April 6, 2010, accessed at www.reuters.com; and Suzanne Vranica, "Nike to Air New Ad Featuring Tiger Woods," *Wall Street Journal*, April 7, 2010, accessed online at www.wsj.com.

Suppose feedback research shows that 80 percent of all shoppers in an area recall seeing the store's ads and are aware of its merchandise and sales. Sixty percent of these aware shoppers have visited a Macy's store in the past month, but only 20 percent of those who visited were satisfied with the shopping experience. These results suggest that although promotion is creating *awareness*, Macy's stores aren't giving consumers the *satisfaction* they expect. Therefore, Macy's needs to improve the shopping experience while staying with the successful communications program. In contrast, suppose research shows that only 40 percent of area consumers are aware of the store's merchandise and events, only 30 percent of those aware have shopped recently, but 80 percent of those who have shopped return soon to shop again. In this case, Macy's needs to strengthen its promotion program to take advantage of its power to create customer satisfaction.

Author Comment | In this section, we'll look at the promotion budget-setting process and how marketers blend the various marketing communication tools into a smooth-functioning integrated promotion mix.

Setting the Total Promotion Budget and Mix (pp 422–427)

We have looked at the steps in planning and sending communications to a target audience. But how does the company determine its total *promotion budget* and the division among the major promotional tools to create the *promotion mix*? By what process does it blend the tools to create integrated marketing communications? We now look at these questions.

Setting the Total Promotion Budget

One of the hardest marketing decisions facing a company is how much to spend on promotion. ◉ John Wanamaker, the department store magnate, once said, "I know that half of my advertising is wasted, but I don't know which half. I spent $2 million for advertising, and I don't know if that is half enough or twice too much." Thus, it is not surprising that industries and companies vary widely in how much they spend on promotion. Promotion spending may be 10–12 percent of sales for consumer packaged goods, 14 percent for cosmetics,

Where imagination saves the day

⦿ **Setting the promotion budget is one of the hardest decisions facing the company. Disney spends hundreds of millions annually on advertising, but is that "half enough or twice too much"?**

Affordable method
Setting the promotion budget at the level management thinks the company can afford.

Percentage-of-sales method
Setting the promotion budget at a certain percentage of current or forecasted sales or as a percentage of the unit sales price.

Competitive-parity method
Setting the promotion budget to match competitors' outlays.

and only 1 percent for industrial machinery products. Within a given industry, both low and high spenders can be found.[14]

How does a company determine its promotion budget? Here, we look at four common methods used to set the total budget for advertising: the *affordable method*, the *percentage-of-sales method*, the *competitive-parity method*, and the *objective-and-task method*.[15]

Affordable Method

Some companies use the **affordable method**: They set the promotion budget at the level they think the company can afford. Small businesses often use this method, reasoning that the company cannot spend more on advertising than it has. They start with total revenues, deduct operating expenses and capital outlays, and then devote some portion of the remaining funds to advertising.

Unfortunately, this method of setting budgets completely ignores the effects of promotion on sales. It tends to place promotion last among spending priorities, even in situations in which advertising is critical to the firm's success. It leads to an uncertain annual promotion budget, which makes long-range market planning difficult. Although the affordable method can result in overspending on advertising, it more often results in underspending.

Percentage-of-Sales Method

Other companies use the **percentage-of-sales method**, setting their promotion budget at a certain percentage of current or forecasted sales. Or they budget a percentage of the unit sales price. The percentage-of-sales method is simple to use and helps management think about the relationships between promotion spending, selling price, and profit per unit.

Despite these claimed advantages, however, the percentage-of-sales method has little to justify it. It wrongly views sales as the *cause* of promotion rather than as the *result*. Although studies have found a positive correlation between promotional spending and brand strength, this relationship often turns out to be effect and cause, not cause and effect. Stronger brands with higher sales can afford the biggest ad budgets.

Thus, the percentage-of-sales budget is based on the availability of funds rather than on opportunities. It may prevent the increased spending sometimes needed to turn around falling sales. Because the budget varies with year-to-year sales, long-range planning is difficult. Finally, the method does not provide any basis for choosing a *specific* percentage, except what has been done in the past or what competitors are doing.

Competitive-Parity Method

Still other companies use the **competitive-parity method**, setting their promotion budgets to match competitors' outlays. They monitor competitors' advertising or get industry promotion spending estimates from publications or trade associations and then set their budgets based on the industry average.

Two arguments support this method. First, competitors' budgets represent the collective wisdom of the industry. Second, spending what competitors spend helps prevent promotion wars. Unfortunately, neither argument is valid. There are no grounds for believing that the competition has a better idea of what a company should be spending on promotion than does the company itself. Companies differ greatly, and each has its own special promotion needs. Finally, there is no evidence that budgets based on competitive parity prevent promotion wars.

Objective-and-task method
Developing the promotion budget by
(1) defining specific promotion objectives,
(2) determining the tasks needed to
achieve these objectives, and (3) estimating
the costs of performing these tasks. The
sum of these costs is the proposed
promotion budget.

Objective-and-Task Method

The most logical budget-setting method is the **objective-and-task method**, whereby the company sets its promotion budget based on what it wants to accomplish with promotion. This budgeting method entails (1) defining specific promotion objectives, (2) determining the tasks needed to achieve these objectives, and (3) estimating the costs of performing these tasks. The sum of these costs is the proposed promotion budget.

The advantage of the objective-and-task method is that it forces management to spell out its assumptions about the relationship between dollars spent and promotion results. But it is also the most difficult method to use. Often, it is hard to figure out which specific tasks will achieve the stated objectives. For example, suppose Sony wants a 95-percent awareness for its latest camcorder model during the six-month introductory period. What specific advertising messages and media schedules should Sony use to attain this objective? How much would these messages and media schedules cost? Sony management must consider such questions, even though they are hard to answer.

Shaping the Overall Promotion Mix

The concept of integrated marketing communications suggests that the company must blend the promotion tools carefully into a coordinated *promotion mix*. But how does it determine what mix of promotion tools to use? Companies within the same industry differ greatly in the design of their promotion mixes. For example, Mary Kay spends most of its promotion funds on personal selling and direct marketing, whereas competitor CoverGirl spends heavily on consumer advertising. We now look at factors that influence the marketer's choice of promotion tools.

The Nature of Each Promotion Tool

Each promotion tool has unique characteristics and costs. Marketers must understand these characteristics in shaping the promotion mix.

Advertising. Advertising can reach masses of geographically dispersed buyers at a low cost per exposure, and it enables the seller to repeat a message many times. For example, television advertising can reach huge audiences. An estimated 106 million Americans watched the most recent Super Bowl, about 41 million people watched at least part of the last Academy Awards broadcast, and 30 million fans tuned in for the debut episode of the ninth season of American Idol. For companies that want to reach a mass audience, TV is the place to be.[16]

Beyond its reach, large-scale advertising says something positive about the seller's size, popularity, and success. Because of advertising's public nature, consumers tend to view advertised products as more legitimate. Advertising is also very expressive; it allows the company to dramatize its products through the artful use of visuals, print, sound, and color. On the one hand, advertising can be used to build up a long-term image for a product (such as Coca-Cola ads). On the other hand, advertising can trigger quick sales (as when Kohl's advertises weekend specials).

Advertising also has some shortcomings. Although it reaches many people quickly, advertising is impersonal and cannot be as directly persuasive as can company salespeople. For the most part, advertising can carry on only a one-way communication with an audience, and the audience does not feel that it has to pay attention or respond. In addition, advertising can be very costly. Although some advertising forms, such as newspaper and radio advertising, can be done on smaller budgets, other forms, such as network TV advertising, require very large budgets.

Personal Selling. Personal selling is the most effective tool at certain stages of the buying process, particularly in building up buyers' preferences, convictions, and actions. It involves personal interaction between two or more people, so each person can observe the other's needs and characteristics and make quick adjustments. Personal selling also allows all kinds of customer relationships to spring up, ranging from matter-of-fact selling relationships to personal friendships. An effective salesperson keeps the customer's interests at heart to

● With personal selling, the customer feels a greater need to listen and respond, even if the response is a polite "No thank-you."

build a long-term relationship by solving a customer's problems. ● Finally, with personal selling, the buyer usually feels a greater need to listen and respond, even if the response is a polite "No thank-you."

These unique qualities come at a cost, however. A sales force requires a longer-term commitment than does advertising—advertising can be turned up or down, but the size of a sales force is harder to change. Personal selling is also the company's most expensive promotion tool, costing companies on average $350 or more per sales call, depending on the industry.[17] U.S. firms spend up to three times as much on personal selling as they do on advertising.

Sales Promotion. Sales promotion includes a wide assortment of tools—coupons, contests, cents-off deals, premiums, and others—all of which have many unique qualities. They attract consumer attention, offer strong incentives to purchase, and can be used to dramatize product offers and boost sagging sales. Sales promotions invite and reward quick response. Whereas advertising says, "Buy our product," sales promotion says, "Buy it now." Sales promotion effects are often short lived, however, and often are not as effective as advertising or personal selling in building long-run brand preference and customer relationships.

Public Relations. PR is very believable—news stories, features, sponsorships, and events seem more real and believable to readers than ads do. PR can also reach many prospects who avoid salespeople and advertisements—the message gets to buyers as "news" rather than as a sales-directed communication. And, as with advertising, PR can dramatize a company or product. Marketers tend to underuse PR or use it as an afterthought. Yet a well-thought-out PR campaign used with other promotion mix elements can be very effective and economical.

Direct Marketing. Although there are many forms of direct marketing—direct mail and catalogs, online marketing, telephone marketing, and others—they all share four distinctive characteristics. Direct marketing is less public: The message is normally directed to a specific person. Direct marketing is immediate and customized: Messages can be prepared very quickly and can be tailored to appeal to specific consumers. Finally, direct marketing is interactive: It allows a dialogue between the marketing team and the consumer, and messages can be altered depending on the consumer's response. Thus, direct marketing is well suited to highly targeted marketing efforts and building one-to-one customer relationships.

Promotion Mix Strategies

Marketers can choose from two basic promotion mix strategies: *push* promotion or *pull* promotion. ● **Figure 14.4** contrasts the two strategies. The relative emphasis given to the specific promotion tools differs for push and pull strategies. A **push strategy** involves "pushing" the product through marketing channels to final consumers. The producer directs its marketing activities (primarily personal selling and trade promotion) toward channel members to induce them to carry the product and promote it to final consumers. For example, John Deere does very little promoting of its lawn mowers, garden tractors, and other residential consumer products to final consumers. Instead, John Deere's sales force works with Lowe's, Home Depot, independent dealers, and other channel members, who in turn push John Deere products to final consumers.

Using a **pull strategy**, the producer directs its marketing activities (primarily advertising and consumer promotion) toward final consumers to induce them to buy the product. For example, Unilever promotes its Axe grooming products directly to its young male target market using TV and print ads, a brand Web site, its YouTube channel, and other channels. If the pull strategy is effective, consumers will then demand the brand from retailers, such as CVS, Walgreens, or Walmart, who will in turn demand it from Unilever. Thus, under a pull strategy, consumer demand "pulls" the product through the channels.

Push strategy

A promotion strategy that calls for using the sales force and trade promotion to push the product through channels. The producer promotes the product to channel members who in turn promote it to final consumers.

Pull strategy

A promotion strategy that calls for spending a lot on consumer advertising and promotion to induce final consumers to buy the product, creating a demand vacuum that "pulls" the product through the channel.

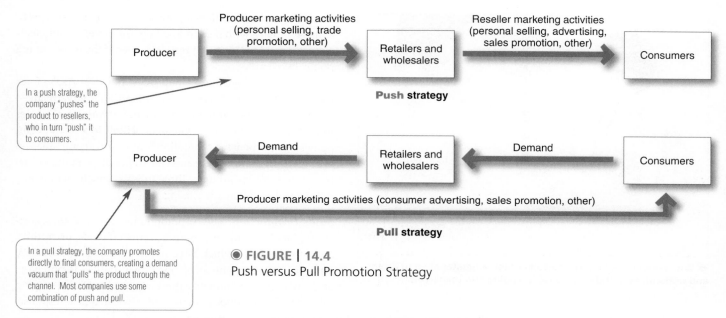

In a push strategy, the company "pushes" the product to resellers, who in turn "push" it to consumers.

In a pull strategy, the company promotes directly to final consumers, creating a demand vacuum that "pulls" the product through the channel. Most companies use some combination of push and pull.

● **FIGURE | 14.4**
Push versus Pull Promotion Strategy

Some industrial-goods companies use only push strategies; some direct-marketing companies use only pull strategies. However, most large companies use some combination of both. For example, Unilever spends $2.4 billion on U.S. media advertising and consumer sales promotions to create brand preference and pull customers into stores that carry its products. At the same time, it uses its own and distributors' sales forces and trade promotions to push its brands through the channels, so that they will be available on store shelves when consumers come calling. In recent years, facing a tight economy and slumping sales, many consumer-goods companies have been decreasing the brand-building pull portions of their mixes in favor of more push. This has caused concern that they may be driving short-run sales at the expense of long-term brand equity.

Companies consider many factors when designing their promotion mix strategies, including the *type of product/market* and the *product life-cycle stage*. For example, the importance of different promotion tools varies between consumer and business markets. Business-to-consumer (B-to-C) companies usually pull more, putting more of their funds into advertising, followed by sales promotion, personal selling, and then PR. In contrast, business-to-business marketers tend to push more, putting more of their funds into personal selling, followed by sales promotion, advertising, and PR. In general, personal selling is used more heavily with expensive and risky goods and in markets with fewer and larger sellers.

The effects of different promotion tools also vary with stages of the product life cycle. In the introduction stage, advertising and PR are good for producing high awareness, and sales promotion is useful in promoting early trial. Personal selling must be used to get the trade to carry the product. In the growth stage, advertising and PR continue to be powerful influences, whereas sales promotion can be reduced because fewer incentives are needed. In the mature stage, sales promotion again becomes important relative to advertising. Buyers know the brands, and advertising is needed only to remind them of the product. In the decline stage, advertising is kept at a reminder level, PR is dropped, and salespeople give the product only a little attention. Sales promotion, however, might continue to be strong.

Integrating the Promotion Mix

Having set the promotion budget and mix, the company must now take steps to see that each promotion mix element is smoothly integrated. Guided by its overall communications strategy, the various promotion elements should work together to carry the firm's unique brand messages and selling points. Integrating the promotion mix starts with customers. Whether it's advertising, personal selling, sales promotion, PR, or direct marketing, communications at each customer touchpoint must deliver consistent messages and positioning. An integrated promotion mix ensures that communications efforts occur when, where, and how *customers* need them.

To achieve an integrated promotion mix, all of the firm's functions must cooperate to jointly plan communications efforts. Many companies even include customers, suppliers, and other stakeholders at various stages of communications planning. Scattered or disjointed promotional activities across the company can result in diluted marketing communications impact and confused positioning. By contrast, an integrated promotion mix maximizes the combined effects of all a firm's promotional efforts.

> **Author** | Marketers should go
> **Comment** | beyond what's "legal"
> and communicate openly and
> responsibly with customers. Good
> customer relationships are built on
> honesty and trust.

Socially Responsible Marketing Communication (pp 427–428)

In shaping its promotion mix, a company must be aware of the large body of legal and ethical issues surrounding marketing communications. Most marketers work hard to communicate openly and honestly with consumers and resellers. Still, abuses may occur, and public policy makers have developed a substantial body of laws and regulations to govern advertising, sales promotion, personal selling, and direct marketing. In this section, we discuss issues regarding advertising, sales promotion, and personal selling. We discuss issues regarding direct marketing in Chapter 17.

Advertising and Sales Promotion

By law, companies must avoid false or deceptive advertising. Advertisers must not make false claims, such as suggesting that a product cures something when it does not. They must avoid ads that have the capacity to deceive, even though no one actually may be deceived. An automobile cannot be advertised as getting 32 miles per gallon unless it does so under typical conditions, and a diet bread cannot be advertised as having fewer calories simply because its slices are thinner.

Sellers must avoid bait-and-switch advertising that attracts buyers under false pretenses. For example, a large retailer advertised a sewing machine at $179. However, when consumers tried to buy the advertised machine, the seller downplayed its features, placed faulty machines on showroom floors, understated the machine's performance, and took other actions in an attempt to switch buyers to a more expensive machine. Such actions are both unethical and illegal.

A company's trade promotion activities also are closely regulated. For example, under the Robinson-Patman Act, sellers cannot favor certain customers through their use of trade promotions. They must make promotional allowances and services available to all resellers on proportionately equal terms.

Beyond simply avoiding legal pitfalls, such as deceptive or bait-and-switch advertising, companies can use advertising and other forms of promotion to encourage and promote socially responsible programs and actions. ◉ For example, Frito-Lay ran TV, print, and online ads promoting the new compostable packaging for its SunChips brand. "They're 100% compostable," said one print ad. "You eat the delicious chips. The earth eats the bag." Frito-Lay also used advertising to promote a program challenging consumers to create videos encouraging positive change in the world. Former vice president Al Gore selected the winner, which Frito-Lay aired on national television during Earth Week.[18]

◉ Promoting socially responsible actions: Frito-Lay ran ads promoting the compostable packaging for its SunChips brand. It also promoted a program challenging consumers to create their own videos encouraging positive change in the world, which it ran on national TV.

Personal Selling

A company's salespeople must follow the rules of "fair competition." Most states have enacted deceptive sales acts that spell out what is not allowed. For example, salespeople may not lie to consumers or mislead them about the advantages of buying a particular product. To avoid bait-and-switch practices, salespeople's statements must match advertising claims.

Different rules apply to consumers who are called on at home or who buy at a location that is not the seller's permanent place of business versus those who go to a store in search of a product. Because people who are called on may be taken by surprise and may be especially vulnerable to high-pressure selling techniques, the Federal Trade Commission (FTC) has adopted a *three-day cooling-off rule* to give special protection to customers who are not seeking products. Under this rule, customers who agree in their own homes, workplace, dormitory, or facilities rented by the seller on a temporary basis—such as hotel rooms, convention centers, and restaurants—to buy something costing more than $25 have 72 hours in which to cancel a contract or return merchandise and get their money back—no questions asked.

Much personal selling involves business-to-business trade. In selling to businesses, salespeople may not offer bribes to purchasing agents or others who can influence a sale. They may not obtain or use technical or trade secrets of competitors through bribery or industrial espionage. Finally, salespeople must not disparage competitors or competing products by suggesting things that are not true.[19]

REVIEWING Objectives AND KEY Terms

In this chapter, you learned how companies use integrated marketing communications (IMC) to communicate customer value. Modern marketing calls for more than just creating customer value by developing a good product, pricing it attractively, and making it available to target customers. Companies also must clearly and persuasively *communicate* that value to current and prospective customers. To do this, they must blend five promotion mix tools, guided by a well-designed and implemented IMC strategy.

Objective 1 Define the five promotion mix tools for communicating customer value. (p 408)

A company's total *promotion mix*—also called its *marketing communications mix*—consists of the specific blend of *advertising, personal selling, sales promotion, public relations,* and *direct-marketing* tools that the company uses to persuasively communicate customer value and build customer relationships. Advertising includes any paid form of nonpersonal presentation and promotion of ideas, goods, or services by an identified sponsor. In contrast, PR focuses on building good relations with the company's various publics by obtaining favorable, unpaid publicity.

Personal selling is any form of personal presentation by the firm's sales force for the purpose of making sales and building customer relationships. Firms use sales promotion to provide short-term incentives to encourage the purchase or sale of a product or service. Finally, firms seeking immediate response from targeted individual customers use nonpersonal direct-marketing tools to communicate with customers and cultivate relationships with them.

Objective 2 Discuss the changing communications landscape and the need for integrated marketing communications. (pp 409–414)

Recent shifts toward targeted or one-to-one marketing, coupled with advances in information and communications technology, have had a dramatic impact on marketing communications. As marketing communicators adopt richer but more fragmented media and promotion mixes to reach their diverse markets, they risk creating a communications hodgepodge for consumers. To prevent this, more companies are adopting the concept of *integrated marketing communications (IMC)*. Guided by an overall IMC strategy, the company works out the roles that the various promotional tools will play and the extent to which each will be used. It carefully coordinates the promotional activities and the timing of when major campaigns take place. Finally, to help implement its integrated marketing strategy, the company can appoint a marketing communications director who has overall responsibility for the company's communications efforts.

Objective 3 Outline the communication process and the steps in developing effective marketing communications. (pp 414–422)

The communication process involves nine elements: two major parties (sender, receiver), two communication tools (message, media), four communication functions (encoding, decoding, response, and feedback), and noise. To communicate effectively, marketers must understand how these elements combine to communicate value to target customers.

In preparing marketing communications, the communicator's first task is to *identify the target audience* and its characteristics. Next, the communicator has to determine the *communication objectives* and define the response sought, whether it be *awareness*, *knowledge*, *liking*, *preference*, *conviction*, or *purchase*. Then a *message* should be constructed with an effective content and structure. *Media* must be selected, both for personal and nonpersonal communication. The communicator must find highly credible sources to deliver messages. Finally, the communicator must collect *feedback* by watching how much of the market becomes aware, tries the product, and is satisfied in the process.

Objective 4 Explain the methods for setting the promotion budget and factors that affect the design of the promotion mix. (pp 422–428)

The company must determine how much to spend for promotion. The most popular approaches are to spend what the company can afford, use a percentage of sales, base promotion on competitors' spending, or base it on an analysis and costing of the communication objectives and tasks. The company has to divide the *promotion budget* among the major tools to create the *promotion mix*. Companies can pursue a *push* or a *pull* promotional strategy—or a combination of the two. The best specific blend of promotion tools depends on the type of product/market, the buyer's readiness stage, and the PLC stage. People at all levels of the organization must be aware of the many legal and ethical issues surrounding marketing communications. Companies must work hard and proactively at communicating openly, honestly, and agreeably with their customers and resellers.

KEY Terms

OBJECTIVE 1

Promotion mix (marketing communications mix) (p 408)
Advertising (p 408)
Sales promotion (p 408)
Personal selling (p 408)
Public relations (PR) (p 408)
Direct marketing (p 408)

OBJECTIVE 2

Integrated marketing communications (IMC) (p 412)

OBJECTIVE 3

Buyer-readiness stages (p 416)
Personal communication channels (p 419)
Word-of-mouth influence (p 419)
Buzz marketing (p 419)
Nonpersonal communication channels (p 419)

OBJECTIVE 4

Affordable method (p 423)
Percentage-of-sales method (p 423)
Competitive-parity method (p 423)
Objective-and-task method (p 424)
Push strategy (p 425)
Pull strategy (p 425)

PEARSON mymarketinglab

- Check your understanding of the concepts and key terms using the mypearsonmarketinglab study plan for this chapter.
- Apply the concepts in a business context using the simulation entitled **Integrated Marketing Communication**.

DISCUSSING & APPLYING THE Concepts

Discussing the Concepts

1. List and briefly describe the five major promotion mix tools. (AASCB: Communication)

2. Define IMC and discuss how marketers implement it. (AACSB: Communication)

3. Name and briefly describe the nine elements of the communications process. Why do marketers need to understand these elements? (AACSB: Communication; Reflective Thinking)

4. Name and describe the six buyer-readiness stages. Discuss why it is important for a marketing communicator to know where the target audience stands and to what stage it needs to be moved. (AACSB: Communication)

5. Discuss the factors to consider with regard to message structure when designing a message. (AACSB: Communication)

6. Compare and contrast personal and nonpersonal communication channels. (AACSB: Communication)

Applying the Concepts

1. Describe the three types of appeals used in marketing communications messages and develop three different ads for the same brand of a product of your choice, each using a different appeal. (AACSB: Communication; Reflective Thinking)

2. Discuss the two basic promotion mix strategies. Form a small group and recommend a promotion mix for a brand of peanut butter implementing primarily a push promotion strategy. Then recommend a promotion mix for the same brand implementing primarily a pull promotion strategy. Explain how your two recommendations differ. (AACSB: Communication; Reflective Thinking)

3. Brands are now starring in movies, television shows, video games, and books. Select three different television programs and identify the brands shown or mentioned in an episode of each program. What product categories seem to be more prevalent? How were the brands presented? Write a report on what you find. (AACSB: Communication; Reflective Thinking)

FOCUS ON Technology

Small businesses account for 90 percent of all companies in the United States, and many do not have resources to spare for promoting their businesses. Newspaper, radio, and the yellow pages have been the mainstay mediums for local businesses, but they can be expensive. As a result, many businesses are turning to the Internet. One survey found that over one-half of small businesses using the Internet are creating or maintaining a social-networking presence on sites such as Facebook, Twitter, and Foursquare. However, social-networking media can be daunting to a small business owner, so MerchantCircle offers a network that brings customers and local businesses together. Founded in 2005, MerchantCircle is now the largest online network of local business owners, with 1.3 million members. Consumers can go to the site to search for local businesses or ask questions and get input from any of MerchantCircle's business members. MerchantCircle business members can interact with each other to help grow their businesses.

1. Visit www.MerchantCircle.com/corporate and search for a jeweler in your city or some other city. What information is provided? Are any jewelers in your city members of MerchantCircle? Search for other products and services and describe the benefits this network provides to the consumer. (AACSB: Communication; Use of IT; Reflective Thinking)

2. Explore the MerchantCircle Web site to learn the benefits and costs for local businesses. Write a brief report of what you learn. (AACSB: Communication; Use of IT; Reflective Thinking)

FOCUS ON Ethics

Imagine a young family driving to Disney World. Along the route, the children see billboards with Mickey, Donald, Kermit the Frog, and other Disney characters. Cinderella, Ariel, and the other princesses are so beautiful. Then come billboards with other beautiful women—only they are scantily clothed and in sexually suggestive poses. These are ads for businesses such as strip clubs, adult bookstores, and other seedy businesses. "There ought to be a law against that," claims the horrified mother of the two young children in the car. In fact, several states have banned such billboards. But in Missouri, South Carolina, and Kansas, federal courts have overturned these laws. Cash-strapped states cannot afford the legal battles and seem to have little chance of winning because of First Amendment protection. The states are losing because they must prove that the purpose of their laws is to prevent "secondary effects," which might include decreased property values or increased crime. Thus, a law recently introduced in Michigan is not attempting to ban the advertising but is instead attempting to restrict the content of ads to list only a business's name, location, and hours of operation.

1. Should these types of ads have the same protection that individual citizens have under the First Amendment? (AACSB: Communication; Ethical Reasoning)

2. Sex sells, and a lot of advertising uses it, even for products or services that are not sexually oriented. Why are lawmakers more concerned with sexually explicit ads on billboards than such ads in other media? (AACSB: Communication; Ethical Reasoning)

MARKETING & THE Economy

Miller Lite

For years, Miller Lite achieved tremendous success with its "Great Taste . . . Less Filling" campaign, which *Advertising Age* ranked as the eighth best campaign in history. But when the recent joint venture MillerCoors took over the Miller Lite brand, it decided to focus exclusively on the "great taste" part, a positioning formula credited for 16 consecutive quarters of growth for competitor Coors Light. Unfortunately, the change in the Miller Lite branding strategy occurred as consumers began to count every penny and demand greater value in the face of new economic realities. In the new economic environment, the single-feature message didn't deliver. Miller Lite immediately began losing sales, posting its worst quarter in more than a decade. With more choices than ever in a beer market flooded with full-flavored crafts, imports, and microbrews, industry insiders have questioned MillerCoors' taste-

only focus. To muddy the waters even further, MillerCoors halted the brand's regular pattern of price cuts and discounts. It has also increased the Miller Lite advertising budget and added some packaging innovations, such as a "Taste-Protector Cap" and a "Taste Activated Bottle." Andy England, chief marketing officer of MillerCoors, is convinced that the company has Miller Lite on the right track. Given that Miller Lite's sales have yet to turn around, observers are not convinced.

1. In your opinion, which factor has had the biggest impact on Miller Lite's sagging sales?

2. Is a single product benefit enough reason to buy in a weak economy?

3. If MillerCoors had retained Miller Lite's previous brand message, would it have suffered a sales decline?

MARKETING BY THE Numbers

Using the percent of sales method, an advertiser sets its budget at a certain percentage of current or forecasted sales. However, determining what percentage to use is not always clear. Many marketers look at industry averages and competitor spending for comparisons. Web sites and trade publications, such as *Advertising Age*, publish data about industry averages and advertising-to-sales ratios for top advertisers.

1. Using information regarding industry advertising-to-sales ratios (see http://company.news-record.com/advertising/

advertising/ratio.html), recommend percentages of sales that advertisers in the following industries should use to set next year's advertising budget: a grocery store, a physician, a cosmetic brand, and malt beverages. (AACSB: Communication; Use of IT)

2. Explain why there is variation in the percentage of sales spent on advertising among the four industries in the previous question. (AACSB: Communication; Reflective Thinking)

VIDEO Case

CP+B

Crispin Porter + Bogusky (Crispin) may not be the oldest advertising agency in the world. It isn't the biggest either. But it has been working over time to prove that it is the most innovative firm at integrating marketing promotions. In fact, Crispin relies very little on the king of all advertising channels, broadcast TV. Instead, Crispin has worked miracles for companies such as Virgin Atlantic Airways, BMW's MINI Cooper, and Burger King by employing non-traditional campaigns on limited budgets.

Crispin attributes its success to the fact that it redefined what an advertisement is. Customer appropriate messages, Crispin discovered, could be delivered in many different ways. So its realm of "ad space" includes things as obscure as the side of a mailbox or

an oversized phone booth in an airport. By communicating a message in many different ways, Crispin has developed a reputation for truly integrating marketing communications.

After viewing the video featuring Crispin, answer the following questions about advertising and promotions:

1. Alex Bogusky once said, "Anything and everything is an ad." What does this mean? How is Crispin demonstrating this mantra?

2. In what ways has Crispin differentiated itself from other advertising agencies?

3. Give some examples as to how Crispin balances strategy with creativity.

COMPANY Case

Pepsi: Can a Soda Really Make the World a Better Place?

This year, PepsiCo did something that shocked the advertising world. After 23 straight years of running ads for its flagship brand on the Super Bowl, it announced that the number-two soft drink maker would be absent from the Big Game. But in the weeks leading up to Super Bowl XLIV, Pepsi was still the second-most discussed advertiser associated with the event. It wasn't so much what Pepsi wasn't doing that created such a stir as much as what it was doing.

Rather than continuing with the same old messages of the past, focusing on the youthful nature of the Pepsi Generation, and using the same old mass-media channels, Pepsi is taking a major gamble by breaking new ground with its advertising program. Its latest campaign, called Pepsi Refresh, represents a major departure from its old promotion efforts in two ways: (1) The message centers on a theme of social responsibility, and (2) the message is being delivered with a fat dose of social media.

At the center of the campaign is the Pepsi Refresh Project. PepsiCo has committed to award $20 million in grants ranging from $5,000 to $250,000 to organizations and individuals with ideas that will make the world a better place. The refresheverything .com Web site greets visitors with the headline, "What do you care about?" PepsiCo accepts up to 1,000 proposals each month in each of six different areas: health, arts and culture, food and shelter, the planet, neighborhoods, and education. Then crowd-sourcing takes over, as consumers vote for their favorites. Pepsi awards the grants each month. One-third of the way through its one-year run, the company had funded more than 100 projects, giving approximately $5 million back to local communities. The company stated that the project was right on target to award the full $20 million by the end of the yearlong effort.

INTEGRATING DIGITAL THROUGHOUT THE PROMOTIONAL MIX

The Pepsi Refresh campaign has been a groundbreaking effort, in part because of its heavy use of social media. PepsiCo is capitalizing on a growing trend in a way that no other major brand has done so far. The company is quick to point out that Pepsi Refresh is not a social media add-on like almost others, where an ad simply directs people to a Web site for reasons that may or may not be relevant to the message. Nor is it a social media campaign as such, where the entire campaign takes place through social media. Rather, social media are the glue that holds together a truly integrated marketing communications effort. "It's not about digital as its own channel anymore," says Bonin Bough, director of digital and social media for PepsiCo. "It's how do we infuse digital across all of our marketing programs?"

For starters, although PepsiCo bypassed the Super Bowl, it is not ditching broadcast media. To the contrary, Pepsi is running spot ads on the main networks as well as 30 different cable channels. The ads initially informed people about the Pepsi Refresh campaign, directing them to the refresheverything.com site. But shortly after the first grants were awarded, ads began highlighting projects that had been funded. Traditional media efforts extend to 10 print publications as well. And PR plays a role through agreements such as the one with NBC Universal for paid pitches on the "Today" show.

But this campaign underscores a shift in how PepsiCo is spending its advertising dollars. According to CEO Indra Nooyi, the world's number two soft drink seller is shifting as much as one-third of its marketing budget to interactive and social media. This move involves not only the Pepsi brand but also Mountain Dew, Doritos, Sobe, and PepsiCo's other brands. Certainly, PepsiCo is not alone in the trend toward digital and social media marketing. But analysts point out that its approach, moving away from high-profile spots in favor of heavy spending on a digitally focused social responsibility campaign, is both compelling and risky. "I applaud Pepsi for embracing social media and technology," said Marc Lucas, an advertising executive. "On the flip side, I think it's very bold to not be in a place where you know you're going to have an audience."

The refresheverything.com Web site is just one component of the brand's online efforts. PepsiCo is spreading the message through the big networks, such as Facebook and Twitter, and even partnering with them for advertising opportunities. For example, Pepsi Refresh held the lead ad position on Facebook during the Super Bowl. Pepsi has also partnered with Hulu to sponsor its first original series, the reality show *If I Can Dream*. "It amplifies an advertising campaign by making it something people talk about, more of a social conversation," said Jean-Paul Colaco, senior vice president for advertising at Hulu. PepsiCo even partnered with Spin magazine, music festival South by Southwest, and two Indie bands in a Web-based contest where music lovers could vote for their favorite. Metric beat out Broken Social Scene for a $100,000 grant that it gave to the Women's Funding Network.

As another component of the integrated campaign, the company has not shied away from using celebrity endorsers. Through clever network spot ads that place celebrities inside a life-sized, three-dimensional laptop made of tagboard, Kevin Bacon appeals to people to vote for his cause, SixDegrees.org. He is quick to point out that this has nothing to do with the cult trivia game, Six Degrees of Kevin Bacon. Rather, he proposes using a $250,000 grant to hand out "good cards" that people can use to donate to any of more than a million different charities. But Bacon goes on to explain that the power of SixDegrees comes from the social networks of good card recipients. They buy more good cards and pass them on to others, and as social networking works its magic, that $250,000 grows into millions.

Among various other celebrities, Pepsi has also recruited Demi Moore; NFL players Mark Sanchez, DeMarcus Ware, and Drew Brees; and NASCAR veterans Jeff Gordon, Dale Earnhardt Jr., and Jimmie Johnson to apply for grants and act as spokespersons for the project. These celebrities are vying for votes to award grants to such organizations as the Girls Education and Mentoring Service, the American Cancer Society, and the Brain Aneurysm Foundation.

PepsiCo is also getting its message out to consumers at the point of purchase. Cans, bottles, and multipacks feature updated graphics that minimize an all lowercase Pepsi logo written vertically and highlights a new Pepsi brand mark: a large circle with swaths of red, white, and blue. That symbol replaces any "o" in Pepsi's packaging and promotional materials. Thus, both "Do Some Good" and "Doing Good 101" each carry four of the new Pepsi circles. To draw people into retailer outlets to see the point-of-purchase (POP) materials and hopefully buy its soft drinks, Pepsi has partnered with Foursquare, the social network that connects people through GPS in real time. Foursquare members are directed to Pepsi retailers and given offers as an incentive for them to visit.

DOING WELL BY DOING GOOD

Despite the growth of cause-related marketing, PepsiCo's effort is perhaps the first example of a major brand making social responsibility the main theme of its campaign, rather than an add-on. This does not downplay the efforts of companies like Target, which has given $273 million to local schools since 1997 through its RedCard program. But PepsiCo's effort is built around a theme that drives the concept of "doing good" as much as it drives the brand. Coca-Cola's response to Pepsi Refresh, donating a dollar to Boys and Girls Clubs of America each time a visitor to Coke's Facebook page shares a virtual Coke gift, illustrates how most advertiser's cause-related marketing efforts are peripheral to other advertising activities.

Nooyi brings the centrality of Pepsi's socially responsible message into perspective.

The Pepsi Refresh Project is a platform, but at the end of the day, what we are doing is awarding the grants, we are enabling connections. It's having a catalytic effect on people who are actually embracing these organizations. So, we're not only benefiting the person who received the grant, we're benefiting the people who are the recipients of the outcome of that idea. With schools, for instance, it's not just one classroom that's benefited. It's all the kids who will be able to go to that classroom. And there have been people who have worked so hard to get this money that others have stepped in and matched the money they receive.

Projects funded thus far are too numerous to list. But they include more than high-profile efforts like the celebrity campaigns. Many awards are being given to everyday people just trying to improve their own little corners of the world. Calvin Cannon received $5,000 for Clothe the N.A.K.E.D. Prom Date, his venture to sponsor low-income, upstanding dudes in Shelbyville, Tennessee, by paying for their tuxedo rentals for the prom. Jeanne Acutanza from Kirkland, Washington, got $5,000 for her children's school so that it could manage a sustainable garden and give the harvest to local food banks. And the Associates of Redlands Bowl received $25,000 to support performing arts in the community of Redlands, California. "I'm proud of every idea we're supporting, but it's the simplicity of [these ideas that is] so innovative," says Nooyi. "You would never have thought that one simple thing could bring about a big change in the community."

IN SEARCH OF THE HOLY GRAIL

All this cutting edge promotion and the effort to change the world are wonderful. But at the end of the day, PepsiCo has to sell soft drinks. After all, it is the fiftieth largest publicly held corporation in the Fortune 500. Pepsi is also the 23rd most valuable brand in the world according to Interbrand. If this experiment fails to support sales of its core brand, PepsiCo will no doubt abandon its innovative promotion efforts and return to its old ways. As one social marketer states, "This is big, new, getting a lot of attention. It's impactful; it's innovative. What the industry is talking about now is, is this a gamble that was worth taking, in terms of a lift in sales? That's the holy grail."

But PepsiCo remains extremely optimistic. In the first few months of the campaign, the number of Facebook fans doubled. The company formerly got a Twitter tweet every five minutes or so. Now, it receives more tweets per minute than a person can read. But just what is the value of a Facebook or a Twitter fan? Although many advocates of social networking say questions like that are irrelevant, budget-strapped chief marketing officers want to see return on investment. That's why Bough and his team have developed a scorecard that ties different elements of the Pepsi Refresh campaign back to the health of the brand. Using standard research methods, PepsiCo will be measuring whether or not this campaign merits the expense.

Pass or fail, many observers inside and outside PepsiCo will learn much from this first-of-its-kind social media and social responsibility campaign. Ana Maria Irazabal, director of marketing for PepsiCo, wants this campaign to become the model of the future. "We want people to be aware that every time you drink a Pepsi you are actually supporting the Pepsi Refresh Project and ideas that are going to move this country forward. We may be the first to do something like this, but hopefully, we're not the last."

Questions for Discussion

1. Consider PepsiCo's advertising throughout its history. (For a list of Pepsi slogans over the years, visit http://en.wikipedia .org/wiki/Pepsi#Slogans.) Identify as many commonalities as possible across its various ad campaigns. How is this campaign consistent with PepsiCo's brand image?

2. List all the promotional mix elements used in the Pepsi Refresh campaign. What grade would you give PepsiCo on integrating these elements into an integration marketing communications campaign?

3. Describe PepsiCo's target audience. Is the Pepsi Refresh campaign consistent with that audience?

4. As completely as possible, analyze the campaign according to the steps listed in the chapter for developing effective marketing communication.

5. Will the Pepsi Refresh campaign be successful? Why or why not?

Sources: Natalie Zmuda, "Pass or Fail, Pepsi's Refresh Will Be Case for Marketing Textbooks," *Advertising Age*, February 8, 2010, p. 1; Stuart Elliott, "Pepsi Invites the Public to Do Good," *New York Times*, January 31, 2010, p. B6; Elaine Wong, "Pepsi Community Effort Finds Fans on Social Nets," *Brandweek*, June 8, 2010, accessed at www.brandweek.com.

Advertising and Public Relations

Chapter Preview

Now that we've looked at overall integrated marketing communications planning, we dig more deeply into the specific marketing communications tools. In this chapter, we explore advertising and public relations. Advertising involves communicating the company's or brand's value proposition by using paid media to inform, persuade, and remind consumers. PR involves building good relations with various company publics—from consumers and the general public to the media, investor, donor, and government publics. As with all the promo-

tion mix tools, advertising and PR must be blended into the overall integrated marketing communications program. In Chapters 16 and 17, we will discuss the remaining promotion mix tools: personal selling, sales promotion, and direct marketing.

Let's start with the question: Does advertising really make a difference? Microsoft and Apple certainly must think so. Each spends more than a half billion dollars a year on it. Here, we examine the long-running advertising battle between the two computer industry giants. As you read, think about the impact of advertising on each brand's fortunes.

Microsoft vs. Apple: Does Advertising Really Make a Difference?

In 2006, Apple launched its now-famous "Get a Mac" ad campaign, featuring two characters—"Mac" and "PC"—sparring over the advantages of the Apple Mac versus a Microsoft Windows-based PC. The ads portrayed Mac as a young, hip, laid back guy in a hoodie, whereas PC was a stodgy, befuddled, error-prone, middle-aged nerd in baggie khakis, a brown sport coat, and unfashionable glasses. Not surprisingly, adroit and modern Mac always got the best of outdated and inflexible PC. Over the years, Apple unleashed a nonstop barrage of Mac vs. PC ads that bashed Windows-based machines—and their owners—as outmoded and dysfunctional.

The "Get a Mac" campaign produced results. When the campaign began, Mac held only a 2–3 percent share of the U.S. computer market. Less than two years later, its share had more than doubled to 6–8 percent and growing. The cool campaign also helped boost customer value perceptions of Apple computers. Even though its computers were widely viewed as more expensive, at one point, Apple scored a whopping 70 on the BrandIndex (which tracks daily consumer perceptions of brand value on a scale of −100 to 100). Microsoft, meanwhile, floundered below zero.

Good advertising wasn't the only thing contributing to Apple's success. The popularity of its iPod, iPhone, and other new products was also converting customers to Mac computers. But the smug ads were consistently hitting their mark. Microsoft needed to do something dramatic to turn the advertising tide. So, two years after the Apple "Get a Mac" onslaught began, conservative Microsoft hired the anything-but-conservative adver-

tising agency Crispin Porter + Bogusky, which is known for its award-winning but cheeky and irreverent campaigns for clients such as Burger King and Coke Zero. Microsoft and Crispin made for an odd mix of corporate personalities. Even Rob Reilly, executive creative director for Crispin, worried a bit about the partnership. After all, Crispin itself was a Mac shop through and through. Still, Reilly was enthused about creating a campaign to blunt Apple's attacks and restore Microsoft's image as an innovative industry leader.

To break from the past, Microsoft and Crispin first launched a set of "teaser ads" designed to "get the conversation going." In the ads, comedian Jerry Seinfeld and Microsoft founder Bill Gates spent time together, shopping for shoes, eating ice cream, and exchanging irrelevant banter, all with little or no mention of Microsoft Windows. Although they made few selling points, the humorous, well-received ads put a more human face on the giant software company.

A few weeks later, Microsoft replaced the teaser commercials with a direct counterpunch to Apple's "Get a Mac" ads. It launched its own "I'm a PC" campaign, featuring a dead-on look-alike of Apple's PC character. In the first ad, dressed in PC's dorky outfit, Microsoft's character opened with the line, "I'm a PC. And I've been made into a stereotype." He was followed by a parade of everyday PC users—from environmentalists, political bloggers, mixed martial arts fighters, and mash-up DJs to budget-conscious laptop shoppers and remarkably tech-savvy preschoolers—each proclaiming, "I'm a PC."

The Microsoft "I'm a PC" campaign struck a chord with Windows users. They no longer had to sit back and take Apple's jibes like the clueless drones they were made out to be. "That's where the whole notion of 'I'm a PC' and putting a face on our users came about," said Reilly. Identifying real PC people "was important to do on behalf of our users, who really aren't like that [Mac vs. PC] guy," says a Microsoft brand marketer.

Off to a successful start, Microsoft and Crispin soon extended the "I'm a PC" campaign with a new pitch, one that was more in tune with the then-troubled economy. Part advertising and part reality TV, the new campaign—called "Laptop Hunters"—tagged along with real consumers as they shopped for new computers. The first ad featured an energetic young redhead named Lauren, who wanted a laptop with "comfortable keys and a 17-inch screen" for under $1,000. Stopping first at a Mac store, she learned that Apple offered only one laptop at $1,000, and it had only a 13-inch screen. To get what she wanted from Apple, she figured, "I'd have to double my budget, which isn't feasible. I guess I'm just not cool enough to be a Mac person." Instead, Lauren giddily buys an HP Pavilion laptop for less than $700. "I'm a PC," she concludes, "only I got just what I wanted."

If previous "I'm a PC" ads started a shift in perceptions, the "Laptop Hunters" series really moved the needle. The ads spoke volumes in a difficult economy, portraying Apple as too expensive, "too cool," and out of touch with mainstream consumers. The provocative ads, in tandem with the nation's economic woes, bumped Microsoft's BrandIndex score from near zero to 46.2, while Apple's score dropped from its previous high of 70 to only 12.4. In a sure sign that Microsoft's revitalized advertising was striking a nerve, Apple's lawyers called Microsoft chief operating officer B. Kevin Turner, demanding that he change the ads because Apple was lowering its prices and the ads were no longer accurate. It was "the greatest single phone call" he'd ever taken, said Turner. "I did cartwheels down the hallway."

To maintain momentum, Microsoft and Crispin launched yet another iteration of the "I'm a PC" campaign—this one introducing Microsoft's new Windows 7 operating system. Consistent with the "I'm a PC" theme, the campaign featured testimonials from everyday folks telling how specific Windows 7 features reflected ideas they'd passed along to Microsoft in an eight million-person beta test of the software. At the end of each ad, customers gloated, "I'm a PC, and Windows 7 was my idea."

Once again, Apple responded. It struck back directly with one of its most negative Mac vs. PC ads yet. Called "Broken Promises," it featured a gloating PC telling Mac that Windows 7 wouldn't have any of the problems associated with the old Window's versions. A bewildered Mac notes that he'd heard such claims before, with each previous Windows generation. In the end, PC says, "Trust me." Many analysts felt that the biting tone of the ad suggested that Apple was feeling the heat and getting defensive. Uncharacteristically, Mac seemed to be losing his cool.

By mid-2010, both companies appeared to be turning down the competitive advertising heat. Apple retired its "Get a Mac" campaign in favor of a more straightforward "Why You'll Love a Mac" campaign,

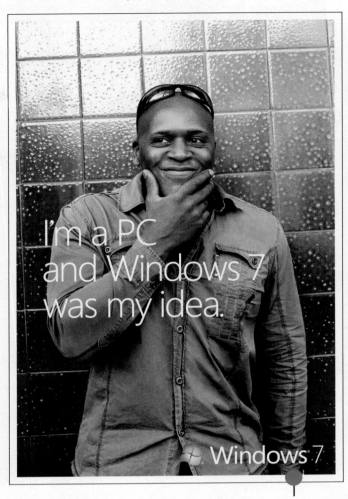

I'm a PC and Windows 7 was my idea.

Windows 7

which listed the reasons for choosing a Mac rather than a PC. Microsoft had long since ditched its "Laptop Hunter" attack ads. Both companies appeared to be focusing more positively on what their products could do, rather than on what the competition couldn't do.

Thanks to the "I'm a PC" campaign, Microsoft has now put itself on equal advertising footing with Apple—perhaps better footing. Consumer value perceptions for Microsoft and Apple are now running pretty much neck and neck. And the campaign has given PC fans everywhere a real boost. "I've never seen more pride at Microsoft," says one Microsoft employee. "You walk through the campus, and you see people's laptops that have 'I'm a PC' stickers on them. I walk in the company store, and there are these huge banners that say 'I'm a PC' and shirts and ties and mugs." Crispin's Reilly now owns not one but two PC laptops and is thrilled with the impact of his agency's efforts. "You are not so embarrassed to take your PC out of the bag on a plane anymore," he says. "It's actually kind of cool that you do. I know this [campaign] is working."[1]

In the long-running advertising battle between Microsoft and Apple, Microsoft's innovative "I'm a PC" campaign has given PC fans everywhere a real boost. Now, it's actually kind of cool to own a PC.

After years of PC bashing by Apple's classic "Get a Mac" campaign, Microsoft is now on equal—perhaps better—footing in the heated advertising battle waged by the two computer industry giants. Microsoft's "I'm a PC" campaign is really working.

As we discussed in the previous chapter, companies must do more than simply create customer value. They must also clearly and persuasively communicate that value to target customers. In this chapter, we take a closer look at two marketing communications tools: *advertising* and *public relations*.

Advertising (pp 436–454)

Author Comment | You already know a lot about advertising—you are exposed to it every day. But here we'll look behind the scenes at how companies make advertising decisions.

Advertising
Any paid form of nonpersonal presentation and promotion of ideas, goods, or services by an identified sponsor.

Advertising can be traced back to the very beginnings of recorded history. Archaeologists working in countries around the Mediterranean Sea have dug up signs announcing various events and offers. The Romans painted walls to announce gladiator fights, and the Phoenicians painted pictures on large rocks to promote their wares along parade routes. During the golden age in Greece, town criers announced the sale of cattle, crafted items, and even cosmetics. An early "singing commercial" went as follows: "For eyes that are shining, for cheeks like the dawn / For beauty that lasts after girlhood is gone / For prices in reason, the woman who knows / Will buy her cosmetics from Aesclyptos."

Modern advertising, however, is a far cry from these early efforts. U.S. advertisers now run up an estimated annual bill of more than $148 billion on measured advertising media; worldwide ad spending exceeds an estimated $450 billion. P&G, the world's largest advertiser, last year spent $4.2 billion on U.S. advertising and $9.7 billion worldwide.[2]

Although advertising is used mostly by business firms, a wide range of not-for-profit organizations, professionals, and social agencies also use advertising to promote their causes to various target publics. In fact, the thirty-third largest advertising spender is a not-for-profit organization—the U.S. government. For example, the federal government recently spent some $300 million on an advertising campaign to motivate Americans to take part in the 2010 Census.[3] Advertising is a good way to inform and persuade, whether the purpose is to sell Coca-Cola worldwide or get people in a developing nation to use birth control.

⊙ FIGURE | 15.1
Major Advertising Decisions

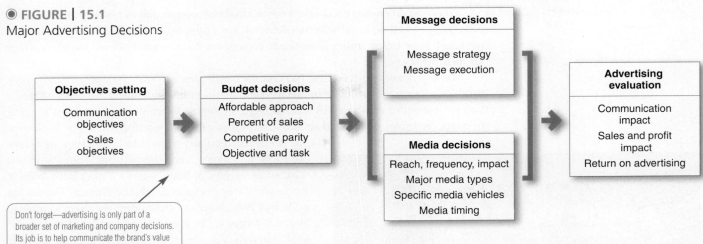

Don't forget—advertising is only part of a broader set of marketing and company decisions. Its job is to help communicate the brand's value proposition to target customers. Advertising must blend well with other promotion and marketing mix decisions.

Marketing management must make four important decisions when developing an advertising program (see ⊙ **Figure 15.1**): *setting advertising objectives, setting the advertising budget, developing advertising strategy (message decisions and media decisions), and evaluating advertising campaigns.*

Setting Advertising Objectives

The first step is to set *advertising objectives*. These objectives should be based on past decisions about the target market, positioning, and the marketing mix, which define the job that advertising must do in the total marketing program. The overall advertising objective is to help build customer relationships by communicating customer value. Here, we discuss specific advertising objectives.

Advertising objective
A specific communication *task* to be accomplished with a specific *target* audience during a specific period of *time*.

An **advertising objective** is a specific communication *task* to be accomplished with a specific *target* audience during a specific period of *time*. Advertising objectives can be classified by their primary purpose—to *inform, persuade,* or *remind*. ⊙ **Table 15.1** lists examples of each of these specific objectives.

Informative advertising is used heavily when introducing a new-product category. In this case, the objective is to build primary demand. Thus, early producers of DVD players first had to inform consumers of the image quality and convenience benefits of the new product.

⊙ **TABLE | 15.1** Possible Advertising Objectives ← *The overall advertising goal is to help build customer relationships by communicating customer value.*

Informative Advertising

Communicating customer value	Suggesting new uses for a product
Building a brand and company image	Informing the market of a price change
Telling the market about a new product	Describing available services and support
Explaining how a product works	Correcting false impressions

Persuasive Advertising

Building brand preference	Persuading customers to purchase now
Encouraging switching to a brand	Persuading customers to receive a sales call
Changing customer perceptions of product value	Convincing customers to tell others about the brand

Reminder Advertising

Maintaining customer relationships	Reminding consumers where to buy the product
Reminding consumers that the product may be needed in the near future	Keeping the brand in a customer's mind during off-seasons

Persuasive advertising becomes more important as competition increases. Here, the company's objective is to build selective demand. For example, once DVD players became established, Sony began trying to persuade consumers that *its* brand offered the best quality for their money.

Some persuasive advertising has become *comparative advertising* (or *attack advertising*), in which a company directly or indirectly compares its brand with one or more other brands. You see examples of comparative advertising in almost every product category, ranging from sports drinks, coffee, and soup to computers, car rentals, and credit cards. For example, Unilever regularly runs ads comparing its Suave products to "overpriced competitors." Says one ad: "Our wide variety of body washes makes Bath & Body Works smell way overpriced." ◉ And Dunkin' Donuts ran a TV and Web campaign comparing the chain's coffee to Starbuck's brews. "In a recent national blind taste test," proclaimed the ads, "more Americans preferred the taste of Dunkin' Donuts coffee over Starbucks. It's just more proof it's all about the coffee (not the couches or music)."

◉ **Comparative advertising:** Dunkin' Donuts ran a TV and Web campaign comparing the chain's coffee to Starbuck's brews. "Try the coffee that won," the ads concluded.

Advertisers should use comparative advertising with caution. All too often, such ads invite competitor responses, resulting in an advertising war that neither competitor can win. Upset competitors might take more drastic action, such as filing complaints with the self-regulatory National Advertising Division of the Council of Better Business Bureaus or even filing false-advertising lawsuits. For example, recently, Verizon Wireless and AT&T fought legal battles over cell phone coverage, Gatorade and Powerade battled over the definition of a "complete sports drink," and Sara Lee's Ball Park sued Oscar Mayer over an advertised taste-test claim.[4]

Reminder advertising is important for mature products; it helps to maintain customer relationships and keep consumers thinking about the product. Expensive Coca-Cola television ads primarily build and maintain the Coca-Cola brand relationship rather than inform or persuade customers to buy it in the short run.

Advertising's goal is to help move consumers through the buying process. Some advertising is designed to move people to immediate action. For example, a direct-response television ad by Weight Watchers urges consumers to pick up the phone and sign up right away, and a Best Buy newspaper insert for a weekend sale encourages immediate store visits. However, many ads focus on building or strengthening long-term customer relationships. For example, a Nike television ad in which well-known athletes work through extreme challenges in their Nike gear never directly asks for a sale. Instead, the goal is to somehow change the way the customers think or feel about the brand.

Setting the Advertising Budget

Advertising budget
The dollars and other resources allocated to a product or a company advertising program.

After determining its advertising objectives, the company next sets its **advertising budget** for each product. Four commonly used methods for setting promotion budgets were discussed in Chapter 14. Here we discuss some specific factors that should be considered when setting the advertising budget.

A brand's advertising budget often depends on its *stage in the product life cycle*. For example, new products typically need relatively large advertising budgets to build awareness and gain consumer trial. In contrast, mature brands usually require lower budgets as a ratio to sales. *Market share* also impacts the amount of advertising needed: Because building market share or taking market share from competitors requires larger advertising spending than does simply maintaining current share, low-share brands usually need more advertising spending as a percentage of sales. Also, brands in a market with many competitors and high advertising clutter must be advertised more heavily to be noticed above the noise in the marketplace. Undifferentiated brands—those that closely resemble other brands in their product class (soft drinks, laundry detergents)—may require heavy advertising to set them apart. When the product differs greatly from competing products, advertising can be used to point out the differences to consumers.

No matter what method is used, setting the advertising budget is no easy task. How does a company know if it is spending the right amount? Some critics charge that large consumer packaged-goods firms tend to spend too much on advertising and that business-to-business marketers generally underspend on advertising. They claim that, on the one hand, large consumer companies use lots of image advertising without really knowing its effects. They overspend as a form of "insurance" against not spending enough. On the other hand, business advertisers tend to rely too heavily on their sales forces to bring in orders. They underestimate the power of company image and product image in preselling to industrial customers. Thus, they do not spend enough on advertising to build customer awareness and knowledge.

Companies such as Coca-Cola and Kraft have built sophisticated statistical models to determine the relationship between promotional spending and brand sales, and to help determine the "optimal investment" across various media. Still, because so many factors affect advertising effectiveness, some controllable and others not, measuring the results of advertising spending remains an inexact science. In most cases, managers must rely on large doses of judgment along with more quantitative analysis when setting advertising budgets.[5]

As a result, advertising is one of the easiest budget items to cut when economic times get tough. Cuts in brand-building advertising appear to do little short-term harm to sales. For example, in the wake of the recent recession, U.S. advertising expenditures plummeted 12 percent from the previous year. In the long run, however, slashing ad spending risks long-term damage to a brand's image and market share. In fact, companies that can maintain or even increase their advertising spending while competitors are decreasing theirs can gain competitive advantage. ● Consider carmaker Audi:[6]

Although Audi's sales slipped during the recession, they fell far less than those of competitors amid a calamitous year for the auto industry. Even more, Audi's brand awareness and buyer consideration are up substantially, with gains outstripping those of

BMW, Mercedes, and Lexus. In short: Audi might be the hottest auto brand on the market right now. And it's strongly positioned for the future as the economy recovers. What is Audi's advantage? The brand spent heavily on advertising and marketing at a time when rivals were retrenching. During the past three years, despite the harsh economy, Audi increased its ad spending fourfold, including high-profile placements such as the last three Super Bowls, the Academy Awards, the NCAA basketball tournament, and Sunday Night Football. Audi "has kept its foot on the pedal while everyone else [was] pulling back," says an Audi ad executive. "Why would we go backward now when the industry [was] generally locking the brakes and cutting spending?" adds Audi's chief marketing executive.

● **Setting the promotion budget:** Promotion spending is one of the easiest items to cut in tough economic times. But Audi has gained competitive advantage by keeping its foot on the promotion pedal as competitors have retrenched.

Developing Advertising Strategy

Advertising strategy

The strategy by which the company accomplishes its advertising objectives. It consists of two major elements: creating advertising messages and selecting advertising media.

Advertising strategy consists of two major elements: creating advertising *messages* and selecting advertising *media*. In the past, companies often viewed media planning as secondary to the message-creation process. The creative department first created good advertisements, and then the media department selected and purchased the best media for carrying those advertisements to desired target audiences. This often caused friction between creatives and media planners.

Today, however, soaring media costs, more-focused target marketing strategies, and the blizzard of new digital and interactive media have promoted the importance of the media-planning function. The decision about which media to use for an ad campaign—television, newspapers, magazines, cell phones, a Web site or an online network, or e-mail—is now sometimes more critical than the creative elements of the campaign. As a result, more and more advertisers are orchestrating a closer harmony between their messages and the media that deliver them. In fact, in a really good ad campaign, you often have to ask "Is that a media idea or a creative idea?"

Creating the Advertising Message

No matter how big the budget, advertising can succeed only if advertisements gain attention and communicate well. Good advertising messages are especially important in today's costly and cluttered advertising environment. In 1950, the average U.S. household received only three network television channels and a handful of major national magazines. Today, the average household receives more than 118 channels, and consumers have more than 20,000 magazines from which to choose.[7] Add in the countless radio stations and a continuous barrage of catalogs, direct mail, e-mail and online ads, and out-of-home media, and consumers are being bombarded with ads at home, work, and all points in between. As a result, consumers are exposed to as many as 3,000 to 5,000 commercial messages every day.[8]

Breaking through the Clutter. If all this advertising clutter bothers some consumers, it also causes huge headaches for advertisers. Take the situation facing network television advertisers. They pay an average of $302,000 to make a single 30-second commercial. Then, each time they show it, they pay an average of $122,000 for 30 seconds of advertising time during a popular prime-time program. They pay even more if it's an especially popular program, such as *American Idol* ($642,000), *Sunday Night Football* ($340,000), *Grey's Anatomy* ($240,000), *Two and a Half Men* ($227,000), or a mega-event such as the Super Bowl (nearly $3 million per 30 seconds!).[9]

Then their ads are sandwiched in with a clutter of other commercials, announcements, and network promotions, totaling nearly 20 minutes of nonprogram material per prime-time hour with commercial breaks coming every six minutes on average. Such clutter in television and other ad media has created an increasingly hostile advertising environment. According to one recent study, more than 70 percent of Americans think there are too many ads on TV, and 62 percent of national advertisers believe that TV ads have become less effective, citing clutter as the main culprit.[10]

Until recently, television viewers were pretty much a captive audience for advertisers. But today's digital wizardry has given consumers a rich new set of information and entertainment choices. With the growth in cable and satellite TV, the Internet, video on demand (VOD), video downloads, and DVD rentals, today's viewers have many more options.

Digital technology has also armed consumers with an arsenal of weapons for choosing what they watch or don't watch. ◉ Increasingly, thanks to the growth of DVR systems, consumers are choosing *not* to watch ads. More than 33 percent of American TV households now have DVRs, and an estimated 44 percent will have them by 2014. One ad agency executive calls these DVR systems "electronic weedwhackers." Research shows that DVR owners view only about 40 percent of the commercials aired. At the same time, VOD and video downloads are exploding, allowing viewers to watch programming on their own time terms—with or without commercials.[11]

Thus, advertisers can no longer force-feed the same old cookie-cutter ad messages to captive consumers through traditional media. Just to gain and hold attention, today's advertising messages must be better planned, more imaginative, more entertaining, and more emotionally engaging. Simply interrupting or disrupting con-

◉ Advertising clutter: Today's consumers, armed with an arsenal of weapons, can choose what they watch and don't watch. Increasingly, they are choosing not to watch ads.

sumers no longer works. Instead, unless ads provide information that is interesting, useful, or entertaining, many consumers will simply skip by them.

Merging Advertising and Entertainment. To break through the clutter, many marketers are now subscribing to a new merging of advertising and entertainment, dubbed "**Madison & Vine**." You've probably heard of Madison Avenue. It's the New York City street that houses the headquarters of many of the nation's largest advertising agencies. You may also have heard of Hollywood & Vine, the intersection of Hollywood Avenue and Vine Street in Hollywood, California, long the symbolic heart of the U.S. entertainment industry. Now, Madison Avenue and Hollywood & Vine are coming together to form a new intersection— Madison & Vine—that represents the merging of advertising and entertainment in an effort to create new avenues for reaching consumers with more engaging messages.

This merging of advertising and entertainment takes one of two forms: advertainment or branded entertainment. The aim of *advertainment* is to make ads themselves so entertaining, or so useful, that people *want* to watch them. There's no chance that you'd watch ads on purpose, you say? Think again. For example, the Super Bowl has become an annual advertainment showcase. Tens of millions of people tune in to the Super Bowl each year, as much to watch the entertaining ads as to see the game.

In fact, DVR systems can actually *improve* viewership of a really good ad. For example, most Super Bowl ads last year were viewed more in DVR households than non-DVR households. Rather than zipping past the ads, many people were skipping back to watch them again and again. Remember the guy who plays football like Betty White until he has a Snickers? Or how about the Doritos ad in which the dog puts the shock collar on its owner? If you've got a DVR, chances are you watched these and other ads several times.

Beyond making their regular ads more entertaining, advertisers are also creating new advertising forms that look less like ads and more like short films or shows. For example, Dove's "Evolution" video wasn't technically an ad, but it drew more—and more meaningful— views than many TV ads do, and the views were initiated by consumers. A range of new brand messaging platforms—from Webisodes and blogs to viral videos—are now blurring the line between ads and entertainment.

Branded entertainment (or *brand integrations*) involves making the brand an inseparable part of some other form of entertainment. The most common form of branded entertainment is product placements—embedding brands as props within other programming. It might be a brief glimpse of the latest LG phone on *Grey's Anatomy*. It could be worked into the show's overall storyline, as it is on *The Big Bang Theory*, whose character Penny works at the Cheesecake Factory. The product placement might even be scripted into an episode. ⦿ For example, one entire episode of *Modern Family* centers around finding geeky father character Phil Dunphy the recently released, hard-to-find Apple iPad he covets as his special birthday present. And in one episode of *30 Rock*, network boss Jack Donaghy blatantly extols the virtues of his Verizon Wireless service. Liz Lemon agrees: "Well sure, that Verizon Wireless service is just unbeatable." She then turns to the camera and deadpans, "Can we have our money now?"[12]

Originally created with TV in mind, branded entertainment has spread quickly into other sectors of the entertainment industry. It's widely used in movies (remember all those GM vehicles in the *Transformers* series, the prominence of Purina Puppy Chow in *Marley & Me*, and the appearance of brands ranging from Burger King, Dr Pepper, 7-Eleven, and Audi to Royal Purple Motor Oil in *Iron Man 2*?). If you look carefully, you'll also see product placements in video games, comic books, Broadway musicals, and even pop music. For example, there's a sandwich-making scene featuring Wonder Bread and Miracle Whip in the middle of Lady Gaga's 10-minute "Telephone" video (which captured more than 50 million YouTube views in less than a month).

Madison & Vine
A term that has come to represent the merging of advertising and entertainment in an effort to break through the clutter and create new avenues for reaching consumers with more engaging messages.

⦿ Madison & Vine: Product placements are often scripted into program episodes. Here, dorky dad Phil on *Modern Family* covets his iPad.

In all, U.S. advertisers shelled out an estimated $10 billion on product placements last year, more than the GDP of Paraguay. In the first three months of the year alone, America's top 11 TV channels produced a massive 117,976 product placements. By itself, Fox's *American Idol* shoehorned in more than 3,000 placements. Old Navy dressed the contestants while Clairol did their hair, Ford supplied the winners with new cars, and Coca-Cola refreshed the judges.[13]

So, Madison & Vine is the new meeting place for the advertising and entertainment industries. The goal is for brand messages to become a part of the entertainment rather than interrupting it. As advertising agency JWT puts it, "We believe advertising needs to stop interrupting what people are interested in and be what people are interested in." However, advertisers must be careful that the new intersection itself doesn't become too congested. With all the new ad formats and product placements, Madison & Vine threatens to create even more of the very clutter that it was designed to break through. At that point, consumers might decide to take yet a different route.

Message Strategy. The first step in creating effective advertising messages is to plan a *message strategy*—the general message that will be communicated to consumers. The purpose of advertising is to get consumers to think about or react to the product or company in a certain way. People will react only if they believe they will benefit from doing so. Thus, developing an effective message strategy begins with identifying customer *benefits* that can be used as advertising appeals.

Ideally, the message strategy will follow directly from the company's broader positioning and customer value strategies. Message strategy statements tend to be plain, straightforward outlines of benefits and positioning points that the advertiser wants to stress. The advertiser must next develop a compelling **creative concept**—or "big idea"—that will bring the message strategy to life in a distinctive and memorable way. At this stage, simple message ideas become great ad campaigns. Usually, a copywriter and an art director will team up to generate many creative concepts, hoping that one of these concepts will turn out to be the big idea. The creative concept may emerge as a visualization, a phrase, or a combination of the two.

The creative concept will guide the choice of specific appeals to be used in an advertising campaign. *Advertising appeals* should have three characteristics. First, they should be *meaningful*, pointing out benefits that make the product more desirable or interesting to consumers. Second, appeals must be *believable*. Consumers must believe that the product or service will deliver the promised benefits.

However, the most meaningful and believable benefits may not be the best ones to feature. Appeals should also be *distinctive*. They should tell how the product is better than competing brands. For example, the most meaningful benefit of owning a wristwatch is that it keeps accurate time, yet few watch ads feature this benefit. Instead, based on the distinctive benefits they offer, watch advertisers might select any of a number of advertising themes. For years, Timex has been the affordable watch. Last Father's Day, for example, Timex ads suggested "Tell Dad more than time this Father's Day. Tell him that you've learned the value of a dollar." Similarly, Rolex ads never talk about keeping time. Instead, they talk about the brand's "obsession with perfection" and the fact that "Rolex has been the preeminent symbol of performance and prestige for more than a century."

Message Execution. The advertiser now must turn the big idea into an actual ad execution that will capture the target market's attention and interest. The creative team must find the best approach, style, tone, words, and format for executing the message. The message can be presented in various **execution styles**, such as the following:

- *Slice of life:* This style shows one or more "typical" people using the product in a normal setting. For example, a Silk soy milk "Rise and Shine" ad shows a young professional starting the day with a healthier breakfast and high hopes.

- *Lifestyle:* This style shows how a product fits in with a particular lifestyle. For example, an ad for Athleta active wear shows a woman in a complex yoga pose and states "If your body is your temple, build it one piece at a time."

Creative concept
The compelling "big idea" that will bring the advertising message strategy to life in a distinctive and memorable way.

Execution style
The approach, style, tone, words, and format used for executing an advertising message.

⊙ **Execution styles: This ad creates a nostalgic mood around the product. "So I baked her the cookies she's loved since she was little."**

- *Fantasy:* This style creates a fantasy around the product or its use. For example, a Travelers Insurance ad features a gentleman carrying a giant red umbrella (the company's brand symbol). The man helps people by using the umbrella to protect them from the rain, sail them across a flooded river, and fly home. The ad closes with "Travelers Insurance. There when you need it."

- *Mood or image:* This style builds a mood or image around the product or service, such as beauty, love, intrigue, or serenity. Few claims are made about the product or service except through suggestion. ⊙ For example, a Nestlé Toll House ad shows a daughter hugging her mother after surprising her with a weekend home from college. "So I baked her the cookies she's loved since she was little."

- *Musical:* This style shows people or cartoon characters singing about the product. For example, FreeCreditReport.com tells its story exclusively through a set of popular singing commercials such as "Dreamgirl" and "Pirate." Similarly, Oscar Mayer's long-running ads show children singing its now classic "I wish I were an Oscar Mayer wiener . . ." jingle.

- *Personality symbol:* This style creates a character that represents the product. The character might be animated (Mr. Clean, Tony the Tiger, the GEICO Gecko, or the Zappos Zappets) or real (Ol' Lonely the Maytag repairman, the E*TRADE babies, Ronald McDonald, or the Aflac duck).

- *Technical expertise:* This style shows the company's expertise in making the product. Thus, natural foods maker Kashi shows its buyers carefully selecting ingredients for its products, and Jim Koch of the Boston Beer Company tells about his many years of experience in brewing Samuel Adams beer.

- *Scientific evidence:* This style presents survey or scientific evidence that the brand is better or better liked than one or more other brands. For years, Crest toothpaste has used scientific evidence to convince buyers that Crest is better than other brands at fighting cavities.

- *Testimonial evidence or endorsement:* This style features a highly believable or likable source endorsing the product. It could be ordinary people saying how much they like a given product. For example, Subway uses spokesman Jared, a customer who lost 245 pounds on a diet of Subway sandwiches. Or it might be a celebrity presenting the product. Olympic gold medal swimmer Michael Phelps also speaks for Subway.

The advertiser also must choose a *tone* for the ad. P&G always uses a positive tone: Its ads say something very positive about its products. Other advertisers now use edgy humor to break through the commercial clutter. Bud Light commercials are famous for this.

The advertiser must use memorable and attention-getting *words* in the ad. For example, rather than claiming simply that its laundry detergent is "superconcentrated," Method asks customers "Are you jug addicted?" The solution: "Our patent-pending formula that's so fricken' concentrated, 50 loads fits in a teeny bottle. . . . With our help, you can get off the jugs and get clean."

Finally, *format* elements make a difference in an ad's impact as well as in its cost. A small change in an ad's design can make a big difference in its effect. In a print ad, the *illustration* is the first thing the reader notices—it must be strong enough to draw attention. Next, the *headline* must effectively entice the right people to read the copy. Finally, the *copy*—the main block of text in the ad—must be simple but strong and convincing. Moreover, these three elements must effectively work *together* to persuasively present customer value.

Consumer-Generated Messages. Taking advantage of today's interactive technologies, many companies are now tapping consumers for message ideas or actual ads. They

● **Consumer-generated advertising: Online crafts marketplace/community Etsy.com ran a contest inviting consumers to tell the Etsy.com story in 30-second videos. The results were "positively remarkable."**

are searching existing video sites, setting up their own sites, and sponsoring ad-creation contests and other promotions. Sometimes the results are outstanding; sometimes they are forgettable. If done well, however, user-generated content can incorporate the voice of the customer into brand messages and generate greater consumer brand involvement (see Real Marketing 15.1).

Many brands develop brand Web sites or hold contests that invite consumers to submit ad message ideas and videos. For example, for the past several years, PepsiCo's Doritos brand has held its annual "Crash the Super Bowl Challenge" contest that invites consumers to create their own video ads about the tasty triangular corn chips. The consumer-generated Doritos ads have been a smashing success. At the other end of the size spectrum, online crafts marketplace/community Etsy.com—"Your best place to buy and sell all things handmade, vintage, and supplies"—ran a contest inviting consumers to tell the Etsy.com story in 30-second videos. ◉ The results were what one well-known former advertising critic called "positively remarkable."[14]

The 10 semifinalists are, as a group, better thought-out and realized than any 10 random commercials running on TV anywhere in the world. The best user-created Etsy ad features a simple, sad, animated robot, consigned to a life of soul-crushing assembly-line production. "See, there's a lot of robots out there," says the voice of the unseen Etsy craftswomen who crafted him. "A lot of these robots are sad because they're stuck making these boring, mass-produced things. Me, I really can believe all that great stuff about how it helps the environment and microeconomics and feeling special about getting something handmade by someone else. But the real reason I make handmade goods is because every time somebody buys something hand-made, a robot gets its wings." The user-made ad "is simply magnificent," concludes the ad critic, "in a way that the agency business had better take note of."

Not all consumer-generated advertising efforts, however, are so successful. As many big companies have learned, ads made by amateurs can be . . . well, pretty amateurish. Done well, however, consumer-generated advertising efforts can produce new creative ideas and fresh perspectives on the brand from consumers who actually experience it. Such campaigns can boost consumer involvement and get consumers talking and thinking about a brand and its value to them.[15]

Selecting Advertising Media

Advertising media
The vehicles through which advertising messages are delivered to their intended audiences.

The major steps in **advertising media** selection are (1) determining on *reach, frequency,* and *impact*; (2) choosing among major *media types*; (3) selecting specific *media vehicles*; and (4) choosing *media timing.*

Determining Reach, Frequency, and Impact. To select media, the advertiser must determine the reach and frequency needed to achieve the advertising objectives. *Reach* is a measure of the *percentage* of people in the target market who are exposed to the ad campaign during a given period of time. For example, the advertiser might try to reach 70 percent of

Real Marketing 15.1

Consumer-Generated Advertising:
When Done Well, It Can Be Really Good

Fueled by the user-generated content craze made popular by the likes of YouTube, Facebook, and other online content-sharing communities, the move toward consumer-generated advertising has spread like wildfire in recent years. Companies large and small—including the likes of PepsiCo, Unilever, P&G, CareerBuilder, and other blue-chip marketers—have fast recognized the benefits (and the drawbacks) of inviting customers to co-create brand messages.

Perhaps no brand has been more successful with user-generated advertising than PepsiCo's Doritos brand. For four years running, the Doritos "Crash the Super Bowl" contest has invited consumers to create their own 30-second video ads featuring the market-leading tortilla chip. A jury of ad pros and Doritos brand managers whittle down the thousands of entries submitted and post the finalists online. Consumers vote for the winners, who receive cash prizes and have their ads run during the Super Bowl.

For last year's Super Bowl, Doritos threw prize money around like a rich uncle home for the holidays. Six finalists each claimed $25,000, and PepsiCo aired the top four ads during the game. To put more icing on the cake, Doritos promised to pay a whopping $1 million to any entrant whose ad placed first in the *USA Today* Ad Meter ratings. Second place was good for $600,000, and third place would take home $400,000. If the winners swept the top three Ad Meter spots, each would receive an additional $1 million. Not surprisingly, the contest attracted more than 4,000 entries.

Although they didn't sweep the top three Ad Meter spots, one ad (called "Underdog") took the number two spot, winning 24-year-old Joshua Svoboda of Raleigh, North Carolina, $600,000—not a bad return for an ad that cost only $200 to produce. Even more notably, the lowest-rated of the four consumer-made Doritos ads came in 17th out of 65 Super Bowl ads. Moreover, the ads finished strongly in virtually every consumer survey. They dominated the "most-watched" ratings in TiVo households, with an ad entitled "House Rules" taking first

and "Underdog" taking fourth. "House Rules" was also the most-liked spot on Hulu.com. And in surveys by Nielsen and Twitter, Doritos was the "most buzzed-about" advertiser during and after the game.

It seems as if everyone is getting into the consumer-generated content act. According to one global report that ranks the world's top creative work, nine of last year's top 10 campaigns involved some kind of consumer input. "This is a big seismic shift in our business," says the former ad agency executive who assembled the report. "We've had 100 years of business-to-consumer advertising, but now the Web has enabled us to get people actively involved in talking to each other. If the idea is interesting enough, consumers will do the work for you." Even more, they'll work for little or no pay.

That kind of talk makes some ad agencies nervous. But the idea isn't that companies should fire their ad agencies and have consumers create their ads instead. In fact, most consumer-generated ad campaigns are coordinated by ad agencies. For example, Unilever is

expanding its "crowdsourcing" efforts with a video ad contest that involves 13 of its brands, including Ben & Jerry's, Dove, Lipton, and Vaseline. However, the company is quick to clarify the role of its user-generated content strategy.

This in no way is a replacement for our ad agencies. It's not really what it's designed to be. The real reason for it is to offer more participation for our consumers, to get closer to consumers, and allow them to be more involved with our brands. It will help them become advocates, help them have more of a connection with the brands if they've been a part of helping to create it. It's not one of our objectives to save money. I mean it's a nice benefit, if we can get great stuff. But it's not really the objective. We believe that marketing will be much more participatory in the next few years and we want to be at the leading edge of that.

Although most consumer-generated content efforts are limited to ad and video messages, Pepsi-Co's Mountain Dew crowdsourcing campaign—called Dewmocracy—involves consumers in decisions across the entire range of marketing for the brand. Now in its second year, Dewmocracy seeks inputs from ardent brand fans on everything from product development to ad messages and ad agency selection.

At the start of the most recent Dewmocracy campaign, Mountain Dew asked loyal fans to submit ideas for three new flavors. It

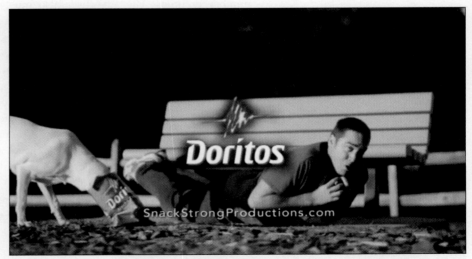

Consumer-generated messages: Last year, the winning ads in the Doritos "Crash the Super Bowl" challenge finished strongly in virtually every consumer survey. The top ad finished second on the *USA Today* Super Bowl Ad Meter.

Continued on next page

sent 50 finalists home-tasting kits and Flip video cameras and encouraged them to upload videos about their experience to YouTube. With three finalists selected, Mountain Dew asked consumers to pick names (Typhoon, Distortion, and White Out rose to the top), colors, and package designs for the new flavors on the Dewmocracy Web site, Facebook, Twitter, and other social media sites. The three flavors were rolled out over the summer, and fans were asked to try them and vote for a favorite, which became a permanent addition to the Mountain Dew lineup.

As for advertising, rather than having consumers submit their own video ads, Mountain Dew invited fans to help choose the ad agencies that would do the job. Consumers "built these products and had a clear idea of the products," said Mountain Dew's director of marketing. They "challenged us to say, who is going to do our advertising, and how do we get some new thinking?" Ad agencies and individuals submitted more than 200 12-second videos outlining their ideas for promoting the three new flavors. Consumers cast 15,000 votes. In the end, three small ad shops landed the jobs.

The Dewmocracy consumer-generated marketing campaigns have produced successful new, customer-approved Mountain Dew flavors at very little cost (the brand didn't spend a dollar on media throughout the process). But they met an even bigger objective. They have "allowed us to have as rich a dialogue as we could with consumers," says the brand's marketing director. The average loyal Mountain Dew drinker is male, between the ages of 18 and 39, with 92 percent on Facebook and 50 percent using YouTube. The digital Dewmocracy campaigns have been incredibly successful at engaging this group and giving them an ownership stake in the brand.

There are downsides to consumer-generated ads, of course. Although it might seem "free," the process of wading through hundreds or even thousands of entries can be difficult, costly, and time consuming. In dealing with user-created content, copyright issues, poor production quality, offensive themes, and even attacks on the brand are all par for the course. And in the end, you never know what you're going to get. For every hit Doritos ad, there are hundreds that are uninspired or just plain dreadful. Many Madison Avenue advertising pros write off consumer-generated efforts as mostly amateurish, crudely produced, and ineffective.

But when it's done well, it can be very good. Despite "a lot of advertising people" playing it down as "a seventh-grader in his backyard with a video camera," says one advertising expert, "it complements efforts by marketers to engage and involve consumers. Consumer-generated content really can work."

Sources: Extracts, quotes, and other information from Stuart Elliott, "Do-It Yourself Super Ads," *New York Times*, February 9, 2010, p. B3; Andrew McMains, "Unilever Embraces UGC," *Adweek*, April 20, 2010, accessed at www.adweek.com; Emma Hall, "Most Winning Creative Work Involves Consumer Participation," *Advertising Age*, January 6, 2010, accessed at http://adage.com/print?article_id=141329; Natalie Zmuda, "Why Mountain Dew Let Skater Dudes Take Control of Its Marketing," *Advertising Age*, February 22, 2010, p. 30; and Rich Thomaselli, "If Consumer Is Your Agency, It's Time for Review," *Advertising Age*, May 17, 2010, p. 2.

the target market during the first three months of the campaign. *Frequency* is a measure of how many *times* the average person in the target market is exposed to the message. For example, the advertiser might want an average exposure frequency of three.

But advertisers want to do more than just reach a given number of consumers a specific number of times. The advertiser also must determine the desired *media impact*—the *qualitative value* of message exposure through a given medium. For example, the same message in one magazine (say, *Newsweek*) may be more believable than in another (say, the *National Enquirer*). For products that need to be demonstrated, messages on television may have more impact than messages on radio because television uses sight *and* sound. Products for which consumers provide input on design or features might be better promoted at an interactive Web site than in a direct mailing.

More generally, the advertiser wants to choose media that will *engage* consumers rather than simply reach them. For example, for television advertising, how relevant an ad is for its audience is often much more important than how many people it reaches. ◉ For example, in an effort to make every advertising dollar count, Ford has recently been selecting TV programs based on viewer engagement ratings:[16]

Ford had little reason to advertise on the Discovery Channel's *Dirty Jobs* series, which stars Mike Rowe. The show delivers puny Nielsen ratings. But when engagement metrics were applied to the program, the viewers most deeply absorbed in the show turned out to be truck-buying men between the ages of 18 and

◉ **Viewer engagement: Viewers most deeply engaged in the Discovery Channel's Dirty Jobs series turned out to be truck-buying men, a ripe demographic for Ford's F-Series pickups.**

49—a ripe demographic for Ford. That prompted Ford to advertise heavily and hire Rowe to appear in highly successful Web videos demonstrating the durability of the F-Series pickup.

Although Nielsen is beginning to measure the levels of television *media engagement*, such measures are hard to come by for most media. Current media measures are things such as ratings, readership, listenership, and click-through rates. However, engagement happens inside the consumer. Notes one expert, "Just measuring the number of eyeballs in front of a television set is hard enough without trying to measure the intensity of those eyeballs doing the viewing."[17] Still, marketers need to know how customers connect with an ad and brand idea as a part of the broader brand relationship.

Choosing Among Major Media Types. Media planners have to know the reach, frequency, and impact of each major media type. As summarized in ⊙ **Table 15.2**, the major media types are television, newspapers, the Internet, direct mail, magazines, radio, and outdoor. Advertisers can also choose from a wide array of new digital media, such as cell phones and other digital devices, which reach consumers directly. Each medium has its advantages and its limitations. Media planners consider many factors when making their media choices. They want to choose media that will effectively and efficiently present the advertising message to target customers. Thus, they must consider each medium's impact, message effectiveness, and cost.

Typically, it's not a question of which one medium to use. Rather, the advertiser selects a mix of media and blends them into a fully integrated marketing communications campaign. Each medium plays a specific role.

The mix of media must be reexamined regularly. For a long time, television and magazines dominated the media mixes of national advertisers, with other media often neglected. However, as discussed previously, the media mix appears to be shifting. As mass-media costs rise, audiences shrink, and exciting new digital and interactive media emerge, many advertisers are finding new ways to reach consumers. They are supplementing the traditional mass media with more-specialized and highly targeted media that cost less, target more effectively, and engage consumers more fully.

For example, in addition to the explosion of online media, cable and satellite television systems are booming. Such systems allow narrow programming formats, such as all sports, all news, nutrition, arts, home improvement and gardening, cooking, travel, history, finance, and others that target select groups. Time Warner, Comcast, and other cable operators are

⊙ **TABLE | 15.2**   Profiles of Major Media Types

Medium	Advantages	Limitations
Television	Good mass-marketing coverage; low cost per exposure; combines sight, sound, and motion; appealing to the senses	High absolute costs; high clutter; fleeting exposure; less audience selectivity
Newspapers	Flexibility; timeliness; good local market coverage; broad acceptability; high believability	Short life; poor reproduction quality; small pass-along audience
The Internet	High selectivity; low cost; immediacy; interactive capabilities	Potentially low impact; the audience controls exposure
Direct mail	High audience selectivity; flexibility; no ad competition within the same medium; allows personalization	Relatively high cost per exposure; "junk mail" image
Magazines	High geographic and demographic selectivity; credibility and prestige; high-quality reproduction; long life and good pass-along readership	Long ad purchase lead time; high cost; no guarantee of position
Radio	Good local acceptance; high geographic and demographic selectivity; low cost	Audio only; fleeting exposure; low attention ("the half-heard" medium); fragmented audiences
Outdoor	Flexibility; high repeat exposure; low cost; low message competition; good positional selectivity	Little audience selectivity; creative limitations

even testing systems that will let them target specific types of ads to specific neighborhoods or individually to specific types of customers. For example, ads for a Spanish-language channel would run in only Hispanic neighborhoods, or only pet owners would see ads from pet food companies.

Advertisers can take advantage of such "narrowcasting" to "rifle in" on special market segments rather than use the "shotgun" approach offered by network broadcasting. Cable and satellite television media seem to make good sense. But, increasingly, ads are popping up in far-less-likely places. In their efforts to find less-costly and more-highly targeted ways to reach consumers, ◉ advertisers have discovered a dazzling collection of "alternative media." These days, no matter where you go or what you do, you will probably run into some new form of advertising.

◉ **Marketers have discovered a dazzling array of alternative media, like this Ben & Jerry's "upside-down bus" ad rolling through Manhattan.**

Tiny billboards attached to shopping carts and advertising decals on supermarket floors urge you to buy JELL-O Pudding Pops or Pampers, while ads roll by on the store's checkout conveyor touting your local Volvo dealer. Step outside and there goes a city trash truck sporting an ad for Glad trash bags. A nearby fire hydrant is emblazoned with advertising for KFC's "fiery" chicken wings. You escape to the ballpark, only to find billboard-size video screens running Budweiser ads while a blimp with an electronic message board circles lazily overhead. How about a quiet trip in the country? Sorry—you find an enterprising farmer using his milk cows as four-legged billboards mounted with ads for Ben & Jerry's ice cream.

These days, you're likely to find ads—well—anywhere. Taxi cabs sport electronic messaging signs tied to GPS location sensors that can pitch local stores and restaurants wherever they roam. Ad space is being sold on DVD cases, parking-lot tickets, airline boarding passes, subway turnstiles, golf scorecards, ATMs, municipal garbage cans, and even police cars, doctors' examining tables, and church bulletins. One agency even leases space on the shaved heads of college students for temporary advertising tattoos ("cranial advertising"). And the group meeting at the office water cooler has a new member—a "coolertising" ad sitting on top of the water cooler jug trying to start up a conversation about the latest episode of *American Idol*.

Such alternative media seem a bit far-fetched, and they sometimes irritate consumers who resent it all as "ad nauseam." But for many marketers, these media can save money and provide a way to hit selected consumers where they live, shop, work, and play. Of course, all this may leave you wondering if there are any commercial-free havens remaining for ad-weary consumers. Public elevators, perhaps, or stalls in a public restroom? Forget it! Each has already been invaded by innovative marketers.

Another important trend affecting media selection is the rapid growth in the number of "media multitaskers," people who absorb more than one medium at a time. One survey found that three-fourths of U.S. TV viewers read the newspaper while they watch TV, and two-thirds of them go online during their TV viewing time. According to another study, Americans between the ages of eight and 18 are managing to cram an average 10.75 hours of media consumption into 7.5 hours.[18] These days it is not uncommon to find a teenage boy chasing down photos of Megan Fox on Google, becoming a fan of a group on Facebook, watching a movie online, and texting a friend on his cell phone—all while trying to complete an essay he's got open in a Word file a few layers down on his desktop. Media planners need to take such media interactions into account when selecting the types of media they will use.

Selecting Specific Media Vehicles. Media planners must also choose the best *media vehicles*— specific media within each general media type. For example, television vehicles include *30 Rock* and *ABC World News Tonight*. Magazine vehicles include *Newsweek*, *Vogue*, and *ESPN the Magazine*.

Media planners must compute the cost per 1,000 persons reached by a vehicle. For example, if a full-page, four-color advertisement in the U.S. national edition of *Newsweek* costs $165,000 and *Newsweek*'s readership is 1.5 million people, the cost of reaching each group of 1,000 persons is about $110. The same advertisement in *BusinessWeek* may cost only $115,600 but reach only 900,000 people—at a cost per 1,000 of about $128. The media planner ranks each magazine by cost per 1,000 and favors those magazines with the lower cost per 1,000 for reaching target consumers.[19]

Media planners must also consider the costs of producing ads for different media. Whereas newspaper ads may cost very little to produce, flashy television ads can be very costly. Many online ads cost little to produce, but costs can climb when producing made-for-the-Web videos and ad series.

In selecting specific media vehicles, media planners must balance media costs against several media effectiveness factors. First, the planner should evaluate the media vehicle's *audience quality*. For a Huggies disposable diapers advertisement, for example, *Parents* magazine would have a high exposure value; *Maxim* would have a low-exposure value. Second, the media planner should consider *audience engagement*. Readers of *Vogue*, for example, typically pay more attention to ads than do *Newsweek* readers. Third, the planner should assess the vehicle's *editorial quality*. *Time* and the *Wall Street Journal* are more believable and prestigious than *Star* or the *National Enquirer*.

Deciding on Media Timing. An advertiser must also decide how to schedule the advertising over the course of a year. Suppose sales of a product peak in December and drop in March (for winter sports gear, for instance). The firm can vary its advertising to follow the seasonal pattern, oppose the seasonal pattern, or be the same all year. Most firms do some seasonal advertising. For example, Mars currently runs M&Ms special ads for almost every holiday and "season," from Easter, Fourth of July, and Halloween to the Super Bowl season and the Oscar season. ◉ The Picture People, the national chain of portrait studios, advertises more heavily before major holidays, such as Christmas, Easter, Valentine's day, and Halloween. Some marketers do *only* seasonal advertising: For instance, P&G advertises its Vicks NyQuil only during the cold and flu season.

Finally, the advertiser must choose the pattern of the ads. *Continuity* means scheduling ads evenly within a given period. *Pulsing* means scheduling ads unevenly over a given time period. Thus, 52 ads could either be scheduled at one per week during the year or pulsed in several bursts. The idea behind pulsing is to advertise heavily for a short period to build awareness that carries over to the next advertising period. Those who favor pulsing feel that it can be used to achieve the same impact as a steady schedule but at a much lower cost. However, some media planners believe that although pulsing achieves minimal awareness, it sacrifices depth of advertising communications.

Evaluating Advertising Effectiveness and the Return on Advertising Investment

Measuring advertising effectiveness and the **return on advertising investment** has become a hot issue for most companies, especially in the tight economic environment. A less friendly

◉ Media Timing: The Picture People, the national chain of family portrait studios, advertises more heavily before special holidays.

Return on advertising investment
The net return on advertising investment divided by the costs of the advertising investment.

economy "has obligated us all to pinch pennies all the more tightly and squeeze blood from a rock," says one advertising executive.[20] That leaves top management at many companies asking their marketing managers, "How do we know that we're spending the right amount on advertising?" and "What return are we getting on our advertising investment?"

Advertisers should regularly evaluate two types of advertising results: the communication effects and the sales and profit effects. Measuring the *communication effects* of an ad or ad campaign tells whether the ads and media are communicating the ad message well. Individual ads can be tested before or after they are run. Before an ad is placed, the advertiser can show it to consumers, ask how they like it, and measure message recall or attitude changes resulting from it. After an ad is run, the advertiser can measure how the ad affected consumer recall or product awareness, knowledge, and preference. Pre- and postevaluations of communication effects can be made for entire advertising campaigns as well.

Advertisers have gotten pretty good at measuring the communication effects of their ads and ad campaigns. However, *sales and profit* effects of advertising are often much harder to measure. For example, what sales and profits are produced by an ad campaign that increases brand awareness by 20 percent and brand preference by 10 percent? Sales and profits are affected by many factors other than advertising—such as product features, price, and availability.

One way to measure the sales and profit effects of advertising is to compare past sales and profits with past advertising expenditures. Another way is through experiments. For example, to test the effects of different advertising spending levels, Coca-Cola could vary the amount it spends on advertising in different market areas and measure the differences in the resulting sales and profit levels. More complex experiments could be designed to include other variables, such as differences in the ads or media used.

However, because so many factors affect advertising effectiveness, some controllable and others not, measuring the results of advertising spending remains an inexact science. For example, dozens of advertisers spend lavishly on high-profile Super Bowl ads each year. Although they sense that the returns are worth the sizable investment, few can actually measure or prove it (see Real Marketing 15.2). A study by the Association of National Advertisers asked advertising managers if they would be able to "forecast the impact on sales" of a 10 percent cut in advertising spending. Sixty-three percent said no. Another recent survey found that more than one-third of the surveyed firms have made no effort at all to measure marketing ROI, and another one-third have been working on it for less than two years.[21]

"Marketers are tracking all kinds of data and they still can't answer basic questions" about advertising accountability, says a marketing analyst, "because they don't have real models and metrics by which to make sense of it." Advertisers are measuring "everything they can, and that ranges from how many people respond to an ad to how many sales are closed and then trying to hook up those two end pieces," says another analyst. "The tough part is, my goodness, we've got so much data. How do we sift through it?"[22] Thus, although the situation is improving as marketers seek more answers, managers often must rely on large doses of judgment along with quantitative analysis when assessing advertising performance.

Other Advertising Considerations

In developing advertising strategies and programs, the company must address two additional questions. First, how will the company organize its advertising function—who will perform which advertising tasks? Second, how will the company adapt its advertising strategies and programs to the complexities of international markets?

Organizing for Advertising

Different companies organize in different ways to handle advertising. In small companies, advertising might be handled by someone in the sales department. Large companies have advertising departments whose job it is to set the advertising budget, work with the ad

Real Marketing 15.2

The Super Bowl: The Mother of All Advertising Events—But Is It Worth It?

The Super Bowl is the mother of all advertising events. Each year, dozens of blue chip advertisers showcase some of their best work to huge audiences around the world. But all this doesn't come cheap. Last year, major advertisers plunked down an average of $2.8 million per 30-second spot—that's almost $100,000 per second! And that's just for the airtime. Throw in ad production costs—which average $2 million per showcase commercial—and running even a single Super Bowl ad becomes a superexpensive proposition. Anheuser-Busch ran *nine* spots last year.

So every year, as the Super Bowl season nears, up pops the big question: Is Super Bowl advertising worth all that money? Does it deliver a high advertising ROI? As it turns out, there's no easy answer to the question, especially when the economy is hurting. These days, in a postrecession economy that has companies watching every penny, spending such big bucks on a single event raises more questions than ever.

Advertiser and industry expert opinion varies widely. Super Bowl stalwarts such as Anheuser-Busch, E*Trade, Bridgestone, CareerBuilder, and Coca-Cola must think it's a good investment—they come back year after year. But what about savvy marketers such as FedEx and P&G, who've opted out in recent years? Last year, for the first time in 20 years, even stalwart PepsiCo ran no Super Bowl ads for its Pepsi, Gatorade, and SoBe brands. In a survey of board members of the National Sports Marketing Network, 31 percent said they would recommend Super Bowl ads. But 41 percent said no—Super Bowl ads just aren't worth the money.

The naysayers make some pretty good arguments. Super Bowl advertising is outrageously expensive. Advertisers pay 85 percent more per viewer than they'd pay using prime-time network programming. Beyond the cost, the competition for attention during the Super Bowl is fierce. Every single ad represents the best efforts of a major marketer trying to design a knock-your-socks-off spectacular that will reap high ratings from both critics and

consumers. Many advertisers feel they can get more for their advertising dollar in venues that aren't so crowded with bigger-than-life commercials.

There is also the issue of product-program fit. Whereas the Super Bowl might be a perfect fit for companies selling beer, snacks, soft drinks, or sporting goods, it simply doesn't fit the creative strategies of many other brands. Consider Unilever's Dove. Some years ago, the company ran a sentimental 45-second commercial from the Dove "Campaign for Real Beauty." The ad was highly rated by consumers, and it created considerable buzz—some 400 million impressions of the ad before and after its single appearance during the Super Bowl. But research showed that the ad produced low levels of involvement with the brand message. Dove got almost equal exposure numbers and more engagement for a lot less money from an outdoor campaign that it ran that same year, and it got a much larger online response from its viral "Dove Evolution" and "Onslaught" films, which incurred no media cost at all. "The Super Bowl really isn't the right environment for Dove," says a Unilever executive.

Finally, although the Super Bowl itself continues to draw bigger and bigger audiences, many advertising critics and viewers bemoan what they view as diminished ad quality in recent Super Bowls. Gone, they say, are the classic, conversation-stopping ads of yesteryear—such as Apple's famous "1984" ad that almost single-handedly launched the Macintosh computer. Rather, recent Big Game ads seem to focus more on grabbing attention with inane gimmicks, fatuous gags, and juvenile humor.

Still, the Super Bowl has a lot to offer to the right advertisers. It's the most-watched TV event of the year. It plays to a huge and receptive audience. In fact, last year's Super Bowl set several records. With 106.5 million U.S. viewers, it was the most watched Super Bowl in history. In fact, it was the most watched *program* in television history, surpassing the previous record of 106 million viewers set by the 1983 series finale of the beloved show *M.A.S.H.*

In addition to sheer numbers of viewers, the Super Bowl stands alone as a TV program during which viewers don't avoid the ads. In fact, to many viewers, the Super Bowl ads are more important than what happens on the gridiron. In one recent year, the game itself drew an average rating (the percent of TV-owning households watching) of 41.6; the ads drew 41.2.

"There is no other platform quite like the Super Bowl," says the chief creative officer at Anheuser-Busch. "It's worth it. When you can touch that many households [with that kind of impact] in one sitting, it's actually efficient." In terms of dollars and cents, a study by one research firm found that consumer

Most Super Bowl ads are just the centerpiece in a much bigger promotional effort. Denny's panicked chickens introduced a popular free breakfast offer, and the chickens generated a flood of positive buzz long after the Super Bowl ad aired.

Continued on next page

packaged-goods firms get a return of $1.25 to $2.74 for every dollar invested in Super Bowl advertising, and one Super Bowl ad is as effective as 250 regular TV spots. "In terms of the audience that you're reaching, . . . I think it makes economic sense," concludes a media research executive. "The reach is incredible, [and whereas] on a lot of other shows . . . there's a real question [of] whether people are fast-forwarding through the commercials or going to grab a drink, . . . here you have people paying attention to the ads."

For most advertisers, the Super Bowl ad itself is only the centerpiece of something much bigger. Long after the game is over, ad critics, media pundits, and consumers are still reviewing, rehashing, and rating the commercials. Last year, for example, ads by Snickers, Doritos, E*Trade, and Google were still on *Advertising Age*'s top ten list of viral ads three weeks after the Super Bowl aired. Advertisers don't usually sit back and just hope that consumers will talk about their ads. They build events that help to boost the buzz.

Denny's, for example, aligned its "Chickens Across America" Super Bowl commercial with a national free Grand Slam breakfast pro-

motion. The ad featured panicked chickens at landmarks across America screeching in terror at the prospect of the eggs needed to support the ad's "Free Grand Slam This Tuesday 6 AM to 2 PM" promise. Concludes the announcer, "Yep, it's going to take a lot of eggs. Great day to be an American. Bad day to be a chicken." The nervous chickens had people flocking to Denny's on Tuesday. Many restaurants had hundreds of people waiting in line at 6 AM as Denny's prepared to serve 2 million free Grand Slams. Moreover, the ad and promotion received massive publicity. According to one study three days after the game, the Denny's ad had generated more positive buzz than any other Super Bowl ad.

And months later, Denny's was still featuring the wacky chickens on its Facebook page and selling "Tough to Be a Chicken" T-shirts on its Web page.

So—back to the original question. Is Super Bowl advertising really worth the huge investment? It seems that there's no definitive answer—for some advertisers it's "yes"; for others, "no." The real trick is in trying to measure the returns. As the title of one article asserts, "Measuring Bowl Return? Good Luck!" The writer's conclusion: "For all the time, energy, and angst marketers spend crafting the perfect Super Bowl spot, [that's] a relative breeze compared to trying to prove its return on investment."

Sources: Quotes and other information from "Denny's, Doritos, Snickers Score Big in Ad Bowl," *Wall Street Journal*, February 8, 2010, accessed at www.wsj.com; Tim Calkins and Derek D. Rucker, "Does a $3M Super Bowl Ad Make Sense In a Recession?" *Advertising Age*, January 12, 2009, p. 17; Brian Steinberg, "Why the Super Bowl Doesn't Loom So Large Any More," *Advertising Age*, February 8, 2010, accessed at http://adage.com/superbowl10/article?article_id=141985; Claire Atkinson, "Measuring Bowl ROI? Good Luck," *Advertising Age*, January 29, 2007, p. 9; Michael Bush, "Which Super Bowl Advertisers Really Bettered Their Buzz?" *Advertising Age*, February 16, 2010, accessed at http://adage.com/superbowl10/article?article_id=142124; and www.facebook.com/dennys#!/dennys?v=app_11007063052, accessed July 2010.

Advertising agency

A marketing services firm that assists companies in planning, preparing, implementing, and evaluating all or portions of their advertising programs.

agency, and handle other advertising not done by the agency. Most large companies use outside advertising agencies because they offer several advantages.

How does an **advertising agency** work? Advertising agencies originated in the mid- to late-1800s by salespeople and brokers who worked for the media and received a commission for selling advertising space to companies. As time passed, the salespeople began to help customers prepare their ads. Eventually, they formed agencies and grew closer to the advertisers than to the media.

Today's agencies employ specialists who can often perform advertising tasks better than the company's own staff can. Agencies also bring an outside point of view to solving the company's problems, along with lots of experience from working with different clients and situations. So, today, even companies with strong advertising departments of their own use advertising agencies.

Some ad agencies are huge; the largest U.S. agency, McCann Erickson Worldwide, has annual gross U.S. revenues of more than $450 million. In recent years, many agencies have grown by gobbling up other agencies, thus creating huge agency holding companies. The largest of these "megagroups," WPP, includes several large advertising, PR, and promotion agencies with combined worldwide revenues of $13.6 billion.[23] Most large advertising agencies have the staff and resources to handle all phases of an advertising campaign for their clients, from creating a marketing plan to developing ad campaigns and preparing, placing, and evaluating ads.

International Advertising Decisions

International advertisers face many complexities not encountered by domestic advertisers. The most basic issue concerns the degree to which global advertising should be adapted to the unique characteristics of various country markets. Some large advertisers have attempted to support their global brands with highly standardized worldwide advertising, with campaigns that work as well in Bangkok as they do in Baltimore. For example, McDonald's unifies its creative elements and brand presentation under the familiar "i'm lovin' it" theme in all its 100-plus markets worldwide. Coca-Cola pulls advertising together for its flagship brand under the theme, "Open Happiness." And VISA coordinates worldwide advertising for its debit and credit cards under the "more people go with Visa" creative platform, which works as well in Korea as it does in the United States or Brazil.

In recent years, the increased popularity of online social networks and video sharing has boosted the need for advertising standardization for global brands. Most big marketing and advertising campaigns include a large online presence. Connected consumers can now zip easily across borders via the Internet, making it difficult for advertisers to roll out adapted campaigns in a controlled, orderly fashion. As a result, at the very least, most global consumer brands coordinate their Web sites internationally. For example, check out the McDonald's Web sites from Germany to Jordan to China. You'll find the golden arches logo, the "i'm lovin' it" logo and jingle, a Big Mac equivalent, and maybe even Ronald McDonald himself.

⊙ **Standardized global advertising: VISA coordinates its worldwide advertising under the theme "more people go with VISA," a theme that works as well in Brazil (middle) or Asia (bottom) as it does in the United States (top).**

Standardization produces many benefits—lower advertising costs, greater global advertising coordination, and a more consistent worldwide image. But it also has drawbacks. Most importantly, it ignores the fact that country markets differ greatly in their cultures, demographics, and economic conditions. Thus, most international advertisers "think globally but act locally." They develop global advertising *strategies* that make their worldwide efforts more efficient and consistent. Then they adapt their advertising *programs* to make them more responsive to consumer needs and expectations within local markets. ⊙ For example, although VISA employs its "more people go with Visa" theme globally, ads in specific locales employ local language and inspiring local imagery that make the theme relevant to the local markets in which they appear.

Global advertisers face several special problems. For instance, advertising media costs and availability differ vastly from country to country. Countries also differ in the extent to which they regulate advertising practices. Many countries have extensive systems of laws restricting how much a company can spend on advertising, the media used, the nature of advertising claims, and other aspects of the advertising program. Such restrictions often require advertisers to adapt their campaigns from country to country.

For example, alcohol products cannot be advertised in India or in Muslim countries. In many countries, such as Sweden and Canada, junk food ads are banned from children's television programming. To play it safe, McDonald's advertises itself as a family restaurant in Sweden. Comparative ads, although acceptable and even common in the United States and Canada, are less commonly used in the United Kingdom and are illegal in India and Brazil. China bans sending e-mail for advertising purposes to people without their permission, and all advertising e-mail that is sent must be titled "advertisement."

China also has restrictive censorship rules for TV and radio advertising; for example, the words *the best* are banned, as are ads that "violate social customs" or present women in "improper ways." McDonald's once avoided government sanctions in China by publicly apologizing for an ad that crossed cultural norms by showing a customer begging for a discount. Similarly, Coca-Cola's Indian subsidiary was forced to end a promotion that offered prizes, such as a trip to Hollywood, because it violated India's established trade practices by encouraging customers to buy to "gamble."

Thus, although advertisers may develop global strategies to guide their overall advertising efforts, specific advertising programs must usually be adapted to meet local cultures and customs, media characteristics, and regulations.

Author | Not long ago, PR was
Comment | considered a marketing
stepchild because of its limited marketing use. That situation is changing fast, however, as more marketers recognize PR's brand-building power.

Public relations (PR)
Building good relations with the company's various publics by obtaining favorable publicity, building up a good corporate image, and handling or heading off unfavorable rumors, stories, and events.

Public Relations (pp 454–457)

Another major mass-promotion tool is **public relations (PR)**—building good relations with the company's various publics by obtaining favorable publicity, building up a good corporate image, and handling or heading off unfavorable rumors, stories, and events. PR departments may perform any or all of the following functions:[24]

- *Press relations or press agency:* Creating and placing newsworthy information in the news media to attract attention to a person, product, or service.
- *Product publicity:* Publicizing specific products.
- *Public affairs:* Building and maintaining national or local community relationships.
- *Lobbying:* Building and maintaining relationships with legislators and government officials to influence legislation and regulation.
- *Investor relations:* Maintaining relationships with shareholders and others in the financial community.
- *Development:* Working with donors or members of nonprofit organizations to gain financial or volunteer support.

Public relations is used to promote products, people, places, ideas, activities, organizations, and even nations. Companies use PR to build good relations with consumers, investors, the media, and their communities. Trade associations have used PR to rebuild interest in declining commodities, such as eggs, apples, potatoes, and milk. For example, the milk industry's popular "Got Milk?" PR campaign featuring celebrities with milk mustaches reversed a long-standing decline in milk consumption. Even government organizations use PR to build awareness. ● For example, the National Heart, Lung, and Blood Institute (NHLBI) of the National Institutes of Health sponsors a long-running PR campaign that builds awareness of heart disease in women:[25]

Heart disease is the number one killer of women; it kills more women each year than all forms of cancer combined. But a 2000 survey by the NHLBI showed that only 34 percent of women knew this, and that most people thought of heart disease as a problem mostly affecting men. So with the help of Ogilvy Public Relations Worldwide, the NHLBI set out to "create a personal and urgent wakeup call to American women." In 2002, it launched a national PR campaign—"The Heart Truth"—to raise awareness of heart disease among women and get women to discuss the issue with their doctors.

The centerpiece of the campaign is the Red Dress, now the national symbol for women and heart disease aware-

● Public relations campaigns: NHLBI's "The Heart Truth" campaign has produced impressive results in raising awareness of the risks of heart disease in women.

ness. The campaign creates awareness through an interactive Web site, mass media placements, and campaign materials—everything from brochures, DVDs, and posters to speaker's kits and airport dioramas. It also sponsors several major national events, such as the National Wear Red Day, an annual Red Dress Collection Fashion Show, and The Heart Truth Road Show, featuring heart disease risk factor screenings in major U.S. cities. Finally, the campaign works with more than three-dozen corporate sponsors, such as Diet Coke, St. Joseph aspirin, Tylenol, Cheerios, CVS Pharmacy, Swarovski, and Bobbi Brown Cosmetics. So far, some 2.65 billion product packages have carried the Red Dress symbol. The results are impressive: Awareness among American women of heart disease as the number one killer of women has increased to 57 percent, and the number of heart disease deaths in women has declined steadily from one in three women to one in four. The American Heart Association has also adopted the Red Dress symbol and introduced its own complementary campaign.

The Role and Impact of PR

Public relations can have a strong impact on public awareness at a much lower cost than advertising can. The company does not pay for the space or time in the media. Rather, it pays for a staff to develop and circulate information and manage events. If the company develops an interesting story or event, it could be picked up by several different media, having the same effect as advertising that would cost millions of dollars. And it would have more credibility than advertising.

PR results can sometimes be spectacular. ⦿ Consider the launch of Apple's iPad:[26]

⦿ The power of PR: Apple's iPad launch created unbounded consumer excitement, a media frenzy, and long lines outside retail stores—all with no advertising, just PR.

Apple's iPad was one of the most successful new-product launches in history. The funny thing: Whereas most big product launches are accompanied by huge prelaunch advertising campaigns, Apple pulled this one off with no advertising. None at all. Instead, it simply fed the PR fire. It built buzz months in advance by distributing iPads for early reviews, feeding the offline and online press with tempting tidbits, and offering fans an early online peek at thousands of new iPad apps that would be available. At launch time, it fanned the flames with a cameo on the TV sitcom *Modern Family*, a flurry of launch-day appearances on TV talk shows, and other launch-day events. In the process, through PR alone, the iPad launch generated unbounded consumer excitement, a media frenzy, and long lines outside retail stores on launch day. Apple sold more than 300,000 of the sleek gadgets on the first day alone and more than two million in the first two months—even as demand outstripped supply.

Despite its potential strengths, public relations is sometimes described as a marketing stepchild because of its often limited and scattered use. The PR department is often located at corporate headquarters or handled by a third-party agency. Its staff is so busy dealing with various publics—stockholders, employees, legislators, and the press—that PR programs to support product marketing objectives may be ignored. Moreover, marketing managers and PR practitioners do not always speak the same language. Whereas many PR practitioners see their jobs as simply communicating, marketing managers tend to be much more interested in how advertising and PR affect brand building, sales and profits, and customer relationships.

This situation is changing, however. Although public relations still captures only a small portion of the overall marketing budgets of most firms, PR can be a powerful brand-building tool. And in this digital age, the lines between advertising and PR are becoming more and more blurred. For example, are brand Web sites, blogs, online social networks, and viral brand videos advertising efforts or PR efforts? All are both. "Blurriness can be good," says one PR executive. "When you have more overlap between PR and other marketing disciplines, it's easier to promote the same message." The point is that advertising and PR should work hand in hand within an integrated marketing communications program to build brands and customer relationships.[27]

Major Public Relations Tools

Public relations uses several tools. One of the major tools is *news*. PR professionals find or create favorable news about the company and its products or people. Sometimes news stories occur naturally; sometimes the PR person can suggest events or activities that would create news. *Speeches* can also create product and company publicity. Increasingly, company executives must field questions from the media or give talks at trade associations or sales meetings, and these events can either build or hurt the company's image. Another common PR tool is *special events*, ranging from news conferences, press tours, grand openings, and fireworks displays to laser light shows, hot air balloon releases, multimedia presentations, or educational programs designed to reach and interest target publics.

Public relations people also prepare *written materials* to reach and influence their target markets. These materials include annual reports, brochures, articles, and company newsletters and magazines. *Audiovisual materials*, such as slide-and-sound programs, DVDs, and online videos are being used increasingly as communication tools. *Corporate identity materials* can also help create a corporate identity that the public immediately recognizes. Logos, stationery, brochures, signs, business forms, business cards, buildings, uniforms, and company cars and trucks—all become marketing tools when they are attractive, distinctive, and memorable. Finally, companies can improve public goodwill by contributing money and time to *public service activities*.

As discussed above, the Web is also an increasingly important PR channel. Web sites, blogs, and social networks such as YouTube, Facebook, and Twitter are providing interesting new ways to reach more people. "The core strengths of public relations—the ability to tell a story and spark conversation—play well into the nature of such social media," says a PR expert. Consider the recent Papa John's "Camaro Search" PR campaign:[28]

● Papa John's "Camaro Search" campaign used traditional PR media plus a host of new social media.

During a road trip this summer to find his long-lost Camaro, John Schnatter, the "Papa John" of Papa John's pizza, set a record for the world's highest pizza delivery (at the Willis Tower's Skydeck in Chicago), rang the closing bell at the Nasdaq stock exchange, and visited a children's hospital. The road trip got solid pickup in the media, with stories in the *New York Times*, the *Wall Street Journal*, and *USA Today*. ABC World News Tonight, CNBC, and CNN also covered the story, which included a $250,000 reward for the person reuniting Schnatter with his beloved Camaro Z28. These were all traditional pre-Web kinds of PR moves.

But unlike the old days, online social media was a key to getting the word out about this Papa John's journey. A Web site dedicated to the trip drew 660,000 unique visitors. On the day of the media conference announcing Schnatter's reunion with his old Chevy classic—Kentuckian Jeff Robinson turned up with the car and took home the cash—there were more than 1,000 tweets about him finding his car, with links galore. In addition, hundreds of people posted photos of themselves on Facebook (in their own Camaros) picking up the free pizza Papa John offered to all Camaro owners as part of the celebration. In all, the Web was buzzing about the Camaro Search story. Pre-Web, "there were different techniques used for [PR]—speeches, publicity, awards," says a PR executive. "Now we're applying the same mindset to social media to build relationships that are critical to any corporate entity."

By itself, a company's Web site is an important PR vehicle. Consumers and other publics often visit Web sites for information or entertainment. Web sites can also be ideal for handling crisis situations. For example, when several bottles of Odwalla apple juice sold on the West Coast were found to contain *E. coli* bacteria, Odwalla initiated a massive product recall. Within only three hours, it set up a Web site laden with information about the crisis and Odwalla's response. Company staffers also combed the Internet looking for newsgroups discussing Odwalla and posted links to the site. In this age where "it's easier to disseminate information through e-mail marketing, blogs, and online chat," notes an analyst, "public relations is becoming a valuable part of doing business in a digital world."[29]

As with the other promotion tools, in considering when and how to use product public relations, management should set PR objectives, choose the PR messages and vehicles, implement the PR plan, and evaluate the results. The firm's PR should be blended smoothly with other promotion activities within the company's overall integrated marketing communications effort.

REVIEWING Objectives AND KEY Terms

Companies must do more than make good products; they have to inform consumers about product benefits and carefully position products in consumers' minds. To do this, they must master *advertising* and *public relations*.

Objective 1 Define the role of advertising in the promotion mix. (pp 436–437)

Advertising—the use of paid media by a seller to inform, persuade, and remind buyers about its products or its organization—is an important promotion tool for communicating the value that marketers create for their customers. American marketers spend more than $163 billion each year on advertising, and worldwide spending exceeds $450 billion. Advertising takes many forms and has many uses. Although advertising is used mostly by business firms, a wide range of not-for-profit organizations, professionals, and social agencies also employ advertising to promote their causes to various target publics. *Public relations*—gaining favorable publicity and creating a favorable company image—is the least used of the major promotion tools, although it has great potential for building consumer awareness and preference.

Objective 2 Describe the major decisions involved in developing an advertising program. (pp 437–454)

Advertising decision making involves making decisions about the advertising objectives, budget, message, media and, finally, the evaluation of results. Advertisers should set clear target, task, and timing *objectives*, whether the aim is to inform, persuade, or remind buyers. Advertising's goal is to move consumers through the buyer-readiness stages discussed in Chapter 14. Some advertising is designed to move people to immediate action. However, many of the ads you see today focus on building or strengthening long-term customer relationships. The advertising *budget* depends on

many factors. No matter what method is used, setting the advertising budget is no easy task.

Advertising strategy consists of two major elements: creating advertising *messages* and selecting advertising *media*. The *message decision* calls for planning a message strategy and executing it effectively. Good messages are especially important in today's costly and cluttered advertising environment. Just to gain and hold attention, today's messages must be better planned, more imaginative, more entertaining, and more rewarding to consumers. In fact, many marketers are now subscribing to a new merging of advertising and entertainment, dubbed *Madison & Vine*. The *media decision* involves defining reach, frequency, and impact goals; choosing major media types; selecting media vehicles; and deciding on media timing. Message and media decisions must be closely coordinated for maximum campaign effectiveness.

Finally, *evaluation* calls for evaluating the communication and sales effects of advertising before, during, and after ads are placed. Advertising accountability has become a hot issue for most companies. Increasingly, top management is asking: "What return are we getting on our advertising investment?" and "How do we know that we're spending the right amount?" Other important advertising issues involve *organizing* for advertising and dealing with the complexities of international advertising.

Objective 3 Define the role of public relations in the promotion mix. (pp 454–456)

Public relations—gaining favorable publicity and creating a favorable company image—is the least used of the major promotion tools, although it has great potential for building consumer awareness and preference. PR is used to promote products, people, places, ideas, activities, organizations, and even nations. Companies use PR to build good relationships with consumers, investors, the media, and their communities. PR can have a strong impact on public awareness at a much lower cost than advertising can, and PR results can sometimes be spectacular. Although PR still captures only a small portion of the overall marketing budgets of most firms, PR is playing an increasingly important brand-building role. In the digital age, the lines between advertising and PR are becoming more and more blurred.

Objective 4 **Explain how companies use public relations to communicate with their publics.**
(pp 456–457)

Companies use public relations to communicate with their publics by setting PR objectives, choosing PR messages and vehicles, imple-

menting the PR plan, and evaluating PR results. To accomplish these goals, PR professionals use several tools, such as *news*, *speeches*, and *special events*. They also prepare *written*, *audiovisual*, and *corporate identity materials* and contribute money and time to *public service activities*. The Web has also become an increasingly important PR channel, as Web sites, blogs, and social networks are providing interesting new ways to reach more people.

KEY Terms

OBJECTIVE 1
Advertising (p 436)

OBJECTIVE 2
Advertising objective (p 437)
Advertising budget (p 438)

Advertising strategy (p 439)
Madison & Vine (p 441)
Creative concept (p 442)
Execution style (p 442)
Advertising media (p 444)

Return on advertising investment (p 449)
Advertising agency (p 452)

OBJECTIVE 3
Public relations (PR) (p 454)

PEARSON mymarketinglab

- Check your understanding of the concepts and key terms using the mypearsonmarketinglab study plan for this chapter.
- Apply the concepts in a business context using the simulation entitled **Advertising**.

DISCUSSING & APPLYING THE Concepts

Discussing the Concepts

1. List the primary types of advertising objectives and discuss the kinds of advertising used to achieve each type. (AASCB: Communication)

2. Why is it important that the advertising media and creative departments work closely together? (AACSB: Communication)

3. Name and describe five of the many execution styles advertisers use when developing ads. For each execution style, describe a television commercial using that style. (AACSB: Communication; Reflective Thinking)

4. How should a company measure the effectiveness of its advertising? (AACSB: Communication)

5. What are the role and functions of public relations within an organization? (AACSB: Communication)

6. Discuss the tools used by public relations professionals. (AACSB: Communication)

Applying the Concepts

1. Select two print ads (such as magazine ads). Based on the three characteristics advertising appeals should possess, evaluate the appeals used in each ad. (AACSB: Communication; Reflective Thinking)

2. Marketers are developing branded Web series to get consumers involved with their brands. One successful series is "Real Women of Philadelphia" from Kraft (www .realwomenofphiladelphia.com). Fans can watch videos of professionals making delicious, simple recipes with one common ingredient—Philadelphia Cream Cheese, of course! The site features a recipe contest and entrants even get training on how to photograph their entries to make them look as yummy as possible. Visit this Web site and find two other branded Web series. Critique the sites and describe how viewers interact with the Web sites. (AACSB: Communication; Use of IT; Reflective Thinking)

3. In a small group, discuss the major public relations tools and develop three public relations items for each of the following: a hospital, a restaurant, and any brand of your choice. (AACSB: Communication; Reflective Thinking)

FOCUS ON Technology

The Internet can pose a public relations nightmare for companies. Venerable P&G found this out firsthand after launching its revolutionary Dry Max technology for its best-selling Pampers diapers. Touted as its most significant innovation in 25 years, the new diapers are 20 percent smaller but much more absorbent than competitive brands because a more-absorbent chemical gel replaced the cottony fluff pulp. Not long after the new product's release, however, customer complaints of severe diaper rash or chemical burns surfaced on the Internet. Angry parents spouted off on P&G's Web sites and several Facebook pages: "Recall Pampers Dry Max Diapers," "Boycott New Pampers Dry Max," and "Bring Back the Old Cruisers/Swaddlers." Mainstream media picked up the discontent and started spreading the news. The CPSC received al-

most 5,000 consumer complaints—85 percent occurring within the first few months of the product launch. The CPSC later reported no link between severe diaper rash and Pampers Dry Max but that did not stop some parents from continuing to use the Internet to call for boycotts or lawyers to solicit lawsuits.

1. Research P&G's problems with its Pampers Dry Max brand. How has P&G responded to this crisis? Write a report on what you learn. (AACSB: Communication; Reflective Thinking)

2. Find examples of other online rumors and discuss how companies can combat negative publicity spread on the Internet. (AACSB: Communication; Reflective Thinking)

FOCUS ON Ethics

The FDA is enlisting doctors in its battle against misleading and deceptive prescription drug ads targeted toward consumers (called direct-to-consumer or DTC ads) and other promotional activities directed at medical professionals. You've seen television commercials for Viagra, Lipitor, Chantix, and other prescription drugs. Since the FDA relaxed the rules regarding broadcast prescription drug advertising in the late 1990s, DTC advertising has increased more than 300 percent, with $4.5 billion spent in 2009. That's actually down from the peak of $5.5 billion in 2006 because of the recession. It's difficult for the FDA to monitor DTC ads and other promotional activity aimed at medical professionals, so it created the "Bad Ad Program" and spent most of 2010 educating doctors about this program.

1. Visit www.fda.gov and search for "Bad Ad Program" to learn more about it. What is the FDA asking medical professionals

to look for in DTC ads and other promotional activities directed toward them? How might this program be abused by the pharmaceutical industry? (AACSB: Communication; Ethical Reasoning; Reflective Thinking)

2. Many consumers are not aware of the FDA's regulations regarding DTC advertising. The agency has a parallel program—called EthicAd—to educate consumers and encourage them to report violations. Search the FDA's Web site for this program, look at examples of correct and incorrect ads, and evaluate two prescription drug advertisements using these guidelines. (AACSB: Communication; Ethical Reasoning; Reflective Thinking)

MARKETING & THE Economy

McDonald's

Despite a down economy—or perhaps because of it—McDonald's has been beating competitors badly in recent years. In fact, the fast-food giant pretty much owns the value menu. But, surprisingly, McDonald's current financial good fortunes are not being driven by its low-price items but rather by its higher-price, higher-margin items. Throughout tough economic times, McDonald's advertising strategy focused on its traditional, full-priced specialties. One month it pushed Big Macs, the next month Chicken McNuggets, and then Quarter Pounders. But McDonald's hasn't forsaken its dollar menu. Instead, it has increased promotional support for its flagship specialties. It's all part of an effort to grab business from diners who are trading down from higher-priced eateries. McDonald's has gambled that people would view the old

favorites as comfort food. Add to this promotional strategy the burger king's migration into a full beverage menu that includes lattes and all-fruit smoothies, and you have a real one-two punch. The company's overall revenues and profits continue to rise, even as the percentage of revenues generated from lower-price items falls. Its promotional, pricing, and product strategies are attracting new customers while also encouraging existing value menu customers to trade up. All this has both executives and franchisees singing "i'm lovin' it."

1. What was McDonald's advertising objective with this promotion campaign?

2. In communicating value during hard times, what elements of McDonald's advertising strategy contributed to its success?

MARKETING BY THE Numbers

Nielsen ratings are very important to both advertisers and television programmers because the cost of television advertising time is based on this rating. A show's *rating* is the number of households in Nielsen's sample tuned to that program divided by the number of television-owning households—115 million in the United States. A show's *share* of the viewing audience is the number of households watching that show divided by the number of households using TV at that time. That is, ratings consider all TV-owning households, whereas share considers only those households that actually have the television on at the time. Ratings and share are usually given together. For example, during one evening hour on September 9, 2010, the following ratings/shares were reported for the major broadcast networks:

Network	Program	Rating/Share
NBC	*Sunday Night Football* (played on Thursday)	13.6/22
CBS	*Big Brother 12*	4.6/8
ABC	*Wipeout*	3.1/5
FOX	*Bones*	2.9/5
The CW	*The Vampire Diaries*	2.0/3

1. If one rating point represents 1 percent of TV households, how many households were watching football that evening? How many households were tuned to *The Vampire Diaries*? (AACSB: Communication; Analytical Reasoning)

2. What total share of the viewing audience was captured by all five networks? Explain why share is higher than the rating for a given program. (AACSB: Communication; Analytical Reasoning; Reflective Thinking)

VIDEO Case

E*TRADE

Super Bowl XXXIV, the first of the new millennium, was known as the Dot-com Bowl for the glut of Internet companies that plopped down an average of $2.2 million per 30-second spot ad. Today, most of the companies that defined the dot-com glory days are gone. But one darling of the dot-com era, E*TRADE, remains one of the few survivors. Although E*TRADE has experienced challenges since the turn of the century, it has also turned profits.

Advertising on the big game hasn't worked out well for everyone. But for E*TRADE, Super Bowl ads have been part of a larger advertising effort that played a role in its survival. In this video, E*TRADE reports on its advertising strategy as well as the advantages and disadvantages of Super Bowl advertising.

After viewing the video featuring E*TRADE, answer the following questions about advertising and promotions:

1. What makes E*TRADE different from now-defunct dot-coms?

2. What has been the role of advertising at E*TRADE?

3. Discuss the factors in E*TRADE's decision to advertise during the Super Bowl.

COMPANY Case

OgilvyOne: It's Not Creative Unless It Sells

These days, there are some extremely creative ads fighting for our attention. Television spots are often on par with feature films in terms of artistic quality. Print ads and billboards rival works of art. Such ads can move our emotions powerfully. They can make us laugh, cry, or sing; they can produce feelings of guilt, fear, or joy. Ads themselves are often as entertaining as the programming in which they appear. However, although highly creative ads might dazzle us and even win awards from advertising critics, they sometimes overlook a very important fundamental truth: Truly creative advertising is advertising that creates sales.

Not all ads have forgotten this truth. But too often, advertisers become so enamored with the artistry of advertising that they forget about the selling part. After all, the ultimate objective of advertising is not to win awards or even to make people like an ad. It's to get people to think, feel, or *act* in some way after being ex-

posed to an ad. Ultimately, no matter how entertaining or artistic an ad, it's not creative unless it sells.

This thinking prompted one of the world's premiere advertising agencies—OgilvyOne Worldwide—to run a unique contest. Part of Ogilvy & Mather Worldwide, OgilvyOne launched a contest to search for the world's greatest salesperson. According to Rory Sutherland, vice chairman for the British operations of Ogilvy & Mather, the goal of the contest is "re-creating the noble art of ka-ching. There's an interesting case to be made that advertising has strayed too far from the business of salesmanship."

"Salesmanship has been lost in the pursuit of art or the dazzle of technology," said Brian Fetherstonhaugh, chairman and CEO at OgilvyOne. "It needs to be rekindled in this postrecession environment, as consumers are making more informed and deliberate choices." But as Fetherstonhaugh also points out, the return to selling through advertising is more challenging today than ever. Technologies such as TiVo, spam filters, and viewing on demand through the Internet have put consumers in control of media more than ever. For this reason, advertisers not only need to become great salespeople, but they also need to be salespeople that get invited into the consumer's environment. According to Fetherstonhaugh, advertising needs to be "less about intrusion and repetition and more about engagement and evangelizing."

THE CONTEST

OgilvyOne chose a popular format for its greatest salesperson contest. Entrants prepared one- to two-minute video clips selling the assigned product and submitted them via YouTube. Viewers voted for their favorite videos, and a panel of judges winnowed the field down to a set of finalists.

But the product that contestants were assigned to sell was anything but the usual. They weren't asked to sell a glitzy new smartphone or super-thin large screen TV. Instead, they had to make a pitch for a brick. That's right, a common, everyday red brick. Why a brick? "If you can sell a red brick, maybe you can sell anything," said Mat Zucker, executive creative director for OgilvyOne and the creator of the contest. Some people at Ogilvy pushed for a more exciting product. But Mish Fletcher, worldwide marketing director at OgilvyOne, pointed out that perhaps those exciting products don't need "the world's greatest salesperson" as much.

A HERITAGE IN SALES

The greatest salesperson contest is a nod to advertising legend David Ogilvy, who founded Ogilvy & Mather more than 60 years ago. Prior to entering the advertising world, Ogilvy sold stoves door-to-door in Scotland. He sold so many stoves that the company asked him to write a manual for other salesmen. That manual was dubbed "the finest sales instruction manual ever written" by the editors of *Fortune* magazine, who still used it as a resource guide thirty years after Ogilvy wrote it. Ogilvy once revealed the secret to his success as a stove salesman. "No sale, no commission. No commission, no eat. That made an impression on me." That notion forms the basis for Ogilvy's credo, "We sell, or else."

David Ogilvy left sales, but sales never left him. He founded Ogilvy & Mather in 1949 based on two principles: (1) The function of advertising is to sell, and (2) successful advertising for any product is based on customer information. Ogilvy's principles worked for major corporation after major corporation. In 1962, *Time* magazine called Ogilvy "the most sought-after wizard in today's advertising industry." He was so successful at expanding the bounds of creativity in advertising that he has often been called "the father of advertising." The list of iconic advertising campaigns that he developed is as long as anyone's in the business.

Based on this heritage, Zucker came up with the idea for the greatest salesperson contest. "If we believe in selling, and our founder was a salesman, we have a special responsibility to reassert the importance of sales," Zucker said.

CREATIVE PITCHES

By May 2010, more 230 videos from entrants in 12 countries had been uploaded to Ogilvy's YouTube contest site. Ogilvy eventually narrowed the entrants down to three finalists. The first finalist was Todd Herman, an international performance coaching and training expert from Edmonton, Canada. Herman pitched a single brick as a symbol of something that can be used as the first step in building something great. He started his video with a brick in hand, saying, "The story of a simple, red brick is one filled with power, struggle, and romance. And now you have the chance to capture some of its magic." From there, Herman summarized various ways that bricks have been used throughout history to build and connect civilizations. His pitch was based on the idea that a red brick is not just a common object but a symbol of a dream that was acted on.

Eric Polins, managing partner of a marketing consulting firm in Tampa, Florida, was the second finalist. Polins, who left broadcast news because of extreme stage fright every time he stepped in front of a camera, sold his brick as an intangible asset—a good luck charm. In a clever way, he pointed out that the classic good luck charms all have problems. A rabbit's foot is too morbid. A four-leaf clover is too hard to come by in a paved-over world. The "knock on wood" gesture is outdated as hardly anything is made out of wood anymore. And a horseshoe . . . who can afford a horse?

The third finalist was Lee Abbas, a former Panasonic marketing executive from Japan. She organized her approach around a reinvention of the classic old brick—a must-have purse with chrome steel handles. She demonstrated this new product from a brick factory and maker of high strength, lightweight bricks. She then related how a friend of hers was mugged. But rather than reaching into her purse for her pepper spray, she simply whacked her assailant over the head with it, knocking him out cold.

All three finalists were winners in one respect. Each received an all-expense paid trip to Cannes, France, for the 57th annual Cannes Lions International Advertising Festival. There, each had to make a live presentation for a second product in front of a studio audience and panel of judges. This time, the finalists had to sell a Motorola Droid phone. They made their presentations, the audience voted, and Todd Herman emerged as the "world's greatest salesperson."

"I honestly can't believe I'm standing here with the World's Greatest Salesperson award . . . it's such an honor to be working with a company whose founder has been such a huge influence on my business philosophy." Perhaps the biggest part of the prize was a job with OgilvyOne. Herman was given the opportunity to fulfill a three-month fellowship with the agency with the express purpose of crafting a sales guide for the 21st century. The principles in the guide will be presented at the Direct Marketing Association's (DMA's) annual conference.

As would be expected of the world's greatest salesperson, Fetherstonhaugh pointed out, Herman "is a true student of persuasion and motivation. It shone through at every stage of the World's Greatest Salesperson competition." Herman's own words seem to reflect the principles of David Ogilvy and the true nature of advertising. "People always think of sales as the in-your-face-used-car salesman. But selling happens all the time. Really great selling is never noticed. You should feel like you just bought something, not like you just got sold."

Questions for Discussion

1. Do you agree with David Ogilvy that the primary function of advertising is selling? How does that fit with the three advertising objectives of informing, persuading, and reminding?

2. If the primary purpose of advertising is to sell, are there any message execution techniques that seem best predisposed to this purpose?

3. As a creator of advertising, what kind of return on investment did OgilvyOne get out of this promotional contest?

4. Do you agree or disagree with the premise that the primary function of advertising is to sell? Give examples of ad campaigns to support your position.

Sources: Stuart Elliott, "In a Test of Sales Savvy, Selling a Red Brick on YouTube," *New York Times*, March 29, 2010, p. B3; "Todd Herman Voted World's Greatest Salesperson," at www.prnewswire.com, accessed July 2010; Robert Trigaux, "To Be 'Greatest Salesperson,' Just Sell a Measly Red Brick," *St. Petersburg Times*, June 15, 2010, p. 1B; Florence Loyie, "Patter to Sell Brick Wins Trip to Cannes," *Edmonton Journal*, June 10, 2010, p. A3.

16

Personal Selling and Sales Promotion

Chapter Preview

In the previous two chapters, you learned about communicating customer value through integrated marketing communications (IMC) and two elements of the promotion mix: advertising and public relations. In this chapter, we examine two more IMC elements: personal selling and sales promotion. Personal selling is the interpersonal arm of marketing communications, in which the sales force interacts with customers and prospects to build relationships and make sales. Sales promotion consists of short-term incentives to encourage the purchase or sale of a product or service. As you read, remember that although this chapter presents personal selling and sales promotion as separate tools, they must be carefully integrated with the other elements of the promotion mix.

First, what is your first reaction when you think of a salesperson or a sales force? Perhaps you think of pushy retail sales clerks, "yell and sell" TV pitchmen, or the stereotypical glad-handing "used-car salesman." But such stereotypes simply don't fit the reality of most of today's salespeople—sales professionals who succeed not by taking advantage of customers but by listening to their needs and helping to forge solutions. For most companies, personal selling plays an important role in building profitable customer relationships. Consider Procter & Gamble, whose customer-focused sales force has long been considered one of the nation's best.

P&G: It's Not Sales, It's Customer Business Development

For decades, Procter & Gamble has been at the top of almost every expert's A-list of outstanding marketing companies. The experts point to P&G's stable of top-selling consumer brands, or that, year in and year out, P&G is the world's largest advertiser. Consumers seem to agree. You'll find at least one of P&G's blockbuster brands in 99 percent of all American households; in many homes, you'll find a dozen or more familiar P&G products. But P&G is also highly respected for something else—its top-notch, customer-focused sales force.

P&G's sales force has long been an American icon for selling at its very best. When it comes to selecting, training, and managing salespeople, P&G sets the gold standard. The company employs a massive sales force of more than 5,000 salespeople worldwide. At P&G, however, they rarely call it "sales." Instead, it's "Customer Business Development" (CBD). And P&G sales reps aren't "salespeople"; they're "CBD managers" or "CBD account executives." All this might seem like just so much "corp-speak," but at P&G the distinction goes to the very core of how selling works.

P&G understands that if its customers don't do well, neither will the company. To grow its own business, therefore, P&G must first grow the business of the retailers that sell its brands to final consumers. And at P&G, the primary responsibility for helping customers grow falls to the sales force. Rather than just selling *to* its retail and wholesale customers, CBD managers partner strategically *with* customers to help develop their business in P&G's product categories. "We depend on them as much as they depend on us," says one CBD manager. By partnering with each other, P&G and its customers create "win-win" relationships that help both to prosper.

Most P&G customers are huge and complex businesses—such as Walgreens, Walmart, or Dollar General—with thousands of stores and billions of dollars in revenues. Working with and selling to such customers can be a very complex undertaking, more than any single salesperson or sales team could accomplish. Instead, P&G assigns a full CBD team to every large customer account. Each CBD team contains not only salespeople but also a full complement of specialists in every aspect of selling P&G's consumer brands at the retail level.

CBD teams vary in size depending on the customer. For example, P&G's largest customer, Walmart, which accounts for an amazing 20 percent of the company's sales, commands a 350-person CBD team. By contrast, the P&G Dollar General team consists of about 30 people. Regardless of size, every CBD team constitutes a complete, multifunctional customer-service unit. Each team includes a CBD manager and several CBD account executives (each responsible for a specific P&G product category), supported by specialists in marketing strategy, product development, operations, information systems, logistics, finance, and human resources.

To deal effectively with large accounts, P&G salespeople must be smart, well trained, and strategically grounded. They deal daily with high-level retail category buyers who may purchase hundreds of millions of dollars worth of P&G and competing brands annually. It takes a lot more than a friendly smile and a firm handshake to interact with such buyers. Yet, individual P&G salespeople can't know everything, and thanks to the CBD sales structure, they don't have to. Instead, as members of a full CBD team, P&G salespeople

have at hand all the resources they need to resolve even the most challenging customer problems. "I have everything I need right here," says a household care account executive. "If my customer needs help from us with in-store promotions, I can go right down the hall and talk with someone on my team in marketing about doing some kind of promotional deal. It's that simple."

Customer Business Development involves partnering with customers to jointly identify strategies that create shopper value and satisfaction and drive profitable sales at the store level. When it comes to profitably moving Tide, Pampers, Gillette, or other P&G brands off store shelves and into consumers' shopping carts, P&G reps and their teams often know more than the retail buyers they advise. In fact, P&G's retail partners often rely on CBD teams to help them manage not only the P&G brands on their shelves but also entire product categories, including competing brands.

Wait a minute. Does it make sense to let P&G advise on the stocking and placement of competitors' brands as well as its own? Would a P&G CBD rep ever tell a retail buyer to stock fewer P&G products and more of a competing brand? Believe it or not, it happens all the time. The CBD team's primary goal is to help the customer win in each product category. Sometimes, analysis shows that the best solution for the customer is "more of the other guy's product." For P&G, that's okay. It knows that creating the best situation for the retailer ultimately pulls in more customer traffic, which in turn will likely lead to increased sales for other P&G products in the same category. Because most of P&G's brands are market share leaders, it stands to benefit more from the increased traffic than competitors do. Again, what's good for the customer is good for P&G—it's a win-win situation.

Honest and open dealings also help to build long-term customer rela-

tionships. P&G salespeople become trusted advisors to their retailer-partners, a status they work hard to maintain. "It took me four years to build the trust I now have with my buyer," says a veteran CBD account executive. "If I talk her into buying P&G products that she can't sell or out of stocking competing brands that she should be selling, I could lose that trust in a heartbeat."

Finally, collaboration is usually a two-way street—P&G gives and customers give back in return. "We'll help customers run a set of commercials or do some merchandising events, but there's usually a return-on-investment," explains another CBD manager. "Maybe it's helping us with distribution of a new product or increasing space for fabric care. We're very willing if the effort creates value for us as well as for the customer and the final consumer."

According to P&G, "Customer Business Development is selling and a whole lot more. It's a P&G-specific approach [that lets us] grow business by working as a 'strategic partner' with our accounts, focusing on mutually beneficial business building opportunities. All customers want to improve their business; it's [our] role to help them identify the biggest opportunities."

Thus, P&G salespeople aren't the stereotypical glad-handers that some people have come to expect when they think of selling. In fact, they aren't even called "salespeople." They are customer business development managers—talented, well-educated, well-trained sales professionals who do all they can to help customers succeed. They know that good selling involves working with customers to solve their problems for mutual gain. They know that if customers succeed, they succeed.[1]

P&G Customer Business Development managers know that to grow P&G's business, they must first help their retail partners to sell P&G's brands.

P&G's sales force has long been an American icon for selling at its very best. But at P&G they rarely call it "sales." Instead, it's "Customer Business Development."

In this chapter, we examine two more promotion mix tools: *personal selling* and *sales promotion*. Personal selling consists of interpersonal interactions with customers and prospects to make sales and maintain customer relationships. Sales promotion involves using short-term incentives to encourage customer purchasing, reseller support, and sales force efforts.

Author Comment | Personal selling is the interpersonal arm of the promotion mix. A company's sales force creates and communicates customer value through personal interactions with customers.

Personal Selling (pp 464–467)

Robert Louis Stevenson once noted, "Everyone lives by selling something." Companies around the world use sales forces to sell products and services to business customers and final consumers. But sales forces are also found in many other kinds of organizations. For example, colleges use recruiters to attract new students, and churches use membership committees to attract new members. Museums and fine arts organizations use fund-raisers to contact donors and raise money. Even governments use sales forces. The U.S. Postal Service, for instance, uses a sales force to sell Express Mail and other services to corporate customers. In the first part of this chapter, we examine personal selling's role in the organization, sales force management decisions, and the personal selling process.

The Nature of Personal Selling

Personal selling
Personal presentations by the firm's sales force for the purpose of making sales and building customer relationships.

Personal selling is one of the oldest professions in the world. The people who do the selling go by many names, including salespeople, sales representatives, agents, district managers, account executives, sales consultants, and sales engineers.

People hold many stereotypes of salespeople—including some unfavorable ones. "Salesman" may bring to mind the image of Arthur Miller's pitiable Willy Loman in *Death of a Salesman* or Dwight Schrute, the opinionated Dunder Mifflin paper salesman from the TV show *The Office*, who lacks both common sense and social skills. And then there are the real-life "yell-and-sell" "pitchmen," who hawk everything from the ShamWow to the Swivel Sweeper and Point 'n Paint in TV infomercials. However, the majority of salespeople are a far cry from these unfortunate stereotypes.

As the opening P&G story shows, most salespeople are well-educated and well-trained professionals who add value for customers and maintain long-term customer relationships. They listen to their customers, assess customer needs, and organize the company's efforts to solve customer problems.[2]

464

Some assumptions about what makes someone a good salesperson are dead wrong. There's this idea that the classic sales personality is overbearing, pushy, and outgoing—the kind of people who walk in and suck all the air out of the room. But the best salespeople are good at one-on-one contact. They create loyalty and customers because people trust them and want to work with them. It's a matter of putting the client's interests first, which is the antithesis of how most people view salespeople. The most successful salespeople are successful for one simple reason: They know how to build relationships. You can go in with a big personality and convince people to do what you want them to do, but that really isn't selling; it's manipulation, and it only works in the short term. A good salesperson can read customer emotions without exploiting them because the bottom line is that he or she wants what's best for the customer.

● **Professional selling: It takes more than fast talk and a warm smile to sell high-tech diesel locomotives. GE's real challenge is to win a buyer's business by building partnerships, day-in, day-out, year-in, year-out, with its customers.**

Consider GE's diesel locomotive business. ● It takes more than fast talk and a warm smile to sell a batch of $2-million high-tech locomotives. A single big sale can easily run into the hundreds of millions of dollars. GE salespeople head up an extensive team of company specialists—all dedicated to finding ways to satisfy the needs of large customers. The selling process can take years from the first sales presentation to the day the sale is announced. The real challenge is to win buyers' business by building day-in, day-out, year-in, year-out partnerships with them based on superior products and close collaboration.

The term **salesperson** covers a wide range of positions. At one extreme, a salesperson might be largely an *order taker*, such as the department store salesperson standing behind the counter. At the other extreme are *order getters*, whose positions demand *creative selling* and *relationship building* for products and services ranging from appliances, industrial equipment, and locomotives to insurance and information technology services. Here, we focus on the more creative types of selling and the process of building and managing an effective sales force.

The Role of the Sales Force

Salesperson
An individual representing a company to customers by performing one or more of the following activities: prospecting, communicating, selling, servicing, information gathering, and relationship building.

Personal selling is the interpersonal arm of the promotion mix. Advertising consists largely of nonpersonal communication with large groups of consumers. By contrast, personal selling involves interpersonal interactions between salespeople and individual customers—whether face-to-face, by telephone, via e-mail, through video or Web conferences, or by other means. Personal selling can be more effective than advertising in more complex selling situations. Salespeople can probe customers to learn more about their problems and then adjust the marketing offer and presentation to fit the special needs of each customer.

The role of personal selling varies from company to company. Some firms have no salespeople at all—for example, companies that sell only online or through catalogs, or companies that sell through manufacturer's reps, sales agents, or brokers. In most firms, however, the sales force plays a major role. In companies that sell business products and services, such as IBM, DuPont, or Boeing, salespeople work directly with customers. In consumer product companies such as P&G and Nike, the sales force plays an important behind-the-scenes role. It works with wholesalers and retailers to gain their support and help them be more effective in selling the company's products.

Linking the Company with Its Customers

The sales force serves as a critical link between a company and its customers. ● In many cases, salespeople serve two masters: the seller and the buyer. First, they *represent the company to customers*. They find and develop new customers and communicate information

● **Salespeople link the company with its customers. To many customers, the salesperson is the company.**

about the company's products and services. They sell products by approaching customers, presenting their offerings, answering objections, negotiating prices and terms, and closing sales. In addition, salespeople provide customer service and carry out market research and intelligence work.

At the same time, salespeople *represent customers to the company*, acting inside the firm as "champions" of customers' interests and managing the buyer-seller relationship. Salespeople relay customer concerns about company products and actions back inside to those who can handle them. They learn about customer needs and work with other marketing and nonmarketing people in the company to develop greater customer value.

In fact, to many customers, the salesperson *is* the company—the only tangible manifestation of the company that they see. Hence, customers may become loyal to salespeople as well as to the companies and products they represent. This concept of "salesperson-owned loyalty" lends even more importance to the salesperson's customer relationship building abilities. Strong relationships with the salesperson will result in strong relationships with the company and its products. Conversely, poor relationships will probably result in poor company and product relationships.

Given its role in linking the company with its customers, the sales force must be strongly customer-solutions focused. In fact, such a customer-solutions focus is a must not only for the sales force but also for the entire organization. Says Anne Mulcahy, successful former CEO and chairman of Xerox, who started her career in sales, a strong customer-service focus "has to be the center of your universe, the heartland of how you run your company" (see Real Marketing 16.1).

Coordinating Marketing and Sales

Ideally, the sales force and other marketing functions (marketing planners, brand managers, and researchers) should work together closely to jointly create value for customers. Unfortunately, however, some companies still treat sales and marketing as separate functions. When this happens, the separate sales and marketing groups may not get along well. When things go wrong, marketers blame the sales force for its poor execution of what they see as an otherwise splendid strategy. In turn, the sales team blames the marketers for being out of touch with what's really going on with customers. Neither group fully values the other's contributions. If not repaired, such disconnects between marketing and sales can damage customer relationships and company performance.

A company can take several actions to help bring its marketing and sales functions closer together. At the most basic level, it can increase communications between the two groups by arranging joint meetings and spelling out communications channels. It can create opportunities for salespeople and marketers to work together. Brand managers and researchers can occasionally tag along on sales calls or sit in on sales planning sessions. In turn, salespeople can sit in on marketing planning sessions and share their firsthand customer knowledge.

A company can also create joint objectives and reward systems for sales and marketing teams or appoint marketing-sales liaisons—people from marketing who "live with the sales force" and help coordinate marketing and sales force programs and efforts. Finally, it can appoint a high-level marketing executive to oversee both marketing and sales. Such a person can help infuse marketing and sales with the common goal of creating value for customers to capture value in return.[3]

Real Marketing 16.1

The Role of the Sales Force— and the Entire Company:
Putting Customers First

When someone says "salesperson," what image comes to mind? Perhaps you think of the stereotypical glad-hander who's out to lighten customers' wallets by selling them something they don't really need. Think again. Today, for most companies, personal selling plays an important role in building profitable customer relationships. In turn, those relationships contribute greatly to overall company success.

Just ask Anne Mulcahy, recently retired CEO and current chairman of the board at Xerox. We talked about Mulcahy in Chapter 3. She took the reins of the then-nearly-bankrupt copier company in early 2001 and transformed it into a successful, modern-day, digital technology and services enterprise. Mulcahy has received much praise from analysts, investors, and others as a transformative leader at Xerox. In 2007, *Fortune* magazine named her the second-most-powerful woman in business, and *Forbes* ranked her as the 13th most powerful woman in the world. In 2008, she became the first female CEO selected by her peers as *Chief Executive* magazine's Chief Executive of the Year.

But the roots of Mulcahy's success go back to the lessons she learned and the skills she honed in sales. The one-time undergraduate English and journalism major began her career in 1976 as a Xerox sales rep in Boston. From there, she worked her way up the sales ladder to become Xerox's vice president of global sales in the late 1990s. Then, 25 years after first knocking on customer doors in New England, she was appointed CEO of Xerox.

As CEO, Mulcahy brought with her a sales and marketing mentality that now permeates the entire Xerox organization. As you may recall from the turnaround story in Chapter 3, the company's transformation started with a new focus solving customer problems. Mulcahy believes that understanding customers is just as important as understanding technology. "Having spent so much time in sales, . . . I knew you have to keep customers in the forefront." Looking back, Mulcahy recalls, Xerox had lost touch with its

markets. To turn things around at Xerox, the company needed to focus on customers. "In a crisis, that is what really matters."

"Sales helps you understand what drives the business and that customers are a critical part of the business," Mulcahy says. "This will be important in any business function, but you learn it [best] in sales management where it is critical, the jewel in the crown." Implementing this customer- first sales philosophy, one of Mulcahy's first actions as CEO was to put on her old sales hat and hit the road to visit customers.

Mulcahy knows that putting customers first isn't just a sales force responsibility; it's an emphasis for everyone in the company. To stress that point at all levels, she quickly set up a rotating "customer officer of the day" program at Xerox, which requires a top executive

to answer customer calls that come to corporate headquarters. As the customer officer of the day, the executive has three responsibilities: listen to the customer, resolve the problem, and take responsibility for fixing the underlying cause. That sounds a lot like sales.

So if you're still thinking of salespeople as fast-talking, ever-smiling peddlers who foist their wares on reluctant customers, you're probably working with an out-of-date stereotype. Good salespeople succeed not by taking customers in but by helping them out—by assessing customer needs and solving customer problems. At Xerox, salespeople are well-trained professionals who listen to customers and win their business by doing what's right for them. In fact, that isn't just good sales thinking—it applies to the entire organization. According to Mulcahy, that "has to be the center of your universe, the heartland of how you run your company."

Sources: Henry Canaday, "Sales Rep to CEO: Anne Mulcahy and the Xerox Revolution," *Selling Power*, November/December 2008, pp. 53–57; "2008 Chief Executive of the Year," *Chief Executive*, September/October 2008, p. 68; Andrea Deckert, "Mulcahy Describes the Keys to Xerox Turnaround," November 2, 2007, p. 3; "Women CEOs, Xerox," *Financial Times*, December 31, 2008, p. 10; and "Anne Mulcahy to Retire as Xerox CEO," *Wireless News*, May 27, 2009.

Putting the customer first: Says transformative former Xerox CEO and chairman, Anne Mulcahy, who started her career in sales, that "has to be the center of your universe, the heartland of how you run your company."

Author | Comment Here's another definition of sales force management: "Planning, organizing, leading, and controlling personal contact programs designed to achieve profitable customer relationships." Once again, the goal of every marketing activity is to create customer value and build customer relationships.

Managing the Sales Force (pp 468–477)

We define **sales force management** as analyzing, planning, implementing, and controlling sales force activities. It includes designing sales force strategy and structure and recruiting, selecting, training, compensating, supervising, and evaluating the firm's salespeople. These major sales force management decisions are shown in ⦿ **Figure 16.1** and are discussed in the following sections.

Designing the Sales Force Strategy and Structure

Marketing managers face several sales force strategy and design questions. How should salespeople and their tasks be structured? How big should the sales force be? Should salespeople sell alone or work in teams with other people in the company? Should they sell in the field, by telephone, or on the Web? We address these issues next.

The Sales Force Structure

A company can divide sales responsibilities along any of several lines. The structure decision is simple if the company sells only one product line to one industry with customers in many locations. In that case the company would use a *territorial sales force structure*. However, if the company sells many products to many types of customers, it might need a *product sales force structure*, a *customer sales force structure*, or a combination of the two.

Sales force management
Analyzing, planning, implementing, and controlling sales force activities.

Territorial sales force structure
A sales force organization that assigns each salesperson to an exclusive geographic territory in which that salesperson sells the company's full line.

Territorial Sales Force Structure. In the **territorial sales force structure**, each salesperson is assigned to an exclusive geographic area and sells the company's full line of products or services to all customers in that territory. This organization clearly defines each salesperson's job and fixes accountability. It also increases the salesperson's desire to build local customer relationships that, in turn, improve selling effectiveness. Finally, because each salesperson travels within a limited geographic area, travel expenses are relatively small.

A territorial sales organization is often supported by many levels of sales management positions. For example, Stanley Black & Decker uses a territorial structure in which each salesperson is responsible for selling all of the company's products—from hand tools to lawn and garden equipment—in assigned territories. Starting at the bottom of the organization are entry-level *territory sales representatives* who report to *territory managers*. Territory sales representatives cover smaller areas, such as Eastern North Carolina, and territory managers cover larger areas such as the Carolinas and Virginia. Territory managers, in turn, report to *regional managers*, who cover regions such as the Southeast or West Coast. Regional managers, in turn, report to a *director of sales*.

Product sales force structure
A sales force organization in which salespeople specialize in selling only a portion of the company's products or lines.

Product Sales Force Structure. Salespeople must know their products, especially when the products are numerous and complex. This need, together with the growth of product management, has led many companies to adopt a **product sales force structure**, in which the sales force sells along product lines. For example, GE employs different sales forces within different product and service divisions of its major businesses. Within GE Infrastructure, for instance, the company has separate sales forces for aviation, energy, transportation, and water processing products and technologies. Within GE Healthcare, it employs different sales forces for diagnostic imaging, life sciences, and integrated IT products and services. In all, a company as large and complex as GE might have dozens of separate sales forces serving its diverse product and service portfolio.

⦿ **FIGURE | 16.1**
Major Steps in Sales Force Management

The goal of this process? You guessed it! The company wants to build a skilled and motivated sales team that will help to create customer value and build strong customer relationships.

| Designing sales force strategy and structure | Recruiting and selecting salespeople | Training salespeople | Compensating salespeople | Supervising salespeople | Evaluating salespeople |

The product structure can lead to problems, however, if a single large customer buys many different company products. For example, several different GE salespeople might end up calling on the same large healthcare customer in a given period. This means that they travel over the same routes and wait to see the same customer's purchasing agents. These extra costs must be compared with the benefits of better product knowledge and attention to individual products.

Customer (or market) sales force structure
A sales force organization in which salespeople specialize in selling only to certain customers or industries.

Customer Sales Force Structure. More and more companies are now using a **customer** (or **market**) **sales force structure**, in which they organize the sales force along customer or industry lines. Separate sales forces may be set up for different industries, serving current customers versus finding new ones, and serving major accounts versus regular accounts. Many companies even have special sales forces to handle the needs of individual large customers. For example, above its territory structure, Stanley Black & Decker has a Home Depot sales organization and a Lowe's sales organization.

Organizing the sales force around customers can help a company build closer relationships with important customers. ⊙ Consider Hill-Rom, a leading supplier of medical equipment, including hospital beds, stretchers, and nurse communication systems, which recently restructured its product-based sales force into a customer-based one:[4]

Hill-Rom divided its sales force into two customer-based teams. One sales force focuses on "key" customers—large accounts that purchase high-end equipment and demand high levels of sales force collaboration. The second sales force focuses on "prime" customers—smaller accounts that are generally more concerned about getting the features and functions they need for the best possible price. Assigning the separate sales forces helps Hill-Rom better understand what the different types of customers need. It also lets the company track how much attention the sales force devotes to each customer group.

⊙ Leading medical-equipment supplier Hill-Rom recently adopted a customer-based sales force structure, which helped it focus more intensely on the needs of large key customers. In the two years following the sales force redesign, sales growth doubled.

For example, prior to restructuring its sales force, Hill-Rom had been treating both key and prime customers the same way. As a result, it was trying to sell smaller prime customers a level of service and innovation that they did not value or could not afford. So the cost of sales for prime customers was four to five times higher than for key customers. Now, a single account manager and team focus intensely on all the areas of each key customer's business, working together to find product and service solutions. Such intensive collaboration would have been difficult under the old product-based sales structure, in which multiple Hill-Rom sales reps serviced the different specialty areas within a single key account. In the two years following the sales force redesign, Hill-Rom's sales growth doubled.

Complex Sales Force Structures. When a company sells a wide variety of products to many types of customers over a broad geographic area, it often combines several types of sales force structures. Salespeople can be specialized by customer and territory; product and territory; product and customer; or territory, product, and customer. For example, Stanley Black & Decker specializes its sales force by customer (with different sales forces calling on Home Depot, Lowe's, and smaller independent retailers) *and* by territory for each key customer group (territory representatives, territory managers, regional managers, and so on). No single structure is best for all companies and situations. Each company should select a sales force structure that best serves the needs of its customers and fits its overall marketing strategy.

Some sales forces are huge. For example, GE employs 16,400 salespeople; American Express, 23,400; PepsiCo, 36,000; and Xerox, 15,000.

A good sales structure can mean the difference between success and failure. Over time, sales force structures can grow complex, inefficient, and unresponsive to customers' needs. Companies should periodically review their sales force organizations to be certain that they serve the needs of the company and its customers.

Sales Force Size

Once the company has set its structure, it is ready to consider *sales force size*. Sales forces may range in size from only a few salespeople to tens of thousands. Some sales forces are huge—for example, PepsiCo employs 36,000 salespeople; American Express, 23,400; GE, 16,400; and Xerox, 15,000.[5] Salespeople constitute one of the company's most productive—and most expensive—assets. Therefore, increasing their numbers will increase both sales and costs.

Many companies use some form of *workload approach* to set sales force size. Using this approach, a company first groups accounts into different classes according to size, account status, or other factors related to the amount of effort required to maintain the account. It then determines the number of salespeople needed to call on each class of accounts the desired number of times.

The company might think as follows: Suppose we have 1,000 A-level accounts and 2,000 B-level accounts. A-level accounts require 36 calls per year, and B-level accounts require 12 calls per year. In this case, the sales force's *workload*—the number of calls it must make per year—is 60,000 calls [(1,000 × 36) + (2,000 × 12) = 36,000 + 24,000 = 60,000]. Suppose our average salesperson can make 1,000 calls a year. Thus, we need 60 salespeople (60,000 ÷ 1,000).[6]

Other Sales Force Strategy and Structure Issues

Sales management must also determine who will be involved in the selling effort and how various sales and sales support people will work together.

Outside sales force (or field sales force)
Salespeople who travel to call on customers in the field.

Inside sales force
Salespeople who conduct business from their offices via telephone, the Internet, or visits from prospective buyers.

Outside and Inside Sales Forces. The company may have an **outside sales force** (or **field sales force**), an **inside sales force**, or both. Outside salespeople travel to call on customers in the field. Inside salespeople conduct business from their offices via telephone, the Internet, or visits from buyers.

Some inside salespeople provide support for the outside sales force, freeing them to spend more time selling to major accounts and finding new prospects. For example, *technical sales support people* provide technical information and answers to customers' questions. *Sales assistants* provide administrative backup for outside salespeople. They call ahead and confirm appointments, follow up on deliveries, and answer customers' questions when outside salespeople cannot be reached. Using such combinations of inside and outside salespeople can help serve important customers better. The inside rep provides daily access and support; the outside rep provides face-to-face collaboration and relationship building.

Other inside salespeople do more than just provide support. *Telemarketers* and *Web sellers* use the phone and Internet to find new leads and qualify prospects or sell and service accounts directly. Telemarketing and Web selling can be very effective, less costly ways to sell to smaller, harder-to-reach customers. Depending on the complexity of the product and customer, for example, a telemarketer can make from 20 to 33 decision-maker contacts a day, compared to the average of four that an outside salesperson can make. And whereas an average B-to-B field sales call costs $350 or more, a routine industrial telemarketing call costs only about $5 and a complex call about $20.[7]

Although the federal government's Do Not Call Registry put a dent in telephone sales to consumers, telemarketing remains a vital tool for many B-to-B marketers. For some smaller companies, telephone and Web selling may be the primary sales approaches. How-

● **For many types of selling situations, phone or Web selling can be as effective as a personal sales call. At Climax Portable Machine Tools, phone reps build surprisingly strong and personal customer relationships.**

ever, larger companies also use these tactics, either to sell directly to small and midsize customers or help out with larger ones. Especially in the leaner times following the recent recession, many companies reduced their in-person customer visits in favor of more telephone, e-mail, and Internet selling.

● For many types of products and selling situations, phone or Web selling can be as effective as a personal sales call:

Climax Portable Machine Tools, which manufactures portable maintenance tools for the metal cutting industry, has proven that telemarketing can save money and still lavish attention on buyers. Under the old system, Climax sales engineers spent one-third of their time on the road, training distributor salespeople and accompanying them on calls. They could make about four contacts a day. Now, each of five sales engineers on Climax's inside sales team calls about 30 prospects a day, following up on leads generated by ads and e-mails. Because it takes about five calls to close a sale, the sales engineers update a prospect's profile after each contact, noting the degree of commitment, requirements, next call date, and personal comments. "If anyone mentions he's going on a fishing trip, our sales engineer enters that in the sales information system and uses it to personalize the next phone call," says Climax's president, noting that this is one way to build good relations.

Another is that the first contact with a prospect includes the sales engineer's business card with his or her picture on it. Climax's customer information system also gives inside reps instant access to customer information entered by the outside sales force and service people. Armed with all the information, inside reps can build surprisingly strong and personal customer relationships. Of course, it takes more than friendliness to sell $15,000 machine tools over the phone (special orders may run $200,000), but the telemarketing approach works well. When Climax customers were asked, "Do you see the sales engineer often enough?" the response was overwhelmingly positive. Obviously, many people didn't realize that the only contact they had with Climax had been on the phone.[8]

Team selling

Using teams of people from sales, marketing, engineering, finance, technical support, and even upper management to service large, complex accounts.

Team Selling. As products become more complex, and as customers grow larger and more demanding, a single salesperson simply can't handle all of a large customer's needs. Instead, most companies now use **team selling** to service large, complex accounts. Sales teams can unearth problems, solutions, and sales opportunities that no individual salesperson could do. Such teams might include experts from any area or level of the selling firm—sales, marketing, technical and support services, R&D, engineering, operations, finance, and others.

In many cases, the move to team selling mirrors similar changes in customers' buying organizations. "Buyers implementing team-based purchasing decisions have necessitated the equal and opposite creation of team-based selling—a completely new way of doing business for many independent, self-motivated salespeople," says a sales force analyst. "Today, we're calling on teams of buying people, and that requires more firepower on our side," agrees one sales vice president. "One salesperson just can't do it all—can't be an expert in everything we're bringing to the customer. We have strategic account teams, led by customer business managers, who basically are our quarterbacks."[9]

Some companies, such as IBM, Xerox, and P&G, have used teams for a long time. In the chapter-opening story, we learned that P&G sales reps are organized into customer business development (CBD) teams. Each CBD team is assigned to a major P&G customer, such as Walmart, Safeway, or CVS Pharmacy. The CBD organization places the focus on serving the complete needs of each major customer. It lets P&G "grow business by working as a 'strategic partner' with our accounts," not just as a supplier.[10]

Team selling does have some pitfalls. For example, salespeople are by nature competitive and have often been trained and rewarded for outstanding individual performance. Salespeople who are used to having customers all to themselves may have trouble learning to work with and trust others on a team. In addition, selling teams can confuse or overwhelm customers who are used to working with only one salesperson. Finally, difficulties in evaluating individual contributions to the team selling effort can create some sticky compensation issues.

Recruiting and Selecting Salespeople

At the heart of any successful sales force operation is the recruitment and selection of good salespeople. The performance difference between an average salesperson and a top salesperson can be substantial. In a typical sales force, the top 30 percent of the salespeople might bring in 60 percent of the sales. Thus, careful salesperson selection can greatly increase overall sales force performance. Beyond the differences in sales performance, poor selection results in costly turnover. When a salesperson quits, the costs of finding and training a new salesperson—plus the costs of lost sales—can be very high. Also, a sales force with many new people is less productive, and turnover disrupts important customer relationships.

● Great salespeople: The best salespeople possess intrinsic motivation, disciplined work style, the ability to close a sale, and perhaps most important, the ability to build relationships with customers.

What sets great salespeople apart from all the rest? In an effort to profile top sales performers, Gallup Consulting, a division of the well-known Gallup polling organization, has interviewed hundreds of thousands of salespeople. ● Its research suggests that the best salespeople possess four key talents: intrinsic motivation, a disciplined work style, the ability to close a sale, and, perhaps most important, the ability to build relationships with customers.[11]

Super salespeople are motivated from within—they have an unrelenting drive to excel. Some salespeople are driven by money, a desire for recognition, or the satisfaction of competing and winning. Others are driven by the desire to provide service and build relationships. The best salespeople possess some of each of these motivations. They also have a disciplined work style. They lay out detailed, organized plans and then follow through in a timely way.

But motivation and discipline mean little unless they result in closing more sales and building better customer relationships. Super salespeople build the skills and knowledge they need to get the job done. Perhaps most important, top salespeople are excellent customer problem solvers and relationship builders. They understand their customers' needs. Talk to sales executives and they'll describe top performers in these terms: good listeners, empathetic, patient, caring, and responsive. Top performers can put themselves on the buyer's side of the desk and see the world through their customers' eyes. They don't want just to be liked; they want to add value for their customers.

When recruiting, a company should analyze the sales job itself and the characteristics of its most successful salespeople to identify the traits needed by a successful salesperson in their industry. Then it must recruit the right salespeople. The human resources department looks for applicants by getting names from current salespeople, using employment agencies, searching the Web, placing classified ads, and working through college placement services. Another source is to attract top salespeople from other companies. Proven salespeople need less training and can be productive immediately.

Recruiting will attract many applicants from which the company must select the best. The selection procedure can vary from a single informal interview to lengthy testing and interviewing. Many companies give formal tests to sales applicants. Tests typically measure sales aptitude, analytical and organizational skills, personality traits, and other characteristics. But test scores provide only one piece of information in a set that includes personal characteristics, references, past employment history, and interviewer reactions.

Training Salespeople

New salespeople may spend anywhere from a few weeks or months to a year or more in training. Then, most companies provide continuing sales training via seminars, sales meetings, and Web e-learning throughout the salesperson's career. In all, U.S. companies spend billions of dollars annually on training salespeople, and sales training typically captures the largest share of the training budget. For example, U.S. technology companies invest 29 percent of their training budgets on sales training. Although training can be expensive, it can also yield dramatic returns. For instance, one recent study showed that sales training conducted by ADP, an administrative services firm, resulted in an ROI of nearly 338 percent in only 90 days.[12]

Training programs have several goals. First, salespeople need to know about customers and how to build relationships with them. So the training program must teach them about different types of customers and their needs, buying motives, and buying habits. It must also teach them how to sell effectively and train them in the basics of the selling process. Salespeople also need to know and identify with the company, its products, and its competitors. So an effective training program teaches them about the company's objectives, organization, products, and the strategies of major competitors.

Today, many companies are adding e-learning to their sales training programs. Online training may range from simple text-based product training and Internet-based sales exercises that build sales skills to sophisticated simulations that re-create the dynamics of real-life sales calls. Training online instead of on-site can cut travel and other training costs, and it takes up less of a salesperson's selling time. It also makes on-demand training available to salespeople, letting them train as little or as much as needed, whenever and wherever needed. Most e-learning is Web-based, but many companies now offer on-demand training via smartphones and iPod-type devices.

Many companies are now using imaginative and sophisticated e-learning techniques to make sales training more efficient—and sometimes even more fun. For example, Bayer Health-Care Pharmaceuticals worked with Concentric RX, a healthcare marketing agency, to create a role-playing simulation video game to train its sales force on a new drug marketing program:[13]

Most people don't usually associate fast-paced rock music and flashy graphics with online sales training tools. ● But Concentric RX's innovative role-playing video game—Rep Race: The Battle for Office Supremacy—has all that and a lot more. Rep Race gives Bayer sales reps far more entertainment than the staid old multiple-choice skills tests it replaces. The game was created to help breathe new life into a mature Bayer product—Betaseron, a 17-year-old multiple sclerosis (MS) therapy treatment. The aim was to find a fresh, more active way to help Bayer sales reps apply the in-depth information they learned about Betaseron to actual selling and objections-handling situations. Bayer also wanted to increase rep engagement through interactive learning and feedback through real-time results. Bayer reps liked Rep Race from the start. According to Bayer, when the game was first launched, reps played it as many as 30 times. In addition to its educational and motivational value, Rep Race allowed Bayer to measure sales reps' individual and collective performance. In the end, Bayer calculated that the Rep Race simulation helped improve the Betaseron sales team's effectiveness by 20 percent.

● **E-training can make sales training more efficient—and more fun. Bayer HealthCare Pharmaceuticals' role-playing video game—Rep Race—helped improve sales rep effectiveness by 20 percent.**

Compensating Salespeople

To attract good salespeople, a company must have an appealing compensation plan. Compensation consists of four elements: a fixed amount, a variable amount, expenses, and fringe benefits. The fixed amount, usually a salary, gives the salesperson some stable income. The variable amount, which might be commissions or bonuses based on sales performance, rewards the salesperson for greater effort and success.

Management must determine what *mix* of these compensation elements makes the most sense for each sales job. Different combinations of fixed and variable compensation give rise to four basic types of compensation plans: straight salary, straight commission, salary plus bonus, and salary plus commission. According to one study of sales force compensation, 18 percent of companies pay straight salary, 19 percent pay straight commission, and 63 percent pay a combination of salary plus incentives. A study showed that the average salesperson's pay consists of about 67 percent salary and 33 percent incentive pay.[14]

A sales force compensation plan can both motivate salespeople and direct their activities. Compensation should direct salespeople toward activities that are consistent with overall sales force and marketing objectives. For example, if the strategy is to acquire new business, grow rapidly, and gain market share, the compensation plan might include a larger commission component, coupled with a new-account bonus to encourage high sales performance and new account development. In contrast, if the goal is to maximize current account profitability, the compensation plan might contain a larger base-salary component with additional incentives for current account sales or customer satisfaction.

In fact, more and more companies are moving away from high commission plans that may drive salespeople to make short-term grabs for business. They worry that a salesperson who is pushing too hard to close a deal may ruin the customer relationship. Instead, companies are designing compensation plans that reward salespeople for building customer relationships and growing the long-run value of each customer.

When the times get tough economically, some companies are tempted to cut costs by reducing sales compensation. However, although some cost-cutting measures make sense when business is sluggish, cutting sales force compensation across the board is usually a "don't-go-there, last-of-the-last-resorts" action, says one sales compensation expert. "Keep in mind that if you burn the salesperson, you might burn the customer relationship." If the company must reduce its compensation expenses, says the expert, a better strategy than across-the-board cuts is to "keep the pay up for top performers and turn the [low performers] loose."[15]

Supervising and Motivating Salespeople

New salespeople need more than a territory, compensation, and training—they need supervision and motivation. The goal of *supervision* is to help salespeople "work smart" by doing the right things in the right ways. The goal of *motivation* is to encourage salespeople to "work hard" and energetically toward sales force goals. If salespeople work smart and work hard, they will realize their full potential—to their own and the company's benefit.

Supervising Salespeople

Companies vary in how closely they supervise their salespeople. Many help salespeople identify target customers and set call objectives. Some may also specify how much time the sales force should spend prospecting for new accounts and set other time management priorities. One tool is the weekly, monthly, or annual *call plan* that shows which customers and prospects to call on and which activities to carry out. Another tool is *time-and-duty analysis*. In addition to time spent selling, the salesperson spends time traveling, waiting, taking breaks, and doing administrative chores.

⦿ **Figure 16.2** shows how salespeople spend their time. On average, active selling time accounts for only 10 percent of total working time! If selling time could be raised from 10 percent to 30 percent, this would triple the time spent selling.[16] Companies are always looking for ways to save time—simplifying administrative duties, developing better sales-call and routing plans, supplying more and better customer information, and using phone, e-mail,

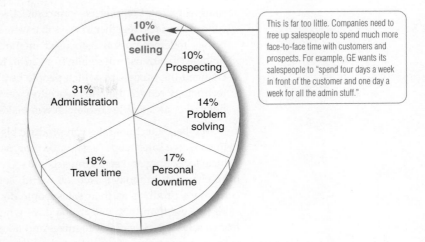

● FIGURE | 16.2
How Salespeople Spend Their Time

Source: Proudfoot Consulting. Data used with permission.

or video conferencing instead of traveling. Consider the changes GE made to increase its sales force's face-to-face selling time.[17]

When Jeff Immelt became GE's new chairman, he was dismayed to find that members of the sales team were spending far more time on deskbound administrative chores than in face-to-face meetings with customers and prospects. "He said we needed to turn that around," recalls Venki Rao, an IT leader in global sales and marketing at GE Power Systems, a division focused on energy systems and products. "[We need] to spend four days a week in front of the customer and one day for all the admin stuff." GE Power's salespeople spent much of their time at their desks because they had to go to many sources for the information needed to sell multimillion-dollar turbines, turbine parts, and services to energy companies worldwide. To fix the problem, GE created a new sales portal, a kind of "one-stop shop" that connects the vast array of GE databases, providing salespeople with everything from sales tracking and customer data to parts pricing and information on planned outages. GE also added external data, such as news feeds. "Before, you were randomly searching for things," says Bill Snook, a GE sales manager. Now, he says, "I have the sales portal as my home page, and I use it as the gateway to all the applications that I have." The sales portal has freed Snook and 2,500 other users around the globe from once time-consuming administrative tasks, greatly increasing their face time with customers.

Many firms have adopted *sales force automation systems*: computerized, digitized sales force operations that let salespeople work more effectively anytime, anywhere. Companies now routinely equip their salespeople with technologies such as laptops, smartphones, wireless Web connections, Webcams for videoconferencing, and customer-contact and relationship management software. Armed with these technologies, salespeople can more effectively and efficiently profile customers and prospects, analyze and forecast sales, schedule sales calls, make presentations, prepare sales and expense reports, and manage account relationships. The result is better time management, improved customer service, lower sales costs, and higher sales performance.[18]

Selling and the Internet

Perhaps the fastest-growing sales technology tool is the Internet. The Internet offers explosive potential for conducting sales operations and interacting with and serving customers. Sales organizations are now both enhancing their effectiveness and saving time and money by using a host of Internet approaches to train sales reps, hold sales meetings, service accounts, and even conduct live sales meetings with customers. Some call it **Sales 2.0**, the merging of innovative sales practices with Web 2.0 technologies to improve sales force effectiveness and efficiency:[19]

Sales 2.0

The merging of innovative sales practices with Web 2.0 technologies to improve sales force effectiveness and efficiency.

Web 2.0 enables a way of interacting, collaborating, and information sharing. With the Internet as a new business platform, now all stakeholders—prospects, customers, salespeople, and marketers—can connect, learn, plan, analyze, engage, collaborate, and conduct business together in ways that were not even imaginable a few years ago. Sales 2.0 brings together customer-focused methodologies and productivity-enhancing technologies that transform selling from an art to an interactive science. Sales 2.0 has forever changed the process by which people buy and companies sell. Will all this new sales technology reduce the role of face-to-face selling? The good news is that Sales 2.0 will not make salespeople obsolete. It will make them a lot more productive and effective.

Web-based technologies can produce big organizational benefits for sales forces. They help conserve salespeople's valuable time, save travel dollars, and give salespeople a new vehicle for selling and servicing accounts. Over the past decade, customer buying patterns have changed. In today's Web 2.0 world, customers often know almost as much about a company's products as their salespeople do. This gives customers more control over the sales process than they had in the days when brochures and pricing were only available from a sales rep. Sales 2.0 recognizes and takes advantage of these buying process changes, creating new avenues for connecting with customers in the Internet age.

For example, sales organizations can now generate lists of prospective customers from online databases and networking sites, such as Hoovers and LinkedIn. They create dialogs when prospective customers visit their Web sites through live chats with the sales team. They can use Web conferencing tools such as WebEx or GoToMeeting to talk live with customers about products and services. Other Sales 2.0 tools allow salespeople to monitor Internet interactions between customers about how they would like to buy, how they feel about a vendor, and what it would take to make a sale.

Today's sales forces are also ramping up their use of social networking media, from proprietary online customer communities to webinars and even Twitter, Facebook, and YouTube applications. A recent survey of business-to-business marketers found that, whereas they have recently cut back on traditional media and event spending, 68 percent are investing more in social media. ⦿ Consider Makino, a leading manufacturer of metal cutting and machining technology:[20]

> Makino complements its sales force efforts through a wide variety of social media initiatives that inform customers and enhance customer relationships. For example, it hosts an ongoing series of industry-specific webinars that position the company as an industry thought leader. Makino produces about three webinars each month and has archived more than 100 on topics ranging from how to get the most out of your machine tools to how metal-cutting processes are done. Webinar content is tailored to specific industries, such as aerospace or medical, and is promoted through carefully targeted banner ads and e-mail invitations. The webinars help to build Makino's customer database, generate leads, build customer relationships, and prepare the way for salespeople by serving up relevant information and educating customers online. Makino even uses Twitter, Facebook, and YouTube to inform customers and prospects about the latest Makino innovations and events and dramatically demonstrate the company's machines in action. "We've shifted dramatically into the electronic marketing area," says Makino's marketing manager. "It speeds up the sales cycle and makes it more efficient—for both the company and the customer. The results have been 'outstanding.'"

⦿ **Selling on the Internet: Machinery manufacturer Makino makes extensive use of online social networking—everything from proprietary online communities and webinars to Twitter, Facebook, and YouTube.**

Ultimately, "Sales 2.0 technologies are delivering instant information that builds relationships and enables sales to be more efficient and cost-effective and more productive," says one sales technology analyst. "Think of it as . . . doing what the best reps always did but doing it better, faster, and cheaper," says another.[21]

But the technologies also have some drawbacks. For starters, they're not cheap. And such systems can intimidate low-tech salespeople or clients. Even more, there are some things you just can't present or teach via the Web—things that require personal interactions. For these reasons, some high-tech experts recommend that sales executives use Web technologies to supplement training, sales meetings, and preliminary client sales presentations but resort to old-fashioned, face-to-face meetings when the time draws near to close the deal.

Motivating Salespeople

Beyond directing salespeople, sales managers must also motivate them. Some salespeople will do their best without any special urging from management. To them, selling may be the most fascinating job in the world. But selling can also be frustrating. Salespeople often work alone, and they must sometimes travel away from home. They may face aggressive competing salespeople and difficult customers. Therefore, salespeople often need special encouragement to do their best.

Management can boost sales force morale and performance through its organizational climate, sales quotas, and positive incentives. *Organizational climate* describes the feeling that salespeople have about their opportunities, value, and rewards for a good performance. Some companies treat salespeople as if they are not very important, so performance suffers accordingly. Other companies treat their salespeople as valued contributors and allow virtually unlimited opportunity for income and promotion. Not surprisingly, these companies enjoy higher sales force performance and less turnover.

Sales quota
A standard that states the amount a salesperson should sell and how sales should be divided among the company's products.

Many companies motivate their salespeople by setting **sales quotas**—standards stating the amount they should sell and how sales should be divided among the company's products. Compensation is often related to how well salespeople meet their quotas. Companies also use various *positive incentives* to increase the sales force effort. *Sales meetings* provide social occasions, breaks from the routine, chances to meet and talk with "company brass," and opportunities to air feelings and identify with a larger group. Companies also sponsor *sales contests* to spur the sales force to make a selling effort above and beyond what is normally expected. Other incentives include honors, merchandise and cash awards, trips, and profit-sharing plans.

Evaluating Salespeople and Sales Force Performance

We have thus far described how management communicates what salespeople should be doing and how it motivates them to do it. This process requires good feedback. And good feedback means getting regular information about salespeople to evaluate their performance.

Management gets information about its salespeople in several ways. The most important source is *sales reports*, including weekly or monthly work plans and longer-term territory marketing plans. Salespeople also write up their completed activities on *call reports* and turn in *expense reports* for which they are partly or wholly reimbursed. The company can also monitor the sales and profit performance data in the salesperson's territory. Additional information comes from personal observation, customer surveys, and talks with other salespeople.

Using various sales force reports and other information, sales management evaluates the members of the sales force. It evaluates salespeople on their ability to "plan their work and work their plan." Formal evaluation forces management to develop and communicate clear standards for judging performance. It also provides salespeople with constructive feedback and motivates them to perform well.

On a broader level, management should evaluate the performance of the sales force as a whole. Is the sales force accomplishing its customer relationship, sales, and profit objectives? Is it working well with other areas of the marketing and company organization? Are sales force costs in line with outcomes? As with other marketing activities, the company wants to measure its *return on sales investment*.

Author | So far, we've examined
Comment | how sales management develops and implements overall sales force strategies and programs. In this section, we'll look at how individual salespeople and sales teams sell to customers and build relationships with them.

The Personal Selling Process (pp 478–481)

We now turn from designing and managing a sales force to the personal selling process. The **selling process** consists of several steps that salespeople must master. These steps focus on the goal of getting new customers and obtaining orders from them. However, most salespeople spend much of their time maintaining existing accounts and building long-term customer *relationships*. We discuss the relationship aspect of the personal selling process in a later section.

Steps in the Selling Process

As shown in ⊙ **Figure 16.3**, the selling process consists of seven steps: prospecting and qualifying, preapproach, approach, presentation and demonstration, handling objections, closing, and follow-up.

Prospecting and Qualifying

Selling process
The steps that salespeople follow when selling, which include prospecting and qualifying, preapproach, approach, presentation and demonstration, handling objections, closing, and follow-up.

The first step in the selling process is **prospecting**—identifying qualified potential customers. Approaching the right potential customers is crucial to the selling success. As one sales expert puts it, "If the sales force starts chasing anyone who is breathing and seems to have a budget, you risk accumulating a roster of expensive-to-serve, hard-to-satisfy customers who never respond to whatever value proposition you have." He continues, "The solution to this isn't rocket science. [You must] train salespeople to actively scout the right prospects." Another expert concludes, "Increasing your prospecting effectiveness is the fastest single way to boost your sales."[22]

Prospecting
A salesperson or company identifies qualified potential customers.

The salesperson must often approach many prospects to get only a few sales. Although the company supplies some leads, salespeople need skill in finding their own. The best source is referrals. Salespeople can ask current customers for referrals and cultivate other referral sources, such as suppliers, dealers, noncompeting salespeople, and Web or other social networks. They can also search for prospects in directories or on the Web and track down leads using telephone and e-mail. Or they can drop in unannounced on various offices (a practice known as *cold calling*).

Salespeople also need to know how to *qualify* leads—that is, how to identify the good ones and screen out the poor ones. Prospects can be qualified by looking at their financial ability, volume of business, special needs, location, and possibilities for growth.

Preapproach

Preapproach
A salesperson learns as much as possible about a prospective customer before making a sales call.

Before calling on a prospect, the salesperson should learn as much as possible about the organization (what it needs, who is involved in the buying) and its buyers (their characteristics and buying styles). This step is known as **preapproach**. "Revving up your sales starts with your preparation," says one sales consultant. "A successful sale begins long before you set foot in the prospect's office." Preapproach begins with good research. The salesperson can consult standard industry and online sources, acquaintances, and others to learn about the company. Then the salesperson must apply the research to develop a customer strategy.

⊙ **FIGURE | 16.3**
Steps in the Selling Process

As shown here, these steps are transaction-oriented—aimed at closing a specific sale with the customer...

...but remember that in the long run, a single sale is only one element of a long-term customer relationship. So the selling process steps must be understood in the broader context of maintaining profitable customer relationships.

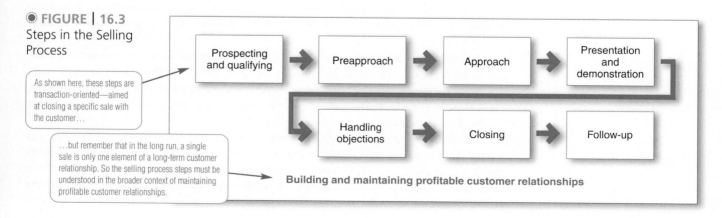

Prospecting and qualifying → Preapproach → Approach → Presentation and demonstration → Handling objections → Closing → Follow-up

Building and maintaining profitable customer relationships

"Being able to recite the prospect's product line in your sleep isn't enough," says the consultant. "You need to translate the data into something useful for your client."[23]

The salesperson should set *call objectives*, which may be to qualify the prospect, gather information, or make an immediate sale. Another task is to determine the best approach, which might be a personal visit, a phone call, or a letter or an e-mail. The best timing should be considered carefully because many prospects are busiest at certain times. Finally, the salesperson should give thought to an overall sales strategy for the account.

Approach

Approach
A salesperson meets the customer for the first time.

During the **approach** step, the salesperson should know how to meet and greet the buyer and get the relationship off to a good start. This step involves the salesperson's appearance, opening lines, and follow-up remarks. The opening lines should be positive to build goodwill from the outset. This opening might be followed by some key questions to learn more about the customer's needs or by showing a display or sample to attract the buyer's attention and curiosity. As in all stages of the selling process, listening to the customer is crucial.

Presentation and Demonstration

Presentation
A salesperson tells the "value story" to the buyer, showing how the company's offer solves the customer's problems.

During the **presentation** step of the selling process, the salesperson tells the "value story" to the buyer, showing how the company's offer solves the customer's problems. The *customer-solution approach* fits better with today's relationship marketing focus than does a hard sell or glad-handing approach. "Stop selling and start helping," advises one sales consultant. "Your goal should be to sell your customers exactly what will benefit them most," says another.[24] Buyers today want answers, not smiles; results, not razzle-dazzle. Moreover, they don't want just products. More than ever in today's economic climate, buyers want to know how those products will add value to their businesses. They want salespeople who listen to their concerns, understand their needs, and respond with the right products and services.

But before salespeople can *present* customer solutions, they must *develop* solutions to present. The solutions approach calls for good listening and problem-solving skills. The qualities that buyers *dislike most* in salespeople include being pushy, late, deceitful, unprepared, disorganized, or overly talkative. The qualities they *value most* include good listening, empathy, honesty, dependability, thoroughness, and follow-through. Great salespeople know how to sell, but more importantly they know how to listen and build strong customer relationships. Says one professional, "You have two ears and one mouth. Use them proportionally." Says another, "Everything starts with listening. I think the magic of these days is we've got so many more ways to listen."[25] ● A classic ad from office products maker Boise Cascade makes the listening point. It shows a Boise salesperson with huge ears drawn on. "With Boise, you'll notice a difference right away, especially with our sales force," says the ad. "At Boise . . . our account representatives have the unique ability to listen to your needs."

Finally, salespeople must also plan their presentation methods. Good interpersonal communication skills count when it comes to making effective sales presentations. However, today's media-rich and cluttered communications environment presents many new challenges for sales presenters. Today's information-overloaded customers

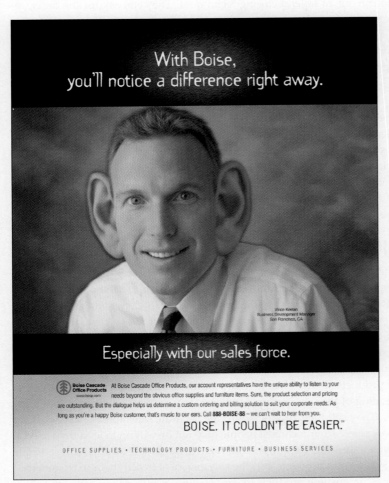

● This classic ad from Boise makes the point that good selling starts with listening. "Our account representatives have the unique ability to listen to your needs."

demand richer presentation experiences. And presenters now face multiple distractions during presentations from cell phones, text messages, and mobile Internet devices. Salespeople must deliver their messages in more engaging and compelling ways.

Thus, today's salespeople are employing advanced presentation technologies that allow for full multimedia presentations to only one or a few people. The venerable old flip chart has been replaced with sophisticated presentation software, online presentation technologies, interactive whiteboards, and handheld computers and projectors.

Handling Objections

Handling objections
A salesperson seeks out, clarifies, and overcomes any customer objections to buying.

Customers almost always have objections during the presentation or when asked to place an order. The problem can be either logical or psychological, and objections are often unspoken. In **handling objections**, the salesperson should use a positive approach, seek out hidden objections, ask the buyer to clarify any objections, take objections as opportunities to provide more information, and turn the objections into reasons for buying. Every salesperson needs training in the skills of handling objections.

Closing

Closing
A salesperson asks the customer for an order.

After handling the prospect's objections, the salesperson now tries to close the sale. Some salespeople do not get around to **closing** or handle it well. They may lack confidence, feel guilty about asking for the order, or fail to recognize the right moment to close the sale. Salespeople should know how to recognize closing signals from the buyer, including physical actions, comments, and questions. For example, the customer might sit forward and nod approvingly or ask about prices and credit terms.

Salespeople can use one of several closing techniques. They can ask for the order, review points of agreement, offer to help write up the order, ask whether the buyer wants this model or that one, or note that the buyer will lose out if the order is not placed now. The salesperson may offer the buyer special reasons to close, such as a lower price or an extra quantity at no charge.

Follow-Up

Follow-up
A salesperson follows up after the sale to ensure customer satisfaction and repeat business.

The last step in the selling process—**follow-up**—is necessary if the salesperson wants to ensure customer satisfaction and repeat business. Right after closing, the salesperson should complete any details on delivery time, purchase terms, and other matters. The salesperson then should schedule a follow-up call after the buyer receives the initial order to make sure proper installation, instruction, and servicing occur. This visit would reveal any problems, assure the buyer of the salesperson's interest, and reduce any buyer concerns that might have arisen since the sale.

Personal Selling and Managing Customer Relationships

The steps in the selling process as just described are *transaction oriented*—their aim is to help salespeople close a specific sale with a customer. But in most cases, the company is not simply seeking a sale. Rather, it wants to serve the customer over the long haul in a mutually profitable *relationship*. The sales force usually plays an important role in customer relationship building. Thus, as shown in Figure 16.3, the selling process must be understood in the context of building and maintaining profitable customer relationships.

Today's large customers favor suppliers who can work with them over time to deliver a coordinated set of products and services to many locations. For these customers, the first sale is only the beginning of the relationship. Unfortunately, some companies ignore these relationship realities. They sell their products through separate sales forces, each working independently to close sales. Their technical people may not be willing to lend time to educate a customer. Their engineering, design, and manufacturing people may have the attitude that "it's our job to make good products and the salesperson's to sell them to customers." Their salespeople focus on pushing products toward customers rather than listening to customers and providing solutions.

Other companies, however, recognize that winning and keeping accounts requires more than making good products and directing the sales force to close lots of sales. If the company wishes only to close sales and capture short-term business, it can do this by simply slashing its prices to meet or beat those of competitors. Instead, most companies want their salespeople to practice *value selling*—demonstrating and delivering superior customer value and capturing a return on that value that is fair for both the customer and the company.

Unfortunately, in the heat of closing sales—especially in a tough economy—salespeople too often take the easy way out by cutting prices rather than selling value. Sales management's challenge is to transform salespeople from customer advocates for price cuts into company advocates for value. Here's how Rockwell Automation sells value and relationships rather than price:[26]

> Facing pressure from Walmart to lower its prices, a condiment producer hastily summoned several competing supplier representatives—including Rockwell Automation sales rep Jeff Policicchio—who were given full access to the plant for one day and asked to find ways to dramatically reduce the customer's operating costs. Policicchio quickly learned that a major problem stemmed from lost production and down time due to poorly performing pumps on 32 huge condiment tanks. Policicchio gathered relevant cost and usage data and then used a Rockwell Automation laptop value-assessment tool to construct the best pump solution for the customer.
>
> The next day, Policicchio and the competing reps presented their solutions to plant management. Policicchio's value proposition: "With this Rockwell Automation pump solution, through less downtime, reduced administrative costs in procurement, and lower spending on repair parts, your company will save at least $16,268 per pump—on up to 32 pumps—relative to our best competitor's solution." It turns out the Policicchio was the only rep to demonstrate tangible cost savings for his proposed solution. Everyone else made fuzzy promises about possible benefits or offered to save the customer money by simply shaving their prices.
>
> The plant managers were so impressed with Policicchio's value proposition that—despite its higher initial price—they immediately purchased one Rockwell Automation pump solution for a trial. When the actual savings were even better than predicted, they placed orders for the remaining pumps. Thus, Policicchio's value-selling approach rather than price-cutting approach not only landed the initial sale but also provided the basis for a profitable long-term relationship with the customer.

Value selling requires listening to customers, understanding their needs, and carefully coordinating the whole company's efforts to create lasting relationships based on customer value.

Author Comment | Sales promotion is the most short-term of the promotion mix tools. Whereas advertising or personal selling says "buy," sales promotions say "buy now."

Sales promotion

Short-term incentives to encourage the purchase or sale of a product or a service.

Sales Promotion (pp 481–488)

Personal selling and advertising often work closely with another promotion tool, sales promotion. **Sales promotion** consists of short-term incentives to encourage the purchase or sales of a product or service. Whereas advertising offers reasons to buy a product or service, sales promotion offers reasons to buy *now*.

Examples of sales promotions are found everywhere. A freestanding insert in the Sunday newspaper contains a coupon offering $1 off Pedigree GoodBites treats for your dog. ● A Bed Bath & Beyond ad in your favorite magazine offers 20 percent off on any single item. The end-of-the-aisle display in the local supermarket tempts impulse buyers with a wall of Coca-Cola cases—four 12-packs for $12. An executive buys a new HP laptop and gets a free memory upgrade. A hardware store chain receives a 10 percent discount on selected Stihl power lawn and garden tools if it agrees to advertise them in local newspapers. Sales promotion includes a wide variety of promotion tools designed to stimulate earlier or stronger market response.

● Sales promotions are found everywhere. For example, your favorite magazine is loaded with offers like this one that promote a strong and immediate response.

The Rapid Growth of Sales Promotion

Sales promotion tools are used by most organizations, including manufacturers, distributors, retailers, and not-for-profit institutions. They are targeted toward final buyers (*consumer promotions*), retailers and wholesalers (*trade promotions*), business customers (*business promotions*), and members of the sales force (*sales force promotions*). Today, in the average consumer packaged-goods company, sales promotion accounts for 77 percent of all marketing expenditures.[27]

Several factors have contributed to the rapid growth of sales promotion, particularly in consumer markets. First, inside the company, product managers face greater pressures to increase current sales, and they view promotion as an effective short-run sales tool. Second, externally, the company faces more competition, and competing brands are less differentiated. Increasingly, competitors are using sales promotion to help differentiate their offers. Third, advertising efficiency has declined because of rising costs, media clutter, and legal restraints. Finally, consumers have become more deal oriented. In the current economy, consumers are demanding lower prices and better deals. Sales promotions can help attract today's more thrift-oriented consumers.

The growing use of sales promotion has resulted in *promotion clutter*, similar to advertising clutter. A given promotion runs the risk of being lost in a sea of other promotions, weakening its ability to trigger an immediate purchase. Manufacturers are now searching for ways to rise above the clutter, such as offering larger coupon values, creating more dramatic point-of-purchase displays, or delivering promotions through new interactive media—such as the Internet or cell phones.

In developing a sales promotion program, a company must first set sales promotion objectives and then select the best tools for accomplishing these objectives.

Sales Promotion Objectives

Sales promotion objectives vary widely. Sellers may use *consumer promotions* to urge short-term customer buying or enhance customer brand involvement. Objectives for *trade promotions* include getting retailers to carry new items and more inventory, buy ahead, or promote the company's products and give them more shelf space. For the *sales force*, objectives include getting more sales force support for current or new products or getting salespeople to sign up new accounts.

Sales promotions are usually used together with advertising, personal selling, direct marketing, or other promotion mix tools. Consumer promotions must usually be advertised and can add excitement and pulling power to ads. Trade and sales force promotions support the firm's personal selling process.

When the economy sours and sales lag, it's tempting to offer deep promotional discounts to spur consumer spending. In general, however, rather than creating only short-term sales or temporary brand switching, sales promotions should help to reinforce the product's position and build long-term *customer relationships*. If properly designed, every sales promotion tool has the potential to build both short-term excitement and long-term consumer relationships. Marketers should avoid "quick fix," price-only promotions in favor of promotions that are designed to build brand equity. Examples include the various "frequency marketing programs" and loyalty cards that have mushroomed in recent years. Most hotels, supermarkets, and airlines offer frequent-guest/buyer/flyer programs that give rewards to regular customers to keep them coming back. All kinds of companies now offer rewards programs. Such promotional programs can build loyalty through added value rather than discounted prices.

For example, Starbucks suffered sales setbacks resulting from the recent economic downturn, coupled with the introduction of cheaper gourmet coffees by a host of fast-food competitors. Starbucks could have lowered its prices or offered promotional discounts. But deep discounts might have damaged the chain's long-term premium positioning. So instead, Starbucks dropped its prices only slightly and ran ads telling customers why its coffee was worth a higher price. With headlines such as "Beware of a cheaper cup of coffee. It comes with a price," the ads laid out what separates Starbucks from the competition, such as its practices of buying fair-trade beans and providing health care for employees who work more than 20 hours a week. ◉ At the same time, to build loyalty, Starbucks promoted its Starbucks Card Rewards program:[28]

◉ **Customer loyalty programs: Rather than offering promotional discounts that might damage its premium positioning, Starbucks ran ads telling customers why its coffee is worth the higher price. Then, to build loyalty, the company promoted the Starbucks Card Rewards program.**

In 1981, when American Airlines was struggling to differentiate itself in a newly deregulated industry, it invented the frequent flyer mile. Ten years later, American Express responded to its own competitive crisis by introducing what we now know as Membership Rewards. So it shouldn't come as any big surprise that Starbucks, facing its own troubled times, would also turn to a loyalty program, Starbucks Card Rewards. To fight off lower-priced competitors, such as Dunkin' Donuts and McDonald's, and keep its loyal customers, well, loyal, Starbucks unveiled a rewards card. Cardholders benefit from perks such as free in-store refills on coffee, paying with an iPhone, complementary in-store Wi-Fi for up to two hours per day, and a free cup of coffee with a purchase of a pound of coffee beans. Such perks increase customer value without big discounts or price reductions. "There is a need for Starbucks to win back customers," says a loyalty marketing consultancy. "The [loyalty] card is a vehicle for doing that."

Major Sales Promotion Tools

Many tools can be used to accomplish sales promotion objectives. Descriptions of the main consumer, trade, and business promotion tools follow.

Consumer Promotions

Consumer promotions

Sales promotion tools used to boost short-term customer buying and involvement or enhance long-term customer relationships.

Consumer promotions include a wide range of tools—from samples, coupons, refunds, premiums, and point-of-purchase displays to contests, sweepstakes, and event sponsorships.

Samples are offers of a trial amount of a product. Sampling is the most effective—but most expensive—way to introduce a new product or create new excitement for an existing one. Some samples are free; for others, the company charges a small amount to offset its cost. The sample might be sent by mail, handed out in a store or at a kiosk, attached to another product, or featured in an ad or an e-mail. Sometimes, samples are combined into sample packs, which can then be used to promote other products and services. Sampling can be a powerful promotional tool.

Coupons are certificates that give buyers a saving when they purchase specified products. Most consumers love coupons. U.S. package-goods companies distributed more than 367 billion coupons last year with an average face value of $1.44. Consumers redeemed more than 3.3 billion of them for a total savings of about $3.5 billion.[29] Coupons can promote early trial of a new brand or stimulate sales of a mature brand. However, as a result of coupon clutter, redemption rates have been declining in recent years. Thus, most major consumer-goods companies are issuing fewer coupons and targeting them more carefully.

Marketers are also cultivating new outlets for distributing coupons, such as supermarket shelf dispensers, electronic point-of-sale coupon printers, and online and mobile coupon programs. According to a recent study, digital coupons now outpace printed newspaper coupons by 10 to 1. Almost one-third of all U.S. coupon users are digital coupon users who get coupons only online or by phone via sites such as Coupons.com, Groupon, McCoupster, and Cellfire (see Real Marketing 16.2).

Cash refunds (or *rebates*) are like coupons except that the price reduction occurs after the purchase rather than at the retail outlet. The customer sends a "proof of purchase" to the manufacturer, which then refunds part of the purchase price by mail. For example, Toro ran a clever preseason promotion on some of its snowblower models, offering a rebate if the snowfall in the buyer's market area turned out to be below average. Competitors were not able to match this offer on such short notice, and the promotion was very successful.

Price packs (also called *cents-off deals*) offer consumers savings off the regular price of a product. The producer marks the reduced prices directly on the label or package. Price packs can be single packages sold at a reduced price (such as two for the price of one) or two related products banded together (such as a toothbrush and toothpaste). Price packs are very effective—even more so than coupons—in stimulating short-term sales.

Premiums are goods offered either free or at low cost as an incentive to buy a product, ranging from toys included with kids' products to phone cards and DVDs. A premium may come inside the package (in-pack), outside the package (on-pack), or through the mail. For example, over the years, McDonald's has offered a variety of premiums in its Happy Meals—from *Avatar* characters to *My Little Pony* and *How to Train Your Dragon* toy figures. Customers can visit www.happymeal.com and play games and watch commercials associated with the current Happy Meal sponsor.[30]

Advertising specialties, also called *promotional products*, are useful articles imprinted with an advertiser's name, logo, or message that are given as gifts to consumers. Typical items include T-shirts and other apparel, pens, coffee mugs, calendars, key rings, mouse pads, matches, tote bags, coolers, golf balls, and caps. U.S. marketers spent more than $18 billion on advertising specialties last year. Such items can be very effective. The "best of them stick around for months, subtly burning a brand name into a user's brain," notes a promotional products expert.[31]

Point-of-purchase (POP) *promotions* include displays and demonstrations that take place at the point of sale. Think of your last visit to the local Safeway, Costco, CVS, or Bed Bath & Beyond. Chances are good that you were tripping over aisle displays, promotional signs, "shelf talkers," or demonstrators offering free tastes of featured food products. Unfortunately, many retailers do not like to handle the hundreds of displays, signs, and posters they receive from manufacturers each year. Manufacturers have responded by offering better POP materials, offering to set them up, and tying them in with television, print, or online messages.

Contests, sweepstakes, and *games* give consumers the chance to win something, such as cash, trips, or goods, by luck or through extra effort. A *contest* calls for consumers to submit an entry—a jingle, guess, suggestion—to be judged by a panel that will select the best entries. A *sweepstakes* calls for consumers to submit their names for a drawing. A *game* presents consumers with something—bingo numbers, missing letters—every time they buy, which may or may not help them win a prize. Such promotions can create considerable brand attention and consumer involvement.[32]

For its 60th birthday, Dunkin' Donuts wanted to celebrate being the world's largest doughnut maker. ◉ At the heart of its "donut domination" campaign is a "Create Dunkin's Next Donut" annual contest that urges people to visit the contest Web site and design their own doughnuts. "Put on your apron and get creative," the campaign urges. At the site, entrants selected from a list of approved ingredients to create the new doughnut, give it a name, and write a 100-word essay about why they think their doughnut creation is the best. Online voting selected a dozen semifinalists, who then cooked up their creations at a bake-off in the company's test kitchens at Dunkin' Donuts University in Braintree, Massachusetts. Last year's grand winner received $12,000, and the winning doughnut—Monkey-see Monkey Donut—was added to the

Real Marketing 16.2

Mobile Coupons: Reaching Customers Where They Are—Now

As cell phones become appendages that many people can't live without, businesses are increasingly eyeing them as prime real estate for marketing messages. Whether it's to build a brand, boost business, or reward loyalty, more merchants are using mobile marketing to tap into the cell-phone's power of immediacy.

"It's cool," said Kristen Palestis at her local Jamba Juice recently after she opted in to receive a 20-percent-off coupon on her cell phone. "I'm spending less money and it was real easy," she said after she used the coupon to buy a smoothie. Palestis received the coupon within seconds of texting a special five-digit code from her cell phone.

Retailers' mobile marketing messages can include text messages with numeric "short codes" that customers dial to receive a promotion, bar-coded digital coupons, Web site links, and display advertisements. "We know the most effective way to reach the customer is to be where they are," says a marketer at Jamba Juice, a national chain that sells smoothies and other "better-for-you" beverages and foods. "For our customers this means both on the Internet and on their mobiles."

Jamba Juice and a growing host of other retailers want to get special offers quickly into the hands of the consumers who are most apt to use them. These mobile social users—as they're called—represent 11 percent of online adults in the United States, but their ranks are growing. They're more likely to respond to ads on their cell phones, buy mobile content and services, and access the mobile Web.

Mobile marketing can be very effective. For example, Fresh Encounter Community Markets, an Ohio grocery chain, uses mobile messages to help customers plan their meals. When Fresh Encounter sends out an urgent same-day offer, as in a chicken promotion, redemptions can exceed 30 percent.

Companies that embrace mobile marketing know they have to be careful not to abuse the access consumers have granted, so permission-based offers are becoming the standard. Trade groups, such as the Mobile Marketing Association in New York, have set guidelines for marketers that are designed to protect the consumer, including opt-in, opt-out, and message delivery frequency standards.

Coupons by phone offer an alluring opportunity. Worldwide, the number of mobile coupon users is forecast to triple by 2014 to more than 300 million people. In the United States alone last year, 45 million consumers used digital coupons, up almost 20 percent over the previous year. Of that group, almost one-third used *only* digital coupons, meaning that they didn't clip coupons from newspapers or magazines.

Still, mobile coupons aren't for everyone. Some consumers just don't want marketing messages delivered to their phones. So many digital coupon marketers include print and e-mail delivery options as well. Challenges aside, companies ranging from Sears and JCPenney to Wendy's and Chick-fil-A are testing the digital couponing waters. For example, Dunkin' Donuts recently sent out free iced coffee coupons to customers living near several Florida stores who'd already opted-in for promotional text messages. The digital promotion generated buzz and also let Dunkin' Donuts learn more about area customers' demographics and shopping psyche.

Over the past few years, a growing list of online coupon sites—such as Coupons.com, MyCoupster, Groupon, and Cellfire—have sprung up and allow consumers to find coupons online and download them to mobile devices, print them out at home, or transfer them to store loyalty cards for later redemption at stores. Consider Cellfire:

Cellfire (www.cellfire.com) distributes digital coupons to the cell phones of consumers nationwide who sign up for its free service. Cellfire's growing list of clients ranges from Domino's Pizza, T.G.I. Friday's, Sears, Kroger, and Hardee's to Kimberly-Clark, Verizon, and Enterprise Rent-A-Car. Cellfire sends an ever-changing assortment of digital coupons to users' cell phones. To use the coupons, users simply call up the stored coupon list, navigate to the coupon they want, press the "Use Now" button, and show the digital coupon to the store cashier.

Coupons distributed through Cellfire offer distinct advantages to both consumers and marketers. Consumers don't have to find and clip paper coupons or print out Web coupons and bring them along when they shop. They always have their cell phone coupons with them.

For marketers, mobile coupons allow more careful targeting and eliminate the costs of printing and distributing paper coupons. The redemption rates can be dazzling—as high as 20 percent—whereas the industry average paper response is less than 1 percent.

Thus, when properly used, mobile coupons can both cost less and be more immediate and effective. When it comes to digital couponing, marketers are increasingly echoing the sentiments of Jamba Juice customer Kristen Palestis. "It's cool."

Sources: Portions adapted from Arlene Satchel, "More Merchants Embrace Mobile Coupons," *McClatchy-Tribune News Service*, February 10, 2010; with information from Erik Sass, "Is Digital Coupons' Rise Print Inserts' Demise?" *MediaDailyNews*, February 17, 2010, accessed at http://tinyurl.com/25vh966. The extract is based on information from Alice Z. Cuneo, "Package-Goods Giants Roll Out Mobile Coupons," *Advertising Age*, March 10, 2008, p. 3; and www.cellfire.com, accessed October 2010.

Mobile coupons: Redemptions of a Fresh Encounter Community Markets urgent same-day offer like this one can exceed 30 percent.

● **Contests can create considerable consumer involvement: The most recent "Create Dunkin's Next Donut" contest generated 90,000 online creations.**

company's menu for a limited time. In all, contestants submitted more than 90,000 creations online. "We were absolutely amazed at the number of entries into our contest," says a Dunkin' Donuts marketing executive.

Finally, marketers can promote their brands through **event marketing** (or **event sponsorships**). They can create their own brand-marketing events or serve as sole or participating sponsors of events created by others. The events might include anything from mobile brand tours to festivals, reunions, marathons, concerts, or other sponsored gatherings. Event marketing is huge, and it may be the fastest-growing area of promotion, especially in tough economic times.

Event marketing can provide a less costly alternative to expensive TV commercials. When it comes to event marketing, sports are in a league of their own. Marketers spent more than $8.7 billion last year to associate their brands with sporting events. For example, Sprint is paying $700 million over 10 years to sponsor the NASCAR Sprint Cup Series. Kraft sponsors NASCAR drivers Tony Stewart and Ryan Newman, and its Oreo and Ritz brands are the official cookie and cracker of NASCAR. Kraft also recently teamed with the NCAA and CBS Sports to make several of its flag-

Event marketing (or event sponsorships)
Creating a brand-marketing event or serving as a sole or participating sponsor of events created by others.

ship brands—including Oreo, Planters, Ritz, and Wheat Thins—the NCAA's official cookie, nut, and cracker partners. The company promotes these sponsorships through in-store promotions and advertising at major NCAA events. According to Kraft's senior director of marketing alliances, the sponsorships give Kraft "an opportunity to connect our . . . snack brands with key audiences in a big way."[33]

Procter & Gamble creates numerous events for its major brands. Consider this example:

> For the past few years, P&G has sponsored a holiday event promotion for its Charmin brand in New York's Times Square, where it can be very difficult to find a public restroom. P&G sets up 20 free, sparkling clean Charmin-themed mini-bathrooms, each with its own sink and a bountiful supply of Charmin. The event is the ultimate in experiential marketing—touching people in places advertising wouldn't dare go. Over the past three holiday seasons, the event has been flush with success. More than one million people have gratefully used the facilities.[34]

Trade Promotions

Trade promotions
Sales promotion tools used to persuade resellers to carry a brand, give it shelf space, promote it in advertising, and push it to consumers.

Manufacturers direct more sales promotion dollars toward retailers and wholesalers (81 percent) than to final consumers (16 percent).[35] **Trade promotions** can persuade resellers to carry a brand, give it shelf space, promote it in advertising, and push it to consumers. Shelf space is so scarce these days that manufacturers often have to offer price-offs, allowances, buy-back guarantees, or free goods to retailers and wholesalers to get products on the shelf and, once there, to keep them on it.

Manufacturers use several trade promotion tools. Many of the tools used for consumer promotions—contests, premiums, displays—can also be used as trade promotions. Or the manufacturer may offer a straight *discount* off the list price on each case purchased during a stated period of time (also called a *price-off*, *off-invoice*, or *off-list*). Manufacturers also may offer an *allowance* (usually so much off per case) in return for the retailer's agreement to feature the manufacturer's products in some way. An advertising allowance compensates retailers for advertising the product. A display allowance compensates them for using special displays.

Manufacturers may offer *free goods*, which are extra cases of merchandise, to resellers who buy a certain quantity or who feature a certain flavor or size. They may offer *push money*—cash or gifts to dealers or their sales forces to "push" the manufacturer's goods. Manufacturers may give retailers free *specialty advertising items* that carry the company's name, such as pens, pencils, calendars, paperweights, matchbooks, memo pads, and yardsticks.

Business Promotions

Business promotions

Sales promotion tools used to generate business leads, stimulate purchases, reward customers, and motivate salespeople.

Companies spend billions of dollars each year on promotion to industrial customers. **Business promotions** are used to generate business leads, stimulate purchases, reward customers, and motivate salespeople. Business promotions include many of the same tools used for consumer or trade promotions. Here, we focus on two additional major business promotion tools: conventions and trade shows and sales contests.

Many companies and trade associations organize *conventions and trade shows* to promote their products. Firms selling to the industry show their products at the trade show. Vendors receive many benefits, such as opportunities to find new sales leads, contact customers, introduce new products, meet new customers, sell more to present customers, and educate customers with publications and audiovisual materials. Trade shows also help companies reach many prospects not reached through their sales forces.

Some trade shows are huge. ◉ For example, at this year's International Consumer Electronics Show, 3,000 exhibitors attracted some 120,000 professional visitors. Even more impressive, at the BAUMA mining and construction equipment trade show in Munich, Germany, more than 3,100 exhibitors from 53 countries presented their latest product innovations to more than 415,000 attendees from more than 200 countries. Total exhibition space equaled about 5.9 million square feet (more than 124 football fields).[36]

A *sales contest* is a contest for salespeople or dealers to motivate them to increase their sales performance over a given period. Sales contests motivate and recognize good company performers, who may receive trips, cash prizes, or other gifts. Some companies award points for performance, which the receiver can turn in for any of a variety of prizes. Sales contests work best when they are tied to measurable and achievable sales objectives (such as finding new accounts, reviving old accounts, or increasing account profitability).

◉ **Some trade shows are huge. At this year's International Consumer Electronics Show, 3,000 exhibitors attracted more than 112,000 professional visitors.**

Developing the Sales Promotion Program

Beyond selecting the types of promotions to use, marketers must make several other decisions in designing the full sales promotion program. First, they must determine the *size of the incentive*. A certain minimum incentive is necessary if the promotion is to succeed; a larger incentive will produce more sales response. The marketer also must set *conditions for participation*. Incentives might be offered to everyone or only to select groups.

Marketers must determine how to *promote and distribute the promotion* program itself. A $2-off coupon could be given out in a package, at the store, via the Internet, or in an advertisement. Each distribution method involves a different level of reach and cost. Increasingly, marketers are blending several media into a total campaign concept. The *length of the promotion* is also important. If the sales promotion period is too short, many prospects (who may not be buying during that time) will miss it. If the promotion runs too long, the deal will lose some of its "act now" force.

Evaluation is also very important. Many companies fail to evaluate their sales promotion programs, and others evaluate them only superficially. Yet marketers should work to measure the returns on their sales promotion investments, just as they should seek to assess the returns on other marketing activities. The most common evaluation method is to compare sales before, during, and after a promotion. Marketers should ask: Did the promotion attract new customers or more purchasing from current customers? Can we hold onto these new customers and purchases? Will the long-run customer relationship and sales gains from the promotion justify its costs?

Clearly, sales promotion plays an important role in the total promotion mix. To use it well, the marketer must define the sales promotion objectives, select the best tools, design the sales promotion program, implement the program, and evaluate the results. Moreover, sales promotion must be coordinated carefully with other promotion mix elements within the overall IMC program.

REVIEWING Objectives AND KEY Terms

This chapter is the third of four chapters covering the final marketing mix element—promotion. The previous two chapters dealt with overall integrated marketing communications and with advertising and public relations. This one investigated personal selling and sales promotion. Personal selling is the interpersonal arm of the communications mix. Sales promotion consists of short-term incentives to encourage the purchase or sale of a product or service.

Objective 1 Discuss the role of a company's salespeople in creating value for customers and building customer relationships. (pp 464–467)

Most companies use salespeople, and many companies assign them an important role in the marketing mix. For companies selling business products, the firm's sales force works directly with customers. Often, the sales force is the customer's only direct contact with the company and therefore may be viewed by customers as representing the company itself. In contrast, for consumer-product companies that sell through intermediaries, consumers usually do not meet salespeople or even know about them. The sales force works behind the scenes, dealing with wholesalers and retailers to obtain their support and helping them become more effective in selling the firm's products.

As an element of the promotion mix, the sales force is very effective in achieving certain marketing objectives and carrying out such activities as prospecting, communicating, selling and servicing, and information gathering. But with companies becoming more market oriented, a customer-focused sales force also works to produce both customer satisfaction and company profit. The sales force plays a key role in developing and managing profitable customer relationships.

Objective 2 Identify and explain the six major sales force management steps. (pp 468–477)

High sales force costs necessitate an effective sales management process consisting of six steps: designing sales force strategy and structure, recruiting and selecting, training, compensating, supervising, and evaluating salespeople and sales force performance.

In designing a sales force, sales management must address various issues, including what type of sales force structure will work

best (territorial, product, customer, or complex structure), how large the sales force should be, who will be involved in the selling effort, and how its various salespeople and sales-support people will work together (inside or outside sales forces and team selling).

To hold down the high costs of hiring the wrong people, salespeople must be recruited and selected carefully. In recruiting salespeople, a company may look to the job duties and the characteristics of its most successful salespeople to suggest the traits it wants in its salespeople. It must then look for applicants through recommendations of current salespeople, employment agencies, classified ads, the Internet, and college recruitment/placement centers. In the selection process, the procedure may vary from a single informal interview to lengthy testing and interviewing. After the selection process is complete, training programs familiarize new salespeople not only with the art of selling but also with the company's history, its products and policies, and the characteristics of its market and competitors.

The sales force compensation system helps to reward, motivate, and direct salespeople. In compensating salespeople, companies try to have an appealing plan, usually close to the going rate for the type of sales job and needed skills. In addition to compensation, all salespeople need supervision, and many need continuous encouragement because they must make many decisions and face many frustrations. Periodically, the company must evaluate their performance to help them do a better job. In evaluating salespeople, the company relies on getting regular information gathered through sales reports, personal observations, customers' letters and complaints, customer surveys, and conversations with other salespeople.

Objective 3 Discuss the personal selling process, distinguishing between transaction-oriented marketing and relationship marketing. (pp 478–481)

The art of selling involves a seven-step selling process: prospecting and qualifying, preapproach, approach, presentation and demonstration, handling objections, closing, and follow-up. These steps help marketers close a specific sale and, as such, are transaction oriented. However, a seller's dealings with customers should be guided by the larger concept of relationship marketing. The company's sales force should help to orchestrate a whole-company effort to develop profitable long-term relationships with key customers based on superior customer value and satisfaction.

Objective 4 **Explain how sales promotion campaigns are developed and implemented.**
(pp 481–488)

Sales promotion campaigns call for setting sales promotions objectives (in general, sales promotions should be *consumer relationship building*); selecting tools; and developing and implementing the sales promotion program by using *consumer promotion tools* (from coupons, refunds, premiums, and point-of-purchase promotions to contests, sweepstakes, and events), *trade promotion tools* (from discounts and allowances to free goods and push money), and *business promotion tools* (conventions, trade shows, and sales contests), as well as determining such things as the size of the incentive, the conditions for participation, how to promote and distribute the promotion package, and the length of the promotion. After this process is completed, the company must evaluate its sales promotion results.

KEY Terms

OBJECTIVE 1

Personal selling (p 464)
Salesperson (p 465)

OBJECTIVE 2

Sales force management (p 468)
Territorial sales force structure (p 468)
Product sales force structure (p 468)
Customer (or market) sales force structure (p 469)
Outside sales force (or field sales force) (p 470)

Inside sales force (p 470)
Team selling (p 471)
Sales 2.0 (p 475)
Sales quota (p 477)

OBJECTIVE 3

Selling process (p 478)
Prospecting (p 478)
Preapproach (p 478)
Approach (p 479)
Presentation (p 479)

Handling objections (p 480)
Closing (p 480)
Follow-up (p 480)

OBJECTIVE 4

Sales promotion (p 481)
Consumer promotions (p 483)
Event marketing (p 486)
Trade promotions (p 486)
Business promotions (p 487)

PEARSON mymarketinglab

- Check your understanding of the concepts and key terms using the mypearsonmarketinglab study plan for this chapter.
- Apply the concepts in a business context using the simulation entitled **Personal Selling**.

DISCUSSING & APPLYING THE Concepts

Discussing the Concepts

1. Discuss the role of personal selling in the promotion mix. In what situations is it more effective than advertising? (AACSB: Communication; Reflective Thinking)

2. Compare and contrast the three sales force structures outlined in the chapter. Which structure is most effective? (AACSB: Communication; Reflective Thinking)

3. What role does an inside sales force play in an organization? (AACSB: Communication)

4. Define *sales promotion* and discuss its objectives. (AACSB: Communication)

5. Name and describe the types of consumer promotions. (AACSB: Communication; Reflective Thinking)

6. Name and describe the types of trade sales promotions. (AACSB: Communication)

Applying the Concepts

1. Although many manufacturers maintain their own sales forces, many use the services of sales agents in the channel of distribution. Discuss the pros and cons of using sales agents compared to a company sales force. Who will best fulfill the channel functions for the manufacturer? (AACSB: Communication; Reflective Thinking)

2. Select a product or service and role-play a sales call—from the approach to the close—with another student. Have one member of the team act as the salesperson with the other member acting as the customer, raising at least three objections. Select another product or service and perform this exercise again with your roles reversed. (AACSB: Communication; Reflective Thinking)

3. Design a sales promotion campaign for your local animal shelter with the goal of increasing pet adoption. Use at least three types of consumer promotions and explain the decisions regarding this campaign. (AACSB: Communication; Reflective Thinking)

FOCUS ON Technology

Want to improve your business's operations? Hold a contest and get some of the best and brightest minds in the world working on it! That's what Netflix did—and it wasn't your everyday contest, either. Netflix, the video streaming and DVD rental company, held a three-year, $1 million contest with the goal of improving its movie-recommendation system by 10 percent. The company wanted to improve its system for predicting what customers might like based on their ratings of previous movies rented or viewed. The contest garnered more than 51,000 contestants from almost 200 countries. The contest attracted entries from scientists, researchers, and engineers, and the winning team consisted of one-time competitors who joined forces to submit the best solution within a few minutes of the contest's deadline. The sequel—Netflix Prize 2—

aimed to improve the movie-recommendation system for Netflix customers who do not regularly rate movies on Netflix, but this contest hit a legal roadblock and was discontinued.

1. Using Google, search for "Netflix Prize" to learn about this contest and the subsequent troubles Netflix experienced with Netflix Prize 2. Write a brief report on what you find and argue for or against cancellation of the second contest. (AACSB: Communication; Use of IT; Reflective Thinking)

2. What other contests or sweepstakes has Netflix sponsored? Discuss the rules of the promotion and winners, if the promotion is complete. (AACSB: Communication; Reflective Thinking)

FOCUS ON Ethics

Hank is a sales representative for a CRM software company and makes several cold calls each day prospecting for customers. He usually starts his call to a technology professional in a company by introducing himself and asking the person if he or she would take a few moments to participate in a survey on technology needs in companies. After a few questions, however, it becomes obvious that Hank is trying to sell software solutions to the potential customer.

1. Is Hank being ethical? Discuss other sales tactics that might be unethical. (AACSB: Communication; Ethical Reasoning; Reflective Thinking)

2. What traits and behaviors should an ethical salesperson possess? What role does the sales manager play in ethical selling behavior? (AACSB: Communication; Ethical Reasoning; Reflective Thinking)

MARKETING & THE Economy

Procter & Gamble

Historically, consumer goods companies fare well during hard economic times. Such items are relatively inexpensive to begin with, brand loyalty is strong, and no one wants to give up clean clothes and healthy teeth. But as the sluggish economy has lasted longer than anticipated, the rules are changing. Consumers remain more price sensitive, even on small purchases. For P&G, that means that even brands such as Tide and Crest are experiencing fallout. To keep volume up, P&G has cut prices on existing products *and* introduced cheaper items. Although this may protect sales volume, both tactics result in thinner margins and lower profits—as much as 18 percent lower. And the new cheaper-item strategy may

cause customers to trade down, eroding profits even more. P&G says it plans to raise prices in 2011. But the price cutting cycle may be hard to stop. Not only do consumers get used to lower prices, but retailers also get into the habit of awarding shelf space to manufacturers who provide lower wholesale prices. There will likely always be manufacturers willing to meet such retailer demands, adding pressure on P&G to continue offering its premium brands at cheaper prices.

1. What can a P&G sales rep do, apart from product and pricing strategies, to boost sales?

2. What should P&G do to boost profits in these and future economic times?

MARKETING BY THE Numbers

FireSpot Inc. is a manufacturer of drop-in household fireplaces sold primarily in the eastern United States. The company has its own sales force that does more than just sell products and services; it manages relationships with retail customers to enable them to better meet consumers' needs. FireSpot's sales reps visit customers several times per year—often for hours at a time. Thus, sales managers must ensure that they have enough salespeople to

adequately deliver value to customers. Refer to Appendix 2 to answer the following questions.

1. Determine the number of salespeople FireSpot needs if it has 1,000 retail customer accounts that need to be called on five times per year. Each sales call lasts approximately 2.5 hours, and each sales rep has approximately 1,250 hours per year to

devote to customers. (AACSB: Communication; Analytical Reasoning)

2. FireSpot wants to expand to the Midwest and western United States and intends to hire ten new sales representatives to secure distribution for its products. Each sales rep earns a salary of $50,000 plus commission. Each retailer generates an average $50,000 in revenue for FireSpot. If FireSpot's

contribution margin is 40 percent, what increase in sales will it need to break even on the increase in fixed costs to hire the new sales reps? How many new retail accounts must the company acquire to break even on this tactic? What average number of accounts must each new rep acquire? (AACSB: Communication; Analytical Reasoning)

VIDEO Case

Nestlé Waters

Who sells more bottled water than any other company? It isn't Coca-Cola with its Dasani line. It isn't PepsiCo with its Aquafina line. Surprisingly, it's Nestlé. With brands like Arrowhead, Poland Spring, Ice Mountain, and Nestlé Pure Life, Nestlé Waters easily outsells its top competitors.

Nestlé Waters hasn't achieved market leadership simply by advertising to consumers. In fact, it does very little advertising. Nestlé Waters understands that for a product like bottled water, success is all about shelf space. The Nestlé Waters video illustrates how the brand's managers developed a sales force strategy that focuses on

maximizing relationships with major retailers. Nestlé Waters has a unique approach to personal selling that has solidified its presence in the marketplace. After viewing the video featuring Nestlé Waters, answer the following questions about the company.

1. How is the sales force at Nestlé Waters structured?

2. Discuss Nestlé Waters' unique approach to personal selling. How does this affect the manner in which the company carries out each step of the selling process?

3. How has Nestlé Waters' unique approach enabled it to maintain customer relationships?

COMPANY Case

HP: Overhauling a Vast Corporate Sales Force

Imagine this scenario: You need a new digital camera. You're not sure which one to buy or even what features you need. So you visit your nearest electronics superstore to talk with a salesperson. You walk through the camera section but can't find anyone to help you. When you finally find a salesperson, he yawns and tells you that he's responsible for selling all the products in the store, so he doesn't really know all that much about cameras. Then he reads some information from the box of one of the models that you ask about, as if he is telling something that you can't figure out for yourself. He then suggests that you should talk to someone else. You finally find a camera-savvy salesperson. However, after answering a few questions, she disappears to handle some other task, handing you off to someone new. And the new salesperson seems to contradict what the first salesperson said, even quoting different prices on a couple of models you like.

That imaginary situation may actually have happened to you. If so, then you can understand what many business buyers face when attempting to buy from a large corporate supplier. This was the case with business customers of technology giant Hewlett-Packard before Mark Hurd took over as HP's CEO a few years ago. Prior to Hurd assuming command, HP's revenues and profits had flattened, and its stock price had plummeted. To find out why, Hurd first talked directly with 400 corporate customers. Mostly what he heard were gripes about HP's corporate sales force.

Customers complained that they had to deal with too many salespeople, and HP's confusing management layers made it hard to figure out whom to call. They had trouble tracking down HP

sales representatives. And once found, the reps often came across as apathetic, leaving the customer to take the initiative. HP reps were responsible for a broad range of complex products, so they sometimes lacked the needed depth of knowledge on any subset of them. Customers grumbled that they received varying price quotes from different sales reps, and it often took weeks for reps to respond to seemingly simple requests. In all, HP's corporate customers were frustrated, not a happy circumstance for a company that gets more than 70 percent of its revenues from businesses.

But customers weren't the only ones frustrated by HP's unwieldy and unresponsive sales force structure. HP was organized into three main product divisions: the Personal Systems Group (PSG), the Technology Solutions Group (TSG), and the Image and Printing Group (IPG). However, HP's corporate sales force was housed in a fourth division, the Customer Sales Group (CSG). All salespeople reported directly to the CSG and were responsible for selling products from all three product divisions. To make matters worse, the CSG was bloated and underperforming. According to one reporter, "of the 17,000 people working in HP's corporate sales, only around 10,000 sold directly to customers. The rest were support staff or in management." HP division executives were frustrated by the CSG structure. They complained that they had little or no direct control over the salespeople who sold their products. And multiple layers of management slowed sales force decision making and customer responsiveness.

Finally, salespeople themselves were frustrated by the structure. They weren't being given the time and support they needed to serve their customers well. Burdened with administrative tasks and bureaucratic red tape, they were spending less than one-third of their time with customers. And they had to work through multiple layers of bureaucracy to get price quotes and sample products for customers. "The customer focus was lacking," says an HP sales vice president. "Trying to navigate inside HP was difficult. It was unacceptable."

As Hurd peeled back the layers, it became apparent that HP's organizational problems went deeper than the sales force. The entire company had become so centralized, with so many layers of management, that it was unresponsive and out of touch with customers. Hurd had come to HP with a reputation for cost-cutting and ruthless efficiency. Prior to his new position, he spent 25 years at NCR, where he ultimately headed the company. Although it was a considerably smaller company than HP, Hurd had it running like a well-oiled machine. Nothing bothered him more than the discoveries he made about HP's inefficient structure.

Thus began what one observer called "one of Hurd's biggest management challenges: overhauling HP's vast corporate sales force." For starters, Hurd eliminated the CSG division, instead assigning salespeople directly to the three product divisions. He also did away with three layers of management and cut hundreds of unproductive sales workers. This move gave divisional marketing and sales executives direct control over a leaner, more efficient sales process, resulting in speedier sales decisions and quicker market response.

Hurd also took steps to reduce salesperson and customer frustrations. Eliminating the CSG meant that each salesperson was responsible for selling a smaller number of products and was able to develop expertise in a specific product area. Hurd urged sales managers to cut back on salesperson administrative requirements and improve sales support so that salespeople could spend more quality time with customers. As a result, salespeople now spend more than 40 percent of their time with customers, up from just 30 percent before. And HP salespeople are noticing big changes in the sales support they receive:

Salesman Richard Ditucci began noticing some of the changes late last year. At the time, Ditucci was trying to sell computer servers to Staples. As part of the process, Staples had asked him to provide a sample server for the company to evaluate. In the past, such requests typically took two to three weeks to fulfill because of HP's bureaucracy. This time, Ditucci got the server he needed within three days. The quick turnaround helped him win the contract, valued at several million dollars.

To ensure that important customers are carefully tended, HP assigned each salesperson three or fewer accounts. The top 2,000 accounts were assigned just one salesperson—"so they'll always know whom to contact." Customers are noticing differences in the attention that they get from HP salespeople:

James Farris, a senior technology executive at Staples, says HP has freed up his salesman to drop by Staples at least twice a month instead of about once a month before. The extra face time enabled the HP salesman to create more valuable interactions, such as arranging a workshop recently for Staples to explain HP's technology to the retailer's executives. As a result, Farris says he is planning to send more business HP's way. Similarly, Keith Morrow, chief information officer of convenience-store chain 7-Eleven, says his HP sales representative is now "here all the time" and has been more knowledgeable in pitching products tailored to his business. As a result, last October, 7-Eleven began deploying in its U.S. stores 10,000 HP pen pads—a mobile device that helps 7-Eleven workers on the sales floor.

A SALESMAN AT HEART

Once the new sales force started to take shape, Hurd began to focus on the role of the client in the sales process. The fact that HP refers to its business buyers as "partners" says a lot about its philosophy. "We heavily rely on [our partners]. We look at them as an extension of the HP sales force," Hurd said. To strengthen the relationship between HP and its partners, HP has partners participating in account planning and strategy development, an activity that teams the partners with HP sales reps and its top executive team.

Because Hurd wants the sales force to have strong relationships with its partners, he practices what he preaches. He spends up to 60 percent of the year on the road with various channel partners and *their* customers. Part of his time is funneled through HP's Executive Connections program, roundtable meetings that take place worldwide. But many of Hurd's interactions with HP partners take place outside that program as well. This demonstration of customer commitment at the highest level has created some fierce customer loyalty toward HP.

"I've probably met Mark Hurd more times in the last three or four years than all the CEOs of our other vendors combined," said Simon Palmer, president of California-based STA, one of HP's fastest growing solution provider partners. "There's no other CEO of any company that size that's even close. He's such a down-to-earth guy. He presents the HP story in very simple-to-understand terms." Mark Sarazin, executive vice president of AdvizeX Technologies, an HP partner for 25 years, sings similar praises. "He spent two-and-a-half hours with our customers. He talked in terms they could relate with, about his own relationship with HP IT. He knocked the ball out of the park with our 25-plus CIOs who were in the room. One said it was the best event he'd been to in his career."

In the four years since Hurd took over as CEO, HP's revenues, profits, and stock price have increased by 44 percent, 123 percent, and 50 percent, respectively. Still, with HP's markets as volatile as they've been, Hurd has taken HP into new equipment markets as well as gaining a substantial presence in service solutions. Each time the company enters a new market and faces new competitors, the HP sales force is at the center of the activity. In an effort to capture market share from Dell, Cisco, and Lexmark in the server market, HP opened a new sales operation in New Mexico called the SMB Exchange. It combines a call center, inside sales, and channel sales teams. Observers have noted that whereas HP's sales force was known for being more passive in the past, it is now much more aggressive—like Cisco's.

Hurd knows that because of HP's enormous size, it walks a fine line. In fact, he refers to the company's size as a "strange friend." On the one hand, it allows the company to offer a tremendous portfolio of products and services with support from a massive sales force. On the other hand, multiple organizational layers can make it more difficult to create solutions for partners and customers. Hurd is doing everything he can to make HP leaner and meaner so that it can operate with the nimbleness and energy of a much smaller company.

The changes that have taken place at HP have made most everyone more satisfied. And happier salespeople are more productive, resulting in happier customers. That should mean a bright future for HP. Hurd knows that there's still much more work to be done. But with a continued focus on the sales force and the sales process, HP is creating a structure that creates better value for its business customers. Now, if your local electronics superstore could only do the same for you. . . .

Questions for Discussion

1. Which of the sales force structures described in the text best describes HP's structure?

2. What are the positive and negative aspects of HP's new sales force structure?

3. Describe some of the differences in the selling process that an HP sales rep might face in selling to a long-term established customer versus a prospective customer.

4. Given that Hurd has an effective sales force, does he really need to meet with HP partners as much as he does?

5. Is it possible for HP to function like a smaller company? Why or why not?

Sources: Quotes and adapted examples from Pui-Wing Tam, "System Reboot: Hurd's Big Challenge at HP: Overhauling Corporate Sales," *Wall Street Journal*, April 3, 2006, p. A1; Christopher Hosford, "Rebooting Hewlett-Packard," *Sales & Marketing Management*, July–August 2006, pp. 32–35; Steven Burke, "HP vs. Cisco: It's Personal," *Computer Reseller News*, November 1, 2009, p. 8; Damon Poeter, "Never Enough," *Computer Reseller News*, April 1, 2010, p. 24.

17 Direct and Online Marketing Building Direct Customer Relationships

Chapter Preview

In the previous three chapters, you learned about communicating customer value through integrated marketing communication and about four elements of the marketing communications mix: advertising, publicity, personal selling, and sales promotion. In this chapter, we examine direct marketing and at its fastest-growing form, online marketing. Actually, direct marketing can be viewed as more than just a communications tool. In many ways it constitutes an overall marketing approach—a blend of communication and distribution channels all rolled into one. As you read this chapter, remember that although direct marketing is presented as a separate tool, it must be carefully integrated with the other elements of the promotion mix.

For starters, let's look at Amazon.com. In only about 15 years, Amazon has blossomed from an obscure dot-com upstart into one of the best-known names on the Internet. According to one estimate, 52 percent of people who shop on the Internet start at Amazon. How has it become such an incredibly successful direct and online marketer? It's all about creating direct, personal, and satisfying online customer experiences. Few direct marketers do that as well as Amazon.com.

Amazon.com: Creating Direct and Satisfying Online Customer Experiences

When you think of shopping on the Web, chances are good that you think first of Amazon. The online pioneer first opened its virtual doors in 1995, selling books out of founder Jeff Bezos's garage in suburban Seattle. Amazon still sells books—*lots and lots* of books. But it now sells just about everything else as well, from music, videos, electronics, tools, housewares, apparel, cell phones, and groceries to loose diamonds and Maine lobsters. Many analysts view Amazon.com as the model for direct marketing in the digital age.

From the start, Amazon has grown explosively. Its annual sales have rocketed from a modest $150 million in 1997 to more than $28 billion today. In the past five years, despite the shaky economy, its sales have more than tripled. Although it took the company eight years to turn its first full-year profit in 2003, Amazon's profits have since surged more than 25-fold. Last year alone, sales grew 28 percent; profits popped nearly 40 percent. This past holiday season, at one point, the online store's more than 88 million active customers worldwide were purchasing 110 items per second.

What has made Amazon one of the world's premier direct marketers? To its core, the company is relentlessly customer driven. "The thing that drives everything is creating genuine value for customers," says Bezos. The company starts with the customer and works backward. "Rather than ask what are we good at and what else can we do with that skill," says Bezos, "we ask, who are our customers? What do they need? And then [we] learn those skills."

For example, when Amazon saw an opportunity to serve its book-buying customers better through access to e-books and other e-content, it developed its own product for the first time ever—the innovative Kindle, a wireless reading device for downloading books, blogs, magazines, newspapers, and other matter. The Kindle took more than four years and a whole new set of skills to develop. But Amazon's start-with-the-customer thinking paid off handsomely. The Kindle is now the company's number one selling product, accounting for 2 percent of total sales; e-books account for another 1.5 percent of sales. The Kindle Store now offers more than 550,000 e-books, including new releases and bestsellers, at $11.99 or less. And various Kindle apps let customers enjoy e-books on devices ranging from BlackBerrys and Droids to iPhones and iPads.

Perhaps more important than *what* Amazon sells is *how* it sells. The company wants to do much more than just sell books or DVDs or digital cameras. It wants to deliver a special *experience* to every customer. "The customer experience really matters," says Bezos. "We've focused on just having a

> Amazon.com excels at creating direct, personalized customer relationships and satisfying online experiences. Many analysts view Amazon as *the* model for direct marketing in the digital age.

better store, where it's easier to shop, where you can learn more about the products, where you have a bigger selection, and where you have the lowest prices. You combine all of that stuff together and people say, 'Hey, these guys really get it.'"

And customers get it, too. Most Amazon.com regulars feel a surprisingly strong relationship with the company, especially given the almost complete lack of actual human interaction. Amazon obsesses over making each customer's experience uniquely personal. For example, the Web site greets customers with their very own personalized home pages, and its "Recommendations for You" feature offers personalized product recommendations. Amazon was first to use "collaborative filtering" technology, which sifts through each customer's past purchases and the purchasing patterns of customers with similar profiles to come up with personalized site content. "We want Amazon.com to be the right store for you as an individual," says Bezos. "If we have 88 million customers, we should have 88 million stores."

Visitors to Amazon.com receive a unique blend of benefits: huge selection, good value, and convenience. But it's the "discovery" factor that makes the buying experience really special. Once on the Web site, you're compelled to stay for a while—looking, learning, and discovering. Amazon.com has become a kind of online community in which customers can browse for products, research purchase alternatives, share opinions and reviews with other visitors, and chat online with authors and experts. In this way, Amazon does much more than just sell goods on the Web. It creates direct, personalized customer relationships and satisfying online experiences. Year after year, Amazon comes in number one or number two on the American Customer Satisfaction Index, regardless of industry.

To create even greater selection and discovery for customers, Amazon.com allows competing retailers—from mom-and-pop operations to Marks & Spencer—to offer their products on Amazon.com, creating a virtual shopping mall of incredible proportions. It even encourages customers to sell used items on the site. The broader selection attracts more customers, and everyone benefits. "We are becoming increasingly important in the lives of our customers," says an Amazon marketing executive.

Based on its powerful growth, many have speculated that Amazon.com will become the Walmart of the Web. In fact, some argue, it already is. As pointed out in Chapter 10, although Walmart's total sales of more than $400 billion dwarf Amazon's $28 billion in sales, Amazon's Internet sales are 12 times greater than Walmart's. So it's Walmart that's chasing Amazon on the Web. Put another way, Walmart wants to become the Amazon.com of the Web, not the other way around. However, despite its mammoth proportions, to catch Amazon online, Walmart

Online pioneer Amazon.com does much more than just sell goods on the Web. It creates direct, personalized customer relationships and online experiences. "The thing that drives everything is creating genuine value for customers," says founder and CEO Jeff Bezos, pictured above.

will have to match the superb Amazon customer experience, and that won't be easy.

Whatever the eventual outcome, Amazon has forever changed the face of online marketing. Most importantly, the innovative direct retailer has set a very high bar for the online customer experience. "The reason I'm so obsessed with . . . the customer experience is that I believe [our success] has been driven exclusively by that experience," says Bezos. "We are not great advertisers. So we start with customers, figure out what they want, and figure out how to get it to them."[1]

Many of the marketing and promotion tools that we've examined in previous chapters were developed in the context of *mass marketing*: targeting broad markets with standardized messages and offers distributed through intermediaries. Today, however, with the trend toward narrower targeting and the surge in digital technology, many companies are adopting *direct marketing*, either as a primary marketing approach, as in Amazon's case, or as a supplement to other approaches. In this section, we explore the exploding world of direct marketing.

Direct marketing
Connecting directly with carefully targeted segments or individual consumers, often on a one-to-one, interactive basis.

Direct marketing consists of connecting directly with carefully targeted consumers, often on a one-to-one, interactive basis. Using detailed databases, companies tailor their marketing offers and communications to the needs of narrowly defined segments or individual buyers.

Beyond brand and relationship building, direct marketers usually seek a direct, immediate, and measurable consumer response. For example, as we learned in the opening story, Amazon interacts directly with customers on its Web site to help them discover and buy almost anything and everything on the Internet. Similarly, GEICO interacts directly with customers—by telephone, through its Web site, or even on its Facebook, Twitter, or YouTube pages—to build individual brand relationships, give insurance quotes, sell policies, or service customer accounts.

Author Comment | For most companies, direct marketing is a supplemental channel or medium. But for many other companies today—such as Amazon, eBay, or GEICO—direct marketing is a complete way of doing business.

The New Direct Marketing Model (pp 496–497)

Early direct marketers—catalog companies, direct mailers, and telemarketers—gathered customer names and sold goods mainly by mail and telephone. Today, however, spurred by rapid advances in database technologies and new marketing media—especially the Internet—direct marketing has undergone a dramatic transformation.

In previous chapters, we discussed direct marketing as direct distribution—as marketing channels that contain no intermediaries. We also include direct marketing as one element of the promotion mix—as an approach for communicating directly with consumers. In actuality, direct marketing is both of these things and more.

Most companies still use direct marketing as a supplementary channel or medium. Thus, Lexus markets mostly through mass-media advertising and its high-quality dealer

Save money.

Get GEICO.

Get a free rate quote today.

GEICO
geico.com
1-800-947-AUTO

Obtenga una cotización gratis
en español en migeico.com.

● The new direct marketing model: Companies such as GEICO have built their entire approach to the marketplace around direct marketing: Just visit geico.com or call 1-800-947-AUTO.

network but also supplements these channels with direct marketing. Its direct marketing includes promotional DVDs and other materials mailed directly to prospective buyers and a Web page (www.lexus.com) that provides customers with information about various models, competitive comparisons, financing, and dealer locations. Similarly, most department stores, such as Sears or Macy's, sell the majority of their merchandise off their store shelves, but they also sell through direct mail and online catalogs.

However, for many companies today, direct marketing is more than just a supplementary channel or advertising medium—it constitutes a complete model for doing business. Firms employing this new *direct model* use it as the *only* approach. ● Companies such as Amazon, eBay, and GEICO have built their entire approach to the marketplace around direct marketing.

Growth and Benefits of Direct Marketing (pp 497–499)

Direct marketing has become the fastest-growing form of marketing. According to the Direct Marketing Association (DMA), U.S. companies spent $149.3 billion on direct marketing last year, 54 percent of the total dollars spent on advertising. In 2009, an investment of $1 in direct marketing advertising expenditures returned, on average, an estimated $11.65 in incremental revenue across all industries. Put another way, these expenditures generated an estimated $1.2 trillion in direct marketing sales, which is about 8 percent of total sales in the U.S. economy. The DMA estimates that direct marketing sales will grow 5.3 percent annually through 2013, compared with a projected 4.1 percent annual growth for total U.S. sales.[2]

Direct marketing continues to become more Web-oriented, and Internet marketing is claiming a fast-growing share of marketing spending and sales. For example, U.S. marketers spent an estimated $23 billion on online advertising last year, 16.2 percent of all media expenditures and more than twice as much as they spent only four years earlier. These efforts generated nearly $300 billion in online consumer spending.[3]

Benefits to Buyers

For buyers, direct marketing is convenient, easy, and private. Direct marketers never close their doors, and customers don't have to trek to and through stores to find products. From their homes, offices, or almost anywhere else, customers can shop the Web at any time of the day or night. Business buyers can learn about products and services without tying up time with salespeople.

Direct marketing gives buyers ready access to a wealth of products. Direct marketers can offer an almost unlimited selection to customers almost anywhere in the world. Just compare the huge selections offered by many Web merchants to the more meager assortments of their brick-and-mortar counterparts. For instance, log onto Bulbs.com, the Web's number one light bulb superstore, and you'll have instant access to every imaginable kind of light bulb or lamp—incandescent bulbs, fluorescent bulbs, projection bulbs, surgical bulbs, automotive bulbs—you name it. Similarly, direct retailer Zappos.com stocks more than 2.7 million shoes, handbags, clothing items, and accessories from more than 1,300 brands. No physical store could offer handy access to such vast selections.

Direct marketing channels also give buyers access to a wealth of comparative information about companies, products, and competitors. Good catalogs or Web sites often provide more information in more useful forms than even the most helpful retail salesperson can provide. For example, Amazon.com offers more information than most of us can digest, ranging from top-10 product lists, extensive product descriptions, and expert and user product descriptions to recommendations based on customers' previous purchases. Catalogs from Sears offer a treasure trove of information about the store's merchandise and services. In fact, you probably wouldn't think it strange to see a Sears' salesperson referring to a catalog in the store for more detailed product information while trying to advise a customer.

Finally, direct marketing is immediate and interactive: Buyers can interact with sellers by phone or on the seller's Web site to create exactly the configuration of information, products, or services they desire and then order them on the spot. Moreover, direct marketing gives consumers a greater measure of control. Consumers decide which catalogs they will browse and which Web sites they will visit.

Benefits to Sellers

For sellers, direct marketing is a powerful tool for building customer relationships. Today's direct marketers can target small groups or individual customers. Because of the one-to-one nature of direct marketing, companies can interact with customers by phone or online, learn more about their needs, and personalize products and services to specific customer tastes. In turn, customers can ask questions and volunteer feedback.

Direct marketing also offers sellers a low-cost, efficient, speedy alternative for reaching their markets. Direct marketing has grown rapidly in business-to-business marketing, partly in response to the ever-increasing costs of marketing through the sales force. When personal sales calls cost an average of $350 or more per contact, they should be made only when necessary and to high-potential customers and prospects.[4] Lower-cost-per-contact media—such as B-to-B telemarketing, direct mail, and company Web sites—often prove more cost effective.

Similarly, online direct marketing results in lower costs, improved efficiencies, and speedier handling of channel and logistics functions, such as order processing, inventory handling, and delivery. Direct marketers such as Amazon or Netflix also avoid the expense of maintaining a store and the related costs of rent, insurance, and utilities, passing the savings along to customers.

Direct marketing can also offer greater flexibility. It allows marketers to make ongoing adjustments to prices and programs or make immediate, timely, and personal announcements and offers. ● For example, in its signature folksy manner, Southwest Airlines uses techie direct marketing tools— including a widget (DING!) and a blog (Nuts about Southwest)—to inject itself directly into customers' everyday lives, at their invitation:[5]

DING! is an application that consumers can download to their computer desktops. Whenever exclusive discount fares are offered, the program emits the familiar in-flight seatbelt-light bell dinging sound. The deep discounts last only 6 to 12 hours and can be accessed only online by clicking on the application. Also available as a phone app, DING! lets Southwest Airlines bypass the reservations system and pass bargain fares directly to interested customers. Eventually, DING! may even allow Southwest Airlines to customize fare offers based on each customer's unique characteristics and travel preferences. In its first two years, the DING! application was downloaded by about two million consumers and generated more than $150 million in ticket sales.

Finally, direct marketing gives sellers access to buyers that they could not reach through other channels. Smaller firms can

● **Southwest Airlines uses techie direct marketing tools—including a widget and a blog—to inject itself directly into customers' everyday lives.**

mail catalogs to customers outside their local markets and post toll-free telephone numbers to handle orders and inquiries. Internet marketing is a truly global medium that allows buyers and sellers to click from one country to another in seconds. A Web user from Paris or Istanbul can access an online L.L.Bean catalog as easily as someone living in Freeport, Maine, the direct retailer's hometown. Even small marketers find that they have ready access to global markets.

> **Author Comment** | Direct marketing begins with a good customer database. A company is no better than what it knows about its customers.

Customer Databases and Direct Marketing (pp 499–500)

Effective direct marketing begins with a good customer database. A **customer database** is an organized collection of comprehensive data about individual customers or prospects. A good customer database can be a potent relationship-building tool. The database gives companies a 360-degree view of their customers and how they behave. A company is no better than what it knows about its customers.

Customer database
An organized collection of comprehensive data about individual customers or prospects, including geographic, demographic, psychographic, and behavioral data.

In consumer marketing, the customer database might contain a customer's geographic data (address, region), demographic data (e.g., age, income, family members, birthdays), psychographic data (activities, interests, and opinions), and buying behavior (buying preferences and the recency, frequency, and monetary value [RFM] of past purchases). In B-to-B marketing, the customer profile might contain the products and services the customer has bought, past volumes and prices, key contacts, competing suppliers, the status of current contracts, estimated future spending, and competitive strengths and weaknesses in selling and servicing the account.

Some of these databases are huge. For example, casino operator Harrah's Entertainment has built a customer database containing 700 terabytes worth of customer information, roughly 70 times the amount of the printed collection in the Library of Congress. It uses these data to create special customer experiences. Similarly, Walmart captures data on every item, for every customer, for every store, every day. Its database contains more than 2.5 petabytes of data—that's equivalent to two billion copies of *Moby Dick*. Google processes an astonishing 20 petabytes of data every day.[6]

Companies use their databases in many ways. They use databases to locate good potential customers and generate sales leads. They mine their databases to learn about customers in detail and then fine-tune their market offerings and communications to the special preferences and behaviors of target segments or individuals. In all, a company's database can be an important tool for building stronger long-term customer relationships.

For example, ◉ financial services provider USAA uses its database to find ways to serve the long-term needs of customers, regardless of immediate sales impact, creating an incredibly loyal customer base:

USAA provides financial services to U.S. military personnel and their families, largely through direct marketing via the telephone and the Internet. It maintains a customer database built from customer purchasing histories and information collected directly through customer surveys, transaction data, and browsing behavior at its Web site. USAA uses the database to tailor direct marketing offers to the specific needs of individual customers. For example, for customers looking toward retirement, it sends information on estate planning. If the family has college-age children, USAA sends those children information on how to manage their credit cards. If the family has younger children, it sends booklets on things such as financing a child's education.

◉ **Customer databases: Financial services provider USAA uses its extensive database to tailor its services to the specific needs of individual customers, creating incredible customer loyalty.**

One delighted reporter, a USAA customer, recounted how USAA even helped him teach his 16-year-old daughter to drive. Just before her birthday, but before she received her driver's license, USAA mailed a "package of materials, backed by research, to help me teach my daughter how to drive, help her practice, and help us find ways to agree on what constitutes safe driving later on, when she gets her license." What's more, marvels the reporter, "USAA didn't try to sell me a thing. My take-away: that USAA is investing in me for the long term, that it defines profitability not just by what it sells today." Through such skillful use of its database, USAA serves each customer uniquely, resulting in high customer loyalty. The $18 billion company retains 98 percent of its customers. For the past four years, *Bloomberg BusinessWeek* magazine has ranked USAA among its top two "Customer Service Champs," highlighting its legendary customer service. And last year, MSN Money ranked USAA number one on its Customer Service Hall of Fame list.[7]

Like many other marketing tools, database marketing requires a special investment. Companies must invest in computer hardware, database software, analytical programs, communication links, and skilled personnel. The database system must be user-friendly and available to various marketing groups, including those in product and brand management, new- product development, advertising and promotion, direct mail, telemarketing, Web marketing, field sales, order fulfillment, and customer service. However, a well-managed database usually results in sales and customer-relationship gains that more than cover these costs.

> **Author** | Direct marketing is rich in
> **Comment** | tools, from traditional old
> favorites such as direct mail, catalogs,
> and telemarketing to the Internet and
> other new digital approaches.

Forms of Direct Marketing (pp 500–508)

The major forms of direct marketing—as shown in ◉ **Figure 17.1**—include personal selling, direct-mail marketing, catalog marketing, telephone marketing, direct-response television (DRTV) marketing, kiosk marketing, new digital direct marketing technologies, and online marketing. We examined personal selling in depth in Chapter 16. Here, we examine the other forms of direct marketing.

◉ **FIGURE | 17.1**
Forms of Direct Marketing

What these many diverse marketing tools have in common is that they reach selected customers directly, and often interactively, building close, one-to-one relationships.

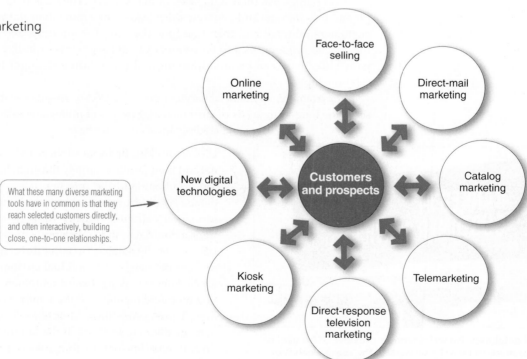

Direct-Mail Marketing

Direct-mail marketing

Direct marketing by sending an offer, announcement, reminder, or other item to a person at a particular physical or virtual address.

Direct-mail marketing involves sending an offer, announcement, reminder, or other item to a person at a particular physical or virtual address. Using highly selective mailing lists, direct marketers send out millions of mail pieces each year—letters, catalogs, ads, brochures, samples, DVDs, and other "salespeople with wings." Direct mail is by far the largest direct marketing medium. The DMA reports that U.S. marketers spent $44.4 billion on direct mail last year (including both catalog and noncatalog mail), which accounted for 32 percent of all direct marketing spending.[8]

Direct mail is well suited to direct, one-to-one communication. It permits high target-market selectivity, can be personalized, is flexible, and allows the easy measurement of results. Although direct mail costs more per thousand people reached than mass media such as television or magazines, the people it reaches are much better prospects. Direct mail has proved successful in promoting all kinds of products, from books, DVDs, insurance, gift items, gourmet foods, clothing, and other consumer goods to industrial products of all kinds. Charities also use direct mail heavily to raise billions of dollars each year.

Some analysts predict a decline in the use of traditional forms of direct mail in coming years, as marketers switch to newer digital forms, such as e-mail and mobile (cell phone) marketing. E-mail, mobile, and other newer forms of direct mail deliver direct messages at incredible speeds and lower costs compared to the post office's "snail mail" pace. We will discuss e-mail and mobile marketing in more detail later in the chapter.

However, even though the new digital forms of direct mail are gaining popularity, the traditional form is still by far the most widely used. Mail marketing offers some distinct advantages over digital forms. It provides something tangible for people to hold and keep. E-mail is easily screened or trashed. "[With] spam filters and spam folders to keep our messaging away from consumers' inboxes," says one direct marketer, "sometimes you have to lick a few stamps."[9]

Traditional direct mail can be used effectively in combination with other media, such as company Web sites. For example, some marketers now send out direct mail featuring personalized URLs (PURLs)—Web addresses such as www.intel.com/JohnDoe—that invite intrigued prospects to individualized Web sites. ● Consider this example:[10]

For companies that had their heads in the clouds when it came time to upgrade their computers, JDA Software Group decided it was time for some skywriting. It teamed with HP and Intel to send out personalized direct mail pieces that featured a man with his arms spread upward, experiencing an epiphany in the form of fluffy words forming above his head: "Bruce Schwartz, The Moment Has Arrived." In reality, the direct mail piece didn't come from out of the blue. Based on customers' upgrade schedules, JDA targeted carefully selected decision makers who were considering buying $500,000 to $1.5 million software suites. These high-value prospects received personalized direct mailings and e-mails with PURLs that led them to individualized Web pages. Once there, prospects learned all about how hardware from HP and Intel would support software from JDA. Customers revealed more information about themselves each time they visited the PURL, which allowed JDA, HP, and Intel to work with them throughout the buying process. The result? The $50,000 campaign yielded a 9.2 percent response rate and $13 million in sales. "Sending specific [information] to specific people does make a huge difference," says Intel's strategic relationships manager.

● **Combining direct mail with PURLs cost JDA only $50,000 but yielded a high response rate and $13 million in sales.**

Direct mail, whether traditional or digital, may be resented as "junk mail" or spam if sent to people who have no interest in it. For this reason, smart marketers are targeting their direct mail carefully so as not to waste their money and recipients' time. They are designing permission-based programs, sending mail, e-mail, and mobile ads only to those who want to receive them.

Catalog marketing
Direct marketing through print, video, or digital catalogs that are mailed to select customers, made available in stores, or presented online.

Catalog Marketing

Advances in technology, along with the move toward personalized, one-to-one marketing, have resulted in exciting changes in **catalog marketing**. *Catalog Age* magazine used to define a *catalog* as "a printed, bound piece of at least eight pages, selling multiple products, and offering a direct ordering mechanism." Today this definition is sadly out of date.

With the stampede to the Internet, more and more catalogs are going digital. A variety of Web-only catalogers have emerged, and most print catalogers have added Web-based catalogs to their marketing mixes. Web-based catalogs eliminate printing and mailing costs. And whereas space is limited in a print catalog, online catalogs can offer an almost unlimited amount of merchandise. Finally, online catalogs allow real-time merchandising; products and features can be added or removed as needed, and prices can be adjusted instantly to match demand.

However, despite the advantages of Web-based catalogs, as your overstuffed mailbox may suggest, printed catalogs are still thriving. U.S. direct marketers mailed out more than 17 billion catalogs past year—about 56 per American. Why aren't companies ditching their old-fashioned paper catalogs in this new digital era? For one thing, paper catalogs create emotional connections with customers that Web-based sales spaces simply can't. "Glossy catalog pages still entice buyers in a way that computer images don't," says an analyst. "Among retailers who rely mainly on direct sales, 62 percent say their biggest revenue generator is a paper catalog."[11]

In addition, printed catalogs are one of the best ways to drive online sales, making them more important than ever in the digital era. According to a recent study, 70 percent of Web purchases are driven by catalogs. Another study found that consumers who received catalogs from the retailer spent 28 percent more on that retailer's Web site than those who didn't get a catalog. ⬤ Thus, even dedicated online-only retailers, such as Zappos.com, have started producing catalogs with the hopes of driving online sales.[12]

⬤ Printed catalogs are one of the best ways to drive online sales. Thus, even dedicated online-only retailer Zappos.com now produces a printed catalog called Zappos Life.

Telephone Marketing

Telephone marketing
Using the telephone to sell directly to customers.

Telephone marketing involves using the telephone to sell directly to consumers and business customers. Last year, telephone marketing accounted for more than 19 percent of all direct marketing-driven sales. We're all familiar with telephone marketing directed toward consumers, but B-to-B marketers also use telephone marketing extensively, accounting for more than 55 percent of all telephone marketing sales.[13] Marketers use *outbound* telephone marketing to sell directly to consumers and businesses. ⬤ They use *inbound* toll-free numbers to receive orders from television and print ads, direct mail, or catalogs.

Properly designed and targeted telemarketing provides many benefits, including purchasing convenience and increased product and service information. However, the explosion in unsolicited outbound telephone marketing over the years has annoyed many consumers, who object to the almost daily "junk phone calls."

Careful...you might sprain a taste bud.

Don't wait another day! Call now to place an order or request a catalog. Also, go on line at **www.carolinacookie.com** to place an order, request a catalog or view our entire selection of products.

1-800-447-5797

CAROLINA COOKIE JUST BAKED COMPANY

⦿ **Marketers use inbound toll-free 800 numbers to receive orders from television and print ads, direct mail, or catalogs. Here, the Carolina Cookie Company urges, "Don't wait another day. Call now to place an order or request a catalog."**

Direct-response television (DRTV) marketing
Direct marketing via television, including direct-response television advertising (or infomercials) and home shopping channels.

In 2003, U.S. lawmakers responded with the National Do Not Call Registry, which is managed by the FTC. The legislation bans most telemarketing calls to registered phone numbers (although people can still receive calls from nonprofit groups, politicians, and companies with which they have recently done business). Consumers responded enthusiastically. To date, more than 191 million phone numbers have been registered at www .donotcall.gov or by calling 888-382-1222. Businesses that break do-not-call laws can be fined up to $11,000 per violation. As a result, reports an FTC spokesperson, the program "has been exceptionally successful."[14]

Do-not-call legislation has hurt the telemarketing industry—but not all that much. Two major forms of telemarketing—inbound consumer telemarketing and outbound B-to-B telemarketing—remain strong and growing. Telemarketing also remains a major fund-raising tool for nonprofit and political groups. In fact, do-not-call regulations appear to be helping most direct marketers more than it's hurting them. Rather than making unwanted calls, many of these marketers are developing "opt-in" calling systems, in which they provide useful information and offers to customers who have invited the company to contact them by phone or e-mail. The opt-in model provides better returns for marketers than the formerly invasive one.

Meanwhile, marketers who violate do-not-call regulations have themselves increasingly become the targets of crusading consumer activist groups, who return the favor by flooding the violating company's phone system with return calls and messages.[15]

Direct-Response Television Marketing

Direct-response television (DRTV) marketing takes one of two major forms. The first is *direct-response television advertising*. Direct marketers air television spots, often 60 or 120 seconds in length, which persuasively describe a product and give customers a toll-free number or a Web site for ordering. Television viewers also often encounter full 30-minute or longer advertising programs, called *infomercials*, for a single product.

Successful DRTV campaigns can ring up big sales. For example, Bowflex has grossed more than $1.3 billion in infomercial sales. And little-known infomercial maker Guthy-Renker has helped propel Proactiv Solution acne treatment into a power brand that pulls in $830 million in sales annually to five million active customers (compare that to only about $150 million in annual drugstore sales of acne products in the United States).[16]

DRTV ads are often associated with somewhat loud or questionable pitches for cleaners, stain removers, kitchen gadgets, and nifty ways to stay in shape without working very hard at it. For example, over the past few years yell-and-sell TV pitchmen like Anthony Sullivan (Swivel Sweeper, Awesome Auger) and Vince Offer (ShamWow, SlapChop) have racked up billions of dollars sales of "As Seen on TV" products. Brands like OxiClean, ShamWow, and the Snuggie (a blanket with sleeves) have become DRTV cult classics.[17]

In recent years, however, a number of large companies—from P&G, Disney, Revlon, Apple, and Kodak to Coca-Cola, Anheuser-Busch, and even the U.S. Navy—have begun using infomercials to sell their wares, refer customers to retailers, recruit members, or attract buyers to their Web sites. For example, Kodak uses direct-response TV to get its message out directly to customers.[18]

The phrase "As Seen on TV" might bring to mind Snuggie, ShamWow, and PedEgg but probably not a venerable American brand that invites you to share the most important moments of your life. Yet for Kodak, DRTV has become an effective and preferred way to reach consumers. ⦿ Short and long infomercials for Kodak printers and low-priced ink, which last two minutes and nearly a half-hour, respectively, focus on the value message Kodak uses in its traditional brand advertising. However, the ads also spell out specific savings, provide testimonials and examples, and even include the tone of a more typical infomercial. One short spot opens with the line "Are you sick of paying ridiculous prices for printer ink?" The Kodak infomercials have produced

● **Large, well-known companies—such as Kodak—are now using direct-response TV to get the message out directly to customers. The infomercials have produced outstanding results, especially in uncertain economic times.**

outstanding results, especially in uncertain economic times—printer and ink sales increased 20 percent after the first airing. "Everybody else in the market [was] down 20 percent, [we were] up 44 percent . . . on both equipment and ink," says Kodak's chief marketing officer. "With 30 printers on a shelf, . . . six different brands, . . . it's hard to stand out," adds an industry analyst. "Talking directly to consumers like that is not a bad idea."

Home shopping channels, another form of DRTV marketing, are television programs or entire channels dedicated to selling goods and services. Some home shopping channels, such as the Quality Value Channel (QVC), Home Shopping Network (HSN), and ShopNBC, broadcast 24 hours a day. Program hosts chat with viewers by phone and offer products ranging from jewelry, lamps, collectible dolls, and clothing to power tools and consumer electronics. Viewers call a toll-free number or go online to order goods. With widespread distribution on cable and satellite television, the top three shopping networks combined now reach 248 million homes worldwide.

Despite their lowbrow images, home shopping channels have evolved into highly sophisticated, very successful marketing operations. For example, HSN has upgraded both its products and its pitches, and its TV operations now work hand in hand with sophisticated Web marketing to build close customer relationships.

HSN now has hosts not so pushy and goods not so schlocky. It has replaced the cheesy baubles and generic electronics once featured with mainstream brands like Sephora cosmetics and 7 for All Mankind jeans. Celebrities and entrepreneurs, including Wolfgang Puck, Tori Spelling, and Joy Mangano, inventor of HSN's curiously popular Huggable Hangers, often get as much airtime as HSN's TV and Web hosts. They chitchat with shoppers who call in to rave about products more often than they push merchandise. HSN wants to be its female audience's "best girlfriend," says HSN's CEO: "It's not just a transactional relationship. It becomes an emotional relationship."[19]

Kiosk Marketing

As consumers become more and more comfortable with digital and touch-screen technologies, many companies are placing information and ordering machines—called *kiosks* (good old-fashion vending machines but so much more)—in stores, airports, hotels, college campuses, and other locations. Kiosks are everywhere these days, from self-service hotel and airline check-in devices to in-store ordering devices that let you order merchandise not carried in the store. "Flashy and futuristic, souped-up machines are popping up everywhere," says one analyst. "They have touch screens instead of buttons, facades that glow and pulse . . . [they] bridge the gap between old-fashioned stores and online shopping."[20]

In-store Kodak, Fuji, and HP kiosks let customers transfer pictures from memory sticks, mobile phones, and other digital storage devices, edit them, and make high-quality color prints. Kiosks in Hilton hotel lobbies let guests view their reservations, get room keys, view prearrival messages, check in and out, and even change seat assignments and print boarding passes for flights on any of 18 airlines. At JetBlue's Terminal Five at New York's John F. Kennedy airport, more than 200 screens throughout the terminal allow travelers to order food and beverages to be delivered to their respective gate. ● And Redbox operates more than 24,000 DVD rental kiosks in McDonald's, Walmart, Walgreens, and other retail outlets. Customers make their selections on a touch screen, then swipe a credit or debit card to rent

● **Kiosk marketing: Redbox operates more than 24,000 DVD rental kiosks in supermarkets and fast-food outlets nationwide.**

DVDs at $1 a day. Customers can even prereserve DVDs online to ensure that their trip to the kiosk will not be a wasted one. Thanks to an ailing economy, even as DVD sales slid last year, wallet-friendly Redbox's sales doubled.[21]

New Digital Direct Marketing Technologies

Today, thanks to a wealth of new digital technologies, direct marketers can reach and interact with consumers just about anywhere, at anytime, about almost anything. Here, we look into several exciting new digital direct marketing technologies: mobile phone marketing, podcasts and vodcasts, and interactive TV (iTV).

Mobile Phone Marketing

With more than 285 million Americans (91 percent) now subscribing to wireless services, many marketers view mobile phones as the next big direct marketing medium. Currently, 21 percent of cell phone subscribers use their phones to access the Web. Some 23 percent of cell phone users have seen advertising on their phones in the last 30 days, and about half of them responded to the ads.[22]

A recent study estimates that worldwide mobile ad spending will grow from the current $3.1 billion annually to $28.8 billion by 2013. About 30 percent of marketers of all kinds—from Pepsi and Nordstrom to nonprofits such as the ASPCA to the local bank or supermarket—are now integrating mobile phones into their direct marketing. Many marketers have created mobile Web sites, optimized for specific phones and mobile service providers. Others have created useful or entertaining apps to engage customers with their brands and help them shop (see Real Marketing 17.1). A mobile marketing effort might be as simple as inviting people to text a number, such as when the Red Cross asked for Haitian relief donations (Text "HAITI" to 90999 to donate $10). Or it might involve texting promotions to consumers—anything from ring-tone giveaways, mobile games and contests, and ad-supported content to retailer announcements of discounts, brand coupons, and gift suggestions.

For example, as noted in Chapter 16, Fresh Encounter Community Market, a Findlay, Ohio, grocery store, uses text messaging to help customers plan their meals:[23]

> Like many food retailers, Fresh Encounter Community Markets stores try to help shoppers resolve their daily dilemma: What to have for dinner? But this 32-store chain has come up with a unique strategy: texting suggestions to the cell phones of shoppers who have opted into its Text-N-Save mobile advertising program. Last month, for example, Fresh Encounter sent text messages at 2 p.m. on a Thursday and Friday offering a deal on a whole rotisserie chickens to shoppers who came in after 5 p.m. on those days. "We asked them, 'What's for dinner?' and if they don't know, then how about this for $3.99?" says Fresh Encounter executive Eric Anderson.
>
> Shoppers in the program receive new text offers each Sunday, ranging from free items (such as milk and soft drinks) to 5 percent off a total purchase of $50 or more. The offers can be customized by store. To cash in, shoppers present their cell phone to the cashier, showing a PLU (price look-up) number in the text message. The redemption rates are "unbelievable," Anderson says—20 percent or more. Takers inevitably buy complementary items as well. When Fresh Encounter sends out a more urgent same-day offer, as in the chicken promotion, redemptions can exceed 30 percent.

As with other forms of direct marketing, however, companies must use mobile marketing responsibly or risk angering already ad-weary consumers. "If you were interrupted every two minutes by advertising, not many people want that," says a mobile marketing

Real Marketing 17.1

Mobile Marketing:
Do Call Me, Please—or I *Will* Call You!

You're at the local Best Buy checking out portable GPS navigation systems. You've narrowed it down to a Garmin nüvi 1200 versus a less-expensive competing model, but you're not certain that Best Buy has the best prices. Also, you'd love to know how other consumers rate the two brands. No problem. Just pull out your iPhone and launch Amazon.com's iPhone app, which lets you browse the brands you're considering, read consumer reviews, and compare prices of portable GPS systems sold by Amazon.com and its retail partners. The application even lets you snap a photo of an item with your phone's camera, and Amazon.com employees will try to find similar items for sale on the Web site. If Amazon.com offers a better deal, you can make the purchase directly from the application.

Welcome to the new world of mobile marketing. Today's new smartphones are changing the way we live—including the way we shop. And as they change how we shop, they also change how marketers sell to us.

A growing number of consumers—especially younger ones—are using their cell phones as a "third screen" for text messaging, surfing the Web, watching downloaded videos and shows, and checking e-mail. According to one expert, "the cell phone . . . is morphing into a content device, a kind of digital Swiss army knife with the capability of filling its owner's every spare minute with games, music, live and on-demand TV, Web browsing, and, oh yes, advertising." Says the president of the Mobile Marketing Association, "It's only a matter of time before mobile is the 'first screen.'" According to another industry insider:

Mobile phones and wireless devices have quietly become the hottest new frontier for marketers, especially those targeting the coveted 18- to 34-year-old set. TV networks are prodding viewers to send text messages to vote for their favorite reality TV character. Wireless Web sites are lacing sports scores and news digests with banner ads for Lexus, Burger King, and Sheraton. A few companies are even customizing 10-second video ads for short, TV-style episodes that are edging their way onto

mobile phones. For advertisers, the young audience is just one selling point. Wireless gadgets are always-on, ever-present accessories. The fact that a phone is tethered to an individual means that ads can be targeted. And users can respond instantly to time-sensitive offers. The mobile phone is very personal, and it's always with you.

Marketers large and small are weaving mobile marketing into their direct marketing mixes. Walmart uses text message alerts to spread the news about sales; you can click on links within the messages to go to the retailer's mobile Web site and check on details. Unilever phones out mobile coupons for Ragu pasta sauce, Dove body wash, Breyers ice cream, and its other brands: Just hold up your cell phone at the checkout, and the cashier will scan the bar-

code off the screen. Tide's Stain Brain app helps customers find ways to remove stains. A Sit or Squat app directs people to nearby public restrooms—it opens with a splash page for Charmin bathroom tissue. Target's "Gift Globe" iPhone app gives you gift recommendations based on the age and gender of recipients—enter the data, shake your phone, and recommended gift items pop up on the screen. You can also use the app to link to Target's Web site to buy the item or find the nearest store.

Beyond helping you buy, other mobile marketing applications provide helpful services, useful information, and entertainment. USAA's iPhone banking app lets you check your balance, transfer funds, and even deposit a check via phone by taking a photo of the front and back of the check and hitting "send." Zipcar's app lets members find and reserve a Zipcar, honk the horn (so you can find it in a crowd), and even lock and unlock the doors—all from your iPhone. REI's The Snow and Ski Report app gives ski slope information for locations throughout the United States and Canada, such as snow depth, snow conditions, and the number of open lifts. The app also links you to "Shop REI," for times "when

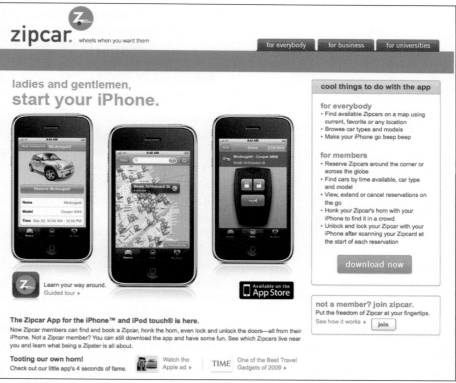

Mobile marketing: Zipcar's iPhone app lets members find and book a Zipcar, honk the horn (so you can find it in a crowd), and even lock and unlock the doors—all from your iPhone.

you decide you can't live without a new set of K2 skis or a two-man Hoo-Doo tent."

For entertainment, carmaker Audi offers the Audi A4 Driving Challenge game, which features a tiny A4 that maneuvers its way through different driving courses—to steer, you tilt your phone right or left. Audi claims that the app has been downloaded nearly three million times since it was introduced, resulting in 400,000 visitors to the Audi A4 iPhone Web site.

One of the most effective mobile marketing applications is Kraft's iFood Assistant, which provides easy-to-prepare recipes for food shoppers on the go. It supplies advice on how to prepare some 7,000 simple but satisfying meals—at three meals a day, that's almost 20 years worth of recipes. The iFood Assistant will even give you directions to local stores. Of course, most of the meals call for ingredients that just happened to be Kraft brands. The iFood Assistant app cost Kraft less than $100,000 to create but has engaged millions of shoppers, providing great marketing opportunities for Kraft and its brands.

Increasingly, consumers are using their phones as in-store shopping aids, and retailers are responding accordingly. For example, while strolling among the bookshelves at the local Barnes & Noble store, you can now snap a photo of any book cover that strikes your interest and use a Barnes & Noble app to learn more about it. The app uses image-recognition software to recognize the book and then almost instantly pulls up user reviews from Barnesandnoble.com to help shoppers decide whether to buy. "We've seen a huge uplift in reservations of books for purchase in physical stores, as well as buying, from the . . . app since we launched it," says the chain's vice president for digital devices.

Most consumers are initially skeptical about receiving mobile ad messages. Their first reaction is likely to be "Don't call me. I'll call you (yeah, right)." But they often change their minds if the ads deliver value in the form of useful brand and shopping information, entertaining content, or discounted prices and coupons for their favorite products and services. Most mobile marketing efforts target only consumers who voluntarily opt in or who download applications. In the increasingly cluttered mobile marketing space, customers just won't do that unless they see real value in it. The challenge for marketers: Develop useful and engaging mobile marketing applications that make customers say "*Do* call me, please. Or, I *will* call you."

Sources: Adapted extract, quotes, and other information from Richard Westlund, "Mobile on Fast Forward," *Brandweek*, March 15, 2010, pp. M1–M5; Joseph De Avila, "Please Hold, My Cell Phone Is Buying a Gift," *Wall Street Journal*, December 9, 2008, p. D1; Todd Wasserman, "I'm on the Phone!" *Adweek*, February 23, 2009, pp. 6–7; Alice Z. Cuneo, "Scramble for Content Drives Mobile," *Advertising Age*, October 24, 2005, p. S6; Jen Arnoff, "Wising Up to Smart Phones," *News & Observer* (Raleigh), April 22, 2009, p. 5B; Carol Angrisani, "Priced to Cell," *Supermarket News*, June 1, 2009, p. 28; Reena Jana, "Retailers Are Learning to Love Smartphones," *Businessweek*, October 26, 2009, p. 49; and www.usaa.com/inet/ent_utils/McStaticPages?key= deposit_at_ mobile_main, accessed November 2010.

expert. "The industry needs to work out smart and clever ways to engage people on mobiles." The key is to provide genuinely useful information and offers that will make consumers want to opt in or call in. One study found that 42 percent of cell phone users are open to mobile advertising if it's relevant.[24]

Podcasts and Vodcasts

Podcasting and vodcasting are on-the-go, on-demand technologies. The name *podcast* derives from Apple's now-everywhere iPod. With podcasting, consumers can download audio files (podcasts) or video files (vodcasts) via the Internet to a handheld device and then listen to or view them whenever and wherever they wish. These days, you can download podcasts or vodcasts on an exploding array of topics, everything from your favorite NPR show, a recent sitcom episode, or current sports features to the latest music video or Snickers commercial.

An estimated 25 percent of the U.S. population has listened to or viewed at least one podcast. A recent study predicts that the U.S. podcast audience will reach 38 million by 2013, up from six million in 2005.[25] As a result, this medium is drawing much attention from marketers. Many are now integrating podcasts and vodcasts into their direct marketing programs in the form of ad-supported podcasts, downloadable ads and informational features, and other promotions.

For example, ⦿ the Walt Disney World Resort offers weekly podcasts on a mix of topics, including behind-the-scenes tours, interviews, upcoming events, and news about new attractions. Nestlé Purina publishes "petcasts" on animal training and behavioral issues. It invites customers to "Take these shows on the road—from

⦿ **Podcasts: The Walt Disney World Resort offers weekly podcasts on topics ranging from behind-the-scenes tours to upcoming events and news about new attractions.**

serious discussions with veterinarians about pet health to wacky animal videos featuring dogs and cats, Purina has a podcast (or two) for you." And HP publishes vodcasts that highlight new business technologies as well as pertinent information for investors.[26]

Interactive TV (iTV)

Interactive TV (iTV) lets viewers interact with television programming and advertising using their remote controls. In the past, iTV has been slow to catch on. However, the technology now appears poised to take off as a direct marketing medium. Research shows that the level of viewer engagement with iTV is much higher than with 30-second spots. A recent poll indicated that 66 percent of viewers would be "very interested" in interacting with commercials that piqued their interest. And broadcasting systems such as DIRECTV, EchoStar, and Time Warner are now offering iTV capabilities.[27]

Interactive TV gives marketers an opportunity to reach targeted audiences in an interactive, more involving way. For example, HSN has launched a "Shop by Remote" iTV service that allows viewers to instantly purchase any item on HSN with their remotes. Viewers who are registered with HSN can complete a purchase in less than 30 seconds.[28]

New York area cable provider Cablevision offers an iTV service by which advertisers can run interactive 30-second spots.[29]

During the ads, a bar at the bottom of the screen lets viewers use their remotes to choose additional content and offers, such as on-demand free product samples, brand channels, or video showcases. For example, a Gillette ad offered to send free samples of its body wash product, Benjamin Moore offered coupons for paint color samples, and Century 21 offered $10 gift cards. Advertisers such as Mattel Barbie and the U.S. Navy invited viewers to select their branded Cablevision channels for optional information and entertainment. So far, response rates for the interactive content have been impressive. For example, in an early test last year, the Disney Travel Channel allowed subscribers to browse information about Disney theme parks and then request a call from an agent. The booking rate for people requesting a call was 25 percent. More broadly, iTV ads slated to run for two weeks apiece had to be shortened, on average, by a week because marketers ran out of materials. For instance, Gillette pulled its on-demand samples offer a week early after maxing out the promotion at 30,000 samples.

Mobile phone marketing, podcasts and vodcasts, and iTV offer exciting direct marketing opportunities. But marketers must be careful to use these new direct marketing approaches wisely. As with other direct marketing forms, marketers who use them risk backlash from consumers who may resent such marketing as an invasion of their privacy. Marketers must target their direct marketing offers carefully, bringing real value to customers rather than making unwanted intrusions into their lives.

Author Comment | Online direct marketing is growing at a blistering pace. By one estimate, the Internet now influences a staggering 50 percent of total retail sales.

Online Marketing (pp 508–513)

As noted earlier, **online marketing** is the fastest-growing form of direct marketing. Widespread use of the Internet is having a dramatic impact on both buyers and the marketers who serve them. In this section, we examine how marketing strategy and practice are changing to take advantage of today's Internet technologies.

Marketing and the Internet

Online marketing
Efforts to market products and services and build customer relationships over the Internet.

Internet
A vast public web of computer networks that connects users of all types around the world to each other and an amazingly large information repository.

Much of the world's business today is carried out over digital networks that connect people and companies. The **Internet**, a vast public web of computer networks, connects users of all types all around the world to each other and an amazingly large information repository. The Internet has fundamentally changed customers' notions of convenience, speed, price, product information, and service. As a result, it has given marketers a whole new way to create value for customers and build relationships with them.

Internet usage and impact continues to grow steadily. Last year, 74 percent of the U.S. population had access to the Internet. The average U.S. Internet user spends some 60 hours a month surfing the Web. Worldwide, more than 1.8 billion people now have Internet access.[30] Moreover, a recent survey found that the Internet has surpassed TV as the medium perceived as most essential in people's lives. When presented with a choice of removing the Internet or television from their lives, 49 percent of respondents chose to drop television, whereas 48 percent chose the Internet. "When we first asked . . . in 2001, the spread was 72 percent for eliminating Internet and 26 percent for eliminating television," says a researcher. "The shift over these nine years has been steady and profound."[31]

All kinds of companies now market online. **Click-only companies** operate on the Internet only. They include a wide array of firms, from *e-tailers* such as Amazon.com and Expedia.com that sell products and services directly to final buyers via the Internet to *search engines and portals* (such as Yahoo!, Google, and MSN), *transaction sites* (eBay, Craigslist), and *content sites* (the *New York Times* on the Web, ESPN.com, and *Encyclopædia Britannica*). Many click-only dot-coms are now prospering in today's online marketplace.

The success of the dot-coms has caused existing *brick-and-mortar* manufacturers and retailers to reexamine how they serve their markets. Now, almost all of these traditional companies have created their own online sales and communications channels, becoming **click-and-mortar companies**. It's hard to find a company today that doesn't have a substantial Web presence.

In fact, many click-and-mortar companies are now having more online success than their click-only competitors. A recent ranking of the world's 10 largest online retail sites contained only one click-only retailer (Amazon.com, which was ranked number one). All the others were multichannel retailers.[32] For example, number two on the list is Staples, the $24 billion office supply retailer. ● Staples operates more than 2,240 superstores worldwide. But you might be surprised to learn that more than half of Staples' North American sales and profits come from its online and direct marketing operations. In fact, whereas Staples' brick-and-mortar store sales in North America have been flat or declining over the past two years, online and direct sales have soared 46 percent.[33]

Selling on the Web lets Staples build deeper, more personalized relationships with customers large and small. A large customer, such as GE or P&G, can create lists of approved office products at discount prices and then let company departments or even individuals do their own online purchasing. This reduces ordering costs, cuts through the red tape, and speeds up the ordering process for customers. At the same time, it encourages companies to use Staples as a sole source for office supplies. Even the smallest companies find 24-hour-a-day online ordering easier and more efficient. In addition, Staples' Web operations complement store sales. The Staples.com site builds store traffic by helping customers find a local store and check stock and prices. In return, the local store promotes the Web site through in-store kiosks. If customers don't find what they need on the shelves, they can quickly order it via the kiosk. Thus, Staples backs its "that was easy" positioning by offering a full range of contact points and delivery modes—online, catalogs, phone or fax, and in the store. No click-only or brick-only seller can match that kind of call, click, or visit convenience and support.

Online Marketing Domains

The four major online marketing domains are shown in ● **Figure 17.2**. They include business-to-consumer (B-to-C), business-to-business (B-to-B), consumer-to-consumer (C-to-C), and consumer-to-business (C-to-B).

Business-to-Consumer

The popular press has paid the most attention to **business-to-consumer (B-to-C) online marketing**—businesses selling goods and services online to final consumers. Today's consumers can buy almost anything online—from clothing, kitchen gadgets, and airline tickets to computers and cars. Even following the recent recession, online consumer buying continues to grow at a healthy double-digit rate. More than half of all U.S. households now regularly shop online. Current U.S. online retail sales of an estimated $279 billion are expected

---

Click-only companies
The so-called dot-coms, which operate online only and have no brick-and-mortar market presence.

Click-and-mortar companies
Traditional brick-and-mortar companies that have added online marketing to their operations.

● Click-and-mortar marketing: Staples backs its "that was easy" positioning by offering a full range of contact points and delivery modes.

Business-to-consumer (B-to-C) online marketing
Businesses selling goods and services online to final consumers.

● **FIGURE | 17.2**
Online Marketing Domains

	Targeted to consumers	Targeted to businesses
Initiated by business	B-to-C (business-to-consumer)	B-to-B (business-to-business)
Initiated by consumer	C-to-C (consumer-to-consumer)	C-to-B (consumer-to-business)

Online marketing can be classified by who initiates it and to whom it is targeted. As consumers, we're most familiar with B-to-C and C-to-C, but B-to-B is also flourishing.

to grow at better than 11 percent a year over the next five years, compared with a growth rate of 2.5 percent in total retail sales.[34]

Perhaps even more important, the Internet now influences an estimated 42 percent of total retail sales—sales transacted online plus those carried out offline but encouraged by online research. Some 97 percent of Web-goers now use the Internet to research products before making purchases. By one estimate, the Internet influences a staggering 50 percent of total retail sales.[35] Thus, smart marketers are employing integrated multichannel strategies that use the Web to drive sales to other marketing channels.

Internet buyers differ from traditional offline consumers in their approaches to buying and their responses to marketing. In the Internet exchange process, customers initiate and control the contact. Traditional marketing targets a somewhat passive audience. In contrast, online marketing targets people who actively select which Web sites they will visit and what marketing information they will receive about which products and under what conditions. Thus, online marketing requires new marketing approaches.

People now go online to order a wide range of goods—clothing from Gap or L.L.Bean, books or electronics or just about anything else from Amazon.com, major appliances from Sears, home mortgages from Quicken Loans, or even a will or divorce from LegalZoom. Where else but the Web could you find a place that specializes in anything and everything bacon?[36]

Americans have a guilty relationship with food, and perhaps no food is more guilt-inducing than bacon—forbidden by religions, disdained by dietitians and doctors. Loving bacon is like shoving a middle finger in the face of all that is healthy and holy. There is something comfortingly unambiguous about a thick slab of bacon. It's bad for you. It tastes fantastic. Any questions?

As Dan Philips says, "Bacon is the ultimate expression of freedom." Philips is the founder of the Grateful Palate, a company whose products have probably done more for the bacon chic movement than anything else. ● At the Grateful Palate, bacon enthusiasts can find everything bacon. It offers a bacon of the month club—Iron Chef Bobby Flay is a member—that includes artisnal bacon from farms across North America cured in a variety of delicious ways—from applewood smoked to hickory smoked with cinnamon sugar. The Grateful Palate also sells bacon-related gifts for people who can't get enough bacon in their day, such as bacon soap, bacon Christmas tree ornaments, bacon toilet paper, bacon air freshener, and even BLT candles—a set of bacon, lettuce, and tomato votives. Says one fan, "You can light them individually, maybe just tomato and lettuce if your vegetarian friends are visiting."

● **B-to-C Web sites: People now go online to buy just about anything. Where else but the Web could you find a place that specializes in anything and everything bacon?**

Business-to-Business

Although the popular press has given the most attention to B-to-C Web sites, **business-to-business (B-to-B) online marketing** is also flourishing. B-to-B marketers use Web sites, e-mail, online product catalogs, online trading networks, and other online resources to reach

Business-to-business (B-to-B) online marketing
Businesses using online marketing to reach new business customers, serve current customers more effectively, and obtain buying efficiencies and better prices.

new business customers, serve current customers more effectively, and obtain buying efficiencies and better prices.

Most major B-to-B marketers now offer product information, customer purchasing, and customer-support services online. For example, corporate buyers can visit networking equipment and software maker Cisco Systems' Web site (www.cisco.com), select detailed descriptions of Cisco's products and service solutions, request sales and service information, attend events and training seminars, view videos on a wide range of topics, have live chats with Cisco staff, and place orders. Some major companies conduct almost all of their business on the Web. For example, Cisco Systems takes more than 80 percent of its orders over the Internet.

Beyond simply selling their products and services online, companies can use the Internet to build stronger relationships with important business customers. For example, Dell has created customized Web sites for more than 100,000 business and institutional customers worldwide. These individualized Premier.Dell.com sites help business customers more efficiently manage all phases of their Dell computer buying and ownership. Each customer's Premier.Dell.com Web site includes a customized online computer store, purchasing and asset management reports and tools, system-specific technical information, links to useful information throughout Dell's extensive Web site, and more. The site makes all the information a customer needs to do business with Dell available in one place, 24/7.[37]

Consumer-to-Consumer

Consumer-to-consumer (C-to-C) online marketing
Online exchanges of goods and information between final consumers.

Much **consumer-to-consumer (C-to-C) online marketing** and communication occurs on the Web between interested parties over a wide range of products and subjects. In some cases, the Internet provides an excellent means by which consumers can buy or exchange goods or information directly with one another. For example, eBay, Overstock.com Auctions, and other auction sites offer popular market spaces for displaying and selling almost anything, from art and antiques, coins and stamps, and jewelry to computers and consumer electronics.

eBay's C-to-C online trading community of more than 90 million active users worldwide (that's more than the total populations of Britain, Egypt, or Turkey) transacted some $60 billion in trades last year. At any given time, the company's Web site lists more than 113 million items up for auction in more than 50,000 categories. Such C-to-C sites give people access to much larger audiences than the local flea market or newspaper classifieds (which, by the way, have also gone online at Web sites such as Craigslist.com and eBay Classifieds). Interestingly, based on its huge success in the C-to-C market, eBay has now attracted more than 500,000 B-to-C sellers, ranging from small businesses peddling their regular wares to large businesses liquidating excess inventory at auction.[38]

Blogs
Online journals where people post their thoughts, usually on a narrowly defined topic.

In other cases, C-to-C involves interchanges of information through Internet forums that appeal to specific special-interest groups. Such activities may be organized for commercial or noncommercial purposes. Web logs, or **blogs**, are online journals where people post their thoughts, usually on a narrowly defined topic. Blogs can be about anything, from politics or baseball to haiku, car repair, or the latest television series. Since 2002, Twitter accounts aside, more than 133 million blogs have been "keyed" in 81 different languages. Currently, 77 percent of online consumers actively read them. Such numbers give blogs—especially those with large and devoted followings—substantial influence.[39]

Many marketers are now tapping into the blogosphere as a medium for reaching carefully targeted consumers. For example, some companies have set up their own blogs. Sports footwear maker Vans has created several blogs—from "Off the Wall" to "Vans Girls"—at which customers can read up on Van's-related news and views about fashion, art, sports, and music. ● Similarly, at Walmart's Check Out blog (www.checkoutblog.com), with the company's blessing, Walmart buyers and

● **Many companies create their own blogs, such as Walmart's Check Out blog, on which Walmart buyers and merchandise managers like Alex Cook above speak candidly, even critically, about the products the chain carries.**

merchandise managers speak candidly, even critically, about the products the chain carries. Says one analyst, the employee-fed blog "has become a forum for [everything from] unfurnished rants about gadgets [and] raves about new video games [to] advice on selecting environmentally sustainable food." The blog also provides a glimpse into the personal lives of the posters. According to Walmart, Check Out helps buyers obtain quick feedback on merchandise from consumers, and it shows a softer side of the giant company.[40]

Companies can also advertise on existing blogs or influence content there. For example, they might encourage "sponsored conversations" by influential bloggers:[41]

As part of its "Living in High Definition" push, Panasonic wanted to build buzz about its brand at the recent Consumer Electronics Show (CES) in Las Vegas. But rather than relying on the usual tech journalists attending the show, Panasonic recruited five influential bloggers—including popular Internet figures Chris Brogan and Steve Garfield—to travel to the CES at its expense. It footed the bill for their travel and passes to the event while also loaning them digital video and still cameras. In return, the bloggers agreed to share their impressions of the show, including Panasonic product previews, with their own powerful distribution networks, in the form of blog posts, Twitter updates, and YouTube videos. The catch: Panasonic had no say on what their guests posted. To maintain credibility, Panasonic kept its distance, and the bloggers fully disclosed the brand's sponsorship. Still, even though Panasonic didn't dictate content—and didn't want to—the "sponsored conversations" allowed the brand to tap into the groundswell of Internet buzz. "When you give [bloggers] equipment and they love it, just like any other consumer they'll evangelize it," says a Panasonic spokesperson. "We're not looking for them to hit message points and in effect shill." Panasonic just wants to be a catalyst for conversations about its brand.

As a marketing tool, blogs offer some advantages. They can offer a fresh, original, personal, and cheap way to enter into consumer Web conversations. However, the blogosphere is cluttered and difficult to control. Blogs remain largely a C-to-C medium. Although companies can sometimes leverage blogs to engage in meaningful customer relationships, consumers remain largely in control.

Whether or not they actively participate in the blogosphere, companies should show up, monitor, and listen to them. For example, Starbucks sponsors its own blog (www.MyStarbucksIdea.com) but also closely follows consumer dialogue on the 30 or more other third-party online sites devoted to the brand. It then uses the customer insights it gains from all these proprietary and third party blogs to adjust its marketing programs.[42]

In all, C-to-C means that online buyers don't just consume product information—increasingly, they create it. As a result, "word of Web" is joining "word of mouth" as an important buying influence.

Consumer to Business

Consumer-to-business (C-to-B) online marketing
Online exchanges in which consumers search out sellers, learn about their offers, and initiate purchases, sometimes even driving transaction terms.

The final online marketing domain is **consumer-to-business (C-to-B) online marketing**. Thanks to the Internet, today's consumers are finding it easier to communicate with companies. Most companies now invite prospects and customers to send in suggestions and questions via company Web sites. Beyond this, rather than waiting for an invitation, consumers can search out sellers on the Web, learn about their offers, initiate purchases, and give feedback. Using the Web, consumers can even drive transactions with businesses, rather than the other way around. For example, using Priceline.com, would-be buyers can bid for airline tickets, hotel rooms, rental cars, cruises, and vacation packages, leaving the sellers to decide whether to accept their offers.

Consumers can also use Web sites such as GetSatisfaction.com, Complaints.com, and PlanetFeedback.com to ask questions, offer suggestions, lodge complaints, or deliver compliments to companies. ◉ GetSatisfaction.com provides "people-powered customer service" by creating a user-driven customer service community. The site provides forums where customers discuss problems they're having with the products and services of 35,000 companies—from Microsoft and P&G to Google and Zappos.com—whether the company participates or not. GetSatisfaction.com also provides tools by which companies

● **C-to-B marketing: GetSatisfaction.com provides "people-powered customer service"** by creating a user-driven customer service community where customers discuss product and service problems.

can adopt GetSatisfaction.com as an official customer service resource.[43]

Setting Up an Online Marketing Presence

In one way or another, most companies have now moved online. Companies conduct online marketing in any of the four ways shown in ● **Figure 17.3**: creating a Web site, placing ads and promotions online, setting up or participating in online social networks, or using e-mail.

Creating a Web Site

For most companies, the first step in conducting online marketing is to create a Web site. However, beyond simply creating a Web site, marketers must design an attractive site and find ways to get consumers to visit the site, stay around, and come back often.

Web sites vary greatly in purpose and content. The most basic type is a **corporate** (or **brand**) **Web site**. These sites are designed to build customer goodwill, collect customer feedback, and supplement other sales channels rather than sell the company's products directly. They typically offer a rich variety of information and other features in an effort to answer customer questions, build closer customer relationships, and generate excitement about the company or brand.

Corporate (or brand) Web site
A Web site designed to build customer goodwill, collect customer feedback, and supplement other sales channels rather than sell the company's products directly.

For example, you can't buy anything at P&G's Old Spice brand site, but you can learn about the different Old Spice products, watch recent ads, enter the latest contest, and post comments on the Old Spice blog. ● Similarly, GE's corporate Web site serves as a global public face for the huge company. It presents a massive amount of product, service, and company information to a diverse audience of customers, investors, journalists, and employees. It's both a B-to-B site and a portal for consumers, whether it's a U.S. consumer researching a microwave, an Indonesian business buyer checking into eco-friendly locomotives, or a German investor looking for shareholder information.

Marketing Web site
A Web site that engages consumers in interactions that will move them closer to a direct purchase or other marketing outcome.

Other companies create a **marketing Web site**. These sites engage consumers in an interaction that will move them closer to a direct purchase or other marketing outcome. For example, MINI USA operates a marketing Web site at www.miniusa.com. Once a potential customer clicks in, the carmaker wastes no time trying to turn the inquiry into a sale and then into a long-term relationship. The site offers a garage full of useful information and interactive selling features, including detailed and fun descriptions of current MINI models, tools for designing your very own MINI, information on dealer locations and services, and even tools for tracking your new MINI from factory to delivery.

Creating a Web site is one thing; getting people to *visit* the site is another. To attract visitors, companies aggressively promote their Web sites in offline print and broadcast advertising and through ads and links on other sites. But today's Web users are quick to abandon

● **FIGURE | 17.3**
Setting Up for Online Marketing

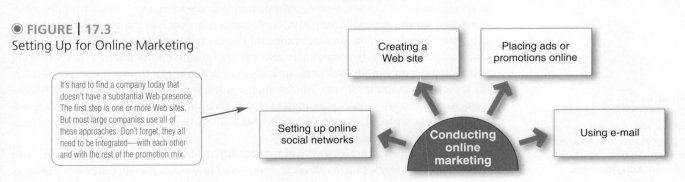

It's hard to find a company today that doesn't have a substantial Web presence. The first step is one or more Web sites. But most large companies use all of these approaches. Don't forget, they all need to be integrated—with each other and with the rest of the promotion mix.

Creating a Web site

Placing ads or promotions online

Setting up online social networks

Using e-mail

Conducting online marketing

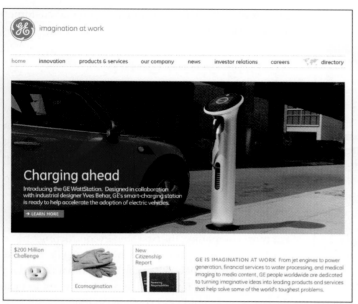

● **Corporate Web sites: You can't buy anything at GE's corporate site. Instead, it serves as a public face for the huge company, presenting a massive amount of information to a diverse global audience.**

Online advertising
Advertising that appears while consumers are browsing the Web, including display ads, search-related ads, online classifieds, and other forms.

Viral marketing
The Internet version of word-of-mouth marketing: Web sites, videos, e-mail messages, or other marketing events that are so infectious that customers will want to pass them along to friends.

any Web site that doesn't measure up. The key is to create enough value and excitement to get consumers who come to the site to stick around and come back again. At the very least, a Web site should be easy to use, professional looking, and physically attractive. Ultimately, however, Web sites must also be *useful*. When it comes to Web browsing and shopping, most people prefer substance over style and function over flash. Thus, effective Web sites contain deep and useful information, interactive tools that help buyers find and evaluate products of interest, links to other related sites, changing promotional offers, and entertaining features that lend relevant excitement.

Placing Ads and Promotions Online

As consumers spend more and more time on the Internet, companies are shifting more of their marketing dollars to **online advertising** to build their brands or attract visitors to their Web sites. Online advertising has become a major medium. Total U.S. Internet advertising spending reached an estimated $24.6 billion last year and is expected to top $34 billion by 2014, making it the second largest medium behind only TV but ahead of newspapers and magazines.[44] Here, we discuss forms of online advertising and promotion and their future.

The major forms of online advertising include search-related ads, display ads, and online classifieds. Online display ads might appear anywhere on an Internet user's screen and are often related to the information being viewed. For instance, while browsing vacation packages on Travelocity.com, you might encounter a display ad offering a free upgrade on a rental car from Enterprise Rent-A-Car. Or while visiting the Yahoo! Finance site, a flashing E*TRADE ad might promise a free BlackBerry smartphone when you open a new account. Internet display ads have come a long way in recent years in terms of attracting and holding consumer attention. New *rich media* ads now incorporate animation, video, sound, and interactivity.

The largest form of online advertising is *search-related ads* (or *contextual advertising*), which accounts for more than 48 percent of all online advertising spending.[45] In search advertising, text-based ads and links appear alongside search engine results on sites such as Google and Yahoo!. For example, search Google for "LCD TVs." At the top and side of the resulting search list, you'll see inconspicuous ads for 10 or more advertisers, ranging from Samsung and Dell to Best Buy, Sears, Amazon.com, Walmart.com, and Nextag.com. Nearly all of Google's $23.6 billion in revenues come from ad sales. Search is an always-on kind of medium. And in today's tight economy, the results are easily measured.

A search advertiser buys search terms from the search site and pays only if consumers click through to its site. For instance, type "Coke" or "Coca-Cola" or even just "soft drinks" or "rewards" into your Google or Yahoo! search engine and almost without fail "My Coke Rewards" comes up as one of the top options. This is no coincidence. Coca-Cola supports its popular online loyalty program largely through search buys. The soft drink giant started first with traditional TV and print advertising but quickly learned that search was the most effective way to bring consumers to www.mycokerewards.com Web site to register. Now, any of dozens of purchased search terms will return MyCokeRewards.com at or near the top of the search list.[46]

Other forms of online promotions include content sponsorships and viral advertising. Using *content sponsorships*, companies gain name exposure on the Internet by sponsoring special content on various Web sites, such as news or financial information or special interest topics. For example, Toyota Tundra sponsors truck-related pages on HowStuffWorks .com. And Marriott sponsors a "Summer to the Rescue!" microsite at Travelocity.com. Sponsorships are best placed in carefully targeted sites where they can offer relevant information or service to the audience.

Finally, online marketers use **viral marketing**, the Internet version of word-of-mouth marketing. Viral marketing involves creating a Web site, video, e-mail, cell phone message, advertisement, or other marketing event that is so infectious that customers will want to pass it along to their friends. Because customers pass the message or promotion along to others, viral marketing can be very inexpensive. And when the information comes from a friend, the recipient is much more likely to view or read it.

Liverpool Street Station

11:00 am

15th January 2009

⊙ Viral marketing: A well-concocted viral campaign can gain vast exposure. T-Mobile's "Life's for Sharing" flash mob viral video "Dance" had more than 21 million views on YouTube.

Sometimes a well-made regular ad can go viral with little help from the company. For example, the clever "Gimme back the Filet-O-Fish" ad from McDonald's, featuring a mechanized singing fish mounted on a wall, grabbed 780,000 YouTube views and a five-star rating in little more than three months. It also inspired a rash of consumer-generated spots posted on YouTube featuring people singing the song while ordering. However, leaving viral efforts to chance rarely works. "It's one of those things you never really know until it's out there," says a McDonald's marketer.[47]

Although marketers usually have little control over where their viral messages end up, ⊙ a well-concocted viral campaign can gain vast exposure. Consider T-Mobile's "Life's for Sharing" flash mob viral video "Dance." The nearly three-minute video features a seemingly "spontaneous" outburst of dancing among hundreds of passengers at London's crowded Liverpool Street railway station. It took months of logistical planning but landed more than 21 million views on YouTube. T-Mobile credits the video for a 29 percent jump in sales in the United Kingdom.[48]

Creating or Participating in Online Social Networks

Online social networks

Online social communities—blogs, social networking Web sites, or even virtual worlds—where people socialize or exchange information and opinions.

As we discussed in Chapters 1 and 5, the popularity of the Internet has resulted in a rash of **online social networks** or *Web communities*. Countless independent and commercial Web sites have arisen that give consumers online places to congregate, socialize, and exchange views and information. These days, it seems, almost everyone is buddying up on Facebook, checking in with Twitter, tuning into the day's hottest videos at YouTube, or checking out photos on Flickr. And, of course, wherever consumers congregate, marketers will surely follow. More and more marketers are now riding the huge social networking wave.

Marketers can engage in online communities in two ways: They can participate in existing Web communities or they can set up their own. Joining existing networks seems the easiest. Thus, many major brands—from Dunkin' Donuts and Harley-Davidson to Volkswagen and Victoria's Secret—have created YouTube channels. GM and other companies have posted visual content on Flickr. Coca-Cola's Facebook page has 5.4 million fans.

Some of the major social networks are huge. The largest social network—Facebook—by itself commands 70 percent of all social network traffic. Forty-seven percent of the online population visits Facebook every day. That rivals the 55 percent who watch any TV channel and trounces the percentage listening to radio (37 percent) and reading newspapers (22 percent) daily. In only a few years, Facebook has signed up more than 400 million members. That's 30 percent greater than the entire U.S. population. And Facebook is adding new members at a rate of five million every week. The massive online network aims to reach one billion members by 2012.[49]

Although large online social networks such as Facebook, YouTube, and Twitter have grabbed most of the headlines, a new breed of more focused niche networks has emerged. These more focused networks cater to the needs of smaller communities of like-minded people, making them ideal vehicles for marketers who want to target special interest groups (see Real Marketing 17.2).

But participating successfully in existing online social networks presents challenges. First, most companies are still experimenting with how to use them effectively, and results

Real Marketing 17.2

Online Social Networks:
Targeting Niches of Like-Minded People

Marketers who think bigger is better may want to reconsider, at least when it comes to online social networks. Although giant networks such as Facebook and Twitter get all the attention these days, social networks focused on topics as remote as knitting or bird watching can present marketers with strong targeting opportunities:

When jet-setters began flocking to an exclusive social-networking Web site reserved for the rich, they got the attention of an online community's most valuable ally: advertisers. The invitation-only site, ASmallWorld.net, has 300,000 select members who have become a magnet for companies that make luxury goods and are trying to reach people who can afford them. The site's biggest advertisers include Burberry, Cartier, and Land Rover. Cognac maker Remy Martin last month threw a tasting party for the site's elite members, at which its top-shelf, $1,800-a-bottle liquor flowed freely.

Thousands of social-networking sites have popped up to cater to specific interests, backgrounds, professions, and age groups. Nightclub frequenters can converge at DontStayIn .com. Wine connoisseurs have formed Snooth .com, and people going through divorce can commiserate at Divorce360.com.

More and more, marketers are taking a chance on smaller sites that could be more relevant to their products. AT&T, for example, recently promoted one of its global cell phones on WAYN.com (short for "Where are you now?"), a social network for international travelers. Although AT&T advertises on the bigger sites like Facebook to reach a large audience quickly, the wireless carrier is also turning to niche networks, "where your ads are more meaningful—those are the real gems," says a social networking expert.

There's at least one social network for just about every interest or hobby. Yub.com and Kaboodle.com are for shopaholics, Fuzzster .com is for pet lovers, moms advise and commiserate at CafeMom.com, Jango.com lets music fans find others with similar tastes, and

PassportStamp.com is one of several sites for avid travelers. Some cater to the obscure. Passions Network is an "online dating niche social network" with 600,000 members and 135 groups for specific interests, including Star Trek fans, truckers, atheists, and people who are shy. The most popular group is a dating site for the overweight. Membership on niche networking sites varies greatly, ranging from a few hundred to a few million. LinkExpats.com, which provides an online haven for U.S. expatriates, has about 200 members. On Ravelry.com, 870,000 registered knitters, crocheters, designers, spinners, and dyers share information about yarn, patterns, methods, and tools.

According to Pew Research Center, 73 percent of teens, 72 percent of young adults, and 40 percent of adults over 30 have an account on at least one social network. A running tally of emerging social networks, now beyond 7,000 by one estimate, suggests an explosive market. That's both a golden opportunity and a colossal headache for brands trying to nail

down the best new network for their campaigns.

Although the niche sites have many fewer members than huge sites such as Facebook, they contain dedicated communities of like-minded people. As on the bigger networks, members can build personalized pages and use them to share information, photos, and news with friends. That makes the niche sites ideal vehicles for marketers who want to target special interest groups.

The niche sites often provide a better marketing message environment. Members of niche social networks share common interests and experiences, so they tend to spend more time on the site and contribute more. On bigger sites, members tend to be less involved and therefore are less attractive to advertisers. Also, notes an online consultant, "the bigger sites have become so cluttered and overrun with advertisers that members are used to tuning stuff out, even personalized ads. . . . But on networking sites that have a self-selecting demographic, people tend to trust the content, including ads."

Not all niche networks welcome marketers. Sermo.com—a social-networking site at which some 112,000 licensed physicians consult with colleagues specializing in areas ranging from dermatology to psychiatry—allows no marketing. However, for a fee, companies can gain access to Sermo.com data and mem-

Thousands of social-networking sites have popped up to cater to specific interests, backgrounds, professions, and age groups. For example, on Ravelry.com, 870,000 registered knitters and crocheters share information about yarn, patterns, methods, and tools.

ber discussions. "They can monitor online discussions, with the doctors' names omitted, or see a tally of topics being discussed at the site to determine what's rising or falling in popularity," notes a health-care industry analyst.

The more focused audiences offered by niche networks are increasingly popular with brands because "relevance," says the consultant, "trumps size." But how brands execute social-networking campaigns is as important as where they do it. Marketers must be careful not to become too commercial or too intrusive. Keeping sites hip and unencumbered by advertising is a balancing act for both brands and social networks. The best approach is not to *market* to network members but *interact* with them on topics of mutual interest. Says one online marketer, "The real way of getting into social media is you don't advertise, you participate in the community."

Sources: Portions adapted from Betsey Cummings, "Why Marketers Love Small Social Networks," *Brandweek*, April 27, 2008, accessed at www.brandweek.com; with adapted extracts, quotes, and other information from Kim Hart, "Online Networking Goes Small, and Sponsors Follow," *Washington Post*, December 29, 2007, p. D1; Brian Morrissey, "Social Media Use Becomes Pervasive," *Adweek*, April 15, 2010, accessed at www.adweek.com; Amanda Lenhardt and others, "Social Media and Young Adults," Pew Research Center, February 3, 2010, www.pewinternet.org/Reports/2010/Social-Media-and-Young-Adults.aspx; and www.sermo.com, accessed October 2010.

are hard to measure. Second, such online networks are largely user controlled. The company's goal is to make the brand a part of consumers' conversations and their lives. However, marketers can't simply muscle their way into consumers' online interactions—they need to earn the right to be there. "You're talking about conversations between groups of friends," says one analyst. "And in those conversations a brand has no right to be there, unless the conversation is already about that brand." Rather than intruding, marketers must learn to become a valued part of the online experience.[50]

To avoid the mysteries and challenges of building a presence on existing online social networks, many companies are now launching their own targeted Web communities. For example, scrapbooking and crafting tools and supplies maker Fiskars created Fiskateers, an exclusive online network of crafters. More than creating sales, the Fiskateers community creates a relationship between the brand and important customers. Similarly, on Nike's Nike Plus Web site, more than 500,000 runners upload, track, and compare their performances. More than half visit the site at least four times a week, and Nike plans eventually to have 15 percent or more of the world's 100 million runners actively participating in the Nike Plus online community.

Using E-Mail

E-mail is an important and growing online marketing tool. A recent study by the DMA found that 79 percent of all direct marketing campaigns employ e-mail. U.S. companies now spend about $600 million a year on e-mail marketing, and spending will reach an estimated $2 billion by 2014.[51]

When used properly, e-mail can be the ultimate direct marketing medium. Most blue-chip marketers use it regularly and with great success. E-mail lets these marketers send highly targeted, tightly personalized, relationship-building messages. For example, the National Hockey League (NHL) sends hypertargeted e-newsletters to fans based on their team affiliations and locations. It sends 62 versions of the e-newsletter weekly—two for each of the 30 teams tailored to fans in both the United States and Canada, and two generic league e-newsletters for the two countries. Another NHL e-mail campaign promoting the start of single-game ticket sales had 930 versions.[52]

Spam

Unsolicited, unwanted commercial e-mail messages.

But there's a dark side to the growing use of e-mail marketing. ⬤ The explosion of **spam**—unsolicited, unwanted commercial e-mail messages that clog up our e-mailboxes—has produced consumer irritation and frustration. According to one research company, spam now accounts for almost 90 percent of all e-mail sent.[53] E-mail marketers walk a fine line between adding value for consumers and being intrusive.

To address these concerns, most legitimate marketers now practice *permission-based e-mail marketing*, sending e-mail pitches only to customers who "opt in." Many companies use configurable e-mail systems that let customers choose what they want to get. Amazon.com targets opt-in customers with a limited number of helpful "we thought you'd like to know" messages based on their expressed preferences and previous purchases. Few customers object

 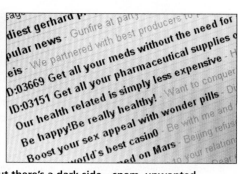

● **E-mail can be an effective marketing tool. But there's a dark side—spam, unwanted commercial e-mail that clogs up our inboxes and causes frustration.**

and many actually welcome such promotional messages. Similarly, Stub-Hub redesigned its e-mail system to make certain that its e-mails go only to consumers who actually *want* to receive them:

> As a start-up almost a decade ago, online ticket merchant Stub-Hub ran "batch-and-blast" e-mail campaigns focused on building awareness. For years, sheer volume far outweighed e-mail relevancy. But StubHub has now learned the value of carefully targeted, relevant e-mail messages. It now lets customers opt in for e-mail at registration, during purchases, and at sign-up modules throughout the StubHub site. Using opt-in customer data, StubHub targets designated consumer segments with ticket and event information closely aligned with their interests. Incorporating customer data produced immediate and stunning results. E-mail click-through rates quickly jumped 30 percent, and the company saw a 79 percent year-over-year increase in ticket sales despite having sent fewer e-mails. "The results speak for themselves," says a StubHub marketer. "These [new targeted campaigns] are driving 2,500 percent more revenue per e-mail than [our] average marketing campaigns."[54]

Given its targeting effectiveness and low costs, e-mail can be an outstanding marketing investment. According to the DMA, e-mail marketing produces the greatest return on investment of all direct-marketing media.[55]

In all, online marketing continues to offer both great promise and many challenges for the future. Its most ardent apostles still envision a time when the Internet and online marketing will replace magazines, newspapers, and even stores as sources for information and buying. Most marketers, however, hold a more realistic view. To be sure, online marketing has become a successful business model for some companies—Internet firms such as Amazon.com and Google and direct marketing companies such as GEICO. However, for most companies, online marketing will remain just one important approach to the marketplace that works alongside other approaches in a fully integrated marketing mix.

> **Author Comment** | Although we mostly benefit from direct marketing, like most other things in life, it has its dark side as well. Marketers and customers alike must guard against irritating or harmful direct marketing practices.

Public Policy Issues in Direct Marketing (pp 518–520)

Direct marketers and their customers usually enjoy mutually rewarding relationships. Occasionally, however, a darker side emerges. The aggressive and sometimes shady tactics of a few direct marketers can bother or harm consumers, giving the entire industry a black eye. Abuses range from simple excesses that irritate consumers to instances of unfair practices or even outright deception and fraud. The direct marketing industry has also faced growing invasion-of-privacy concerns, and online marketers must deal with Internet security issues.

Irritation, Unfairness, Deception, and Fraud

Direct marketing excesses sometimes annoy or offend consumers. Most of us dislike direct-response TV commercials that are too loud, long, and insistent. Our mailboxes fill up with unwanted junk mail, our e-mailboxes bulge with unwanted spam, and our computer screens flash with unwanted display or pop-under ads.

Beyond irritating consumers, some direct marketers have been accused of taking unfair advantage of impulsive or less-sophisticated buyers. Television shopping channels and program-long infomercials targeting television-addicted shoppers seem to be the worst culprits. They feature smooth-talking hosts, elaborately staged demonstrations, claims of drastic price reductions, "while they last" time limitations, and unequaled ease of purchase to inflame buyers who have low sales resistance. Worse yet, so-called heat merchants design mailers and write copy intended to mislead buyers.

Internet fraud has multiplied in recent years. The FBI's IC3 provides consumers with a convenient way to alert authorities of suspected violations.

Fraudulent schemes, such as investment scams or phony collections for charity, have also multiplied in recent years. *Internet fraud*, including identity theft and financial scams, has become a serious problem. Last year alone, the FBI's Internet Crime Complaint Center (IC3) received more than 336,650 complaints related to Internet fraud involving monetary loss, with a total dollar loss of $560 million.[56]

One common form of Internet fraud is *phishing*, a type of identity theft that uses deceptive e-mails and fraudulent Web sites to fool users into divulging their personal data. For example, consumers may receive an e-mail, supposedly from their bank or credit card company, saying that their account's security has been compromised. The sender asks them to log onto a provided Web address and confirm their account number, password, and perhaps even their social security number. If they follow the instructions, they are actually turning this sensitive information over to scam artists. Although many consumers are now aware of such schemes, phishing can be extremely costly to those caught in the net. It also damages the brand identities of legitimate online marketers who have worked to build user confidence in Web and e-mail transactions.

Many consumers also worry about *online security*. They fear that unscrupulous snoopers will eavesdrop on their online transactions, picking up personal information or intercepting credit and debit card numbers. Although online shopping has grown rapidly, in one survey, 75 percent of participants said they still do not like sending personal or credit card information over the Internet.[57] Internet shoppers are also concerned about contracting annoying or harmful viruses, spyware, and other malware (malicious software).

Another Internet marketing concern is that of *access by vulnerable or unauthorized groups*. For example, marketers of adult-oriented materials and sites have found it difficult to restrict access by minors. In a recent survey, for instance, one in four children ages 8 to 12 admitted to having an account on a social network site such as Facebook or MySpace, which supposedly do not allow children under 13 to have a profile. The survey also found that 17 percent of their parents did not know they had a social network account.[58]

Invasion of Privacy

Invasion of privacy is perhaps the toughest public policy issue now confronting the direct marketing industry. Consumers often benefit from database marketing; they receive more offers that are closely matched to their interests. However, many critics worry that marketers may know *too* much about consumers' lives and that they may use this knowledge to take unfair advantage of consumers. At some point, they claim, the extensive use of databases intrudes on consumer privacy.

These days, it seems that almost every time consumers enter a sweepstakes; apply for a credit card; visit a Web site; or order products by mail, telephone, or the Internet, their names are entered into some company's already bulging database. Using sophisticated computer technologies, direct marketers can use these databases to "microtarget" their selling efforts. *Online privacy* causes special concerns. Most online marketers have become highly skilled at collecting and analyzing detailed consumer information. As Web tracking technology grows in sophistication, digital privacy experts worry that some marketers will use such information to take unfair advantage of unknowing customers:[59]

> The problem is what economists call "information asymmetry." In simple terms, on one side of your screen is grandma searching for arthritis treatments or a birthday gift for her granddaughter, and on the other side of the screen is a black-belt quant-jock working for a data-mining start-up. The consumer can't be expected to understand—and follow—all that happens with his or her data. In the realm of online data collection, the notion of "consumer empowerment" tends to ring hollow.

Some consumers and policy makers worry that the ready availability of information may leave consumers open to abuse. For example, they ask, should Web sellers be allowed to plant cookies in the browsers of consumers who visit their sites and use tracking information to target ads and other marketing efforts? Should credit card companies be allowed to make data on their millions of cardholders worldwide available to merchants who accept their cards? Or is it right for states to sell the names and addresses of driver's license holders, along with height, weight, and gender information, allowing apparel retailers to target tall or overweight people with special clothing offers?

A Need for Action

To curb direct marketing excesses, various government agencies are investigating not only do-not-call lists but also "do-not-mail" lists, "do-not-track" lists, and "Can Spam" legislation. In response to online privacy and security concerns, the federal government has considered numerous legislative actions to regulate how Web operators obtain and use consumer information. For example, Congress is drafting legislation that would give consumers more control over how Web information is used. And the FTC is taking a more active role in policing online privacy.

All of this calls for strong actions by marketers to prevent privacy abuses before legislators step in to do it for them. For example, to head off increased government regulation, four advertiser groups—the American Association of Advertising Agencies, the Association of National Advertisers, the DMA, and the Interactive Advertising Bureau—recently issued new guidelines for Web sites. Among other measures, the guidelines call for Web marketers to alert consumers if their activities are being tracked. The ad industry has agreed on an "advertising option icon"—a little "i" inside a triangle—that it will add to most behaviorally targeted online ads to tell consumers why they are seeing a particular ad and allowing them to opt out.[60]

Of special concern are the privacy rights of children. In 2000, Congress passed the Children's Online Privacy Protection Act (COPPA), which requires Web site operators targeting children to post privacy policies on their sites. They must also notify parents about any information they're gathering and obtain parental consent before collecting personal information from children under age 13. With the subsequent advent of online social networks, mobiles phones, and other new technologies, privacy groups are now urging the U.S. Senate to extend COPPA to include both the new technologies and teenagers. The main concern is the amount of data mined by third parties from social networks as well as the social networks' own hazy privacy policies.[61]

Many companies have responded to consumer privacy and security concerns with actions of their own. Still others are taking an industry-wide approach. For example, TRUSTe, a nonprofit self-regulatory organization, works with many large corporate sponsors, including Microsoft, Yahoo!, AT&T, Facebook, Disney, and Apple, to audit privacy and security measures and help consumers navigate the Web safely. According to the company's Web site, "TRUSTe believes that an environment of mutual trust and openness will help make and keep the Internet a free, comfortable, and richly diverse community for everyone." To reassure consumers, the company lends its TRUSTe privacy seal to Web sites that meet its privacy and security standards.[62]

The direct marketing industry as a whole is also addressing public policy issues. For example, in an effort to build consumer confidence in shopping direct, the DMA—the largest association for businesses practicing direct, database, and interactive marketing, including nearly half of the Fortune 100 companies—launched a "Privacy Promise to American Consumers." The Privacy Promise requires that all DMA members adhere to a carefully developed set of consumer privacy rules. Members must agree to notify customers when any personal information is rented, sold, or exchanged with others. They must also honor consumer requests to "opt out" of receiving further solicitations or having their contact information transferred to other marketers. Finally, they must abide by the DMA's Preference Service by removing the names of consumers who do not wish to receive mail, telephone, or e-mail offers.[63]

Direct marketers know that, left untended, such direct marketing abuses will lead to increasingly negative consumer attitudes, lower response rates, and calls for more restrictive state and federal legislation. Most direct marketers want the same things that consumers want: honest and well-designed marketing offers targeted only toward consumers who will appreciate and respond to them. Direct marketing is just too expensive to waste on consumers who don't want it.

REVIEWING Objectives AND KEY Terms

This chapter is the last of three chapters covering the final marketing mix element—promotion. The previous chapters dealt with advertising, public relations, personal selling, and sales promotion. This one investigated the burgeoning field of direct and online marketing.

Objective 1   Define direct marketing and discuss its benefits to customers and companies. (pp 496–500)

Direct marketing consists of direct connections with carefully targeted segments or individual consumers. Beyond brand and relationship building, direct marketers usually seek a direct, immediate, and measurable consumer response. Using detailed databases, direct marketers tailor their offers and communications to the needs of narrowly defined segments or even individual buyers.

For buyers, direct marketing is convenient, easy to use, and private. It gives buyers ready access to a wealth of products and information, at home and around the globe. Direct marketing is also immediate and interactive, allowing buyers to create exactly the configuration of information, products, or services they desire and then order them on the spot. For sellers, direct marketing is a powerful tool for building customer relationships. Using database marketing, today's marketers can target small groups or individual customers, tailor offers to individual needs, and promote these offers through personalized communications. It also offers them a low-cost, efficient alternative for reaching their markets. As a result of these advantages to both buyers and sellers, direct marketing has become the fastest-growing form of marketing.

Objective 2   Identify and discuss the major forms of direct marketing. (pp 500–508)

The main forms of direct marketing include personal selling, *direct-mail marketing*, *catalog marketing*, *telephone marketing*, *DRTV marketing*, kiosk marketing, and *online marketing*. We discussed personal selling in the previous chapter.

Direct-mail marketing, the largest form of direct marketing, consists of the company sending an offer, announcement, reminder, or other item to a person at a specific address. Recently, new forms of mail delivery have become popular, such as e-mail and mobile marketing. Some marketers rely on catalog marketing—selling through catalogs mailed to a select list of customers, made available in stores, or accessed on the Web. Telephone marketing consists of using the telephone to sell directly to consumers. DRTV marketing has two forms: direct-response advertising (or infomercials) and home shopping channels. Kiosks are information and ordering machines that direct marketers place in stores, airports, hotels, and other locations. In recent years, a number of new digital direct marketing technologies have emerged, including mobile marketing, podcasts and vodcasts, and interactive TV. Online marketing involves online channels that digitally link sellers with consumers.

Objective 3   Explain how companies have responded to the Internet and other powerful new technologies with online marketing strategies. (pp 508–513)

Online marketing is the fastest-growing form of direct marketing. The *Internet* enables consumers and companies to access and share huge amounts of information with just a few mouse clicks. In turn, the Internet has given marketers a whole new way to create value for customers and build customer relationships. It's hard to find a company today that doesn't have a substantial Web marketing presence.

Online consumer buying continues to grow at a healthy rate. Most American online users now use the Internet to shop. Perhaps more importantly, the Internet influences offline shopping. Thus, smart marketers are employing integrated multichannel strategies that use the Web to drive sales to other marketing channels.

Objective 4   Discuss how companies go about conducting online marketing to profitably deliver more value to customers. (pp 513–518)

Companies of all types are now engaged in online marketing. The Internet gave birth to the *click-only companies* that operate online only. In addition, many traditional brick-and-mortar companies have added online marketing operations, transforming themselves into *click-and-mortar companies*. Many click-and-mortar companies are now having more online success than their click-only companies.

Companies can conduct online marketing in any of the four ways: creating a Web site, placing ads and promotions online, setting up or participating in Web communities and online social networks, or using e-mail. The first step typically is to create a Web site. Beyond simply creating a site, however, companies must make their sites engaging, easy to use, and useful to attract visitors, hold them, and bring them back again.

Online marketers can use various forms of online advertising and promotion to build their Internet brands or attract visitors to their Web sites. Forms of online promotion include online display advertising, search-related advertising, content sponsorships, and *viral marketing*, the Internet version of word-of-mouth marketing. Online marketers can also participate in online social networks and other Web communities, which take advantage of the *C-to-C* properties of the Web. Finally, e-mail marketing has become a fast-growing tool for both *B-to-C* and *B-to-B* marketers. Whatever direct marketing tools they use, marketers must work hard to integrate them into a cohesive marketing effort.

Objective 5   Overview the public policy and ethical issues presented by direct marketing. (pp 518–520)

Direct marketers and their customers usually enjoy mutually rewarding relationships. Sometimes, however, direct marketing presents a darker side. The aggressive and sometimes shady tactics of a few direct marketers can bother or harm consumers, giving the entire industry a black eye. Abuses range from simple excesses that irritate consumers to instances of unfair practices or even outright deception and fraud. The direct marketing industry has also faced growing concerns about invasion-of-privacy and Internet security issues. Such concerns call for strong action by marketers and public policy makers to curb direct marketing abuses. In the end, most direct marketers want the same things that consumers want: honest and well-designed marketing offers targeted only toward consumers who will appreciate and respond to them.

KEY Terms

OBJECTIVE 1

Direct marketing (p 496)
Customer database (p 499)

OBJECTIVE 2

Direct-mail marketing (p 501)
Catalog marketing (p 502)
Telephone marketing (p 502)
Direct-response television (DRTV) marketing (p 503)

OBJECTIVE 3

Online marketing (p 508)
Internet (p 508)
Click-only companies (p 509)
Click-and-mortar companies (p 509)
Business-to-consumer (B-to-C) online marketing (p 509)
Business-to business (B-to-B) online marketing (p 510)
Consumer-to-consumer (C-to-C) online marketing (p 511)

Blogs (p 511)
Consumer-to-business (C-to-B) online marketing (p 512)

OBJECTIVE 4

Corporate (or brand) Web site (p 513)
Marketing Web site (p 513)
Online advertising (p 514)
Viral marketing (p 514)
Online social networks (p 515)
Spam (p 517)

PEARSON mymarketinglab

- Check your understanding of the concepts and key terms using the mypearsonmarketinglab study plan for this chapter.
- Apply the concepts in a business context using the simulation entitled **Online Marketing**.

DISCUSSING & APPLYING THE Concepts

Discussing the Concepts

1. Discuss the importance of customer databases in direct marketing. (AACSB: Communication)

2. Describe the four major online marketing domains and give an example of each. (AACSB: Communication)

3. Name and describe the major forms of direct marketing. (AACSB: Communication)

4. Explain the ways in which companies can establish an online marketing presence. (AACSB: Communication)

5. Compare and contrast the different forms of online advertising. What factors should a company consider in deciding among these different forms? (AACSB: Communication)

6. What is *phishing*? How does it harm consumers and marketers? (AACSB: Communication; Reflective Thinking)

Applying the Concepts

1. In a small group, design a viral marketing campaign targeted to teens for a brand of soft drink. Discuss the challenges marketers might encounter when implementing this viral campaign. (AACSB: Communication; Use of IT; Reflective Thinking)

2. Visit Nike's Web site at http://nikeid.nike.com/nikeid/index.jsp and design your own shoe. Print out your shoe design and bring it to class. Do you think the price is appropriate for the value received from being able to customize your shoe? Identify and describe two other Web sites that allow buyers to customize products. (AACSB: Communication; Use of IT; Reflective Thinking)

3. Find news articles about two recent data security breaches. How did the breaches occur? Who was potentially affected by them? (AACSB: Communication; Reflective Thinking)

FOCUS ON Technology

The Internet opened the door for explosive growth in direct marketing, and much of that growth is through applications for mobile devices. For example, for $12.99 per month, Schlage, a lock manufacturer, now offers a wireless, keyless door lock system integrated with cell phones. And Zipcar, a car-sharing service, launched an app for the iPhone enabling customers to not only reserve and locate a car but also unlock it and drive it away—all without contacting a customer service representative. Honking the virtual horn on an iPhone triggers the horn on the reserved car so the member can locate it in the Zipcar lot. The app even looks

like a key fob, prompting the user to push the button to unlock the door. Once in the car, swiping a membership card allows access to the keys in the car.

1. What key benefits do these forms of direct marketing offer for consumers and for marketers? (AACSB: Communication; Use of IT; Reflective Thinking)

2. Find or conceive of other applications in which the Internet and mobile devices create direct marketing opportunities. (AACSB: Communication; Reflective Thinking)

FOCUS ON Ethics

The World Wide Web is often referred to as the Wild West. Unlike advertising, which openly identifies the sponsor, much product and brand information seen on the Internet does not reveal sponsorship. You might read about a product in a blog, see it in a YouTube video, or follow it in Twitter, often unaware that the person was paid or provided free merchandise or goodies to say positive things. These undercover company shills are difficult to detect. Kmart, Sony Pictures, HP, and other marketers use companies like IZEA to develop sponsored conversations using its network of bloggers. Sponsored conversations generated by IZEA disclose sponsorships, but many others do not. However, that could be changing soon. The FTC recently updated its endorsement guidelines requiring bloggers to disclose sponsorships. Violators could be slapped with an $11,000 fine per violation, but with almost 30 million bloggers out there—80 percent of whom occasionally or frequently post product or brand reviews—it will be difficult, if not impossible, to enforce this rule. Even with the new rules, sponsored conversations grew almost 14 percent to $46 million in 2009.

1. Find examples of product information posted in blogs. Did the blogger indicate in the post that he or she was paid or provided free products? Should the government enact laws to require bloggers and others on the Internet to disclose sponsorship from marketers? Explain. (AACSB: Communication; Ethical Reasoning)

2. Review the FTC's revised guidelines on endorsements and testimonials in advertising (www.ftc.gov/os/2009/10/091005revisedendorsementguides.pdf) and visit the Word of Mouth Marketing Association's Web site (http://womma.org/main) and the Web site of a social marketing company, such as (http://izea.com). Write a report on how marketers can effectively use sponsored conversations within the FTC's guidelines. (AACSB: Communication; Reflective Thinking)

MARKETING & THE Economy

Dell

Not long ago, Dell was the PC industry darling, turning the industry upside down with its direct marketing approach. At one point, it was the world's leading PC maker. But in recent years, Dell has been hit hard by a combination of factors. One is competition: HP took Dell's "top-seller" status away by providing a better one-stop shop for equipment and services to businesses, where Dell gets three-fourths of its sales. At the same time, Taiwanese competitor Acer took a bite out of Dell's low-cost advantage. By selling cheaper machines, Acer bumped Dell out of the number-two market share spot. The final blow came from the weak economic environment, which has made consumers and businesses more reluctant to upgrade to newer, faster models. Dell's PC sales fell by 13 percent in 2010, and its net profits fell by 44 percent. The company has cut costs and is also looking to its other businesses to shore up sagging PC sales. But for the most part, Dell appears to just be hanging on while waiting for an improved economy and a predicted powerful PC replacement cycle to reboot the industry.

1. What is wrong with Dell's strategy to increase PC sales?

2. How can Dell overcome this problem, particularly as consumer frugality persists? What would you recommend?

MARKETING BY THE Numbers

Many companies are realizing the efficiency of telemarketing in the face of soaring sales force costs. Whereas the average cost of a B-to-B sales call by an outside salesperson costs more than $300, the cost of a telemarketing sales call can be as little as $5 to $20. In addition, telemarketers can make up to 33 decision maker contacts per day compared to a salesperson's four per day. This has gotten the attention of many B-to-B marketers, where telemarketing can be very effective.

1. Refer to Appendix 2 to determine the marketing return on sales (marketing ROS) and marketing ROI for each company in the chart below. Which company is performing better? Explain. (AACSB: Communication; Analytical Reasoning; Reflective Thinking)

	Company A (sales force only)	Company B (telemarketing only)
Net sales	$2,000,000	$1,000,000
Cost of goods sold	$800,000	$500,000
Sales expenses	$700,000	$200,000

2. Should all companies consider reducing their sales forces in favor of telemarketing? Discuss the pros and cons of this action. (AACSB: Communication; Reflective Thinking)

VIDEO Case

Zappos.com

Zappos.com spends almost no money on advertising—it doesn't have to. Customers are so enamored with the company, they keep coming back. And they keep telling their friends. Instead of mass media advertising, Zappos.com focuses on strengthening customer relationships through marketing directly to customers. Like its impeccable customer service, the company's unique promotional methods are valued by customers. When Zappos.com sends out an e-mail or Tweet, customers listen. Its strength in direct marketing, combined with user-friendly Web design, have made Zappos one of the strongest retailers anywhere.

After viewing the video featuring Zappos, answer the following questions:

1. What benefits has Zappos.com gained by marketing directly to customers rather than engaging heavily in mass-market advertising?

2. What role does database technology play in Zappos.com's ability to connect with its customers?

3. Discuss Zappos.com's Web site in terms of effective Web design. What are its strengths and weaknesses?

COMPANY Case

EBay: Fixing an Online Marketing Pioneer

Pop quiz: Name the high-tech company that got its start in someone's living room, grew from zero revenue to a multibillion dollar corporation in less than a decade, and pioneered the model for an entire industry to follow. If you're thinking that the companies that fit this description make a list that is a mile long, you're right. But in this case, we're talking about eBay.

EBay is one of the biggest Web success stories in the history of, well, the World Wide Web. But sooner or later, every high-growth company hits a speed bump and experiences growing pains. After amazing growth for its first 15 years, eBay has hit that speed bump. Current CEO John Donahoe is faced with the difficult challenge of putting eBay back on the superhighway to prosperity.

EBay started in 1995 as an auction house. Unlike most dot-coms, eBay was based on a model that produced profits, not just revenue. Whenever a user posted an item for auction, eBay collected a fee. The more products that went up for auction, the more money eBay made. EBay has tinkered with its fee structure over the years. But the basic idea has remained the same. The online auction formula took off like wildfire, and eBay dominated the industry. EBay's revenue, stock price, profits, and number of employees soared. By the year 2000, eBay was the number one e-commerce site in the world by sales revenue.

THE CHANGING FACE OF A GROWING COMPANY

With explosive growth, change was inevitable. According to many industry observers, the face of eBay slowly began to change based on two dynamics. The first was expansion. EBay's list of categories and subcategories grew into the hundreds. The e-commerce giant also added international sites for different countries. And it began to launch subsites (such as eBay Motors) and acquire other dot .coms relevant to its business. Such acquisitions ultimately included Half.com, PayPal, StubHub, Shopping.com, and Skype.

The second dynamic driving change in eBay was the addition of fixed-price selling options. During its early years, open auction was the only option buyers and sellers had. Sellers put up an item for sale with a designated starting price for a period of one to 10 days and sold to the highest bidder. In 1999, eBay augmented that core

method with a fixed-price, "Buy It Now" option. Two years later, it took that concept further with the introduction of eBay stores. With eBay stores, a seller could create an online "storefront" within eBay. The feature allowed sellers to post items more quickly, making it easier for high volume sellers to do business. It also gave fixed-price options with no bidding whatsoever and virtually eliminated the sales period for an item.

Both of these dynamics continued to fuel eBay's steady, strong growth for years. In 2006, $52.5 billion worth of goods were sold on eBay. Those sales were generated by 222 million users posting 610 million new listings. EBay's take was $5.97 billion in revenue and $1.12 billion in net income. These numbers were tremendous for a company that had been doing business only for a single decade; they also marked a zenith for the company.

A NEW DIRECTION

In 2007, eBay began to show signs of slowing down. In early 2008, John Donahoe took over as CEO, replacing Meg Whitman, the mastermind behind the company's success for 10 of its 13 years. Donahoe acknowledged that eBay faced issues, including the fact that it had been resting on its laurels. "We were the biggest and the best. EBay has a storied past. But frankly, it's a past we've held onto too much." Consumer behavior was shifting. When eBay was new, many users were thrilled by the uncertainty of bidding against other buyers for a bargain. But as online shopping went mainstream, more people opted for the tried-and-true method of finding the best price on a new piece of merchandise and buying it from a reputable retailer.

The consumer shift to buying new products at fixed prices was evident in the growth experienced by online retailers such as Amazon.com, Buy.com, and Walmart.com, companies that eBay had previously refused to recognize as competitors. Amazon passed eBay as the largest online retailer a number of years earlier by continuing to expand its selection of fixed-price items, often with free shipping.

Shortly after taking over from Whitman, Donahoe said at a public event, "We need to redo our playbook, we need to redo it fast, and we need to take bold actions." He unveiled the details of a new strategy for eBay's turnaround. The strategy focused on changing the identity of the eBay marketplace. Donahoe specified that the new strategy would focus on building the site's business in the secondary market, the $500-billion-a-year slice of retail that includes out-of-season and overstock items as well as the used and antique items for which eBay had always been known. The new strategy included the following tactics:

- Fixed-price listings would be favored over auctions.
- A new fee structure would drop the cost of listing an item but increase eBay's cut when an item sold.
- A new search engine algorithm would give top billing to items based on price and customer satisfaction rating.
- Seller feedback to buyers would be eliminated.
- Fee reductions for highly rated sellers, fixed-price listings, and sellers offering free shipping would be implemented.

Donahoe claimed that all these tactics helped align eBay's interests with those of its best sellers. But the moves also created tension between two groups of sellers that had been growing apart for years. The traditional eBay seller sold typical flea market wares, including used, vintage, antique, and homemade items. These sellers typically included mom and pop operations that dealt in low to moderate volumes. These merchants gave eBay its start and continued to be a sizable portion of eBay's business. Such sellers were a sharp contrast to eBay's high volume Powersellers. These sellers were often major operations employing dozens if not hundreds of people. They most often sold new, refurbished, or overstock items in bulk. High volume sellers sold tens of thousands, hundreds of thousands, and even millions of items on eBay every year.

Traditional sellers complained that the new strategy favored the big merchants and made it harder for the little sellers to do business. Lower volume sellers could not afford to invest the time or money to raise their ratings. Because the items sold by traditional merchants were difficult to price accurately, open auctions were much more effective. And whereas the new fee structure decreased the selling costs for high-volume sellers, it increased the selling costs for most traditional vendors.

As a result, many sellers began to look for other venues to peddle their merchandise. Traditional sellers voiced their concerns to executives at shareholder meetings and seller conventions. Some sellers even organized a brief boycott. It became increasingly clear that eBay's turnaround strategy had generated an identity crisis, with its 25 million sellers caught between the images of the classic seller that had made eBay an e-commerce giant and the more corporate merchant that was thriving on the new eBay. "EBay used to have a very distinct community culture," said Skip McGrath, author of nine books on how to make money on eBay. "Now, it's like eBay doesn't know who it is."

Donahoe responded that the managers at eBay knew there would be fallout, but that the transformation was essential. "We have to create a marketplace where we're helping our sellers give our buyers what they want," he said. He added that he strongly believed that buyers wanted a fixed price, quick service, and free shipping.

FROM BAD TO WORSE

All that may have ended well had eBay's numbers turned around. But in 2008, eBay's financials slid badly. In the last quarter of that year, typically eBay's strongest with holiday shopping, eBay experienced its first ever quarterly decline. For its core marketplace, revenue was down 16 percent from the previous year, while net income dropped a whopping 31 percent. Even the increasing strength of its PayPal business couldn't offset the losses in its marketplace business.

It would have been very easy for Donahoe and his team to blame the company's woes on the economic downturn. After all, with consumers concerned about job losses and the economy, retail sales during the 2008 holiday season were the worst in decades. But as eBay experienced a drop in traffic, Amazon.com and Walmart enjoyed increases. It was also no secret that eBay had shown signs of weakness even before the Great Recession reared its ugly head. And during the tech bust and economic slowdown of 2001, eBay's revenue had grown 74 percent and its stock more than doubled as consumers dumped used goods on the site. It was apparent that eBay's problems were deeper than a bad economy.

More than a year after Donahoe revealed his turnaround strategy, he made public statements about eBay's direction and performance. His statements did not indicate a shift in strategy but rather a refining of the strategy the company had been executing. He promised that the eBay site would be easier to use, offer even better deals, and provide a more satisfying experience. "The 'buyer beware' experience has run its course," he said. He reiterated eBay's plans to focus on the secondary market. "We're going to focus where we can win," Donahoe said, indicating that the shift away from new merchandise where its biggest competitors dominated would give eBay a strong point of differentiation. "We have begun significant change. The eBay you knew is not the eBay we are, or the eBay we will become."

Donahoe also asked that the eBay community and its investors be patient; the plan would take three or four years to produce fruit. In addition to the strategy laid out for marketplace business, Donahoe announced that eBay would also divest itself of businesses that did not perform well or that were not relevant to its core mission of connecting buyers and sellers. He also noted that PayPal would be a core component of eBay's growth and that it would produce an increasing proportion of the company's revenue and profits.

Although few doubted that the nonmarketplace aspects of eBay's strategy would likely strengthen the company, Donahoe gave few new details as to how the company would correct its marketplace issues. Acknowledging the discontent of many eBay sellers, he asserted that eBay's strategy wasn't based on a zero-sum game between big merchants and traditional eBay sellers. "We aren't dictating who's successful and not successful on eBay. All we're doing is ensuring that the sellers who provide the things that buyers want get exposure and positive reinforcement."

Things have improved somewhat since Donahoe's statements. But while its 2009 revenue increase of 2.2 percent was better than a decline, it paled in comparison to the 28 percent increase achieved by Amazon. And although eBay's profits shot up 34 percent, much of that was from the sale of Skype and came in lower than analysts had expected. None of this goes against the promises made by Donahoe. The question is, will investors have enough patience to wait for his plan to work?

Questions for Discussion

1. Analyze the marketing environment and the forces shaping eBay's business over the years.

2. How has the change in the nature of eBay sellers affected the creation of value for buyers?

3. Do you agree or disagree with Donahoe that eBay's current strategy doesn't mean that certain sellers will lose?

4. Is eBay doing the right thing by sticking to its current strategy? What changes, if any, would you recommend to Donahoe?

Sources: Geoffrey Fowler, "EBay Profit Rises, Outlook Disappoints," *Wall Street Journal*, April 22, 2010, accessed at www.wsj.com; Fowler, "Auctions Fade in eBay's Bid for Growth," *Wall Street Journal*, May 26, 2009, p. A1; Fowler, "EBay Retreats in Web Retailing," *Wall Street Journal*, March 12, 2009, accessed at www.wsj.com; Peter Burrows, "EBay Outlines Three-Year Revival Plan," *BusinessWeek*, March 12, 2009, accessed at www.businessweek.com.

Creating Competitive Advantage

Chapter Preview

In previous chapters, you explored the basics of marketing. You learned that the aim of marketing is to create value *for* customers in order to capture value *from* them in return. Good marketing companies win, keep, and grow customers by understanding customer needs, designing customer-driven marketing strategies, constructing value-delivering marketing programs, and building customer and marketing partner relationships. In the final three chapters, we'll extend this concept to three special areas: creating competitive advantage, global marketing, and social and environmental marketing sustainability.

In this chapter, we pull all the marketing basics together. Understanding customers is an important first step in developing profitable customer relationships, but it's not enough. To gain competitive advan-

tage, companies must use this understanding to design marketing offers that deliver more value than the offers of competitors seeking to win the same customers. In this chapter, we look first at competitor analysis—the process companies use to identify and analyze competitors. Then we examine competitive marketing strategies by which companies position themselves against competitors to gain the greatest possible competitive advantage.

Let's first look at Korean carmaker Hyundai (rhymes with Sunday). When the Great Recession of 2008 battered the automobile industry, most car companies slashed their marketing budgets and battened down the hatches to weather the economic storm. But one company—Hyundai—did just the opposite. It *increased* its marketing spending as rivals were cutting back. And it found just the right value proposition for the changing economic times and marketplace.

Hyundai: Hitting the Accelerator When Competitors Throttle Down

Consider the state of affairs when viewers tuned into the Super Bowl in February 2009. Banks had failed, the stimulus package still hadn't been announced, and unemployment was surging. Escapism was the order of the day, and most advertisers played right along, with brands like Bud Lite and Coke offering happy-happy, joy-joy ads that jarred with reality. There was one advertiser, however, that didn't. In the third quarter, in an otherwise standard-issue, cars-rolling-through-the-landscape spot, a voice-over brought into the light of day something that most people didn't want to talk about. "Now finance or lease a new Hyundai, and if you lose your income in the next year, you can return it with no impact on your credit."

With that bold stroke, Hyundai—yes, Hyundai—an automaker not historically known for fearless marketing, began in earnest a frontal assault on a recession that was not only dampening consumer enthusiasm but also drowning it. Then, in sharp contrast to the tail-between-the-legs mode of Hyundai's rivals, many of whom had slashed their marketing budgets, the Korean carmaker put the pedal to the marketing metal by repeating the Hyundai Assurance

promise in an eye-popping nine high-profile spots on the Academy Awards.

Hyundai's aggressive, customer-focused marketing strategy in the face of the economic downturn produced stunning results. The Hyundai Assurance program resonated with debt-wary consumers, and Hyundai's sales rocketed 59 percent for January and February 2009 as compared with the previous year. Nielsen's postgame survey showed that 43 percent of participants who saw the ads improved their opinion of Hyundai. The Hyundai Assurance program, "made people feel Hyundai cared about their situation—that they were sympathetic," said one analyst. The ads said, "We hear you. We understand. We're in this together."

Hyundai's competitive marketing strategy is all about opportunity, aggressiveness, and speed. In 1986, then virtually unknown Hyundai entered the U.S. market with its small, entry-level Hyundai Excel, priced at an incredibly low $5,000. After some early success, Hyundai hit a speed bump with design and quality. The car's outdated looks, underpowered engine, and flimsy engineering made it the butt of jokes by late-night comics. David Letterman once joked that if you wanted to really frighten the astronauts in space, just place a Hyundai logo on the space shuttle's control panel.

Undeterred, however, Hyundai stepped up its investments in quality, new model introductions, and marketing. In late 1998, Hyundai introduced the industry's first 10-year, 100,000-mile drivetrain warranty, and by 2007 it had substantially improved both its quality and its reputation. In 2008, the company introduced its new Genesis upmarket sedan—a step up from its best-selling midsize Sonata model and the priciest Hyundai ever.

Then came the Great Recession and the virtual implosion of the U.S. auto industry. But rather than throttling down, Hyundai hit the accelerator. As rivals were cutting their marketing budgets, an opportunistic Hyundai *increased* its spending. More spending, however, means little without good marketing ideas. With the economy down, what could Hyundai possibly say that would get reluctant consumers buying again?

Joel Ewanick, Hyundai's chief marketing officer, asked consumers directly. "You can only learn so much by reading research numbers," he said. "It's another thing to have them look you in the eye and say how they feel." In focus groups, Ewanick kept asking, "Why aren't you buying a car right now? You say you want to buy one, but you aren't doing it." As he pressed the question, people began to open up. "We realized the elephant in the room was the fear of losing your job," Ewanick recounts. "This was a recession of fear."

Hyundai acted quickly on this insight. Within only 37 days, it had fashioned the Hyundai Assurance program and produced TV ads. It purchased two spots in the 2009 Super Bowl, along with sponsorship of the pregame show, followed by those nine Academy Award spots. These bold marketing moves and Hyundai's customer-focused value proposition helped the brand turn the corner on customer perceptions. Even though only about 100 customers returned their cars, the Hyundai Assurance program won Hyundai enormous amounts of attention and goodwill. The ads alerted customers that Hyundai stood behind its brands and with its buyers. "The idea of giving people the option to give the car back if they were struggling . . . seemed to make customers comfortable and increase our market share in an economy like this," said Ewanick.

Moving forward, despite the still-slowed economy, Hyundai showed no signs of slowing down. In 2010, it introduced a new premium luxury model called Equus (with a price tag of about $60,000), designed to compete with top-of-the-line models marketed by Mercedes, BMW, and Audi that cost $20,000 more. It also introduced the Sonata Hybrid and the Sonata Turbo models. Although it continued its Hyundai Assurance program through 2010, in line with a changing economy,

Hyundai's more recent ads have shifted from "the safety of purchasing a Hyundai to the safety of driving one." And whatever the economy, Hyundai continues to pour resources into marketing.

Customers seem to be getting a new message about Hyundai. "Five years ago, Hyundai was known for its low prices, so-so quality, and a 100,000-mile power-train warranty," says an industry observer. "Today, . . . Hyundai stands for softer, more positive qualities like smart, fresh, and high-tech." Sixty percent of U.S. consumers are now aware of the brand and willing to buy it, up from 40 percent two years ago. Astonished Hyundai dealers are seeing consumers trade in Acura, BMW, and even Mercedes vehicles for the Hyundai Genesis and Equus models. "We're really eroding other brands," crows one dealer.

Thanks to its marketing hustle, improved quality, and aggressive tactics, Hyundai is now one of world's fastest-growing major auto manufacturers. Its U.S. market share has climbed to 4.3 percent, up from 3.1 percent a year earlier, making it the nation's sixth biggest brand by sales. Last year, Hyundai passed Ford to move into fourth place globally. Moreover, Hyundai ranked seventh in last year's J.D. Power's Annual Initial Quality Survey—right up there with Honda and Lexus and well ahead of Toyota. And to top things off, the brand ranked number one last year in the well-respected Brand Keys customer loyalty ratings, surpassing even perennial front-runners Toyota and Honda. "Fans show their loyalty in all kinds of ways," says one ad. "Ours just buy another Hyundai."

Thus, Hyundai has the right competitive marketing strategy for its customers, the changing economy, and the competitive marketplace. "Hyundai is for real," concludes an analyst. "Competitors hate them. Customers love them."[1]

> "Hyundai is for real," says one analyst. "Competitors hate them. Customers love them."

> **Hyundai's marketing hustle and aggressive competitive marketing strategy have made it the world's fastest-growing major car maker. When rivals throttled down on marketing, Hyundai hit the accelerator.**

Competitive advantage
An advantage over competitors gained by offering consumers greater value than competitors do.

Competitor analysis
The process of identifying key competitors; assessing their objectives, strategies, strengths and weaknesses, and reaction patterns; and selecting which competitors to attack or avoid.

Competitive marketing strategies
Strategies that strongly position the company against competitors and give the company the strongest possible strategic advantage.

Author Comment | Creating competitive advantage begins with a thorough understanding of competitors' strategies. But before a company can analyze its competitors, it must first identify them—a task that's not as simple as it seems.

Today's companies face their toughest competition ever. In previous chapters, we argued that to succeed in today's fiercely competitive marketplace, companies must move from a product-and-selling philosophy to a customer-and-marketing philosophy.

This chapter spells out in more detail how companies can go about outperforming competitors to win, keep, and grow customers. To win in today's marketplace, companies must become adept not only in managing products but also in managing customer relationships in the face of determined competition and a difficult economic environment. Understanding customers is crucial, but it's not enough. Building profitable customer relationships and gaining **competitive advantage** requires delivering more value and satisfaction to target customers than competitors do. Customers will see competitive advantages as *customer advantages*, giving the company an edge over its competitors.

In this chapter, we examine competitive marketing strategies—how companies analyze their competitors and develop successful, customer value-based strategies for building and maintaining profitable customer relationships. The first step is **competitor analysis**, the process of identifying, assessing, and selecting key competitors. The second step is developing **competitive marketing strategies** that strongly position the company against competitors and give it the greatest possible competitive advantage.

Competitor Analysis (pp 528–535)

To plan effective marketing strategies, the company needs to find out all it can about its competitors. It must constantly compare its marketing strategies, products, prices, channels, and promotions with those of close competitors. In this way, the company can find areas of potential competitive advantage and disadvantage. As shown in ◉ **Figure 18.1**, competitor analysis involves first identifying and assessing competitors and then selecting which competitors to attack or avoid.

Identifying Competitors

Normally, identifying competitors would seem to be a simple task. At the narrowest level, a company can define its competitors as other companies offering similar products and services to the same customers at similar prices. Thus, Abercrombie & Fitch might see the Gap as a major competitor, but not Macy's or Target. The Ritz-Carlton might see the Four Seasons hotels as a major competitor, but not Holiday Inn, the Hampton Inn, or any of the thousands of bed-and-breakfasts that dot the nation.

However, companies actually face a much wider range of competitors. The company might define its competitors as all firms with the same product or class of products. Thus, the Ritz-Carlton would see itself as competing against all other hotels. Even more broadly, competitors might include all companies making products that supply the same service.

● FIGURE | 18.1
Steps in Analyzing Competitors

| Identifying the company's competitors | ➡ | Assessing competitors' objectives, strategies, strengths and weaknesses, and reaction patterns | ➡ | Selecting which competitors to attack or avoid |

Identifying competitors isn't as easy as it seems. For example, now bankrupt music superstore Tower Records saw other music stores as its only major competitors. But its real competitors turned out to be discounters, such as Best Buy and Walmart, and digital download services, such as iTunes.

Here the Ritz-Carlton would see itself competing not only against other hotels but also against anyone who supplies rooms for weary travelers. Finally, and still more broadly, competitors might include all companies that compete for the same consumer dollars. Here the Ritz-Carlton would see itself competing with travel and leisure services, from cruises and summer homes to vacations abroad.

Companies must avoid "competitor myopia." A company is more likely to be "buried" by its latent competitors than its current ones. For example, it wasn't direct competitors that put an end to Western Union's telegram business after 161 years; it was cell phones and the Internet. Music superstore Tower Records didn't go bankrupt at the hands of other traditional music stores; it fell victim to unexpected competitors such as Best Buy, Walmart, and iTunes and other digital download services. ● Another classic example of competitor myopia is the United States Postal Service (USPS):[2]

● **Identifying competitors: It's not direct competitors such as FedEx or UPS that are causing problems for the U.S. Postal Service. It's the soaring personal and business use of e-mail and online transactions.**

> The USPS is losing money at a mind-boggling rate— billions of dollars per year. But it's not direct competitors such as FedEx or UPS that are the problem. Instead, it's a competitor that the USPS could hardly have even imagined a decade and a half ago—the soaring use of personal and business e-mail and online transactions, what the USPS calls "electronic diversion." As Internet usage has surged, personal and business letter mail have plunged. Last year alone, the USPS delivered an eye-popping 25.6 billion fewer mail pieces compared with the previous year. That's *billion*! The USPS's response: Proposed increases in postage stamp prices and a reduction from five-day delivery to three-day delivery, moves that will almost certainly reduce mail volume further. The solution? When I figure it out, I'll e-mail you.

Companies can identify their competitors from an *industry* point of view. They might see themselves as being in the oil industry, the pharmaceutical industry, or the beverage industry. A company must understand the competitive patterns in its industry if it hopes to be an effective player in that industry. Companies can also identify competitors from a *market* point of view. Here they define competitors as companies that are trying to satisfy the same customer need or build relationships with the same customer group.

From an industry point of view, Pepsi might see its competition as Coca-Cola, Dr Pepper, 7UP, and the makers of other soft drink brands. From a market point of view, however, the customer really wants "thirst quenching"—a need that can be satisfied by bottled water, energy drinks, fruit juice, iced tea, and many other fluids. Similarly, Hallmark's Crayola crayons might define its competitors as other makers of crayons and children's drawing supplies. But from a market point of view, it would include all firms making recreational and educational products for children. In general, the market concept of competition opens the company's eyes to a broader set of actual and potential competitors.

Assessing Competitors

Having identified the main competitors, marketing management now asks: What are the competitors' objectives? What does each seek in the marketplace? What is each competitor's strategy? What are various competitor's strengths and weaknesses, and how will each react to actions the company might take?

Determining Competitors' Objectives

Each competitor has a mix of objectives. The company wants to know the relative importance that a competitor places on current profitability, market share growth, cash flow, technological leadership, service leadership, and other goals. Knowing a competitor's mix of objectives reveals whether the competitor is satisfied with its current situation and how it might react to different competitive actions. For example, a company that pursues low-cost leadership will react much more strongly to a competitor's cost-reducing manufacturing breakthrough than to the same competitor's advertising increase.

A company also must monitor its competitors' objectives for various segments. If the company finds that a competitor has discovered a new segment, this might be an opportunity. If it finds that competitors plan new moves into segments now served by the company, it will be forewarned and, hopefully, forearmed.

Identifying Competitors' Strategies

The more that one firm's strategy resembles another firm's strategy, the more the two firms compete. In most industries, the competitors can be sorted into groups that pursue different strategies. A **strategic group** is a group of firms in an industry following the same or a similar strategy in a given target market. For example, in the major appliance industry, GE and Whirlpool belong to the same strategic group. Each produces a full line of medium-price appliances supported by good service. ◉ In contrast, Sub-Zero and Viking belong to a different strategic group. They produce a narrower line of higher-quality appliances, offer a higher level of service, and charge a premium price.

Strategic group
A group of firms in an industry following the same or a similar strategy.

Some important insights emerge from identifying strategic groups. For example, if a company enters a strategic group, the members of that group become its key competitors. Thus, if the company enters a group containing GE and Whirlpool, it can succeed only if it develops strategic advantages over these two companies.

Although competition is most intense within a strategic group, there is also rivalry among groups. First, some strategic groups may appeal to overlapping customer segments. For example, no matter what their strategy, all major appliance manufacturers will go after the apartment and homebuilders segment. Second, customers may not see much difference in the offers of different groups; they may see little difference in quality between GE and Whirlpool. Finally, members of one strategic group might expand into new strategy segments. Thus, GE's Monogram and Profile lines of appliances compete in the premium-quality, premium-price line with Viking and Sub-Zero.

The company needs to look at all the dimensions that identify strategic groups within the industry. It must understand how each competitor delivers value to its customers. It needs to know each competitor's product quality, features, and mix; customer services; pricing policy; distribution coverage; sales force strategy; and advertising and sales promotion programs. And it must study the details of each competitor's R&D, manufacturing, purchasing, financial, and other strategies.

IMAGINE YOUR LIFE IN A VIKING KITCHEN. 1-888-845-4641 vikingrange.com

◉ Strategic groups: Viking belongs to an appliance industry strategic group that offers a narrow line of high-quality appliances supported by good service.

Assessing Competitors' Strengths and Weaknesses

Marketers need to carefully assess each competitor's strengths and weaknesses to answer a critical question: What *can* our competitors do? As a first step, companies can gather data on each competitor's goals, strategies, and performance over the past few years. Admittedly, some of this information will be hard to obtain. For example, B-to-B marketers find it hard to estimate competitors' market shares because they do not have the same syndicated data services that are available to consumer packaged-goods companies.

Companies normally learn about their competitors' strengths and weaknesses through secondary data, personal experience, and word of mouth. They can also conduct primary marketing research with customers, suppliers, and dealers. Or they can **benchmark** themselves against other firms, comparing one company's products and processes to those of competitors or leading firms in other industries to identify best practices and find ways to improve quality and performance. Benchmarking has become a powerful tool for increasing a company's competitiveness.

Estimating Competitors' Reactions

Next, the company wants to know: What *will* our competitors do? A competitor's objectives, strategies, and strengths and weaknesses go a long way toward explaining its likely actions. They also suggest its likely reactions to company moves, such as price cuts, promotion increases, or new-product introductions. In addition, each competitor has a certain philosophy of doing business, a certain internal culture and guiding beliefs. Marketing managers need a deep understanding of a given competitor's mentality if they want to anticipate how the competitor will act or react.

Each competitor reacts differently. Some do not react quickly or strongly to a competitor's move. They may feel their customers are loyal, they may be slow in noticing the move, or they may lack the funds to react. Some competitors react only to certain types of moves and not to others. Other competitors react swiftly and strongly to any action. Thus, P&G does not allow a competitor's new detergent to come easily into the market. Many firms avoid direct competition with P&G and look for easier prey, knowing that P&G will react fiercely if it is challenged.

In some industries, competitors live in relative harmony; in others, they fight constantly. Knowing how major competitors react gives the company clues on how best to attack competitors or how best to defend its current positions.

Selecting Competitors to Attack and Avoid

A company has already largely selected its major competitors through prior decisions on customer targets, distribution channels, and its marketing-mix strategy. Management now must decide which competitors to compete against most vigorously.

Strong or Weak Competitors

The company can focus on one of several classes of competitors. Most companies prefer to compete against weak competitors. This requires fewer resources and less time. But in the process, the firm may gain little. You could argue that the firm also should compete with strong competitors to sharpen its abilities. Moreover, even strong competitors have some weaknesses, and succeeding against them often provides greater returns.

A useful tool for assessing competitor strengths and weaknesses is **customer value analysis**. The aim of customer value analysis is to determine the benefits that target customers value and how customers rate the relative value of various competitors' offers. In conducting a customer value analysis, the company first identifies the major attributes that customers value and the importance customers place on these attributes. Next, it assesses its performance and the performance of its competitors on those valued attributes.

The key to gaining competitive advantage is to take each customer segment and examine how the company's offer compares to that of its major competitors. The company wants to find the place in the market where it meets customers' needs in a way that rivals can't. If the company's offer delivers greater value by exceeding the competitor's offer on important attributes, the company can charge a higher price and earn higher profits, or it can charge the same price and gain more market share. But if the company is seen as performing at a lower level than its major competitors on some important attributes, it must invest in strengthening those attributes or finding other important attributes where it can build a lead on its competitors.

Benchmarking
The process of comparing the company's products and processes to those of competitors or leading firms in other industries to identify best practices and find ways to improve quality and performance.

Customer value analysis
An analysis conducted to determine what benefits target customers value and how they rate the relative value of various competitors' offers.

Close or Distant Competitors

Most companies will compete with close competitors—those that resemble them most—rather than distant competitors. Thus, Nike competes more against Adidas than against Timberland or Keen. And Target competes against Walmart rather than Neiman Marcus or Nordstrom.

At the same time, the company may want to avoid trying to "destroy" a close competitor. For example, in the late 1970s, Bausch & Lomb moved aggressively against other soft lens manufacturers with great success. However, this forced weak competitors to sell out to larger firms such as Johnson & Johnson (J&J). As a result, Bausch & Lomb then faced much larger competitors—and it suffered the consequences. J&J acquired Vistakon, a small nicher with only $20 million in annual sales. Backed by J&J's deep pockets, the small but nimble Vistakon developed and introduced its innovative Acuvue disposable lenses. With Vistakon leading the way, J&J is now the dominant U.S. contact lens maker, while Bausch & Lomb lags in third place. In this case, success in hurting a close rival brought in tougher competitors.[3]

Good or Bad Competitors

A company really needs and benefits from competitors. The existence of competitors results in several strategic benefits. Competitors may share the costs of market and product development and help legitimize new technologies. They may serve less-attractive segments or lead to more product differentiation. Finally, competitors may help increase total demand. For example, you might think that an independent coffeehouse surrounded by Starbucks stores might have trouble staying in business. But that's often not the case:[4]

> Coffee shop owners around the country have discovered that the corporate steamroller known as Starbucks is actually good for their business. It turns out that when a Starbucks comes to the neighborhood, the result is new converts to the latte-drinking fold. When all those converts overrun the local Starbucks, the independents are there to catch the spillover. In fact, some independent storeowners now actually try to open their stores near a Starbucks if they can. That's certainly not how the coffee behemoth planned it. "Starbucks is actually *trying* to be ruthless," says the owner of a small coffeehouse chain in Los Angeles. But "in its predatory store-placement strategy, Starbucks has been about as lethal a killer as a fluffy bunny rabbit."

However, a company may not view all its competitors as beneficial. An industry often contains *good competitors* and *bad competitors*. Good competitors play by the rules of the industry. Bad competitors, in contrast, break the rules. They try to buy share rather than earn it, take large risks, and play by their own rules.

For example, the nation's traditional newspapers face a lot of bad competitors these days. Digital services that overlap with traditional newspaper content are bad competitors because they offer for free real-time content that subscription-based newspapers printed once a day can't match. An example is Craigslist, the online community that lets local users post largely free classified ads. Started as a hobby about 15 years ago by Craig Newmark, Craigslist has never cared all that much about profit margins, and that's about as bad as the competitor can get. ⦿ Another example is *Examiner .com*, the "insider source for everything local." The hyperlocal online newspaper is authored by "pro-am contributors," referred to as "Examiners," who are paid based on page views instead of a flat rate per article. The ad-supported site is free to users, versus the subscription rates charged by traditional newspapers. Such unorthodox digital competitors have helped to drive many traditional newspapers into bankruptcy in recent years.

⦿ **Bad competitors: Unorthodox digital competitors, such as *Examiner.com*, have helped to drive many traditional newspapers into bankruptcy in recent years.**

Finding Uncontested Market Spaces

Rather than competing head to head with established competitors, many companies seek out unoccupied positions in uncontested market spaces. They try to create products and services for which there are no direct competitors. Called a "blue ocean strategy," the goal is to make competition irrelevant:[5]

> Companies have long engaged in head-to-head competition in search of profitable growth. They have flocked for competitive advantage, battled over market share, and struggled for differentiation. Yet in today's overcrowded industries, competing head-on results in nothing but a bloody "red ocean" of rivals fighting over a shrinking profit pool. In their book *Blue Ocean Strategy*, two marketing professors contend that although most companies compete within such red oceans, the strategy isn't likely to create profitable growth in the future. Tomorrow's leading companies will succeed not by battling competitors but by creating "blue oceans" of uncontested market space. Such strategic moves—termed *value innovation*—create powerful leaps in value for both the firm and its buyers, creating all new demand and rendering rivals obsolete. By creating and capturing blue oceans, companies can largely take rivals out of the picture.

One example of a company exhibiting blue-ocean thinking is Allegiant Air, the profitable low-cost airline that avoids direct competition with major airline rivals by targeting smaller, neglected markets and new flyers. Allegiant "goes where they ain't" (see Real Marketing 18.1). Another example is Cirque du Soleil, which reinvented the circus as a higher form of modern entertainment. At a time when the circus industry was declining, Cirque du Soleil innovated by eliminating high cost and controversial elements such as animal acts and instead focused on the theatrical experience. Cirque du Soleil did not compete with then market leader Ringling Bros. and Barnum & Bailey; it was altogether different from anything that preceded it. Instead, it created an uncontested new market space that made existing competitors irrelevant. The results have been spectacular. Thanks to its blue-ocean strategy, in only its first 20 years, Cirque du Soleil achieved more revenues than Ringling Brothers and Barnum & Bailey achieved in its first 100 years.

Designing a Competitive Intelligence System

We have described the main types of information that companies need about their competitors. This information must be collected, interpreted, distributed, and used. Gathering competitive intelligence can cost considerable money and time, so the company must design a cost-effective competitive intelligence system.

The competitive intelligence system first identifies the vital types of competitive information needed and the best sources of this information. Then, the system continuously collects information from the field (sales force, channels, suppliers, market research firms, Web sites, and trade associations) and published data (government publications, speeches, and online databases). Next the system checks the information for validity and reliability, interprets it, and organizes it in an appropriate way. Finally, it sends key information to relevant decision makers and responds to inquiries from managers about competitors.

With this system, company managers receive timely intelligence information about competitors in the form of reports, phone calls, e-mails, bulletins, and newsletters. Managers can also connect with the system when they need to interpret a competitor's sudden move, when they want to know a competitor's weaknesses and strengths, or when they need to know how a competitor will respond to a planned company move.

Smaller companies that cannot afford to set up formal competitive intelligence offices can assign specific executives to watch specific competitors. Thus, a manager who used to work for a competitor might follow that competitor closely; he or she would be the "in-house expert" on that competitor. Any manager needing to know the thinking of a given competitor could contact the assigned in-house expert.

Real Marketing 18.1

Allegiant Air: "Going Where They Ain't"

In July 2001, Maurice Gallagher wanted to start a new airline. Conventional wisdom suggested that, to be successful, a new airline needed to follow the JetBlue model: Invest a lot of cash and fly from a large urban hub with lots of brand-new planes. It needed to meet competitors head-on, wresting frequent flyers from rival airlines in the hypercompetitive commercial airspace. Unfortunately, Gallagher didn't have much cash, and he had only one aging, gas-guzzling, 150-seat MD-80 airplane. So he needed to find a different model—a blue ocean strategy—that would give him an uncontested place in the chronically overcrowded skies.

The result was Allegiant Air, arguably today's most successful American airline. Over the past five years, as other airlines struggled through the worst recession in recent history, Allegiant has seen five straight years of profits—something no other airline can claim. Last year alone, Allegiant's revenue soared 11 percent and profits more than doubled, with operating margins of 22 percent, which were triple the industry average. As other airlines were cutting back, the budding Allegiant Air launched 27 new routes and ended the year with 46 planes.

So, what makes Allegiant different? In an industry littered with failing, low-cost initiatives, "we needed a strategy that was low-cost and could make money from day one," says Gallagher. "Slowly, we figured it out: Go where they ain't." By "go where they ain't," Gallagher means a new kind of airline—one that serves customers now neglected by major competitors in a whole new way. According to one analyst, unlike other airlines, Allegiant "eschews business travelers, daily flights, even service between major cities." Allegiant is the "un-airline."

First, Allegiant Air looks for uncontested turf—routes neglected by larger, more established competitors. In their efforts to cut costs, the major airlines have abandoned many smaller markets, and Allegiant is filling the gap. It began by connecting its home city, Las Vegas—and later other popular tourist destinations such as Los Angeles, Orlando, and Phoenix—with dozens of otherwise empty airports in third-string cities such as Fresno, California; Bozeman, Montana; Peoria, Illinois; and Toledo, Ohio. These smaller markets,

many of which are served by no other scheduled airline, welcomed Allegiant with open arms and runways. "These small cities have been neglected over the years," Gallagher notes. "We're the circus coming to town, but we don't ever leave." As a result of flying where other airlines don't, Allegiant has direct competition on only 7 of its 136 routes.

Second, Allegiant doesn't just target the usual frequent business and leisure flyers coveted by rival airlines. Instead, rather than trying to steal competitors' passengers, Allegiant also targets customers who might not otherwise fly—those who are used to driving an hour or two to some vacation spot but now want to go on a real vacation. Allegiant's idea is to entice that person in Peoria, who doesn't fly all that much, to get off the couch and take a weekend vacation at a more distant destination, such as Las Vegas or Orlando. Allegiant also offers charter flights, so the local Kiwanis Club can charter a plane and take its members and their families on a group vacation.

To entice these more-reluctant travelers, Allegiant offers rock-bottom fares and direct flights. It "provides a complete travel experience with great value and without all the

hassle," says the airline. Allegiant lures passengers on board with really low teaser fares—as low as $9. Of course, you have to pay extra to book online or phone a call center. You also have to pay to check your bags, for priority boarding, or for a reserved seat. But add it all up, and you'll still pay less than you would for a ticket on a competing airline. And Allegiant's à la carte pricing structure provides psychological advantages. "If I tried to charge you $110 up front, you wouldn't pay it," observes Gallagher. "But if I sell you a $75 ticket and you self-select the rest, you will."

What's more, Allegiant doesn't just sell airline tickets; it encourages customers to buy an entire vacation package at its Web site. Last year, it sold 400,000 hotel rooms, along with extras such as rental cars, show tickets, and even beach towels and suntan oil. These extra revenues per passenger comprise nearly one-third of the company's business.

To support its lower fares, Allegiant prides itself on being one of the industry's lowest-cost, most-efficient operators. Even though its old MD-80 airplanes slurp gas, Allegiant buys used ones for as little as $4 million, a tenth of what it costs Southwest Airlines to buy a new 737. And rather than running three-times-a-day service to its smaller markets, Allegiant offers about three flights a week. Passengers don't seem to mind the less-frequent service, especially because they can fly nonstop. Whereas flying Allegiant nonstop from Peoria to Las Vegas takes a little less than seven hours, the same trip

Allegiant Air's blue ocean strategy: "Go where they ain't" by serving customers in neglected smaller markets in a whole new way.

using other airlines with connecting flights (and layovers) might take 19 hours—and you pay more for the ticket.

Less frequent flights make for more efficient use of Allegiant's fleet. For example, the low-cost airline serves 40 destinations from Las Vegas with only 14 planes, with an average occupancy of 90 percent. Greater efficiency results in higher margins, despite lower fares.

Under its blue ocean "go where they ain't" strategy, nicher Allegiant is thriving in an otherwise supercompetitive airline environment. Whereas the major airlines are battling it out with one another for the same passengers in major markets, Allegiant has found its own uncluttered space. In a mature industry that's struggling just to stay in the air, Allegiant has found a profitable place to land. According to Gallagher, Allegiant Air has identified 300 more potential routes in the United States, Canada, Mexico, and the Caribbean.

And it recently agreed to acquire 18 more MD-80s from another airline.

"They're very much one of a kind," says an airline analyst. Forget talk about milking secondary markets, cutting costs, or flying all-but-vintage airplanes. "The truth is, [Allegiant Air] is a totally new business model."

Sources: Quotes and other information from Jerome Greer Chandler, "Pledging Allegiant Ascendance of the Un-Airline," *Air Transport World*, February, 2010, p. 60; Greg Lindsay, "Flying for Fun and Profit," *Fast Company*, September 2009, p. 48; Charisse Jones, "Airline Caters to Passengers in Small Communities Rather Than Business Travelers," *USA Today*, October 19, 2009; "Allegiant Air's Success Comes with No Frills," Morning Edition, National Public Radio, April 17, 2009, www.npr.org/templates/rundowns/rundown.php?prgId=3&prgDate=4-17-2009; and www.allegiantair.com, accessed September 2010.

> **Author Comment** | Now that we've identified competitors and know all about them, it's time to design a strategy for gaining competitive advantage.

Competitive Strategies (pp 535–544)

Having identified and evaluated its major competitors, the company now must design broad competitive marketing strategies by which it can gain competitive advantage through superior customer value. But what broad marketing strategies might the company use? Which ones are best for a particular company or for the company's different divisions and products?

Approaches to Marketing Strategy

No one strategy is best for all companies. Each company must determine what makes the most sense given its position in the industry and its objectives, opportunities, and resources. Even within a company, different strategies may be required for different businesses or products. Johnson & Johnson uses one marketing strategy for its leading brands in stable consumer markets, such as BAND-AID, Tylenol, Listerine, or J&J's baby products, and a different marketing strategy for its high-tech health-care businesses and products, such as Monocryl surgical sutures or NeuFlex finger joint implants.

Companies also differ in how they approach the strategy-planning process. Many large firms develop formal competitive marketing strategies and implement them religiously. However, other companies develop strategy in a less formal and orderly fashion. Some companies, such as Harley-Davidson, Virgin Atlantic Airways, and BMW's MINI Cooper unit succeed by breaking many of the rules of marketing strategy. Such companies don't operate large marketing departments, conduct expensive marketing research, spell out elaborate competitive strategies, and spend huge sums on advertising. Instead, they sketch out strategies on the fly, stretch their limited resources, live close to their customers, and create more satisfying solutions to customer needs. They form buyer's clubs, use buzz marketing, and focus on winning customer loyalty. It seems that not all marketing must follow in the footsteps of marketing giants such as IBM and P&G.

In fact, approaches to marketing strategy and practice often pass through three stages: entrepreneurial marketing, formulated marketing, and intrepreneurial marketing.

- *Entrepreneurial marketing:* Most companies are started by individuals who live by their wits. For example, in the beginning, Robert Ehrlich, founder and CEO of Pirate Brands, a snack food company, didn't believe in formal marketing—or formal anything else. Pirate Brands markets a pantry full of all-baked, all-natural, trans fat and gluten-free snacks, including favorites such as Pirate's Booty, Potato Flyers, Smart Puffs, and Tings. Over the past two decades, founder Robert Ehrlich has built Pirate Brands into a thriving $50 million empire that's become a thorn in the paw of snack food lions like Nabisco

● **Entrepreneurial marketing:** Initially, Pirate Brands founder and CEO Robert Ehrlich built a thriving $50 million empire with little or no formal marketing. "We do no marketing," he used to say proudly. "Zero."

and Frito-Lay. ● But until only a few years ago, he did that with virtually no formal marketing. According to one account at the time:[6]

"We do no marketing," says Ehrlich proudly. "Zero." New product R&D? It's whatever pops into Ehrlich's head on a given day. Product names and taglines? He cooks them all up himself while driving, flying, sleeping—whatever. Focus groups? Are you *kidding*? Package design? Ehrlich phones a cartoonist chum from *Mad* magazine and tells him what to draw. The snack bags sport a scribbled look that's reminiscent of a doodle pad. In fact, Ehrlich's carefree packaging is as close as the company has come to formal marketing, unless you count the 20 guys that Ehrlich employs around the country to dress up in pirate costumes and hand out free bags of its chips at grocery stores. When it comes to marketing, shrugs Ehrlich, "I'm influenced by a lot of different things. There's no real thought to it. We're not Exxon Mobil, thank you very much. We don't want to be."

- *Formulated marketing:* As small companies achieve success, they inevitably move toward more-formulated marketing. They develop formal marketing strategies and adhere to them closely. For example, as Pirate Brands has grown, it now takes a more formal approach to product development and its PR and distributor relations strategies. It has also developed more formal customer outreach efforts, such as a full-feature Web page, a Facebook page, a "Booty Blog," and a Captain's Newsletter, which features product updates, coupons, special offers, and event listings. Although Pirate Brands will no doubt remain less formal in its marketing than the Frito-Lays of the marketing world, as it grows, it will adopt more-developed marketing tools.

- *Intrepreneurial marketing:* Many large and mature companies get stuck in formulated marketing. They pore over the latest Nielsen numbers, scan market research reports, and try to fine-tune their competitive strategies and programs. These companies sometimes lose the marketing creativity and passion they had at the start. They now need to reestablish within their companies the entrepreneurial spirit and actions that made them successful in the first place. They need to encourage more initiative and "intrepreneurship" at the local level. They need to refresh their marketing strategies and try new approaches. Their brand and product managers need to get out of the office, start living with their customers, and visualize new and creative ways to add value to their customers' lives.

The bottom line is that there are many approaches to developing effective competitive marketing strategy. There will be a constant tension between the formulated side of marketing and the creative side. It is easier to learn the formulated side of marketing, which has occupied most of our attention in this book. But we have also seen how marketing creativity and passion in the strategies of many of the companies studied—whether small or large, new or mature—have helped to build and maintain success in the marketplace. With this in mind, we now look at the broad competitive marketing strategies companies can use.

Basic Competitive Strategies

Three decades ago, Michael Porter suggested four basic competitive positioning strategies that companies can follow—three winning strategies and one losing one.[7] The three winning strategies are as follows:

- *Overall cost leadership:* Here the company works hard to achieve the lowest production and distribution costs. Low costs let it price lower than its competitors and win a large market share. Texas Instruments and Walmart are leading practitioners of this strategy.

- *Differentiation:* Here the company concentrates on creating a highly differentiated product line and marketing program so that it comes across as the class leader in the industry. Most customers would prefer to own this brand if its price is not too high. IBM and Caterpillar follow this strategy in information technology services and heavy construction equipment, respectively.

- *Focus:* Here the company focuses its effort on serving a few market segments well rather than going after the whole market. For example, Ritz-Carlton focuses on the top 5 percent of corporate and leisure travelers. Tetra Food supplies 80 percent of pet tropical fish food. Similarly, Hohner owns a stunning 85 percent of the harmonica market.

Companies that pursue a clear strategy—one of the above—will likely perform well. The firm that carries out that strategy best will make the most profits. But firms that do not pursue a clear strategy—*middle-of-the-roaders*—do the worst. Sears and Holiday Inn encountered difficult times because they did not stand out as the lowest in cost, highest in perceived value, or best in serving some market segment. Middle-of-the-roaders try to be good on all strategic counts but end up being not very good at anything.

Two marketing consultants, Michael Treacy and Fred Wiersema, offer a more customer-centered classification of competitive marketing strategies.[8] They suggest that companies gain leadership positions by delivering superior value to their customers. Companies can pursue any of three strategies—called *value disciplines*—for delivering superior customer value.

- *Operational excellence:* The company provides superior value by leading its industry in price and convenience. It works to reduce costs and create a lean and efficient value-delivery system. It serves customers who want reliable, good-quality products or services but want them cheaply and easily. Examples include Walmart, Costco, and Southwest Airlines.

- *Customer intimacy:* The company provides superior value by precisely segmenting its markets and tailoring its products or services to exactly match the needs of targeted customers. It specializes in satisfying unique customer needs through a close relationship with and intimate knowledge of the customer. It builds detailed customer databases for segmenting and targeting and empowers its marketing people to respond quickly to customer needs. Customer-intimate companies serve customers who are willing to pay a premium to get precisely what they want. They will do almost anything to build long-term customer loyalty and to capture customer lifetime value. Examples include Nordstrom, Lexus, British Airways, and Ritz-Carlton. As we learned in the very first chapter, at fast-growing Web retailer Zappos.com, customer intimacy starts with a deep-down obsession with customer service.

- *Product leadership:* The company provides superior value by offering a continuous stream of leading-edge products or services. It aims to make its own and competing products obsolete. Product leaders are open to new ideas, relentlessly pursue new solutions, and work to get new products to market quickly. They serve customers who want state-of-the-art products and services, regardless of the costs in terms of price or inconvenience. Examples include Apple and Nokia.

Some companies successfully pursue more than one value discipline at the same time. For example, FedEx excels at both operational excellence and customer intimacy. However, such companies are rare; few firms can be the best at more than one of these disciplines. By trying to be *good at all* value disciplines, a company usually ends up being *best at none*.

Treacy and Wiersema found that leading companies focus on and excel at a single value discipline, while meeting industry standards on the other two. Such companies design their entire value delivery network to single-mindedly support the chosen discipline. For example, Walmart knows that customer intimacy and product leadership are important. Compared with other discounters, it offers very good customer service and an excellent product assortment. Still, it purposely offers less customer service and less product depth than does Nordstrom or Williams-Sonoma, which pursue customer intimacy. Instead, Walmart focuses obsessively on operational excellence—on reducing costs and streamlining its order-to-delivery process to make it convenient for customers to buy just the right products at the lowest prices.

By the same token, the Ritz-Carlton wants to be efficient and employ the latest technologies. But what really sets the luxury hotel chain apart is its customer intimacy. The Ritz-Carlton creates custom-designed experiences to coddle its customers.

Classifying competitive strategies as value disciplines is appealing. It defines marketing strategy in terms of the single-minded pursuit of delivering superior value to customers. Each value discipline defines a specific way to build lasting customer relationships.

Competitive Positions

Firms competing in a given target market, at any point in time, differ in their objectives and resources. Some firms are large; others are small. Some have many resources; others are strapped for funds. Some are mature and established; others new and fresh. Some strive for rapid market share growth; others for long-term profits. And these firms occupy different competitive positions in the target market.

We now examine competitive strategies based on the roles firms play in the target market—leader, challenger, follower, or nicher. Suppose that an industry contains the firms shown in ◉ **Figure 18.2**. Forty percent of the market is in the hands of the **market leader**, the firm with the largest market share. Another 30 percent is in the hands of **market challengers**, runner-up firms that are fighting hard to increase their market share. Another 20 percent is in the hands of **market followers**, other runner-up firms that want to hold their share without rocking the boat. The remaining 10 percent is in the hands of **market nichers**, firms that serve small segments not being pursued by other firms.

◉ **Table 18.1** shows specific marketing strategies that are available to market leaders, challengers, followers, and nichers.[9] Remember, however, that these classifications often do not apply to a whole company but only to its position in a specific industry. Large companies such as GE, Microsoft, P&G, or Disney might be leaders in some markets and nichers in others. For example, P&G leads in many segments, such as laundry detergents and shampoo. But it challenges Unilever in hand soaps and Kimberly-Clark in facial tissues. Such companies often use different strategies for different business units or products, depending on the competitive situations of each.

Market Leader Strategies

Most industries contain an acknowledged market leader. The leader has the largest market share and usually leads the other firms in price changes, new-product introductions, distribution coverage, and promotion spending. The leader may or may not be admired or respected, but other firms concede its dominance. Competitors focus on the leader as a company to challenge, imitate, or avoid. Some of the best-known market leaders are Walmart (retailing), McDonald's (fast food), Verizon (wireless), Coca-Cola (beverages), Microsoft (computer software), Caterpillar (earth-moving equipment), Nike (athletic footwear and apparel), and Google (Internet search services).

A leader's life is not easy. It must maintain a constant watch. Other firms keep challenging its strengths or trying to take advantage of its weaknesses. The market leader can easily miss a turn in the market and plunge into second or third place. A product innovation may come along and hurt the leader (as when Apple developed the iPod and took the market lead from Sony's Walkman portable audio devices). The leader might grow arrogant or complacent and misjudge the competition (as when Sears lost its lead to Walmart). Or the leader might look old-fashioned against new and peppier

> Each market position calls for a different competitive strategy. For example, the market leader wants to expand total demand and protect or expand its share. Market nichers seek market segments that are big enough to be profitable but small enough to be of little interest to major competitors.

Market leader
The firm in an industry with the largest market share.

Market challenger
A runner-up firm that is fighting hard to increase its market share in an industry.

Market follower
A runner-up firm that wants to hold its share in an industry without rocking the boat.

Market nicher
A firm that serves small segments that the other firms in an industry overlook or ignore.

◉ **FIGURE | 18.2**
Competitive Market Positions and Roles

Market leader	Market challengers	Market followers	Market nichers
40%	30%	20%	10%

● **TABLE | 18.1** Strategies for Market Leaders, Challengers, Followers, and Nichers

Market Leader Strategies	Market Challenger Strategies	Market Follower Strategies	Market Nicher Strategies
Expand total market	Full frontal attack	Follow closely	By customer, market, quality-price, service
Protect market share	Indirect attack	Follow at a distance	Multiple niching
Expand market share			

rivals (as when Gap lost serious ground to stylish niche brands such as 7 for all Mankind and American Apparel and mall brands such as Abercrombie & Fitch, Aeropostale, and J. Crew).

To remain number one, leading firms can take any of three actions. First, they can find ways to expand total demand. Second, they can protect their current market share through good defensive and offensive actions. Third, they can try to expand their market share further, even if market size remains constant.

Expanding Total Demand

The leading firm normally gains the most when the total market expands. If Americans eat more fast food, McDonald's stands to gain the most because it holds more than three times the fast-food market share of nearest competitors Subway and Burger King. If McDonald's can convince more Americans that fast food is the best eating-out choice in these economic times, it will benefit more than its competitors.

Market leaders can expand the market by developing new users, new uses, and more usage of its products. They usually can find *new users* or untapped market segments in many places. For example, Nutrisystem has typically targeted its weight loss programs toward women. Recently, however, it stepped up its efforts to attract male customers by advertising in media such as ESPN and *Men's Health*. The ads feature Dan Marino and Don Shula, who talk about how they "ate like a man and still lost weight" with Nutrisystem. The company also created dedicated online features for men, such as a dedicated chat room. Since the launch of the targeted ads, the male share of Nutrisystem jumped from 13 percent to 32 percent.[10]

Marketers can expand markets by discovering and promoting *new uses* for the product. For example, ● Nintendo is now expanding into classrooms with its popular handheld Nintendo DS game system:[11]

● **Creating new uses: Nintendo is now expanding into classrooms with its popular handheld Nintendo DS game system.**

A giggly class of 32 seventh graders uses plastic pens to spell words like "hamburger" and "cola" on the touch panel screen—the key feature of the Nintendo DS— following an electronic voice from the handheld console. It's a sort of high-tech spelling bee. When the student gets the spelling right, the word *good* pops up on the screen, and the student proceeds to the next exercise. "It's fun," says a 12-year-old student. The instructor acknowledges that she has never before seen the kind of enthusiastic concentration the DS classes have inspired in her students.

Nintendo, never content to create gaming products that are simply for gaming, is taking its portable DS system to school. Using a PC, teachers can interact with students via Wi-Fi, beaming questions, visual aids, and other information to a special DS Classroom cartridge in students' handheld devices. Teachers can receive responses from students in real time, instantly monitoring which students answered correctly and which are falling behind. The system can even help grade tests as they are happening, letting students see their performance immediately after finishing a test. Nintendo DS Classroom will kick off next year in Japan, with 60 programs covering everything from spelling and math to physics and civics for elementary, junior high, and high school students. Creating classroom uses substantially expands the market for market leader Nintendo's gaming products.

Finally, market leaders can encourage *more usage* by convincing people to use the product more often or use more per occasion. For example, Campbell urges people to eat soup and other Campbell's products more often by running ads containing new recipes. It also offers a toll-free hotline (1-888-MM-MM-GOOD), staffed by live recipe representatives who offer recipes to last-minute cooks at a loss for meal ideas. And the Campbell's Kitchen Web site (www.campbellskitchen.com) lets visitors search for or exchange recipes, ~~_____ recipe box~~, sign up for a daily or weekly Meal Mail program, and ~~_____~~ of 23 recipes on Campbell's

[handwritten note: Business Name Ideas / Cartsy / Cartify / Carthaven]

so must protect its current business ~~_____~~ guard against Target; Caterpil-

~~_____~~ first, it must prevent or fix weak-~~_____~~ always fulfill its value promise. ~~_____~~ tomers see in the brand. It must ~~_____~~ stomers. The leader should "plug

~~_____~~ response is *continuous innovation*. ~~_____~~ ngs are and leads the industry in ~~_____~~ ess, promotion, and cost cutting. ~~_____~~ alue to customers. And when attacked by challengers, ~~the___~~ ~~_____~~ ly. ● For example, in the laundry products category, market leader P&G has been relentless in its offense against challengers such as Unilever.

In one of the most fabled marketing battles of the past century, P&G won the laundry war because it was bigger, better, more focused, and more aggressive than challenger Unilever. Entering this millennium, even though its U.S. laundry detergent market share was well over 50 percent, P&G kept raining blows on Unilever and all other comers with stepped-up product launches. By 2007, P&G was outgunning Unilever on U.S. media spending for laundry brands by $218 million to $25 million. New products such as Tide with Downey, Tide Coldwater, and the scent-focused Simple Pleasures lineup for Tide and Downey helped P&G steadily gain a share point or two per year, so that by 2008, it owned a 62.5 percent share of the $3.6 billion laundry-detergent market to Unilever's 12.9 percent (including Unilever's All, Wisk, and Surf brands). It had an even bigger lead in fabric softeners—66 percent to Unilever's 8.4 percent (Unilever's Snuggle brand). Globally, P&G went from being the number two laundry player in the early 1990s to a dominant market leader, with a global market share of 34 percent to Unilever's 17 percent. In the face of P&G's relentless assault, in mid-2008, Unilever finally threw in the towel and sold its North American detergents business.[12]

● **Protecting market share: In the face of market leader P&G's relentless assault in the laundry war, Unilever finally threw in the towel by putting its U.S. detergents business up for sale.**

Expanding Market Share

Market leaders also can grow by increasing their market shares further. In many markets, small market share increases mean very large sales increases. For example, in the U.S. digital camera market, a 1 percent increase in market share is worth $66 million; in carbonated soft drinks, $739 million![13]

Studies have shown that, on average, profitability rises with increasing market share. Because of these findings, many companies have sought expanded market shares to improve profitability. GE, for example, declared that it wants to be at least number one or two in each of its markets or else get out. GE shed its computer, air-conditioning, small appliances, and television businesses because it could not achieve top-dog position in those industries.

However, some studies have found that many industries contain one or a few highly profitable large firms, several profitable and more focused firms, and a large number of medium-sized firms with poorer profit performance. It appears that profitability increases as a business gains share relative to competitors in its *served market*. For example, Lexus holds only a small share of the total car market, but it earns a high profit because it is the leading brand in the luxury-performance car segment. And it has achieved this high share in its served market because it does other things right, such as producing high-quality products, creating good service experiences, and building close customer relationships.

Companies must not think, however, that gaining increased market share will automatically improve profitability. Much depends on their strategy for gaining increased share. There are many high-share companies with low profitability and many low-share companies with high profitability. The cost of buying higher market share may far exceed the returns. Higher shares tend to produce higher profits only when unit costs fall with increased market share or when the company offers a superior-quality product and charges a premium price that more than covers the cost of offering higher quality.

Market Challenger Strategies

Firms that are second, third, or lower in an industry are sometimes quite large, such as PepsiCo, Ford, Lowe's, Hertz, and AT&T Mobility. These runner-up firms can adopt one of two competitive strategies: They can challenge the market leader and other competitors in an aggressive bid for more market share (market challengers). Or they can play along with competitors and not rock the boat (market followers).

A market challenger must first define which competitors to challenge and its strategic objective. The challenger can attack the market leader, a high-risk but potentially high-gain strategy. Its goal might be to take over market leadership. Or the challenger's objective may simply be to wrest more market share.

Although it might seem that the market leader has the most going for it, challengers often have what some strategists call a "second-mover advantage." The challenger observes what has made the market leader successful and improves on it. For example, Home Depot invented the home-improvement superstore. However, after observing Home Depot's success, number two Lowe's, with its brighter stores, wider aisles, and arguably more helpful salespeople, has positioned itself as the friendly alternative to Big Bad Orange. Over the past 10 years, follower Lowe's has consistently grown faster and more profitably than Home Depot.

In fact, challengers often become market leaders by imitating and improving on the ideas of pioneering processors. For example, Chrysler invented the modern minivan and led in that market for more than a decade. However, then-followers Honda and Toyota improved on the concept and now dominate the minivan market. Similarly, McDonald's first imitated and then mastered the fast-food system first pioneered by White Castle. And founder Sam Walton admitted that Walmart borrowed most of its practices from discount pioneer Sol Price's FedMart and Price Club chains and then perfected them to become today's dominant retailer.[14]

Alternatively, the challenger can avoid the leader and instead challenge firms its own size or smaller local and regional firms. These smaller firms may be underfinanced and not serving their customers well. Several of the major beer companies grew to their present size not by challenging large competitors but by gobbling up small local or regional competitors. If the challenger goes after a small local company, its objective may be to put that company out of business. The important point remains: The challenger must choose its opponents carefully and have a clearly defined and attainable objective.

How can the market challenger best attack the chosen competitor and achieve its strategic objectives? It may launch a full *frontal attack*, matching the competitor's product, advertising, price, and distribution efforts. It attacks the competitor's strengths rather than its weaknesses. The outcome depends on who has the greater strength and endurance. PepsiCo challenges Coca-Cola in this way.

If the market challenger has fewer resources than the competitor, however, a frontal attack makes little sense. Thus, many new market entrants avoid frontal attacks, knowing that market leaders can head them off with ad blitzes, price wars, and other retaliations. Rather than challenging head-on, the challenger can make an *indirect attack* on the competitor's weaknesses or on gaps in the competitor's market coverage. It can carve out toeholds using tactics that established leaders have trouble responding to or choose to ignore. ⊙ For example, compare the vastly different strategies of two different European challengers—Virgin Drinks and Red Bull—when they entered the U.S. soft drink market in the late 1990s against market leaders Coca-Cola and PepsiCo.[15]

Virgin Drinks took on the leaders head-on, launching its own cola, advertising heavily, and trying to get into all the same retail outlets that stocked the leading brands. At Virgin Cola's launch, Virgin CEO Richard Branson even drove a tank through a wall of rivals' cans in New York's Times Square to symbolize the war he wished to wage on the big, established rivals. However, Coca-Cola's and PepsiCo's viselike grip on U.S. shelf space proved impossible for Virgin Drinks to break. Although Virgin Drinks is still around, it has never gained more than a 1 percent share of the U.S. cola market.

Red Bull, by contrast, tackled the leaders indirectly. It entered the U.S. soft drink market with a niche product: a carbonate energy drink retailing at about twice what you would pay for a Coke or Pepsi. It started by selling Red Bull through unconventional outlets not dominated by the market leaders, such as bars and nightclubs, where twenty-somethings gulped down the caffeine-rich drink so they could dance all night. After gaining a loyal following, Red Bull used the pull of high margins to elbow its way into the corner store, where it now sits in refrigerated bins within arm's length of Coke and Pepsi. Despite rapidly intensifying competition in the United States, Red Bull captures a 33 percent share of the energy drink market.

⊙ Market challenger strategies: Virgin Drinks mounted a full frontal attack on Coca-Cola and PepsiCo but couldn't break the leaders' viselike grip on U.S. shelf space.

Market Follower Strategies

Not all runner-up companies want to challenge the market leader. The leader never takes challenges lightly. If the challenger's lure is lower prices, improved service, or additional product features, the market leader can quickly match these to defuse the attack. The leader probably has more staying power in an all-out battle for customers. For example, a few years ago, when Kmart launched its renewed low-price "bluelight special" campaign, directly challenging Walmart's everyday low prices, it started a price war that it couldn't win. Walmart had little trouble fending off Kmart's challenge, leaving Kmart worse off for the attempt. Thus, many firms prefer to follow rather than challenge the market leader.

A follower can gain many advantages. The market leader often bears the huge expenses of developing new products and markets, expanding distribution, and educating the market. By contrast, as with challengers, the market follower can learn from the market leader's experience. It can copy or improve on the leader's products and programs, usually with much less investment. Although the follower will probably not overtake the leader, it often can be as profitable.

Following is not the same as being passive or a carbon copy of the market leader. A follower must know how to hold current customers and win a fair share of new ones. It must find the right balance between following closely enough to win customers from the market leader but following at enough of a distance to avoid retaliation. Each follower tries to bring distinctive advantages to its target market—location, services, financing. A follower is often a major target of attack by challengers. Therefore, the market follower must keep its manufacturing costs and prices low or its product quality and services high. It must also enter new markets as they open up.

Market Nicher Strategies

Almost every industry includes firms that specialize in serving market niches. Instead of pursuing the whole market or even large segments, these firms target subsegments. Nichers are often smaller firms with limited resources. But smaller divisions of larger firms also may pursue niching strategies. Firms with low shares of the total market can be highly successful and profitable through smart niching.

Why is niching profitable? The main reason is that the market nicher ends up knowing the target customer group so well that it meets their needs better than other firms that casually sell to that niche. As a result, the nicher can charge a substantial markup over costs because of the added value. Whereas the mass marketer achieves high volume, the nicher achieves high margins.

Nichers try to find one or more market niches that are safe and profitable. An ideal market niche is big enough to be profitable and has growth potential. It is one that the firm can serve effectively. Perhaps most importantly, the niche is of little interest to major competitors. And the firm can build the skills and customer goodwill to defend itself against a major competitor as the niche grows and becomes more attractive. For example, computer mouse and interface device maker Logitech is only a fraction of the size of giant Microsoft. Yet, through skillful niching, it dominates the PC mouse market, with Microsoft as its runner-up. ⬤ Another example is pet insurer Veterinary Pet Insurance (VPI):

Health insurance for pets? Most large insurance companies haven't paid much attention to the still small but fast-growing segment. And that leaves room for focused nichers like VPI. Pet ownership is big business. Collectively, Americans own some 61 million dogs, 69 million cats, 24 million small animals, 13 million reptiles, and 14 million horses. These pets are very important to most owners. More than two-thirds have included their pets in holiday celebrations, and one-third characterize their pet as a child. Some 42 percent of dogs now sleep in the same bed as their owners.

Americans spend a whopping $41 billion a year on their pets, more than the gross domestic product of all but 64 countries in the world. They spend $12.2 billion of that on pet health care. Pet medical procedures can be costly. If not diagnosed quickly, even a mundane ear infection in a dog can result in $1,000 worth of medical treatment. Ten days of dialysis treatment can reach $12,000, and cancer treatment as much as $40,000. All of this adds up to a lot of potential growth for pet health insurers. VPI covers mostly dogs and cats but also a menagerie of other exotic critters, from birds, rabbits, ferrets, rats, and guinea pigs to snakes, iguanas, turtles, hedgehogs, and potbellied pigs. VPI is growing like a newborn puppy in its niche, now providing more than 60 percent of all U.S. pet insurance policies and insures more than 460,000 pets. That might not amount to much for the likes of MetLife, Prudential,

FAMILY *Redefined.*

Enroll Today at **PETINSURANCE.COM** or **800-944-1649**

He's not just a dog. He's your baby and deserves the best medical care. VPI Pet Insurance helps pay for your pet's lab fees, medications, surgeries, X-rays, and more. We even offer coverage for routine care, including vaccinations and prescription flea control. Plus, you're free to use any veterinarian. That's the kind of protection you need for all your family members. Call today for a free quote.

VPI PET insurance

⬤ **Nichers: Market nicher VPI is growing faster than a newborn puppy. Its mission is to "empower pet owners to work with their veterinarians in making optimal healthcare decisions for their pets."**

or Northwestern Mutual, but it's profitable business for nicher VPI. And there's room to grow. Only about 3 percent of U.S. pet owners currently buy pet insurance.[16]

The key idea in niching is specialization. A market nicher can specialize along any of several market, customer, product, or marketing mix lines. For example, it can specialize in serving one type of *end user*, as when a law firm specializes in the criminal, civil, or business law markets. The nicher can specialize in serving a given *customer-size* group. Many nichers specialize in serving small and midsize customers who are neglected by the majors.

Some nichers focus on one or a few *specific customers*, selling their entire output to a single company, such as Walmart or GM. Still other nichers specialize by *geographic market*, selling only in a certain locality, region, or area of the world. *Quality-price* nichers operate at the low or high end of the market. For example, HP specializes in the high-quality, high-price end of the hand-calculator market. Finally, *service nichers* offer services not available from other firms. For example, LendingTree provides online lending and realty services, connecting homebuyers and sellers with national networks of mortgage lenders and realtors who compete for the customer's business. "When lenders compete," it proclaims, "you win."

Niching carries some major risks. For example, the market niche may dry up, or it might grow to the point that it attracts larger competitors. That is why many companies practice *multiple niching*. By developing two or more niches, a company increases its chances for survival. Even some large firms prefer a multiple niche strategy to serving the total market. For example, as discussed in Chapter 7, apparel maker VF Corporation markets more than 30 lifestyle brands in niche markets ranging from jeanswear, sportswear, and contemporary styles to outdoor gear and imagewear (workwear). For example, VF's Vans unit creates footwear, apparel, and accessories for skate-, surf-, and snowboarders. Its 7 for All Mankind brand offers premium denim and accessories sold in boutiques and high-end department stores. In contrast, the company's Red Kap, Bulwark, and Chef Designs workwear brands provide an array of uniforms and protective apparel for businesses and public agencies, whether it's outfitting a police force or a chef's crew. Together, these separate niche brands combined to make VF a $7.6 billion apparel powerhouse.[17]

Balancing Customer and Competitor Orientations (pp 544–545)

Whether a company is the market leader, challenger, follower, or nicher, it must watch its competitors closely and find the competitive marketing strategy that positions it most effectively. And it must continually adapt its strategies to the fast-changing competitive environment. This question now arises: Can the company spend *too* much time and energy tracking competitors, damaging its customer orientation? The answer is yes. A company can become so competitor centered that it loses its even more important focus on maintaining profitable customer relationships.

Competitor-centered company

A company whose moves are mainly based on competitors' actions and reactions.

A **competitor-centered company** is one that spends most of its time tracking competitors' moves and market shares and trying to find strategies to counter them. This approach has some pluses and minuses. On the positive side, the company develops a fighter orientation, watches for weaknesses in its own position, and searches out competitors' weaknesses. On the negative side, the company becomes too reactive. Rather than carrying out its own customer relationship strategy, it bases its own moves on competitors' moves. As a result, it may end up simply matching or extending industry practices rather than seeking innovative new ways to create more value for customers.

Customer-centered company

A company that focuses on customer developments in designing its marketing strategies and delivering superior value to its target customers.

A **customer-centered company**, by contrast, focuses more on customer developments in designing its strategies. Clearly, the customer-centered company is in a better position to identify new opportunities and set long-run strategies that make sense. By watching customer needs evolve, it can decide what customer groups and what emerging needs are the most important to serve. Then it can concentrate its resources on delivering superior value to target customers.

● FIGURE | 18.3
Evolving Company Orientations

Customer-centered

Market-centered companies understand both customers and competitors. They build profitable customer relationships by delivering more customer value than competitors do.

Market-centered company
A company that pays balanced attention to both customers and competitors in designing its marketing strategies.

In practice, today's companies must be **market-centered companies**, watching both their customers and their competitors. But they must not let competitor watching blind them to customer focusing.

● **Figure 18.3** shows that companies might have any of four orientations. First, they might be product oriented, paying little attention to either customers or competitors. Next, they might be customer oriented, paying attention to customers. In the third orientation, when a company starts to pay attention to competitors, it becomes competitor oriented. Today, however, companies need to be market oriented, paying balanced attention to both customers and competitors. Rather than simply watching competitors and trying to beat them on current ways of doing business, they need to watch customers and find innovative ways to build profitable customer relationships by delivering more customer value than competitors do.

REVIEWING Objectives AND KEY Terms

Today's companies face their toughest competition ever. Understanding customers is an important first step in developing strong customer relationships, but it's not enough. To gain competitive advantage, companies must use this understanding to design market offers that deliver more value than the offers of *competitors* seeking to win over the same customers. This chapter examined how firms analyze their competitors and design effective competitive marketing strategies.

Objective 1 Discuss the need to understand competitors as well as customers through competitor analysis. (pp 528–535)

To prepare an effective marketing strategy, a company must consider its competitors as well as its customers. Building profitable customer relationships requires satisfying target consumer needs *better than competitors do*. A company must continuously analyze competitors and develop *competitive marketing strategies* that position it effectively against competitors and give it the strongest possible *competitive advantage*.

Competitor analysis first involves identifying the company's major competitors, using both an industry-based and a market-based analysis. The company then gathers information on competitors' objectives, strategies, strengths and weaknesses, and reaction patterns. With this information in hand, it can select competitors to attack or avoid. Competitive intelligence must be collected, interpreted, and distributed continuously. Company marketing managers should be able to obtain full and reliable information about any competitor affecting their decisions.

Objective 2 Explain the fundamentals of competitive marketing strategies based on creating value for customers. (pp 535–544)

Which competitive marketing strategy makes the most sense depends on the company's industry and on whether it is the market leader, challenger, follower, or nicher. The *market leader* has to mount strategies to expand the total market, protect market share, and expand market share. A *market challenger* is a firm that tries aggressively to expand its market share by attacking the leader, other runner-up companies, or smaller firms in the industry. The challenger can select from a variety of direct or indirect attack strategies.

A *market follower* is a runner-up firm that chooses not to rock the boat, usually from fear that it stands to lose more than it might gain. But the follower is not without a strategy and seeks to use its particular skills to gain market growth. Some followers enjoy a higher rate of return than the leaders in their industry. A *market nicher* is a smaller firm that is unlikely to attract the attention of larger firms. Market nichers often become specialists in some end use, customer size, specific customer, geographic area, or service.

Objective 3 Illustrate the need for balancing customer and competitor orientations in becoming a truly market-centered organization. (pp 544–545)

A competitive orientation is important in today's markets, but companies should not overdo their focus on competitors. Companies are more likely to be hurt by emerging consumer needs and new competitors than by existing competitors. *Market-centered companies* that balance customer and competitor considerations are practicing a true market orientation.

KEY Terms

OBJECTIVE 1

Competitive advantage (p 528)
Competitor analysis (p 528)
Competitive marketing strategies
   (p 528)
Strategic group (p 530)

Benchmarking (p 531)
Customer value analysis (p 531)

OBJECTIVE 2

Market leader (p 538)
Market challenger (p 538)

Market follower (p 538)
Market nicher (p 538)

OBJECTIVE 3

Competitor-centered company (p 544)
Customer-centered company (p 544)
Market-centered company (p 545)

PEARSON
mymarketinglab

- Check your understanding of the concepts and key terms using the mypearsonmarketinglab study plan for this chapter.
- Apply the concepts in a business context using the simulation entitled **New Product Development**.

DISCUSSING & APPLYING THE Concepts

Discussing the Concepts

1. Which point of view is best for identifying competitors—industry or market? (AACSB: Communication)

2. Explain how having strong competitors can benefit a company. (AACSB: Communication; Reflective Thinking)

3. Name and describe the three basic winning competitive strategies espoused by Michael Porter. (AACSB: Communication)

4. Describe the three value disciplines for delivering superior customer value and explain why classifying competitive strategies in this way is appealing. (AACSB: Communication)

5. Discuss the advantages of being a market follower and the factors to consider when pursuing this strategy. (AACSB: Communication)

6. Compare and contrast product-oriented, competitor-centered, customer-centered, and market-centered

companies. Which orientation is the best? (AACSB: Communication; Reflective Thinking)

Applying the Concepts

1. Form a small group and discuss the differences between increasing market share and increasing customer share. What factors should a company consider when deciding on which to focus? (AACSB: Communication; Reflective Thinking)

2. Research "blue ocean strategy" and discuss examples of companies that have succeeded in pursuing this strategy. Do companies developing uncontested marketspaces necessarily have to be innovative upstarts? (AACSB: Communication; Reflective Thinking)

3. Identify a company following a market niche strategy in each of the following industries: higher education, apparel, soft drinks, and rental cars. (AACSB: Communication; Reflective Thinking)

FOCUS ON Technology

Apple has hit three home runs in less than ten years—the iPod, iPhone, and iPad. Apple sold three million iPads within 80 days of its release, and there were 25,000 iPad-specific apps in Apple's App Store within six months. Like iPhone apps, many iPad apps are free because they display ads that produce revenues for developers. So far, Apple is not taking a cut on the ad revenues, and developers keep 70 percent of the money that they take in from paid-for consumer applications. Publishers in Apple's iBook app keep 70 percent of the money they take in. Consequently, Barnes and Noble's Nook and Amazon's Kindle increased the percentage of revenue publishers earn to 70 percent as well. Forecasters are

predicting that iPad sales in 2011 will reach 20 to 30 million, which has competitors worried.

1. Who are Apple's iPad competitors? What is Apple's competitive position in this industry? (AACSB: Communication; Reflective Thinking)

2. Why is Apple virtually giving away this platform to third-party applications developers? Wouldn't it be more profitable for Apple to generate more revenue from its App Store? (AACSB: Communication; Reflective Thinking)

FOCUS ON Ethics

Deconstruction experts eagerly anticipated the release of Apple's iPad. Some, like Luke Soules, wanted to be the first to get his hands on the device so he could take it apart and analyze it, called

teardowns in the industry. He even spread video of his purchase and teardown on the Internet and bragged about feeding intimate information about the device's innards to folks before stores even opened in California. Although Soules' company, iFixit, makes teardown information public, most deconstruction firms provide data only to paying clients. Apple's gadgets are particularly tricky to crack; there are no screws. The tool of choice for prying open the iPhone was a dental pick. Apple is very secretive of the components that make up its gadgets; some components carry the Apple name rather than the manufacturer's name. However, experts armed with X-ray machines and scanning electron microscopes, with a little bit of sleuthing mixed in, are often able to determine the origins and cost of parts.

1. Using Google, search for "iPad teardown" to find what information is available on the iPad. Is it ethical to tear down a product and share that information publicly or sell it to other firms? (AACSB: Communication; Ethical Reasoning; Reflective Thinking)

2. iFixit used the iPad teardown as a publicity stunt to promote its repair business. Apple is a "closed company" and doesn't want users repairing its products. In fact, users cannot replace a battery on an iPad; they have to return it to Apple and purchase a refurbished device for $99 plus shipping. Replacing a battery is not as simple as popping in a new one because the batteries are soldered in. Is it right for Apple to be so restrictive regarding what customers can do with the product? (AACSB: Communication; Ethical Reasoning; Reflective Thinking)

MARKETING & THE Economy

British Airways

British Airways offers airline services in all segments. Yet a significant portion of its business targets first-class and business-class travelers. Private "demi-cabins" are available on its 747s, each with 6.6-foot beds, an LCD wide screen for in-flight entertainment, and power outlets. Last year, British Airways launched a business-class only service between New York and London City, with planes configured with only 32 roomy seats that spread fully flat.

The travel industry has suffered amidst a weak economy. Low-fare airlines have struggled, and premium services have felt significant air travel reductions. British Airways has seen first- and business-classes seats decline as a percentage of overall tickets sold. Passengers flying premium services have opted to pay less and settle for nonrefundable tickets. As a result, British Airways endured an 11 percent sales decline in 2009 and a net loss of over $800 million, which was its worst performance since it went public in 1987. The travel industry is seeing signs of renewed life, which has flyers returning to premium services to some extent. But British Airways has yet to experience a return to its prerecession financial performance.

1. How should British Airways handle a decline in premium air travel?

2. After such an extended economic downturn, when the economy does recover, will air travelers fully return to their prerecession travel spending habits?

3. Should British Airways be content with signs that the airline industry is recovering? What could it do to better position itself for similar cycles in the future?

MARKETING BY THE Numbers

The base Wi-Fi 16 GB iPad was introduced at $499; like all electronic products, Apple will likely lower the price within a year or two of introduction. The 16 GB iPad's cost of goods sold is $250. Refer to Appendix 2 to answer the following questions.

1. Calculate Apple's gross margin per unit and gross margin as a percentage of sales for the 16 GB iPad. What is Apple's gross margin if the company sells 10 million iPads? (AACSB: Communication; Analytical Reasoning)

2. What will happen to the gross margin generated by the iPad if Apple reduces the price by $100? (AACSB: Communication; Analytical Reasoning)

VIDEO Case

Umpqua Bank

The retail banking industry has become very competitive. And with a few powerhouses dominating the market, how is a small bank to thrive? By differentiating itself through a competitive advantage that the big guys can't touch.

That's exactly what Umpqua has done. Step inside a branch of this Oregon-based community bank and you'll see immediately that this is not your typical Christmas club savings account/free toaster bank. Umpqua's business model has transformed banking from retail drudgery into a holistic experience. Umpqua has created an environment in which people just love to hang out. It not only has its own music download service featuring local artists, it even has its own blend of coffee.

But beneath all these bells and whistles lies the core of what makes Umpqua so different—a rigorous service culture where every branch and employee gets measured on how well they serve customers. That's why every customer feels like they get the help and attention they need from employees.

After viewing the video featuring Umpqua Bank, answer the following questions about creating competitive advantage:

1. With what companies does Umpqua compete?

2. What is Umpqua's competitive advantage?

3. Will Umpqua be able to maintain this advantage in the long run? Why or why not?

COMPANY Case

Ford: Resurrecting an Iconic Company

The old phrase, "The bigger they are, the harder they fall," perfectly describes what has happened to the U.S. auto industry over the past decade. Consider the Ford Motor Company. In 1998, the iconic company accounted for 25 percent of all cars and trucks sold. Its F-series pickup was the best selling vehicle on the planet, with more than 800,000 units rolling off assembly lines. The Ford Explorer held the top slot in the hot SUV market. And the Ford Taurus had been a perennial contender for the top selling sedan. Ford was number two on the Fortune 500 (GM was number one) with $153 billion in revenues. A strong stock price gave Ford a market value of $73 billion. And according to Interbrand, the company was the sixth most valuable brand in the world, worth $36 billion.

But in only 10 years, its position at the top fell apart like a rusting old jalopy. In 2008, its market share sat at just 14 percent. Revenues had dropped to $146 billion, and the company lost $14.7 billion, the biggest loss in its history. Its stock price had plummeted to only $2 a share, erasing 93 percent of its market value. And it was no longer a top ten brand. It had dropped to the 49th position on the Interbrand top-100 list, worth only $7 billion. The company verged on collapse.

Ford could try to explain its misfortunes by pointing out that the entire auto industry was reeling by 2008. High gas prices and the weakest global economy in over 70 years had made a mess of automobile sales. But that wouldn't explain its drastic drop in market share or the magnitude of its losses relative to the rest of the industry. The company was in far worse shape than most car companies.

Looking back, it's clear that Ford had taken its eye off the market. It had become too dependent on gas-guzzling trucks and SUVs and could not shift quickly enough to more fuel-efficient vehicles. Its vehicle quality had suffered, and its operations were bloated with excessive costs. In a quest to serve every customer segment—acquiring Land Rover, Volvo, Aston Martin, and Jaguar—the company had lost touch with the needs of any specific customer segment. All those luxury brands were sapping valuable company resources as well. Finally, the company's innovation was at an all-time low. Mark Fields, president for the Americas, adds, "We used to have a saying in the company that we were a fast follower. Which meant we were slow."

A NEW DIRECTION

Even as the company's financials looked their worst in years, a strategy was already underway to resurrect the company. In 2006, Ford had brought in an industry outsider to perform cardiac resuscitation on the ailing giant. Alan Mulally, who had led Boeing through its most ambitious product launch in decades with the 767 Dreamliner, took the reins as the new CEO. Cheerful and fresh faced, he exuded optimism. "I am here to save an American and global icon," Mulally declared.

Mulally got to work right away. He cut labor costs by almost 22 percent, bringing the company more in line with new industry leader Toyota. He shuttered unprofitable factories and cut out as much operational fat as possible. In 2008, as GM and Chrysler held their hats out for a government bailout, Ford managed to raise cash the old-fashioned way—by borrowing from a bank to the tune of $23.5 billion. By remaining financially independent,

Ford avoided giving Uncle Sam a say in how the company was run. It also avoided bankruptcy, a fate that befell its two Detroit siblings.

But the move that put Ford back on the highway was the crafting of a good old-fashioned mission statement. Mulally ordered up small plastic cards that Ford's 200,000 employees could carry in their wallets featuring what he called "Expected Behaviors." Those expectations were really four goals that Mulally fully believed would make the company competitive again. To Mulally, this was sacred text. "This is me," he said. "I wrote it. It's what I believe in. You can't make this shit up."

Focus on the Ford Brand. According to Mulally, "Nobody buys a house of brands." It was the Ford name and the legacy of the Ford family that had propelled the company to greatness. Mulally considered the conglomeration of automotive companies a failed experiment and immediately set out to divest the company of Jaguar, Volvo, Aston Martin, and Land Rover. He even went one step further. Ford's storied Mercury division had always had the mission of providing Ford with a mid-priced car that fit between inexpensive Ford models and its more luxurious Lincolns. But Mercury was a dying brand, so Mulally gave it the axe.

Compete in Every Market Segment with Carefully Defined Products. Even with only the Ford and Lincoln divisions left, Mulally was convinced that Ford could compete in all major industry segments: cars, SUVs, and trucks, in sizes small through large. Mulally loves to tell the story of how he started revamping Ford's product line:

> I arrive here, and the first day I say, "Let's go look at the product lineup." And they lay it out, and I said, "Where's the Taurus?" They said, "Well, we killed it." I said, "What do you mean, you killed it?" "Well, we made a couple that looked like a football. They didn't sell very well, so we stopped it." "You stopped the Taurus?" I said. "How many billions of dollars does it cost to build brand loyalty around a name?" "Well, we thought it was so damaged that we named it the Five Hundred." I said, "Well, you've got until tomorrow to find a vehicle to put the Taurus name on because that's why I'm here. Then you have two years to make the coolest vehicle that you can possibly make."

Mulally had good reason to insist on the Taurus. It was the fourth best-selling vehicle in the history of the company, behind the Model T, F-Series, and Mustang. But Mulally's biggest news in the product department was a shift to small "world" cars that can be sold in every country with little change. Ford had tried the "world" car idea various times in the past and failed. But that was largely because the regional divisions of the company couldn't agree on what kinds of cars to build. Mulally has reorganized the company around the world car. If it works, the benefits of reduced costs based on economies of scale are obvious.

The "small" part of Mulally's product strategy is a bit foreign to Ford's truck-heavy culture. "Everybody says you can't make money off small cars," he says. "Well, you'd better damn well figure out how to make money, because that's where the world is going." Mulally's plan isn't just to make more small cars but to make nicer small cars. The 2010 Fiesta and Focus were designed in Europe and are the first vehicles that are part of Mulally's "One Ford" program.

More fuel-efficient vehicles (including electrics) will also help position Ford to meet stricter government fuel-economy standards.

Market Fewer Nameplates. According to Mulally, the "more is better" rule is not a good branding strategy. When he arrived at Ford, the company sold 97 nameplates around the world. To him, that was just an indication of how unfocused and uncool the Ford brand had become. "I mean, we had 97 of these, for God's sake! How you gonna make 'em all cool? You gonna come in at 8 AM and say, 'From 8 until noon, I'm gonna make No. 64 cool? And then I'll make No. 17 cool after lunch?' It was ridiculous!" Mulally's goal was to bring the number of nameplates down to 40 by 2013. But instead, it has been trimmed to just 20 as of 2010. This thrills Mulally.

Become Best in Class in Quality, Fuel Efficiency, Safety, and Value. The smaller cars are certainly achieving the fuel efficiency goal. But Mulally has the Ford culture once again thinking along the lines of its old slogan, "Quality is Job One." This focus has paid off. Last year, *Consumer Reports* recommended more Ford models than Toyota vehicles. The Fusion beat the Toyota Camry in the magazine's reliability survey. And Ford took both "Car of the Year" and "Truck of the Year" honors at the Detroit Auto show with its Fusion Hybrid and Transit Connect. "Our product lineup is stronger than ever, and our leadership in quality, fuel, safety, smart design, and value is resonating with consumers," Mulally says as if reciting his own mission statement.

A NEW COMPETITIVE ADVANTAGE

In his quest to redefine Ford's image, thrill young customers, and even revolutionize the car itself, Mulally may very well have stumbled on a competitive advantage that will carry Ford into the future. He wants to connect his autos to the Internet and the souls of the people who surf it. "Look, it's cool to connect. But it's past cool. It's a reason to buy. Tech is why people are going to buy Ford! We're going to be the coolest, most useful app you've ever had, seamlessly keeping you connected."

Mulally is talking about Ford's Sync option. In short, a Sync-equipped vehicle connects the driver to the Internet through the smartphone in his or her pocket. Unlike GM's OnStar and other similar systems, Sync is an interface, not a system that is hardwired to the car. Those other systems are obsolete by the time they hit the showroom and are not upgradable. With Sync, the connection is to whatever technology the driver is carrying. And folks tend to keep their gadgets pretty up-to-date.

But Sync takes existing technologies and makes them even better. With two LCD panels on either side of the speedometer, the user interface is bigger, in the driver's field of vision, and customizable. If you don't need to know about the car's climate but you're lost, the climate-control readout can be replaced with navigation. If you're on a long stretch of highway and don't need navigation help, the display can connect the driver to phone controls or music (including satellite radio and even Pandora). Drivers can even watch video on these screens, but only when the car is in park.

The latest Sync system also brings voice recognition to the cockpit, transforming the car into *2001: A Space Odyssey's* HAL 9000 (only without the evil desire to take over the universe). All the driver has to do is speak normally to the car instead of fumbling with buttons or navigating through screen-based menus. Simple commands like "I'm hungry" produce spoken restaurant advice matched to the GPS location. If the driver is in the mood for some Dave Brubeck, "I'd like to hear some jazz," brings up every piece of jazz attached to the car, whether it's on a smartphone, iPod, or netbook.

All this is not only cool, "it makes you a better driver," claims Mulally. His first commandment is, "We won't do it unless it lets you keep your eyes on the road and your hands on the wheel." This will actually make people less likely to fumble with their tech gadgets or even look down to adjust the radio or air conditioning.

Sync was already in development when Mulally took over. But he surprised everyone when he announced that Sync would be the future of the company. And he insisted that it be available in all Ford vehicles, not just the high-end luxury products. In this respect, Mulally sees Sync as a way to do what Henry Ford did in the beginning. "Democratize a brand new technology. Make it available to the masses."

SIGNS OF LIFE

Mulally's original goal was to turn an annual profit by 2011. That profit came two years early in the form of $2.1 billion for 2009. Ford's market share is on the rise. Its stock price has increased 700 percent from a 52-week low. And customers are paying more for Fords without the huge discount incentives that the company ran for many years. As just one indication, Taurus sales were up by 109 percent in 2010 over the prior year. Customers paid an average of $30,322 for each one, a transaction price that was $850 higher than a Toyota Avalon and a whopping $6,300 higher than the prior Taurus model.

Ford is back on track but far from out of the woods. Because it didn't take the government's bailout, it has a heavy debt burden. GM and Chrysler are emerging from bankruptcy with clean balance sheets and are on the warpath. And it isn't clear whether Ford can make as much profit on small cars as it did in the past on high dollar trucks. As positive as he is, Mulally also worries about the global competitive environment. "Global economic conditions are improving but remain fragile," he said, pointing out that labor markets are weak, credit is tight, consumer spending is depressed, and oil and other commodity prices are rising. All this leaves industry observers and consumers wondering whether or not Ford can return to the prominent position that it held for decades.

Questions for Discussion

1. Where would you put Ford in terms of competitive position? Why?

2. Is Ford a market-centered company? How can it improve in this area?

3. How does Ford's Sync contribute to its competitive advantage? Is this a sustainable advantage?

4. Can Mulally succeed with small world cars?

5. What other recommendations would you make to Mulally and Ford?

Sources: Paul Hochman, "Ford's Big Reveal," *Fast Company*, April 2010, pp. 90–97; Alex Taylor, "Fixing Up Ford," *Fortune*, May 25, 2009, p. 44; Joann Muller, "Ford's Rebound Is for Real," *Forbes*, April 27, 2010, accessed at www.forbes.com/2010/04/27/ford-alan-mulally-business-autos-ford.html; Joann Muller, "Ford's Neat Trick," *Forbes*, January 28, 2010, accessed at www.forbes.com/2010/01/28/ford-motor-earnings-business-autos-ford.html.

The Global Marketplace

Chapter Preview

You've now learned the fundamentals of how companies develop competitive marketing strategies to create customer value and build lasting customer relationships. In this chapter, we extend these fundamentals to global marketing. Although we discussed global topics in each previous chapter—it's difficult to find an area of marketing that doesn't contain at least some international applications—here we'll focus on special considerations that companies face when they market their brands globally. Advances in communication, transportation, and other technologies have made the world a much smaller place. Today, almost every firm, large or small, faces international marketing issues. In this chapter, we will examine six major decisions marketers make in going global.

To start our exploration of global marketing, let's look again at Google. Google is a truly global operation. It's accessible just about anywhere in the world and in hundreds of different languages. But just as international markets provide opportunities, they sometimes present daunting challenges. Here, we examine Google's odyssey into mainland China—and back out again.

Google in China: Running the Global Marketing Gauntlet

Google's mission is "to organize the world's information and make it universally accessible and useful." Almost by definition, this suggests that Google needs to operate internationally. What's more, international markets are a key to Google's expansion, as growth slows in domestic search advertising, Google's strongest business.

True to its mission and growth model, Google has, in fact, gone global. International markets now make up more than one-half of the company's revenues. Whereas Google controls 60 percent of the U.S. Internet search market, it controls an even more impressive 80 percent of the European market. Google is available in hundreds of languages—from Korean to Arabic to Zulu—almost anywhere in the world. Anywhere, that is, except China. After a long-running feud with the Chinese government over censorship and other issues, Google has all but shut down—at least for now—its operations in mainland China and its Google.cn search engine.

Google's experiences in China vividly illustrate the prospects and perils of going global. The world's most populous country and third-largest economy, China represents a huge potential market for Google. Although only 23 percent of Chinese now use the Internet, the number of Internet users in China reached 330 million last year, more than the entire population of the United States. The Internet in China, especially for young people, offers an outlet for enormous pent-up demand for entertainment, amusement, and social interaction. More than 70 percent of Chinese Internet users are under 30 years old. Moreover, online advertising in China generates an estimated $3 billion in annual revenues.

To access all that potential, however, Google has had to run against a gauntlet of local competitors and government restrictions. Google began in early 2000 by building a Chinese language version of its search engine, one that mirrored the English language content on Google.com. In 2002, however, the Chinese government shut down Google's site in China, claiming that people were using it to access forbidden content. To the disappointment of many, Google revised the site to self-censor content deemed taboo by the Chinese government. It argued that it was blocking only a small proportion of the sites that Chinese users visit. Users still would be able to get uncensored information on most important topics.

By early 2006, Google had received Chinese government approval to launch Google.cn. The company wanted to locate its own servers in China—inside the so-called "Great Firewall of China," the government's system of censoring electronic information that enters or leaves the country. Although Chinese Internet users could access Google.com, having servers inside the country would help Google to compete more effectively with Chinese-owned market leader Baidu and with Yahoo and Microsoft's MSN, which had already established local Chinese operations.

Google was especially interested in providing services for the potentially lucrative Chinese mobile phone market. China has more than 500 million mobile-phone users—more than the United States, Japan, Germany, and the United Kingdom combined. The Chinese use their phones to buy ringtones, pictures, and other content from Internet portals such as KongZhong and TOM Online. Although such downloads sell for only a few cents each, when multiplied by hundreds of millions, the revenues add up quickly. Mobile users also like to play online multiplayer games, providing substantial subscription and accessories revenues.

With Google.cn established, Google began a bruising competitive battle for the hearts, minds, and wallets of Chinese consumers. Its most formidable rival was Baidu, which successfully targeted less-educated, lower-income users, the fastest-growing Chinese subscriber segment. Baidu had a six-year head start on Google in China. And as a local company, Baidu had a better understanding of the nuances of the Chinese market and language. Mandarin Chinese is a character-based language in which characters can have multiple meanings. Google had to learn how to "talk" to users—how to interpret the correct meaning of characters in search requests. Still, by late 2009, Google's share of the China search market had increased to 35.6 percent, while Baidu's share had fallen to 58 percent.

Despite this success, however, Google was growing increasingly uncomfortable with China's censorship restrictions. Chinese law banned the spread of "content subverting State power, undermining national unity, infringing upon national honor and interest, inciting ethnic hatred and secession," or supporting pornography or terrorism. By 2010, the Chinese government was enforcing strict interpretations of these laws on foreign IT companies operating in China. But knuckling under to government censorship just didn't fit well with Google's culture of free and open expression. To top things off, while Google was struggling with self-censorship issues, it suffered what it called a "highly sophisticated" cyber attack by Chinese hackers who stole some proprietary code and infiltrated the Google e-mail accounts of Chinese human-rights activists.

In early 2010, Google had seen enough of what it saw as the Chinese government's heavy-handed tactics. It announced that it would remove its technical operations from mainland China and route www.google.com.cn users to an uncensored version of its www.google.com.hk site in Hong Kong, which is not subject to the restrictions. Despite the Chinese government's displeasure with Google's evasive action, in mid-2010 it renewed Google's operating license, allowing Google to continue serving Chinese users with the uncensored Hong Kong service. Still, the cat-and-mouse game continued, and Google's Chinese connection remained shaky.

In pulling its search operations out of mainland China, Google doesn't lose all that much current business—analysts estimated that Google earned only 1–2 percent of its global revenue from China, between $250 and $300 million. And about 30–40 percent of that revenue comes from Chinese companies that place ads on Google sites outside China, which will likely continue. However, leaving mainland China cedes the country's huge search advertising potential to competitors. It also threatens Google's mobile phone business in China. Thus, many analysts think that Google will eventually resolve its feud with the Chinese government and once again enter this important market directly. By the time you read this, that might already have happened.

For now, however, Google's mainland China pullout has won praise on moral grounds. Beyond its mission to make the world's information universally accessible, Google was founded on a simple code of conduct: "Don't be evil." According to Google founders Larry Page and Sergey Brin, that means "we believe strongly that in the long term, we will be better served—as shareholders and in all other ways—by a company that does good things for the world, even if we forego some short term gains." In the eyes of many Google fans—even those in China—the company's strong stand against censorship is simply the right thing to do. Says one prominent Chinese blogger, it was "high time to change [Google's policy in China] back to the right track."[1]

> The challenges of global marketing: After a long-running feud with the Chinese government over censorship, Google pulled out of mainland China.

> **Just as international markets provide opportunities, they sometimes present challenges. Google's odyssey into mainland China—and back out again—vividly illustrates the prospects and perils of going global.**

In the past, U.S. companies paid little attention to international trade. If they could pick up some extra sales via exports, that was fine. But the big market was at home, and it teemed with opportunities. The home market was also much safer. Managers did not need to learn other languages, deal with strange and changing currencies, face political and legal uncertainties, or adapt their products to different customer needs and expectations. Today, however, the situation is much different. Organizations of all kinds, from Google, Coca-Cola, and HP to MTV and even the NBA, have gone global.

Author Comment | The rapidly changing global environment provides both opportunities and threats. It's difficult to find a marketer today that isn't affected in some way by global developments.

Global Marketing Today (pp 552–553)

The world is shrinking rapidly with the advent of faster communication, transportation, and financial flows. Products developed in one country—Gucci purses, Sony electronics, McDonald's hamburgers, Japanese sushi, German BMWs—have found enthusiastic acceptance in other countries. It would not be surprising to hear about a German businessman wearing an Italian suit meeting an English friend at a Japanese restaurant who later returns home to drink Russian vodka and watch *Dancing with the Stars* on TV.

International trade has boomed over the past three decades. Since 1990, the number of multinational corporations in the world has grown from 30,000 to more than 63,000. Some of these multinationals are true giants. In fact, of the largest 150 "economies" in the world, only 81 are countries. The remaining 69 are multinational corporations. Walmart, the world's largest company, has annual revenues greater than the GDP of all but the world's 21 largest countries.[2]

Between 2000 and 2008, total world trade grew more than 7 percent per year, easily outstripping GDP output, which was about 3 percent. Despite a dip in world trade caused by the recent worldwide recession, the world trade of products and services last year was valued at more than $12 trillion, about 17 percent of GDP worldwide.[3]

● Many U.S. companies have long been successful at international marketing: McDonald's, Coca-Cola, Starbucks, GE, IBM, Colgate, Caterpillar, Boeing, and dozens of other American firms have made the world their market. In the United States, names such as Sony, Toyota, Nestlé, IKEA, Canon, and Nokia have become household words. Other products and services that appear to be American are, in fact, produced or owned by foreign companies, such

● **Many American companies have now made the world their market.**

as Bantam books, Baskin-Robbins ice cream, GE and RCA televisions, Carnation milk, Universal Studios, and Motel 6. Michelin, the oh-so-French tire manufacturer, now does 34 percent of its business in North America; J&J, the maker of quintessentially all-American products such as BAND-AIDs and Johnson's Baby Shampoo, does 50 percent of its business abroad. And America's own Caterpillar belongs more to the wider world, with 61 percent of its sales coming from outside the United States.[4]

But as global trade grows, global competition is also intensifying. Foreign firms are expanding aggressively into new international markets, and home markets are no longer as rich in opportunity. Few industries are now safe from foreign competition. If companies delay taking steps toward internationalizing, they risk being shut out of growing markets in western and eastern Europe, China and the Pacific Rim, Russia, India, and elsewhere. Firms that stay at home to play it safe might not only lose their chances to enter other markets but also risk losing their home markets. Domestic companies that never thought about foreign competitors suddenly find these competitors in their own backyards.

Ironically, although the need for companies to go abroad is greater today than in the past, so are the risks. Companies that go global may face highly unstable governments and currencies, restrictive government policies and regulations, and high trade barriers. The recently dampened global economic environment has also created big global challenges. And corruption is an increasing problem; officials in several countries often award business not to the best bidder but to the highest briber.

A **global firm** is one that, by operating in more than one country, gains marketing, production, R&D, and financial advantages that are not available to purely domestic competitors. The global company sees the world as one market. It minimizes the importance of national boundaries and develops global brands. It raises capital, obtains materials and components, and manufactures and markets its goods wherever it can do the best job. For example, Otis Elevator, the world's largest elevator maker, achieves 80 percent of its sales from outside the United States. It gets its elevator door systems from France, small geared parts from Spain, electronics from Germany, and special motor drives from Japan. It uses the United States only for systems integration.[5] Many of today's global corporations—both large and small—have become truly borderless.

This does not mean that small- and medium-sized firms must operate in a dozen countries to succeed. These firms can practice global niching. But the world is becoming smaller, and every company operating in a global industry—whether large or small—must assess and establish its place in world markets.

The rapid move toward globalization means that all companies will have to answer some basic questions: What market position should we try to establish in our country, in our economic region, and globally? Who will our global competitors be and what are their strategies and resources? Where should we produce or source our products? What strategic alliances should we form with other firms around the world?

As shown in **●** **Figure 19.1**, a company faces six major decisions in international marketing. We discuss each decision in detail in this chapter.

Global firm

A firm that, by operating in more than one country, gains R&D, production, marketing, and financial advantages in its costs and reputation that are not available to purely domestic competitors.

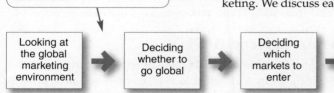

It's a big and beautiful but threatening world out there for marketers! Most large American firms have made the world their market. For example, once all-American McDonald's now captures 65 percent of its sales from outside the United States.

| Looking at the global marketing environment | → | Deciding whether to go global | → | Deciding which markets to enter | → | Deciding how to enter the market | → | Deciding on the global marketing program | → | Deciding on the global marketing organization |

● **FIGURE | 19.1**
Major International Marketing Decisions

Author | As if operating within a
Comment | company's own borders
wasn't difficult enough, going global
adds many layers of complexities. For
example, Coca-Cola markets its
products in hundreds of countries
around the globe. It must understand
the varying trade, economic, cultural,
and political environments in each
market.

Looking at the Global Marketing Environment (pp 554–560)

Before deciding whether to operate internationally, a company must understand the international marketing environment. That environment has changed a great deal in the past two decades, creating both new opportunities and new problems.

The International Trade System

U.S. companies looking abroad must start by understanding the international *trade system*. When selling to another country, a firm may face restrictions on trade between nations. Governments may charge *tariffs*, taxes on certain imported products designed to raise revenue or protect domestic firms. Tariffs are often used to force favorable trade behaviors from other nations. ◉ For example, the United States recently threatened high tariffs on—of all things—Roquefort cheese in retaliation to a European Union (EU) ban on U.S. hormone-treated beef.[6]

◉ **Trade barriers: In retaliation for a European Union ban on U.S. hormone-treated beef, the United States threatened high tariffs on—of all things—Roquefort cheese and other popular European food imports.**

Roquefort cheese and some other popular European food imports could have disappeared from U.S. gourmet shops and fancy food departments thanks to a threatened 100–300 percent import tax. The imports were hostages in a long-running trans-Atlantic food fight over the EU's French-led refusal to import hormone-treated U.S. beef. By the tit-for-tat logic of playground and world trade disputes, if the EU didn't lift its 20-year beef ban, the United States would impose punishing World Trade Organization (WTO)-sanctioned tariffs on selected products that EU members sold in the United States. No one would have starved as a result, but the 300 percent duty on Roquefort would have driven its price into the unheard-of, demand-stifling range of $60 a pound. Although Roquefort was the most harshly attacked, other U.S. tariffs would have doubled the retail prices of 34 items, ranging from Italian mineral water to Irish oatmeal, French chestnuts, and other regional foodie delights from 26 EU countries. In the end, it's was hard to tell who won this battle. The United States dropped the threatened tariff increases after the EU agreed to quadruple its U.S. non-hormone-treated beef imports over the next four years. But the EU still bans hormone-treated beef.

Countries may set *quotas*, limits on the amount of foreign imports that they will accept in certain product categories. The purpose of a quota is to conserve on foreign exchange and protect local industry and employment. Firms may also face *exchange controls*, which limit the amount of foreign exchange and the exchange rate against other currencies.

A company also may face *nontariff trade barriers*, such as biases against its bids, restrictive product standards, or excessive host-country regulations. For example, non-Chinese companies trying to crack the huge and fast-growing Chinese life insurance market have found the going tough. Domestic companies, such as China Life, Ping An, and others, enjoyed tremendous name recognition. But they also benefit from protectionist regulations. For instance, whereas domestic firms can obtain nationwide licenses, foreign firms need separate permissions for every new city or province in which they want to do business—a daunting hurdle. "There is clearly an uneven playing field," says an American insurance executive.[7]

At the same time, certain other forces can *help* trade between nations. Examples include the General Agreement on Tariffs and Trade (GATT) and various regional free trade agreements.

The World Trade Organization and GATT

GATT is a 62-year-old treaty designed to promote world trade by reducing tariffs and other international trade barriers. Since the treaty's inception in 1947, member nations (currently numbering 153) have met in eight rounds of GATT negotiations to reassess trade barriers and establish new rules for international trade. The first seven rounds of negotiations reduced the average worldwide tariffs on manufactured goods from 45 percent to just 5 percent.[8]

The most recently completed GATT negotiations, dubbed the Uruguay Round, dragged on for seven long years before concluding in 1994. The benefits of the Uruguay Round will be felt for many years as the accord promotes long-term global trade growth. It reduced the world's remaining merchandise tariffs by 30 percent. The agreement also extended GATT to cover trade in agriculture and a wide range of services, and it toughened the international protection of copyrights, patents, trademarks, and other intellectual property. Although the financial impact of such an agreement is difficult to measure, research suggests that cutting agriculture, manufacturing, and services trade barriers by one-third would boost the world economy by $613 billion, the equivalent of adding another Poland to the world economy.[9]

Beyond reducing trade barriers and setting global standards for trade, ◉ the Uruguay Round created the WTO to enforce GATT rules. In general, the WTO acts as an umbrella organization, overseeing GATT, mediating global disputes, helping developing countries build trade capacity, and imposing trade sanctions. The previous GATT organization never had such authorities. A new round of GATT negotiations, the Doha round, began in Doha, Qatar, in late 2001 and was set to conclude in 2005, but the discussions still continued through 2010.[10]

◉ **The WTO and GATT: GATT promotes world trade by reducing tariffs and other international trade barriers. The WTO oversees GATT, imposes trade sanctions, and mediates global disputes.**

Regional Free Trade Zones

Economic community
A group of nations organized to work toward common goals in the regulation of international trade.

Certain countries have formed *free trade zones* or **economic communities**. These are groups of nations organized to work toward common goals in the regulation of international trade. One such community is the *European Union (EU)*. Formed in 1957, the EU set out to create a single European market by reducing barriers to the free flow of products, services, finances, and labor among member countries and developing policies on trade with nonmember nations. ◉ Today, the EU represents one of the world's largest single markets. Currently, it has 27 member countries containing close to half a billion consumers and accounting for more than 20 percent of the world's exports.[11]

European unification offers tremendous trade opportunities for U.S. and other non-European firms. However, it also poses threats. As a result of increased unification, European companies have grown bigger and more competitive. Perhaps an even greater concern, however, is that lower barriers *inside* Europe will create only thicker *outside* walls. Some observers envision a "Fortress Europe" that heaps favors on firms from EU countries but hinders outsiders by imposing obstacles.

Progress toward European unification has been slow. In recent years, however, 16 member nations have taken a significant step toward unification by adopting the euro as a common currency. Many other countries are expected to follow within the next few years. Widespread adoption of the euro will decrease much of the currency risk associated with doing business in Europe, making member countries with previously weak currencies more attractive markets.[12]

However, even with the adoption of the euro, it is unlikely that the EU will ever go against 2,000 years of tradition and become the "United States of Europe." A community with more than two-dozen different languages and cultures will always have difficulty coming together and acting as a single entity. Still, with a combined annual GDP of more than $16.1 trillion, the EU has become a potent economic force.[13]

In 1994, the *North American Free Trade Agreement (NAFTA)* established a free trade zone among the United States, Mexico, and Canada. The agreement created a single market of 452 million people who produce and consume almost $17 trillion worth of goods and services annually. Over the past 15 years, NAFTA has eliminated trade barriers and investment restrictions among the three countries. According to the International Monetary Fund, total

● **Economic communities: The European Union represents one of the world's single largest markets. Its current member countries contain more than half a billion consumers and account for 20 percent of the world's exports.**

trade among the three countries has more than doubled from $306 billion in 1993 to $637 billion in 2009.[14]

Following the apparent success of NAFTA, in 2005 the Central American Free Trade Agreement (CAFTA-DR) established a free trade zone between the United States and Costa Rica, the Dominican Republic, El Salvador, Guatemala, Honduras, and Nicaragua. Other free trade areas have formed in Latin America and South America. For example, the Union of South American Nations (UNASUR), modeled after the EU, was formed in 2004 and formalized by a constitutional treaty in 2008. Consisting of 12 countries, UNASUR makes up the largest trading bloc after NAFTA and the EU, with a population of 361 million, a combined economy of more than $973 billion, and exports worth $181 billion. Similar to NAFTA and the EU, UNASUR aims to eliminate all tariffs between nations by 2019.[15]

Each nation has unique features that must be understood. A nation's readiness for different products and services and its attractiveness as a market to foreign firms depend on its economic, political-legal, and cultural environments.

Economic Environment

The international marketer must study each country's economy. Two economic factors reflect the country's attractiveness as a market: its industrial structure and its income distribution.

The country's *industrial structure* shapes its product and service needs, income levels, and employment levels. The four types of industrial structures are as follows:

- *Subsistence economies:* In a subsistence economy, the vast majority of people engage in simple agriculture. They consume most of their output and barter the rest for simple goods and services. They offer few market opportunities.

- *Raw material exporting economies:* These economies are rich in one or more natural resources but poor in other ways. Much of their revenue comes from exporting these resources. Some examples are Chile (tin and copper), the Democratic Republic of the Congo (copper, cobalt, and coffee), and Saudi Arabia (oil). These countries are good markets for large equipment, tools and supplies, and trucks. If there are many foreign residents and a wealthy upper class, they are also a market for luxury goods.

- *Emerging economies (industrializing economies):* In an emerging economy, fast growth in manufacturing results in rapid overall economic growth. Examples include the BRIC countries—Brazil, Russia, India, and China. As manufacturing increases, the country needs more imports of raw textile materials, steel, and heavy machinery, and fewer imports of finished textiles, paper products, and automobiles. Industrialization typically creates a new rich class and a small but growing middle class, both demanding new types of imported goods.

- *Industrial economies:* Industrial economies are major exporters of manufactured goods, services, and investment funds. They trade goods among themselves and also export them to other types of economies for raw materials and semifinished goods. The varied manufacturing activities of these industrial nations and their large middle class make them rich markets for all sorts of goods. Examples include the United States, Japan, and Norway.

The second economic factor is the country's *income distribution*. Industrialized nations may have low-, medium-, and high-income households. In contrast, countries with subsistence economies consist mostly of households with very low family incomes. Still other countries may have households with only either very low or very high incomes. Even poor or emerging economies may be attractive markets for all kinds of goods. These days, com-

● **Economic environment: In India, Ford's $7,700 Figo targets low- to middle-income consumers who want to move off their motorbikes.**

panies in a wide range of industries—from cars to computers to candy—are increasingly targeting even low- and middle-income consumers in emerging economies. ● For example, in India, Ford recently introduced a new model targeted to consumers who are only now able to afford their first car:[16]

In an effort to boost its presence in Asia's third-largest auto market behind Japan and China, Ford introduced the Figo, a $7,700 hatchback design for a hypothetical twenty-something Indian named Sandeep. He works in IT, finance, or another service industry and tools around on a motorcycle. But now that he's enjoying the first fruits of affluence, Sandeep wants four wheels. "There are huge numbers of people wanting to move off their motorbikes," says Ford's India general manager. Some 70 percent of cars sold in India are in the Figo's size and price range. In fact, GM beat Ford to the punch by two months with its new $7,600 Chevy Beat, which is so popular in India that there's now a two-month waiting list.

Political-Legal Environment

Nations differ greatly in their political-legal environments. In considering whether to do business in a given country, a company should consider factors such as the country's attitudes toward international buying, government bureaucracy, political stability, and monetary regulations.

Some nations are very receptive to foreign firms; others are less accommodating. For example, India has tended to bother foreign businesses with import quotas, currency restrictions, and other limitations that make operating there a challenge. In contrast, neighboring Asian countries, such as Singapore and Thailand, court foreign investors and shower them with incentives and favorable operating conditions. Political and regulatory stability is another issue. For example, Venezuela's government is notoriously volatile—due to economic factors such as inflation and steep public spending—which increases the risk of doing business there. Although most international marketers still find the Venezuelan market attractive, the unstable political and regulatory situation will affect how they handle business and financial matters.[17]

Companies must also consider a country's monetary regulations. Sellers want to take their profits in a currency of value to them. Ideally, the buyer can pay in the seller's currency or in other world currencies. Short of this, sellers might accept a blocked currency—one whose removal from the country is restricted by the buyer's government—if they can buy other goods in that country that they need themselves or can sell elsewhere for a needed currency. In addition to currency limits, a changing exchange rate also creates high risks for the seller.

Most international trade involves cash transactions. Yet many nations have too little hard currency to pay for their purchases from other countries. They may want to pay with other items instead of cash. For example, *barter* involves the direct exchange of goods or services: China recently agreed to help the Democratic Republic of Congo develop $6 billion of desperately needed infrastructure—2,400 miles of roads, 2,000 miles of railways, 32 hospitals, 145 health centers, and 2 universities—in exchange for natural resources needed to feed China's booming industries—10 million tons of copper and 400,000 tons of cobalt.[18]

Cultural Environment

Each country has its own folkways, norms, and taboos. When designing global marketing strategies, companies must understand how culture affects consumer reactions in each of its world markets. In turn, they must also understand how their strategies affect local cultures.

The Impact of Culture on Marketing Strategy

Sellers must understand the ways that consumers in different countries think about and use certain products before planning a marketing program. There are often surprises. For example, the average French man uses almost twice as many cosmetics and grooming aids as his wife. The Germans and the French eat more packaged, branded spaghetti than Italians do. Some 49 percent of Chinese eat on the way to work. Most American women let down their hair and take off makeup at bedtime, whereas 15 percent of Chinese women style their hair at bedtime and 11 percent put *on* makeup.[19]

Companies that ignore cultural norms and differences can make some very expensive and embarrassing mistakes. Here are two examples:

Nike inadvertently offended Chinese officials when it ran an ad featuring LeBron James crushing a number of culturally revered Chinese figures in a kung fu–themed television ad. ● The Chinese government found that the ad violated regulations to uphold national dignity and respect the "motherland's culture" and yanked the multimillion-dollar campaign. With egg on its face, Nike released a formal apology.

Burger King made a similar mistake when it created in-store ads in Spain showing Hindu goddess Lakshmi atop a ham sandwich with the caption "a snack that is sacred." Cultural and religious groups worldwide objected strenuously—Hindus are vegetarian. Burger King apologized and pulled the ads.[20]

● **Overlooking cultural differences can result in embarrassing mistakes. China imposed a nationwide ban on this "blasphemous" kung fu–themed television ad featuring LeBron James crushing a number of culturally revered Chinese figures.**

Business norms and behavior also vary from country to country. For example, American executives like to get right down to business and engage in fast and tough face-to-face bargaining. However, Japanese and other Asian businesspeople often find this behavior offensive. They prefer to start with polite conversation, and they rarely say no in face-to-face conversations. As another example, South Americans like to sit or stand very close to each other when they talk business—in fact, almost nose-to-nose. An American business executive tends to keep backing away as the South American moves closer. Both may end up being offended. American business executives need to understand these kinds of cultural nuances before conducting business in another country.

By the same token, companies that understand cultural nuances can use them to their advantage when positioning products and preparing campaigns internationally. Consider LG Electronics, the $22 billion South Korean electronics, telecommunications, and appliance powerhouse. LG now operates in more than 60 countries and captures 87 percent of its sales from markets outside its home country. LG's global success rests on understanding and catering to the unique characteristics of each local market through in-country research, manufacturing, and marketing.[21]

If you've got kimchi in your fridge, it's hard to keep it a secret. Made from fermented cabbage seasoned with garlic and chili, kimchi is served with most meals in Korea. But when it's stored inside a normal refrigerator, its pungent odor taints nearby foods. That's why, two decades ago, LG introduced the kimchi refrigerator, featuring a dedicated compartment that isolates smelly kimchi from other foods. Kimchi refrigerators have become a fixture in 65 percent of Korean homes, and LG is the country's top-selling manufacturer.

LG's mission is to make customers happy worldwide by creating products that fit perfectly into their lives, no matter where they live. In India, LG rolled out refrigerators with larger vegetable- and water-storage compartments, surge-resistant power supplies, and brightly colored finishes that reflect local preferences (red in the south, green in Kashmir). Some of LG's Indian microwaves have dark-colored interiors to hide masala stains. In Iran, LG offers a microwave oven with a preset button for reheating shish kebabs—a favorite dish. In the Middle East, the company unveiled a gold-plated 71-inch flat-screen television that sells for $80,000—a tribute to the region's famous affinity for gilded opulence. And in Russia, where many people entertain at home during the country's long winters, LG developed a karaoke phone that can be programmed with the top 100 Russian songs, whose lyrics scroll across the screen when they're played. The phone sold more than 220,000 handsets in the first year.

Thus, understanding cultural traditions, preferences, and behaviors can help companies not only avoid embarrassing mistakes but also take advantage of cross-cultural opportunities.

The Impact of Marketing Strategy on Cultures

Whereas marketers worry about the impact of culture on their global marketing strategies, others may worry about the impact of marketing strategies on global cultures. For example, social critics contend that large American multinationals, such as McDonald's, Coca-Cola, Starbucks, Nike, Microsoft, Disney, and MTV, aren't just "globalizing" their brands; they are "Americanizing" the world's cultures.[22]

There are now as many people studying English in China (or playing basketball, for that matter) as there are people in the United States. Seven of the 10 most watched TV shows around the world are American, *Avatar* is the top-grossing film of all time in China, and the world is as fixated on U.S. brands as ever, which is why U.S. multinationals from McDonald's to Nike book more than half their revenues overseas. If you bring together teenagers from Nigeria, Sweden, South Korea, and Argentina—to pick a random foursome—what binds these kids together in some kind of community is American culture—the music, the Hollywood fare, the electronic games, Google, American consumer brands. The only thing they will likely have in common that doesn't revolve around the United States is an interest in soccer. The . . . rest of the world is becoming [evermore] like us—in ways good and bad.

"Today, globalization often wears Mickey Mouse ears, eats Big Macs, drinks Coke or Pepsi, and does its computing with Windows," says Thomas Friedman, in his book *The Lexus and the Olive Tree: Understanding Globalization.*[23] Critics worry that, under such "McDomination," countries around the globe are losing their individual cultural identities. Teens in India watch MTV and ask their parents for more westernized clothes and other symbols of American pop culture and values. Grandmothers in small European villas no longer spend each morning visiting local meat, bread, and produce markets to gather the ingredients for dinner. Instead, they now shop at Walmart Supercenters. Women in Saudi Arabia see American films and question their societal roles. In China, most people never drank coffee before Starbucks entered the market. Now Chinese consumers rush to Starbucks stores "because it's a symbol of a new kind of lifestyle." Similarly, in China, where McDonald's operates more than 80 restaurants in Beijing alone, nearly half of all children identify the chain as a domestic brand.

Such concerns have sometimes led to a backlash against American globalization. Well-known U.S. brands have become the targets of boycotts and protests in some international markets. As symbols of American capitalism, companies such as Coca-Cola, McDonald's, Nike, and KFC have been singled out by antiglobalization protestors in hot spots around the world, especially when anti-American sentiment peaks.

Despite such problems, defenders of globalization argue that concerns of "Americanization" and the potential damage to American brands are overblown. U.S. brands are doing very well internationally. In the most recent Millward Brown Optimor brand value survey of global consumer brands, 16 of the top 20 brands were American owned, including megabrands such as Google, IBM, Apple, Microsoft, Coca-Cola, McDonald's, GE, Amazon .com, and Walmart.[24] ● Many iconic American brands are prospering globally, even in some of the most unlikely places:[25]

It's lunchtime in Tehran's tiny northern suburbs, and around the crowded tables at Nayeb Restaurant, elegant Iranian women in Jackie O sunglasses and designer jeans let their table chatter glide effortlessly between French, English, and their native Farsi. The only visual clues that these lunching ladies aren't dining at some smart New York City eatery but in the heart of Washington's axis of evil are the expensive Hermès scarves covering their blonde-tipped hair in deference to the mullahs. And the drink of choice? This being revolutionary Iran, where alcohol is banned, the women are making do with Coca-Cola. Yes, Coca-Cola. It's a hard fact for some of Iran's theocrats to swallow. They want Iranians to shun "Great Satan" brands like Coke and Pepsi, and the Iranian government has recently pressured Iranian soft drink companies to clarify their "ties with the Zionist company Coca-Cola." Yet, Coke and Pepsi have grabbed about half the national soft drink sales in Iran, one of the Middle East's biggest drink markets. "I joke with customers not to buy this stuff because it's American," says a Tehran storekeeper, "but they don't care. That only makes them want to buy it more."

⦿ **Many iconic American brands are prospering globally, even in some of the most unlikely places. At this Tehran restaurant, American colas are the drink of choice. Coca-Cola and PepsiCo have grabbed about half the national soft drink sales in Iran.**

More fundamentally, the cultural exchange goes both ways: America gets as well as gives cultural influence. True, Hollywood dominates the global movie market, but British TV gives as much as it gets in dishing out competition to U.S. shows, spawning such hits as *The Office*, *American Idol*, and *Dancing with the Stars*. Although Chinese and Russian youth are donning NBA superstar jerseys, the increasing popularity of American soccer has deep international roots. Even American childhood has been increasingly influenced by European and Asian cultural imports. Most kids know all about imports such as Hello Kitty, the Bakugan Battle Brawler, or any of a host of Nintendo or Sega game characters. And J. K. Rowling's so-very-British Harry Potter books have shaped the thinking of a generation of American youngsters, not to mention the millions of American oldsters who've fallen under their spell as well. For the moment, English remains the dominant language of the Internet, and having Web access often means that third-world youth have greater exposure to American popular culture. Yet these same technologies let Eastern European students studying in the United States hear Webcast news and music from Poland, Romania, or Belarus.

Thus, globalization is a two-way street. If globalization has Mickey Mouse ears, it is also wearing a French beret, talking on a Nokia cell phone, buying furniture at IKEA, driving a Toyota Camry, and watching a Samsung plasma TV.

Deciding Whether to Go Global (pp 560–561)

Not all companies need to venture into international markets to survive. For example, most local businesses need to market well only in their local marketplace. Operating domestically is easier and safer. Managers don't need to learn another country's language and laws. They don't have to deal with unstable currencies, face political and legal uncertainties, or redesign their products to suit different customer expectations. However, companies that operate in global industries, where their strategic positions in specific markets are affected strongly by their overall global positions, must compete on a regional or worldwide basis to succeed.

Any of several factors might draw a company into the international arena. Global competitors might attack the company's home market by offering better products or lower prices.

● **Going global: Coca-Cola has emphasized international growth in recent years to offset stagnant or declining U.S. soft drink sales.**

The company might want to counterattack these competitors in their home markets to tie up their resources. The company's customers might be expanding abroad and require international servicing. Or, most likely, international markets might simply provide better opportunities for growth. ● For example, Coca-Cola has emphasized international growth in recent years to offset stagnant or declining U.S. soft drink sales. "It's been apparent that Coke's signature cola can't grow much on its home turf anymore," states an industry analyst. Today, about 80 percent of Coke's profits come from outside North America.[26]

Before going abroad, the company must weigh several risks and answer many questions about its ability to operate globally. Can the company learn to understand the preferences and buyer behavior of consumers in other countries? Can it offer competitively attractive products? Will it be able to adapt to other countries' business cultures and deal effectively with foreign nationals? Do the company's managers have the necessary international experience? Has management considered the impact of regulations and the political environments of other countries?

Deciding Which Markets to Enter (pp 561–562)

Before going abroad, the company should try to define its international *marketing objectives and policies*. It should decide what *volume* of foreign sales it wants. Most companies start small when they go abroad. Some plan to stay small, seeing international sales as a small part of their business. Other companies have bigger plans, seeing international business as equal to or even more important than their domestic business.

The company also needs to choose in *how many* countries it wants to market. Companies must be careful not to spread themselves too thin or expand beyond their capabilities by operating in too many countries too soon. Next, the company needs to decide on the *types* of countries to enter. A country's attractiveness depends on the product, geographical factors, income and population, political climate, and other factors. The seller may prefer certain country groups or parts of the world. In recent years, many major new markets have emerged, offering both substantial opportunities and daunting challenges.

After listing possible international markets, the company must carefully evaluate each one. It must consider many factors. For example, P&G's decision to enter the Chinese toothpaste market with its Crest is a no-brainer: China's huge population makes it the world's largest toothpaste market. And given that only 20 percent of China's rural dwellers now brush daily, this already huge market can grow even larger. Yet P&G must still question whether market size *alone* is reason enough for investing heavily in China.

P&G should ask some important questions: Can Crest compete effectively with dozens of local competitors, Colgate, and a state-owned brand managed by Unilever? Will the Chinese government remain stable and supportive? Does China provide for the needed production and distribution technologies? Can the company master China's vastly different cultural and buying differences? Crest's current success in China suggests that it can answer yes to every question.[27]

"Just 10 years ago, P&G's Crest brand was unknown to China's population, most of whom seldom—if ever—brushed their teeth," says one analyst. "Now P&G . . . sells more tubes of toothpaste there than it does in America, where Crest has been on store shelves for 52 years." P&G achieved this by sending researchers to get a feel for what urban and rural Chinese were willing to spend and what flavors they preferred. These researchers discovered that urban Chinese are happy to pay more than $1 for tubes of Crest with exotic flavors such as Icy Mountain Spring and Morning Lotus Fragrance. But Chinese living in the countryside prefer the 50-cent Crest Salt White because many rural Chinese believe that salt whitens teeth. Armed with such insights, Crest now leads all competitors in China with a 25 percent market share. Some users even believe it's a Chinese brand. P&G hopes to find similar success in other emerging markets across its entire product mix. Such markets now account for 30 percent of the company's total sales.

Possible global markets should be ranked on several factors, including market size, market growth, the cost of doing business, competitive advantage, and risk level. The goal is to determine the potential of each market, using indicators such as those shown in ◉ **Table 19.1**. Then the marketer must decide which markets offer the greatest long-run return on investment.

> **Author Comment** | A company has many options for entering an international market, from simply exporting its products to working jointly with foreign companies to holding its own foreign-based operations.

Deciding How to Enter the Market (pp 562–565)

Once a company has decided to sell in a foreign country, it must determine the best mode of entry. Its choices are *exporting*, *joint venturing*, and *direct investment*. ◉ **Figure 19.2** shows three market entry strategies, along with the options each one offers. As the figure shows, each succeeding strategy involves more commitment and risk but also more control and potential profits.

Exporting

Exporting
Entering a foreign market by selling goods produced in the company's home country, often with little modification.

The simplest way to enter a foreign market is through **exporting**. The company may passively export its surpluses from time to time, or it may make an active commitment to expand exports to a particular market. In either case, the company produces all its

---

◉ **TABLE | 19.1**   Indicators of Market Potential

Demographic Characteristics	Sociocultural Factors
Education	Consumer lifestyles, beliefs, and values
Population size and growth	Business norms and approaches
Population age composition	Cultural and social norms
	Languages

Geographic Characteristics	Political and Legal Factors
Climate	National priorities
Country size	Political stability
Population density—urban, rural	Government attitudes toward global trade
Transportation structure and market accessibility	Government bureaucracy
	Monetary and trade regulations

Economic Factors

GDP size and growth

Income distribution

Industrial infrastructure

Natural resources

Financial and human resources

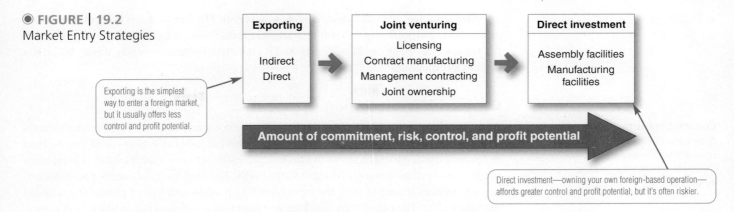

● FIGURE | 19.2
Market Entry Strategies

Exporting is the simplest way to enter a foreign market, but it usually offers less control and profit potential.

Direct investment—owning your own foreign-based operation—affords greater control and profit potential, but it's often riskier.

Joint venturing
Entering foreign markets by joining with foreign companies to produce or market a product or service.

Licensing
A method of entering a foreign market in which the company enters into an agreement with a licensee in the foreign market.

● Licensing: In Japan, the Moringa Milk Company produces Sunkist fruit juices, drinks, and dessert items.

goods in its home country. It may or may not modify them for the export market. Exporting involves the least change in the company's product lines, organization, investments, or mission.

Companies typically start with *indirect exporting*, working through independent international marketing intermediaries. Indirect exporting involves less investment because the firm does not require an overseas marketing organization or network. It also involves less risk. International marketing intermediaries bring know-how and services to the relationship, so the seller normally makes fewer mistakes. Sellers may eventually move into *direct exporting*, whereby they handle their own exports. The investment and risk are somewhat greater in this strategy, but so is the potential return.

Joint Venturing

A second method of entering a foreign market is by **joint venturing**—joining with foreign companies to produce or market products or services. Joint venturing differs from exporting in that the company joins with a host country partner to sell or market abroad. It differs from direct investment in that an association is formed with someone in the foreign country. There are four types of joint ventures: licensing, contract manufacturing, management contracting, and joint ownership.

Licensing

Licensing is a simple way for a manufacturer to enter international marketing. The company enters into an agreement with a licensee in the foreign market. For a fee or royalty payments, the licensee buys the right to use the company's manufacturing process, trademark, patent, trade secret, or other item of value. The company thus gains entry into a foreign market at little risk; the licensee gains production expertise or a well-known product or name without having to start from scratch.

In Japan, Budweiser beer flows from Kirin breweries, and Moringa Milk Company produces ● Sunkist fruit juice, drinks, and dessert items. Coca-Cola markets internationally by licensing bottlers around the world and supplying them with the syrup needed to produce the product. Its global bottling partners range from the Coca-Cola Bottling Company of Saudi Arabia to Europe-based Coca-Cola Hellenic, which bottles and markets Coca-Cola products to 560 million people in 28 countries, from Italy and Greece to Nigeria and Russia.

Licensing has potential disadvantages, however. The firm has less control over the licensee than it would over its own operations. Furthermore, if the licensee is very successful, the firm has given up these profits, and if and when the contract ends, it may find it has created a competitor.

Contract Manufacturing

Contract manufacturing
A joint venture in which a company contracts with manufacturers in a foreign market to produce the product or provide its service.

Another option is **contract manufacturing**—the company contracts with manufacturers in the foreign market to produce its product or provide its service. Sears used this method in opening up department stores in Mexico and Spain, where it found qualified local manufacturers to produce many of the products it sells. The drawbacks of contract manufacturing are decreased control over the manufacturing process and loss of potential profits on manufacturing. The benefits are the chance to start faster, with less risk, and the later opportunity either to form a partnership with or buy out the local manufacturer.

Management Contracting

Management contracting
A joint venture in which the domestic firm supplies the management know-how to a foreign company that supplies the capital; the domestic firm exports management services rather than products.

Under **management contracting**, the domestic firm supplies management know-how to a foreign company that supplies the capital. The domestic firm exports management services rather than products. Hilton uses this arrangement in managing hotels around the world. For example, the hotel chain recently opened a Doubletree by Hilton in the United Arab Emirates. The property is locally owned, but Hilton manages the hotel with its world-renowned hospitality expertise.[28]

Management contracting is a low-risk method of getting into a foreign market, and it yields income from the beginning. The arrangement is even more attractive if the contracting firm has an option to buy some share in the managed company later on. The arrangement is not sensible, however, if the company can put its scarce management talent to better uses or if it can make greater profits by undertaking the whole venture. Management contracting also prevents the company from setting up its own operations for a period of time.

Joint Ownership

Joint ownership
A joint venture in which a company joins investors in a foreign market to create a local business in which the company shares joint ownership and control.

Joint ownership ventures consist of one company joining forces with foreign investors to create a local business in which they share joint ownership and control. A company may buy an interest in a local firm, or the two parties may form a new business venture. Joint ownership may be needed for economic or political reasons. The firm may lack the financial, physical, or managerial resources to undertake the venture alone. Or a foreign government may require joint ownership as a condition for entry.

● Best Buy recently formed a 50/50 joint venture with UK-based Carphone Warehouse to open its first European Best Buy stores, starting in Britain:[29]

● **Joint ventures: Best Buy formed a joint venture with UK retailer Carphone Warehouse to jointly introduce Best Buy stores in Europe. Having "experience and connections in Europe is a huge, huge benefit."**

A new Best Buy store in Britain is exactly like its American counterpart. Even the carpets and the fittings have been imported from the United States. But the management team and senior employees are from the United Kingdom. To learn the Best Buy way of retailing, the locals receive nine weeks of training at Best Buy's "Blue Shirt Academy" in the United States. Best Buy is betting that this combination of its proven superstore concept with Carphone's local market savvy will differentiate Best Buy from the largely price-driven UK competition. Whereas other U.S. retail chains, such as Walmart, have struggled in the United Kingdom, partnering with Carphone will help. "Best Buy has a much better chance of being successful in Europe by partnering with Carphone than it would opening stores there all by itself," says a retailing analyst. "Having a management team that already has experience and connections in Europe is a huge, huge benefit."

Joint ownership has certain drawbacks, however. The partners may disagree over investment, marketing, or other policies. Whereas many U.S. firms like to reinvest earnings for growth, local firms often prefer to take out these earnings; whereas U.S. firms emphasize the role of marketing, local investors may rely on selling.

Direct Investment

Direct investment
Entering a foreign market by developing foreign-based assembly or manufacturing facilities.

The biggest involvement in a foreign market comes through **direct investment**—the development of foreign-based assembly or manufacturing facilities. For example, HP has made direct investments in several major markets abroad, including India. It has opened two factories that make PCs for the Indian market, along with HP-owned retail outlets in 150 Indian cities. Thanks to such commitments, HP is a market leader in India and now controls more than 16 percent of the market in India.[30]

If a company has gained experience in exporting and if the foreign market is large enough, foreign production facilities offer many advantages. The firm may have lower costs in the form of cheaper labor or raw materials, foreign government investment incentives, and freight savings. The firm may improve its image in the host country because it creates jobs. Generally, a firm develops a deeper relationship with the government, customers, local suppliers, and distributors, allowing it to adapt its products to the local market better. Finally, the firm keeps full control over the investment and therefore can develop manufacturing and marketing policies that serve its long-term international objectives.

The main disadvantage of direct investment is that the firm faces many risks, such as restricted or devalued currencies, falling markets, or government changes. In some cases, a firm has no choice but to accept these risks if it wants to operate in the host country.

Deciding on the Global Marketing Program (pp 565–573)

Author Comment | The major global marketing decision usually boils down to this: How much, if at all, should a company adapt its marketing strategy and programs to local markets? How might the answer differ for Boeing versus McDonald's?

Companies that operate in one or more foreign markets must decide how much, if at all, to adapt their marketing strategies and programs to local conditions. At one extreme are global companies that use **standardized global marketing**, essentially using the same marketing strategy approaches and marketing mix worldwide. At the other extreme is **adapted global marketing**. In this case, the producer adjusts the marketing strategy and mix elements to each target market, bearing more costs but hoping for a larger market share and return.

Standardized global marketing
An international marketing strategy that basically uses the same marketing strategy and mix in all of the company's international markets.

Adapted global marketing
An international marketing strategy that adjusts the marketing strategy and mix elements to each international target market, bearing more costs but hoping for a larger market share and return.

The question of whether to adapt or standardize the marketing strategy and program has been much debated over the years. On the one hand, some global marketers believe that technology is making the world a smaller place, and consumer needs around the world are becoming more similar. This paves the way for "global brands" and standardized global marketing. Global branding and standardization, in turn, result in greater brand power and reduced costs from economies of scale.

On the other hand, the marketing concept holds that marketing programs will be more effective if tailored to the unique needs of each targeted customer group. If this concept applies within a country, it should apply even more across international markets. Despite global convergence, consumers in different countries still have widely varied cultural backgrounds. They still differ significantly in their needs and wants, spending power, product preferences, and shopping patterns. Because these differences are hard to change, most marketers today adapt their products, prices, channels, and promotions to fit consumer desires in each country.

However, global standardization is not an all-or-nothing proposition. It's a matter of degree. Most international marketers suggest that companies should "think globally but act locally"—that they should seek a balance between standardization and adaptation. The company's overall strategy should provide global strategic direction. Then regional or local units should focus on adapting the strategy to specific local markets.

Collectively, local brands still account for the overwhelming majority of consumers' purchases. "The vast majority of people still lead very local lives," says a global analyst. "By all means go global, but the first thing you have to do is win on the ground. You have to go local." Another analyst agrees: "You need to respect local culture and become part of it." A global brand must "engage with consumers in a way that feels local to them." Simon Clift, head of marketing for global consumer-goods giant Unilever, puts it this way: "We're trying to strike a balance between being mindlessly global and hopelessly local."[31]

McDonald's operates this way: It uses the same basic fast-food look, layout, and operating model in its restaurants around the world but adapts its menu to local tastes. In Japan, it offers Ebi Filet-O-Shrimp burgers and fancy Salad Macs salad plates. In Korea it sells the Bulgogi Burger, a grilled pork patty on a bun with a garlicky soy sauce. In India, where cows are considered sacred, McDonald's serves McChicken, Filet-O-Fish, McVeggie (a vegetable burger), Pizza McPuffs, McAloo Tikki (a spiced-potato burger), and the Maharaja Mac—two all-chicken patties, special sauce, lettuce, cheese, pickles, onions on a sesame-seed bun. In all, McDonald's serves local markets with a global brand (see Real Marketing 19.1).

Product

Five strategies allow for adapting product and marketing communication strategies to a global market (see ◉ **Figure 19.3**).[32] We first discuss the three product strategies and then turn to the two communication strategies.

Straight product extension
Marketing a product in a foreign market without any change.

Straight product extension means marketing a product in a foreign market without any change. Top management tells its marketing people, "Take the product as is and find customers for it." The first step, however, should be to find out whether foreign consumers use that product and what form they prefer.

Straight extension has been successful in some cases and disastrous in others. Apple iPads, Gillette razors, Black & Decker tools, and even 7–11 Slurpees are all sold successfully in about the same form around the world. But when General Foods introduced its standard powdered JELL-O in the British market, it discovered that British consumers prefer a solid wafer or cake form. Likewise, Philips began to make a profit in Japan only after it reduced the size of its coffeemakers to fit into smaller Japanese kitchens and its shavers to fit smaller Japanese hands. Straight extension is tempting because it involves no additional product development costs, manufacturing changes, or new promotion. But it can be costly in the long run if products fail to satisfy consumers in specific global markets.

Product adaptation
Adapting a product to meet local conditions or wants in foreign markets.

Product adaptation involves changing the product to meet local conditions or wants. For example, Finnish cell phone maker Nokia customizes its cell phones for every major market. To meet the needs of less-affluent consumers in large developing countries such as India, China, and Kenya, the company has created full-featured but rugged and low-cost phones especially designed for harsher living conditions. For instance, it developed dustproof keypads—crucial in dry, hot countries with many unpaved roads. Some phones have built-in radio antennas for areas where radio is the main source of entertainment. Thanks to such adaptation, Nokia commands a whopping 62.3 percent share of the market in Africa and the Middle East, 48.5 percent in Eastern Europe, and 41.8 percent in Asia.[33]

The real question buried in this figure is this: How much should a company standardize or adapt its products and marketing across global markets?

◉ **FIGURE | 19.3**
Five Global Product and Communications Strategies

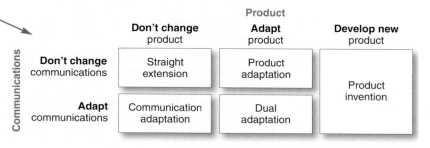

	Product		
Communications	**Don't change** product	**Adapt** product	**Develop new** product
Don't change communications	Straight extension	Product adaptation	Product invention
Adapt communications	Communication adaptation	Dual adaptation	

Real Marketing 19.1

McDonald's: Serving Local Markets with a Global Brand

Most Americans think of McDonald's as their very own. The first McDonald's stand popped up in California in 1954, and what could be more American than burger-and-fries fast food? But as it turns out, the quintessentially all-American company now sells more burgers and fries outside the country than within. Nearly 65 percent of McDonald's $23 billion of sales last year came from outside the United States, and its international sales grew at close to twice the rate of domestic sales growth.

McDonald's today is a sprawling global enterprise. Its 32,000 restaurants serve more than 60 million people in more than 100 countries each day. Few firms have more international marketing experience than McDonald's. Its restaurants around the world employ a common global strategy—convenient food at affordable prices. And no matter where you go in the world—from Moscow to Montreal or Shanghai to Cheboygan, Michigan—you'll find those good old golden arches and a menu full of Quarter Pounders, Big Macs, fries, milkshakes, and other familiar items. But within that general strategic framework, McDonald's adapts to the subtleties of each local market.

Adapting its proven formula to local markets hasn't always been easy, and McDonald's has learned many important lessons in its journeys overseas. Consider its experiences in Russia, a market that's very different culturally, economically, and politically from our own.

McDonald's first set its sights on Russia (then a part of the Soviet Union) in 1976, when George Cohon, head of McDonald's in Canada, took a group of Soviet Olympics officials to a McDonald's while they were in town for the Montreal Olympic Games. Cohon was struck by how much the Soviets liked McDonald's hamburgers, fries, and other fare. Over the next 14 years, Cohon flew to Russia more than 100 times, first to get Soviet permission for McDonald's to provide food for the 1980 Moscow Olympics and later to be allowed to open McDonald's restaurants in the country. He quickly learned that no one in Russia had any idea what a McDonald's was. The Soviets turned Cohon down flat on both requests.

Finally in 1988, as Premier Mikhail Gorbachev began to open the Russian economy, Cohon forged a deal with the city of Moscow to launch the first Russian McDonald's in Moscow's Pushkin Square. But obtaining permission was only the first step. Actually opening the restaurant brought a fresh set of challenges. Thanks to Russia's large and bureaucratic government structure, McDonald's had to obtain some 200 separate signatures just to open the single location. It had difficulty finding reliable suppliers for even such basics as hamburgers and buns. So McDonald's forked over $45 million to build a facility to produce these things itself. It even brought in technical experts from Canada with special strains of disease-resistant seed to teach Russian farmers how to grow Russet Burbank potatoes for french fries, and it built its own pasteurizing plant to ensure a plentiful supply of fresh milk.

When the Moscow McDonald's at Pushkin Square finally opened its doors in January 1990, it quickly won the hearts of Russian consumers. However, the company faced still more hurdles. The Pushkin Square restaurant is huge—26 cash registers (more than you'll find in a typical Walmart supercenter) and 900 seats (compared with 40 to 50 seats in a typical U.S. McDonald's). The logistics of serving customers on such a scale was daunting, made even more difficult by the fact that few employees or customers understood the fast-food concept.

Although American consumers were well acquainted with McDonald's, the Russians were clueless. So, to meet its high standards for customer satisfaction in this new market, the U.S. fast feeder had to educate employees about the time-tested McDonald's way of doing things. It trained Russian managers at Hamburger University in Illinois and subjected each of 630 new employees (most of whom didn't know a chicken McNugget from an Egg McMuffin) to 16 to 20 hours of training on such essentials as cooking meat patties, assembling Filet-O-Fish sandwiches, and giving service with a smile. Back in those days, McDonald's even had to train consumers—most Muscovites had never seen a fast-food restaurant. Customers waiting in line were shown videos telling them everything—from how to order and pay at the counter, to how to put their coats over the backs of their seats, to how to handle a Big Mac.

However, the new Moscow McDonald's got off to a spectacular start. An incredible

McDonald's is a "global brand serving local markets." Its Pushkin Square location in Russia is the busiest McDonald's in the world.

Continued on next page

50,000 customers swarmed the restaurant during its first day of business. And in its usual way, McDonald's began immediately to build community involvement. On opening day, it held a kickoff party for 700 Muscovite orphans and then donated all the opening-day proceeds to the Moscow Children's Fund.

Today, just over 20 years after opening its first restaurant there, McDonald's is thriving in Russia. The Pushkin Square location is now the busiest McDonald's in the world, and Russia is the crown jewel in McDonald's global empire. The company's 245 restaurants in Russia each serve an average of 900,000 diners a year—twice the per-store traffic of any of the other 122 countries in which McDonald's operates.

Despite the long lines of customers, McDonald's has been careful about how rapidly it expands in Russia. In recent years, it has reined in its rapid growth strategy and focused instead on improving product and service quality and profitability. The goal is to squeeze more business out of existing restaurants and grow slowly but profitably. One way to do that is to add new menu items to draw in consumers at different times of the day. So, as it did many years ago in the United States, McDonald's in Russia has now added breakfast items.

Although only about 5 percent of Russians eat breakfast outside the home, more commuters in the big cities are leaving home earlier to avoid heavy traffic. The company hopes that the breakfast menu will encourage commuters to stop off at McDonald's on their way to work. However, when the fast-food chain added breakfast items, it stopped offering its traditional hamburger fare during the morning hours. When many customers complained of "hamburger withdrawal," McDonald's introduced the Fresh McMuffin, an English muffin with a sausage patty topped with cheese, lettuce, tomato, and special sauce. The new sandwich became an instant hit.

To reduce the lines inside restaurants and attract motorists, McDonald's is also introducing Russian consumers to drive-thru windows. At first, many Russians didn't get the concept.

Instead, they treated the drive-thru window as just another line, purchasing their food there, parking, and going inside to eat. Also, Russian cars often don't have cup holders, so drive-thru customers bought fewer drinks. However, as more customers get used to the concept, McDonald's is putting drive-thru and walk-up windows in about half of its new stores.

As McDonald's has tweaked its formula in Russia, it also adjusts its marketing and operations to meet the special needs of local consumers in other major global markets. To be sure, McDonald's is a global brand. But to consumers around the world, McDonald's is rapidly becoming their very own. Says a McDonald's Europe executive, "Across Europe with 40 different markets, there are 40 sets of tastes. There are also differences within each market. We are a local market but a global brand."

Sources: Quotes and other information from Janet Adamy, "Steady Diet: As Burgers Boom in Russia, McDonald's Touts Discipline," *Wall Street Journal*, October 16, 2007, p. A1; Fern Glazer, "NPD: QSR Chains Expanding Globally Must Also Act Locally," *Nation's Restaurant News*, October 22, 2007, p. 18; "McDonald's Eyes Russia with 40 New Stores," Reuters.com, February 27, 2009, http://uk.reuters.com/article/idUKLQ86281720090226; Nataliya Vasilveya, "McDonalds Fast-food Giant a Success Story in Russia with More Plans to Expand," *Associated Press*, February 2, 2010, www.encyclopedia.com/doc/1G1-218074550.html; and information from www.aboutmcdonalds.com/mcd, accessed November 2010.

Campbell found out the hard way that it couldn't just slap new labels on its products and peddle them abroad:[34]

In its first foray into China in the early 1990s, Campbell essentially slapped a Chinese label on its classic U.S. condensed soups. They sold well for a while, but when the novelty wore off, sales fell and Campbell withdrew. The company returned to China in 2007, but only after two years of thorough research with Chinese consumers. It found that in China, as well as Russia, there's a cultural disposition to cooking soup from scratch. In both countries, about 98 percent of soup is homemade. So, in both countries, Campbell has now introduced products that reduce the time to make homemade soup from 2.5 hours to about 45 minutes. Getting the product right is important. Consumers in each country typically eat soup four to five times per week, compared with once a week in the United States. Campbell estimates that if it could capture just 3 percent of the soup market in the two countries combined, it would create a business as big as the entire U.S. soup market.

Product invention

Creating new products or services for foreign markets.

Product invention consists of creating something new to meet the needs of consumers in a given country. For example, companies ranging from computer and carmakers to candy producers have developed products that meet the special purchasing needs of low-income consumers in developing economies such as India and China. Ford developed the economical, low-priced Figo model especially for entry-level consumers in India. And Cadbury, long known for its premium chocolates, is now developing products for less affluent consumers in India and other developing economies:[35]

As more Indians begin to treat themselves to little luxuries, Cadbury hopes to capture millions of new customers with chocolates that sell for only a few pennies. The candy maker has been in India for more than 60 years and dominates the chocolate market there with a 70 percent market share. For years, however, Cadbury was considered a luxury brand purchased only by the elite. But now Cadbury is taking aim at India's huge population of lower-income consumers by offering cheaper products. India constitutes a vast untapped market—less than half of India's 1.1 billion people have ever tasted chocolate. The premium candy maker's latest product for the low end of the Indian market is Cadbury Dairy Milk Shots—pea-sized chocolate balls sold for just two rupees, or about four U.S. cents, for a packet of two. Cadbury has also developed other small, low-cost candies, such as Eclair caramels, which cost about two cents each. Last year, emerging markets accounted for 35 percent of Cadbury's sales and about 60 percent of its sales growth.

Promotion

Companies can either adopt the same communication strategy they use in the home market or change it for each local market. Consider advertising messages. Some global companies use a standardized advertising theme around the world. For example, Apple sold millions of iPods with a single global campaign featuring silhouetted figures dancing against a colorful background. And other than for language, the Apple Web site looks about the same for any of the more than 70 countries in which Apple markets its products, from Australia to Senegal to the Czech Republic.

campaignforrealbeauty.com ➤ *Dove*

☐ plain?
☐ perfect?

Do only made up faces attract
attention? Join the beauty debate.

⦿ **Even highly standardized global ad campaigns must be adapted to meet cultural differences. In Western markets, Dove's Campaign for Real Beauty featured images of everyday women in their underwear. But in the Middle East, where attitudes toward nudity are more conservative, the ads were modified to simply reveal the face behind a woman's veil.**

Of course, even in highly standardized communications campaigns, some adjustments might be required for language and cultural differences. ⦿ For example, in Western markets, Dove's high-impact Campaign for Real Beauty campaign featured images of everyday women in their underwear. In the Middle East, however, where attitudes toward nudity are more conservative, the campaign was modified to simply reveal the face behind a woman's veil.[36]

Global companies often have difficulty crossing the language barrier, with results ranging from mild embarrassment to outright failure. Seemingly innocuous brand names and advertising phrases can take on unintended or hidden meanings when translated into other languages. For example, an Italian company's Traficante mineral water received an interesting reception in Spain, where the name translates as "drug dealer." And Motorola's Hellomoto ring tone sounds like "Hello, Fatty" in India. (See Real Marketing 19.2 for more language blunders in international marketing.)

Other companies follow a strategy of **communication adaptation**, fully adapting their advertising messages to local markets. Kellogg ads in the United States promote the taste and nutrition of Kellogg's cereals versus competitors' brands. In France, where consumers drink little milk and eat little for breakfast, Kellogg's ads must convince consumers that cereals are a tasty and healthful breakfast. In India, where many consumers eat heavy, fried breakfasts, Kellogg's advertising convinces buyers to switch to a lighter, more nutritious breakfast diet.

Similarly, Coca-Cola sells its low-calorie beverage as Diet Coke in North America, the United Kingdom, and the Middle and Far East but as Coke Light elsewhere. According to Diet Coke's global brand manager, in Spanish-speaking countries Coke Light ads "position the soft drink as an object of desire, rather than as a way to feel good about yourself, as Diet Coke is positioned in the United States." This "desire positioning" plays off research showing that "Coca-Cola Light is seen in other parts of the world as a vibrant brand that exudes a sexy confidence." (Check out this ad and others on YouTube: www.youtube.com/watch?v=Tu5dku6YkHA.)[37]

Communication adaptation
A global communication strategy of fully adapting advertising messages to local markets.

Real Marketing 19.2

Global Marketing: Watch Your Language!

Many global companies have had difficulty crossing the language barrier, with results ranging from mild embarrassment to outright failure. Seemingly innocuous brand names and advertising phrases can take on unintended or hidden meanings when translated into other languages. Careless translations can make a marketer look downright foolish to foreign consumers.

The classic language blunders involve standardized brand names that do not translate well. When Coca-Cola first marketed Coke in China in the 1920s, it developed a group of Chinese characters that, when pronounced, sounded like the product name. Unfortunately, the characters actually translated as "bite the wax tadpole." Now the characters on Chinese Coke bottles translate as "happiness in the mouth."

Several modern-day marketers have had similar problems when their brand names crashed into the language barrier. Chevy's Nova translated into Spanish as *no va*—"it doesn't go." GM changed the name to Caribe (Spanish for Caribbean), and sales increased. Rolls-Royce avoided the name Silver Mist in German markets, where *mist* means "manure." Sunbeam, however, entered the German market with its Mist Stick hair-curling iron. As should have been expected, the Germans had little use for a "manure wand." IKEA marketed a children's workbench named FARTFULL (the word means "speedy" in Swedish); it soon discontinued the product.

Interbrand of London, the firm that created household names such as Prozac and Acura, recently developed a brand name "hall of shame" list, which contained these and other foreign brand names you're never likely to see inside the local Kroger supermarket: Krapp toilet paper (Denmark), Plopp chocolate (Scandinavia), Crapsy Fruit cereal (France), Poo curry powder (Argentina), and Pschitt lemonade (France).

Travelers often encounter well-intentioned advice from service firms that takes on meanings very different from those intended. The menu in one Swiss restaurant proudly stated, "Our wines leave you nothing to hope for." Signs in a Japanese hotel pronounced, "You are invited to take advantage of the chambermaid." At a laundry in Rome, it was, "Ladies, leave your clothes here and spend the afternoon having a good time."

Advertising themes often lose—or gain—something in the translation. The Coors beer slogan "get loose with Coors" in Spanish came out as "get the runs with Coors." Coca-Cola's "Coke adds life" theme in Japanese translated into "Coke brings your ancestors back from the dead." The milk industry learned too late that its American advertising question "Got Milk?" translated in Mexico as a more provocative "Are you lactating?" And in Chinese, the KFC slogan "finger-lickin' good" came out as "eat your fingers off." And Motorola's Hellomoto ring tone sounds like "Hello, Fatty" in India. Even when the language is the same, word usage may differ from country to country. Thus, the classic British ad line for Electrolux vacuum cleaners—"Nothing sucks like an Electrolux"—would capture few customers in the United States.

So, crossing the language barrier involves much more than simply translating names and slogans into other languages. Beyond just word meanings and nuances, international marketers must also consider things such as phonetic appeal and even associations with historical figures, legends, and other factors. "You can't uproot a concept and just translate it and put it into another market," says one translation consultant. "It's not really about translating word for word, but actually adapting a certain meaning." Says another, "If you fail to review what your brand is saying to a foreign market, you may wish you stayed home."

Sources: Quotes, examples, and other information from Neil Payne, "Cross-Cultural Marketing Blunders," July 28, 2008, accessed at www.proz.com/translation-articles/articles/1909/1/Cross-Cultural-Marketing-Blunders-; Randall Frost, "Lost in Translation," *Brandchannel.com*, November 13, 2006, www.brandchannel.com/features_effect.asp?pf_id=340; David A. Ricks, "Perspectives: Translation Blunders in International Business," *Journal of Language for International Business* 7, No. 2, 1996, pp. 50–55; Martin Croft, "Mind Your Language," *Marketing*, June 19, 2003, pp. 35–39; Eric Pfanner, "Marketers Take a Fresh Look at the Language Barrier," *New York Times*, July 22, 2007, www.nytimes.com/2007/07/22/business/worldbusiness/22iht-ad23.1.6765550.html; and Mark Young, "Don't Let Your Brand Get Lost in Translation," *Brandweek*, February 8, 2010, p. 34.

Global language barriers: Some standardized names do not translate well globally. You won't likely find this French lemonade brand at your local Kroger.

Media also need to be adapted internationally because media availability and regulations vary from country to country. TV advertising time is very limited in Europe, for instance, ranging from four hours a day in France to none in Scandinavian countries. Advertisers must buy time months in advance, and they have little control over airtimes. However, cell phone ads are much more widely accepted in Europe and Asia than in the United States. Magazines also vary in effectiveness. For example, magazines are a major medium in Italy but a minor one in Austria. Newspapers are national in the United Kingdom but only local in Spain.[38]

Price

Companies also face many considerations in setting their international prices. For example, how might Stanley Black & Decker price its tools globally? It could set a uniform price globally, but this amount would be too high a price in poor countries and not high enough in rich ones. It could charge what consumers in each country would bear, but this strategy ignores differences in the actual costs from country to country. Finally, the company could use a standard markup of its costs everywhere, but this approach might price Stanley Black & Decker out of the market in some countries where costs are high.

Regardless of how companies go about pricing their products, their foreign prices probably will be higher than their domestic prices for comparable products. An Apple iPad that sells for $600 in the United States goes for $750 in the United Kingdom. Why? Apple faces a *price escalation* problem. It must add the cost of transportation, tariffs, importer margin, wholesaler margin, and retailer margin to its factory price. Depending on these added costs, the product may have to sell for two to five times as much in another country to make the same profit.

To overcome this problem when selling to less-affluent consumers in developing countries, many companies make simpler or smaller versions of their products that can be sold at lower prices. For example, in China and other emerging markets, Dell sells its simplified Vostro PC for $399, and Unilever and P&G sell consumer goods—everything from shampoo to toothpaste—in less costly formulations and smaller packages at more affordable prices.

Another problem involves setting a price for goods that a company ships to its foreign subsidiaries. If the company charges its foreign subsidiary too much, it may end up paying higher tariff duties even while paying lower income taxes in that country. If the company charges its subsidiary too little, it can be charged with *dumping*. Dumping occurs when a company either charges less than its costs or less than it charges in its home market.

For example, the United States has been slapping duties on a growing list of Chinese products—from tires to chickens—found to be unfairly priced. One such product is pipes used in oil and gas wells. It might not sound glamorous, but it's an $11 billion market, with Chinese imports accounting for about 10 percent. When a group of American companies complained that Chinese firms were pricing these goods below market value, the U.S. Commerce Department agreed and imposed duties as high as 99 percent on oil field pipe imports from China.[39] Various governments are always watching for dumping abuses, and they often force companies to set the price charged by other competitors for the same or similar products.

Recent economic and technological forces have had an impact on global pricing. ⬤ For example, the Internet is making global price differences more obvious. When firms sell their wares over the Internet, customers can see how much products sell for in different countries. They can even order a given product directly from the company location or dealer offering the lowest price. This is forcing companies toward more standardized international pricing.

⬤ The Internet is making global price differences more obvious, forcing companies toward more standardized international pricing.

Distribution Channels

Whole-channel view
Designing international channels that take into account the entire global supply chain and marketing channel, forging an effective global value delivery network.

An international company must take a **whole-channel view** of the problem of distributing products to final consumers. ● **Figure 19.4** shows the two major links between the seller and the final buyer. The first link, *channels between nations*, moves company products from points of production to the borders of countries within which they are sold. The second link, *channels within nations*, moves products from their market entry points to the final consumers. The whole-channel view takes into account the entire global supply chain and marketing channel. It recognizes that to compete well internationally, the company must effectively design and manage an entire *global value delivery network*.

Channels of distribution within countries vary greatly from nation to nation. There are large differences in the numbers and types of intermediaries serving each country market and in the transportation infrastructure serving these intermediaries. For example, whereas large-scale retail chains dominate the U.S. scene, most of the retailing in other countries is done by small, independent retailers. In India, millions of retailers operate tiny shops or sell in open markets. Thus, in its efforts to sell those rugged, affordable phones discussed earlier to Indian consumers, Nokia has had to forge its own distribution structure.[40]

● Distribution channels vary greatly from nation to nation. In its efforts to sell rugged, affordable phones to Indian consumers, Nokia forged its own distribution structure, including a fleet of distinctive blue Nokia-branded vans that prowl rutted country roads to visit remote villages.

In India, Nokia has a presence in almost 90 percent of retail outlets selling mobile phones. It estimates there are 90,000 points-of-sale for its phones, ranging from modern stores to makeshift kiosks. That makes it difficult to control how products are displayed and pitched to consumers. "You have to understand where people live, what the shopping patterns are," says a Nokia executive. "You have to work with local means to reach people—even bicycles or rickshaws." ● To reach rural India, Nokia has outfitted its own fleet of distinctive blue Nokia-branded vans that prowl the rutted country roads. Staffers park these advertisements-on-wheels in villages, often on market or festival days. There, with crowds clustering around, Nokia reps explain the basics of how the phones work and how to buy them. Nokia has extended the concept to minivans, which can reach even more remote places. Thanks to smart product development and innovative channels, Nokia now owns an astounding 50 percent share of India's mobile device market.

Similarly, Coca-Cola adapts its distribution methods to meet local challenges in global markets. For example, in Montevideo, Uruguay, where larger vehicles are challenged by traffic, parking, and pollution difficulties, Coca-Cola purchased 30 small, efficient three-wheeled ZAP alternative transportation trucks. The little trucks average about one-fifth the fuel consumption and scoot around congested city streets with greater ease. In rural areas, Coca-Cola uses a manual delivery process. In China, an army of more than 10,000 Coca-Cola sales reps

Distribution channels between and within nations can vary dramatically around the world. For example, in the United States, Nokia distributes phones through a network of sophisticated retailers. In rural India, it maintains a fleet of Nokia-branded vans that prowl the rutted country roads.

● **FIGURE** | 19.4
Whole-Channel Concept for International Marketing

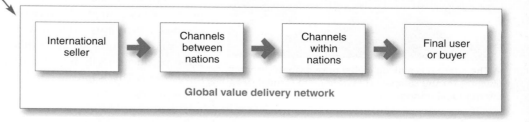

| International seller | → | Channels between nations | → | Channels within nations | → | Final user or buyer |

Global value delivery network

make regular visits to small retailers, often on foot or bicycle. To reach the most isolated spots, the company even relies on teams of delivery donkeys. In Tanzania, 93 percent of Coca-Cola's products are manually delivered via pushcarts and bicycles.[41]

Author Comment | Many large companies, regardless of their "home country," now think of themselves as truly *global* organizations. They view the entire world as a single borderless market. For example, although headquartered in Chicago, Boeing is as comfortable selling planes to Lufthansa or Air China as to American Airlines.

Deciding on the Global Marketing Organization (pp 573–574)

Companies manage their international marketing activities in at least three different ways: Most companies first organize an export department, then create an international division, and finally become a global organization.

A firm normally gets into international marketing by simply shipping out its goods. If its international sales expand, the company will establish an *export department* with a sales manager and a few assistants. As sales increase, the export department can expand to include various marketing services so that it can actively go after business. If the firm moves into joint ventures or direct investment, the export department will no longer be adequate.

Many companies get involved in several international markets and ventures. A company may export to one country, license to another, have a joint ownership venture in a third, and own a subsidiary in a fourth. Sooner or later it will create *international divisions* or subsidiaries to handle all its international activity.

International divisions are organized in a variety of ways. An international division's corporate staff consists of marketing, manufacturing, research, finance, planning, and personnel specialists. It plans for and provides services to various operating units, which can be organized in one of three ways. They can be *geographical organizations*, with country managers who are responsible for salespeople, sales branches, distributors, and licensees in their respective countries. Or the operating units can be *world product groups*, each responsible for worldwide sales of different product groups. Finally, operating units can be *international subsidiaries*, each responsible for their own sales and profits.

Many firms have passed beyond the international division stage and are truly *global organizations*. ● For example, consider Reckitt Benckiser (RB), an $11 billion European producer of household, health, and personal care products and consumer goods with a stable full of familiar brands (Air Wick, Lysol, Woolite, Calgon, Mucinex, Clearasil, French's, and many others—see www.rb.com):[42]

RB has operations in more than 60 countries. It's top 400 managers represent 53 different nationalities. Although headquartered in the United Kingdom, an Italian runs its UK business, an American runs the German business, and a Dutchman runs the U.S. business. An Indian runs the Chinese business, a Belgian the Brazilian business, a Frenchman the Russian business, an Argentine the Japanese business, a Brit the Middle East North Africa business and a Czech the South Africa business. "Most of our top managers . . . view themselves as global citizens rather than as citizens of any given nation," says RB's chief executive officer.

The company has spent the past decade building a culture of global mobility because it thinks that's one of the best ways to generate new ideas and create global entrepreneurs. And it has paid

● European household, health, and personal and consumer goods producer Reckitt Benckiser has a truly global organization. "Most of our top managers . . . view themselves as global citizens rather than as citizens of any given nation."

off. Products launched in the past three years—all the result of global cross-fertilization—account for 35–40 percent of net revenue. Over the past few years, even during the economic downturn, the company has outperformed its rivals—P&G, Unilever, and Colgate—in growth.

Global organizations don't think of themselves as national marketers who sell abroad but as global marketers. The top corporate management and staff plan worldwide manufacturing facilities, marketing policies, financial flows, and logistical systems. The global operating units report directly to the chief executive or the executive committee of the organization, not to the head of an international division. Executives are trained in worldwide operations, not just domestic *or* international operations. Global companies recruit management from many countries, buy components and supplies where they cost the least, and invest where the expected returns are greatest.

Today, major companies must become more global if they hope to compete. As foreign companies successfully invade their domestic markets, companies must move more aggressively into foreign markets. They will have to change from companies that treat their international operations as secondary to companies that view the entire world as a single borderless market.

REVIEWING Objectives AND KEY Terms

Companies today can no longer afford to pay attention only to their domestic market, regardless of its size. Many industries are global industries, and firms that operate globally achieve lower costs and higher brand awareness. At the same time, global marketing is risky because of variable exchange rates, unstable governments, protectionist tariffs and trade barriers, and several other factors. Given the potential gains and risks of international marketing, companies need a systematic way to make their global marketing decisions.

Objective 1 **Discuss how the international trade system and the economic, political-legal, and cultural environments affect a company's international marketing decisions.** (pp 552–562)

A company must understand the *global marketing environment*, especially the international trade system. It must assess each foreign market's *economic*, *political-legal*, and *cultural characteristics*. The company must then decide whether it wants to go abroad and consider the potential risks and benefits. It must decide on the volume of international sales it wants, how many countries it wants to market in, and which specific markets it wants to enter. These decisions call for weighing the probable rate against the level of risk.

Objective 2 **Describe three key approaches to entering international markets.** (pp 562–565)

The company must decide how to enter each chosen market—whether through *exporting*, *joint venturing*, or *direct investment*. Many companies start as exporters, move to joint ventures, and finally make a direct investment in foreign markets. In *exporting*, the company enters a foreign market by sending and selling products through international marketing intermediaries (indirect exporting) or the company's own department, branch, or sales representative or agents (direct exporting). When establishing a *joint venture*, a company enters foreign markets by joining with foreign companies to produce or market a product or service. In *licensing*, the company enters a foreign market by contracting with a licensee in the foreign market, offering the right to use a manufacturing process, trademark, patent, trade secret, or other item of value for a fee or royalty.

Objective 3 **Explain how companies adapt their marketing mixes for international markets.** (pp 565–573)

Companies must also decide how much their products, promotion, price, and channels should be adapted for each foreign market. At one extreme, global companies use *standardized global marketing* worldwide. Others use *adapted global marketing*, in which they adjust the marketing strategy and mix to each target market, bearing more costs but hoping for a larger market share and return. However, global standardization is not an all-or-nothing proposition. It's a matter of degree. Most international marketers suggest that companies should "think globally but act locally"—that they should seek a balance between globally standardized strategies and locally adapted marketing mix tactics.

Objective 4 **Identify the three major forms of international marketing organization.** **(pp 573–574)**

The company must develop an effective organization for international marketing. Most firms start with an *export department* and graduate to an *international division*. A few become *global organizations*, with worldwide marketing planned and managed by the top officers of the company. Global organizations view the entire world as a single, borderless market.

KEY Terms

OBJECTIVE 1

Global firm (p 553)
Economic community (p 555)

OBJECTIVE 2

Exporting (p 563)
Joint venturing (p 563)
Licensing (p 563)

Contract manufacturing (p 564)
Management contracting (p 564)
Joint ownership (p 564)
Direct investment (p 565)

OBJECTIVE 3

Standardized global marketing (p 565)
Adapted global marketing (p 565)

Straight product extension (p 566)
Product adaptation (p 566)
Product invention (p 568)
Communication adaptation (p 569)
Whole-channel view (p 572)

PEARSON mymarketinglab™

- Check your understanding of the concepts and key terms using the mypearsonmarketinglab study plan for this chapter.
- Apply the concepts in a business context using the simulation entitled **Global Marketing**.

DISCUSSING & APPLYING THE Concepts

Discussing the Concepts

1. Explain what is meant by the term *global firm* and list the six major decisions involved in international marketing. (AACSB: Communication)

2. Discuss the types of restrictions governments might impose on trade between nations. (AACSB: Communication)

3. Name and define the four types of country industrial structures. (AACSB: Communication)

4. What factors do companies consider when deciding on possible global markets to enter? (AACSB: Communication; Reflective Thinking)

5. Discuss the three ways to enter foreign markets. Which is the best? (AACSB: Communication; Reflective Thinking)

6. Discuss how global distribution channels differ from domestic channels. (AACSB: Communication)

Applying the Concepts

1. Visit www.transparency.org and click on "corruption perception index." What is the most recent Corruption Perceptions Index (CPI) for the following countries: Denmark, Jamaica, Malaysia, Myanmar, New Zealand, Somali, and the United States? What are the implications of this index for U.S.-based companies doing business in these countries? (AACSB: Communication; Use of IT; Reflective Thinking)

2. The United States restricts trade with Cuba. Visit the U.S. Department of the Treasury Web site at www.ustreas.gov/offices/enforcement/ofac to learn more about economic and trade sanctions. Click on the "Cuba Sanctions" link to learn more about the trade restrictions on Cuba. Are these tariff, quota, or embargo restrictions? To what extent do these trade restrictions allow U.S. businesses to export their products to Cuba? (AACSB: Communication; Use of IT; Reflective Thinking)

3. Visit the Central Intelligence Agency's World Factbook at www.cia.gov/library/publications/the-world-factbook. In a small group, select a country and describe the information provided about that country on this site. How is this information useful to marketers? (AACSB: Communication; Use of IT; Reflective Thinking)

FOCUS ON Technology

"Reverse innovation," "innovation blowback," and "trickle-up innovation" are terms used to describe the process by which innovations developed to meet the needs of emerging markets make their way into developed markets. Traditionally, innovations are birthed in developed countries, with older models later offered in lower-income markets, such as India and China. Although many "bottom of the pyramid" emerging markets are low on the economic food chain, they are large in numbers, providing opportunities for businesses that meet growing needs at an affordable price. GE, the dominant maker of expensive electrocardiograph (ECG) machines sold to hospitals, developed a lower-priced, small, battery-powered ECG machine for use in India and China. GE then marketed this product to primary care doctors, visiting nurses, and rural hospitals and clinics in the United States. Reverse innovation is not limited to technological products; it can apply to products as basic as yogurt.

1. Learn more about how GE used reverse innovation to capitalize on opportunities in the United States. Find two other examples of reverse innovation for technological products. (AACSB: Communication; Reflective Thinking)

2. Discuss two examples of reverse innovation for nontechnology products. (AACSB: Communication; Reflective Thinking)

FOCUS ON Ethics

Imagine Ford building a passenger van in Turkey, shipping it to the United States, and then ripping out the back windows and seats to convert it into a delivery van. The fabric and foam from the seats are shredded and become landfill cover, while the steel and glass are recycled in other ways. Seems like a waste, doesn't it? Well, that's actually cheaper than paying the 25 percent tariff Ford would have to pay to import its own delivery vans. The windows and seats are there just to get around an ongoing trade spat with Europe, known as the "chicken tax." In the 1960s, Europe imposed high tariffs on imported chicken due to increased U.S. poultry sales to West Germany. In retaliation, U.S. President Johnson imposed a tax on imports of foreign-made trucks and commercial vans—specifically targeting German-made Volkswagens. The chicken tax has long pestered automakers. Even U.S. automobile companies such as Ford must pay the tariff, which is ironic because U.S. trade rules have protected the U.S. automakers' truck market for years. However, converting the vehicle into a delivery truck after reaching our shores represents costs of 2.5 percent, significantly lower than the 25 percent tariff if the vehicle came into the country that way.

1. Should U.S. companies be penalized for importing their own products from other countries? (AACSB: Communication; Ethical Reasoning)

2. Although Ford is complying "with the letter of the law," are Ford's actions proper? (AACSB: Communication; Ethical Reasoning)

MARKETING & THE Economy

SPAM

For decades, SPAM (the Hormel canned meat product, not unwanted e-mail) has been the brunt of bad jokes. But it's all in good fun, as consumers all around the world gobble up hundreds of millions of dollars worth of the pork concoction every year. In the United Kingdom, deep-fried SPAM slices—known as SPAM fritters—adorn menus at fish and chips shops. In Japan, it's an ingredient in a popular stir-fry dish. South Koreans eat the meat with rice or wrap it up in sushi rolls. In Hawaii, even McDonald's and Burger King sell SPAM specialties.

But here's one of the most interesting things about SPAM: the "SPAM Index." Over the years, SPAM sales have been very strongly and inversely correlated with economic indicators that some analysts consider the canned meat's revenues themselves as an index of economic conditions. The Great Recession was no exception. SPAM experienced double-digit increases in sales after economists officially announced the beginning of the recession. Hormel responded by launching SPAM's first major advertising campaign in five years. Radio, TV, and print ads carry a "Break the Monotony" message, showing how SPAM can breathe new life into home-cooked meals. The Hormel Web site boasts 350 new SPAM recipes, including Cheesy Country SPAM Puff, SPAMaroni, and SPAM Lettuce Wraps. A little bit of SPAM goes a long way.

1. Why does SPAM have such universal appeal to global consumers?

2. What recommendations would you make to Hormel to keep SPAM sales high when the economy is once again strong?

MARKETING BY THE Numbers

A country's import/export activity is revealed in its balance-of-payments statement. This statement includes three accounts: the current account, the capital account, and the reserves account. The current account is most relevant to marketing because it is a record of all merchandise exported from and imported into a country. The latter two accounts record financial transactions. The U.S. Department of Commerce's Bureau of Economic Analysis provides yearly and monthly figures on the country's trade in goods and services.

1. Visit www.bea.gov and find the U.S. international trade in goods and services for the most recent year available. What does that number mean? (AACSB: Communication; Use of IT; Reflective Thinking)

2. Search the Internet for China's balance of trade information for the same year. How does it compare to that of the United States? (AACSB: Communication; Use of IT; Reflective Thinking)

VIDEO Case

Monster

In 1994, Monster Worldwide pioneered job recruiting on the Internet with Monster.com. Today, it is the only online recruitment provider that can service job seekers and job posters on a truly global basis. With a presence in 50 countries around the world, Monster has unparalleled international reach. And although global economic woes have hindered the growth of corporations everywhere, Monster is investing heavily with plans to become even bigger worldwide. Most recently, Monster's international expansion has included the purchase of ChinaHR.com giving it a strong presence in the world's largest country. Monster already gets about 45 percent of its annual revenue of $1.3 billion from outside the United States. But it expects to become even more

global in the coming years. To back that geographic expansion, Monster is also inventing heavily in search technologies and Web design in order to appeal to clients everywhere.

After viewing the video featuring Monster Worldwide, answer the following questions about the company and the global marketplace:

1. Which of the five strategies for adapting products and promotion for global markets does Monster employ?

2. Which factors in the global marketing environment have challenged Monster's global marketing activities most? How has Monster met those challenges?

COMPANY Case

Nokia: Envisioning a Connected World

What brand of cell phone do you own? If you're living in the United States, chances are it isn't a Nokia. But if you're living anywhere else in the world, it probably is. The Finnish electronics company grabs only a single-digit slice of the U.S. cell phone pie, but it dominates the global cell phone market with close to a 40 percent share. Few companies lead their industries the way that Nokia does. Half of the world's population holds an active cell phone, and more than one in three of those phones is a Nokia. That's over one billion people holding a cell phone with a Nokia logo. Perhaps even more amazing, the company sells half-again that many—about half a billion—phones every year. In fact, Nokia sells more cell phones each year than its three closest rivals—Samsung, Motorola, and Sony-Ericsson—combined!

You might think that Nokia has accomplished this feat by being the product leader, always introducing the latest cutting-edge gadget. But Nokia has actually been slow to take advantage of design trends, such as clamshell phones; "candy-bar" phones that slide open and closed; and ultrathin, blingy, multifunction phones. Rather, Nokia has risen to global dominance based on a simple, age-old strategy: sell basic products at low prices. Although Nokia markets a huge variety of cell phone models, it is best known for its trademarked easy-to-use block handset. Nokia mass produces this basic reliable hardware cheaply and ships it in huge volumes to all parts of the world.

GAINING STRENGTH AS THE VOLUME LEADER

Based in Finland, Nokia's single most profit- and revenue-generating region is Europe. But the company's global strategy has been likened to that of Honda decades ago. Honda started by focusing on developing markets with small motorbikes. As the economies of such countries emerged and people could afford cars, they were already loyal to Honda.

Nokia has followed that same model. It sells phones in more than 150 countries, and in most of those countries, it is the market leader. Nokia has a real knack for forging regional strategies based on the overall needs of its consumers. But Nokia has filled its coffers by understanding the growth dynamics of specific emerging markets. Soren Peterson, Nokia's senior vice president of mobile phones, understands that concept more than anyone. He spends a great deal of his time studying the needs of consumers in emerging markets. And for the most part, these consumers need cheap phones.

To that end, Petersen has led Nokia on a crusade to bring down costs and make its phones even less expensive. Petersen cites an example of one cost-cutting tactic that sparked a chain of events at Nokia. While on a visit to Kenya, he stopped by an "excessively rural storefront," where he noticed that all products were displayed in plastic bags. When he asked the merchant where the boxes and manuals had gone, the man replied, "Make good fire." Petersen quickly realized that packaging for many areas of the world barely needed to "last the journey." Packaging changes resulted in a savings of $147 million a year.

Among other notable discoveries for emerging markets, Nokia developed an icon-based interface to replace text, a welcome innovation for many people in the world who don't know how to read. Nokia also added multiple phonebooks to its devices, based on the fact that many people in less-developed countries share their phones with up to a half-dozen other people. Nokia has even developed an inexpensive charging kit for bicycles with a dynamo that attaches to the wheel and a phone holder for the handlebars. At 7.5 miles per hour, it charges as fast as a traditional wall charger.

CAPITALIZING ON MARKET LEADERSHIP

Just as Honda used strength gained from selling motorbikes in emerging countries to establish itself as a manufacturer of virtually every kind of passenger vehicle, Nokia aims to do the same in the mobile industry. Although Nokia remains committed to the entry-level market and emerging nations, it has developed a comprehensive global strategy. According to Nokia's vision statement, that strategy has three facets: growing the number of people using Nokia devices, transforming the devices people use, and building new businesses.

For the first part of this plan, Nokia projects that global cell phone usage will reach five billion users by 2015. That means Nokia can significantly increase the number of phones it sells, even if it doesn't increase its market share. In fact, if Nokia simply holds its current share of the market, that means that approximately 1.7 billion people will be holding Nokia phones, 67 percent more than today. That's good news for Nokia. According to one analyst, given the number of players in the global market, it will be almost impossible for Nokia to maintain a 40 percent share.

As for transforming the devices that people use, Nokia is aiming to become more than just an entry-level phone provider. Of its 123,000 employees, almost one-third work in R&D, and R&D expenses account for approximately 10 percent of net sales. Nokia invests heavily in developing more cutting-edge devices in hopes that as its customers in developing nations gain the resources, they will trade-up and stay with Nokia. Nokia may have an advantage here. Beyond selling lots of phones, Nokia is also one of the most trusted brands in the world. With a brand value of $35 billion, it's the fifth-most-valuable brand in the world. "The trust is so high, it has less trouble than other brands getting a customer back who may have tried out a competing brand," says a branding expert.

Nokia also recognizes that the biggest trends in mobile devices are music, navigation, and gaming. Focusing on these activities, it is collaborating with the best minds in the business to find ways to add value for the consumer. Nokia appears poised to take advantage of the convergence of the Internet, media, and the cell phone. Last year, Nokia sold more than 200 million camera phones (far more cameras than Canon) and more than 140 million music phones (Apple only sold 52 million iPods). Thus, through its mobile handsets, Nokia can claim to sell more computers, portable music players, and cameras than any other company. However, it has yet to find a way to secure a steady income stream from its devices once they are in place.

This creates a logical transition to the third leg of Nokia's strategy, building new businesses. In an effort to gain income from existing devices, Nokia has opened its "Ovi Store." The goal is to accomplish something that has eluded many mobile network operators—building a profitable business in mobile services. The Ovi Store is a one-stop shop that connects consumers with content providers through their Nokia phones. Users can access apps, games, videos, widgets, podcasts, location-based services, and personalized content. Nokia customers all over the planet now download more than one million apps per day; that's not close to the 30 million apps downloaded from Apples iTunes store, but it's a start.

Nokia continues to develop a host of mobile services, including Point & Find (a service that lets users gain relevant Internet content by simply pointing a camera phone at a real-world object), Nokia Home Control Center (lets users interact with home appliances and devices), and various satellite location services. Not only has the cell phone giant invested a great deal of money in these projects, it is has also lured executives from Yahoo!, Microsoft, eBay, and IBM and is collaborating with numerous other corporations to help build these business ventures.

STORM ON THE HORIZON

Regardless of the fact that Nokia dominates the cell phone market, it seems that the latest wares from smaller competitors have been the darlings of the press. In an attempt to downplay the initial success of Apple's iPhone after it sold four million units its first year out, one Nokia vice president was heard to say, "We've done that since we've had dinner last Friday." That statement was meant to draw attention to the fact that Apple has only 4 percent of the global cell phone market. But given the shifting tides of consumer preference, it is now apparent that Nokia has a serious threat on its hands.

Growth in smartphones is fast outpacing the growth of the overall market. Although global sales of mobile handsets surged 17 percent in the first quarter of 2010, most of that was due to the increasing hunger for smartphones, which grew by a whopping 40 percent, the strongest annual increase for the category since 2006. Despite Nokia's R&D efforts to expand its portfolio of high-end devices, the company still lags in that area. Smartphones are the only phones that Apple makes, so it is poised to enjoy the lion's share of market growth. For example, Apple sold 83 percent more iPhones in 2009 than it did the year before, a bigger bump than any other company. In terms of market share, that translates to a jump from 3 percent of the global smartphone market to more than 13 percent.

Nokia still holds the title not only for the most phones sold but also for the most smartphones, with a 39 percent share. But Apple has hit another home run with its new iPhone4. On the first day of preorders, the company sold 600,000 units (a company record) despite the fact that higher than expected volume crashed the servers at both Apple's online store and AT&T. Close on the heels of Apple's new "must have," Samsung's Galaxy S and Sony Ericsson's Xperia X10 will also be on the market. And Google's open-platform Android now boasts the fourth most widely used mobile-operating system.

Falling behind in this rapidly growing market segment is taking its toll on Nokia's financial performance. Halfway through 2010, the Finnish giant announced that its market share by volume would be flat for the year. Given that smartphones have higher prices and higher margins, this means that Nokia's share of the market by revenue would actually drop. Nokia dropped another bomb on investors by admitting that its profits would also be lower than previously forecasted.

But Nokia is determined to stay in the battle. Months following the release of the latest gadgets by its competitors, Nokia will launch it's impressive new N8, complete with a 12-megapixel camera, high definition video, and streaming TV services. But given its competitors' head start, many analysts question just how much of a splash Nokia's top-end model will make.

Questions for Discussion

1. Does Nokia have a truly global strategy or just a series of regional strategies? Explain.

2. Consider the different global marketing environments discussed in the text. How do these environments differ in developing versus developed countries?

3. Discuss Nokia's global strategy in terms of the five global product and communications strategies.

4. Can competitors easily replicate Nokia's global strategy? Why or why not?

5. Based on the most recent competitive threats, what do you predict for Nokia in the coming years?

Sources: Kit Eaton, "Nokia Profit Warning: It's Been Outmaneuvered by Apple," *Fast Company*, June 16, 2010, accessed at www.fastcompany.com; Ruth Bender, "Apple, RIM Gain Ground in Handset Market," *Wall Street Journal*, May 20, 2010, accessed at http://online.wsj.com; Matt Kapko, "Nokia World: Strategies for the U.S., Emerging Markets," *RCR Wireless News*, December 17, 2007, p. 16; James Ashton, "Emerging Markets Help Nokia to Win Race for Mobile Supremacy," *Sunday Times* (London), January 27, 2008, p. 11.

Sustainable Marketing
Social Responsibility and Ethics

Chapter Preview

In this final chapter, we'll examine the concepts of sustainable marketing, meeting the needs of consumers, businesses, and society—now and in the future—through socially and environmentally responsible marketing actions. We'll start by defining sustainable marketing and then look at some common criticisms of marketing as it impacts individual consumers and public actions that promote sustainable marketing. Finally, we'll see how companies themselves can benefit from proactively pursuing sustainable marketing practices that bring value to not only individual customers but also society as a whole. Sustainable marketing actions are more than just the right thing to do; they're also good for business.

First, let's visit the concept of social and environmental sustainability in business. Perhaps no one gets more fired up about corporate social responsibility than Jeffrey Swartz, CEO of footwear-and-apparel maker Timberland. He's on a passionate mission to use the resources of his company to combat the world's social ills. But he knows that to do this, his company must also be profitable. Swartz firmly believes that companies actually can do both—that they can do well by doing good.

Timberland: Pursuing Sustainable Value—Doing Well by Doing Good

Timberland is no ordinary for-profit company. Sure, it makes and sells rugged, high-quality boots, shoes, clothes, and other outdoor gear. But Timberland's corporate mission is about more than just making good products; it's about "trying to make a difference in the communities where we live and work."

Similarly, Timberland's Jeff Swartz is no ordinary CEO. He sees Timberland's place in the world as much bigger than the products it puts into it. He fervently believes that making money should go hand in hand with making the world a better place. Swartz is so passionate about this concept that he's sometimes referred to as a "prophet-CEO," a messiah for a new age of social awareness. He's spreading the word about corporate citizenship to anyone who will listen, whether it's customers, suppliers, or employees.

For example, when Swartz recently met with McDonald's executives to pitch providing the fast-food giant with new uniforms, he didn't bring along any designs. In fact, he didn't even talk about clothing. Instead, he made an impassioned speech about how Timberland could help McDonald's create a more unified, motivated, purposeful workforce that would benefit both the company and the world at large. He preached the virtues of Timberland's corporate culture, which encourages employees to do volunteer work by giving them 40 hours of paid leave every year. He talked about Serv-a-palooza, Timberland's annual single-day volunteer-fest, which hosts hundreds of service projects in dozens of countries and provides tens of thousands of volunteer work hours.

Then, rather than trying to close the sale, Swartz left the McDonald's executives with the charge of truly helping every community in which it does business. In the end, Timberland didn't land the McDonald's uniform business, but Swartz was elated all the same. "I told my team to find me 10 more places where I can have this conversation," he said. "No one believes in this more than we do, and that is our competitive advantage."

Founded by Jeff's grandfather, cobbler Nathan Swartz, in 1952, the now publicly traded company is out to show that it can make profits *and* combat social ills, help the environment, and improve labor conditions around the world. Swartz isn't talking charity—he's an avowed capitalist. He's just passionately committed to the notion that a company can do well by doing good. Swartz refers to this as the beautiful—and profitable—nexus between "commerce and justice."

For years, Swartz's do-good philosophy paid off. Between 1992 and 2005, Timberland's market capitalization grew eightfold, and annual sales hit $1.6 billion. During that period, Swartz implemented social and environmental initiatives galore. He also implemented some of the toughest worker protection standards in global manufacturing. The combination of financial performance and corporate responsibility won Swartz praise from both Wall Street and social activists.

But on the way to the awards ceremonies, Timberland stalled. Over the next four years, earnings slipped almost 20 percent. And the company was forced to cut product lines and close stores. This left many analysts wondering: Has Timberland put too much emphasis on justice and not enough on commerce? Is it possible for a company to serve a double bottom line of both values and profits?

In this time of company crisis, Swartz learned some valuable lessons about the commerce side of the business. Especially during tough economic times, Swartz discovered, not all Timberland consumers place a high value on the sustainability part of the brand. "Do good" works well in good times. But when things get tough, customers want a lot more. Swartz explains today's more demanding customers:

These days, customers are saying, "I'll have a conversation with you; [but] it will be all on my terms. Your product is going to have to be visually beautiful, technically perfect, and distinctive. And it has to be available where I shop at a price I'm willing to pay." Now, if it is all of those things, you gain the permission, in the one minute the consumer deals with your brand, to devote about 10 seconds to the issue of values. And if you miss any step along the way, you are talking to yourself, which is a terribly sad place to be.

Despite the challenging times, Swartz remains firmly committed to Timberland's mission of making a difference. Instead of backing off on Timberland's sustainable practices, he's ramping them up. And despite recent sales declines, profits are up over the past two years. Looking beyond the world's current economic difficulties, Swartz insists that it is only a matter of time until consumers refuse to patronize companies that do not serve their communities. "I believe that there's a storm coming against the complacent who say good enough is good enough," he says.

To inspire consumers to make more sustainable decisions, Timberland puts Green Index tags on its products. Modeled after the nutritional labels found on food products, the index provides a 0-to-10 rating of each product's ecological footprint in terms of climate impact, chemicals used, and resources consumed. The lower the score, the smaller the environmental footprint.

Timberland is doing everything it can to reduce the footprint of the products it makes and sells. But the company's sustainability efforts go far beyond environmental responsibility. Swartz recently commissioned a new long-term strategy for both environmental and social corporate responsibility. The plan lays out short- and long-term goals supported by key initiatives in line with four strategic pillars: *energy* (reduce greenhouse emissions), *products* (design environmentally responsible, recyclable products), *workplaces* (establish fair, safe, and nondiscriminatory workplaces), and *service* (energize and engage Timberland's employees in service).

Timberland is moving along on these initiatives at a rapid pace. It has a solar-powered distribution center in California and a wind-powered factory in the Dominican Republic. It's currently installing energy-efficient lighting and equipment retrofits in its facilities and educating workers about production efficiency. And it has launched two new footwear collections featuring outsoles made from recycled car tires. Timberland's new Earthkeeper line of boots, made from recycled and organic materials, has given rise to its Earthkeeper's campaign, an online social-networking effort that seeks to inspire one million people to take actions to lighten their environmental footprints.

Thus, despite recent setbacks, Swartz and Timberland continue in their quest of "caring capitalism," doing well by doing good. Swartz has an advantage not held by many for-profit chief executives: Although Timberland is a public company, the Swartz family controls 69 percent of shareholder voting rights. Therefore, Swartz can pursue his own corporate values while being less accountable to Wall Street. Still, he has no illusion that he's untouchable. For Timberland, "commerce" funds "justice." "No one's performance, especially in this age, will get supported through time if it's substandard," Swartz says. "Maybe I am self-indulgent, and if I am and our performance suffers, I will get fired. All I continue to say to shareholders is that I believe I am pursuing sustainable value."[1]

"We started out as bootmakers," says Timberland, "but we're about much more. Like you, we care about the strength of our neighborhoods, the well-being of our environment, and the quality of life in our communities."

Timberland is no ordinary for-profit company. Its corporate mission is about more than just making good products and profits. It's about trying to make a difference in the world.

Responsible marketers discover what consumers want and respond

with market offerings that create value for buyers and capture value in return. The *marketing concept* is a philosophy of customer value and mutual gain. Its practice leads the economy by an invisible hand to satisfy the many and changing needs of millions of consumers.

Not all marketers follow the marketing concept, however. In fact, some companies use questionable marketing practices that serve their own rather than consumers' interests. Moreover, even well-intentioned marketing actions that meet the current needs of some consumers may cause immediate or future harm to other consumers or the larger society. Responsible marketers must consider whether their actions are sustainable in the longer run.

Consider the sale of SUVs. These large vehicles meet the immediate needs of many drivers in terms of capacity, power, and utility. However, SUV sales involve larger questions of consumer safety and environmental responsibility. For example, in accidents, SUVs are more likely to kill both their own occupants and the occupants of other vehicles. Research shows that SUV occupants are three times more likely to die from their vehicle rolling than are occupants of sedans. Moreover, gas-guzzling SUVs use more than their fair share of the world's energy and other resources and contribute disproportionately to pollution and congestion problems, creating costs that must be borne by both current and future generations.[2]

This chapter examines sustainable marketing and the social and environmental effects of private marketing practices. First, we address the question: What is sustainable marketing and why is it important?

Author Comment | Marketers must think beyond immediate customer satisfaction and business performance toward strategies that preserve the world for future generations.

Sustainable Marketing (pp 582–584)

Sustainable marketing calls for socially and environmentally responsible actions that meet the present needs of consumers and businesses while also preserving or enhancing the ability of future generations to meet their needs. ◉ **Figure 20.1** compares the sustainable marketing concept with marketing concepts we studied in earlier chapters.[3]

The *marketing concept* recognizes that organizations thrive from day to day by determining the current needs and wants of target group customers and fulfilling those needs and

◉ FIGURE | 20.1
Sustainable Marketing

The marketing concept means meeting the current needs of both customers and the company. But that can sometimes mean compromising the future of both.

	Now	Future
Now	Marketing concept	Strategic planning concept
Future	Societal marketing concept	**Sustainable marketing concept**

Needs of Consumers (vertical axis) / **Needs of Business** (horizontal axis)

Sustainable marketing means meeting current needs in a way that preserves the rights and options of future generations of consumers and businesses.

Sustainable marketing
Socially and environmentally responsible marketing that meets the present needs of consumers and businesses while also preserving or enhancing the ability of future generations to meet their needs.

wants more effectively and efficiently than competitors do. It focuses on meeting the company's short-term sales, growth, and profit needs by giving customers what they want now. However, satisfying consumers' immediate needs and desires doesn't always serve the future best interests of either customers or the business.

For example, McDonald's early decisions to market tasty but fat- and salt-laden fast foods created immediate satisfaction for customers and sales and profits for the company. However, critics assert that McDonald's and other fast-food chains contributed to a longer-term national obesity epidemic, damaging consumer health and burdening the national health system. In turn, many consumers began looking for healthier eating options, causing a slump in the sales and profits of the fast-food industry. Beyond issues of ethical behavior and social welfare, McDonald's was also criticized for the sizable environmental footprint of its vast global operations, everything from wasteful packaging and solid waste creation to inefficient energy use in its stores. Thus, McDonald's strategy was not sustainable in terms of either consumer or company benefit.

Whereas the *societal marketing concept* identified in Figure 20.1 considers the future welfare of consumers and the *strategic planning concept* considers future company needs, the *sustainable marketing concept* considers both. Sustainable marketing calls for socially and environmentally responsible actions that meet both the immediate and future needs of customers and the company.

For example, as we discussed in Chapter 2, in recent years, McDonald's has responded with a more sustainable "Plan to Win" strategy of diversifying into salads, fruits, grilled chicken, low-fat milk, and other healthy fare. Also, after a seven-year search for healthier cooking oil, McDonald's phased out traditional artery-clogging trans fats without compromising the taste of its french fries. And the company launched a major multifaceted education campaign—called "it's what i eat and what i do . . . i'm lovin' it"—to help consumers better understand the keys to living balanced, active lifestyles.

◉ The McDonald's "Plan to Win" strategy also addresses environmental issues. For example, it calls for food-supply sustainability, reduced and environmentally sustainable packaging, reuse and recycling, and more responsible store designs. McDonald's has even developed an environmental scorecard that rates its suppliers' performance in areas such as water use, energy use, and solid waste management.

McDonald's more sustainable strategy is benefiting the company as well as its customers. Since announcing its Plan to Win strategy, McDonald's sales have increased by more than 50 percent, and profits have more than quadrupled. And for the past five years, the company has been included in the Dow Jones Sustainability Index, recognizing its commitment to sustainable economic, environmental, and social performance. Thus, McDonald's is well positioned for a sustainably profitable future.[4]

◉ Sustainable marketing: McDonald's "Plan to Win" strategy has both created sustainable value for customers and positioned the company for a profitable future.

Truly sustainable marketing requires a smooth-functioning marketing system in which consumers, companies, public policy makers, and others work together to ensure socially and environmentally responsible marketing actions. Unfortunately, however, the marketing system doesn't always work smoothly. The following sections examine several sustainability questions: What are the most frequent social criticisms of marketing? What steps have private citizens taken to curb marketing ills? What steps have legislators and government agencies taken to promote sustainable marketing? What steps have enlightened companies taken to carry out socially responsible and ethical marketing that creates sustainable value for both individual customers and society as a whole?

> **Author** | In most ways, we all
> **Comment** | benefit greatly from
> marketing activities. However, like
> most other human endeavors,
> marketing has its flaws. Here we
> present both sides of some of the most
> common criticisms of marketing.

Social Criticisms of Marketing (pp 584–592)

Marketing receives much criticism. Some of this criticism is justified; much is not. Social critics claim that certain marketing practices hurt individual consumers, society as a whole, and other business firms.

Marketing's Impact on Individual Consumers

Consumers have many concerns about how well the American marketing system serves their interests. Surveys usually show that consumers hold mixed or even slightly unfavorable attitudes toward marketing practices. Consumer advocates, government agencies, and other critics have accused marketing of harming consumers through high prices, deceptive practices, high-pressure selling, shoddy or unsafe products, planned obsolescence, and poor service to disadvantaged consumers. Such questionable marketing practices are not sustainable in terms of long-term consumer or business welfare.

High Prices

Many critics charge that the American marketing system causes prices to be higher than they would be under more "sensible" systems. Such high prices are hard to swallow, especially when the economy takes a downturn. Critics point to three factors—*high costs of distribution*, *high advertising and promotion costs*, and *excessive markups*.

High Costs of Distribution. A long-standing charge is that greedy channel intermediaries mark up prices beyond the value of their services. Critics charge that there are too many intermediaries, that intermediaries are inefficient, or that they provide unnecessary or duplicate services. As a result, distribution costs too much, and consumers pay for these excessive costs in the form of higher prices.

How do resellers answer these charges? They argue that intermediaries do work that would otherwise have to be done by manufacturers or consumers. Markups reflect services that consumers themselves want—more convenience, larger stores and assortments, more service, longer store hours, return privileges, and others. In fact, they argue, retail competition is so intense that margins are actually quite low. If some resellers try to charge too much relative to the value they add, other resellers will step in with lower prices. Low-price stores such as Walmart, Costco, and other discounters pressure their competitors to operate efficiently and keep their prices down. In fact, in the wake of the recent recession, only the most efficient retailers have survived profitably.

High Advertising and Promotion Costs. Modern marketing is also accused of pushing up prices to finance heavy advertising and sales promotion. ● For example, a few dozen tablets of a heavily promoted brand of pain reliever sell for the same price as 100 tablets of less-promoted brands. Differentiated products—cosmetics, detergents, toiletries—include promotion and packaging costs that can amount to 40 percent or more of the manufacturer's price to the retailer. Critics charge that much of the packaging and promotion adds only psychological, not functional, value to the product.

Marketers respond that although advertising adds to product costs, it also adds value by informing potential buyers of the availability and merits of a brand. Brand name products may

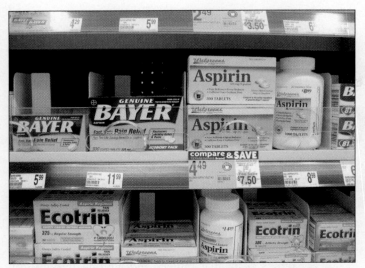

● A heavily promoted brand of aspirin sells for much more than a virtually identical, nonbranded or store-branded product. Critics charge that promotion adds only psychological, not functional, value to the product.

cost more, but branding gives buyers assurances of consistent quality. Moreover, consumers can usually buy functional versions of products at lower prices. However, they *want* and are willing to pay more for products that also provide psychological benefits—that make them feel wealthy, attractive, or special. Also, heavy advertising and promotion may be necessary for a firm to match competitors' efforts; the business would lose "share of mind" if it did not match competitive spending.

At the same time, companies are cost conscious about promotion and try to spend their funds wisely. Today's increasingly more frugal consumers are demanding genuine value for the prices they pay. The continuing shift toward buying store brands and generics suggests that when it comes to value, consumers want action, not just talk.

Excessive Markups. Critics also charge that some companies mark up goods excessively. They point to the drug industry, where a pill costing five cents to make may cost the consumer $2 to buy. They point to the pricing tactics of funeral homes that prey on the confused emotions of bereaved relatives and the high charges for auto repairs and other services.

Marketers respond that most businesses try to deal fairly with consumers because they want to build customer relationships and repeat business and that most consumer abuses are unintentional. When shady marketers take advantage of consumers, they should be reported to Better Business Bureaus and state and federal agencies. Marketers also respond that consumers often don't understand the reasons for high markups. For example, pharmaceutical markups must cover the costs of purchasing, promoting, and distributing existing medicines plus the high R&D costs of formulating and testing new medicines. As pharmaceuticals company GlaxoSmithKline has stated in its ads, "Today's medicines finance tomorrow's miracles."

Deceptive Practices

Marketers are sometimes accused of deceptive practices that lead consumers to believe they will get more value than they actually do. Deceptive practices fall into three groups: pricing, promotion, and packaging. *Deceptive pricing* includes practices such as falsely advertising "factory" or "wholesale" prices or a large price reduction from a phony high retail list price. *Deceptive promotion* includes practices such as misrepresenting the product's features or performance or luring customers to the store for a bargain that is out of stock. *Deceptive packaging* includes exaggerating package contents through subtle design, using misleading labeling, or describing size in misleading terms.

Deceptive practices have led to legislation and other consumer protection actions. For example, in 1938 Congress reacted to such blatant deceptions as Fleischmann's Yeast's claim to straighten crooked teeth by enacting the Wheeler-Lea Act, which gave the Federal Trade Commission power to regulate "unfair or deceptive acts or practices." The FTC has published several guidelines listing deceptive practices. Despite new regulations, some critics argue that deceptive claims are still the norm. Consider the glut of "environmental responsibility" claims marketers are now making:

Are you a victim of "greenwashing"? Biodegradable, eco-friendly, recycled, green, carbon neutral, carbon offsets, made from sustainable resources—such phrases are popping up more and more on products worldwide, leading many to question their validity. Over the past few years, the FTC has been updating its "Green Guides"—voluntary guidelines that it asks companies to adopt to help them avoid breaking laws against deceptive marketing. "We have seen a surge in environmental claims," says a lawyer at the FTC's Bureau of Consumer Protection. Last year, TerraChoice Environmental Marketing, which advises companies on green positioning, reviewed claims

Green-wash (green'wash', -wôsh') – verb: the act of misleading consumers regarding the environmental practices of a company or the environmental benefits of a product or service.

● **Deceptive practices:** Consider "green marketing" claims. A recent TerraChoice study found that 98 percent of products making green claims committed "at least one of the Sins of Greenwashing."

companies made about 2,219 widely sold goods. ● Using measures created by government agencies, TerraChoice concluded that 98 percent of the products committed "at least one of the Sins of Greenwashing." "There is a lot going on there that just isn't right," says one environmental trend-watcher. "If truly green products have a hard time differentiating themselves from fake ones, then this whole notion of a green market will fall apart," says a TerraChoice executive.[5]

The toughest problem is defining what is "deceptive." For instance, an advertiser's claim that its chewing gum will "rock your world" isn't intended to be taken literally. Instead, the advertiser might claim, it is "puffery"—innocent exaggeration for effect. However, others claim that puffery and alluring imagery can harm consumers in subtle ways. Think about the popular and long-running MasterCard Priceless commercials that painted pictures of consumers fulfilling their priceless dreams despite the costs. The ads suggested that your credit card can make it happen. But critics charge that such imagery by credit card companies encouraged a spend-now-pay-later attitude that caused many consumers to *over*use their cards. They point to statistics showing that Americans took on record amounts of credit card debt—often more than they could repay—contributing heavily to the nation's recent financial crisis.

Marketers argue that most companies avoid deceptive practices. Because such practices harm a company's business in the long run, they simply aren't sustainable. Profitable customer relationships are built on a foundation of value and trust. If consumers do not get what they expect, they will switch to more reliable products. In addition, consumers usually protect themselves from deception. Most consumers recognize a marketer's selling intent and are careful when they buy, sometimes even to the point of not believing completely true product claims.

High-Pressure Selling

Salespeople are sometimes accused of high-pressure selling that persuades people to buy goods they had no thought of buying. It is often said that insurance, real estate, and used cars are *sold*, not *bought*. Salespeople are trained to deliver smooth, canned talks to entice purchase. They sell hard because sales contests promise big prizes to those who sell the most. Similarly, TV infomercial pitchmen use "yell and sell" presentations that create a sense of consumer urgency that only those with the strongest willpower can resist.

But in most cases, marketers have little to gain from high-pressure selling. Such tactics may work in one-time selling situations for short-term gain. However, most selling involves building long-term relationships with valued customers. High-pressure or deceptive selling can seriously damage such relationships. For example, imagine a P&G account manager trying to pressure a Walmart buyer or an IBM salesperson trying to browbeat an information technology manager at GE. It simply wouldn't work.

Shoddy, Harmful, or Unsafe Products

Another criticism concerns poor product quality or function. One complaint is that, too often, products and services are not made or performed well. A second complaint concerns product safety. Product safety has been a problem for several reasons, including company indifference, increased product complexity, and poor quality control. A third complaint is that many products deliver little benefit or that they might even be harmful.

For example, think again about the fast-food industry. Many critics blame the plentiful supply of fat-laden, high calorie, fast-food fare for the nation's rapidly growing obesity epidemic. Studies show that some 34 percent of American adults are obese, with another

⊙ **Harmful products: Is Hardee's being socially irresponsible or simply practicing good marketing by giving customers a big juicy burger that clearly pings their taste buds? Judging by the nutrition calculator at its Web site, the company certainly isn't hiding the nutritional facts.**

34 percent considered overweight. Some 32 percent of children are obese. This national weight issue continues despite repeated medical studies showing that excess weight brings increased risks for heart disease, diabetes, and other maladies, even cancer.[6]

The critics are quick to fault what they see as greedy food marketers who are cashing in on vulnerable consumers, turning us into a nation of overeaters. Some food marketers are looking pretty much guilty as charged. ⊙ Take Hardee's, for example. At a time when other fast-food chains, such as McDonald's, Wendy's, and Subway, have been pushing healthier meals, Hardee's has launched one artery-clogging burger after another—gifts to consumers fed up with "healthy," low-fat menu items. Its Monster Thickburger contains two-thirds of a pound of Angus beef, four strips of bacon, and three slices of American cheese, all nestled in a buttered sesame-seed bun slathered with mayonnaise. The blockbuster burger weighs in at an eye-popping 1,320 calories and 95 grams of fat, far greater than the government's recommended fat intake for an entire day (65 grams). Although it appears to be bucking the trends, since introducing the mouthwatering Thickburger line, Hardee's has experienced healthy sales increases and even fatter profits.

Is Hardee's being socially irresponsible by aggressively promoting overindulgence to ill-informed or unwary consumers? Or is it simply practicing good marketing, creating more value for its customers by offering big juicy burgers that ping their taste buds and let them make their own eating choices? Hardee's claims the latter. It says that its target consumers—young men between the ages of 18 and 34—are capable of making their own decisions about health and well-being.

And Hardee's certainly doesn't hide the nutritional facts—they are clearly posted on the company's Web site. The site describes the Monster Thickburger as "a monument to decadence—the only thing that can slay the hunger of a young guy on the move." And the CEO of CKE, Hardee's parent company, notes that the chain has salads and low-carb burgers on its menus, but "we sell very few of them." So, is Hardee's being irresponsible or simply responsive? As in many matters of social responsibility, what's right and wrong may be a matter of opinion.

However, most manufacturers *want* to produce quality goods. The way a company deals with product quality and safety problems can damage or help its reputation. Companies selling poor-quality or unsafe products risk damaging conflicts with consumer groups and regulators. Unsafe products can result in product liability suits and large awards for damages. More fundamentally, consumers who are unhappy with a firm's products may avoid future purchases and talk other consumers into doing the same. Thus, quality missteps are not consistent with sustainable marketing. Today's marketers know that good quality results in customer value and satisfaction, which in turn creates sustainable customer relationships.

Planned Obsolescence

Critics also have charged that some companies practice *planned obsolescence*, causing their products to become obsolete before they actually should need replacement. They accuse some producers of using materials and components that will break, wear, rust, or rot sooner than they should. And if the products themselves don't wear out fast enough, other companies are charged with *perceived obsolescence*—continually changing consumer concepts of acceptable styles to encourage more and earlier buying.[7] An obvious example is constantly changing clothing fashions.

Still others are accused of introducing planned streams of new products that make older models obsolete. Critics claim that this occurs in the consumer electronics and computer industries. If you're like most people, you probably have a drawer full of yesterday's

● **Planned obsolescence:** Most people have a drawer full of yesterday's hottest technological gadgets—from cell phones and cameras to iPods and flash drives—now reduced to the status of fossils.

hottest technological gadgets—from cell phones and cameras to iPods and flash drives—now reduced to the status of fossils. ● It seems that anything more than a year or two old is hopelessly out of date. For example, here's one critic's tongue-in-cheek take on Apple's methods for getting customers to ditch the old iPod and buy the latest and greatest version:[8]

> Apple has probably already developed iPods that double as jetpacks that allow you to orbit the moon. But you won't see those anytime soon. And when they come out, they'll first just have iPods that can fly you to your neighbor's house. Then a few months later they'll introduce ones that can fly you across the country. And that'll seem pretty amazing compared to the ones that could only go down the street, but they won't be amazing three months later, when the iPod Sputnik hits the market.

Marketers respond that consumers *like* style changes; they get tired of the old goods and want a new look in fashion. Or they *want* the latest high-tech innovations, even if older models still work. No one has to buy the new product, and if too few people like it, it will simply fail. Finally, most companies do not design their products to break down earlier because they do not want to lose customers to other brands. Instead, they seek constant improvement to ensure that products will consistently meet or exceed customer expectations. Much of the so-called planned obsolescence is the working of the competitive and technological forces in a free society—forces that lead to ever-improving goods and services.

Poor Service to Disadvantaged Consumers

Finally, the American marketing system has been accused of poorly serving disadvantaged consumers. For example, critics claim that the urban poor often have to shop in smaller stores that carry inferior goods and charge higher prices. The presence of large national chain stores in low-income neighborhoods would help to keep prices down. However, the critics accuse major chain retailers of "redlining," drawing a red line around disadvantaged neighborhoods and avoiding placing stores there.

For example, the nation's poor areas have 30 percent fewer supermarkets than affluent areas do. ● As a result, many low-income consumers find themselves in what one expert calls "food deserts," which are awash with small markets offering frozen pizzas, Cheetos, Twinkies, and Cokes, but fruits and vegetables or fresh fish or chicken are out of reach. "In low-income areas, you can go for miles without being able to find a fresh apple or a piece of broccoli," says the executive director of The Food Trust, a group that's trying to tackle the problem. In turn, the lack of access to healthy, affordable fresh foods has a negative impact on the health of underserved consumers in these areas.[9]

Similar redlining charges have been leveled at the insurance, consumer lending, banking, and health-care industries. Most recently, however, consumer advocates charged that banks and mortgage lenders were practicing "reverse-redlining." Instead of staying away from people in poor urban areas, they targeted and exploited them by offering them risky subprime mortgages rather than safer mortgages with better terms. These subprime mortgages often featured adjustable interest rates that started out very low but quickly increased. When interest rates went up, many owners could no longer afford their mortgage payments. And as housing prices dropped, these owners were trapped in debt and owed more than their houses were worth, leading to bankruptcies, foreclosures, and the subprime mortgage crisis.

● **Underserved consumers:** Because of the lack of supermarkets in low-income areas, many disadvantaged consumers find themselves in "food deserts," with little or no access to healthy, affordable fresh foods.

Clearly, better marketing systems must be built to service disadvantaged consumers. In fact, many marketers profitably target such consumers with legitimate goods and services that create real value. In cases in which marketers do not step in to fill the void, the government likely will. For example, the FTC has taken action against sellers who advertise false values, wrongfully deny services, or charge disadvantaged customers too much.

Marketing's Impact on Society as a Whole

The American marketing system has been accused of adding to several "evils" in American society at large, such as creating too much materialism, too few social goods, and a glut of cultural pollution.

False Wants and Too Much Materialism

Critics have charged that the marketing system urges too much interest in material possessions, and America's love affair with worldly possessions is not sustainable. Too often, people are judged by what they *own* rather than by who they *are*. The critics do not view this interest in material things as a natural state of mind but rather as a matter of false wants created by marketing. Marketers, they claim, stimulate people's desires for goods and create materialistic models of the good life. Thus, marketers have created an endless cycle of mass consumption based on a distorted interpretation of the "American Dream."

The Constitution speaks of life, liberty, and the pursuit of happiness, not an automatic chicken in every pot. One sociologist attributes consumer overspending to a growing "aspiration gap"—the gap between what we have and what we want, between the lifestyles we can afford and those to which we aspire. This aspiration gap results at least partly from a barrage of marketing that encourages people to focus on the acquisition and consumption of goods. Advertising encourages consumers to aspire to celebrity lifestyles, to keep up with the Joneses by acquiring more stuff. Some marketing-frenzied consumers will let nothing stand between them and their acquisitions. Recently, at a Walmart store in New York, a mob of 2,000 eager shoppers broke through a glass door in their rush to get to post-Thanksgiving sales items, trampling a store employee to death in the process.[10]

Thus, marketing is seen as creating false wants that benefit industry more than consumers. "In the world of consumerism, marketing is there to promote consumption," says one marketing critic. It is "inevitable that marketing will promote overconsumption and, from this, a psychologically, as well as ecologically, unsustainable world." Says another critic: "For most of us, our basic material needs are satisfied, so we seek in ever-growing consumption the satisfaction of wants, which consumption cannot possibly deliver. More is not always better; it is often worse."[11]

Some critics have taken their concerns to the public, via the Web or even straight to the streets. For example, consumer activist Annie Leonard founded The Story of Stuff project with a 20-minute Web video about the social and environmental consequences of America's love affair with stuff; the video has been viewed more than 10 million times online and in thousands of schools and community centers around the world.[12] ● And for more than a decade Bill Talen, also known as Reverend Billy, has taken to the streets, exhorting people to resist temptation—the temptation to shop.[13]

● **Materialism: With the zeal of a street-corner preacher and the schmaltz of a street-corner Santa, Reverend Billy—founder of the Church of Life After Shopping—will tell anyone who will listen that people are walking willingly into the hellfire of consumption.**

With the zeal of a street-corner preacher and the schmaltz of a street-corner Santa, Reverend Billy will tell anyone willing to listen that people are walking willingly into the hellfire of consumption. Reverend Billy, leader of the Church of Life After Shopping, believes that shoppers have almost no resistance to media messages that encourage them, around the clock, to want things and buy them. He sees a population lost in consumption, the meaning of individual existence vanished in a fog of wanting, buying, and owning too many things, ultimately leading to "Shopocalypses"—such as the recent world economic collapse. Sporting a televangelist's pompadour, a priest's collar, and a white megaphone, Reverend Billy is often accompanied by his gospel choir when he strides into stores he considers objectionable or shows up at protests. When the choir, made up of volunteers, erupts in song, it is hard to ignore: "Stop shopping! Stop shopping! We will never shop again!"

Marketers respond that such criticisms overstate the power of business to create needs. People have strong defenses against advertising and other marketing tools. Marketers are most effective when they appeal to existing wants rather than when they attempt to create new ones. Furthermore, people seek information when making important purchases and often do not rely on single sources. Even minor purchases that may be affected by advertising messages lead to repeat purchases only if the product delivers the promised customer value. Finally, the high failure rate of new products shows that companies are not able to control demand.

On a deeper level, our wants and values are influenced not only by marketers but also by family, peer groups, religion, cultural background, and education. If Americans are highly materialistic, these values arose out of basic socialization processes that go much deeper than business and mass media could produce alone.

Moreover, consumption patterns and attitudes are also subject to larger forces, such as the economy. As discussed in Chapter 1, the recent recession put a damper on materialism and conspicuous spending. In one consumer survey, 75 percent of respondents agreed that "the downturn is encouraging me to evaluate what is really important in life." Many observers predict a new age of consumer thrift. "The American dream is on pause," says one analyst. "The majority of Americans still believe they can achieve the dream in their lifetimes but, for [now], it's all about shoring up the foundations." Says another, shoppers "now are taking pride in their newfound financial discipline." As a result, far from encouraging today's more frugal consumers to overspend their means, marketers are working to help them find greater value with less.[14]

Too Few Social Goods

Business has been accused of overselling private goods at the expense of public goods. As private goods increase, they require more public services that are usually not forthcoming. For example, an increase in automobile ownership (private good) requires more highways, traffic control, parking spaces, and police services (public goods). The overselling of private goods results in "social costs." For cars, some of the social costs include traffic congestion, gasoline shortages, and air pollution. For example, American travelers lose, on average, 36 hours a year in traffic jams, costing the United States more than $87 billion a year. In the process, they waste 2.8 billion gallons of fuel and emit millions of tons of greenhouse gases.[15]

A way must be found to restore a balance between private and public goods. One option is to make producers bear the full social costs of their operations. For example, the government is requiring automobile manufacturers to build cars with more efficient engines and better pollution-control systems. Automakers will then raise their prices to cover the extra costs. If buyers find the price of some cars too high, however, the producers of these cars will disappear. Demand will then move to those producers that can support the sum of the private and social costs.

A second option is to make consumers pay the social costs. ● For example, many cities around the world are now charging "congestion tolls" in an effort to reduce traffic congestion. To unclog its streets, the city of London levies a congestion charge of £8 per day per car to drive in an eight-square-mile area downtown. The charge has not only reduced traffic congestion within the zone by 21 percent (70,000 fewer vehicles per day) and increased bicycling

● **Balancing private and public goods: In response to lane-clogging traffic congestion, London now levies a congestion charge. The charge has reduced congestion by 21 percent and raised money to shore up the city's public transportation system.**

by 43 percent but also raises money to shore up London's public transportation system.[16]

Cultural Pollution

Critics charge the marketing system with creating *cultural pollution*. Our senses are being constantly assaulted by marketing and advertising. Commercials interrupt serious programs; pages of ads obscure magazines; billboards mar beautiful scenery; spam fills our inboxes. These interruptions continually pollute people's minds with messages of materialism, sex, power, or status. One study found that 70 percent of Americans think there are too many TV ads, and some critics call for sweeping changes.[17]

Marketers answer the charges of "commercial noise" with these arguments: First, they hope that their ads primarily reach the target audience. But because of mass-communication channels, some ads are bound to reach people who have no interest in the product and are therefore bored or annoyed. People who buy magazines addressed to their interests—such as *Vogue* or *Fortune*—rarely complain about the ads because the magazines advertise products of interest.

Second, ads make much of television and radio free to users and keep down the costs of magazines and newspapers. Many people think commercials are a small price to pay for these benefits. Consumers find many television commercials entertaining and seek them out; for example, ad viewership during the Super Bowl usually equals or exceeds game viewership. Finally, today's consumers have alternatives. For example, they can zip or zap TV commercials on recorded programs or avoid them altogether on many paid cable or satellite channels. Thus, to hold consumer attention, advertisers are making their ads more entertaining and informative.

Marketing's Impact on Other Businesses

Critics also charge that a company's marketing practices can harm other companies and reduce competition. Three problems are involved: acquisitions of competitors, marketing practices that create barriers to entry, and unfair competitive marketing practices.

Critics claim that firms are harmed and competition reduced when companies expand by acquiring competitors rather than by developing their own new products. The large number of acquisitions and the rapid pace of industry consolidation over the past several decades have caused concern that vigorous young competitors will be absorbed, so competition will be reduced. In virtually every major industry—retailing, entertainment, financial services, utilities, transportation, automobiles, telecommunications, health care—the number of major competitors is shrinking.

Acquisition is a complex subject. Acquisitions can sometimes be good for society. The acquiring company may gain economies of scale that lead to lower costs and lower prices. A well-managed company may take over a poorly managed company and improve its efficiency. An industry that was not very competitive might become more competitive after the acquisition. But acquisitions can also be harmful and, therefore, are closely regulated by the government.

Critics have also charged that marketing practices bar new companies from entering an industry. Large marketing companies can use patents and heavy promotion spending or tie up suppliers or dealers to keep out or drive out competitors. Those concerned with antitrust regulation recognize that some barriers are the natural result of the economic advantages of doing business on a large scale. Existing and new laws can challenge other barriers. For example, some critics have proposed a progressive tax on advertising spending to reduce the role of selling costs as a major barrier to entry.

Finally, some firms have, in fact, used unfair competitive marketing practices with the intention of hurting or destroying other firms. They may set their prices below costs, threaten to cut off business with suppliers, or discourage the buying of a competitor's products. Various laws work to prevent such predatory competition. It is difficult, however, to prove that the intent or action was really predatory.

In recent years, Walmart has been accused of using predatory pricing in selected market areas to drive smaller, mom-and-pop retailers out of business. Walmart has become a lightning rod for protests by citizens in dozens of towns who worry that the megaretailer's unfair practices will choke out local businesses. However, whereas critics charge that Walmart's actions are predatory, others assert that its actions are just the healthy competition of a more efficient company against less efficient ones.

For instance, ◉ when Walmart began a program to sell generic drugs at $4 a prescription, local pharmacists complained of predatory pricing. They charged that at those low prices, Walmart must be selling under cost to drive them out of business. But Walmart claimed that, given its substantial buying power and efficient operations, it could make a profit at those prices. The $4 pricing program, the retailer claimed, was not aimed at putting competitors out of business. Rather, it was simply a good competitive move that served customers better and brought more of them in the door. Moreover, Walmart's program drove down prescription prices at the pharmacies of other supermarkets and discount stores, such as Kroger and Target. Currently more than 300 prescription drugs are available for $4 at the various chains.[18]

◉ **Walmart prescription pricing: Is it predatory pricing or just good business?**

> **Author Comment** | Sustainable marketing isn't the province of businesses and governments only. Through consumerism and environmentalism, consumers themselves can play an important role.

Consumer Actions to Promote Sustainable Marketing (pp 592–599)

Sustainable marketing calls for more responsible actions by both businesses and consumers. Because some people view businesses as the cause of many economic and social ills, grassroots movements have arisen from time to time to keep businesses in line. Two major movements have been *consumerism* and *environmentalism*.

Consumerism

Consumerism
An organized movement of citizens and government agencies to improve the rights and power of buyers in relation to sellers.

Consumerism is an organized movement of citizens and government agencies to improve the rights and power of buyers in relation to sellers. Traditional *sellers' rights* include the following:

- The right to introduce any product in any size and style, provided it is not hazardous to personal health or safety, or, if it is, to include proper warnings and controls
- The right to charge any price for the product, provided no discrimination exists among similar kinds of buyers
- The right to spend any amount to promote the product, provided it is not defined as unfair competition
- The right to use any product message, provided it is not misleading or dishonest in content or execution
- The right to use buying incentive programs, provided they are not unfair or misleading

  Traditional *buyers' rights* include the following:

- The right not to buy a product that is offered for sale

- The right to expect the product to be safe
- The right to expect the product to perform as claimed

Comparing these rights, many believe that the balance of power lies on the seller's side. True, the buyer can refuse to buy. But critics feel that the buyer has too little information, education, and protection to make wise decisions when facing sophisticated sellers. Consumer advocates call for the following additional consumer rights:

- The right to be well informed about important aspects of the product
- The right to be protected against questionable products and marketing practices
- The right to influence products and marketing practices in ways that will improve "quality of life"
- The right to consume now in a way that will preserve the world for future generations of consumers

Each proposed right has led to more specific proposals by consumerists and consumer protection actions by government. ◉ The right to be informed includes the right to know the true interest on a loan (truth in lending), the true cost per unit of a brand (unit pricing), the ingredients in a product (ingredient labeling), the nutritional value of foods (nutritional labeling), product freshness (open dating), and the true benefits of a product (truth in advertising). Proposals related to consumer protection include strengthening consumer rights in cases of business fraud, requiring greater product

◉ Consumer desire for more information led to packaging labels with useful facts, from ingredients and nutrition facts to recycling and country of origin information. Jones Soda even puts customer-submitted photos on its labels.

safety, ensuring information privacy, and giving more power to government agencies. Proposals relating to quality of life include controlling the ingredients that go into certain products and packaging and reducing the level of advertising "noise." Proposals for preserving the world for future consumption include promoting the use of sustainable ingredients, recycling and reducing solid wastes, and managing energy consumption.

Sustainable marketing applies not only to consumers but also to businesses and governments. Consumers have not only the *right* but also the *responsibility* to protect themselves instead of leaving this function to the government or someone else. Consumers who believe they got a bad deal have several remedies available, including contacting the company or the media; contacting federal, state, or local agencies; and going to small-claims courts. Consumers should also make good consumption choices, rewarding companies that act responsibly while punishing those that don't. Ultimately, the move from irresponsible consumption to sustainable consumption is in the hands of consumers.

Environmentalism

Whereas consumerists consider whether the marketing system is efficiently serving consumer wants, environmentalists are concerned with marketing's effects on the environment and the environmental costs of serving consumer needs and wants. **Environmentalism** is an organized movement of concerned citizens, businesses, and government agencies to protect and improve people's current and future living environment.

Environmentalism
An organized movement of concerned citizens and government agencies to protect and improve people's current and future living environment.

Environmentalists are not against marketing and consumption; they simply want people and organizations to operate with more care for the environment. "Too often the environment is seen as one small piece of the economy," says one activist. "But it's not just one little thing; it's what every single thing in our life depends upon."[19] The marketing system's goal, the environmentalists assert, should not be to maximize consumption, consumer choice, or consumer satisfaction but rather maximize life quality. "Life quality" means not only the quantity and quality of consumer goods and services but also the quality of the environment.

The first wave of modern environmentalism in the United States was driven by environmental groups and concerned consumers in the 1960s and 1970s. They were concerned with damage to the ecosystem caused by strip-mining, forest depletion, acid rain, global warming, toxic and solid wastes, and litter. They were also concerned with the loss of recreational areas and the increase in health problems caused by bad air, polluted water, and chemically treated food.

The second environmentalism wave was driven by the federal government, which passed laws and regulations during the 1970s and 1980s governing industrial practices impacting the environment. This wave hit some industries hard. Steel companies and utilities had to invest billions of dollars in pollution control equipment and costlier fuels. The auto industry had to introduce expensive emission controls in cars. The packaging industry had to find ways to improve recyclability and reduce solid wastes. These industries and others have often resented and resisted environmental regulations, especially when they have been imposed too rapidly to allow companies to make proper adjustments. Many of these companies claim they have had to absorb large costs that have made them less competitive.

The first two environmentalism waves have now merged into a third and stronger wave in which companies are accepting more responsibility for doing no harm to the environment. They are shifting from protest to prevention and from regulation to responsibility. More and more companies are adopting policies of **environmental sustainability**. Simply put, environmental sustainability is about generating profits while helping to save the planet. Environmental sustainability is a crucial but difficult societal goal.

Some companies have responded to consumer environmental concerns by doing only what is required to avert new regulations or keep environmentalists quiet. Enlightened companies, however, are taking action not because someone is forcing them to or to reap short-run profits but because it's the right thing to do—for both the company and the planet's environmental future.

● **Figure 20.2** shows a grid that companies can use to gauge their progress toward environmental sustainability. In includes both internal and external "greening" activities that will pay off for the firm and environment in the short run and "beyond greening" activities that will pay off in the longer term. At the most basic level, a company can practice *pollution prevention*. This involves more than pollution control—cleaning up waste after it has been created. Pollution prevention means eliminating or minimizing waste before it is created. Companies emphasizing prevention have responded with internal "green marketing" programs—designing and developing ecologically safer products, recyclable and biodegradable packaging, better pollution controls, and more energy-efficient operations.

For example, Nike makes shoes out of "environmentally preferred materials," recycles old sneakers, and educates young people about conservation, reuse, and recycling. General Mills shaved 20 percent off the paperboard packaging for Hamburger Helper, resulting in 500 fewer distribution trucks on the road each year. UPS has been developing its "green fleet," which now boasts more than 1,900 low-carbon-emissions vehicles, including electric, hybrid-electric, compressed natural gas, liquefied natural gas, and propane trucks. Intel is installing solar power systems at four of its offices; the new solar panels for just one office

Environmental sustainability
A management approach that involves developing strategies that both sustain the environment and produce profits for the company.

● **FIGURE | 20.2**
The Environmental Sustainability Portfolio

Sources: Stuart L. Hart, "Innovation, Creative Destruction, and Sustainability," *Research Technology Management*, September–October 2005, pp. 21–27.

	Today: Greening	**Tomorrow: Beyond Greening**
Internal	**Pollution prevention** Eliminating or reducing waste before it is created	**New clean technology** Developing new sets of environmental skills and capabilities
External	**Product stewardship** Minimizing environmental impact throughout the entire product life cycle	**Sustainability vision** Creating a strategic framework for future sustainability

How does "environmental sustainability" relate to "marketing sustainability"? Environmental sustainability involves preserving the natural environment, whereas marketing sustainability is a broader concept that involves both the natural and social environments—pretty much everything in this chapter.

As it turns out...
It is easy to be green.

On May 4, 2004, Subaru of Indiana Automotive became the first auto manufacturing plant in the U.S. to become zero landfill. And we did it two years ahead of schedule.

As it turns out, being a good steward of the environment isn't that hard to do. And if a big auto plant can do it...so can you. For more information, log onto www.subaru-earth.com

SIA
SUBARU of INDIANA AUTOMOTIVE, INC.
www.subaru-sia.com

● **Pollution prevention: Subaru of Indiana claims that it now sends less trash to the landfill each year than the average American family.**

will reduce carbon dioxide emissions by 32.8 million pounds.[20]

● Subaru of Indiana (SIA), which manufactures all North American Subarus and some Toyota Camrys, brags that it now sends less trash to the landfill each year than the average American family:[21]

In 2000, SIA generated 459 pounds of waste for every car built. By the end of 2009, it was down to 245 pounds per unit. Of that, 190 pounds were easily recycled steel. The remaining 55 pounds were pallets, cardboard, and plastic, which were also recycled in various ways. The result: The SIA manufacturing plant sends zero waste to the landfill. "Whenever we looked at plant efficiency and quality, we also looked to see if we could reduce waste, recycle materials, and cut back gas, water, and energy use," recalls Denise Coogan, SIA's safety and environmental compliance manager. "Every section manager on the floor had a piece of this and a target. They were held equally accountable for quality, safety, and environmental targets." According to Coogan, although waste reduction was "the right thing to do," it was also "very cost-effective when done right. Every time you throw something away, you've paid to bring it in and you're paying to throw it out. Cut waste and you cut costs." Last year the plant earned $2.3 million on waste reduction.

At the next level, companies can practice *product stewardship*—minimizing not only pollution from production and product design but also all environmental impacts throughout the full product life cycle, while at the same time reducing costs. Many companies are adopting *design for environment (DFE)* and *cradle-to-cradle* practices. This involves thinking ahead to design products that are easier to recover, reuse, recycle, or safely return to nature after usage, becoming part of the ecological cycle. Design for environment and cradle-to-cradle practices not only help to sustain the environment, they can also be highly profitable for the company.

For example, more than a decade ago, IBM started a business designed to reuse and recycle parts from its mainframe computers returned from lease. Today, IBM takes in 40,000 pieces of used IBM and other equipment per week, strips them down to their chips, and recovers valuable metals. "We find uses for more than 99 percent of what we take in and have a return-to-landfill rate of [less than 1 percent]," says an IBM spokesperson. What started out as an environmental effort has now grown into a $2 billion IBM business that profitably recycles electronic equipment at 22 sites worldwide.[22]

Today's "greening" activities focus on improving what companies already do to protect the environment. The "beyond greening" activities identified in Figure 20.2 look to the future. First, internally, companies can plan for *new clean technology*. Many organizations that have made good sustainability headway are still limited by existing technologies. To create fully sustainable strategies, they will need to develop innovative new technologies. For example, Coca-Cola is investing heavily in research addressing many sustainability issues:[23]

From a sustainability viewpoint for Coca-Cola, an aluminum can is an ideal package. Aluminum can be recycled indefinitely. Put a Coke can in a recycling bin, and the aluminum finds its way back to a store shelf in about six weeks. The trouble is, people prefer clear plastic bottles with screw-on tops. Plastic bottles account for nearly 50 percent of Coke's global volume, three times more than aluminum cans. And they are not currently sustainable. They're made from oil, which is a finite resource. Most wind up in landfills or, worse, as roadside trash. They can't be recycled indefinitely because the plastic discolors. To attack this waste problem, Coca-Cola is investing more than $60 million to build the world's largest state-of-the-art plastic-bottle-to-bottle recycling plant. The new recycling plant will produce approximately 100 million pounds of PET plastic for reuse each year.

⬤ **New clean technologies: Coca-Cola is investing heavily to develop new solutions to environmental issues. To reduce packaging waste problems, it's now testing new contour bottles made from corn, bioplastics, or more easily recycled aluminum.**

As a more permanent solution, Coke is also investing in new clean technologies that address these and other environmental issues. ⬤ For example, it's researching and testing new bottles made from aluminum, corn, or bioplastics. It's also designing more eco-friendly distribution alternatives. Currently, some 10 million vending machines and refrigerated coolers gobble up energy and use potent greenhouse gases called hydrofluorocarbons (HFCs) to keep Cokes cold. To eliminate them, the company invested $40 million in research and recently began installing sleek new HFC-free coolers that use 30 to 40 percent less energy. Coca-Cola also aims to become "water neutral" by researching ways to help its bottlers waste less water and protect or replenish watersheds around the world.

Finally, companies can develop a *sustainability vision*, which serves as a guide to the future. It shows how the company's products and services, processes, and policies must evolve and what new technologies must be developed to get there. This vision of sustainability provides a framework for pollution control, product stewardship, and new environmental technology for the company and others to follow.

Most companies today focus on the upper-left quadrant of the grid in Figure 20.2, investing most heavily in pollution prevention. Some forward-looking companies practice product stewardship and are developing new environmental technologies. Few companies have well-defined sustainability visions. However, emphasizing only one or two quadrants in the environmental sustainability grid can be shortsighted. Investing only in the left half of the grid puts a company in a good position today but leaves it vulnerable in the future. In contrast, a heavy emphasis on the right half suggests that a company has good environmental vision but lacks the skills needed to implement it. Thus, companies should work at developing all four dimensions of environmental sustainability.

Walmart, for example, is doing just that. Through its own environmental sustainability actions and its impact on the actions of suppliers, Walmart has emerged in recent years as the world's super "eco-nanny" (see Real Marketing 20.1). Unilever is also setting a high sustainability standard. For six years running it has been named one of the most sustainable corporations in the annual "Global 100 Most Sustainable Corporations in the World" ranking:[24]

Unilever has multiple programs in place to manage the environmental impacts of its own operations. But that's only the start. "The world faces enormous environmental pressures," says the company. "Our aim is to make our activities more sustainable and also encourage our customers, suppliers, and others to do the same." On the "upstream side," more than two-thirds of Unilever's raw materials come from agriculture, so the company helps suppliers develop sustainable farming practices that meet its own high expectations for environmental and social impacts. The long-term goal is to source all key raw materials sustainably by 2015. On the "downstream side"— when consumers use its products—Unilever reduces the environmental impacts of its products during use through innovative product development and consumer education. For example, almost one-third of households worldwide use Unilever laundry products to do their washing—approximately 125 billion washes every year. So the company launched the Cleaner Planet Plan project, which aims to reduce the impact of laundry on the environment by designing sustainable products and manufacturing them efficiently. But up to 70 percent of the total greenhouse gas footprint and 95 percent of the water footprint of Unilever's laundry products occur during consumer use. So the Cleaner Planet Plan also engages consumers directly to educate

Real Marketing 20.1

Walmart: The World's Super Eco-Nanny

When you think of the corporate "good guys"—companies that are helping to save the world through sustainable actions—you probably think of names like Patagonia, Timberland, Ben & Jerry's, Whole Foods Market, or Stonyfield Farm. But hold onto your seat. When it comes to sustainability, perhaps no company in the world is doing more good these days than Walmart. That's right—big, bad, Walmart. Notes one incredulous reporter: "The company whose 2,600 supercenters take up at least 46,000 acres of earth, whose 117 square miles of asphalt parking lots add up to the size of Tampa, Florida, and who in 2004 faced fines for violating environmental laws in nine states, has . . . found green religion."

Critics have long bashed Walmart for a broad range of alleged social misdeeds, from unfair labor practices to destroying small communities. So, many consumers are surprised to learn that the world's largest company is also the world's biggest crusader for the cause of saving the world for future generations. When it comes to sustainability, Walmart is rapidly emerging as the world's super "eco-nanny." In the long run, Walmart's stated environmental goals are to use 100 percent renewable energy, create zero waste, and sell only products that sustain the world's environment. Toward that goal, Walmart is not only greening up its own operations but also working with its vast networks of 100,000 suppliers, 2.2 million employees, and the 200 million customers who walk through its doors every week to get them to do the same.

Walmart operates almost 7,900 stores around the world, and its huge stores are gluttons for energy and other resources. So even small steps toward making stores more efficient can add up to huge environmental savings. For example, just removing the lights from vending machines across Walmart stores saves $1.4 million worth of energy per year. But Walmart isn't settling for small steps; it's moving in large leaps to develop new eco-technologies. In 2005, the giant retailer opened two experimental superstores in McKinney, Texas, and Aurora, Colorado, that were designed to test dozens of environmentally friendly and energy-efficient technologies:

A 143-foot-tall wind turbine stands outside a Walmart Supercenter in Aurora, Colorado. In-

congruous as it might seem, it's a clear sign that something about this particular store is different. On the outside, the store's façade features row after row of windows to allow in as much natural light as possible. The landscaping uses native, drought-tolerant plants well adapted to the hot, dry Colorado summers, cutting down on watering, mowing, and the amount of fertilizer and other chemicals needed. Inside the store, an efficient high-output linear fluorescent lighting system saves enough electricity annually from this store alone to supply the needs of 52 single-family homes. The store's heating system burns recovered cooking oil from the deli's fryers; the oil is collected, mixed with waste engine oil from the store's Tire and Lube Express, and burned in the waste-oil boiler. All organic waste, including produce, meats, and paper, is placed in an organic waste compactor, which is then hauled off to a company that turns it into mulch for the garden. These and dozens more technological touches make the supercenter a laboratory for efficient and Earth-friendly retail operations.

After evaluating these experimental stores, Walmart is now rolling out new high-efficiency stores, each one saving more energy than the last. A recently opened Las Vegas store uses 45 percent less energy than a standard Walmart. Moreover, Walmart is eagerly spreading the word by encouraging visitors and sharing what it learns—even with competing companies such as Target and Home Depot.

At the same time that Walmart presses forward with its own sustainability initiatives, it's also affecting the environmental behaviors of its customers, employees, and suppliers. For example, it puts

its marketing muscle behind eco-friendly products, regularly promoting brands such as Sun Chips, PUR water filters, and GE fluorescent bulbs. "If Walmart can galvanize its regular shopper base into green purchasing and eco-friendly habits, it's succeeded in reducing the ecological footprint of 200 million people," says one analyst. The giant retailer has also launched an employee program called the "personal sustainability project" (PSP), in which employees commit to responsible acts in front of their coworkers—anything from quitting smoking to converting the lights in their house to energy-efficient bulbs. The company now has more than 200,000 PSPs.

Walmart is also laying down the eco-law to suppliers. It recently announced plans to cut some 20 million metric tons of greenhouse gas emissions from its supply chain by the end of 2015—the equivalent of removing more than 3.8 million cars from the road for a year. To

For Walmart, sustainability is about more than just doing the right thing. Above all, it makes good business sense—"driving out hidden costs, conserving our natural resources for future generations, and providing sustainable and affordable products for our customers so they can save money and live better."

Continued on next page

accomplish this and other sustainability goals, Walmart is asking its huge corps of suppliers to examine the carbon life cycles of their products and rethink how they source, manufacture, package, and transport these goods.

Walmart is even developing a Sustainability Index—based on information provided by suppliers—that tracks the life cycle of every product it sells, measuring it on everything from water use and greenhouse gas emissions to fair labor practices. Within a few years, Walmart wants to place a Sustainability Index tag on all its goods that details each product's eco-friendliness and social impact. High-scoring products will earn preferential treatment—and likely more shelf space—in Walmart stores.

Because of Walmart's size, even small supplier product and packaging changes have a substantial environmental impact. For example, to meet Walmart's requests, P&G developed a mega roll technology for its Charmin brand, which combines the sheets of four regular toilet paper rolls into one small roll. The seemingly minor change saves 89.5 million cardboard rolls and 360,000 pounds of plastic packaging wrap a year. It also allows Walmart

to ship 42 percent more units on its trucks, saving about 54,000 gallons of fuel a year.

Although some suppliers are grumbling about Walmart's heavy-handed sustainability requirements, most are joining in. With its immense buying power, Walmart can humble even the mightiest supplier. When imposing its environmental demands on suppliers, Walmart "has morphed into . . . a sort of privatized Environmental Protection Agency, only with a lot more clout," says an industry observer. "The EPA can levy [only] a seven-figure fine; Walmart can wipe out more than a quarter of a business in one fell swoop."

So there you have it—Walmart the eco-nanny. Walmart's sustainability efforts have earned praise from even its harshest critics. As

one skeptic begrudgingly admits, "Walmart has more green clout than anyone." But for Walmart, leading the eco-charge is about more than just doing the right thing. Above all, it also makes good business sense. More efficient operations and less wasteful products are not only good for the environment but also save Walmart money. Lower costs, in turn, let Walmart do more of what it has always done best—save customers money.

Says a Walmart executive, "We've laid the foundation for a long-term effort that will transform our business by driving out hidden costs, conserving our natural resources for future generations, and providing sustainable and affordable products for our customers so they can save money and live better."

Sources: Quotes, adapted extract, and other information from "Walmart," *Fast Company*, March 2010, p. 66; Eve Lazarus, "Walmart's Green Business Summit Builds Business Case for Sustainability," *Canadian Grocer*, March 2010, p. 11; Jack Neff, "Why Walmart Has More Green Clout Than Anyone," *Advertising Age*, October 15, 2007, p. 1; Denise Lee Yohn, "A Big, Green, Reluctant Hug for Retailing's 800-lb. Gorilla," *Brandweek*, May 5, 2008, p. 61; Kate Rockwood, "Will Walmart's 'Sustainability Index' Actually Work?" *Fast Company*, February 1, 2010, accessed at www.fastcompany.com; and "Sustainable Value Networks," at http://walmartstores.com/Sustainability/7672.aspx, accessed November 2010.

them on better laundry habits to reduce their environmental impact. Thus, Unilever leads the entire value chain—from suppliers to consumers—in the cause of saving the environment.

Environmentalism creates some special challenges for global marketers. As international trade barriers come down and global markets expand, environmental issues are having an ever-greater impact on international trade. Countries in North America, Western Europe, and other developed regions are generating strict environmental standards. In the United States, for example, more than two dozen major pieces of environmental legislation have been enacted since 1970, and recent events suggest that more regulation is on the way. A side accord to the North American Free Trade Agreement established the Commission for Environmental Cooperation for resolving environmental matters. And the European Union's Eco-Management and Audit Scheme (EMAS) provides guidelines for environmental self-regulation.[25]

However, environmental policies still vary widely from country to country. Countries such as Denmark, Germany, Japan, and the United States have fully developed environmental policies and high public expectations. But major developing countries such as China, India, Brazil, and Russia are only in the early stages of developing such policies. Moreover, environmental factors that motivate consumers in one country may have no impact on consumers in another. For example, PVC soft-drink bottles cannot be used in Switzerland or Germany. However, they are preferred in France, which has an extensive recycling process for them. Thus, international companies have found it difficult to develop standard environmental practices that work globally. Instead, they are creating general policies and then translating these policies into tailored programs that meet local regulations and expectations.

FIGURE | 20.3
Major Marketing Decision Areas
That May Be Called into Question
under the Law

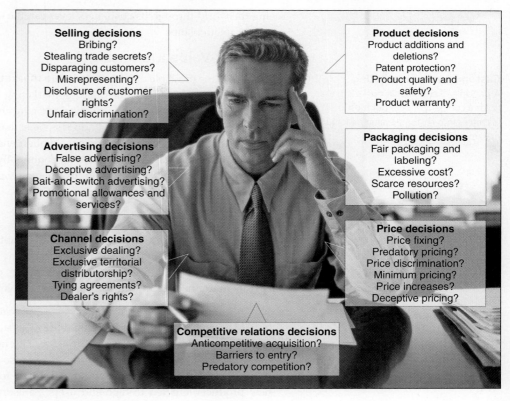

Selling decisions
Bribing?
Stealing trade secrets?
Disparaging customers?
Misrepresenting?
Disclosure of customer
rights?
Unfair discrimination?

Product decisions
Product additions and
deletions?
Patent protection?
Product quality and
safety?
Product warranty?

Advertising decisions
False advertising?
Deceptive advertising?
Bait-and-switch advertising?
Promotional allowances and
services?

Packaging decisions
Fair packaging and
labeling?
Excessive cost?
Scarce resources?
Pollution?

Channel decisions
Exclusive dealing?
Exclusive territorial
distributorship?
Tying agreements?
Dealer's rights?

Price decisions
Price fixing?
Predatory pricing?
Price discrimination?
Minimum pricing?
Price increases?
Deceptive pricing?

Competitive relations decisions
Anticompetitive acquisition?
Barriers to entry?
Predatory competition?

Public Actions to Regulate Marketing

Citizen concerns about marketing practices will usually lead to public attention and legislative proposals. Many of the laws that affect marketing were identified in Chapter 3. The task is to translate these laws into a language that marketing executives understand as they make decisions about competitive relations, products, price, promotion, and distribution channels. **Figure 20.3** illustrates the major legal issues facing marketing management.

Author Comment | In the end, marketers themselves must take responsibility for sustainable marketing. That means operating in a responsible and ethical way to bring both immediate and future value to customers.

Business Actions Toward Sustainable Marketing (pp 599–608)

At first, many companies opposed consumerism, environmentalism, and other elements of sustainable marketing. They thought the criticisms were either unfair or unimportant. But by now, most companies have grown to embrace sustainability marketing principles as a way to create greater immediate and future customer value and strengthen customer relationships.

Sustainable Marketing Principles

Under the sustainable marketing concept, a company's marketing should support the best long-run performance of the marketing system. It should be guided by five sustainable marketing principles: *consumer-oriented marketing*, *customer-value marketing*, *innovative marketing*, *sense-of-mission marketing*, and *societal marketing*.

Consumer-Oriented Marketing

Consumer-oriented marketing
A principle of sustainable marketing that holds a company should view and organize its marketing activities from the consumer's point of view.

Consumer-oriented marketing means that the company should view and organize its marketing activities from the consumer's point of view. It should work hard to sense, serve, and satisfy the needs of a defined group of customers—both now and in the future. The good marketing companies that we've discussed in this text have had this in common: an all-consuming passion for delivering superior value to carefully chosen customers. Only by seeing the world through its customers' eyes can the company build lasting and profitable customer relationships.

Customer-Value Marketing

Customer-value marketing

A principle of sustainable marketing that holds a company should put most of its resources into customer-value-building marketing investments.

According to the principle of **customer-value marketing**, the company should put most of its resources into customer-value-building marketing investments. Many things marketers do—one-shot sales promotions, cosmetic packaging changes, direct-response advertising—may raise sales in the short run but add less *value* than would actual improvements in the product's quality, features, or convenience. Enlightened marketing calls for building long-run consumer loyalty and relationships by continually improving the value consumers receive from the firm's market offering. By creating value *for* consumers, the company can capture value *from* consumers in return.

Innovative Marketing

Innovative marketing

A principle of sustainable marketing that requires a company seek real product and marketing improvements.

The principle of **innovative marketing** requires that the company continuously seek real product and marketing improvements. The company that overlooks new and better ways to do things will eventually lose customers to another company that has found a better way. An excellent example of an innovative marketer is Nintendo:[26]

> Not too many years ago, Samsung was a copycat consumer electronics brand you bought if you couldn't afford Sony. But today, the brand holds a high-end, cutting-edge aura. In 1996, Samsung Electronics turned its back on making cheap knock-offs and set out to overtake rival Sony, not just in size but also in style and innovation. It hired a crop of fresh, young designers who unleashed a torrent of sleek, bold, and beautiful new products targeted to high-end users. Samsung called them "lifestyle works of art"—from brightly colored cell phones to large-screen TVs that hung on walls like paintings. Every new product had to pass the "Wow!" test: if it didn't get a "Wow!" reaction during market testing, it went straight back to the design studio. Thanks to its strategy of innovation, the company quickly surpassed its lofty goals—and more. Samsung Electronics is now, by far, the world's largest consumer electronics company, with 50 percent greater sales than Sony. It's the world's largest TV manufacturer and second-largest cell phone producer. And its designs are coveted by consumers. Samsung recently bagged eight awards at the International Design Excellence Awards (IDEA); design darling Apple took home only seven awards. Says a Samsung designer, "We are not el cheapo anymore."[27]

Sense-of-Mission Marketing

Sense-of-mission marketing

A principle of sustainable marketing that holds a company should define its mission in broad social terms rather than narrow product terms.

Sense-of-mission marketing means that the company should define its mission in broad *social* terms rather than narrow *product* terms. When a company defines a social mission, employees feel better about their work and have a clearer sense of direction. Brands linked with broader missions can serve the best long-run interests of both the brand and consumers.

For example, PEDIGREE makes good dog food, but that's not what the brand is really all about. Instead, the brand came up with the tagline "Dogs rule." The tagline "is the perfect encapsulation of everything we stand for," says a PEDIGREE marketer. "Everything that we do is because we love dogs, because dogs rule. It's just so simple." This mission-focused positioning drives everything the brand does—internally and externally. ● One look at a PEDIGREE ad or a visit to the PEDIGREE.com Web site confirms that the people behind the PEDIGREE brand really do believe the "Dogs rule" mission. An internal manifesto called "Dogma" even encourages employees to take their dogs to work and on sales calls. To further fulfill the "Dogs rule" brand promise, the company created The PEDIGREE Adoption Drive Foundation, which has raised millions of dollars for helping "shelter dogs" find good homes. Sense-of-mission marketing has made PEDIGREE the world's number one dog food brand.[28]

Some companies define their overall corporate missions in broad societal terms. For example, defined in narrow product terms, the mission of outdoor gear and apparel maker Patagonia might be "to sell clothes and outdoor equipment." However, Patagonia states its

Meet Echo.

Echo lives in a shelter.

She was the loser in a divorce.

Echo isn't used to her new home—the cement feels strange on her paws. When people walk past, she runs to the front of her cage and smiles. Then they move on. And Echo doesn't understand where they went. When you buy Pedigree, we make a donation to help dogs like Echo find loving homes.

Help us help dogs.

The PEDIGREE Adoption Drive

Pedigree   Dogsrule.com

● **Sense-of-mission marketing: One look at a PEDIGREE ad or a visit to the PEDIGREE.com Web site confirms that the people behind the PEDIGREE brand really do believe the "Dogs rule" mission.**

mission more broadly, as one of producing the highest quality products while doing the least harm to the environment. From the start, Patagonia has pursued a passionately held social responsibility mission:[29]

> For us at Patagonia, "a love of wild and beautiful places demands participation in the fight to save them, and to help reverse the steep decline in the overall environmental health of our planet." Our reason for being is to "build the best product and cause no unnecessary harm—to use business to inspire and implement solutions to the environmental crisis." Yet we're keenly aware that everything we do as a business—or have done in our name—leaves its mark on the environment. As yet, there is no such thing as a sustainable business, but every day we take steps to lighten our footprint and do less harm.

Each year since 1985, the company has given away 10 percent of its pretax profits to support environmental causes. Today, it donates its time, services, and at least 1 percent of sales or 10 percent pretax profits to hundreds of grassroots environmental groups all over the world who work to help reverse the environmental tide.

However, having a "double bottom line" of values and profits isn't easy. Over the years, companies such as Patagonia, Ben & Jerry's, The Body Shop, and Burt's Bees—all known and respected for putting "principles before profits"—have at times struggled with less-than-stellar financial returns. In recent years, however, a new generation of social entrepreneurs has emerged, well-trained business managers who know that to "do good," they must first "do well" in terms of profitable business operations. As we learned in the chapter-opening story, Timberland CEO Jeff Swartz refers to this as the beautiful—and profitable—nexus between "commerce" and "justice." Timberland's mission is to make profits while at the same time making a difference in the world. Moreover, today, socially responsible business is no longer the sole province of small, socially conscious entrepreneurs. Many large, established companies and brands—from Walmart and Nike to PepsiCo—have adopted substantial social and environmental responsibility missions (see Real Marketing 20.2).

Societal Marketing

Societal marketing

A principle of sustainable marketing that holds a company should make marketing decisions by considering consumers' wants, the company's requirements, consumers' long-run interests, and society's long-run interests.

Following the principle of **societal marketing**, a company makes marketing decisions by considering consumers' wants, the company's requirements, consumers' long-run interests, and society's long-run interests. Companies should be aware that neglecting consumer and societal long-run interests is a disservice to consumers and society. Alert companies view societal problems as opportunities.

Sustainable marketing calls for products that are not only pleasing but also beneficial. The difference is shown in ● **Figure 20.4**. Products can be classified according to their degree of immediate consumer satisfaction and long-run consumer benefit.

● **FIGURE | 20.4**
Societal Classification of Products

Immediate Satisfaction

	Low	High
High	Salutary products	**Desirable products**
Low	Deficient products	Pleasing products

Long-run Consumer Benefit

The goal? Create desirable products—those that create both immediate customer satisfaction and a long-run customer benefit. An example is Haworth's Zody chair, which is both good for your body and good for the environment.

Real Marketing 20.2

Socially Responsible Marketing:
Making the World a Better Place

Chances are, when you hear the term *socially responsible business*, a handful of companies leap to mind, companies such as Ben & Jerry's, The Body Shop, Burt's Bees, Stonyfield Farms, Patagonia, and TOMS Shoes, to name a few. Such companies pioneered the concept of "values-led business" or "caring capitalism." Their mission: Use business to make the world a better place.

The classic "do good" pioneer is Ben & Jerry's. Ben Cohen and Jerry Greenfield founded the company in 1978 as a firm that cared deeply about its social and environmental responsibilities. Ben & Jerry's bought only hormone-free milk and cream and used only organic fruits and nuts to make its ice cream, which it sold in environmentally friendly containers. It went to great lengths to buy from minority and disadvantaged suppliers. From its early Rainforest Crunch to its more recent Chocolate Macadamia (made with sustainably-sourced macadamias and fair trade certified cocoa and vanilla), Ben & Jerry's has championed a host of social and environmental causes over the years. From the start, Ben & Jerry's donated a whopping 7.5 percent of pre-tax profits to support projects that exhibited "creative problem solving and hopefulness . . . relating to children and families, disadvantaged groups, and the environment." By the mid-1990s, Ben & Jerry's had become the nation's number two superpremium ice cream brand.

However, as competitors not shackled by Ben & Jerry's "principles before profits" mission invaded its markets, growth and profits flattened. After several years of lackluster financial returns, Ben & Jerry's was acquired by consumer goods giant Unilever. What happened to the founders' lofty ideals of caring capitalism? Looking back, Ben & Jerry's may have focused too much on social issues at the expense of sound business management. Ben Cohen never really wanted to be a businessperson. In fact, according to one analyst, Cohen "saw businesspeople as tools of the military-industrial complex and profits as a dirty word." Cohen once commented, "There came a time [when I had to admit] 'I'm a busi-

nessman.' And I had a hard time mouthing those words."

Having a "double bottom line" of values and profits is no easy proposition. Operating a business is tough enough. Adding social goals to the demands of serving customers and making a profit can be daunting and distracting. You can't take good intentions to the bank. In fact, many of the pioneering values-led businesses have since been acquired by bigger companies. For example, Unilever absorbed Ben & Jerry's, Clorox bought out Burt's Bees, L'Oreal acquired The Body Shop, and Dannon ate up Stonyfield Farms.

The experiences of pioneers like Ben & Jerry's, however, taught the socially responsible business movement some hard lessons. As a result, a new generation of mission-driven entrepreneurs emerged—not social activists with big hearts who hate capitalism but well-trained business managers and company

builders with a passion for a cause. These new double-bottom-line devotees know that to "do good," they must first "do well" in terms of viable and profitable business operations.

For example, home and cleaning products company Method is on a mission to "inspire a happy, healthy home revolution." All of Method's products are derived from natural ingredients, such as soy, coconut, and palm oils. The products come in environmentally responsible, biodegradable packaging. But Method knows that just doing good things won't make it successful. In fact, it's the other way around—being successful will let it do good things. "Business is the most powerful agent for positive change on the planet," says Method cofounder and "chief greenskeeper" Adam Lowry. "Mere sustainability is not our goal. We want to go much farther than that. We want to become restorative and enriching in everything we do so that the bigger we get, the more good we can create. We are striving for sustainable abundance. That's why at Method, we are always looking for ways to not just make our products greener, but our company better."

Beyond its social responsibility mission, Method is a well-run business and savvy marketer. Instead of touting the eco-friendly prop-

Method's mission is to inspire a happy, healthy home revolution. Says Method cofounder and "chief greenskeeper" Adam Lowry, "Business is the most powerful agent for positive change on the planet."

erties of its products, Method emphasizes product performance and innovation. Its products really work. And Method's marketing is on par with that of large blue chip competitors, such as P&G or Unilever. For example, through solid marketing, Method has attained mainstream distribution in Kroger, Safeway, Target, Whole Foods Market, Bed Bath & Beyond, Staples, Amazon.com, and a growing list of other big retailers. In only a few short years, through smart business practices, Method has become one of the nation's fastest growing companies, with more than $100 million in annual revenues. In the process, it's achieving its broader social goals.

Small companies with big social goals are one thing. However, today, socially responsible missions are no longer the exclusive domain of well-intentioned start-ups. Social responsibility has gone mainstream, with large corporations—from Walmart and Nike to Starbucks, Mars, and PepsiCo—adopting broad-based "change the world" initiatives. For example, Walmart is fast becoming the world's leading eco-nanny. Starbucks created C.A.F.E. Practices, guidelines for achieving product quality, economic accountability, social responsibility, and environmental leadership.

Nike supports a broad social and environmental responsibility agenda, everything from eco-friendly product designs and manufacturing processes to improving conditions for the nearly 800,000 workers in its global supply chain to programs that engage the world's youth in the fight against AIDS in Africa. Sounding more like Ben & Jerry's or Method than a large, uncaring corporation, Nike states "We can use the power of our brand, the energy and passion of our people, and the scale of our business to create meaningful change." Says one Nike manager, "Our customers expect this from us. It's not about two or three green shoes—it's about changing the way our company does things in general."

Some brands are building their very identities around social responsibility missions. For example, as previously discussed, Mars Inc.'s Pedigree brand is on a "Dogs rule" mission to urge people to adopt homeless dogs and support the care of these animals in shelters. Last year, it distributed $1.5 million in grants to 1,000 animal shelters. Pedigree donates one bowl of dog food to shelters every time it gets a Facebook fan. Last year, that added up to more than four million bowls of dog food, enough to feed every shelter dog in America for one day.

Similarly, through its Pepsi Refresh campaign, PepsiCo redefines its flagship brand as not just a soft drink but as an agent for world change. In a year-long effort, the Pepsi Refresh Project is awarding $20 million in grants to hundreds of individuals and organizations in local communities that propose ideas that will "make the world a better place." Pepsi is backing the effort with a big-budget traditional and social marketing campaign. This is no mere cause-related marketing effort: The Pepsi Refresh Project makes "doing good" a major element of Pepsi's mission and positioning. Says Pepsi's director of marketing, "We want people to be aware that every time you drink a Pepsi you are actually supporting the Pepsi Refresh Project and ideas that are going to move this country forward."

Sources: Quotes and other information from Bob Liodice, "10 Companies with Social Responsibility at the Core," *Advertising Age*, April 19, 2010, p. 88; Mike Hoffman, "Ben Cohen: Ben & Jerry's Homemade, Established in 1978," *Inc*, April 30, 2001, p. 68; Sindya N. Bhanoo, "Products That Are Earth-and-Profit Friendly," *New York Times*, June 12, 2010, p. B3; Elaine Wong, "Pepsi Community Effort Finds Fans on Social Nets," *Brandweek*, June 9, 2010, accessed at www.brandweek.com; and www.methodhome.com/behind-the-bottle/, www.benjerry.com/company/history/, and www.nikebiz.com/responsibility/, accessed November 2010.

Deficient products
Products that have neither immediate appeal nor long-run benefits.

Pleasing products
Products that give high immediate satisfaction but may hurt consumers in the long run.

Salutary products
Products that have low appeal but may benefit consumers in the long run.

Desirable products
Products that give both high immediate satisfaction and high long-run benefits.

Deficient products, such as bad-tasting and ineffective medicine, have neither immediate appeal nor long-run benefits. **Pleasing products** give high immediate satisfaction but may hurt consumers in the long run. Examples include cigarettes and junk food. **Salutary products** have low immediate appeal but may benefit consumers in the long run; for instance, bicycle helmets or some insurance products. **Desirable products** give both high immediate satisfaction and high long-run benefits, such as a tasty *and* nutritious breakfast food.

Examples of desirable products abound. GE's Energy Smart compact fluorescent lightbulb provides good lighting at the same time that it gives long life and energy savings. Maytag's front-loading Neptune washer provides superior cleaning along with water savings and energy efficiency. And Haworth's Zody office chair is not only attractive and functional but also environmentally responsible. It's made without PVC, chlorofluorocarbons (CFCs), chrome, or any other toxic materials. Ninety-eight percent of the chair can be recycled; some 50 percent of it already has been. The energy used in the manufacturing process is completely offset by wind-power credits. When the chair is ready to be retired, the company will take it back and reuse its components.[30]

Companies should try to turn all of their products into desirable products. The challenge posed by pleasing products is that they sell very well but may end up hurting the consumer. The product opportunity, therefore, is to add long-run benefits without reducing the product's pleasing qualities. The challenge posed by salutary products is to add some pleasing qualities so that they will become more desirable in consumers' minds.

Desirable products: PepsiCo has hired a team of scientists to help it develop a larger portfolio of healthy product options, such as the new Trop50 brand.

For example, PepsiCo recently hired a team of "idealistic scientists," headed by a former director of the World Health Organization, to help the company create attractive new healthy product options while "making the bad stuff less bad."[31] The group of physicians, PhDs, and other health advocates, under the direction of PepsiCo's vice president for global health policy, looks for healthier ingredients that can go into multiple products. For example, their efforts led to an all-natural zero-calorie sweetener now featured in several new PepsiCo brands, including the $100-million Trop50 brand, a Tropicana orange juice variation that contains no artificial sweeteners and half the sugar and calories.

Marketing Ethics

Good ethics are a cornerstone of sustainable marketing. In the long run, unethical marketing harms customers and society as a whole. Further, it eventually damages a company's reputation and effectiveness, jeopardizing its very survival. Thus, the sustainable marketing goals of long-term consumer and business welfare can be achieved only through ethical marketing conduct.

Conscientious marketers face many moral dilemmas. The best thing to do is often unclear. Because not all managers have fine moral sensitivity, companies need to develop *corporate marketing ethics policies*—broad guidelines that everyone in the organization must follow. These policies should cover distributor relations, advertising standards, customer service, pricing, product development, and general ethical standards.

The finest guidelines cannot resolve all the difficult ethical situations the marketer faces. **Table 20.1** lists some difficult ethical issues mar-

TABLE | 20.1   Some Morally Difficult Situations in Marketing

Your R&D department has slightly changed one of your company's products. It is not really "new and improved," but you know that putting this statement on the package and in advertising will increase sales. What would you do?

You have been asked to add a stripped-down model to your line that could be advertised to pull customers into the store. The product won't be very good, but salespeople will be able to switch buyers up to higher-priced units. You are asked to give the green light for the stripped-down version. What would you do?

You are thinking of hiring a product manager who has just left a competitor's company. She would be more than happy to tell you all the competitor's plans for the coming year. What would you do?

One of your top dealers in an important territory recently has had family troubles, and his sales have slipped. It looks like it will take him a while to straighten out his family trouble. Meanwhile you are losing many sales. Legally, on performance grounds, you can terminate the dealer's franchise and replace him. What would you do?

You have a chance to win a big account that will mean a lot to you and your company. The purchasing agent hints that a "gift" would influence the decision. Your assistant recommends sending a large-screen television to the buyer's home. What would you do?

You have heard that a competitor has a new product feature that will make a big difference in sales. The competitor will demonstrate the feature in a private dealer meeting at the annual trade show. You can easily send a snooper to this meeting to learn about the new feature. What would you do?

You have to choose between three advertising campaigns outlined by your agency. The first (a) is a soft-sell, honest, straight-information campaign. The second (b) uses sex-loaded emotional appeals and exaggerates the product's benefits. The third (c) involves a noisy, somewhat irritating commercial that is sure to gain audience attention. Pretests show that the campaigns are effective in the following order: c, b, and a. What would you do?

You are interviewing a capable female applicant for a job as salesperson. She is better qualified than the men who have been interviewed. Nevertheless, you know that in your industry some important customers prefer dealing with men, and you will lose some sales if you hire her. What would you do?

keters could face during their careers. If marketers choose immediate sales-producing actions in all these cases, their marketing behavior might well be described as immoral or even amoral. If they refuse to go along with *any* of the actions, they might be ineffective as marketing managers and unhappy because of the constant moral tension. Managers need a set of principles that will help them figure out the moral importance of each situation and decide how far they can go in good conscience.

But *what* principle should guide companies and marketing managers on issues of ethics and social responsibility? One philosophy is that the free market and the legal system should decide such issues. Under this principle, companies and their managers are not responsible for making moral judgments. Companies can in good conscience do whatever the market and legal systems allow.

A second philosophy puts responsibility not on the system but in the hands of individual companies and managers. This more enlightened philosophy suggests that a company should have a "social conscience." Companies and managers should apply high standards of ethics and morality when making corporate decisions, regardless of "what the system allows." History provides an endless list of examples of company actions that were legal but highly irresponsible.

Each company and marketing manager must work out a philosophy of socially responsible and ethical behavior. Under the societal marketing concept, each manager must look beyond what is legal and allowed and develop standards based on personal integrity, corporate conscience, and long-run consumer welfare.

Dealing with issues of ethics and social responsibility in an open and forthright way helps to build strong customer relationships based on honesty and trust. In fact, many companies now routinely include consumers in the social responsibility process. ● Consider toy maker Mattel:[32]

● **When the discovery of lead paint on several of its best-selling products forced Mattel to recall millions of toys worldwide, the company's forthright response helped it maintain customer confidence. Mattel even involved its panel of 400 moms as "brand advisors" to help shape its response.**

In fall 2007, the discovery of lead paint on several of its best-selling products forced Mattel to make worldwide recalls on millions of toys. Threatening as this was, rather than hesitating or hiding the incident, the company's brand advisors were up to the challenge. Their quick, decisive response helped to maintain consumer confidence in the Mattel brand, even contributing to a 6 percent sales increase over the same period from the year before. Just who were these masterful "brand advisors"? They were the 400 moms with kids ages 3 to 10 who constitute The Playground community, a private online network launched by Mattel's worldwide consumer insights department in June 2007 to "listen to and gain insight from moms' lives and needs." Throughout the crisis, The Playground community members kept in touch with Mattel regarding the product recalls and the company's forthright response plan, even helping to shape the postrecall promotional strategy for one of the affected product lines. Even in times of crisis, "brands that engage in a two-way conversation with their customers create stronger, more trusting relationships," says a Mattel executive.

As with environmentalism, the issue of ethics presents special challenges for international marketers. Business standards and practices vary a great deal from one country to the next. For example, bribes and kickbacks are illegal for U.S. firms, and a variety of treaties against bribery and corruption have been signed and ratified by more than 60 countries. Yet these are still standard business practices in many countries. The World Bank estimates that bribes totaling more than $1 trillion per year are paid out worldwide. One studied showed that the most flagrant bribe-paying firms were from India, Russia, and China. Other countries where corruption is common include Iraq, Myanmar, and Haiti. The least corrupt were companies from Sweden, New Zealand, and Denmark.[33] The question arises as to whether a company must lower its ethical standards to compete effectively in countries with lower standards. The answer is no. Companies should make a commitment to a common set of shared standards worldwide.

Many industrial and professional associations have suggested codes of ethics, and many companies are now adopting their own codes. For example, the American Marketing Association, an international association of marketing managers and scholars, developed the code of ethics shown in ● **Table 20.2**. Companies are also developing programs to teach managers about important ethical issues and help them find the proper responses. They hold ethics workshops and seminars and create ethics committees. Furthermore, most major U.S. companies have appointed high-level ethics officers to champion ethical issues and help resolve ethics problems and concerns facing employees.

PricewaterhouseCoopers (PwC) is a good example. In 2002, PwC established a global ethics office and comprehensive ethics program, headed by a high-level global ethics officer. The ethics program begins with a code of conduct called "The Way We Do Business." PwC employees learn about the code of conduct and about how to handle thorny ethics issues in comprehensive ethics training programs, which start when the employee joins the company and continue throughout the employee's career. The program also includes an ethics help line and regular communications at all levels. "It is obviously not enough to distribute a document," says PwC's former CEO, Samuel DiPiazza. "Ethics is in everything we say and do."[34]

Still, written codes and ethics programs do not ensure ethical behavior. Ethics and social responsibility require a total corporate commitment. They must be a component of the overall corporate culture. According to DiPiazza, "I see ethics as a mission-critical issue . . . deeply embedded in who we are and what we do. It's just as important as our product development cycle or our distribution system. . . . It's about creating a culture based on integrity and respect, not a culture based on dealing with the crisis of the day. . . . We ask ourselves every day, 'Are we doing the right things?'"[35]

● **TABLE | 20.2**   American Marketing Association Code of Ethics

Ethical Norms and Values for Marketers

Preamble

The American Marketing Association commits itself to promoting the highest standard of professional ethical norms and values for its members. Norms are established standards of conduct that are expected and maintained by society and/or professional organizations. Values represent the collective conception of what communities find desirable, important and morally proper. Values also serve as the criteria for evaluating our own personal actions and the actions of others. As marketers, we recognize that we not only serve our organizations but also act as stewards of society in creating, facilitating and executing the transactions that are part of the greater economy. In this role, marketers are expected to embrace the highest professional ethical norms and the ethical values implied by our responsibility toward multiple stakeholders (e.g., customers, employees, investors, peers, channel members, regulators and the host community).

Ethical Norms

As Marketers, we must:

1. **Do no harm.** This means consciously avoiding harmful actions or omissions by embodying high ethical standards and adhering to all applicable laws and regulations in the choices we make.

2. **Foster trust in the marketing system.** This means striving for good faith and fair dealing so as to contribute toward the efficacy of the exchange process as well as avoiding deception in product design, pricing, communication, and delivery of distribution.

3. **Embrace ethical values.** This means building relationships and enhancing consumer confidence in the integrity of marketing by affirming these core values: honesty, responsibility, fairness, respect, transparency and citizenship.

● TABLE | 20.2   American Marketing Association Code of Ethics—*continued*

Ethical Values

Honesty—to be forthright in dealings with customers and stakeholders. To this end, we will:

- Strive to be truthful in all situations and at all times.
- Offer products of value that do what we claim in our communications.
- Stand behind our products if they fail to deliver their claimed benefits.
- Honor our explicit and implicit commitments and promises.

Responsibility—to accept the consequences of our marketing decisions and strategies. To this end, we will:

- Strive to serve the needs of customers.
- Avoid using coercion with all stakeholders.
- Acknowledge the social obligations to stakeholders that come with increased marketing and economic power.
- Recognize our special commitments to vulnerable market segments such as children, seniors, the economically impoverished, market illiterates and others who may be substantially disadvantaged.
- Consider environmental stewardship in our decision-making.

Fairness—to balance justly the needs of the buyer with the interests of the seller. To this end, we will:

- Represent products in a clear way in selling, advertising and other forms of communication; this includes the avoidance of false, misleading and deceptive promotion.
- Reject manipulations and sales tactics that harm customer trust.
- Revise to engage in price fixing, predatory pricing, price gouging or "bait-and-switch" tactics.
- Avoid knowing participation in conflicts of interest.
- Seek to protect the private information of customers, employees and partners.

Respect—to acknowledge the basic human dignity of all stakeholders. To this end, we will:

- Value individual differences and avoid stereotyping customers or depicting demographic groups (e.g., gender, race, sexual orientation) in a negative or dehumanizing way.
- Listen to the needs of customers and make all reasonable efforts to monitor and improve their satisfaction on an ongoing basis.
- Make every effort to understand and respectfully treat buyers, suppliers, intermediaries and distributors from all cultures.
- Acknowledge the contributions of others, such as consultants, employees and coworkers, to marketing endeavors.
- Treat everyone, including our competitors, as we would wish to be treated.

Transparency—to create a spirit of openness in marketing operations. To this end, we will:

- Strive to communicate clearly with all constituencies.
- Accept constructive criticism from customers and other stakeholders.
- Explain and take appropriate action regarding significant product or service risks, component substitutions or other foreseeable eventualities that could affect customers or their perception of the purchase decision.
- Disclose list prices and terms of financing as well as available price deals and adjustments.

Citizenship—to fulfill the economic, legal, philanthropic, and societal responsibilities that serve stakeholders. To this end, we will:

- Strive to protect the ecological environment in the execution of marketing campaigns.
- Give back to the community through volunteerism and charitable donations.
- Contribute to the overall betterment of marketing and its reputation.
- Urge supply chain members to ensure that trade is fair for all participants, including producers in developing countries.

Implementation

We expect AMA members to be courageous and proactive in leading and/or aiding their organizations in the fulfillment of the explicit and implicit promises made to those stakeholders. We recognize that every industry sector and marketing sub-discipline (e.g., marketing research, e-commerce, Internet selling, direct marketing, and advertising) has its own specific ethical issues that require policies and commentary. An array of such codes can be accessed through links on the AMA Web site. Consistent with the principle of subsidiarity (solving issues at the level where the expertise resides), we encourage all such groups to develop and/or refine their industry and discipline-specific codes of ethics to supplement these guiding ethical norms and values.

Source: Reprinted with permission of the American Marketing Association, www.marketingpower.com/AboutAMA/Pages/Statement%20of%20Ethics.aspx#.

The Sustainable Company

At the foundation of marketing is the belief that companies that fulfill the needs and wants of customers will thrive. Companies that fail to meet customer needs or that intentionally or unintentionally harm customers, others in society, or future generations will decline. Says one observer, "Sustainability is an emerging business megatrend, like electrification and mass production, that will profoundly affect companies' competitiveness and even their survival."[36]

Sustainable companies are those that create value for customers through socially, environmentally, and ethically responsible actions. Sustainable marketing goes beyond caring for the needs and wants of today's customers. It means having concern for tomorrow's customers in assuring the survival and success of the business, shareholders, employees, and the broader world in which they all live. Sustainable marketing provides the context in which companies can build profitable customer relationships by creating value *for* customers in order to capture value *from* customers in return—now and in the future.

REVIEWING Objectives AND KEY Terms

In this chapter, we addressed many of the important *sustainable marketing* concepts related to marketing's sweeping impact on individual consumers, other businesses, and society as a whole. Sustainable marketing requires socially, environmentally, and ethically responsible actions that bring value to not only present-day consumers and businesses but also future generations and society as a whole. Sustainable companies are those that act responsibly to create value for customers in order to capture value from customers in return—now and in the future.

Objective 1   Define sustainable marketing and discuss its importance.   (pp 582–584)

Sustainable marketing calls for meeting the present needs of consumers and businesses while preserving or enhancing the ability of future generations to meet their needs. Whereas the marketing concept recognizes that companies thrive by fulfilling the day-to-day needs of customers, sustainable marketing calls for socially and environmentally responsible actions that meet both the immediate and future needs of customers and the company. Truly sustainable marketing requires a smooth-functioning marketing system in which consumers, companies, public policymakers, and others work together to ensure responsible marketing actions.

Objective 2   Identify the major social criticisms of marketing.   (pp 584–592)

Marketing's *impact on individual consumer welfare* has been criticized for its high prices, deceptive practices, high-pressure selling, shoddy or unsafe products, planned obsolescence, and poor ser-

vice to disadvantaged consumers. Marketing's *impact on society* has been criticized for creating false wants and too much materialism, too few social goods, and cultural pollution. Critics have also denounced marketing's *impact on other businesses* for harming competitors and reducing competition through acquisitions, practices that create barriers to entry, and unfair competitive marketing practices. Some of these concerns are justified; some are not.

Objective 3   Define consumerism and environmentalism and explain how they affect marketing strategies.   (pp 592–599)

Concerns about the marketing system have led to *citizen action movements*. *Consumerism* is an organized social movement intended to strengthen the rights and power of consumers relative to sellers. Alert marketers view it as an opportunity to serve consumers better by providing more consumer information, education, and protection. *Environmentalism* is an organized social movement seeking to minimize the harm done to the environment and quality of life by marketing practices. The first wave of modern environmentalism was driven by environmental groups and concerned consumers; the second wave was driven by the federal government, which passed laws and regulations governing industrial practices impacting the environment. The first two environmentalism waves are now merging into a third and stronger wave, in which companies are accepting responsibility for doing no environmental harm. Companies now are adopting policies of *environmental sustainability*—developing strategies that both sustain the environment and produce profits for the company. Both consumerism and environmentalism are important components of sustainable marketing.

Objective 4 **Describe the principles of sustainable marketing.** (pp 599–604)

Many companies originally resisted these social movements and laws, but most now recognize a need for positive consumer information, education, and protection. Under the sustainable marketing concept, a company's marketing should support the best long-run performance of the marketing system. It should be guided by five sustainable marketing principles: *consumer-oriented marketing*, *customer-value marketing*, *innovative marketing*, *sense-of-mission marketing*, and *societal marketing*.

Objective 5 **Explain the role of ethics in marketing.** (pp 604–608)

Increasingly, companies are responding to the need to provide company policies and guidelines to help their managers deal with questions of *marketing ethics*. Of course, even the best guidelines cannot resolve all the difficult ethical decisions that individuals and firms must make. But there are some principles from which marketers can choose. One principle states that the free market and the legal system should decide such issues. A second and more enlightened principle puts responsibility not on the system but in the hands of individual companies and managers. Each firm and marketing manager must work out a philosophy of socially responsible and ethical behavior. Under the sustainable marketing concept, managers must look beyond what is legal and allowable and develop standards based on personal integrity, corporate conscience, and long-term consumer welfare.

KEY Terms

OBJECTIVE 1
Sustainable marketing (p 583)

OBJECTIVE 3
Consumerism (p 592)
Environmentalism (p 593)
Environmental sustainability (p 594)

OBJECTIVE 4
Consumer-oriented marketing (p 599)
Customer-value marketing (p 600)
Innovative marketing (p 600)
Sense-of-mission marketing (p 600)

Societal marketing (p 601)
Deficient products (p 603)
Pleasing products (p 603)
Salutary products (p 603)
Desirable products (p 603)

PEARSON mymarketinglab

- Check your understanding of the concepts and key terms using the mypearsonmarketinglab study plan for this chapter.
- Apply the concepts in a business context using the simulation entitled **Ethics**.

DISCUSSING & APPLYING THE Concepts

Discussing the Concepts

1. What is sustainable marketing? Explain how the sustainable marketing concept differs from the marketing concept and the societal marketing concept. (AACSB: Communication)

2. Discuss the issues relevant to marketing's impact on society as a whole and how marketers respond to these criticisms. (AACSB: Communication)

3. Discuss the types of harmful impact that marketing practices can have on competition and the associated problems. (AACSB: Communication)

4. What is consumerism? Describe the rights of sellers and buyers. (AACSB: Communication)

5. Describe the five sustainable marketing principles and explain how companies benefit from adhering to them. (AACSB: Communication)

6. Describe the two philosophies regarding what principle should guide companies and marketing managers on issues of ethics and social responsibility. (AACSB: Communication)

Applying the Concepts

1. Visit www.causemarketingforum.com and learn about the Halo Awards for outstanding cause-related marketing programs. Describe an award-winning case that exemplifies the sustainable marketing concept. (AACSB: Communication; Use of IT; Reflective Thinking)

2. In a small group, discuss each of the morally difficult situations in marketing presented in Table 20.1. Which philosophy is guiding your decision in each situation? (AACSB: Communication; Ethical Reasoning)

   KGOY stands for "kids getting older younger," and marketers are getting much of the blame, especially for young girls. Critics describe clothing designed for young girls ages 8–11 as floozy and sexual, with department stores selling thongs for youngsters and T-shirts that say "Naughty Girl!" Although Barbie's sexuality has never been subtle, she was originally targeted to girls 9–12 years old. Now, Barbie dolls target primarily 3–7 year-old girls. In a small group, discuss other examples of this phenomenon and debate whether marketers are to blame. Are any companies countering this trend by offering age-appropriate products for children? (AACSB: Communication; Reflective Thinking)

FOCUS ON Technology

Marketers are hungry for customer information, and the electronic tracking industry is answering the call by gathering consumer Internet behavior data. A recent investigation by the *Wall Street Journal* found that the fifty most popular U.S. Web sites installed more than 3,000 tracking files on the computer used in the study. The total was even higher—4,123 tracking files—for the top fifty sites popular with children and teens. Many sites installed more than 100 tracking tools each during the tests. Tracking tools include files placed on users' computers and on Web sites. You probably know about cookies, small information files that are placed on your computer. Newer technology, such Web beacons (also known as Web bugs, tracking bugs, pixel tags, and clear GIFs) are invisible graphic files placed on Web sites and in e-mails that, when combined with cookies, can tell a lot about the user. For example, beacons can tell a marketer if a page was viewed and for how long and can even tell if you read the e-mail sent to you.

Such tracking has become aggressive to the point where keystrokes can be analyzed for clues about a person, and "flash cookies" can reappear after a user deletes them. Although the data do not identify users by name, data-gathering companies can construct consumer profiles that include demographic, geographic, and lifestyle information. Marketers use this information to target online ads.

1. Critics claim that Internet tracking infringes consumer privacy rights. Should marketers have access to such information? Discuss the advantages and disadvantages of this activity for marketers and consumers. (AACSB: Communication; Ethical Reasoning)

2. Discuss the position of the FTC on this activity. Is it right to track a computer user's online search behavior? (AACSB: Communication; Ethical Reasoning)

FOCUS ON Ethics

Many companies, such as Timberland, which was profiled at the beginning of this chapter, take sustainable marketing seriously. Consumers might soon be able to use the Outdoor Industry Association's (OIA) Eco Index to help them identify such companies. The OIA has guided brand manufacturers and retailers, such as Nike, Levi Strauss, Timberland, Target, Patagonia, and many others in developing of a software tool to measure the eco-impact of their products. A product as simple as a pair of jeans has considerable environmental impact. A pair of Levis jeans moves from cotton grown in Louisiana; to fabric woven in North Carolina; to jeans cut in the Dominican Republic, sewn in Haiti, and finished in Jamaica; to the final product distributed in the store where you purchase them. And that's just for jeans sold in the United States; Levi's are sold all over the world. The Eco Index takes all this into account and more. It factors in other environmental things, such as washing methods, the amount of water used in the life of the

jeans, and the disposal of the product. The holdup on the Eco Index, however, is that all the information is self-reported, and manufacturers have to obtain information from their suppliers as well.

1. Learn more about this initiative by visiting the OIA's Web site at www.outdoorindustry.org. If implemented, will this index help marketers who score well on it develop a sustainable competitive advantage? Would you be more willing to purchase a product from a company that scores well on this index? (AACSB: Communication; Use of IT; Reflective Thinking)

2. The Eco Index is an industry-led initiative; all information is self-reported with no proof required. Is there a potential to abuse the system and possibly deceive consumers? Explain. (AACSB: Communication; Ethical Reasoning; Reflective Thinking)

MARKETING & THE Economy

Thrift Stores

It makes sense that as unemployment rates rise and incomes weaken, more middle-class shoppers turn to thrift stores in search of bargains. But in recent times, thrift stores have benefited from more than just a new consumer frugality. The negative stigma of shopping at musty, second-hand shops has diminished. For fashionistas everywhere, the line between "thrift" and "vintage" has grown razor thin. Today, people aren't just buying any old rags at thrift stores. They're finding treasures in some top-name brands. Goodwill Industries is taking advantage of this trend. It promotes its wares to hipster trendsetters through fashion shows and apparel blogs and by offering store credit for apparel donations.

Goodwill's overall sales have gone up by about 7 percent in the face of a weaker economy. Other thrift stores report increases of

up to 35 percent. But the industry's good fortunes present a unique dilemma. The same forces that are driving thrift sales up are driving donations down. People are keeping their own old stuff longer. And rather than donating old apparel, people are selling it elsewhere for cash. As a result, the two-bag donor is now bringing in only one bag. And the goods that are donated tend to be lower in quality. This unusual dynamic could make it difficult for thrift stores to stock their shelves in the future.

1. In what ways does the thrift store industry present solutions to the common social criticisms of marketing outlined in the text?

2. How might the thrift store industry overcome its supply problems in the current environment of more frugal consumers?

MARKETING BY THE Numbers

One element of sustainability is organic farming. But if you've priced organic foods, you know they are more expensive. For example, a dozen conventionally farmed eggs costs consumers $1.50, whereas a dozen organic eggs costs $2.80. Organic farming costs much more than conventional farming, and those costs are passed onto consumers. However, if prices get too high, consumers will not purchase the organic eggs. Suppose that the average fixed costs per year for conventionally farmed eggs are $1 million per year, but they are twice that amount for organic eggs. Organic farmers' variable costs per dozen are twice as much as well—$1.80 per dozen. Refer to Appendix 2 to answer the following questions.

1. Most large egg farmers sell eggs directly to retailers. What is the farmer's price per dozen to the retailer for conventional and organic eggs if the retailer's margin is 20 percent based on the retail price? (AACSB: Communication; Analytical Reasoning)

2. How many dozen eggs does a conventional farmer need to sell to break even? How many does an organic farmer need to sell to break even? (AACSB: Communication; Analytical Reasoning)

VIDEO Case

Land Rover

The automotive industry has seen better days. Many auto companies are now facing declining revenues and negative profits. Additionally, because of its primary dependence on products that consume petroleum, the auto industry has a big environmental black eye, especially companies that primarily make gas-guzzling trucks and SUVs.

During the past few years, however, Land Rover has experienced tremendous growth in revenues and profits. It is currently selling more vehicles than ever worldwide. How is this possible for a company that only sells SUVs? One of the biggest reasons is Land Rover's strategic focus on social responsibility and environmentalism. Land Rover believes that it can meet consumer needs for luxury all-terrain vehicles while at the same time providing a vehicle that is kinder to the environment. As a corporation, it is also working feverishly to reduce its carbon emissions, reduce waste,

and reduce water consumption and pollution. With actions like this, Land Rover is successfully repositioning its brand away from the standard perceptions of SUVs as environmental enemies.

After viewing the video featuring Land Rover, answer the following questions about the company's efforts toward social responsibility:

1. Make a list of social criticisms of the automotive industry. Discuss all of the ways that Land Rover is combating those criticisms.

2. By the textbook's definition, does Land Rover practice "sustainable marketing"?

3. Do you believe that Land Rover is sincere in its efforts to be environmentally friendly? Is it even possible for a large SUV to be environmentally friendly?

COMPANY Case

International Paper:
Combining Industry and Social Responsibility

What image comes to mind when you hear the words *industrial corporation*? Pollution-belching smoke stacks? Strip-mined landscapes? Chemicals seeping into water supplies? Now think about the words *environmental steward*. What comes to mind? Although that label might not seem compatible, the truth is that changes in regulations, combined with pressure from environmental and consumer groups, have forced most industrial companies to become more socially responsible. But at least one company has had social responsibility as a core value since it started business more than 110 years ago. That company is International Paper (IP). Today, it is considered by many to be the most socially responsible company in the world.

You may not know much about IP, but it makes products that you use every day. It makes products such as paper for printers, envelopes for mail, cardboard clamshells and paper bags for fast food, and the boxes that hold your cold cereal, to name a few. And IP makes lots of those products. Last year, it sold over $23 billion worth of paper, packaging, and wood products, placing it in the number 104 slot on the Fortune 500. With operations all over the world, the company employs more than 50,000 people. Those are pretty big numbers for a company that most people know little about.

But International Paper is more than just big. For many years, it has also ranked consistently among *Fortune* magazine's most admired companies. Not only has it grabbed the number one spot on that list in its industry over the past six years; out of more than 600 contending companies from all industries, IP recently ranked number one in social responsibility. That's right—a paper and lumber company leading in initiatives to make the world a better place.

At the heart of IP's admirable actions, we have to look at the comprehensive, integrated plan that the company labels "sustainability."

The company sums up the program with the slogan, "Sustaining a better world for generations, the IP way." That's not just a catch phrase. It lies at the heart of IP's corporate mission statement and has created a culture based on a set of supporting principles. According to company literature, "We have always taken a sustainable approach to business that balances environmental, social, and economic needs. This approach has served our company and society well." IP constantly maintains this balance by adhering to three key pillars that transform the concepts into action: managing natural resources, reducing the environmental footprint, and building strategic partnerships.

MANAGING NATURAL RESOURCES

According to David Liebetreu, IP's vice president of global sourcing, "Sustainability means that we can take care of the environment and our businesses—those two concepts are not mutually exclusive." By taking care of the environment, Liebetreu refers to the systems that IP has in place to ensure that every phase of the corporate global supply chain—manufacturing, distribution, sales, and recycling—is carried out in a way that safely and responsibly cares for natural resources.

For example, International Paper has been a leader in promoting the planting and growing of trees. It believes that if forest resources are properly managed, they provide an infinite supply of raw materials for the company's products while supporting clean water, diverse wildlife habitats, recreational opportunities, and aesthetic beauty. To this end, the company actively supports research, innovation, and third-party certification to improve the management of forest resources.

Another way that the company manages natural resources is through conservation. But it has proven time and time again that conservation doesn't have to be a sunk cost. It can be an investment that provides cost savings for a company.

Pulp and paper mills are complex, energy intensive operations. Finding ways to reduce, reuse, and recycle energy at each of its facilities reduces the consumption of fossil fuels and reduces air emissions, including carbon dioxide.

Typically gas, coal, or bark fuels are fired in boilers to produce steam to power operations throughout the mill. Capturing steam in one area and reusing it in another reduces the amount of fresh steam required and reduces the amount of fuel needed to power the plant.

[The IP] mill in Vicksburg, Mississippi, is recovering and reusing 38,000 pounds of steam per hour. A one-time investment of $2.8 million in capital improvements will save an estimated $2.4 million in fuel costs annually. At [an IP] mill in Savannah, Georgia, an investment of $900,000 in capital improvements reduced the demand for steam and, consequently, the coal needed to produce it, by 25,000 pounds per hour. The annual savings are estimated at more than $600,000.

REDUCING THE ENVIRONMENTAL FOOTPRINT

By reducing its environmental footprint, International Paper means that it is committed to transparently reporting its activities to the public for any of its activities that impact the environment, health, or safety. "At International Paper, we've been routinely sharing our environmental, economic, and social performance with the public for over a decade," said David Struhs, vice president of environment, health, and safety. "Over the years, these reports have offered a level of transparency unmatched in our industry." This reporting philosophy applies to any company activity that leaves a footprint, including air emissions, environmental performance, health and safety, solid waste, and environmental certifications.

With transparency comes accountability. Because of its reporting practices, IP is more motivated to reduce its environmental footprint. Over a recent two-year period, the company cut its hazardous waste by almost 8 percent. It reduced the amount that it put in landfills by 10 percent by finding beneficial ways to recycle those materials. It made similar improvements in virtually every company footprint area. A recent account of company activities in Brazil illustrates this concept well.

Nature, once tamed, is again growing wild along Brazil's Mogi Guacu River, which means "large river of snakes" in the native language of Tupi. This year, seven constructed lagoons running along the banks of the Mogi Guacu designed to filter used water from the nearby IP plant were replaced by a more modern wastewater facility.

Although the lagoons are no longer needed for water treatment, IP recognized their potential environmental benefits. Five of the ponds were restored with native vegetation to establish a vast expanse of natural wetland habitat. Two of the ponds were preserved to sustain wildlife that had made their home in the area—snakes included.

To better manage the future impact of mill operations on the lush tropical landscape, the mill also installed technology at the river's edge to continuously measure and report water quality. The results are monitored remotely by facility managers as well as by government regulators. This unprecedented access to information on environmental performance has set a standard for other industries along this large river of snakes.

BUILDING STRATEGIC PARTNERSHIPS

To most efficiently carry out its sustainability efforts, IP enlists the help of numerous organizations. Building strategic partnerships is, therefore, critical. The company has a long tradition of partnering with a broad range of governmental, academic, environmental, and customer organizations. These partnerships are guided by the objectives of making progress in sustainability, providing solutions for customers, making a positive impact on the environment, and supporting social responsibility.

IP has partnered with some of the biggest sustainability organizations to make big differences. Partners include the National Park Foundation, the National Recycling Coalition, and the Conservation Fund. But the following story from a company press release illustrates how even a minor partnership oriented around a small product can make a "latte" difference in the world.

Coffee is one of the world's most popular drinks. Coffee houses—long a fixture in cultures and countries around the globe—sprang up across America over the last 20 years. Every year, as many as 15 billion "cups of joe" are served on the go in paper cups, and that number is expected to grow to 23 billion by the end of the decade.

As coffee connoisseurs savored the flavors of new varieties of beans and brews, engineers and scientists at IP were thinking about how to improve the cup. Though cups are made of fiber grown and harvested from sustainable forests, conventional paper cups are lined with a petroleum-based plastic. The plastic lining is a small part of the cup made from nonrenewable resources that inhibits the decomposition of the underlying paper. As a result, disposable cups once filled with coffee are filling up our landfills.

But what if disposable coffee cups could join coffee grounds in the compost heap? To achieve that vision, IP, with partners DaniMer Scientific and NatureWorks LLC, developed a new type of cup lining made from plants instead of petrochemicals.

The revolutionary new cup, dubbed the ecotainer, is coated with a resin made from a modified biopolymer. When discarded in commercial and municipal operations, cups with the new lining become compost, which can then be used for gardening, landscaping, and farming.

Since the launch of the ecotainer with Green Mountain Coffee Roasters in 2006, large and small companies alike have adopted this new cup. More than half a billion cups have eliminated over a million pounds of petrochemical plastic from the marketplace—enough petroleum to heat more than 32,000 homes for one year.

Coffee cups are just the beginning. IP is exploring opportunities to expand the technology to other products used in food-service disposable packaging. So next time you order an espresso with steamed milk, ask for one in an ecotainer so you too can make a "latte" difference in the world.

International Paper hasn't been one of the high-growth juggernauts of the corporate world. Then again, it operates in a very mature industry. But IP makes innovative products that meet the needs of consumers. It employs tens of thousands of people throughout the world, contributing substantially to the communities in which it does business. It has grown in size to become one of the 100 largest companies in the United States. It has been consistently profitable. And it does all these things while sustaining the world for future generations. Indeed, IP proves that good business and good corporate citizenship can go hand in hand.

Questions for Discussion

1. Give as many examples as you can for how International Paper defies the common social criticisms of marketing.

2. Why is IP successful in applying concepts of sustainability?

3. Analyze IP according to the environmental sustainability portfolio in Figure 20.2.

4. Does IP practice enlightened marketing? Support your answer with as many examples as possible.

5. Would IP be more financially successful if it were not so focused on social responsibility? Explain.

Sources: Extracts and other case information are from International Paper's corporate Web site, at www.internationalpaper.com/US/EN/Company/Sustainability/index.html, accessed September 2010; with additional information from money.cnn.com/magazines/fortune/mostadmired/2010/snapshots/229.html.

Marketing Plan

The Marketing Plan: An Introduction (pp A1–A2)

As a marketer, you'll need a good marketing plan to provide direction and focus for your brand, product, or company. With a detailed plan, any business will be better prepared to launch a new product or build sales for existing products. Nonprofit organizations also use marketing plans to guide their fund-raising and outreach efforts. Even government agencies develop marketing plans for initiatives such as building public awareness of proper nutrition and stimulating area tourism.

The Purpose and Content of a Marketing Plan

Unlike a business plan, which offers a broad overview of the entire organization's mission, objectives, strategy, and resource allocation, a marketing plan has a more limited scope. It serves to document how the organization's strategic objectives will be achieved through specific marketing strategies and tactics, with the customer as the starting point. It is also linked to the plans of other departments within the organization.

Suppose a marketing plan calls for selling 200,000 units annually. The production department must gear up to make that many units, the finance department must arrange funding to cover the expenses, the human resources department must be ready to hire and train staff, and so on. Without the appropriate level of organizational support and resources, no marketing plan can succeed.

Although the exact length and layout will vary from company to company, a marketing plan usually contains the elements described in Chapter 2. Smaller businesses may create shorter or less formal marketing plans, whereas corporations frequently require highly structured marketing plans. To effectively guide implementation, every part of the plan must be described in great detail. Sometimes a company will post its marketing plan on an internal Web site, which allows managers and employees in different locations to consult specific sections and collaborate on additions or changes.

The Role of Research

Marketing plans are not created in a vacuum. To develop successful strategies and action programs, marketers require up-to-date information about the environment, the competition, and the market segments to be served. Often, an analysis of internal data is the starting point for assessing the current marketing situation; this is supplemented by marketing intelligence and research investigating the overall market, the competition, key issues, and threats and opportunities. As the plan is implemented, marketers use a variety of research techniques to measure progress toward objectives and identify areas for improvement if the results fall short of projections.

Finally, marketing research helps marketers learn more about their customers' requirements, expectations, perceptions, and satisfaction levels. This deeper understanding is the foundation for building competitive advantage through well-informed segmenting, targeting, differentiating, and positioning decisions. Thus, the marketing plan should outline what marketing research will be conducted and how the findings will be applied.

The Role of Relationships

The marketing plan shows how the company will establish and maintain profitable customer relationships. It also shapes several internal and external relationships. First, it affects how marketing personnel work with each other and with other departments to deliver value and satisfy customers. Second, it affects how the company works with suppliers, distributors, and strategic alliance partners to achieve the objectives in the plan. Third, it influences the company's dealings with other stakeholders, including government regulators, the media, and the community at large. All of these relationships are important to the organization's success, so they should be considered when a marketing plan is being developed.

From Marketing Plan to Marketing Action

Companies generally create yearly marketing plans, although some plans cover longer periods of time. Marketers start planning well in advance of the implementation date to allow time for marketing research, thorough analysis, management review, and coordination between departments. Then, after each action program begins, marketers monitor ongoing results, compare them with projections, analyze any differences, and take corrective steps as needed. Some marketers also prepare contingency plans if certain conditions emerge. Because of inevitable and sometimes unpredictable environmental changes, marketers must be ready to update and adapt marketing plans at any time.

For effective implementation and control, the marketing plan should define how progress toward objectives will be measured. Managers typically use budgets, schedules, and performance standards for monitoring and evaluating results. With budgets, they can compare planned expenditures with actual expenditures for a given week, month, or other time period. Schedules allow management to see when tasks were supposed to be completed and when they were actually completed. Performance standards track the outcomes of marketing programs to see whether the company is moving toward its objectives. Some examples of performance standards are market share, sales volume, product profitability, and customer satisfaction.

Sample Marketing Plan for Sonic (pp A2–A10)

This section takes you inside the sample marketing plan for Sonic, a hypothetical start-up company. The company's first product is the Sonic 1000, a multimedia, cellular/Wi-Fi–enabled smartphone. Sonic will be competing with Apple, Nokia, Research in Motion, Motorola, Samsung, and other well-established rivals in a crowded, fast-changing marketplace for smartphones that combine communication, entertainment, and storage functionality. The marginal definitions explain the purpose and function of each section of the plan.

Executive Summary

Executive summary
This section summarizes and overviews the main goals, recommendations, and points for senior managers who will read and approve the marketing plan. For management convenience, a table of contents usually follows this section.

Sonic is preparing to launch a new multimedia, dual-mode smartphone, the Sonic 1000, in a mature market. Our product offers a competitively unique combination of advanced features and functionality at a value-added price. We are targeting specific segments in the consumer and business markets, taking advantage of opportunities indicated by higher demand for easy-to-use smartphones with expanded communications, entertainment, and storage functionality.

The primary marketing objective is to achieve first-year U.S. sales of 500,000 units. The primary financial objectives are to achieve first-year sales revenues of $75 million, keep first-year losses under $8 million, and break even early in the second year.

Current Marketing Situation

Current marketing situation
In this section, marketing managers discuss the overall market, identify the market segments they will target, and provide information about a company's current situation.

Sonic, founded 18 months ago by two entrepreneurs with experience in the PC market, is about to enter the mature smartphone market. Multifunction cell phones, e-mail devices, and wireless communication devices are commonplace for both personal and professional use. Research shows that the United States has 262 million wireless phone subscribers, and 85 percent of the population owns a cell phone.

Competition is therefore more intense even as demand flattens, industry consolidation continues, and pricing pressures squeeze profitability. Worldwide, Nokia is the smartphone leader, with 38 percent of the global market. The runner-up is Research in Motion, maker of the BlackBerry, with 18 percent of the global market. In the U.S. market, Research in Motion is the market leader (with a 32.1 percent share) and Apple, maker of the iPhone, is the runner-up (with a 21.7 percent share). To gain market share in this dynamic environment, Sonic must carefully target specific segments with features that deliver benefits valued by each customer group.

Market Description

Market description

Describes the targeted segments in detail and provides context for the marketing strategies and detailed action programs discussed later in the plan.

Sonic's market consists of consumers and business users who prefer to use a single device for communication, information storage and exchange, and entertainment on the go. Specific segments being targeted during the first year include professionals, corporations, students, entrepreneurs, and medical users. ◉ **Table A1.1** shows how the Sonic 1000 addresses the needs of targeted consumer and business segments.

Buyers can choose among models based on several different operating systems, including systems from Microsoft, Symbian, BlackBerry, and Linux variations. Sonic licenses a Linux-based system because it is somewhat less vulnerable to attack by hackers and viruses. Hard drives and removable memory cards are popular smartphone options. Sonic is equipping its first entry with an ultrafast, 20-gigabyte removable memory card for information and entertainment storage. This will allow users to transfer photos and other data from the smartphone to a home or office computer. Technology costs are decreasing even as capabilities are

Benefits and product features

Table A1.1 clarifies the benefits that product features will deliver to satisfy the needs of customers in each targeted segment.

◉ **TABLE | A1.1** Segment Needs and Corresponding Features/Benefits

Targeted Segment	Customer Needs	Corresponding Features/Benefits
Professionals (consumer market)	• Stay in touch conveniently and securely while on the go • Perform many functions hands-free without carrying multiple gadgets	• Built-in cell phone and push-to-talk feature to communicate anywhere at any time • Wireless e-mail/Web access from anywhere • Linux operating system that is less vulnerable to hackers • Voice-activated applications are convenient • GPS functionality and camera add value
Students (consumer market)	• Perform many functions hands-free without carrying multiple gadgets • Express style and individuality	• Compatible with numerous applications and peripherals for convenient, cost-effective communication and entertainment • Variety of smartphone cases
Corporate users (business market)	• Security and adaptability for proprietary tasks • Obtain driving directions to business meetings	• Customizable to fit corporate tasks and networks • Linux-based operating system less vulnerable to hackers • Built-in GPS allows voice-activated access to directions and maps
Entrepreneurs (business market)	• Organize and access contacts, schedule details, and business and financial files • Get in touch fast	• Hands-free, wireless access to calendar, address book, information files for checking appointments and data, and connecting with contacts • Push-to-talk instant calling speeds up communications
Medical users (business market)	• Update, access, and exchange medical records • Photograph medical situations to maintain a visual record	• Removable memory card and hands-free, wireless information recording reduces paperwork and increases productivity • Built-in camera allows fast and easy photography and stores images for later retrieval

increasing, which makes value-priced models more appealing to consumers and business users with older devices who want to trade up to new, high-end multifunction units.

Product Review

Product review

The product review summarizes the main features for all of a company's products, organized by product line, type of customer, market, and/or order of product introduction.

Our first product, the Sonic 1000, offers the following standard features with a Linux operating system:

- Built-in dual cell phone/Internet phone functionality and push-to-talk instant calling
- Digital music/video/television recording, wireless downloading, and playback
- Wireless Web, e-mail, text messaging, and instant messaging
- 3.5-inch color screen for easy viewing
- Organization functions, including calendar, address book, and synchronization
- GPS for directions and maps
- Integrated 4-megapixel digital camera
- Ultrafast, 20-gigabyte removable memory card with upgrade potential
- Interchangeable case wardrobe of different colors and patterns
- Voice recognition functionality for hands-free operation

First-year sales revenues are projected to be $75 million, based on sales of 500,000 Sonic 1000 units at a wholesale price of $150 each. During the second year, we plan to introduce the Sonic 2000, also with a Linux operating system, as a higher-end smartphone product offering the following standard features:

- Global phone and messaging compatibility
- Translation capabilities to send English text as Spanish text (other languages to be offered as add-on options)
- Integrated 8-megapixel camera with flash

Competitive Review

Competitive review

The purpose of a competitive review is to identify key competitors, describe their market positions, and briefly discuss their strategies.

The emergence of lower-priced smartphones, including the Apple iPhone, has increased competitive pressure. Competition from specialized devices for text and e-mail messaging, such as BlackBerry devices, is a major factor, as well. Key competitors include the following:

- *Nokia.* The market leader in smartphones, Nokia offers a wide range of products for personal and professional use. It purchased the maker of the Symbian operating system and made it into a separate foundation dedicated to improving and promoting this mobile software platform. Many of Nokia's smartphones offer full keyboards, similar to Research in Motion models. Nokia also offers stripped-down models for users who do not require the full keyboard and full multimedia capabilities.

- *Apple.* The stylish and popular iPhone 4 has a 3.5-inch color screen and is well equipped for music, video, and Web access; it also has communication, calendar, contact management, and file management functions. Its global positioning system technology can pinpoint a user's location. Also, users can erase data with a remote command if the smartphone is lost or stolen. However, AT&T was for years the only U.S. network provider. Apple has only recently added new providers. The iPhone 4 is priced at $199 for the 16GB model and $299 for the 32GB model.

- *RIM.* Lightweight BlackBerry wireless multifunction products are manufactured by Research in Motion and are especially popular among corporate users. RIM's continuous innovation and solid customer service strengthen its competitive standing as it introduces smartphones with enhanced features and communication capabilities. Its newest Blackberry, the Torch 9800, is the company's first touch-screen smartphone that includes a full keyboard. Priced at $199 with a two-year AT&T contract, the Torch competes with its iPhone and Android rivals.

- *Motorola.* Motorola, a global giant, has been losing U.S. market share to Apple and Research in Motion because it has slowed the pace of new product introduction. However,

Motorola is now showing signs of improvement as it taps into the Android operating system market with its newest smartphone, the Droid X. Boasting an 8-megapixel camera, 4.3-inch screen, and Google services ranging from voice search to Gmail, the Droid X is priced at $200 (after $100 mail-in rebate and a two-year Verizon Wireless contract).

- *Samsung.* Value, style, function—Samsung is a strong competitor and offers a variety of smartphones for consumer and business segments. Some of its smartphones are available for specific telecommunications carriers, and some are "unlocked," ready for any compatible telecommunications network. Its newest smartphones, the Galaxy S series, are available with the top four U.S. wireless carriers. The Captivate model features a 4-inch AMOLED touch screen and a 5-megapixel camera for $199 with a two-year contract.

Despite this strong competition, Sonic can carve out a definite image and gain recognition among the targeted segments. Our voice-recognition system for completely hands-free operation is a critical point of differentiation for competitive advantage. Also, offering GPS as a standard feature gives us a competitive edge compared with similarly priced smartphones. Moreover, our product is speedier than most and runs on the Linux operating system, which is an appealing alternative for customers concerned about security. ◉ **Table A1.2** shows a sample of competitive products and prices.

Channels and Logistics Review

Channels and logistics review
In this section, marketers list the most important channels, overview each channel arrangement, and identify developing issues in channels and logistics.

Sonic-branded products will be distributed through a network of retailers in the top 50 U.S. markets. Some of the most important channel partners are as follows:

- *Office supply superstores.* Office Max and Staples will both carry Sonic products in stores, in catalogs, and online.
- *Computer stores.* Independent computer retailers will carry Sonic products.
- *Electronics specialty stores.* Circuit City and Best Buy will feature Sonic products.
- *Online retailers.* Amazon.com will carry Sonic products and, for a promotional fee, will give Sonic prominent placement on its homepage during the introduction.

Initially, our channel strategy will focus on the United States; according to demand, we plan to expand into Canada and beyond, with appropriate logistical support.

◉ **TABLE | A1.2** Sample of Competitive Products and Pricing

Competitor	Model	Features	Price
Nokia	E71 classic	Quad-band for worldwide phone, e-mail and Internet access; monoblock with full keyboard; corporate and personal e-mail integration; 2.36-inch screen; 3.2-megapixel camera; media player; Symbian operating system	$249 without phone contract
Apple	iPhone 4	Sleek styling; 3.5-inch screen; fast Internet functions; one-touch calling; GPS navigation; voice commands; integrated personal and corporate e-mail; open and edit Microsoft Office files; 5-megapixel camera; no keyboard; Apple operating system	$199 for 16GB model; $299 for 32GB model
RIM	BlackBerry Torch 9800	High-resolution, 3.2-inch touch screen display; slide-out full keyboard; wireless e-mail and Internet access; 5-megapixel camera; built-in maps and GPS; camera and video recording; expandable memory; Blackberry operating system	$199 with two-year contract
Motorola	Droid X	4.3-inch high-resolution touch screen; 8-megapixel camera with video capabilities; no keyboard; voice activated dialing; Google mobile services; FM radio; Android operating system	$299 with two-year phone contract
Samsung	Captivate	Social network integration; embedded GPS; 4-inch AMOLED touch screen; 5-megapixel camera; audio and HD video capabilities; Android operating system	$199.99 with two-year phone contract

Strengths, Weaknesses, Opportunities, and Threat Analysis

Sonic has several powerful strengths on which to build, but our major weakness is a lack of brand awareness and image. The major opportunity is the demand for multimedia smartphones that deliver a number of valued benefits, eliminating the need for customers to carry more than one device. We also face the threat of ever-higher competition from consumer electronics manufacturers, as well as downward pricing pressure. ◉ **Table A1.3** summarizes Sonic's main strengths, weaknesses, opportunities, and threats.

Strengths

Strengths
Strengths are internal capabilities that can help a company reach its objectives.

Sonic can build on three important strengths:

1. *Innovative product.* The Sonic 1000 offers a combination of features that would otherwise require customers to carry multiple devices: speedy, hands-free, dual-mode cell/Wi-Fi telecommunications capabilities; GPS functionality; and digital video/music/television program storage and playback.

2. *Security.* Our smartphone uses a Linux-based operating system that is less vulnerable to hackers and other security threats that can result in stolen or corrupted data.

3. *Pricing.* Our product is priced lower than many competing multifunction models—none of which offer the same bundle of features—which gives us an edge with price-conscious customers.

Weaknesses

Weaknesses
Weaknesses are internal elements that may interfere with a company's ability to achieve its objectives.

By waiting to enter the smartphone market until some consolidation of its competitors has occurred, Sonic has learned from the successes and mistakes of others. Nonetheless, we have two main weaknesses:

1. *Lack of brand awareness.* Sonic has no established brand or image, whereas Apple and others have strong brand recognition. We will address this issue with aggressive promotion.

2. *Physical specifications.* The Sonic 1000 is slightly heavier and thicker than most competing models because it incorporates multiple features, offers sizable storage capacity, and is compatible with numerous peripheral devices. To counteract this weakness, we will emphasize our product's benefits and value-added pricing, which are two compelling competitive strengths.

Opportunities

Opportunities
Opportunities are external elements that a company may be able to exploit to its advantage.

Sonic can take advantage of two major market opportunities:

1. *Increasing demand for multimedia smartphones with multiple functions.* The market for multimedia, multifunction devices is growing much faster than the market for single-

◉ **TABLE | A1.3**   Sonic's Strengths, Weaknesses, Opportunities, and Threats

Strengths	Weaknesses
• Innovative combination of functions in one portable, voice-activated device	• Lack of brand awareness and image
• Security due to a Linux-based operating system	• Heavier and thicker than most competing models
• Value pricing	
Opportunities	**Threats**
• Increased demand for multimedia, multifunction smartphones	• Intense competition
• Cost-efficient technology	• Downward pricing pressure
	• Compressed product life cycle

use devices. Growth will accelerate as dual-mode capabilities become mainstream, giving customers the flexibility to make phone calls over cell or Internet connections. Smartphones are already commonplace in public, work, and educational settings, which is boosting primary demand. Also, customers who bought entry-level models are replacing older models with more advanced models.

2. *Cost-efficient technology.* Better technology is now available at a lower cost than ever before. Thus, Sonic can incorporate advanced features at a value-added price that allows for reasonable profits.

Threats

We face three main threats with the introduction of the Sonic 1000:

1. *Increased competition.* More companies are entering the U.S. market with smartphone models that offer some but not all the features and benefits provided by Sonic's product. Therefore, Sonic's marketing communications must stress our clear differentiation and value-added pricing.

2. *Downward pressure on pricing.* Increased competition and market-share strategies are pushing smartphone prices down. Still, our objective of seeking a 10 percent profit on second-year sales of the original model is realistic, even given the lower margins in this market.

3. *Compressed product life cycle.* Smartphones have reached the maturity stage of their life cycle more quickly than earlier technology products. We have contingency plans to keep sales growing by adding new features, targeting additional segments, and adjusting prices as needed.

Objectives and Issues

We have set aggressive but achievable objectives for the first and second years of market entry.

- *First-year objectives.* During the Sonic 1000's initial year on the market, we are aiming for unit sales volume of 500,000.

- *Second-year objectives.* Our second-year objectives are to sell a combined total of one million units of our two models and break even early in this period.

Issues

In relation to the product launch, our major issue is the ability to establish a well-regarded brand name linked to meaningful positioning. We will invest heavily in marketing to create a memorable and distinctive brand image projecting innovation, quality, and value. We also must measure awareness and response so we can adjust our marketing efforts as necessary.

Marketing Strategy

Sonic's marketing strategy is based on a positioning of product differentiation. Our primary consumer target is middle- to upper-income professionals who need one portable device to coordinate their busy schedules, communicate with family and colleagues, get driving directions, and be entertained on the go. Our secondary consumer target is high school, college, and graduate students who want a multimedia, dual-mode device. This segment can be described demographically by age (16–30) and educational attainment level.

Our primary business target is mid- to large-sized corporations that want to help their managers and employees stay in touch and be able to input or access critical data when not in the office. This segment consists of companies with more than $25 million in annual sales and more than 100 employees. We are also targeting entrepreneurs and small-business owners as well as medical users who want to update or access patients' medical records while reducing paperwork.

Threats
Threats are current or emerging external elements that could potentially challenge a company's performance.

Objectives and issues
A company's objectives should be defined in specific terms so management can measure progress and plan corrective action, if needed, to stay on track. This section describes any major issues that might affect a company's marketing strategy and implementation.

Positioning

Positioning built on meaningful differentiation, supported by appropriate strategy and implementation, can help a company build competitive advantage.

Marketing tools

This section summarizes the broad logic that will guide decisions made during the period covered by the plan.

Marketing research

This section shows how marketing research will be used to support development, implementation, and evaluation of strategies and action programs.

Marketing organization

The marketing department may be organized by function, as in this sample, geography, product, or customer (or some combination thereof).

Positioning

Using product differentiation, we are positioning the Sonic as the most versatile, convenient, and value-added model for personal and professional use. Our marketing will focus on hands-free operation of multiple communication, entertainment, and information capabilities that differentiate the Sonic 1000 from its competitors.

Product Strategy

The Sonic 1000, including all the features described earlier, will be sold with a one-year warranty. We will introduce a more compact, powerful high-end model (the Sonic 2000) in the second year. Building the Sonic brand is an integral part of our product strategy. The brand and logo (Sonic's distinctive yellow thunderbolt) will be displayed on the product and its packaging and reinforced by its prominence in the introductory marketing campaign.

Pricing Strategy

The Sonic 1000 will be introduced at $150 wholesale/$199 estimated retail price per unit. We expect to lower the price of this first model when we expand the product line by launching the Sonic 2000, whose wholesale price will be $175 per unit. These prices reflect a strategy of attracting desirable channel partners and taking share from Nokia, Research in Motion, Motorola, and other established competitors.

Distribution Strategy

Our channel strategy is to use selective distribution, marketing Sonic smartphones through well-known stores and online retailers. During the first year, we will add channel partners until we have coverage in all major U.S. markets and the product is included in the major electronics catalogs and Web sites. We will also investigate distribution through cell-phone outlets maintained by major carriers, such as Verizon Wireless. In support of our channel partners, Sonic will provide demonstration products, detailed specification handouts, and full-color photos and displays featuring the product. Finally, we plan to arrange special payment terms for retailers that place volume orders.

Marketing Communications Strategy

By integrating all messages in all media, we will reinforce the brand name and the main points of product differentiation. Research about media consumption patterns will help our advertising agency choose appropriate media and timing to reach prospects before and during product introduction. Thereafter, advertising will appear on a pulsing basis to maintain brand awareness and communicate various differentiation messages. The agency will also coordinate public relations efforts to build the Sonic brand and support the differentiation message. To create buzz, we will host a user-generated video contest on our Web site. To attract, retain, and motivate channel partners for a push strategy, we will use trade sales promotions and personal selling. Until the Sonic brand has been established, our communications will encourage purchases through channel partners rather than from our Web site.

Marketing Research

Using research, we are identifying the specific features and benefits that our target market segments value. Feedback from market tests, surveys, and focus groups will help us develop the Sonic 2000. We are also measuring and analyzing customers' attitudes toward competing brands and products. Brand awareness research will help us determine the effectiveness and efficiency of our messages and media. Finally, we will use customer satisfaction studies to gauge market reaction.

Marketing Organization

Sonic's chief marketing officer, Jane Melody, holds overall responsibility for all marketing activities. ● **Figure A1.1** shows the structure of the eight-person marketing organization. Sonic has hired Worldwide Marketing to handle national sales campaigns, trade and consumer sales promotions, and public relations efforts.

● FIGURE | A1.1
Sonic's Marketing Organization

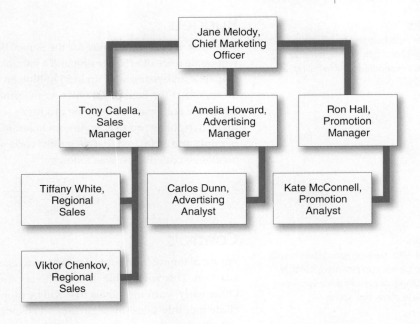

Action Programs

The Sonic 1000 will be introduced in February. The following are summaries of the action programs we will use during the first six months of next year to achieve our stated objectives.

- *January.* We will launch a $200,000 trade sales promotion campaign and exhibit at the major industry trade shows to educate dealers and generate channel support for the product launch in February. Also, we will create buzz by providing samples to selected product reviewers, opinion leaders, influential bloggers, and celebrities. Our training staff will work with retail sales personnel at major chains to explain the Sonic 1000's features, benefits, and advantages.

- *February.* We will start an integrated print/radio/Internet advertising campaign targeting professionals and consumers. The campaign will show how many functions the Sonic smartphone can perform and emphasize the convenience of a single, powerful handheld device. This multimedia campaign will be supported by point-of-sale signage as well as online-only ads and video tours.

- *March.* As the multimedia advertising campaign continues, we will add consumer sales promotions, such as a contest in which consumers post videos to our Web site showing how they use the Sonic in creative and unusual ways. We will also distribute new point-of-purchase displays to support our retailers.

- *April.* We will hold a trade sales contest offering prizes for the salesperson and retail organization that sells the most Sonic smartphones during the four-week period.

- *May.* We plan to roll out a new national advertising campaign this month. The radio ads will feature celebrity voices telling their Sonic smartphones to perform various functions, such as initiating a phone call, sending an e-mail, playing a song or video, and so on. The stylized print and online ads will feature avatars of these celebrities holding their Sonic smartphones.

- *June.* Our radio campaign will add a new voice-over tagline promoting the Sonic 1000 as a graduation gift. We will also exhibit at the semiannual electronics trade show and provide channel partners with new competitive comparison handouts as a sales aid. In addition, we will tally and analyze the results of customer satisfaction surveys for use in future promotions and provide feedback for product and marketing activities.

Budgets
Managers use budgets to project profitability and plan for each marketing program's expenditures, scheduling, and operations.

Budgets

Total first-year sales revenue for the Sonic 1000 is projected at $75 million, with an average wholesale price of $150 per unit and a variable cost per unit of $100 for 500,000 units. We anticipate a first-year loss of up to $8 million on the Sonic 1000 model. Break-even calculations indicate that the Sonic 1000 will become profitable after the sales volume exceeds 650,000, which we anticipate early in the product's second year. Our break-even analysis of Sonic's first smartphone product assumes wholesale revenue of $150 per unit, variable cost of $100 per unit, and estimated first-year fixed costs of $32,500,000. Based on these assumptions, the break-even calculation is as follows:

$$\frac{\$32,500,000}{\$150/\text{unit} - \$100/\text{unit}} = 650,000 \text{ units}$$

Controls
Controls help management assess results after the plan is implemented, identify any problems or performance variations, and initiate corrective action.

Controls

We are planning tight control measures to closely monitor quality and customer service satisfaction. This will enable us to react very quickly to correct any problems that may occur. Other early warning signals that will be monitored for signs of deviation from the plan include monthly sales (by segment and channel) and monthly expenses. Given the market's volatility, we are developing contingency plans to address fast-moving environmental changes, such as new technology and new competition.

Marketing Plan Tools

Prentice Hall offers two valuable resources to assist you in developing a marketing plan:

- *The Marketing Plan Handbook* by Marian Burk Wood explains the process of creating a marketing plan and includes detailed checklists and dozens of real-world examples.

- *Marketing Plan Pro* is an award-winning software package that includes sample plans, step-by-step guides, an introductory video, help wizards, and customizable charts for documenting a marketing plan.

Sources: Background information and market data adapted from Matt Gallagher, "Blackberry Gets Smarter," *Red Herring*, August 3, 2010, p. 5; Dan Moren and Jason Snell, "Meet the iPhone 4," *Macworld*, August 2010, pp. 22–23; Walter S. Mossberg, "Galaxy Phones from Samsung Are Worthy iPhone Rivals," *Wall Street Journal* (Eastern Edition), July 22, 2010, pp. D1–D5; Hester Plumridge, "Nokia Dials New Number for Success," *Wall Street Journal* (Eastern Edition), July 21, 2010, p. C16; Rich Jaroslovsky, "Motorola's New Mojo," *Bloomberg Businessweek*, July 12, 2010, p. 72; Edward C. Baig, "Droid X Marks All the Right Spots; Android Phone Could Challenge iPhone 4," *USA Today*, July 1, 2010, p. 3B; Arik Hesseldahl, "Nokia's Kallasvuo: We Must 'Move Even Faster,'" *Businessweek Online*, March 17, 2010, p. 1; Ginny Miles, "The Hottest Smartphones of the Season," *PC World*, September 2009, pp. 44–48; "Android Smart Phone Shipments Grow 886% Year-on-Year in Q2 2010," www.canalys.com/pr/2010/r2010081 .html, accessed August 2010.

Marketing by the Numbers

Marketing managers are facing increased accountability for the financial implications of their actions. This appendix provides a basic introduction to measuring marketing financial performance. Such financial analysis guides marketers in making sound marketing decisions and in assessing the outcomes of those decisions.

The appendix is built around a hypothetical manufacturer of consumer electronics products—ConnectPhone. In the past, ConnectPhone has concentrated on making Internet modems. However, the company is now introducing a new type of product—a *media phone* that replaces a household's telephone and provides "always-on" Internet connectivity and wireless phone access through VoIP (Voice over Internet Protocol) technology. In this appendix, we will analyze the various decisions ConnectPhone's marketing managers must make before and after the new-product launch.

The appendix is organized into *three sections*. The *first section* introduces pricing, break-even, and margin analysis assessments that will guide the introduction of ConnectPhone's new product. The *second section* discusses demand estimates, the marketing budget, and marketing performance measures. It begins with a discussion of estimating market potential and company sales. It then introduces the marketing budget, as illustrated through a *pro forma* profit-and-loss statement followed by the actual profit-and-loss statement. Next, we discuss marketing performance measures, with a focus on helping marketing managers to better defend their decisions from a financial perspective. In the *third section*, we analyze the financial implications of various marketing tactics.

Each of the three sections ends with a set of quantitative exercises that provide you with an opportunity to apply the concepts you learned to situations beyond ConnectPhone.

Pricing, Break-Even, and Margin Analysis (pp A11–A16)

Pricing Considerations

Determining price is one of the most important marketing-mix decisions. The limiting factors are demand and costs. Demand factors, such as buyer-perceived value, set the price ceiling. The company's costs set the price floor. In between these two factors, marketers must consider competitors' prices and other factors such as reseller requirements, government regulations, and company objectives.

Current competing media phone products sell at retail prices between $500 and $1,000. ConnectPhone plans to introduce its new product at a lower price in order to expand the market and to gain market share rapidly. We first consider ConnectPhone's pricing decision from a cost perspective. Then, we consider consumer value, the competitive environment, and reseller requirements.

Determining Costs

Fixed costs
Costs that do not vary with production or sales level.

Recall from Chapter 10 that there are different types of costs. **Fixed costs** do not vary with production or sales level and include costs such as rent, interest, depreciation, and clerical and management salaries. Regardless of the level of output, the company must pay these

A11

Variable costs

Costs that vary directly with the level of production.

Total costs

The sum of the fixed and variable costs for any given level of production.

costs. Whereas total fixed costs remain constant as output increases, the fixed cost per unit (or average fixed cost) will decrease as output increases because the total fixed costs are spread across more units of output. **Variable costs** vary directly with the level of production and include costs related to the direct production of the product (such as costs of goods sold—COGS) and many of the marketing costs associated with selling it. Although these costs tend to be uniform for each unit produced, they are called variable because their total varies with the number of units produced. **Total costs** are the sum of the fixed and variable costs for any given level of production.

ConnectPhone has invested $10 million in refurbishing an existing facility to manufacture the new media phone product. Once production begins, the company estimates that it will incur fixed costs of $20 million per year. The variable cost to produce each device is estimated to be $250 and is expected to remain at that level for the output capacity of the facility.

Setting Price Based on Costs

Cost-plus pricing (or markup pricing)

A standard markup to the cost of the product.

ConnectPhone starts with the cost-based approach to pricing discussed in Chapter 10. Recall that the simplest method, **cost-plus pricing** (or **markup pricing**), simply adds a standard markup to the cost of the product. To use this method, however, ConnectPhone must specify expected unit sales so that total unit costs can be determined. Unit variable costs will remain constant regardless of the output, but *average unit fixed costs* will decrease as output increases.

To illustrate this method, suppose ConnectPhone has fixed costs of $20 million, variable costs of $250 per unit, and expects unit sales of one million media phones. Thus, the cost per unit is given by:

$$\text{Unit cost} = \text{variable cost} + \frac{\text{fixed costs}}{\text{unit sales}} = \$250 + \frac{\$20,000,000}{1,000,000} = \$270$$

Relevant costs

Costs that will occur in the future and that will vary across the alternatives being considered.

Note that we do *not* include the initial investment of $10 million in the total fixed cost figure. It is not considered a fixed cost because it is not a *relevant* cost. **Relevant costs** are those that will occur in the future and that will vary across the alternatives being considered. ConnectPhone's investment to refurbish the manufacturing facility was a one-time cost that will not reoccur in the future. Such past costs are *sunk costs* and should not be considered in future analyses.

Break-even price

The price at which total revenue equals total cost and profit is zero.

Also notice that if ConnectPhone sells its product for $270, the price is equal to the total cost per unit. This is the **break-even price**—the price at which unit revenue (price) equals unit cost and profit is zero.

Suppose ConnectPhone does not want to merely break even but rather wants to earn a 25 percent markup on sales. ConnectPhone's markup price is:[1]

$$\text{Markup price} = \frac{\text{unit cost}}{(1 - \text{desired return on sales})} = \frac{\$270}{1 - .25} = \$360$$

This is the price at which ConnectPhone would sell the product to resellers such as wholesalers or retailers to earn a 25 percent profit on sales.

Return on investment (ROI) pricing (or target-return pricing)

A cost-based pricing method that determines price based on a specified rate of return on investment.

Another approach ConnectPhone could use is called **return on investment (ROI) pricing** (or **target-return pricing**). In this case, the company *would* consider the initial $10 million investment, but only to determine the dollar profit goal. Suppose the company wants a 30 percent return on its investment. The price necessary to satisfy this requirement can be determined by:

$$\text{ROI price} = \text{unit cost} + \frac{\text{ROI} \times \text{investment}}{\text{unit sales}} = \$270 + \frac{0.3 \times \$10,000,000}{1,000,000} = \$273$$

That is, if ConnectPhone sells its product for $273, it will realize a 30 percent return on its initial investment of $10 million.

In these pricing calculations, unit cost is a function of the expected sales, which were estimated to be one million units. But what if actual sales were lower? Then the unit cost would be higher because the fixed costs would be spread over fewer units, and the realized percentage markup on sales or ROI would be lower. Alternatively, if sales are higher than the estimated one million units, unit cost would be lower than $270, so a lower price would produce the desired markup on sales or ROI. It's important to note that these cost-based pricing methods are *internally* focused and do not consider demand, competitors' prices, or reseller requirements. Because ConnectPhone will be selling this product to consumers through wholesalers and retailers offering competing brands, the company must consider markup pricing from this perspective.

Setting Price Based on External Factors

Whereas costs determine the price floor, ConnectPhone also must consider external factors when setting price. ConnectPhone does not have the final say concerning the final price of its media phones to consumers—retailers do. So it must start with its suggested retail price and work back. In doing so, ConnectPhone must consider the markups required by resellers that sell the product to consumers.

Markup
The difference between a company's selling price for a product and its cost to manufacture or purchase it.

In general, a dollar **markup** is the difference between a company's selling price for a product and its cost to manufacture or purchase it. For a retailer, then, the markup is the difference between the price it charges consumers and the cost the retailer must pay for the product. Thus, for any level of reseller:

$$\text{Dollar markup} = \text{selling price} - \text{cost}$$

Markups are usually expressed as a percentage, and there are two different ways to compute markups—on *cost* or on *selling price*:

$$\text{Markup percentage on cost} = \frac{\text{dollar markup}}{\text{cost}}$$

$$\text{Markup percentage on selling price} = \frac{\text{dollar markup}}{\text{selling price}}$$

To apply reseller margin analysis, ConnectPhone must first set the suggested retail price and then work back to the price at which it must sell the product to a wholesaler. Suppose retailers expect a 30 percent margin and wholesalers want a 20 percent margin based on their respective selling prices. And suppose that ConnectPhone sets a manufacturer's suggested retail price (MSRP) of $599.99 for its product.

Recall that ConnectPhone wants to expand the market by pricing low and generating market share quickly. ConnectPhone selected the $599.99 MSRP because it is lower than most competitors' prices, which can be as high as $1,000. And the company's research shows that it is below the threshold at which more consumers are willing to purchase the product. By using buyers' perceptions of value and not the seller's cost to determine the MSRP, ConnectPhone is using **value-based pricing**. For simplicity, we will use an MSRP of $600 in further analyses.

Value-based pricing
Offering just the right combination of quality and good service at a fair price.

To determine the price ConnectPhone will charge wholesalers, we must first subtract the retailer's margin from the retail price to determine the retailer's cost ($600 − ($600 × 0.30) = $420). The retailer's cost is the wholesaler's price, so ConnectPhone next subtracts the wholesaler's margin ($420 − ($420 × 0.20) = $336). Thus, the **markup chain** representing the sequence of markups used by firms at each level in a channel for ConnectPhone's new product is:

Markup chain
The sequence of markups used by firms at each level in a channel.

Suggested retail price:	$600
minus retail margin (30%):	− $180
Retailer's cost/wholesaler's price:	$420
minus wholesaler's margin (20%):	− $ 84
Wholesaler's cost/ConnectPhone's price:	$336

By deducting the markups for each level in the markup chain, ConnectPhone arrives at a price for the product to wholesalers of $336.

Break-Even and Margin Analysis

The previous analyses derived a value-based price of $336 for ConnectPhone's product. Although this price is higher than the break-even price of $270 and covers costs, that price assumed a demand of 1 million units. But how many units and what level of dollar sales must ConnectPhone achieve to break even at the $336 price? And what level of sales must be achieved to realize various profit goals? These questions can be answered through break-even and margin analysis.

Determining Break-Even Unit Volume and Dollar Sales

Break-even analysis

Analysis to determine the unit volume and dollar sales needed to be profitable given a particular price and cost structure.

Based on an understanding of costs, consumer value, the competitive environment, and reseller requirements, ConnectPhone has decided to set its price to wholesalers at $336. At that price, what sales level will be needed for ConnectPhone to break even or make a profit on its media phones? **Break-even analysis** determines the unit volume and dollar sales needed to be profitable given a particular price and cost structure. At the break-even point, total revenue equals total costs and profit is zero. Above this point, the company will make a profit; below it, the company will lose money. ConnectPhone can calculate break-even volume using the following formula:

$$\text{Break-even volume} = \frac{\text{fixed costs}}{\text{price} - \text{unit variable cost}}$$

Unit contribution

The amount that each unit contributes to covering fixed costs—the difference between price and variable costs.

The denominator (price − unit variable cost) is called **unit contribution** (sometimes called contribution margin). It represents the amount that each unit contributes to covering fixed costs. Break-even volume represents the level of output at which all (variable and fixed) costs are covered. In ConnectPhone's case, break-even unit volume is:

$$\text{Break-even volume} = \frac{\text{fixed cost}}{\text{price} - \text{variable cost}} = \frac{\$20,000,000}{\$336 - \$250} = 232,558.1 \text{ units}$$

Thus, at the given cost and pricing structure, ConnectPhone will break even at 232,559 units.

To determine the break-even dollar sales, simply multiply unit break-even volume by the selling price:

$$\text{BE sales} = \text{BE}_{vol} \times \text{price} = 232,559 \times \$336 = \$78,139,824$$

Contribution margin

The unit contribution divided by the selling price.

Another way to calculate dollar break-even sales is to use the percentage contribution margin (hereafter referred to as **contribution margin**), which is the unit contribution divided by the selling price:

$$\text{Contribution margin} = \frac{\text{price} - \text{variable cost}}{\text{price}} = \frac{\$336 - \$250}{\$336} = 0.256 \text{ or } 25.6\%$$

Then,

$$\text{Break-even sales} = \frac{\text{fixed costs}}{\text{contribution margin}} = \frac{\$20,000,000}{0.256} = \$78,125,000$$

Note that the difference between the two break-even sales calculations is due to rounding.

Such break-even analysis helps ConnectPhone by showing the unit volume needed to cover costs. If production capacity cannot attain this level of output, then the company should not launch this product. However, the unit break-even volume is well within ConnectPhone's capacity. Of course, the bigger question concerns whether ConnectPhone can sell this volume at the $336 price. We'll address that issue a little later.

Understanding contribution margin is useful in other types of analyses as well, particularly if unit prices and unit variable costs are unknown or if a company (say, a retailer) sells many products at different prices and knows the percentage of total sales variable costs represent. Whereas unit contribution is the difference between unit price and unit variable costs, total contribution is the difference between total sales and total variable costs. The overall contribution margin can be calculated by:

$$\text{Contribution margin} = \frac{\text{total sales} - \text{total variable costs}}{\text{total sales}}$$

Regardless of the actual level of sales, if the company knows what percentage of sales is represented by variable costs, it can calculate contribution margin. For example, ConnectPhone's unit variable cost is $250, or 74 percent of the selling price ($250 ÷ $336 = 0.74). That means for every $1 of sales revenue for ConnectPhone, $0.74 represents variable costs, and the difference ($0.26) represents contribution to fixed costs. But even if the company doesn't know its unit price and unit variable cost, it can calculate the contribution margin from total sales and total variable costs or from knowledge of the total cost structure. It can set total sales equal to 100 percent regardless of the actual absolute amount and determine the contribution margin:

$$\text{Contribution margin} = \frac{100\% - 74\%}{100\%} = \frac{1 - 0.74}{1} = 1 - 0.74 = 0.26 \text{ or } 26\%$$

Note that this matches the percentage calculated from the unit price and unit variable cost information. This alternative calculation will be very useful later when analyzing various marketing decisions.

Determining "Breakeven" for Profit Goals

Although it is useful to know the break-even point, most companies are more interested in making a profit. Assume ConnectPhone would like to realize a $5 million profit in the first year. How many must it sell at the $336 price to cover fixed costs and produce this profit? To determine this, ConnectPhone can simply add the profit figure to fixed costs and again divide by the unit contribution to determine unit sales:

$$\text{Unit volume} = \frac{\text{fixed cost} - \text{profit goal}}{\text{price} - \text{variable cost}} = \frac{\$20,000,000 + \$5,000,000}{\$336 - \$250} = 290,697.7 \text{ units}$$

Thus, to earn a $5 million profit, ConnectPhone must sell 290,698 units. Multiply by price to determine dollar sales needed to achieve a $5 million profit:

$$\text{Dollar sales} = 290,698 \text{ units} \times \$336 = \$97,674,528$$

Or use the contribution margin:

$$\text{Sales} = \frac{\text{fixed cost} + \text{profit goal}}{\text{contribution margin}} = \frac{\$20,000,000 + \$5,000,000}{0.256} = \$97,656,250$$

Again, note that the difference between the two break-even sales calculations is due to rounding.

As we saw previously, a profit goal can also be stated as a return on investment goal. For example, recall that ConnectPhone wants a 30 percent return on its $10 million investment. Thus, its absolute profit goal is $3 million ($10,000,000 × 0.30). This profit goal is treated the same way as in the previous example:[2]

$$\text{Unit volume} = \frac{\text{fixed cost} + \text{profit goal}}{\text{price variable cost}} = \frac{\$20,000,000 + \$3,000,000}{\$336 - \$250} = 267,442 \text{ units}$$

$$\text{Dollar sales} = 267,442 \text{ units} \times \$336 = \$89,860,512$$

Or

$$\text{Dollar sales} = \frac{\text{fixed cost} + \text{profit goal}}{\text{contribution margin}} = \frac{\$20,000,000 + \$3,000,000}{0.256} = \$89,843,750$$

Finally, ConnectPhone can express its profit goal as a percentage of sales, which we also saw in previous pricing analyses. Assume ConnectPhone desires a 25 percent return on sales. To determine the unit and sales volume necessary to achieve this goal, the calculation is a little different from the previous two examples. In this case, we incorporate the profit goal into the unit contribution as an additional variable cost. Look at it this way: If 25 percent of each sale must go toward profits, that leaves only 75 percent of the selling price to cover fixed costs. Thus, the equation becomes:

$$\text{Unit volume} = \frac{\text{fixed cost}}{\text{price} - \text{variable cost} - (0.25 \times \text{price})} \text{ or } \frac{\text{fixed cost}}{(0.75 \times \text{price}) - \text{variable cost}}$$

So,

$$\text{Unit volume} = \frac{\$20,000,000}{(0.75 \times \$336) - \$250} = 10,000,000 \text{ units}$$

$$\text{Dollar sales necessary} = 10,000,000 \text{ units} \times \$336 = \$3,360,000,000$$

Thus, ConnectPhone would need more than $3 billion in sales to realize a 25 percent return on sales given its current price and cost structure! Could it possibly achieve this level of sales? The major point is this: Although break-even analysis can be useful in determining the level of sales needed to cover costs or to achieve a stated profit goal, it does not tell the company whether it is *possible* to achieve that level of sales at the specified price. To address this issue, ConnectPhone needs to estimate demand for this product.

Before moving on, however, let's stop here and practice applying the concepts covered so far. Now that you have seen pricing and break-even concepts in action as they related to ConnectPhone's new product, here are several exercises for you to apply what you have learned in other contexts.

Marketing by the Numbers Exercise Set One

Now that you've studied pricing, break-even, and margin analysis as they relate to ConnectPhone's new-product launch, use the following exercises to apply these concepts in other contexts.

1.1 Sanborn, a manufacturer of electric roof vents, realizes a cost of $55 for every unit it produces. Its total fixed costs equal $2 million. If the company manufactures 500,000 units, compute the following:

   a. unit cost

   b. markup price if the company desires a 10 percent return on sales

   c. ROI price if the company desires a 25 percent return on an investment of $1 million

1.2 An interior decorator purchases items to sell in her store. She purchases a lamp for $125 and sells it for $225. Determine the following:

   a. dollar markup

   b. markup percentage on cost

   c. markup percentage on selling price

1.3 A consumer purchases a toaster from a retailer for $60. The retailer's markup is 20 percent, and the wholesaler's markup is 15 percent, both based on selling price. For what price does the manufacturer sell the product to the wholesaler?

1.4 A vacuum manufacturer has a unit cost of $50 and wishes to achieve a margin of 30 percent based on selling price. If the manufacturer sells directly to a retailer who then adds a set margin of 40 percent based on selling price, determine the retail price charged to consumers.

1.5 Advanced Electronics manufactures DVDs and sells them directly to retailers who typically sell them for $20. Retailers take a 40 percent margin based on the retail selling price. Advanced's cost information is as follows:

DVD package and disc	$2.50/DVD
Royalties	$2.25/DVD
Advertising and promotion	$500,000
Overhead	$200,000

Calculate the following:

   a. contribution per unit and contribution margin

   b. break-even volume in DVD units and dollars

   c. volume in DVD units and dollar sales necessary if Advanced's profit goal is 20 percent profit on sales

   d. net profit if 5 million DVDs are sold

Demand Estimates, the Marketing Budget, and Marketing Performance Measures (pp A17–A18)

Market Potential and Sales Estimates

ConnectPhone has now calculated the sales needed to break even and to attain various profit goals on its new product. However, the company needs more information regarding demand in order to assess the feasibility of attaining the needed sales levels. This information is also needed for production and other decisions. For example, production schedules need to be developed and marketing tactics need to be planned.

Total market demand
The total volume that would be bought by a defined consumer group, in a defined geographic area, in a defined time period, in a defined marketing environment, under a defined level and mix of industry marketing effort.

The **total market demand** for a product or service is the total volume that would be bought by a defined consumer group in a defined geographic area in a defined time period in a defined marketing environment under a defined level and mix of industry marketing effort. Total market demand is not a fixed number but a function of the stated conditions. For example, next year's total market demand for media phones will depend on how much other producers spend on marketing their brands. It also depends on many environmental factors, such as government regulations, economic conditions, and the level of consumer confidence in a given market. The upper limit of market demand is called **market potential**.

Market potential
The upper limit of market demand.

One general but practical method that ConnectPhone might use for estimating total market demand uses three variables: (1) the number of prospective buyers, (2) the quantity purchased by an average buyer per year, and (3) the price of an average unit. Using these numbers, ConnectPhone can estimate total market demand as follows:

$$Q = n \times q \times p$$

where

Q = total market demand

n = number of buyers in the market

q = quantity purchased by an average buyer per year

p = price of an average unit

Chain ratio method
Estimating market demand by multiplying a base number by a chain of adjusting percentages.

A variation of this approach is the **chain ratio method**. This method involves multiplying a base number by a chain of adjusting percentages. For example, ConnectPhone's product is designed to replace a household's telephone as well as provide "always on" Internet access. Thus, only households with broadband Internet access will be able to use the product. Finally, not all Internet households will be willing and able to purchase the new product. ConnectPhone can estimate U.S. demand using a chain of calculations like the following:

Total number of U.S. households
$\times$ The percentage of U.S. households with broadband Internet access
$\times$ The percentage of these households willing and able to buy this device

The U.S. Census Bureau estimates that there are approximately 113 million households in the United States.[3] Research also indicates that 50 percent of U.S. households have broadband Internet access.[4] Finally, ConnectPhone's own research indicates that 33.1 percent of households possess the discretionary income needed and are willing to buy a device such as this. Then, the total number of households willing and able to purchase this product is:

113 million households $\times$ 0.50 $\times$ 0.331 = 18.7 million households

Households will need only one media phone. Assuming the average retail price across all brands is $750 for this product, the estimate of total market demand is as follows:

18.7 million households $\times$ 1 device per household $\times$ $750 = $14 billion

This simple chain of calculations gives ConnectPhone only a rough estimate of potential demand. However, more detailed chains involving additional segments and other qualifying factors would yield more accurate and refined estimates. Still, these are only *estimates* of market potential. They rely heavily on assumptions regarding adjusting percentages, average quantity, and average price. Thus, ConnectPhone must make certain that its assumptions are reasonable and defendable. As can be seen, the overall market potential in dollar sales can vary widely given the average price used. For this reason, ConnectPhone will use unit sales potential to determine its sales estimate for next year. Market potential in terms of units is 18.7 million (18.7 million households × 1 device per household).

Assuming that ConnectPhone wants to attain 2 percent market share (comparable to its share of the Internet modem market) in the first year after launching this product, then it can forecast unit sales at 18.7 million units × 0.02 = 374,000 units. At a selling price of $336 per unit, this translates into sales of $125,664,000 (374,000 units × $336 per unit). For simplicity, further analyses will use forecasted sales of $125 million.

This unit volume estimate is well within ConnectPhone's production capacity and exceeds not only the break-even estimate (232,559 units) calculated earlier, but also the volume necessary to realize a $5 million profit (290,698 units) or a 30 percent return on investment (267,442 units). However, this forecast falls well short of the volume necessary to realize a 25 percent return on sales (10 million units!) and may require that ConnectPhone revise expectations.

To assess expected profits, we must now look at the budgeted expenses for launching this product. To do this, we will construct a pro forma profit-and-loss statement.

The Profit-and-Loss Statement and Marketing Budget (pp A18–A19)

Pro forma (or projected) profit-and-loss statement (or income statement or operating statement)
A statement that shows projected revenues less budgeted expenses and estimates the projected net profit for an organization, product, or brand during a specific planning period, typically a year.

All marketing managers must account for the profit impact of their marketing strategies. A major tool for projecting such profit impact is a **pro forma** (or projected) **profit-and-loss statement** (also called an **income statement** or **operating statement**). A pro forma statement shows projected revenues less budgeted expenses and estimates the projected net profit for an organization, product, or brand during a specific planning period, typically a year. It includes direct product production costs, marketing expenses budgeted to attain a given sales forecast, and overhead expenses assigned to the organization or product. A profit-and-loss statement typically consists of several major components (see ◉ **Table A2.1**):

- *Net sales*—gross sales revenue minus returns and allowances (for example, trade, cash, quantity, and promotion allowances). ConnectPhone's net sales for 2011 are estimated to be $125 million, as determined in the previous analysis.

- *Cost of goods sold*—(sometimes called *cost of sales*)—the actual cost of the merchandise sold by a manufacturer or reseller. It includes the cost of inventory, purchases, and other costs associated with making the goods. ConnectPhone's cost of goods sold is estimated to be 50 percent of net sales, or $62.5 million.

- *Gross margin (or gross profit)*—the difference between net sales and cost of goods sold. ConnectPhone's gross margin is estimated to be $62.5 million.

- *Operating expenses*—the expenses incurred while doing business. These include all other expenses beyond the cost of goods sold that are necessary to conduct business. Operating expenses can be presented in total or broken down in detail. Here, ConnectPhone's estimated operating expenses include *marketing expenses* and *general and administrative expenses*.

Marketing expenses include sales expenses, promotion expenses, and distribution expenses. The new product will be sold through ConnectPhone's sales force, so the company budgets $5 million for sales salaries. However, because sales representatives earn a 10 percent commission on sales, ConnectPhone must also add a variable component to sales expenses of $12.5 million (10 percent of $125 million net sales), for a total budgeted sales

● TABLE | A2.1   Pro Forma Profit-and-Loss Statement for the 12-Month Period Ended December 31, 2011

			% of Sales
Net Sales		$125,000,000	100%
Cost of Goods Sold		62,500,000	50%
Gross Margin		$62,500,000	50%
Marketing Expenses			
Sales expenses	$17,500,000		
Promotion expenses	15,000,000		
Freight	12,500,000	45,000,000	36%
General and Administrative Expenses			
Managerial salaries and expenses	$2,000,000		
Indirect overhead	3,000,000	5,000,000	4%
Net Profit Before Income Tax		$12,500,000	10%

expense of $17.5 million. ConnectPhone sets its advertising and promotion to launch this product at $10 million. However, the company also budgets 4 percent of sales, or $5 million, for cooperative advertising allowances to retailers who promote ConnectPhone's new product in their advertising. Thus, the total budgeted advertising and promotion expenses are $15 million ($10 million for advertising plus $5 million in co-op allowances). Finally, ConnectPhone budgets 10 percent of net sales, or $12.5 million, for freight and delivery charges. In all, total marketing expenses are estimated to be $17.5 million + $15 million + $12.5 million = $45 million.

General and administrative expenses are estimated at $5 million, broken down into $2 million for managerial salaries and expenses for the marketing function and $3 million of indirect overhead allocated to this product by the corporate accountants (such as depreciation, interest, maintenance, and insurance). Total expenses for the year, then, are estimated to be $50 million ($45 million marketing expenses + $5 million in general and administrative expenses).

- *Net profit before taxes*—profit earned after all costs are deducted. ConnectPhone's estimated net profit before taxes is $12.5 million.

In all, as Table A2.1 shows, ConnectPhone expects to earn a profit on its new product of $12.5 million in 2011. Also note that the percentage of sales that each component of the profit-and-loss statement represents is given in the right-hand column. These percentages are determined by dividing the cost figure by net sales (that is, marketing expenses represent 36 percent of net sales determined by $45 million ÷ $125 million). As can be seen, ConnectPhone projects a net profit return on sales of 10 percent in the first year after launching this product.

Marketing Performance Measures (pp A19–A23)

Now let's fast-forward a year. ConnectPhone's product has been on the market for one year and management wants to assess its sales and profit performance. One way to assess this performance is to compute performance ratios derived from ConnectPhone's **profit-and-loss statement** (or **income statement** or **operating statement**).

Whereas the pro forma profit-and-loss statement shows *projected* financial performance, the statement given in ● **Table A2.2** shows ConnectPhone's *actual* financial performance based on actual sales, cost of goods sold, and expenses during the past year. By comparing the profit-and-loss statement from one period to the next, ConnectPhone can gauge performance against goals, spot favorable or unfavorable trends, and take appropriate corrective action.

The profit-and-loss statement shows that ConnectPhone lost $1 million rather than making the $12.5 million profit projected in the pro forma statement. Why? One obvious

Profit-and-loss statement (or income statement or operating statement)
A statement that shows actual revenues less expenses and net profit for an organization, product, or brand during a specific planning period, typically a year.

⊙ TABLE | A2.2   Profit-and-Loss Statement for the 12-Month Period Ended December 31, 2011

			% of Sales
Net Sales		$100,000,000	100%
Cost of Goods Sold		55,000,000	55%
Gross Margin		$45,000,000	45%
Marketing Expenses			
Sales expenses	$15,000,000		
Promotion expenses	14,000,000		
Freight	10,000,000	39,000,000	39%
General and Administrative Expenses			
Managerial salaries and expenses	$2,000,000		
Indirect overhead	5,000,000	7,000,000	7%
Net Profit Before Income Tax		($1,000,000)	(1%)

reason is that net sales fell $25 million short of estimated sales. Lower sales translated into lower variable costs associated with marketing the product. However, both fixed costs and the cost of goods sold as a percentage of sales exceeded expectations. Hence, the product's contribution margin was 21 percent rather than the estimated 26 percent. That is, variable costs represented 79 percent of sales (55 percent for cost of goods sold, 10 percent for sales commissions, 10 percent for freight, and 4 percent for co-op allowances). Recall that contribution margin can be calculated by subtracting that fraction from one ($1 - 0.79 = 0.21$). Total fixed costs were $22 million, $2 million more than estimated. Thus, the sales that ConnectPhone needed to break even given this cost structure can be calculated as:

$$\text{Break-even sales} = \frac{\text{fixed costs}}{\text{contribution margin}} = \frac{\$22,000,000}{0.21} = \$104,761,905$$

If ConnectPhone had achieved another $5 million in sales, it would have earned a profit.

Although ConnectPhone's sales fell short of the forecasted sales, so did overall industry sales for this product. Overall industry sales were only $2.5 billion. That means that ConnectPhone's **market share** was 4 percent ($100 million ÷ $2.5 billion = 0.04 = 4%), which was higher than forecasted. Thus, ConnectPhone attained a higher-than-expected market share but the overall market sales were not as high as estimated.

Market share
Company sales divided by market sales.

Analytic Ratios

The profit-and-loss statement provides the figures needed to compute some crucial **operating ratios**—the ratios of selected operating statement items to net sales. These ratios let marketers compare the firm's performance in one year to that in previous years (or with industry standards and competitors' performance in that year). The most commonly used operating ratios are the gross margin percentage, the net profit percentage, and the operating expense percentage. The inventory turnover rate and return on investment (ROI) are often used to measure managerial effectiveness and efficiency.

The **gross margin percentage** indicates the percentage of net sales remaining after cost of goods sold that can contribute to operating expenses and net profit before taxes. The higher this ratio, the more a firm has left to cover expenses and generate profit. ConnectPhone's gross margin ratio was 45 percent:

Operating ratios
The ratios of selected operating statement items to net sales.

Gross margin percentage
The percentage of net sales remaining after cost of goods sold—calculated by dividing gross margin by net sales.

$$\text{Gross margin percentage} = \frac{\text{gross margin}}{\text{net sales}} = \frac{\$45,000,000}{\$100,000,000} = 0.45 = 45\%$$

Note that this percentage is lower than estimated, and this ratio is seen easily in the percentage of sales column in Table A2.2. Stating items in the profit-and-loss statement as a percent of sales allows managers to quickly spot abnormal changes in costs over time. If there was previous history for this product and this ratio was declining, management should examine it more closely to determine why it has decreased (that is, because of a decrease in sales volume or price, an increase in costs, or a combination of these). In ConnectPhone's case, net sales were $25 million lower than estimated, and cost of goods sold was higher than estimated (55 percent rather than the estimated 50 percent).

Net profit percentage

The percentage of each sales dollar going to profit—calculated by dividing net profits by net sales.

The **net profit percentage** shows the percentage of each sales dollar going to profit. It is calculated by dividing net profits by net sales:

$$\text{Net profit percentage} = \frac{\text{net profit}}{\text{net sales}} = \frac{-\$1,000,000}{\$100,000,000} = -0.01 = -1.0\%$$

This ratio is easily seen in the percent of sales column. ConnectPhone's new product generated negative profits in the first year, not a good situation given that before the product launch net profits before taxes were estimated at more than $12 million. Later in this appendix, we will discuss further analyses the marketing manager should conduct to defend the product.

Operating expense percentage

The portion of net sales going to operating expenses—calculated by dividing total expenses by net sales.

The **operating expense percentage** indicates the portion of net sales going to operating expenses. Operating expenses include marketing and other expenses not directly related to marketing the product, such as indirect overhead assigned to this product. It is calculated by:

$$\text{Operating expense percentage} = \frac{\text{total expenses}}{\text{net sales}} = \frac{\$46,000,000}{\$100,000,000} = 0.46 = 46\%$$

This ratio can also be quickly determined from the percent of sales column in the profit-and-loss statement by adding the percentages for marketing expenses and general and administrative expenses (39% + 7%). Thus, 46 cents of every sales dollar went for operations. Although ConnectPhone wants this ratio to be as low as possible, and 46 percent is not an alarming amount, it is of concern if it is increasing over time or if a loss is realized.

Inventory turnover rate (or stockturn rate)

The number of times an inventory turns over or is sold during a specified time period (often one year)—calculated based on costs, selling price, or units.

Another useful ratio is the **inventory turnover rate** (also called **stockturn rate** for resellers). The inventory turnover rate is the number of times an inventory turns over or is sold during a specified time period (often one year). This rate tells how quickly a business is moving inventory through the organization. Higher rates indicate that lower investments in inventory are made, thus freeing up funds for other investments. It may be computed on a cost, selling price, or unit basis. The formula based on cost is:

$$\text{Inventory turnover rate} = \frac{\text{cost of goods sold}}{\text{average inventory at cost}}$$

Assuming ConnectPhone's beginning and ending inventories were $30 million and $20 million, respectively, the inventory turnover rate is:

$$\text{Inventory turnover rate} = \frac{\$55,000,000}{(\$30,000,000 + \$20,000,000)/2} = \frac{\$55,000,000}{\$25,000,000} = 2.2$$

That is, ConnectPhone's inventory turned over 2.2 times in 2011. Normally, the higher the turnover rate, the higher the management efficiency and company profitability. However, this rate should be compared to industry averages, competitors' rates, and past performance to determine if ConnectPhone is doing well. A competitor with similar sales but a higher inventory turnover rate will have fewer resources tied up in inventory, allowing it to invest in other areas of the business.

Return on investment (ROI)

A measure of managerial effectiveness and efficiency—net profit before taxes divided by total investment.

Companies frequently use **return on investment (ROI)** to measure managerial effectiveness and efficiency. For ConnectPhone, ROI is the ratio of net profits to total investment required to manufacture the new product. This investment includes capital investments in land, buildings, and equipment (here, the initial $10 million to refurbish the manufacturing facility) plus inventory costs (ConnectPhone's average inventory totaled $25 million), for a total of $35 million. Thus, ConnectPhone's ROI for this product is:

$$\text{Return on investment} = \frac{\text{net profit before taxes}}{\text{investment}} = \frac{-\$1,000,000}{\$35,000,000} = -0.286 = -2.86\%$$

ROI is often used to compare alternatives, and a positive ROI is desired. The alternative with the highest ROI is preferred to other alternatives. ConnectPhone needs to be concerned with the ROI realized. One obvious way ConnectPhone can increase ROI is to increase net profit by reducing expenses. Another way is to reduce its investment, perhaps by investing less in inventory and turning it over more frequently.

Marketing Profitability Metrics

Given the above financial results, you may be thinking that ConnectPhone should drop this new product. But what arguments can marketers make for keeping or dropping this product? The obvious arguments for dropping the product are that first-year sales were well below expected levels and the product lost money, resulting in a negative return on investment.

So what would happen if ConnectPhone did drop this product? Surprisingly, if the company drops the product, the profits for the total organization will decrease by $4 million! How can that be? Marketing managers need to look closely at the numbers in the profit-and-loss statement to determine the *net marketing contribution* for this product. In ConnectPhone's case, the net marketing contribution for the product is $4 million, and if the company drops this product, that contribution will disappear as well. Let's look more closely at this concept to illustrate how marketing managers can better assess and defend their marketing strategies and programs.

Net Marketing Contribution

Net marketing contribution (NMC)

A measure of marketing profitability that includes only components of profitability controlled by marketing.

Net marketing contribution (NMC), along with other marketing metrics derived from it, measures *marketing* profitability. It includes only components of profitability that are controlled by marketing. Whereas the previous calculation of net profit before taxes from the profit-and-loss statement includes operating expenses not under marketing's control, NMC does not. Referring back to ConnectPhone's profit-and-loss statement given in Table A2.2, we can calculate net marketing contribution for the product as:

$$\text{NMC} = \text{net sales} - \text{cost of goods sold} - \text{marketing expenses} =$$
$$\$100 \text{ million} - \$55 \text{ million} - \$41 \text{ million} = \$4 \text{ million}$$

The marketing expenses include sales expenses ($15 million), promotion expenses ($14 million), freight expenses ($10 million), and the managerial salaries and expenses of the marketing function ($2 million), which total $41 million.

Thus, the product actually contributed $4 million to ConnectPhone's profits. It was the $5 million of indirect overhead allocated to this product that caused the negative profit. Further, the amount allocated was $2 million more than estimated in the pro forma profit-and-loss statement. Indeed, if only the estimated amount had been allocated, the product would have earned a *profit* of $1 million rather than losing $1 million. If ConnectPhone drops the product, the $5 million in fixed overhead expenses will not disappear—it will simply have to be allocated elsewhere. However, the $4 million in net marketing contribution *will* disappear.

Marketing Return on Sales and Investment

To get an even deeper understanding of the profit impact of marketing strategy, we'll now examine two measures of marketing efficiency—*marketing return on sales* (marketing ROS) and *marketing return on investment* (marketing ROI).[5]

Marketing return on sales (or marketing ROS)

The percent of net sales attributable to the net marketing contribution—calculated by dividing net marketing contribution by net sales.

Marketing return on sales (or **marketing ROS**) shows the percent of net sales attributable to the net marketing contribution. For our product, ROS is:

$$\text{Marketing ROS} = \frac{\text{net marketing contribution}}{\text{net sales}} = \frac{\$4,000,000}{\$100,000,000} = 0.04 = 4\%$$

Thus, out of every $100 of sales, the product returns $4 to ConnectPhone's bottom line. A high marketing ROS is desirable. But to assess whether this is a good level of performance, ConnectPhone must compare this figure to previous marketing ROS levels for the product, the ROSs of other products in the company's portfolio, and the ROSs of competing products.

Marketing return on investment (or marketing ROI)
A measure of the marketing productivity of a marketing investment—calculated by dividing net marketing contribution by marketing expenses.

Marketing return on investment (or **marketing ROI**) measures the marketing productivity of a marketing investment. In ConnectPhone's case, the marketing investment is represented by $41 million of the total expenses. Thus, marketing ROI is:

$$\text{Marketing ROI} = \frac{\text{net marketing contribution}}{\text{marketing expenses}} = \frac{\$4,000,000}{\$41,000,000} = 0.0976 = 9.76\%$$

As with marketing ROS, a high value is desirable, but this figure should be compared with previous levels for the given product and with the marketing ROIs of competitors' products. Note from this equation that marketing ROI could be greater than 100 percent. This can be achieved by attaining a higher net marketing contribution and/or a lower total marketing expense.

In this section, we estimated market potential and sales, developed profit-and-loss statements, and examined financial measures of performance. In the next section, we discuss methods for analyzing the impact of various marketing tactics. However, before moving on to those analyses, here's another set of quantitative exercises to help you apply what you've learned to other situations.

Marketing by the Numbers Exercise Set Two

2.1 Determine the market potential for a product that has 50 million prospective buyers who purchase an average of 3 per year and price averages $25. How many units must a company sell if it desires a 10 percent share of this market?

2.2 Develop a profit-and-loss statement for the Westgate division of North Industries. This division manufactures light fixtures sold to consumers through home improvement and hardware stores. Cost of goods sold represents 40 percent of net sales. Marketing expenses include selling expenses, promotion expenses, and freight. Selling expenses include sales salaries totaling $3 million per year and sales commissions (5 percent of sales). The company spent $3 million on advertising last year, and freight costs were 10 percent of sales. Other costs include $2 million for managerial salaries and expenses for the marketing function and another $3 million for indirect overhead allocated to the division.
  a. Develop the profit-and-loss statement if net sales were $20 million last year.
  b. Develop the profit-and-loss statement if net sales were $40 million last year.
  c. Calculate Westgate's break-even sales.

2.3 Using the profit-and-loss statement you developed in question 2.2b, and assuming that Westgate's beginning inventory was $11 million, ending inventory was $7 million, and total investment was $20 million including inventory, determine the following:
  a. gross margin percentage
  b. net profit percentage
  c. operating expense percentage
  d. inventory turnover rate
  e. return on investment (ROI)
  f. net marketing contribution
  g. marketing return on sales (marketing ROS)
  h. marketing return on investment (marketing ROI)
  i. Is the Westgate division doing well? Explain your answer.

Financial Analysis of Marketing Tactics (pp A23–A28)

Although the first-year profit performance for ConnectPhone's new product was less than desired, management feels that this attractive market has excellent growth opportunities. Although the sales of ConnectPhone's product were lower than initially projected, they were not unreasonable given the size of the current market. Thus, ConnectPhone wants to explore new marketing tactics to help grow the market for this product and increase sales for the company.

For example, the company could increase advertising to promote more awareness of the new product and its category. It could add salespeople to secure greater product distribution. ConnectPhone could decrease prices so that more consumers could afford its product. Finally, to expand the market, ConnectPhone could introduce a lower-priced model in addition to the higher-priced original offering. Before pursuing any of these tactics, ConnectPhone must analyze the financial implications of each.

Increase Advertising Expenditures

Although most consumers understand the Internet and telephones, they may not be aware of media phones. Thus, ConnectPhone is considering boosting its advertising to make more people aware of the benefits of this device in general and of its own brand in particular.

What if ConnectPhone's marketers recommend increasing national advertising by 50 percent to $15 million (assume no change in the variable cooperative component of promotional expenditures)? This represents an increase in fixed costs of $5 million. What increase in sales will be needed to break even on this $5 million increase in fixed costs?

A quick way to answer this question is to divide the increase in fixed cost by the contribution margin, which we found in a previous analysis to be 21 percent:

$$\text{Increase in sales} = \frac{\text{increase in fixed cost}}{\text{contribution margin}} = \frac{\$5,000,000}{0.21} = \$23,809,524$$

Thus, a 50 percent increase in advertising expenditures must produce a sales increase of almost $24 million to just break even. That $24 million sales increase translates into an almost 1 percentage point increase in market share (1 percent of the $2.5 billion overall market equals $25 million). That is, to break even on the increased advertising expenditure, ConnectPhone would have to increase its market share from 4 percent to 4.95 percent ($123,809,524 ÷ $2.5 billion = 0.0495 or 4.95% market share). All of this assumes that the total market will not grow, which might or might not be a reasonable assumption.

Increase Distribution Coverage

ConnectPhone also wants to consider hiring more salespeople in order to call on new retailer accounts and increase distribution through more outlets. Even though ConnectPhone sells directly to wholesalers, its sales representatives call on retail accounts to perform other functions in addition to selling, such as training retail salespeople. Currently, ConnectPhone employs 60 sales reps who earn an average of $50,000 in salary plus 10 percent commission on sales. The product is currently sold to consumers through 1,875 retail outlets. Suppose ConnectPhone wants to increase that number of outlets to 2,500, an increase of 625 retail outlets. How many additional salespeople will ConnectPhone need, and what sales will be necessary to break even on the increased cost?

Workload method
An approach to determining sales force size based on the workload required and the time available for selling.

One method for determining what size sales force ConnectPhone will need is the **workload method**. The workload method uses the following formula to determine the salesforce size:

$$NS = \frac{NC \times FC \times LC}{TA}$$

where

NS = number of salespeople

NC = number of customers

FC = average frequency of customer calls per customer

LC = average length of customer call

TA = time an average salesperson has available for selling per year

ConnectPhone's sales reps typically call on accounts an average of 20 times per year for about 2 hours per call. Although each sales rep works 2,000 hours per year (50 weeks per year $\times$ 40 hours per week), they spent about 15 hours per week on nonselling activities such as administrative duties and travel. Thus, the average annual available selling time per sales rep per year is 1,250 hours (50 weeks $\times$ 25 hours per week). We can now calculate how many sales reps ConnectPhone will need to cover the anticipated 2,500 retail outlets:

$$NS = \frac{2,500 \times 20 \times 2}{1,250} = 80 \text{ salespeople}$$

Therefore, ConnectPhone will need to hire 20 more salespeople. The cost to hire these reps will be $1 million (20 salespeople $\times$ $50,000 salary per sales person).

What increase in sales will be required to break even on this increase in fixed costs? The 10 percent commission is already accounted for in the contribution margin, so the contribution margin remains unchanged at 21 percent. Thus, the increase in sales needed to cover this increase in fixed costs can be calculated by:

$$\text{Increase in sales} = \frac{\text{increase in fixed cost}}{\text{contribution margin}} = \frac{\$1,000,000}{0.21} = \$4,761,905$$

That is, ConnectPhone's sales must increase almost $5 million to break even on this tactic. So, how many new retail outlets will the company need to secure to achieve this sales increase? The average revenue generated per current outlet is $53,333 ($100 million in sales divided by 1,875 outlets). To achieve the nearly $5 million sales increase needed to break even, ConnectPhone would need about 90 new outlets ($4,761,905 $\div$ $53,333 = 89.3 outlets), or about 4.5 outlets per new rep. Given that current reps cover about 31 outlets apiece (1,875 outlets $\div$ 60 reps), this seems very reasonable.

Decrease Price

ConnectPhone is also considering lowering its price to increase sales revenue through increased volume. The company's research has shown that demand for most types of consumer electronics products is elastic—that is, the percentage increase in the quantity demanded is greater than the percentage decrease in price.

What increase in sales would be necessary to break even on a 10 percent decrease in price? That is, what increase in sales will be needed to maintain the total contribution that ConnectPhone realized at the higher price? The current total contribution can be determined by multiplying the contribution margin by total sales:[6]

$$\text{Current total contribution} = \text{contribution margin} \times \text{sales} =$$
$$.21 \times \$100 \text{ million} = \$21 \text{ million}$$

Price changes result in changes in unit contribution and contribution margin. Recall that the contribution margin of 21 percent was based on variable costs representing 79 percent of sales. Therefore, unit variable costs can be determined by multiplying the original price by this percentage: $336 $\times$ 0.79 = $265.44 per unit. If price is decreased by 10 percent, the new price is $302.40. However, variable costs do not change just because price decreased, so the contribution and contribution margin decrease as follows:

	Old	New (reduced 10%)
Price	$336	$302.40
− Unit variable cost	$265.44	$265.44
= Unit contribution	$70.56	$36.96
Contribution margin	$70.56/$336 = 0.21 or 21%	$36.96/$302.40 = 0.12 or 12%

So a 10 percent reduction in price results in a decrease in the contribution margin from 21 percent to 12 percent.[7] To determine the sales level needed to break even on this price reduction, we calculate the level of sales that must be attained at the new contribution margin to achieve the original total contribution of $21 million:

$$\text{New contribution margin} \times \text{new sales level} = \text{original total contribution}$$

So,

$$\text{New sales level} = \frac{\text{original contribution}}{\text{new contribution margin}} = \frac{\$21,000,000}{0.12} = \$175,000,000$$

Thus, sales must increase by $75 million ($175 million − $100 million) just to break even on a 10 percent price reduction. This means that ConnectPhone must increase market share to 7 percent ($175 million ÷ $2.5 billion) to achieve the current level of profits (assuming no increase in the total market sales). The marketing manager must assess whether or not this is a reasonable goal.

Extend the Product Line

Cannibalization

The situation in which one product sold by a company takes a portion of its sales from other company products.

As a final option, ConnectPhone is considering extending its product line by offering a lower-priced model. Of course, the new, lower-priced product would steal some sales from the higher-priced model. This is called **cannibalization**—the situation in which one product sold by a company takes a portion of its sales from other company products. If the new product has a lower contribution than the original product, the company's total contribution will decrease on the cannibalized sales. However, if the new product can generate enough new volume, it is worth considering.

To assess cannibalization, ConnectPhone must look at the incremental contribution gained by having both products available. Recall in the previous analysis we determined that unit variable costs were $265.44 and unit contribution was just over $70. Assuming costs remain the same next year, ConnectPhone can expect to realize a contribution per unit of approximately $70 for every unit of the original product sold.

Assume that the first model offered by ConnectPhone is called MP1 and the new, lower-priced model is called MP2. MP2 will retail for $400, and resellers will take the same markup percentages on price as they do with the higher-priced model. Therefore, MP2's price to wholesalers will be $224 as follows:

Retail price:	$400
minus retail margin (30%):	−$120
Retailer's cost/wholesaler's price:	$280
minus wholesaler's margin (20%):	−$ 56
Wholesaler's cost/ConnectPhone's price	$224

If MP2's variable costs are estimated to be $174, then its contribution per unit will equal $50 ($224 − $174 = $50). That means for every unit that MP2 cannibalizes from MP1, ConnectPhone will *lose* $20 in contribution toward fixed costs and profit (that is, contribution$_{MP2}$ − contribution$_{MP1}$ = $50 − $70 = −$20). You might conclude that ConnectPhone should not pursue this tactic because it appears as though the company will be worse off if it introduces the lower-priced model. However, if MP2 captures enough *additional* sales, ConnectPhone will be better off even though some MP1 sales are cannibalized. The company must examine what will happen to *total* contribution, which requires estimates of unit volume for both products.

Originally, ConnectPhone estimated that next year's sales of MP1 would be 600,000 units. However, with the introduction of MP2, it now estimates that 200,000 of those sales will be cannibalized by the new model. If ConnectPhone sells only 200,000 units of the new MP2 model (all cannibalized from MP1), the company would lose $4 million in total contribution

(200,000 units × −$20 per cannibalized unit = −$4 million)—not a good outcome. However, ConnectPhone estimates that MP2 will generate the 200,000 of cannibalized sales plus an *additional* 500,000 unit sales. Thus, the contribution on these additional MP2 units will be $25 million (i.e., 500,000 units × $50 per unit = $25 million). The net effect is that ConnectPhone will gain $21 million in total contribution by introducing MP2.

The following table compares ConnectPhone's total contribution with and without the introduction of MP2:

	MP1 only	**MP1 and MP2**
MP1 contribution	600,000 units × $70 = $42,000,000	400,000 units × $70 = $28,000,000
MP2 contribution	0	700,000 units × $50 = $35,000,000
Total contribution	$42,000,000	$63,000,000

The difference in the total contribution is a net gain of $21 million ($63 million − $42 million). Based on this analysis, ConnectPhone should introduce the MP2 model because it results in a positive incremental contribution. However, if fixed costs will increase by more than $21 million as a result of adding this model, then the net effect will be negative and ConnectPhone should not pursue this tactic.

Now that you have seen these marketing tactic analysis concepts in action as they related to ConnectPhone's new product, here are several exercises for you to apply what you have learned in this section in other contexts.

Marketing by the Numbers Exercise Set Three

3.1 Kingsford, Inc. sells small plumbing components to consumers through retail outlets. Total industry sales for Kingsford's relevant market last year were $80 million, with Kingsford's sales representing 10 percent of that total. Contribution margin is 25 percent. Kingsford's sales force calls on retail outlets and each sales rep earns $45,000 per year plus 1 percent commission on all sales. Retailers receive a 40 percent margin on selling price and generate average revenue of $10,000 per outlet for Kingsford.

    a. The marketing manager has suggested increasing consumer advertising by $300,000. By how much would dollar sales need to increase to break even on this expenditure? What increase in overall market share does this represent?

    b. Another suggestion is to hire three more sales representatives to gain new consumer retail accounts. How many new retail outlets would be necessary to break even on the increased cost of adding three sales reps?

    c. A final suggestion is to make a 20 percent across-the-board price reduction. By how much would dollar sales need to increase to maintain Kingsford's current contribution? (See endnote 13 to calculate the new contribution margin.)

    d. Which suggestion do you think Kingsford should implement? Explain your recommendation.

3.2 PepsiCo sells its soft drinks in approximately 400,000 retail establishments, such as supermarkets, discount stores, and convenience stores. Sales representatives call on each retail account weekly, which means each account is called on by a sales rep 52 times per year. The average length of a sales call is 75 minutes (or 1.25 hours). An average salesperson works 2,000 hours per year (50 weeks per year × 40 hours per week), but each spends 10 hours a week on nonselling activities, such as administrative tasks and travel. How many sales people does PepsiCo need?

3.3 Hair Zone manufactures a brand of hair-styling gel. It is considering adding a modified version of the product—a foam that provides stronger hold. Hair Zone's variable
costs and prices to wholesalers are:

	Current Hair Gel	**New Foam Product**
Unit selling price	2.00	2.25
Unit variable costs	.85	1.25

Hair Zone expects to sell 1 million units of the new styling foam in the first year after introduction, but it expects that 60 percent of those sales will come from buyers who normally purchase Hair Zone's styling gel. Hair Zone estimates that it would sell 1.5 million units of the gel if it did not introduce the foam. If the fixed cost of launching the new
foam will be $100,000 during the first year, should Hair Zone add the new product to its
line? Why or why not?

References

Chapter 1

1. Portions adapted from Natalie Zmuda, "Zappos: Customer Service First—and a Daily Obsession," *Advertising Age*, October 20, 2008, p. 36; with additional information and quotes from Jeffrey M. O'Brien, "Zappos Knows How to Kick It," February 2, 2009, p. 54; Masha Zager, "Zappos Delivers Service . . . with Shoes on the Side," *Apparel Magazine*, January 2009, pp. 10–13; Kelly Holman, "For Amazon, the Shoe Fits," *The Investment Dealer's Digest*, January 29, 2010, p. 28; "Zappos.com Salutes Customer Loyalty Team in New Ad Campaign," *Marketing Business Weekly*, April 4, 2010, p. 691; Barbara Lippert, "Zappos Brilliantly Goes Small to Show How Customer Service Is a Big Deal," *BrandWeek*, March 22, 2010, p. 9; and www.youtube.com/zappos and www.zappos.com, accessed November 2010.

2. See "U.S. Market Leaders," *Advertising Age*, June 21, 2010, p. 18.

3. As quoted in John J. Burnett, *Nonprofit Marketing Best Practices* (New York: John Wiley & Sons, 2008), p. 21.

4. The American Marketing Association offers the following definition: "Marketing is an organizational function and a set of processes for creating, communicating, and delivering value to customers and for managing customer relationships in ways that benefit the organization and its stakeholders." www.marketingpower.com/_layouts/Dictionary.aspx?dLetter=M, accessed November 2010.

5. Jeffrey M. O'Brien, "Zappos Knows How to Kick It," *Fortune*, January 22, 2009, accessed at http://money.cnn.com/2009/01/15/news/companies/Zappos_best_companies_obrien.fortune/index.htm; and Roland T. Rust, Christine Moorman, and Gaurav Bhalla, "Rethinking Marketing," *Harvard Business Review*, January–February 2010, pp. 94–101.

6. See www.michigan.org and www.adcouncil.org/default.aspx?id=602, accessed July 2010.

7. See Theodore Levitt's classic article, "Marketing Myopia," *Harvard Business Review*, July–August 1960, pp. 45–56. For more recent discussions, see "What Business Are You In?" *Harvard Business Review*, October 2006, pp. 127–137; Lance A. Bettencourt, "Debunking Myths about Customer Needs," *Marketing Management*, January/February 2009, pp. 46–51, here p. 50; and N. Craig Smith, Minette E. Drumright, and Mary C. Gentile, "The New Marketing Myopia," *Journal of Public Policy & Marketing*, Spring 2010, pp. 4–11.

8. Information from a recent "The Computer Is Personal Again" ad and www.hp.com/united-states/personal_again/index.html, accessed August 2010.

9. See *Sustainability at UPS*, www.responsibility.ups.com/community/Static%20Files/sustainability/2008_CSR_PDF_Report.pdf, pp. 13–18; "UPS Corporate Sustainability: Everyone Matters," www.responsibility.ups.com/Sustainability?WT.svl=Footer, accessed August 2010; "World's Most Admired Companies," http://money.cnn.com/magazines/fortune/mostadmired/2010/best_worst/best4.html, August 2010; and http://sustainability.ups.com/, accessed November 2010.

10. See David Kiley, "How to Sell Luxury to Penny-Pinchers," *BusinessWeek*, November 10, 2008, p. 60.

11. For more on how to measure customer satisfaction, see D. Randall Brandt, "For Good Measure," *Marketing Management*, January–February 2007, pp. 21–25.

12. Based on information from Michael Bush, "Why You Should Be Putting on the Ritz," *Advertising Age*, June 21, 2010, p. 1; Julie Barker, "Power to the People," *Incentive*, February 2008, p. 34; and Carmine Gallo, "Employee Motivation the Ritz-Carlton Way," *BusinessWeek*, February 29, 2008, accessed at www.businessweek.com/smallbiz/content/feb2008/sb20080229_347490.htm. Also see http://corporate.ritzcarlton.com/en/About/Awards.htm#Hotel, accessed November 2010.

13. Information about the Harley Owners Group, www.harley-davidson.com/wcm/Content/Pages/HOG/HOG.jsp?locale=en_US, accessed November 2010.

14. Elizabeth A. Sullivan, "Just Say No," *Marketing News*, April 15, 2008, p. 17; and Raymund Flandez, "It Just Isn't Working? Some File for Customer Divorce," *Wall Street Journal*, November 16, 2009, p. B7.

15. Sullivan, "Just Say No," p. 17.

16. Josh Hyatt, "Playing Favorites," *CFO Magazine*, January 1, 2009, accessed at http://www.cfo.com/article.cfm/12835154?f. The Sprint example is adapted from information found in Vikas Mittal, Matthew Sarkees, and Feisal Murshed, "The Right Way to Manage Unprofitable Customers," *Harvard Business Review*, April 2008, pp. 95–102. For another example, see Whitney Hess, "Fire Your Worst Customers," *Pleasure & Pain*, February 21, 2010, http://whitneyhess.com/blog/2010/02/21/fire-your-worst-customers/.

17. Quotes from Andrew Walmsley, "The Year of Consumer Empowerment," *Marketing*, December 20, 2006, p. 9; and Jeff Heilman, "Rules of Engagement: During a Recession, Marketers Need to Have *Their* Keenest Listening-to-Customers Strategy in Place," *The Magazine of Branded Content*, Winter 2009, p. 7. Also see Frank's Striefler, "5 Marketing Principles Brands Should Embrace in 2010," *Adweek*, January 13, 2010, accessed at www.adweek.com.

18. See James Rainey, "On the Media: Twitter's Charms Sort of Grow on You," *Los Angeles Times*, February 18, 2009, p. A1; B. L. Ochman, "Debunking Six Social Media Myths," *BusinessWeek*, February 19, 2009, accessed at www.businessweek.com; Brian Morrissey, "Brand Sweepstakes Get Twitterized," *Adweek*, November 22, 2009, accessed at www.adweek.com; and Alicia Wallace, "Owing Social: Businesses Dial in to Facebook, Twitter to Build Business," *McClatchy-Tribune Business News*, April 26, 2010.

19. See www.facebook.com/Honda and http://apps.facebook.com/wholovesahonda/, accessed September 2010.

20. See "Successful IKEA Facebook Campaign Shows Importance of Offering Deals to Consumers on Social Media," *Illuminea*, November 27, 2009, http://illuminea.com/social-media/ikea-facebook-social-media/; Chris Matyszczyk, "IKEA's Brilliant Facebook Campaign," *CNET News*, November 24, 2009, http://news.cnet.com/8301-17852_3-10404937-71.html; and www.youtube.com/watch?v=P_K1ti4RU78&feature=player_embedded, accessed August 2010.

21. Sullivan, "We Were Right!" p. 17.

22. Joel Rubenstein, "Marketers, Researchers, and Your Ears," *Brandweek*, February 15, 2010, p. 34.

23. "Doritos Fan-Created Super Bowl Ad 'Underdog,' Created for $200, Scores No. 2 on *USA Today* Ad Meter and $600,000 Prize," February 8, 2010, http://www.fritolay.com/about-us/press-release-20100208.html; Stuart Elliott, "Do-It-Yourself Super Ads," *New York Times*, February 9, 2010, www.nytimes.com; and "*USA Today* 2010 Ad Meter Tracks Super Bowl XLIV Ads," *USA Today*, February 15, 2010, accessed at www.usatoday.com/money/advertising/admeter/2010admeter.htm.

24. Gavin O'Malley, "Entries Pour in for Heinz Ketchup Commercial Contest," August 13, 2007, accessed at http://publications.mediapost.com.

25. Philip Kotler and Kevin Lane Keller, *Marketing Management*, 14th ed. (Upper Saddle River, NJ: Prentice Hall, 2012), p. 17.

26. "Consumer 'New Frugality'' May Be an Enduring Feature of Post-Recession Economy, Finds Booz & Company Survey," *Business-Wire*, February 24, 2010.

27. "Stew Leonard's," *Hoover's Company Records*, July 15, 2010, pp. 104–226; and www.stew-leonards.com/html/about.cfm, accessed August 2010.

28. Graham Brown, "MobileYouth Key Statistics," March 28, 2008, www.mobileyouth.org/?s=MobileYouth+Key+Statistics. For interesting discussions on customer lifetime value, see Sunil Gupta, et al., "Modeling Customer Lifetime Value," *Journal of Service Research*, November 2006, pp. 139–146; Nicolas Glady, Bart Baesens, and Christophe Croux, "Modeling Churn Using Customer Lifetime Value," *European Journal of Operational Research*, August 16, 2009, p. 402; and Jason Q. Zhang, Ashutosh Dixit, and Roberto Friedman, "Customer Loyalty and Lifetime Value: An Empirical Investigation of Consumer Packaged Goods," *Journal of Marketing Theory and Practice*, Spring 2010, p. 127.

29. Heather Green, "How Amazon Aims to Keep You Clicking," *BusinessWeek*, March 2, 2009, pp. 34–40; and Geoffrey A. Fowler, "Corporate News: Amazon's Sales Soar, Lifting Profit," *Wall Street Journal*, April 23, 2010, p. B3.

30. Don Peppers and Martha Rogers, "Customers Don't Grow on Trees," *Fast Company*, July 2005, p. 26.

31. For more discussion on customer equity, see Roland T. Rust, Valerie A. Zeithaml, and Katherine A. Lemon, *Driving Customer Equity* (New York: Free Press 2000); Rust, Lemon, and Zeithaml, "Return on Marketing: Using Customer Equity to Focus Marketing Strategy," *Journal of Marketing*, January 2004, pp. 109–127; Dominique M. Hanssens, Daniel Thorpe, and Carl Finkbeiner, "Marketing When Customer Equity Matters," *Harvard Business Review*, May 2008, pp. 117–124; Thorsten Wiesel, Bernd Skieram, and Julián Villanueva, "Customer Equity: An Integral Part of Financial Reporting," *Journal of Marketing*, March 8, 2008, pp. 1–14; and V. Kumar and Denish Shaw, "Expanding the Role of Marketing: From Customer Equity to Market Capitalization," *Journal of Marketing*, November 2009, p. 119.

32. This example is adapted from information found in Rust, Lemon, and Zeithaml, "Where Should the Next Marketing Dollar Go?" *Marketing Management*, September–October 2001, pp. 24–28; and Jeff Green and David Welch, "What Cadillac Is Learning from the Ritz," *Bloomberg BusinessWeek*, June 17, 2010, p. 1.

33. Werner Reinartz and V. Kumar, "The Mismanagement of Customer Loyalty," *Harvard Business Review*, July 2002, pp. 86–94. Also see Stanley F. Slater, Jakki J. Mohr, and Sanjit Sengupta, "Know Your Customer," *Marketing Management*, February 2009, pp. 37–44.

34. "Consumer "New Frugality" May Be an Enduring Feature of Post-Recession Economy."

35. Layura Petrecca, "Marketers Try to Promote Value without Cheapening Image," *USA Today*, November 17, 2008, p. B1. Also see Kenneth Hein," Why Price Isn't Everything," *Brandweek*, March 2, 2009, p. 6; and Judann Pollack, "Now's Time to Reset Marketing for Post-Recession," February 1, 2010, p. 1.

36. Quotes from Natalie Zmuda, "Target to Put More Focus on Value," *Advertising Age*, August 19, 2008, accessed at http://adage .com/print?article_id=130419; and Stuart Elliott, "With Shoppers Pinching Pennies, Some Big Retailers Get the Message," *New York Times*, April 13, 2009, www.nytimes.com. Also see Sharon Edelson, "Target to Bring Message Back to Quality," *WWD*, January 22, 2010, p. 2.

37. Emily Thornton, "The New Rules," *BusinessWeek*, January 19, 2009, pp. 30–34.

38. Information from www.starbucks.com and www.mcdonalds.com, accessed August 2010.

39. Adapted from information in Brad Stone, "Breakfast Can Wait. Today's First Stop Is Online," *New York Times*, August 10, 2009, p. A1.

40. Internet usage stats from www.internetworldstats.com/stats.htm, accessed August 2010; James Lewin, "Pew Internet and the American Life Project: Trend Data," www.pewinternet.org/Trend-Data .aspx, accessed August 2010; and Pew/Internet, "The Future of the Internet III," December 14, 2008, accessed at www.pewinternet. org/Reports/2008/The-Future-of-the-Internet-III.aspx.

41. For more discussion, see "Research and Markets: Semantic Wave Report: Industry Roadmap to Web 3.0 and Multibillion Market Opportunities," *M2 Presswire*, January 20, 2009; Greg Smith, "Web 3.0: 'Vague, but Exciting,'" *Adweek*, June 15, 2009, p. 19; and Michael Baumann, "Pew Report: Expert Opinion Divided on Web 3.0," *Information Today*, July/August 2010, p. 11.

42. Laurie Rowell, "In Search of Web 3.0," *netWorker*, September 2008, pp. 18–24. Also see "Research and Markets: Web 3.0 Manifesto," *Business Wire*, January 21, 2009; and Jessi Hempel, "Web 2.0 Is So Over. Welcome to Web 3.0," *Fortune*, January 19, 2009, p. 36.

43. "Pew Internet and the American Life Project: Trend Data."

44. www.aboutmcdonalds.com/mcd and www.nikebiz.com, accessed August 2010.

45. Quotes and information found at www.patagonia.com/web/us/ contribution/patagonia.go?assetid=2329, accessed August 2010.

46. For examples and for a good review of nonprofit marketing, see Philip Kotler and Alan R. Andreasen, *Strategic Marketing for Nonprofit Organizations*, 7th ed. (Upper Saddle River, NJ: Prentice Hall, 2008); Philip Kotler and Karen Fox, *Strategic Marketing for Educational Institutions* (Upper Saddle River, NJ: Prentice Hall, 1995); Philip Kotler, John Bowen, and James Makens, *Marketing for Hospitality and Tourism*, 4th ed. (Upper Saddle River, NJ: Prentice Hall, 2006); and Philip Kotler and Nancy Lee, *Marketing in the Public Sector: A Roadmap for Improved Performance* (Philadelphia: Wharton School Publishing, 2007).

47. Adapted from information in Stephanie Strom, "Ad Featuring Singer Proves Bonanza for A.S.P.C.A.," *New York Times*, December 26, 2008, p. 20.

48. "Leading National Advertisers," *Advertising Age*, June 21, 2010, pp. 10–12. For more on social marketing, see Philip Kotler, Ned Roberto, and Nancy R. Lee, *Social Marketing: Improving the Quality of Life*, 2nd ed. (Thousand Oaks, CA: Sage Publications, 2002).

Chapter 2

1. Quotes and other information from Barbara Lippert, "Game Changers," *Adweek*, November 17–24, 2008, p. 20; Mark Borden, "Nike," *Fast Company*, March 2008, p. 93; Michael McCarthy, "Nike's Swoosh Is Under Wraps," *USA Today*, January 7, 2009, www.USAToday.com; Jonathon Birchall, "Nike Seeks 'Opportunities' in Turmoil," *Financial Times*, March 16, 2009, p. 20; Brian Morrissey, "Nike Plus Starts to Open Up to Web," *Adweek*, July 20–27, 2009, p. 8; John Kell, "Corporate News: Nike's Quarterly Profit Jumps 53%," *Wall Street Journal*, June 24, 2010, p. B4; and annual reports and other sources at www.nikebiz.com, accessed November 2010.

2. Mission statements are from Under Armour, http://investor .underarmour.com/investors.cfm and Chipotle, www.chipotle.com, accessed September 2010.

3. Jack and Suzy Welch, "State Your Business; Too Many Mission Statements Are Loaded with Fatheaded Jargon. Play It Straight," *BusinessWeek*, January 14, 2008, p. 80. Also see Nancy Lublin, "Do Something," *Fast Company*, November 2009, p. 86; and Jack Neff, "P&G, Walmart, Lever, General Mills Are Major Marketers on a Mission," *Advertising Age*, November 16, 2009, pp. 1, 45.

4. See "Kohler Mulls Second Manufacturing Plant in Guj," *Economic Times*, November 18, 2009, http://economictimes.indiatimes.com; and the Kohler Press Room, "IBS Press Kit," www.us.kohler.com/ pr/presskit.jsp?aid=1194383270995, accessed January 2010.

5. The following discussion is based in part on information found at www.bcg.com/documents/file13904.pdf, accessed December 2010.

6. Matthew Garrahan, "Disney Profits Fall as Recession Hits," *Financial Times*, February 4, 2009, p. 25; Richard Siklos, "Bob Iger Rocks Disney," *Fortune*, January 19, 2009, pp. 80–86; and Ben Fritz, "Company Town; Disney Profit Increases 55%," *Los Angeles Times*, May 12, 2010, p. B3.

7. H. Igor Ansoff, "Strategies for Diversification," *Harvard Business Review*, September–October 1957, pp. 113–124.

8. Information about Under Armour in this section is from Alexandria Steigrad, "Apparel, Accessories Boost Under Armour Profits," April 28, 2010, p. 14; Liz Farmer, "Apparel Lifts Baltimore-Based Under Armour's Quarter," *Daily Record (Baltimore)*, January 28, 2010, http://findarticles.com/p/articles/mi_qn4183/is_20100128/ai_n52472257/; Andrea K. Walker, "Under Armour Plans Major New Investments," *McClatchy-Tribune Business News*, January 29, 2010; and Under Armour annual reports and other documents, www.underarmour.com, accessed July 2010.

9. See Michael E. Porter, *Competitive Advantage: Creating and Sustaining Superior Performance* (New York: Free Press, 1985); and Michel E. Porter, "What Is Strategy?" *Harvard Business Review*, November–December 1996, pp. 61–78. Also see "The Value Chain," www.quickmba.com/strategy/value-chain, accessed July 2010; and Philip Kotler and Kevin Lane Keller, *Marketing Management*, 13th ed. (Upper Saddle River, NJ: Prentice Hall, 2009), pp. 35–36 and pp. 252–253.

10. Nirmalya Kumar, "The CEO's Marketing Manifesto," *Marketing Management*, November–December 2008, pp. 24–29.

11. Rebecca Ellinor, "Crowd Pleaser," *Supply Management*, December 13, 2007, pp. 26–29; and information from www.loreal.com/_en/_ww/html/suppliers/index.aspx, accessed August 2010.

12. See www.nikebiz.com/company_overview/, accessed July 2010.

13. "100 Leading National Advertisers," *Advertising Age*, June 21, 2010, p. 10.

14. The four Ps classification was first suggested by E. Jerome McCarthy, *Basic Marketing: A Managerial Approach* (Homewood, IL: Irwin, 1960). For the 4Cs, other proposed classifications, and more discussion, see Robert Lauterborn, "New Marketing Litany: 4P's Passé C-Words Take Over," *Advertising Age*, October 1, 1990, p. 26; Phillip Kotler, "Alphabet Soup," *Marketing Management*, March–April 2006, p. 51; Nirmalya Kumer, "The CEO's Marketing Manifesto," *Marketing Management*, November/December 2008, pp. 24–29; and Roy McClean, Marketing 101—4 C's versus the 4 P's of Marketing," www.customfitfocus.com/marketing-1.htm, accessed July 2010.

15. For more discussion of the chief marketing officer position, see Philip Kotler and Kevin Lane Keller, *Marketing Management*, 13th ed., pp. 11–12; Terry H. Grapentine and David Dwight, "Lay the Foundation for CMO Success," *Marketing Management*, May/June 2009, pp. 24–30; and Todd Wasserman, "The Evolving CMO," *AdweekMedia*, June 8, 2009, p. 13.

16. Adapted from information found in Diane Brady, "Making Marketing Measure Up," *BusinessWeek*, December 13, 2004, pp. 112–113; Gray Hammond, "You Gotta Be Accountable," *Strategy*, December 2008, p. 48; and Kate Maddox, "Optimism, Accountability, Social Media Top Trends," *BtoB*, January 18, 2010, p. 1.

17. See Kenneth Hein, "CMOs Pressured to Show ROI," *Brandweek*, December 12, 2008, p. 6; Lance Richard, "The Paradox of ROI and Decreased Spending in the Ad Industry," *American Journal of Business*, Fall 2009, www.bsu.edu/mcobwin/majb/?p=599; and Kevin J. Clancy and Peter C. Krieg, "Getting a Grip," *Marketing Management*, Spring 2010, pp. 18–23.

18. Mark McMaster, "ROI: More Vital Than Ever," *Sales & Marketing Management*, January 2002, pp. 51–52. Also see Steven H. Seggie, Erin Cavusgil, and Steven Phelan, "Measurement of Return on Marketing Investment: A Conceptual Framework and the Future of Marketing Metrics," *Industrial Marketing Management*, August 2007, pp. 834–841; and David Armano, "The New Focus Group: The Collective," *BusinessWeek*, January 8, 2009, accessed at www.businessweek.com/innovate/content/jan2009/id2009017_198183.htm.

19. See Hein, "CMOs Pressured to Show ROI," p. 6; Hammond, "You Gotta Be Accountable," p. 48; and Lawrence A. Crosby, "Getting Serious about Marketing ROI," *Marketing Management*, May/June 2009, pp. 10–11.

20. See "We Believe Research Should Lead to Action," *Marketing News*, November 15, 2009, p. 30.

21. For a full discussion of this model and details on customer-centered measures of return on marketing investment, see Roland T. Rust, Katherine N. Lemon, and Valerie A. Zeithaml, "Return on Marketing: Using Customer Equity to Focus Marketing Strategy," *Journal of Marketing*, January 2004, pp. 109–127; Roland T. Rust, Katherine N. Lemon, and Das Narayandas, *Customer Equity Management* (Upper Saddle River, NJ: Prentice Hall, 2005); Roland T. Rust, "Seeking Higher ROI? Base Strategy on Customer Equity," *Advertising Age*, September 10, 2007, pp. 26–27; Thorsen Wiesel, Bernd Skiera, and Julián Villanueva, "Customer Equity: An Integral Part of Financial Reporting," *Journal of Marketing*, March 2008, pp. 1–14.

22. Elizabeth A. Sullivan, "Measure Up," *Marketing News*, May 30, 2009, pp. 8–17; and "Marketing Strategy: Diageo CMO: 'Workers Must Be Able to Count,'" *Marketing Week*, June 3, 2010, p. 5.

Chapter 3

1. Quotes and other information from or adapted from Richard Waters, "Xerox Chief Sets Out the Big Picture," *Financial Times*, May 6, 2010, p. 16; "Copy This Advice: Xerox's CEO Says 'Let's Get Personal,'" *Marketing News*, October 15, 2008, pp. 18–19; Geoff Colvin, "Ursula Burns Launches Xerox into the Future," *Fortune*, May 3, 2010, p. 5; William M. Bulkeley, "Xerox Tries to Go Beyond Copiers," *Wall Street Journal*, February 24, 2009, p. B5; and annual reports and other information at www.xerox.com, accessed October 2010.

2. "Copy This Advice: Xerox's CEO Says 'Let's Get Personal,'" p. 18.

3. Quotes and other information from Jeffery K. Liker and Thomas Y. Choi, "Building Deep Supplier Relationships," *Harvard Business Review*, December 2004, pp. 104–113; Lindsay Chappell, "Toyota Aims to Satisfy Its Suppliers," *Automotive News*, February 21, 2005, p. 10; and David Hannon, "Automotive Rebrands Procurement," *Purchasing*, March 11, 2010, p. 45; and www.toyotasupplier.com, accessed November 2010.

4. Information from Robert J. Benes, Abbie Jarman, and Ashley Williams, "2007 NRA Sets Records," at www.chefmagazine.com, accessed September 2007; and www.thecoca-colacompany.com/presscenter/presskit_fs.html and www.cokesolutions.com, accessed November 2010.

5. See "About Tide Loads of Hope," www.tide.com/en-US/loads-of-hope/about.jspx, accessed November 2010.

6. World POPClock, U.S. Census Bureau, at www.census.gov, accessed August 2010. This Web site provides continuously updated projections of the U.S. and world populations.

7. See Clay Chandler, "Little Emperors," *Fortune*, October 4, 2004, pp. 138–150; "China's 'Little Emperors,'" *Financial Times*, May 5, 2007, p. 1; "Me Generation Finally Focuses on US," *Chinadaily.com.cn*, August 27, 2008, www.chinadaily.com.cn/china/2008-08/27/content_6972930.htm; Melinda Varley, "China: Chasing the Dragon," *Brand Strategy*, October 6, 2008, p. 26; Clifford Coonan, "New Rules to Enforce Chain's One-Child Policy," *Irish Times*, January 14, 2009, p. 12; and David Pilling, "Reflections of Life in China's Fast Lane," *Financial Times*, April 19, 2010, p. 10.

8. Adapted from information in Janet Adamy, "Different Brew: Eyeing a Billion Tea Drinkers, Starbucks Pours It On in China," *Wall Street Journal*, November 29, 2006, p. A1; and Justine Lau, "Coffee, the New Tea?" *Financial Times*, July 2, 2010, p. 6.

9. U.S. Census Bureau projections and POPClock Projection, at www.census.gov, accessed August 2010.

10. Noreen O'Leary, "Squeeze Play," *Adweek*, January 12, 2009, pp. 8–9; David Court, "The Downturn's New Rules for Marketers," *The McKinsey Quarterly*, December 2008, accessed at www.mckinseyquarterly.com/the_downturn_new_rules_for_marketers_2262; Emily Brandon, "Planning to Retire: 10 Things You Didn't Know about Baby Boomers," *USNews.com*, January 15, 2009, accessed at http://money.usnews.com; and Iris Taylor, "Impact of Baby Boomers Delaying Retirement Explored," *McClatchy-Tribune Business News*, April 5, 2010.

11. Emily Brandon, "Planning to Retire: 10 Things You Didn't Know about Baby Boomers"; and Rick Ferguson and Bill Brohaugh, "The Aging of Core Areas," *Journal of Consumer Marketing*, Vol. 27, No. 1, 2010, p. 76.

12. See Simon Hudson, "Wooing Zoomers: Marketing to the Mature Traveler," *Marketing Intelligence & Planning*, Vol. 28, No. 4, 2010, pp. 444–461.

13. Hudson, "Wooing Zoomers: Marketing to the Mature Traveler."

14. Dee Depass, "Designed with a Wink, Nod at Boomers," *Minneapolis-St. Paul Star Tribune*, April 1, 2006, p. 1. Also see Linda Stern, "It's Not All Downhill," *Newsweek*, December 1, 2008, www.newsweek.com/2008/11/30/it-s-not-all-downhill.html; and Sheldon Marks, "Empty Nests and Full Purses Make Boomer Women Prime Marketing Targets," *National Jeweler*, May 16, 2010, p. 60.

15. Based on information from Todd Wasserman, "Merrill Lynch Asks Jittery Boomers to Vent Via Text," *Brandweek*, January 25, 2010, www.brandweek.com; and Tanya Irwin, "Merrill Lynch Launches $20 Million Effort," *MediaPostNews*, January 27, 2010, accessed at www.mediapost.com/publications/?fa=Articles.showArticle&art_aid=121313.

16. For more discussion, see R. K. Miller and Kelli Washington, *Consumer Behavior 2009* (Atlanta, GA: Richard K. Miller & Associates, 2009), chapter 27.

17. Based on information found in Donna C. Gregory, "Virginia Tourism Corp. Marketing to Generation X," December 29, 2009, www.virginiabusiness.com/index.php/news/article/romancing-generation-x. Also see www.virginia.org/home.asp, accessed November 2010.

18. R. K. Miller and Kelli Washington, *Consumer Behavior 2009*; and Piet Levy, "The Quest for Cool," *Marketing News*, February 28, 2009, p. 6.

19. Jessica Tsai, "Who, What, Where, When, Y," *Customer Relationship Management*, November 2008, pp. 24–28; and John Austin, "Automakers Try to Reach Gen Y: Carmakers Look for New Marketing Approaches, Technological Advances to Attract Millennials," *McClatchy-Tribune Business News*, February 1, 2009.

20. Example adapted from Peter Feld, "What Obama Can Teach You about Millennial Marketing," *Advertising Age*, August 11, 2008, p. 1; Eric Greenberg and Karl Weber, "Why the Youth Vote Is the Big Story—for 2008 and for Decades to Come," *Huffington Post*, January 15, 2009, www.huffingtonpost.com/eric-greenberg-and-karl-weber/why-the-youth-vote-is-the_b_158273.html; Andrew Hampp, "Inauguration Pairing a Watershed Moment," *Advertising Age*, March 30, 2009, p. 12; and www.barackobama.com, accessed May 2010.

21. See U.S. Census Bureau, "Families and Living Arrangements: 2009," at www.census.gov/population/www/socdemo/hh-fam.html, accessed May 2010.

22. U.S. Census Bureau, "Families and Living Arrangements: 2009"; "Census Bureau News—2009 America's Families and Living Arrangements," *PR Newswire*, January 15, 2010; and U.S. Census Bureau, "Facts for Features," March 2010, accessed at https://www.census.gov/newsroom/releases/archives/facts_for_features_special_editions/cb10-ff03.html.

23. See Marissa Miley and Ann Mack, "The New Female Consumer: The Rise of the Real Mom," *Advertising Age*, November 16, 2009, p. A1.

24. U.S. Census Bureau, "Geographical Mobility/Migration," at www.census.gov/population/www/socdemo/migrate.html, accessed April 2010.

25. See U.S. Census Bureau, "Metropolitan and Micropolitan Statistical Areas," www.census.gov/population/www/estimates/aboutmetro.html, accessed January 2010; Gordon F. Mulligan and Alexander C. Vias, "Growth and Change in Micropolitan Areas," *The Annals of Regional Science*, June 2006, p. 203; and Madeline Johnson, "Devilish Definitions as Urban Masses Evolve, New Terms and Labels Are Emerging to Try to Describe and Distinguish Them," *Financial Times*, December 29, 2007.

26. Jennifer Schramm, "At Work in the Virtual World," *HRMagazine*, June 2010, p. 152; and Marcia Heroux Pounds, "$400 Billion Savings Could Result from Telework, Report Says," *McClatchy-Tribune Business News*, May 19, 2010.

27. See "About WebEx," at www.webex.com/about-webex/index.html, accessed November 2010.

28. U.S. Census Bureau, "Educational Attainment," at www.census.gov/population/www/socdemo/educ-attn.html, accessed April 2010.

29. See U.S. Census Bureau, *The 2010 Statistical Abstract: Labor Force, Employment, and Earnings,"* table 603, accessed at www.census.gov/compendia/statab/cats/labor_force_employment_earnings.html; and U.S. Department of Labor, *Occupational Outlook Handbook, 2010–11 Edition*, accessed at www.bls.gov/oco/.

30. See U.S. Census Bureau, "U.S. Population Projections," www.census.gov/population/www/projections/summarytables.html, accessed August 2010; and "Characteristics of the Foreign-Born Population by Nativity and US Citizenship Status," www.census.gov/population/www/socdemo/foreign/cps2008.html.

31. Based on "Hispanic Creative Advertising Awards: TV Silver Winners," *Advertising Age*, September 19, 2009, p. 36; and Jean Halliday, "Courageous Clients: Steve Neder," *Advertising Age*, September 19, 2009, p. 36.

32. For these and other statistics, see Witeck-Combs Communications, "Buying Power of Gay Men and Lesbians in 2008," June 2008; www.rivendellmedia.com/ngng/executive_summary/NGNG.PPT and www.gaymarket.com/ngng/ngng_reader.html, accessed April 2009; and Paul Morrissette, "Market to LGBT Community," *American Agent & Broker*, July 2010, p. 50.

33. See Brandon Miller, "And the Winner Is . . ." *Out Traveler*, Winter 2008, pp. 64–65; and www.aa.com/rainbow, accessed August 2010.

34. Andrew Adam Newman, "Web Marketing to a Segment Too Big to Be a Niche," *New York Times*, October 30, 2007, p. 9; Kenneth Hein, "The Invisible Demographic," *Brandweek*, March 3, 2008, p. 20; and Tanya Mohn, "Smoothing the Way," *New York Times*, April 26, 2010, www.nytimes.com.

35. See Chris Taylor, "Opening New Worlds: The Disability Boom," *Fortune Small Business*, September 15, 2008, http://money.cnn.com/2008/09/11/smallbusiness/disability_boom.fsb/index.htm; and information from Ford, July 2009; and www.disaboom.com, accessed August 2010.

36. Gavin Rabinowitz, "India's Tata Motors Unveils $2,500 Car, Bringing Car Ownership within Reach of Millions," *Associated Press*, January 10, 2008; Jessica Scanlon, "What Can Tata's Nano Teach Detroit?" *BusinessWeek*, March 19, 2009, accessed at www.businessweek.com/innovate/content/mar2009/id20090318_012120.htm; Mark Phelan, "Engineers Study the Magic Behind Tata Nano," *Pittsburgh Tribune Review*, April 17, 2010, http://www.pittsburghlive.com; and http://tatanano.inservices.tatamotors.com/tatamotors/nano_brochure.pdf, accessed August 2010.

37. Noreen O'Leary, "Squeeze Play," *Adweek*, January 12, 2009, pp. 8–9. Also see Alessandra Stanley, "For Hard Times, Softer Sells," *New York Times*, February 6, 2009, www.nytimes.com; and Kenneth Hein, "Why Price Isn't Everything," *Brandweek*, March 2, 2009, p. 6.

38. U.S. Census Bureau, "Income, Poverty, and Health Insurance Coverage in the United States: 2008," September 2009, table 3, www.census.gov/prod/2009pubs/p60-236.pdf.

39. Christopher Muther, "Designer Alex Carleton Has Been Handed a Tall Order: Give Maine-Based L.L.Bean Some Edge," *Boston Globe*, October 29, 2009, p. G18.

40. Andrew Zolli, "Business 3.0," *Fast Company*, March 2007, pp. 64–70.

41. See www.ge.com and www.getransportation.com/na/en/hybrid.html, accessed August 2010.

42. Facts from www.pepsico.com/Purpose/Environmental-Sustainability.html, accessed November 2010.

43. See David Blanchard, "The Five Stages of RFID," *Industry Week*, January 2009, p. 50; Mary Hayes Weier, "Slow and Steady Progress,"

InformationWeek, November 16, 2009, p. 31; and information at www.autoidlabs.org, accessed August 2010.

44. See "Martin Grueber, "Re-Emerging U.S. R&D," *R&D Mag,* December 22, 2009, www.rdmag.com/Featured-Articles/2009/12/Policy-and-Industry-Re-Emerging-U-S-R-D/.

45. See Elaine Wong, "Q&A: Pepsi's Ana Maria Irazabal," *Adweek,* June 9, 2010, accessed at www.adweek.com; and www.refresheverything .com, accessed August 2010.

46. See "The Growth of Cause Marketing," at www.causemarketingforum .com/page.asp?ID=188, accessed November 2010.

47. Karen Von Hahn, "Plus ça Change: Get Set for Cocooning 2.0," *Globe and Mail* (Toronto), January 3, 2008, p. L1; and Liza N. Burby, "Tips for Making Your Home a Cozy Nest, or 'Hive,'" *Newsday,* January 23, 2009, www.newsday.com.

48. Based on information from Beth Snyder Bulik, "Stay-at-Home Trend Feathers Samsung Nest," *Advertising Age,* November 3, 2008, p. 18: and Alessandra Stanley, "For Hard Times, Softer Sells," *New York Times,* February 6, 2009.

49. Laura Feldmann, "After 9/11 Highs, America's Back to Good Ol' Patriotism," *Christian Science Monitor,* July 5, 2006, p. 1; and "Lifestyle Statistics: Very Proud of Their Nationality," at www .nationmaster.com, accessed April 2010.

50. Sarah Mahoney. "Report: LOHAS Market Nears $300 Billion," *Marketing Daily,* April 26, 2010, www.mediapost.com/publications/ ?art_aid=126836&fa=Articles.showArticle; and www.lohas.com, accessed November 2010.

51. Information from "Food to Live By," Earthbound Farm 2010 media kit, at www.ebfarm.com/AboutUs/EarthboundFarm-2010MediaKit.pdf, accessed August 2010; and "Earthbound Farms, Inc.," *BNET,* accessed at www.bnet.com/company/earthbound+farm+inc. August 2010.

52. See Organic Trade Association, "U.S. Organic Product Sales Reach $26.6 Billion in 2009," April 22, 2010, www.organicnewsroom.com.

53. The Pew Forum on Religion & Public Life, "U.S. Religious Landscape Survey," http://religions.pewforum.org/reports#, accessed August 2010.

54. Dan Harris, "America Is Becoming Less Christian, Less Religious," *ABC News,* March 9, 2009, accessed at http://abcnews.go.com.

55. W. Chan Kim and Renée Mauborgne, "How Strategy Shaped Structure," *Harvard Business Review,* September 2009, pp. 73–80.

56. Based on information found at www.breakthechain.org/exclusives/ oscarmayer.html and www.kraftfoods.com, accessed November 2009. Also see David Emery, "Urban Legend: Oscar Meyer Refuses to Send Hotdogs to Marines," *About.com,* at http:// urbanlegends.about.com/od/business/a/oscar_mayer.htm, accessed August 2010.

Chapter 4

1. Quotes and other information from Christina Saunders and Liza Martindale, "Tide Celebrates the Diverse, Individual Style of Americans in New Advertising Campaign," P&G press release, January 20, 2010, http://multivu.prnewswire.com/mnr/tide/ 42056/; Elaine Wong, "Marketer of the Year: Team Tide," *Adweek,* September 14, 2009, p. 20; "Case Study: Tide Knows Fabrics Best," *ARF Ogilvy Awards,* 2007, accessed at http://thearf.org; Stuart Elliot, "A Campaign Linking Clean Clothes with Stylish Living," *New York Times,* January 8, 2010, p. B3; and "P&G: Our Purpose, Values, and Principles," www.pg.com/company/who_we_are/ ppv.jhtml, accessed November 2010.

2. Unless otherwise noted, quotes in this section are from the excellent discussion of customer insights found in Mohanbir Sawhney, "Insights into Customer Insights," www.redmond.nl/hro/upload/ Insights_into_Customer_Insights.pdf, accessed April 2009. The Apple iPod example is also adapted from this article. Also see "Corporate News: Demands for Macs, iPhones Fuels Apple," *Wall Street Journal Asia,* January 27, 2010, p. 22.

3. Alan Mitchell, "Consumer Data Gathering Has Changed from Top to Bottom," *Marketing,* August 12, 2009, pp. 26–27.

4. Carey Toane, "Listening: The New Metric," *Strategy,* September 2009, p. 45.

5. Warren Thayer and Michael Sansolo, "Walmart: Our Retailer of the Year," *R&FF Retailer,* June 2009, pp. 14–20.

6. Ian C. MacMillan and Larry Seldon, "The Incumbent's Advantage," *Harvard Business Review,* October 2008, pp. 111–121.

7. Arianne Cohen, "Barneys and Friend," *Fast Company,*" May 2008, www.fastcompany.com/magazine/125/barneys-and-friend.html. See also Alex Wright, "Mining the Web for Feelings, Not Facts," *New York Times,* August 24, 2009, www.nytimes.com.

8. Example based on information from "PacSun to Surf the Social Web with Radian6," Radian6 press release, March 24, 2009, www .radian6.com/blog/2009/03/pacsun-set-to-surf-the-social-web-with-radian6/; Jessica Tsai, "Taking the Measure of Social Media," *Customer Relationship Management,* July 2009, pp. 17–18; "Microsoft and Radian6: Tools, Analytics, and Strategy," October 5, 2009, www .radian6.com and www.Radian6.com, accessed November 2010.

9. For more on research firms that supply marketing information, see Jack Honomichl, "Honomichl Top 50," special section, *Marketing News,* June 30, 2009. Other information from http://en-us.nielsen. com/expertise; www.smrb.com/web/guest/core-solutions/ national-consumer-study; and www.yankelovich.com, accessed August 2010.

10. See http://symphonyiri.com/?TabId=159&productid=84 accessed June 2010.

11. Example adapted Dana Flavelle, "Kraft Goes inside the Kitchen of the Canadian Family," *Toronto Star,* January 16, 2010, www.thestar. com/business/article/751507.

12. See Pradeep K. Tyagi, "Webnography: A New Tool to Conduct Marketing Research," *Journal of American Academy of Business,* March 2010, pp. 262–268.

13. Spencer E. Ante, "The Science of Desire," *BusinessWeek,* June 5, 2006, p. 100; Rhys Blakely, "You Know When It Feels Like Somebody's Watching You . . .," *Times,* May 14, 2007, p. 46; and Jack Neff, "Marketing Execs: Researchers Could Use a Softer Touch," *Advertising Age,* January 27, 2009, http://adage.com/article?article_ id=134144.

14. Emily Spensieri, "A Slow, Soft Touch," *Marketing,* June 5, 2006, pp. 15–16. Also see information at www.femqb.com, accessed February 2010.

15. Jack Neff, "Marketing Execs: Researchers Could Use a Softer Touch," *Advertising Age,* January 27, 2009, http://adage.com/article ?article_id=134144.

16. "E-Rewards Rakes in $60M in New Funding," October 17, 2008, http://dallas.bizjournals.com/dallas/stories/2008/10/20/story5 .html; and Gary Langer, "Study Finds Trouble for Opt-in Internet Surveys," ABCNews.com, September 1, 2009, http://blogs .abcnews.com/thenumbers/2009/09/study-finds-trouble-for-internet-surveys.html.

17. See "Study Finds Trouble for Opt-in Internet Surveys"; and Internet penetration statistics found at www.internetworldstats.com/ stats14.htm, accessed July 2010.

18. Based on information found www.channelm2.com/ HowOnlineQualitativeResearch.html, accessed December 2010.

19. See "Online Panel," www.zoomerang.com/online-panel/, accessed June 2010.

20. Adapted from Jeremy Nedelka, "Adidas Relies on Insiders for Insight," *1to1 Media,* November 9, 2009, www.1to1media.com/ view.aspx?DocID=31963&m=n.

21. Stephen Baker, "The Web Knows What You Want," *BusinessWeek,* July 27, 2009, p. 48.

22. For more on Internet privacy, see "What Would You Reveal on the Internet?" *Privacy Journal,* January 2009, p. 1; Jayne O'Donnell, "Cookies Sound Sweet, But They Can Be Risky," *USA Today,* October 26, 2009, www.usatoday.com; and James Temple, "All Eyes on Online Privacy," *San Francisco Chronicle,* January 29, 2010, p. D1.

23. Adapted from Brooks Barnes, "Lab Watches Web Surfers to See Which Ads Work," *New York Times*, July 26, 2009.

24. Jessica Tsai, "Are You Smarter Than a Neuromarketer?" *Customer Relationship Management*, January 2010, pp. 19–20.

25. This and the other neuromarketing examples are adapted from Laurie Burkitt, "Neuromarketing: Companies Use Neuroscience for Consumer Insights," *Forbes*, November 16, 2009, www.forbes.com/forbes/2009/1116/marketing-hyundai-neurofocus-brain-waves-battle-for-the-brain.html.

26. See Barney Beal, "Gartner: CRM Spending Looking Up," *SearchCRM.com*, April 29, 2008, http://searchcrm.techtarget.com/news/article/0,289142,sid11_gci1311658,00.html; David White, "CRM Magazine Announces Winners of 2009 CRM Service Awards," *Business Wire*, April 1, 2009; and "Research and Markets: Global Customer Relationship Management (CRM) Sales Automation Software Market 2008–2012," *M2 Presswire*, January 14, 2010.

27. Mike Freeman, "Data Company Helps Walmart, Casinos, Airlines Analyze Customers," *San Diego Union Tribune*, February 24, 2006, http://ww.uniontrib.com/uniontrib/20060224/news_1b24teradata.html. For another good CRM example, see "SAS Helps 1-800-Flowers.com Grow Deep Roots with Customers," http://www.sas.com/success/1800flowers.html, accessed February 2010.

28. Example adapted from information found in Dan Sewell, "Kroger User Shopper Data to Target Coupons," *Huffington Post*, January 6, 2009, www.huffingtonpost.com/2009/01/06/kroger-uses-shopper-data_n_155667.html. Also see Chris Blackhurst, "Tesco at Top of Its Game As Leahy Plays His Cards Right," December 14, 2009, www.thisislondon.co.uk/standard-business/article-23783269-tesco-at-top-of-its-game-as-leahy-plays-his-cards-right.do.

29. Gillian S. Ambroz, "CRM: Getting Back to Basics," *Folio*, January 2010, p. 97.

30. "SAS helps 1-800-Flowers.com Grow Deep Roots with Customers," www.sas.com/success/1800flowers.html, accessed February 2010.

31. See "Penske Launches Improved Extranet," *Refrigerated Transporter*, March 2009, p. 47; and information found at www.pensketruckleasing.com/leasing/precision/precision_features.html, accessed September 2010.

32. Adapted from information in Ann Zimmerman, "Small Business; Do the Research," *Wall Street Journal*, May 9, 2005, p. R3; with information from John Tozzi, "Market Research on the Cheap," *BusinessWeek*, January 9, 2008, www.businessweek.com/smallbiz/content/jan2008/sb2008019_352779.htm; and www.bibbentuckers.com, accessed July 2010.

33. Zimmerman, "Small Business; Do the Research," *Wall Street Journal*, p. R3.

34. For some good advice on conducting market research in a small business, see "Marketing Research . . . Basics 101," www.sba.gov/smallbusinessplanner/index.html, accessed August 2010; and "Researching Your Market," U.S. Small Business Administration, www.sba.gov/idc/groups/public/documents/sba_homepage/pub_mt8.pdf, accessed November 2010.

35. See www.nielsen.com/, accessed July 2010.

36. Internet stats are from www.worldbank.org/, accessed July 2010. Also see www.iwcp.hpg.ig.com.br/communications.html, accessed February 2010.

37. Subhash C. Jain, *International Marketing Management*, 3rd ed. (Boston: PWS-Kent, 1990), p. 338. For more discussion on international marketing research issues and solutions, see Warren J. Keegan and Mark C. Green, *Global Marketing*, 6th ed. (Upper Saddle River, NJ: Prentice Hall, 2011) pp. 170–201.

38. See Stephanie Clifford, "Many See Privacy on the Web as Big Issue, Survey Says," *New York Times*, March 16, 2009, www.nytimes.com; and Mark Davis, "Behavioral Targeting of Online Ads Is Growing," *McClatchy-Tribune Business News*, December 19, 2009. Also see "Consumers Encouraged to Protect Their Privacy Online," *PR Newswire*, January 27, 2010.

39. "ICC/ESOMAR International Code of Marketing and Social Research Practice," www.esomar.org/index.php/codes-guidelines.html, accessed July 2010. Also see "Respondent Bill of Rights," www.mra-net.org/ga/billofrights.cfm, accessed November 2010.

40. See Jaikumar Vijayan, "Disclosure Laws Driving Data Privacy Efforts, Says IBM Exec," *Computerworld*, May 8, 2006, p. 26; "Facebook Chief Privacy Officer—Interview," *Analyst Wire*, February 18, 2009; and Rita Zeidner, "New Face in the C-Cuite," *HRMagazine*, January 2010, pp. 39–41.

41. Federal Trade Commission, "Kellogg Settles FTC Charges That Ads for Frosted Mini-Wheats Were False," April 20, 2009, www.ftc.gov/opa/2009/04/kellogg.shtm; Kellogg's Frosted Mini-Wheats Neuroscience: The FTC Reckoning," http://rangelife.typepad.com/rangelife/2009/04/kelloggs-frosted-miniwheats-neuro-science-the-ftc-reckoning.html, April 21, 2009; and Todd Wasserman, "New FTC Asserts Itself," *Brandweek*, April 27, 2009, p. 8.

42. Information at http://www.casro.org/codeofstandards.cfm#intro, accessed December 2010.

Chapter 5

1. Jefferson Graham, "Apple Reports Best Earnings Ever," *USA Today*, January 26, 2010, p. B1; "Macolyte," *Urban Dictionary*, www.urbandictionary.com/define.php?term=Macolyte, accessed October 2010; Katie Hafner, "Inside Apple Stores, a Certain Aura Enchants the Faithful," *New York Times*, December 27, 2007, www.nytimes.com/2007/12/27/business/27apple.html; "Apple," the American Consumer Satisfaction Index, www.theacsi.org/index.php?option=com_content&task=view&id=149&Itemid=157&c=Apple+, accessed March 2010; Steve Maich, "Nowhere to Go But Down," *Maclean's*, May 9, 2005, p. 32; Steven H. Wildstrom, "The Stubborn Luxury of Apple," *BusinessWeek*, November 23, 2009, p. 82; Adam Lashinsky, "The Decade of Steve," *Fortune*, November 23, 2009, pp. 93–114; Philip Michaels, "Apple: What Recession?" *MacWorld*, January 2010, p. 16; and financial information found at www.apple.com, accessed May 2010.

2. GDP figures from *The World Fact Book*, April 2, 2010, https://www.cia.gov/library/publications/the-world-factbook/index.html; and "Research and Markets: Evaluate the U.S. Consumer Behavior 2010 Market: Accounting for 71% of the U.S. Gross Domestic Product, or Over $10 Trillion," *Business Wire*, December 18, 2009. Population figures from the World POPClock, U.S. Census Bureau, www.census.gov/main/www/popclock.html, accessed May 2010. This Web site provides continuously updated projections of U.S. and world populations.

3. Don E. Schultz, "Lines or Circles" *Marketing News*, November 5, 2007, p. 21; and Elizabeth A. Sullivan, "Pick Your Brain," *Marketing News*, March 15, 2009, pp. 10–13.

4. See U.S. "Hispanic Spending Growth Dwarfs the General Market," *PRNewswire*, January 5, 2010; and Noreen O'Leary, "Latin Flavor," *Next*, November 2, 2009, pp. 10–11. For detailed information on the buying power of the subcultures discussed in this section see Jeffrey M. Humphreys, *The Multicultural Economy 2008* (Athens, GA: Selig Center for Economic Growth, 2008), www.terry.uga.edu/selig/buying_power.html.

5. Jonathan Birchall, "Walmart Focuses on Smaller Format," *Financial Times*, October 19, 2009, p. 18; and "Burger King Wraps Up Its Annual FÚTBOL KINGDOM National Tour with Scores of Success," *BusinessWire*, December 10, 2009.

6. Adapted from information found in Della de Lafuente, "The New Weave," *Adweek*, March 3, 2008, pp. 26–28; with additional information from "Latino Subcultures: A Rising Force of Cultural Inspiration," Conill, http://conill.com/assets/whitepapers/Latino_Subcultures_Booklet_low.pdf, accessed March 2010. For lots of other good examples, see "Hispanic Creative Advertising Awards," *Advertising Age*, September 21, 2009, pp. 31–38.

7. See Todd Wasserman, "Report Shows Are Shifting African-American Population," *Brandweek*, January 11, 2000, p. 6; R. Thomas Umstead, "BET: African-Americans Grow in Numbers, Buying Power,"

January 26, 2010, www.multichannel.com/article/446028-BET_African_Americans_Grow_in_Numbers_Buying_Power.php; and Mark Dolliver, "How to Reach Affluent African Americans," *Adweek*, February 2, 2010, www.adweek.com/aw/content_display/news/strategy/e3i8decb5ca03594f57dadfad445ed35524; and U.S. Census Bureau reports, www.census.gov, accessed February 2010.

8. See "Top 10 Advertisers across All African American Media," *Adweek*, February 9, 2009, p. 16; and "About the Covergirl Queen Collection," www.covergirl.com/products/collections/queen/, accessed April 2010.

9. Michael Bush, "P&G Unveils 'My Black Is Beautiful,' Campaign," *PRweek*, December 3, 2007; David Holthaus, "P&G, BET Team Up on TV," *Cincinnati Enquirer*, January 22, 2009, www.cincinnati.com; Kelly Parker, "Capturing the Essence of 'My Black Is Beautiful' Campaign," *Louisiana Weekly*, July 13–19, 2009, www.louisianaweekly.com/news.php?viewStory=1557; and www.myblackisbeautiful.com, accessed November 2010.

10. See Lynn Russo Whylly, "Marketing to Asian Americans," advertising supplement to *Brandweek*, May 26, 2008, pp. S1–S3; Jeffrey M. Humphreys, *The Multicultural Economy 2008*; and U.S. Census Bureau reports www.census.gov, accessed October 2010.

11. Bill Imada, "Why State Farm Tries to Be a Good Neighbor to Asian American Community," *Advertising Age*, September 1, 2009, http://adage.com/bigtent/post?article_id=138735; and Imada, "Top 10 Corporate Marketers in the U.S. Asian Market in 2009," *Advertising Age*, January 20, 2010, http://adage.com/bigtent/post?article_id=141595.

12. See Gene Epstein, "Boomer Consumer," *Barron's*, October 5, 2009, http://online.barrons.com/article/SB125452437207860627.html; Stuart Elliott, "The Older Audiences Looking Better Than Ever," *New York Times*, April 20, 2009, www.nytimes.com/2009/04/20/business/20adcol.html; Ellen Byron, Seeing Store Shelves through Senior Eyes," *Wall Street Journal*, September 14, 2009, p. B1; and Brent Bouchez, "Super Bowl Ads Need to Age Gracefully," *BusinessWeek*, February, 2010, www.businessweek.com/bwdaily/dnflash/content/feb2010/db2010028_715748.htm.

13. Elliott, "The Older Audiences Looking Better Than Ever."

14. "Boom Time of America's New Retirees Feel Entitled to Relax—and Intend to Spend," *Financial Times*, December 6, 2007, p. 9.

15. Mark Dolliver, "Marketing to Today's 65-Plus Consumers," *Adweek*, July 27, 2009, www.adweek.com/aw/content_display/news/client/e3i4d0a69ad29e1cca567f0f1f59beac1f7?imw=Y.

16. "Research Reveals Word-of-Mouth Campaigns on Customer Networks Double Marketing Results," *Business Wire*, October 27, 2009.

17. See "JetBlue Lovers Unite to Share Brand Perks with Peers," WOOMA Case, www.womma.org/casestudy/examples/create-an-evangelism-program/jetblue-lovers-unite-to-share/, accessed March 2010; Joan Voigt, "The New Brand Ambassadors," *Adweek*, December 31, 2007, pp. 18–19, 26; Rebecca Nelson, "A Citizen Marketer Talks," *Adweek*, December 31, 2007, p. 19; Holly Shaw, "Buzzing Influencers," *National Post*, March 13, 2009, pp. FP 12; and information from www.repnation.com, accessed October 2010.

18. See Brian Morrissey, "Social Rings," *Brandweek*, January 18, 2010, p. 20.

19. Beth Krietsch, "YouTube Channel for Congress Builds Dialogue, Transparency," *PR Week*, January 19, 2009, p. 9; "*Death* of TV Advertising," *Business and Finance*, June 24, 2008; Samir Balwani, "Presenting: 10 of the Smartest Big Brands in Social Media," *Mashable*, February 6, 2009, http://mashable.com/2009/02/06/social-media-smartest-brands/; and Gerald C. Kane and others, "Community Relations 2.0," *Harvard Business Review*, November 2009, pp. 45–50; and "Harnessing the Power of Online Marketing and Social Media," *Business Wire*, January 25, 2010.

20. See Eleftheria Parpis, "She's in Charge," *Adweek*, October 6–13, 2008, p. 38; Abigail Posner, "Why Package-Goods Companies Should Market to Men," *Advertising Age*, February 9, 2009,

http://adage.com/print?article_id=134473; and Marissa Miley and Ann Mark, "The New Female Consumer: The Rise of the Real Mom," *Advertising Age*, November 16, 2009, pp. A1–A27.

21. Adapted from Michel Marriott, "Gadget Designers Take Aim at Women," *New York Times*, June 7, 2007, p. C7. Also see Dean Takahashi, "Philips Focuses on TVs Women Buyers," *McClatchy-Tribune Business News*, January 6, 2008.

22. Examples from Michael J. Silverstein and Kate Sayre, "The Female Economy"; and Andrea Learned and Carolyn Hadlock, "Reaching Recession Dads," *Adweek*, June 15, 2009, p. AM20.

23. R. K. Miller and Kelli Washington, *Consumer Behavior 2009* (Atlanta, GA: Richard K. Miller & Associates, 2009), chapter 27. Also see Michael R. Sullivan, *Consumer Behavior: Buying, Having, and Being* (Upper Saddle River, New Jersey: Prentice Hall, 2011), pp. 439–445.

24. Ron Ruggless, "Casual Chains Cater to Kids as Way to Lure *Back* Families," *Nation's Restaurant News*, July 13, 2009, pp. 1, 29–30.

25. For this quote and other information on Acxiom's PersonicX segmentation system, see "Acxiom Study Reveals Insight on Evolving Consumer Shopping Behaviors in Trying Economic Times," www.acxiom.com/news/press_releases/2009/Pages/AcxiomStudyRevealsInsightsonEvolvingConsumerShoppingBehaviorsinTryingEconomicTimes.aspx; accessed January 13, 2009; "Acxiom Study Offers Insight into Leisure Travelers Who Still Spend Freely Despite a Down Economy," *Business Wire*, November 18, 2009; and "Acxiom PersonicX" and "Intelligent Solutions for the Travel Industry: Life-Stage Marketing," www.acxiom.com, accessed April 2010.

26. Quotes and examples from www.carhartt.com, July 2010.

27. Quotes from Kenneth Hein, "Target Tries Price Point Play," *Adweek.com*, January 15, 2009, www.adweek.com/aw/content_display/creative/news/e3i0b84325122066ed9830db4ccb41e7ecf; and "Target Introduces The Great Save," *Business Wire*, January 4, 2010.

28. Beth J. Harpaz, "New Book Connects Political and Lifestyle Choices," November 4, 2006, www.seattlepi.com/lifestyle/291052_lifestylevote04.html. For more on lifestyle and consumer behavior, see Michael R. Solomon, *Consumer Behavior: Buying, Having, and Being* (Upper Saddle River, NJ: Prentice Hall, 2011), pp. 226–233.

29. Based on "Mix It Up," *Home Furnishings Business*, February 2010, pp. 36–40; Laura Compton, "Seducing Us Softly: Why Women Love Anthropologie," *San Francisco* and *Chronicle*, September 12, 2004, www.sfgate.com/cgi-bin/article.cgi?f=/c/a/2004/09/12/CMG1L890631.DTL; with information from http://urbanoutfittersinc.com, accessed November 2010.

30. See Jennifer Aaker, "Dimensions of Measuring Brand Personality," *Journal of Marketing Research*, August 1997, pp. 347–356; Kevin Lane Keller, *Strategic Brand Management*, 3rd ed. (Upper Saddle River, New Jersey, 2008), pp. 66–67; and Vanitha Swaminathan, Karen M. Stilley, and Rohini Ahluwalla, "When Brand Personality Matters: The Moderating Role of Attachment Styles," *Journal of Consumer Research*, April 2009, pp. 985–1002.

31. See www.apple.com/ca/getamac/ads/, accessed May 2010.

32. See Abraham. H. Maslow, "A Theory of Human Motivation," *Psychological Review*, 50 (1943), pp. 370–396. Also see Maslow, *Motivation and Personality*, 3rd ed. (New York: HarperCollins Publishers, 1987); and Leon G. Schiffman, Leslie Lazar Kanuk, *Consumer Behavior* (Upper Saddle River, NJ: Prentice Hall, 2010), pp. 98–106.

33. See Louise Story, "Anywhere the Eye Can See, It's Now Likely to See an Ad," *New York Times*, January 15, 2007, www.nytimes.com/2007/01/15/business/media/15everywhere.html; Matthew Creamer, "Caught in the Clutter Crossfire: Your Brand," *Advertising Age*, April 1, 2007, p. 35; and Ruth Mortimer, "Consumer Awareness: Getting the Right Attention," *Brand Strategy*, December 10, 2008, p. 55.

34. See Bob Garfield, "'Subliminal' Seduction and Other Urban Myths," *Advertising Age*, September 18, 2000, pp. 4, 105; Lewis Smith, "Subliminal Advertising May Work, But Only If You're Paying Attention," *Times*, March 9, 2007, www.timesonline.co.uk/tol/

news/science/article1490199.ece; and Cahal Milmo, "Power of the Hidden Message Is Revealed," *Independent* (London), September 28, 2009, p. 8.

35. Quotes and information from Yubo Chen and Jinhong Xie, "Online Consumer Review: Word-of-Mouth as a New Element of Marketing Communication Mix," *Management Science*, March 2008, pp. 477–491; "Leo J. Shapiro & Associates: User-Generated Content Three Times More Influential Than TV Advertising on Consumer Purchase Decisions," *Marketing Business Weekly*, December 28, 2008, p. 34; and "Word of Mouth Influences Most Apparel Purchases," *Army/Navy Store & Outdoor Merchandiser*, January 15, 2010, p. 6.

36. See Leon Festinger, *A Theory of Cognitive Dissonance* (Stanford, CA: Stanford University Press, 1957); Cynthia Crossen, "'Cognitive Dissonance' Became a Milestone in the 1950s Psychology," *Wall Street Journal*, December 12, 2006, p. B1; and Anupam Bawa and Purva Kansal, "Cognitive Dissonance and the Marketing of Services: Some Issues," *Journal of Services Research*, October 2008–March 2009, p. 31.

37. The following discussion draws from the work of Everett M. Rogers. See his *Diffusion of Innovations*, 5th ed. (New York: Free Press, 2003).

38. Nick Bunkley, "Hyundai, Using a Safety Net, Wins Market Share," *New York Times*, February 5, 2009; Chris Woodyard and Bruce Horvitz, "GM, Ford Are Latest Offering Help to Those Hit by Job Loss," *USA Today*, April 1, 2009; and "Hyundai Assurance Enhanced for 2010," *PR Newswire*, December 29, 2009.

39. "Two-Thirds of U.S. Consumers Own HDTVs," *Business Wire*, January 28, 2010.

Chapter 6

1. Peter Sanders, "Boeing Overhauls Commercial Planes Unit," *Wall Street Journal*, January 28, 2010, http://online.wsj.com; "Upwards and Onwards; Maiden Flights for Boeing and Airbus," *Economist*, December 19, 2009; p. 117; Peter Sanders, "Long Overdue, Boeing Dreamliner Taxis toward Its First Flight," *Wall Street* Journal, December 7, 2009, p. B1; John Loughmiller, "Boeing's Dreamliner Struggles: Surprise or Predictable," *Design News*, August 2009, p. 44; "All Nippon Airways Orders 10 Boeing Jets," December 21, 2009, www.komonews.com/news/boeing/79848202.html; Peter Sanders, "Boeing Dreamliner to Fly in 2009," *Wall Street Journal*, August 28, 2009, p. B3; Mariko Sanchanta, "Executive Salvages Relationships," *Wall Street Journal Asia*, December 21, 2009, p. 12; "Boeing Company News," *The New York Times*, February 12, 2010, http://topics.nytimes.com/topics/reference/timestopics/index.html; and "Boeing in Brief," January 25, 2010, www.boeing.com.

2. See Theresa Ooi, "Amazing Key to IKEA Success," *Australian*, September 22, 2008; Kerry Capell, "How the Swedish Retailer Became a Global Cult Brand," *BusinessWeek*, November 14, 2005, p. 103; IKEA, *Hoover's Company Records*, April 1, 2010, p. 42925; and information from www.ikea.com, accessed September 2010.

3. This classic categorization was first introduced in Patrick J. Robinson, Charles W. Faris, and Yoram Wind, *Industrial Buying Behavior and Creative Marketing* (Boston: Allyn & Bacon, 1967). Also see James C. Anderson and James A. Narus, *Business Market Management*, 2nd ed. (Upper Saddle River, NJ: Prentice Hall, 2004), chapter 3; and Philip Kotler and Kevin Lane Keller, *Marketing Management*, 13th ed. (Upper Saddle River, NJ: Prentice Hall, 2009), chapter 7.

4. Example adapted from information found in "Nikon Focuses on Supply Chain Innovation—and Makes New Product Distribution a Snap," UPS case study, www.ups-scs.com/solutions/case_studies/cs_nikon.pdf, accessed November 2010.

5. See Frederick E. Webster Jr. and Yoram Wind, *Organizational Buying Behavior* (Upper Saddle River, NJ: Prentice Hall, 1972), pp. 78–80. Also see Jorg Brinkman and Markus Voeth, "An Analysis of Buying Center Decisions Through the Sales Force," *Industrial Marketing Management*, October 2007, p. 998; and Philip Kotler and Kevin Lane Keller, *Marketing Management*, 13th ed., pp. 188–191.

6. See "Our Company," accessed at www.peterbilt.com/company.aspx, accessed June 2010.

7. Robinson, Faris, and Wind, *Industrial Buying Behavior*, p. 14. Also see Philip Kotler and Kevin Lane Keller, *Marketing Management*, pp. 192–198.

8. For this and other examples, see "10 Great Web Sites," *BtoB Online*, September 15, 2008, and 10 Great Web Sites," *BtoB Online*, September 14, 2009, both accessed at www.btobonline.com. Other information from www.cisco.com/cisco/web/solutions/small_business/index.html, accessed October 2010.

9. See William J. Angelo, "E-Procurement Process Delivers Best Value for Kodak," *Engineering News-Record*, March 17, 2008, p. 22.

10. Information from www.shrine-bowl.com/shrine/shriners_hospitals.htm; and www.tenethealth.com/about/pages/default.aspx, accessed January 2010.

11. Michael Myser, "The Hard Sell," *Business 2.0*, December 2006, pp. 62–65; and Solomon Moore, "Prison Spending Outpaces All But Medicaid," *New York Times*, March 2, 2009, accessed at www.nytimes.com/2009/03/03/us/03prison.html.

12. See www.gmifs.com, accessed April 2010.

13. Henry Canaday, "Government Contracts," *Selling Power*, June 2008, pp. 59–62.

14. Jill R. Aitoro, "Federal IT Spending to Increase Almost 4 Percent in Fiscal 2010," *Nextgov*, January 12, 2010, www.nextgov.com/nextgov/ng_20100112_7868.php; U.S. Department of Homeland Security Transportation Security Administration, "Statement of Gale D. Rossides, Acting Administrator," June 10, 2009, www.dhs.gov/.../TSA_EBSP_Recovery_Act_Plan_Final_2009-05-15.pdf; and "Programs and Services to Help You Start, Grow, and Succeed," U.S. Small Business Administration, www.sba.gov/contractingopportunities/index.html, accessed November 2010.

15. Based on communications with Ari Vidali, CEO of Envisage Technologies, July 2006 and January 2010.

16. See "GSA Organization Overview," www.gsa.gov/Portal/gsa/ep/contentView.do?contentType=GSA_OVERVIEW&contentId=8054, accessed January 2010; and Department of Veterans Affairs Office of Acquisition & Material Management, accessed at www1.va.gov/oamm, accessed November 2010.

Chapter 7

1. Quotes and extracts from "Connected World," Best Buy Fiscal 2008 Annual Report, pp. 1–3, www.bby.com; Jonathan Birchall, "Personal Approach to Expansion," *Financial Times*, May 13, 2008, p. 14; and Gary McWilliams, "Analyzing Customers, Best Buy Decides Not All Are Welcome," *Wall Street Journal*, November 8, 2004, p. A1. Other information from Laura Spinali and Jeff O'Heir, "Top 101," *Dealerscope*, March 2009, p. 38; "Consumer Survey: Best Buy, Walmart Top CE Chains," *TWICE*, April 6, 2009, p. 6; Philippe Gohier, "Best Buy Isolates Its 'Demons,'" *MacLean's*, April 7, 2009, p. 40; Andrew Nusca, "In Wake of Circuit City's Demise, Best Buy Rivals Gain Share," *ZDNet.com*, January 12, 2010, www.zdnet.com/blog/gadgetreviews/in-wake-of-circuit-citys-demise-best-buy-rivals-gain-share/11060; and annual reports and other documents found at www.bestbuyinc.com, accessed October 2010.

2. See "Less Is More," *Progressive Grocer*, January/February 2009, p. 46; Jonathan Birchall, "Walmart Looks to Hispanic Market in Expansion Drive," *Financial Times*, March 13, 2009, p. 18; Jonathan Birchall, "Walmart Focuses on Smaller Front," *Financial Times*, October 19, 2009, p. 18, and http://walmartstores.com/AboutUs/7606.aspx, accessed July 2010.

3. For these and other examples, see Philip Kotler and Kevin Lane Keller, *Marketing Management*, 13th ed. (Upper Saddle River, NJ: Prentice Hall, 2009), pp. 210–211; and www.zipcar.com/about/, accessed October 2010.

4. Elaine Wong, "P&G, Dial, Unilever Target the Middle Man," *Brandweek*, May 18, 2009, p. 8; and www.niveaformen.com, accessed October 2010.

5. Adapted from information found in Elizabeth A. Sullivan, "H.O.G: Harley-Davidson Shows Brand Strength as It Navigates Down New Roads—and Picks Up More Female Riders along the Way," *Marketing News*, November 1, 2008, p. 8: "Harley-Davidson Hosts Special Rides to Kick Off Women Riders Month," *PR Newswire*, March 23, 2009; "Women Riders to Rev for a Cure at Daytona Bike Week," *PRNewswire*, February 5, 2010; and www.harley-davidson.com/wcm/Content/Pages/women_riders/landing.jsp, accessed October 2010.

6. See "Guide to Hotel Packages," *Travel + Leisure*, www.travelandleisure.com/articles/the-suspicious-package/sidebar/1, accessed February 2009.

7. Examples from Richard Baker, "Retail Trends—Luxury Marketing: The End of a Mega-Trend," *Retail*, June/July 2009, pp. 8–12.

8. John Waggoner, "Even the Wealthy Feel Tapped Out," *USA Today*, February 2, 2009, p. B1; and Piet Levy, "How to Reach the New Consumer," *Marketing News*, February 28, 2010, pp. 16–20.

9. Information from www.rssc.com, and http://nationofwhynot.com, accessed November 2010.

10. See Louise Story, "Finding Love and the Right Linens," *New York Times*, December 13, 2006, www.nytimes.com; and www.williams-sonoma.com/customer-service/store-events.html?cm_src=OLDLINK, accessed September 2010.

11. Blair Chancey, "King, Meet the World," *QSR Magazine*, February 2009, www.qsrmagazine.com/articles/interview/112/shaufelberger-3.phtml; and Julie Jargon, "As Sales Drop, Burger King Draws Critics for Courting 'Super Fans,'" *Wall Street Journal*, February 1, 2010, p. B1.

12. For more on the PRIZM Lifestyle Segmentation System, see http://en-us.nielsen.com/tab/product_families/nielsen_claritas/prizm and www.MyBestSegments.com, accessed October 2010.

13. Information from www.201.americanexpress.com/business-credit-cards/home?us_nu=subtab&intlink=opennav_main, accessed August 2010.

14. See Michael Porter, *Competitive Advantage* (New York: Free Press, 1985), pp. 4–8, 234–236. For more recent discussions, see Stanley Slater and Eric Olson, "A Fresh Look at Industry and Market Analysis," *Business Horizons*, January–February 2002, pp. 15–22; Kenneth Sawka and Bill Fiora, "The Four Analytical Techniques Every Analyst Must Know: 2. Porter's Five Forces Analysis," *Competitive Intelligence Magazine*, May–June 2003, p. 57; and Philip Kotler and Kevin Lane Keller, *Marketing Management*, 13th ed., pp. 342–343.

15. See Suzanne Kapner, "How Fashion's VF Supercharges Its Brands," *Fortune*, April 14, 2008, pp. 108–110; and www.vfc.com, accessed October 2010.

16. Store information found at www.walmartstores.com, www.wholefoodsmarket.com; and www.kroger.com, accessed July 2010.

17. See Gerry Khermouch, "Call It the Pepsi Blue Generation," *BusinessWeek*, February 3, 2003, p. 96; Valerie Bauerlein, "Soda-Pop Sales Fall at Faster Rate," *Wall Street Journal*, March 31, 2009, p. B7; and D. Gail Fleenor, "Energetic Sales?" *Progressive Grocer*, November/December 2009, pp. 80, 82.

18. Adapted from information found in Linda Tischler, "The Fast Company 50 – 2009: Etsy," *Fast Company*, February 11, 2009, www.fastcompany.com/fast50_09/profile/list/etsy; and www.etsy.com, accessed July 2010.

19. Examples from Darell K. Rigby and Vijay Vishwanath, "Localization: The Revolution in Consumer Markets," *Harvard Business Review*, April 2006, pp. 82–92. Also see Jenny McTaggart, "Walmart Unveils New Segmentation Scheme," *Progressive Grocer*, October 1, 2006, pp. 10–11; and Jonathan Birchall, "Walmart Looks to Hispanic Market in Expansion Drive," *Financial Times*, March 13, 2009, p. 18.

20. Adapted from Claire Cain Miller, "Take a Step Closer for an Invitation to Shop," *New York Times*, February 23, 2010, www.nytimes.com.

21. Adapted from information found in "When You Watch These Ads, the Ads Check You Out," *New York Times*, January 31, 2009, www.nytimes.com; Leonard Goh, "Soon, Billboards That Know Male from Female," June 17, 2009, http://news.cnet.com/8301-17938_105-10266755-1.html; and www.tru-media.com, accessed March 2010.

22. Adapted from portions of Fae Goodman, "Lingerie Is Luscious and Lovely," *Chicago Sun-Times*, February 19, 2006, p. B2; and Stacy Weiner, "Goodbye to Girlhood," *Washington Post*, February 20, 2007, p. HE01. Also see Suzanne C. Ryan and Betsy Cummings, "Tickled Pink," *Brandweek*, September 8, 2008, pp. MO26–MO28; and India Knight, "Relax: Girls Will Be Girls," *Sunday Times* (London), February 21, 2010, p. 4.

23. See "IC3 2008 Annual Report on Internet Crime Released," March 31, 2010, www.ic3.gov/media/2010/100312.aspx.

24. SUV sales data furnished by www.WardsAuto.com, accessed March 2010. Price data from www.edmunds.com, accessed March 2010.

25. Based on information found in Michael Myser, "Marketing Made Easy," *Business 2.0*, June 2006, pp. 43–44; "Staples, Inc." *Hoover's Company Records*, http://premium.hoovers.com/subscribe/co/factsheet.xhtml?ID=rcksfrhrfjcxtr, April 2010; and www.staples.com, accessed April 2010.

26. Quote from "Singapore Airlines: Company Information," accessed at www.singaporeair.com, November 2010.

27. See Bobby J. Calder and Steven J. Reagan, "Brand Design," in Dawn Iacobucci, ed. *Kellogg on Marketing* (New York: John Wiley & Sons, 2001), p. 61. For more discussion, see Philip Kotler and Kevin Lane Keller, *Marketing Management*, 13th ed., pp. 315–316.

28. See Stuart Elliott, "With the Car Industry in Trouble, Nissan Rolls Out the Mobile Device," *New York Times*, April 6, 2009, www.nytimes.com; Dan Neil, "Nissan's Cube Is Coolness in a Box," *Los Angeles Times*, March 6, 2009, p. 1; and www.nissanusa.com/cube, accessed November 2010.

Chapter 8

1. Quotes and other information from Mary Jane Mash, "ESPN Founder Shares Secrets of Success," *Targeted News Service*, October 14, 2008; "How Do You View?" *Economist*, August 2, 2008; Jessica E. Vascellaro and Elizabeth Holmes, "YouTube Seals Deal on ABC, ESPN Clips," *Wall Street Journal*, March 31, 2009, p. B3; Lynn Zinser, "ESPN Outbids Fox Sports and Wins B.C.S. Rights," *New York Times*, November 19, 2008, p. 16; Matthew Futterman, "ESPN Hauls in Rights to Top College Bowl Games," *Wall Street Journal*, November 18, 2008, p. B4; Anthony Crupi, "ESPN Tops Beta Research Again," *Mediaweek*, January 10, 2010, www.mediaweek.com; and information from www.espn.com, http://espnmediazone3.com/wpmu, and www.collegefanz.com/index.jspa, accessed November 2010.

2. Adapted from information found in Chuck Salter, "Why America Is Addicted to Olive Garden," *Fast Company*, July–August 2009, pp. 102–106; and "Culinary Institute of Tuscany," www.olivegarden.com/culinary/cit/, accessed November 2010.

3. R. K. Krishna Kumar, "Effective Marketing Must Begin with Customer Engagement," *Marketing News*, April 15, 2009, p. 15.

4. Example based on information from Nicole Alper, "Recipe for Success: Food Network Phenomenon," *Celebrated Living*, Fall 2007, www.celebratedliving.com/tabid/3097/tabidext/3247/default.aspx; and www.foodnetwork.com, www.rachaelray.com, and www.target.com/Giada, accessed November 2010.

5. Information from www.discoverireland.com/us, accessed May 2010. Also see www.iloveny.com and www.visitcalifornia.com, accessed October 2010.

6. Accessed at www.social-marketing.org/aboutus.html, November 2010.

7. See Rob Gould and Karen Gutierrez, "Social Marketing Has a New Champion," *Marketing News*, February 7, 2000, p. 38. Also see Alan R. Andreasen, *Social Marketing in the 21st Century* (Thousand Oaks, CA: Sage Publications, 2006); Philip Kotler and Nancy Lee, *Social Marketing: Improving the Quality of Life*, 3rd ed. (Thousand Oaks, CA: Sage Publications, 2008); and www.social-marketing.org, accessed October 2010.

8. Quotes and definitions from Philip Kotler, *Kotler on Marketing* (New York: Free Press, 1999), p. 17; and www.asq.org/glossary/q.html, accessed November 2010.

9. Quotes and other information from Regina Schrambling, "Tool Department; The Sharpest Knives in the Drawer," *Los Angeles Times*, March 8, 2006, p. F1; "Alex Lee at Gel 2008," video and commentary at http://vimeo.com/3200945, accessed June 2009; Reena Jana and Helen Walters, "OXO Gets a Grip on New Markets," *BusinessWeek*, October 5, 2009, p. 71; and www.oxo.com/about.jsp, accessed November 2010.

10. Andy Goldsmith, "Coke vs. Pepsi: The Taste They Don't Want You to Know About," *The 60-Second Marketer*, www.60secondmarketer.com/60SecondArticles/Branding/cokevs.pepsitast.html, accessed May 2009.

11. See "Supermarket facts," www.fmi.org/facts_figs/?fuseaction=superfact, accessed April 2010; "Walmart Facts," www.walmartfacts.com/StateByState/?id=2, accessed April 2010; "FMI—Supermarket Facts," http://www.fmi.org/facts_figs/?fuseaction=superfact, accessed July 2010; and "Shopper Decisions Made In-Store by OgilvyAction," www.wpp.com, accessed July 2010.

12. See Brennon Slattery, "Amazon Offers Easy-to-Open Packaging," *PC World*, January 2009, p. 36; Peter Clarke, "This Holiday, Help Fight the Dangers of Wrap Rage," December 23, 2009, www.fastcompany.com; and "Amazon Frustration-Free packaging," www.amazon.com/gp/help/customer/display.html?nodeId=200285450, accessed November 2010.

13. Sonja Reyes, "Ad Blitz, Bottle Design Fuel Debate over Heinz's Sales," *Brandweek*, February 12, 2007, www.brandweek.com/bw/news/recent_display.jsp?vnu_content_id=1003544497.

14. Natalie Zmuda, "What Went into the Updated Pepsi Logo," *Advertising Age*, October 27, 2008, p. 6; Natalie Zmuda, "Pepsi, Coke Tried to Outdo Each Other with Rays of Sunshine," *Advertising Age*, January 19, 2009, p. 6; Todd Wasserman, "Grim Times Prompt More Upbeat Logos," *Brandweek*, February 23, 2009, p. 9; and "New Pepsi Logo Kicks off Campaign," *McClatchy-Tribune Business News*, January 15, 2010.

15. For these and other stories, see Bob Janet, "Customers Never Tire of Great Service," *Dealerscope*, July 2008, p. 40; and Greta Schulz, "Nordstrom Makes Customer Service Look Easy," December 11, 2009, http://amazingserviceguy.com/2370/2370/.

16. See the HP Total Care site at http://h71036.www7.hp.com/hho/cache/309717-0-0-225-121.html, accessed November 2010.

17. Information at www.marriott.com/corporateinfo/glance.mi, accessed August 2010.

18. Information on Colgate's product mix from www.colgate.com/app/Colgate/US/HomePage.cvsp, accessed April 2010.

19. See Stuart Elliott, "A Strategy When Times Are Tough: 'It's New,'" *New York Times*, March 25, 2009, accessed at www.nytimes.com; and John A. Quelch and Katherine E. Jocz, "How to Market in a Downturn," *Harvard Business Review*, April 2009, pp. 52–62.

20. See CIA, *The World Factbook*, https://www.cia.gov/library/publications/the-world-factbook/geos/xx.html and https://www.cia.gov/library/publications/the-world-factbook/fields/2012.html, accessed August 2010; and information from the Bureau of Labor Statistics, www.bls.gov, accessed August 2010.

21. Portions adapted from information in Leonard Berry and Neeli Bendapudi, "Clueing in Customers," *Harvard Business Review*, February 2003, pp. 100–106; with additional information and quotes from Jeff Hansel, "Mayo Hits the Blogosphere," *McClatchy-Tribune Business News*, January 22, 2009; and www.mayoclinic.org, accessed August 2010.

22. See James L. Heskett, W. Earl Sasser Jr., and Leonard A. Schlesinger, *The Service Profit Chain: How Leading Companies Link Profit and Growth to Loyalty, Satisfaction, and Value* (New York: Free Press, 1997); Heskett, Sasser, and Schlesinger, *The Value Profit Chain: Treat Employees Like Customers and Customers Like Employees* (New York:

Free Press, 2003); Christian Homburg, Jan Wieseke, and Wayne D. Hoyer, "Social Identity and the Service-Profit Chain," *Journal of Marketing*, March 2009, pp. 38–54; and Rachael W. Y. Yee and others, "The Service-Profit Chain: A Review and Extension," *Total Quality Management & Business Excellence*, 2009, pp. 617–632.

23. Based on quotes and information from Pete Blackshaw, "Zappos Shows How Employees Can Be Brand-Builders," *Advertising Age*, September 2, 2008, http://adage.com/print?article_id=130646; Jeremy Twitchell, "Fun Counts with Web Retailer," *Fort Wayne Journal-Gazette*, February 16, 2009, p. C5; Jeffrey M. O'Brien, "Zappos Knows How to Kick It," *Fortune*, February 2, 2009, pp. 55–60; and http://about.zappos.com/jobs, accessed August 2010.

24. See "United States: Prescription Drums," www.statehealthfacts.org/profileind.jsp?sub=66&rgn=1&cat=5, accessed April 2010; and "Postal Facts," www.usps.com/communications/newsroom/postalfacts.htm, accessed June 2010.

25. Portions adapted from Jena McGregor, "Customer Service Champs," *BusinessWeek*, March 5, 2007, pp. 52–64; with information from Daniel B. Honigman, "10 Minutes with . . . Fred Taylor," *Marketing News*, May 1, 2008, pp. 8–27.

26. See "McAtlas Shrugged," *Foreign Policy*, May–June 2001, pp. 26–37; and Philip Kotler and Kevin Lane Keller, *Marketing Management*, 13th ed. (Upper Saddle River, NJ: Prentice Hall, 2009), p. 254.

27. Quotes from Jack Trout, "'Branding' Simplified," *Forbes*, April 19, 2007, www.forbes.com; and a presentation by Jason Kilar at the Kenan-Flagler Business School, University of North Carolina at Chapel Hill, Fall 2009.

28. For more on Young & Rubicam's Brand Asset Valuator, see "Brand Asset Valuator," Value Based Management.net, www.valuebasedmanagement.net/methods_brand_asset_valuator.html, accessed May 2010; www.brandassetconsulting.com, accessed May 2010; and W. Ronald Lane, Karen Whitehill King, and Tom Reichert, *Kleppner's Advertising Procedure*, 18th ed. (Upper Saddle River, NJ: Pearson Prentice Hall, 2011), pp. 83–84.

29. See Millward Brown Optimor, "BrandZ Top 100 Most Powerful Brands 2009," www.millwardbrown.com/brandz/.

30. See Scott Davis, *Brand Asset Management*, 2nd ed. (San Francisco: Jossey-Bass, 2002). For more on brand positioning, see Philip Kotler and Kevin Lane Keller, *Marketing Management*, 13th ed., Chapter 10.

31. Adapted from information found in Geoff Colvin, "Selling P&G," *Fortune*, September 17, 2007, pp. 163–169; "For P&G, Success Lies in More Than Merely a Dryer Diaper," *Advertising Age*, October 15, 2007, p. 20; Jack Neff, "Stengel Discusses Transition at P&G," *Advertising Age*, July 21, 2008, p. 17; and www.jimstengel.com, accessed June 2010.

32. Susan Wong, "Foods OK, But Some Can't Stomach More Ad Increases," *Brandweek*, January 5, 2009, p. 7. Also see "Brand Names Need to Reward Consumers to Keep Them According to Study," *PR Newswire*, October 23, 2009; "IDDBA Study Shows Store Brands Spiking," *Dairy Foods*, January 2010, p. 38; and "Consumers Praise Store Brands," *Adweek*, April 8, 2010, www.adweek.com.

33. See Jack Neff, "Private Label Winning Battle of Brands," *Advertising Age*, February 23, 2009, p. 1; Chris Burritt and Carol Wolf, "Walmart's Store-Brand Groceries to Get New Emphasis," *Bloomberg.com*, February 19, 2009; Jenn Abelson, "Seeking Savings, Some Ditch Brand Loyalty," *Boston Globe*, January 29, 2010, p. B1.

34. See information from www.kroger.com and www.wholefoodsmarket.com/products/365-everyday-value.php, accessed November 2010.

35. Nirmalya Kumar and Jan-Benedict E. M. Steenkamp, *Private Label Strategy* (Boston, MA: Harvard Business School Press, 2007), p. 5.

36. "Nickelodeon Expands Product Offerings and Debuts New Properties for Kids and Teens at Licensing 2008 International Show," *PR Newswire*, June 10, 2008; Gary Strauss, "Sponge Bob: A Hit from Square One," *USA Today*, July 15, 2009; David Benady, "Using Licensing to Build a Megabrand," *Marketing*, February 3, 2010, p. 32;

and Alan Feldman and others, "Corporate and Brand Licensing: Year in Review," *Licensing Journal*, February 2010, pp. 1–6.

37. "Tim Hortons and Cold Stone: Co-Branding Strategies," *Business-Week*, July 10, 2009, www.businessweek.com/smallbiz/content/jul2009/sb20090710_574574.htm; and Steve McKee, "The Pros and Cons of Co-Branding," *BusinessWeek*, July 10, 2009, www.businessweek.com/smallbiz/content/jul2009/sb20090710_255169.htm.

38. Quote from www.apple.com/ipod/nike/, accessed August 2010.

39. The quote and the best/worst examples are from "TippingSprung Publishes Results from Fifth Annual Brand-Extensions Survey," January 6, 2009, www.tippingsprung.com/images/pdf/TS_08_brand_ext_survey_pr_r02.pdf.

40. "Leading National Advertisers," *Advertising Age*, June 22, 2009, p. 12.

41. Quotes from Stephen Cole, "Value of the Brand," *CA Magazine*, May 2005, pp. 39–40; and Lawrence A. Crosby and Sheree L. Johnson, "Experience Required," *Marketing Management*, July/August 2007, pp. 21–27.

42. See Kevin Lane Keller, *Strategic Brand Management* (Upper Saddle River, NJ: Prentice Hall, 2008), chapter 10.

Chapter 9

1. Extracts and quotes from or adapted from information found in Chuck Salter, "Google: The Faces and Voices of the World's Most Innovative Company," *Fast Company*, March 2008, pp. 74–88; "The World's Most Innovative Companies," *Fast Company*, March 2009, p. 52; "The World's Most Innovative Companies," *Fast Company*, February 22, 2010, p. 60; "Google Shines a Light on Innovation," *Computer Weekly*, September 9–September 15, 2008, p. 3; David Pogue, "Geniuses at Play, On the Job," *New York Times*, February 26, 2009, p. B1; Quentin Hardy, "When Google Runs Your Life," *Forbes*, December 28, 2009, pp. 88–93; Tom Krazit, "Slight Dip in Google's January Search Market Share," *CNET News*, February 11, 2010, http://news.cnet.com/8301-30684_3-10452235-265.html; and www.google.com and www.googlelabs.com, accessed September 2010.

2. "In a Tough Economy, Innovation Is King," *Marketing News*, April 15, 2009, p. 14.

3. Calvin Hodock, "Winning the New-Products Game," *Advertising Age*, November 12, 2007, p. 35; Neale Martin, "Force of Habit," *Brandweek*, October 13, 2008, pp. 18–20; "How P&G Plans to Clean up," *BusinessWeek*, April 13, 2009, pp. 44–45; and "Top 10 Reasons for New-Product Failure," *The Marketing Fray*, January 7, 2010, www.marketingfray.com/2010/01/top-10-reasons-for-new-product-failure.html.

4. Information and examples from Robert M. McMath and Thom Forbes, *What Were They Thinking? Money-Saving, Time-Saving, Face-Saving Marketing Lessons You Can Learn from Products That Flopped* (New York: Times Business, 1999), various pages; Beatriz Cholo, "Living with Your 'Ex': A Brand New World," *Brandweek*, December 5, 2005, p. 4; and www.gfkamerica.com/newproductworks, accessed October 2010.

5. John Peppers and Martha Rogers, "The Buzz on Customer-Driven Innovation," *Sales & Marketing Management*, June 2007, p. 13.

6. See Richard Martin, "Collaboration Cisco Style," *InformationWeek*, January 28, 2008, p. 30; and Guido Jouret, "Inside Cisco's Search for the Next Big Idea," *Harvard Business Review*, September 2009, pp. 43–45.

7. See http://mystarbucksidea.force.com/ideaHome, accessed November 2010.

8. Mary Tripsas, "Seeing Customers as Partners in Invention," *New York Times*, December 27, 2009, www.nytimes.com.

9. Elisabeth A. Sullivan, "A Group Effort: More Companies Are Turning to the Wisdom of the Crowd to Find Ways to Innovate," *Marketing News*, February 28, 2010, pp. 22–29.

10. Adapted from Sullivan, "A Group Effort," p. 26.

11. See Brian Morrissey, "The Social Sell?" *Brandweek*, February 14, 2010, www.brandweek.com; and www.ideastorm.com, accessed November 2010.

12. Jeff Howe, "Join the Crowd," *Independent (London)*, September 2, 2008, p. 2; "P&G Leads 2010 Edison Best New Product Award Finalists with Five Nods," *PR Newswire*, February 11, 2010; and "About Us," www.innocentive.com, accessed September 2010.

13. Guido Jouret, "Inside Cisco's Search for the Next Big Idea," *Harvard Business Review*, September 2009, pp. 43–45.

14. Kevin O'Donnell, "Where Do the Best Ideas Come From? The Unlikeliest Sources," *Advertising Age*, July 14, 2008, p. 15.

15. See George S. Day, "Is It Real? Can We Win? Is It Worth Doing?" *Harvard Business Review*, December 2007, pp. 110–120.

16. Information for this example obtained from www.teslamotors.com, accessed June 2010.

17. Information from www.hpproducttest.com/index.cfm, accessed November 2010.

18. "KFC Fires Up Grilled Chicken," March 23, 2008, www.money.cnn.com; "KFC Serves Up a Second Secret Recipe: Kentucky Grilled Chicken," *PR Newswire*, April 14, 2009; and Noreen O'Leary, "KFC's Grilled Chicken Tops Most-Recalled '09 Launches," *Brandweek*, December 14, 2009, p. 4.

19. Information on BehaviorScan accessed at http://www.symphonyiri.com/ProductsSolutions/AllProducts/AllProductsDetail/tabid/159/productid/75/Default.aspx, accessed August 2010.

20. Example developed from information found in "Decision Insight: Simushop," www.decisioninsight.com/content/simushop.shtml, accessed September 2010; and Allison Enright, "Best Practices: Frito-Lay Get Real Results from a Virtual World," *Marketing News*, December 15, 2006, p. 20. Also see Piet Levy, "10 Minutes with . . . Brad Barash, Vice President of Decision Insight, Inc.," *Marketing News*, February 28, 2009, p. 28.

21. Dan Sewell, "Procter & Gamble to Test Web Sales," *Associated Press*, January 15, 2010.

22. See Emily Bryson York, "McD's Serves Up $100M McCafé Ad Blitz," *Crain's Chicago Business*, May 4, 2009, www.chicagobusiness.com; John Letzing, "Bing's Share Rises Again," *Wall Street Journal*, June 18, 2009, http://online.wsj.com; and Rita Chang, "With $100M Saturation Campaign, Droid Will Be Impossible to Avoid," *Advertising Age*, November 9, 2009, p. 3.

23. Jeremy Mullman, "Copying Corona: Miller, Bud Want Their Fun in the Sun," *Advertising Age*, January 29, 2007, p. 1; David Kesmodel, "Miller to Bring 'Chill' to Australia," *Wall Street Journal*, November 12, 2007, p. B6; and Tom Daykin, "Miller Chill Makeover Squeezes in More Lime Flavor," *McClatchy-Tribune Business News*, February 19, 2009.

24. See Robert G. Cooper, "Formula for Success," *Marketing Management*, March–April 2006, pp. 19–23; Barry Jaruzelski and Kevin Dehoff, "The Global Innovation of 1000," *Strategy + Business*, Issue 49, fourth quarter, 2007, pp. 68–83; and Shu-Hua Chien and Jyh-jye Chen, "Supplier Involvement in Customer Involvement Effect on New Product Development Success in the Financial Service Industry," *Service Industries Journal*, February 2010, p. 185.

25. Robert Berner, "How P&G Pampers New Thinking," *BusinessWeek*, April 14, 2008, pp. 73–74; "How P&G Plans to Clean Up," *BusinessWeek*, April 13, 2009, pp. 44–45; and "Procter & Gamble Company," www.wikinvest.com/stock/Procter_&_Gamble_Company_ (PG), accessed April 2010.

26. "PNC's Virtual Wallet Takes Online Banking to the Next Level," *PRNewswire*, August 5, 2008; Todd Wasserman, "Thinking by Design," *Brandweek*, November 3, 2008, pp. 18–21; and Daniel Wolfe, "New PNC Virtual Wallet Has Two Targets: Students, Parents," *American Banker*, July 28, 2009, p. 12.

27. Adapted from Darrell K. Rigby, Karen Gruver, and James Allen, "Innovation in Turbulent Times," *Harvard Business Review*, June 2009, pp. 79–86. Also see John Hayes, "In a Tough Economy, Innovation Is King," *Marketing News*, April 15, 2009, pp. 14–17.

28. Ibid.; and Judann Pollock, "Now's the Time to Reset Marketing for Post-Recession," *Advertising Age*, February 1, 2010, p. 1.

29. This definition is based on one found in Bryan Lilly and Tammy R. Nelson, "Fads: Segmenting the Fad-Buyer Market," *Journal of Consumer Marketing*, vol. 20, no. 3, 2003, pp. 252–265.

30. See Katya Kazakina and Robert Johnson, "A Fad's Father Seeks a Sequel," *New York Times*, May 30, 2004, www.nytimes.com; John Schwartz, "The Joy of Silly," *New York Times*, January 20, 2008, p. 5; and www.crazyfads.com, accessed November 2010.

31. Example adapted from information found in Patrick J. Sauer, "I Just IM'd to say 'I Love You,'" *Fast Company*, May 2008, p. 52. Also see "American Greetings Introduces New 'Ideas' Online," *PR Newswire*, November 28, 2008; and www.aginteractive.com/products_overview brands-Kiwee.html and www.kiwee.com, accessed November 2010.

32. See www.1000uses.com, accessed September 2010.

33. For a more comprehensive discussion of marketing strategies over the course of the PLC, see Philip Kotler and Kevin Lane Keller, *Marketing Management*, 13th ed. (Upper Saddle River, NJ: Prentice Hall, 2009), pp. 278–290.

34. See "Year-by-Year Analysis Reveals an Overall Compensatory Award of $1,500,000 for Products Liability Cases," *Personal Injury Verdict Reviews*, July 3, 2006; Administrative Office of the U.S. Courts, "Judicial Facts and Figures: Multi-Year Statistical Compilations on the Federal Judiciary's Caseload Through Fiscal Year 2008," September 2009, www.uscourts.gov/judicialfactsfigures/2008/all2008judicialfactsfigures.pdf; and Rachanee Srisavasdi, "Rules Set For Toyota Out-of-Control Cars Case," *McClatchy-Tribune Business News*, June 23, 2010.

35. Example based on information provided by Nestle Japan Ltd., May 2008; with additional information from Laurel Wentz, "Kit Kat Wins Cannes Media Grand Prix for Edible Postcard," *Advertising Age*, June 23, 2009, http://adage.com/cannes09/article?article_id=137520; and http://en.wikipedia.org/wiki/Kit_Kat; and the Japanese Wikipedia discussion of Kit Kat at http://ja.wikipedia.org, accessed November 2010.

36. Information accessed online at www.db.com, September 2010.

37. Information accessed online at www.interpublic.com and www.mccann.com, accessed September 2010.

38. See "Global Powers of Retailing 2010," www.deloitte.com; "Walmart Corporate International," http://walmartstores.com/AboutUs/246.aspx, February 2010; and information accessed at www.carrefour.com, February 2010.

Chapter 10

1. Quotes and extracts from Brad Stone and Stephanie Rosenbloom, "The Gloves Come Off at Amazon and Walmart," *New York Times*, November 24, 2009, p. 1; Gayle Feldman, "Behind the US Price War," *Bookseller*, November 13, 2009, p. 16; and Jeffrey A. Trachtenberg and Miguel Bustillo, "Amazon, Walmart Cut Deeper in Book Duel," *Wall Street Journal*, October 19, 2009, p. B1. Also see Brad Stone, "Can Amazon Be Walmart of the Web," *New York Times*, September 20, 2009, p. 1; Jonathan Birchall, "Walmart Tweaks Price in Amazon Battle," *Financial Times*, October 17, 2009, www.ft.com; and information from www.walmart.com and www.amazon.com, accessed September 2010.

2. See Allen Adamson, "Marketers: Expect a Return to Core Brand Value—and Values—in 2010," *Forbes*, January 4, 2010, www.forbes.com; and "Consumer 'New Frugality' May Be an Enduring Feature of Post-Recession Economy, Finds Booz & Company Survey," *Business Wire*, February 24, 2010.

3. For more on the importance of sound pricing strategy, see Thomas T. Nagle, John Hogan, and Joseph Zale, *The Strategy and Tactics of Pricing: A Guide to Growing More Profitably* (Upper Saddle River, NJ: Prentice Hall, 2011), chapter 1.

4. Based on information from Anne Marie Chaker, "For a Steinway, I Did It My Way," *Wall Street Journal*, May 22, 2008, www.wsj.com; and www.steinway.com/steinway and www.steinway.com/steinway/quotes.shtml, accessed November 2010.

5. See Kevin Done, "Runway Success—Ryanair," *Financial Times*, March 20, 2009, www.ft .com; Matthew Maier, "A Radical Fix for Airlines: Make Flying Free," *Business 2.0*, April 2006, pp. 32–34; "Ryanair Lures 14% More Passengers with Price Cuts," *Financial Times*, February 2, 2010, www.financialtimes.com; and www.ryanair.com/en, accessed September 2010.

6. Example adapted from Anupam Mukerji, "Monsoon Marketing," *Fast Company*, April 2007, p. 22. Also see www.stagumbrellas.com, accessed September 2010.

7. Elizabeth A. Sullivan, "Value Pricing: Smart Marketers Know Cost-Plus Can Be Costly," *Marketing News*, January 15, 2008, p. 8. Also see Peter J. Williamson and Ming Zeng, "Value-for-Money Strategies," *Harvard Business Review*, March 2009, pp. 66–74.

8. Accumulated production is drawn on a semilog scale so that equal distances represent the same percentage increase in output.

9. The arithmetic of markups and margins is discussed in Appendix 2, Marketing by the Numbers.

10. Comments from www.yelp.com/biz/annie-blooms-books-portland (3/23/2008), accessed June 2010.

11. Adapted from information found in Joseph Weber, "Over a Buck for Dinner? Outrageous," *BusinessWeek*, March 9, 2009, p. 57.

12. See Nagle, Hogan, and Zale, *The Strategy and Tactics of Pricing*, Chapter 7.

13. Susan Mires, "The New Economy of Frugality: Cost-Seating Skills Going up in Value," *McClatchy-Tribune Business News*, March 19, 2009; Laura Petrecca, "Marketers Try to Promote Value without Cheapening Image," *USA Today*, November 17, 2008, p. B1; and Allen Adamson, "Marketers: Expect a Return to Core Brand Value—and Values—in 2010," *Forbes*, January 4, 2010, www.forbes.com.

14. Petrecca, "Marketers Try to Promote Value without Cheapening Image," *USA Today*, November 17, 2008, p. B1; Anne D'Innocenzio, "Butter, Kool-Aid in Limelight in Advertising Shift," April 21, 2009, www.azcentral.com/business/articles/2009/04/21/20090421biz-NewFrugality0421.html; and Judann Pollack, "Now's the Time to Reset Marketing for Post-Recession," *Advertising Age*, February 1, 2010, p. 1.

15. Kenneth Hein, "Study: Value Trumps Price among Shoppers," *Brandweek*, March 2, 2009, p. 6.

Chapter 11

1. Quotes and other information from Anna Sowa, "Trader Joe's: Why the Hype?" *McClatchy-Tribune Business News*, March 27, 2008; Deborah Orr, "The Cheap Gourmet," *Forbes*, April 10, 2006, pp. 76–77; Monica Chen, "'Crew' Readies Trader Joe's," Durham *Herald-Sun*, November 29, 2007, p. 1; "Affordable Luxury: Trader Joe's Carries Unique Products That It Says Won't Break the Bank," *Richmond Times-Dispatch*, September 21, 2008, p. D1; "Wegmans, Trader Joe's, Publix Top *Consumer Reports* Supermarket Survey," April 6, 2009, http://consumeraffairs.com/news04/2009/04/cr_supers.html; "SN's Top 75 Retailers for 2010," *Supermarket News*, http://supermarketnews.com/profiles/top75/2010/; and www.traderjoes.com, accessed November 2010.

2. For comprehensive discussions of pricing strategies, see Thomas T. Nagle, John E. Hogan, and Joseph Zale, *The Strategy and Tactics of Pricing*, 5th ed. (Upper Saddle River, New Jersey: Prentice Hall, 2011).

3. Adapted from information found in Mei Fong, "IKEA Hits Home in China; The Swedish Design Giant, Unlike Other Retailers, Slashes Prices for the Chinese," *Wall Street Journal*, March 3, 2006, p. B1; "Beijing Loves IKEA—But Not for Shopping," *Los Angeles Times*, http://articles.latimes.com/2009/aug/25/business/fi-china-ikea25; and www.ikea.com/ms/en_US/about_ikea/factandfigures/index.html, accessed April 2010.

4. Paul Miller, "Sony Losing Mad Loot on Each PS3," *Engadet*, November 16, 2006, www.engadget.com/2006/11/16/sony-losing-mad-loot-on-each-ps3/; Sam Kennedy, "Sony Has Lost More on

the PS3 Than It Made on PS2," *1UP News*, August 19, 2008, www.1up.com/do/newsStory?cId=3169439; and Don Reisinger, "Sony Still Losing on Every PlayStation 3 It Sells," *CNET News*, February 5, 2010, http://news.cnet.com/8301-13506_3-10448137-17.html?tag=hotTopicsBody.1.

5. Information from "What Happens to All That Poo at the Zoo . . .," www.youtube.com/watch?v=kjfNVEvRI3w&feature=player_embedded#, accessed April 2010; "Zoo Doo® at Woodland Park Zoo," www.zoo.org/zoo-doo, accessed November 2010.

6. Peter Coy, "Why the Price Is Rarely Right," *Bloomberg BusinessWeek*, February 1 & 8, 2010, pp. 77–78.

7. See Eric Anderson and Duncan Simester, "Mind Your Pricing Cues," *Harvard Business Review*, September 2003, pp. 96–103; and Peter J. Boyle and E. Scott Lathrop, "Are Consumers' Perceptions of Price-Quality Relationships Well Calibrated?" *International Journal of Consumer Studies*, January 2009, p. 58.

8. Anthony Allred, E. K. Valentin, and Goutam Chakraborty, "Pricing Risky Services: Preference and Quality Considerations," *Journal of Product and Brand Management*, vol. 19, no. 1, 2010, p. 54. Also see Kenneth C. Manning and David E. Sprott, "Price Endings, Left-Digit Effects, and Choice," *Journal of Consumer Research*, August 2009, pp. 328–336.

9. Adapted from information found in Elizabeth A. Sullivan, "Stay on Course," *Marketing News*, February 15, 2009, pp. 11–13. Also see Stuart Elliott, "Never Mind What It Costs. Can I Get It 70 Percent Off?" *New York Times*, April 27, 2009, www.nytimes.com; and "Consumer 'New Frugality' May Be an Enduring Feature of Post-Recession Economy, Finds Booz & Company Survey," *Business Wire*, February 24, 2010.

10. Example adapted from Louise Story, "Online Pitches Made Just for You," *New York Times*, March 6, 2008, www.nytimes.com. Also see Lucy Soto, "Cookies Bite Back: Those Little Computer Chromes Keep Track of Your Spending Habits," *Atlanta Journal-Constitution*, January 31, 2010, p. B1.

11. Based on information found in "The World's Most Influential Companies: Unilever," *BusinessWeek*, December 22, 2008, p. 47; and www.unilever.com/sustainability/, accessed November 2009.

12. Example adapted from information found in Ellen Byron, "Fashion Victim: To Refurbish Its Image, Tiffany Risks Profits," *Wall Street Journal*, January 10, 2007, p. A1; and Aliza Rosenbaum and John Christy, "Financial Insight: Tiffany's Boutique Risk; By Breaking Mall Fast, High-End Exclusivity May Gain Touch of Common," *Wall Street Journal*, October 20, 2007, p. B14. Also see Brian Burnsed, "Where Discounting Can Be Dangerous," *BusinessWeek*, August 3, 2009, p. 49.

13. Andrea Sachs, "We Were There: BoltBus's Inaugural Run to NYC," *Washington Post*, March 27, 2008, http://voices.washingtonpost.com; and https://www.boltbus.com and www.greyhound.com, accessed November 2010.

14. See Ellen Byron, "Tide Turns 'Basic' for P&G in Slump," *Wall Street Journal*, August 6, 2009, http://online.wsj.com/article/SB124946926161107433.html; Mark Ritson, "Should You Launch a Fighter Brand?" *Harvard Business Review*, October 2009, pp. 87–94; and Stuart Elliott, "A Campaign Linking Clean Clothes with Stylish Living," *New York Times*, January 8, 2010, www.nytimes.com.

15. For discussions of these issues, see Dhruv Grewel and Larry D. Compeau, "Pricing and Public Policy: A Research Agenda and Overview of the Special Issue," *Journal of Public Policy and Marketing*, Spring 1999, pp. 3–10; Michael V. Marn, Eric V. Roegner, and Craig C. Zawada, *The Price Advantage* (Hoboken, New Jersey: John Wiley & Sons, 2004), appendix 2; and Thomas T. Nagle, John E. Hogan, and Joseph Zale, *The Strategy and Tactics of Pricing*, 5th ed.

16. See Mark A. Fox, "Market Power in Music Retailing: The Case of Wal-Mart," *Popular Music and Society*, October 2005, pp. 501–519; Ed Christman, "Blue Christmas," *Billboard*, January 6, 2007, www.billboard.com; and Ed Christman, "Solutions for Sale," *Billboard*, January 23, 2010, www.billboard.com.

17. "FTC Guides Against Deceptive Pricing," www.ftc.gov/bcp/guides/decptprc.htm, accessed December 2010.

Chapter 12

1. Percentages are based on revenues as presented in Hertz, "Hertz Acquires Dollar Thrifty," April 26, 2010, slide 5.

2. The "e" logo, Enterprise, and "We'll Pick You Up" are registered trademarks of Enterprise Rent-A-Car Company. Quotes and other information from "Enter Enterprise," *Business Travel News*, April 23, 2007; Carol J. Loomis, "Enterprise Pulls Up at the Airport," *Fortune*, July 23, 2007, p. 50; Stephan Stern, "Revealed: The Secret to Survival in 2009 (Pass It On)," *Financial Times*, December 23, 2008, p. 12; Michael B. Baker, "Wreckers Again on Her Enterprise," *Business Travel News*, December 14, 2009, p. 4; Andrew Ross Sorkin, "Hertz Aims to Push Forward with Dollar Thrifty," *New York Times*, April 6, 2010, accessed at http://dealbooks.blogs.nytimes.com.; Gary Stoller, "Hertz to Acquire Rental Car Rival Dollar Thrifty in $1.2B Deal," *USA Today*, April 26, 2010, accessed at www.usastoday.com; "Update 1—Car Rental Shares Rise After Hertz Bid," Reuters, September 13, 2010, accessed at www.reuters.com/article/idUSN1321335120100913; and www.enterprise.com; www.enterpriseholdings.com, www.wecar.com, http:// aboutus.enterprise.com/press_room/fact_sheets.html, accessed October 2010.

3. Example adapted from Richard Gibson, "Burger King Franchisees Can't Have It *Their* Own Way," *Wall Street Journal*, January 21, 2010, p. B1; with additional information from Emily Bryson York, "BK Swears Off Sex in Ads to Quell Franchisee Freak Out," *Advertising Age*, July 13, 2009, p. 1; and York, "Burger King, Franchisees Start Making Nice," *Advertising Age*, February 17, 2010, http://adage.com/article?article_id=142158.

4. Information accessed at www.kroger.com and www.luxottica.com/en/company/quick_view, accessed October 2010.

5. Franchising facts from *2010 Franchise Business Economic Outlook*, December 21, 2009, www.franchise.org/uploadedFiles/Franchise_Industry/Resources/Education_Foundation/2010%20Franchise%20Business%20Outlook%20Report_Final%202009.12.21.pdf; and www.azfranchises.com/franchisefacts.htm, accessed March 2010.

6. Brent Kendall and Scott Morrison, "Regulators Clear Microsoft-Yahoo Alliance," *Wall Street Journal*, February 19, 2010, p. B5.

7. Quotes and other information from Matthew Boyle, "Reed Hastings," *Fortune*, May 28, 2007, p. 30; "Nick Wingfield, "Netflix vs. Naysayers," *Wall Street Journal*, March 27, 2007, p. B1; Michael V. Copeland, "Netflix Lives!" *Fortune*, April 28, 2008, p. 40; Terrence O'Brien, "Netflix to Let Users 'Watch Instantly' on Windows Phone 7 Series," March 15, 2010, www.switched.com; and www.netflix.com, accessed November 2010.

8. Information from www.marykay.com/company/default.aspx, accessed April 2010.

9. Quotes and information from Normandy Madden, "Two Chinas," *Advertising Age*, August 16, 2004, pp. 1, 22; Russell Flannery, "China: The Slow Boat," *Forbes*, April 12, 2004, p. 76; Jeff Berman, "U.S. Providers Say Logistics in China on the Right Track," *Logistics Management*, March 2007, p. 22; Jamie Bolton, "China: The Infrastructure Imperative," *Logistics Management*, July 2007, p. 63; and China trade facts from http:// cscmp.org/press/fastfacts.asp, accessed March 2010.

10. Nanette Byrnes, "Avon Calls. China Opens the Door," *BusinessWeek Online*, February 28, 2006, p. 19; Mei Fong, "Avon's Calling, But China Opens Door Only a Crack," *Wall Street Journal*, February 26, 2007, p. B1; "Cosmetic Changes in China Market," October 11, 2007, www.chinadaily.com.cn; and David Barboza, "Direct Selling Flourishes in China," *New York Times*, December 26, 2009, p. B1.

11. Jack Neff, "Walmart Food-Bag Consolidation Wipes Glad, Hefty from Shelves," *Advertising Age*, February 4, 2010, http://adage.com/print?article_id=141918.

12. Quotes and other information from Alex Taylor III, "Caterpillar," *Fortune*, August 20, 2007, pp. 48–54; Donald V. Fites, "Make Your

Dealers Your Partners," *Harvard Business Review*, March–April 1996, pp. 84–95; and information at www.cat.com, accessed November 2010.

13. John D. Schultz, "Logistics News: U.S. Logistics Costs Drop for the First Time in Six Years," *Supply Chain Management Review*, June 18, 2009; Larry Rohter, "Shipping Costs Start to Crimp Globalization," *New York Times*, August 3, 2008, p. A1; and supply chain facts from http://cscmp.org/press/fastfacts.asp, accessed June 2010.

14. William B. Cassidy, "Walmart Squeezes Costs from Supply Chain," *Journal of Commerce*, January 5, 2010.

15. Shlomo Maital, "The Last Frontier of Cost Reduction," *Across the Board*, February 1994, pp. 51–52; and information http://walmartstores .com, accessed June 2010.

16. Bill Mongrelluzzo, "Supply Chain Expert Sees Profits in Sustainability," *Journal of Commerce*, March 11, 2010, www.joc.com/logistics-economy/sustainability-can-lead-profits- says-expert.

17. Gail Braccidiferro, "One Town's Rejection Is Another's 'Let's Do Business,'" *New York Times*, June 15, 2003, p. 2; Dan Scheraga, "Wal-Smart," *Chain Store Age*, January 2006 supplement, pp. 16A–21A; and facts from www.walmart.com, accessed August 2010.

18. Example adapted from Evan West, "These Robots Play Fetch," *Fast Company*, July/ August 2007, pp. 49–50. See also John Teresko, "Getting Lean with Armless Robots," *Industry Week*, September 2008, p. 26; and www.kivasystems.com/video.htm, accessed February 2010.

19. See "A Worldwide Look at RFID," *Supply Chain Management Review*, April 2007, pp. 48–55; "Walmart Says Use RFID Tags or Pay Up," *Logistics Today*, March 2008, p. 4; David Blanchard, "The Five Stages of RFID," *Industry Week*, January 1, 2009, p. 50; and Maida Napolitano, "RFID Revisited," *Modern Materials Handling*, February 2010, p. 45.

20. Michael Margreta, Chester Ford, and M. Adhi Dipo, "U.S. Freight on the Move: Highlights from the 2007 Commodity Flow Survey Preliminary Data," September 30, 2009, www.bts.gov/publications/bts_special_report/2009_09_30/html/entire.html; Bureau of Transportation Statistics, "Pocket Guide to Transportation 2009," January 2010, www.bts.gov/publications/pocket_guide_to_transportation/2010/; and American Trucking Association, www.truckline.com, accessed February 2010.

21. See Walmart's supplier requirements at http://walmartstores .com/Suppliers/248.aspx, accessed June 2010. Also see Sriram Narayanan, Ann S. Marucheck, and Robert B. Handfield, "Electronic Data Interchange: Research Review and Future Directions," *Decision Sciences*, February 2009, p. 121.

22. See Bob Trebilcock, "Top 20 Supply Chain Management Software Suppliers," *Modern Material Handling*, August 12, 2009, www .logisticsmgmt.com/article/331247-Top_20_supply_chain_management_software_suppliers_2009.php; and "The 2009 Supply & Demand Chain Executive 100," *Supply & Demand Chain Executive*, June–July 2009, www.sdcexec.com.

23. "Whirlpool: Outsourcing Its National Service Parts Operation Provides Immediate Benefits," www.ryder.com/pdf/MCC633_Whirlpool_single.pdf, accessed October 2010.

24. Jeff Berman, "2009 3PL Revenue Down 15.2 Percent Year-Over-Year," *Logistics Management*, February 2010, p. 21; and David Biederman, "3PL Slowdown Goes Global," *Journal of Commerce*, February 8, 2010, www.joc.com/logistics-economy/3pl-slowdown-goes-global.

Chapter 13

1. Quotes and other information from "The Fortune 500," *Fortune*, May 3, 2010, pp. F1–F51; Jack Neff, "Stuck-in-the Middle Walmart Starts to Lose Share," *Advertising Age*, March 8, 2010, p. 1; "A Promise of Value When Shoppers Need It Most," *Advertising Age*, November 9, 2009, p. 1; Michael Barbaro and Stuart Elliot, "Clinging to Its Roots, Walmart Steps Back from an Edgy, New Image," *International Herald Tribune*, December 10, 2006, accessed at http://

tinyurl.com/2454pb9; Justin Willet, "Walmart Launches New Format at Older Store," *McClatchy-Tribune Business News*, April 30, 2009; Jack Neff, "Why Walmart Is Getting Serious about Marketing," *Advertising Age*, June 8, 2009, p. 1; and various fact sheets and other reports found at www.walmartstores.com, accessed November 2010.

2. Quotes and other information on OgilvyAction from Katy Bachman, "Suit Your Shelf," *AdweekMedia*, January 19, 2009, pp. 10–12; "OgilvyAction Takes Regional Marketers to the Last Mile," January 23, 2008, accessed at www.entrepreneur.com/tradejournals/article/173710015.html; and Jack Neff, "Trouble in Store for Shopper Marketing," *Advertising Age*, March 2, 2009, pp. 3–4. Retail sales statistics from "Monthly and Annual Retail Trade," U.S. Census Bureau, www.census.gov/retail/, accessed February 2010.

3. Jack Neff, "P&G Pushes Design in Brand-Building Strategy," April 12, 2010, accessed at http://adage.com/print?article_id=143211.

4. Store shopping statistics from Bachman, "Suit Your Shelf," p. 10. For more on shopper marketing, see Grocery Manufacturers Association and Deloitte Consulting, *Delivering the Promise of Shopper Marketing: Mastering Execution of Competitive Advantage*, 2008, accessed at www.deloitte.com/dtt/article/0,1002,cid%253D226237,00 .html; Featherstone, "'The Last Mile' of Marketing," *AdweekMedia*, May 4, 2009, p. 17; and "Where to for Shopper Marketing?" *Retail World*, February 1, 2010, p. 20.

5. Richard Westlund, "Bringing Brands to Life: The Power of In-Store Marketing," *Brandweek*, January 18, 2010, pp. IS1–IS2.

6. Jo-Ann Heslin, "Supermarkets—Are They on the Endangered Species List?" *HealthNewsDigest.com*, March 30, 2008, accessed at www .healthnewsdigest.com.

7. Mark Hamstra, "In Tune," *Supermarket News*, October 13, 2008, p. 14; "Kroger Profits as It Woos Shoppers," *Los Angeles Times*, March 10, 2010, p. B2; and www.thekrogerco.com, accessed November 2010.

8. "Convenience Store Industry Sales, Profits Show Gains in 2008," April 7, 2009, accessed at www.nacsonline.com/NACS/News/Daily/Pages/ND0407091.aspx; and "Industry Resources: Fact Sheets," www.nacsonline.com/NACS/News/FactSheets/Pages/default.aspx, accessed April 2010.

9. See "Stan Sheetz Recognized Among Most Influential Retail Leaders in the World," *PR Newswire*, January 29, 2008; "Sheetz, Inc.," *Hoover's Company Records*, March 15, 2010, p. 43078; and www .sheetz.com/main/about/definition.cfm, accessed November 2010.

10. Statistics based on information from "SN Top 75 2010," http://supermarketnews.com/profiles/top75/walmart_stores10/, accessed April 2010; Elliot Zwiebach, "Wal-Mart Trims HQ Office Staff," *Supermarket News*, February 16, 2009, p. 4; and "Supermarket Facts," www.fmi.org/facts_figs/?fuseaction=superfact, accessed March 2010.

11. Extract adapted from information found in Sandra M. Jones, "Outlets Proved Promising for High-End Retailers: Luxury Goods for Less Attract Shoppers," *McClatchy-Tribune Business News*, April 11, 2009. Also see Karen Talley, "Bloomingdale's to Open Outlet Stores," *Wall Street Journal*, January 21, 2010; and David Moin, "VCs Considering Outlets," *WWD*, January 22, 2010, p. 2.

12. Quotes and other information from "Costco Outshines the Rest," *Consumer Reports*, May 2009, p. 8; Matthew Boyle, "Why Costco Is So Addictive," *Fortune*, October 25, 2006, pp. 126–132; Andrew Bary, "Everybody's Store," *Barron's*, February 12, 2007, pp. 29–32; Jeff Chu and Kate Rockwood, "Thinking Outside the Big Box," *Fast Company*, November 2008, pp. 128–131; "Top 10 U.S. Retailers," *RIS News*, December 15, 2009, accessed at www.risnews.com; and www.costco.com, accessed September 2010.

13. Company information from http://www.aboutmcdonalds.com/mcd and www.subway .com/subwayroot/AboutSubway/index .aspx, accessed November 2010.

14. "Ten Brands, Ten Challenges," *Chain Store Age*, August 2008, p. 6A; and Jeremy Lee, "Gap," *Marketing*, August 27, 2008, p. 19; Marianne

Wilson, "Talking Retail," *Chain Store Age*, May 2009, p. 14; and www.gapinc.com/public/Investors/inv_financials.shtml, accessed June 2010.

15. "Whole Foods Market, Inc.," *Hoover's Company Records*, March 25, 2010, p. 10952, p.1; "First: Planet Walmart," *Fortune*, May 3, 2010, p. 27; and www.wholefoodsmarket.com, accessed June 2010.

16. See www.wikinvest.com/stock/J.C._Penney_(JCP), accessed April 2010.

17. See Sandy Smith "Scents and Sellability," *Stores*, July 2009, http://www.stores.org/stores-magazine-july-2009/scents-and-sellability and www.scentair.com, accessed November 2010.

18. For definitions of these and other types of shopping centers, see "Dictionary," American Marketing Association, www.marketingpower.com/_layouts/Dictionary.aspx, accessed December 2010.

19. Paul Grimaldi, "Shopping for a New Look: Lifestyle Centers Are Replacing Enclosed Malls," *Providence Journal (Rhode Island)*, April 29, 2007, p. F10; Neil Nisperos, "Lifestyle Centers Offer More Than Fresh Air," *Inland Valley Daily Bulletin*, January 5, 2009; and Courtenay Edelhart, "Malls Can't Take Customers for Granted As New Outdoor Centers Pop Up," *McClatchy-Tribune Business News*, January 16, 2010.

20. Ken Favaro, Tim Romberger, and David Meer, "Five Rules for Retailing in a Recession," *Harvard Business Review*, April 2009, pp. 64–72.

21. Kenneth Hein, "Target Tries First Price Point Driven TV Ads," *Brandweek*, January 14, 2009, accessed at www.brandweek.com.

22. Hein, p. 1.

23. See Sharon Edelson, "Target to Bring Message Back to Quality," *WWD*, January 22, 2010, p. 2.

24. See www.rpminc.com/consumer.asp, accessed April 2010.

25. U.S. Census Bureau News, "Quarterly Retail E-Commerce Sales, 4th Quarter 2009," February 16, 2010, accessed at www.census.gov/retail/mrts/www/data/html/09Q4.html.

26. Mark Penn, "New Info Shoppers," *Wall Street Journal*, January 8, 2009, accessed at http://online.wsj.com/article/SB123144483005365353.html.

27. The online shopper statistics and extract example are from or adapted from Mark Penn, "New Info Shoppers."

28. "Facts about America's Top 500 E-Retailers," *Internet Retailer*, http://69.67.214.151/top500/facts.asp, accessed September 2010.

29. See Don Davis, "M Is for Multi-channel," *Internet Retailer*, June 2007, www.internetretailer .com/2007/06/01/m-is-for-multi-channel; Macy's, Inc., Online Selling Sites Enhance Integration with Bricks-and-Mortar Stores, *Business Wire*, December 8, 2008; and information from www.macys.com, accessed November 2010.

30. See Deena M. Amato McCoy, "Connecting with Customers," *Grocery Headquarters*, December 1, 2009, http://groceryheadquarters.com/articles/2009-12-01/Connecting-with-customers; and Bob Greenberg, "Reinventing Retail," *Brandweek*, February 15, 2010, p. 16.

31. See Jordan Cooke, "McDonald's Eco-Friendly Seal," *McClatchy-Tribune Business News*, January 13, 2010; "The Golden Arches Go Green: McDonald's First LEED Certified Restaurant," December 11, 2008, accessed at www.greenbeanchicago.com; "McDonald's Green Prototype Uses 25 Percent Less Energy," *Environmental Leader*, April 8, 2009, accessed at www.environmentalleader.com; and D. Gail Fleenor, "Green Light," *Stores*, October 2009, p. 52.

32. Quotes and other information from Berlinski, "Green Keeps Growing," *Private Label Magazine*, www.privatelabelmag.com/feature.cfm, accessed March 31, 2010, p. 1; and www.jcpenney.com, accessed November 2010.

33. See Alan Wolf, "Chains Embrace Eco Strategies," *Twice*, March 30, 2009, p. 1; and information from www.staples.com and www.bestbuy.com, accessed November 2010.

34. Peter Berlinski, "Green Keeps Growing." Also see Kee-hung Lai, T.C.E. Cheng, and Ailie K.Y. Tang, "Green Retailing: Factors for Success," *California Management Review*, Winter 2010, pp. 6+.

35. "Walmart: International Data Sheet," http://walmartstores.com/pressroom/news/9705.aspx, accessed February 2010; and http://investors.target.com/phoenix.zhtml?c=65828&p=irol-IRHome, accessed April 2010.

36. See "Emerging from the Downturn: Global Powers of Retailing 2010," *Stores*, January 2010, accessed at www.deloitte.com/assets/Dcom-Global/Local%20Assets/Documents/Consumer%20Business/dtt_globalpowersofretailing2010.pdf.

37. Information from http://walmartstores.com//default.aspx and www.carrefour.com, accessed June 2010.

38. See the *Grainger 2010 Fact Book* and other information accessed at http://pressroom.grainger.com/phoenix.zhtml?c=76754&p=irol-irFactBook and www.grainger.com.

39. *Grainger 2009 Fact Book*, accessed at http://pressroom.grainger.com/phoenix.zhtml?c=76754&p=irol-irFactBook.

40. See Dale Buss, "The New Deal," *Sales & Marketing Management*, June 2002, pp. 25–30; Colleen Gourley, "Redefining Distribution," *Warehousing Management*, October 2000, pp. 28–30; Stewart Scharf, "Grainger: Tooled Up for Growth," *BusinessWeek Online*, April 25, 2006, p. 8; and *Grainger 2010 Fact Book*, accessed at www.grainger.com.

41. Information from "About Us" www.mckesson.com and "Supply Management Online," www.mckesson.com/en_us/McKesson.com/For+Pharmacies/Retail+National+ Chains/Ordering+and +Inventory+Management/Supply+Management+Online.html, accessed November 2010.

42. Facts from www.supervalu.com, accessed June 2010.

43. See McKesson "Form 10-K," May 5, 2009, accessed at http://www.mckesson.com/en_us/McKesson.com/Investors/Financial%2BInformation/SEC%2BFilings.html, accessed September 2010.

Chapter 14

1. See "Integrated Campaigns: Häagen-Dazs," *Communication Arts Advertising Annual 2009*, pp. 158–159; Tiffany Meyers, "Marketing 50: Häagen-Dazs, Katty Pien," *Advertising Age*, November 17, 2008, p. S15; Barbara Lippert, "Häagen-Dazs Tries Beekeeping," *Adweek*, May 5, 2008, accessed at www.adweek.com/aw/content_display/creative/critique/e3i26f1bfd408799a2088db93460922ea3f; Ted McKenna, "The Right Message," *PR Week*, July 28, 2008, p. 17; Karen Egolf, "Häagen-Dazs Extends Social Media Effort," *Advertising Age*, November 10, 2009, accessed at http://adage.com/goodworks/post?article_id=140412; "Häagen-Dazs Loves Honey Bees," April 28, 2010, a summary video accessed at http://limeshot.com/2010/haagen-dazs-loves-honey-bees-titanium-silver-lion-cannes-2009; and information from www.helpthehoneybees.com, accessed October 2010.

2. For other definitions, see www.marketingpower.com/_layouts/Dictionary.aspx, accessed December 2010.

3. Piet Levy, "Touching the Dial," *Marketing News*, March 3, 2010, pp. 16–18. Also see Bob Garfield, *The Chaos Scenario* (Franklin, TN: Stielstra Publishing, 2009); Garfield, "Future May Be Brighter But It's Apocalypse Now," *Advertising Age*, March 23, 2009, pp. 1, 14; and James Othmer, "When I Knew Advertising Had Completely Changed," *Advertising Age*, January 4, 2010, pp. 4, 23.

4. Burt Helm, "TV Commercials: Who Needs Them," *BusinessWeek*, May 25, 2009, p. 24; and Elizabeth A. Sullivan, "Targeting to the Extreme," *Marketing News*, June 15, 2009, pp. 17–19.

5. Jack Neff, "'Passion for Digital' Pumps P&G's Spending," *Advertising Age*, June 8, 2009, accessed at http://adage.com/digital/article?article_id=137134.

6. Quote from Michael Schneider, "Nielsen: Traditional TV Still King," *Variety*, December 7, 2009. TV advertising stats from "U.S. Ad Spending Totals by Medium," *Advertising Age*, June 21, 2010, p. 22.

7. "Integrated Campaigns," Advertising Annual 2008, *Communication Arts*, pp. 72–73; Emily Bryson York, "'Whopper Freakout' Wins Grand Effie," *Advertising Age*, June 4, 2009, accessed at http://adage.com/article?article_id=137066; and www.bk.com/en/us/campaigns/whopper-freakout.html, accessed December 2010.

8. Based on information from "Kia Unveils Super Bowl Ad with Popular Life-Size Children's Characters Taking Cross-Country Joyride in the All-New 2011 Sorento," *PRNewswire*, February 5, 2010.

9. See "Brand Design: Cracking the Colour Code," *Marketing Week*, October 11, 2007, p. 28; and Joe Tradii, "Available for Your Brand: Burnt Umber! Any Takers?" *Brandweek*, November 17, 2009, accessed at www.brandweek.com.

10. Jonah Bloom, "The Truth Is: Consumers Trust Fellow Buyers Before Marketers," *Advertising Age*, February 13, 2006, p. 25; and "Global Advertising: Consumers Trust Real Friends and Virtual Strangers the Most," *Nielsen Wire*, July 7, 2009.

11. See www.tremor.com/revealing-case-studies/crest-weekly-clean/, accessed June 2010.

12. See Lacey Rose, "The 10 Most Trusted Celebrities," *Forbes*, January 25, 2010, accessed at www.forbes.com; Robert Klara, "I'm with the Celebrity, Get Me Out of Here!" *Brandweek*, March 8, 2010, p. 13; and "Which Athletes Can Lift Brands?" *Mediaweek*, April 19, 2010, p. 23.

13. T. L. Stanley, "Dancing with the Stars," *Brandweek*, March 8, 2010, pp. 10–12.

14. For more on advertising spending by company and industry, see http://adage.com/ datacenter/datapopup.php?article_id=119881, accessed September 2010.

15. For more on setting promotion budgets, see W. Ronald Lane, Karen Whitehill King, and J. Thomas Russell, *Kleppner's Advertising Procedure*, 18th ed. (Upper Saddle River, NJ: Prentice Hall, 2011), chapter 6.

16. See "Super Bowl Dethrones 'M*A*S*H,' Sets All-Time Record!" *Hollywood Reporter*, February 8, 2010, www.thrfeed.com/2010/02/super-bowl-xliv-ratings-.html; Bill Gorman, "Academy Awards Averages 41.3 Million Viewers; Most Since 2005," *TV by the Numbers*, March 8, 2010, www.tvbythenumbers.com; and Denise Martin, "Ratings: 'American Idol' Premiere Draws 29.8 Million Viewers," *Los Angeles Times*, January 13, 2010, http://latimesblogs.latimes.com.

17. Susan Greco, "How to Reduce Your Cost of Sales," *Inc.*, March 5, 2010, accessed at www.inc.com/guide/reducing-cost-of-sales.html#.

18. Dianna Dilworth, "Sun Chips Promotes Compostable Chip Bag with Pre-Earth Day Campaign," *DMNews*, March 31, 2010, accessed at www.dmnews.com/sunchips-promotes-compostable-chip-bag-with-pre-earth-day-campaign/article/167069/.

19. For more on the legal aspects of promotion, see Lane, King, and Russell, *Kleppner's Advertising Procedure*, chapter 25; and William L. Cron and Thomas E. DeCarlo, *Dalrymple's Sales Management*, 10th ed. (New York: Wiley, 2009), chapter 10.

Chapter 15

1. See Devin Leonard, "Hey, PC, Who Taught You to Fight Back?" *New York Times*, August 30, 2009, p. BU1; Eleftheria Parpis, "Microsoft Fetes Windows 7 'Creators,'" *Adweek*, October 22, 2009, accessed at www.adweek.com/aw/content_display/esearch/e3i92ec830f3865d5c0c7438cad8708e49e; Noreen O'Leary, "Amid Transition, Rivals Are Descending on Apple," *Brandweek*, November 7, 2009, p. 4; Abbey Klaassen, "In Mac vs. PC Battle, Microsoft Winning in Value Perception," *Advertising Age*, May 18, 2009, accessed at http://adage.com/digital/article?article_id=136731; Rupal Parekh, "Microsoft vs. Apple Fight Enters New Round," *Advertising Age*, September 18, 2008, accessed at http://adage.com/article?article_id=131102; and Josh Smith, "Apple Ends 'Get a Mac' Ads: Goodbye Mac, Goodbye PC," May 26, 2010, accessed at www.walletpop.com/blog/2010/05/26/apple-ends-get-a-mac-ads-goodbye-mac-goodbye-pc/.

2. Data on U.S. and global advertising spending obtained at "Leading National Advertisers," *Advertising Age*, June 21, 2010, pp. 10–12; "Top 50 Global Marketers," *Advertising Age*, December 28, 2009, p. 15.

3. See http://2010.census.gov/mediacenter/paid-ad-campaign/new-ads/index.php?v n11, accessed June 2010.

4. For these and other examples of comparative advertising, see Emily Bryson York and Natalie Zmuda, "So Sue Me: Why Big Brands Are Taking Claims to Court," *Advertising Age*, January 4, 2010, pp. 1, 23; Marin Perez, "AT&T Ends Verizon Ad Lawsuit," *InformationWeek*, December 2, 2009, http://www.informationweek.com/news/mobility/ 3G/showArticle.jhtml?articleID=222000326; "Pepsi Suing Coca-Cola Over Powerade Ads," *New York Times*, April 13, 2009, accessed at www.nytimes.com; Emily Bryson York, "Book of Tens: Nasty Comparative Campaigns of 2009," *Advertising Age*, December 14, 2009, accessed at http://adage.com/print?article_id=141025; and Isabella Soscia, Simona Girolamo, and Bruno Busacca, "The Effect of Comparison Advertising on Consumer Perceptions: Similarity or Differentiation?" *Journal of Business and Psychology*, March 2010, pp. 109–118.

5. For more on advertising budgets, see Ronald Lane, Karen King, and Thomas Russell, *Kleppner's Advertising Procedure*, 18th ed. (Upper Saddle River, NJ: Prentice Hall, 2011), chapter 6.

6. Example adapted from Jean Halliday, "Thinking Big Takes Audi from Obscure to Awesome," *Advertising Age*, February 2, 2009, accessed at http://adage.com/print ?article_id=134234. Also see Jack Neff, "Study: Cutting Spending Hurts Brands in Long-Term: Following Boom/Bust Cycle Flirts with Danger," *Advertising Age*, April 6, 2009, accessed at http://adage.com/article?article_id=135790; and Nat Ives, "Ad Spending Dropped 12% in 2009, But Things Are Looking Up," *Advertising Age*, March 17, 2010, accessed at http://adage.com/print?article_id=142832.

7. "Average U.S. Home Now Receives a Record 118.6 TV Channels, According to Nielsen" June 6, 2008, http://en-us.nielsen.com/content/nielsen/en_us/news/news_releases/2008/june/average_u_s__home.html; and "Number of Magazines by Category," http://www.magazine.org/asme/editorial%5Ftrends, accessed August 2010.

8. Louise Story, "Anywhere the Eye Can See, It's Likely to See an Ad," *New York Times*, January 15, 2007, p. A12; and James Othmer, "Persuasion Gives Way to Engagement," *Vancouver Sun*, August 20, 2009, p. A13.

9. See Bill Carter, "An 'Idol' Ratings Loss, But Not in Its Pocketbook," *New York Times*, April 6, 2010, www.nytimes.com; "Executive Summary of the 4A's Television Production Cost Survey," December 15, 2009, www.aaaa.org/news/bulletins/Documents/2008TVPCSExecSumcosts.pdf; Bill Gorman, "Fox's Average Ad Price in Q4 2009: $122,000," March 16, 2010, www.tvbytheNumbers.com; Brian Steinberg, "'Sunday Night Football' Remains Costliest TV Show," *Advertising Age*, October 26, 2009, p. 8; and "Sluggish Economy Pinches Super Bowl Ad Prices," *Associated Press*, January 11, 2010.

10. "Advertising in the U.S.: Synovate Global Survey Shows Internet, Innovation and Online Privacy a Must," December 3, 2009, accessed at http://www.synovate.com/news/article/2009/12/advertising-in-the-us-synovate-global-survey-shows-internet-innovation-and-online-privacy-a-must.html; and Katy Bachman, "Survey: Clutter Causing TV Ads to Lack Effectiveness," *MediaWeek*, February 8, 2010.

11. "Report: Ad Execs Stymied by DVR Ad Skipping," *Mediaweek*, June 29, 2009, accessed at http://www.adweek.com/aw/content_display/news/e3i4fe3d67e44c8b3aded206ae7b29cd20b; Nielsen, *How DVRs Are Changing the Television Landscape*, April 2009, http://blog.nielsen.com/nielsenwire/wp-content/uploads/2009/04/dvr_tvlandscape_043009.pdf; Bill Carter, "DVR, Once TVs Mortal Foe, Helps Ratings," *New York Times*, November 2, 2009, www.nytimes.com; and Andrew O'Connell, Advertisers: Learn to Love the DVR," *Harvard Business Review*, April 2010, p. 22.

12. See Alessandra Stanley, "Commercials You Can't Zap," *New York Times*, June 7, 2009, p. MT1; Sam Schechner and Suzanne Vranica, "IPad Gets Star Turn in Television Comedy," *Wall Street Journal*, April 2, 2010, p. B8; and Rupal Parekh, "Why Long-Form Ads Are the Wave of the Future," *Advertising Age*, May 3, 2010, accessed at http://adage.com/madisonandvine/article?article_id=143603.

13. For more on product placements, see Randee Dawn and Alex Ben Block, "Brands Take 'American Idol' Stage," *Adweek*, May 12, 2009,

accessed at http://www.adweek.com/aw/content_display/news/strategy/e3if21dd856cfb9103e5d9128faa8ed6740; Richard Huff, "Product Placement Outsells Ads," *Daily News*, December 27, 2007, p. 73; Ravi Somaiya, "Chloe, It's Kac. Who Does Our Phones?" *Guardian*, June 16, 2008, accessed at www.guardian.com; Stanley, "Commercials You Can't Zap"; and T. L. Stanley, "A Place for Everything," *Brandweek*, March 1, 2010, pp. 12–14.

14. Adapted from information found in Bob Garfield, "How Etsy Made Us Rethink Consumer-Generated Ads," *Advertising Age*, September 21, 2009, p. 4.

15. For more on consumer-generated advertising, see Emma Hall, "Most Winning Creative Work Involves Consumer Participation," *Advertising Age*, January 6, 2010, accessed at http://adage.com/print?article_id=141329; Stuart Elliott, "Do-It-Yourself Super Ads," *New York Times*, February 8, 2010, www.nytimes.com; Michael Learmonth, "Brands Team Up for User-Generated-Ad Contests," *Advertising Age*, March 23, 2009, p. 8; and Rich Thomaselli, "If Consumer Is Your Agency, It's Time for Review," *Advertising Age*, May 17, 2010, p. 2.

16. See David Kiley, "Paying for Viewers Who Pay Attention," *BusinessWeek*, May 18, 2009, p. 56.

17. Brian Steinberg, "Viewer-Engagement Rankings Signal Change for TV Industry," *Advertising Age*, May 10, 2010, p. 12.

18. See Claudia Wallis, "The Multitasking Generation," *Time*, March 27, 2006, accessed at www.time.com/time/magazine/article/0,9171,1174696,00.html; Tanya Irwin, "Study: Kids Are Master Multitaskers on TV, Web, Mobile," *MediaPost Publications*, March 10, 2008, accessed at www.mediapostpublications.com; Jon Lafayette, "Integrated Campaigns Worth Overcoming Hurdles," April 29, 2009, accessed at http://www.tvweek.com/news/2009/04/integrated_campaigns_worth_ove.php; and Henry J. Kaiser Family Foundation, *Generation M2: Media in the Lives of 8- to 18-Year-Olds*, January 20, 2010, accessed at www.kff.org/entmedia/mh012010pkg.cfm.

19. *Newsweek* and *BusinessWeek* cost and circulation data online at http://mediakit.businessweek.com and www.newsweekmediakit.com, accessed October 2010.

20. Kate Maddox, "Optimism, Accountability, Social Media Top Trends," *BtoB*, January 18, 2010, p. 1.

21. See Lawrence A. Crosby, "Getting Serious about Marketing ROI," *Marketing Management*, May/June 2009, pp. 10–17.

22. Stuart Elliott, "How Effective Is This Ad, in Real Numbers? Beats Me," *New York Times*, July 20, 2005, p. C8; and "Taking Measure of Which Metrics Matter," *BtoB*, May 5, 2008, http://www.btobonline.com/apps/pbcs.dll/article?AID=/20080505/FREE/137926423/1150/ISSUENEWS.

23. Information on advertising agency revenues from "Agency Report 2010," *Advertising Age*, April 26, 2010, pp. 22+.

24. Adapted from Scott Cutlip, Allen Center, and Glen Broom, *Effective Public Relations*, 10th ed. (Upper Saddle River, NJ: Prentice Hall, 2009), chapter 1.

25. Information from "The Heart Truth: Making Healthy Hearts Fashionable," Ogilvy Public Relations Worldwide, accessed at www.ogilvypr.com/en/case-study/heart-truth?page=0, accessed June 2010; and www.nhlbi.nih.gov/educational/hearttruth/about/index.htm, accessed November 2010.

26. See Geoffrey Fowler and Ben Worthen, "Buzz Powers iPad Launch," *Wall Street Journal*, April 2, 2010; "Apple iPad Sales Top 2 Million Since Launch," *Tribune-Review* (Pittsburgh), June 2, 2010; and "PR Pros Must Be Apple's iPad as a True Game-Changer," *PRweek*, May 2010, p. 23.

27. Matthew Schwartz, "New Influence," *Advertising Age*, October 26, 2009, p. S4.

28. Adapted from information in "PR in the Driver's Seat," *Advertising Age*, October 26, 2009, pp. S6–S7.

29. Paul Holmes, "Senior Marketers Are Sharply Divided about the Role of PR in the Overall Mix," *Advertising Age*, January 24, 2005, pp. C1–C2. For another example, see Jack Neff, "How Pampers Battled Diaper Debacle," *Advertising Age*, May 10, 2010, accessed at http://adage.com/article?article_id=143777.

Chapter 16

1. Based on information from numerous P&G managers; with information from "500 Largest Sales Forces in America," *Selling Power*, October 2009, pp. 43–60; and www.pg.com/jobs/jobs_us/cac/f_cbd_home.shtml, accessed December 2010.

2. Adapted from information in Kim Wright Wiley, "For the Love of Sales," *Selling Power*, October 2008, pp. 70–73.

3. See Philip Kotler, Neil Rackham, and Suj Krishnaswamy, "Ending the War Between Sales and Marketing," *Harvard Business Review*, July–August 2006, pp. 68–78; Christian Homburg, Ove Jensen, and Harley Krohmer, "Configurations of Marketing and Sales: A Taxonomy," *Journal of Marketing*, March 2008, pp. 133–154; Paul Greenberg, "The Shotgun Marriage of Sales and Marketing," *Customer Relationship Management*, February 2010, pp. 30–36; and Elizabeth A. Sullivan, "The Ties That Bind," *Marketing News*, May 15, 2010.

4. Example based on Ernest Waaser and others, "How You Slice It: Smarter Segmentation for Your Sales Force," *Harvard Business Review*, March 2004, pp. 105–111.

5. "Selling Power 500: The Largest Sales Force in America," http://www.sellingpower.com/content/article.php?a=7823, accessed September/October 2010.

6. For more on this and other methods for determining sales force size, see Mark W. Johnston and Greg W. Marshall, *Sales Force Management*, 9th ed. (Boston: McGraw-Hill Irwin, 2009), pp. 152–156.

7. Susan Greco, "How to Reduce Your Cost of Sales," *Inc.*, March 5, 2010, accessed at www.inc.com/guide/reducing-cost-of-sales.html#.

8. See "Case Study: Climax Portable Machine Tools," www.selltis.com/products/SalesCaseStudyClimax.aspx, accessed December 2010.

9. Jennifer J. Salopek, "Bye, Bye, Used Car Guy," *T+D*, April 2007, pp. 22–25; William F. Kendy, "No More Lone Rangers," *Selling Power*, April 2004, pp. 70–74; Michelle Nichols, "Pull Together—Or Fall Apart," *BusinessWeek*, December 2, 2005, accessed at www.businessweek.com/smallbiz/content/may2005/sb20050513_6167.htm; and John Boe, "Cross-Selling Takes Teamwork," *American Salesman*, March 2009, pp. 14–16.

10. "Customer Business Development," www.pg.com/jobs/jobs_us/cac/f_cbd_home.shtml, accessed November 2010.

11. For this and more information and discussion, see www.gallup.com/consulting/1477/Sales-Force-Effectiveness.aspx, accessed October 2009; Benson Smith, *Discover Your Strengths: How the World's Greatest Salespeople Develop Winning Careers* (New York: Warner Business Books, 2003); Tom Reilly, "Planning for Success," *Industrial Distribution*, May 2007, p. 25; Dave Kahle, "The Four Characteristics of Successful Salespeople," *Industrial Distribution*, April 2008, p. 54; and "The 10 Skills of 'Super' Salespeople," www.businesspartnerships.ca/articles/the_10_skills_of_super_salespeople.phtml, accessed May 2010.

12. "2008 Corporate Learning Factbook Values U.S. Training at $58.5B," *Business Wire*, January 29, 2008; and "ADP Case Study," Corporate Visions, Inc., www.corporatevisions.com/client_result.html, accessed August 2010.

13. Based on information found in Sara Donnelly, "Staying in the Game," *Pharmaceutical Executive*, May 2008, pp. 158–159; "Improving Sales Force Effectiveness: Bayer's Experiment with New Technology," Bayer Healthcare Pharmaceuticals, Inc., 2008, www.icmrindia.org/casestudies/catalogue/Marketing/MKTG200.htm; and Tanya Lewis, "Concentric," *Medical Marketing and Media*, July 2008, p. 59. For more on e-learning, see "Logging on for Sale School," *CustomRetailer*, November 2009, p. 30; and Sarah Boehle, "Global Sales Training's Balancing Act," *Training*, January 2010, p. 29.

14. See Joseph Kornak, "07 Compensation Survey: What's It All Worth?" *Sales & Marketing Management*, May 2007, pp. 28–39; and William L. Cron and Thomas E. DeCarlo, *Dalrymple's Sales Management*, 10th edition (New York: John Wiley & Sons Inc., 2009), p. 303.

15. Susan Greco, "How to Reduce Your Cost of Sales."

16. See Henry Canady, "How to Increase the Time Reps Spend Selling," *Selling Power*, March 2005, p. 112; David J. Cichelli, "Plugging Sales 'Time Leaks,'" *Sales & Marketing Management*, April 2006, p. 23; and Rebecca Aronauer, "Time Well Spent," *Sales & Marketing Management*, January–February 2007, p. 7.

17. See Gary H. Anthes, "Portal Powers GE Sales," *Computerworld*, June 2, 2003, pp. 31–32. Also see Henry Canaday, "How to Boost Sales Productivity and Save Valuable Time," *Agency Sales*, November 2007, p. 20; and "According to IDC, One-Third of Potential Selling Time Is Wasted Due to Poor Sales Enhancement," *Business Wire*, November 13, 2008.

18. For extensive discussions of sales force automation, see the May 2005 issue of *Industrial Marketing Management*, which is devoted to the subject; Anupam Agarwal, "Bringing Science to Sales," *Customer Relationship Management*, March 2008, p. 16; and, Robert M. Barker, Stephen F. Gohmann, Jian Guan, and David J. Faulds, "Why Is My Sales Force Automation System Failing?" *Harvard Business Review*, May/June 2009, p. 233.

19. Adapted from information found in Pelin Wood Thorogood, "Sales 2.0: How Soon Will It Improve Your Business?" *Selling Power*, November/December 2008, pp. 58–61; and Gerhard Gschwandtner, "What Is Sales 2.0, and Why Should You Care?" *Selling Power*, March/April 2010, p. 9.

20. Adapted from information in Elizabeth A. Sullivan, "B-to-B Marketers: One-to-One Marketing," *Marketing News*, May 15, 2009, pp. 11–13. Also see "Social Media to Lead Growth in Online B2B Marketing," *Min's b2b*, February 8, 2010, accessed at www.minonline.com/b2b/13441.html; and "Eye on Advertising: Social Media Taps Its Way into B2B Marketing Plans," *Min's b2b*, February 1, 2010, accessed at www.minonline.com/b2b/13378.html.

21. Quotes from David Thompson, "Embracing the Future: A Step by Step Overview of Sales 2.0," *Sales and Marketing Management*, July/August 2008, p. 21; and "Ahead of the Curve: How Sales 2.0 Will Affect Your Sales Process—For the Better," *Selling Power*, March/April 2010, pp. 14–17.

22. Quotes from Bob Donath, "Delivering Value Starts with Proper Prospecting," *Marketing News*, November 10, 1997, p. 5; and Bill Brooks, "Power-Packed Prospecting Pointers," *Agency Sales*, March 2004, p. 37. Also see Maureen Hrehocik, "Why Prospecting Gets No Respect," *Sales & Marketing Management*, October 2007, p. 7; and "Referrals," *Partner's Report*, January 2009, p. 8.

23. Quotes in this paragraph from Lain Ehmann, "Prepare to Win," *Selling Power*, April 2008, pp. 27–29.

24. John Graham, "Salespeople under Siege: The Profession Redefined," *Agency Sales*, January 2010, pp. 20–25; and Rick Phillips, "Don't Pressure, Persuade," *Selling Power*, January/February 2010, p. 22.

25. "For B-to-B, Engagement, Retention Are Key," *Marketing News*, April 15, 2009, p. 9; and Nancy Peretsman, "Stop Talking and Start Listening," *Fortune*, November 9, 2009, p. 24.

26. Example based on information from James C. Anderson, Nirmalya Kumar, and James A. Narus, "Become a Value Merchant," *Sales & Marketing Management*, May 6, 2008, pp. 20–23; and "Business Market Value Merchants," *Marketing Management*, March/April 2008, pp. 31+. Also see John A. Quelch and Katherine E. Jocz, "How to Market in a Downturn," *Harvard Business Review*, April 2009, pp. 52–62.

27. *Transforming Trade Promotion/Shopper-Centric Approach* (Wilton, CT: Kantar Retail, June 2010), p. 8.

28. Based on information and quotes from Richard H. Levey, "A Slip Between Cup and Lip," *Direct*, May 1, 2008, http://directmag.com/

roi/0508-starbucks-loyalty-program/index.html; Emily Bryson York, "Starbucks: Don't Be Seduced by Lower Prices," *Advertising Age*, April 30, 2009, accessed at http://adage.com/print?article_id=136389; and Emily Bryson York, "Starbucks Gets Its Business Brewing Again with Social Media," *Advertising Age*, February 22, 2010, p. 34.

29. See "Coupon Use Skyrocketed in 2009," *Promo*, January 27, 2010.

30. See www.happymeal.com/en_US/, accessed April 2010.

31. See "2010 Promotion Products Fact Sheet," www.ppa.org/NR/rdonlyres/35235FB0-A367-4498-B0AF-E88085C3A60B/0/PPAIProProFactSheet.pdf, accessed August 2010.

32. Based on information found in "Dunkin' Donuts Returns to Its Roots—Doughnuts—in $10 Million Campaign," *Promo*, March 18, 2009, accessed at http://promomagazine.com/contests/dunkindonutscampaign/; "Time to Judge the Donuts," *PR Newswire*, May 18, 2009; Steve Adams, "Dunkin Donuts Contest Finalists Cooked Their Unique Creations in Bake-Off," *Patriot Ledger*, May 29, 2009, accessed at http://www.patriotledger.com/business/x1594716181/Doughnut-design-101; and www.dunkindonuts.com/donut/, August 2010.

33. "Kraft Foods Scores Multi-Season Partnership with the NCAA and CBS Sports," *Business Wire*, March 11, 2010.

34. "The Charmin Restrooms Return to Times Square This Holiday Season to Help Consumers Really 'Enjoy the Go,'" *PR Newswire*, November 23, 2009; and http://www.charmin.com/en_US/enjoy-the-go/nyc-restrooms.php, accessed March 2010.

35. *Transforming Trade Promotion/Shopper-Centric Approach*, p. 8.

36. See Erica Ogg, "CES Attendance Bounces Back," *Circuit Breaker—CNET News*, January 11, 2010, accessed at http://news.cnet.com/8301-31021_3-10432369-260.html; and the Bauma Web site, www.bauma.de, accessed October 2010.

Chapter 17

1. See Daniel Lyons, "The Customer Is Always Right," *Newsweek*, January 4, 2010, p. 85; Brad Stone, "Can Amazon Be the Walmart of the Web?" *New York Times*, September 20, 2009, p. BU1; Heather Green, "How Amazon Aims to Keep You Clicking," *BusinessWeek*, March 2, 2009, pp. 34–40; Joe Nocera, "Putting Buyers First? What a Concept," *New York Times*, January 5, 2008, www.nytimes.com; Brian Morrissey, "Marketer of the Year: Jeff Bezos," *Brandweek*, September 14, 2009, p. 30; Geoffrey A. Fowler, "Corporate News: Amazon's Sales Soar, Lifting Profit," *Wall Street Journal*, April 23, 2010, p. B3; and annual reports and other information found at www.amazon.com, accessed October 2010.

2. For these and other direct marketing statistics in this section, see Direct Marketing Association, *The DMA 2010 Statistical Fact Book*, *32nd edition*, February 2010; and Direct Marketing Association, *The Power of Direct Marketing: 2008–2009 Edition*, June 2009; "DMA's Power to Direct Marketing Report Finds DM Ad Expenditures Climb to Over 54% of All Advertising Expenditures," October 19, 2009, accessed at www.the-dma.org/cgi/dispannouncements?article=1335; and a wealth of other information at www.the-dma.org, accessed November 2010.

3. See "Advertising Age's Digital Market Facts 2010," foldout in *Advertising Age*, February 22, 2010.

4. Susan Greco, "How to Reduce Your Cost of Sales," *Inc.*, March 5, 2010, accessed at www.inc.com/guide/reducing-cost-of-sales.html#.

5. Portions adapted from Mike Beirne, "A Wing—and a Ding," *Brandweek*, October 23, 2006, p. 22; and Jason Voight, "Southwest Keeps Fans from Straying," *Adweek*, August 20, 2007, accessed at www.adweek.com/aw/esearch/article_display.jsp? vnu_content_id=1003627839. Other information from "Southwest Airlines Celebrates Anniversary of DING!" *PR Newswire*, February 28, 2008; Bob Garfield, "What's the Big Deal with Widgets?" *Advertising Age*, December 1, 2008, p. 1; www.blogsouthwest.com and "What Is DING!?" www.southwest.com/ding, accessed December 2010.

6. Mike Freeman, "Data Company Helps Wal-Mart, Casinos, Airlines Analyze Data," *Knight Ridder Business Tribune News*, February 24, 2006, p. 1; Eric Lai, "Teradata Creates Elite Club for Petabyte-Plus Data Warehouse Customers," *Computer World*, October 14, 2008, http://www.computerworld.com/s/article/9117159/Teradata_creates_elite_club_for_petabyte_plus_data_warehouse_customers; and "Data, Data Everywhere," *Economist*, February 27, 2010, p. 3.

7. See Scott Horstein, "Use Care with That Database," *Sales & Marketing Management*, May 2006, p. 22; "USAA Announces Mobile RDC App for Android Phones," *TechWeb*, January 27, 2010; "USAA," *Hoover's Company Records*, June 15, 2010, http://premium.hoovers.com/subscribe/co/factsheet.xhtml?ID=cfhfxffksyjscr; Jean McGregor, "Customer Service Champs: USAA's Battle Plan," *Bloomberg BusinessWeek*, March 1, 2010, pp. 40–43; "Largest U.S. Corporations," *Fortune*, May 3, 2010, p. F7; and www.usaa.com, accessed November 2010.

8. See DMA, *The Power of Direct Marketing, 2009–2010 Edition*; and "Mail Spend to Rise," *Deliver Magazine*, January 7, 2010, https://www.delivermagazine.com/the-magazine/2010/01/07/mail-spend-to-rise.

9. Julie Liesse, "When Times Are Hard, Mail Works," *Advertising Age*, March 30, 2009, p. 14; and Sarah O'Leary, "Thanks to Spam, It's Not Junk Mail Anymore," *Huffington Post*, April 19, 2010, http://www.huffingtonpost.com/sarah-oleary/thanks-to-spam-its-not-ju_b_542024.html; For counterpoints, see Gavin O'Malley, "Direct-Mail Doomed, Long Live E-Mail," *MediaPost News*, May 20, 2009, accessed at www.mediapost.com/publications.

10. Based on information from "JDA, HP, and Intel Team Up with Mahoney to Yield Outstanding Quantifiable Results," The Mahoney Company, www.mahoneyprint.com/caseStudies/jda.pdf; and Heather Fletcher, "PURLs of Wisdom," *Target Marketing*, January 2009, pp. 27–29.

11. Jeffrey Ball, "Power Shift: In Digital Era, Marketers Still Prefer a Paper Trail," *Wall Street Journal*, October 16, 2009, p. A3.

12. Ball, "Power Shift: In Digital Era, Marketers Still Prefer a Paper Trail"; and "Report: Catalogs Increasingly Drive Online Sales," RetailCustomerExperience.com, March 17, 2010, www.retailcustomerexperience.com/article/21521/Report-Catalogs-increasingly-drive-online-sales.

13. DMA, *The Power of Direct Marketing, 2009–2010 Edition*.

14. "Off the Hook," *Marketing Management*, January–February 2008, p. 5; Jeff Gelles, "Consumer 10.0: Calls Persist Despite List," *Philadelphia Inquirer*, January 24, 2010, p. D2; and www.donotcall.gov, accessed October 2010.

15. See Geoffrey A. Fowler, "Peeved at Auto Warranty Calls, a Web Posse Strikes Back," *Wall Street Journal*, May 15, 2009, A1.

16. See Brian Steinberg, "Read This Now!; But Wait! There's More! The Infomercial King Explains," *Wall Street Journal*, March 9, 2005, p. 1; Rachel Brown, "Perry, Fischer, Lavigne Tapped for Proactiv," *WWD*, January 13, 2010, p. 3; and www.proactiv.com, accessed November 2010.

17. Brian O'Keefe, "Secrets of the TV Pitchmen," *Fortune*, April 13, 2009, pp. 82–90; and Andrew Adam Newman, "Snuggie Rode Silly Ads to Stardom Over Rivals," *New York Times*, February 26, 2009, http://www.nytimes.com/2009/02/27/business/media/27adco.html.

18. Example adapted from Beth Snyder Bulik, "Act Now, and Will Double Your Market Share!" *Advertising Age*, August 27, 2009, accessed at http://adage.com/article?article_id=138693.

19. Adapted from Allison Fass, "Extreme Makeover," *Forbes*, September 1, 2008, pp. 64–66. Also see Richard Mullins, "TV, Web Sales Have HSN Clicking," *Tampa Tribune*, May 6, 2010, p. 8.

20. Stephanie Rosenbloom, "The New Touch-Face of Vending Machines," *New York Times*, May 25, 2010, accessed at www.nytimes.com/2010/05/26/business/26vending.html.

21. Beth Snyder Bulik, "Redbox Rakes in Green in Tough Times," *Advertising Age*, February 23, 2009, p. 6; Jessica Mintz, "Redbox's Machines Take on Netflix's Red Envelopes," *USA Today*, June 22, 2009, accessed at www.usatoday.com/tech/news/2009-06-22-redbox_N.htm; Brad Tuttle, "Movies for Cheap," *Time*, March 8, 2010, p. 50; and www.redbox.com, accessed November 2010.

22. Daniel B. Honigman, "On the Verge: Mobile Marketing Will Make Strides," *Marketing News*, January 15, 2008, pp. 18–21; "Mobile Search Ads to Grow 130% by 2013," *TechWeb*, February 25, 2009; "Mobile Web Use Leaps 34%," *Adweek*, September 30, 2009, www.adweek.com; Carol Flammer, "Cell Phones, Texting and Your Customers," January 9, 2010, www.carolflammer.com/2010/01/cell-phones-text-messaging-marketing-to-consumers/; and "Wireless Quick Facts," http://www.ctia.org/advocacy/research/index.cfm/AID/10323, accessed July 2010.

23. Adapted from Michael Garry, "Going Mobile," *Supermarket News*, January 12, 2009, p. 65.

24. See Emily Burg, "Acceptance of Mobile Ads on the Rise," *MediaPost Publications*, March 16, 2007, accessed at www.mediapost.com/publications; Steve Miller and Mike Beirne, "The iPhone Effect," Adweek.com, April 28, 2008, www.adweek.com; Altmeyer, "Smart Phones, Social Networks to Boost Mobile Advertising," *Reuters.com*, June 29, 2009; and Richard Westlund, "Mobile on Fast Forward," *Brandweek*, March 15, 2010, pp. M1–M5.

25. Arbitron/Edison Internet and Multimedia Study, "The Podcast Consumer Revealed 2009," accessed at www.edisonresearch.com/home/archives/2009/05/the_podcast_consumer_2009.php; and "Marketing News' Digital Handbook," *Marketing News*, April 3, 2009, pp. 9–18.

26. "Disney Online Podcasts," http://disney.go.com/music/podcasts/today/index.html, accessed December 2010; "HP Audio and Video Podcasts," www.hp.com/hpinfo/podcasts.html, accessed December 2010; and "Take These Shows on the Road," http://www.purina.com/downloads/Podcasts/Index.aspx, accessed December 2010.

27. Shahnaz Mahmud, "Survey: Viewers Crave TV Ad Fusion," Adweek.com, January 25, 2008, www.adweek.com; Andrew Hampp, "Addressable Ads Are Here; Who's Ready?" *Advertising Age*, April 13, 2009, p. 9; and Hampp, "Scorecard: Were We Wrong or Almost Right on ITV?" *Advertising Age*, April 12, 2010, http://adage.com/cabletv10/article?article_id=143163.

28. Mark Albright, "With HSN and FIOS, You Can Sit ad Shop," *St. Petersburg Times*, December 4, 2009, p. 4B; and "Shopping HSN via TV Remote Control Now in 20 Million Homes," InternetRetailer.com, January 2010.

29. Adapted from information in Zachary Rodgers, "Cablevision's Interactive TV Ads Pay Off for Gillette," *ClickZ*, October 21, 2009, accessed at www.clickz.com/3635413/print; and David Goetzl, "Interactive Ads Pay Off for Cablevision," *MediaPost News*, January 12, 2010, accessed at www.mediapost.com/publications.

30. For these and other statistics on Internet usage, see "Nielsen Online Reports Topline U.S. Web Data for February 2010," *Nielsen Online*, March 15, 2009, accessed at http://blog.nielsen.com/nielsenwire/online_mobile/nielsen-provides-topline-u-s-web-data-for-february-2010/; and www.internetworldstats.com, accessed July 2010.

31. See "Study Finds Internet More Important Than TV," *Radio Business Report*, March 25, 2010, http://www.rbr.com/media-news/research/22765.html.

32. See "Internet Retailer: Top 500 Guide," www.internetretailer.com/top500/list, accessed October 2010.

33. Staples data from annual reports and other information found at www.staples.com, accessed July 2010.

34. See "U.S. Web Retail Sales to Reach $249 Billion by '14—Study," *Reuters*, March 8, 2010, accessed at www.reuters.com/article/idUSN0825407420100308; and "Retail and Travel Spending," *Advertising Age's Digital Marketing Facts 2010* section, February 22, 2010.

35. Erick Schonfeld, "Forrester Forecast: Online Retail Sales Will Grow to $250 Billion by 2014," *Tech Crunch.com*, March 8, 2010, accessed

at http://techcrunch.com/2010/03/08/forrester-forecast-online-retail-sales-will-grow-to-250-billion-by-2014/; and Anna Johnson, "Local Marketing: 97 Percent of Consumers Use Online Media for Local Shopping," *Kikabink News*, March 17, 2010, accessed at www.kikabink.com/news/local-marketing-97-percent-of-consumers-use-online-media-for-local-shopping/.

36. Information for this example from Sarah Hepola, "A Divine Cut of Swine," *National Post* (Canada), July 14, 2008, p. AL4; Laura Giovanelli, "Silly Stuff for the Season," *McClatchy- Tribune Business News*, December 11, 2008; and www.gratefulpalate.com, accessed November 2010.

37. Information for this example at www.dell.com/content/topics/topic.aspx/global/ premier/login/signin?c=us&l=en, accessed August 2010.

38. See "eBay Inc.," *Hoover's Company Records*, April 19, 2009, p. 56307; and facts from eBay annual reports and other information at www.ebayinc.com, accessed July 2010.

39. Nigel Hollis, "Going Global? Better Think Local Instead," *Brandweek*, December 1, 2008 p. 14; Jeff Vandam, "Blogs Find Favor as Buying Guides," *New York Times*, December 22, 2008, p. B3; and "State of the Blogosphere 2009," *Technorati*, May 2009, accessed at http://technorati.com/blogging/feature/state-of-the-blogosphere-2009/.

40. See Michael Barbaro, "Wal-Mart Tastemakers Write Unfiltered Blog," *New York Times*, March 3, 2008, www.nytimes.com; Jack Neff, "Owning the Concept of Value Online," *Advertising Age*, March 30, 2009, p. 22; http://thevansblog.blogspot.com/ and http://offthewallvansgirls.wordpress.com/, accessed May 2010; and Bianca Male, "How to Make an Awesome Corporate Blog," *Business Insider*, February 8, 2010, accessed at www.businessinsider.com/how-to-build-an-awesome-corporate-blog-2010-2.

41. Adapted from information found in Brian Morrissey, "Brands Tap into Web Elite for Advertorial 2.0: Well-Connected Bloggers Are Creating Content on Behalf of Sponsors Thirsty for Buzz," *Adweek*, January 12, 2009, p. 9. Also see Elizabeth A. Sullivan, "Blog Savvy," *Marketing News*, November 15, 2009, p. 8; and Michael Bush, "All Marketers Use Online Influencers to Boost Branding Efforts," *Advertising Age*, December 21, 2009, accessed at http://adage.com/digital/article?article_id=141147.

42. See Michael Bush, "Starbucks Gets Web 2.0 Religion, But Can It Convert Nonbelievers?" *Advertising Age*, March 24, 2008, p. 1; and B. L. Bachman, "Starbucks Social Media Monitoring & Community Help It Survive Brand Attack," *WhatNextBlog.com*, June 3, 2009, accessed at www.whatsnextblog.com/archives/2009/06/starbucks_social_ media_community_helps_it_survive_brand_attack.asp.

43. See "Get Satisfaction Connects Customer Support and the Social Web," *PRNewswire*, April 21, 2010; and www.getsatisfaction.com, accessed November 2010.

44. Lauren Goode, "Internet Is Set to Overtake Newspapers in Ad Revenue," *Wall Street Journal*, June 15, 2010, accessed at http://blogs.wsj.com/digits/2010/06/15/internet-is-set-to-overtake-newspapers-in-ad-revenue/?mod=rss_WSJBlog&mod.

45. "U.S. Online Advertising Forecast by Format," *Advertising Age's Digital Marketing Facts 2010* section, February 22, 2010; and Internet Advertising Bureau, *IAB Internet Advertising Revenue Report*, April 7, 2010, www.iab.net/insights_research/947883/adrevenuereport.pdf.

46. See Elaine Wong, "Coke, ConAgra, Kellogg Cozy Up with Search Buys," *Brandweek*, October 12, 2008, accessed at www.brandweek.com.

47. Leftheria Parpis, "Behind McD's Flashy New Spot: Mounted Musical Mouthpiece Makes a Splash on the Net," *Adweek*, March 10, 2009, accessed at www.adweek.com.

48. Noreen O'Leary, "Does Viral Pay?" *Adweek*, March 29, 2010; and www.youtube.com/watch?v=VQ3d3KigPQM, accessed November 2010.

49. Brian Morrissey, "Social Media Use Becomes Pervasive," *Adweek*, April 15, 2010, accessed at www.adweek.com.

50. Chaddus Bruce, "Big Biz Buddies Up to Gen Y," *Wired*, December 20, 2006, accessed at www.wired.com; and Brian Morrissey, "Kraft Gives Facebook Users Reason to Share," *Adweek*, December 30, 2008, accessed at www.adweek.com.

51. See Ken Magill, "E-mail ROI Still Stunning, Still Slipping: DMA," *Direct Magazine*, October 20, 2009, accessed at http://directmag.com/magilla/1020-e-mail-roi-still-slipping/; "E-Mail," *Advertising Age's Digital Marketing Facts 2010* section, February 22, 2010; and Success Stories in E-Mail Marketing," *Brandweek*, February 1, 2010, pp. EM2–EM6.

52. Elizabeth A. Sullivan, "Targeting to the Extreme," *Marketing News*, June 15, 2010, pp. 17–19.

53. Symantec, *The State of Spam and Phishing: Home of the Monthly Report—April 2010*, accessed at www.symantec.com/business/theme.jsp?themeid=state_of_spam.

54. Jessica Tsai, "How Much Marketing Is Too Much?" *DestinationCRM.com*, October 1, 2008, http://www.destinationcrm.com; "StubHub Increases Revenue Per E-mail by Over 2,500 Percent with Responsys Interact and Omniture Recommendations," February 18, 2009, www.responsys.com/company/press/2009_02_18.php.

55. Carroll Trosclair, "Direct Marketing, Advertising and ROI: Commercial E-Mail Delivers Highest DM Return on Investment," *Suite101.com*, April 2, 2010, http://advertising.suite101.com/article.cfm/direct-marketing-advertising-and-roi.

56. See Internet Crime Complaint Center, "IC3 2009 Annual Report on Internet Crime Released," March 12, 2010, accessed at www.ic3.gov/media/2010/100312.aspx.

57. See Greg Sterling, "Pew: Americans Increasingly Shop Online But Still Fear Identity Theft," *SearchEngineLand.com*, February 14, 2008, accessed at http://searchengineland.com/pew-americans-increasingly-shop-online-but-still-fear-identity-theft-13366. See also http://www.ftc.gov/bcp/edu/microsites/idtheft/, accessed November 2010.

58. See "A Quarter of Internet Users Aged 8–12 Say They Have Under-Age Social Networking Profiles," Ofcom, Marcy 26, 2010, www.ofcom.org.uk/media/news/2010/03/nr_ 20100326a.

59. Steve Lohr, "Privacy Concerns Limit Online Ads, Study Says," *New York Times*, April 30, 2010.

60. Emily Steel, "Web Privacy Efforts Targeted—Facing Rules, Ad Firms to Give, Consumers More Control," *Wall Street Journal*, June 26, 2009, B10; Michael Learmonth, "Since Incoming Regulation, Online Ad Groups Unite," *Advertising Age*, January 13, 2009, accessed at http://adage.com/print?article_id=133730; Stephanie Clifford, "A Little 'i' to Teach about Online Privacy," *New York Times*, January 26, 2010, www.nytimes.com, and Tanzina Vega, "Ad Group Unveils Plan to Improve Web Policy," *New York Times*, Ocbtober 4, 2010, accessed at www.nytimes.com.

61. See Mark Rotenberg, "An Examination of Children's Privacy: New Technologies and the Children's Online Privacy Protection Act (COPPA)," April 29, 2010, http://epic.org/privacy/kids/EPIC_COPPA_Testimony_042910.pdf; and "FTC to Study Children's Online Privacy Protection Act," April 21, 2010, accessed at www.aaaa.org/advocacy/gov/news/Pages/042110_children.aspx.

62. Information on TRUSTe at www.truste.com, accessed October 2010.

63. Information on the DMA Privacy Promise at http://www.the-dma.org/cgi/dispissue? article=129, accessed November 2010.

Chapter 18

1. Extracts, quotes, and other information from or adapted from Alex Taylor III, "Hyundai Smokes the Competition," *Fortune*, January 18, 2010, pp. 63–71; Jean Halliday, "Marketer of the Year: Hyundai," *Advertising Age*, November 9, 2009, pp. 1, 11–12; Todd Wasserman, "Why Hyundai's Dead Serious about Its SB Ads," *Adweek*, February 2, 2010, accessed at www.adweek.com; "Hyundai Marketer Ewanick Goes Face to Face with the Customer," *Automotive News*, October 26, 2009, p. 16; Janet Stilson, "Passing Lane," *Brandweek*,

April 6, 2009, p. A7; and "Hyundai Launches FIFA 'Loyalty' Campaign," *MediaPostNews*, June 10, 2010, accessed at http://tinyurl.com/2c636kr.

2. Example adapted from information found in Frank James "Postal Service Quarterly Losses Surge; Internet Gets Blamed," August 5, 2009, accessed at www.NPR.org; and "Postal Facts 2010" and other information from www.usps.com, accessed May 2010.

3. See "Bausch & Lomb," www.wikinvest.com/wiki/Bausch_&_Lomb, accessed May 2010.

4. Adapted from Taylor Clark, "Who's Afraid of the Big Bad Starbucks?" *The Week*, January 18, 2008, p. 46.

5. Adapted from information found in W. Chan Kim, "Blue Ocean Strategy: Making the Competition Irrelevant," Fall 2008, accessed at http://www.blueoceanstrategy.com/abo/Links/Academy_magazine_Autumn08.pdf; and W. Chan Kim and Renée Mauborgne, *Blue Ocean Strategy: How to Create Uncontested Market Space and Make Competition Irrelevant* (Boston: Harvard Business Press, 2005). For other discussion and examples, see Kim and Mauborgne, "How Strategy Shapes Structure," *Harvard Business Review*, September, 2009, pp. 72–90; and Mioke Mallaro, "Is HME Retailing a Blue Ocean? Could Be," *HME News*, March 2010, p. S7.

6. Adapted from information found in Robert Klara, "Puff Daddy," *Brandweek*, May 19, 2008, pp. 25–27; and Eric Slack, "Pirate Brands: Healthy Treasure," *Retail Merchandisers*, March/April 2010, pp. 125–127.

7. Michael E. Porter, *Competitive Strategy: Techniques for Analyzing Industries and Competitors* (New York: Free Press, 1980), chapter 2; and Porter, "What Is Strategy?" *Harvard Business Review*, November–December 1996, pp. 61–78. Also see Stefan Stern, "May the Force Be with You and Your Plans for 2008," *Financial Times*, January 8, 2008, p. 14; and "Porter's Generic Strategies," www.quickmba.com/strategy/generic.shtml, accessed May 2010.

8. See Michael Treacy and Fred Wiersema, "Customer Intimacy and Other Value Disciplines," *Harvard Business Review*, January–February 1993, pp. 84–93; Treacy and Wiersema, *The Discipline of Market Leaders: Choose Your Customers, Narrow Your Focus, Dominate Your Market* (New York: Perseus Press, 1997); Wiersema, *Customer Intimacy: Pick Your Partners, Shape Your Culture, Win Together* (Santa Monica, CA: Knowledge Exchange, 1998); Wiersema, *Double-Digit Growth: How Great Companies Achieve It—No Matter What* (New York: Portfolio, 2003); and Edward M. Hindin, "Learning from Leaders: Questions to Ask and Rules to Follow," *Health Care Strategic Management*, August 2006, pp. 11–13.

9. For more discussion, see Philip Kotler and Kevin Lane Keller, *Marketing Management*, 13th ed. (Upper Saddle River, NJ: Prentice Hall, 2009), chapter 11.

10. Based on information found in Andrew Adam Newman, "The Skinny on Males Dieting," *Adweek*, April 7–April 14, 2008, pp. 24–27; and www.nutrisystem.com, accessed September 2008.

11. Adapted from information found in Clay Dillow, "Nintendo Goes to School: DS Classroom Turns Handheld Console into Teaching Tool," *Fast Company*, June 12, 2009, accessed at http://www.fastcompany.com; Yuri Kageyama, "In Tokyo School, Nintendo DS Is an English Teacher," *USA Today*, June 27, 2008, www.USAToday.com; Matt Peckham, "The Great Nintendo DS Invasion," *PC World*, March 19, 2010, www.pcworld.com; and Raphael G. Slatter, "Nintendo Aims to Get Consoles in Schools," *Associated Press*, March 19, 2010, http://www.msnbc.msn.com/id/35952226/ns/technology_and_science-games/.

12. Adapted from information found in Jack Neff, "Why Unilever Lost the Laundry War," *Advertising Age*, August 6, 2007, pp. 1, 25; "Bidders Eye Unilever's US Detergent Arm," *Financial Times*, April 9, 2008, p. 24; "Unilever Sells North American Detergents Unit," July 28, 2008, accessed at www.msnbc.msn.com/id/25884712.

13. See "Jefferson Graham, "Digital Camera Prices Won't Go Much Lower," *USA Today*, February 22, 2010, www.USAToday.com; and "Soft Drink Sales Volume Drops 2.1 Percent in 2009," *Associated Press*, March 24, 2010, http://finance.yahoo.com/news/Soft-drink-sales-volume-drops-apf-705895836.html?x=0&.v=1.

14. See Oded Shenkar, "Defend Your Research: Imitation Is More Valuable Than Innovation," *Harvard Business Review*, April 2010, pp. 28–29.

15. Adapted from David J. Bryce and Jeffrey H. Dyer, "Strategies to Crack Well-Guarded Markets," *Harvard Business Review*, May 2007, pp. 84–91; with information from Matthew Futterman, "Red Bull's Latest Buzz: New Soccer Stadium," *Wall Street Journal*, March 18, 2010, www.online.wsj.com.

16. See Anna Wilde Mathews, "Polly Want an Insurance Policy?" *Wall Street Journal*, December 9, 2009, p. D1; Diane Brady and Christopher Palmeri, "The Pet Economy," *BusinessWeek*, August 6, 2007, pp. 45–54; "New National Pet Owners Survey Details Two Decades of Evolving American Pet Ownership," American Pet Products Manufacturers Association, June 18, 2007, accessed at http://media.americanpetproducts.org/press.php?include=138671; "All in the Family," *Marketing Management*, January/February 2008, p. 7; and information at http://press.petinsurance.com, accessed September 2010.

17. Information from www.vfc.com, accessed September 2010.

Chapter 19

1. Quotes and other information from Matthew Fomey and Arthur Kroeber, "Google's Business Reason for Leaving China," *Wall Street Journal*, April 6, 2010, p. 15; Aaron Back and Loretta Chao, "Google Weaves a Tangled Chinese Web," *Wall Street Journal*, March 25, 2010, http://online.wsj.com; Jessica E. Vascellaro, "Brin Drove Google's Pullback," *Wall Street Journal*, March 25, 2010, p. A1; Normandy Madden, "Whether It Stays or Goes, Google Wasn't Winning in China Anyway," *Advertising Age*, January 18, 2010, p. 2; Bruce Einhorn, "Google in China: A Win for Liberty—and Strategy," *Bloomberg BusinessWeek*, January 25, 2010, p. 35; Wang Xing and Chen Limin, "Multinationals 'Should Respect Laws in China,'" *China Daily*, June 16, 2010; and David Gelles, "Google Blames China 'Blockage' on Miscalculation," *Financial Times*, July 29, 2010, accessed at www.ft.com.

2. Data from Michael V. Copeland, "The Mighty Micro-Multinational," *Business 2.0*, July 28, 2006, accessed at http://cnnmoney.com; "List of Countries by GDP: List by the CIA World Factbook," *Wikipedia*, http://en.wikipedia.org/wiki/List_of_countries_by_GDP_(nominal), accessed July 2010; and "Fortune 500," *Fortune*, May 3, 2010, pp. F1–F26.

3. "Global Economic Prospects 2010: Crisis, Finance, and Growth," *World Bank*, January 21, 2010, accessed at http://tinyurl.com/2bfgrd6; and "Trade to Expand by 9.5% in 2010 after a Dismal 2009, WTO Reports," *World Trade Organization*, March 26, 2010, accessed at www.wto.org/english/news_e/pres10_e/pr598_e.htm.

4. Information from www.michelin.com/corporate, www.jnj.com, and www.mcdonalds.com, accessed October 2010.

5. See Otis Elevator Company," *Hoover's Company Records*, June 15, 2010, p. 56332; and www.otisworldwide.com, accessed August 2010.

6. Frank Greve, "International Food Fight Could Spell End to Roquefort Dressing," *McClatchy-Tribune Business News*, April 9, 2009; James Hagengruber, "A Victory for Cheese Eaters?" *Christian Science Monitor*, May 7, 2009, www.csmonitor.com.

7. Frederik Balfour, "A Slog in China for Foreign Insurers," *BusinessWeek*, November 23, 2009, p. 24; and Research and Markets: Analyzing China's Insurance Industry—Comprehensive Report, *Business Wire*, April 19, 2010.

8. "What Is the WTO?" www.wto.org/english/thewto_e/whatis_e/whatis_e.htm, accessed November 2010.

9. See *WTO Annual Report 2009*, www.wto.org/english/res_e/publications_e/anrep09_e.htm, accessed September 2010; and World Trade Organization, "10 Benefits of the WTO Trading System," www.wto.org/english/thewto_e/whatis_e/10ben_e/10b00_e.htm, accessed September 2010.

10. Pascal Lamy, "Europe and Recovery: Now Is the Time to Conclude Doha," *Wall Street Journal* (Europe edition), February 11, 2009, p. 13; and Tim Colebatch, "No Sign of Giving Ground in Doha Trade Talks," *Age* (Melbourne, Australia), March 4, 2010, p. B4.

11. "The EU at a Glance," http://europa.eu/abc/index_en.htm, accessed September 2010.

12. "Economic and Monetary Affairs," http://europa.eu/pol/emu/index_en.htm, accessed September 2010.

13. CIA, *The World Factbook*, https://www.cia.gov/library/publications/the-world-factbook, accessed June 2010.

14. Statistics and other information from CIA, *The World Factbook*, https://www.cia.gov/library/publications/the-world-factbook/, accessed June 2010; "NAFTA Analysis 2007" and "North American FTA," Office of the U.S. Trade Representative, www.ustr.gov/Trade_Agreements/Regional/NAFTA/Section_Index.html, accessed July 2010; and Thomas L. Gallagher, "NAFTA Trade Dropped 23 Percent in 2009," *Journal of Commerce*, March 18, 2010, www.joc.com/logistics-economy/nafta-trade-dropped-historic-23-percent-2009.

15. See CIA, *The World Factbook*, https://www.cia.gov/library/publications/ the-world-factbook/, accessed June 2010; and www.comunidadandina.org/ingles/sudamerican.htm, accessed July 2010.

16. Adapted from information found in Bruce Einhorn, "Alan Mulally's Asian Sales Call," *Bloomberg BusinessWeek*, April 12, 2010, pp. 41–43.

17. See Leticia Lozano, "Trade Disputes Roil South American Nations," *Journal of Commerce*, January 18, 2010, http://www.joc.com/breakbulk/trade-disputes-roil-south-american-nations; and "Welcome to the U.S. Commercial Service Venezuela," www.buyusa.gov/venezuela/en/, accessed September 2010.

18. "$9 Billion Barter Deal," *BarterNews.com*, April 19, 2008, accessed at www.barternews.com/9_billion_dollar_barter_deal.htm; and David Pilling, "Africa Builds as Beijing Scrambles to Invest," *Financial Times*, December 10, 2009, p. 11.

19. For these and other examples, see Emma Hall, "Do You Know Your Rites? BBDO Does," *Advertising Age*, May 21, 2007, p. 22.

20. Jamie Bryan, "The Mintz Dynasty," *Fast Company*, April 2006, pp. 56–61; Viji Sundaram, "Offensive Durga Display Dropped," *India-West*, February 2006, p. A1; and Emily Bryson York and Rupal Parekh, "Burger King's MO: Offend, Earn Media, Apologize, Repeat," *Advertising Age*, July 8, 2009, accessed at http://adage.com/print? article_id=137801.

21. See Elizabeth Esfahani, "Thinking Locally, Succeeding Globally," *Business 2.0*, December 2005, pp. 96–98; Evan Ramstas, "LG Electronics' Net Surges 91 Percent as Cell Phone Margins Improve," *Wall Street Journal*, January 25, 2006, p. B2; and www.lg.com, accessed November 2010.

22. Andres Martinez, "The Next American Century," *Time*, March 22, 2010, p. 1.

23. Thomas L. Friedman, *The Lexus and the Olive Tree: Understanding Globalization* (New York: Anchor Books, 2000).

24. "Top 100 Most Valuable Global Brands 2010," Millward Brown Optimor, accessed at www.millwardbrown.com/Sites/mbOptimor/Ideas/BrandZTop100/BrandZTop100.aspx.

25. Eric Ellis, "Iran's Cola War," *Fortune*, March 5, 2007, pp. 35–38; and "Iran Pressures Firm over Coca-Cola Links," January 19, 2009, *World News Network*, accessed at www.google.com/hostednews/afp/article/ALeqM5i0vWNjBSFX67GiiSk01zDDUwtY1w.

26. Betsy McKay, "Coke Bets on Russia for Sales Even as Economy Falls Flat," *Wall Street Journal*, January 28, 2009, p. A1; and William Neuman, "Coke Profit Edges Up; American Sales Stall," *New York Times*, October 21, 2009, p. B2.

27. See Noreen O'Leary, "Bright Lights, Big Challenge," *Adweek*, January 15, 2007, pp. 22–28; Dexter Roberts, "Scrambling to Bring Crest to the Masses," *BusinessWeek*, June 25, 2007, p. 72; Jonathan Birchall, "P&G Set to Expand in Emerging Markets," *Financial Times*, December 12, 2008, p. 22; and Jonathan Birchall, "P&G Set to Regain Market Share," *Financial Times*, January 29, 2010, p. 17.

28. "Hilton Introduces Prestigious Doubletree Brand to the Region," *Gulf News*, May 4, 2009, http://gulfnews.com.

29. Alex Armitage, "Best Buy Acquires Stake in Carphone Warehouse," *Bloomberg.com*, May 8, 2008, http://www.bloomberg.com/apps/news?sid=ar.QDJ3wZ6og&pid= newsarchive; and Jenny Davey and James Ashton, "American Invader Aims to Topple Comet and Currys," *Sunday Times* (London), February 28, 2010, p. 7.

30. Bruce Einhorn and Nandini Lakshman, "PC Makers Are Racing to India," *BusinessWeek*, October 1, 2007, p. 48; "HP in Aggressive Move to Expand Market Presence in India," June 9, 2008, www.Digi-Help.com; and Rahul Sachitanand, "The Rise and Rise of Dell," *Business Today*, March 21, 2010, http://businesstoday.intoday.in/.

31. Quotes from Andrew McMains, "To Compete Globally, Brands Must Adapt," *Adweek*, September 25, 2008, accessed at www.adweek.com; Pankaj Ghemawat, "Regional Strategies for Global Leadership," *Harvard Business Review*, December 2005, pp. 97–108; Eric Pfanner, "The Myth of the Global Brand," *New York Times*, January 11, 2009, www.nytimes.com; Also see Pankej Ghemawat, "Finding Your Strategy in the New Landscape," *Harvard Business Review*, March 2010, pp. 54–60.

32. See Warren J. Keegan and Mark C. Green, *Global Marketing*, 6th ed. (Upper Saddle River, NJ: Prentice Hall, 2011), pp. 314–321.

33. See Jack Ewing, "First Mover in Mobile: How It's Selling Cell Phones to the Developing World," *BusinessWeek*, May 14, 2007, p. 60; and Nelson D. Schwartz, "Can Nokia Recapture Its Glory Days?" *New York Times*, December 12, 2009, accessed at www.nytimes.com/2009/12/13/business/13nokia.html?pagewanted=1&_r=2.

34. Mike Hughlett, "Packaged Food Is Taking Off in Emerging Markets," *Charleston Gazette*, March 23, 2010, p. A10.

35. Adapted from information found in Sonya Misquitta, "Cadbury Redefines Cheap Luxury—Marketing to India's Poor, Candy Makers Sells Small Bites for Pennies," *Wall Street Journal*, June 8, 2009, p. B4.

36. See McMains, "To Compete Globally, Brands Must Adapt."

37. Kate MacArthur, "Coca-Cola Light Employs Local Edge," *Advertising Age*, August 21, 2000, pp. 18–19; "Case Studies: Coke Light Hottest Guy," MSN India, accessed at http://in.msn.com/, March 15, 2004; and www.youtube.com/watch?v= Tu5dku6YkHA, accessed July 2010.

38. See George E. Belch and Michael A. Belch, *Advertising and Promotion: An Integrated Marketing Communications Perspective*, 7th ed. (New York: McGraw Hill, 2007), chapter 20; Shintero Okazaki and Charles R. Taylor, "What Is SMS Advertising and Why Do Multinationals Adopt It?" *Journal of Business Research*, January 2008, pp. 4–12; and Warren J. Keegan and Mark C. Green, *Global Marketing*, 6th ed. (Upper Saddle River, NJ: Prentice Hall, 2011), pp. 413–415.

39. Howard Schneider, "U.S. Sets Tariff on Chinese Oil Field Pipes of Up to 99%," *Washington Post*, April 11, 2010, p. A10.

40. Adapted from Jack Ewing, "First Mover in Mobile: How It's Selling Cell Phones to the Developing World," *BusinessWeek*, May 14, 2007, p. 60; with information from Anshul Gupta, "Mobile Handsets: Hand Set Growth to Be Flat in 2009," March 9, 2009, accessed at www.expresscomputeronline.com/20090309/2009anniversary14.shtml.

41. See "Coca-Cola Rolls Out New Distribution Model with ZAP," *ZAP*, January 23, 2008, www.zapworld.com/zap-coca-cola-truck; and Jane Nelson, Eriko Ishikawa, and Alexis Geaneotes, "Developing Inclusive Business Models: A Review of Coca-Cola's Manual Distribution Centers in Ethiopia and Tanzania," Harvard Kennedy School, 2009, www.hks.harvard.edu/ m-rcbg/CSRI/publications/other_10_MDC_report.pdf. For some interesting photos of Coca-Cola distribution methods in third-world and emerging markets, see www.flickr.com/photos/73509998@N00/sets/72157594299144032/, accessed November 2010.

42. Adapted from information found in Bart Becht, "Building a Company without Borders," *Harvard Business Review*, April 2010, pp. 103–106.

Chapter 20

1. Mark Borden and Anya Kamenetz, "The Prophet CEO," *Fast Company*, September 2008, p. 126; Jennifer Reingold, "Walking the Walk," *Fast Company*, November 2005, pp. 81–85; Elaine Wong, "Timberland Kicks Off Earth Day Effort," *Adweek*, March 24, 2009, accessed at www.adweek.com; "From the Power of One to the Effort of Many," *Business Wire*, April 19, 2009; Andrew Clark, "Timberland Boss Jeffrey Swartz Puts the Boot In—Over His Own Failures," *Guardian UK*, March 18, 2010, www.guardian.co.uk/business/2010/mar/18/jeffrey-swartz-timberland; and information from www.timberland.com, accessed September 2010.

2. For lots of information on SUV safety and environmental performance, see www.citizen .org/autosafety/suvsafety, accessed September 2010.

3. The figure and the discussion in this section are adapted from Philip Kotler, Gary Armstrong, Veronica Wong, and John Saunders, *Principles of Marketing: European Edition*, 5th ed. (London: Pearson Publishing, 2009), chapter 2.

4. McDonald's financial information and other facts from www .aboutmcdonalds.com/mcd/investors.html and www.about mcdonalds.com/mcd, accessed July 2010. Also see "Dow Jones Sustainability World 80 Index," May 2010, accessed at www .sustainability-index.com/djsi_pdf/publications/Factsheets/SAM_ IndexesMonthly_DJSIWorld80.pdf.

5. Heather Green, "How Green Is That Gizmo?" *BusinessWeek*, December 31, 2007, p. 36; Tom Wright, "False 'Green' Ads Draw Global Scrutiny," *Wall Street Journal*, January 30, 2008, p. B4; Benjamin Heath, "FTC Updating Green Guides," *GlobalClimateLaw.com*, April 7, 2009, www.globalclimatelaw.com/2009/04/articles/environmental/ftc-updating-green-guides-which-govern-environmental-building-claims; and http://sinsofgreenwashing.org and www.terrachoice .com, accessed July 2010.

6. See Jennifer Corbett Dooren, "One-Third of American Adults Are Obese, but Rate Slows," *Wall Street Journal*, February 8, 2010; and "Overweight and Obesity," Centers for Disease Control and Prevention, www.cdc.gov/nccdphp/dnpa/obesity/trend/index.htm, accessed July 2010.

7. For more on perceived obsolescence, see Annie Leonard, *The Story of Stuff* (New York: Free Press, 2010), pp. 162–163; and www .storyofstuff.com, accessed September 2010.

8. Dan Pashman, "Planned Obsolescence-Induced Insanity (Or: Damn You Steve Jobs! Why Must You Torment Me?!), *National Public Radio*, September 6, 2007, www.npr.org/blogs/bryantpark/2007/09/planned_obsolescenceinduced_in_1.html. For more discussion, see Joseph Guiltinan, "Creative Destruction and Destructive Creations: Environmental Ethics and Planned Obsolescence," *Journal of Business Ethics*, May 2009, pp. 19–28; and "American Dream of Home Ownership Morphs into Nightmare," *Irish Times*, November 7, 2009, p. 11.

9. See Karen Auge, "Planting Seed in Food Deserts: Neighborhood Gardens, Produce in Corner Stores," *Denver Post*, April 18, 2010, p. 1; and "Supermarket Campaign: Improving Access to Supermarkets in Underserved Communities," *The Food Trust*, www .thefoodtrust.org/php/programs/super.market.campaign.php, accessed July 2010.

10. Adapted from information found in John A. Quelch, "Selling Out the American Dream," *Harvard Business School Working Knowledge*, November 6, 2008, accessed at http://hbswk.hbs.edu/item/6071.html; Leonard Stern, "Aspiration Gap behind Downward Cycle in U.S.," *Calgary Herald* (Canada), November 9, 2008, p. A11; and Keilo Morris, "Brief: OSHA Cites Walmart in Trampling Death," *McClatchy-Tribune Business News*, May 26, 2009.

11. Oliver James, "It's More Than Enough to Make You Sick," *Marketing*, January 23, 2008, pp. 26–28; and Richard J. Varey, "Marketing Means and Ends for a Sustainable Society: A Welfare Agenda for Transformative Change," *Journal of Macromarketing*, June 2010, pp. 112–126.

12. See "Overconsumption Is Costing Us the Earth and Human Happiness," *Guardian*, June 21, 2010, accessed at www.guardian.co .uk/environment/2010/jun/21/overconsumption-environment-relationships-annie-leonard; and "The Story of Stuff," www .storyofstuff.com, accessed July 2010.

13. Portions of the Reverend Billy example based on information from Constance L. Hays, "Preaching to Save Shoppers from 'Evil' of Consumerism," *New York Times*, January 1, 2003, p. C1; "A Preacher's Plea to Stop the 'Shopocalypse,'" *Knight Ridder Tribune Business News*, December 11, 2006; "Rev and Choir on CNN's Campbell Brown, Christmas 2009," accessed at www.revbilly.com/press/2010/02/rev-and-choir-on-cnns-campbell-brown-christmas-2009; and www.revbilly.com, accessed July 2010.

14. "The American Dream Has Been Revised Not Reversed," *Business Wire*, March 9, 2009; and Conor Dougherty and Elizabeth Holmes, "Consumer Spending Perks up Economy," *Wall Street Journal*, March 13, 2010, p. A1.

15. See "Traffic Congestion and Urban Mobility," *Texas Transportation Institute*, http://tti.tamu.edu/infofor/media/topics/congestion_mobility .htm, accessed July 2010.

16. See www.tfl.gov.uk/roadusers/congestioncharging/6710.aspx, accessed July 2010.

17. See "Advertising in the U.S.: Synovate Global Survey Shows Internet, Innovation and Online Privacy a Must," December 3, 2009, accessed at www.synovate.com; and Katy Bachman, "Survey: Clutter Causing TV Ads to Lack Effectiveness," *MediaWeek*, February 8, 2010, www.mediaweek.com.

18. See Martin Sipkoff, "Four-Dollar Pricing Considered Boom or Bust," *Drug Topics*, August 2008, p. 4S; and Sarah Bruyn Jones, "Economic Survival Guide: Drug Discounts Common Now," *McClatchy-Tribune Business News*, February 23, 2009.

19. "Overconsumption Is Costing Us the Earth and Human Happiness."

20. See Jack Neff, "Green-Marketing Revolution Defies Economic Downturn," *Advertising Age*, April 20, 2009, accessed at http://adage.com/print?article_id=136091; Ben Jacklet, "Energy Hog Intel Hones Green-Power Strategy," *Oregon Business*, March 2010, p. 14; and "UPS Adds 245 CNG Trucks to the Company's Green Fleet," *GreenBiz*, January 19, 2010, accessed at www.greenbiz.com/news/2010/01/19/ups-adds-245-cng-trucks-green-fleet.

21. Based on information from Alan S. Brown, "The Many Shades of Green," *Mechanical Engineering*, January 2009, http://memagazine.asme.org/Articles/2009/January/Many_Shades_Green.cfm; Sara Snow, "Green Eyes On: A Visit to a Zero Landfill Subaru Plant," *Treehugger*, May 4, 2010, accessed at www.treehugger.com/files/2010/05/green-eyes-on-subaru-plant.php; and information supplied by Subaru of Indiana, August 2010.

22. See Brown, "The Many Shades of Green."

23. Based on information from Marc Gunther, "Coca-Cola's Green Crusader," *Fortune*, April 28, 2008, p. 150; "Cold Test Markets Aluminum Bottles," February 20, 2008, accessed at www.bevnet.com/news/2008/02-20-2008-Coke.asp; "Coca-Cola to Install 1,800 CO_2 Coolers in North America," April 30, 2009, accessed at www.r744 .com/articles/2009-04-30-coca-cola-to-install-1800-co2-coolers-in-north-america.php; and "The Business of Recycling," www.thecoca-colacompany.com/citizenship/environment_ case_studies.html, accessed September 2010.

24. See "2010 Global 100 List," www.global100.org/annual-reviews/2010-global-100-list.html?sort=company; and www.unileverusa .com/sustainability/environment/, accessed September 2010.

25. See Geoffrey Garver and Aranka Podhora, "Transboundary Environmental Impact Assessment as Part of the North American

Agreement on Environmental Cooperation," *Impact Assessment & Project Appraisal*, December 2008, pp. 253–263; http://ec.europa.eu/environment/index_en.htm, accessed July 2010; and "What Is EMAS?" http://ec.europa.eu/environment/emas/index_en.htm, accessed October 2010.

26. Based on information found in Chuck Salter, "Fast 50: The World's Most Innovative Companies," *Fast Company*, March 2008, pp. 73+. Also see Yukari Iwatani Kane and Daisuke Wakabayashi, "Nintendo Looks Outside the Box," *Wall Street Journal*, May 27, 2009, p. B5.

27. Information from Mark Borden, "The World's 50 Most Innovative Companies: #36: Samsung," *Fast Company*, February 17, 2010, p. 90; Laurie Burkitt, "Samsung Courts Consumers, Marketers," *Forbes*, June 7, 2010, accessed at www.forbes.com/global/2010/0607/marketing-apps-consumer-electronics-apple-samsungs-big-spend.html; and Choi He-suk, "Samsung Renews Resolve to Reform," *Korea Herald*, June 8, 2010, accessed at www.koreaherald.com/national/Detail.jsp?newsMLId=20100607001598.

28. Information from Eleftheria Parpis, "Must Love Dogs," *Adweek*, February 18, 2008, accessed at www.adweek.com; and "The PEDIGREE Adoption Drive Partners with Dog Lover Carrie Underwood to Help Homeless Dogs," February 12, 2010, accessed at www.mars.com/global/news-and-media/press-releases/news-releases.aspx?SiteId=94&Id=1767.

29. See "Our Reason for Being," www.patagonia.com/web/us/patagonia.go?slc=en_US&sct=US&assetid=2047, accessed November 2010.

30. Information from www.haworth.com/en-us/Products/Furniture/Seating/Desk/Pages/Zody.aspx, accessed October 2010.

31. Nanette Byrnes, "Pepsi Brings in the Health Police," *Bloomberg BusinessWeek*, January 25, 2010, pp. 50–51.

32. Adapted from material found in Jeff Heilman, "Rules of Engagement," *The Magazine of Branded Engagement*, Winter 2009, pp. 7–8.

33. See The World Bank, "The Costs of Corruption," April 8, 2004, accessed at http://tinyurl.com/ytavm; "Bribe Payers Index 2008," *Transparency International*, www.transparency.org/policy_research/surveys_indices/bpi; and "Global Corruption Report 2009," *Transparency International*, accessed at www.transparency.org/publications/ gcr/gcr_2009.

34. See Samuel A. DiPiazza, Jr., "Ethics in Action," *Executive Excellence*, January 2002, pp. 15–16; Samuel A. DiPiazza Jr., "It's All Down to Personal Values," August 2003, accessed at http://www.hollywoodreporter.com/hr/search/article_display.jsp?vnu_content_id=2000910; and "Ethics and Business Conduct," www.pwc.com/ethics, accessed November 2010.

35. DiPiazza, "Ethics in Action," p. 15.

36. David A. Lubin and Daniel C. Esty, "The Sustainability Imperative," *Harvard Business Review*, May 2010, pp. 41–50.

Appendix

1. This is derived by rearranging the following equation and solving for price: Percentage markup = (price − cost) ÷ price.

2. Again, using the basic profit equation, we set profit equal to ROI × I: $ROI \times I = (P \times Q) - TFC - (Q \times UVC)$. Solving for Q gives $Q = (TFC + (ROI \times I)) \times (P - UVC)$.

3. U.S. Census Bureau, available at http://www.census.gov/prod/1/pop/p25-1129.pdf accessed October 26, 2009.

4. "Broadband Internet to Reach 77 Percent of Households by 2012," available at www.tmcnet.com/voip/ip-communications/articles/35393-gartner-broadband-internet-reach-77-percent-households-2012.htm, accessed August 25, 2008.

5. See Roger J. Best, *Market-Based Management*, 4th ed. (Upper Saddle River, NJ: Prentice Hall, 2005).

6. Total contribution can also be determined from the unit contribution and unit volume: Total contribution = unit contribution × unit sales. Total units sold in were 297,619 units, which can be determined by dividing total sales by price per unit ($100 million × $336). Total contribution = $70 contribution per unit × 297,619 units = $20,833,330 (difference due to rounding).

7. Recall that the contribution margin of 21 percent was based on variable costs representing 79 percent of sales. Therefore, if we do not know price, we can set it equal to $1.00. If price equals $1.00, 79 cents represents variable costs and 21 cents represents unit contribution. If price is decreased by 10 percent, the new price is $0.90. However, variable costs do not change just because price decreased, so the unit contribution and contribution margin decrease as follows:

	Old	New (reduced 10%)
Price	$1.00	$0.90
— Unit variable cost	$0.79	$0.79
= Unit contribution	$0.21	$0.11
Contribution margin	$0.21/$1.00 = 0.21 or 21%	$0.11/$0.90 = 0.12 or 12%

Glossary

Adapted global marketing An international marketing strategy that adjusts the marketing strategy and mix elements to each international target market, bearing more costs but hoping for a larger market share and return.

Administered VMS A vertical marketing system that coordinates successive stages of production and distribution, not through common ownership or contractual ties but through the size and power of one of the parties.

Adoption process The mental process through which an individual passes from first hearing about an innovation to final adoption.

Advertising Any paid form of nonpersonal presentation and promotion of ideas, goods, or services by an identified sponsor.

Advertising agency A marketing services firm that assists companies in planning, preparing, implementing, and evaluating all or portions of their advertising programs.

Advertising budget The dollars and other resources allocated to a product or a company advertising program.

Advertising media The vehicles through which advertising messages are delivered to their intended audiences.

Advertising objective A specific communication *task* to be accomplished with a specific *target* audience during a specific period of *time*.

Advertising strategy The strategy by which the company accomplishes its advertising objectives. It consists of two major elements: creating advertising messages and selecting advertising media.

Affordable method Setting the promotion budget at the level management thinks the company can afford.

Age and life-cycle segmentation Dividing a market into different age and life-cycle groups.

Agent A wholesaler who represents buyers or sellers on a relatively permanent basis, performs only a few functions, and does not take title to goods.

Allowance Promotional money paid by manufacturers to retailers in return for an agreement to feature the manufacturer's products in some way.

Alternative evaluation The stage of the buyer decision process in which the consumer uses information to evaluate alternative brands in the choice set.

Approach A salesperson meets the customer for the first time.

Attitude A person's consistently favorable or unfavorable evaluations, feelings, and tendencies toward an object or idea.

Baby boomers The 78 million people born during years following World War II and lasting until 1964.

Basing-point pricing A geographical pricing strategy in which the seller designates some city as a basing point and charges all customers the freight cost from that city to the customer.

Behavioral segmentation Dividing a market into segments based on consumer knowledge, attitudes, uses, or responses to a product.

Belief A descriptive thought that a person holds about something.

Benchmarking The process of comparing the company's products and processes to those of competitors or leading firms in other industries to identify best practices and find ways to improve quality and performance.

Benefit segmentation Dividing the market into segments according to the different benefits that consumers seek from the product.

Blogs Online journals where people post their thoughts, usually on a narrowly defined topic.

Brand A name, term, sign, symbol, design, or a combination of these, that identifies the products or services of one seller or group of sellers and differentiates them from those of competitors.

Brand equity The differential effect that knowing the brand name has on customer response to the product or its marketing.

Brand extension Extending an existing brand name to new product categories.

Break-even pricing (target return pricing) Setting price to break even on the costs of making and marketing a product or setting price to make a target return.

Broker A wholesaler who does not take title to goods and whose function is to bring buyers and sellers together and assist in negotiation.

Business analysis A review of the sales, costs, and profit projections for a new product to find out whether these factors satisfy the company's objectives.

Business buyer behavior The buying behavior of organizations that buy goods and services for use in the production of other products and services that are sold, rented, or supplied to others.

Business buying process The decision process by which business buyers determine which products and services their organizations need to purchase and then find, evaluate, and choose among alternative suppliers and brands.

Business portfolio The collection of businesses and products that make up the company.

Business promotions Sales promotion tools used to generate business leads, stimulate purchases, reward customers, and motivate salespeople.

Business-to-business (B-to-B) online marketing Businesses using online marketing to reach new business customers, serve current customers more effectively, and obtain buying efficiencies and better prices.

Business-to-consumer (B-to-C) online marketing Businesses selling goods and services online to final consumers.

Buyer-readiness stages The stages consumers normally pass through on their way to a purchase, including awareness, knowledge, liking, preference, conviction, and, finally, the actual purchase.

Buyers People in an organization's buying center who make an actual purchase.

Buying center All the individuals and units that play a role in the purchase decision-making process.

Buzz marketing Cultivating opinion leaders and getting them to spread information about a product or service to others in their communities.

By-product pricing Setting a price for by-products to make the main product's price more competitive.

Captive product pricing Setting a price for products that must be used along with a main product, such as blades for a razor and games for a videogame console.

Catalog marketing Direct marketing through print, video, or digital catalogs that are mailed to select customers, made available in stores, or presented online.

Category killer A giant specialty store that carries a very deep assortment of a particular line and is staffed by knowledgeable employees.

Causal research Marketing research to test hypotheses about cause-and-effect relationships.

Chain stores Two or more outlets that are commonly owned and controlled.

Channel conflict Disagreement among marketing channel members on goals, roles, and rewards—who should do what and for what rewards.

Channel level A layer of intermediaries that performs some work in bringing the product and its ownership closer to the final buyer.

Click-and-mortar companies Traditional brick-and-mortar companies that have added online marketing to their operations.

Click-only companies The so-called dot-coms, which operate online only and have no brick-and-mortar market presence.

Closing A salesperson asks the customer for an order.

Co-branding The practice of using the established brand names of two different companies on the same product.

Cognitive dissonance Buyer discomfort caused by postpurchase conflict.

Commercial online databases Collections of information available from online commercial sources or accessible via the Internet.

Commercialization Introducing a new product into the market.

Communication adaptation A global communication strategy of fully adapting advertising messages to local markets.

Competition-based pricing Setting prices based on competitors' strategies, prices, costs, and market offerings.

Competitive advantage An advantage over competitors gained by offering greater customer value, either by having lower prices or providing more benefits that justify higher prices.

Competitive marketing intelligence The systematic collection and analysis of publicly available information about consumers, competitors, and developments in the marketing environment.

Competitive marketing strategies Strategies that strongly position the company against competitors and give the company the strongest possible strategic advantage.

Competitive-parity method Setting the promotion budget to match competitors' outlays.

Competitor analysis The process of identifying key competitors; assessing their objectives, strategies, strengths and weaknesses, and reaction patterns; and selecting which competitors to attack or avoid.

Competitor-centered company A company whose moves are mainly based on competitors' actions and reactions.

Complex buying behavior Consumer buying behavior in situations characterized by high consumer involvement in a purchase and significant perceived differences among brands.

Concentrated (niche) marketing A market-coverage strategy in which a firm goes after a large share of one or a few segments or niches.

Concept testing Testing new-product concepts with a group of target consumers to find out if the concepts have strong consumer appeal.

Consumer buyer behavior The buying behavior of final consumers—individuals and households that buy goods and services for personal consumption.

Consumer market All the individuals and households that buy or acquire goods and services for personal consumption.

Consumer product A product bought by final consumers for personal consumption.

Consumer promotions Sales promotion tools used to boost short-term customer buying and involvement or enhance long-term customer relationships.

Consumer-generated marketing Brand exchanges created by consumers themselves—both invited and uninvited—by which consumers are playing an increasing role in shaping their own brand experiences and those of other consumers.

Consumer-oriented marketing A principle of sustainable marketing that holds a company should view and organize its marketing activities from the consumer's point of view.

Consumer-to-business (C-to-B) online marketing Online exchanges in which consumers search out sellers, learn about their offers, and initiate purchases, sometimes even driving transaction terms.

Consumer-to-consumer (C-to-C) online marketing Online exchanges of goods and information between final consumers.

Consumerism An organized movement of citizens and government agencies to improve the rights and power of buyers in relation to sellers.

Contract manufacturing A joint venture in which a company contracts with manufacturers in a foreign market to produce the product or provide its service.

Contractual VMS A vertical marketing system in which independent firms at different levels of production and distribution join together through contracts to obtain more economies or sales impact than they could achieve alone.

Convenience product A consumer product that customers usually buy frequently, immediately, and with minimal comparison and buying effort.

Convenience store A small store, located near a residential area, that is open long hours seven days a week and carries a limited line of high-turnover convenience goods.

Conventional distribution channel A channel consisting of one or more independent producers, wholesalers, and retailers, each a separate business seeking to maximize its own profits, even at the expense of profits for the system as a whole.

Corporate (or brand) Web site A Web site designed to build customer goodwill, collect customer feedback, and supplement other sales channels rather than sell the company's products directly.

Corporate VMS A vertical marketing system that combines successive stages of production and distribution under single ownership—channel leadership is established through common ownership.

Cost-based pricing Setting prices based on the costs for producing, distributing, and selling the product plus a fair rate of return for effort and risk.

Cost-plus pricing (markup pricing) Adding a standard markup to the cost of the product.

Creative concept The compelling "big idea" that will bring the advertising message strategy to life in a distinctive and memorable way.

Crowdsourcing Inviting broad communities of people—customers, employees, independent scientists and researchers, and even the public at large—into the new-product innovation process.

Cultural environment Institutions and other forces that affect society's basic values, perceptions, preferences, and behaviors.

Culture The set of basic values, perceptions, wants, and behaviors learned by a member of society from family and other important institutions.

Customer (or market) sales force structure A sales force organization in which salespeople specialize in selling only to certain customers or industries.

Customer database An organized collection of comprehensive data about individual customers or prospects, including geographic, demographic, psychographic, and behavioral data.

Customer equity The total combined customer lifetime values of all of the company's customers.

Customer insights Fresh understandings of customers and the marketplace derived from marketing information that become the basis for creating customer value and relationships.

Customer lifetime value The value of the entire stream of purchases that the customer would make over a lifetime of patronage.

Customer relationship management The overall process of building and maintaining profitable customer relationships by delivering superior customer value and satisfaction.

Customer relationship management (CRM) Managing detailed information about individual customers and carefully managing customer touch points to maximize customer loyalty.

Customer satisfaction The extent to which a product's perceived performance matches a buyer's expectations.

Customer value analysis An analysis conducted to determine what benefits target customers value and how they rate the relative value of various competitors' offers.

Customer value-based pricing Setting price based on buyers' perceptions of value rather than on the seller's cost.

Customer-centered company A company that focuses on customer developments in designing its marketing strategies and delivering superior value to its target customers.

Customer-centered new-product development New-product development that focuses on finding new ways to solve customer problems and create more customer-satisfying experiences.

Customer-managed relationships Marketing relationships in which customers, empowered by today's new digital technologies, interact with companies and with each other to shape their relationships with brands.

Customer-perceived value The customer's evaluation of the difference between all the benefits and all the costs of a marketing offer relative to those of competing offers.

Customer-value marketing A principle of sustainable marketing that holds a company should put most of its resources into customer-value-building marketing investments.

Deciders People in an organization's buying center who have formal or informal power to select or approve the final suppliers.

Decline stage The PLC stage in which a product's sales decline.

Deficient products Products that have neither immediate appeal nor long-run benefits.

Demand curve A curve that shows the number of units the market will buy in a given time period, at different prices that might be charged.

Demands Human wants that are backed by buying power.

Demographic segmentation Dividing the market into segments based on variables such as age, gender, family size, family life cycle, income, occupation, education, religion, race, generation, and nationality.

Demography The study of human populations in terms of size, density, location, age, gender, race, occupation, and other statistics.

Department store A retail organization that carries a wide variety of product lines—each line is operated as a separate department managed by specialist buyers or merchandisers.

Derived demand Business demand that ultimately comes from (derives from) the demand for consumer goods.

Descriptive research Marketing research to better describe marketing problems, situations, or markets, such as the market potential for a product or the demographics and attitudes of consumers.

Desirable products Products that give both high immediate satisfaction and high long-run benefits.

Differentiated (segmented) marketing A market-coverage strategy in which a firm decides to target several market segments and designs separate offers for each.

Differentiation Actually differentiating the market offering to create superior customer value.

Direct investment Entering a foreign market by developing foreign-based assembly or manufacturing facilities.

Direct marketing Direct connections with carefully targeted individual consumers to both obtain an immediate response and cultivate lasting customer relationships.

Direct marketing channel A marketing channel that has no intermediary levels.

Direct-mail marketing Direct marketing by sending an offer, announcement, reminder, or other item to a person at a particular physical or virtual address.

Direct-response television marketing Direct marketing via television, including direct-response television advertising (or infomercials) and home shopping channels.

Discount A straight reduction in price on purchases during a stated period of time or of larger quantities.

Discount store A retail operation that sells standard merchandise at lower prices by accepting lower margins and selling at higher volume.

Disintermediation The cutting out of marketing channel intermediaries by product or service producers or the displacement of traditional resellers by radical new types of intermediaries.

Dissonance-reducing buying behavior Consumer buying behavior in situations characterized by high involvement but few perceived differences among brands.

Distribution center A large, highly automated warehouse designed to receive goods from various plants and suppliers, take orders, fill them efficiently, and deliver goods to customers as quickly as possible.

Diversification Company growth through starting up or acquiring businesses outside the company's current products and markets.

Dynamic pricing Adjusting prices continually to meet the characteristics and needs of individual customers and situations.

E-procurement Purchasing through electronic connections between buyers and sellers—usually online.

Economic community A group of nations organized to work toward common goals in the regulation of international trade.

Economic environment Economic factors that affect consumer purchasing power and spending patterns.

Environmental sustainability A management approach that involves developing strategies that both sustain the environment and produce profits for the company.

Environmentalism An organized movement of concerned citizens and government agencies to protect and improve people's current and future living environment.

Ethnographic research A form of observational research that involves sending trained observers to watch and interact with consumers in their "natural environments."

Event marketing (event sponsorships) Creating a brand-marketing event or serving as a sole or participating sponsor of events created by others.

Exchange The act of obtaining a desired object from someone by offering something in return.

Exclusive distribution Giving a limited number of dealers the exclusive right to distribute the company's products in their territories.

Execution style The approach, style, tone, words, and format used for executing an advertising message.

Experience curve (learning curve) The drop in the average per-unit production cost that comes with accumulated production experience.

Experimental research Gathering primary data by selecting matched groups of subjects, giving them different treatments, controlling related factors, and checking for differences in group responses.

Exploratory research Marketing research to gather preliminary information that will help define problems and suggest hypotheses.

Exporting Entering a foreign market by selling goods produced in the company's home country, often with little modification.

Factory outlet An off-price retailing operation that is owned and operated by a manufacturer and normally carries the manufacturer's surplus, discontinued, or irregular goods.

Fad A temporary period of unusually high sales driven by consumer enthusiasm and immediate product or brand popularity.

Fashion A currently accepted or popular style in a given field.

Fixed costs (overhead) Costs that do not vary with production or sales level.

FOB-origin pricing A geographical pricing strategy in which goods are placed free on board a carrier; the customer pays the freight from the factory to the destination.

Focus group interviewing Personal interviewing that involves inviting six to ten people to gather for a few hours with a trained interviewer to talk about a product, service, or organization. The interviewer "focuses" the group discussion on important issues.

Follow-up A salesperson follows up after the sale to ensure customer satisfaction and repeat business.

Franchise A contractual association between a manufacturer, wholesaler, or service organization (a franchisor) and independent businesspeople (franchisees) who buy the right to own and operate one or more units in the franchise system.

Franchise organization A contractual vertical marketing system in which a channel member, called a franchisor, links several stages in the production-distribution process.

Freight-absorption pricing A geographical pricing strategy in which the seller absorbs all or part of the freight charges to get the desired business.

Gatekeepers People in an organization's buying center who control the flow of information to others.

Gender segmentation Dividing a market into different segments based on gender.

General need description The stage in the business buying process in which a buyer describes the general characteristics and quantity of a needed item.

Generation X The 45 million people born between 1965 and 1976 in the "birth dearth" following the baby boom.

Geographic segmentation Dividing a market into different geographical units, such as nations, states, regions, counties, cities, or even neighborhoods.

Geographical pricing Setting prices for customers located in different parts of the country or world.

Global firm A firm that, by operating in more than one country, gains R&D, production, marketing, and financial advantages in its costs and reputation that are not available to purely domestic competitors.

Good-value pricing Offering the right combination of quality and good service at a fair price.

Government market Governmental units—federal, state, and local—that purchase or rent goods and services for carrying out the main functions of government.

Group Two or more people who interact to accomplish individual or mutual goals.

Growth stage The PLC stage in which a product's sales start climbing quickly.

Growth-share matrix A portfolio-planning method that evaluates a company's SBUs in terms of its market growth rate and relative market share.

Habitual buying behavior Consumer buying behavior in situations characterized by low-consumer involvement and few significantly perceived brand differences.

Handling objections A salesperson seeks out, clarifies, and overcomes any customer objections to buying.

Horizontal marketing system A channel arrangement in which two or more companies at one level join together to follow a new marketing opportunity.

Idea generation The systematic search for new-product ideas.

Idea screening Screening new-product ideas to spot good ideas and drop poor ones as soon as possible.

Income segmentation Dividing a market into different income segments.

Independent off-price retailer An off-price retailer that is either independently owned and run or is a division of a larger retail corporation.

Individual marketing Tailoring products and marketing programs to the needs and preferences of individual customers—also called *one-to-one marketing, customized marketing,* and *markets-of-one marketing.*

Indirect marketing channel Channel containing one or more intermediary levels.

Industrial product A product bought by individuals and organizations for further processing or for use in conducting a business.

Influencers People in an organization's buying center who affect the buying decision; they often help define specifications and also provide information for evaluating alternatives.

Information search The stage of the buyer decision process in which the consumer is aroused to search for more information; the consumer may simply have heightened attention or may go into an active information search.

Innovative marketing A principle of sustainable marketing that requires a company seek real product and marketing improvements.

Inside sales force Salespeople who conduct business from their offices via telephone, the Internet, or visits from prospective buyers.

Institutional market Schools, hospitals, nursing homes, prisons, and other institutions that provide goods and services to people in their care.

Integrated logistics management The logistics concept that emphasizes teamwork—both inside the company and among all the marketing channel organizations—to maximize the performance of the entire distribution system.

Integrated marketing communications (IMC) Carefully integrating and coordinating the company's many communications channels to deliver a clear, consistent, and compelling message about the organization and its products.

Intensive distribution Stocking the product in as many outlets as possible.

Interactive marketing Training service employees in the fine art of interacting with customers to satisfy their needs.

Intermarket segmentation (cross-market segmentation) Forming segments of consumers who have similar needs and buying behavior even though they are located in different countries.

Intermodal transportation Combining two or more modes of transportation.

Internal databases Electronic collections of consumer and market information obtained from data sources within the company network.

Internal marketing Orienting and motivating customer-contact employees and supporting service people to work as a team to provide customer satisfaction.

Internet A vast public web of computer networks that connects users of all types around the world to each other and an amazingly large information repository.

Introduction stage The PLC stage in which a new product is first distributed and made available for purchase.

Joint ownership A joint venture in which a company joins investors in a foreign market to create a local business in which the company shares joint ownership and control.

Joint venturing Entering foreign markets by joining with foreign companies to produce or market a product or service.

Learning Changes in an individual's behavior arising from experience.

Licensing A method of entering a foreign market in which the company enters into an agreement with a licensee in the foreign market.

Lifestyle A person's pattern of living as expressed in his or her activities, interests, and opinions.

Line extension Extending an existing brand name to new forms, colors, sizes, ingredients, or flavors of an existing product category.

Local marketing Tailoring brands and promotions to the needs and wants of local customer segments—cities, neighborhoods, and even specific stores.

Macroenvironment The larger societal forces that affect the microenvironment—demographic, economic, natural, technological, political, and cultural forces.

Madison & Vine A term that has come to represent the merging of advertising and entertainment in an effort to break through the clutter and create new avenues for reaching consumers with more engaging messages.

Management contracting A joint venture in which the domestic firm supplies the management know-how to a foreign company that supplies the capital; the domestic firm exports management services rather than products.

Manufacturers' sales branches and offices Wholesaling by sellers or buyers themselves rather than through independent wholesalers.

Market The set of all actual and potential buyers of a product or service.

Market challenger A runner-up firm that is fighting hard to increase its market share in an industry.

Market development Company growth by identifying and developing new market segments for current company products.

Market follower A runner-up firm that wants to hold its share in an industry without rocking the boat.

Market leader The firm in an industry with the largest market share.

Market nicher A firm that serves small segments that the other firms in an industry overlook or ignore.

Market offerings Some combination of products, services, information, or experiences offered to a market to satisfy a need or want.

Market penetration Company growth by increasing sales of current products to current market segments without changing the product.

Market segment A group of consumers who respond in a similar way to a given set of marketing efforts.

Market segmentation Dividing a market into smaller segments with distinct needs, characteristics, or behavior that might require separate marketing strategies or mixes.

Market targeting (targeting) The process of evaluating each market segment's attractiveness and selecting one or more segments to enter.

Market-centered company A company that pays balanced attention to both customers and competitors in designing its marketing strategies.

Market-penetration pricing Setting a low price for a new product to attract a large number of buyers and a large market share.

Market-skimming pricing (price skimming) Setting a high price for a new product to skim maximum revenues layer by layer from the segments willing to pay the high price; the company makes fewer but more profitable sales.

Marketing The process by which companies create value for customers and build strong customer relationships in order to capture value from customers in return.

Marketing channel (or distribution channel) A set of interdependent organizations that help make a product or service available for use or consumption by the consumer or business user.

Marketing channel design Designing effective marketing channels by analyzing customer needs, setting channel objectives, identifying major channel alternatives, and evaluating those alternatives.

Marketing channel management Selecting, managing, and motivating individual channel members and evaluating their performance over time.

Marketing concept A philosophy that holds that achieving organizational goals depends on knowing the needs and wants of target markets and delivering the desired satisfactions better than competitors do.

Marketing control Measuring and evaluating the results of marketing strategies and plans and taking corrective action to ensure that the objectives are achieved.

Marketing environment The actors and forces outside marketing that affect marketing management's ability to build and maintain successful relationships with target customers.

Marketing implementation Turning marketing strategies and plans into marketing actions to accomplish strategic marketing objectives.

Marketing information system (MIS) People and procedures for assessing information needs, developing the needed information, and helping decision makers to use the information to generate and validate actionable customer and market insights.

Marketing intermediaries Firms that help the company to promote, sell, and distribute its goods to final buyers.

Marketing logistics (or physical distribution) Planning, implementing, and controlling the physical flow of materials, final goods, and related information from points of origin to points of consumption to meet customer requirements at a profit.

Marketing management The art and science of choosing target markets and building profitable relationships with them.

Marketing mix The set of tactical marketing tools—product, price, place, and promotion—that the firm blends to produce the response it wants in the target market.

Marketing myopia The mistake of paying more attention to the specific products a company offers than to the benefits and experiences produced by these products.

Marketing research The systematic design, collection, analysis, and reporting of data relevant to a specific marketing situation facing an organization.

Marketing strategy development Designing an initial marketing strategy for a new product based on the product concept.

Marketing strategy The marketing logic by which the company hopes to create customer value and achieve profitable customer relationships.

Marketing Web site A Web site that engages consumers in interactions that will move them closer to a direct purchase or other marketing outcome.

Maturity stage The PLC stage in which a product's sales growth slows or levels off.

Merchant wholesaler An independently owned wholesaler business that takes title to the merchandise it handles.

Microenvironment The actors close to the company that affect its ability to serve its customers—the company, suppliers, marketing intermediaries, customer markets, competitors, and publics.

Micromarketing Tailoring products and marketing programs to the needs and wants of specific individuals and local customer segments; It includes *local marketing* and *individual marketing*.

Millennials (or Generation Y) The 83 million children of the baby boomers, born between 1977 and 2000.

Mission statement A statement of the organization's purpose—what it wants to accomplish in the larger environment.

Modified rebuy A business buying situation in which the buyer wants to modify product specifications, prices, terms, or suppliers.

Motive (drive) A need that is sufficiently pressing to direct the person to seek satisfaction of the need.

Multichannel distribution system A distribution system in which a single firm sets up two or more marketing channels to reach one or more customer segments.

Natural environment Natural resources that are needed as inputs by marketers or that are affected by marketing activities.

Need recognition The first stage of the buyer decision process, in which the consumer recognizes a problem or need.

Needs States of felt deprivation.

New product A good, service, or idea that is perceived by some potential customers as new.

New task A business buying situation in which the buyer purchases a product or service for the first time.

New-product development The development of original products, product improvements, product modifications, and new brands through the firm's own product development efforts.

Nonpersonal communication channels Media that carry messages without personal contact or feedback, including major media, atmospheres, and events.

Objective-and-task method Developing the promotion budget by (1) defining specific promotion objectives, (2) determining the tasks needed to achieve these objectives, and (3) estimating the costs of performing these tasks. The sum of these costs is the proposed promotion budget.

Observational research Gathering primary data by observing relevant people, actions, and situations.

Occasion segmentation Dividing the market into segments according to occasions when buyers get the idea to buy, actually make their purchase, or use the purchased item.

Off-price retailer A retailer that buys at less-than-regular wholesale prices and sells at less than retail. Examples are factory outlets, independents, and warehouse clubs.

Online advertising Advertising that appears while consumers are browsing the Web, including display ads, search-related ads, online classifieds, and other forms.

Online focus groups Gathering a small group of people online with a trained moderator to chat about a product, service, or organization and gain qualitative insights about consumer attitudes and behavior.

Online marketing Efforts to market products and services and build customer relationships over the Internet.

Online marketing research Collecting primary data online through Internet surveys, online focus groups, Web-based experiments, or tracking consumers' online behavior.

Online social networks Online social communities—blogs, social networking Web sites, or even virtual worlds—where people socialize or exchange information and opinions.

Opinion leader A person within a reference group who, because of special skills, knowledge, personality, or other characteristics, exerts social influence on others.

Optional product pricing The pricing of optional or accessory products along with a main product.

Order-routine specification The stage of the business buying process in which the buyer writes the final order with the chosen supplier(s), listing the technical specifications, quantity needed, expected time of delivery, return policies, and warranties.

Outside sales force (or field sales force) Salespeople who travel to call on customers in the field.

Packaging The activities of designing and producing the container or wrapper for a product.

Partner relationship management Working closely with partners in other company departments and outside the company to jointly bring greater value to customers.

Percentage-of-sales method Setting the promotion budget at a certain percentage of current or forecasted sales or as a percentage of the unit sales price.

Perception The process by which people select, organize, and interpret information to form a meaningful picture of the world.

Performance review The stage of the business buying process in which the buyer assesses the performance of the supplier and decides to continue, modify, or drop the arrangement.

Personal communication channels Channels through which two or more people communicate directly with each other, including face to face, on the phone, via mail or e-mail, or even through an Internet "chat."

Personal selling Personal presentations by the firm's sales force for the purpose of making sales and building customer relationships.

Pleasing products Products that give high immediate satisfaction but may hurt consumers in the long run.

Political environment Laws, government agencies, and pressure groups that influence and limit various organizations and individuals in a given society.

Portfolio analysis The process by which management evaluates the products and businesses that make up the company.

Positioning Arranging for a product to occupy a clear, distinctive, and desirable place relative to competing products in the minds of target consumers.

Positioning statement A statement that summarizes company or brand positioning. It takes this form: To (target segment and need) our (brand) is (concept) that (point of difference).

Postpurchase behavior The stage of the buyer decision process in which consumers take further action after purchase based on their satisfaction or dissatisfaction with a purchase.

Preapproach A salesperson learns as much as possible about a prospective customer before making a sales call.

Presentation A salesperson tells the "value story" to the buyer, showing how the company's offer solves the customer's problems.

Price The amount of money charged for a product or service; the sum of the values that customers exchange for the benefits of having or using the product or service.

Price elasticity A measure of the sensitivity of demand to changes in price.

Primary data Information collected for the specific purpose at hand.

Problem recognition The first stage of the business buying process in which someone in the company recognizes a problem or need that can be met by acquiring a good or a service.

Product Anything that can be offered to a market for attention, acquisition, use, or consumption that might satisfy a want or need.

Product adaptation Adapting a product to meet local conditions or wants in foreign markets.

Product bundle pricing Combining several products and offering the bundle at a reduced price.

Product concept A detailed version of the new-product idea stated in meaningful consumer terms.

Product concept The idea that consumers will favor products that offer the most quality, performance, and features and that the organization should therefore devote its energy to making continuous product improvements.

Product development Company growth by offering modified or new products to current market segments.

Product development Developing the product concept into a physical product to ensure that the product idea can be turned into a workable market offering.

Product invention Creating new products or services for foreign markets.

Product life cycle (PLC) The course of a product's sales and profits over its lifetime. It involves five distinct stages: product development, introduction, growth, maturity, and decline.

Product line A group of products that are closely related because they function in a similar manner, are sold to the same customer groups, are marketed through the same types of outlets, or fall within given price ranges.

Product line pricing Setting the price steps between various products in a product line based on cost differences between the products, customer evaluations of different features, and competitors' prices.

Product mix (or product portfolio) The set of all product lines and items that a particular seller offers for sale.

Product position The way the product is defined by consumers on important attributes—the place the product occupies in consumers' minds relative to competing products.

Product quality The characteristics of a product or service that bear on its ability to satisfy stated or implied customer needs.

Product sales force structure A sales force organization in which salespeople specialize in selling only a portion of the company's products or lines.

Product specification The stage of the business buying process in which the buying organization decides on and specifies the best technical product characteristics for a needed item.

Product/market expansion grid A portfolio-planning tool for identifying company growth opportunities through market penetration, market development, product development, or diversification.

Production concept The idea that consumers will favor products that are available and highly affordable and that the organization should therefore focus on improving production and distribution efficiency.

Promotion mix (or marketing communications mix) The specific blend of promotion tools that the company uses to persuasively communicate customer value and build customer relationships.

Promotional pricing Temporarily pricing products below the list price, and sometimes even below cost, to increase short-run sales.

Proposal solicitation The stage of the business buying process in which the buyer invites qualified suppliers to submit proposals.

Prospecting A salesperson or company identifies qualified potential customers.

Psychographic segmentation Dividing a market into different segments based on social class, lifestyle, or personality characteristics.

Psychological pricing Pricing that considers the psychology of prices, not simply the economics; the price says something about the product.

Public Any group that has an actual or potential interest in or impact on an organization's ability to achieve its objectives.

Public relations (PR) Building good relations with the company's various publics by obtaining favorable publicity, building up a good corporate image, and handling or heading off unfavorable rumors, stories, and events.

Pull strategy A promotion strategy that calls for spending a lot on consumer advertising and promotion to induce final consumers to buy the product, creating a demand vacuum that "pulls" the product through the channel.

Purchase decision The buyer's decision about which brand to purchase.

Push strategy A promotion strategy that calls for using the sales force and trade promotion to push the product through channels. The producer promotes the product to channel members who in turn promote it to final consumers.

Reference prices Prices that buyers carry in their minds and refer to when they look at a given product.

Retailer A business whose sales come *primarily* from retailing.

Retailing All the activities involved in selling goods or services directly to final consumers for their personal, nonbusiness use.

Return on advertising investment The net return on advertising investment divided by the costs of the advertising investment.

Return on marketing investment (or marketing ROI) The net return from a marketing investment divided by the costs of the marketing investment.

Sales 2.0 The merging of innovative sales practices with Web 2.0 technologies to improve sales force effectiveness and efficiency.

Sales force management Analyzing, planning, implementing, and controlling sales force activities.

Sales promotion Short-term incentives to encourage the purchase or sale of a product or a service.

Sales quota A standard that states the amount a salesperson should sell and how sales should be divided among the company's products.

Salesperson An individual representing a company to customers by performing one or more of the following activities: prospecting, communicating, selling, servicing, information gathering, and relationship building.

Salutary products Products that have low appeal but may benefit consumers in the long run.

Sample A segment of the population selected for marketing research to represent the population as a whole.

Secondary data Information that already exists somewhere, having been collected for another purpose.

Segmented pricing Selling a product or service at two or more prices, where the difference in prices is not based on differences in costs.

Selective distribution The use of more than one but fewer than all the intermediaries who are willing to carry the company's products.

Selling concept The idea that consumers will not buy enough of the firm's products unless it undertakes a large-scale selling and promotion effort.

Selling process The steps that salespeople follow when selling, which include prospecting and qualifying, preapproach, approach, presentation and demonstration, handling objections, closing, and follow-up.

Sense-of-mission marketing A principle of sustainable marketing that holds a company should define its mission in broad social terms rather than narrow product terms.

Service An activity, benefit, or satisfaction offered for sale that is essentially intangible and does not result in the ownership of anything.

Service inseparability Services are produced and consumed at the same time and cannot be separated from their providers.

Service intangibility Services cannot be seen, tasted, felt, heard, or smelled before they are bought.

Service perishability Services cannot be stored for later sale or use.

Service profit chain The chain that links service firm profits with employee and customer satisfaction.

Service retailer A retailer whose product line is actually a service, including hotels, airlines, banks, colleges, and many others.

Service variability The quality of services may vary greatly depending on who provides them and when, where, and how.

Share of customer The portion of the customer's purchasing that a company gets in its product categories.

Shopper marketing Using in-store promotions and advertising to extend brand equity to "the last mile" and encourage favorable in-store purchase decisions.

Shopping center A group of retail businesses built on a site that is planned, developed, owned, and managed as a unit.

Shopping product A consumer product that the customer, in the process of selecting and purchasing, usually compares on such attributes as suitability, quality, price, and style.

Social class Relatively permanent and ordered divisions in a society whose members share similar values, interests, and behaviors.

Social marketing The use of commercial marketing concepts and tools in programs designed to influence individuals' behavior to improve their well-being and that of society.

Societal marketing A principle of sustainable marketing that holds a company should make marketing decisions by considering consumers' wants, the company's requirements, consumers' long-run interests, and society's long-run interests.

Societal marketing concept The idea that a company's marketing decisions should consider consumers' wants, the company's requirements, consumers' long-run interests, and society's long-run interests.

Spam Unsolicited, unwanted commercial e-mail messages.

Specialty product A consumer product with unique characteristics or brand identification for which a significant group of buyers is willing to make a special purchase effort.

Specialty store A retail store that carries a narrow product line with a deep assortment within that line.

Standardized global marketing An international marketing strategy that basically uses the same marketing strategy and mix in all of the company's international markets.

Store brand (or private brand) A brand created and owned by a reseller of a product or service.

Straight product extension Marketing a product in a foreign market without any change.

Straight rebuy A business buying situation in which the buyer routinely reorders something without any modifications.

Strategic group A group of firms in an industry following the same or a similar strategy.

Strategic planning The process of developing and maintaining a strategic fit between the organization's goals and capabilities and its changing marketing opportunities.

Style A basic and distinctive mode of expression.

Subculture A group of people with shared value systems based on common life experiences and situations.

Supermarket A large, low-cost, low-margin, high-volume, self-service store that carries a wide variety of grocery and household products.

Superstore A store much larger than a regular supermarket that offers a large assortment of routinely purchased food products, non-food items, and services.

Supplier development Systematic development of networks of supplier-partners to ensure an appropriate and dependable supply of products and materials for use in making products or reselling them to others.

Supplier search The stage of the business buying process in which the buyer tries to find the best vendors.

Supplier selection The stage of the business buying process in which the buyer reviews proposals and selects a supplier or suppliers.

Supply chain management Managing upstream and downstream value-added flows of materials, final goods, and related information among suppliers, the company, resellers, and final consumers.

Survey research Gathering primary data by asking people questions about their knowledge, attitudes, preferences, and buying behavior.

Sustainable marketing Socially and environmentally responsible marketing that meets the present needs of consumers and businesses while also preserving or enhancing the ability of future generations to meet their needs.

SWOT analysis An overall evaluation of the company's strengths (S), weaknesses (W), opportunities (O), and threats (T).

Systems selling (or solutions selling) Buying a packaged solution to a problem from a single seller, thus avoiding all the separate decisions involved in a complex buying situation.

Target costing Pricing that starts with an ideal selling price and then targets costs that will ensure that the price is met.

Target market A set of buyers sharing common needs or characteristics that the company decides to serve.

Team selling Using teams of people from sales, marketing, engineering, finance, technical support, and even upper management to service large, complex accounts.

Team-based new-product development An approach to developing new products in which various company departments work closely together, overlapping the steps in the product development process to save time and increase effectiveness.

Technological environment Forces that create new technologies, creating new product and market opportunities.

Telephone marketing Using the telephone to sell directly to customers.

Territorial sales force structure A sales force organization that assigns each salesperson to an exclusive geographic territory in which that salesperson sells the company's full line.

Test marketing The stage of new-product development in which the product and its proposed marketing program are tested in realistic market settings.

Third-party logistics (3PL) provider An independent logistics provider that performs any or all of the functions required to get a client's product to market.

Total costs The sum of the fixed and variable costs for any given level of production.

Trade promotions Sales promotion tools used to persuade resellers to carry a brand, give it shelf space, promote it in advertising, and push it to consumers.

Undifferentiated (mass) marketing A market-coverage strategy in which a firm decides to ignore market segment differences and go after the whole market with one offer.

Uniform-delivered pricing A geographical pricing strategy in which the company charges the same price plus freight to all customers, regardless of their location.

Unsought product A consumer product that the consumer either does not know about or knows about but does not normally consider buying.

Users Members of the buying organization who will actually use the purchased product or service.

Value chain The series of internal departments that carry out value-creating activities to design, produce, market, deliver, and support a firm's products.

Value delivery network A network composed of the company, suppliers, distributors, and, ultimately, customers who "partner" with each other to improve the performance of the entire system in delivering customer value.

Value proposition The full positioning of a brand—the full mix of benefits on which it is positioned.

Value-added pricing Attaching value-added features and services to differentiate a company's offers and charging higher prices.

Variable costs Costs that vary directly with the level of production.

Variety-seeking buying behavior Consumer buying behavior in situations characterized by low consumer involvement but significant perceived brand differences.

Vertical marketing system (VMS) A distribution channel structure in which producers, wholesalers, and retailers act as a unified system. One channel member owns the others, has contracts with them, or has so much power that they all cooperate.

Viral marketing The Internet version of word-of-mouth marketing: Web sites, videos, e-mail messages, or other marketing events that are so infectious that customers will want to pass them along to friends.

Wants The form human needs take as they are shaped by culture and individual personality.

Warehouse club An off-price retailer that sells a limited selection of brand name grocery items, appliances, clothing, and a hodgepodge of other goods at deep discounts to members who pay annual membership fees.

Wheel-of-retailing concept A concept that states that new types of retailers usually begin as low-margin, low-price, low-status operations but later evolve into higher-priced, higher-service operations, eventually becoming like the conventional retailers they replaced.

Whole-channel view Designing international channels that take into account the entire global supply chain and marketing channel, forging an effective global value delivery network.

Wholesaler A firm engaged *primarily* in wholesaling activities.

Wholesaling All the activities involved in selling goods and services to those buying for resale or business use.

Word-of-mouth influence Personal communications about a product between target buyers and neighbors, friends, family members, and associates.

Zone pricing A geographical pricing strategy in which the company sets up two or more zones. All customers within a zone pay the same total price; the more distant the zone, the higher the price.

Credits

CHAPTER 1 3 © 2010 Zappos.com, Inc. or its affiliates. 6 Courtesy of the US Forest Service. Shrek ® & © 2001 DreamWorks Animation LLC, used with permission of DreamWorks Animation LLC. 9 Courtesy of smart USA. 11 Courtesy of www.istock.com. 13 Rough Guides Dorling Kindersley. 14 Newscom. 16 © Jeff Greenberg/Alamy. 16 S4Carlisle. 17 © 2010 Zappos.com, Inc. or its affiliates. 18 © AJ Mast/The New York Times/Redux. 20 Courtesy of Stew Leonard's. 21 © CORBIS. All Rights Reserved. 24 © 2008 De Beers Group. 23 Justin Sullivan/Getty Images. 26 Getty Images. 27 Sinopix Photo Agency Limited. 28 Courtesy of Patagonia, Inc. 28 Courtesy of the ASPCA, Sarah McLauchlan, and Eagle-Com.

CHAPTER 2 37 Riza Ayson. 41 Bloomberg via Getty Images. 44 Beth A. Keiser/CORBIS. 45 Larry French/Getty Images for Under Armour. 47 Teh Eng Koon/Agence France Presse/Getty Images; PRNews Foto/L'Oreal Paris. 50 Newscom. 51 The BURGER KING® trademarks and advertisements are used with permission from Burger King Corporation. 56 PM Images/Stone/Getty Images. 58 © MarketingNPV LLC. All rights reserved. Used with permission.

CHAPTER 3 65 Courtesy of Xerox Corporation. 68 © James Kirkikis. 69 Courtesy of Procter & Gamble. 70 REUTERS/Claro Cortes IV (CHINA). 71 Courtesy of Merrill Lynch Wealth Management, Bank of America Corporation. Photographer: Chris Buck. 72 Courtesy of Virginia Tourism Corporation. 73 Amanda Kamen. 75 © 2010 Cisco Systems, Inc. 76 GEPA/Imago/Icon SMI 429/Newscom. 77 Courtesy of Tata Motors Limited. 79 AP Photo/Mary Altaffter. 80 AP Wide World Photos. 84 PR NEWSWIRE/Newscom. 85 Pepsi-Cola Company. Photographer: Martin Wonnocott. 86 Kenneth Cole Productions, Inc. 88 Courtesy of Earthbound Farm. 90 Courtesy of Michael Whitford. Used with permission.

CHAPTER 4 97 Courtesy of Procter & Gamble. 98 AP Wide World Photos. 101 Courtesy of Barneys New York, Inc. 102 Courtesy of Radian6 Technologies Inc. 104 Courtesy of Red Bull North America. 107 Amanda Kamen. 108 Lauren Pond/The Photo Pond. 111 Corbis RF. 112 Courtesy of Zoomerang, a MarketTools Company. 113 Courtesy of adidas AG. 115 © Frank and Helena/Cultural Corbis. 117 ERICH SCHLEGEL/The New York Times. 120 Courtesy of The Kroger Co. 121 Courtesy of Penske Truck Leasing Co., LP. 122 Copyright © 2010 Bibbentuckers. All rights reserved. Reprinted with permission. 123 Courtesy of The Nielsen Company. 125 Eric Meyerson/Rangelife.

CHAPTER 5 133 © Michael Nagle/Liaison/Getty Images. 136 The BURGER KING® trademarks and advertisements are used with permission from Burger King Corporation. 137 Courtesy of Procter & Gamble. 138 Courtesy of State Farm Mutual Automobile Insurance Company. 139 Courtesy of Chrysler Group LLC. 140 Courtesy of Mr. Youth, LLC | the generation of ideas. 141 Courtesy of Blendtec. 142 Pepsi-Cola Company. 144 © Randy Faris/CORBIS. 144 © Jochen Sand/Digital Vision/Getty Images Inc. 145 Courtesy of Acxiom Corporation. 146 Courtesy of Triumph Motorcycles Ltd. 147 Bounce/Getty Images. 149 Courtesy of the American Association of Advertising Agencies. 150 Pepsi-Cola Company. 153 Courtesy of Campbell Soup Company. 155 Copyright ©2010 Lexus. All rights reserved. Used with permission. 157 Courtesy of Hyundai Motor America.

CHAPTER 6 165 Getty Images, Inc./Stephen Brashear/Stringer/Getty Images News. 168 Courtesy of W. L. Gore & Associates, Inc. GORE-TEX is a trademark of W.L. Gore & Associates, Inc. 2010. 169 Courtesy of The Dow Chemical Company. 169 © Bill Varie/Somos Images/Corbis. 170 Newscom. 172 © Caro/Alamy. 172 Newscom. 172 C3472 Frank/May/Newscom. 173 © Steve Prezant/CORBIS. All Rights Reserved. 173 © 2010 Peterbilt Motors Company. All rights reserved. Used with permission. 175 © Golden Pixels LLC/Alamy. 177 Courtesy of Makino, Inc. 179 Courtesy of Cisco Systems Inc. 180 Getty Images, Inc. Getty News. 182 Courtesy Federal Business Opportunities.

CHAPTER 7 189 © Najlah Feanny/CORBIS. All Rights Reserved. 191 Allicia Strickland/Everyday Images Photography. 193 © Disney Enterprises Inc. 193 ANWAR AMRO/APF/GETTY IMAGES. 195 Courtesy of Zipcar. 196 M&M'S is a registered trademark of Mars, Incorporated and its affiliates. This trademark is used with permission. Mars, Incorporated is not associated with Pearson. Advertisement printed with permission of Mars, Incorporated. 197 © James Leynse/CORBIS. All Rights Reserved. 198 Courtesy of The Nielsen Company. 199 Superstock/Art Life Images. 200 Courtesy of Anything Left-Handed. 202 © 2010 VF Corporation. Image used with permission of VF Corporation. 203 Courtesy of Etsy, Inc. and The Clay Collection. 204 Newscom. 205 Courtesy of TruMedia. 206 © Bebeto Matthews/AP Wide World. 209 © Bumper De Jesus/Star Ledger/CORBIS. 212 Courtesy of The Dial Corporation, a Henkel Company. 214 Getty Images, Inc.—Getty News. 215 Courtesy of SABERTOOTH and Nissan. © 2010 Nissan. Nissan model names and the Nissan logo are registered trademarks of Nissan.

CHAPTER 8 223 Jeremy Brevard/Icon SMI. 225 Courtesy of Darden Restaurants, Inc. 225 © Greg Hinsdale/Corbis. 228 Newscom. 228 Chris Gordon/WireImage. 231 © 2010 OXO International Inc. All rights reserved. Used with permission. 232 © 2010 Amazon, Inc or its affiliates. All rights reserved. 233 Pepsi-Cola Company. 234 © Vibe Images/Alamy. 235 PR NEWSWIRE/Newscom. 237 Courtesy of the Mayo Foundation for Medical Education and Research. 239 Robyn Twomey. 240 © 2010 Zappos.com , Inc. or its affiliates. 241 Adron Gardner/MCT/Newscom. 242 Courtesy of Southwest Airlines. 244 Kurtis Meyers. 245 Courtesy of Michael Schwab and Amtrak. 247 Amanda Kamen. 249 PR News Foto/Nickelodeon. 250 Courtesy of The Procter & Gamble Company. 252 Mickey Mouse © Disney Enterprises, Inc./Joe Raedle/Getty

CHAPTER 9 259 Eros Hoagland/Redux. 261 Courtesy of NewProductWorks, a division of GFK Strategic Innovation. Used with permission. www.gfkamerica.com/newproductworks. 262 Courtesy of the 3M Company. 263 Reproduced by permission of Netflix, Inc. Copyright © 2010 Netflix, Inc. All rights reserved. 264 Courtesy of Tesla Motors. 266 © Adrian-Sherratt/Alamy. 267 Kentucky Grilled Chicken® and related images courtesy of KFC Corporation. 271 Courtesy of LEGO Systems, Inc. LEGO MINDSTORMS® is a registered trademark of LEGO Systems, Inc. LEGO, the LEGO, logo, LEGO MINDSTORMS® are trademarks of the LEGO Group. © 2010 The LEGO Group. 274 TABASCO® is a registered trademark for sauces and other goods and services; TABASCO, the TABASCO bottle design and label designs are the exclusive property of McIlhenny Company, Avery Island, LA, USA 70513. www.TABASCO.com. 276 Amanda Kamen. 278 Reproduced by Permission. American Greetings Corporation. © AGC, Inc. 281 NESTLÉ and KIT KAT are registered trademarks of Société des Produits Nestlé S.A., Switzerland and are reproduced with the consent of the trademark owner.

CHAPTER 10 289 Christopher Schall/Impact Photo. 290 Shutterstock. 292 Courtesy of Steinway Musical Instruments, Inc. 293 Courtesy of Ryanair Holdings Plc. 293 Raghu Rai. 294 AP Wide World Photos. 299 Reprinted with permission of the artist, Kaye Synoground. Courtesy of Annie Blooms Books. 301 Courtesy of Titus Cycles. 302 Colby Lysne. 304 Courtesy of The Home Depot, Inc. 305 Librado Romero/The New York Times.

CHAPTER 11 313 © Michael Nagle/Getty Images. 315 © Romain Degoul/REA/Redux. 316 © 2010 Six Flags Theme Parks Inc. All rights reserved. Used with permission. 317 © 2010 Eastman Kodak Company. All rights reserved. Used with permission. 318 Courtesy of Biz Kid$ and Woodland Park Zoo. 320 Christopher Schall/Impact Photo. 321 PhotoEdit Inc. 322 AP Wide World Photos. 323 Courtesy of Priceline.com Incorporated. 324 TENGKU BAHAR/Agence France Presse/Getty Images. 325 © Louis DeLuca/Dallas Morning News/CORBIS. All Rights Reserved. 326 Amanda Kamen. 328 Courtesy of BoltBus. 329 Lilli Day/Getty Images. 331 AP Photo/Reed Saxon.

CHAPTER 12 339 © 2010 Enterprise Rent-a-Car Company. All rights reserved. Used with permission. 341 Courtesy of Ford Motor Company. 345 The BURGER KING® trademarks and advertisements are used with permission from Burger King Corporation. 346 Courtesy of Service Brands International, LLC. 347 © Kevin Foy/Alamy. 349 AP Wide World Photos. 350 Reproduced by permission of Netflix, Inc. Copyright © 2010 Netflix, Inc. All rights reserved. Photographer: Remy Haynes Photography. 351 AP Wide World Photos. 353 Courtesy of Bentley Houston. 354 Lou Linwei/Alamy. 356 David Boily/Agence France Presse/Getty Images. 358 Richard Ross/Photographer's Choice/Getty Images. 359 Courtesy of Con-way Inc. 361 Redux

Indexes

Name, Organization, Brand, Company

Note: Italicized page numbers indicate illustrations

Subject

Note: Italicized page numbers indicate illustrations.